T0181516

Lecture Notes in Computer Science   13007

Founding Editors

Gerhard Goos
  Karlsruhe Institute of Technology, Karlsruhe, Germany

Juris Hartmanis
  Cornell University, Ithaca, NY, USA

Editorial Board Members

Elisa Bertino
  Purdue University, West Lafayette, IN, USA

Wen Gao
  Peking University, Beijing, China

Bernhard Steffen
  TU Dortmund University, Dortmund, Germany

Gerhard Woeginger
  RWTH Aachen, Aachen, Germany

Moti Yung
  Columbia University, New York, NY, USA

More information about this subseries at http://www.springer.com/series/7410

Yu Yu · Moti Yung (Eds.)

Information Security and Cryptology

17th International Conference, Inscrypt 2021
Virtual Event, August 12–14, 2021
Revised Selected Papers

 Springer

Editors
Yu Yu 🆔
Shanghai Jiao Tong University
Shanghai, China

Moti Yung 🆔
Columbia University
New York, NY, USA

ISSN 0302-9743　　　　　　　ISSN 1611-3349 (electronic)
Lecture Notes in Computer Science
ISBN 978-3-030-88322-5　　　　ISBN 978-3-030-88323-2 (eBook)
https://doi.org/10.1007/978-3-030-88323-2

LNCS Sublibrary: SL4 – Security and Cryptology

© Springer Nature Switzerland AG 2021, corrected publication 2022
This work is subject to copyright. All rights are reserved by the Publisher, whether the whole or part of the material is concerned, specifically the rights of translation, reprinting, reuse of illustrations, recitation, broadcasting, reproduction on microfilms or in any other physical way, and transmission or information storage and retrieval, electronic adaptation, computer software, or by similar or dissimilar methodology now known or hereafter developed.
The use of general descriptive names, registered names, trademarks, service marks, etc. in this publication does not imply, even in the absence of a specific statement, that such names are exempt from the relevant protective laws and regulations and therefore free for general use.
The publisher, the authors and the editors are safe to assume that the advice and information in this book are believed to be true and accurate at the date of publication. Neither the publisher nor the authors or the editors give a warranty, expressed or implied, with respect to the material contained herein or for any errors or omissions that may have been made. The publisher remains neutral with regard to jurisdictional claims in published maps and institutional affiliations.

This Springer imprint is published by the registered company Springer Nature Switzerland AG
The registered company address is: Gewerbestrasse 11, 6330 Cham, Switzerland

Preface

The 17th International Conference on Information Security and Cryptology (Inscrypt 2021) was originally planned as a hybrid event to take place in Qingdao, China, during August 12–14, 2021. Due to the COVID-19 pandemic, it was eventually held online (virtually). The conference was organized by the State Key Laboratory of Information Security (SKLOIS) of the Institute of Information Engineering of the Chinese Academy of Sciences and the School of Cyber Science and Technology, Shandong University, in cooperation with the IACR.

Inscrypt is an annual international conference held in China, targeting research advances in all areas of information security, cryptology, and their applications. Inscrypt 2021 received 81 submissions from Canada, China, Japan, Morocco, Romania, Slovenia, Switzerland, and the UK. The program committee (PC) was composed of 58 members, who are leading experts on cryptology and security from six countries or regions. The PC team selected 28 papers as full papers. Each submission underwent a double-blind peer-review process and was scrutinized by at least three PC members or sub-reviewers. All the accepted papers are included in this conference proceedings.

We note that the program of Inscrypt 2021 included four excellent invited academic keynote talks by Shengli Liu (China), Ran Canetti (USA), Sanjam Garg (USA), and François-Xavier Standaert (Belgium); we thank the invited speakers for their important contributions to the program. In addition to these keynotes, the program included nine regular presentation sessions on Signatures, System Security, Symmetric Cryptanalysis, Asymmetric Cryptanalysis, Cryptographic Protocols, Mathematical Foundations, Symmetric Cryptography, Public Key Cryptography, and Real World Cryptography.

It would not have been possible to have a successful Inscrypt 2021 without the significant contributions of many people. First, we would like to thank all the authors for submitting their research results to the conference. We are also very grateful to the PC members and external reviewers for contributing their knowledge, expertise, and hard work to assuring the quality of the conference. Secondly, we are greatly indebted to the honorary chairs, Dongdai Lin and Xiaoyun Wang, and to the general co-chairs, Yu Chen and Chun Guo, for their organizational efforts. Thirdly, we thank Puwen Wei for organizing the online conference program. Last but not least, we thank Anna Kramer, Ronan Nugent, and their Springer colleagues for handling the publication of the conference proceedings.

August 2021

Yu Yu
Moti Yung

Organization

Honorary Chairs

Dongdai Lin   Chinese Academy of Sciences, China
Xiaoyun Wang   Tsinghua University, China

General Chairs

Yu Chen   Shandong University, China
Chun Guo   Shandong University, China

Technical Program Chairs

Yu Yu   Shanghai Jiao Tong University, China
Moti Yung   Google LLC and Columbia University, USA

Organizing Chair

Puwen Wei   Shandong University, China

Steering Committee

Feng Bao   Huawei International, Singapore
Kefei Chen   Hangzhou Normal University, China
Dawu Gu   Shanghai Jiao Tong University, China
Xinyi Huang   Fujian Normal University, China
Hui Li   Xidian University, China
Dongdai Lin   Chinese Academy of Sciences, China
Peng Liu   Pennsylvania State University, USA
Zhe Liu   Nanjing University of Aeronautics and Astronautics, China
Wen-Feng Qi   National Digital Switching System Engineering
         and Technological Research Center, China
Meiqin Wang   Shandong University, China
Xiaofeng Wang   Indiana University at Bloomington, USA
Xiaoyun Wang   Tsinghua University, China
Jian Weng   Jinan University, China
Moti Yung   Google LLC and Columbia University, USA
Fangguo Zhang   Sun Yat-sen University, China
Huanguo Zhang   Wuhan University, China

Program Committee

Man Ho Au	The University of Hong Kong, China
Shi Bai	Florida Atlantic University, USA
Davide Bellizia	Université catholique de Louvain, Belgium
Zhenzhen Bao	Nanyang Technological University, Singapore
Qi Chen	Guangzhou University, China
Long Chen	New Jersey Institute of Technology, USA
Rongmao Chen	National University of Defense Technology, China
Xiaofeng Chen	Xidian University, China
Yi Deng	Chinese Academy of Sciences, China
Haixin Duan	Tsinghua University, China
Thanassis Giannetsos	Ubiquitous Technologies Limited, USA
Jian Guo	Nanyang Technological University, Singapore
Qian Guo	Lund University, Sweden
Shuai Han	Shanghai Jiao Tong University, China
Itamar Levi	Bar Ilan University, Israel
Jian Liu	Zhe Jiang University, China
Kaitai Liang	TU Delft, Netherlands
Jingqiang Lin	University of Science and Technology of China, China
Joseph Liu	Monash University, Australia
Juanru Li	Shanghai Jiao Tong University, China
Zhen Ling	Southeast University, China
Meicheng Liu	Chinese Academy of Sciences, China
Qipeng Liu	Princeton University, USA
Junzuo Lai	Jinan University, China
Abe Masayuki	NTT and Kyoto University, Japan
Weizhi Meng	Technical University of Denmark, Denmark
Khoa Nguyen	Nanyang Technological University, Singapore
Jianting Ning	National University of Singapore, Singapore
Emmanouil Panaousis	University of Greenwich, UK
Christophe Petit	Université libre de Bruxelles, Belgium
Thomas Peters	UCLouvain, Belgium
Longjiang Qu	National University of Defense Technology, China
Chao Shen	Xi'an Jiaotong University, China
Ron Steinfeld	Monash University, Australia
Ling Song	Jinan University, China
Ling Sun	Shandong University, China
Siwei Sun	Chinese Academy of Sciences, China
Qiang Tang	The University of Sydney, Australia
Anyu Wang	Tsinghua University, China
Qian Wang	Wuhan University, China
Qingju Wang	University of Luxembourg, Luxembourg
Weijia Wang	Shandong University, China
Xiao Wang	Northwestern University, USA

Xiang Xie	Shanghai Key Laboratory of Privacy-Preserving Computation, China
Peng Xu	Huazhong University of Science and Technology, China
Liang Xiao	Xiamen University, China
Moti Yung	Google LLC and Columbia University, USA
Yu Yu	Shanghai Jiao Tong University, China
Yang Yu	Tsinghua University, China
Bingsheng Zhang	Zhejiang University, China
Jiaheng Zhang	UC Berkeley, USA
Jiang Zhang	State Key Laboratory of Cryptology, China
Lei Zhang	Fudan University, China
Yupeng Zhang	Texas A&M University, USA
Yang Zhang	CISPA Helmholtz Center for Information Security, Germany
Xiaohan Zhang	Fudan University, China
Zhenfeng Zhang	Chinese Academy of Sciences, China
Hong-Sheng Zhou	Virginia Commonwealth University, USA

Sub-reviewers

Weihao Bai
Alessandro Budroni
Hongrui Cui
Nan Cui
Xiaoyang Dong
Xuejun Fan
Boris Fouotsa
Junqing Gong
Haihua Gu
Kaiwen Guo
Xiaojie Guo
Debiao He
Haodong Jiang
Mingming Jiang
Peter Kutas
Chunlei Li

Ming Li
Shun Li
Xiangxue Li
Yiming Li
Guozhen Liu
Hanlin Liu
Xiangyu Liu
Zhen Liu
Yonglin Hao
Guifang Huang
Erik Mårtensson
Phuong Pham
Joost Renes
Yao Sun
Phuc Thai
Song Tian

Yi Wang
Haiyang Xue
Jing Yang
Kang Yang
Qianqian Yang
Rupeng Yang
Li Yao
Bin Zhang
Lulu Zhang
Shuoyao Zhao
Zhongxiang Zheng
Tanping Zhou
Yu Zhou
Yuqing Zhu

Sponsor

Contents

Public Key Cryptography

Real World Cryptography

Signatures

Concurrent Signatures from a Variety of Keys

George Teşeleanu[1,2]([envelope]) [ORCID]

[1] Advanced Technologies Institute, 10 Dinu Vintilă, Bucharest, Romania
tgeorge@dcti.ro
[2] Simion Stoilow Institute of Mathematics of the Romanian Academy,
21 Calea Grivitei, Bucharest, Romania

Abstract. Concurrent signatures allow two entities to produce two ambiguous signatures that become binding once an extra piece of information (called the keystone) is released. Such a signature is developed by Chen *et al.*, but it restricts signers to using the same public parameters. We describe and analyse a new concurrent signature that allows users to sign documents even if they use different underlying hard problems when generating their public parameters.

1 Introduction

The fair exchange of signatures between two mutually distrustful parties is a fundamental and well-studied problem in cryptography. Ideally, we would like the exchange of signatures to be done in fair way, *i.e.* each participant receives the other's signature, or neither does. We would also like to have some sort of guarantee that is impossible for one party to terminate the protocol and to leave the other participant committed when they are not.

To achieve a form of the properties mentioned above, several authors have put forth three main categories:

- Gradual release schemes: Using the idea of time release, the output is gradually revealed (*e.g.* bit per bit). Usually, this solution is highly interactive and may not work if the adversary is more computationally powerful [8,10,16].
- Optimistic schemes: Using a trusted third party, this approach can restore fairness if a dispute rises. In some cases, the infrastructure requirements and trusting a third party are not appropriate [2,5,14].
- Concurrent or legally fair schemes: The exchanged signatures become binding only when an extra piece of information (the keystone) is revealed. To enforce a signed contract, a participant has to present it in a court of law. Note that the keystone offers enough information to restore fairness. This approach does not require a trusted arbitrator or a high degree of interaction between parties [6,7,12].

Chen *et al.* [6] constructed their concurrent signature protocol based on a 1-out-of-n signature scheme proposed by Abe *et al.* [1]. An 1-out-of-n signature is

© Springer Nature Switzerland AG 2021
Y. Yu and M. Yung (Eds.): Inscrypt 2021, LNCS 13007, pp. 3–22, 2021.
https://doi.org/10.1007/978-3-030-88323-2_1

constructed so that once a signature is computed, then any verifier is convinced that the signature was generated by one of n signers. Hence, using a slight modification of Abe *et al.* signature, Chen *et al.* are able to guarantee ambiguity before revealing the keystone.

In their paper, Abe *et al.* presented both a non-separable scheme where all n key pairs correspond to the same scheme, and a separable scheme where each key pair can be generated by a different scheme, under a different hardness assumption. For the discrete logarithm assumption, the authors of [1] also propose an non-separable schemes that is more efficient than the generic one. The concurrent signature proposed by Chen *et al.* was based on the efficient non-separable variant. Hence, it is based on the discrete logarithm assumption. Furthermore, the security of this protocol can be proven in the random oracle model, assuming the hardness of computing discrete logarithms in a cyclic group of prime order. Using a variation of Abe *et al.*'s 1-out-of-n signature with key separation, we introduce a concurrent signature in the separable model.

The efficient 1-out-of-n signature without key separation proposed in [1] is an adaptation of the Schnorr signature [17]. Maurer [13] introduced a construction that unifies the Schnorr zero-knowledge protocol [17] and the Guillou-Quisquater protocol [11]. A consequence of Maurer's construction is the introduction of other novel protocols whose security is based on other hardness assumptions.[1] Based on Maurer's approach, we describe a generic 1-out-of-n signature that can be seen as an adaptation of the signature described in [12]. Based on this signature we also generalize Chen *et al.*'s signature.

Note that in [1] the authors also describe a 1-out-of-n signature with key separation based on the full domain RSA signature scheme [4]. We chose to use only the zero-knowledge version, since working in a general framework[2] may reduce implementation errors, and save application development and maintenance time.

Remark that concurrent signatures are not abuse-free in the sense of [3,9], since the party *Bob* who holds the keystone can always determine whether to complete the protocol or not. But, there are situations where it is not in *Bob*'s interest to try and cheat *Alice*. One interesting scenario is that of fair tendering of contracts. Suppose *Alice* has a building contract that she wishes to put out to tender. Also, suppose that *Bob* and *Charlie* are two competing companies that put forward signed proposals to win the contract. If *Alice* whats to accept *Bob*'s offer, she returns a signed payment instruction to *Bob* and he in turn releases the keystone. A common form of abuse is to show *Charlie Bob*'s proposal and thus enabling *Charlie* to make a better offer. But, in the case of concurrent signatures, *Charlie* sees an ambiguous signature that might have been crafted by *Alice*. Hence, *Alice* gains no advantage in revealing *Bob*'s proposal.

Our Contributions. In their paper, Chen *et al.* [6] claim that their scheme can be extended to other ring signatures as long as the scheme is compatible to the keystone idea. Hence, different hard problems could be used to construct such

---

[1] Different from the discrete logarithm and e^{th}-root assumptions.

[2] Guillou-Quisquater's signature is also included in this framework.

schemes. Also, they claim that concurrent signatures that work in the separable model can be build using the techniques developed in [1]. Unfortunately, they do not provide such examples. Our aim is to fill this gap. Hence, the main contributions of our paper are the following:

- Adjusting the construction of Chen *et al.* to support signatures with separable keys. To achieve this, we first introduce a modification to Abe *et al.*'s separable 1-out-of-*n* signature.
- Generalizing the non-separable 1-out-of-*n* signature of Abe *et al.* to other hardness assumptions. We also implicitly prove the security of Abe *et al.*'s signature[3].
- Generalizing Chen *et al.*'s original concurrent signature to support additional hardness assumptions.

Structure of the Paper. We introduce notations, definitions, schemes and protocols used throughout the paper in Sect. 2. We present a variation of Abe *et al.*'s signature scheme in Sect. 3. In Sect. 4 we present our main result, namely a concurrent signature in the separable model. We conclude in Sect. 5. In Appendices A and B we generalize the non-separable signature from [1] and the concurrent signature from [6].

2 Preliminaries

Notations. Throughout the paper, the notation $|S|$ denotes the cardinality of a set S. The action of selecting a random element x from a sample space X is denoted by $x \xleftarrow{\$} X$, while $x \leftarrow y$ represents the assignment of value y to variable x. The probability of the event E to happen is denoted by $Pr[E]$. The subset $\{0, \ldots, s-1\} \in \mathbb{N}$ is denoted by $[0, s)$. Note we further consider that all of $\mathcal{N}$'s subsets are of the form $[0, s)$ and have more than one element. A vector v of length n is denoted either $v = (v_0, \ldots, v_{n-1})$ or $v = \{v_i\}_{i \in [0,n)}$. Also, we use the notations C_k^n to denote binomial coefficients and exp to denote Euler's constant.

2.1 Groups

Let $(\mathbb{G}, \star)$ and $(\mathbb{H}, \otimes)$ be two groups. We assume that the group operations $\star$ and $\otimes$ are efficiently computable.

Let $f : \mathbb{G} \to \mathbb{H}$ be a function (not necessarily one-to-one). We say that f is a homomorphism if $f(x \star y) = f(x) \otimes f(y)$. Throughout the paper we consider f to be a one-way function, *i.e.* it is infeasible to compute x from $f(x)$. To be consistent with [13], we denote by $[x]$ the value $f(x)$. Note that given $[x]$ and $[y]$ we can efficiently compute $[x \star y] = [x] \otimes [y]$, due to the fact that f is a homomorphism.

---

[3] The original authors give an idea of how to prove that their signature is secure, but do not provide a concrete proof.

2.2   1-out-of-n Signatures

Definition 1 (1-out-of-n Signature). *An 1-out-of-n signature scheme is a digital signature comprised of the following algorithms*

Setup(λ): On input a security parameter λ, this algorithm outputs the private and public keys (sk_i, pk_i) of all the participants and the public parameters $pp = (\mathcal{M}, \mathcal{S})$, where $\mathcal{M}$ is the message space and $\mathcal{S}$ is the signature space.

Sign(m, sk_k, L): A PPT algorithm that on input a message $m \in \mathcal{M}$, the private key sk_k and a list of public keys L such that $pk_k \in L$, outputs a signature σ.

Verify(m, σ, L) An algorithm that on input a message m, a signature σ and a list of public keys L outputs either true *or* false.

We further present the security models presented in [1] for 1-out-of-n signature schemes.

Definition 2 (Signer Ambiguity). *Let $\mathcal{L} = \{pk_i\}_{i \in [0,n)}$, where pk_i are generated by the Setup algorithm. An 1-out-of-n signature is perfectly signer ambiguous if for any message m, any $L \subseteq \mathcal{L}$, any $sk_k \in L$ and any signature σ generated by the Sign(m, sk_k, L), any unbound adversary $\mathcal{A}$ outputs an sk such that $sk = sk_k$ with probability exactly $1/|L|$.*

Definition 3 (Existential Unforgeability against Adaptive Chosen Message and Chosen Public Key Attacks - EUF-CMCPA). *The notion of unforgeability for signatures is defined in terms of the following security game between the adversary $\mathcal{A}$ and a challenger:*

1. *The Setup algorithm is run and all the public parameters are provided to $\mathcal{A}$.*
2. *For any message and any subset of $\mathcal{L} = \{pk_i\}_{i \in [0,n)}$, $\mathcal{A}$ can perform signature queries to the challenger.*
3. *Finally, $\mathcal{A}$ outputs a signature (m, σ, L), where $L \subseteq \mathcal{L}$.*

$\mathcal{A}$ wins the game if Verify(m, σ, L) = true, $L \subseteq \mathcal{L}$ and $\mathcal{A}$ did not query the challenger on (m, L). We say that a signature scheme is unforgeable when the success probability of $\mathcal{A}$ in this game is negligible.

Note that when $n = 1$ Definitions 1 and 3 are equivalent with the classical signature definition and, respectively, the existential unforgeability against adaptive chosen message attack.

We further introduce the notions of a Boolean matrix and of a heavy row in such a matrix [15]. These definitions are then used in stating the heavy row lemma [15].

Definition 4 (Boolean Matrix of Random Tapes). *Let us consider a matrix M whose rows consist of all possible random choices of an adversary and the columns consist of all possible random choices of a challenger. Its entries are 0 if the adversary fails the game and 1 otherwise.*

Definition 5 (Heavy Row). *A row of M is heavy if the fraction of 1's along the row is at least $\varepsilon/2$, where ε is the adversary's success probability.*

Lemma 1 (Heavy Row Lemma). *The 1's in M are located in heavy rows with a probability of at least $1/2$.*

2.3   Concurrent Signatures

Definition 6 (Concurrent Signature). *A concurrent signature scheme is a digital signature comprised of the following algorithms*

Setup(λ): On input a security parameter λ, this algorithm outputs the private and public keys (x_i, y_i) of all participants and the public parameters $pp = (\mathcal{M}, \mathcal{S}, \mathcal{K}, \mathcal{F}, KeyGen)$, where $\mathcal{M}$ is the message space, $\mathcal{S}$ is the signature space, $\mathcal{K}$ is the keystone space, $\mathcal{F}$ the keystone fix space and $KeyGen : \mathcal{K} \to \mathcal{F}$ is a function.

aSign(y_i, y_j, x_i, f, m): On input the public keys $y_i \neq y_j$, the private key x_i corresponding to y_i, an element $f \in \mathcal{F}$ and a message $m \in \mathcal{M}$, this algorithm outputs an ambiguous signature $\sigma = \langle s, e, f \rangle$, where $s \in \mathcal{S}$ and $e \in \mathcal{F}$.

aVerify(σ, y_i, y_j, m): On input an ambiguous signature $\sigma = \langle s, e, f \rangle$, public keys y_i, y_j and a message m this algorithm outputs a boolean value.

Verify(k, σ, y_i, y_j, m): On input $k \in \mathcal{K}$, $\sigma = \langle s, e, f \rangle$, public keys y_i, y_j and message m, this algorithm checks whether $KeyGen(k) = f$ and outputs false *if not; otherwise it outputs the result of aVerify(σ, y_i, y_j, m).*

Concurrent signatures are used by two parties *Alice* and *Bob* as depicted in Fig. 1. At the end of the protocol, both $\langle k, \sigma_A \rangle$ and $\langle k, \sigma_B \rangle$ are binding, and accepted by the *Verify* algorithm.

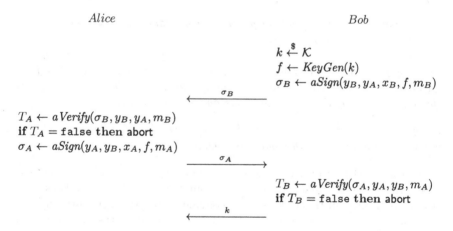

Fig. 1. The concurrent signature of messages m_A and m_B.

According to the security notions presented in [6], a PPT adversary $\mathcal{A}$ for a concurrent signature can perform the following queries

- *KeyGen* queries: $\mathcal{A}$ can request the value $f \leftarrow KeyGen(k)$, where k is selected by the challenger $\mathcal{T}$. If $\mathcal{A}$ whants to choose his own k, he can compute $KeyGen(k)$ by himself.

- *KeyReveal* queries: $\mathcal{A}$ can requests $\mathcal{T}$ to reveal the keystone k associated to f. If f was not previously computed by the challenger, then $\mathcal{T}$ outputs invalid, otherwise he returns k.
- *aSign* queries: $\mathcal{A}$ can request a valid *aSign* signature σ for two public keys $y_i \neq y_j$, an element $f \in \mathcal{F}$ and a message m of his choosing. Note that using *aSign* queries in conjunction with *KeyGen* queries, the adversary can obtain concurrent signatures for messages and pairs of users of his choice.
- *SKExtract* queries: $\mathcal{A}$ can request the private key corresponding to a public key.
- Directory queries: $\mathcal{A}$ can request the public key of any user.

The following definition captures the notion of unforgeability in the concurrent context.

Definition 7 (Concurrent Signature Unforgeability - EUF-CS). *The notion of unforgeability for concurrent signatures is defined in terms of the following security game between the adversary $\mathcal{A}$ and a challenger $\mathcal{T}$:*

1. *The Setup algorithm is run and all the public parameters are provided to $\mathcal{A}$.*
2. *$\mathcal{A}$ can perform any number of queries to the challenger, as described above.*
3. *Finally, $\mathcal{A}$ outputs a tuple (m, y_C, y_D, s, e, f).*

$\mathcal{A}$ wins the game if $aVerify(s, e, f, y_C, y_D, m) = \mathtt{true}$ and either of the following holds

- *$\mathcal{A}$ did not query SKExtract on y_C nor on y_D, and did not query aSign on either (y_C, y_D, f, m) or (y_D, y_C, f, m).*
- *$\mathcal{A}$ did not query SKExtract on y_D, and did not query aSign on (y_D, y_i, f, m) for any $y_i \neq y_D$ and $\mathcal{A}$ produces a keystone k such that $KeyGen(k) = f$.*
- *$\mathcal{A}$ did not query SKExtract on y_C, and did not query aSign on (y_C, y_i, f, m) for any $y_i \neq y_C$ and f was a previous output from a KeyGen query.*

We say that a concurrent signature scheme is existentially unforgeable when the success probability of $\mathcal{A}$ in this game is negligible.

Note that in Definition 7 the first output condition corresponds to an outside attacker that tries to create a forgery without knowing the secret keys of the participants. Hence, in this case *Alice* is convinced that the signature originates from *Bob*. The second and third conditions correspond to the case where the attacker and one of the participants are one and the same.

The next definition captures the notion of ambiguity for concurrent signatures. Note that the security notion is slightly weaker than Definition 2 due to the fact f is generated by *KeyGen* that in practice approximates as best as possible a random oracle.

Definition 8 (Concurrent Signature Ambiguity). *The notion of ambiguity for concurrent signatures is defined in terms of the following security game between the adversary $\mathcal{A}$ and a challenger $\mathcal{T}$:*

1. *The Setup algorithm is run and all the public parameters are provided to $\mathcal{A}$.*
2. *$\mathcal{A}$ can perform any number of queries to the challenger, as described above.*
3. *$\mathcal{A}$ selects a message m and two public keys y_C and y_D.*
4. *In response, the challenger randomly computes $\sigma \leftarrow aSign(y_C, y_D, x_C, f, m)$ or $\sigma \leftarrow aSign(y_D, y_C, x_D, f, m)$, where $k \xleftarrow{\$} \mathcal{K}$ and $f \leftarrow KeyGen(k)$, and sends σ to $\mathcal{A}$.*
5. *Finally, $\mathcal{A}$ guesses $\mathcal{T}$'s choice.*

A concurrent signature is signer ambiguous if $\mathcal{A}$ cannot guess $\mathcal{T}$'s choice with a probability non-negligible greater than $1/2$.

The following definition captures the intuitive notion of fairness. More precisely, that the person that generated the keystone is the only one that can use it to create a binding signature and that any ambiguous signature produced using the same keystone fix f will all become binding. Note that the definition does not guarantee that *Alice* will receive the necessary keystone k.

Definition 9 (Fairness). *The notion of fairness for concurrent signatures is defined in terms of the following security game between the adversary $\mathcal{A}$ and a challenger $\mathcal{T}$:*

1. *The Setup algorithm is run and all the public parameters are provided to $\mathcal{A}$.*
2. *$\mathcal{A}$ can perform any number of queries to the challenger, as described above.*
3. *$\mathcal{A}$ chooses two public keys y_C and y_D and outputs a tuple (m, y_C, y_D, σ, k), where $\sigma = \langle s, e, f \rangle$ and $f = KeyGen(k)$.*

The adversary wins the game if $aVerify(s, e, f, y_C, y_D, m) = \text{true}$ and either of the following holds

- *f was a previous output from a KeyGen query, $\mathcal{A}$ did not query KeyReveal on f and (k, σ) is accepted by the Verify algorithm.*
- *$\mathcal{A}$ also outputs a tuple (m, y_D, y_C, σ'), where $\sigma' = \langle s', e', f \rangle$, such that aVerify accepts σ' and Verify accepts (k, σ), but (k, σ') is not accepted by Verify.*

We say that a concurrent signature scheme is fair when the success probability of $\mathcal{A}$ in this game is negligible.

3   1-out-of-n Signatures with Key Separation

3.1   Description

We present a variation of the 1-out-of-n signature scheme presented in [1]. This variation will be used later to develop a concurrent signature protocol that allows users with different flavors of public keys (*i.e.* discrete logarithm based, e^{th} root problem based) to produce two binding and ambiguous signatures. In practice, each user can generate their own public parameters and key pair. To simplify description we present the *Setup* algorithm as a centralized algorithm. We will denote the following signature with 1n-KSS.

Setup(λ): Let $i \in [0, n)$. Choose for each user two groups $\mathbb{G}_i$, $\mathbb{H}_i$, a homomorphism $[\cdot]_i : \mathbb{G}_i \to \mathbb{H}_i$ and a hash function $H_i : \{0,1\}^* \to \mathcal{C} \subseteq \mathbb{N}$. Note that we require that $|\mathbb{G}_i| \geq 2^\lambda$. Choose $x_i \xleftarrow{\$} \mathbb{G}_i$ and compute $y_i \leftarrow [x_i]_i$. Output the public key $pk_i = y_i$. The secret key is $sk_i = x_i$.

Listing(): Collect the public keys and randomly shuffle them. Store the result into a list $\mathcal{L} = \{y_j\}_{j \in [0,n)}$ and output $\mathcal{L}$.

Sign($m, sk_k, \mathcal{L}$): To sign a message $m \in \{0,1\}^*$, first generate two random elements $\alpha \xleftarrow{\$} \mathbb{G}_k$, $\beta \xleftarrow{\$} \mathcal{C}$ and compute $c_{k+1} \leftarrow H_{k+1}(\mathcal{L}, m, [\alpha]_k)$ and $c'_{k+1} \leftarrow c_{k+1} - \beta \bmod c$, where $|\mathcal{C}| = c$. For $j \in [k+1, n) \cup [0, k)$, select $s_j \xleftarrow{\$} \mathbb{G}_j$ and then compute $c_{j+1} \leftarrow H_{j+1}(\mathcal{L}, m, [s_j]_j \otimes_j y_j^{c'_j})$ and $c'_{j+1} \leftarrow c_{j+1} - \beta \bmod c$. Compute $s_k \leftarrow \alpha \star_k x_k^{-c'_k}$. Output the signature $(c_0, \beta, \mathcal{S})$, where $\mathcal{S} = \{s_j\}_{j \in [0,n)}$.

Verify($m, c_0, \beta, \mathcal{S}, \mathcal{L}$): For $j \in [0, n)$, compute $e_j \leftarrow [s_j]_j \otimes_j y_j^{c_j - \beta}$ and then $c_{j+1} \leftarrow H_{j+1}(\mathcal{L}, m, e_j)$ if $j \neq n - 1$. Output **true** if and only if $c_0 = H_0(\mathcal{L}, m, e_{n-1})$. Otherwise, output **false**.

Correctness. If the pair $(c_0, \beta, \mathcal{S})$ is generated according to the scheme, it is easy to see that the c_j values from the *Sign* and *Verification* coincide when when $j \neq k$. When $j = k$ we observe that

$$e_k = [s_k]_k \otimes_k y_k^{c_k - \beta} = [\alpha \star_k x_k^{-c_k + \beta}]_k \otimes_k y_k^{c_k - \beta}$$
$$= [\alpha]_k \otimes_k [x_k]_k^{-c_k + \beta} \otimes_k y_k^{c_k - \beta} = [\alpha]_k$$

and thus we obtain the same c_k as in the signing phase.

Remark 1. In practice hash functions have $\mathcal{C} = \{0,1\}^\kappa$, where κ is for example 256, 384 or 512. So, if the users from $\mathcal{L}$ have hash functions with different output sizes the simplest method for obtaining a common challenge space $\mathcal{C}$ is to lengthen the function's output by running it several times[4] until we obtain c bits. If efficiency is desired, another method for obtaining a common $\mathcal{C}$ is to truncate all the outputs to the smallest size. Note this method decreases security for some users.

3.2 Security Analysis

Theorem 1. *The 1n-KSS scheme is perfectly signer ambiguous.*

Proof. Note that all s_j are taken randomly from $\mathbb{G}_j$, except for s_k. Since α is a random element from $\mathbb{G}_k$, then s_k is also randomly distributed in $\mathbb{G}_k$. Also, β is a random element from $\mathcal{C}$. Hence, for a fixed $(m, \mathcal{L})$ the probability of $(\beta, \mathcal{S})$ is always $1/(|\mathcal{C}| \cdot \prod |\mathbb{G}_i|)$, regardless of the closing point s_k. The remaining c_0 is uniquely determined from $(m, \mathcal{L})$ and $(\beta, \mathcal{S})$.   □

---

[4] *e.g.* for each run we can add a different prefix to the message.

Theorem 2. *If the following statements are true*

- *an* EUF-CMCPA *attack on the* $1n$-*KSS has non-negligible probability of success in the ROM,*
- *an* $\ell \in \mathbb{Z}$ *is known such that* $\gcd(c_0 - c_1, \ell) = 1$ *for all* $c_0, c_1 \in \mathcal{C}$ *with* $c_0 \neq c_1$,
- *for all* i *values,* $u_i \in \mathbb{G}_i$ *are known such that* $[u_i]_i = y_i^\ell$,

then at least a homomorphism $[\cdot]_i$ *can be inverted in polynomial time.*

Proof. Let $\mathcal{A}$ be an efficient EUF-CMCPA attacker for $1n$-KSS that requests at most q_s and q_h signing and, respectively, random oracle queries. Also, let ε be its success probability and τ its running time.

In order to make $\mathcal{A}$ work properly we simulate the random oracles that correspond to each hash function (see Algorithm 1) and the signing oracle (see Algorithm 2). For simplicity we treat all the random oracles as one big random oracle $\mathcal{O}_H$ that takes as input the j-th query (i, L_j, m_j, r_j) and returns a random value corresponding to $H_i(L_j, m_j, r_j)$. Also, to avoid complicated suffixes y_0, for example, refers to the first public key from the current L_j.

Algorithm 1: Hashing oracle $\mathcal{O}_H$ simulation for all H_i.

Input: A hashing query (i, L_j, m_j, r_j) from $\mathcal{A}$

1 **if** $\exists h_j$ such that $\{L_j, m_j, r_j, h_j\} \in T_i$ **then**
2 $\quad$ $e \leftarrow h_j$
3 **else**
4 $\quad$ $e \xleftarrow{\$} \mathcal{C}$
5 $\quad$ Append $\{L_j, m_j, r_j, e\}$ to T_i
6 **end if**
7 **return** e

The signing oracle $\mathcal{O}_S$ fails and returns $\perp$ only if we cannot assign c_0 to $(L_j, m_j, e_{|L_j|-1})$ without causing an inconsistency in T_0. This event happens with probability at most q_h/q, where $q = 2^\lambda$. Thus, $\mathcal{O}_S$ is successful with probability at least $(1 - q_h/q)^{q_s} \geq 1 - q_h q_s/q$.

Let Θ and Ω be the random tapes given to $\mathcal{O}_S$ and $\mathcal{A}$. The adversary's success probability is taken over the space defined by Θ, Ω and $\mathcal{O}_H$. Let Σ be the set of $(\Theta, \Omega, \mathcal{O}_H)$ with which $\mathcal{A}$ successfully creates a forgery, while having access to a real signing oracle. Let $(m, c_0, \beta, \{s_i\}_{i \in [0,n')}, L)$ be $\mathcal{A}$'s forgery, where $|L| = n'$. Then T_{i+1} contains a query for (L, m, e_i) for all $i \in [0, n')$ with probability at least $1 - 1/c$, due to the ideal randomness of $\mathcal{O}_H$. Let $\Sigma' \subseteq \Sigma$ be the set of $(\Theta, \Omega, \mathcal{O}_H)$ with which $\mathcal{A}$ successfully creates a forgery, while having access only to the simulated oracle $\mathcal{O}_S$. Then, $Pr[(\Theta, \Omega, \mathcal{O}_H) \in \Sigma'] \geq \varepsilon'$, where $\varepsilon' = (1 - q_h q_s/q)(1 - 1/c)\varepsilon$.

Since the queries form a ring, there exists at least an index $k \in [0, n')$ such that the u query $Q_u = (k+1, L, m, e_k)$ and the v query $Q_v = (k, L, m, e_{k-1})$

Algorithm 2: Signing oracle $\mathcal{O}_S$ simulation.

Input: A signature query (m_j, L_j) from $\mathcal{A}$

1 $c_0, \beta \xleftarrow{\$} \mathcal{C}$
2 **for** $i \in [0, |L_j|)$ **do**
3 $\quad$ $s_i \xleftarrow{\$} \mathbb{G}_i$
4 $\quad$ $e_i \leftarrow [s_i]_i \otimes_i y_i^{c_i - \beta}$
5 $\quad$ **if** $i \neq |L_j| - 1$ **then**
6 $\quad$ $\quad$ $c_{i+1} \leftarrow H_{i+1}(L_j, m_j, e_i)$
7 $\quad$ **end if**
8 **end for**
9 **if** $\nexists h$ such that $\{L_j, m_j, e_{|L_j|-1}, h\} \in T_0$ **then**
10 $\quad$ Append $\{L_j, m_j, e_{|L_j|-1}, c_0\}$ to T_0
11 $\quad$ **return** $(c_0, \beta, \{s_i\}_{i \in [0, |L_j|)})$
12 **else**
13 $\quad$ **return** $\bot$
14 **end if**

---

satisfy $u \leq v$. Such a pair (u, v) is called a gap index. Remark that $u = v$ only when $n' = 1$. If there are two or more gap indices with regard to a signature, we only consider the smallest one.

We denote by $\Sigma'_{u,v}$ the set of $(\Theta, \Omega, \mathcal{O}_H)$ that yield the gap index (u, v). There are at most $C_2^{q_h} + C_1^{q_h} = q_h(q_h + 1)/2$ such sets. If we invoke $\mathcal{A}$ with randomly chosen $(\Theta, \Omega, \mathcal{O}_H)$ at most $1/\varepsilon'$ times, then we will find at least one $(\Theta, \Omega, \mathcal{O}_H) \in \Sigma'_{u,v}$ for some gap index (u, v) with probability $1 - (1 - \varepsilon')^{1/\varepsilon'} > 1 - exp(-1) > 3/5$.

We define the sets $GI = \{(u, v) \mid |\Sigma'_{u,v}|/|\Sigma'| \geq 1/(q_h(q_h + 1))\}$ and $B = \{(\Theta, \Omega, \mathcal{O}_H) \in \Sigma'_{u,v} \mid (u, v) \in GI\}$. Then, we have $Pr[B|\Sigma'] \geq 1/2$. Using the heavy row lemma we obtain that a triplet $(\Theta, \Omega, \mathcal{O}_H)$ that yields a successful run of $\mathcal{A}$ is in B with probability at least $1/2$.

Let $\mathcal{O}_{H'}$ be the identical to $\mathcal{O}_H$ except for the Q_v query to which $\mathcal{O}_{H'}$ responds with a random element $c'_k \neq c_k$. Then according to the heavy row lemma, with probability $1/2$, $(\Theta, \Omega, \mathcal{O}_{H'})$ satisfies $Pr[(\Theta, \Omega, \mathcal{O}_{H'}) \in \Sigma'_{u,v}] = \varepsilon''/2$, where $\varepsilon'' = \varepsilon'/(2q_h(q_h + 1))$. Hence, if we run $\mathcal{A}$ at most $2/\varepsilon''$ times, then with probability $1/2 \cdot [1 - (1 - \varepsilon''/2)^{2/\varepsilon''}] > 1/2 \cdot (1 - exp(-1)) > 3/10$ we will find at least one c'_k such that $(\Theta, \Omega, \mathcal{O}_{H'}) \in \Sigma'_{u,v}$. Since Q_u is queried before Q_v, e_k remains unchanged. Therefore we can compute

$$\tilde{x}_k = u_k^a \star_k \left(s_k'^{-1} \star_k s_k\right)^b,$$

where a and b are computed using Euclid's algorithm such that $\ell a + (c'_k - c_k)b = 1$. Note that

$$[s_k'^{-1} \star_k s_k]_k = [s_k'^{-1}]_k \otimes_k [s_k]_k$$
$$= y_k^{c'_k - \beta} \otimes_k ([\alpha]_k)^{-1} \otimes_k [\alpha]_k \otimes_k y_k^{-c_k + \beta}$$
$$= y_k^{c'_k - c_k}$$

and thus

$$
\begin{aligned}
[\tilde{x}_k]_k &= [u_k^a \star_k (s_k'^{-1} \star_k s_k)^b]_k \\
&= ([u_k]_k)^a \otimes_k ([s_k'^{-1} \star_k s_k]_k)^b \\
&= (y_k^\ell)^a \otimes_k (y_k^{c_k' - c_k})^b \\
&= y_k.
\end{aligned}
$$

The overall success probability is $9/100 = 3/5 \cdot 1/2 \cdot 3/10$ and $\mathcal{A}$ is invoked at most $1/\varepsilon' + 2/\varepsilon''$ times. □

3.3 Concrete Examples

All Discrete Logarithm Case. Let $p = 2q + 1$ be a prime number such that q is also prime. Select an element $h \in \mathbb{H}_p$ of order q in some multiplicative group of order $p - 1$. The discrete logarithm of an element $z \in \mathbb{H}_p$ is an exponent x such that $z = h^x$. We further describe the parameters of the all discrete logarithm signature.

Define $(\mathbb{G}_i, \star_i) = (\mathbb{Z}_{q_i}, +)$ and $\mathbb{H}_i = \langle h_i \rangle$. The one-way group homomorphism is defined by $[x_i]_i = h_i^{x_i}$ and the challenge space $\mathcal{C}$ can be any arbitrary subset of $[0, q)$, where q is the smallest q_i from $\mathcal{L}$. Let 1_i be the neutral element of $\mathbb{H}_i$. Then the conditions of Theorem 2 are satisfied for

- $\ell = \prod_{i=0}^{n-1} q_i$, since for all $c \in \mathcal{C}$ we have $c < q \leq q_i$ and q_i are primes,
- for $u = 0$ we have $[u]_i = [0]_i = 1_i = y_i^\ell = (y_i^{\ell/q_i})^{q_i}$ since every element of $\mathbb{H}_i$ raised to the group order q_i is the neutral element 1_i.

All e^{th}-root Case. Let p and q be two safe prime numbers such that $(p - 1)/2$ and $(q - 1)/2$ are also prime. Compute $N = pq$ and choose a prime e such that $\gcd(e, \varphi(N)) = 1$. An eth-root of an element $z \in \mathbb{Z}_N^*$ is a base x such that $z = x^e$. Note that the eth-root is not unique. We further describe the parameters of the all e^{th}-root signature.

Define $(\mathbb{G}_i, \star_i) = (\mathbb{H}_i, \otimes_i) = (\mathbb{Z}_{N_i}^*, \cdot)$, where $N_i = p_i q_i$ and $\gcd(N_i, N_j) = 1$ for $i \neq j$. The one-way group homomorphism is defined by $[x_i]_i = x_i^{e_i}$ and the challenge space $\mathcal{C}$ can be any arbitrary subset of $[0, e)$, where e is the smallest e_i in $\mathcal{L}$. The conditions of Theorem 2 are satisfied for

- $\ell = \prod_{i=0}^{n-1} e_i$, since for all $c \in \mathcal{C}$ we have $c < e \leq e_i$ and e_i are primes,
- for $u_i = y_i^{\ell/e_i}$ we have $[u_i]_i = [y_i^{\ell/e_i}]_i = y_i^\ell$.

Mixture of Discrete Logarithm and e^{th}-root. For simplicity, we consider the case $n = 2$. Let $(\mathbb{G}_0, \star_0) = (\mathbb{Z}_q, +)$, $\mathbb{H}_0 = \langle h \rangle$ and $(\mathbb{G}_1, \star_1) = (\mathbb{H}_1, \otimes_1) = (\mathbb{Z}_N^*, \cdot)$. The one-way group homomorphisms are defined by $[x_0]_0 = h^{x_0}$ and $[x_1]_1 = x_1^e$. The challenge space $\mathcal{C}$ can be any arbitrary subset of $[0, s)$, where s is the smallest of q and e. The conditions of Theorem 2 are satisfied for

- $\ell = eq$, since for all $c \in \mathcal{C}$ we have $c < s \leq e$, $c < s \leq q$ and e, q are primes,
- for $u_0 = 0$ we have $[0]_0 = 1 = (y_0^e)^q$,
- for $u_1 = y_1^q$ we have $[y_1^q]_1 = y_1^\ell$.

All Discrete Logarithm Representation Case. Consider again a group of prime order $\mathbb{H}_p$ and select t elements $h_1, \ldots, h_t \in \mathbb{H}_p$ of order q. A discrete logarithm representation of an element $z \in \langle h_1, \ldots, h_t \rangle$ is a list of exponents $(x_1, \ldots, x_t)$ such that $z = h_1^{x_1} \ldots h_t^{x_t}$. Note that discrete logarithm representations are not unique. We further describe the parameters of the all discrete logarithm representation signature.

We define $\mathbb{G}_i = \mathbb{Z}_{q_i}^{t_i}$ with $\star$ defined as addition applied component-wise and $\mathbb{H}_i = \langle h_{i1}, \ldots, h_{it} \rangle$. Let $x_i = (x_{i1}, \ldots, x_{it})$. The one-way group homomorphism is defined by $[x_i]_i = h_{i1}^{x_{i1}} \ldots h_{it}^{x_{it}}$ and the challenge space $\mathcal{C}$ can be any arbitrary subset of $[0, q]$, where q is the smallest q_i from $\mathcal{L}$. Let 1_i be the neutral element of $\mathbb{H}_i$. Then the conditions of Theorem 2 are satisfied for $\ell = \prod_{i=0}^{n-1} q_i$ and for $u = (0, \ldots, 0)$.

Remark that if some t_is are one, we obtain a signature based on mixture of discrete logarithm and discrete logarithm representation problems.

All e^{th}-root Representation Case. Let again $N = pq$ and choose primes $e_1, \ldots, e_t$ such that $\gcd(e_i, \varphi(N)) = 1$, for $1 \le i \le t$. An eth-root representation of an element $z \in \mathbb{Z}_N^*$ is a list of bases $(x_1, \ldots, x_t)$ such that $z = x_1^{e_1} \ldots x_t^{e_t}$. Note that e^{th}-root representations are not unique. We further describe the parameters of the all e^{th}-root representation signature.

Let $N_i = p_i q_i$ and $\gcd(N_i, N_j) = 1$ for $i \ne j$. We define $\mathbb{G}_i = (\mathbb{Z}_{N_i}^*)^{t_i}$ with $\star_i$ defined as multiplication applied component-wise and $(\mathbb{H}_i, \otimes_i) = (\mathbb{Z}_{N_i}^*, \cdot)$. The one-way group homomorphism is defined by $[(x_{i1}, \ldots, x_{it})] = x_{i1}^{e_{i1}} \ldots x_{it}^{e_{it}}$ and the challenge space $\mathcal{C}$ can be any arbitrary subset of $[0, e)$, where e is a prime such that $\gcd(e, \phi(N_i)) = 1$. Since all exponents are coprime then we can compute integers such that $\alpha_{i1} e_{i1} + \ldots + \alpha_{it} e_{it} = 1$. The conditions of Theorem 2 are satisfied for

- $\ell = 1$,
- for $u_i = (y_i^{\alpha_{i1}}, \ldots, y_i^{\alpha_{im}})$ we have $[u_i]_i = y_i^{\alpha_{i1} e_{i1} + \ldots + \alpha_{it} e_{it}} = y_i$.

4 Concurrent Signatures with Key Separation

4.1 Description

Concurrent signatures allow *Alice* and *Bob* to produce two signatures such that both signatures are ambiguous from the eyes of a third party, but once Alice releases a secret keystone, both signatures become binding to their true signer. Such signatures are useful for contract signing and fair exchange protocols. Based on $1n$-KSS we introduce such a concurrent signature scheme denoted with $1n$-KSCS. Note that when both users use the same group for defining their underlying homomorphisms a more efficient construction is presented in Appendix B.

As before, $\mathcal{C}$ denotes the challenge space and c its cardinality. The $1n$-KSCS scheme uses three cryptographic hash functions $H_k, H_A, H_B : \{0,1\}^* \to \mathcal{C}$. The detailed protocol is presented in Fig. 2

Alice

Bob

$$k \xleftarrow{\$} \{0,1\}^*$$
%*KeyGen*
$$f \leftarrow H_k(k)$$
%*aSign*
$$t \xleftarrow{\$} \mathbb{G}_B, s_A \xleftarrow{\$} \mathbb{G}_A$$
$$f_A \leftarrow H_B\left(m_B, [t]_B\right)$$
$$e_A \leftarrow f_A - f \bmod c$$
$$f_B \leftarrow H_A\left(m_B, [s_A]_A \otimes_A y_A^{e_A}\right)$$
$$e_B \leftarrow f_B - f \bmod c$$
$$s_B \leftarrow t \star_B x_B^{-e_B}$$
$$\sigma_B \leftarrow \langle s_A, s_B, e_A, f \rangle$$

$\xleftarrow{\quad \sigma_B \quad}$

%*aVerify*
$$T_A \leftarrow H_A\left(m_B, [s_A]_A \otimes_A y_A^{e_A}\right)$$
$$S \leftarrow T_A - f \bmod c$$
$$T_B \leftarrow H_B\left(m_B, [s_B]_B \otimes_B y_B^{S}\right)$$
if $T_B \neq e_A + f \bmod c$ then **abort**
%*aSign*
$$u \xleftarrow{\$} \mathbb{G}_A, v_B \xleftarrow{\$} \mathbb{G}_B$$
$$g_B \leftarrow H_A\left(m_A, [u]_A\right)$$
$$h_B \leftarrow g_B - f \bmod c$$
$$g_A \leftarrow H_B\left(m_A, [v_B]_B \otimes_B y_B^{h_b}\right)$$
$$h_A \leftarrow g_A - f \bmod c$$
$$v_A \leftarrow u \star_A x_A^{-h_A}$$
$$\sigma_A \leftarrow \langle v_A, v_B, h_A, f \rangle$$

$\xrightarrow{\quad \sigma_A \quad}$

%*aVerify*
$$W_A \leftarrow H_A\left(m_A, [v_A]_A \otimes_A y_A^{h_A}\right)$$
$$Z \leftarrow W_A - f \bmod c$$
$$W_B \leftarrow H_B\left(m_B, [v_B]_B \otimes_B y_B^{Z}\right)$$
if $W_B \neq h_A + f \bmod c$ then **abort**

$\xleftarrow{\quad k \quad}$

Fig. 2. Key separation concurrent signature.

Correctness. If the signature $\langle s_A, e_A, f \rangle$ is generated according to the scheme, it is easy to see that

$$[v_A]_A \otimes_A y_B^{h_A} = [u]_A \otimes_A [x_A]_A^{-g_A+f} \otimes y_A^{g_A-f} = [u]_A.$$

Similarly, we can show correctness for *Bob*'s side.

4.2   Security Analysis

The following theorem is a direct consequence of Theorem 1.

Theorem 3. *The 1n-KSCS scheme satisfies the concurrent signature ambiguity property in the ROM.*

Theorem 4. *If the following statements are true*

- *an* EUF-CS *attack on the 1n-KSCS has non-negligible probability of success in the ROM,*
- *an* $\ell \in \mathbb{Z}$ *is known such that* $\gcd(c_0 - c_1, \ell) = 1$ *for all* $c_0, c_1 \in \mathcal{C}$ *with* $c_0 \neq c_1$,
- *for* $i \in \{A, B\}$, $u_i \in \mathbb{G}_i$ *are known such that* $[u_i]_i = y_i^\ell$,

then either $[\cdot]_A$ *or* $[\cdot]_B$ *can be inverted in polynomial time.*

Proof. Let $\mathcal{A}$ be an efficient EUF-CS attacker for 1n-KSCS and let ε be its success probability. We split the proof into three cases: $\mathcal{A}$ does not have access to the participants' secret keys, $\mathcal{A} = Bob$ and $\mathcal{A} = Alice$.

First Case. The challenger generates a set of participants U, where $|U| = \rho$ and ρ is the result of a polynomial function in λ. Then the challenger chooses $\gamma_A \neq \gamma_B \xleftarrow{\$} [0, \rho)$. For each participant P_i, $i \neq \gamma_a, \gamma_B$, $\mathcal{T}$ selects the associated public parameters (in accordance to the security parameter λ) and generates their secret and public keys (x_i, y_i). For $C = P_{\gamma_A}$ the challenger sets the public parameters to $(\mathbb{G}_A, [\cdot]_A, H_A)$ and the public key $y_{\gamma_A} = y_A$. Similarly for we set $D = P_{\gamma_B}$'s parameters.

To make $\mathcal{A}$ work properly we must simulate all the oracles which $\mathcal{A}$ can query. Hence, the random oracles H_A and H_B can be simulated using Algorithm 1, where we set $\mathcal{L} = \emptyset$, $i = 0$ for A and $i = 1$ for B. We change the list notations from T_0 and T_1 to T_A and T_B. In the case of H_k, the simulation is similar to Algorithm 1. Thus, instead of querying (i, L_j, m_j, r_j), the adversary can query any message M and the algorithm will store its answers in list denoted T_k. When $\mathcal{A}$ makes a *KeyGen* query, $\mathcal{T}$ randomly generates a k and return $f \leftarrow H_k(k)$. Note that the *KeyGen* oracle is actually a sublist of T_k, but the challenger is required to answer *KeyReveal* queries. Hence, when $\mathcal{A}$ requests the keystone associated to an $f \in \mathcal{C}$, we search T_k for a pair $\{k, f\}$ and if it exists we return k, otherwise we return invalid. The simulation of *aSign* queries can be achieved using Algorithm 2 where β is not chosen randomly, but is set to f. Finally, when an *SKExtract* query for a public key is made, $\mathcal{T}$ respond with the associated secret key, except in the case y_C, y_D, when he aborts.

There are two possible situations where our simulation fails. When $\mathcal{O}_S$ causes inconsistencies in $\mathcal{O}_H$ or $\mathcal{A}$ asks the secret keys for user C or user D. The first event does not happen with probability $1 - q_h q_s / q$, where $q = 2^\lambda$, and q_s and q_h are the number of signing queries and random oracle queries to H_A and H_B. The probability for the second event not happening is $1 - 2/\rho$. Let $\varepsilon' = 2/\rho(1 - q_h q_s / q)(1 - 2/\rho)(1 - 1/c)\varepsilon$. Then, if we run $\mathcal{A}$ at most $1/\varepsilon'$ with probability $3/5$ $\mathcal{A}$ will output a forgery $\sigma = \langle s_C, s_D, e, f \rangle$, for a message m.

Note that in this case $\mathcal{A}$ did not make *SKExtract* queries for C and D, and the signature is not produced by an *aSign* query. In other words $\mathcal{A}$ breaks the unforgeability of the 1n-KSS scheme. Hence, according to Theorem 1 $\mathcal{A}$ inverted either $[\cdot]_A$ or $[\cdot]_B$.

Second Case. Now, let us see what happens when $\mathcal{A}$ plays the role of *Alice*. In contrast with the first case, the challenger only chooses $\gamma_B \xleftarrow{\$} [0, \rho)$ and then sets D's public parameters to $(\mathbb{G}_B, [\cdot]_B, H_B)$ and the public key $y_{\gamma_B} = y_B$.

The probability of $\mathcal{A}$ not asking the secret key for user D is $1 - 1/\rho$. Let $\varepsilon'' = 1/\rho(1 - q_h q_s/q)(1 - 1/\rho)(1 - 1/c)\varepsilon$. Then, if we run $\mathcal{A}$ at most $1/\varepsilon''$ with probability $3/5$ $\mathcal{A}$ will output a forgery $\sigma = \langle s_A, s_D, e_A, f \rangle$, for a message m. According to the heavy row lemma with probability $1/2$ we are on situated on a heavy row $\mathcal{H}$.

Let $T_A \leftarrow H_A(m, [s_A]_A \otimes_A y_A^{e_A})$. Define $\mathcal{O}_{H'}$ as a random oracle identical to $\mathcal{O}_H$ except for the $(0, m, [s_A]_A \otimes_A y_A^{e_A})$ query to which $\mathcal{O}_{H'}$ responds with a random element $T'_A \neq T_A$. We restart $\mathcal{A}$ at most $2/\varepsilon'$ and with a probability of $1/2 \cdot (1 - (1 - \varepsilon'/2)^{2/\varepsilon'}) > 3/10$ we will be situated on $\mathcal{H}$. Hence, we obtain a new forgery $\sigma' = \langle s'_A, s'_D, e'_A, f' \rangle$.

Note that $T_A = e_A + f \neq e'_A + f' = T'_A$. If $e_A = e'_A$ then $f \neq f'$, so these values must have been computed before the relevant H queries and satisfy $f = T_A - e_A$ and $f' = T'_A - e'_A$. However, f is also an output of H_K and the probability that an output from some H_K query and some H query matches is at most $q_h q_k/q$, where q_k is the number of random oracle queries to H_K. Hence, with probability $1 - q_h q_k/q$ we have $f = f'$ and $e_A \neq e'_A$. In this case, using techniques similar to Theorem 2's proof we manage to find a preimage of $[\cdot]_B$.

Third Case. The proof is similar to the second case and thus is omitted.   □

Theorem 5. *The 1n-KSCS scheme is fair in the ROM.*

Proof. The challenger generates a set of participants U, where $|U| = \rho$ and ρ is a polynomial function in λ. For each participant $\mathcal{T}$ selects the associated public parameters (in accordance to the security parameter λ) and generates their secret and public keys (x_i, y_i). We simulate the adversary's random oracles, and the *KeyGen* and *KeyReveal* algorithms as in Theorem 4's proof. Also, the challenger responds to *aSign* and *SKExtract* queries using its knowledge of the private keys. In the final stage of the fairness game, $\mathcal{A}$ outputs a signature $\sigma = \langle s, e, f \rangle$.

In the first case f was obtained by a *KeyGen* query, but no *KeyReveal* query was made for f. Since H_K is a random oracle, this event happens with probability q_k/q. Thus, is negligible.

In the second case (k, σ) is accepted by the *Verify* algorithm and $\mathcal{A}$ manages to produce a second signature $\sigma' = \langle s', e', f \rangle$ that is accepted by the *aVerify* algorithm, but (k, σ') is rejected by the *Verify* algorithm. Since, (k, σ) is accepted by *Verify*, we have $f = KeyGen(k)$. Since σ and σ' share the value f, we must have that (k, σ') is also accepted by the *Verify* algorithm. This is a contradiction.

□

5   Conclusion

Our concurrent signature protocol is the abstraction of a large class of protocols that allow users with independently selected underlying problems to commonly produce an ambiguous signature. We have managed to relate the presented protocol's security to the hardness of inverting one-way homomorphisms. Note that the presented list of homomorphisms examples is by no means exhaustive.

A   1-out-of-n Signatures Without Key Separation

A.1   Description

In this section we present a more efficient 1-out-of-n signature. This signature only works when all the participants use the same underlying commutative group. We will denote the following signature with $1n$-NKSS.

$Setup(\lambda)$: Choose two commutative groups $\mathbb{G}$, $\mathbb{H}$, a homomorphism $[\cdot] : \mathbb{G} \to \mathbb{H}$ and a hash function $H : \{0,1\}^* \to C \subseteq \mathbb{N}$. Note that we require that $|\mathbb{G}| \geq 2^\lambda$.

For each user, choose $x_i \xleftarrow{\$} \mathbb{G}$ and compute $y_i \leftarrow [x_i]$. Output the public key $pk_i = y_i$. The secret key is $sk_i = x_i$.

$Listing()$: Collect the public keys and randomly shuffle them. Store the result into a list $\mathcal{L} = \{y_j\}_{j \in [0,n)}$ and output $\mathcal{L}$.

$Sign(m, sk_k, \mathcal{L})$: To sign a message $m \in \{0,1\}^*$, first generate the random elements $\alpha \xleftarrow{\$} \mathbb{G}$ and $c_j \xleftarrow{\$} C$, where $j \in [0,n) \setminus \{k\}$. Then compute

$$z \leftarrow [\alpha] \otimes y_0^{c_0} \otimes \ldots \otimes y_{k-1}^{c_{k-1}} \otimes y_{k+1}^{c_{k+1}} \otimes \ldots \otimes y_{n-1}^{c_{n-1}}$$

$$c \leftarrow H(\mathcal{L}, m, z)$$

$$c_k \leftarrow c - c_0 - \ldots - c_{k-1} - c_{k+1} - \ldots - c_{n-1} \bmod c$$

$$s \leftarrow \alpha \star x_k^{-c_k}.$$

Output the signature $(s, \mathcal{W})$, where $\mathcal{W} = \{c_j\}_{j \in [0,n)}$.

$Verify(m, s, \mathcal{W}, \mathcal{L})$: Compute the values $u \leftarrow \sum_{j=0}^{n-1} c_j \bmod c$ and $v \leftarrow [s] \otimes (\otimes_{j=0}^{n-1} y_j^{c_j})$. Output true if and only if $u \equiv H(\mathcal{L}, m, v) \bmod c$. Otherwise, output false.

Correctness. If the pair $(s, \mathcal{W})$ is generated according to the scheme, it is easy to see that

$$v = [s] \otimes (\otimes_{j=0}^{n-1} y_j^{c_j}) = [\alpha] \otimes [x_k]^{-c_k} \otimes (\otimes_{j=0}^{n-1} y_j^{c_j}) = z$$

and

$$u \equiv \sum_{j=0}^{n-1} c_j \equiv c \equiv H(\mathcal{L}, m, z) \equiv H(\mathcal{L}, m, v) \bmod c.$$

A.2   Security Analysis

Theorem 6's proof is similar to Theorem 1's proof and thus is omitted.

Theorem 6. *The 1n-NKSS scheme is perfectly signer ambiguous.*

Theorem 7. *If the following statements are true*

- *an EUF-CMCPA attack on the 1n-NKSS has non-negligible probability of success in the ROM,*
- *an $\ell \in \mathbb{Z}$ is known such that $\gcd(c_0 - c_1, \ell) = 1$ for all $c_0, c_1 \in \mathcal{C}$ with $c_0 \neq c_1$,*
- *for all i values, $u_i \in \mathbb{G}$ are known such that $[u_i] = y_i^\ell$,*

then the homomorphism $[\cdot]$ can be inverted in polynomial time.

Proof (sketch). In order to make $\mathcal{A}$ work properly we simulate the random oracle that correspond to the hash function (see Algorithm 1 with i always set to 0) and the signing oracle (see Algorithm 3). Note that $\mathcal{A}$ requests at most q_s and q_h signing and, respectively, random oracle queries.

The signing oracle $\mathcal{O}_S$ fails and returns $\perp$ only if we cannot assign c to (L_j, m_j, e) without causing an inconsistency in T_0. Thus, $\mathcal{O}_S$ is successful with probability at least $(1 - q_h/q)^{q_s} \geq 1 - q_h q_s/q$. The success probability of $\mathcal{A}$ in the simulated environment is $(1 - q_h q_s/q)\varepsilon$, where ε is $\mathcal{A}$'s success probability.

Let $(m, s, \{c_i\}_{i \in [0, n')}, L)$ be $\mathcal{A}$'s forgery, where $|L| = n'$. Define $z \leftarrow [s] \otimes (\otimes_{i=0}^{n'-1} y_i^{c_i})$. Due to the ideal randomness of $\mathcal{O}_H$, $\mathcal{A}$ queries $\mathcal{O}_H$ on (L, m, z) with probability $1 - 1/c$. Let $k \in [0, n')$ be the index of the user associated with the forgery. Then, according to Theorem 6, $\mathcal{A}$ will guess k with a probability of $1/n'$. If we invoke $\mathcal{A}$ at most $1/\varepsilon'$ times, where $\varepsilon' = n'(1 - q_h q_s/q)(1 - 1/c)\epsilon$, then we will find at least one $(\Theta, \Omega, \mathcal{O}_H)$ for which $\mathcal{A}$ knows k with probability $3/5$. According to the heavy row lemma we are situated on a heavy row $\mathcal{H}$ with probability $1/2$.

Define $\mathcal{O}_{H'}$ as a random oracle identical to $\mathcal{O}_H$ except for the (L, m, z) query to which $\mathcal{O}_{H'}$ responds with a random element $c' \neq c$. We rewind the simulation and run $\mathcal{A}$ at most $2/\varepsilon'$ times, but with access to $\mathcal{O}_{H'}$ instead of $\mathcal{O}_H$. We will be situated on $\mathcal{H}$ with a probability of $3/10$. Now we can compute

$$\tilde{x}_k = u^a \star (s'^{-1} \star s)^b,$$

where a and b are computed using Euclid's algorithm such that $\ell a + (c' - c)b = 1$. As in Theorem 2's proof, we obtain $[\tilde{x}_k] = y_k$.

The overall success probability is $9/200 = 3/5 \cdot 3/10$ and $\mathcal{A}$ is invoked at most $3/\varepsilon'$ times. $\square$

Algorithm 3: Signing oracle $\mathcal{O}_S$ simulation.

Input: A signature query (m_j, L_j) from $\mathcal{A}$

1 **for** $i \in [0, |L_j|)$ **do**
2     $s_i \xleftarrow{\$} \mathbb{G}$
3     $c_i \xleftarrow{\$} \mathcal{C}$
4     $e_i \leftarrow [s_i] \otimes y_i^{c_i}$
5 **end for**
6 $s \leftarrow s_0 \star \ldots \star s_{|L_j|-1}$
7 $c \leftarrow c_0 + \ldots + c_{|L_j|-1}$
8 $e \leftarrow e_0 \otimes \ldots \otimes e_{|L_j|-1}$
9 **if** $\nexists h$ such that $\{L_j, m_j, e, h\} \in T_0$ **then**
10   Append $\{L_j, m_j, e, c\}$ to T_0
11   **return** $(s, \{c_i\}_{i \in [0,|L_j|)})$
12 **else**
13   **return** $\bot$
14 **end if**

B   Same Group 1-out-of-n Concurent Signature

B.1   Description

Based on the $1n$-NKSS signature we introduce a more efficient concurrent signature ($1n$-NKSCS) in the non-separable model. In this case, the scheme only uses two cryptographic hash functions $H_1, H_2 : \{0,1\}^* \to \mathcal{C}$. The detailed protocol is presented in Fig. 3.

Correctness. If the signature $\langle s_A, e_A, f \rangle$ is generated according to the scheme, it is easy to see that

$$[s_A] \otimes y_A^{e_A} \otimes y_B^f = [t_A] \otimes [x_A]^{-e_A} \otimes y_A^{e_A} \otimes y_B^f = [t_A] \otimes y_B^f.$$

Similarly, we can show correctness for *Bob*'s side.

B.2   Security Analysis

Theorem 8 is a direct consequence of Theorem 6 and Theorems 9 and 10's proofs are omitted due to their similarity to Theorems 4 and 5's proofs.

Theorem 8. *The $1n$-NKSCS scheme satisfies the concurrent signature ambiguity property in the ROM.*

Theorem 9. *Let $i \in \{A, B\}$. If the following statements are true*

- *an EUF-CS attack on the $1n$-NKSCS has non-negligible probability of success in the ROM,*
- *an $\ell \in \mathbb{Z}$ is known such that $\gcd(c_0 - c_1, \ell) = 1$ for all $c_0, c_1 \in \mathcal{C}$ with $c_0 \neq c_1$,*
- *for all i values, $u_i \in \mathbb{G}$ are known such that $[u_i] = y_i^\ell$,*

then the homomorphism $[\cdot]$ can be inverted in polynomial time.

Theorem 10. *The $1n$-NKSCS scheme is fair in the ROM.*

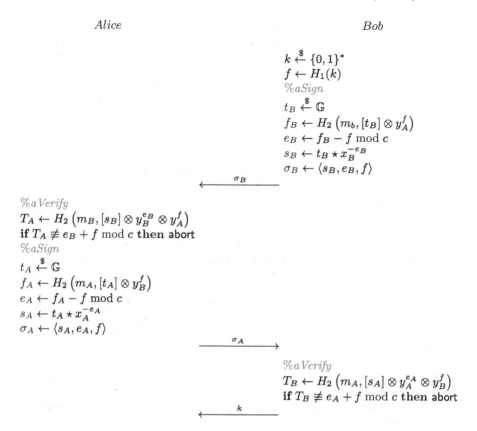

Fig. 3. Same group concurrent signature.

References

1. Abe, M., Ohkubo, M., Suzuki, K.: 1-out-of-n Signatures from a Variety of Keys. In: Zheng, Y. (ed.) ASIACRYPT 2002. LNCS, vol. 2501, pp. 415–432. Springer, Heidelberg (2002). https://doi.org/10.1007/3-540-36178-2_26
2. Asokan, N., Schunter, M., Waidner, M.: Optimistic protocols for fair exchange. In: CCS 1997, pp. 7–17. ACM (1997)
3. Baum-Waidner, B., Waidner, M.: Round-optimal and abuse-free optimistic multi-party contract signing. In: Montanari, U., Rolim, J.D.P., Welzl, E. (eds.) ICALP 2000. LNCS, vol. 1853, pp. 524–535. Springer, Heidelberg (2000). https://doi.org/10.1007/3-540-45022-X_44
4. Bellare, M., Rogaway, P.: Random oracles are practical: a paradigm for designing efficient protocols. In: CCS 1993, pp. 62–73. ACM (1993)
5. Cachin, C., Camenisch, J.: Optimistic fair secure computation. In: Bellare, M. (ed.) CRYPTO 2000. LNCS, vol. 1880, pp. 93–111. Springer, Heidelberg (2000). https://doi.org/10.1007/3-540-44598-6_6
6. Chen, L., Kudla, C., Paterson, K.G.: Concurrent signatures. In: Cachin, C., Camenisch, J.L. (eds.) EUROCRYPT 2004. LNCS, vol. 3027, pp. 287–305. Springer, Heidelberg (2004). https://doi.org/10.1007/978-3-540-24676-3_18

7. Ferradi, H., Géraud, R., Maimuţ, D., Naccache, D., Pointcheval, D.: Legally fair contract signing without keystones. In: Manulis, M., Sadeghi, A.-R., Schneider, S. (eds.) ACNS 2016. LNCS, vol. 9696, pp. 175–190. Springer, Cham (2016). https://doi.org/10.1007/978-3-319-39555-5_10

8. Garay, J., MacKenzie, P., Prabhakaran, M., Yang, K.: Resource fairness and composability of cryptographic protocols. In: Halevi, S., Rabin, T. (eds.) TCC 2006. LNCS, vol. 3876, pp. 404–428. Springer, Heidelberg (2006). https://doi.org/10.1007/11681878_21

9. Garay, J.A., Jakobsson, M., MacKenzie, P.: Abuse-free optimistic contract signing. In: Wiener, M. (ed.) CRYPTO 1999. LNCS, vol. 1666, pp. 449–466. Springer, Heidelberg (1999). https://doi.org/10.1007/3-540-48405-1_29

10. Goldwasser, S., Levin, L.: Fair computation of general functions in presence of immoral majority. In: Menezes, A.J., Vanstone, S.A. (eds.) CRYPTO 1990. LNCS, vol. 537, pp. 77–93. Springer, Heidelberg (1991). https://doi.org/10.1007/3-540-38424-3_6

11. Guillou, L.C., Quisquater, J.-J.: A practical zero-knowledge protocol fitted to security microprocessor minimizing both transmission and memory. In: Barstow, D., et al. (eds.) EUROCRYPT 1988. LNCS, vol. 330, pp. 123–128. Springer, Heidelberg (1988). https://doi.org/10.1007/3-540-45961-8_11

12. Maimuţ, D., Teşeleanu, G.: A unified security perspective on legally fair contract signing protocols. In: Lanet, J.-L., Toma, C. (eds.) SECITC 2018. LNCS, vol. 11359, pp. 477–491. Springer, Cham (2019). https://doi.org/10.1007/978-3-030-12942-2_35

13. Maurer, U.: Unifying zero-knowledge proofs of knowledge. In: Preneel, B. (ed.) AFRICACRYPT 2009. LNCS, vol. 5580, pp. 272–286. Springer, Heidelberg (2009). https://doi.org/10.1007/978-3-642-02384-2_17

14. Micali, S.: Simple and fast optimistic protocols for fair electronic exchange. In: PODC 2003, pp. 12–19. ACM (2003)

15. Ohta, K., Okamoto, T.: On concrete security treatment of signatures derived from identification. In: Krawczyk, H. (ed.) CRYPTO 1998. LNCS, vol. 1462, pp. 354–369. Springer, Heidelberg (1998). https://doi.org/10.1007/BFb0055741

16. Pinkas, B.: Fair secure two-party computation. In: Biham, E. (ed.) EUROCRYPT 2003. LNCS, vol. 2656, pp. 87–105. Springer, Heidelberg (2003). https://doi.org/10.1007/3-540-39200-9_6

17. Schnorr, C.P.: Efficient identification and signatures for smart cards. In: Brassard, G. (ed.) CRYPTO 1989. LNCS, vol. 435, pp. 239–252. Springer, New York (1990). https://doi.org/10.1007/0-387-34805-0_22

A Generic Construction of Fuzzy Signature

Jie Song[1] and Yunhua Wen[1,2(✉)]

[1] School of Computer Science and Technology, Donghua University,
Shanghai 200240, China
2202559@mail.dhu.edu.cn, yhwen@dhu.edu.cn
[2] State Key Laboratory of Information Security, Institute of Information
Engineering, Chinese Academy of Sciences, Beijing 100093, China

Abstract. *Fuzzy signature* is a signature scheme in which the signing key is no longer uniformly generated nor precisely reproducible but a fuzzy string with enough entropy such as biometric information. In this paper, we give a variant definition of fuzzy signature and propose a generic construction of fuzzy signature which uses a fuzzy extractor and a signature scheme with simple key generation process as building blocks. Meanwhile, we give two instantiations of our generic construction. The first instantiation results in a fuzzy signature scheme which is secure under the computational Diffie-Hellman (CDH) assumption over bilinear groups in the standard model. The second instantiation results in a fuzzy signature that is secure in the random oracle model under the worst-case hardness of the $\widetilde{O}(n^{1.5})$-SIVP problem in general lattices. Moreover, compared with previous work, our fuzzy signatures have weaker requirements for the fuzzy signing key, which makes our fuzzy signatures more practical.

Keywords: Digital signature · Fuzzy extractor · Fuzzy signature

1 Introduction

The security of cryptographic primitives depends on the security of private key. The private key generally needs to be uniformly distributed and carefully kept. Once the private key is leaked, there is no security at all. Private key is hard to remember, and securely keeping it puts a burden on the user. Since biometric information is inherent and unique, one of the promising approaches to fundamentally solve this problem is to use biometric information (e.g., fingerprint [11], face and iris [4]) as a cryptographic private key. However, since biometric data is not uniformly distributed and fluctuates each time when it is captured, it cannot be used directly as a cryptographic key.

A lot of works has been devoted to researching the application of biometric information in cryptography. For example, fuzzy extractor [6], fuzzy signature [14] and biometric-based remote user authentication [1,2,7].

In this paper, we will focus on the study of fuzzy signature [13]. *Fuzzy signature* is a digital signature in which the signing key need not to be uniformly

© Springer Nature Switzerland AG 2021
Y. Yu and M. Yung (Eds.): Inscrypt 2021, LNCS 13007, pp. 23–41, 2021.
https://doi.org/10.1007/978-3-030-88323-2_2

distributed or accurate reproducible. We call such signing key as fuzzy signing key. With fuzzy signature people can use his/her biometric characteristics (such as retina, iris, face and fingerprint) as the fuzzy signing key to sign messages. In fuzzy signature, the key generation algorithm $\mathsf{KeyGen_F}$ takes the fuzzy signing key sk (a sample of a user's biometric characteristic) as input and outputs a verification key vk. The signing algorithm $\mathsf{Sign_F}$ takes the fuzzy signing key sk' (another sample of the same biometric characteristic) and a message m as input, and outputs a signature σ. The verification algorithm $\mathsf{Verify_F}$ on input vk, m, σ outputs 0/1 meaning σ is invalid or valid. If the two fuzzy signing keys sk' and sk are close enough, the signature σ will be verified as valid by the verification key vk, where vk is generated by sk.

Takahashi et al. [13] gave the formal definition of fuzzy signature. They gave a generic construction of fuzzy signature based on a signature scheme with certain homomorphic properties regarding keys and signatures, and a tool called linear sketch. They showed a concrete instantiation of their generic construction based on the Waters signature scheme [15]. However, the resulting fuzzy signature has a weakness that the fuzzy signing key sk needs to be uniformly distributed. In another word, if a user wants to use his/her biometric characteristic such as fingerprint as the fuzzy signing key, then the sample of his/her fingerprint is assumed to be uniformly distributed. It seems impossible that samples from biometric characteristics follow the uniform distribution. In order to solve this problem, in paper [9], Matsuda et al. gave a new construction of fuzzy signature by relaxing the requirements of the building blocks in [13]. By instantiation, they got a fuzzy signature which does not need the fuzzy signing key uniform anymore, but the resulting fuzzy signature is secure only in the random oracle model.

Takahashi et al. also defined the security model of fuzzy signature [13]. Recall that the key generation algorithm of fuzzy signature $\mathsf{KeyGen_F}$ on input a fuzzy signing key sk outputs a verification key vk and the signing algorithm $\mathsf{Sign_F}$ on input the fuzzy signing key sk' and a message m outputs a signature σ, where sk and sk' are two different samples of the same biometric characteristic. In their security model, it is required that the error distribution e between the two different samples sk and sk' is independent of the biometric characteristic. This requirement makes the fuzzy signature far from practical application because it seems impossible that the error distribution between two different samples is independent of the biometric characteristic. A natural question arises:

Is it possible to design a fuzzy signature which has a more practical requirement for the fuzzy signing key?

1.1 Our Contributions

We answer the above question in the affirmative. Our contributions can be listed as follows:

- We give a formal definition of fuzzy signature which is a little different from that by Takahashi et al. [14]. The difference between our fuzzy signature and Takahashi et al. is that when generating a signature of a message m, our signature algorithm needs both the fuzzy signing key sk and the verification key vk as input while Takahashi et al.'s does not need vk.

- We define a new security model of fuzzy signature which is called m-existentially unforgeable under chosen message attack (m-EUF-CMA) security. In this security model, we only require that the fuzzy signing key sk has entropy larger than m and the error distribution between different samples sk and sk' can be arbitrary depend on the biometric characteristic.

- We provide a generic construction of fuzzy signature based on a fuzzy extractor (FE) and a signature scheme (SIG) with a simple key generation process. The simple key generation process says that the key generation algorithm first picks a secret key uniformly at random from the secret key space, then computes the corresponding verification key deterministically from the secret key.

- We give two instantiations of our generic construction.
  - When instantiating SIG with the Waters signature scheme [15] and FE constructed in [6], we obtain a fuzzy signature scheme which is secure in the standard model under the computational Diffie-Hellman (CDH) assumption in bilinear groups and only assumes that the fuzzy signing key has enough entropy.
  - When instantiating SIG with the lattice-based signature constructed in [8] and FE constructed in [6], we obtain a fuzzy signature scheme which is secure in the random oracle model based on the worst-case hardness of the $\widetilde{O}(n^{1.5})$-SIVP problem in general lattices and only assumes that the fuzzy signing key has enough entropy.

Our fuzzy signatures have a weaker requirement for the fuzzy signing key, which makes the fuzzy signature more practical. In Table 1, we compare our work with previous fuzzy signature schemes.

Table 1. Comparison with some known fuzzy signature schemes. Let SK be the distribution of the fuzzy signing key and $|\mathcal{SK}|$ be the size of key space $\mathcal{SK}$. "Entropy Requirement" asks what is the entropy requirement for the fuzzy signing key. "Correlation" asks the relationship of error distribution e and the biometric characteristic W, where e is the error distribution between the fuzzy signing key sk and sk' (two samples of the same biometric characteristic W). "Assumption" asks which assumption the fuzzy signature is based on. "Standard Model" asks whether the fuzzy signature is secure in the standard model.

Fuzzy Signature Schemes	Entropy Requirement	Correlation	Assumption	Stantard Model
TMMHN[13]	$H_\infty(SK) = log\|\mathcal{SK}\|$	Independent	CDH	Yes
MTMH [9]	$H_\infty(SK) \geq$ m	Independent	DL	No
Our first instantiation	$H_\infty(SK) \geq$ m	Arbitrary	CDH	Yes
Our second instantiation	$H_\infty(SK) \geq$ m	Arbitrary	$\widetilde{O}(n^{1.5})$-SIVP	No

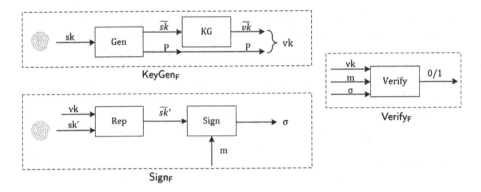

Fig. 1. The construction of fuzzy signature

1.2 Our Approach

Our construction makes use of a fuzzy extractor and a signature scheme with a simple key generation process. Recall that a fuzzy extractor consists of two efficient algorithms (Gen, Rep). The generation algorithm Gen on input a sample w of a biometric characteristic $\mathcal{W}$ (such as retina, iris, face and fingerprint) outputs a public helper string P together with an extracted string R. The reproduction algorithm Rep on input w' and the public helper string P will reproduce R if w' is close enough to w. The security of fuzzy extractor guarantees that R is (pseudo-)random if $\mathcal{W}$ has enough entropy. A signature scheme with a simple key generation process says that there exists a deterministic PPT algorithm KG such that the key generation algorithm KeyGen can be written as follows:

$$\mathsf{KeyGen} : [\ sk \leftarrow_\$ \mathcal{SK}; vk \leftarrow \mathsf{KG}(sk); \mathrm{Return}(vk, sk).\ ],$$

where $\mathcal{SK}$ is the secret key space of the signature.

Our generic construction of fuzzy signature is shown in Fig. 1 in which we omit the public parameters. More precisely,

- The key generation algorithm KeyGen$_\mathsf{F}$ on input the fuzzy signing key sk which is a sample of a biometric characteristic (e.g., fingerprint), outputs the verification key vk. It proceeds as follow, the fuzzy signing key sk is fed to the generation algorithm Gen of fuzzy extractor. The generation algorithm Gen outputs a public helper string P and a uniformly random string which will be served as the signing key $\widetilde{sk}$ of the underlying signature scheme (not fuzzy). The deterministic PPT algorithm KG on input $\widetilde{sk}$ outputs $\widetilde{vk}$. The verification key is $vk = (\widetilde{vk}, P)$.
- The signature algorithm Sign$_\mathsf{F}$ on input a fuzzy signing key sk' and the verification key vk will invoke the reproduction algorithm Rep to reproduce the signing key $\widetilde{sk}$ of the underlying signature scheme(not fuzzy) with the help of P, then use $\widetilde{sk}$ to sign the message m.

– The verification algorithm $\mathsf{Verify_F}$ on input (vk, m, σ), parses $vk = (\widetilde{vk}, P)$ and invokes the verification algorithm of the underlying signature scheme $b \leftarrow \mathsf{Verify}(\widetilde{vk}, m, \sigma)$.

Correctness. The key generation algorithm on input sk outputs a verification key vk. We need to show that for any sk' close enough to sk, the signature generated by sk' will be verified as valid. Observe that the signature algorithm $\mathsf{Sign_F}$ on input a fuzzy signing key sk' and the verification key vk will invoke the reproduction algorithm Rep to reproduce the signing key $\widetilde{sk}$ and use $\widetilde{sk}$ as the signing key to sign the message m. By the correctness of fuzzy extractor, if sk and sk' are close enough, then $\widetilde{sk}$ can be accurately reproduced, then by the correctness of the underlying signature scheme, the signature by sk' can be verified valid.

Security. The security of our generic construction of fuzzy signature scheme can be reduced to the security of the underlying signature scheme and the underlying fuzzy extractor. The security of underlying fuzzy extractor guarantees that if the input sk has enough entropy, then the extracted signing key $\widetilde{sk}$ is uniformly distributed. By the correctness of fuzzy extractor, if sk' is close enough to sk, then $\widetilde{sk}$ will always be accurately reproduced. Then the security of the fuzzy signature can be reduced to the security of the underlying signature scheme.

2 Preliminaries

Let $\mathbb{N}$, $\mathbb{Z}$ and $\mathbb{R}$ denote the sets of natural numbers, integers and real numbers, respectively. For a natural number $n \in \mathbb{N}$, we define $[n] := \{1, \cdots, n\}$. The notion "$x \leftarrow y$" denotes that y is (deterministically) assigned to x. For a finite set S, the notion "$|S|$" refers to the size of S, and the notion "$x \leftarrow_{\$} S$" refers to that x is uniformly chosen from S. For two bit-strings x and y, the notion $|x|$ refers to the bit length of x, and the notion $x \parallel y$ refers to the concatenation of x and y. "PPT" is short for probabilistic polynomial-time. If $\mathcal{A}$ is a probabilistic algorithm, the notion $y \leftarrow \mathcal{A}(x; r)$ refers to that $\mathcal{A}$ runs with input x and randomness r and outputs y. For a primitive XX and a security notion YY, by $\mathsf{Expt}^{\mathrm{YY}}_{\mathrm{XX}, \mathcal{A}}(k) \Rightarrow 1$, we mean that the security experiment outputs 1 after interacting with an adversary $\mathcal{A}$. By $\mathsf{Adv}^{\mathrm{YY}}_{\mathrm{XX}, \mathcal{A}}(k)$, we denote the advantage of a PPT adversary $\mathcal{A}$ and define $\mathsf{Adv}^{\mathrm{YY}}_{\mathrm{XX}}(\lambda) := \max_{\mathrm{PPT}\mathcal{A}} \mathsf{Adv}^{\mathrm{YY}}_{\mathrm{XX}, k}(k)$.

Definition 1 (Negligible function). *A function f is negligible if for every polynomial $p(\cdot)$ there exists an N such that for all integers $n > N$ it holds that $f(n) < \frac{1}{p(n)}$.*

Definition 2 (Metric spaces). *A metric space is a set $\mathcal{W}$ with a distance function $\mathsf{dis} : \mathcal{W} \times \mathcal{W} \rightarrow \mathbb{R}^+ = [0, \infty)$. For all $x, y, z \in \mathcal{W}$, the distance function should satisfy the following conditions:*

1. Reflexivity : $\mathsf{dis}(x, y) = 0$ if and only if $x = y$;

2. *Symmetry* : $\mathsf{dis}(x, y) = \mathsf{dis}(y, x)$;
3. *Triangle inequality* : $\mathsf{dis}(x, z) \leq \mathsf{dis}(x, y) + \mathsf{dis}(y, z)$.

We usually consider multi-dimensional metric spaces of form $\mathcal{W} = \mathcal{F}^n$ for some alphabet $\mathcal{F}$ (usually a finite filed $\mathcal{F}^p$) equipped with the Hamming distance. For any two element $x, y \in \mathcal{W}$, the Hamming distance $\mathsf{dis}(x, y)$ is the number of coordinates in which they differ. For an element $x \in \mathcal{W}$, let $\mathsf{dis}(x) := \mathsf{dis}(x, 0)$.

Definition 3 (Min-entropy). *[12] For a random variable* X, *the min-entropy of* X, *denoted by* $H_\infty(\mathsf{X})$, *is defined by*

$$H_\infty(\mathsf{X}) := -log_2(max_x \Pr[\mathsf{X} = x]).$$

Definition 4 (Average min-entropy). *[12] For two random variables* X *and* Y, *the average min-entropy of* X *given* Y, *denoted by* $\widetilde{H}_\infty(\mathsf{X}|\mathsf{Y})$, *is defined by*

$$\widetilde{H}_\infty(\mathsf{X}|\mathsf{Y}) := -log_2(\underset{y \leftarrow \mathsf{Y}}{E}[\underset{x \in \mathsf{X}}{max} \Pr[\mathsf{X} = x|\mathsf{Y} = y]]).$$

Definition 5 (Statistical distance). *The statistical distance between two probability distributions* A *and* B *is*

$$\mathbf{SD}(A, B) = \frac{1}{2}\sum_v |\Pr(A = v) - \Pr(B = v)|.$$

Definition 6 (Universal hash functions). *[3] A family of hash functions* $\mathcal{H}_\mathcal{I} = \{\mathsf{H}_i : \mathcal{X} \to \mathcal{Y}\}$ *is universal, if for all distinct* $x, x' \in \mathcal{X}$,

$$\Pr[\mathsf{H}_i : \mathsf{H}_i(x) = \mathsf{H}_i(x')] \leq \frac{1}{|\mathcal{Y}|},$$

where i *is uniformly chosen from* $\mathcal{I}$.

Definition 7 (Strong extractor). *[10] A function* $\mathsf{Ext} : \mathcal{X} \times \mathcal{I} \to \mathcal{T}$ *is an average-case* $(\mathcal{X}, \mathfrak{m}, \mathcal{T}, \varepsilon)$-*strong extractor with seed* $I \in \mathcal{I}$, *if for any variable* X *over* $\mathcal{X}$ *and any variable* Y *such that* $\widetilde{H}_\infty(X|Y) \geq \mathfrak{m}$, *we have*

$$\mathbf{SD}((\mathsf{Ext}(X, I), Y, I), (U, Y, I)) \leq \varepsilon,$$

where I *and* U *are uniformly distributed over* $\mathcal{I}$ *and* $\mathcal{T}$, *respectively.*

In particular, universal hash functions are average-case $(\mathcal{X}, \mathfrak{m}, \mathcal{T}, \varepsilon)$-strong extractors.

Definition 8 (Secure sketch). *[6] A* $(\mathcal{W}, \mathfrak{m}, \widetilde{\mathfrak{m}}, t)$-*secure sketch consists of a pair of PPT algorithms* $(\mathsf{SS}, \mathsf{Rec})$ *with the following specifications:*

- $\mathsf{SS}(w)$ *on input* $w \in \mathcal{W}$ *outputs a sketch* s.
- $\mathsf{Rec}(w', s)$ *on input* $w' \in \mathcal{W}$ *and a sketch* s *outputs* $\widetilde{w}$.

It also satisfies the following properties:

Correctness. *If* $\mathsf{dis}(w, w') \leq t$, *then* $w = \mathsf{Rec}(w', \mathsf{SS}(w))$.

Privacy. *For any distribution* W *over* $\mathcal{W}$, *if* $H_\infty(W) \geq \mathfrak{m}$, *then* $\tilde{H}_\infty(W|\mathsf{SS}(W)) \geq \tilde{\mathfrak{m}}$.

An instantiation of secure sketch is the syndrome-based secure sketch [5]. Recall that an efficiently decodable $[n, k, 2t + 1]_{\mathcal{F}}$-linear error correcting code $\mathcal{C}$ can correct up to t errors and it is a linear subspace of $\mathcal{F}^n$ of dimension k. The parity-check matrix of $\mathcal{C}$ is an $(n - k) \times n$ matirx H whose rows generate the orthogonal space $\mathcal{C}^\perp$. For any $v \in \mathcal{F}^n$, the syndrome of v is defined by $\mathsf{syn}(v) := Hv$. Note that $v \in \mathcal{C} \Leftrightarrow \mathsf{syn}(v) = 0$. For any $c \in \mathcal{C}$, $\mathsf{syn}(c + e) = \mathsf{syn}(c) + \mathsf{syn}(e) = \mathsf{syn}(e)$. A linear error-correcting code implies a syndrome-based secure sketch as shown below.

- $\mathsf{SS}(w) := \mathsf{syn}(w) = s$.
- $\mathsf{Rec}(w', s) := w' - \mathsf{Decode}(\mathsf{syn}(w') - s)$.

2.1 Bilinear Groups

We say that $\mathcal{BG} = (p, \mathbb{G}, \mathbb{G}_T, g, e)$ constitutes (symmetric) bilinear groups if p is a prime, $\mathbb{G}$ and $\mathbb{G}_T$ are cyclic groups with order p, g is a generator of $\mathbb{G}$, and $e : \mathbb{G} \times \mathbb{G} \rightarrow \mathbb{G}_T$ is an efficiently (in $|p|$) computable mapping satisfying the following two properties:

- **Bilinearity:** For all $g \in \mathbb{G}$ and $a, b \in \mathbb{Z}_p$, it holds that $e(g^a, g^b) = e(g, g)^{ab}$.
- **Non-degeneracy:** For all generators g of $\mathbb{G}$, $e(g, g) \in \mathbb{G}_T$ is not the identity element of $\mathbb{G}_T$.

For convenience, we denote by BGGen an algorithm (referred to as a "bilinear group generator") that, on input 1^k, outputs a description of bilinear groups $\mathcal{BG} = (p, \mathbb{G}, \mathbb{G}_T, g, e)$ such that $|p| = \Theta(k)$.

2.2 Signature Scheme

Definition 9 (Signature scheme). *A signature scheme* SIG *is a tuple of PPT algorithms* (Setup, KeyGen, Sign, Verify) *satisfying the following:*

- Setup(k) $\rightarrow$ pp. *The setup algorithm* Setup *takes a security parameter* k *as input, and outputs the public parameter* pp.
- KeyGen(pp) $\rightarrow$ (vk, sk). *The key generation algorithm* KeyGen *takes the public parameter* pp *as input, and outputs a verification/signing key pair* (vk, sk).
- Sign(pp, sk, m) $\rightarrow \sigma$. *The signing algorithm* Sign *takes the public parameter* pp, *the signing key* sk *and a message* m *from message space* $\mathcal{M}$ *as input, and outputs a signature* σ.
- Verify(pp, vk, m, σ) $\rightarrow$ 1/0. *The (deterministic) verification algorithm* Verify *takes the public parameter* pp, *a verification key* vk, *a message* m *and a signature* σ *as input, and outputs a bit* b, *with* b = 1 *meaning valid and* b = 0 *meaning invalid.*

Correctness. We require that for all $pp \leftarrow \mathsf{Setup}(k)$, $(vk, sk) \leftarrow \mathsf{KeyGen}(pp)$, and messages $m \in \mathcal{M}$, we have

$$\mathsf{Verify}(pp, vk, m, \mathsf{Sign}(pp, sk, m)) = 1.$$

Definition 10 (EUF-CMA security). *A signature scheme* SIG *is said to be existentially unforgeable under non-adaptive chosen message attack (EUF-CMA), if for all PPT adversaries* $\mathcal{A}$,

$$\mathsf{Adv}_{\mathsf{SIG},\mathcal{A}}^{EUF\text{-}CMA}(k) := \Pr[\ \mathsf{Expt}_{\mathsf{SIG},\mathcal{A}}^{EUF\text{-}CMA}(k) \Rightarrow 1\ ] \leqslant \mathsf{negl}(k).$$

Here $\mathsf{Expt}_{\mathsf{SIG},\mathcal{A}}^{EUF\text{-}CMA}(k)$ *is an experiment played between an adversary* $\mathcal{A}$ *and a challenger* $\mathcal{C}$ *as follows.*

$\underline{\mathsf{Expt}_{\mathsf{SIG},\mathcal{A}}^{EUF\text{-}CMA}(k):}$

1. *The challenger* $\mathcal{C}$ *invokes* $pp \leftarrow \mathsf{Setup}(k)$, *generates* $(vk, sk) \leftarrow \mathsf{KeyGen}(pp)$ *and initializes the set of chosen-message queries* $\mathcal{Q} = \emptyset$ *issued by the adversary. Subsequently, it returns* pp *and* vk *to* $\mathcal{A}$.
2. *The adversary* $\mathcal{A}$ *may adaptively make signing oracle queries of the following form*
   - $\mathcal{A}$ *sends a message* $m_i \in \mathcal{M}$ *to the challenger* $\mathcal{C}$.
   - $\mathcal{C}$ *invokes* $\sigma_i \leftarrow \mathsf{Sign}(pp, sk, m_i)$, *adds* m_i *to the set* $\mathcal{Q}$ *and returns* σ_i *to* $\mathcal{A}$.
3. *Finally,* $\mathcal{A}$ *submits a message-signature pair* (m^*, σ^*). *The experiment outputs 1 if* $m^* \notin \mathcal{Q} \wedge \mathsf{Verify}(pp, vk, m^*, \sigma^*) = 1$ *and 0 otherwise.*

Simple Key Generation Process. We will use signature schemes with a structural property which is called the *simple key generation process* property. Simple key generation process property says that the key generation algorithm KeyGen first picks a secret key sk uniformly at random from the secret key space, then computes the corresponding verification key vk deterministically from sk.

Definition 11 (Simple key generation process, [14]). *Let* $\mathsf{SIG} =$ $(\mathsf{Setup}, \mathsf{Ke\text{-}yGen}, \mathsf{Sign}, \mathsf{Verify})$ *be a signature scheme. We say* SIG *has a simple key generation process if each* pp *output by* Setup *specifies the secret key space* $\mathcal{SK}_{pp}$, *and there exists a deterministic PPT algorithm* KG *such that the key generation algorithm* $\mathsf{KeyGen}(pp)$ *can be written as follows:*

$$\mathsf{KeyGen}(pp) : [\ sk \leftarrow_\$ \mathcal{SK}_{pp}; vk \leftarrow \mathsf{KG}(pp, sk); Return\ (vk, sk).\ ].$$

2.3 Fuzzy Extractor

Definition 12 (Fuzzy extractor). *[6] An* $(\mathcal{W}, \mathfrak{m}, \mathcal{R}, t, \epsilon)$-*fuzzy extractor* $\mathsf{FE} =$ $(\mathsf{Init}, \mathsf{Gen}, \mathsf{Rep})$ *consists of three PPT algorithms:*

- $\mathsf{Init}(k) \rightarrow pp$. *The initialization algorithm* Init *takes a security parameter* k *as input, and outputs the public parameter* pp.

- $\mathsf{Gen}(pp, w) \rightarrow (P, R)$. *The generation algorithm* Gen *takes the public parameter* pp *and* $w \in \mathcal{W}$ *as input, and outputs a public helper string* P *and an extracted string* $R \in \mathcal{R}$.
- $\mathsf{Rep}(pp, P, w') \rightarrow R/\bot$. *The reproduction algorithm* Rep *takes* pp, P *and* $w' \in \mathcal{W}$ *as input, and outputs an extracted string* R *or* $\bot$.

Correctness. If $\mathsf{dis}(w, w') \leq t$, then for all $(R, P) \leftarrow \mathsf{Gen}(pp, w)$, it holds that $R \leftarrow \mathsf{Rep}(pp, P, w')$.

Security. Let W be a distribution on $\mathcal{W}$, if $H_\infty(W) \geq m$, then for all PPT adversaries $\mathcal{A}$,

$$\mathsf{Adv}^{\mathsf{ind}}_{\mathsf{FE}, \mathcal{A}}(k) = |\Pr[\mathcal{A}(P, R) \Rightarrow 1] - \Pr[\mathcal{A}(P, U) \Rightarrow 1]| \leq \epsilon,$$

where $(P, R) \leftarrow \mathsf{Gen}(pp, w)$, $w \leftarrow W$ and $U \leftarrow_\$ \mathcal{R}$.

3   Fuzzy Signature

A fuzzy signature scheme is a special signature scheme whose signing key is no longer required to be uniformly random, but can be a noise random string such as biometric data. We call such signing key as fuzzy signing key. Here, we give the formal definition of fuzzy signature, which is a little different from the definition by Takahashi et al. [14]. The difference between our fuzzy signature and Takahashi et al.'s is that when generating a signature of a message m, our signature algorithm not only needs the fuzzy signing key but also needs vk as input while Takahashi et al.'s does not need vk.

Definition 13 (Fuzzy signature). *Let* $\mathcal{SK}$ *be the fuzzy signing key space and* $\mathcal{M}$ *be the message space. An* $(\mathcal{SK}, \mathcal{M}, t)$-*fuzzy signature scheme* SIG_F *consists of the following four PPT algorithms* $(\mathsf{Setup}_\mathsf{F}, \mathsf{KeyGen}_\mathsf{F}, \mathsf{Sign}_\mathsf{F}, \mathsf{Verify}_\mathsf{F})$:

- $\mathsf{Setup}_\mathsf{F}(k) \rightarrow pp$. *The setup algorithm* $\mathsf{Setup}_\mathsf{F}$ *takes a security parameter* k *as input, and outputs a public parameter* pp.
- $\mathsf{KeyGen}_\mathsf{F}(pp, sk) \rightarrow vk$. *The key generation algorithm* $\mathsf{KeyGen}_\mathsf{F}$ *takes the public parameter* pp *and a fuzzy signing key* $sk \in \mathcal{SK}$ *as input, and outputs a verification key* vk.
- $\mathsf{Sign}_\mathsf{F}(pp, vk, sk', m) \rightarrow \sigma$. *The signing algorithm* Sign_F *takes the public parameter* pp, *the verification key* vk, *a new fuzzy signing key* $sk' \in \mathcal{SK}$ *and a message* $m \in \mathcal{M}$ *as input, and outputs a signature* σ.
- $\mathsf{Verify}_\mathsf{F}(pp, vk, m, \sigma) \rightarrow 0/1$. *The verification algorithm* $\mathsf{Verify}_\mathsf{F}$ *takes the public parameter* pp, *the verification key* vk, *the message* m *and the signature* σ *as input, and outputs a bit* 1 *(accept) or* 0 *(reject).*

Correctness. We require that for all $pp \leftarrow \mathsf{Setup}_\mathsf{F}(k)$, $vk \leftarrow \mathsf{KeyGen}_\mathsf{F}(pp, sk)$, and messages $m \in \mathcal{M}$, if $\mathsf{dis}(sk, sk') \leq t$, it holds that

$$\mathsf{Verify}_\mathsf{F}(pp, vk, m, \mathsf{Sign}_\mathsf{F}(pp, vk, sk', m)) = 1.$$

In [14], Takahashi et al. assumed that the error distribution between sk and sk' (two samples of the same biometric characteristic) are independent of the biometric characteristic. More precisely, they assume that for all objects W that produce the fuzzy data (which will be used as the fuzzy signing key), if W produces a data sk at the first measurement, and if the same object is measured next time, then the measured data sk' follows the distribution $\{e \leftarrow \Phi; sk' \leftarrow sk + e : sk'\}$, and error distribution Φ is independent of W. This requirement is too strong since it seems impossible that error distribution between different samples is independent of the biometric characteristic. So we try to relax the requirement in [14] and define the following security model of fuzzy signature.

Definition 14 (m-EUF-CMA security). *An $(\mathcal{SK}, \mathcal{M}, t)$- fuzzy signature scheme is said to be m-existentially unforgeable under non-adaptive chosen message attack (m-EUF-CMA) secure, if for any distribution SK over metric space $\mathcal{SK}$ with $H_\infty(SK) \geq m$, for any PPT adversaries $\mathcal{A}$, it holds that*

$$\mathsf{Adv}_{\mathsf{SIG}_F, \mathcal{A}}^{m\text{-}EUF\text{-}CMA}(k) := \Pr[\mathsf{Expt}_{\mathsf{SIG}_F, \mathcal{A}}^{m\text{-}EUF\text{-}CMA}(k) \Rightarrow 1] \leqslant \mathsf{negl}(k).$$

Here $\mathsf{Expt}_{\mathsf{SIG}, \mathcal{A}}^{m\text{-}EUF\text{-}CMA}(k)$ is an experiment played between an adversary $\mathcal{A}$ and a challenger $\mathcal{C}$ as follows.

$\underline{\mathsf{Expt}_{\mathsf{SIG}, \mathcal{A}}^{m\text{-}EUF\text{-}CMA}(k):}$

1. *The challenger $\mathcal{C}$ invokes $pp \leftarrow \mathsf{Setup}_F(k)$, samples $sk \leftarrow SK$, generates $vk \leftarrow \mathsf{KenGen}_F(pp, sk)$ and initializes the set of chosen-message queries $\mathcal{Q} = \emptyset$ issued by the adversary. Subsequently, it returns pp and vk to $\mathcal{A}$.*
2. *The adversary $\mathcal{A}$ may adaptively make signing oracle queries of the following form*
   - *$\mathcal{A}$ sends a message $m_i \in \mathcal{M}$ and a function $f_i \in \Phi$ to challenger $\mathcal{C}$, where $\Phi := \{\forall sk \in \mathcal{SK}, f(sk) < t | f : \mathcal{SK} \rightarrow \mathcal{SK}\}$.*
   - *$\mathcal{C}$ invokes $\sigma_i \leftarrow \mathsf{Sign}_F(pp, vk, sk + f_i(sk), m_i)$, adds m_i to the set $\mathcal{Q}$ and returns σ_i to $\mathcal{A}$.*
3. *Finally, $\mathcal{A}$ submits a message-signature pair (m^*, σ^*). The experiment outputs 1 if $m^* \notin \mathcal{Q} \wedge \mathsf{Verify}_F(pp, vk, m^*, \sigma^*) = 1$ and 0 otherwise.*

Remark 1. In our security model, when adversary $\mathcal{A}$ making a signing oracle query of message m_i, $\mathcal{A}$ will send a function $f_i \in \Phi$ to challenger $\mathcal{C}$ as well. Note that $\Phi := \{\forall sk \in \mathcal{SK}, f(sk) < t | f : \mathcal{SK} \rightarrow \mathcal{SK}\}$. In this way, we model that the error distribution between different samples of the same biometric characteristic can be arbitrary depend on the biometric characteristic except the error is bound by t. It is reasonable to bound the error, because different samples of the same biometric characteristic are similar. Meanwhile, it is necessary to bound the error, otherwise there is no security at all.

4   Construction of Fuzzy Signature

Figure 2 illustrates our construction of fuzzy signature $\mathsf{SIG_F} = (\mathsf{Setup_F}, \mathsf{KeyGen_F}, \mathsf{Sign_F}, \mathsf{Verify_F})$ which makes use of the following building blocks:

- A signature scheme $\mathsf{SIG}=(\mathsf{Setup}, \mathsf{KeyGen}, \mathsf{Sign}, \mathsf{Verify})$ with a simple key generation process (i.e., there exists a deterministic PPT algorithm KG). Let its secret key space be $\widetilde{\mathcal{SK}}$ and message space be $\mathcal{M}$.
- An $(\mathcal{SK}, \mathfrak{m}, \widetilde{\mathcal{SK}}, t, \epsilon)$-fuzzy extractor $\mathsf{FE}=(\mathsf{Init}, \mathsf{Gen}, \mathsf{Rep})$.

$\mathsf{Setup_F}(k)$:	$\mathsf{KeyGen_F}(pp, sk)$:	$\mathsf{Sign_F}(pp, vk, sk', m)$:	$\mathsf{Verify_F}(pp, vk, m, \sigma)$:
$pp_1 \leftarrow \mathsf{Init}(k)$	$(pp_1, pp_2) \leftarrow pp$	$(pp_1, pp_2) \leftarrow pp$	$(pp_1, pp_2) \leftarrow pp$
$pp_2 \leftarrow \mathsf{Setup}(k)$	$(P, \widetilde{sk}) \leftarrow \mathsf{Gen}(pp_1, sk)$	$(\widetilde{vk}, P) \leftarrow vk$	$(\widetilde{vk}, P) \leftarrow vk$
$pp \leftarrow (pp_1, pp_2)$	$\widetilde{vk} \leftarrow \mathsf{KG}(pp_2, \widetilde{sk})$	$\widetilde{sk'} \leftarrow \mathsf{Rep}(pp_1, P, sk')$	$b \leftarrow \mathsf{Verify}(pp_2, \widetilde{vk}, m, \sigma)$
Return pp	$vk \leftarrow (\widetilde{vk}, P)$	$\sigma \leftarrow \mathsf{Sign}(pp_2, \widetilde{sk'}, m)$	Return b
	Return vk	Return σ	

Fig. 2. Our generic construction of fuzzy signature scheme $\mathsf{SIG_F}$.

4.1   Correctness

The correctness of our fuzzy signature scheme $\mathsf{SIG_F}$ is guaranteed as follows.

Theorem 1. *The correctness of* $\mathsf{SIG_F}$ *follows from the correctness of the underlying signature scheme* SIG *and the underlying* $(\mathcal{SK}, \mathfrak{m}, \widetilde{\mathcal{SK}}, t, \epsilon)$-*fuzzy extractor* FE.

Proof. By the correctness of FE, if $\mathsf{dis}(sk, sk') \leq t$, then $\widetilde{sk'} = \widetilde{sk}$, where $(P, \widetilde{sk}) \leftarrow \mathsf{Gen}(pp_1, sk)$, $\widetilde{sk'} \leftarrow \mathsf{Rep}(pp_1, P, sk')$. Note that $\widetilde{vk} \leftarrow \mathsf{KG}(pp_2, \widetilde{sk})$, by the correctness of SIG, for any message $m \in \mathcal{M}$, it follows that

$$\mathsf{Verify}(pp_2, \widetilde{vk}, m, \mathsf{Sign}(pp_2, \widetilde{sk}, m)) = 1.$$

More precisely,

$$
\begin{aligned}
&\mathsf{Verify_F}(pp, vk, m, \mathsf{Sign_F}(pp, vk, sk', m)) \\
={}& \mathsf{Verify}(pp_2, \widetilde{vk}, m, \mathsf{Sign_F}(pp, vk, sk', m)) && \text{(by the construction)} \\
={}& \mathsf{Verify}(pp_2, \widetilde{vk}, m, \mathsf{Sign}(pp_2, \widetilde{sk'}, m)) && \text{(by the construction)} \\
={}& \mathsf{Verify}(pp_2, \widetilde{vk}, m, \mathsf{Sign}(pp_2, \widetilde{sk}, m)) && \text{(by the correctness of } \mathsf{FE}) \\
={}& 1 && \text{(by the correctness of } \mathsf{SIG})
\end{aligned}
$$

∎

4.2   Security

The security of our fuzzy signature scheme $\mathsf{SIG_F}$ is guaranteed as follows.

Theorem 2. *If the underlying signature scheme* SIG *with secret key space* $\widetilde{\mathcal{SK}}$ *and message space* $\mathcal{M}$ *satisfies EUF-CMA security and the underlying* FE *is an* $(\mathcal{SK}, \mathsf{m}, \widetilde{\mathcal{SK}}, t, \epsilon)$-*fuzzy extractor, our construction* $\mathsf{SIG_F}$ *is an* $(\mathcal{SK}, \mathcal{M}, t)$-*fuzzy signature that satisfies* m-*EUF-CMA security.*

Proof. Let $\mathcal{A}$ be an arbitrary PPT algorithm adversary that attacks the m-EUF-CMA security of $\mathsf{SIG_F}$. We will consider three indistinguishable games, where the first game Game 0 is the original game $\mathsf{Expt}_{\mathsf{SIG_F},\mathcal{A}}^{\mathsf{m}\text{-}\mathsf{EUF\text{-}CMA}}(k)$. For $i \in \{0, 1, 2\}$, denote by S_i the event that $\mathcal{A}$ wins (i.e., the experiment returns 1) in Game i. Our goal is to show that $\mathsf{Adv}_{\mathsf{SIG_F},\mathcal{A}}^{\mathsf{m}\text{-}\mathsf{EUF\text{-}CMA}}(k) := \Pr[\mathsf{Expt}_{\mathsf{SIG_F},\mathcal{A}}^{\mathsf{m}\text{-}\mathsf{EUF\text{-}CMA}}(k) \Rightarrow 1]$ is negligible.

Game 0. Game 0 is just the experiment $\mathsf{Expt}_{\mathsf{SIG_F},\mathcal{A}}^{\mathsf{m}\text{-}\mathsf{EUF\text{-}CMA}}(k)$. More precisely,

1. The challenger $\mathcal{C}$ invokes $pp_1 \leftarrow \mathsf{Init}(k)$ and $pp_2 \leftarrow \mathsf{Setup}(k)$, samples $sk \leftarrow \mathcal{SK}$, invokes $(P, \widetilde{sk}) \leftarrow \mathsf{Gen}(pp_1, sk)$ and $\widetilde{vk} \leftarrow \mathsf{KG}(pp_2, \widetilde{sk})$, sets $pp \leftarrow (pp_1, pp_2)$ and $vk \leftarrow (\widetilde{vk}, P)$ and initializes the set of chosen-message queries $\mathcal{Q} = \emptyset$ issued by the adversary. Subsequently, it returns pp and vk to $\mathcal{A}$.
2. The adversary $\mathcal{A}$ may adaptively make signing oracle queries of the following form
   - $\mathcal{A}$ sends a message $m_i \in \mathcal{M}$ and a function $f_i \in \Phi$ to challenger $\mathcal{C}$, where $\Phi := \{\forall sk \in \mathcal{SK}, f(sk) < t | f : \mathcal{SK} \to \mathcal{SK}\}$.
   - $\mathcal{C}$ parses pp as pp_1 and pp_2, parses vk as $\widetilde{vk}$ and P, invokes $\widetilde{sk}'_i \leftarrow \mathsf{Rep}(pp_1, P, sk + f_i(sk))$, $\sigma_i \leftarrow \mathsf{Sign}(pp_2, \widetilde{sk}'_i, m_i)$, adds m_i to the set $\mathcal{Q}$ and returns σ_i to $\mathcal{A}$.
3. Finally, $\mathcal{A}$ submits a message-signature pair (m^*, σ^*). Then, challenger $\mathcal{C}$ parses pp as pp_1 and pp_2, parses vk as $\widetilde{vk}$ and P, invokes $b \leftarrow \mathsf{Verify}(pp_2, \widetilde{vk}, m^*, \sigma^*)$. The experiment outputs 1 if $m^* \notin \mathcal{Q} \wedge b = 1$ and 0 otherwise.

Obviously,

$$\mathsf{Adv}_{\mathsf{SIG_F},\mathcal{A}}^{\mathsf{m}\text{-}\mathsf{EUF\text{-}CMA}}(k) = \Pr[\mathsf{Expt}_{\mathsf{SIG_F},\mathcal{A}}^{\mathsf{m}\text{-}\mathsf{EUF\text{-}CMA}}(k) \Rightarrow 1] = \Pr[S_0].$$

Game 1. This game is identical to Game 0, except that in step 2, when the challenger answers the signing oracle queries, it uses $\widetilde{sk}$ as the signing key of the underlying signature scheme other than $\widetilde{sk}'_i \leftarrow \mathsf{Rep}(pp_1, P, sk'_i)$. More precisely,

1. The challenger $\mathcal{C}$ invokes $pp_1 \leftarrow \mathsf{Init}(k)$ and $pp_2 \leftarrow \mathsf{Setup}(k)$, samples $sk \leftarrow \mathcal{SK}$, invokes $(P, \widetilde{sk}) \leftarrow \mathsf{Gen}(pp_1, sk)$ and $\widetilde{vk} \leftarrow \mathsf{KG}(pp_2, \widetilde{sk})$, sets $pp \leftarrow (pp_1, pp_2)$ and $vk \leftarrow (\widetilde{vk}, P)$ and initializes the set of chosen-message queries $\mathcal{Q} = \emptyset$ issued by the adversary. Subsequently, it returns pp and vk to $\mathcal{A}$.
2. The adversary $\mathcal{A}$ may adaptively make signing oracle queries of the following form
   - $\mathcal{A}$ sends a message $m_i \in \mathcal{M}$ and a function $f_i \in \Phi$ to challenger $\mathcal{C}$, where $\Phi := \{\forall sk \in \mathcal{SK}, f(sk) < t | f : \mathcal{SK} \to \mathcal{SK}\}$.

- $\mathcal{C}$ parses pp as pp_1 and pp_2, invokes $\sigma_i \leftarrow \mathsf{Sign}(pp_2, \widetilde{sk}, m_i)$, adds m_i to the set $\mathcal{Q}$ and returns σ_i to $\mathcal{A}$.

3. Finally, $\mathcal{A}$ submits a message-signature pair (m^*, σ^*). Then, challenger $\mathcal{C}$ parses pp as pp_1 and pp_2, parses vk as $\widetilde{vk}$ and P and invokes $b \leftarrow \mathsf{Verify}(pp_2, \widetilde{vk}, m^*, \sigma^*)$. The experiment outputs 1 if $m^* \notin \mathcal{Q} \wedge b = 1$ and 0 otherwise.

Lemma 1. $\Pr[S_1] = \Pr[S_0]$.

Proof. The only difference between Game 0 and Game 1 is the signing key used in the signing oracle. In Game 1 the challenger uses $\widetilde{sk}$ as the signing key, while in Game 0 the challenger uses $\widetilde{sk}'_i$ where $\widetilde{sk}'_i \leftarrow \mathsf{Rep}(pp_1, P, sk + f_i(sk))$.

Since the function f_i is chosen by the adversary $\mathcal{A}$ from the set $\varPhi$, where $\varPhi := \{\forall sk \in \mathcal{SK}, f(sk) < t | f : \mathcal{SK} \rightarrow \mathcal{SK}\}$, we have $\mathsf{dis}(sk, sk + f_i(sk)) \leq t$. By the correctness of the underlying $(\mathcal{SK}, \mathfrak{m}, \widetilde{\mathcal{SK}}, t, \epsilon)$-fuzzy extractor FE, we have $\widetilde{sk}'_i = \widetilde{sk}$. Therefore, the change between Game 0 and Game 1 is just conceptual. It follows that

$$\Pr[S_1] = \Pr[S_0]. \qquad \square$$

Game 2. This game is identical to Game 1, except that the signing key $\widetilde{sk}$ is uniformly chosen from $\widetilde{\mathcal{SK}}$ other than $(P, \widetilde{sk}) \leftarrow \mathsf{Gen}(pp_1, sk)$. More precisely,

1. The challenger $\mathcal{C}$ invokes $pp_1 \leftarrow \mathsf{Init}(k)$ and $pp_2 \leftarrow \mathsf{Setup}(k)$, samples $sk \leftarrow SK$, invokes $(P, \widetilde{sk}) \leftarrow \mathsf{Gen}(pp_1, sk)$, samples $U \leftarrow_\$ \widetilde{\mathcal{SK}}$, set $\widetilde{sk} \leftarrow U$, invokes $\widetilde{vk} \leftarrow \mathsf{KG}(pp_2, \widetilde{sk})$, sets $pp \leftarrow (pp_1, pp_2)$ and $vk \leftarrow (\widetilde{vk}, P)$ and initializes the set of chosen-message queries $\mathcal{Q} = \emptyset$ issued by the adversary. Subsequently, it returns pp and vk to $\mathcal{A}$.
2. The adversary $\mathcal{A}$ may adaptively make signing oracle queries of the following form
   - $\mathcal{A}$ sends a message $m_i \in \mathcal{M}$ and a function $f_i \in \varPhi$ to challenger $\mathcal{C}$, where $\varPhi := \{\forall sk \in \mathcal{SK}, f(sk) < t | f : \mathcal{SK} \rightarrow \mathcal{SK}\}$.
   - $\mathcal{C}$ parses pp as pp_1 and pp_2, invokes $\sigma_i \leftarrow \mathsf{Sign}(pp_2, \widetilde{sk}, m_i)$, adds m_i to the set $\mathcal{Q}$ and returns σ_i to $\mathcal{A}$.
3. Finally, $\mathcal{A}$ submits a message-signature pair (m^*, σ^*). Then, challenger $\mathcal{C}$ parses vk as $\widetilde{vk}$ and P and invokes $b \leftarrow \mathsf{Verify}(pp_2, \widetilde{vk}, m^*, \sigma^*)$. The experiment outputs 1 if $m^* \notin \mathcal{Q} \wedge b = 1$ and 0 otherwise.

Lemma 2. $|\Pr[S_1] - \Pr[S_2]| \leq \epsilon$.

Proof. The only difference between Game 1 and Game 2 is the way of generating the signing key $\widetilde{sk}$ (not fuzzy). In Game 1, $\widetilde{sk}$ is generated by $(P, \widetilde{sk}) \leftarrow \mathsf{Gen}(pp_1, sk)$, while in Game 2, $\widetilde{sk}$ is uniformly chosen from $\widetilde{\mathcal{SK}}$.

By the security of the underlying $(\mathcal{SK}, \mathfrak{m}, \widetilde{\mathcal{SK}}, t, \epsilon)$-fuzzy extractor FE, if SK is a distribution over $\mathcal{SK}$ with $H_\infty(SK) \geq \mathfrak{m}$, then

$$|\Pr[\mathcal{A}(P, \widetilde{sk}) \Rightarrow 1] - \Pr[\mathcal{A}(P, U) \Rightarrow 1]| \leq \epsilon,$$

where $(P, \widetilde{sk}) \leftarrow \mathsf{Gen}(pp_1, sk)$, $sk \leftarrow SK$ and $U \leftarrow_\$ \widetilde{SK}$. Therefore, we have

$$|\Pr[S_1] - \Pr[S_2]| \leq \epsilon.$$

$\square$

Lemma 3. $\Pr[S_2] \leq \mathsf{Adv}_{\mathsf{SIG}}^{EUF\text{-}CMA}(k)$.

Proof. We will reduce the EUF-CMA security of the underlying signature scheme SIG to the altered game as described in Game 2. To this end, we assume a PPT adversary $\mathcal{A}$ winning Game 2 and show how to construct a PPT adversary $\mathcal{B}$ attacking the underlying EUF-CMA secure signature SIG.

On receiving pp_2 and $\widetilde{vk}$ from its own challenger, adversary $\mathcal{B}$ invokes $pp_1 \leftarrow \mathsf{Init}(k)$, samples $sk \leftarrow SK$, invokes $(P, \widetilde{sk}) \leftarrow \mathsf{Gen}(pp_1, sk)$, sets $pp \leftarrow (pp_1, pp_2)$ and $vk \leftarrow (\widetilde{vk}, P)$. Finally, $\mathcal{B}$ returns pp and vk to $\mathcal{A}$.

Upon receiving the signing oracle queries $m_i \in \mathcal{M}$ and a function $f_i \in \Phi$ from $\mathcal{A}$, adversary $\mathcal{B}$ answers $\mathcal{A}$'s query as follows:

1. $\mathcal{B}$ sends m_i to its own challenger.
2. Upon receiving σ_i from its own challenger, $\mathcal{B}$ returns σ_i to $\mathcal{A}$.

Finally, $\mathcal{A}$ submits a message-signature pair (m^*, σ^*) to $\mathcal{B}$. $\mathcal{B}$ submits (m^*, σ^*) to its own challenger and returns what its challenger returns.

Note that $\mathcal{B}$ simulates Game 2 perfectly. If $\mathcal{A}$ wins in Game 2, then $\mathcal{B}$ wins in the EUF-CMA game. By the security of the underlying EUF-CMA secure signature scheme SIG, we have

$$\Pr[S_2] = \mathsf{Adv}_{\mathsf{SIG}, \mathcal{B}}^{EUF\text{-}CMA}(k) \leq \mathsf{Adv}_{\mathsf{SIG}}^{EUF\text{-}CMA}(k).$$

$\square$

From Lemmas 1, 2 and 3, we have

$$\mathsf{Adv}_{\mathsf{SIG_F}}^{m\text{-}EUF\text{-}CMA}(k) \leq \mathsf{Adv}_{\mathsf{SIG}}^{EUF\text{-}CMA}(k) + \epsilon,$$

and Theorem 2 follows. ∎

5 Instantiation

Let us recall the fuzzy extractor in [6] which uses a $(\mathcal{W}, \mathfrak{m}, \widetilde{\mathfrak{m}}, t)$-secure sketch (SS, Rec) and an average-case $(\mathcal{W}, \widetilde{\mathfrak{m}}, \mathcal{R}, \epsilon)$-strong extractor Ext with seed set $\mathcal{I}$ as building blocks. The construction is as follows.

– $\mathsf{Init}(k)$: $i \leftarrow_\$ \mathcal{I}$, $pp = i$.
– $\mathsf{Gen}(pp, w)$: Compute $s = \mathsf{SS}(w)$, set $P = s$, $R = \mathsf{Ext}(w, i)$. Output (P, R).
– $\mathsf{Rep}(pp, w', P)$: Recover $w = \mathsf{Rec}(w', s)$ and output $R = \mathsf{Ext}(w, i)$.

It was shown by Dodis et.al. [6] the above construction is an $(\mathcal{W}, \mathfrak{m}, \mathcal{R}, t, \epsilon)$-fuzzy extractor.

5.1 First Instantiation

Our first concrete instantiation of a fuzzy signature scheme is based on the Waters signature scheme [15], and thus we review it here. We consider the version where the setup and the key generation for each user are separated so that the scheme fits our syntax. Let $l = l(k)$ be a positive polynomial, and let BGGen be a bilinear group generator. The Waters signature scheme $\mathsf{SIG}_{\mathsf{Wat}}$ is shown in Fig. 3, which is EUF-CMA secure if the CDH assumption holds with respect to BGGen.

$\mathsf{Setup}_{\mathsf{Wat}}(k)$:	$\mathsf{KeyGen}_{\mathsf{Wat}}(pp)$:
$\mathcal{BG} := (p, \mathbb{G}, \mathbb{G}_T, g, e) \leftarrow \mathsf{BGGen}(1^k)$	$sk \leftarrow_\$ \mathbb{Z}_p$
$h, u', u_1, \cdots, u_l \leftarrow_\$ \mathbb{G}$	$vk \leftarrow g^{sk}$
$pp \leftarrow (\mathcal{BG}, h, u', (u_i)_{i \in [l]})$	Return (vk, sk)
Return pp	
$\mathsf{Sign}_{\mathsf{Wat}}(pp, sk, m)$:	$\mathsf{Verify}_{\mathsf{Wat}}(pp, vk, m, \sigma)$:
Parse m as $(m_1\|\cdots\|m_l) \in \{0,1\}^l$	$(\sigma_1, \sigma_2) \leftarrow \sigma$
$r \leftarrow_\$ \mathbb{Z}_p$	Parse m as $(m_1\|\cdots\|m_l) \in \{0,1\}^l$
$\sigma_1 \leftarrow h^{sk} \cdot (u' \cdot \prod_{i \in [l]} u_i^{m_i})^r$, $\sigma_2 \leftarrow g^r$	If $e(\sigma_2, u' \cdot \prod_{i \in [l]} u_i^{m_i}) \cdot e(vk, h) = e(\sigma_1, g)$
Return $\sigma \leftarrow (\sigma_1, \sigma_2)$	Then return 1 else return 0

Fig. 3. The waters signature scheme $\mathsf{SIG}_{\mathsf{Wat}}$

Theorem 3. [15] *The signature scheme is (t, q, ϵ) existentially unforgeable assuming the decisional $(t, \frac{\epsilon}{16(n+1)q})$ BDH assumption holds, where $\lambda = \frac{1}{8(n+1)q}$.*

Obviously, the signature scheme $\mathsf{SIG}_{\mathsf{Wat}}$ in Fig. 3 has the *simple key generation process* property in which $vk = g^{sk}$.

Note that the secret key space of Waters signature scheme is $\mathbb{Z}_p$. We want to construct a fuzzy extractor with extracted string space $\mathbb{Z}_p$. Let Ext be a universal hash function, i.e., $\mathsf{Ext}(\cdot, i) := \mathsf{H}_i(\cdot) : \mathbb{Z}_p^l \to \mathbb{Z}_p$, [1] where $i = (i_1, \cdots, i_l) \in \mathbb{Z}_p^l$, $x = (x_0, x_1, \cdots, x_l) \in \mathbb{Z}_p^{l+1}$, and

$$\mathsf{Ext}(x, i) = \mathsf{H}_i(x) = x_0 + i_1 x_1 + \cdots + i_l x_l, \tag{1}$$

and H is a family of universal hash functions according to [12]. If we instantiate the secure sketch by the syndrome-based secure sketch introduced in Sect. 2.3 and extractor by $\mathsf{Ext}(x, i)$ (Eq. 1), then we get a fuzzy extractor FE_1. And the extracted string by FE_1 is uniformly distributed over $\mathbb{Z}_p$. Note that the secret key space of Waters signature $\mathsf{SIG}_{\mathsf{Wat}}$ is $\mathbb{Z}_p$.

By instantiating the signature scheme SIG in Fig. 2 with Waters signature $\mathsf{SIG}_{\mathsf{Wat}}$, the fuzzy extractor FE in Fig. 2 with the above fuzzy extractor FE_1,

---

[1] One can always translate a binary string to an element in $\mathbb{Z}_p^l$ for a proper l.

we get a fuzzy signature scheme which is m-EUF-CMA secure under the computational Diffie-Hellman (CDH) assumption in bilinear groups in the standard model (See Fig. 4).

Setup$_{F1}(k)$:	KeyGen$_{F1}(pp, sk)$:
$i \leftarrow_\$ \mathbb{Z}_p^l,\ pp_1 \leftarrow i$	$(pp_1, pp_2) \leftarrow pp$
$\mathcal{BG} := (p, \mathbb{G}, \mathbb{G}_T, g, e) \leftarrow \mathsf{BGGen}(1^k)$	$s \leftarrow \mathsf{SS}(sk),\ P \leftarrow s$
$h, u', u_1, \cdots, u_l \leftarrow_\$ \mathbb{G}$	$\widetilde{sk} \leftarrow \mathsf{Ext}(sk, i)$
$pp_2 \leftarrow (\mathcal{BG}, h, u', (u_i)_{i \in [l]})$	$\widetilde{vk} \leftarrow g^{\widetilde{sk}}$
$pp \leftarrow (pp_1, pp_2)$	$vk \leftarrow (\widetilde{vk}, P)$
Return pp	Return vk.
Sign$_{F1}(pp, vk, sk', m)$:	**Verify$_{F1}(pp, vk, m, \sigma)$:**
$(pp_1, pp_2) \leftarrow pp,\ (\widetilde{vk}, P) \leftarrow vk$	$(pp_1, pp_2) \leftarrow pp$
$\widetilde{sk}' \leftarrow \mathsf{Ext}(\mathsf{Rec}(sk', P), i)$	$(\widetilde{vk}, P) \leftarrow vk$
Parse m as $(m_1 \| \cdots \| m_l) \in \{0,1\}^l$	$(\sigma_1, \sigma_2) \leftarrow \sigma$
$r \leftarrow_\$ \mathbb{Z}_p$	Parse m as $(m_1 \| \cdots \| m_l) \in \{0,1\}^l$
$\sigma_1 \leftarrow h^{\widetilde{sk}'} \cdot (u' \cdot \prod_{i \in [l]} u_i^{m_i})^r,\ \sigma_2 \leftarrow g^r$	If $e(\sigma_2, u' \cdot \prod_{i \in [l]} u_i^{m_i}) \cdot e(\widetilde{vk}, h) = e(\sigma_1, g)$
Return $\sigma \leftarrow (\sigma_1, \sigma_2)$	Then return 1 else return 0

Fig. 4. Our first instantiation SIG_{F1}

Corollary 1. *The construction in Fig. 4 is an m-EUF-CMA secure fuzzy signature under the computational Diffie-Hellman (CDH) assumption in bilinear groups in the standard model.*

5.2 Second Instantiation

Our second concrete instantiation of a fuzzy signature scheme is based on the Lattice-based Signatures [8], and thus we review it here. Let $\mathcal{D}_\theta^m$ be the m-dimensional discrete Gaussian distribution for some standard deviation θ. The lattice-based signature scheme SIG_{Lat} based on SIS is shown in Fig. 5, which is secure in the random oracle model based on the worst-case hardness of the $\widetilde{O}(n^{1.5})$-SIVP problem in general lattices.

Theorem 4. *[8] If there is a polynomial-time forger, who makes at most s queries to the signing oracle and h queries to the random oracle H, who breaks the signature (with proper parameters) with probability δ, then there is a polynomial-time algorithm who can solve the $l_2\text{-SIS}_{q,u,v,\beta}$ problem for $\beta = (4\theta + 2dk)\sqrt{v} = \widetilde{O}(du)$ with probability $\approx \frac{\delta^2}{2(h+s)}$.*

$\mathsf{Setup}_{\mathsf{Lat}}(k):$	$\mathsf{Sign}_{\mathsf{Lat}}(pp, \mathbf{sk}, m):$	$\mathsf{Verify}_{\mathsf{Lat}}(pp, \mathbf{vk}, m, \sigma):$
Random Oracle: $\mathsf{H} : \{0,1\}^* \to \{-1,0,1\}^k$	$\mathbf{y} \leftarrow \mathcal{D}_\theta^v$	$(\mathbf{c}, \mathbf{z}) \leftarrow \sigma$
$\mathbf{A} \leftarrow_\$ \mathbb{Z}_q^{u \times v}$	$\mathbf{c} \leftarrow \mathsf{H}(\mathbf{Ay}, m)$	If $\|\mathbf{z}\| \leq \eta\theta\sqrt{v}$
Return $pp \leftarrow (\mathsf{H}, \mathbf{A})$	$\mathbf{z} \leftarrow \mathbf{sk} \cdot \mathbf{c} + \mathbf{y}$	$\wedge\ \mathbf{z} = \mathsf{H}(\mathbf{Az} - \mathbf{vk} \cdot \mathbf{c}, m)$
	Return $\sigma \leftarrow (\mathbf{c}, \mathbf{z})$	Return 1, Else, Return 0
$\mathsf{KeyGen}_{\mathsf{Lat}}(pp):$		
$\mathbf{sk} \leftarrow_\$ \{-d, 0, d\}^{v \times k}$		
$\mathbf{vk} \leftarrow \mathbf{A} \cdot \mathbf{sk}$		
Return $(\mathbf{vk}, \mathbf{sk})$		

Fig. 5. Lattice-based signatures $\mathsf{SIG}_{\mathsf{Lat}}$

Obviously, the signature scheme $\mathsf{SIG}_{\mathsf{Lat}}$ in Fig. 5 has the *simple key generation process* property in which $\mathbf{vk} = \mathbf{A} \cdot \mathbf{sk}$.

Note that the secret key space of the signature scheme $\mathsf{SIG}_{\mathsf{Lat}}$ is $\{-d, 0, d\}^{v \times k}$. We want to construct a fuzzy extractor with extracted string space $\{-d, 0, d\}^{v \times k}$. Lyubashevsky [8] gave parameters choices for the lattice-based signature scheme in which d can be equal to 1 or 31. Here we consider the case $d = 1$.

For $x \in \mathbb{Z}_3^l$, $i \in \mathbb{Z}_3^{n \times l}$, define

$$\mathsf{H}_i(x) := ix,$$

then $\mathcal{H} = \{\mathsf{H}_i : \mathbb{Z}_3^l \to \mathbb{Z}_3^n | i \in \mathbb{Z}_3^{n \times l}\}$ is a family of universal hash functions. Let $n = v \times k$, we can readily interpret a vector in $\mathbb{Z}_3^n$ as a matrix in $\mathbb{Z}_3^{v \times k}$. Given $y \in \mathbb{Z}_3^{v \times k}$, we can get a matrix $y' \in \{-1, 0, 1\}^{v \times k}$ by subtracting 2 from each component of the matrix y. Define the above two operation as $f_1 : \mathbb{Z}_3^n \to \mathbb{Z}_3^{v \times k}$ and $f_2 : \mathbb{Z}_3^{v \times k} \to \{-1, 0, 1\}^{v \times k}$ separately. We can easily get a family of universal hash functions

$$\mathcal{H}' = \{f_2 \circ f_1 \circ \mathsf{H}_i : \mathbb{Z}_3^l \to \{-1, 0, 1\}^{v \times k} | i \in \mathbb{Z}_3^{n \times l}\}. \qquad (2)$$

If we instantiate the secure sketch by the syndrome-based secure sketch introduced in Sect. 2.3 and extractor by the universal hash function $\mathcal{H}'$ (Eq. 2), then we get a fuzzy extractor FE_2. The extracted string by FE_2 is uniformly distributed over $\{-1, 0, 1\}^{v \times k}$.

By instantiating the signature scheme SIG in Fig. 2 with $\mathsf{SIG}_{\mathsf{Lat}}$ (with proper parameters), the fuzzy extractor FE in Fig. 2 with above fuzzy extractor FE_2, we get a fuzzy signature scheme which is m-EUF-CMA secure in the random oracle model based on the worst-case hardness of the $\widetilde{O}(n^{1.5})$-SIVP problem in general lattices (See Fig. 6).

$\mathsf{Setup}_{\mathsf{F2}}(k)$:	$\mathsf{Sign}_{\mathsf{F2}}(pp, sk', m)$:	$\mathsf{Verify}_{\mathsf{F2}}(pp, vk, m, \sigma)$:
$i \leftarrow_{\$} \mathbb{Z}_3^{n \times l},\ pp_1 \leftarrow i$	$(pp_1, pp_2) \leftarrow pp$	$(\mathbf{c}, \mathbf{z}) \leftarrow \sigma$
Random Oracle: $\mathsf{H} : \{0,1\}^* \rightarrow \{-1,0,1\}^k$	$(\widetilde{\mathbf{vk}}, P) \leftarrow vk$	$(\widetilde{\mathbf{vk}}, P) \leftarrow vk$
$\mathbf{A} \leftarrow_{\$} \mathbb{Z}_q^{u \times v},\ pp_2 \leftarrow (\mathsf{H}, \mathbf{A})$	$\widetilde{\mathbf{sk}}' \leftarrow \mathsf{Ext}(\mathsf{Rec}(sk', P), i)$	If $\|\mathbf{z}\| \leq \eta\theta\sqrt{v}$
Return $pp \leftarrow (pp_1, pp_2)$	$\mathbf{y} \leftarrow \mathcal{D}_\theta^v,\ \mathbf{c} \leftarrow \mathsf{H}(\mathbf{Ay}, m)$	$\wedge\ \mathbf{z} = \mathsf{H}(\mathbf{Az} - \widetilde{\mathbf{vk}} \cdot \mathbf{c}, m)$
	$\mathbf{c} \leftarrow \widetilde{\mathbf{sk}}' \cdot \mathbf{c} + \mathbf{y}$	Return 1, Else, Return 0
$\mathsf{KeyGen}_{\mathsf{F2}}(pp, sk)$:	Return $\sigma \leftarrow (\mathbf{c}, \mathbf{z})$	
$(pp_1, pp_2) \leftarrow pp$		
$s \leftarrow \mathsf{SS}(sk),\ P \leftarrow s$		
$\widetilde{\mathbf{sk}} \leftarrow \mathsf{Ext}(sk, i),\ \widetilde{\mathbf{vk}} \leftarrow \mathbf{A} \cdot \widetilde{\mathbf{sk}}$		
Return $vk \leftarrow (\widetilde{\mathbf{vk}}, P)$		

Fig. 6. Our second instantiation $\mathsf{SIG}_{\mathsf{F2}}$

Corollary 2. *The construction in Fig. 6 is an* m-*EUF-CMA secure fuzzy signature based on the worst-case hardness of the* $\tilde{O}(n^{1.5})$-*SIVP problem in general lattices in the random oracle model.*

Acknowledgement. We would like to thank the reviewers for their valuable comments. The authors are supported by the Shanghai Sailing Program (Grant No. 21YF1401200), Fundamental Research Funds for the Central Universities (Grant No. 2232020D-34) and Open Fund Program for State Key Laboratory of Information Security of China (Grant No. 2021-MS-05).

References

1. Boyen, X.: Reusable cryptographic fuzzy extractors. In: Atluri, V., Pfitzmann, B., McDaniel, P.D. (eds.) Proceedings of the 11th ACM Conference on Computer and Communications Security, CCS 2004, Washington, DC, USA, October 25–29, 2004. pp. 82–91. ACM (2004). https://doi.org/10.1145/1030083.1030096, https://doi.org/10.1145/1030083.1030096

2. Boyen, X., Dodis, Y., Katz, J., Ostrovsky, R., Smith, A.: Secure remote authentication using biometric data. In: Cramer, R. (ed.) EUROCRYPT 2005. LNCS, vol. 3494, pp. 147–163. Springer, Heidelberg (2005). https://doi.org/10.1007/11426639_9

3. Carter, L., Wegman, M.N.: Universal classes of hash functions. J. Comput. Syst. Sci. **18**(2), 143–154 (1979)

4. Connaughton, R., Bowyer, K.W., Flynn, P.J.: Fusion of face and iris biometrics. In: Burge, M.J., Bowyer, K.W. (eds.) Handbook of Iris Recognition. Advances in Computer Vision and Pattern Recognition, , pp. 219–237. Springer, London (2013). https://doi.org/10.1007/978-1-4471-4402-1_12

5. Cramer, R., Dodis, Y., Fehr, S., Padró, C., Wichs, D.: Detection of algebraic manipulation with applications to robust secret sharing and fuzzy extractors. In: Smart, N. (ed.) EUROCRYPT 2008. LNCS, vol. 4965, pp. 471–488. Springer, Heidelberg (2008). https://doi.org/10.1007/978-3-540-78967-3_27

6. Dodis, Y., Reyzin, L., Smith, A.: Fuzzy extractors: how to generate strong keys from biometrics and other noisy data. In: Cachin, C., Camenisch, J.L. (eds.) EUROCRYPT 2004. LNCS, vol. 3027, pp. 523–540. Springer, Heidelberg (2004). https://doi.org/10.1007/978-3-540-24676-3_31

7. Li, N., Guo, F., Mu, Y., Susilo, W., Nepal, S.: Fuzzy extractors for biometric identification. In: Lee, K., Liu, L. (eds.) 37th IEEE International Conference on Distributed Computing Systems, ICDCS 2017, Atlanta, GA, USA, June 5–8, 2017, pp. 667–677. IEEE Computer Society (2017). https://doi.org/10.1109/ICDCS.2017.107

8. Lyubashevsky, V.: Lattice signatures without trapdoors. In: Pointcheval, D., Johansson, T. (eds.) EUROCRYPT 2012. LNCS, vol. 7237, pp. 738–755. Springer, Heidelberg (2012). https://doi.org/10.1007/978-3-642-29011-4_43

9. Matsuda, T., Takahashi, K., Murakami, T., Hanaoka, G.: Fuzzy signatures: relaxing requirements and a new construction. In: Manulis, M., Sadeghi, A.-R., Schneider, S. (eds.) ACNS 2016. LNCS, vol. 9696, pp. 97–116. Springer, Cham (2016). https://doi.org/10.1007/978-3-319-39555-5_6

10. Nisan, N., Zuckerman, D.: Randomness is linear in space. J. Comput. Syst. Sci. 52(1), 43–52 (1996)

11. Raghavendra, R., Raja, K.B., Surbiryala, J., Busch, C.: A low-cost multimodal biometric sensor to capture finger vein and fingerprint. In: IEEE International Joint Conference on Biometrics, Clearwater, IJCB 2014, FL, USA, Sept 29–Oct 2, 2014, pp. 1–7. IEEE (2014). https://doi.org/10.1109/BTAS.2014.6996225

12. Shoup, V.: A Computational Introduction to Number Theory and Algebra. Cambridge University Press, Cambridge (2006)

13. Takahashi, K., Matsuda, T., Murakami, T., Hanaoka, G., Nishigaki, M.: A signature scheme with a fuzzy private key. In: Malkin, T., Kolesnikov, V., Lewko, A.B., Polychronakis, M. (eds.) ACNS 2015. LNCS, vol. 9092, pp. 105–126. Springer, Cham (2015). https://doi.org/10.1007/978-3-319-28166-7_6

14. Takahashi, K., Matsuda, T., Murakami, T., Hanaoka, G., Nishigaki, M.: Signature schemes with a fuzzy private key. Int. J. Inf. Sec. 18(5), 581–617 (2019)

15. Waters, B.: Efficient identity-based encryption without random oracles. In: Cramer, R. (ed.) EUROCRYPT 2005. LNCS, vol. 3494, pp. 114–127. Springer, Heidelberg (2005). https://doi.org/10.1007/11426639_7

Identity Based Linkable Ring Signature with Logarithmic Size

Mohamed Nassurdine[1,2], Huang Zhang[3], and Fangguo Zhang[1,2(✉)]

[1] School of Computer Science and Engineering, Sun Yat-sen University,
Guangzhou 510006, China
[2] Guangdong Province Key Laboratory of Information Security Technology,
Guangzhou 510006, China
`isszhfg@mail.sysu.edu.cn`
[3] School of Computer and Communication Engineering,
Changsha University of Science and Technology, Changsha 410114, China

Abstract. Anonymity is an inevitable and sensitive matter of concern, especially in the age where people are willing to use digital devices and Internet to deal with almost all things in their work and daily life. To support anonymity, modern cryptography is one of the most suitable choices in the algorithm level. Particularly, in the scenarios, such as e-voting, crypto-currency, and smart grid *etc.*, a cryptographic primitive, called linkable ring signature, has shown its ability to handle anonymity problems. However, signature schemes will introduce additional costs to those e-commerce systems, so that they should be as efficient as possible. On the other side, a signature scheme that requires the public key infrastructure (PKI) brings much unnecessary inconvenience to its users, since typically, users of the aforementioned systems are not familiar with cryptographic skills and the system establishers are trusted by them in some sense. As a result, an identity-based (ID-based) signature scheme with small size fulfills the visible requirements of e-commerce systems. In this paper, we proposed an ID-based linkable ring signature scheme with logarithmic size from pairing and elliptic curve discrete logarithm problem (ECDLP), and gave all the security proofs in detail. Besides that, the scheme needs no trusted setup, except that the key generation center knows the secret key of each user and it is a property of ID-based cryptography in nature.

Keywords: Anonymity · ID-based linkable ring signature · Logarithmic size · Pairing

1 Introduction

Linkable ring signature, as a variant of ring signature [24], has been studied for many years [20]. It is significantly useful in several e-commerce systems, such as e-voting, smart grid, *etc.*. In recent years, linkable ring signatures receives a lot of attentions, due to the fast development of blockchain-based crypto-currencies.

© Springer Nature Switzerland AG 2021
Y. Yu and M. Yung (Eds.): Inscrypt 2021, LNCS 13007, pp. 42–60, 2021.
https://doi.org/10.1007/978-3-030-88323-2_3

Researchers suggest to use such a signature to handle anonymity problems and keep the block-chain system lightweight [25]. Informally speaking, (linkable) ring signatures grants a system the ability to anonymously authenticate their users, while keep the costs at a low level. Comparing to a system that employs general purpose zero-knowledge proof protocols to support anonymity [26], a (linkable) ring signature based one is typically more efficient. Consequently, efficiency is an important index to measure the performance of a (linkable) ring signature, and a small signature size would be a desirable property for such a scheme. On the other side, as linkable ring signatures are very suitable for e-commerce systems, and such a system is efficiency sensitive, it is nature to consider that the association between a standard signature scheme and the PKI would bring much unnecessary inconvenience. For instance, sometime the group of an e-voting event is organized temporary so that to get a certificate from the PKI is a boring work for group members to do. As for smart grid, such a system is typically established by an authority party, and thus users delivers enough trusts to the system holder in some sense. Since ID-based cryptography is one of the directions to avoid the PKI [8], it is nature for us to equip our linkable ring signature with an ID-based property. That will make an e-commerce system more flexible to deploy a cryptographic scheme for security consideration.

Now, we have a common sense on that a (linkable) ring signature scheme in e-commerce system should be efficient and convenient. However, generally speaking, a traditional (linkable) ring signature usually features a signature size of $O(n)$, where n is the cardinality of the ring. A more satisfactory result would be $O(\log n)$ or $O(1)$, which means the signature size is slightly influenced by or independent of the number of participants. The first ID-based ring signature is in [28], and several works appears since then [4,13]. They were all proved in the random oracle model, and the signature size is linear in the cardinality of the ring. Only a few works were constructed in the standard model [3,6,12], but at least their signature size is not desirable enough, except those in [5,10,16, 18]. Fortunately, by using accumulator, constant size (ID-based linkable) ring signatures could be designed [1,2,11,14,22,27]. When considering no trusted setup, there are two original $O(\log n)$ ring signatures based on number-theoretic assumptions [9,15], and the logarithmic-size ring signatures with Tight Security [17]. Currently, some elegant short ring signature schemes were proposed relying on various assumptions [7,21]. However, neither of them is ID-based or contains the property of linking. To fill a vacancy in this area, in this paper, we design an ID-based linkable ring signature with logarithmic size, by using the strategies from [15] and parings. Amounts of proof skills are inspired by their work, so that if readers are familiar with the framework of [15], they can better understand the construction and proofs in the current paper.

In the literature [15], Groth *et al.*. designed a ring signature with logarithmic size, but in fact, this signature scheme is a Fiat-Shamir transformation of a Sigma-protocol for one-out-many-proofs. An underlying cryptographic primitive is a homomorphic commitment scheme, such as the Pedersen commitment in DLP (Discrete Logarithm Problem) settings. To finish their one-out-of-many proofs, they also introduced a Sigma-protocol for proving in zero knowledge that such a commitment is opened to 1 or 0. Our major work is to improve the ECDLP-based version of that in [29] to an ID-based one, and because of the new problems brought by the modifications, we redesigned the corresponding security proofs, so that the scheme could convince users that it is unforgeable under the adaptively chosen message and ID attack in the random oracle model and so on.

The remaining of this paper is organized as follows: in Sect. 2 we introduce notations and concepts used in this work. The details of the construction and the security proofs are described in Sect. 3. Finally, we give a short conclusion and further consideration in Sect. 4.

2   Preliminaries

This section gives a brief introduction to the notations, definitions adopted in this paper.

2.1   Notations

We use $\mathbb{Z}$, $\mathbb{N}$ to denote the set of all integers, and the set natural numbers. If $a, b \in \mathbb{Z}$ and $a < b$, then $[a, b]$ is the set $\{x \in \mathbb{Z} : a \leq x \leq b\}$ and $[a, b)$ is the set $\{x \in \mathbb{Z} : a \leq x < b\}$. For an integer i, i_j symbolizes the j-th bit of i. $\delta_{i\ell}$ is Kronecker's delta, i.e., $\delta_{\ell\ell} = 1$ and $\delta_{i\ell} = 0$ for $i \neq \ell$. A set $\{x_1, \ldots, x_n\}$ will be denoted by $\{x_i\}_{i=1}^n$ for short. We use $|S|$ to indicate the cardinality of a set finite S, and $a \leftarrow S$ means a is chosen from S uniformly at random. We use the standard big O notation and write $\mathrm{negl}(n)$ as a negligible function (probability) and $1 - \mathrm{negl}(n)$ is called overwhelming probability.

2.2   Bilinear Map

Definition 1. Let $\mathbb{G} = \langle G \rangle$, $\mathbb{G}_T$ be two (additive) cyclic groups of prime order p. A map $e : \mathbb{G} \times \mathbb{G} \rightarrow \mathbb{G}_T$ is a bilinear map (pairing) if it satisfies the following properties.

- BILINEARITY: For any $x, y \in \mathbb{Z}_p$, we have $e(xG, yG) = xy \cdot e(G, G)$.
- NON-DEGENERACY: If $P, Q \in \mathbb{G}$ are two generators of $\mathbb{G}$, then $e(P, Q)$ generates $\mathbb{G}_T$.
- COMPUTABILITY: There is an efficient algorithm to compute $e(P, Q)$, for all $P, Q \in \mathbb{G}$.

The security of most paring-based schemes relying on the hardness of the following problems.

Definition 2. Let $\mathbb{G}$, G, p be as in Definition 1. the computational Diffie-Hellman problem (CDH) is to computes abG, for any given triple (G, aG, bG).

Definition 3. *Let* $\mathbb{G}$, G, p, e *be as in Definition 1. For given two distributions* $(G, aG, bG, cG, w \cdot e(G, G))$, $(G, aG, bG, cG, abc \cdot e(G, G))$, *where* $a, b, c, w \leftarrow \mathbb{Z}_p$ *are independently chosen from uniform distribution, the problem which distinguishes the two distributions is called the decisional bilinear Diffie-Hellman problem (DBDH).*

The DBDH problem is not harder than the CDH problem. The CDH assumption and the DBDH assumption states that all PPT algorithms can only solve the corresponding problems with negligible probabilities.

2.3   Pedersen Commitment

The Pedersen commitment [23] allows a user to construct a commitment to a value and any party could check whether the value opened, later is the one which was committed at the beginning. The scheme involves a pair of efficient algorithms (**Gen, Com**)

- **Gen**(1^λ): On input a security parameter λ, the algorithm generates a cyclic group $\mathbb{G}$ of prime order p. It then selects two generators, $G, H \in \mathbb{G}$ at random. $\{\mathbb{G}, p, G, H\}$ will be published as the public parameters.
- **Com**(x, y): On input a value $x \in \mathbb{Z}_p$, and a randomly chosen $y \leftarrow \mathbb{Z}_p$, this algorithm computes and outputs a commitment $c = xH + yG$. The commitment c can later be opened by giving x, y.

Pedersen commitment is perfectly hiding and computationally binding under the discrete logarithm assumption.

2.4   ID-Based Linkable Ring Signature

According to the definition in [1], an ID-based linkable ring signature scheme consists of a quintuple of PPT algorithms (**Setup, Ext, Sign, Vfy, Link**).

- $(v, pp) \leftarrow$ **Setup**(1^λ): On input a security parameter λ, the algorithm outputs a master secret key v and a list of system parameters pp that includes λ and the descriptions of a user secret key space $\mathcal{D}$, a message space $\mathcal{M}$, an event-id space $\mathcal{EID}$ as well as a signature space Ψ. The system parameters pp will be a default input for the remaining algorithms.
- $V \leftarrow$ **Ext**(ID, v): On input an identity $\text{ID} \in \{0, 1\}^*$ for a user and the master secret key v, this algorithm outputs the user's secret key $V \in \mathcal{D}$. This algorithm is usually executed by a trusted party called Private Key Generator (PKG).
- $\sigma \leftarrow$ **Sign**$(n, V, M, event, L)$: On input group size $n \in \mathbb{N}$, a set L of n identities, a message $M \in \mathcal{M}$, and an event-id $event \in \mathcal{EID}$, a secret key $V \in \mathcal{D}$ whose corresponding identity is in L, the algorithm returns a signature $\sigma \in \Psi$.
- $b \leftarrow$ **Vfy**$(n, M, event, L, \sigma)$: The algorithm verifies a purported signature $\sigma \in \Psi$ on message $M \in \mathcal{M}$, group L of n identities and event-id $event \in \mathcal{EID}$. The algorithm outputs $b = 1$ if accepting and outputs $b = 0$ if rejecting the signature.

– $b \leftarrow \textbf{Link}(\sigma_1, \sigma_2)$: On input two accepting signatures σ_1, $\sigma_2 \in \Psi$ on the same event-id, output $b = 1$ if the signatures are linked, and output $b = 0$ otherwise.

As a variant of ring signature, the quintuple (**Setup, Ext, Sign, Vfy, Link**) should satisfy several requirements as introduced in [1] and [19]. Those requirements include on correctness, unforgeability, anonymity, linkability, and nonslanderability.

Definition 4 (Perfect verification correctness). *An ID-based linkable ring signature scheme* (**Setup, Ext, Sign, Vfy, Link**) *is of perfect verification correctness, if for all adversaries* $\mathcal{A}$

$$\left[\begin{array}{l} (v, pp) \leftarrow \textbf{Setup}(1^\lambda); \\ \text{ID} \leftarrow \mathcal{A}(pp); V \leftarrow \textbf{Ext}(\text{ID}, v); \\ (n, M, event, L) \leftarrow \mathcal{A}(pp, \text{ID}, V); \\ \sigma \leftarrow \textbf{Sign}(n, V, M, event, L) \end{array} : \begin{array}{c} \textbf{Vfy}(n, M, event, L, \sigma) = 1 \\ \vee \\ \text{ID} \notin L \end{array} \right] = 1 .$$

Definition 5 (Perfect linking correctness). *An ID-based linkable ring signature scheme* (**Setup, Ext, Sign, Vfy, Link**) *has perfect linking correctness, if for all adversaries* $\mathcal{A}$

$$\left[\begin{array}{l} (v, pp) \leftarrow \textbf{Setup}(1^\lambda); \\ \text{ID} \leftarrow \mathcal{A}(pp); V \leftarrow \textbf{Ext}(\text{ID}, v); \\ \begin{pmatrix} n_1, M_1, L_1 \\ event \\ n_2, M_2, L_2 \end{pmatrix} \leftarrow \mathcal{A}(pp, \text{ID}, V); \\ \sigma_1 \leftarrow \textbf{Sign}(n_1, V, M_1, event, L_1); \\ \sigma_2 \leftarrow \textbf{Sign}(n_2, V, M_2, event, L_2); \end{array} : \begin{array}{c} \textbf{Link}(\sigma_1, \sigma_2) = 1 \\ \vee \\ \textbf{Vfy}(n_1, M_1, event, L_1, \sigma_1) = 0 \\ \vee \\ \textbf{Vfy}(n_2, M_2, event, L_2, \sigma_2) = 0 \end{array} \right] = 1 .$$

The remaining requirements are for security concerns. Most of them employ the following oracles to specify the abilities of an attacking adversary $\mathcal{A}$.

– $V \leftarrow \mathcal{EO}(\text{ID})$: The stateful *Extraction Oracle*, on input $\text{ID} \in \{0, 1\}^*$, returns the corresponding secret key $V \in \mathcal{D}$.
– $\sigma \leftarrow \mathcal{SO}(n, \text{ID}_\pi, M, event, L)$: The *Signing Oracle*, on input a group size n, an event-id $event \in \mathcal{EID}$, a set L of n identities, the identity of the signer $\text{ID}_\pi \in L$, and a message $M \in \mathcal{M}$, returns a valid signature σ. The extraction oracle could be queried during the process.

If hash functions are modeled as random oracles, then $\mathcal{A}$ can ask for the values of the hash functions for any input.

Definition 6 (Unforgeability). *An ID-based linkable ring signature scheme* (**Setup, Ext, Sign, Vfy, Link**) *is unforgeable if for all PPT adversaries* $\mathcal{A}$

$$\Pr \left[\begin{array}{l} (v, pp) \leftarrow \textbf{Setup}(1^\lambda); \\ (n, M, L, event, \sigma) \leftarrow \mathcal{A}^{\mathcal{EO}, \mathcal{SO}}(pp) \end{array} : \textbf{Vfy}(n, M, event, L, \sigma) = 1 \right] \leq \text{negl}(\lambda) ,$$

where $(n, *, M, event, L)$ *has not been queried to* $\mathcal{SO}$, *and all identities in* L *have not been queried to* $\mathcal{EO}$

Definition 7 (Computational anonymity). *An ID-based linkable ring signature scheme* (**Setup, Ext, Sign, Vfy, Link**) *has computational anonymity, if for any PPT adversary* $\mathcal{A}$

$$\Pr\left[\begin{array}{c} (v, pp) \leftarrow \textbf{Setup}(1^\lambda); \\ (n, M, L, event) \leftarrow \mathcal{A}^{\mathcal{EO}, \mathcal{SO}}(pp); \\ i \leftarrow [0, n); \\ \sigma \leftarrow \textbf{Sign}(n, V_i, M, event, L); \end{array} : \mathcal{A}(\sigma) = i \right] \leq \frac{1}{n} + \mathrm{negl}(\lambda) \ ,$$

where all identities in L *has not been queried to* $\mathcal{EO}$.

Definition 8 (Linkability). *An ID-based linkable ring signature scheme* (**Setup, Ext, Sign, Vfy, Link**) *is of linkability if for all PPT adversaries* $\mathcal{A}$

$$\Pr\left[\begin{array}{c} (v, pp) \leftarrow \textbf{Setup}(1^\lambda); \\ \begin{pmatrix} n_1, M_1, L_1, \sigma_1 \\ event \\ n_2, M_2, L_2, \sigma_2 \end{pmatrix} \leftarrow \mathcal{A}^{\mathcal{EO}, \mathcal{SO}}(pp) \end{array} : \begin{array}{c} \textbf{Link}(\sigma_1, \sigma_2) = 0 \\ \wedge \\ \textbf{Vfy}(n_1, M_1, event, L_1, \sigma_1) = 1 \\ \wedge \\ \textbf{Vfy}(n_2, M_2, event, L_2, \sigma_2) = 1 \end{array} \right] \leq \mathrm{negl}(\lambda) \ ,$$

where σ_1, σ_2 *are not returned by* $\mathcal{SO}$, *and no more than 1 identity in* $L_1 \cap L_2$ *has been submitted to* $\mathcal{CO}$.

Definition 9 (Nonslanderability). *An ID-based linkable ring signature scheme* (**Setup, Ext, Sign, Vfy, Link**) *has nonslanderability if for any PPT adversary* $\mathcal{A}$

$$\Pr\left[\begin{array}{c} (v, pp) \leftarrow \textbf{Setup}(1^\lambda); \\ (n_1, \mathrm{ID}, M_1, event, L_1) \leftarrow \mathcal{A}^{\mathcal{EO}, \mathcal{SO}}(pp); \\ \sigma_1 \leftarrow \textbf{Sign}(n_1, V_i, M_1, event, L_1); \\ (n_2, M_2, L_2, \sigma_2) \leftarrow \mathcal{A}^{\mathcal{EO}, \mathcal{SO}}(pp, \sigma_1) \end{array} : \begin{array}{c} \textbf{Link}(\sigma_1, \sigma_2) = 1 \\ \wedge \\ \textbf{Vfy}(n_2, M_2, event, L_2, \sigma_2) = 1 \end{array} \right] \leq \mathrm{negl}(\lambda) \ ,$$

where σ_2 *is not an output of* $\mathcal{SO}$, *and* $\mathrm{ID} \in L_1$ *has not been queried to* $\mathcal{EO}$.

3 ID-based Linkable Ring Signature Scheme

As we mentioned before, our ID-based linkable ring signature scheme was inspired by the spirits of [15], so that it is essentially a non-interactive argument protocol for one-out-of-many relations, and the Fiat-Shamir heuristic is adopted also (see App B).

In our scheme, a signer proves to verifiers that she knows the secret key of one of the public keys (identities) in $L = (\mathrm{ID}_0, \ldots, \mathrm{ID}_{n-1})$, but the strategy is somewhat different Since the signer could duplicate some ring members, without loss of generality let us assume $n = 2^m$, for $m \in \mathbb{Z}^+$. Let the signer's public key be ID_ℓ, and write $\ell = \ell_1, \ldots \ell_m$ in binary. To make the signature size logarithmic in n, the knowledge of the index of the signer's public key in L is used. In brief, a signer will first demonstrate that she is the identity indexed by ℓ and also show her knowledge on the secret key of ID_ℓ, both in zero-knowledge ways. Consequently, in the signing step, the signer will make commitments A_j to the bits ℓ_j, and reveals w_j of the form $w_j = \ell_j x + a_j$, for $j \in [1, m]$. Subsequently, to say that the signer knows the secret key of ID_ℓ is equivalent to say $\sum_{i=0}^{n-1} \delta_{i\ell} Q_i$ is the hash digest of her identity, where $Q_i = \mathcal{H}_1(ID_i)$, and $\delta_{i\ell}$ is the Kronecker's delta, i.e., $\delta_{\ell\ell} = 1$ and $\delta_{i\ell} = 0$ for $i \neq \ell$. If writing i and ℓ in binary, we further have $\delta_{i\ell} = \prod_{j=1}^{m} \delta_{i_j \ell_j}$.

However, the foregoing approach shows the knowledge of ℓ directly, so that we seek for the help of w_j which contains the information of ℓ_j secretly. Define $w_{j,1} = w_j = \ell_j x + a_j = \delta_{1\ell_j} x + a_j$, and $w_{j,0} = x - w_j = (1-\ell_j)x - a_j = \delta_{0\ell_j} x - a_j$. For every $i \in [0, n)$ the product $\prod_{j=1}^{m} w_{j,i_j}$ is a polynomial in the indeterminate x of the form

$$p_i(x) = \prod_{j=1}^{m} w_{j,i_j} = \prod_{j=1}^{m} (\delta_{i_j \ell_j} x) + \sum_{k=0}^{m-1} p_{i,k} x^k = \delta_{i\ell} x^m + \sum_{k=0}^{m-1} p_{i,k} x^k . \quad (1)$$

Here, $p_{i,k}$ is the coefficient of the kth degree term of the polynomial $p_i(x)$, and can be efficiently computed when $(a_j)_{j=1}^{m}$, i and ℓ are given. On the other side, only if $i = \ell$, the mth degree term of $p_i(x)$ in (1) is not 0, so that if we use w_{j,i_j} to substitute the function of $\delta_{i_j \ell_j}$, we have

$$\sum_{i=0}^{n-1} \left(\prod_{j=1}^{m} w_{j,i_j} \right) Q_i = x^m Q_\ell + \sum_{i=0}^{n-1} \left(\sum_{k=1}^{m-1} p_{i,k} x^k \right) Q_i ,$$

where the mth degree term merely contains the hash digest of the signer's public key, and that is the key point in proving the signer knows the secret key of ID_ℓ secretly.

3.1 Construction

The details of our ID-based linkable ring signature (**Setup, Ext, Sign, Vfy, Link**) is as follows.

Setup(1^λ): The input of this procedure is a security parameter λ. Let E be an elliptic curve defined over a finite field $\mathbb{F}_q$. Let $G \in E$ be a point of prime order p, here $\log p = O(\lambda)$ and let $\mathbb{G}$ be the prime order subgroup of E generated by G. Let $\mathcal{H} : \{0,1\}^* \to \mathbb{Z}_p$, $\mathcal{H}_1 : \{0,1\}^* \to \mathbb{G}$, $\mathcal{H}_2 : \{0,1\}^* \to \mathbb{G}$, be three cryptographic hash functions, and $e : \mathbb{G} \times \mathbb{G} \to \mathbb{G}_T$ a pairing. Select a master secret key $v \leftarrow \mathbb{Z}_p$ and compute the master public key $P = vG$. Independently pick a group element $H \leftarrow \mathbb{G}$. The list of system parameters $pp = (\lambda, \mathbb{G}, G, H, P, p, q, \mathcal{H}, \mathcal{H}_1, \mathcal{H}_2, e)$ is published as an implicit input for the other algorithms and the master secret key v is kept by the PKG secretly.

Ext(ID, v): Given an identity $ID \in \{0,1\}^*$, the algorithm generates the associated secret key $V = vQ$ by using the hash digest $Q = \mathcal{H}_1(ID)$.

Sign($n, V_\ell, M, event, L$): Parse $L = (ID_0, \ldots, ID_{n-1})$ and write $\ell = \ell_1 \ldots \ell_m$ in binary. Without loss of generality assume $n = 2^m$.

- compute $(Q_0, \ldots, Q_{n-1}) = (\mathcal{H}_1(\text{ID}_0), \ldots, \mathcal{H}_1(\text{ID}_{n-1}))$.
- compute $K = \mathcal{H}_2(event)$, $I = e(V_\ell, K)$.
- For j from 1 to m,
  - choose $r_j, a_j, s_j, t_j \leftarrow \mathbb{Z}_p$ uniformly at random,
  - compute $A_j = \ell_j H + r_j G$,
  - compute $B_j = a_j H + s_j G$,
  - compute $C_j = a_j \ell_j H + t_j G$.
- For k from 0 to $m-1$,
  - choose $\rho_k \leftarrow \mathbb{Z}_p$ uniformly at random,
  - compute $D_k = (\sum_{i=0}^{n-1} p_{i,k} Q_i) + \rho_k G$, where $p_{i,k}$ is introduced later (1),
  - compute $E_k = e(P, \rho_k K)$.
- Let $cmt = (A_j, B_j, C_j, D_{j-1} E_{j-1})_{j=1}^m$ and compute $x = \mathcal{H}(M, L, cmt, I, event)$.
- For j from 1 to m, compute
  - $w_j = x\ell_j + a_j \bmod p$,
  - $y_j = xr_j + s_j \bmod p$,
  - $z_j = (x - w_j)r_j + t_j \bmod p$.
- $Z = x^m V_\ell - \sum_{k=0}^{m-1} \rho_k x^k P \bmod p$.
- Let $rsp = (w_j, y_j, z_j)_{j=1}^m$. Return $\sigma = (cmt, x, rsp, Z, I)$ as a signature on M, L and $event$.

Vfy$(n, M, event, L, \sigma)$:
Parse $L = (\text{ID}_0, \ldots, \text{ID}_{n-1})$, and $\sigma = (cmt, x, rsp, Z, I)$. Let $K = \mathcal{H}_2(event)$, and $(Q_0, \ldots, Q_{n-1}) = (\mathcal{H}_1(\text{ID}_0), \ldots, \mathcal{H}_1(\text{ID}_{n-1}))$. The algorithm returns 1 only if all the following conditions hold.

- $x = \mathcal{H}(M, L, cmt, I, event)$.
- For j from 1 to m
  - $xA_j + B_j = w_j H + y_j G$,
  - $(x - w_j)A_j + C_j = z_j G$.
- $x^m I - \sum_{k=0}^{m-1} x^k E_k = e(Z, K)$.
- $e(Z, G) = e\left(\sum_{i=0}^{n-1}(\prod_{j=1}^m w_{j,i_j})Q_i + \sum_{k=0}^{m-1}(-x^k)D_k, P\right)$.

Link(σ_1, σ_2): For $s \in \{0, 1\}$, parse $\sigma_s = (cmt_s, x_s, rsp_s, Z_s, I_s)$. The algorithm returns 1 only if $I_1 = I_2$, and returns 0 otherwise.

Theorem 1. *The scheme* (**Setup, Ext, Sign, Vfy, Link**) *is of perfect verification and linking correctness.*

The conclusion is obvious so that we left the brief explanation in Appendix A.

3.2   Security Proofs

Theorem 2. *The scheme* (**Setup, Ext, Sign, Vfy, Link**) *is computationally anonymous in the random oracle model, if the DBDH assumption holds and the Pedersen is perfectly hiding.*

Proof. Suppose $\mathcal{A}$ is a PPT adversary breaking computational anonymity with probability ϵ.

Let $\mathbb{G} = \langle G \rangle$ be a cyclic group of prime order p, e be a corresponding bilinear map, and $T_1 = (G, aG, bG, cG, w \cdot e(G,G))$, $T_2 = (G, aG, bG, cG, abc \cdot e(G,G))$ be an instance of the DBDH problem. According to the DBDH assumption we have for all PPT challenger $\mathcal{C}$

$$| \Pr[\mathcal{C}(T_1) = 1] - \Pr[\mathcal{C}(T_2) = 1]| \leq \mathrm{negl}(\lambda) \ .$$

When $\mathcal{C}$ is given T_s, for $s \in \{0,1\}$, it does as follows to simulate an anonymity game for $\mathcal{A}$. For simplicity, we use T_{si} to denote the ith component of T_s.

$\mathcal{C}$ first provides the public system parameter to $\mathcal{A}$. To this end, $\mathcal{C}$ selects $H \leftarrow \mathbb{G}$, and set the master public key $P = T_{s2}$. $\mathcal{C}$ sends $pp = (\mathbb{G}, G, P, p, q, \mathcal{H}, \mathcal{H}_1, \mathcal{H}_2, e)$ to $\mathcal{A}$, where the hash functions are modeled as random oracles. Additionally, we assume that $\mathcal{A}$ will check whether an obtained signature is valid which simplifies the proof, since it guarantees $\mathcal{A}$ does at some point access the random oracle to have the necessary hash digests.

After receiving pp, $\mathcal{A}$ contacts with all oracles (simulated by $\mathcal{C}$) adaptively. Assume that $\mathcal{A}$ queries $\mathcal{H}_1, \mathcal{H}_2$ for at most $\mathcal{Q}_1, \mathcal{Q}_2$ times, respectively.

Oracle simulation: $\mathcal{C}$ will randomly picks integers $\eta_1 \leftarrow [1, \mathcal{Q}_1]$, $\eta_2 \leftarrow [1, \mathcal{Q}_2]$.

- *Random oracle* $\mathcal{H}(M, L, cmt, I, event)$: if $\mathcal{H}(s)$ was queried before, return the recorded element. Else, $\mathcal{C}$ randomly picks and returns $x \leftarrow \mathbb{Z}_p$. It models the random oracle to have $\mathcal{H}(M, L, cmt, I, event) = x$.
- *Random oracle* $\mathcal{H}_1(\mathrm{ID})$: if $\mathcal{H}_1(\mathrm{ID})$ was queried before, return the recorded element. Else if it is the η_1th query, return $Q = T_{s3}$. Otherwise, $\mathcal{C}$ randomly picks $\alpha \leftarrow \mathbb{Z}_p$ and computes $Q = \alpha G$. Thus, $V = \alpha P$ is the corresponding secret key. The random oracle return Q and is modeled to have $\mathcal{H}_1(\mathrm{ID}) = Q$.
- *Random oracle* $\mathcal{H}_2(event)$: if $\mathcal{H}_2(event)$ was queried before, return the recorded element. Else if it is the η_2th query, return $K = T_{s4}$. Otherwise, randomly select and return $K \leftarrow \mathbb{G}$. It models the random oracle to have $\mathcal{H}_2(event) = K$.
- *Extracting oracle* $\mathcal{EO}(\mathrm{ID})$: if $H_1(\mathrm{ID}) = T_{s3}$, the oracle aborts. Else if $\mathcal{H}_1(\mathrm{ID})$ was not queried before, $\mathcal{C}$ queries it. The oracle returns $V = \alpha P$.
- *Signing oracle* $\mathcal{SO}(n, \mathrm{ID}, M, event, L)$: if $\mathrm{ID} \notin L$, $\mathcal{C}$ refuses to answer. If $\mathcal{H}_1(\mathrm{ID})$ or $\mathcal{H}_2(event)$ were not queried before, $\mathcal{C}$ queries them and use $V = \alpha P$ as the corresponding secret key. Then $\mathcal{C}$ runs **Sign**$(n, V, M, event, L)$ to generate and return an accepting signature σ.

After interacting with the oracles, $\mathcal{A}$ specifies a target $(n, M, L, event)$. If $T_{s3} \in L$ and $event = T_{s4}$, $\mathcal{C}$ uses the SHVZK simulator (see Appendix B) to generate a valid signature (proof transcript) $\sigma_s = (cmt, x, rsp, Z, I = T_{s5})$ for ID $= T_{s3}$. Let the index of ID $= T_{s3} \in L$ is $\pi \in [0, n)$. Please note that the probabilities that $\mathcal{EO}$ aborts, $T_{s3} \notin L$ and $event \neq T_s$ is $1/\mathcal{Q}_1$, $1 - n/\mathcal{Q}_1$, and $1/\mathcal{Q}_2$, respectively.

Finally, $\mathcal{A}$ returns an index $j \in [0, n)$, after receiving σ. If $j = \pi$, $\mathcal{C}$ outputs 1, otherwise $\mathcal{C}$ outputs 0. If $\mathcal{C}$ is fed with T_1, then $\mathcal{A}$ is in a real anonymity game. According to the hypothesis to $\mathcal{A}$, we have

$$\Pr[\mathcal{C}(T_1) = 1] = \Pr[\mathcal{A}(\sigma_1) = \pi] \geq \epsilon - \frac{1 + \mathcal{Q}_1 - n}{\mathcal{Q}_1} - \frac{1}{\mathcal{Q}_2} = \epsilon - \frac{1}{\text{poly}(\lambda)} \ .$$

On the other side, if $\mathcal{C}$ is fed with T_2, then the advantage for $\mathcal{A}$ to find the correct π is no better than random guessing, since the underlying Sigma-protocol is SHVZK (see Appendix B) and the linking tag I is independent of every pubic key in L. Thus,

$$\Pr[\mathcal{C}(T_2) = 1] = \Pr[\mathcal{A}(\sigma_2) = \pi] = 1/n - \frac{1}{\text{poly}(\lambda)} \ .$$

Consequently, depending on the DBDH assumption

$$\text{negl}(\lambda) \geq |\Pr[\mathcal{C}(T_1) = 1] - \Pr[\mathcal{C}(T_2) = 1]| = |\Pr[\mathcal{A}(\sigma_1) = \pi] - \Pr[\mathcal{A}(\sigma_2) = \pi]|$$
$$\geq |\Pr[\mathcal{A}(\sigma_1) = \pi]| - |\Pr[\mathcal{A}(\sigma_2) = \pi]| \geq \epsilon - 1/n \ .$$

Thus we have $\epsilon \leq 1/n + \text{negl}(\lambda)$, which means the advantage for $\mathcal{A}$ to break the computational anonymity of our scheme is negligible. $\qquad\square$

Theorem 3. *The scheme* (**Setup, Ext, Sign, Vfy, Link**) *is unforgeable in the random oracle model, if the Computational Diffie-Hellman (CDH) assumption hold, and the Pedersen commitment is perfectly hiding and computationally binding.*

Proof. Suppose $\mathcal{A}$ is a PPT adversary breaking unforgeability with probability ϵ. Let $\mathbb{G} = \langle G \rangle$ be a cyclic group of prime order p, e be a corresponding bilinear map, and $T = (G, aG, bG)$ be an instance of the the CDH problem. According to the CDH assumption we have for all PPT challenger $\mathcal{C}$

$$\Pr[\mathcal{C}(T) = abG] \leq \text{negl}(\lambda) \ .$$

When $\mathcal{C}$ is given T, it does as follows to simulate an unforgeability game for $\mathcal{A}$. For simplicity, we use T_i to denote the ith component of T.

$\mathcal{C}$ first provides the public system parameter to $\mathcal{A}$. To this end, $\mathcal{C}$ selects $H \leftarrow \mathbb{G}$, and set the master public key $P = T_2$. $\mathcal{C}$ sends $pp = (\mathbb{G}, G, P, p, q, \mathcal{H}, \mathcal{H}_1, \mathcal{H}_2, e)$ to $\mathcal{A}$, where the hash functions are modeled as random oracles. Additionally, we assume that $\mathcal{A}$ will check whether an obtained signature is valid which simplifies the proof, since it guarantees $\mathcal{A}$ does at some point access the random oracle to have the necessary hash digests.

After receiving pp, $\mathcal{A}$ contacts with all oracles (simulated by $\mathcal{C}$) adaptively. Assume that $\mathcal{A}$ queries $\mathcal{H}_1$ for at most $\mathcal{Q}_1$ times, respectively.

Oracle simulation: $\mathcal{C}$ will randomly picks integers $\eta_1 \leftarrow [1, \mathcal{Q}_1]$.

- *Random oracle* $\mathcal{H}(M, L, cmt, I, event)$: the random oracle is simulated the same as in the proof of Theorem 2.
- *Random oracle* $\mathcal{H}_1(\text{ID})$: If $\mathcal{H}_1(\text{ID})$ was queried before, return the recorded element. Else if it is the η_1th query, return $Q = T_3$ Otherwise, $\mathcal{C}$ randomly picks $\alpha \leftarrow \mathbb{Z}_p$ and computes $Q = \alpha G$. The random oracle is modeled to have $\mathcal{H}_1(\text{ID}) = Q$. Notice that $V = \alpha P$ is the corresponding secret key.
- *Random oracle* $\mathcal{H}_2(event)$: if $\mathcal{H}_2(event)$ was queried before, return the recorded element. Otherwise, randomly select $\beta \leftarrow \mathbb{Z}_p$ and compute $K = \beta G$. The random oracle is modeled to have $\mathcal{H}_2(event) = K$ and return K.
- *Extracting oracle* $\mathcal{EO}(\text{ID})$: If $\mathcal{H}_1(\text{ID}) = T_2$, abort. Else if $\mathcal{H}_1(\text{ID})$ was not queried before, C queries it. The oracle returns $V = \alpha P$.
- *Signing oracle* $\mathcal{SO}(n, \text{ID}, M, event, L)$: if $\text{ID} \notin L$, $\mathcal{C}$ refuses to answer. If $\mathcal{H}_1(\text{ID})$ or $\mathcal{H}_2(event)$ were not queried before, $\mathcal{C}$ queries them and use $V = \alpha P$ as the corresponding secret key. If $\mathcal{H}_1(\text{ID}) \neq T_2$, $\mathcal{C}$ runs **Sign**$(n, V, M, event, L)$ to return an accepting signature σ. Else if $\mathcal{H}_1(\text{ID}) = T_2$, $\mathcal{C}$ randomly picks challenge $x \leftarrow \mathbb{Z}_p$, and uses $I = e(T_2, \beta P)$ as the linking tag. It invokes the SHVZK simulator to return an accepting signature $\sigma = (cmt, x, rsp, Z, I)$ and models the random oracle to have $\mathcal{H}_1(M, L, cmt, I, event) = x$. If $\mathcal{H}_1(M, L, cmt, I, event)$ was queried and the recorded element is not x, abort.

After interacting with the oracles, $\mathcal{A}$ outputs a forgery $(n, M, L, event, \sigma)$ such that σ is not an output of $\mathcal{SO}$ and all identities in L have not been queried to $\mathcal{EO}$.

According to the analysis in Theorem 4 of [15], $\mathcal{C}$ is able to obtain $n + 1$ distinct challenge-response pairs to the same initial message with probability near $\epsilon/2$, so that the $(n+1)$-special soundness extractor (see Appendix B) could extract a secret key V, and since the Pedersen commitment is perfectly hiding, with probability $1/\mathcal{Q}_1$, V is the secret key of ID, for $\mathcal{H}_1(\text{ID}) = T_2$. In this case, we have

$$\log_{T_2} V = \log_G P$$
$$\Downarrow$$
$$\log_{bG} V = \log_G aG$$
$$\Downarrow$$
$$V = abG$$

Hence, V is a correct answer for the instance of the CDH problem, and the proof is a PPT algorithm to find it with probability close to or higher than $\epsilon/2\mathcal{Q}_1$. Based on the CDH assumption, we have $\epsilon \leq \text{negl}(\lambda)$, so that the ID-based linkable ring signature scheme is unforgeable. $\square$

Theorem 4. *The scheme* (**Setup, Ext, Sign, Vfy, Link**) *has linkability in the random oracle model if the CDH assumption holds, and the Pedersen commitment is perfectly hiding and computationally binding.*

Proof. Suppose $\mathcal{A}$ is a PPT adversary breaking linkability with probability ϵ. Let $\mathbb{G} = \langle G \rangle$ be a cyclic group of prime order p, e be a corresponding bilinear map, and $T = (G, aG, bG)$ be an instance of the the the CDH problem. $\mathcal{C}$ simulates a linkability game for $\mathcal{A}$ when given T.

To this end, $\mathcal{C}$ generates the system parameters, and simulates the oracles the same as in the proof of Theorem 3, where $P = T_2$, $Q = T_3$.

Assume that $\mathcal{A}$ queries $\mathcal{H}_1$, $\mathcal{H}_2$ for at most $\mathcal{Q}_1$, $\mathcal{Q}_2$ times, respectively. After receiving public system parameters and interacting with the oracles, $\mathcal{A}$ returns two tuples $(n_1, M_1, L_1, \sigma_1)$, $(n_2, M_2, L_2, \sigma_2)$ on the same *event*, such that the signatures are accepting and not the outputs of $\mathcal{SO}$, $\mathbf{Link}(\sigma_1, \sigma_2) = 0$ and no more than 1 identity in $L_1 \cup L_2$ was queried to $\mathcal{EO}$.

As all the simulation are the same as in Theorem 3, we state that $\mathcal{C}$ could rewind $\mathcal{A}$ to obtain $n + 1$ distinct challenge-response pairs for at least one of the initial messages of σ_1 and σ_2 with probability near $\epsilon/2$. Without loss of generality, let σ_1 be the one, so that $\mathcal{C}$ can extract a secret key V for one of the identities in L_1 with probability close to or higher than $\epsilon/2$. With this in mind, let us consider the following two cases.

Case 1, no identity in $L_1 \cup L_2$ has been submitted to $\mathcal{EO}$. This case will yield a contradiction to the unforgeability of the scheme, as the extracted V is the secret key of Q with probability near $\epsilon/2\mathcal{Q}_1$, and acts as a correct answer for the instance of the CDH problem.

Case 2, only one identity in L_2 was queried to $\mathcal{EO}$, and $L_1 \cap L_2 = \emptyset$. This case is similar to Case 1, and yields a contraction to unforgeability.

Case 3, only one identity in $L_1 \cap L_2$ was submitted to $\mathcal{EO}$. Writing $\sigma_1 = (\ldots, I_1)$, $\sigma_2(\ldots, I_2)$, since $\mathbf{Link}(\sigma_1, \sigma_2) = 0$, we have $I_1 \neq I_2$. Let $L_1 = (\mathrm{ID}_i)_{i=1}^{n_1-1}$, and $L_1' = (Q_i)_{i=0}^{n_1-1} = (\mathcal{H}_1(\mathrm{ID}_i))_{i=0}^{n-1}$. Similar to the introduction in Theorem 3, by rewinding $\mathcal{A}$, $\mathcal{C}$ is able to extract a secret key V for $\overline{Q} \in L'$ such that

$$\log_{\overline{Q}} V = \log_G P = \log_{e(\overline{Q}, H_2(event^*))} I_1 .$$

Moreover, with probability near $\epsilon/2\mathcal{Q}_1$, we have $Q = \overline{Q}$, so that $V = Q \cdot \log_G P = abG$. Since $I_1 \neq I_2$, for all $\mathrm{ID} \in L_2$

$$\log_{\mathcal{H}_1(\mathrm{ID})} \overline{V} = \log_{e(\mathcal{H}_1(\mathrm{ID}), \mathcal{H}_2(event))} e(\overline{V}, H_2(event))$$
$$\neq \log_{e(Q, H_2(event))} I = \log_Q V . \qquad (2)$$

Hence, $\overline{V} \neq V$, which means V is a valid solution for the instance of the CDH problem and $\mathcal{A}$ did not hold it in advance. With the CDH assumption, $\mathcal{A}$ does not exist, so that the scheme is of linkability. $\qquad \square$

Theorem 5. *The ID-based linkable ring signature scheme is nonslanderable in the random oracle model if it is unforgeable on adaptively chosen message and ID attacks and is of linkability.*

Proof. Theorem 3 showed that if an PPT adversary $\mathcal{A}$ does not hold one of secret key of the corresponding ring, it barely can generate an accepting signature. Thus, conditioned on $\mathcal{A}$ outputs an accepting signature $\sigma = (cmt, x, rsp, I)$ on behalf of L and event description *event*, it is with overwhelming probability that $\mathcal{A}$ made use the knowledge of its key pair (V, Q), such that $V \in L$. Then, by the proof of Theorem 4, the linking tag $I = e(V, \mathcal{H}_2(event))$ with overwhelming probability. To summarize, an PPT adversary $\mathcal{A}$ has negligible probability to output an accepting signature such that the linking tag is equivalent to the one belongs to another signer. $\square$

4   Conclusions and Future Works

In this paper, we proposed an ID-based linkable ring signature with logarithmic size and gave a complete security proof to it. Without public key infrastructure, e-commerce parties are more flexible to deploy our signature in there system, and due to the logarithmic size, anonymity problems could be handled at the relatively low cost. In the future works, we are going to widely utilize the advantages of the current signature scheme.

Acknowledgements. This work is supported by Guangdong Major Project of Basic and Applied Basic Research (2019B030302008) and the National Natural Science Foundation of China (No. 61972429).

Appendix

A   Proof of Theorem 1

Proof. It is easy to see that an honestly generated signature can always pass the verification algorithm. We only explicitly deduce the two equations whose correctness are not shown directly. The first equation is responsible for checking that the linking tag is generated honestly.

$$x^m I - \sum_{k=0}^{m-1} x^k E_k = x^n \cdot e(V_\ell, K) - e(P, \sum_{k=0}^{n-1} x^k \rho_k K)$$

$$= e(x^n V_\ell, K) - e(\sum_{k=0}^{n-1} x^k \rho_k P, K)$$

$$= e(x^n V_\ell - \sum_{k=0}^{n-1} x^k \rho_k P, K)$$

$$= e(Z, K) \ .$$

The second equation is to show that the signer hold the corresponding signing key.

$$e\left(\sum_{i=0}^{n-1}(\prod_{j=1}^{m}w_{j,i_j})Q_i + \sum_{k=0}^{m-1}(-x^k)D_k, P\right)$$

$$= e\left(\sum_{i=0}^{n-1}(\delta_{i\ell}x^m + \sum_{k=1}^{m-1}p_{i,k}x^k)Q_i - \sum_{k=0}^{m-1}((\sum_{i=0}^{n-1}p_{i,k}Q_i) + \rho_k G)x^k, P\right)$$

$$= e\left(\sum_{i=0}^{n-1}\delta_{i\ell}x^m Q_i - \sum_{k=0}^{m-1}\rho_k x^k G, P\right)$$

$$= e\left(x^m Q_\ell - \sum_{k=0}^{m-1}\rho_k x^k G, vG\right)$$

$$= e\left(x^m V_\ell - \sum_{k=0}^{m-1}\rho_k x^k P, G\right)$$

$$= e(Z, G)$$

The correctness of the other equations could be verified easily.   □

B   The Underlying Sigma-Protocol

We have noticed before that the current ID-based linkable ring signature scheme is the non-interactive version of a one-out-of many Sigma-protocol which we call it Σ_2. The only difference between them is that in the Sigma-protocol, the hash digest $x \in \mathbb{Z}_p$ is chosen uniformly at random by the verifier rather than computed from some predetermined values. Such a framework is inspired by [15], and actually, to build the aforementioned one-out-of-many Sigma-Protocol, another Sigma-Protocol (which we call it Σ_1 for short) for proving that a commitment is opened to 1 or 0 is needed. As Σ_1 is the same to the one in Sect. 2.3 in [15], we omit its description here. The only thing we need to know is that σ_1 is perfect 2-special sound and perfect special honest verifier zero-knowledge.

Given the public parameters pp, public keys $Q_0, \ldots, Q_{n-1}$, linking tag $I = e(V_\ell, K)$, and the event description $event$ which fixes $K = \mathcal{H}_2(event)$, the NP relation to be proved by the prover (signer) who hold $V_\ell = vQ_\ell$ is

$$\mathcal{R} = \left\{(pp, (Q_0, \ldots, Q_{n-1}, K, I), (\ell, V_\ell)) : \begin{array}{c} Q_1, \ldots, Q_n, \in \mathbb{G} \wedge \ell \in [0, n) \wedge \\ I \in \mathbb{G}_T \wedge \log_{Q_\ell} V_\ell = \log_G P \wedge \\ \log_{e(Q_\ell, K)} I = \log_G P \end{array}\right\}.$$

In simple terms, the prover should convince the verifier that 1) his/her knowledge to the NP witness involves an integer $\ell \in [0, n)$ and a group element $V_\ell \in \mathbb{G}$; 2) the discrete logarithm between V_ℓ and the ℓth public key Q_ℓ is equal to that between the master public key P and the group generator G; 3) The linking tag is uniquely determined by V_ℓ under the same pp and $event$.

Theorem 6. Σ_2 *is of* $(m+1)$-*special soundness.*

Proof. Suppose the adversary creates $m+1$ accepting responses

$$\{w_1^{(\alpha)}, \ldots, w_m^{(\alpha)}, y_1^{(\alpha)}, \ldots, y_m^{(\alpha)}, z_1^{(\alpha)}, \ldots, z_m^{(\alpha)}, Z^{(\alpha)}\}_{\alpha \in [0,m]}$$

to $m+1$ distinct challenges $x^{(0)}, \ldots, x^{(m)}$. Using any two of the challenge-response pairs, the 2-special soundness of Σ_1 ensures that we are able to extract an opening $(\ell_j, r_j) \in \{0,1\} \times \mathbb{Z}_p$ to A_j such that for $j \in [1, m]$, $A_j = \ell_j H + r_j G$. Additionally, from the first equation in the verification, we have

$$x^{(\alpha)} A_j + B_j = w_j^{(\alpha)} H + y_j^{(\alpha)} G$$
$$\Downarrow$$
$$B_j = w_j^{(\alpha)} H + y_j^{(\alpha)} G - x^{(\alpha)} A_j$$
$$\Downarrow$$
$$B_j = w_j^{(\alpha)} H + y_j^{(\alpha)} G - x^{(\alpha)}(\ell_j H + r_j G)$$
$$\Downarrow$$
$$B_j = (w_j^{(\alpha)} - x^{(\alpha)} \ell_j) H + (y_j^{(\alpha)} - x^{(\alpha)} r_j) G.$$

Define $a_j^{(\alpha)} = w_j^{(\alpha)} - x^{(\alpha)} \ell_j$, and it is with overwhelming probability that $a_j^{(\alpha)} = a_j^{(\alpha')} \stackrel{\text{def}}{=} a_j$ for all $\alpha, \alpha' \in [0, m]$ (otherwise, we obtain at least one pair of distinct openings to B_j). Consequently, we have that $w_j^{(\alpha)} = \ell_j x^{(\alpha)} + a_j$ for all $\alpha \in [0, m]$ and $j \in [1, m]$. For $i \neq \ell$, we can see that $\prod_{j=1}^{m} w_{j,i_j}^{(\alpha)}$ is a degree $m-1$ polynomial in determinate x and for $i = \ell$, it is a polynomial of degree m. So, from the last equation in the verification procedure, we have

$$e\left(\sum_{i=0}^{n-1}\sum_{j=1}^{m}(\prod w_{j,i_j}^{(\alpha)})Q_i + \sum_{k=0}^{m-1}(-(x^{(\alpha)})^k)D_k, P\right)$$
$$= e\left((x^{(\alpha)})^m Q_\ell + \sum_{i=0}^{n-1}\sum_{k=0}^{m-1} P_{i,k}(x^{(\alpha)})^k Q_i - \sum_{k=0}^{m-1}(x^{(\alpha)})^k D_k, P\right)$$
$$= e\left((x^{(\alpha)})^m Q_\ell + \sum_{k=0}^{m-1}(x^{(\alpha)})^k D_k', P\right)$$
$$= e\left(Z^{(\alpha)}, G\right) ,$$

where the third line of the above equation could be viewed as a polynomial of degree m with indeterminate $x^{(\alpha)}$, and D_k' is the coefficient of the k-th degree term. Since $x^{(0)}, \ldots, x^{(m)}$ are all different, we can find $\beta_0, \beta_1, \ldots, \beta_m$ so that the following equation holds.

$$\begin{pmatrix} (x^{(0)})^0 & (x^{(1)})^0 & \cdots & (x^{(m)})^0 \\ (x^{(0)})^1 & (x^{(1)})^1 & \cdots & (x^{(m)})^1 \\ \vdots & \vdots & \ddots & \vdots \\ (x^{(0)})^m & (x^{(1)})^m & \cdots & (x^{(m)})^m \end{pmatrix} \cdot \begin{pmatrix} \beta_0 \\ \beta_1 \\ \vdots \\ \beta_m \end{pmatrix} = \begin{pmatrix} 0 \\ 0 \\ \vdots \\ 0 \\ 1 \end{pmatrix}.$$

Define $V'_\ell = \sum_{\alpha=0}^m \beta_\alpha Z^{(\alpha)}$. Notice that

$$
\begin{aligned}
e(V'_\ell, G) &= e\left(\sum_{\alpha=0}^m \beta_\alpha \cdot Z^{(\alpha)}, G\right) \\
&= e\left(\sum_{\alpha=0}^m \beta_\alpha \left((x^{(\alpha)})^m Q_\ell + \sum_{k=0}^{m-1} (x^{(\alpha)})^k D'_k\right), P\right) \\
&= e\left(\sum_{\alpha=0}^m \left(\beta_\alpha (x^{(\alpha)})^m\right) Q_\ell + \sum_{k=0}^{m-1} \left(\sum_{\alpha=0}^m \beta_\alpha (x^{(\alpha)})^k\right) D'_k, P\right) \\
&= e\left(Q_\ell, P\right) \\
&= e\left(vQ_\ell, G\right).
\end{aligned}
$$

So we conclude that $V'_\ell = vQ_\ell$. On the other side, from the equation which is responsible for checking the validity of linking tag, we have

$$
\left(x^{(\alpha)}\right)^n I - e\left(P, \sum_{k=0}^{n-1} \left(x^{(\alpha)}\right)^k E_k\right) = e(Z^{(\alpha)}, K) \ ,
$$

so that with the $m + 1$ accepting transcripts, we obtain

$$
\begin{pmatrix}
1 & (x^{(0)})^1 & \cdots & (x^{(0)})^m \\
1 & (x^{(1)})^1 & \cdots & (x^{(1)})^m \\
\vdots & \vdots & \ddots & \vdots \\
1 & (x^{(m)})^1 & \cdots & (x^{(m)})^m
\end{pmatrix}
\begin{pmatrix}
E_0 \\
E_1 \\
\vdots \\
I
\end{pmatrix}
=
\begin{pmatrix}
e(Z^{(0)}, K) \\
e(Z^{(1)}, K) \\
\vdots \\
e(Z^{(m)}, K)
\end{pmatrix} . \tag{3}
$$

By left multiplying (3) with $(\beta_0, \beta_1, \ldots, \beta_m)$, we observe that

$$
I = \sum_{\alpha=0}^m \beta_\alpha \cdot e\left(Z^{(\alpha)}, K\right) = e\left(\sum_{\alpha=0}^m \beta_\alpha \cdot Z^{(\alpha)}, K\right) = e(V'_\ell, K) = v \cdot e(Q_\ell, K) \ .
$$

The above facts show that (ℓ, V'_ℓ) is a valid witness for the statement in $\mathcal{R}$. $\square$

Theorem 7. Σ_2 *is of special honest verifier zero-knowledge (SHVZK) if the commitment scheme is perfectly hiding.*

Proof. On input a challenge $x \in \mathbb{Z}_p$, the simulator first chooses $w_j, y_j, z_j \leftarrow \mathbb{Z}_p$, for $j \in [1, m]$. It is obvious that the distributions of these simulated responses are statistically close to that in a real proof. The simulator then picks $\ell \leftarrow [0, n)$, $r_j \leftarrow \mathbb{Z}_p$ and computes $A_j = \ell_j H + r_j G$. Due to the properties of the commitment scheme $(A_j)_{j=1}^\tau$ are statistically indistinguishable from that of a real proof.

Subsequently, for $j \in [1, \tau]$, let $a_j = f_j - \ell_j x$, and compute $(p_{i,j})_{i \in [0,n), k \in [1,m)}$. For $k \in [1, \tau)$, it picks $\rho_k \leftarrow \mathbb{Z}_p$ and computes $D_k = \sum_{i=0}^{n-1} p_{i,k} Q_i + \rho_k G$, $E_k = e(P, \rho_k K)$. The distributions of D_k and E_k are statistically close to uniform distribution in G and they are pairwise dependent since they use the same randomness as in a real proof.

Since $(B_j)_{j=1}^m$, $(C_j)_{j=1}^m$, D_0, E_0 are uniquely determined by the correspond-ing verification equations and the above generated parameters, the simulator computes

$$B_j = w_j H + y_j G - x A_j \ , \ \text{for } j \in [1, m]$$
$$C_j = z_j G - (x - w_j) A_j \ , \ \text{for } j \in [1, m]$$
$$D_0 = \sum_{i=0}^{n-1} (\prod_{j=1}^{m} w_{j,i_j}) Q_i + \sum_{k=1}^{m-1} (-x^k) D_k - rG$$
$$E_0 = x^m I - \sum_{k=1}^{m-1} x^k E_k - e(Z, K) \ .$$

By the foregoing discussion, the distribution of the outputting transcript

$$\left((A_j, B_j, C_j), D_{j-1}, E_{j=1}^m, x, (w_j)_{j=1}^m, (y_j)_{j=1}^m, (z_j)_{j=1}^m, Z \right)$$

is totally indistinguishable from that of a real proof. As a result, Σ_2 is SHVZK.

□

References

1. Au, M.H., Liu, J.K., Susilo, W., Yuen, T.H.: Constant-size ID-based linkable and revocable-iff-linked ring signature. In: Barua, R., Lange, T. (eds.) INDOCRYPT 2006. LNCS, vol. 4329, pp. 364–378. Springer, Heidelberg (2006). https://doi.org/10.1007/11941378_26
2. Au, M.H., Liu, J.K., Susilo, W., Yuen, T.H.: Secure ID-based linkable and revocable-iff-linked ring signature with constant-size construction. Theor. Comput. Sci. **469**, 1–14 (2013)
3. Au, M.H., Liu, J.K., Yuen, T.H., Wong, D.S.: ID-based ring signature scheme secure in the standard model. In: Yoshiura, H., Sakurai, K., Rannenberg, K., Murayama, Y., Kawamura, S. (eds.) IWSEC 2006. LNCS, vol. 4266, pp. 1–16. Springer, Heidelberg (2006). https://doi.org/10.1007/11908739_1
4. Awasthi, A.K., Lal, S.: ID-based ring signature and proxy ring signature schemes from bilinear pairings. Int. J. Netw. Secur. **4**(2), 187–192 (2007)
5. Backes, M., Döttling, N., Hanzlik, L., Kluczniak, K., Schneider, J.: Ring signatures: logarithmic-size, no setup—from standard assumptions. In: Ishai, Y., Rijmen, V. (eds.) EUROCRYPT 2019. LNCS, vol. 11478, pp. 281–311. Springer, Cham (2019). https://doi.org/10.1007/978-3-030-17659-4_10
6. Bender, A., Katz, J., Morselli, R.: Ring signatures: stronger definitions, and constructions without random oracles. In: Halevi, S., Rabin, T. (eds.) TCC 2006. LNCS, vol. 3876, pp. 60–79. Springer, Heidelberg (2006). https://doi.org/10.1007/11681878_4
7. Beullens, W., Katsumata, S., Pintore, F.: Calamari and Falafl: logarithmic (link-able) ring signatures from isogenies and lattices. In: Moriai, S., Wang, H. (eds.) ASIACRYPT 2020. LNCS, vol. 12492, pp. 464–492. Springer, Cham (2020). https://doi.org/10.1007/978-3-030-64834-3_16

8. Boneh, D., Franklin, M.: Identity-based encryption from the weil pairing. In: Kilian, J. (ed.) CRYPTO 2001. LNCS, vol. 2139, pp. 213–229. Springer, Heidelberg (2001). https://doi.org/10.1007/3-540-44647-8_13

9. Bootle, J., Cerulli, A., Chaidos, P., Ghadafi, E., Groth, J., Petit, C.: Short accountable ring signatures based on DDH. In: Pernul, G., Ryan, P.Y.A., Weippl, E. (eds.) ESORICS 2015. LNCS, vol. 9326, pp. 243–265. Springer, Cham (2015). https://doi.org/10.1007/978-3-319-24174-6_13

10. Chatterjee, R., et al.: Compact ring signatures from learning with errors. Cryptology ePrint Archive, Report 2021/942 (2021). https://ia.cr/2021/942

11. Hu, C., Liu, P.: An enhanced constant-size identity-based ring signature scheme. In: 2nd IEEE International Conference on Computer Science and Information Technology, pp. 587–590. IEEE (2009)

12. Chow, S.S.M., Wei, V.K., Liu, J.K., Yuen, T.H.: Ring signatures without random oracles. In: Symposium on Information, Computer and Communications Security, ASIACCS 2006, ACM, New York, NY, USA, pp. 297–302 (2006)

13. Chow, S.S.M., Yiu, S.-M., Hui, L.C.K.: Efficient identity based ring signature. In: Ioannidis, J., Keromytis, A., Yung, M. (eds.) ACNS 2005. LNCS, vol. 3531, pp. 499–512. Springer, Heidelberg (2005). https://doi.org/10.1007/11496137_34

14. Dodis, Y., Kiayias, A., Nicolosi, A., Shoup, V.: Anonymous identification in Ad Hoc groups. In: Cachin, C., Camenisch, J.L. (eds.) EUROCRYPT 2004. LNCS, vol. 3027, pp. 609–626. Springer, Heidelberg (2004). https://doi.org/10.1007/978-3-540-24676-3_36

15. Groth, J., Kohlweiss, M.: One-out-of-many proofs: or how to leak a secret and spend a coin. In: Oswald, E., Fischlin, M. (eds.) EUROCRYPT 2015. LNCS, vol. 9057, pp. 253–280. Springer, Heidelberg (2015). https://doi.org/10.1007/978-3-662-46803-6_9

16. Haque, A., Krenn, S., Slamanig, D., Striecks, C.: Logarithmic-size (linkable) threshold ring signatures in the plain model. Cryptology ePrint Archive, Report 2020/683 (2020), https://ia.cr/2020/683

17. Libert, B., Peters, T., Qian, C.: Logarithmic-size ring signatures with tight security from the DDH assumption. In: Lopez, J., Zhou, J., Soriano, M. (eds.) ESORICS 2018. LNCS, vol. 11099, pp. 288–308. Springer, Cham (2018). https://doi.org/10.1007/978-3-319-98989-1_15

18. Libert, B., Nguyen, K., Peters, T., Yung, M.: One-shot fiat-shamir-based nizk arguments of composite residuosity in the standard model. Cryptology ePrint Archive, Report 2020/1334 (2020), https://ia.cr/2020/1334

19. Liu, J.K., Au, M.H., Susilo, W., Zhou, J.: Linkable ring signature with unconditional anonymity. IEEE Trans. Knowl. Data Eng. 26(1), 157–165 (2014)

20. Liu, J.K., Wong, D.S.: Linkable ring signatures: security models and new schemes. In: Gervasi, O., et al. (eds.) ICCSA 2005. LNCS, vol. 3481, pp. 614–623. Springer, Heidelberg (2005). https://doi.org/10.1007/11424826_65

21. Lyubashevsky, V., Nguyen, N.K., Seiler, G.: Smile: set membership from ideal lattices with applications to ring signatures and confidential transactions. Cryptology ePrint Archive, Report 2021/564 (2021). https://ia.cr/2021/564

22. Nguyen, L.: Accumulators from bilinear pairings and applications. In: Menezes, A. (ed.) CT-RSA 2005. LNCS, vol. 3376, pp. 275–292. Springer, Heidelberg (2005). https://doi.org/10.1007/978-3-540-30574-3_19

23. Pedersen, T.P.: Non-interactive and information-theoretic secure verifiable secret sharing. In: Feigenbaum, J. (ed.) CRYPTO 1991. LNCS, vol. 576, pp. 129–140. Springer, Heidelberg (1992). https://doi.org/10.1007/3-540-46766-1_9

24. Rivest, R.L., Shamir, A., Tauman, Y.: How to leak a secret. In: Boyd, C. (ed.) ASIACRYPT 2001. LNCS, vol. 2248, pp. 552–565. Springer, Heidelberg (2001). https://doi.org/10.1007/3-540-45682-1_32
25. Saberhagen, N.V.: CryptoNote v2.0 (2013). https://cryptonote.org/whitepaper.pdf
26. Sasson, E.B., et al.: Zerocash: decentralized anonymous payments from Bitcoin. In: Symposium on Security and Privacy–SP 2014, pp. 459–474. IEEE (2014)
27. Zhang, F., Chen, X.: Cryptanalysis and improvement of an ID-based ad-hoc anonymous identification scheme at CT-RSA 05. Inf. Process. Lett. **109**(15), 846–849 (2009). https://doi.org/10.1016/j.ipl.2009.04.002
28. Zhang, F., Kim, K.: ID-based blind signature and ring signature from pairings. In: Zheng, Y. (ed.) ASIACRYPT 2002. LNCS, vol. 2501, pp. 533–547. Springer, Heidelberg (2002). https://doi.org/10.1007/3-540-36178-2_33
29. Zhang, H., Zhang, F., Tian, H., Au, M.H.: Anonymous post-quantum cryptocash. In: Meiklejohn, S., Sako, K. (eds.) FC 2018. LNCS, vol. 10957, pp. 461–479. Springer, Heidelberg (2018). https://doi.org/10.1007/978-3-662-58387-6_25

Security Analysis of DGM and GM Group Signature Schemes Instantiated with XMSS-T

Mahmoud Yehia[✉], Riham AlTawy[✉], and T. Aaron Gulliver

Department of Electrical and Computer Engineering, University of Victoria, Victoria, BC, Canada
{mahmoudyehia,raltawy}@uvic.ca

Abstract. Group Merkle (GM) (PQCrypto 2018) and Dynamic Group Merkle (DGM) (ESORICS 2019) are recent proposals for post-quantum hash-based group signature schemes. They are designed as generic constructions that employ any stateful Merkle hash-based signature scheme. XMSS-T (PKC 2016, RFC8391) is the latest stateful Markle hash-based signature scheme where (almost) optimal parameters are provided. In this paper, we show that the setup phase of both GM and DGM does not enable drop-in instantiation by XMSS-T which limits both designs in employing earlier XMSS versions with sub-optimal parameters which negatively affects the performance of both schemes. Thus, we provide a tweak to the setup phase of GM and DGM to overcome this limitation and enable the adoption of XMSS-T. Moreover, we analyze the bit security of DGM when instantiated with XMSS-T and show that it is susceptible to multi-target attacks because of the parallel Signing Merkle Trees (SMT) approach. More precisely, when DGM is used to sign 2^{64} messages, its bit security is 44 bits less than that of XMSS-T. Finally, we provide a DGM variant that mitigates multi-target attacks and show that it attains the same bit security as XMSS-T.

Keywords: Digital signatures · Hash-based signature schemes · Group signature schemes · Post-quantum cryptography · Merkle trees

1 Introduction

A group signature scheme (GSS) incorporates N members in a signing scheme with a single public key. GSS allows any group member to sign anonymously on behalf of the whole group [16]. A group manager is assigned to perform system setup, reveal the identity of a given signer when needed, add new members, and revoke memberships when required. Remote attestation protocols, e-commerce, e-voting, traffic management, and privacy preserving techniques in blockchain applications [3, 8, 35] are applications that utilize group signature schemes. There have been several proposals for group signature schemes [6, 8, 14, 15, 28, 29]. However, the majority rely on number theoretic assumptions that are not secure against post-quantum attacks.

© Springer Nature Switzerland AG 2021
Y. Yu and M. Yung (Eds.): Inscrypt 2021, LNCS 13007, pp. 61–81, 2021.
https://doi.org/10.1007/978-3-030-88323-2_4

There is now an imperative need to replace the current public key infrastructure with quantum-secure algorithms. This is evidenced by the current NIST post-quantum cryptography standardization competition (PQC) [33]. GSS is a public key infrastructure primitive which has attracted research attention to provide quantum security. The first post-quantum lattice-based group signature scheme was proposed in [20], and other schemes were proposed in [17,25–27,30,32]. However, unlike the lattice-based signature scheme PQC finalists, their group signature structures are not as efficient [36]. Code-based group signature schemes were developed to provide another alternative for quantum secure GSSs [1,2,19], but they have very large signature sizes on the order of Megabytes [4].

In 2018, El Bansarkhani and Misoczki introduced Group Merkle (GM), the first post-quantum stateful hash-based group signature scheme [18]. A year Later, Dynamic Group Merkle (DGM), the latest hash-based group signature scheme, was introduced to solve some of the limitations of GM [12]. GM and DGM provide quantum security with reasonable signature sizes on the order of KBytes and both are general constructions that can be instantiated with any stateful Merkle hash-based signature scheme. The security analysis of both schemes included standard security notions of group signature schemes (anonymity and full-traceability) [5,13], but no bit security analysis was provided. XMSS$^+$ [21], XMSS^{MT} [23], and XMSS-T [24] are stateful hash-based signature schemes that overcome the performance drawbacks of Merkle Signature Scheme (MSS) [31]. The last version of XMSS-T given in Internet Engineering Task Force (IETF) RFC8391 [22] provides (almost) optimal parameters and mitigates multi-target attacks [9].

Our Contributions. The contributions of this work are as follows.

- We show that the setup phase of both GM and DGM restricts them from being directly instantiated by XMSS-T which negatively affects the performance of both schemes because they may use earlier XMSS versions with sub-optimal parameters.
- We introduce simple tweaks to the GM and DGM setup phases that enable their instantiation with XMSS-T.
- We analyze the bit security of DGM when instantiated with XMSS-T and show that it is vulnerable to multi-target attacks due to allowing multiple signing trees to branch out from the same intermediate initial Merkle tree node. Concretely, when the scheme is used to sign 2^{64} messages under the same public key (similar to the NIST PQC requirement [34]), DGM has bit security that is 44 bits less than that of the utilized Merkle signing scheme, i.e. 212 bit security when instantiated with XMSS-T-SHA2 at 256 bit security.
- We propose a DGM variant that mitigates the described multi-target attacks and show that such a variant maintains the same bit security as the utilized Merkle signing scheme.

2 Preliminaries

In this section, we provide the security definitions of hash functions that will be used throughout the paper and introduce the notion of unforgeability in GSSs. In addition to the standard one wayness, and strong and weak collision resistance security notions, we consider the security notions of hash function families introduced in [9,24]. In what follows, let $n \in \mathbb{N}$ be the security parameter, $k = poly(n)$, $m = poly(n)$, $\mathcal{H}_n = \{H_K(M) : \{0,1\}^k \times \{0,1\}^m \to \{0,1\}^n$ be a keyed hash function family where $K \in \{0,1\}^k$ is the hash key and $M \in \{0,1\}^m$ is the message. Hash-based signature schemes usually adopt parameterized hash functions with $m, k \geq n$. Note that the success probability of quantum adversaries assumes a Quantum Accessible Random Oracle Model [7].

Definition 1 (Post-Quantum) Distinct-function, Multi-target Second Preimage Resistance (PQ-DM-SPR). *Given a (quantum) adversary $\mathcal{A}$ who is provided with p message-key pairs (M_i, K_i), $1 \leq i \leq p$, the success probability that $\mathcal{A}$ finds a second preimage of a pair (j), $1 \leq j \leq p$ using the corresponding hash function key (K_j) is given by,*

$$Succ_{\mathcal{H}_n,p}^{\mathsf{PQ\text{-}DM\text{-}SPR}}(\mathcal{A}) = \Pr[K_i \leftarrow \{0,1\}^k; M_i \leftarrow \{0,1\}^m, 1 \leq i \leq p;$$
$$(j, M') \leftarrow \mathcal{A}((K_1, M_1), \ldots, (K_p, M_p)) :$$
$$M' \neq M_j \wedge H(K_j, M_j) = H(K_j, M')]$$

A generic attack by a classical (resp. quantum) DM-SPR adversary who makes q_h queries to an n bit hash function has success probability of $\frac{q_h+1}{2^n}$ (resp. $\Theta(\frac{(q_h+1)^2}{2^n})$). Note that if the keys of the hash function family are chosen randomly, then the security notion in Definition 1 is referred to as *Multi-Function, Multi-target Second-Preimage Resistance (*MM-SPR*).

Definition 2 (Post-Quantum) Multi-target Extended Target Collision Resistance (PQ-M-eTCR). *Given a (quantum) adversary $\mathcal{A}$ who is given a target set of p key-message pairs (K_i, M_i), $1 \leq i \leq p$ and is required to find a different message-key pair (with possibly the same key), whose image collides with any of the pairs in the target set, the success probability of $\mathcal{A}$ is given by,*

$$Succ_{\mathcal{H}_n,p}^{\mathsf{PQ\text{-}M\text{-}eTCR}}(\mathcal{A}) = \Pr[K_i \leftarrow \{0,1\}^k; M_i \leftarrow \{0,1\}^m, 1 \leq i \leq p;$$
$$(j, K', M') \leftarrow \mathcal{A}((K_1, M_1), \ldots, (K_p, M_p)) :$$
$$M' \neq M_j \wedge H(K_j, M_j) = H(K', M')]$$

A generic attack by a classical (quantum) M-eTCR adversary who is given p targets and makes q_h queries to an n bit hash function has a success probability of $\frac{p(q_h+1)}{2^n} + \frac{pq_h}{2^k}$ (resp. $\Theta(\frac{p(q_h+1)^2}{2^n} + \frac{pq_h^2}{2^k})$) when $k \geq n$.

Definition 3 ((Post-Quantum) M-eTCR with Nonce (PQ-NM-eTCR)). *Given a (quantum) adversary $\mathcal{A}$ who is given a target set of p key-message-nonce* *tuples (K_i, M_i, i), $1 \leq i \leq p$, and are required to find a different key-message-nonce tuple (K', M', j) whose image collides with the j-th tuple in the target set (with possibly the same key), the success probability of $\mathcal{A}$ is given by,*

$$Succ_{\mathcal{H}_{n,p}}^{PQ\text{-}NM\text{-}eTCR}(\mathcal{A}) = \Pr[K_i \leftarrow \{0,1\}^k; M_i \leftarrow \{0,1\}^m, 1 \leq i \leq p;$$
$$(K', M', j) \leftarrow \mathcal{A}((K_1, M_1, 1), \dots, (K_p, M_p, p)) :$$
$$M' \neq M_j \wedge H(K_j || j, M_j) = H(K' || j, M')]$$

A generic attack by a classical (quantum) NM-eTCR adversary who is given p targets and makes q_h queries to an n bit hash function has a success probability of $\frac{(q_h+p)}{2^n} + \frac{pq_h}{2^k}$ (resp. $\Theta(\frac{(q_h+p)^2}{2^n} + \frac{pq_h^2}{2^k})$) when $k \geq n$.

Definition 4 ((Post Quantum) Pseudorandom Function (PQ-PRF)). $\mathcal{H}_n$ *is called a PRF function family if it is efficiently computable and for any (quantum) adversary $\mathcal{A}$ who can query a black-box oracle $\mathcal{O}$ that is initialized with either $\mathcal{H}_n$ function or a random function $\mathcal{G}$, where $\mathcal{G} : \{0,1\}^m \rightarrow \{0,1\}^n$, the success probability of $\mathcal{A}$ distinguishing the output of $\mathcal{O}$ by determining which function it is initialized with, is negligible. Such a success probability is given by,*

$$Succ_{\mathcal{H}_n}^{PQ\text{-}PRF}(\mathcal{A}) = |\Pr[\mathcal{O} \leftarrow \mathcal{H}_n : \mathcal{A}^{\mathcal{O}(\cdot)} = 1] - \Pr[\mathcal{O} \leftarrow \mathcal{G} : \mathcal{A}^{\mathcal{O}(\cdot)} = 1]|$$

A generic attack by a classical (resp. quantum) PQ-PRF adversary who makes q_h queries to an $\mathcal{H}_n$ has a success probability of $\frac{q_h+1}{2^n}$ (resp. $\Theta(\frac{(q_h+1)^2}{2^n})$).

Unforgeability in Group Signature Schemes. A basic security notion of a (group) digital signature scheme is that signatures cannot be forged. More precisely, it is computationally infeasible for an adversary $\mathcal{A}$ who does not know the secret key and is allowed unrestricted queries to the signing oracle to generate a message signature pair (M', Σ') that passes as valid by the verification algorithm.

In what follows, we give the definition of the unforgeability game $\mathsf{EXP}_{\mathcal{GS},\mathcal{A}}^{forge}(n, N)$ for a group signature scheme, $\mathcal{GS}$, with N members and security parameter n. Such a game was described by Bellare *et al.* in [5] as an adaptation from the traceability game where $\mathcal{A}$ is not allowed to corrupt members. Intuitively, $\mathcal{A}$ is successful in winning $\mathsf{EXP}_{\mathcal{GS},\mathcal{A}}^{forge}$ if the forged message is either traced to a group member or cannot be traced to a member.

Definition 5 (Unforgeability). *A group signature scheme $\mathcal{GS}$ is unforgeable if for any ppt adversary $\mathcal{A}$ that is given unrestricted access to the signing and opening oracles, $\mathcal{A}$ cannot generate a valid signature for a message that was not previously queried. $\mathcal{A}$ has a negligible advantage in the experiment $Exp_{\mathcal{GS},\mathcal{A}}^{forge}$ as given in Fig. 1*

$$Adv_{\mathcal{GS},\mathcal{A}}^{forge}(n, N) = |\Pr[Exp_{\mathcal{GS},\mathcal{A}}^{forge}(n, N) = 1]| \leq negl(n)$$

$Exp_{GS,A}^{forge}(n, N)$

- $(GPK, sk^*) \leftarrow G.KGen(1^n, N)$
- Unrestricted queries:
  * $Sign(M, \cdot)$
  * $G.Open(M, \Sigma)$
- Generate (M', Σ')
- **If** $G.Verify(\Sigma', M', gpk) == 1$ **Return** 1
  Else Return 0

Fig. 1. Unforgeability experiment

3   Specification of Related Schemes

In this section, we provide a brief description of XMSS-T, GM and DGM, the related signing schemes used throughout this paper. Details are given only for the procedures that are relevant to our analysis. For more information, the reader is referred to [12, 18, 22, 24].

3.1   Extended Merkle Signature Scheme-Tightened (XMSS-T)

XMSS-T is a multi Merkle tree construction where the tree leaf nodes are the public keys of the Winternitz One-Time Signature Scheme with Tightened security (WOTS-T) [10]. In what follows, we consider the specification of one tree instance of XMSS-T because this is used in GM and DGM. XMSS-T has a public addressing mapping scheme, $ADRS$, that maps a public seed, $pk.seed$, a leaf/internal node index, i, and a level, j, to generate a (distinct) new hash randomizer, r, and bit-mask, q, for each hash call in the scheme (the hashing in the WOTS-T scheme and the Merkel tree hashing). Such a distinct randomizer enables the scheme to mitigate multi-target attacks. Precisely, a Merkle tree of height h has 2^h leaf nodes (WOTS-T.pk) and the i-th node at level j is denoted by $X_{i,j}$, where $0 \leq i < 2^{h-j}, 0 \leq j \leq h$. The internal nodes are generated by $X_{i,j} = H(r_{i,j}, (X_{2i,j-1}||X_{2i+1,j-1}) \oplus q_{i,j})$, where $r_{i,j}$ and $q_{i,j}$ are the hash randomizer and bit-mask generated by the addressing scheme $(r_{i,j}, q_{i,j}) \leftarrow ADRS(pk.seed, i, j)$. The XMSS-T addressing scheme (see Appendix A for details), takes the leaf index, i, and calculates j according to the hashing sub-structure i.e., OTS hash chains, L-tree hashing or Merkle tree hashing. Then, it generates the required hash randomizer and bit mask. For simplicity, $ADRS$ takes the node level j as input.

The nodes at level 0, $X_{i,0}$, are the leaf nodes, and they are the public keys of the WOTS-T which also utilizes the addressing scheme, $ADRS$, to evaluate the required hash randomizers and bit masks for its hashing. For details of the WOTS-T signing scheme and addressing schemes, the reader is referred to [24] and Appendix A, respectively. Figure 2 depicts a simplified example of XMSS-T with one tree of 8 signing leaves $L_0, \cdots, L_7$. A signature by leaf L_2 (colored in black) has all the gray nodes in its authentication path.

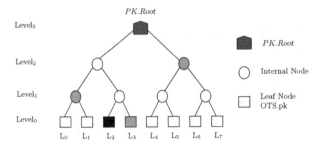

Fig. 2. A one layer XMSS-T, where the leaf nodes are the WOTS-T public keys. The nodes colored in gray are the authentication path for signing with leaf node L_2. (Color figure online)

3.2   Group Merkle (GM)

Group Merkle (GM) is the first post-quantum hash-based group signature scheme. It is a one Merkle tree construction that can be instantiated by any stateful one-tree Merkle hash-based signature scheme that employs a One-Time Signing (OTS) scheme as the underlying signing algorithm. The group manager in GM is responsible for the setup procedure of N group members. In this phase, a member j, $1 \leq j \leq N$, generates their own B OTS keys and sends the corresponding public keys $(OTS.pk_{(j-1)B+1}, OTS.pk_{(j-1)B+2}, \ldots, OTS.pk_{jB})$ to the group manager who labels all the received NB keys from the N members by $(1, 2, \cdots, NB)$, where each consecutive $(j-1)B+1, (j-1)B+2, \ldots, jB$ set of keys belongs to the j-th member.

To ensure signer anonymity, the OTS public keys are shuffled by encrypting the corresponding labels by a symmetric encryption algorithm, $pos_i = Enc(i, sk_{gm})$, where sk_{gm} is the group manager's secret key, and $1 \leq i \leq NB$. Thus, the group manager has the pairs $(OTS.pk_1, pos_1), \cdots, (OTS.pk_{N \cdot B}, pos_{N \cdot B})$. These pairs are reordered in ascending order of the encrypted positions to perform the pair permutation. Then, the GM tree is constructed where a leaf node, denoted by $L_i = X_{i,0}$ contains the pair $(OTS.pk_j, pos_j)$ and i is the new permuted position of $OTS.pk_j$. Accordingly, the p-th node at level 1 is calculated by $X_{p,1} = H(X_{2p,0} || X_{2p+1,0}) = H(OTS.pk_x, pos_x || OTS.pk_z, pos_z)$ for $0 \leq p \leq \frac{NB}{2} - 1$, i.e. $L_{2p} = X_{2p,0} = (OTS.pk_x, pos_x)$ and $L_{2p+1} = X_{2p+1,0} = (OTS.pk_z, pos_z)$, because after the permutation, position x is mapped to $2p$ and position z is mapped to $2p + 1$. Hashing neighboring nodes continues up the levels until the tree root is evaluated which is the group public key $GM.gpk$. Note that the encrypted position is included in the signature, and is used by to group manager to reveal the identity of the signer. Figure 3 shows a simplified example of a GM tree of two members colored in red and blue where each has 2 OTS key pairs.

3.3   Dynamic Group Merkle (DGM)

DGM [12] combines two types of Merkle trees, one Initial Merkle Tree (IMT) and multiple Signing Merkle Trees (SMTs). The IMT has height 20 and random

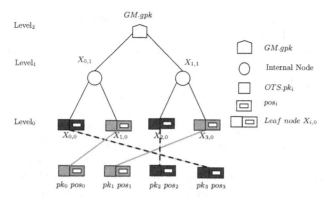

Fig. 3. GM with two members colored in red and blue, each of which has two signing leaves, the leaf Permutation is done by sorting the encrypted positions. (Color figure online)

values for its leaves in order to build the tree whose root is the group public key $DGM.gpk$. The SMTs have variable height and their leaves are OTSs which are used by group members to sign messages. Initially, a group member asks the group manager for B OTS signing keys the group manager randomly chooses B internal nodes from the IMT, i.e. nodes at levels $1, 2, \ldots, 19$, and assigns an OTS from each SMT that is linked to these internal nodes. If all the OTSs of an existing SMT are assigned or an IMT internal node does not have an SMT yet, then a new SMT is generated. The height of an SMT is equal to the level of the internal node that it is linked to.

SMT Generation. The SMT is constructed in the same manner as the GM tree. However, in DGM, the OTS secret and public key pairs are generated by the group manager and the whole SMT is built without input from the group members. Let $OTS.pk_i$ denote the i-th OTS public key, $0 \leq i \leq z$, where z denotes the total number of signatures supported by the scheme. Let $i = (v, u)$ where u denotes the OTS number within the v-th SMT.

All the OTS public keys are generated and indexed by $DGM.i = (v, u)$. Such indexes are then encrypted with a symmetric encryption algorithm to generate $DGM.pos_i = Enc(DGM.i, sk_{gm})$, where sk_{gm} is the group manger secret key. The OTS public keys are then shuffled by sorting the encrypted positions $DGM.pos$. Afterwards, the SMT leaves are generated, precisely, the j-th SMT leaf node is the hashing of the concatenation of the i-th OTS public key and their encrypted position, $L_j = H(OTS.pk_i \| DGM.pos_i)$, where j is the new position of the i-th OTS after the permutation. These leaves are used to build the SMT and evaluate its root r_{SMT} which is then linked to an IMT internal node called the fallback node, Fn, using a symmetric encryption algorithm. More precisely, r_{SMT}, is linked to Fn by evaluating the fallback key as $Fk = Dec(Fn, r_{SMT})$ which is included in the signature. Note that the verifier has to communicate with the group manager to check the validity of the received Fk and then calculate $Fn = Enc(Fk, r_{SMT})$ to complete the verification process. After all the leaves of an SMT are used, a new SMT is generated and linked to the same Fn. Note that different SMTs linked to the same fallback node Fn have different fallback keys.

Figure 4 depicts a simplified DGM example where the IMT, colored in blue, has height 4. The figure has one SMT colored in red which is linked to the IMT first internal node at level 3, $Fn = X_{0,3}$. When L_2 is used to sign a message M, the resulting signature is given by $\Sigma = (indx, OTS.\sigma_{indx}, DGM.pos_i, Auth)$, where $indx = 2$ is the signing leaf index with respect to the IMT to enable calculating which node is concatenated on its right and left in both the SMT and IMT from the authentication path in the verification process. $OTS.\sigma_{indx}$ denotes the OTS signature by the leaf index $indx$, $Auth = Auth_{SMT}, Fk, Auth_{IMT}$, where $Auth_{SMT} = L_3, SMT.X_{0,1}, SMT.X_{1,2}$ is the SMT authentication path (colored in pink), and $Auth_{IMT} = IMT.X_{1,3}$, colored in light blue, is the IMT authentication path for the fallback node Fn.

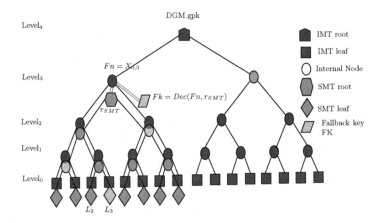

Fig. 4. DGM example.

4 Instantiating GM and DGM with XMSS-T

In both GM and DGM, the signing leaves which contain the public keys of the OTS used by the group members are first generated and then permuted. Afterwards, the Merkle tree (SMT in DGM) is built using the permuted leaves. In GM, the group members generate their own OTS keys and send the corresponding OTS public keys to the group manager who permutes them and then builds the GM tree. Finally, the group manager distributes all GM tree signing leaves to all the members. On the other hand, in DGM, the group manager generates the OTSs on behalf of the group members, evaluates the signing leaves and permutes them, then constructs the SMTs, and assigns OTSs at random from randomly chosen SMTs.

XMSS-T is the latest stateful MSS variant and has (almost) optimal parameters when compared to other MSS variants which translates to smaller signatures. For instance, with the same parameters (SHA-256 hash function, Winternetiz parameter $w=16$, tree height 20), the bit security of XMSS-T (resp. XMSS [11]) is 256 (resp. 196). With a bit security of 196, XMSS-T (resp. XMSS) has a signature size of 14,328 (resp. 22,296) bits. XMSS-T uses WOTS-T as the underlying OTS signing scheme which requires the signing leaf index, i, within the Merkle tree to generate the OTS public keys. More precisely, XMSS-T uses an addressing scheme that utilizes the signing leaf index within the Merkle tree as input to generate a distinct hash randomizer and bit mask for each hash call in the hash chains of WOTS-T [24] (see Appendix A). These hash randomizers and bit masks are used in evaluating the WOTS-T public keys which represent the signing leaves (see Sect. 3.1).

Instantiating GM and DGM by XMSS-T is not directly achievable because in the specifications of these schemes, a signing leaf index, i, is known only after its corresponding OTS public key has been generated and the associated leaf permuted, while in XMSS-T, WOTS-T requires the leaf index i to evaluate the OTS public key and generate its corresponding leaf. One solution is to employ an earlier XMSS version with an OTS variant that does not require the position of the leaf within the Merkle tree to evaluate the OTS public keys. Such a solution results in using OTS with larger parameters than WOTS-T which negatively affects the performance of the group signature scheme.

GM and DGM with XMSS-T. We provide a tweak in the setup phase of both GM and DGM which enables their instantiation with XMSS-T. In GM, the setup phase is interactive so we add an extra communication step between the group manager and the group members where the permuted indexes are first sent to the members who can then generate their WOTS-T public keys. More precisely, the permutation in GM is done by encrypting a given position that is associated with an OTS public key, but the encryption itself is independent from the value of the public key, i.e. $pos_i = Enc(i, sk_{gm})$. Accordingly, the group manger can initially permute the indexes of the leaves for all group members before the OTS keys are generated. Afterwards, the permuted indexes are assigned to group members in a manner similar to the original setup phase (see Sect. 3.2). Each group member uses the assigned indexes within the whole tree as an input to the WOTS-T addressing scheme, $ADRS$, to generate the required hash randomizers and bit masks which are required to generate their WOTS-T public keys. Finally, the WOTS-T public keys are sent back to the group manager who constructs the GM tree using XMSS-T.

In DGM, no extra communication is needed because the group manger generates the OTS signing keys for the group members and their corresponding public keys. Accordingly, the manager may first permute the indexes using symmetric encryption then generate the OTS public keys using the permuted indexes.

In other words, the specification of the setup phase stays the same with only the permutation and OTS key generation order swapped.

5 DGM with XMSS-T Security Analysis

In [12], DGM was analyzed with respect to security notions of group digital signature schemes, i.e. anonymity and traceability. However, since DGM was not instantiated with a specific Merkle signing scheme, no bit security analysis for its unforgeability was provided. In this section, we analyze the bit security of the unforgeability of DGM when it is instantiated with XMSS-T. Note that the same analysis is valid if DGM is instantiated with earlier XMSS versions. Henceforth, we refer to DGM when instantiated with XMSS-T as simply DGM.

5.1 Multi-target Attacks and XMSS-T

If an n bit hash function is used once in a cryptographic primitive with a security parameter λ whose security is dependent on the second preimage resistance of the hash function, then finding a second preimage of the generated digest requires 2^n computations, thus it suffices that $n = \lambda$. However, if the same hash function is used t times in the cryptographic primitive, i.e. an adversary has access to t digests generated with the same hash function, then a second preimage may be obtained on any of these t targets with $2^n/t$ computations. Assuming that $n = \lambda$, the security of the scheme is reduced from n to $n - \log t$. A naive remedy to reach n bit security is to use message digests of length $n + \log t$. Alternatively, one may enforce that each hash application is different such that each digest for the t targets is evaluated using a different hash function so that finding a second preimage for any function, i.e. using the same hash key, requires 2^n computations.

In XMSS-T, the addressing scheme, $ADRS$, generates a hash randomizer and bit mask for each hash function call depending on the hash node index in the tree or WOTS-T chain iteration. For a tree with height h, the i-th node at level j is denoted by $X_{i,j}$ where $0 \leq i < 2^{h-j}$, $0 \leq j \leq h$. $ADRS$ is given by $(r_{i,j}, q_{i,j}) \leftarrow ADRS(pk.seed, i, j)$ where $r_{i,j}$ and $q_{i,j}$ are the hash randomizer and bit mask used. The internal nodes are generated as $X_{i,j} = H(r_{i,j}, (X_{2i,j-1}||X_{2i+1,j-1}) \oplus q_{i,j})$, i.e., $H_{r_{i,j}}$ is unique for $X_{i,j}$. Accordingly, if an adversary collects all the signatures supported by the scheme, each element in the WOTS-T signatures and each node in any authentication path is generated by a different hash function. Consequently, finding a forgery requires finding a second preimage of a given node using the corresponding hash function where other nodes are no longer applicable targets.

5.2 Multi-target Attacks on DGM

DGM allows multiple SMT trees to branch out of any IMT internal node, fallback node. Accordingly, one may regard DGM as several overlapping parallel trees

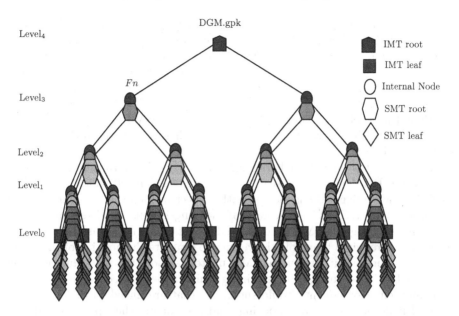

Fig. 5. Simplified DGM example of height 4 with 42 SMTs, 112 signing leaves, and fallback nodes uniformly distributed across the internal IMT nodes (Color figure online)

with heights ranging from 1 to 20. The IMT tree is the only tree with height 20 and the SMTs have heights ranging from 1 to 19. To visualize such a structure, Fig. 5 depicts a reduced DGM instance with an IMT, colored in blue, of height 4 and 42 SMTs, colored red, yellow and green. We assume a uniform distribution in the selection of the IMT internal nodes from which keys are assigned from the linked SMTs. Hence, each IMT internal node has the same number of assigned OTS keys (i.e. leaf nodes), and the number of SMTs per node in level j is double the number of SMTs per node in level $(j + 1)$. There are 4, 2, and 1 SMTs branching out from internal IMT nodes at levels 1, 2, and 3, respectively, and their respective colors are green, yellow, and red. This simplified example has 112 signing leaves which can be used to sign 112 messages under the same public key (IMT root). Note that there is no maximum number of SMTs so if more signing leaves are needed, new SMTs can be constructed and linked to a random internal node.

Following the NIST PQC recommendation, a signature scheme should be secure to sign up to 2^{64} messages under the same public key [33]. In what follows, we assume that DGM is used to sign 2^{64} messages. According to the design specifications, when a group member needs B signing keys (leaves), the group manager randomly selects B internal nodes of the IMT and assigns to that member the next unassigned OTS of each SMT linked to that internal node. The total number of internal nodes excluding the root in an IMT of height 20 is $2^{19} + 2^{18} + \cdots + 4 + 2 = 2^{20} - 2$. Recall that if the SMT OTS leaves linked to any randomly chosen internal node are used up, then a new SMT tree is generated, linked to that fallback node and one of its leaves is assigned. Accordingly, assuming a uniform distribution in the random fallback node selection, to assign 2^{64} OTSs to all group members, each IMT internal node is chosen $2^{64}/(2^{20} - 2) > 2^{44}$ times. This means that each IMT internal node at level j, $1 \leq j \leq 19$, has $2^{44-(j-1)-1} = 2^{44-j}$ SMT trees each of height j, i.e. 2^{43} SMTs of height 1 for each IMT internal node at level 1, 2^{42} SMTs of height 2 for each IMT internal node at level 2, up to 2^{25} SMTs of height 19 for each IMT internal node at level 19.

When DGM is instantiated with XMSS-T, to enable verification of a given signature, a DGM instance is seen as one tree of height 20 which means that wherever the signing SMT is located with respect to the IMT, the leaf indexing is in the set $\{0, 1, \ldots, 2^{20} - 1\}$, i.e. leaf indexing is considered relevant to the IMT where the signing SMT is considered a part of the IMT. Such an indexing restriction is required to enable the verifier to evaluate the position of the nodes in the authentication path of the IMT up to its root (the pale blue nodes in Fig. 4), which is essential in determining which nodes are concatenated on its right and left. Consequently, different SMTs that are linked to the same IMT internal node have the same indexing, and accordingly their parallel nodes at the same position are evaluated with the same hash function, i.e. the same hash randomizer and bit mask. For instance, in Fig. 5, any 4 green SMT roots branching from the same level 1 IMT blue node are evaluated with the same hash function as they share the same index within the IMT. Moreover, there are SMT nodes that share the same indexes and nodes of the SMTs that are connected to upper IMT internal nodes, for example, in Fig. 5, any 4 green SMT roots at an IMT level one intermediate node share the same indexes with 2 intermediate yellow SMT nodes and one intermediate red SMT node. Therefore, even though XMSS-T is secure against multi-target attacks, employing several parallel instances of it with the same indexing in the form of SMTs makes DGM vulnerable to multi-target attacks. Intuitively, a forgery adversary who collects a set of message-signature pairs, can group them in t-target sets that share common indexes, and then they can find another message whose digest collides with any of the message digests in the set. Note that such sets have t messages with authentication paths that share nodes with the same IMT indexes, so with complexity $2^n/t$ a forgery is obtained.

5.3 DGM Bit Security

Consider that DGM is used to sign 2^y messages where $y > 20$. Accordingly, each internal IMT node is chosen $2^y/(2^{20} - 2)$ times by the group manager to assign the next available OTS from the linked SMT. Assume an adversary $\mathcal{A}$ is able to collect all 2^y signatures generated by the scheme. The signature given by $\Sigma = (R, indx, OTS.\sigma_{indx}, DGM.pos_i, Auth)$ is signed with the i-th OTS key pair and has index $indx$ relative to its IMT position, i.e. $indx \in \{0, 1, \ldots, 2^{20} - 1\}$ (see Sect. 3.3). $\mathcal{A}$ can then group the signatures along with their corresponding messages in sets that share the same signing index, $indx$, where each set is expected to have t target message-signatures pairs, i.e. a given target set is denoted by $ts = \{(M_0, \Sigma_0), (M_1, \Sigma_1), \ldots, (M_{t-1}, \Sigma_{t-1})\}$. Assuming a uniform distribution in selecting IMT Fn positions, the number of targets t per set is given by,

$$t = \sum_{j=1}^{j=19} \frac{2^y/(2^{20} - 2)}{2^j} < 2^{y-20} \tag{1}$$

We assume a fully filled tree similar to the example in Fig. 5 where all IMT internal nodes have an equal number of assigned leaves, e.g. $2^y/(2^4 - 2) = 112/14 = 8$. Otherwise, the index that has the maximum number of signatures is considered. The maximum number of overlapping SMT nodes is given by $\frac{8}{2} + \frac{8}{2^2} + \frac{8}{2^3} = 7$, so $t = 7$.

In XMSS-T, to sign a message M, its message digest md is initially calculated as $md = H_{msg}(R||DGM.root||indx, M)$ where $H_{msg} : \{H(K, M) : \{0, 1\}^m \times \{0, 1\}^* \to \{0, 1\}^n$, R is the hash randomizer chosen by the signer and $index$ is the leaf index relative to the IMT. Since ts has t (M, Σ) pairs all with the same $indx$, $\mathcal{A}$ can search for (M', R') pair such that $M' \notin ts$, and the corresponding md' collides with a message digest of any of the messages in ts. Specifically, $\mathcal{A}$ finds (M', R') such that

$$H_{msg}(R'||DGM.root||indx, M') \in \{(H_{msg}(R_0||DGM.root||indx, M_0)), \ldots,$$
$$(H_{msg}(R_{t-1}||DGM.root||indx, M_{t-1}))\}.$$

Thus, $\mathcal{A}$ can successfully find a forgery for (M', R') with probability $2^{-n+\log_2 t}$. Similar multi-taget attacks can be applied on the OTS public keys or authentication paths in ts. In what follows, we give the security reduction of DGM when it is used to sign 2^y messages with $y > 20$. For completeness and consistency with XMSS-T notation [24], the hash functions used in different contexts within the signature scheme are defined as follows.

- $F : \{F(K, M) : \{0, 1\}^n \times \{0, 1\}^n \to \{0, 1\}^n$ used in OTS hash chains
- $H : \{H(K, M) : \{0, 1\}^n \times \{0, 1\}^{2n} \to \{0, 1\}^n$ used to calculate the Merkle tree hash nodes
- $H_{msg} : \{H(K, M) : \{0, 1\}^m \times \{0, 1\}^* \to \{0, 1\}^n$ used to calculate the message digests
- $\mathcal{F}_n$ (resp. $\mathcal{F}_m$) is a pseudorandom function family that takes a secret seed as input and outputs the OTS secret keys (resp. the message digest hash randomizer R) each of n bits (resp. m bits ($m = n + y$)).

Theorem 1. *For security parameter $n \in \mathbb{N}$ and parameters y, t as defined above, DGM is unforgeable against an adaptive chosen message attacks if*

- *F and H are PQ-DM-SPR hash function families,*
- *$\mathcal{F}_n$ and $\mathcal{F}_m$ are post-quantum pseudorandom function families, and*
- *H_{msg} is a PQ-NM-eTCR hash function family.*

The insecurity function, $\mathsf{InSec}^{PQ\text{-}forge}(DGM, \xi, 2^y)$, that describes the maximum success probability over all adversaries running in time $\leq \xi$ against the PQ-forge security of DGM and making a maximum of $qs = 2^y$ queries is bounded by

$$\mathsf{InSec}^{PQ\text{-}forge}(DGM, \xi, 2^y) \leq \mathsf{InSec}^{PQ\text{-}PRF}(\mathcal{F}_n, \xi) + \mathsf{InSec}^{PQ\text{-}PRF}(\mathcal{F}_m, \xi) +$$

$$max[t \times (\mathsf{InSec}^{PQ\text{-}DM\text{-}SPR}(H, \xi) + \mathsf{InSec}^{PQ\text{-}DM\text{-}SPR}(F, \xi) + \mathsf{InSec}^{PQ\text{-}NM\text{-}eTCR}(H_{msg}, \xi))]$$

Proof. The proof is based on the approach of the proof given in [24]. Note that we do not include the proof of $\mathcal{F}_n$ and $\mathcal{F}_m$ with respect to PQ-PRF because they are not affected by instantiating DGM with XMSS-T, hence, the proof is similar to that of XMSS-T in [24]. Assume the adversary $\mathcal{A}$ is allowed to make 2^y queries to a signing oracle running DGM with XMSS-T. $\mathcal{A}$ wins the $\mathsf{EXP}_{GS,\mathcal{A}}^{forge}$, as shown in Fig. 1, if they find a valid forgery (M', Σ') where the message M' is not in the queried set of 2^y messages. $\mathcal{A}$ initially groups the signatures that share a given $indx$ in a set ts. Forgery occurs in the following three mutually exclusive cases.

- The message digest of M' under $indx$ results in M' being a second preimage of one of the message digests of the messages in ts. More precisely

$$md = H_{msg}(R' || DGM.root || indx, M') = H_{msg}(R_j || DGM.root || indx, M_j)$$

where $M_j \in ts$. This occurs with success probability $t \times \mathsf{InSec}^{PQ\text{-}NM\text{-}eTCR}(H_{msg})$ (see Definition 3), i.e. $\mathcal{A}$ is able to break the security of NM-eTCR of the message hash function used, H_{msg}.
- The OTS public key of the forged signature, $OTS.pk'$, exists in the set of OTS public keys of the signatures in ts, i.e. $OTS.pk' \in \{OTS.pk_0, \cdots, OTS.pk_{t-1}\}$. This occurs with success probability $t \times \mathsf{InSec}^{PQ\text{-}DM\text{-}SPR}(F)$ (see Definition 1), i.e. $\mathcal{A}$ is able to break the security of DM-SPR of hash function F.
- The forged signature contains a node in the authentication path ($X'_{i,j}$, the i-th node in level j), that collides with a node at the same position in the set of authentication paths in ts ($X_{i,j}$, the i-th node in level j), e.g. $H(r_{i,j}, (X'_{2i,j-1} || X'_{2i+1,j-1}) \oplus q_{i,j}) = H(r_{i,j}, (X_{2i,j-1} || X_{2i+1,j-1}) \oplus q_{i,j})$, where the nodes $(X'_{2i,j-1}, X'_{2i+1,j-1})$ are from the forged signature authentication path, the nodes $(X_{2i,j-1}, X_{2i+1,j-1})$ are from an authentication path of a signature in ts, and $r_{i,j}, q_{i,j}$ are the hash randomizer and bit mask used for hashing. This occurs with success probability $t \times \mathsf{InSec}^{PQ\text{-}DM\text{-}SPR}(H)$ (see Definition 1). Thus, $\mathcal{A}$ is able to break the security of the second preimage resistance of hash function H.

The above proof shows that if DGM is instantiated with the parameters of XMSS-T (RFC 8391), i.e. the message digest length equals the security parameter n, then DGM does not achieve the same bit security level as XMSS-T. In particular, the bit security of DGM decreases by $\log_2 t$ bits compared to that of XMSS-T, so for XMSS-T with security parameter $n = 256$ and DGM used to sign 2^{64} messages, the DGM bit security decreases by $\log_2(\sum_{j=0}^{j=18} 2^{43-j}) = 44$ bits, i.e. DGM achieves 212 bits of security. Therefore, if DGM is required to achieve n bits of security, then XMSS-T should use a hash function with output size $n + \log_2 t$ which decreases the signing performance and increases the signature size. In the following section, we propose a solution that allows DGM to attain optimal parameters whereas XMSS-T attains (almost) optimal parameters [9].

6   DGM$^+$ with Optimal Parameters

In this section we propose DGM$^+$, a DGM-XMSS-T variant that mitigates multitarget attacks (per index) as discussed in Sect. 5. We modify the addressing scheme such that it outputs different hash randomizers and bit masks for the same hash call location in different SMTs branching from the same IMT internal node, and for overlapped SMTs that share the same indexing for some leaves.

The DGM public parameters contain two values $DGM.root$ and $DGM.seed$, where $DGM.root$ is the IMT root (group public key), and $DGM.seed$ is the public key seed that is used in the XMSS-T addressing scheme to generate the hash randomizers r_i and bit masks q_i for each hash call at address ad_i in the IMT, i.e. $(r_i, q_i) \leftarrow ADRS(DGM.seed, ad_i)$. To enable opening, each SMT leaf has index (v, u) which is encrypted to generate $DGM.pos$, where v is the SMT number and u is the leaf index within the SMT. Note that both u and v are secrets but $DGM.pos$ is not because it is sent in the signature. If we assume that the bit size of v is equal to the block length, b, of the encryption algorithm used, then we can get ev as the first b bits from $DGM.pos$, where ev denotes the encryption of v. Accordingly, we propose the following.

- IMT uses $DGM.seed$ directly as the seed to generate the hash randomizers and bit masks for each hash call within the IMT.
- Each SMT utilizes (publicly calculated) a different seed, SMT.$seed_v$ for its hash randomizer and bit mask generation. SMT.$seed_v$ is unique for the v-th SMT and is calculated by SMT.$seed_v = PRF(DGM.seed, ev)$.

For all SMTs that share indexing, we utilize different seed values with each SMT and keep the XMSS-T addressing scheme unchanged [22] (see Sect. A). Thus, different hash randomizers and bit masks are used at the same IMT location but for different SMTs. Note that for signing, the IMT utilizes $DGM.seed$ in its construction, while the v-th SMT utilizes SMT.$seed_v = PRF(DGM.seed, ev)$ in its construction. Let $SMT.root.level$ denote the level of the fallback node for a given signing SMT. The signature authentication path, $Auth$, contains the whole SMT authentication path, $Auth.SMT_v$ and the top $20 - SMT.root.level$ nodes from the IMT. The latter authentication path starts from the neighboring node of the fallback node linked to the SMT root and up to $DGM.root$.

For verification, the verifier uses two seeds. $DGM.seed$ is used for hash evaluations of the authentication path from the fallback node and up. Moreover, the verifier calculates STM.$seed_v = PRF(DGM.seed, ev)$ which is used in the WOTS-T hash iterations and the SMT authentication path, $Auth.SMT_v$, hash evaluations.

6.1   Message Hashing with DM-SPR

It was shown in Sect. 5 that the security of DGM depends on the NM-eTCR of the hash function used where the number of targets, t, is considered per index. We tweak the message hashing such that the security of DGM depends on the DM-SPR of the hash function used (see Definition 1), to prevent multi-targets attacks. This is achieved by using the message hash randomizer $R = F^{w-1}(sk_1)$ as follows

$$md = H_{msg}(R||DGM.root||idx, M) = H_{msg}(F^{w-1}(sk_1)||DGM.root||indx, M)$$

where $F^{w-1}(sk_1)$ is the last iteration, $w - 1$, of the first secret key of WOTS-T (see [24] for the details of WOTS-T).

Message Hashing Tweak Rationale. The elements $(R||DGM.root||idx)$ serve as the hash key where R is chosen at random for each new message hashing and $DGM.root$ is fixed. If an adversary $\mathcal{A}$ who has access to the signing oracle is able to get the hash randomizer R before querying the signing oracle, then $\mathcal{A}$ can search to find two messages that have the same image using the same R, i.e. $\mathcal{A}$ looks for a collision. Therefore, $\mathcal{A}$ queries the signing oracle with one message and the other message has the same signature. Nevertheless, as R is chosen randomly and is known to the adversary only after querying the signing oracle, $\mathcal{A}$ works to find a second primage of any of the queried messages when any hash randomizer R' is used, i.e. for a valid forgery the adversary needs to break the NM-eTCR security of the hash function used.

   If we replace the hash randomizer R with the last iteration of the first secret key of the OTS used, $pk_1 = F^{w-1}(sk_1)$ (see [24] for details), then R is not chosen at random and is known publicly only after signing. Accordingly, for a valid forgery, the adversary is restricted to using the same message hash randomizer, $R = F^{w-1}(sk_1)$ (that is sent in the signature), to find a message digest collision with the queried set. Hence, the adversary is required to break the security of MM-SPR of the hash function used which has a lower probability of success than breaking the NM-eTCR security of the hash function. Note that the last chain iteration of the first OTS secret key, $F^{w-1}(sk_1)$, is not a public parameter and is known only after signing with the corresponding leaf node, i.e. it is different than the OTS public key which is the root of the L-Tree (see [24] for the details of the L-Tree).

   In the verification procedure, the verifier checks if $pk_1 = F^{w-a_1-1}(\sigma_1) \stackrel{?}{=} R$, where σ_1 is the first signature element in the OTS signature, otherwise, it returns invalid signature. Accordingly, for a valid forgery the adversary is required to find a second primage using the hash key $F^{w-1}(sk_1)||DGM.root||idx$, i.e. break the MM-SPR of the hash function (see Definition 1).

   Note that using the above message hashing to generate R from the OTS public keys may be used to enable XMSS-T [9] to attain optimal parameters. Specifically, when R is bound to a specific signing leaf, it suffices that R is n bits to provide n bit security.

6.2   DGM and DGM$^+$ Comparison

This section provides a comparison between DGM and DGM$^+$ when both are instantiated with XMSS-T to provide n bit security and support 2^y messages where $y \geq 20$, and the IMT height is 20.

Secret and Public Keys Sizes. For DGM to achieve n bit security requires a hash output size of $n + \log_2 t$ bits where t is given by Eq. 1. Thus, its tree nodes and secret keys will also be $n + \log_2 t$ bits. The DGM public key is the pair $(pk.seed, IMT.root)$ each of $n + \log_2 t$ bits, and the secret key contains $sk.prf$ to generate the message hash randomizer and $sk.seed$ to generate the WOTS-T secret keys. Accordingly, the secret key size is $2(n + \log_2 t)$ bits.

For DGM$^+$, the size of the tree nodes and secret keys is n bits. The DGM$^+$ public key size is $2n$ bits, i.e. $(pk.seed, IMT.root)$ each of n bits. The secret key contains only $sk.seed$ of n bits because it does not require $sk.prf$ as the message hash randomizer is the last hash iteration of the first WOTS-T secret key.

Signature Size. A DGM signature contains the message hash randomizer, R, the leaf index, the encrypted position, the WOTS-T signature, the authentication path, and the fallback key. The signature element sizes in DGM$^+$ is n bits while in DGM it is $n + \log_2 t$ bits. This has another impact as the message digest size is increased, the number of WOTS-T elements, l, is increased. This increases both the signature size and the computational cost.

Table 1 provides the size of the keys and signature for both DGM$^+$and DGM at 128, 192, and 256 bit security when they are used to support up to 2^{64} signatures where the signature size is $(22 + l)n + 4$ Bytes and l is the number of elements in the OTS signature. The index is 4 Bytes and we consider the encrypted position and message hash randomizer, R, equal to the node size in the scheme.

Table 1. DGM and DGM$^+$ keys and signature sizes in Bytes at 128, 192, and 256 bit security and 2^{64} signatures.

Algorithm	Bit security	Node size	pk	sk	l	Signature size
DGM	128	22	44	44	47	1522
	192	30	60	60	63	2554
	256	38	76	76	79	3842
DGM$^+$	128	16	32	16	35	916
	192	24	48	24	51	1756
	256	32	64	32	67	2852

7   Conclusion

In this paper, we discussed the challenges of instantiating GM and DGM with XMSS-T and provided a tweak in the setup phases of GM and DGM to overcome the discussed challenges. Moreover, we analyzed the bit security of DGM when instantiated with XMSS-T and showed that because of the parallel multiple XMSS-T instances construction, DGM is vulnerable to multi-target attacks that may enable forgery with 44 bits less effort than that of XMSS-T when the scheme is used to sign 2^{64} messages. Finally, we proposed a solution that mitigates these multi-target attacks and presented a new message hashing mechanism that reduces the associated signature and secret key sizes.

Acknowledgment. The authors would like to thank the reviewers for their valuable comments that helped improve the quality of the paper.

A   XMSS-T Addressing Scheme

XMSS-T utilizes a hash function addressing scheme that enumerates each hash call in the scheme and outputs a distinct hash randomizer r and bit mask q for each hash call to mitigate multi-target attacks [22]. XMSS-T has three main substructures, WOTS-T, L-tree, and Merkle tree hash. The first substructure requires for each hash call a hash randomizer and bit mask, each of n bits. The other two substructures require a hash randomizer of n bits and $2n$ bits for the bit mask. The hash function address consists of 256 bits. There are three address types for the three substructure mentioned above which are described below.

1. WOTS-T hash address: The first field (32 bits) is the tree layer address which indexes a given layer in which the WOTS-T exists (this value is set to zero for DGM). The tree address (64 bits) indexes a tree within the layer (this value is set to zero for DGM), and the addressing type (32 bits) which is equal to zero. The key pair address (32 bits) denotes the index of the WOTS-T within the hash tree. The chain address (32 bits) denotes the number of the WOTS-T secret key on which the chain is applied. The hash address (32 bits) denotes the number of the hash function iterations within a chain. The last field is KeyAndMask (32 bits) which is used to generate two different addresses for one hash function call (it is set to zero to get the hash randomizer R and it is set to one to get the bit mask, each of n bits).
2. L-tree hash address: The first field (32 bits) is the layer address which indexes the layer in which the WOTS-T exists (this value is set to zero for DGM). The tree address (64 bits) indexes a tree within the layer (this value is set to zero for DGM), and the addressing type (32 bits) which is equal to one. The L-tree address (32 bits) denotes the leaf index that is used to sign the message. The tree height (32 bits) encodes the node height in the L-tree, and the tree index (32 bits) refers to the node index within that height. The last field is KeyAndMask (32 bits) which in this substructure is used to generate three different addresses for one hash function call (it is set to zero to get the hash randomizer R, one to get the first bit mask and two to get the second bit mask, each of n bits).
3. Merkle tree hash: The first field (32 bits) is the layer address which indexes the layer in which the WOTS-T exists (this value is set to zero for DGM).

The tree address (64 bits) indexes a tree within the layer (this value is set to zero for DGM), and the addressing type (32 bits) which is equal to two. Then a padding of zeros (32 bits). The tree height (32 bits) encodes the node height in the main Merkle tree and the tree index (32 bits) refers to the node index within that height. As the L-tree addressing, the last field is KeyAndMask (32 bits) which is used to generate three different addresses for one hash function call (it is set to zero to get the hash randomizer R, one to get the first bit mask and two to get the second bit mask, each of n bits).

References

1. Alamélou, Q., Blazy, O., Cauchie, S., Gaborit, P.: A practical group signature scheme based on rank metric. In: Duquesne, S., Petkova-Nikova, S. (eds.) WAIFI 2016. LNCS, vol. 10064, pp. 258–275. Springer, Cham (2016). https://doi.org/10.1007/978-3-319-55227-9_18
2. Alamélou, Q., Blazy, O., Cauchie, S., Gaborit, P.: A code-based group signature scheme. Des. Codes Crypt. **82**(1–2), 469–493 (2017)
3. AlTawy, R., Gong, G.: Mesh: a supply chain solution with locally private blockchain transactions. Proc. Priv. Enhancing Technol. **2019**(3), 149–169 (2019)
4. Ayebie, B.E., Assidi, H., Souidi, E.M.: A new dynamic code-based group signature scheme. In: El Hajji, S., Nitaj, A., Souidi, E.M. (eds.) C2SI 2017. LNCS, vol. 10194, pp. 346–364. Springer, Cham (2017). https://doi.org/10.1007/978-3-319-55589-8_23
5. Bellare, M., Micciancio, D., Warinschi, B.: Foundations of group signatures: formal definitions, simplified requirements, and a construction based on general assumptions. In: Biham, E. (ed.) EUROCRYPT 2003. LNCS, vol. 2656, pp. 614–629. Springer, Heidelberg (2003). https://doi.org/10.1007/3-540-39200-9_38
6. Boneh, D., Boyen, X., Shacham, H.: Short group signatures. In: Franklin, M. (ed.) CRYPTO 2004. LNCS, vol. 3152, pp. 41–55. Springer, Heidelberg (2004). https://doi.org/10.1007/978-3-540-28628-8_3
7. Boneh, D., Dagdelen, Ö., Fischlin, M., Lehmann, A., Schaffner, C., Zhandry, M.: Random oracles in a quantum world. In: Lee, D.H., Wang, X. (eds.) ASIACRYPT 2011. LNCS, vol. 7073, pp. 41–69. Springer, Heidelberg (2011). https://doi.org/10.1007/978-3-642-25385-0_3
8. Boneh, D., Shacham, H.: Group signatures with verifier-local revocation. In: Proceedings of the ACM Conference on Computer and Communications Security, pp. 168–177 (2004)
9. Bos, J.W., Hülsing, A., Renes, J., van Vredendaal, C.: Rapidly verifiable XMSS signatures. IACR Trans. Cryptogr. Hardware Embed. Syst. **2021**, 137–168 (2021)
10. Buchmann, J., Dahmen, E., Ereth, S., Hülsing, A., Rückert, M.: On the security of the Winternitz one-time signature scheme. In: Nitaj, A., Pointcheval, D. (eds.) AFRICACRYPT 2011. LNCS, vol. 6737, pp. 363–378. Springer, Heidelberg (2011). https://doi.org/10.1007/978-3-642-21969-6_23
11. Buchmann, J., Dahmen, E., Hülsing, A.: XMSS - a practical forward secure signature scheme based on minimal security assumptions. In: Yang, B.-Y. (ed.) PQCrypto 2011. LNCS, vol. 7071, pp. 117–129. Springer, Heidelberg (2011). https://doi.org/10.1007/978-3-642-25405-5_8

12. Buser, M., Liu, J.K., Steinfeld, R., Sakzad, A., Sun, S.-F.: DGM: a dynamic and revocable group Merkle signature. In: Sako, K., Schneider, S., Ryan, P.Y.A. (eds.) ESORICS 2019. LNCS, vol. 11735, pp. 194–214. Springer, Cham (2019). https://doi.org/10.1007/978-3-030-29959-0_10

13. Camenisch, J., Groth, J.: Group signatures: better efficiency and new theoretical aspects. In: Blundo, C., Cimato, S. (eds.) SCN 2004. LNCS, vol. 3352, pp. 120–133. Springer, Heidelberg (2005). https://doi.org/10.1007/978-3-540-30598-9_9

14. Camenisch, J., Lysyanskaya, A.: Dynamic accumulators and application to efficient revocation of anonymous credentials. In: Yung, M. (ed.) CRYPTO 2002. LNCS, vol. 2442, pp. 61–76. Springer, Heidelberg (2002). https://doi.org/10.1007/3-540-45708-9_5

15. Camenisch, J., Lysyanskaya, A.: Signature schemes and anonymous credentials from bilinear maps. In: Franklin, M. (ed.) CRYPTO 2004. LNCS, vol. 3152, pp. 56–72. Springer, Heidelberg (2004). https://doi.org/10.1007/978-3-540-28628-8_4

16. Chaum, D., van Heyst, E.: Group signatures. In: Davies, D.W. (ed.) EUROCRYPT 1991. LNCS, vol. 547, pp. 257–265. Springer, Heidelberg (1991). https://doi.org/10.1007/3-540-46416-6_22

17. Del Pino, R., Lyubashevsky, V., Seiler, G.: Lattice-based group signatures and zero-knowledge proofs of automorphism stability. In: Proceedings of the ACM SIGSAC Conference on Computer and Communications Security, pp. 574–591 (2018)

18. El Bansarkhani, R., Misoczki, R.: G-Merkle: a hash-based group signature scheme from standard assumptions. In: Lange, T., Steinwandt, R. (eds.) PQCrypto 2018. LNCS, vol. 10786, pp. 441–463. Springer, Cham (2018). https://doi.org/10.1007/978-3-319-79063-3_21

19. Ezerman, M.F., Lee, H.T., Ling, S., Nguyen, K., Wang, H.: Provably secure group signature schemes from code-based assumptions. IEEE Trans. Inf. Theor. 66(9), 5754–5773 (2020)

20. Gordon, S.D., Katz, J., Vaikuntanathan, V.: A group signature scheme from lattice assumptions. In: Abe, M. (ed.) ASIACRYPT 2010. LNCS, vol. 6477, pp. 395–412. Springer, Heidelberg (2010). https://doi.org/10.1007/978-3-642-17373-8_23

21. Hülsing, A., Busold, C., Buchmann, J.: Forward secure signatures on smart cards. In: Knudsen, L.R., Wu, H. (eds.) SAC 2012. LNCS, vol. 7707, pp. 66–80. Springer, Heidelberg (2013). https://doi.org/10.1007/978-3-642-35999-6_5

22. Hülsing, A., Butin, D., Gazdag, S.-L., Rijneveld, J., Mohaisen, A.: XMSS: extended Merkle signature scheme. In: RFC 8391. IRTF (2018)

23. Hülsing, A., Rausch, L., Buchmann, J.: Optimal parameters for $XMSS^{MT}$. In: Cuzzocrea, A., Kittl, C., Simos, D.E., Weippl, E., Xu, L. (eds.) CD-ARES 2013. LNCS, vol. 8128, pp. 194–208. Springer, Heidelberg (2013). https://doi.org/10.1007/978-3-642-40588-4_14

24. Hülsing, A., Rijneveld, J., Song, F.: Mitigating multi-target attacks in hash-based signatures. In: Cheng, C.-M., Chung, K.-M., Persiano, G., Yang, B.-Y. (eds.) PKC 2016. LNCS, vol. 9614, pp. 387–416. Springer, Heidelberg (2016). https://doi.org/10.1007/978-3-662-49384-7_15

25. Laguillaumie, F., Langlois, A., Libert, B., Stehlé, D.: Lattice-based group signatures with logarithmic signature size. In: Sako, K., Sarkar, P. (eds.) ASIACRYPT 2013. LNCS, vol. 8270, pp. 41–61. Springer, Heidelberg (2013). https://doi.org/10.1007/978-3-642-42045-0_3

26. Langlois, A., Ling, S., Nguyen, K., Wang, H.: Lattice-based group signature scheme with verifier-local revocation. In: Krawczyk, H. (ed.) PKC 2014. LNCS, vol. 8383, pp. 345–361. Springer, Heidelberg (2014). https://doi.org/10.1007/978-3-642-54631-0_20

27. Libert, B., Ling, S., Mouhartem, F., Nguyen, K., Wang, H.: Signature schemes with efficient protocols and dynamic group signatures from lattice assumptions. In: Cheon, J.H., Takagi, T. (eds.) ASIACRYPT 2016. LNCS, vol. 10032, pp. 373–403. Springer, Heidelberg (2016). https://doi.org/10.1007/978-3-662-53890-6_13
28. Libert, B., Peters, T., Yung, M.: Group signatures with almost-for-free revocation. In: Safavi-Naini, R., Canetti, R. (eds.) CRYPTO 2012. LNCS, vol. 7417, pp. 571–589. Springer, Heidelberg (2012). https://doi.org/10.1007/978-3-642-32009-5_34
29. Libert, B., Peters, T., Yung, M.: Scalable group signatures with revocation. In: Pointcheval, D., Johansson, T. (eds.) EUROCRYPT 2012. LNCS, vol. 7237, pp. 609–627. Springer, Heidelberg (2012). https://doi.org/10.1007/978-3-642-29011-4_36
30. Ling, S., Nguyen, K., Wang, H.: Group signatures from lattices: simpler, tighter, shorter, ring-based. In: Katz, J. (ed.) PKC 2015. LNCS, vol. 9020, pp. 427–449. Springer, Heidelberg (2015). https://doi.org/10.1007/978-3-662-46447-2_19
31. Merkle, R.C.: A certified digital signature. In: Brassard, G. (ed.) CRYPTO 1989. LNCS, vol. 435, pp. 218–238. Springer, New York (1990). https://doi.org/10.1007/0-387-34805-0_21
32. Nguyen, P.Q., Zhang, J., Zhang, Z.: Simpler efficient group signatures from lattices. In: Katz, J. (ed.) PKC 2015. LNCS, vol. 9020, pp. 401–426. Springer, Heidelberg (2015). https://doi.org/10.1007/978-3-662-46447-2_18
33. NIST. Post-quantum cryptography project. http://csrc.nist.gov/groups/ST/post-quantum-crypto
34. NIST. Submission requirements and evaluation criteria for the post-quantum cryptography standardization process. https://csrc.nist.gov/Projects/post-quantum-cryptography/post-quantum-cryptography-standardization/Call-for-Proposals
35. Traoré, J.: Group signatures and their relevance to privacy-protecting offline electronic cash systems. In: Pieprzyk, J., Safavi-Naini, R., Seberry, J. (eds.) ACISP 1999. LNCS, vol. 1587, pp. 228–243. Springer, Heidelberg (1999). https://doi.org/10.1007/3-540-48970-3_19
36. Yang, R., Au, M.H., Zhang, Z., Xu, Q., Yu, Z., Whyte, W.: Efficient lattice-based zero-knowledge arguments with standard soundness: construction and applications. In: Boldyreva, A., Micciancio, D. (eds.) CRYPTO 2019. LNCS, vol. 11692, pp. 147–175. Springer, Cham (2019). https://doi.org/10.1007/978-3-030-26948-7_6

System Security

UC-Secure Cryptographic Reverse Firewall–Guarding Corrupted Systems with the Minimum Trusted Module

Geng Li[1], Jianwei Liu[2], Zongyang Zhang[2(✉)], and Yanting Zhang[2]

[1] National Computer Network Emergency Response Technical Team/Coordination Center of China, Beijing, China
ligeng@buaa.edu.cn
[2] School of Cyber Science and Technology, Beihang University, Beijing, China
{liujianwei,zongyangzhang,yantingzhang}@buaa.edu.cn

Abstract. Nowadays, mass-surveillance is becoming an increasingly severe threat to the public's privacy. The PRISM and a series of other events showed that inner attacks such as subversion attacks may exist in the current network extensively. As an important strategy to defend users' privacy against these attacks, cryptographic reverse firewall (CRF) is designed to be a middle-box, modifying all the messages coming in and out of a computer. However, the current formal definition of CRFs merely considers a single protocol session. If such a CRF applies to multiple entities, the security of every entity could not be deduced directly, which leads to an application limitation. In this work, we re-define the notion of CRF from a new perspective based on UC-emulation. Our new definition expresses all expected properties of a CRF in a more brief way, under the universal composition environment. We present a composition theorem which enables deploying one CRF for a local area of network rather than a single computer, and this can significantly reduce the number of CRFs used in practical applications.

As another part of this work, under the new definition, we present the first deterministic CRF construction. Compared with existing CRFs, our construction only requires secure randomness in its initial phase rather than every protocol session, and such randomness can be acquired from a public resource. Noting that the probabilistic algorithms are the main targets of subversion attacks, our work makes it much easier to realize a trusted CRF, and thus, pushes CRFs from a concept to application with one more step.

Keywords: Post-Snowden cryptography · Subversion attack · Cryptographic reverse firewall · Universal composition · Security implementation

---

G. Li—The research in this paper is mainly done when the first author was a Ph. D candidate in Beihang University.

© Springer Nature Switzerland AG 2021
Y. Yu and M. Yung (Eds.): Inscrypt 2021, LNCS 13007, pp. 85–110, 2021.
https://doi.org/10.1007/978-3-030-88323-2_5

1   Introduction

The PRISM has attracted great attention to the risk of mass-surveillance. A series of events implied that some powerful institutions may monitor people's private conversation and other online activities, via some special methods which are out of the consideration of conventional cryptography. Subversion attack is a typical attack method in the mass-surveillance, which deviates the implementations of cryptographic algorithms from the corresponding specifications in an undetectable way, and only the backdoor holder is able to recognize the subverted implementations and acquire user's private information based on their outputs. Due to the effectiveness and concealment, the subversion attack has been explored by a lot of works, and it serves as an essential foundation for Post-Snowden cryptography.

To deal with subversion attacks, researchers have proposed several defending strategies, such as the split-program [17], multi-source components [13], public random resources [1], and cryptographic reverse firewalls (CRFs) [8,10,15]. CRF is a machine sitting between a user's computer and the outside world, modifying all the incoming and outgoing messages to guard the protocol against information leakage. On the one hand, a CRF is assumed to be a trusted module, i.e., the implementation should completely obey its specification. On the other hand, however, a CRF is still a public entity, saying, it can only access public information such as public-keys and ciphertexts. Mironov and Stephens-Davidowitz [15] formally defined a CRF with three important properties: functionality-maintaining, security-preserving, and exfiltration-resistance.

Assumed to be trusted, a CRF seems to exclude the risk of subversion attacks in an ideal way. However, the current theory is a little imperfect from the view of practical applications. Following the definition in work [15], we need to deploy a CRF for every entity in the reality (as shown in Fig. 1). This may imply a logical contradiction: we worry about the credibility of user's computer, but at the same time, we directly assume the existence of the same amount of trusted modules (CRF). Therefore, the idea of CRF just bypasses the difficulty in the mass-surveillance, and the tricky problem remains unsolved.

We claim that in a reasonable design, the number of CRFs should be much less than the number of users' computers, thus, we can concentrate to achieving these small amount of trusted modules to protect the whole system. Concretely, as shown in Fig. 2, a CRF serves for a local area of network containing multiple computers. It is straightforward that this framework is much more practical than the previous "one-one" pattern. However, this "one-many" framework is actually out of the consideration of the current definition. Here, several entities share a CRF, and a CRF may serve for multiple kinds of protocol. It is inevitable that different protocol sessions may have shared information or joint state. We cannot ensure that a CRF under the current definition is able to protect every entity in such a compositional setting. Thus, we call for a new definition of CRFs to adapt to this setting.

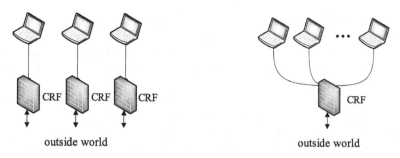

Fig. 1. The "one-one" pattern   **Fig. 2.** The "one-many" pattern

Besides, another factor that inspires us to revisit the formalization of CRF is the redundancy of the current definition [15], where the relationship between security-preserving and exfiltration-resistance is much complex. These two properties sometimes are equivalent, but sometimes have subtle differences. Including both of them as basic requirements of a CRF seems redundant, while omitting either one will render the definition incomplete. Therefore, it is meaningful if we could find a method to conclude all the expected properties of a CRF with only one expression.

Under the current definition [15], researchers now have proposed a series of constructions of CRF. To the best of our knowledge, all these CRFs need to generate the same amount of randomness to the underlying protocol. We should note that achieving the credibility of probabilistic implementations is far more difficult than deterministic implementations, thus, generating such a large amount of randomness increases the difficulty of realizing a trusted CRF. If we could construct a CRF with only deterministic algorithms, the meaning of CRFs will be significantly increased. This work may also initialize another line of research, i.e., removing the assumption that CRFs are trusted modules, and including CRFs also under the consideration of subversion attacks.

1.1   Our Contribution

The main purpose of this paper about CRF is "guarding corrupted systems with the minimum trusted module", and this keynote can be interpreted from two levels. In the first level, we propose the scenario that using one CRF to guard multiple computers. We re-define the notion of CRF based on the UC framework, which is more compatible with such compositional settings. In the second level, we try to further shrink the trusted element of CRF, by designing a CRF only using deterministic algorithms.

Re-definition of a CRF Based on UC-emulation. Based on the UC-emulation [5,6], we re-define the notion of CRF. All analyses in this paper are under the precondition that the specification of a protocol can emulate the ideal functionality perfectly. We say a CRF guards the protocol, if either it could detect the subverted implementations, or it could correct the corrupted protocol to emulate the ideal functionality, with no environment being able to distinguish between these two cases. We build the new definition by three steps: Firstly, we specify the formalization of a protocol using the language of UC framework; Then, we formulate the deployment and operation of a CRF; Finally, we present the security definition of a CRF.

Compared with the current one, our new definition has at least two advantages. Firstly, this definition is designed from the view of composition. We present a composition theorem, which demonstrates that the CRF's security property for every single session does not decline in any compositional setting. That is to say, when a CRF deals with multiple sessions or multiple protocols at the same time, even though different sessions have shared information or joint state, every protocol session can still UC-emulate the ideal functionality. Thus, such definition provides a basis for the "one-many" deployment in applications as shown in Fig. 2. Secondly, the new definition incorporates the three basic requirements (functionality-maintaining, security-preserving and exfiltration-resistance) into one property, which makes the expression far more clear. We make a rigorous comparison between the two definitions of a CRF, proving that the new definition implies the current one in a general sense.

Construction of a Deterministic CRF. Our construction is based on the classical framework of CRF in work [10], but transfers the probabilistic algorithms to deterministic algorithms. Noting that probabilistic algorithms are main targets of subversion attacks, this modification will significantly weaken the assumption that a CRF is a trusted module.

Unlike the existing CRFs which need to generate randomness during every run of protocol, our CRF only requires a small amount of randomness as its keys in the initial phase. The keys should remain confidential to the protocol parties, however, may be a little surprising, they are unnecessary to stay secure against external adversaries. Such property provides us with a possible operation pattern of CRF, i.e., injecting a public randomness into a CRF, after the implementations of protocol parties are deployed.

We achieve such a deterministic CRF by replacing the coins in the former CRFs, via hashing input messages along with the CRF key. Observing that even if being subverted, an implementation of protocol party should still ensure its output to have high min-entropy, otherwise it can be detected from its specification easily. Taking use of this point, we prove that for both subverted implementations and external adversaries, the input of the hash function is inaccessible, thus, the acquired coins can serve as uniform randomness.

1.2   Related Work

Post-Snowden Cryptography. The notion of kleptography was introduced by Young and Yung in a series of researches [18–21]. They considered the scenario where implementations of cryptographic algorithms are maliciously designed by adversaries. They also designed several detailed attacks aimed at some commonly used schemes such as RSA, Elgamal, Diffie-Hellman key-exchange protocol, et al.

Bellare, Paterson and Rogaway [4] formally established the security model for encryption schemes under subversion attacks. This model consists of a pair of games, the surveillance game and the detection game, to characterize the advantage of a surveillant and the probability of detecting a subverted implementation. Work [9] and work [3] made partial progresses on the model in work [4], to adopt to several special cases such as input-trigger attacks. Using a similar framework, Ateniese, Magri and Venturi [2] formulated the security model for signature schemes. Russell et al. [16] proposed the notion of cliptography. They introduced an entity named "watchdog" which checks all implementations provided by an adversary. If all implementations agreed by the watchdog could run without any difference to the specification even from the view of the adversary itself, then we say the scheme is stego-freeness.

A series of defending strategies have been proposed against the subversion attack. Russell et al. [17] gave the idea of split-program methodology, dividing one algorithm into several components. All implementations with respect to the components are probably subverted and modeled as blackboxes, but users could ensure the security of the whole system with the help of the watchdog's checking and a trusted amalgamation. Fischlin and Mazaheri [11] presented a defending strategy named "self-guarding protocol". They assumed that users can set up a secure initial phase for the protocol, in which a number of randomness are generated, and all algorithms executed after the initial phase are designed to be deterministic. Ateniese et al. [1] showed how to correct subverted implementations using a public (secure) randomness generator which is accessible to both users and adversaries. Li, Liu and Zhang [13,14] proposed a defending strategy where users could construct a system using implementations from multiple sources. When multiple adversaries are isolated [13] or only able to communicate in a limited way [14], users can take certain designs to achieve a secure system against all adversaries, only using untrusted implementations.

Cryptographic Reverse Firewall. The notion of cryptographic reverse firewall (CRF) was first proposed by Mironov and Stephens-Davidowitz [15]. They characterized a robust CRF by three properties: functionality-maintaining, security-preserving and exfiltration-resistance. To demonstrate the achievability of this definition, they also showed how to convert an arbitrary protocol into a protocol with exfiltration-resistant reverse firewalls for all parties.

Dodis, Mironov and Stephens-Davidowitz [10] researched the security of message-transmission protocols under subversion attacks. They designed a CRF for a type of interactive and concurrent CCA-secure message-transmission. Chen et al. [8] extended the notion of smooth projective hash function (SPHF) to malleable smooth projective hash function, based on which they proposed a general construction of CRF for some widely used cryptographic protocols. Especially, considering conventional oblivious transfer (OT) protocol is not compatible with the above modular way of CRF construction, they developed a new OT framework from graded rings and showed how to construct OT-CRFs by modifying the malleable SPHF framework.

Universal Composition. First proposed by Canetti [5], universal composition is a general framework to describe cryptographic protocols and analyze their security in complex environments. Canetti defined the security of a protocol by the indifference between an execution of the real protocol with an adversary, and an execution of the ideal functionality with a PPT simulator. Within this framework, protocols are guaranteed to maintain their security in any context, even in the presence of an unbounded number of arbitrary protocol sessions that run concurrently in an adversarially controlled manner.

The composition theorem in work [5] assumed the composed protocol instances have disjoint internal states and are independent completely. To relax this restriction, Canetti and Rabin [7] extended the framework and proposed the universal composition with joint state (JUC). This work considered the case where different protocol instances may have joint state and randomness. Following the line of work [7], Canetti et al. [6] further explored the composition theorem in the scenario where we cannot ensure that the set-up phase of a protocol provides the expected security guarantee. Hofheinz and Shoup [12] proposed a new framework named GNUC, which deviate from UC in several important aspects such as the formalization of protocols and the notion of corruptions.

Organization. Section 2 introduces the main notations and preliminaries. Section 3 presents a formal description of protocols, and gives a definition of CRFs from a new prospective. Section 4 presents the composition theorem of protocol instances equipped with a CRF. Section 5 demonstrates that the new definition implies the current one. Section 6 presents a construction of deterministic CRF under the new definition.

2 Preliminary

2.1 Notations

We use $s \xleftarrow{\$} S$ to denote that s is a uniformly random element in set S. U_ℓ denotes a ℓ-bit uniformly random string. $[1, r]$ is short for set $\{1, 2, \cdots, r\}$. $s_1 \| s_2$ means the concatenation of two bit strings s_1 and s_2. $\mathsf{poly}(x)$ represents a polynomial function of x. Let λ be a security parameter. $\mathsf{negl}(\lambda)$ is a negligible function in λ if it vanishes faster than the inverse of any polynomial in λ. $\mathsf{A}(x)$ is a probabilistic polynomial-time (PPT) algorithm if for any input x, $\mathsf{A}(x)$ terminates at most $\mathsf{poly}(|x|)$ steps. If the algorithm A outputs y upon the input x, we write $y \leftarrow \mathsf{A}(x)$. We use $\mathsf{G} \twoheadleftarrow \mathsf{A}(\cdot)$ to represent that A generates the implementation G.

For two distributions $\mathcal{X} = \{X_\lambda\}$ and $\mathcal{Y} = \{Y_\lambda\}$, let $\mathsf{Dist_D}(\mathcal{X}, \mathcal{Y}) \stackrel{def}{=} |\Pr[\mathsf{D}(X_\lambda) = 1] - \Pr[\mathsf{D}(Y_\lambda) = 1]|$. If $\mathsf{Dist_D}(\mathcal{X}, \mathcal{Y}) \leq \mathsf{negl}(\lambda)$ for all PPT algorithm D, we call $\mathcal{X}$ and $\mathcal{Y}$ are computational indistinguishable and denote it by $\mathcal{X} \approx \mathcal{Y}$ for simplicity.

2.2 Proud-but-Malicious Adversary

"Proud-but-malicious" adversaries are the main issue considered in Post-Snowden cryptography. This kind of adversary tries to compromise security by providing subverted implementations of cryptographic algorithms. The important thing is that, a "proud-but-malicious" adversary prefers subversions to be "under the radar" of any possible detection [17]. Russell et al. established the notion of watchdog $\mathcal{W}$ which is a PPT detector aiming at distinguishing subversion from the specification. Concretely, for $\mathsf{G_{impl}} \longleftarrow \mathcal{A}(\mathsf{G_{spec}})$, and any PPT watchdog $\mathcal{W}$, we call $\mathcal{A}$ is a proud-but-malicious adversary against offline watchdog if

$$\left| \Pr[\mathcal{W}^{\mathsf{G_{impl}}}(1^\lambda) = 1] - \Pr[\mathcal{W}^{\mathsf{G_{spec}}}(1^\lambda) = 1] \right| \leq \mathsf{negl}(\lambda).$$

Similarly, we call $\mathcal{A}$ is a proud-but-malicious adversary against online watchdog if

$$\left| \Pr[\mathcal{W}^{\mathsf{G_{impl}}}(\tau) = 1] - \Pr[\mathcal{W}^{\mathsf{G_{spec}}}(\tau) = 1] \right| \leq \mathsf{negl}(\lambda),$$

where τ denotes all the transcripts accessible to $\mathcal{A}$ in the same time. When $\mathcal{W}$ is clear, we simply say $\mathcal{A}$ is a proud-but-malicious adversary. And for simplicity, in this paper we call it a *PM-adversary*.

2.3 The Current Definition of a CRF

The notion of cryptographic reverse firewall (CRF) was first proposed by Mironov and Stephens-Davidowitz [15]. A CRF is a trusted module sitting between a user's computer and the outside world, intercepting all the messages coming in and out. A formal description of CRF is presented in Definition 1

Definition 1. *A cryptographic reverse firewall (CRF) is a stateful algorithm* crf *that takes as input its state and a message, and outputs an updated state and a modified message. For simplicity, we do not write the state of* crf *explicitly.*

For a cryptographic reverse firewall crf *and a party* A = {receive, next, output}, *where* receive *is the function to receive messages from outside,* next *is the function to generate outputting message, and* output *is the function to generate the final result of the protocol. The composed party* A ∘ crf *is defined as:*

$$\mathsf{A} \circ \mathsf{crf} \overset{def}{=} \Big(\mathsf{receive}_{\mathsf{A} \circ \mathsf{crf}}(\sigma, m) = \mathsf{receive}_{\mathsf{A}}(\sigma, \mathsf{crf}(m)),$$

$$\mathsf{next}_{\mathsf{A} \circ \mathsf{crf}}(\sigma) = \mathsf{crf}(\mathsf{next}_{\mathsf{A}}(\sigma)),$$

$$\mathsf{output}_{\mathsf{A} \circ \mathsf{crf}}(\sigma) = \mathsf{output}_{\mathsf{A}}(\sigma) \Big),$$

where σ *denotes the state of the party* A, *and* m *denotes the transcript received.*

According to work [15], a CRF is characterized by three properties: functionality-maintaining, security-preserving, and exfiltration-resistance. Readers are referred to Appendix A for the formal definitions.

3 Security Model

Based on the notion of UC-emulation, this section presents a new definition of CRFs, which is totally different from the current definition consisting of functionality-maintaining, security-preserving and exfiltration-resistance. We first make a formal characterization of protocols in the view of the subversion attacks in Sect. 3.1. Next, we state the deployment and operation of a CRF in Sect. 3.2. Based on the above works, we present the security definition of a CRF in Sect. 3.3.

3.1   Protocol Framework

Our characterization of protocols mainly follows the idea in work [5], but with a deep simplification. We simplify the model mainly because the intention of this paper concentrates on CRFs, rather than protocols themselves. Thus, it is unnecessary to analyze a protocol in such a complicated way. The subversion attack could be regarded as "inner attack", i.e., an adversary compromises the security by corrupting the implementations inside a user's system. Considering such a property, we divide a protocol into several inner parts (main machines) and an external part (channel machine).

We consider an n-party protocol $\mathcal{P}$, an adversary $\mathcal{A}$ and an environment $\mathcal{E}$, all of which are modeled as interactive Turing machines (ITMs). Each instance of ITM is labeled by a protocol identity fid, a party identity pid and a session identity sid, which remain unchanged throughout. The messages transmitted between instances of ITM are interpreted as a tuple:

$$(fid, sid, pid_s, pid_r, m||ad, type).$$

pid_s and pid_r are identities of the sender and the receiver, respectively. $m||ad$ is the message and its associated data. $type \in \{$"$input$", "$internal\text{-}output$", "$output$", "$backdoor$"$\}$ is the label of the message; "$input$" represents the initial input of the protocol from environment $\mathcal{E}$; "$internal\text{-}output$" represents the information transmitted among machines of protocol $\mathcal{P}$; "$output$" represents the final output of protocol $\mathcal{P}$ from party π_i to $\mathcal{E}$; "$backdoor$" is used to represent backdoor information come from the adversary, or disclosed to it.

We simplify the structure of a protocol in work [5] and define $\mathcal{P}$ only as a channel machine and several main machines: $\mathcal{P} = \{\pi_1, \cdots, \pi_n, \mathsf{ch}\}$. Formally,

- π_i ($i \in [1, n]$) represents the program executed by each party in the protocol. π_i receives information from $\mathcal{E}$ in type of "$input$", and returns information in type of "$output$". π_i also has interface with ch to transmit messages in type of "$internal\text{-}output$", and has interface with $\mathcal{A}$ to transmit messages in type of "$backdoor$". Especially, there is no direct interface between π_i and π_j ($i, j \in [1, n]$). All their communication is via channel machine or adversaries.
- ch represents the message transmission during the execution of the protocol. Besides interacting with π_i, it is also accessible to the adversary $\mathcal{A}$. For example, for an authenticated channel, when ch receives $(fid, sid, pid_{\pi_i}, pid_{\mathsf{ch}}, m||$"$pid_{\pi_i}$ to pid_{π_j}", "$internal\text{-}output$"), it sends $(fid, sid, pid_{\mathsf{ch}}, pid_{\mathcal{A}}, m||$"$pid_{\pi_i}$ to pid_{π_j}", "$backdoor$") to $\mathcal{A}$. After receiving $(fid, sid, pid_{\mathcal{A}}, pid_{\mathsf{ch}},$ "ok", "$backdoor$") from $\mathcal{A}$, it sends $(fid, sid, pid_{\mathsf{ch}}, pid_{\pi_j}, m||$"$pid_{\pi_i}$ to pid_{π_j}", "$internal\text{-}output$") to party π_j.

3.2 Protocol Equipped with a CRF

Now we present the formalization of a cryptographic reverse firewall. A CRF is an interactive Turing machine which intercepts and modifies all the messages sent between main machines π_i and channel machine ch. Especially, if the protocol is executed normally, the CRF seems "transparent". A CRF is regarded as a trusted model, saying, different with the protocol $\mathcal{P}$, it should be executed honestly according to its specification in any case. Another important difference between the CRF and machines of $\mathcal{P}$ is that a CRF instance is designed to operate across multiple sessions or even multiple protocols, while every ITM instance of protocol is corresponding to only one session.

Credibility and Session-Units. The adversary is not allowed to corrupt crf. All the messages transmitted between π_i and crf are inaccessible to the adversary. As a CRF operates across multiple sessions, we interpret crf as a basic-program and several session-units. Every session-unit is marked by a triple (fid, sid, pid), where fid and sid are protocol identity and session identity, and pid denotes the protocol party this unit serves. The session-units store the relative information with respect to the corresponding session and party.

The Authority to Alarm. We allow CRFs to "alarm". If a CRF perceives any abnormality of inputting messages implying that the implementation of the protocol is likely to be subverted, the CRF is able to alarm directly, and the whole protocol breaks off at the same time. To ensure the reasonability, the current definition (see Appendix A) imposes an adversary with some special limitations, e.g., it must provide functionality-maintaining implementations. Our design of "alarm" provides a possibility to remove these limitations and solve the problem by CRF itself.

The Notion of Shell Machine. To capture the feature of transparency of crf, we introduce the notion of shell machine to characterize a protocol deployed with a CRF. A shell machine operates like a "shell", modifying the string fields of the identities of sender and receiver, when transmitting messages coming in or out of the inner machine. We denote the shell of π_i, ch and crf by SH_{π_i}, $\mathsf{SH}_{\mathsf{ch}}$ and $\mathsf{SH}_{\mathsf{crf}}$, respectively, and denote the shelled machine of X by X^{SH}. The shell machines operate as in Fig. 3. Formally:

- SH_{π_i} filters all the messages coming in/out of π_i. It changes outgoing messages $(\cdot, \cdot, pid_{\pi_i}, pid_{\mathsf{ch}}, \cdot, \cdot)$ to $(\cdot, \cdot, pid_{\pi_i}, pid_{\mathsf{crf}}, \cdot, \cdot)$, and forwards other messages without modification.
- $\mathsf{SH}_{\mathsf{ch}}$ filters all the messages coming in/out of ch. It changes outgoing messages $(\cdot, \cdot, pid_{\mathsf{ch}}, pid_{\pi_i}, m||ad, \cdot)$ to $(\cdot, \cdot, pid_{\mathsf{ch}}, pid_{\mathsf{crf}}, m||ad||\text{"to } pid_{\pi_i}\text{"}, \cdot)$, and forwards other messages without modification.
- $\mathsf{SH}_{\mathsf{crf}}$ filters all the messages coming in/out of crf. It changes outgoing messages $(\cdot, \cdot, pid_{\mathsf{crf}}, pid_{\pi_i}, \cdot, \cdot)$ to $(\cdot, \cdot, pid_{\mathsf{ch}}, pid_{\pi_i}, \cdot, \cdot)$, and changes outgoing messages $(\cdot, \cdot, pid_{\mathsf{crf}}, pid_{\mathsf{ch}}, \cdot, \cdot)$ corresponding to the session-unit marked by (fid, sid, pid_{π_i}) to $(\cdot, \cdot, pid_{\pi_i}, pid_{\mathsf{ch}}, \cdot, \cdot)$. It forwards other messages without modification.

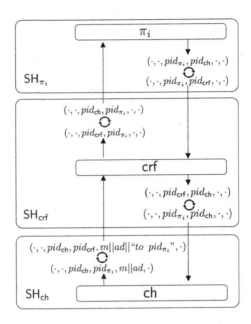

Fig. 3. Operation of the protocol deployed with a CRF. The round arrows represent the transfer operations of shells.

Now we are ready to formalize the operation of cryptographic reverse firewall crf when it composed with protocol $\mathcal{P}$. Following the work [15], we use $\mathcal{P} \circ \mathsf{crf}$ to denote a the protocol $\mathcal{P}$ equipped with a CRF crf. The cryptographic reverse firewall crf runs as follows:

- At the very beginning, the basic unit of crf is invoked.
- When perceiving any abnormality of the inputting messages, crf outputs ($\perp$, $\perp$, $pid_{\mathsf{crf}}, \mathcal{E}$, "alarm", "output"), and the protocol aborts.
- On receiving $(fid, sid, pid_{\pi_i}, pid_{\mathsf{crf}}, m||ad,$ "internal-output") from a main machine, crf checks if there exists a session-unit marked as (fid, sid, pid_{π_i}). If not, such a new session-unit is generated. Based on the information in the session-unit, crf generates the modified $m'||ad'$ and outputs $(fid, sid, pid_{\mathsf{crf}}, pid_{\mathsf{ch}}, m'||ad',$ "internal-output").
- Similarly, on receiving $(fid, sid, pid_{\mathsf{ch}}, pid_{\mathsf{crf}}, m||ad,$ "internal-output") from a channel machine, crf interprets ad as $ad^*||$"to pid_{π_j}", and checks if there exists a session-unit marked as (fid, sid, pid_{π_j}). If not, such a new session-unit is generated. Based on the information in the session-unit, crf generates the modified $m'||ad'$ and outputs $(fid, sid, pid_{\mathsf{crf}}, pid_{\mathsf{ch}}, m'||ad',$ "internal-output").
- On receiving messages in type of "backdoor", crf handles it as above, and returns messages in type of "backdoor".

3.3   Define a CRF by UC-emulation

Based on the above works, we present the new definition of the security of a CRF. Post-Snowden cryptography mainly focuses on the security of the implementations of cryptographic algorithms when they deviate from the corresponding specifications. Such analysis is meaningless if the specifications themselves do not satisfy the required security. Thus, all works in this paper are based on the premise that the protocol specification is secure, saying, it UC-emulates an ideal functionality $\mathcal{F}$.

The basic idea of the security definition of CRF is that, a CRF can either detect subverted implementations, or it could correct a subverted protocol to UC-emulate the ideal functionality $\mathcal{F}$. We use $\widehat{\mathsf{X}}$ to denote the subverted implementation of X. We first present the game of protocol execution in conventional settings. Readers are referred to Fig. 4 for the game of protocol execution. The machines in dashed boxes may be subverted by adversary $\mathcal{A}$, and the solid lines represent direct communications between ITMs. Concretely,

1. $\mathcal{E}$ is the first Turing machine to be invoked.
2. $\mathcal{E}$ invokes the adversary $\mathcal{A}$.
3. $\mathcal{E}$ generates the inputs of the protocol, and invokes the target protocol $\mathcal{P}$.
4. The target protocol ends when the main machines return their outputs to $\mathcal{E}$.
5. $\mathcal{E}$ outputs its one bit decision $\mathsf{EXEC}_{\mathcal{P},\mathcal{A},\mathcal{E}}$.

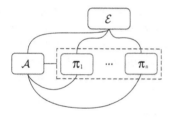

Fig. 4. Execution of protocol in conventional settings.

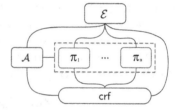

Fig. 5. Execution of protocol equipped with a CRF.

As a special case, when the target protocol is an ideal functionality $\mathcal{F}$, and the adversary is replaced by a simulator $\mathcal{S}$, we denote the output of $\mathcal{E}$ by $\mathsf{EXEC}_{\mathcal{F},\mathcal{S},\mathcal{E}}$. The security of protocol $\mathcal{P}$ in the conventional setting is defined based on the notion of "UC-emulation" [5]. Formally,

Definition 2. *Let $\mathcal{P}$ be a PPT protocol and $\mathcal{F}$ be an ideal functionality. We say that $\mathcal{P}$ UC-emulates $\mathcal{F}$, if for any PPT adversary $\mathcal{A}$, there exists a PPT simulator $\mathcal{S}$ such that for any PPT environment $\mathcal{E}$, we have*

$$\mathsf{EXEC}_{\mathcal{F},\mathcal{S},\mathcal{E}} \approx \mathsf{EXEC}_{\mathcal{P},\mathcal{A},\mathcal{E}}.$$

That is, for any input, the probability that $\mathcal{E}$ outputs 1 after interacting with $\mathcal{A}$ and $\mathcal{P}$ differs by at most a negligible amount from the probability that $\mathcal{E}$ outputs 1 after interacting with $\mathcal{S}$ and $\mathcal{F}$.

Next, we formulate the game of a protocol in the subversion setting. The main difference here is that the implementations of the target protocol are provided by an adversary, and the protocol is executed with the protection of a CRF. Readers are referred to Fig. 5 for detail. Concretely,

1. $\mathcal{E}$ is the first Turing machine to be invoked.
2. $\mathcal{E}$ invokes the adversary $\mathcal{A}$.
3. $\mathcal{A}$ generates the subverted implementations $\widehat{\mathcal{P}} = \{\widehat{\pi}_1, \cdots, \widehat{\pi}_n, \mathsf{ch}\}$, and submits them to $\mathcal{E}$.
4. $\mathcal{E}$ generates the inputs of the protocol, and invokes the target protocol $\widehat{\mathcal{P}} \circ \mathsf{crf}$.
5. The target protocol ends when crf alarms or the main machines return their outputs to $\mathcal{E}$.
6. $\mathcal{E}$ outputs its one bit decision $\mathsf{EXEC}_{\widehat{\mathcal{P}} \circ \mathsf{crf}, \mathcal{A}, \mathcal{E}}$.

Before presenting the security definition of a CRF, we define the notion of *robust CRFs*, which refers to that the CRF hardly alarms if all the implementations of protocol obey the specification honestly. Formally,

Definition 3. *A cryptographic reverse firewall* crf *is* robust[1], *if for any PPT adversary $\mathcal{A}$ and PPT environment $\mathcal{E}$,* crf *alarms only in a negligible probability when combines with the specification* $\{\pi_1, \cdots, \pi_n\}$ *of protocol $\mathcal{P}$.*

Now we are prepared for the definition of the security of a CRF.

Definition 4. *Let $\mathcal{P}$ be a PPT protocol which UC-emulates an ideal functionality $\mathcal{F}$ in conventional setting. We say a cryptographic reverse firewall* crf *guards $\mathcal{P}$ for $\mathcal{F}$, if (1)* crf *is robust; (2) for all the PPT adversary $\mathcal{A}$, the combined protocol $\widehat{\mathcal{P}} \circ \mathsf{crf}$ aborts with* crf *alarming in a non-negligible probability, or there exists a PPT simulator $\mathcal{S}$ such that for any PPT environment $\mathcal{E}$, we have:*

$$\mathsf{EXEC}_{\mathcal{F}, \mathcal{S}, \mathcal{E}} \approx \mathsf{EXEC}_{\widehat{\mathcal{P}} \circ \mathsf{crf}, \mathcal{A}, \mathcal{E}}.$$

4   Universal Composition of Protocols Deployed with a CRF

As we expect a CRF to serve multiple protocols and multiple sessions, it is necessary to analyze the compositional conditions of protocols with a CRF. Without an explicit formal theorem about composition, even if we prove a CRF is able to guard every protocol session independently, its security in practical application is still unguaranted. Fortunately, Canetti et al. [6] have proposed the notion of universally composable security with a global setup, which could provide a reference to our work, although their work focused on another topic.

Before presenting our composition theorem, we first introduce the notions of *CRF-subroutine respecting* and *honesty CRF*. These two properties actually

---

[1] Note that the definition of "robust" in this paper is totally different from the notion of "robust" in work [15].

achieve that any two sessions have no communication except using a same CRF, which is a little similar to the $\overline{\mathcal{G}}$-subroutine respecting proposed by Canetti et al. [6].

Definition 5. *A protocol $\mathcal{P}$ is CRF-subroutine respecting, if for the instance of $\mathcal{P}$ labeled as $fid_{\mathcal{P}}$ and sid_s, the shell machines SH_{π_i} reject all the incoming messages $(fid, sid, \cdot, \cdot, \cdot, \cdot)$ that $\{fid, sid\} \neq \{fid_{\mathcal{P}}, sid_s\}$.*

Definition 6. *A CRF is called* honest *if it does not change the protocol identity fid and session identity sid in the transmitted messages.*

Assume the ideal functionality $\mathcal{F}$ is a subroutine of protocol ρ. $\rho^{\mathcal{F} \to \widehat{\mathcal{P}}\text{ocrf}}$ denotes the protocol which is acquired by replacing the $\mathcal{F}$ in ρ by $\widehat{\mathcal{P}} \circ \mathsf{crf}$. Now we are prepared to present the composition theorem.

Theorem 1. *Let ρ and $\mathcal{P}$ be PPT protocols, and $\mathcal{F}$ be an ideal functionality. If an honest reverse firewall crf guards $\mathcal{P}$ for $\mathcal{F}$, and $\mathcal{P}$ is crf-subroutine respecting, then for any PPT adversary $\mathcal{A}$, $\rho^{\mathcal{F} \to \widehat{\mathcal{P}}\text{ocrf}}$ aborts with crf alarming in a non-negligible probability, or there exists a PPT adversary $\mathcal{S}$ such that for any PPT environment $\mathcal{E}$,*

$$\mathsf{EXEC}_{\rho, \mathcal{S}, \mathcal{E}} \approx \mathsf{EXEC}_{\rho^{\mathcal{F} \to \widehat{\mathcal{P}}\text{ocrf}}, \mathcal{A}, \mathcal{E}}.$$

Proof. We need only consider the case when crf does not alarm.

Following the idea in work [5], we take the language of "dummy adversary" to express the CRF's property in a substitutive way. A dummy adversary $\mathcal{D}$ just acts as a "transparent channel" between $\mathcal{E}$ and the machines in protocol. It forwards the backdoor type messages from $\mathcal{E}$ to main machines of protocol $\mathcal{P}$, and forwards the returned message from protocol machines to $\mathcal{E}$. Work [5] provides a rigorous proof that such adjustment from adversary $\mathcal{A}$ to "dummy adversary" $\mathcal{D}$ makes no change to the essence of the protocol security. That is to say, if there exists a PPT environment $\mathcal{E}$ being able to distinguish between an execution of protocol $\widehat{\mathcal{P}} \circ \mathsf{crf}$ with $\mathcal{A}$, and an execution of ideal functionality $\mathcal{F}$ with any PPT simulator $\mathcal{S}$, we can construct another PPT environment $\mathcal{E}'$ being able to distinguish between an execution of protocol $\widehat{\mathcal{P}} \circ \mathsf{crf}$ with dummy adversary $\mathcal{D}$, and an execution of ideal functionality $\mathcal{F}$ with any PPT simulator $\mathcal{S}_{\mathcal{D}}$. Of course, if there is no such $\mathcal{E}$, such $\mathcal{E}'$ does not exist either .

Following the assumption in Theorem 1, we have that if crf does not alarm, for dummy adversary $\mathcal{D}$ and any PPT environment $\mathcal{E}_{\mathcal{P}}$, there exists a PPT $\mathcal{S}_{\mathcal{D}}$ such that

$$\mathsf{EXEC}_{\mathcal{F}, \mathcal{S}_{\mathcal{D}}, \mathcal{E}_{\mathcal{P}}} \approx \mathsf{EXEC}_{\widehat{\mathcal{P}}\text{ocrf}, \mathcal{D}, \mathcal{E}_{\mathcal{P}}}. \tag{1}$$

Next, we construct a simulator $\mathcal{S}$ out of $\mathcal{S}_{\mathcal{D}}$, such that for any PPT environment $\mathcal{E}$ and adversary $\mathcal{A}$,

$$\mathsf{EXEC}_{\rho, \mathcal{S}, \mathcal{E}} \approx \mathsf{EXEC}_{\rho^{\mathcal{F} \to \widehat{\mathcal{P}}\text{ocrf}}, \mathcal{A}, \mathcal{E}}.$$

Readers are referred to Fig. 6 for the operation of S. Concretely, we divide $\rho^{\mathcal{F}\to\widehat{\mathcal{P}}\text{ocrf}}$ into $\widehat{\mathcal{P}}\text{ocrf}$ and the rest part of ρ (we use ρ' to denote it). The adversary $\mathcal{A}$ is geared to interact with $\rho^{\mathcal{F}\to\widehat{\mathcal{P}}\text{ocrf}}$. S channels the communication between $\mathcal{A}$ and the environment $\mathcal{E}$, and the communication between $\mathcal{A}$ and ρ' without any change. The important operation of S is that the communication between $\mathcal{A}$ and every instance of $\mathcal{F}$ is "pipelined" with an instance of $S_{\mathcal{D}}$, saying, messages generated by $\mathcal{A}$ aimed for $\widehat{\mathcal{P}}\text{ocrf}$ is sent to $S_{\mathcal{D}}$ as messages from the environment. Incoming messages from $\mathcal{F}$ to $S_{\mathcal{D}}$ are forwarded without any change. Outputs of $S_{\mathcal{D}}$ to environment are forwarded to $\mathcal{A}$ as messages from $\widehat{\mathcal{P}} \circ \text{crf}$.

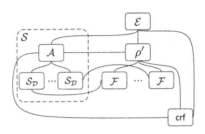

Fig. 6. Construction of simulator S in the proof of Theorem 1. Full lines denote direct communication between ITMs.

Now we demonstrate that the above construction of S is available. Based on the "dummy adversary" setting, the adversary $\mathcal{A}$ run by S behaves exactly like the environment that $S_{\mathcal{D}}$ expects. We assume that there exists an environment $\mathcal{E}$ which is able to distinguish an execution of $\{S, \rho\}$ and an execution of $\{\mathcal{A}, \rho^{\mathcal{F}\to\widehat{\mathcal{P}}\text{ocrf}}\}$, then we can deduce another environment $\mathcal{E}_{\mathcal{P}}$ which is competent to violate Formula (1). Assume that ρ involves n instances of $\mathcal{F}$, we design $n+1$ hybrids of the game. Concretely,

- **Game** 0: $\mathcal{E}$ aims at distinguishing between a execution of $\{S, \rho\}$ and an execution of $\{\mathcal{A}, \rho^{\mathcal{F}\to\widehat{\mathcal{P}}\text{ocrf}}\}$, where S is exactly like the case in Fig. 6.
- **Game** $i+1$: is same with **Game** i except that an instance of $\mathcal{F}$ in ρ is replaced by $\widehat{\mathcal{P}} \circ \text{crf}$, the corresponding $S_{\mathcal{D}}$ connected with such $\mathcal{F}$ in S is replaced by $\mathcal{D}$.

It is straightforward that $\mathcal{E}$' advantage in **Game** n equals to 0, as the two objects for judging are completely consistent. If there exists an environment $\mathcal{E}$ being able to distinguish an execution of $\{S, \rho\}$ and an execution of $\{\mathcal{A}, \rho^{\mathcal{F}\to\widehat{\mathcal{P}}\text{ocrf}}\}$ with a non-negligible probability, there must exists a pair of game **Game** i and **Game** $i+1$, in which $\mathcal{E}$'s outputs are different in a non-negligible probability.

As shown in Fig. 7, we design $\mathcal{E}_{\mathcal{P}}$ which invokes environment $\mathcal{E}$, adversary $\mathcal{A}$, the caller part of protocol ρ', i executions of $\mathcal{D}$ associated with $\widehat{\mathcal{P}} \circ \text{crf}$, and $(n-i-1)$ executions of $S_{\mathcal{D}}$ associated with $\mathcal{F}$. The adversary $\mathcal{A}$ and ρ' just operate as normal, except that one pair of their subroutine, i.e., an execution of $\{\mathcal{D}, \widehat{\mathcal{P}} \circ \mathsf{crf}\}$, or an execution of $\{\mathcal{S}_{\mathcal{D}}, \mathcal{F}\}$, is chosen randomly. If $\mathcal{E}$ succeed in the game to distinguish $\{\mathcal{A}, \rho^{\mathcal{F} \to \widehat{\mathcal{P}} \circ \mathsf{crf}}\}$ and $\{\mathcal{S}, \rho\}$ (or its hybrid), $\mathcal{E}_{\mathcal{P}}$ outputs 1; Otherwise $\mathcal{E}_{\mathcal{P}}$ outputs 0. In this case, if $\mathcal{E}_{\mathcal{P}}$ deals with $\{\mathcal{S}_{\mathcal{D}}, \mathcal{F}\}$, $\mathcal{E}$ is operates in **Game** i; Else if $\mathcal{E}_{\mathcal{P}}$ deals with $\{\mathcal{D}, \widehat{\mathcal{P}} \circ \mathsf{crf}\}$, $\mathcal{E}$ actually operates in **Game** $i+1$. Thus, if $\mathcal{E}$'s outputs are different with a non-negligible probability when in **Game** i and **Game** $i+1$, $\mathcal{E}_{\mathcal{P}}$ is able to distinguish $\{\mathcal{S}_{\mathcal{D}}, \mathcal{F}\}$ and $\{\mathcal{D}, \widehat{\mathcal{P}} \circ \mathsf{crf}\}$. This is contradiction to Formula (1).

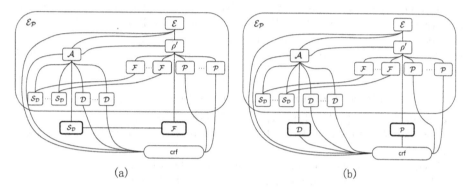

(a)   (b)

Fig. 7. Construction of $\mathcal{E}_{\mathcal{P}}$ in the proof of Theorem 1. The lines denote direct communication between ITMs. If there exists a PPT $\mathcal{E}$ in the Fig. 6 which is able to distinguish the pair $\{\mathcal{S}, \rho\}$ and $\{\mathcal{A}, \rho^{\mathcal{F} \to \widehat{\mathcal{P}} \circ \mathsf{crf}}\}$, we can construct a $\mathcal{E}_{\mathcal{P}}$ in this figure to violate the security property of crf, i.e., make different output in non-negligible probability when operating in case (a) and case (b).

5   From the New Definition to the Current Definition

In this section we demonstrate that the new definition actually implies the current one. This means that the new definition does not change the basic intuition of CRF, while characterizing the expected properties of a CRF under the idea that "guarding a corrupted system with the minimum trusted module".

For simplicity, here we only consider the PM-adversaries (readers are referred to Sect. 2.2 for details). The reason for this simplification is that we have allowed a CRF to alarm, in some sense, a CRF can serve as an online watchdog, and implementations provided by adversaries other than PM-adversaries can be easily detected. In this section, we will prove that our definition implies the current definition, that is to say, considering typical subversion attacks, the new definition is at least as strong as the current one. Formally,

Theorem 2. *If a CRF guards protocol $\mathcal{P}$ as defined in Definition 4, then it also satisfies functionality-maintaining, security-preserving, and exfiltration-resistance for PM-adversaries.*

Proof. It is straightforward that for a PM-adversary, the probability that the CRF alarms is negligible. Otherwise we can simply recognize a subverted implementation when the CRF alarms, as it only alarms with a negligible probability when combined with unsubverted implementations as defined.

The functionality and security of a protocol are defined by the indifference between an execution of protocol $\widehat{\mathcal{P}} \circ \mathsf{crf}$ with $\mathcal{A}$, and an execution of ideal functionality $\mathcal{F}$ with $\mathcal{S}$. Now that if a CRF is able to ensure such indifference despite the implementations are corrupted by the adversary, it is straightforward that this CRF satisfies functionality-maintaining and security-preserving.

Assume that there exists a PM-adversary $\mathcal{A}$ being able to break the exfiltration-resistance of a CRF. Then we can build a PPT adversary $\mathcal{B}$ and environment $\mathcal{E}$, for which no PPT simulator $\mathcal{S}$ achieves $\mathsf{EXEC}_{\mathcal{F},\mathcal{S},\mathcal{E}} \approx \mathsf{EXEC}_{\widehat{\mathcal{P}}\circ\mathsf{crf},\mathcal{B},\mathcal{E}}$, which means the CRF does not guards $\mathcal{P}$. Concretely, when $\mathcal{E}$ operates with $\mathcal{B}$ and $\mathcal{P} \circ \mathsf{crf}$:

1. $\mathcal{E}$ invokes $\mathcal{A}$ to get the subverted implementation $\widehat{\mathcal{P}} = \{\widehat{\pi}_1, \cdots, \widehat{\pi}_n, \mathsf{ch}\}$.
2. $\mathcal{E}$ generates $b \xleftarrow{\$} \{0,1\}$. If $b = 1$, $\mathcal{P}^* \leftarrow \widehat{\mathcal{P}}$; else $\mathcal{P}^* \leftarrow \mathcal{P}$.
3. $\mathcal{E}$ invokes $\mathcal{B}$ and forwards $\mathcal{P}^*$ to $\mathcal{B}$. $\mathcal{B}$ submits them back to $\mathcal{E}$. $\mathcal{E}$ invokes $\mathcal{P}^* \circ \mathsf{crf}$.
4. $\mathcal{B}$ acquires all transcripts of $\widehat{\pi}_i$, and forwards them back to $\mathcal{E}$.
5. $\mathcal{E}$ forwards the transcripts to $\mathcal{A}$, and acquires $\mathcal{A}$'s final output b'.
6. $\mathcal{E}$ returns its final output $(b' = b)$.

Thus, if $\mathcal{E}$ interacts with $\{\mathcal{P}^* \circ \mathsf{crf}, \mathcal{B}\}$, according to the definition of exfiltration-resistance (Appendix A) $\Pr[b' = b] = \mathsf{Adv}^{\mathsf{exf}}_{\mathcal{A},\mathsf{crf}}(\lambda) + 1/2$.

Now we consider the case where $\mathcal{E}$ interacts with $\{\mathcal{F}, \mathcal{S}\}$. Since $\mathcal{A}$ is proud-but-malicious, $\widehat{\mathcal{P}}$ and $\mathcal{P}$ are indistinguishable to any PPT simulator $\mathcal{S}$. Thus b has no influence on the returned information from $\mathcal{F}$ and $\mathcal{S}$, i.e., $\Pr[b' = b] = 1/2$. Thus, we have that for any PPT simulator $\mathcal{S}$,

$$\Pr[\mathsf{EXEC}_{\mathcal{F},\mathcal{S},\mathcal{E}} \neq \mathsf{EXEC}_{\mathcal{P}^*\circ\mathsf{crf},\mathcal{B},\mathcal{E}}] \geq \mathsf{Adv}^{\mathsf{exf}}_{\mathcal{A},\mathsf{crf}}(\lambda),$$

which completes the proof that the CRF is exfiltration-resistant for PM-adversaries.

6   Construction of a Deterministic CRF

This section presents a detailed construction of CRF. To the best of our knowledge, all of the existing CRFs need to generate a new randomness, to deal with every randomness generated by the underlying protocol. This implies a assumption that a CRF is competent to produce the same amount of randomness to the protocol being protected. Those designs could be regarded as transferring a tough task from users' computers to CRFs.

Our basic framework of CRF construction is more reasonable than existing ones. It takes the idea that although the CRF is still assumed to be unsubverted, it is not expected to generate such a large amount of randomness. Instead, a CRF just needs to get a small amount of fresh and trusted randomness as its keys during the initial phase, and all the following operations are designed to be deterministic. Further more, our construction can even achieve that the CRF's key is allowed to opened to external adversaries, as long as it stays confidential to the implementations of inner protocol parties. In such a situation, the credibility of a CRF is much easier to be realized, as the main source of the risk, probabilistic modules, are shrunken as much as possible. We observe that although an implementation of a probabilistic algorithm is subverted, its output should still have high min-entropy. Otherwise, this subverted implementation will easily be detected in black-box testing. In this case, a CRF can simply alarm when observes a collision, causing the protocol to break off. We take use of this point to achieve our design, which guards a protocol merely using deterministic algorithms, including a module serving as an online watchdog [16].

In this section we only consider the CRF for a class of two-round message-transmission protocol, but under the UC-based definition, the CRF is designed in an extendible setting. Our construction is based on the framework proposed by work [10], which presents a general CRF construction method for message-transmission protocols based on public encryption schemes with special properties.

Preliminary. In order to present a comprehensible introduction of our construction, it is necessary to present several basic notions as a foundation. Considering the page limitation, we put them to appendix. Appendix B.1 introduces a two-round message-transmission protocol based on public-key encryption. Appendix B.2 reviews the notion of rerandomizable encryption and key malleability. Appendix B.3 presents a brief introduction of the CRF construction in work [10].

Our CRF serves for the message-transmission protocol presented in Appendix B.1. We also require that the involved public-key encryption scheme should satisfy (1) *rerandomizable*, with rerandomize function $\mathsf{Rerand} : \mathcal{PK} \times \mathcal{C} \times \{0,1\}^{\ell} \to \mathcal{C}$; (2) *key malleable*, with rerandomize function $\mathsf{KeyMaul} : \mathcal{PK} \times \{0,1\}^{\kappa} \to \mathcal{PK}$, and $\mathsf{CKeyMaul} : \mathcal{C} \times \{0,1\}^{\kappa} \to \mathcal{C}$.

The Ideal Functionality. In order to analyze the CRF in the new definition, we need to specify the ideal functionality $\mathcal{F}$ corresponding to the message-transmission protocol with an authenticated encryption channel. On receiving the message *"ready"* from Bob, $\mathcal{F}$ informs simulator $\mathcal{S}$, and transfers *"ready"* to Alice after getting $\mathcal{S}$'s agreement. On receiving a message m from Alice, $\mathcal{F}$ informs $\mathcal{S}$, and after receiving a returned agreement, $\mathcal{F}$ forwards m to Bob. Readers are referred to Fig. 8 for details.

Construction. The significant progress of our construction comparing to the design in Appendix B.3 is the acquirement of the coins for rerandomization. We extract r_1 and r_2 from the fixed key of CRF along with the inputs via RO. This transfers the CRF from a probabilistic algorithm to a deterministic one. We present the formal CRF's operation for $\mathcal{P}$ in Fig. 10, and readers are referred to Fig. 9 for a sketch map.

> 1. Upon receiving *"ready"* from Bob, $\mathcal{F}$ sends *"ready"* to the simulator $\mathcal{S}$.
> 2. After receiving *"ready-agree"* from $\mathcal{S}$, $\mathcal{F}$ sends *"ready"* to Alice.
> 3. Upon receiving m from Alice, $\mathcal{F}$ sends *"transmit"* to the simulator $\mathcal{S}$.
> 4. After receiving *"transmit-agree"* from $\mathcal{S}$, $\mathcal{F}$ sends m to Bob.

Fig. 8. Operation of $\mathcal{F}$ for message-transmission protocol $\mathcal{P}$

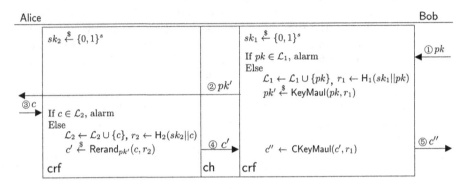

Fig. 9. A sketch map for CRF construction

Remark. In logical sense, we characterize the CRF as a single part as in Sect. 3.2, but actually in the reality, the CRF is realized by several modules which composed with different protocol parties. It is unpractical and unnecessary to require all the modules to acquire a same key. Thus, in the construction of Fig. 10, the CRF is injected with two keys sk_1 and sk_2, to enable the two parts composed with Bob and Alice, respectively.

We claim that in our construction, the CRF's key sk_1 and sk_2 can be opened to the adversary, as long as it is uniformly random to the subverted parties $\widehat{\text{Alice}}$ and $\widehat{\text{Bob}}$. This property provides us with a possible operation pattern of CRF, i.e., injecting public randomness into the CRF after the deployment of implementations of protocol parties.

Theorem 3. *The CRF in Fig. 10 guards $\mathcal{P}$ for $\mathcal{F}$, if H_1 and H_2 are modeled as random oracles.*

Proof. We first demonstrate that crf is robust. Given that PE is a probabilistic encryption scheme, for $(pk_0, sk_0), (pk_1, sk_1) \leftarrow \mathsf{KeyGen}(\lambda)$ and $m_0, m_1 \xleftarrow{\$} \mathcal{M}$, where $\mathcal{M}$ is the plaintext space, we have $\Pr[pk_0 = pk_1] \leq \mathsf{negl}(\lambda)$, and $\Pr[\mathsf{Enc}_{pk_a}(m_b) = \mathsf{Enc}_{pk_c}(m_d)] \leq \mathsf{negl}(\lambda)$ $(a, b, c, d \in \{0, 1\}$ and $(a, b) \neq (c, d))$. As crf only alarms when the inputting messages is not consistent to the standard form, or there is collision among the input public-keys or ciphertexts, when combining with the specification, it alarms in a negligible probability.

Cryptographic reverse firewall for protocol $\mathcal{P}$

Initial phase(sk_1, sk_2) $\backslash\backslash sk_1 \xleftarrow{\$} \{0,1\}^s$, $sk_2 \xleftarrow{\$} \{0,1\}^s$

Establish two empty list $\mathcal{L}_1$ and $\mathcal{L}_2$

Unavaliable message$(\cdot)$

When receiving messages not consistent to the forms of outputs from the specification, alarm

Key malleation $(fid_\mathcal{P}, sid_n, pid_{\mathsf{Bob}}, pid_{\mathsf{crf}}, pk\|\text{"}public\text{-}key\ to\ \mathsf{Alice}\text{"}, \text{"}internal\text{-}output\text{"})$

Generate a session-unit marked as $(fid_\mathcal{P}, sid_n, pid_{\mathsf{Bob}})$

If $pk \in \mathcal{L}_1$, alarm

Else

$\quad \mathcal{L}_1 \leftarrow \mathcal{L}_1 \cup \{pk\}$, $r_1 \leftarrow \mathsf{H}_1(sk_1\|pk)$, store r_1 in the session-unit.

$\quad pk' \leftarrow \mathsf{KeyMaul}(pk, r_1)$

$\quad$ Output $(fid_\mathcal{P}, sid_n, pid_{\mathsf{crf}}, pid_{\mathsf{ch}}, pk'\|\text{"}public\text{-}key\ to\ \mathsf{Alice}\text{"}, \text{"}internal\text{-}output\text{"})$

Receive key $(fid_\mathcal{P}, sid_n, pid_{\mathsf{ch}}, pid_{\mathsf{crf}}, pk'\|\text{"}public\text{-}key\ to\ \mathsf{Alice}\text{"}, \text{"}internal\text{-}output\text{"})$

Generate a session-unit marked as $(fid_\mathcal{P}, sid_n, pid_{\mathsf{Alice}})$

Record pk' in the session-unit

Output $(fid_\mathcal{P}, sid_n, pid_{\mathsf{crf}}, pid_{\mathsf{Alice}}, pk'\|\text{"}public\text{-}key\ to\ \mathsf{Alice}\text{"}, \text{"}internal\text{-}output\text{"})$

Ciphertext rerandomization $(fid_\mathcal{P}, sid_n, pid_{\mathsf{Alice}}, pid_{\mathsf{crf}}, c\|\text{"}ciphertext\ to\ \mathsf{Bob}\text{"},$
$\text{"}internal\text{-}output\text{"})$

If there is no session-unit marked as $\{fid_\mathcal{P}, sid_n, pid_{\mathsf{Alice}}\}$, return $\perp$

Else

$\quad$ Invoke the public-key pk' from the session-unit marked as $(fid_\mathcal{P}, sid_n, pid_{\mathsf{Alice}})$

$\quad$ If $c \in \mathcal{L}_2$, alarm

$\quad$ Else

$\quad\quad \mathcal{L}_2 \leftarrow \mathcal{L}_2 \cup \{c\}$, $r_2 \leftarrow \mathsf{H}_2(sk_2\|c)$

$\quad\quad c' \leftarrow \mathsf{Rerand}_{pk'}(c, r_2)$

$\quad\quad$ Output $(fid_\mathcal{P}, sid_n, pid_{\mathsf{crf}}, pid_{\mathsf{ch}}, c'\|\text{"}ciphertext\ to\ \mathsf{Bob}\text{"}, \text{"}internal\text{-}output\text{"})$

Inverse key malleation $(fid_\mathcal{P}, sid_n, pid_{\mathsf{ch}}, pid_{\mathsf{crf}}, c'\|\text{"}ciphertext\ to\ \mathsf{Bob}\text{"},$
$\text{"}internal\text{-}output\text{"})$

If there is no session-unit marked as $(fid_\mathcal{P}, sid_n, pid_{\mathsf{Bob}})$, returns $\perp$

Else

$\quad$ Invoke r_1 from the session-unit marked as $(fid_\mathcal{P}, sid_n, pid_{\mathsf{Bob}})$

$\quad c'' \leftarrow \mathsf{CKeyMaul}(c', r_1)$

$\quad$ Output $(fid_\mathcal{P}, sid_n, pid_{\mathsf{crf}}, pid_{\mathsf{Bob}}, c''\|\text{"}ciphertext\ to\ \mathsf{Bob}\text{"}, \text{"}internal\text{-}output\text{"})$

Fig. 10. Operation of crf for protocol $\mathcal{P}$

Thus, we only need to consider the case where CRF does not alarm. Following the proof of Theorem 1, here we still take the method of "dummy adversary", saying, we will design a PPT simulator $\mathcal{S}$ such that any PPT environment $\mathcal{E}$ is unable to distinguish an execution of protocol $\widehat{\mathcal{P}} \circ \mathsf{crf}$ with dummy adversary $\mathcal{D}$, and an execution of ideal functionality $\mathcal{F}$ with $\mathcal{S}$. Work [5] has presented a complete proof that such adjustment from adversary to dummy adversary actually makes no influence to the security property of protocols.

We construct a PPT simulator $\mathcal{S}$ which takes the following strategy in a session.

1. On receiving *"ready"* from $\mathcal{F}$, $\mathcal{S}$ generates $(pk^*, sk^*) \leftarrow \mathsf{KeyGen}(1^\lambda)$, passes pk^* to $\mathcal{E}$, and sends *"ready-agree"* to $\mathcal{F}$.
2. On receiving *"transmit"* from $\mathcal{F}$, $\mathcal{S}$ generates $\mathsf{Rerand}_{pk^*}(\mathsf{Enc}(0), U_\ell)$, passes it to $\mathcal{E}$, and sends *"transmit-agree"* to $\mathcal{F}$.

We present the following hybrids of the CRF:

- **Hybrid 0**: It is identical to Fig. 10.
- **Hybrid 1**: It runs in the same way as **Hybrid 0**, except that r_1 in Key malleation and Inverse key malleation are substituted by $r_1' \xleftarrow{\$} \{0,1\}^\kappa$.
- **Hybrid 2**: It runs in the same way as **Hybrid 1**, except that r_2 in Ciphertext rerandomization is substituted by $r_2' \xleftarrow{\$} \{0,1\}^\ell$.
- **Hybrid 3**: It runs in the same way as **Hybrid 2**, except that in Key malleation, pk' is replaced by pk^*, and $(pk^*, sk^*) \leftarrow \mathsf{KeyGen}(1^\lambda)$.
- **Hybrid 4**: It runs in the same way as **Hybrid 3**, except that in Ciphertext rerandomization, c' is replaced by $c^* \leftarrow \mathsf{Rerand}_{pk'}(\mathsf{Enc}_{pk'}(0), U_\ell)$.

We denote the environment $\mathcal{E}$'s output after interacting with $\mathcal{D}$ and protocol equipped **Hybrid i** as $\mathsf{EXEC}_{\mathcal{P}\circ\mathsf{Hybi},\mathcal{D},\mathcal{E}}$, and the corresponding advantage as

$$\mathsf{Adv}_{\mathcal{E}}^i(\lambda) = \frac{1}{2} \Big| \Pr[\mathsf{EXEC}_{\mathcal{F},\mathcal{S}_P,\mathcal{E}} = 1] - \Pr[\mathsf{EXEC}_{\mathcal{P}\circ\mathsf{Hybi},\mathcal{D},\mathcal{E}} = 1] \Big|.$$

Lemma 1. *For any PPT environment $\mathcal{E}$, we have*

$$\left| \mathsf{Adv}_{\mathcal{E}}^1(\lambda) - \mathsf{Adv}_{\mathcal{E}}^0(\lambda) \right| \leq \frac{n_1}{2^s} + \frac{n_2}{2^\delta},$$

where n_1 and n_2 are numbers of queries from the subverted implementation and the environment/dummy adversary. δ is the min-entropy of public-key $\widehat{pk}$ produced by the potentially subverted party $\widehat{\mathrm{Bob}}$.

Proof. (of Lemma 1). Based on the definition of RO, **Hybrid 1** only differs from **Hybrid 0** when

- Event 1: subverted implementation submits $sk_1 \| pk$ to RO;
- Event 2: environment $\mathcal{E}$ or dummy adversary $\mathcal{D}$ submits $sk_1 \| pk$ to RO.

As sk_1 is generated at the initial phase of CRF, thus, it stays uniformly random to the implementations of protocol parties. So we have

$$\Pr[\text{Event 1}] \leq \frac{n_1}{2^s}.$$

Now we explore the probability of Event 2. We claim that although the protocol party Bob is subverted, its output pk should still reach a high min-entropy, otherwise, crf will alarm in a non-negligible probability. Concretely, if we assume that

$$\max_{pk^*} \Pr[pk = pk^*, (pk, sk_1) \leftarrow \widehat{\mathsf{Keygen}}(\lambda)] = 2^{-\delta} = \frac{1}{\mathsf{ploy}(\lambda)},$$

then, within q rounds of the protocol, the probability of crf alarms:

$$\Pr[\text{crf alarms}] \geq \frac{1}{2}q(q-1) \cdot 2^{-2\delta} = \frac{q(q-1)}{2 \cdot \mathsf{ploy}^2(\lambda)}$$

Thus, if crf only alarms in a negligible probability, we have $\delta \leq \mathsf{negl}(\lambda)$. In this case,

$$\Pr[\text{Event 2}] \leq n_2 2^{-\delta} < \mathsf{negl}(\lambda).$$

So we have

$$\left| \mathsf{Adv}^1_{\mathcal{E}}(\lambda) - \mathsf{Adv}^0_{\mathcal{E}}(\lambda) \right| \leq \Pr[\text{Event 1}] + \Pr[\text{Event 2}] < \frac{n_1}{2^s} + \frac{n_2}{2^\delta}. \quad (2)$$

Based on the same idea, we present Lemma 2 without detailed proof.

Lemma 2. *For any PPT environment $\mathcal{E}$, we have*

$$\left| \mathsf{Adv}^2_{\mathcal{E}}(\lambda) - \mathsf{Adv}^1_{\mathcal{E}}(\lambda) \right| \leq \frac{n_3}{2^s} + \frac{n_4}{2^\sigma},$$

where n_3 and n_4 are numbers of queries from the subverted implementation and the environment/dummy adversary, respectively; σ is the min-entropy of ciphertext c produced by the potentially subverted party $\widehat{\mathsf{Alice}}$.

Based on the property of key malleable encryption in Definition 11, when the coin used in KeyMaul is a uniformly randomness, the output key from KeyMaul is uniformly random distributed over the public-key space. Thus, we could present Lemma 3 directly,

Lemma 3. *For any PPT environment $\mathcal{E}$, we have $\mathsf{Adv}^3_{\mathcal{E}}(\lambda) = \mathsf{Adv}^2_{\mathcal{E}}(\lambda)$.*

Based on the property of rerandomizable encryption in Definition 10, when the coin used in Rerand is a uniformly randomness, $(c; \mathsf{Rerand}_{pk}(c, U_\kappa))$ is computationally indistinguishable from $(c; \mathsf{Rerand}_{pk}(\mathsf{Enc}_{pk}(0), U_\kappa))$, Thus. we could present Lemma 4 directly,

Lemma 4. *For any PPT environment $\mathcal{E}$, $\left| \mathsf{Adv}^4_{\mathcal{E}}(\lambda) - \mathsf{Adv}^3_{\mathcal{E}}(\lambda) \right| \leq \mathsf{negl}(\lambda)$.*

It is obviously that $\mathsf{Adv}^4_{\mathcal{E}}(\lambda) = 0$. Summing up Lemma 1–4, we reach the conclusion

$$\mathsf{EXEC}_{\mathcal{F}, \mathcal{S}_P, \mathcal{E}} \approx \mathsf{EXEC}_{\mathcal{P}_{\mathsf{ocrf}}, \mathcal{D}, \mathcal{E}},$$

which means that $(\mathcal{S}, \mathcal{F})$ makes an ideal emulation to $(\mathcal{D}, \widehat{\mathcal{P}} \circ \mathsf{crf})$.

Acknowledgment. This work is partly supported by the National Natural Science Foundation of China (61972017) and the Fundamental Research Funds for the Central Universities (YWF-21-BJ-J-1040).

A   The Current Definition of a CRF

Mironov and Stephens-Davidowitz [15] characterized the expect properties of a CRF by functionality-maintaining, security-preserving and exfiltration-resistance.

Definition 7. *(Functionality-maintaining) For any CRF* crf *and any party* A, *let* $A \circ crf^1 = A \circ crf$, *and for* $k \geq 2$, $A \circ crf^k = (A \circ crf^{k-1}) \circ crf$. *For a protocol* P *that satisfies functionality requirement* $\mathcal{FR}$, *for any polynomial bounded* $k > 1$, *if* $A \circ crf^k$ *maintains* $\mathcal{FR}$ *for* A *in* P, *we say that* crf *maintains* $\mathcal{FR}$ *for* A *in* P.

$P_{A \to \overline{A} \circ crf}$ denotes the protocol in which party A is replaced by the combination of crf and a subverted party $\overline{A}$. Besides, we denote a functionality-maintaining party by $\widehat{A}$ and an arbitrary subverted party by $\overline{A}$.

Definition 8. *(Security-preserving) For a protocol* P *that satisfies security requirements* $\mathcal{SR}$, *and a CRF* crf, *we say that*

- crf *strongly preserves* $\mathcal{SR}$ *for* A *in* P *if the protocol* $P_{A \to \overline{A} \circ crf}$ *satisfies* $\mathcal{SR}$;
- crf *weakly preserves* $\mathcal{SR}$ *for* A *in* P *if the protocol* $P_{A \to \widehat{A} \circ crf}$ *satisfies* $\mathcal{SR}$.

The exfiltration-resistance is defined based on the leakage game which is presented in Fig. 11. We assume the protocol has two parties A and B. The advantage of an adversary $\mathcal{A}$ in **Game** LEAK is defined as

$$\mathsf{Adv}_{\mathcal{A},crf}^{\mathsf{LEAK}}(\lambda) \stackrel{def}{=} \left| \Pr\left[\mathsf{LEAK}(P, A, B, crf, \lambda) = 1\right] - \frac{1}{2} \right|.$$

Definition 9. *(Exfiltration-resistance) For a protocol that satisfies functionality requirements* $\mathcal{FR}$ *and a reverse firewall* crf, *we say that*

- crf *is* strongly exfiltration-resistant *for party* A *against party* B *in the protocol* P *if for any PPT adversary* $\mathcal{A}$, $\mathsf{Adv}_{\mathcal{A},crf}^{\mathsf{LEAK}}(\lambda)$ *is negligible in the security parameter* λ; *and*
- crf *is* weakly exfiltration-resistant *for party* A *against party* B *in the protocol* P *if for any PPT adversary* $\mathcal{A}$, $\mathsf{Adv}_{\mathcal{A},crf}^{\mathsf{LEAK}}(\lambda)$ *is negligible in the security parameter* λ *provided that* $\overline{A}$ *maintains* $\mathcal{FR}$ *for party* A.

In the special case where B is empty, we say that crf is exfiltration-resistant against eavesdroppers.

$$\boxed{\begin{array}{l} \textbf{Game LEAK } (\mathcal{P}, \mathsf{A}, \mathsf{B}, \mathsf{crf}, \lambda) \\ \hline (st_{\overline{\mathsf{A}}}, \overline{\mathsf{A}}, \overline{\mathsf{B}}, I) \leftarrow \mathcal{A}(1^\lambda) \\ b \xleftarrow{\$} \{0, 1\} \\ \text{IF } b = 1, \mathsf{A}^* \leftarrow \overline{\mathsf{A}} \circ \mathsf{crf} \\ \text{ELSE}, \mathsf{A}^* \leftarrow \mathsf{A} \circ \mathsf{crf} \\ \Gamma^* \leftarrow \mathcal{P}_{\mathsf{A} \to \mathsf{A}^*, \mathsf{B} \to \overline{\mathsf{B}}}(I) \\ b^* \leftarrow \mathcal{A}(\Gamma^*, st_{\overline{\mathsf{B}}}) \\ \text{RETURN } (b = b^*) \end{array}}$$

Fig. 11. The leakage game LEAK. $st_{\overline{\mathsf{A}}}$ and $st_{\overline{\mathsf{B}}}$ are the state of $\overline{\mathsf{A}}$ and $\overline{\mathsf{B}}$. I is a valid input for $\mathcal{P}$, and Γ^* is the transcript produced by protocol $\mathcal{P}_{\mathsf{A} \to \mathsf{A}^*, \mathsf{B} \to \overline{\mathsf{B}}}(I)$.

B   CRF Construction in Work [10]

B.1   Two-round Message-Transmission Protocol

Let $\mathsf{PE} = (\mathsf{Keygen}, \mathsf{Enc}, \mathsf{Dec})$ be a public-key encryption scheme. $\mathsf{Keygen} : 1^\lambda \to (\mathcal{PK}, \mathcal{SK})$ is key generation algorithm, where $\mathcal{PK}$ and $\mathcal{SK}$ are public-key space and secret-key space, respectively. $\mathsf{Enc} : \mathcal{PK} \times \mathcal{M} \to \mathcal{C}$ is encryption algorithm, where $\mathcal{M}$ and $\mathcal{C}$ are plaintext space and ciphertext space, respectively. $\mathsf{Dec} : \mathcal{SK} \times \mathcal{C} \to \mathcal{M}$ is decryption algorithm. We define the correctness of PE as: for any $m \in \mathcal{M}$ and $(pk, sk) \leftarrow \mathsf{Keygen}(1^\lambda)$, we have $\mathsf{Dec}_{sk}(\mathsf{Enc}_{pk}(m)) = m$. And we define the CPA-security of PE as for any adversarially chosen pair of plaintexts (m_0, m_1), $(pk, \mathsf{Enc}_{pk}(m_0))$ and $(pk, \mathsf{Enc}_{pk}(m_1))$ are computational indistinguishable.

The basic form of a two-round public-key based message-transmission protocol is like this: Bob generates $(pk, sk) \leftarrow \mathsf{KeyGen}(1^\lambda)$, and sends pk to Alice. Alice encrypts massage m by $c \leftarrow \mathsf{Enc}_{pk}(m)$. After getting c, Bob decrypts it via $m \leftarrow \mathsf{Dec}_{sk}(c)$.

B.2   Rerandomizable Encryption and Key Malleability Encryption

Rerandomizable encryption refers to the public-key encryption whose ciphertexts can be rerandomized to a new one, without bringing influence to the normal decryption. Formally,

Definition 10. *[10] A public-key encryption scheme is* rerandomizable *if there is a PPT algorithm* $\mathsf{Rerand} : \mathcal{PK} \times \mathcal{C} \times \{0,1\}^\kappa \to \mathcal{C}$, *for any ciphertext c such that* $\mathsf{Dec}_{sk}(c) \neq \perp$, *we have: (1)* $\mathsf{Dec}_{sk}(\mathsf{Rerand}_{pk}(c, U_\kappa)) = \mathsf{Dec}_{sk}(c)$, *(2)* $(c; \mathsf{Rerand}_{pk}(c, U_\kappa))$ *is computationally indistinguishable from* $(c; \mathsf{Rerand}_{pk}(\mathsf{Enc}_{pk}(0), U_\kappa))$.

Key malleable encryption refers to encryption whose public-key can be transfered to a new one, and there exists an efficient algorithm mapping ciphertexts under the new key-pair to ciphertexts under initial key-pair. Formally,

Definition 11. *[10] A public-key encryption scheme is key malleable if: (1) the output of* KeyGen *is distributed uniformly over the space of valid keys; (2) for each public-key pk there is a unique associated private key sk; and (3) there is a pair of efficient algorithms* KeyMaul *and* CKeyMaul *that behave as follows.* KeyMaul *takes as inputs a public-key pk and a randomness* $r \overset{\$}{\leftarrow} \{0,1\}^\ell$ *and returns a new public-key pk' whose distribution is uniformly random over the public-key space. Let (sk, pk) be a private-key/public-key pair, and let (sk', pk') be the unique pair associated with randomness r such that $pk' = $* KeyMaul$(pk, r)$. *Then,* CKeyMaul *takes as inputs a ciphertext c and randomness r and returns c' such that* $\mathsf{Dec}_{sk'}(c) = \mathsf{Dec}_{sk}(c')$.

For example, Elgamal encryption is both rerandomizable and key malleable. Such encryption can also be achieved via universal hash proof function [10].

B.3   CRF Construction for Two-round Message-Transmission Protocols

The work [10] presents a CRF construction, which takes the idea that rerandomizing the public-key and the ciphertext by KeyMaul and Rerand, respectively. After receiving a processed ciphertext, the CRF adjusts it to match the original secret key. Readers are referred to Fig. 12 for detailed formalization. Concretely,

1. When receiving pk from Bob, if pk is not in the standard form, CRF alarms; else, it generates $r_1 \overset{\$}{\leftarrow} \{0,1\}^\ell$ and $pk' \overset{\$}{\leftarrow}$ KeyMaul(pk, r_1), and outputs pk' to channel.
2. When receiving c from Alice, if c is not in the standard form, CRF alarms; else, it generates $r_2 \overset{\$}{\leftarrow} \{0,1\}^\kappa$ and $c' \overset{\$}{\leftarrow}$ Rerand$_{pk'}(c, r_2)$, and outputs c' to channel.
3. When receiving c' from channel, if c' is not in the standard form, CRF alarms; else, it invokes r_1, generates $c'' \leftarrow$ CKeyMaul(c', r_1), and outputs c'' to Bob.

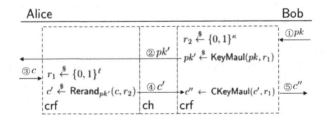

Fig. 12. CRF based on rerandomizable encryption

References

1. Ateniese, G., Francati, D., Magri, B., Venturi, D.: Public immunization against complete subversion without random oracles. In: Deng, R.H., Gauthier-Umaña, V., Ochoa, M., Yung, M. (eds.) ACNS 2019. LNCS, vol. 11464, pp. 465–485. Springer, Cham (2019). https://doi.org/10.1007/978-3-030-21568-2_23
2. Ateniese, G., Magri, B., Venturi, D.: Subversion-resilient signature schemes. In: ACM CCS, pp. 364–375 (2015)
3. Bellare, M., Jaeger, J., Kane, D.: Mass-surveillance without the state: strongly undetectable algorithm-substitution attacks. In: ACM CCS, pp. 1431–1440 (2015)
4. Bellare, M., Paterson, K.G., Rogaway, P.: Security of symmetric encryption against mass surveillance. In: Garay, J.A., Gennaro, R. (eds.) CRYPTO 2014. LNCS, vol. 8616, pp. 1–19. Springer, Heidelberg (2014). https://doi.org/10.1007/978-3-662-44371-2_1
5. Canetti, R.: Universally composable security: a new paradigm for cryptographic protocols. In: FOCS, pp. 136–145 (2001)
6. Canetti, R., Dodis, Y., Pass, R., Walfish, S.: Universally composable security with global setup. In: Vadhan, S.P. (ed.) TCC 2007. LNCS, vol. 4392, pp. 61–85. Springer, Heidelberg (2007). https://doi.org/10.1007/978-3-540-70936-7_4
7. Canetti, R., Rabin, T.: Universal composition with joint state. In: Boneh, D. (ed.) CRYPTO 2003. LNCS, vol. 2729, pp. 265–281. Springer, Heidelberg (2003). https://doi.org/10.1007/978-3-540-45146-4_16
8. Chen, R., Mu, Y., Yang, G., Susilo, W., Guo, F., Zhang, M.: Cryptographic reverse firewall via malleable smooth projective hash functions. In: Cheon, J.H., Takagi, T. (eds.) ASIACRYPT 2016. LNCS, vol. 10031, pp. 844–876. Springer, Heidelberg (2016). https://doi.org/10.1007/978-3-662-53887-6_31
9. Degabriele, J.P., Farshim, P., Poettering, B.: A more cautious approach to security against mass surveillance. In: Leander, G. (ed.) FSE 2015. LNCS, vol. 9054, pp. 579–598. Springer, Heidelberg (2015). https://doi.org/10.1007/978-3-662-48116-5_28
10. Dodis, Y., Mironov, I., Stephens-Davidowitz, N.: Message transmission with reverse firewalls - secure communication on corrupted machines. In: CRYPTO, vol. 9814, pp. 341–372 (2016)
11. Fischlin, M., Mazaheri, S.: Self-guarding cryptographic protocols against algorithm substitution attacks. In: CSF, pp. 76–90 (2018)
12. Hofheinz, D., Shoup, V.: GNUC: a new universal composability framework. J. Cryptol. 28(3), 423–508 (2015)
13. Li, G., Liu, J., Zhang, Z.: Security against subversion in a multi-surveillant setting. In: Jang-Jaccard, J., Guo, F. (eds.) ACISP 2019. LNCS, vol. 11547, pp. 419–437. Springer, Cham (2019). https://doi.org/10.1007/978-3-030-21548-4_23
14. Li, G., Liu, J., Zhang, Z.: A more realistic analysis of mass surveillance - security in multi-surveillant settings. IET Inf. Secur. 2020, 643–651 (2020)
15. Mironov, I., Stephens-Davidowitz, N.: Cryptographic reverse firewalls. In: Oswald, E., Fischlin, M. (eds.) EUROCRYPT 2015. LNCS, vol. 9057, pp. 657–686. Springer, Heidelberg (2015). https://doi.org/10.1007/978-3-662-46803-6_22
16. Russell, A., Tang, Q., Yung, M., Zhou, H.-S.: Cliptography: clipping the power of kleptographic attacks. In: Cheon, J.H., Takagi, T. (eds.) ASIACRYPT 2016. LNCS, vol. 10032, pp. 34–64. Springer, Heidelberg (2016). https://doi.org/10.1007/978-3-662-53890-6_2

17. Russell, A., Tang, Q., Yung, M., Zhou, H.: Generic semantic security against a kleptographic adversary. In: ACM CCS, pp. 907–922 (2017)

18. Young, A.L., Yung, M.: The dark side of "black-box" cryptography or: should we trust capstone? In: CRYPTO, vol. 1109, pp. 89–103 (1996)

19. Young, A., Yung, M.: Kleptography: using cryptography against cryptography. In: Fumy, W. (ed.) EUROCRYPT 1997. LNCS, vol. 1233, pp. 62–74. Springer, Heidelberg (1997). https://doi.org/10.1007/3-540-69053-0_6

20. Young, A., Yung, M.: The prevalence of kleptographic attacks on discrete-log based cryptosystems. In: Kaliski, B.S. (ed.) CRYPTO 1997. LNCS, vol. 1294, pp. 264–276. Springer, Heidelberg (1997). https://doi.org/10.1007/BFb0052241

21. Young, A., Yung, M.: Malicious cryptography: kleptographic aspects. In: Menezes, A. (ed.) CT-RSA 2005. LNCS, vol. 3376, pp. 7–18. Springer, Heidelberg (2005). https://doi.org/10.1007/978-3-540-30574-3_2

A Message Franking Channel

Loïs Huguenin-Dumittan[1,2(✉)] and Iraklis Leontiadis[1,2]

[1] LASEC, EPFL, Lausanne, Switzerland
`lois.huguenin-dumittan@epfl.ch`
[2] Inpher, New York, USA
`iraklis@inpher.io`

Abstract. We pursue to formalize and instantiate a secure bidirectional channel with message franking properties. Under this model a sender may send an abusive message to the receiver and the latter wish to open it in a verifiable way to a third party. Potential malicious behavior of a sender requires message franking protocols resistant to sending messages that cannot be opened later by the receiver. An adversary impersonated by the receiver may also try to open messages that have not been sent by the sender. Wrapping a message franking protocol in a secure channel requires a more delicate treatment in order to avoid drops or replay of messages and out-of-order delivery. To the best of our knowledge we are the first to model the security of a message franking channel, which apart from integrity, confidentiality, resistance to drops, relays and out-of-order delivery is *sender* and *receiver binding*: a sender cannot send a message which cannot be opened in a verifiable way later by the receiver, and the receiver cannot claim a message that had not been truly sent by the receiver. Finally, we instantiate a bidirectional message franking channel from symmetric primitives and analyze its security.

Keywords: Message franking channel · Secure communication · Channel security · Abusive verifiable reports

1 Introduction

The most popular messaging services such as Facebook Messenger, Whatsapp, Telegram or Signal offer end-to-end encryption, preventing anyone apart from the recipients from reading the messages. While preserving privacy, such schemes increase the difficulty of filtering spam or reporting abusive messages. Indeed, without the capacity to read the plaintexts, the router (e.g. Facebook) cannot check for abusive content, malware, malicious links, etc. The problem of abuse reporting was recently tackled by Facebook, which introduced the concept of *message franking* [Fac16]. With this proposed protocol, a user can report abusive messages to Facebook and can prove that an abusive message was sent by another user. More recently, Grubbs et al. initiated the formal analysis of such schemes [GLR17]. In particular, they introduced a new cryptographic primitive called committing authenticated encryption with associated data (committing AEAD) along with new security definitions. In the same paper, they analyze the security

© Springer Nature Switzerland AG 2021
Y. Yu and M. Yung (Eds.): Inscrypt 2021, LNCS 13007, pp. 111–128, 2021.
https://doi.org/10.1007/978-3-030-88323-2_6

of Facebook's scheme and present a more efficient construction. In a follow up work Dodis, Grubbs, Ristenpart and Woodage [DGRW18] revealed a flaw in Facebook message franking protocol for attachment delivery. The authors showed compromisation of sender binding, letting a malicious sender to send messages that cannot be reported. To circumvent that flaw they suggest a new design for message franking based on hashing encryption which provides the requiring commitment properties on the ciphertext with only one pass.

The security of communication protocols though depends not only on the underlying cryptographic primitives but also on the behavior of the protocol itself. For instance, a protocol based on secure primitives accepting out-of-order messages or an adversary being able to drop or replay messages renders communication between two end points vulnerable to such malicious behaviors. More generally, traditional cryptographic primitives cannot model real-world attacks beyond basic confidentiality and integrity. In particular, the integrity of the communication channel (e.g. security against out-of-order messages, message drops or replay attacks) is not captured by traditional security definitions. These reasons led to the study of communication protocols as stateful encryption schemes, so called: cryptographic channels [BKN02,KPB03,Mar17,PR18].

Cryptographic Channel. Consider a messaging protocol where several participants share a key with each other and want to send and receive end-to-end encrypted messages. Once all the keys are fixed, a channel with confidentality, integrity–which includes resistance to replay attacks, out-of-order delivery and drops–must be established between each pair of participants. The cryptographic primitive that models the channels and the interaction between the participants is called a *cryptographic channel*. A channel where the only actions available to the clients are *send* and *receive* (i.e. as in a traditionnal message exchange protocol) will be referred to as a *standard cryptographic channel*.

A standard cryptographic channel $\mathsf{Ch} = (\mathsf{init}, \mathsf{snd}, \mathsf{rcv})$ is a tuple of three efficient algorithms that allows the participants to send and receive encrypted messages. If there are two participants and only one can send and only one can receive, the channel is unidirectional while if both can send and receive, the channel is bidirectional.

One could imagine that a bidirectional channel made up of two secure unidirectional channels should be secure. However, as shown in [MP17] this does not hold. In the same paper, the authors show several security results on bidirectional channels constructed from unidirectional channels in a special construction called the *canonic composition*. The more interesting ones concerning confidentality, are the following:

$$\text{IND-1CPA} + \text{IND-1CPA} \iff \text{IND-2CPA} \tag{1}$$

$$\text{IND-1CCA} + \text{IND-1CCA} \impliedby \text{IND-2CCA} \tag{2}$$

$$\text{IND-1CCA} + \text{IND-1CCA} \not\implies \text{IND-2CCA} \tag{3}$$

where IND-1CPA, IND-2CPA are the IND-CPA security for unidirectional and bidirectional channels, respectively, and IND-1CCA, IND-2CCA are the

IND-CCA security for unidirectional and bidirectional channels, respectively [MP17]. One can see that if a unidirectional channel is CPA secure, a CPA secure bidirectional channel can be constructed. On the other hand, two CCA secure unidirectional channels are not sufficient to create a CCA secure bidirectional channel. Intuitively, one can understand this result by considering the following example. We consider a bidirectional channel made up of two independent confidential unidirectional channels that do not guarantee integrity. Let the protocol be such that if an adversary sends a special ciphertext c' to Alice, she sends her password to Bob without a handshake. Note that this contradicts integrity but not confidentiality. Then, since Bob does not expect this message, he outputs the message (i.e. the password) in clear for everyone. Obviously, this does not contradict the confidentiality of the $B \to A$ channel. Now, we assume that Alice sends her password to Bob without a handshake if and only if she receives c'. Then, the $A \to B$ channel can still be confidential since unidirectional confidentiality (IND-1CCA) does not model the fact that Alice can receive messages in the $A \to B$ channel, in particular c'. Thus, these results show the importance of considering protocols in bidirectional cryptographic channels.

Recent results analyze security of secure communication channel over TLS [BHMS15, BH17, GM17], but without sender and receiver binding guarantees. In this work we aim to close the gap in the existing literature with the definitions, design and analysis of a secure communication channel with message franking properties: sender and receiver binding.

Our Contributions. The contributions of this work are summarized as follows:

1. We first define a message franking channel (MFC) that models a messaging protocol where users can report abusive messages.
2. Then, we present unidirectional and bidirectional security definitions for our construction. The most challenging are the uni/bi-directional sender and receiver binding notions, which were introduced by Grubbs et al. [GLR17]. Specifically, binding definitions guarantee that a delivered message can be reported and a forged message cannot be reported.
3. We prove that a special construction called hereafter the *canonical composition*, made from two binding unidirectional MFC, is sufficient to build a secure binding bidirectional MFC.
4. Finally we present an instantiation of a message franking channel made from a secure committing AEAD scheme and a message authentication code.

Outline. In Sect. 2 we introduce some notation for the manuscript. In Sect. 3 we recap the reader the message franking protocol definitions and Facebook message franking protocol. We continue in Sect. 4 with the syntactical definition of a message franking channel and in Sect. 5 with the security properties thereof. A concrete instantiation is presented in Sect. 6. Finally, we conclude our work in Sect. 7.

2 Notation

A participant is referred to interchangeably as a client, a user or a party. We write $A \parallel B$ to denote the concatenation of A with B and $|A|$ to denote the length of A. We write $\Pr[G \Rightarrow x]$ to denote the probability a game G outputs x. If $\mathcal{X}$ is a set, then $X \leftarrow_\$ \mathcal{X}$ means that X is uniformly sampled from $\mathcal{X}$. If G is a randomized algorithm, we write $x \leftarrow_\$ G$ to denote the fact that x takes the value output by G. If G is deterministic, we write $x \leftarrow G$.

In the different games, we denote the initialization of an array A by $A \leftarrow []$. At each position i, an array can be assigned a single value x or a tuple of values $(x_1, \ldots, x_n)$. We denote these events by $A[i] \leftarrow x$ and $A[i] \leftarrow (x_1, \ldots, x_n)$, respectively. We write **abort** for "Stop the game and return 0 as a failure". If G is a game that returns a value n, we denote by $\Pr[G \Rightarrow n]$ the probability that G returns n.

Finally, when this is clear from the context, we denote by $*$ any value that could fit. For example, if $T \in \mathcal{X} \times \mathcal{Y}$ is a tuple of two values and $X \in \mathcal{X}$, we write $T == (X, *)$ to denote the event that there exists some $Y \in \mathcal{Y}$ such that T is equal to (X, Y).

3 Commiting AEAD

Grubbs et al. [GLR17] formalized the concept of message franking into the definition of *committing AEAD*. Roughly, the idea is to define a cryptographic primitive that creates a ciphertext and a commitment on the plaintext. Then, one can decrypt to retrieve the plaintext and an opening key, which is used to verify the commitement on the plaintext. We present here the definition of committing AEAD where all randomness is defined by a public nonce. Formally, a nonce-based committing AEAD is defined as follows:

Definition 1 (Nonce-based Committing AEAD). *A nonce-based committing AEAD scheme* $\mathsf{nCE} = (\mathsf{init}, \mathsf{enc}, \mathsf{dec}, \mathsf{vrf})$ *is a set of four algorithms. Associated to this scheme is a key space* $\mathcal{K}$, *a header space* $\mathcal{H}$, *a message space* $\mathcal{M}$, *a ciphertext space* $\mathcal{C}$, *an opening space* $\mathcal{K}_f$, *a franking tag space* $\mathcal{T}$ *and a nonce space* $\mathcal{N}$. *An error symbol* $\perp$ *is also required. The four algorithms are as follows:*

- $K \leftarrow_\$ \mathsf{init}$: *The initialization algorithm* init *outputs a random key* $K \in \mathcal{K}$.
- $(C_1, C_2) \leftarrow \mathsf{enc}_K(N, H, M)$: *The encryption algorithm* enc *takes a key* $K \in \mathcal{K}$, *a nonce* $N \in \mathcal{N}$, *a header* $H \in \mathcal{H}$ *and a message* $M \in \mathcal{M}$, *and it outputs a ciphertext* $C_1 \in \mathcal{C}$ *and a franking tag* $C_2 \in \mathcal{T}$.
- $(M, K_f) \leftarrow \mathsf{dec}_K(N, H, C_1, C_2)$: *The decryption algorithm* dec *takes a key* $K \in \mathcal{K}$, *a nonce* $N \in \mathcal{N}$, *a header* $H \in \mathcal{H}$, *a ciphertext* $C_1 \in \mathcal{C}$ *and a franking tag* $C_2 \in \mathcal{T}$, *and it outputs a message* $M \in \mathcal{M}$ *and an opening* $K_f \in \mathcal{K}_f$ *or an error symbol* $\perp$.
- $b \leftarrow \mathsf{vrf}(H, M, K_f, C_2)$: *The verification algorithm* vrf *takes a header* $H \in \mathcal{H}$, *a message* $M \in \mathcal{M}$, *an opening value* $K_f \in \mathcal{K}_f$ *and a franking tag* $C_2 \in \mathcal{T}$, *and it outputs a verification bit* b, *regarding the correctness of the reporting procedure.*

The first procedure init is randomized while the others are deterministic, since the randomness is defined by the nonce value N.

Correctness. For the correctness of the scheme, we require that for any $K \in \mathcal{K}$, $N \in \mathcal{N}$, $H \in \mathcal{H}$ and $M \in \mathcal{M}$ and $(C_1, C_2) = \mathsf{enc}_K(N, H, M)$

$$\Pr[\mathsf{dec}_K(N, H, C_1) = (M, K_f)] = 1$$

for some $K_f \in \mathcal{K}_f$.

Also, if we let $(C_1, C_2) = \mathsf{enc}_K(N, H, M)$ and $(M, K_f) = \mathsf{dec}_K(N, H, C_1, C_2)$ then we require that

$$\Pr[\mathsf{vrf}(H, M, K_f, C_2) = 1] = 1$$

for any $K \in \mathcal{K}$, $N \in \mathcal{N}$, $H \in \mathcal{H}$ and $M \in \mathcal{M}$.

Finally, we require the length of the ciphertexts (C_1, C_2) to be deterministic given H and M. In other words, there is a deterministic function $len(H, M)$ s.t. $(|C_1|, |C_2|) = len(H, M)$.

Due to space constraints security definitions for AEAD are deferred in Appendix A.

4   Cryptographic Channel for Message Franking (MFC)

A cryptographic channel is a set of algorithms that allows several participants to exchange messages (i.e. send and receive) with confidentiality, message integrity, resistance to replay attacks, out-of-order delivery and message drops. For the reasons exposed above and the fact that a bidirectional channel is more generic than a unidirectional one, we are going to focus on a bidirectional channel where two participants (Alice and Bob) exchange messages. However, in the message franking case, the participants do not only exchange messages but they also report them as abusive to a third entity, which we refer to as *router*. Therefore, we need to define a new model for a cryptographic channel, which we call a message franking channel (MFC). Informally, we raise the nonce-based committing AEAD concept to the channel level, in the context of message franking.

We define a message franking channel (MFC), using the syntax used by Marson et al. [MP17]:

Definition 2 (Message Franking Channel). *A message franking channel* $\mathsf{Ch} = (\mathsf{init}, \mathsf{snd}, \mathsf{tag}, \mathsf{rcv}, \mathsf{rprt})$ *is a five-tuple of algorithms. Associated to this channel is a key space* $\mathcal{K}$, *a nonce space* $\mathcal{N}$, *a header space* $\mathcal{H}$, *a message space* $\mathcal{M}$, *a ciphertext space* $\mathcal{C}$, *an opening space* $\mathcal{K}_f$, *a franking tag space* $\mathcal{T}$, *a router tag space* $\mathcal{T}_R$ *and a state space* $\mathcal{S}$. *The participants space is* $\mathcal{P} = \{A, B\}$ *(for Alice and Bob). We also require a special rejection symbol* $\perp \notin (\mathcal{K}_f \times \mathcal{M}) \cup \mathcal{S}$. *The five procedures are defined as follows:*

- $(st_A, st_B, st_R) \leftarrow_{\$} \mathsf{init}$: *The initialization algorithm* init *samples a key* $K \in \mathcal{K}$ *and a key* $K_R \in \mathcal{K}$, *and it outputs initial states* $st_A, st_B, st_R \in \mathcal{S}$. *K is the shared key resulting from a secure and authenticated key exchange protocol between both clients and* K_R *is the secret key of the router.*

- $(st'_u, H, C_1, C_2) \leftarrow$ snd(st_u, N, M): *The sending algorithm* snd *takes the sender's state* $st_u \in \mathcal{S}$, *a nonce* $N \in \mathcal{N}$ *and a message* $M \in \mathcal{M}$, *and it outputs an updated state* $st'_u \in \mathcal{S}$, *a header* $H \in \mathcal{H}$ *and a pair of ciphertext and franking tag* $(C_1, C_2) \in \mathcal{C} \times \mathcal{T}$.
- $(st'_R, T_R) \leftarrow$ tag(st_R, id_s, H, C_2): *The router tagging algorithm* tag *takes the router's state* $st_R \in \mathcal{S}$, *the sender's identity* $id_s \in \mathcal{P}$, *a header* $H \in \mathcal{H}$ *and a franking tag* $C_2 \in \mathcal{T}$, *and it outputs an updated state* $st'_R \in \mathcal{S}$ *and a router tag* $T_R \in \mathcal{T}_R$.
- $(st'_u, M, K_f) \leftarrow$ rcv(st_u, N, H, C_1, C_2): *The receiving algorithm* rcv *takes the receiver's state* $st_u \in \mathcal{S}$, *a nonce* $N \in \mathcal{N}$, *a header* $H \in \mathcal{H}$, *a ciphertext* $C_1 \in \mathcal{C}$ *and a franking tag* $C_2 \in \mathcal{T}$, *and it outputs an updated state* $st'_u \in \mathcal{S} \cup \{\bot\}$, *and an opening value pair* $(M, K_f) \in \mathcal{M} \times \mathcal{K}_f$ *or* $\bot$. *We require* $st'_u = \bot$ *if* $(M, K_f) = \bot$.
- $(st'_R, b) \leftarrow$ rprt$(st_R, id_r, H, M, K_f, C_2, T_R)$: *The router's verification algorithm* rprt *takes the router's state* $st_R \in \mathcal{S}$, *the reporter's identity* $id_r \in \mathcal{P}$, *a header* $H \in \mathcal{H}$, *a message* $M \in \mathcal{M}$, *an opening* $K_f \in \mathcal{K}_f$, *a franking tag* $C_2 \in \mathcal{T}$ *and a router tag* $T_R \in \mathcal{T}_R$, *and it outputs an updated router's state* $st'_R \in \mathcal{S} \cup \{\bot\}$ *and a verification bit* $b \in \{0, 1\}$. *We require* $st'_R = \bot$ *if* $b = 0$.

We assume the channel is stateful, i.e. the participants save their state between send/tag/receive/report calls. The rcv procedure can verify the commitment C_2 and outputs $\bot$ if the verification fails. Also, note that the rprt procedure does not depend on the nonce N nor on the ciphertext C_1. In particular, this means that the router must be able to verify the validity of the router tag T_R given only its state st_R, the header H and the franking tag C_2. The channel uses $\bot$ to indicate an error. Once a state is marked as bogus (i.e. $st = \bot$), it cannot be used anymore in the invokation of the functions snd, rcv and rprt, since $\bot \notin \mathcal{S}$. This corresponds to the reasonable behaviour of an application refusing to process any more data once an error has been detected. Error management in channels is a full topic in itself (e.g. [BDPS13]) and can lead to vulnerabilities (e.g. padding oracle attack [Vau02]). Here, we assume that an adversary does not learn anything from an error apart from the failure of the corresponding procedure. The randomness is uniquely determined by public nonces N. Nonces can be used to perform randomized encryption but also to generate a random opening key K_f, as in Facebook's scheme. The role of the nonce is determined by the underlying schemes used by the different algorithms.

Remarks. The key K_R is the router's secret key that can be used to generate the router tags T_R. In a real-life message franking protocol, all messages go through the router, where they get tagged. Otherwise, clients could bypass the tagging procedure and messages would not be reportable. Therefore, one could imagine that a unique procedure for sending and tagging would be sufficient. While making the MFC definition simpler, this would render the instantiation of a real MFC difficult. Indeed, snd is meant to be executed by a client while tag is run by the router. Thus, such a simplification would be impractical. However, in the oracles of adversarial models used in the following sections, snd and tag procedures will sometimes be considered as one operation, to model the fact that a message sent is always seen by the router.

It is important for the security of the scheme, in particular for the receiver-binding property, that the router knows the identity of the sender and the identity of the receiver. This is why these identities id_s and id_r are passed as arguments in the tag and rprt procedures, respectively. Obviously, the router should be able to verify these identities in order for the whole protocol to be secure, otherwise one could tag messages on behalf of another user. However, throughout this paper we assume that the parties and the router have established secure keys and that the router can authenticate the sender and the reporter in the corresponding procedures. It is a fair assumption since messaging protocols usually encrypt and authenticate the communications between a client and the server. For example, TextSecure (Signal's ancestor) used to encrypt client-to-router communications with TLS and it used to authenticate the client with the phone number concatenated with some secret key [FMB+14]. Whatsapp encrypts communications to its servers with the Noise Protocol Framework and it stores the client's Curve25519 public key, allowing the router to authenticate the user during the Diffie-Hellman key exchange protocol [Per18,Wha17].

4.1   Correctness of the Channel

As in a standard bidirectional channel [MP17], we require a MFC to have certain properties. In short, we want messages sent by a client to be decryptable by the other participant without errors, assuming that the ciphertexts are not modified in the channel and that the order of the messages is preserved. Also, a message sent by a honest participant in the channel and correctly deciphered at the receiving end should be reportable, assuming that all messages sent on the channel are not modified (i.e. no active adversary).

Such requirements can be represented as a game, where only passive external adversaries (i.e. adversaries that can only see and relay messages) are allowed and where the participants are honest. The adversary can schedule snd/tag, rcv and rprt procedures and it wins if a message sent can not be decrypted or reported (i.e. rprt fails). This game is represented in Fig. 1. We assume $u \in \{A, B\}$, $N \in \mathcal{N}$, $H \in \mathcal{H}$, $M \in \mathcal{M}$, $C_1 \in \mathcal{C}$, $C_2 \in \mathcal{T}$, $K_f \in \mathcal{K}_f$ and $T_R \in \mathcal{T}_R$. The variables s_A, s_B, r_A, r_B keep track of the number of messages sent and received by each participant. The variables h_A and h_B keep track of the state of each participant (whether it has received modified/out-of-order messages). Note that an adversary can be external and try to modify the messages on the channel or it can be a participant who communicates with the other benign participant and/or the router. If a participant u receives out-of-order/modified data, (i.e. if the adversary actively attacks u), its variable h_u is set to false. If $h_u = true$ we say that u is clean. Observe that the adversary can win only if the participant u used in the oracle query is clean. $M_{A,B}[]$, $M_{B,A}[]$, $C_{A,B}[]$ and $C_{B,A}[]$ record the messages and ciphertexts exchanged. The adversary has access to three oracles:

- $\mathcal{O}^{snd}(u, N, M)$: The $\mathcal{O}^{snd}$ oracle takes the client identity u, a message and a nonce, and it calls the snd and tag procedures on behalf of the participant

u. Then, it records the resulting ciphertext and franking/router tags, if the client is still clean. This prevents the adversary from winning if the client u had previously received out-of-order/modified messages.

- $\mathcal{O}^{rcv}(u, N, H, C_1, C_2)$: With the oracle $\mathcal{O}^{rcv}$, an adversary can make a user u receive (i.e. decrypt). Now, if this participant is still clean and the ciphertext is delivered without modification (and in the right order) compared to the one sent (condition in line 4), then the message recovered should be the one sent. If this is not the case (condition in line 6), then the adversary wins. Otherwise, if the condition at line 4 is not respected, then the ciphertext/tags have been modified and the participant is flagged as not clean.

- $\mathcal{O}^{rprt}(u, n, H, M, K_f, C_2, T_R)$: The adversary can use also the $\mathcal{O}^{rprt}$ oracle to report a given message on behalf of a user u, by providing the message along with the tags. It also must specify the index n of the message (we assume the adversary records the number of messages sent). As before, if the user is clean and the header, the franking tag, the router tag and the message were not modified compared to the one sent (conditions at lines 2–3), then the participant/adversary should be able to report the message. If this is not the case, the adversary wins. Otherwise, if the condition in line 3 is not respected (i.e. the message, ciphertext or tags have been tampered with), the participant is flagged as not clean.

Now, for any adversary $\mathcal{A}$ playing CORR and any channel Ch, we denote the advantage of $\mathcal{A}$ as

$$\mathsf{Adv}_{\mathsf{Ch}}^{\mathrm{corr}}(\mathcal{A}) = \Pr[\mathrm{CORR}_{\mathsf{Ch}}(\mathcal{A}) \Rightarrow \mathsf{true}]$$

Definition 3 (Bidirectional Message Franking Channel Correctness).
We say that a message franking bidirectional channel Ch is correct if for any adversary $\mathcal{A}$ playing the CORR game

$$\mathsf{Adv}_{\mathsf{Ch}}^{\mathrm{corr}}(\mathcal{A}) = 0$$

In Appendix B, we give the unidirectional correctness definition.

5   Security for Message Franking Channel

5.1   Confidentiality

We elevate the MO-nRAND confidentiality game for nonce-based committing AEAD schemes to the bidirectional MFC case. Confidentiality means that no adversary is able to retrieve information about the messages exchanged by the participants. This notion concerns the exchange of messages and not the reporting phase. In addition, we note that once an abusive message is reported, it becomes public, in the sense that we do not specify how the message is sent to the router for reporting (e.g. it could be sent in clear).

$\text{CORR}_{\text{Ch}}(\mathcal{A})$

1: $win \leftarrow$ false
2: $(st_A, st_B, st_R) \leftarrow\$ \text{init}$
3: $s_A \leftarrow 0; s_B \leftarrow 0$
4: $r_A \leftarrow 0; r_B \leftarrow 0$
5: $h_A \leftarrow$ true$; h_B \leftarrow$ true
6: $M_{A,B} \leftarrow []; M_{B,A} \leftarrow []$
7: $C_{A,B} \leftarrow []; C_{B,A} \leftarrow []$
8: $\mathcal{A}^{\mathcal{O}^{snd}, \mathcal{O}^{rcv}, \mathcal{O}^{rprt}}$
9: **return** win

Oracle $\mathcal{O}^{rprt}(u, n, H, M, K_f, C_2, T_R)$

1: $(st_R, b) \leftarrow \text{rprt}(st_R, u, H, M, K_f, C_2, T_R)$
2: **if** h_u :
3:    **if** $C_{v,u}[n] = (*, H, *, C_2, T_R)$ and $M_{v,u}[n] = M$:
4:      **if** $b = 0$:
5:        $win \leftarrow$ true
6:    **else** :
7:      $h_u \leftarrow$ false
8: **return** b

Oracle $\mathcal{O}^{snd}(u, N, M)$

1: $(st_u, H, C_1, C_2) \leftarrow \text{snd}(st_u, N, M)$
2: $(st_R, T_R) \leftarrow \text{tag}(st_R, u, H, C_2)$
3: $v \leftarrow \{A, B\} \setminus \{u\}$
4: **if** h_u :
5:    $M_{u,v}[s_u] \leftarrow M$
6:    $C_{u,v}[s_u] \leftarrow (N, H, C_1, C_2, T_R)$
7:    $s_u \leftarrow s_u + 1$
8: **return** (C_1, C_2, T_R)

Oracle $\mathcal{O}^{rcv}(u, N, H, C_1, C_2)$

1: $(st_u, M, K_f) \leftarrow \text{rcv}(st_u, N, H, C_1, C_2)$
2: $v \leftarrow \{A, B\} \setminus \{u\}$
3: **if** h_u :
4:    **if** $r_u < s_u$ and $C_{v,u}[r_u] = (N, H,$
5:                    $C_1, C_2, *)$:
6:      **if** $(M, K_f) = \perp$ or $M_{v,u}[r_u] \neq M$:
7:        $win \leftarrow$ true
8:      $r_u \leftarrow r_u + 1$
9:    **else** :
10:      $h_u \leftarrow$ false
11: **return** (M, K_f)

Fig. 1. Correctness game for a bidirectional message franking channel.

While in a standard channel the adversary is external to the participants, in the message franking case the adversary can also be the router. Therefore, in the following games we give the adversary access to the router's state st_R. This means the adversary does not need a tag and report oracle, as it is able to run these procedures on its own.

The MO-2nREAL and MO-2nRAND games of Fig. 2 are adapted from the MO-nREAL and MO-nRAND games. In both games, we assume the adversary is nonce-respecting (i.e. it cannot query $\mathcal{O}^{snd}$ or $\mathcal{O}^{chal}$ twice with the same nonce N).

The adversary wins if it can differentiate with non-negligible probability between the encryption of a message M and the encryption of a random bit-string. The h_u variables, as in the correctness games, let the adversary decrypt ciphertexts as long as it remains passive: the adversary only relays messages. In particular, this prevents the adversary from winning by decrypting the ciphertexts obtained from the $\mathcal{O}^{chal}$ oracle.

MO-2nREAL$_{\text{Ch}}(\mathcal{A})$	MO-2nRAND$_{\text{Ch}}(\mathcal{A})$
$(st_A, st_B, st_R) \leftarrow_\$ \text{init}$	$(st_A, st_B, st_R) \leftarrow_\$ \text{init}$
$s_A \leftarrow 0; s_B \leftarrow 0; r_A \leftarrow 0; r_B \leftarrow 0$	$s_A \leftarrow 0; s_B \leftarrow 0; r_A \leftarrow 0; r_B \leftarrow 0$
$h_A \leftarrow \text{true}; h_B \leftarrow \text{true}$	$h_A \leftarrow \text{true}; h_B \leftarrow \text{true}$
$C_{A,B} \leftarrow []; C_{B,A} \leftarrow []$	$C_{A,B} \leftarrow []; C_{B,A} \leftarrow []$
$b' \leftarrow \mathcal{A}^{\mathcal{O}^{snd}, \mathcal{O}^{rcv}, \mathcal{O}^{chal}, st_R}$	$b' \leftarrow \mathcal{A}^{\mathcal{O}^{snd}, \mathcal{O}^{rcv}, \mathcal{O}^{chal}, st_R}$
return b'	**return** b'

Oracle $\mathcal{O}^{snd}(u, N, M)$	**Oracle** $\mathcal{O}^{snd}(u, N, M)$
$(st_u, H, C_1, C_2) \leftarrow \text{snd}(st_u, N, M)$	$(st_u, H, C_1, C_2) \leftarrow \text{snd}(st_u, N, M)$
$v \leftarrow \{A, B\} \setminus \{u\}$	$v \leftarrow \{A, B\} \setminus \{u\}$
if h_u :	**if** h_u :
$\quad C_{u,v}[s_u] \leftarrow (N, H, C_1, C_2)$	$\quad C_{u,v}[s_u] \leftarrow (N, H, C_1, C_2)$
$\quad s_u \leftarrow s_u + 1$	$\quad s_u \leftarrow s_u + 1$
return (H, C_1, C_2)	**return** (H, C_1, C_2)

Oracle $\mathcal{O}^{rcv}(u, N, H, C_1, C_2)$	**Oracle** $\mathcal{O}^{rcv}(u, N, H, C_1, C_2)$
$(st_u, M, K_f) \leftarrow \text{rcv}(st_u, N, H, C_1, C_2)$	$(st_u, M, K_f) \leftarrow \text{rcv}(st_u, N, H, C_1, C_2)$
$v \leftarrow \{A, B\} \setminus \{u\}$	$v \leftarrow \{A, B\} \setminus \{u\}$
if $r_u < s_v$ and $C_{v,u}[r_u] = (N, H, C_1, C_2)$:	**if** $r_u < s_v$ and $C_{v,u}[r_u] = (N, H, C_1, C_2)$:
$\quad r_u \leftarrow r_u + 1$	$\quad r_u \leftarrow r_u + 1$
else :	**else** :
$\quad h_u \leftarrow \text{false}$	$\quad h_u \leftarrow \text{false}$
if h_u: **return** (M, K_f)	**if** h_u: **return** (M, K_f)
else : **return** $\perp$	**else** : **return** $\perp$

Oracle $\mathcal{O}^{chal}(u, N, M)$	**Oracle** $\mathcal{O}^{chal}(u, N, M)$
$(st_u, H, C_1, C_2) \leftarrow \text{snd}(st_u, N, M)$	$M_r \leftarrow_\$ \{0, 1\}^{|M|}$
return (C_1, C_2)	$(st_u, H, C_1, C_2) \leftarrow \text{snd}(st_u, N, M_r)$
	return (C_1, C_2)

Fig. 2. Confidentality games for nonce-based bidirectional message franking channels.

For a bidirectional MFC channel Ch, we define the nonce-based multiple opening real-or-random (MO-2nRoR) advantage of any algorithm $\mathcal{A}$ as

$$\text{Adv}_{\text{Ch}}^{\text{mo-2nror}}(\mathcal{A}) = |\Pr[\text{MO-2nREAL}_{\text{Ch}}(\mathcal{A}) \Rightarrow 1] - \Pr[\text{MO-2nRAND}_{\text{Ch}}(\mathcal{A}) \Rightarrow 1]|$$

5.2 Integrity

We adapt the MO-nCTXT integrity notions of committing AEAD to the bidirectional MFC. Ciphertext integrity means that a receiver can only receive and decrypt in-order and legitimate ciphertexts, which have been sent by another participant. As in the MO-2nROR confidentiality notion, the adversary can be the router and thus we give access to the state st_R.

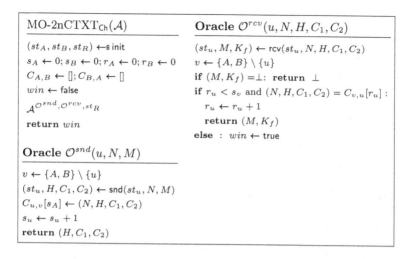

Fig. 3. Integrity game for nonce-based committing AEAD

Let MO-2nCTXT be the game in Fig. 3. By observing the $\mathcal{O}^{rcv}$ oracle, one can see that the adversary wins if the rcv procedure is successful but the ciphertexts are not legitimate or they are received out-of-order. For a bidirectional MFC Ch, we define the nonce-based multiple opening integrity advantage of any algorithm $\mathcal{A}$ playing the MO-2nCTXT game as

$$\mathsf{Adv}_{\mathsf{Ch}}^{\mathrm{mo\text{-}2nctxt}}(\mathcal{A}) = \Pr[\text{MO-2nCTXT}_{\mathsf{Ch}}(\mathcal{A}) \Rightarrow \mathrm{true}]$$

5.3 Binding Security Notions

In order to guarantee verifiable reporting of abusive messages, a MFC should adhere to sender and receiver binding notions as with message franking protocols [Fac16, GLR17]. One difference between the committing AEAD binding definitions and the ones defined here, is that in a channel the participants are stateful and their behavior may evolve over time, whereas such concepts do not exist in the security definitions of cryptographic primitives like committing AEAD. The threat in such security definitions is a malicious participant and not an external adversary. Therefore, in all the binding games of this section, we assume that the adversary can modify the states of the participants (Alice and Bob). In particular, this allows the adversary to control sthe encryption key K.

Sender Binding. Sender binding for MFC guarantees that any message received without error by a client can be successfully reported to the router. This notion is defined with the game s-2BIND presented in Fig. 4.

The adversary has access to three oracles in addition to the states of Alice and Bob. Here is a description of the s-2BIND game:

s-2BIND$_{Ch}(\mathcal{A})$	Oracle $\mathcal{O}^{rprt}(u, H, M, K_f, C_2, T_R)$
1: $win \leftarrow$ false	1: $id_r \leftarrow u$
2: $(st_A, st_B, st_R) \leftarrow\!\!\$ \, init$	2: $v \leftarrow \{A, B\} \setminus \{u\}$
3: $s_A \leftarrow 0; s_B \leftarrow 0$	3: $(st_R, b) \leftarrow rprt(st_R, id_r, H, M, K_f, C_2, T_R)$
4: $r_A \leftarrow 0; r_B \leftarrow 0$	4: if (H, M, K_f, C_2, T_R) in $R_{v,u}$ and $b = 0$:
5: $S_{A,B} \leftarrow []; S_{B,A} \leftarrow []$	5: $win \leftarrow$ true
6: $R_{A,B} \leftarrow []; R_{B,A} \leftarrow []$	6: return b
7: $\mathcal{A}^{\mathcal{O}^{tag}, \mathcal{O}^{rcv}, \mathcal{O}^{rprt}, st_A, st_B}$	
8: return win	

Oracle $\mathcal{O}^{rcv}(u, N, H, C_1, C_2)$	Oracle $\mathcal{O}^{tag}(u, H, C_2)$
1: $v = \{A, B\} \setminus \{u\}$	1: $id_s \leftarrow u$
2: if (H, C_2, T_R) in $S_{v,u}$ for some T_R:	2: $(st_R, T_R) \leftarrow tag(st_R, id_s, H, C_2)$
3: $(st_u, M, K_f) \leftarrow rcv(st_u, N, H, C_1, C_2)$	3: $v = \{A, B\} \setminus \{u\}$
4: if $(M, K_f) \neq \perp$	4: $S_{u,v}[s_u] = (H, C_2, T_R)$
5: $R_{v,u}[r_u] \leftarrow (H, M, K_f, C_2, T_R)$	5: $s_u \leftarrow s_u + 1$
6: $r_u \leftarrow r_u + 1$	6: return T_R

Fig. 4. Game for message franking channel sender-binding security definition.

- s-2BIND$_{Ch}(\mathcal{A})$: The r_A, r_B, s_A, s_B variables keep track of the number of messages received and sent by each party. The arrays $S_{A,B}[], S_{B,A}[]$ store the franking tags C_2, the headers H and the associated router tags T_R sent from A to B and from B to A, respectively. The arrays $R_{A,B}[]$ and $R_{B,A}[]$ store the tags and messages corresponding to ciphertexts when the rcv procedure outputs a valid pair (M, K_f), after decryption.
- $\mathcal{O}^{tag}(u, H, C_2)$: This oracle is used to modify the router state st_R and to obtain a router tag for a tuple (H, C_2), with u as the sender. The header H, the franking tag C_2 and the router tag obtained T_R are stored in the corresponding array $S_{u,v}[]$ (line 4). This array is needed to ensure that a router tag T_R really corresponds to a header,franking tag pair (H, C_2). Then, the number of messages sent by the participant is incremented (line 5). Finally, the router tag is returned to the adversary (line 6).
- $\mathcal{O}^{rcv}(u, N, H, C_1, C_2)$: The $\mathcal{O}^{rcv}$ oracle first checks that H and C_2 corresponds to a router tag T_R (line 2) computed for a message sent by client v. If this is the case, the rcv procedure is called and it outputs a plaintext, opening key pair (M, K_f). If this pair is valid (i.e. not equal to $\perp$), it is stored in the appropriate array $R_{v,u}$ alongside with the header and the tags (C_2, T_R) (line 5). This means that these values correspond to a ciphertext that decrypts to a valid message. Finally, the number of valid messages received by u is incremented (line 6).
- $\mathcal{O}^{rprt}(u, H, M, K_f, C_2, T_R)$: The oracle $\mathcal{O}^{rprt}$ calls the rprt procedure on the the header, the message, the opening key and the tags, with u as the reporter.

r-2BIND$_{Ch}(\mathcal{A})$	**Oracle** $\mathcal{O}^{snd}(u, N, H, M)$
1: $win \leftarrow$ false	1: $id_s \leftarrow u$
2: $(st_A, st_B, st_R) \leftarrow \$ \text{ init}$	2: $(st_u, \_, C_1, C_2) \leftarrow \text{snd}(st_u, N, M)$
3: $s_A \leftarrow 0; s_B \leftarrow 0$	3: $(st_R, T_R) \leftarrow \text{tag}(st_R, id_s, H, C_2)$
4: $M_{A,B} \leftarrow []; M_{B,A} \leftarrow []$	4: $v = \{A, B\} \setminus \{u\}$
5: $\mathcal{A}^{\mathcal{O}^{snd}, \mathcal{O}^{rprt}, st_A, st_B}$	5: $M_{u,v}[s_u] \leftarrow M$
6: **return** win	6: $s_u \leftarrow s_u + 1$
	7: **return** (C_1, C_2, T_R)

Oracle $\mathcal{O}^{rprt}(u, H, M, K_f, C_2, T_R)$

1: $id_r \leftarrow u; v = \{A, B\} \setminus \{u\}$
2: $(st_R, b) \leftarrow \text{rprt}(st_R, id_r, H, M, K_f, C_2, T_R)$
3: **if** M **not** in $M_{v,u}$ and $b = 1$:
4:    $win \leftarrow$ true
5: **return** b

Fig. 5. Game for franking channel receiver-binding security definition.

This allows an adversary to update the router state st_R. Then, if the input values correspond to some ciphertext that outputs a valid message but the report procedure fails (line 4), the adversary wins.

The adversary can use the $\mathcal{O}^{rprt}$ oracle to report a message on behalf of a user u. If the message was actually sent and correctly decrypted by u then it is in $R_{v,u}$ with the corresponding header and tags. Therefore, if the message is in $R_{v,u}$ but the rprt procedure fails, the adversary wins. Indeed, we ask an adversary to win if the decryption is successful but the report procedure fails. We need to use a second pair of arrays $(S_{A,B}, S_{B,A})$ to store the router tag T_R corresponding to a pair (H, C_2). Otherwise, one could not store T_R in the array $R_{v,u}$ at line 5 of $\mathcal{O}^{rcv}$. Indeed, if T_R was not stored in $R_{v,u}$, the adversary could specify a random T_R when reporting with legit values, making the verification fail. Finally, we note that despite the fact the adversary has access to both user states, in a real-life threat model the adversary would be only one of the participants (e.g. Alice). However, since both participants share everything, it does not matter if the adversary has access to one or both states. For any adversary $\mathcal{A}$ playing s-2BIND and any channel Ch, the advantage of $\mathcal{A}$ is:

$$\text{Adv}_{Ch}^{s-2bind}(\mathcal{A}) = \Pr[\text{s-2BIND}_{Ch}(\mathcal{A}) \Rightarrow \text{true}]$$

Receiver Binding. We recall that receiver binding assures that a malicious participant cannot report an abusive message that was never sent. Receiver binding for message franking channels is defined with the game r-2BIND$_{Ch}$ presented in Fig. 5. In this game, the adversary represents two colluding participants that can schedule snd/tag/rprt operations for message exchanges and then one of the participants tries to report a message never sent to her/him. Since the adversary controls the users states, it would need only access to tag/rprt oracles since it can run the other algorithms by itself. However, the game should store the sent messages (i.e. the ones the adversary requested a router tag for) in order to compare them with the reported message in the $\mathcal{O}^{rprt}$ oracle. Therefore, we let the $\mathcal{O}^{snd}$ oracle run the snd procedure as well as the tag procedure. Here is a description of the game:

- r-2BIND$_{Ch}(\mathcal{A})$: The s_A, s_B variables keep track of the number of messages sent by each party. They are used as indexes for the arrays $M_{A,B}[], M_{B,A}[]$ that store all messages sent by A to B and B to A, respectively.
- $\mathcal{O}^{snd}(u, N, H, M)$: In the $\mathcal{O}^{snd}$ oracle, the message sent M is recorded in the corresponding array (line 5) and the number of messages sent by the participant is incremented (line 6). The ciphertext, franking tag and router tag are returned to the adversary (line 7). In short, this oracle allows an adversary to obtain the router tag for any header/message tuple, while recording the message. We let the adversary pass the header H as an argument since we want the adversary to be able to get a router tag for any header.
- $\mathcal{O}^{rprt}(u, H, M, K_f, C_2, T_R)$: The $\mathcal{O}^{rprt}$ takes a header H, the message to be reported M, an opening key K_f, a franking tag C_2, a router tag T_R and the identity of the reporter u. At line 3, the condition checks that the submitted message was not sent to the reporting participant and that the message passes the rprt procedure. If this is the case, the adversary wins.

In order to respect this receiver binding notion, the router must be able to check the sender and receiver of a message. Indeed, if this is not the case, one can construct an adversary $\mathcal{A}^{r\text{-}2\text{BIND}}$ that always wins, as shown in Fig. 6. Let Alice be the malicious participant. She picks a random message and a random nonce and sends the corresponding ciphertext to Bob using the sending oracle. Thus, the message is in the array $M_{A,B}$. Note that Alice can compute the opening key K_f since she controls st_A, N, H and M. Finally, she reports Bob as the sender of the message by calling the $\mathcal{O}^{rprt}$ oracle. Since the message is in $M_{A,B}$ but not in $M_{B,A}$, the first part of the condition in line 3 of $\mathcal{O}^{rprt}$ is fulfilled. Thus, since all values used to report are legitimate, the report procedure will succeed unless the router knows the message was actually sent by Alice to Bob.

One solution to this problem is to incorporate the receiver/sender identities in the router tag T_R. This is done in the Facebook protocol by putting the sender and receiver identities in some context data. The router tag T_R becomes $T_R = \mathsf{HMAC}_{K_R}(C_2 \parallel sender \parallel receiver)$ and the router can check whether the participant A reporting an abusive message from participant A is telling the truth or not and accept or reject accordingly. This shows the importance to correctly manage the identity of the participants.

For any adversary $\mathcal{A}$ playing r-2BIND and any channel Ch, we write the advantage of $\mathcal{A}$ as

$$\mathsf{Adv}_{Ch}^{r-2bind}(\mathcal{A}) = \Pr[\text{r-2BIND}_{Ch}(\mathcal{A}) \Rightarrow \mathsf{true}]$$

In other words, in addition to the control of participants' states, the adversary must be able to modify the state of the router, as in a real exchange of messages.

In Appendix B, we give the unidirectional binding definitions.

$$
\begin{array}{l}
\hline
\mathcal{A}^{\text{r-2BIND}} \\
\hline
1: \quad M \leftarrow_\$ \mathcal{M}; N \leftarrow_\$ \mathcal{N} \\
2: \quad \text{compute next } K_f \text{ from } (N, H, M, st_A) \\
3: \quad (H, C_1, C_2, T_R) \leftarrow \mathcal{O}^{snd}(A, N, M) \\
4: \quad \mathcal{O}^{rprt}(A, H, M, K_f, C_2, T_R) \\
\hline
\end{array}
$$

Fig. 6. Attack on r-BIND game.

6   MFC Instantiation

Now that the security properties of a MFC have been defined, we wish to instantiate a practical MFC that fulfills these properties. Our construction is based on two cryptographic primitives, namely a committing AEAD and a message authentication code (MAC) scheme. We show how to combine these primitives with some message counters to obtain a practical bidirectional MFC.

6.1   Construction

Let $\mathsf{nCE} = (\mathsf{init}_{\mathsf{nCE}}, \mathsf{enc}, \mathsf{dec}, \mathsf{vrfy}_{\mathsf{nCE}})$ be a secure nonce-based committing AEAD and $\mathsf{MAC} = (\mathsf{init}_{\mathsf{mac}}, \mathsf{tag}_{\mathsf{mac}}, \mathsf{vrfy}_{\mathsf{mac}})$ be a secure MAC scheme. Our MFC construction is given in Fig. 7. We refer to it as MF. The channel operates as follows:

- $(st_A, st_B, st_R) \leftarrow_\$ \mathsf{init}$: The initialization procedure samples the keys and creates the states. Alice and Bob states are made of their identity, the secret key and the send and receive counters. The router's state is made of the router key.
- $(st, H, C_1, C_2) \leftarrow \mathsf{snd}(st, N, M)$: The sending procedure computes the header H as the identity concatenated with the number of sent messages. Then, the ciphertexts are computed, the sent counter is incremented and the values are returned.
- $(st_R, T_R) \leftarrow \mathsf{tag}(st_R, id_s, H, C_2)$: The router tag is computed as a MAC on the sender/receiver identities, the header and the franking tag, with the router key K_R.
- $(st, M, K_f) \leftarrow \mathsf{rcv}(st, N, H, C_1, C_2)$: The sender identity and the message sequence number are extracted from the header and the ciphertext is decrypted. If this fails or if the number of received messages is not equal to the message sequence number, an error is returned. Otherwise, the number of received messages is incremented and the new state, the plaintext and the opening key are returned.
- $(st_R, b) \leftarrow \mathsf{rprt}(st_R, id_r, H, M, K_f, C_2, T_R)$: The reporter's identity u and the alleged sender's identity v are extracted. Then, the router's tag T_R is verified with the identities v and u along with the header H and the franking tag C_2. Finally, the message is verified to be legit using the franking tag and the opening key K_f. If everything is successful, the procedure returns 1, as a success.

init	$snd(st, N, M)$	$tag(st_R, id_s, H, C_2)$
$K \leftarrow_\$ \mathcal{K}; K_R \leftarrow_\$ \mathcal{K}$	$u\|K\|s_u\|r_u \leftarrow st; H \leftarrow u\|s_u$	$K_R \leftarrow st_R; u \leftarrow id_s$
$s_A \leftarrow 0; s_B \leftarrow 0$	$(C_1, C_2) \leftarrow enc_K(N, H, M);$	if $u \notin \{A, B\}$:
$r_A \leftarrow 0; r_B \leftarrow 0$	$s_u \leftarrow s_u + 1; st \leftarrow u\|K\|s_u\|r_u$	return $(\bot, \bot)$
$st_A \leftarrow A\|K\|s_A\|r_A$	return (st, H, C_1, C_2)	$v \leftarrow \{A, B\} \setminus \{u\}$
$st_B \leftarrow B\|K\|s_B\|r_B$		$T_R \leftarrow tag_{mac}(K_R, u\|v\|H\|C_2)$
$st_R \leftarrow K_R$		return (st_R, T_R)
return (st_A, st_B, st_R)		

$rcv(st, N, H, C_1, C_2)$	$rprt(st_R, id_r, H, M, K_f, C_2, T_R)$
$u\|K\|s_u\|r_u \leftarrow st; v\|s_v \leftarrow H$	$K_R \leftarrow st_R; u \leftarrow id_r$
$(M, K_f) \leftarrow dec_K(N, H, C_1, C_2)$	if $u \notin \{A, B\}$:
if $r_u \neq s_v$ or $(M, K_f) = \bot$:	return $(\bot, 0)$
return $(\bot, \bot)$	$v \leftarrow \{A, B\} \setminus \{u\}$
$r_u \leftarrow r_u + 1$	if $vrfy_{mac}(K_R, v\|u\|H\|C_2, T_R) = 0$:
$st \leftarrow u\|K\|s_u\|r_u$	return $(\bot, 0)$
return (st, M, K_f)	if $vrfy_{nCE}(H, M, K_f, C_2) = 0$:
	return $(\bot, 0)$
	return $(st_R, 1)$

Fig. 7. Instantiation of a real MFC.

6.2 Security Analysis

Confidentiality. The ciphertexts sent by MF are output by the nonce-base committing AEAD nCE. Then, if an adversary can differentiate between real and random ciphertexts output by MF, then it can differentiate between real and random ciphertexts output by nCE. Therefore, if nCE is MO-nRoR secure, then MF is MO-2nRoR secure. We state this formally in Theorem 1, skipping the proof that simply follows from the observation given above.

Theorem 1. (MF confidentiality). *Let* MF *be the* MFC *given in Fig. 7, based on a secure committing AEAD scheme* nCE. *Then, for any adversary* $\mathcal{A}$ *playing the MO-2nRoR game there exists an adversary* $\mathcal{B}$ *such that*

$$\mathsf{Adv}_{\mathsf{MF}}^{mo\text{-}2nror}(\mathcal{A}) \leq \mathsf{Adv}_{\mathsf{nCE}}^{mo\text{-}nror}(\mathcal{B})$$

Integrity. The integrity property of MF follows from the use of send and receive counters and from the integrity of nCE. Formally, the following theorem holds:

Theorem 2. *Let* MF *be the* MFC *given in Fig. 7, based on a committing AEAD scheme* nCE. *Then, for any adversary* $\mathcal{A}$ *playing the MO-2nCTXT game there exists an adversary* $\mathcal{B}$ *such that*

$$\mathsf{Adv}_{\mathsf{MF}}^{mo\text{-}2nctxt}(\mathcal{A}) \leq \mathsf{Adv}_{\mathsf{nCE}}^{mo\text{-}nctxt}(\mathcal{B})$$

Sender Binding. The sender binding property follows directly from the sender binding property of nCE. Formally, we state the following theorem:

Theorem 3. *Let* MF *be the* MFC *given in Fig. 7, based on a committing AEAD scheme* nCE. *Then, for any adversary* $\mathcal{A}$ *playing the S-2BIND game there exists an adversary* $\mathcal{B}$ *such that*

$$\mathsf{Adv}_{\mathsf{MF}}^{s\text{-}2bind}(\mathcal{A}) \leq \mathsf{Adv}_{\mathsf{nCE}}^{s\text{-}bind}(\mathcal{B})$$

Receiver Binding. The receiver binding property of our construction is a consequence of the receiver binding property of the committing AEAD scheme and of the security against forgery of the MAC scheme used. We state the following theorem:

Theorem 4. *Let* MF *be the* MFC *given in Fig. 7, based on a committing AEAD scheme* nCE *and a MAC scheme* MAC. *Then, for any adversary* $\mathcal{A}$ *playing the S-2BIND game there exists an adversary* $\mathcal{B}$ *and an adversary* $\mathcal{C}$ *such that*

$$\mathsf{Adv}_{\mathsf{MF}}^{r\text{-}2bind}(\mathcal{A}) \leq \mathsf{Adv}_{\mathsf{nCE}}^{r\text{-}bind}(\mathcal{B}) + \mathsf{Adv}_{\mathsf{MAC}}^{uf\text{-}cma}(\mathcal{C})$$

Due to space limits the proofs for Theorems 2, 3, 4 are given in the full version.

7   Conclusion

In this paper, we introduced a *message franking channel* (MFC) which apart from message confidentiality/integrity, resistance to message drops, out of order delivery and replay attacks guarantees sender and receiver binding: Namely, the sender cannot send an abusive message, which cannot be reported to a third party and the receiver cannot report a fake message. Even if all of the definitions were presented in the unidirectional and bidirectional case, we focused mainly on bidirectional security definitions. We presented two results on binding properties in the canonic composition of two unidirectional MFC. In particular, we proved that two unidirectional receiver binding MFC are sufficient to create a bidirectional receiver binding MFC. In addition, we stressed that these results do not necessarily hold in general but only in the canonic composition. Finally, we gave an instantiation of a bidirectional MFC given a secure nonce based committing AEAD [GLR17] and a message authentication code.

References

[BDPS13] Alexandra, B., Jean, P.D., Kenneth, G.P., Martijn, S.: On symmetric encryption with distinguishable decryption failures. In: International Workshop on Fast Software Encryption, pp. 367–390. Springer (2013). https://doi.org/10.1007/978-3-662-43933-3_19

[BH17] Colin, B., Britta, H.: Secure channels and termination: The last word on tls. Cryptology ePrint Archive, Report 2017/784 (2017). https://eprint.iacr.org/2017/784

[BHMS15] Colin, B., Britta, H., Stig, F.M., Douglas, S.: From stateless to stateful: Generic authentication and authenticated encryption constructions with application to TLS. Cryptology ePrint Archive, Report 2015/1150 (2015). https://eprint.iacr.org/2015/1150

[BKN02] Mihir, B., Tadayoshi, K., Chanathip, N.: Authenticated encryption in SSH: provably fixing the ssh binary packet protocol. In: Proceedings of the 9th ACM Conference on Computer and Communications Security, pp. 1–11. ACM (2002)

[DGRW18] Dodis, Y., Grubbs, P., Ristenpart, T., Woodage, J.: Fast message franking: from invisible salamanders to encryptment. In: Shacham, H., Boldyreva, A. (eds.) CRYPTO 2018. LNCS, vol. 10991, pp. 155–186. Springer, Cham (2018). https://doi.org/10.1007/978-3-319-96884-1_6

[Fac16] Facebook. Messenger secret conversations (2016). https://fbnewsroomus.files.wordpress.com/2016/07/secret_conversations_whitepaper-1.pdf

[FMB+14] Tilman, F., Christian, M., Christoph, B., Florian, B., Joerg, S., Thorsten, H.: How secure is textsecure? Cryptology ePrint Archive, Report 2014/904 (2014). https://eprint.iacr.org/2014/904

[GLR17] Paul, G., Jiahui, L., Thomas, R.: Message franking via committing authenticated encryption. Cryptology ePrint Archive, Report 2017/664 (2017). https://eprint.iacr.org/2017/664

[GM17] Felix, G., Sogol, M.: A formal treatment of multi-key channels. Cryptology ePrint Archive, Report 2017/501 (2017). https://eprint.iacr.org/2017/501

[KPB03] Tadayoshi, K., Adriana, P., John, B.: Building secure cryptographic transforms, or how to encrypt and mac. Cryptology ePrint Archive, Report 2003/177 (2003). https://eprint.iacr.org/2003/177

[Mar17] Giorgia, A.M.: Real-World Aspects of Secure Channels: Fragmentation, Causality, and Forward Security. PhD thesis, Technische Universität Darmstadt (2017)

[MP17] Giorgia, A.M., Bertram, P.: Security notions for bidirectional channels. Cryptology ePrint Archive, Report 2017/161 (2017). https://eprint.iacr.org/2017/161

[Per18] Trevor, P.: The noise protocol framework (2018). http://noiseprotocol.org/noise.html. Accessed on 03 Sept 2018

[PR18] Bertram, P., Paul, R.: Ratcheted key exchange, revisited. Cryptology ePrint Archive, Report 2018/296 (2018). https://eprint.iacr.org/2018/296

[Vau02] Serge, V.: Security flaws induced by cbc padding – applications to SSL, IPSEC, WTLS... In; Lars, R.K. (ed.) Advances in Cryptology – EUROCRYPT 2002, pp. 534–545. Springer, Berlin, Heidelberg (2002). https://doi.org/10.1007/3-540-46035-7_35

[Wha17] Whatsapp. Whatsapp encryption overview (2017). https://www.whatsapp.com/security/WhatsApp-Security-Whitepaper.pdf

SPARROWHAWK: Memory Safety Flaw Detection via Data-Driven Source Code Annotation

Yunlong Lyu[1(✉)], Wang Gao[2], Siqi Ma[3], Qibin Sun[1], and Juanru Li[2(✉)]

[1] University of Science and Technology of China, Hefei, China
lyl2019@mail.ustc.edu.cn
[2] Shanghai Jiao Tong University, Shanghai, China
{gaowang,jarod}@sjtu.edu.cn
[3] The University of Queensland, Brisbane, Australia
slivia.ma@uq.edu.au

Abstract. Detecting code flaws in programs is a vital aspect of software maintenance and security. Classic code flaw detection techniques rely on program analysis to check whether the code logic violates certain pre-define rules. In many cases, however, program analysis falls short of understanding the semantics of a function (e.g., the functionality of an API), and thus is difficult to judge whether the function and its related behaviors would lead to a security bug. In response, we propose an automated data-driven annotation strategy to enhance the understanding of the semantics of functions during flaw detection. Our designed SPARROWHAWK source code analysis system utilizes a programming language aware text similarity comparison to efficiently annotate the attributes of functions. With the annotation results, SPARROWHAWK makes use of the Clang static analyzer to guide security analyses.

To evaluate the performance of SPARROWHAWK, we tested SPARROWHAWK for memory corruption detection, which relies on the annotation of customized memory allocation/release functions. The experiment results show that by introducing function annotation to the original source code analysis, SPARROWHAWK achieves more effective and efficient flaw detection, and successfully discovers 51 new memory corruption vulnerabilities in popular open source projects such as FFmpeg and kernel of OpenHarmony IoT operating system.

Keywords: Objective function recognition · Programming language understanding · Neural network · Vulnerability discovery

1 Introduction

Due to a variety of cyber attacks targeting on software flaws, pursuing secure programming becomes one of the most essential requirements for all programmers. However, a software is commonly comprised by thousands of lines of code, which is not easy for programmers to be aware of all flaws timely. In the real

© Springer Nature Switzerland AG 2021
Y. Yu and M. Yung (Eds.): Inscrypt 2021, LNCS 13007, pp. 129–148, 2021.
https://doi.org/10.1007/978-3-030-88323-2_7

world, hackers attack softwares every 39 s, averagely 2,244 times per day[1]. The software with security breaches may be exploited by the hackers and finally data breaches will expose sensitive information and vulnerable users to hackers. Hence, it is crucial to identify and fix software flaws in time.

To reduce human efforts on analyzing project source code, automated approaches are propose to explore software flaws. Two types of techniques for source code analysis, program analysis [28,39,48,50] and machine learning [23,24,36], are mainly introduced. For program analysis based approaches, they commonly analyze the entire source code and learn the control/data dependencies by conducting abstract interpretation, pattern matching, symbolic execution to identify. Although such a technique can ensure a significant code coverage, it is inefficient to construct control/data dependencies among functions when a large amount of code with complex dependencies are involved. To solve this issue, some researchers proposed machine learning algorithms to learn patterns of the vulnerable code and then rely on the trained models to discover software flaws. Different from the program analysis techniques that have to be executed every time of flaw detection, model training is a one-time effort; thus it only needs to be trained once and then used for the following detection.

However, the existed machine learning based approaches have a common drawback—a vast dataset of millions of open source functions that are labeled appropriately. Since the programming languages are unlike natural languages, it is impractical to understand how a function behaves by simply regarding each function as a bag of words. Generally two steps are proceeded: 1) extracting inter- and intra-dependencies at a fine-grained level. 2) taking the dependency graph as input for model training. Even though the model training is a one-time effort, it is time consuming to label millions of open source functions manually and study the inter- and intra-dependencies of every function.

To address the limitations of the previous machine learning based approaches, we observe that operations implemented in the function bodies can be inferred via the function prototypes. Hence, we propose an automated function annotating inspired approach for flaw detection. Since function prototypes consist of multiple informal terms (e.g., abbreviation, programming-specified words), we first construct a programming corpus with the posts from StackOverflow [41]. Within the programming corpus, it not only contains the informal terms used in programming languages, but also includes natural languages that are commonly used in project programming. In order to extract meaningful word units (subwords) from programming corpus, we further utilize Byte Pair Encode (BPE) [38] and BPE-dropout [33] algorithms to collect a subword collection with occurrence frequencies. According to the subword collection, function prototypes are segmented with meaningful subwords through a Probabilistic Language Model (PLM). Then we train a Siamese network [3] to embed function prototypes into vectors, and the annotations of unknown function prototypes will be obtained by comparing the vectors with a certain type of function prototypes.

---

[1] https://www.varonis.com/blog/cybersecurity-statistics/.

Based on the function annotating inspired approach, we build a flaw detection tool, SPARROWHAWK. To validate the effectiveness of SPARROWHAWK, we conducted experiments targeting on memory-specified flaws, namely, null pointer dereference and double free. We labeled functions that are collected from real-world open source projects including OpenHarmony [32] IoT operating system and FFmpeg [11] and evaluated the performance of SPARROWHAWK. With the enhancement of function annotation, SPARROWHAWK successfully reported 51 previously unknown memory corruption flaws. We also evaluated whether the performance of SPARROWHAWK was influenced when various input data were provided. We found SPARROWHAWK still annotated functions effectively and efficiently even if only a small amount of training material (3,579 functions) were provided.

Contributions of this Paper:

- We proposed an automated annotation-based analysis system that recognizes the targeted functions accurately without the need of analyzing the corresponding function implementations. While training the annotation model, only a few labeled dataset are required, which is helpful to reduce the involved human efforts.
- We implemented an efficient flaw detection tool, SPARROWHAWK, to explore certain types of flaws based on function annotation. Instead of analyzing the entire source code of a project, SPARROWHAWK pinpoints specific target functions by checking their function names and further identifies whether the target functions are properly invoked. This function annotation based flaw detection is data driven and flexible.
- We evaluated the performance of function annotation by providing various amount of input data and observed that SPARROWHAWK could still identify memory operation functions effectively. Moreover, SPARROWHAWK reported 51 previously unknown flaws from eight open source projects, which indicates that function annotation enhances classical flaw detection.

Availability. We provided the SPARROWHAWK executable, instructions of our experiments, and the tested projects at https://sparrowhawk.code-analysis.org.

2   Motivation

The existing program analysis based approaches are heavyweight while analyzing the program source code. We aim to design a system that can annotate each function accurately without checking the corresponding implementations of the function body. Lack of the semantic information of function prototypes, the following challenges are required to be addressed to implement an efficient and effective annotation based flaw detection.

2.1   Challenges

In order to annotate the targeted functions from source code, the following three aspects are generally processed:

- **Function Name.** By analyzing the semantic meaning of the function name, it is easily to determine what operations might be performed in its body.
- **Function Arguments.** According to the input arguments including argument types and argument names, the attributes of operation objects and operation types can be retrieved.
- **Function Body.** Reference to each function body including the implementation and annotations, the implemented functionalities can be determine.

Although the three aspects are precisely defined for function recognition, several challenges need to be resolved to determine whether a function is relevant to memory operation automatically. Details are demonstrated as below.

Challenge I: Natural Language Gap. Instead of using the completed and formal semantic words, function names are normally comprised by abbreviations, informal terms, programming-specific terms and project-specific terms. As these characters are barely appeared in the natural languages, it is difficult to determine the semantic meaning of a function name automatically.

Challenge II: Function Prototype Correlations. Since there exist strong correlations between each part of function prototype, it makes the entire semantics extraction form function prototype even more challenging. Even though some association patterns exist in function prototype, the workload for modeling the relationships for each type of function by human effort can be unacceptable. Therefore, for extracting the entire semantics from function prototype automatically, we need a method which can capture different relationships exist in different function prototypes.

Challenge III: Complex Logical Structures in Function Implementation. Sometimes, determining the functionality of a function only by its function prototype is not enough, and the complex logical structures in function implementation hinder automated tools to identify its main functionality.

2.2   Insights

Programming Language Aware Word Segmentation. The variety of naming styles and the usage of informal terms make it difficult to segment each function name into meaning units. To address Challenge I, we construct a programming corpus which contains not only the context in natural languages, but also programming-specified terms. Such a programming corpus provides a channel to connect the programming-specified terms with the natural language context.

Additionally, function names commonly consist of multiple terms. We further learn how function names are constructed by utilizing a pair encoding algorithm, which learns the frequent word units appeared in the programming corpus. Based on the frequent word units, we adopt PLM to conduct function segmentation.

Self-Attention Based Function Prototype Embedding. For each word unit of the function prototype, it is inaccurate and inefficient to extract its semantic meaning by designing a rule to match the word unit with natural language context. To address this issue (Challenge II), we propose a self-attention based neural network encoder to generate function prototype embedding.

Semantic-Aware Call Graph. Generally, analyzing the function body and determining its main functionality is a hard work. But fortunately, by analyzing the function implementation manually, we observe that the functionality information about a function can be conveyed by its callee functions. As the semantics of function prototype can be extracted by the self-attention neural network and the nodes in call graph structure are function prototypes, thus we can give the call graph with some semantic information.

Therefore, to solve Challenge III, we propose a method to annotate targeted function in call graph, and utilize these annotations to understand the implementation of function.

3   SPARROWHAWK

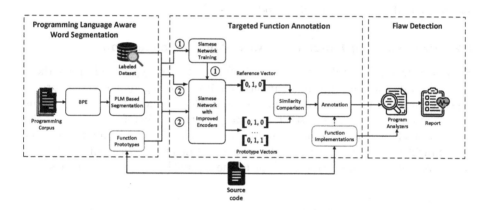

Fig. 1. Workflow of SPARROWHAWK

For most original flaw detection tools, they generally identify the specific flaws by analyzing the entire source code, which is inefficient. To resolve this issue, we propose an annotating inspired detection system, SPARROWHAWK, which automatically learns the functionality of each function through the function prototype and further identifies flaws by analyzing the source code of the target function.

3.1   Overview

The workflow of SPARROWHAWK is shown in Fig. 1, which include three components, *Programming Language Aware Word Segmentation*, *Targeted Function Annotation*, *Flaw Detection*. We introduce each component in detail as below:

Programming Language Aware Word Segmentation. Functions are named variously and each function name might consist of multiple informal terms and programming-specific words, thus it is difficult to learn the functionality of a function via its name precisely (Challenge I). Instead of analyzing the function name as a whole, SPARROWHAWK takes as input a programming corpus to build a segmentation model. It further splits each function name into several units of words (subwords).

Targeted Function Annotation. Taken the subwords as input, SPARROWHAWK trains a function annotation model and generates a *reference vector* from the target functions in labeled dataset. To annotate unknown function prototypes, SPARROWHAWK executes the annotation model to generate function prototype vectors. It then computes cosine similarities between the *reference vector* and the function prototype vectors. If the cosine similarities are higher than a threshold, or their function implementations are matched by annotation rules, SPARROWHAWK labeled them as targeted functions.

Flaw Detection. After recognizing the targeted functions, SPARROWHAWK conducts a source code based program analysis to examine whether the input source code files contain potential code flaws.

3.2   Programming Language Aware Word Segmentation

SPARROWHAWK first takes as input the function prototypes and splits them into subwords for the following semantic analysis. To segment function prototypes accurately, it is essential to build a corpus that includes the informal terms and programming languages used for naming functions. Therefore, we collect the posts of StackOverflow forum containing the context of programming languages from StackExchange Archive Site [40] which contains rich lexical information of programming languages. Figure 2 depicts the detailed process of word segmentation.

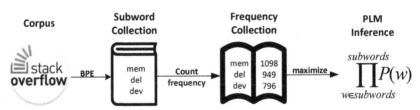

Fig. 2. Programming language aware word segmentation

Programming Corpus Construction. The significant difference between programming language and natural language determines that SPARROWHAWK could not rely on the materials with natural languages to guide the following segmentation. However, directly using source code as corpus is neither suitable since it only contains limited semantic information. Therefore, we created a programming corpus for SPARROWHAWK using the posts of StackOverflow forum, which contains both meaningful natural language materials and programming language texts.

Subwords Collection. With the created corpus, SPARROWHAWK collects meaningful units from it as subwords. Note that a subword may not be a vocabulary, thus SPARROWHAWK utilizes the BPE algorithm to collect subwords from the corpus by merging the most frequent items at character level. BPE initializes the input with a sequence of characters and iteratively replace each occurrence of the most frequent pair with a new item. Figure 3 gives an example of BPE merge operation. In this example, input text contains three words: *memory, mempool,* and *memmap.* The BPE processing first splits each word to separate characters, then merges the most frequent item *mem* and adds the item and its occurrence frequency to the subword collection.

For efficiency consideration, SPARROWHAWK only returns a subword that contains less than 15 characters. To provide a robust subword collecting, SPARROWHAWK additionally adopt BPE-dropout [33] algorithm to add stochastic noise during BPE merge operation.

```
1  Input text:        memory,mempool,memmap
2  Preprocess: m e m o r y, m e m p o o l, m e m m a p
3  m e → me : me m o r y, me m p o o l, me m m a p
4  me m → mem: mem o r y, mem p o o l, mem m a p
5  ...
```

Fig. 3. An example of BPE merging operations

PLM Based Word Segmentation. The collection of subwords (and their occurrence frequencies) is used by SPARROWHAWK to employ a PLM based word segmentation. SPARROWHAWK first splits a function prototype using the item appeared in the subword collection. If there exists only one segmentation result, then this result is accepted. Otherwise, SPARROWHAWK uses Eq. (1) to determine which segmentation result should be chosen. For instance, for a segmentation result with subwords A, B, and C, the occurrence frequency probability of each subword is multiplied to obtain the probability of the segmentation result. Then SPARROWHAWK chooses the one with the highest probability.

$$P(segmentation) = \prod_{w \in subwords}^{subwords} P(w) \tag{1}$$

3.3 Targeted Function Annotation

SPARROWHAWK *identifies* certain types of a function (e.g., crypto function, encoding function) with an automated function annotation. To annotate a function , SPARROWHAWK compares its prototype to a labeled dataset, which contains manually labeled target functions and non-target functions. SPARROWHAWK first trains a Siamese network combined with two identical Transformer encoders [44], who share the same parameters. The training starts from randomly generating either a *target pair* (two prototypes of target functions) or a *non-target pair* (one prototype of target function and the other non-target function) from the labeled dataset. Pairs of prototypes are sent to two encoders to calculate the similarity between two functions.

After the training, SPARROWHAWK uses one of the improved encoder to generate embedding vectors for all target functions in labeled dataset, and derives a *reference vector* by computing the mean vector of these embedding vectors. This reference vector helps SPARROWHAWK efficiently identify a new target function: if the prototype vector of an analyzed function is similar to the reference vector (using cosine similarity, 0.5 as the similarity threshold), it belongs to the type of labeled dataset and is annotated as a target function by SPARROWHAWK.

In the following, we illustrate the annotation process in detail.

Siamese Architecture. Given a set of function prototype pairs (f_i, f_i') with ground truth pairing information $y_i \in \{+1, -1\}$, where $y_i = +1$ indicates that f_i and f_i' are similar, or $y_i = -1$ otherwise. We define the embedding of function prototype f_i as $\overrightarrow{e}_i$, and the output of Siamese architecture for each pair as

$$cosine(f, f') = \frac{\overrightarrow{e}^\top \overrightarrow{e}'}{||\overrightarrow{e}|| \times ||\overrightarrow{e}'||} \tag{2}$$

Then the parameters of function prototype encoder will be trained by minimize the Mean Squared Error Loss Function [31].

Function Prototype Embedding. A function prototype generally consists of four parts: return type, function name, argument types and argument names. And all these four parts changing the semantic of function prototype to different degrees. In order to encode a function prototype to a meaningful embedding vector, SPARROWHAWK adopts the Transformer encoder as the function prototype encoder.

Transformer is a powerful attention model whose attention mechanism can learn the association of words forwardly and backwardly in a sequence. However, the output of the Transformer Encoder is a context matrix, different to Recurrent Neural Network, and it does not provide a sentence embedding directly. To address this issue, we add a pooling layer after the output layer of Transformer Encoder, introduced by the CLS-token pooling strategy in Sentence-BERT [35], to take a function prototype as the input, and output a function prototype embedding.

Similarity Inference. After the Siamese network training is completed, we generate the embedding vectors $e_1, ..., e_n$ for all target function prototypes in the label dataset, and compute their arithmetic mean $\overrightarrow{e}_m$ as *reference vector*. For a given new function prototype f_t and its embedding vector $\overrightarrow{e}_t$, we obtain its similarity score by calculating cosine similarity with *reference vector*.

$$Score(f_t) = cos(\overrightarrow{e}_t, \overrightarrow{e}_m) = \frac{\overrightarrow{e}_t^\top \overrightarrow{e}_m}{||\overrightarrow{e}_t|| \times ||\overrightarrow{e}_m||} \in [-1, 1] \tag{3}$$

Targeted Function Annotation. Based on the similarity scores, SPAR-ROWHAWK provides two ways to annotate targeted functions. The straightforward way only needs function prototype to make inference, whereas another way needs function body and customize the heuristic rules but provides more accurate annotation.

With Only Function Prototype. SPARROWHAWK simply makes inference by comparing the similarity scores of the given functions with the threshold *infer-threshold*. If the similarity scores are greater than the threshold, then SPAR-ROWHAWK annotates the these functions as targeted functions.

With Function Implementation and Heuristic Rules. As our observation that the functionality information of a function can be conveyed through its callee function, and SPARROWHAWK has the ability to attribute a function only by its function prototype, thus SPARROWHAWK is able to achieve a more accurate annotation with well-designed heuristic rules on call graph.

```
1 int hl_ctx_create(struct h1_device *hdv,struct h1_fpriv
2 *hpriv) {
3       ...
4       ctx = kzalloc(sizeof(*ctx), GFP_KERNEL);
5       ...
6       return 0;
7 }
8  static inline void *kzalloc(size_t size, gfp_t flags){
9      return kmalloc(size, flags | __GFP_ZERO);
10}
```

Fig. 4. An example of user-defined memory allocation function

Figure 4 is an intuitive example for the memory allocation function annotation task. As we observe the body of function hl_ctx_create, it is easy to find that its main functionality of memory allocation is implemented by its callee function kzalloc. As seeing the body of function kzalloc, kzalloc also calls a memory allocation function kmalloc to allocate memory. This common phenomenon exists in many projects, that because developers usually hope to wrapper lower level functions to achieve performance improvements and bring convenience by using custom memory allocators and de-allocators,

Therefore, we can take advantage of this property to design some heuristic rules and provide more accurate annotation about memory operation functions. More specifically, we set two different similarity thresholds, *recall-threshold* and *precision-threshold*. The functions whose similarity score lower than *recall-threshold* are filtered out, and the remaining functions are annotated as targeted functions only if they have a callee function whose similarity score is greater than *precision-threshold*.

3.4 Flaw Detection

SPARROWHAWK creates a flaw report for source code projects by comparing the usages of targeted functions with the predefined function misuse rules of program analyzers. First, SPARROWHAWK extracts function prototypes from source code files and generates call graphs. Then, according to the function prototypes and call graphs, SPARROWHAWK annotates the targeted functions and passes them to program analyzers to guide the function misuses detection. Here, SPARROWHAWK implements a program analyzer to detect null pointer dereference and double free vulnerabilities in source code.

Having the targeted functions, SPARROWHAWK performs a flow-sensitive and inter-procedural static analysis based on symbolic execution. SPARROWHAWK maintains two symbolic variables sets, allocation set and deallocation set, to record the status of memory chunks during the symbolic execution. Once symbolic execution reaches a memory operation function, the symbolic variables of allocated or deallocated memory chunks will be added to allocation set or deallocation set, respectively. When the same symbolic variable is added to deallocation set more than once, SPARROWHAWK will report a double free vulnerability. Or the dereference operation related symbolic variable exists in allocation set and its value of constraint solving equals to zero, then SPARROWHAWK will report a null pointer dereference vulnerability.

3.5 Implementation

We relied on several existing tools and modules to fulfil the certain functionalities in SPARROWHAWK. Clang [6] is embedded as part of the function prototype extractor to distinguish function prototypes during compiling. The used programming corpus is an 80 GB raw XML dataset and the size of meaningful text is 18 GB after our normalization. To retrieve subwords, SPARROWHAWK uses the *CharBPETokenizer* module in Tokenizers [43] which relies on the BPE and BPE-Dropout algorithms to segment and regularize words into sequences of subword units. The Siamese network is trained relying on Gensim[13] with the implemented Word2vec [30] for subword embedding training. We further built the Siamese network in TensorFlow [2]. Once the interested function is retrieved, we adopted Clang Static Analyzer [1] to analyze the source code of each software and identify potential vulnerabilities.

4 Real-World Evaluation

We evaluated SPARROWHAWK from three perspective, function segmentation, function annotation, and flaw detection. In specific, the following three research questions (RQs) are answered:

RQ1: Function Prototype Segmentation. The first step of SPARROWHAWK is to segment function prototypes, thus we are curious about how accurate SPARROWHAWK is during function prototype segmentation.

RQ2: Function Annotation. As SPARROWHAWK relies on the customized memory operation functions, how effective and efficient is SPARROWHAWK in recognizing customized memory operation functions, i.e., memory allocation functions and memory deallocation functions.

RQ3: Flaw Detection. As SPARROWHAWK is introduced to detect the specific flaws (i.e., null pointer dereference and double free), how effective is SPARROWHAWK in detecting these flaws?

Since the goal for each research question is different, we collected different sets of dataset to conduct our experiment.

4.1   RQ 1: Function Prototype Segmentation

To evaluate the segmentation accuracy of SPARROWHAWK, we compared its segmentation result with a state-of-the-art tool, NLP-EYE [46], which is proposed with function prototype segmentation.

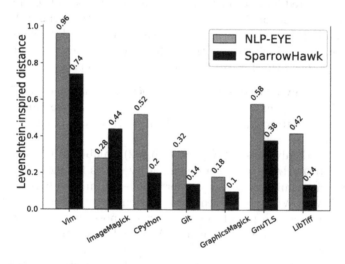

Fig. 5. Function name segmentation results comparison between NLP-EYE and SPARROWHAWK

Setup. We randomly collected 350 function names from seven programs, i.e., Vim [45], ImageMagick [20], GraphicsMagic [17], CPython [7], LibTIFF [27], GnuTLS[15], and Git [14], 50 function names from each program. Given the 350 function names, we built our ground truth by manually segmenting each function name. Then we evaluated the segmentation accuracy of SPARROWHAWK and NLP-EYE relying on Levenshtein-inspired distance [22,37] in which a lower distance represents a higher accuracy.

Results. The segmentation results of SPARROWHAWK and NLP-EYE are demonstrated in Fig. 5. We observed that SPARROWHAWK achieves a lower Levenstein distance, i.e., performs better than NLP-EYE. By manually inspecting the segmentation results, we realized that NLP-EYE fails to distinguish the function names with abbreviation, information terms and programming-specification words. Although a large corpus (i.e., GWTWC [16]) and an adaptive corpus with a number of program annotations is being used for segmentation, the semantic meanings of certain informal terms are unable to be learned precisely. For SPARROWHAWK, we firstly constructed the programming corpus and then applied BPE and BPE-Dropout to collect subwords, which enable SPARROWHAWK to segment function name precisely with the knowledge of programming language.

4.2   RQ 2: Function Annotation

SPARROWHAWK aims to identify the customized memory operation function, i.e., memory allocation functions and memory deallocation functions. We first evaluated the effectiveness of function annotation and then assessed the improvement with designed heuristic rules.

Setup. We collected 35,794 functions from the source code of ten Linux kernel drivers including `bluetooth`, `devfreq`, `mm`, `memory`, `media`, `memstick`, `message`, `mfd`, `misc`, and `mmc`. Obviously, it is time-consuming and infeasible to manually verify all functions to build ground truth, Hence, we conducted a semi-automatic annotating approach which takes the following three steps:

1. We first manually labeled 591 memory allocation functions and 778 memory deallocation functions in 5,342 functions (15% of the entire functions) as the initial labeled dataset, and utilized them to train the Siamese network of SPARROWHAWK.
2. Next, we randomly chose 19% (5,800/30,492) unlabeled functions and executed SPARROWHAWK to generate similarity scores for these functions. For functions with similarity scores smaller than -0.9 (around 90% in our experiment), SPARROWHAWK labeled them as non-target functions but need to inspect their function prototypes to select the possible target functions and exam their implementations manually. And the left functions were verified by both examining their prototypes and implementations manually.
3. With the labeled $5342 + 5,800$ functions, we then repeated step 2 again. This time we sent the rest unlabeled 24,652 functions as inputs of SPARROWHAWK.

Finally, all 35,795 functions were labeled which include 2,008 memory allocation functions and 3,001 memory deallocation functions, and the other functions as non-target functions. Although our semi-automatic annotation may not strictly reflect the ground truth (85% of the functions were annotated relying on a computer-aided labeling), it significantly increases the scale of the labeled dataset by introducing a small portion of inaccuracy. Given the labeled dataset, all the labelled 35,794 functions were used to train the Siamese network again and the evaluation of function annotation of SPARROWHAWK was performed on the trained Siamese network.

Effectiveness. As different developers might have various styles to name functions in their projects, we investigated whether the previous trained Siamese

Table 1. Comparison of memory operation function annotation with and without heuristic rules of SPARROWHAWK

Function type	Allocation function annotation		Deallocation function annotation		Memory operation function annotation	
	Allocation	Others	Deallocation	Others	Target	Others
# of functions	117	2,883	135	2,865	252	5,748
# of correct annotation	73/86	2,853/2,875	123/127	2,786/2,815	196/213	5,639/5,690
# of error annotation	44/31	30/8	12/8	79/50	56/39	109/58
Precision	70.8%/91.4%		60.8%/71.7%		64.2%/78.9%	
Recall	62.9%/73.5%		91.1%/94.0%		77.7%/84.5%	
F1-score	**66.3%/81.5%**		**72.9%/81.4%**		**70.3%/81.4%**	

∗ The **left** side of slash represent the results **with only function prototype**.
∗ The **right** side of slash represent the results **with function implementations and heuristic rules**.

network can annotate memory operation functions in a different project. Therefore, we set up a testing dataset by randomly selecting 3,000 functions from the OpenHarmony [32] IoT operating system and labeled them manually. As a result, 117 memory allocation functions and 135 memory deallocation functions were identified.

The experiment result is listed in Table 1. SPARROWHAWK successfully annotated 196 memory operation functions out of the 252 memory operation functions, with precision of 62.4%, recall of 77.7% and F1-score of 70.3%. Specifically, SPARROWHAWK separately achieved F1-score of 66.3% and 72.9% when it identified memory allocation functions and memory deallocation functions, respectively. The accuracy to annotate memory allocation functions is lower because the implementations of memory allocation functions are more complicated.

By analyzing the function prototypes collected from Linux kernel and Open-Harmony OS, we found that the performance drop is mainly caused by the inconsistent naming style. Consider the word "get" as an example, it indicates to fetch an object from a structure in Linux kernel, whereas developers of OpenHarmony use it to allocate a memory chunk sometimes. Alternatively, the word "release" in Linux kernel functions usually represents deallocating a memory space. However in OpenHarmony OS, it is usually used to release a lock, clean up an object, or set a flag bit to zero.

Improvement with Heuristic Rules. Due to the inconsistent naming style among projects, SPARROWHAWK cannot annotate functions accurately based on function prototypes only. To resolve this issue, we improved SPARROWHAWK by embedding customized heuristic rules which analyzes function prototypes as well as each function bodies. In order to balance the candidate retrieving and precision improvement, we set the *recall-threshold* and *precision-thresholds* as −0.9 and 0.95, respectively.

The results in Table 1 show that the effectiveness of SPARROWHAWK is improved significantly with the help of the customized heuristic rules. In terms of the precision, recall, and F1-score of memory operation, SPARROWHAWK with the customized heuristic rules improves over SPARROWHAWK by 22.9%, 8.7% and 15.7%. Relying on the recall threshold, SPARROWHAWK can label more functions as the potential memory operation functions; thus it achieves a higher recall value. Besides, the precision threshold filtered out the function that did not invoke any memory operation functions in its function body.

Time Cost. We conducted our experiment on a server running 64-bit Ubuntu 18.04 with an AMD 3970X CPU (32 cores) running at 2.2GHz, 256 GB RAM and a GeForce GTX 2080Ti GPU card. We computed the efficiency of SPARROWHAWK by considering the worst case. Hence, we trained the Siamese network by using 90% of labeled functions. Finally, SPARROWHAWK averagely cost 5 h 7 min to train the model for memory allocation function and 7 h 21 min to train the model for memory deallocation functions. The time cost for model training is reasonable because it can be completed within one day and it is a one-time effort.

4.3   RQ 3: Flaw Detection

According to the annotated memory operation functions, SPARROWHAWK analyzes the corresponding functions to check whether there is any memory-related flaws, i.e., null pointer dereference and double free.

Table 2. Details about collected projects

	Number of functions	Number of allocators	Number of de-allocator
OpenHarmony	17,893	539	930
Cpython	11,347	436	228
FFmpeg	19,905	227	469
Gnutls	4,478	27	137
Vim	6,090	113	237
BusyBox	4,134	82	134
Curl	2,877	120	327
Gravity	916	60	62

*All collected in the master branch in May 2021.

Setup. We executed SPARROWHAWK on eight open source projects, i.e., OpenHarmony [32], Cpython [7], FFmpeg [11], Gnutls [15], Vim [45], BusyBox [5], Curl [8], Gravity [18]. SPARROWHAWK first pinpointed the customized memory operation functions. Table 2 lists the result of the annotated memory operation functions in each project. Reference to the customized memory operation functions, SPARROWHAWK conducted code analysis to detect flaws.

Table 3. Detection results

	Null pointer dereference			Double free		
	Reported	Identified	Confirmed	Reported	Identified	Confirmed
OpenHarmony	41	16	**12**	128	0	0
Cpython	16	5	**5**	0	0	0
FFmpeg	37	9	**5**	43	0	0
Gnutls	4	2	**2**	10	3	**1**
Vim	41	0	0	46	4	**1**
BusyBox	114	1	**1**	15	1	**1**
Curl	0	0	0	6	1	0
Gravity	87	9	–	8	0	0
Total	340	42	**25**	256	9	**3**

Results. The detection result is presented in Table 3. In total, SPARROWHAWK reported 596 vulnerabilities from the eight projects including 340 null pointer dereference and 256 double free. By manually inspected the results, we identified 42 null pointer dereference vulnerabilities and 9 double free vulnerabilities.

To further verify the identification correctness, we contacted the project developers and reported the manual-confirmed vulnerabilities. Finally, 28 vulnerabilities (i.e., 25 null pointer dereference and 3 double free) are confirmed by SPARROWHAWK.

Case Study. We demonstrated a representative example to discuss how SPARROWHAWK detects flaws. The source code snippet of Vim is shown in Fig. 6 which contains a double free flaw.

Given the File1, SPARROWHAWK first extracted all function prototypes and corresponding function implementations and conducted function annotation to identify memory operation functions. As a result, it identified a memory allocation functions (i.e., mem_realloc (line 1)) and two memory deallocation functions (i.e., mem_realloc (line 1) and vim_free (line 8)).

Having the identified memory operation functions, SPARROWHAWK executed Clang Static Analyzer to analyze File2 and identified whether the identified memory operation functions were being properly invoked. Since there exists a feasible execution path from vim_realloc (line 20) to vim_free (line 24) and the two deallocation function freed the same memory chunk, where the macro function vim_realloc is expanded to function mem_realloc in File3, SPARROWHAWK reports a double free vulnerability.

As we observed that if the argument bufno is can be controlled, function vim_realloc will free the variable buf_list and return NULL, thus the same memory address will be freed twice by function vim_free. According to the feedback of Vim developers, the argument bufno can be controlled by a netbeans command, and the vulnerability is patched with a patch number 8.2.1843.

File1:Vim/src/misc2.c

```
1   void *mem_realloc(void *ptr, size_t size){
2       void *p;
3       mem_pre_free(&ptr);
4       p = realloc(ptr, size);
5       mem_post_alloc(&p, size);
6       return p;
7   }
8   void vim_free(void *x){
9       ...
10      free(x);
11      ...
12  }
```

File2:Vim/src/netbeans.c

```
13  static nbbuf_T *nb_get_buf(int bufno){
14      buf_list_size = 100;
15      ...
16      if (bufno >= buf_list_size){
17          nbbuf_T *t_buf_list = buf_list;
18          incr = bufno - buf_list_size + 90;
19          buf_list_size += incr;
20          buf_list = vim_realloc(buf_list,
21              buf_list_size * sizeof(nbbuf_T));
22          if (buf_list == NULL)
23            {
24              vim_free(t_buf_list);
25              buf_list_size = 0;
26              return NULL;
27            }
28      }
29  }
```

File3:Vim/src/vim.h

```
30  # define vim_realloc(ptr, size)
31  mem_realloc((ptr), (size))
```

Fig. 6. A double free vulnerability in Vim

5   Related Work

We classify the related prior work into two categories: deep learning based flaw detection and program analysis based flaw detection.

5.1   Deep Learning Based Flaw Detection

Recently, deep learning based approaches are being widely used to detect code flaw automatically. These approaches aim to learn syntactic and semantic representations [9,25,26,36] or learn graph structure representations [10,51] from source code, and then utilize these representations to detect code flaws.

To learn syntactic and semantic representations, Khanh Dam *et al.* [9] parses methods of Java source files into sequences of code tokens and uses Long Short-Term Memory networks [19] to generate syntactic and semantics features of a file. Russell *et al.* [36] creates a custom C/C++ lexer to tokenize source code and adopts Convolutional Neural Network (CNN) to learn function-level representations. In order to provide more fine-grained detection, VulDeePecker [26] and SySeVR [25] extract code slices based on data dependency and convert them to vector of symbolic representation, and then apply deep learn models to predict vulnerabilities.

As the aforementioned approaches have limitations on capturing logic and structure from source code, some works have attempted to learn representations from graph structures. Based on Code Property Graph (CPG) [47], VulSniper [10] utilize attention mechanism to encode CPG to a feature tensor and Devign [51] uses Graph Neural Network [21] to learn node representations.

However, these deep learning based approaches need the heavy efforts of gathering and labeling a large number flaw dataset, and can not give the precise reasons about how flaws are caused.

5.2   Program Analysis Based Flaw Detection

Program analysis based methods find flaws in source code by detecting unexpected behaviors. K-Miner [12] utilizes data-flow analysis to uncover memory corruption vulnerabilities in Linux kernel. It requires human effort to mark memory operation functions and performs a source-sink analysis on marked memory operation functions. Dr.checker [29] focus on control flow and has found diverse bugs in Linux kernel drivers by using a soundy pointer and taint analysis based on abstract representation. Moreover, SVF [42] is a static analysis framework which applies sparse value-flow analysis to detect flaws. Developers can use SVF to write their own checkers and detect flaws in source code.

To reduce the false positive of static analysis, symbolic execution based approaches utilize constraint solving to reason feasible paths. As the number of feasible paths in programs grows exponentially with an increase in program size, whole-program symbolic execution could encounter the problem of path explosion. Thus, under-constrained methods like UCKLEE [34], sys [4] and UBI-TECT [49] are proposed to overcome this problem by executing individual functions instead of whole programs.

6   Conclusion

In this paper, we present SPARROWHAWK, an automated annotation-based source code flaw detection system. SPARROWHAWK includes a function prototype segmentation tool with the state-of-the-art accuracy, a targeted function annotation model requires only a few labeled dataset and an efficient source code flaw detection tool for detecting null pointer dereference and double free vulnerabilities. We demonstrated that SPARROWHAWK successfully identified 51 unknown flaws with the help of annotated memory operation functions. Furthermore, SPARROWHAWK is not limited to detect memory corruptions. Developers can easily customize SPARROWHAWK to annotate other types of function, and thus detect new types of flaws efficiently.

Acknowledgment. We would like to thank the anonymous reviewers for their helpful comments. This work was partially supported by the National Natural Science Foundation of China (U19B2023), the National Key Research and Development Program of China (Grant No.2020AAA0107800), and the National Natural Science Foundation of China (Grant No.62002222).

References

1. Clang Static Analyzer. http://clang-analyzer.llvm.org
2. Abadi, M., et al.: Tensorflow: A system for large-scale machine learning. In: Proceedings of the 12th USENIX Conference on Operating Systems Design and Implementation, pp. 265–283. USENIX Association (2016)
3. Bromley, J., Guyon, I., LeCun, Y., Säckinger, E., Shah, R.: Signature verification using a "siamese" time delay neural network. In: Proceedings of the 6th International Conference on Neural Information Processing Systems, pp. 737–744. Morgan Kaufmann Publishers Inc (1993)
4. brown, F., Deian, S., Dawson, E.: Sys: A static/symbolic tool for finding good bugs in good (browser) code. In: 29th USENIX Security Symposium (USENIX Security 20), pp. 199–216. USENIX Association (2020)
5. Busybox. https://github.com/mirror/busybox
6. Clang. https://clang.llvm.org/
7. Cpython. https://github.com/python/cpython
8. Curl. https://github.com/curl/curl
9. Dam, H.K., Tran, T., Pham, T., Ng, S.W., Grundy, J., Ghose, A.: Automatic feature learning for vulnerability prediction. arXiv:1708.02368 (2017)
10. Duan, X., et al.: Vulsniper: Focus your attention to shoot fine-grained vulnerabilities. In: Proceedings of the Twenty-Eighth International Joint Conference on Artificial Intelligence, IJCAI-19, pp. 4665–4671. International Joint Conferences on Artificial Intelligence Organization (2019)
11. Ffmpeg. https://github.com/FFmpeg/FFmpeg
12. Gens, D., Schmitt, S., Davi, L., Sadeghi, A.R.: K-miner: Uncovering memory corruption in linux. (2018)
13. Gensim. https://radimrehurek.com/gensim/
14. Git. https://github.com/git/git
15. Gnutls. https://gitlab.com/gnutls/gnutls/

16. Google web trillion word corpus. http://googleresearch.blogspot.com/2006/08/all-our-n-gram-are-belong-to-you.html
17. Graphicsmagick. http://www.graphicsmagick.org/
18. Gravity. https://github.com/marcobambini/gravity
19. Hochreiter, S., Schmidhuber, J.: Long short-term memory. Neural Comput. **9**, 1735–1780 (1997)
20. Imagemagick. https://github.com/ImageMagick/ImageMagick
21. Li, Y., Tarlow, D., Brockschmidt, M., Zemel, R.: Gated graph sequence neural networks. arXiv:1511.05493 (2017)
22. Li, Y., Liu, B.: A normalized levenshtein distance metric. IEEE Trans. Pattern Anal. Mach. Intell. **29**, 1091–1095 (2007)
23. Li, Z., Zou, D., Tang, J., Zhang, Z., Sun, M., Jin, H.: A comparative study of deep learning-based vulnerability detection system. IEEE Access **7**, 103184–103197 (2019)
24. Li, Z., Zou, D., Xu, S., Jin, H., Qi, H., Hu, J.: Vulpecker: an automated vulnerability detection system based on code similarity analysis. In: Proceedings of the 32nd Annual Conference on Computer Security Applications, pp. 201–213 (2016)
25. Li, Z., Zou, D., Xu, S., Jin, H., Zhu, Y., Chen, Z.: Sysevr: A framework for using deep learning to detect software vulnerabilities. arXiv:1807.06756 (2018)
26. Li, Z., et al.: Vuldeepecker: A deep learning-based system for vulnerability detection (2018)
27. Libtiff. http://www.libtiff.org/
28. Ma, S., Thung, F., Lo, D., Sun, C., Deng, R.H.: Vurle: automatic vulnerability detection and repair by learning from examples. In: European Symposium on Research in Computer Security. pp. 229–246. Springer (2017). https://doi.org/10.1007/978-3-319-66399-9_13
29. Machiry, A., Spensky, C., Corina, J., Stephens, N., Kruegel, C., Vigna, G.: DR. CHECKER: A soundy analysis for linux kernel drivers. In: 26th USENIX Security Symposium (USENIX Security 17), pp. 1007–1024. USENIX Association (2017)
30. Mikolov, T., Sutskever, I., Chen, K., Corrado, G.S., Dean, J.: Distributed representations of words and phrases and their compositionality. Adv. Neural Inf. Process. Syst. **26**, 3111–3119 (2013)
31. Mean squared error. https://en.wikipedia.org/wiki/Mean_squared_error
32. Openharmony. https://openharmony.gitee.com/openharmony
33. Provilkov, I., Emelianenko, D., Voita, E.: BPE-dropout: Simple and effective subword regularization. In: Proceedings of the 58th Annual Meeting of the Association for Computational Linguistics, pp. 1882–1892. Association for Computational Linguistics (2020)
34. Ramos, D.A., Engler, D.: Under-constrained symbolic execution: Correctness checking for real code. In: 24th USENIX Security Symposium (USENIX Security 15), pp. 49–64. USENIX Association (2015)
35. Reimers, N., Gurevych, I.: Sentence-bert: sentence embeddings using siamese bert-networks. In: Proceedings of the 2019 Conference on Empirical Methods in Natural Language Processing and the 9th International Joint Conference on Natural Language Processing (EMNLP-IJCNLP), pp. 3982–3992. Association for Computational Linguistics (2019)
36. Russell, R., et al.: Automated vulnerability detection in source code using deep representation learning. In: 2018 17th IEEE International Conference on Machine Learning and Applications (ICMLA), pp. 757–762. IEEE (2018)

37. Schwartz, E.J., Cohen, C.F., Duggan, M., Gennari, J., Havrilla, J.S., Hines, C.: Using logic programming to recover C++ classes and methods from compiled executables. In: Proceedings of the 2018 ACM SIGSAC Conference on Computer and Communications Security (CCS) (2018)

38. Sennrich, R., Haddow, B., Birch, A.: Neural machine translation of rare words with subword units. In: Proceedings of the 54th Annual Meeting of the Association for Computational Linguistics (Volume 1: Long Papers), pp. 1715–1725. Association for Computational Linguistics (2016)

39. Shen, Z., Chen, S.: A survey of automatic software vulnerability detection, program repair, and defect prediction techniques. Security and Communication Networks 2020 (2020)

40. Stackexchange archive site. https://archive.org/download/stackexchange/stackoverflow.com-Posts.7z

41. Stackoverflow forum. https://stackoverflow.com/

42. Sui, Y., Xue, J.: Svf: Interprocedural static value-flow analysis in LLVM. In: Proceedings of the 25th International Conference on Compiler Construction, pp. 265–266. Association for Computing Machinery (2016)

43. Tokenizers. https://github.com/huggingface/tokenizers

44. Vaswani, A., et al.: Attention is all you need. In: Advances in Neural Information Processing Systems 30, pp. 5998–6008 (2017)

45. Vim. https://github.com/vim/vim

46. Wang, J., et al.: Nlp-eye: Detecting memory corruptions via semantic-aware memory operation function identification. In: 22nd International Symposium on Research in Attacks, Intrusions and Defenses (RAID 2019), pp. 309–321. USENIX Association (2019)

47. Yamaguchi, F., Golde, N., Arp, D., Rieck, K.: Modeling and discovering vulnerabilities with code property graphs. In: 2014 IEEE Symposium on Security and Privacy, pp. 590–604. IEEE (2014)

48. Yan, H., Sui, Y., Chen, S., Xue, J.: Spatio-temporal context reduction: a pointer-analysis-based static approach for detecting use-after-free vulnerabilities. In: 2018 IEEE/ACM 40th International Conference on Software Engineering (ICSE), pp. 327–337. IEEE (2018)

49. Zhai, Y., yzhai: Ubitect: a precise and scalable method to detect use-before-initialization bugs in linux kernel. In: 28th ACM Joint European Software Engineering Conference and Symposium on the Foundations of Software Engineering (ESEC/FSE 2020). ACM (2020)

50. Zhang, Y., Ma, S., Li, J., Li, K., Nepal, S., Gu, D.: Smartshield: automatic smart contract protection made easy. In: 2020 IEEE 27th International Conference on Software Analysis, Evolution and Reengineering (SANER), pp. 23–34. IEEE (2020)

51. Zhou, Y., Liu, S., Siow, J., Du, X., Liu, Y.: Devign: effective vulnerability identification by learning comprehensive program semantics via graph neural networks. Adv. Neural Inf. Process. Syst. 32, 10197–10207 (2019)

Symmetric Cryptanalysis

A New Approach for Finding Low-Weight Polynomial Multiples

Laila El Aimani[✉]

University of Cadi Ayyad - ENSA Safi, Route Sidi Bouzid BP 63, 46000 Safi, Morocco

Abstract. We consider the problem of finding low-weight multiples of polynomials over binary fields, which arises in stream cipher cryptanalysis or in finite field arithmetic. We first devise memory-efficient algorithms based on the recent advances in techniques for solving the knapsack problem. Then, we tune our algorithms using the celebrated Parallel Collision Search (PCS) method to decrease the time cost at the expense of a slight increase in space. Both our memory-efficient and time-memory trade-off algorithms improve substantially the state-of-the-art. The gain is for instance remarkable for large weights; a situation which occurs when the available keystream is small, e.g. the Bluetooth keystream.

Keywords: Low-weight polynomial multiple · Stream cipher cryptanalysis · Knapsack · Collision-finding algorithm · Time-memory trade-off

1 Introduction

We consider the following problem:

Definition 1 (The Low-Weight Polynomial Multiple (LWPM) problem). *Given a binary polynomial $P \in \mathbb{F}_2[X]$ of degree d and a bound n, find a multiple of P with degree less than n and with the least possible weight ω, where the weight of a multiple is the number of its nonzero coefficients.*

The LWPM arises in stream cipher cryptanalysis, and in efficient finite field arithmetic.

Fast correlation attacks [19,23] against LFSR-based (Linear Feedback Shift Register) stream ciphers first precompute a low-weight multiple of the constituent LFSR connection polynomial. In fact, low-weight polynomial multiples are required to keep the bias, of the linear approximation in a correlation attack, as high as possible so as to reduce the cost of key-recovery or distinguishing attacks.

Low-weight polynomial multiples find also application in finite field arithmetic. Actually, von zur Gathen and Nöker [13] found that $\mathbb{F}_{2^d} = \mathbb{F}_2[x]/(g)$, where g is a low-weight irreducible polynomial of degree d, is the most efficient representation of finite fields. However, such polynomials do not always exist.

© Springer Nature Switzerland AG 2021
Y. Yu and M. Yung (Eds.): Inscrypt 2021, LNCS 13007, pp. 151–170, 2021.
https://doi.org/10.1007/978-3-030-88323-2_8

Brent and Zimmerman [3] proposed an interesting solution: take an irreducible polynomial $f \in \mathbb{F}_2[X]$ of degree d but possibly large weight, a multiple g of f with small weight, and work in the ring $\mathbb{F}_2[X]/(g)$ most of the time, going back to the field $\mathbb{F}_{2^d}$ only when necessary.

1.1   Related Work

There have been several approaches for computing low-weight multiples of polynomials. Most methods first estimate the minimal possible weight ω of multiples, of the given polynomial P, with degree at most n and with nonzero constant term, then look for multiples of weight at most ω. To estimate the minimal weight, one solves for ω_e the following inequality

$$\binom{n}{\omega_e - 1} \geq 2^d \tag{1}$$

where d is the degree of P; the minimal weight ω is the smallest solution. In fact, if multiples are uniformly distributed, then one expects the inequality to hold. It is worth noting that the number of such multiples can be approximated by $\mathcal{N}_M = 2^{-d}\binom{n}{\omega-1}$.

Given a polynomial $P \in \mathbb{F}_2[X]$ of degree d and a bound n, we summarize below the strategies used to find a multiple of P of degree at most n and with the least possible weight ω. We describe theitemi time or space complexity using the Big-O notation, which denotes the worst case complexity of the algorithms. Also, we use the approximation $\binom{n}{\omega} \approx O(n^\omega)$.

Standard Techniques. The standard Time/Memory Trade-Off (TMTO) method runs in $O(n^{\lceil \frac{\omega-1}{2} \rceil})$ and uses $O(n^{\lfloor \frac{\omega-1}{2} \rfloor})$ of memory. Chose et al. [7] cut down the memory utilization to $O(n^{\lfloor \frac{\omega-1}{4} \rfloor})$ using a *match-and-sort* approach. Canteaut and Trabbia [6] introduced a memory-efficient method for solving the LWPM problem that runs in $O(n^{\omega-1})$ and requires only linear memory. When the degree of the multiple gets very large and there are many low-weight multiples, but it is sufficient to find only one, *Wagner's generalized birthday paradox* [25] becomes more efficient. For instance, if $n \geq 2^{d/(1+\log_2(\omega-1))}$, then this method finds a weight-ω multiple of P of degree at most n in $O((\omega-1)n)$ and uses $O(n)$ memory.

Discrete-Log-Based Techniques. They were introduced in [21], then improved and generalized in [8,22]. They work with discrete logarithms in the multiplicative group of $\mathbb{F}_{2^d}$ instead of the direct representation of the polynomials. [8] use a time/memory trade-off to solve the problem in time $O(n^{\lceil \frac{\omega-2}{2} \rceil})$ and memory $O(n^{\lfloor \frac{\omega-2}{2} \rfloor})$. [22] provide a memory-efficient algorithm that runs in approximately $O(\frac{2^d}{n})$. The methods assume however a constant cost of the discrete logarithm computations, using precomputed tables that do not require excessive storage. This is not the case if $2^d - 1$ is not smooth. Also, the methods assume some conditions on the input polynomial: primitive in case of [8] or product of powers of irreducible polynomials with coprime orders in case of [22].

Syndrome Decoding. This technique reduces LWPM to finding a low-weight codeword in a linear code; a popular problem for which there exist known algorithms to solve it, e.g. the so-called information-set decoding algorithms [2,5,15,17,18,24]. These algorithms introduce many parameters to optimize the running time and the memory consumption according to the problem instance, however, we can approximate the running time by $O(\text{Poly}(n) \cdot (\frac{n}{d})^{\omega})$, and the memory complexity by $O(d^{\omega})$.

Lattice-Based Techniques. This technique, introduced in [10], reduces the LWPM problem to finding short vectors in an n-dimensional lattice. The method uses the LLL reduction [14] to solve the problem in time $O(n^6)$ and space $O(n \cdot d)$. Unfortunately, this technique gives inaccurate results, i.e. fails to find a multiple with the least possible weight, as soon as the bound n exceeds few hundreds.

1.2 Our Approach

We view the LWPM problem as a special instance of the following subset sum problem:

Definition 2 (Group Subset Sum Problem). *Let $(G, +)$ be an abelian group. Given $a_0, a_1, \ldots, a_n \in G$ together with $\omega, 0 < \omega \leq \frac{n}{2}$ such that there exists some solution $\mathbf{z} = (z_1, \ldots, z_n) \in \{0, 1\}^n$ satisfying*

$$\sum_{i=1}^{n} z_i a_i = a_0 \quad \text{with} \quad \text{weight}(z) = \omega$$

The goal is to recover $\mathbf{z}$ (or some other weight-ω solution $\mathbf{z}$).

This definition generalizes that in [11] as it does not impose the group order to be of bitsize n. It captures then the LWPM problem as follows. Let P be a degree-d polynomial in $\mathbb{F}_2[X]$. Consider further the group $(\mathbb{F}_2^d, +)$ of d-dimensional vectors over $\mathbb{F}_2$, where the group law is the bitwise addition over $\mathbb{F}_2$. A weight-ω multiple $1 + \sum_{i=1}^{n} z_i X^i$ of P, with nonzero constant term and degree at most n satisfies:

$$\sum_{i=1}^{n} z_i a_i = a_0 \quad \text{with } a_i = X^i \bmod P, \ 0 \leq i \leq n$$

Note that the condition on the weight ($\omega \leq \frac{n}{2}$) is not restrictive. Actually, the searched weight ω is obviously smaller than the weight of P, which is often smaller than $\frac{d}{2}$, and thus smaller than $\frac{n}{2}$. Also, for convenience purposes, we consider throughout the document the relative weight $\omega_n = \omega/n$.

The (group) subset sum problem is one of the most popular and ubiquitous problems in cryptography. It has undergone an extensive analysis with a focus on polynomial-memory algorithms to solve it. In fact, it is known that random-access memory is usually more expensive than time. Most algorithms for solving the subset sum problem [1,11] try to find as many representations as possible of the solution; in fact, the more representations there exist the faster the solution can be found. For example, the folklore algorithm, described in [12], represents the solution $z = x \parallel y$ as a concatenation of two $\frac{n}{2}$-dimensional vectors x and y with weight(x) = weight(y) = $\frac{\omega}{2}$. In the same spirit, [1] split the solution z into two n-dimensional vectors x and y , with weight(x) = weight(y) = $\frac{\omega}{2}$, that add up to z. Recently, [11] further increase the number of representations by splitting z into a sum *over* $\mathbb{Z}$, of two integers of smaller weight, and exploiting the carry propagation.

Contributions. We view the solution z to LWPM as a collision (x, y) of some random function f mapping from a set $\mathcal{T}$ to itself (in order to use known cycle-finding algorithms to compute collisions). The set $\mathcal{T}$ is determined by how z splits into (x, y). Also, $\mathcal{T}$ ought to allow for many "representations" (x, y) of the solution z, so as to reduce the number of function calls needed before finding a collision. More precisely, we make the following contributions.

First, we present two memory-efficient algorithms for LWPM that improve the state-of-the-art in polynomial-memory algorithms for LWPM. The idea behind the algorithms consists in splitting the solution z into two n-dimensional vectors x and y that add up to z over $\mathbb{F}_2$. The weight of both x and y is some function of ω to be determined.

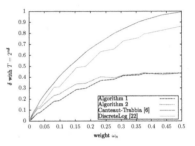

More precisely, Algorithm 1 assumes and puts in place a Bernoulli distribution on the representation of z, then determines the optimal weight $\phi(\omega)$ to be used for x and y. As a result, we significantly improve the running time offered by the state-of-the-art methods, i.e. the standard and the discrete-log methods

Fig. 1. Comparison between the memory-efficient techniques and our algorithms

(see Fig. 1; the x-axis represents the relative weight $\omega_n = \omega/n$, and the y-axis represents the relative exponent $\log(T)/n$ of the time cost T).

Since Algorithm 1 uses a pseudo-random number generator to establish the desired Bernoulli distribution, it incurs a slight overhead in the computations. Therefore, we reinforce our contribution with Algorithm 2 which gets rid of the Bernoulli distribution; the result still substantively outperforms the state-of-the-art (see Fig. 1).

We show the practicality of our technique with an implementation of the algorithms that confirm our theoretical estimates.

Second, we tune our algorithms via the Parallel Collision Search (PCS) technique [20] to decrease the running time at the expense of memory. Again, we achieve a nice time/memory trade-off compared to the state-of-the-art (see Fig. 2; the x-axis represents the relative weight $\omega_n = \omega/n$, whereas the y-axis represents the relative exponent $\log(T)/n$ (resp. $\log(M)/n$) of the time (resp. memory) cost T (resp. M)).

The rest of the paper is organized as follows. Section 2 recalls the necessary background and establishes the notation that will be used throughout the

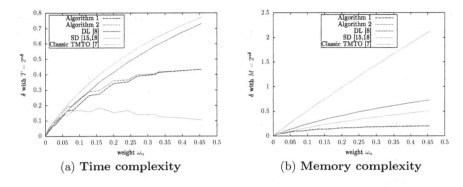

(a) **Time complexity**   (b) **Memory complexity**

Fig. 2. Time/Memory costs of the state-of-the-art and our trade-off algorithms

document. Sections 3 and 4 respectively describe, analyze, and experimentally validate our algorithms. Section 5 compares the performance of our algorithms with the state-of-the-art. Finally, the time/memory trade-off tuning of the proposed algorithms is given in Sect. 6.

2   Theoretical Background

2.1   Notations and Conventions

Let $a, b \in \mathbb{N}$ with $a < b$. We conveniently write $[a, b] := \{a, a + 1 \ldots, b\}$. For a vector $z = (z_1, \ldots, z_n) \in \{0, 1\}^n$, we denote by $\text{weight}(z) := |\{i \in [1, n] \colon z_i = 1\}|$. $\mathbb{Z}_N$ denotes the ring of integers modulo N. $\mathbb{F}_2$ denotes the field of two elements where the additive identity and the multiplicative identity are denoted 0 and 1, as usual. $\mathbb{F}_2[X]$ refers to the ring of polynomials with coefficients in $\mathbb{F}_2$. $\mathbb{R}^+$ denotes the set of positive real numbers.

Let $P \in \mathbb{F}_2[X]$. $\deg(P)$ and $\text{weight}(P)$ refer to the degree and weight of P respectively; the weight of a polynomial in $\mathbb{F}_2[X]$ corresponds to the number of its non-zero coefficients. In the text, we identify polynomials in $\mathbb{F}_2[X]$ with their coefficient vectors. For instance, the sum of two polynomials in $\mathbb{F}_2[X]$ is the sum over $\mathbb{F}_2$ of their coefficient vectors termwise.

Suppose $\deg(P) = d$. $\mathbb{F}_2[X]/P$ denotes the ring of polynomials modulo P; addition and multiplication are performed modulo P. Finally, $(\mathbb{F}_2^d, +)$ refers to the group of d-dimensional vectors over $\mathbb{F}_2$, where the group law $+$ is the bitwise addition and the identity is referred to as $0_{\mathbb{F}_2^d}$.

The Big-O, Θ, and $\tilde{\Theta}$ Notations. The Big-O notation represents the upper bound of the running time of an algorithm; it gives then the worst case complexity of an algorithm.

$$O(g) = \left\{ f \colon \exists \, c, x_0 \in \mathbb{R}^+ \colon 0 \leq f(x) \leq cg(x) \; \forall x \geq x_0 \right\}$$

The Θ notation represents the upper and the lower bound of the running time of an algorithm. It is useful when studying the average case complexity of algorithms.

$$\Theta(g) = \left\{ f : \exists\, c_1, c_2, x_0 \in \mathbb{R}^+ : 0 \le c_1 g(x) \le f(x) \le c_2 g(x)\ \forall x \ge x_0 \right\}$$

The $\tilde{\Theta}$ notation suppresses the polynomial factors in the input. For example $\tilde{\Theta}(2^n)$ suppresses the polynomial factors in n.

Binomial Coefficient. The binomial coefficient $\binom{n}{k}$ refers to the number of distinct choices of k elements within a set of n elements. We have: $\binom{n}{k} = \frac{n!}{k! \cdot (n-k)!}$. Often, we need to obtain asymptotic approximations for binomials of the form $\binom{n}{\alpha\, n}$ or $\binom{n}{\lfloor \alpha\, n \rfloor}$ for values $\alpha \in\,]0, 1[$. This is easily achieved using Stirling's formula: $n! = (1 + o(1))\sqrt{2\pi n}\left(\frac{n}{e}\right)^n$. Thus $\binom{n}{\alpha n} \approx \frac{1}{\sqrt{2\pi\, n\alpha(1-\alpha)}} \cdot 2^{nH(\alpha)}$, where H is the binary entropy function defined as $H(x) := -x \log_2(x) - (1-x) \log_2(1-x)$; $\log_2$ is the logarithm in base 2. We can then write

$$\binom{n}{\alpha n} = \Theta\left(n^{-1/2} 2^{nH(\alpha)}\right) \quad \text{or} \quad \binom{n}{\alpha n} = \tilde{\Theta}\left(2^{nH(\alpha)}\right)$$

Probability Laws. For a finite set E, $e \in_R E$ refers to drawing uniformly at random an element e from E. The PMF of a random variable denotes its probability mass function.

Let X be a random variable, $p \in [0, 1]$, and $n \in \mathbb{N}$. $X \sim \text{Bernoulli}(p)$ signifies that X takes the value 1 with probability p and the value 0 with probability $1 - p$.

$X := (X_1, \ldots, X_n) \sim \text{Bernoulli}(p, n)$ means that the X_i are independent and identically distributed with $X_i \sim \text{Bernoulli}(p)$, for $i \in [1, n]$. $X \sim \text{Binomial}(p, n)$ means that X follows the Binomial distribution with PMF: $\Pr[X = k] = \binom{n}{k} p^k (1 - p)^{n-k}$, $k \in [0, n]$. Finally, if $X \sim \text{Bernoulli}(p, n)$, then the random variable Y corresponding to the number of successes of X follows the binomial distribution, i.e. $Y := \text{weight}(X) \sim \text{Binomial}(p, n)$.

2.2   Random Functions

Birthday Paradox. Let E be a finite set of n elements. If elements are sampled uniformly at random from E, then the expected number of samples to be taken before some element is sampled twice is less than $\sqrt{\pi n / 2} = \Theta(\sqrt{n})$. The element that is sampled twice is called a **collision**. See [12] for the details.

Expected Number of Collisions. Let $f : E \to F$ be a random function. We are interested in the expected number of collisions of f, i.e. the number of distinct pairs $\{x, y\}$ with $f(x) = f(y)$. For instance, if k elements have the same value, this counts as $\binom{k}{2}$ collisions.

Fact 1. *Let $f : E \to F$ be a random function, with $|E| = n$ and $|F| = m$. The expected number of f collisions is $\Theta\left(\frac{n^2}{2m}\right)$.*

Proof. For each pair $\{x, y\}$ ($x \neq y$), we define the following indicator random variable:

$$I_{\{x,y\}} = \begin{cases} 1 & \text{if } f(x) = f(y) \\ 0 & \text{otherwise} \end{cases}$$

Let C denote the number of collisions of f. The expectation $E(C)$ is given by:

$$E(C) = \sum_{\{x,y\} \in E \times E, x \neq y} E(I_{\{x,y\}}) = \frac{1}{m} \sum_{\{x,y\} \in E \times E, x \neq y} 1 = \frac{1}{m}\binom{n}{2} = \Theta\left(\frac{n^2}{2m}\right)$$

$\square$

Collision-Finding Algorithms. Let $f : E \to F$, with $F \subseteq E$, be a random function. According to the birthday paradox, a collision of f can be found in roughly $\Theta(\sqrt{|F|})$ evaluations. Common search algorithms, e.g. Brent's cycle-finding algorithm [4], achieve this by computing a chain of invocations of f from a random starting point s until a collision occurs. In the text, the notation $(x, y) \longleftarrow \text{Rho}(f, s)$ refers to the collision (x, y) returned by f from starting point s, using a cycle-finding algorithm.

In [20], van Oorschot and Wiener extend this idea to search collisions between two functions f_1 and f_2 (both have the same domain E and range F, with $F \subseteq E$). The construction defines a new function f that alternates between f_1 and f_2 depending on the input. The new function f is a random function, thus any cycle-finding algorithm applies and finds a collision for the new function in $\Theta(\sqrt{|F|})$ and polynomial memory. The found collision is a collision between f_1 and f_2 with probability $\frac{1}{2}$. Therefore the running time will roughly double if collisions are random. This is achieved by randomizing the output of the algorithm. In fact, Brent's cycle-finding algorithm is likely to produce always the same collision. To remediate this problem, [1,11] consider a family of permutations $(P_k)_{k \in \mathbb{N}}$ in E addressed by k: they apply the collision-finding algorithm to $g : E \to E$ with $g(x) = P_k(f(x))$, where P_k is a random permutation from the considered family. I.e., a new permutation is used with each invocation of the collision-finding algorithm, which ensures that the produced collisions are uniformly distributed.

3 First Algorithm

Let P be a degree-d polynomial over $\mathbb{F}_2$ with nonzero constant term, and $n > d$ be an integer. Our goal is to compute a multiple of P with the least possible weight, and with nonzero constant term and degree at most n. We proceed as follows.

We first determine the minimal weight using Inequality Eq. (1). Let ω be the found weight, and $1 + z = 1 + \sum_{i=1}^{n} z_i X^i$ be a weight-ω solution to the LWPM problem. We decompose z to $z = x + y$, with $x, y \in (\mathbb{F}_2^n, +)$ and weight$(x) =$ weight$(y) = \phi = n * \phi_n$, where ϕ is a weight to be determined as a function of ω. Then, we compute x and y as a collision to a random function f, using any collision-finding algorithm, e.g. [4].

To compute ϕ, we assume and put in place a Bernoulli distribution on x and y. That is, we ensure the coordinates (of x and y) are independent and equal to 1 with the constant probability $\phi_n = \phi/n$.

This section is organized as follows. Subsection 3.1 defines the building blocks that will be used in the algorithm, namely the weight ϕ, the random function f and a further function that puts in place the Bernoulli distribution. Subsection 3.2 describes our first algorithm for solving LWPM. Finally, Subsect. 3.3 is dedicated to the experimental validation of the presented algorithm.

3.1 Building Blocks

Computation of ϕ. Assume a Bernoulli distribution on x and y. I.e. the coordinates of both x and y are considered independent trials with the constant probability of success $\Pr(x_i = 1) = \Pr(y_i = 1) = \phi_n = \frac{\phi}{n}$ for $i \in [1, n]$.

Therefore $z = x + y$ follows also a Bernoulli law with PMF $\Pr(z_i = 1) = 2\phi_n(1 - \phi_n)$, for $i \in [1, n]$. Moreover, weight$(z) \sim \text{Binomial}(2\phi_n(1 - \phi_n), n)$. Since weight$(z) = \omega - 1$, thus $\omega - 1 = 2n\phi_n(1 - \phi_n)$, which is equivalent to $\phi_n = \frac{1}{2}(1 \pm \sqrt{1 - 2\omega_n})$, where $\omega_n := \frac{\omega-1}{n}$. Note that we assumed $\omega \leq \frac{n}{2}$, thus $\omega_n \leq \frac{1}{2}$.

Random Function f. Let ϕ and ϕ_n be the quantities computed in the previous paragraph. Define the set $\mathcal{T}$:

$$\mathcal{T} = \{x \in \{0, 1\}^n : \text{weight}(x) = \phi = n * \phi_n\} \qquad (2)$$

Let further $a_i = X^i \mod P$ for $i \in [0, n]$. Consider the functions f_0, f_1:

$$f_0, f_1 : \mathcal{T} \longrightarrow \mathbb{F}_2^d$$

$$f_0(x) = \sum_{i=1}^{n} x_i a_i \quad \text{and} \quad f_1(x) = a_0 + \sum_{i=1}^{n} x_i a_i \qquad (3)$$

Define further the function f:

$$f : \mathcal{T} \longrightarrow \mathbb{F}_2^d$$

$$x \longmapsto \begin{cases} f_0(x) & \text{if } h(x) = 0 \\ f_1(x) & \text{if } h(x) = 1 \end{cases} \qquad (4)$$

where $h : \{0, 1\}^n \to \{0, 1\}$ is a random bit function. In other terms, f alternates between applications of f_0 and f_1 depending on the input. It is clear that a collision (x, y) of the function f will lead to a multiple of P with expected weight less than ω. In fact, a collision of type $f_i(x) = f_i(y)$, $i = 0,1$ gives a multiple with expected weight $\omega - 1$, and a collision of type $f_i(x) = f_{1-i}(y)$, $i = 0,1$ gives a multiple with expected weight ω.

Finally, since we will use a cycle-finding algorithm to search collisions of f, we need the function range and domain to be the same. To achieve this, we consider an injective map $\tau \colon \mathbb{F}_2^d \longrightarrow \mathcal{T}$ (provided $2^d \leq |\mathcal{T}|$). Therefore, all collisions (x, y) of f satisfy

$$f(x) = f(y) \iff \tau \circ f(x) = \tau \circ f(y)$$

In this way, any cycle-finding technique can be applied to $\tau \circ f$ to search for collisions of f.

In the rest of the text, we conveniently identify $\tau \circ f$ with f; that is we assume that f outputs elements in $\mathcal{T}$, provided that $2^d \leq |\mathcal{T}|$, but we keep in mind that $|f(\mathcal{T})| = 2^d$.

Bernoulli Distribution on the Input of f. Recall that function f inputs vectors of $\mathcal{T}$ that follow a Bernoulli distribution with parameters ϕ_n and n. That is, coordinates of the input vectors are independent and identically distributed with the constant probability ϕ_n of being equal to one. With this assumption, a collision of f leads to a multiple of P with expected weight less than ω.

We achieve such a distribution by using a random function σ

$$\sigma \colon \{0,1\}^n \longrightarrow \{0,1\}^n$$
$$x \longmapsto \sigma(x) \colon \sigma(x) \sim \mathrm{Bernoulli}(\phi_n, n)$$

More precisely, σ uses the input elements as a seed to produce n-bit vectors that satisfy the Bernoulli distribution. Therefore, the input elements are only used to "remember" the state of the function, so that when it is called with the same value, it produces the same output.

Note that σ outputs elements with weight ϕ with non-negligible probability:

$$\Pr[\sigma(x) \in \mathcal{T}, x \in_R \{0,1\}^n] = \binom{n}{\phi} \phi_n^\phi (1 - \phi_n)^{n-\phi} = \binom{n}{n\phi_n} 2^{-nH(\phi_n)}$$

$$\approx \frac{1}{\sqrt{2\pi n \phi_n (1 - \phi_n)}}$$

On other note, σ induces a uniform distribution on $\mathcal{T}$. In fact, let $y \in \mathcal{T}$ be a given element in $\mathcal{T}$, and x a random input element to σ

$$\Pr[\sigma(x) = y \mid \sigma(x) \in \mathcal{T}] = \frac{\Pr[\sigma(x) = y, \sigma(x) \in \mathcal{T}]}{\Pr[\sigma(x) \in \mathcal{T}]} = \frac{\phi_n^\phi (1 - \phi_n)^{n-\phi}}{\binom{n}{\phi} \phi_n^\phi (1 - \phi_n)^{n-\phi}} = \frac{1}{|\mathcal{T}|}$$

Therefore, we conveniently assume in the rest of this section that σ has range $\mathcal{T}$ on which it induces a uniform probability distribution.

3.2 The Algorithm

Consider the following map:

$$g\colon \{0,1\}^n \longrightarrow \mathcal{T}(\subset \{0,1\}^n)$$
$$x \longmapsto f \circ \sigma(x)$$

g is well defined as we assumed that σ has range $\mathcal{T}$. Moreover, g is a random function from $\{0,1\}^n$ to $\{0,1\}^n$, and thus we can apply any cycle-finding algorithm to search collisions for g. Note that σ will introduce some unnecessary collisions as we are only interested in collisions of f. We explain later how we compute this fraction of "useful" collisions among the total number of g collisions.

Now therefore, in consideration of the foregoing, a cycle-finding algorithm for g picks a random starting point $s \in_R \{0,1\}^n$, then computes a chain of invocations of g, i.e. $g(s), g^2(s) := g \circ g(s), \ldots$ until finding a repetition. If such a repetition leads to a valid collision (x, y), i.e. $g(x) = g(y)$ and $x \neq y$, return it otherwise start again with a new starting point. Termination of the algorithm is guaranteed if the execution paths from different starting points are independent. In other words, a random collision should be returned for each new starting point.

To randomize collisions, we introduce our last ingredient, a family of permutations P_k addressed by integer k:

$$P_k\colon \{0,1\}^n \longrightarrow \{0,1\}^n$$

The new function subject to collision search is

$$g^{[k]} = g \circ P_k \colon \mathcal{T} \longrightarrow \mathcal{T}$$

Note that the restriction of P_k to $\mathcal{T}$ is still a permutation from $\mathcal{T}$ to $P_k(\mathcal{T})(\subset \{0,1\}^n)$.

$g^{[k]}$ is a random function, with domain and range $\mathcal{T}$, which satisfies the randomness requirement on the computed collisions. In fact, for each new starting point s, a freshly random element $P_k(s)$ is obtained thanks to P_k (the permutation P_k is picked new with each new starting point), which is then used as a seed to σ to produce a random n-bit vector in $\mathcal{T}$ (with non-negligible probability) that satisfies the Bernoulli distribution. Therefore, execution paths, in cycle-searching algorithms for $g^{[k]}$, from different starting points are independent.

Also, (x, y) is a collision for $g^{[k]}$ if and only if $(P_k(x), P_k(y))$ is a collision for g. We can then apply any cycle-finding algorithm to $g^{[k]}$ to search collisions for g.

We can now describe Algorithm 1 for solving the LWPM problem.

Remark 1. Algorithm 1 finds weight-ω multiples provided they exist. When Inequality Eq. (1) predicts a weight that does not exist, the algorithm runs indefinitely. As a safety valve, one can allow a margin in the breaking condition, and accept multiples with weights within that margin.

Algorithm 1. for LWPM

Input A polynomial P with degree d, and a bound n

Output A multiple M of P such that $\deg(M) \leq n$ and with the least possible weight.

Compute the expected minimal weight ω by solving Inequality 1

$\omega_n \longleftarrow (\omega - 1)/n$; $\mu \longleftarrow \omega - 1$

repeat

    $\mu_n \longleftarrow \mu/n$; $\mu \longleftarrow \mu + 1$

    $\phi_n \longleftarrow \frac{1}{2}(1 \pm \sqrt{1 - 2 * \mu_n})$; $\phi \longleftarrow n * \phi_n$

until $\binom{n}{\phi} \geq 2^d$ ▷ to ensure that f has range $f(\mathcal{T}) \subseteq \mathcal{T}$

repeat

    choose a random permutation P_k

    choose a random starting point $s \in_R \mathcal{T}$

    $(x, y) \longleftarrow \mathrm{Rho}(g^{[k]}, s)$

    $(p, q) \longleftarrow (\sigma \circ P_k(x), \sigma \circ P_k(y))$

    $M \longleftarrow \begin{cases} X * (p + q) & \text{if } f_i(p) = f_i(q), \ i = 0, 1 \\ 1 + X * (p + q) & \text{if } f_i(p) = f_{1-i}(q), \ i = 0, 1 \end{cases}$

until $M \equiv 0 \bmod P$ and weight$(M) \in [1, \omega]$

return M

Remark 2. The μ_n's considered in the first loop are all less than $\frac{1}{2}$. In fact, they satisfy $\mu_n = 2\phi_n(1 - \phi_n)$, and the function $x \longmapsto 2x(1 - x)$ is upper bounded by $\frac{1}{2}$ for $x \in [0, 1]$.

Remark 3. Both the values $\frac{1}{2}(1 + \sqrt{1 - 2\mu_n})$ and $\frac{1}{2}(1 - \sqrt{1 - 2\mu_n})$ for ϕ_n give the same expected time in terms of function calls, however, the latter value finds the solution faster as it is easier to manipulate sparse vectors.

Theorem 1. *Algorithm 1 runs in time $\Theta(2^{C_t})$ with*

$$C_t = \frac{d}{2} + n(-H(w_n) + H_1(\omega_n)) + \frac{3}{2}\log_2(2\pi n\omega_n(1 - \omega_n))$$

where $H_1(\omega_n) = -\omega_n \log_2(2\omega_n(1 - \omega_n)) - (1 - \omega_n)\log_2(1 - 2\omega_n(1 - \omega_n))$.

□

The proof is given in the full version [9].

3.3 Experimental Results

We run Algorithm 1 on the following polynomial P for $n \in [30, 1100]$. The results are depicted in Fig. 3.

$$P = X^{19} + X^{11} + X^{10} + X^8 + X^7 + X^5 + X^4 + X^3 + X^2 + X^1 + 1$$

Further experiments are given in [9].

We used the the $\tilde{\Theta}$ notation for the estimated time, which explains the differences between the estimates and the experiments; the polynomial factor $(2\pi n\omega_n(1 - \omega_n))^{\frac{3}{2}}$ is ignored in the estimated time.

4 Second Algorithm

Algorithm 1 in Sect. 3 incurs an overhead in the computations due to function
σ. Actually, with each invocation of the
function f, we make a call to σ which
uses a pseudo-random number generator
to establish the Bernoulli distribution on
the input.

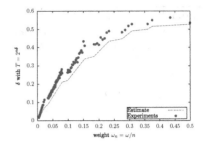

Fig. 3. Averaged function calls T for
Algorithm 1 run on Polynomial P

We remediate this problem in this
section. Therefore, we decompose the
solution z of LWPM into a pair (x, y),
where x, y are n-bit vectors that do not enjoy any specific properties except
having the same weight ϕ to be determined. We then look for such pairs by
searching collisions of f.

Consider the set $\mathcal{T}$ defined in Statement 2, and let $x, y \in_R \mathcal{T}$. We proceed as
follows. We first determine the PMF of the random variable $Y = \text{weight}(x + y)$
and compute ϕ as a function of ω. Then, we describe, analyze and experimentally
validate our second algorithm in the subsequent subsections.

4.1 Computation of ϕ

Probability Law of $Y = \text{weight}(x + y)$. We first note the following facts.

Fact 2 $\Pr[Y = 2k + 1] = 0, \forall k \in \mathbb{N}$.   □

Fact 3 $\Pr[Y = k] = 0$, for $k \notin [0, \min(2\phi, n)]$.   □

The proofs are given in [9].

Let now, $k \le \min(\phi, n/2)$ be an integer. $\Pr[Y = 2k]$ is given by the number
of strings x and y that disagree on $2k$ positions, divided by the size of the
probability space. The number of such strings is given by the product of:

- $\binom{n}{2k}$: the number of ways to choose the positions where x and y disagree.
- $\binom{2k}{k}$: the number of ways to distribute k ones in those $2k$ positions. In fact,
  let $\bar{x}$ and $\bar{y}$ be the $(2k)$-bit strings extracted from x and y respectively, and
  composed of the bits where x and y disagree. Then, $\bar{x}$ and $\bar{y}$ have the same
  weight, namely k, as x and y have the same weight ϕ, and agree on the
  remaining $n - 2k$ positions. Thus, the $2k$ ones must be equally distributed
  among $\bar{x}$ and $\bar{y}$.
- $\binom{n-2k}{\phi-k}$: the number of ways to choose $(n - 2k)$-bit strings with weight $(\phi - k)$.
  I.e. the number of sub-strings where x and y agree.

The size of the probability space is given by $|\mathcal{T}|^2 = \binom{n}{\phi}^2$. Thus

$$\Pr[Y = 2k, k \le \min(\phi, n/2)] = \binom{n}{2k}\binom{2k}{k}\binom{n-2k}{\phi-k} \bigg/ \binom{n}{\phi}^2 = \binom{\phi}{k}\binom{n-\phi}{k} \bigg/ \binom{n}{\phi}$$

We conclude that:

$$\Pr[\text{weight}(x+y) = 2k] = \begin{cases} \binom{\phi}{k}\binom{n-\phi}{k}/\binom{n}{\phi} & \text{if } 0 \le k \le \min(\phi, n/2) \\ 0 & \text{otherwise} \end{cases}$$

Computation of ϕ Note that the PMF of $Y = \text{weight}(x+y)$ is reminiscent of the hypergeometric distribution G given by PMF:

$$\Pr[G = k] = \begin{cases} \binom{t}{k}\binom{n-t}{\phi-k}/\binom{n}{\phi} & \text{if } 0 \le t, \phi \le n \text{ and } 0 \le k \le \min(\phi, t) \\ 0 & \text{otherwise} \end{cases}$$

and expectation $E(G) = \frac{t \cdot \phi}{n}$. Actually, for $t = \phi$, we get

$$\Pr[G = k] = \begin{cases} \binom{\phi}{k}\binom{n-\phi}{\phi-k}/\binom{n}{\phi} & \text{if } 0 \le \phi \le n \text{ and } 0 \le k \le \phi \\ 0 & \text{otherwise} \end{cases}$$

Therefore $\Pr[\text{weight}(x+y) = 2k] = \Pr[G = \phi - k]$. We derive the expectation of $Y = \text{weight}(x+y)$ as follows.

$$E(Y) = \sum_{k=0, k=2p}^{2\phi} k \Pr[Y = k] = \sum_{k=0}^{\phi} 2k \Pr[Y = 2k]$$

$$= \sum_{k=0}^{\phi} 2k \Pr[G = \phi - k] = 2\sum_{k=0}^{\phi} (\phi - k)\Pr[G = k]$$

$$= 2\phi - 2E(G) = 2\phi(1 - \phi/n)$$

Therefore, if we conserve our previous notations: $\phi = n * \phi_n$, and $\omega - 1 = \omega_n * n$, and solve for ϕ_n the equation $\omega_n * n = 2\phi(1 - \phi/n)$. We get $\phi_n = \frac{1}{2}(1 \pm \sqrt{1 - 2\omega_n})$ ($\omega_n \le \frac{1}{2}$). Note that we get the same value we found for ϕ in Sect. 3, when we assumed a Bernoulli distribution on x and y, and consequently a binomial distribution on $\text{weight}(x + y)$ ($x + y \sim \text{Bernoulli}(\phi_n(1 - \phi_n), n)$ and thus $\text{weight}(x+y) \sim \text{Binomial}(2\phi_n(1 - \phi_n), n)$). This is not surprising; we know that for increasing n, the hypergeometric law converges to the binomial law.

4.2   The Algorithm

Let (P, d, n) be a LWPM instance. We compute the minimal weight ω as usual by solving Inequality (1), then we compute ϕ_n as $\frac{1}{2}(1 \pm \sqrt{1 - 2(\omega - 1)/n})$ and ϕ as $n\phi_n$.

To compute a weight-ω multiple of P with degree less than n, we similarly search for collisions (p, q) of the function f defined earlier, where p and q are n-bit vectors with weight ϕ. There is a small particularity of this algorithm depending on the parity of ω. In fact, collisions of f are of two types:

Type 1 collisions   that correspond to $f_i(p) = f_{1-i}(q)$, $i = 0, 1$. These collisions produce multiples of type $1 + X(p + q)$, with weight $1 + 2k$, $1 \le k \le \min(\phi, n/2)$.

Type 2 collisions that correspond to $f_i(x) = f_i(y)$, $i = 0, 1$. These collisions produce multiples of type $X(p + q)$, with weight $2k$, $1 \leq k \leq \min(\phi, n/2)$

Therefore, if $\omega = 1 + 2k$, we set $\mu =: \omega - 1$ and $\phi = n\phi_n$, with $\phi_n = \frac{1}{2}(1 \pm \sqrt{1 - 2\mu/n})$. As in Algorithm 1, we ensure that f outputs values in $\mathcal{T}$ (using the injective map $\tau \colon \mathbb{F}_2^d \longrightarrow \mathcal{T}$) by satisfying the condition $|\mathcal{T}| \geq 2^d$, where $|\mathcal{T}| = \binom{n}{\phi}$: we keep increasing μ until the inequality holds. Similarly, if $\omega = 2k$, then we initially set $\mu := \omega$ and keep increasing it until $\binom{n}{\phi} \geq 2^d$, where $\phi = n\phi_n$ and $\phi_n = \frac{1}{2}(1 \pm \sqrt{1 - 2\mu/n})$. We note again that both $\frac{1}{2}(1 + \sqrt{1 - 2\mu/n})$ and $\frac{1}{2}(1 - \sqrt{1 - 2\mu/n})$ lead to the same expected function calls, however, the latter value finds the solution faster as it is easier to manipulate sparse vectors.

Finally, to randomize collisions, it is enough to use any family of permutations $P_k \colon \mathcal{T} \longrightarrow \mathcal{T}$. The collision-finding algorithm is then applied to $f^{[k]} := P_k \circ f$.

We are now ready to give the pseudo-code description of our second algorithm for LWPM in Algorithm 2.

Algorithm 2. for LWPM

Input A polynomial P with degree d, and a bound n

Output A multiple M of P such that $\deg(M) \leq n$ and with the least possible weight.

Compute the expected minimal weight ω by solving Inequality 1

if $\omega\%2 = 1$ **then**

  $\omega_n \longleftarrow (\omega - 1)/n$; $\mu \longleftarrow \omega - 1$

else

  $\omega_n \longleftarrow \omega/n$; $\mu \longleftarrow \omega$

end if

repeat

  $\mu_n \longleftarrow \mu/n$; $\mu \longleftarrow \mu + 1$

  $\phi_n \longleftarrow \frac{1}{2}(1 \pm \sqrt{1 - 2 * \mu_n})$; $\phi \longleftarrow n * \phi_n$

until $\binom{n}{\phi} \geq 2^d$ ▷ to ensure that f has range $f(\mathcal{T}) \subseteq \mathcal{T}$

repeat

  choose a random permutation $P_k \colon \mathcal{T} \longrightarrow \mathcal{T}$

  choose a random starting point $s \in_R \mathcal{T}$

  $(p, q) \longleftarrow \mathrm{Rho}(f^{[k]}, s)$

  $M \longleftarrow \begin{cases} X * (p + q) & \text{if } f_i(p) = f_i(q), \ i = 0, 1 \\ 1 + X * (p + q) & \text{if } f_i(p) = f_{1-i}(q), \ i = 0, 1 \end{cases}$

until $M \equiv 0 \bmod P$ and $\mathrm{weight}(M) \in [1, \omega]$

return M

First, we note that Remarks 1 and 2 and 3 for Algorithm 1 apply also here. Moreover, for even ω, Algorithm 2 finds multiples of the form $X * (p + q)$, where $p + q$ is a polynomial with degree at most $n - 1$. That is, the algorithm finds a weight-ω multiple with nonzero constant term and degree at most $n - 1$ (since P has nonzero constant term) provided it exists. One could change, in this case, the definition of $\mathcal{T}$ and f and manipulate $(n + 1)$-bit vectors instead of n-bit vectors in order to find multiples of degree at most n, but we opted for the above description to keep the algorithm simple.

Theorem 2. *Algorithm 2 runs in time* $\tilde{\Theta}(2^{C_t})$ *where* $C_t = \frac{d}{2} + n\left(- H_2(\omega_n) + H(\omega_n)\right)$, *with* $H_2(\omega_n) = \omega_n + (1 - \omega_n)H\left(\frac{\omega_n}{2(1-\omega_n)}\right)$. □

The proof is given in [9].

4.3   Experimental Results

We consider the same test polynomial in Subsect. 3.3 for the same range of values $n \in [30, 1100]$; the results are depicted in Fig. 4. Note that we used the $\tilde{\Theta}$ notation for the estimated time, which explains the slight differences between the estimates and the experiments. Further experiments are given in [9].

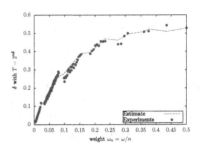

Fig. 4. Averaged function calls T for Algorithm 2

5   Comparison with the State-of-the-art

In this section, we compare the performance of our algorithms with existing memory-efficient methods for LWPM (discrete-log [22] and Canteaut-Trabbia [6]). These lasts run in $\tilde{\Theta}(2^d)$ and $\tilde{\Theta}(2^{nH(\omega_n)})$ respectively. Actually, we discard the lattice method as it becomes inaccurate with increasing n (few hundreds) (Table 1).

Table 1. Comparison between the memory-efficient techniques and our algorithms

Method	DL [22]	[6]	Algorithm 1	Algorithm 2
$\log_2(\tilde{\Theta}(T))$	d	$nH(\omega_n)$	$\frac{d}{2} + n(-H(w_n) + H_1(\omega_n))$	$\frac{d}{2} + n\left(-H_2(\omega_n) + H(\omega_n)\right)$

Figure 5 depicts the performance of our algorithms in comparison with the state-of-the-art methods. Note that our algorithms apply to any polynomial, and do not use any precomputed tables of discrete logarithms, unlike some existing memory-efficient methods (discrete-log-based ones).

Cryptanalytic Application I: The Bluetooth Summation Generator Polynomial. The Bluetooth polynomial is the product of the four constituent LFSRs feedback polynomials; $P_{BT} = P_1 \cdot P_2 \cdot P_3 \cdot P_4$ where:

$$P_1(x) = x^{25} + x^{20} + x^{12} + x^8 + 1;$$
$$P_2(x) = x^{31} + x^{24} + x^{16} + x^{12} + 1;$$
$$P_3(x) = x^{33} + x^{28} + x^{24} + x^4 + 1;$$
$$P_4(x) = x^{39} + x^{36} + x^{28} + x^4 + 1;$$

P_{BT} has degree 128 and weight 49; at degree $n = 668$, the authors in [16] found a multiple of weight $\omega = 31$. Note that the max-

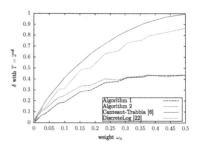

Fig. 5. Comparison between the memory-efficient techniques and our algorithms

imum keystream length for the Bluetooth combiner is 2745. That is, the maximum value for n is 2745. We note in Table 2 the performances of the different polynomial memory algorithms on this instance.

Table 2. Time costs of the memory-efficient techniques and our algorithms on the Bluetooth polynomial

Method	DL [22]	Canteaut-Trabbia [6]	Algorithm 1	Algorithm 2
$\log_2(\tilde{\Theta}(T))$	128	177	76	108

Cryptanalytic Application II. [8] We consider the test polynomial used in [8]

$$P_{53} = X^{53} + X^{47} + X^{45} + X^{44} + X^{42} + X^{40} + X^{39} + X^{38} + X^{36} + X^{33} + X^{32}$$
$$+ X^{31} + X^{30} + X^{28} + X^{27} + X^{26} + X^{25} + X^{21} + X^{20} + X^{17} + X^{16} + X^{15}$$
$$+ X^{13} + X^{11} + X^{10} + X^7 + X^6 + X^3 + X^2 + X^1 + 1.$$

The authors in [8] found multiples of weight $\omega = 5$ at degree $n = 2^{13}$. We note in Table 3 the performances of the different polynomial memory algorithms on this instance.

At degree $n \geq 2^{20}$, the authors found multiples with weight $\omega = 4$. However, at this degree, the condition $n \geq 2^{d/(1+\log_2(\omega-1))}$ is satisfied; thus, the generalized birthday method [25] outperforms with a time and a memory cost linear in n.

Table 3. Time costs of the memory-efficient techniques and our algorithms on the [8] instance

Method	Discrete Log [22]	Canteaut-Trabbia [6]	Algorithm 1	Algorithm 2
$\log_2(\tilde{\Theta}(T))$	53	50	28	45

6   Time-Memory Trade-Off Variants

Our previously described algorithms allow fortunately for a time/memory trade-off, thanks to van Oorschot-Wiener's Parallel Collision Search (PCS) technique [20]. This technique has been extensively used in cryptanalysis since its introduction; it allows to efficiently find multiple collisions, of a random function, at a low amortized cost per collision. More precisely, let C be the time complexity to find a collision with polynomial memory, then PCS finds $\tilde{\Theta}(2^m)$ collisions in time $\tilde{\Theta}(2^{\frac{m}{2}}C)$ using $\tilde{\Theta}(2^m)$ memory.

In the following, we apply PCS to Algorithms 1 and 2 in order to decrease their time complexity at the expense of memory.

Algorithm 1 Trade-off. According to the analysis in Sect. 3, Algorithm 1 requires to find $\tilde{\Theta}(2^{n(-H(w_n)+H_1(\omega_n))})$ collisions. In fact, this value corresponds to the number of examined collisions before coming across a so-called *useful collision*, i.e. a collision that leads to a solution to the LWPM problem. Each collision comes at the cost of $\tilde{\Theta}(2^{\frac{d}{2}})$. Therefore, using $M_{\text{tmto-1}} = \tilde{\Theta}(2^{n(-H(w_n)+H_1(\omega_n))})$ memory, the time complexity of the trade-off variant of Algorithm 1 reduces to $T_{\text{tmto-1}} = \tilde{\Theta}(2^{\frac{n(-H(\omega_n)+H_1(\omega_n))}{2}} \cdot 2^{\frac{d}{2}})$.

Algorithm 2 Trade-off. Algorithm 2 requires to find $\tilde{\Theta}(2^{n(H(\omega_n)-H_2(\omega_n))})$ collisions, each at the cost of $\tilde{\Theta}(2^{\frac{d}{2}})$. Therefore, using $M_{\text{tmto-2}} = \tilde{\Theta}(2^{n(H(\omega_n)-H_2(\omega_n))})$ memory, the time complexity of the trade-off variant of Algorithm 2 reduces to $T_{\text{tmto-2}} = \tilde{\Theta}(2^{\frac{n(H(\omega_n)-H_2(\omega_n))}{2}} \cdot 2^{\frac{d}{2}})$.

We depict in Table 4 and Fig. 6 the time/memory costs of the trade-off variants of Algorithms 1 and 2 and of the state-of-the-art. We omit the generalized birthday method [25] which is linear in time and memory ($O(n)$) if the condition $n \geq d/(1 + \log_2(\omega - 1))$ is satisfied.

Our trade-off variants outperform obviously the state-of-the-art in memory, however, they loose the lead in the running time as the weights get smaller. Note however that when the weights get very small, then the generalized birthday method [25] imposes itself as we will see below in Cryptanalytic application II.

Table 4. Comparison between the time/memory trade-off techniques and our algorithms

	DL [8]	SD [15,18]	TMTO [7]	Algo1	Algo2
$\frac{\log_2(T)}{n}$	$H(\frac{\omega-2}{2n})$	$\omega_n(\log_2 n - \log_2 d)$	$H(\frac{\omega-1}{2n})$	$\frac{1}{2}(\frac{d}{n} - H(\omega_n) + H_1(\omega_n))$	$\frac{1}{2}(\frac{d}{n} + H(\omega_n) - H_2(\omega_n))$
$\frac{\log_2(M)}{n}$	$H(\frac{\omega-2}{2n})$	$\omega_n \log_2 d$	$H(\frac{\omega-1}{4n})$	$-H(\omega_n) + H_1(\omega_n)$	$H(\omega_n) - H_2(\omega_n)$

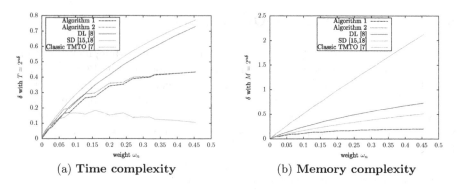

(a) **Time complexity**   (b) **Memory complexity**

Fig. 6. Time/Memory costs of the state-of-the-art and our trade-off algorithms

Cryptanalytic Application I: The Bluetooth Polynomial. We note in Table 5 the performances of the time/memory trade-off methods on the Bluetooth instance considered in Sect. 5. We discard the generalized birthday method as the condition $n \geq d/(1 + \log_2(\omega - 1))$ is not satisfied.

Table 5. Time/memory costs of the trade-off techniques on the Bluetooth polynomial

	DL [8]	SD [15,18]	TMTO [7]	Algo1	Algo2
$\log_2(T)$	101	73	103	70	86
$\log_2(M)$	101	217	59	12	44

Cryptanalytic Application II. [8] We consider the instance polynomial P_{53} defined earlier in Sect. 5. We provide in Table 6 the performances of the time/memory trade-off methods on this polynomial at degree $n = 2^{13}$ and weight $\omega = 5$.

It is clear that, despite requiring a big precomputation step and applying only to primitive polynomials with smooth orders, the DL [8] method provides the best time/memory trade-off on this instance. However, we remark that if go up to degree $n = 2^{20}$, we can get a 4-weight multiple using Wagner's generalized birthday, in time and memory linear in 2^{20}. This is of course only possible when the available keystream allows it (since n is upper bounded by the available keystream length).

Table 6. Time/memory costs of the trade-off techniques on the [8] instance

	DL [8]	SD [15,18]	TMTO [7]	Algo1	Algo2
$\log_2(T)$	21	36	27	27	36
$\log_2(M)$	21	29	14	13	19

Acknowledgments. I thank the anonymous reviewers of Inscrypt 2021, for their useful remarks and suggestions that substantially improved the quality of the present paper.

References

1. Becker, A., Coron, J.S., Joux, A.: Improved generic algorithms for hard knapsacks. In: Advances in Cryptology - EUROCRYPT 2011, pp. 364–385 (2011)
2. Becker, A., Joux, A., May, A., Meurer, A.: Decoding random binary linear codes in $2^{n/20}$: How 1+1=0 improves information set decoding. In: EUROCRYPT 2012, pp. 520–536 (2012)
3. Brent, R.P., Zimmermann, P.: Algorithms for finding almost irreducible and almost primitive trinomials (2003), lectures in Honour of the Sixtieth Birthday of Hugh Cowie Williams (2003)
4. Brent, R.P.: an improved monte carlo factorization algorithm. BIT Numerical Mathematics, pp. 176–184 (1980)
5. Canteaut, A., Chabaud, F.: A new algorithm for finding minimum-weight words in a linear code: application to mceliece's cryptosystem and to narrow-sense BCH codes of length 511. IEEE Trans. Inf. Theory **44**, 367–378 (1998)
6. Canteaut, A., Trabbia, M.: Improved fast correlation attacks using parity-check equations of weight 4 and 5. In: Preneel, B. (ed.) Advances in Cryptology - Eurocrypt 2000. LNCS, vol. 1807, pp. 573, 588. Springer (2000). https://doi.org/10.1007/3-540-45539-6_40
7. Chose, P. Joux, A., Mitton, M.: Fast correlation attacks: an algorithmic point of view. In: Knudsen, L.R. (ed.) Advances in Cryptology - Eurocrypt 2002. LNCS, vol. 2332, pp. 209, 221. Springer (2002). https://doi.org/10.1007/3-540-46035-7_14
8. Didier, J., Laigle-Chapuy, Y.: finding low-weight polynomial multiples using discrete logarithm. In: IEEE International Symposium on Information Theory ISIT'07. p. to appear. Nice, France (2007)
9. El Aimani, L.: A new approach for finding low-weight polynomial multiples. IACR Cryptol. ePrint Arch. **2021**, 586 (2021)
10. El Aimani, L., von zur Gathen, J.: Finding low weight polynomial multiples using lattices. Poster session of the LLL + 25 conference (2007), full version available at the Cryptology ePrint Archive, Report 2007/423
11. Esser, A., May, A.: Low weight discrete logarithm and subset sum in $2^{0.65n}$ with polynomial memory. In: Advances in Cryptology - EUROCRYPT 2020, pp. 94–122 (2020)
12. Galbraith, S.D.: Mathematics of Public Key Cryptography. Cambridge University Press (2012)
13. von zur Gathen, J., Nöcker, M.: Polynomial and normal bases for finite fields. J. Cryptol. **18**(4), 337–355 (2005), http://gatnoe03b.pdf
14. Lenstra, A., Lenstra, H., Lovasz, L.: Factoring polynomials with rational coefficients. Mathematische Annalen **261**(4), 515–534 (1982)
15. Löndahl, C., Johansson, T.: Improved algorithms for finding low-weight polynomial multiples in $F_2[x]$ and some cryptographic applications. Des. Codes Cryptogr. **73**, 625–640 (2014)
16. Lu, Y., Vaudenay, S.: Faster correlation attack on Bluetooth keystream generator E0. In: Franklin, M.K. (ed.) Advances in Cryptology - Crypto 2004. LNCS, vol. 3152, pp. 407, 425. Springer (2004). https://doi.org/10.1007/978-3-540-28628-8_25

17. May, A., Meurer, A., Thomae, E.: Decoding random linear codes in $\tilde{\mathcal{O}}(2^{0.054n})$. In: Advances in Cryptology - ASIACRYPT 2011 (2011)
18. May, A., Ozerov, I.: On computing nearest neighbors with applications to decoding of binary linear codes. In: Advances in Cryptology - EUROCRYPT 2015, pp. 203–228 (2015)
19. Meier, W., Staffelbach, O.: Fast correlation attacks on certain stream ciphers. J. Cryptol. **1**, 159–176 (1989)
20. van Oorschot, P.C., Wiener, M.J.: Parallel collision search with cryptanalytic applications. J. Cryptol. **12**, 1–28 (1999)
21. Penzhorn, W.T., Kühn, G.J.: Computation of low-weight parity checks for correlation attacks on stream ciphers. In: Cryptography and Coding, pp. 74–83 (1995)
22. Peterlongo, P., Sala, M., Tinnirello, C.: A discrete logarithm-based approach to compute low-weight multiples of binary polynomials. Finite Fields Their Appl. **38**, 57–71 (2016)
23. Siegenthaler, T.: Decrypting a class of stream ciphers using ciphertext only. IEEE Trans. Comput. **C-34**(1), 81–84 (1985)
24. Stern, J.: A method for finding codewords of small weight. In: Coding Theory and Application, pp. 106–113 (1988)
25. Wagner, D.: A generalized birthday problem. In: Yung, M. (ed.) Advances in Cryptology - Crypto 2002. LNCS, vol. 2442, pp. 288–304. Springer (2002). https://doi.org/10.1007/3-540-45708-9_19

Differential-Linear Cryptanalysis of the Lightweight Cryptographic Algorithm KNOT

Shichang Wang[1,2], Shiqi Hou[1,2], Meicheng Liu[1,2(✉)], and Dongdai Lin[1,2(✉)]

[1] State Key Laboratory of Information Security,
Institute of Information Engineering, Chinese Academy of Sciences,
Beijing 100093, China
{wangshichang,houshiqi,liumeicheng,ddlin}@iie.ac.cn
[2] School of Cyber Security, University of Chinese Academy of Sciences,
Beijing 100049, China

Abstract. KNOT is one of the 32 candidates in the second round of NIST's lightweight cryptography standardization process. The KNOT family consists of bit-slice lightweight Authenticated Encryption with Associated Data (AEAD) and hashing algorithms. In this paper, we evaluate the security for the initialization phase of two members of the KNOT-AEAD family by differential-linear cryptanalysis.

More exactly, we analyze KNOT-AEAD(128,256,64) and KNOT-AEAD(128,384,192) which have 128-bit secret keys. As a result, for 15-round KNOT-AEAD(128,256,64), our attack takes $2^{48.8}$ time complexity and $2^{47.5}$ blocks to recover the full 128-bit key. To the best of our knowledge, this is the first full key-recovery attack on 15-round KNOT-AEAD(128,256,64), and it achieves three more rounds compared with the existing work. Regarding 17-round KNOT-AEAD(128,384,192), time complexity of $2^{59.2}$ and data complexity of $2^{58.2}$ are required to launch a key-recovery attack, which is five rounds better than the known result. We stress here that our attacks do not threaten the security of KNOT-AEAD.

Keywords: Differential-linear cryptanalysis · Lightweight cryptography · KNOT

1 Introduction

The National Institute of Standards and Technology (NIST) is selecting and standardizing lightweight authenticated encryption and hashing algorithms that are suitable for use in constrained environments (e.g. sensor networks, healthcare,

This work was supported by the National Natural Science Foundation of China (Grant No. 61872359 and 62122085), the National Key R&D Program of China (Grant No. 2020YFB1805402), and the Youth Innovation Promotion Association of Chinese Academy of Sciences.

The original version of this chapter was revised: an orthographical error in the title was corrected. The correction to this chapter is available at
https://doi.org/10.1007/978-3-030-88323-2_29

© Springer Nature Switzerland AG 2021, corrected publication 2022
Y. Yu and M. Yung (Eds.): Inscrypt 2021, LNCS 13007, pp. 171–190, 2021.
https://doi.org/10.1007/978-3-030-88323-2_9

the Internet of Things). Of the 56 Round 1 candidates, 32 algorithms are selected by NIST to Round 2, such as [1, 4, 5, 13, 29]. The designers of cryptographic primitives always use the minimum of active S-boxes as the indicator for resistance against differential or linear (hull) attacks. However, this ignores some powerful variants of differential and linear cryptanalyses, for example, differential-linear attacks. It is necessary to carefully evaluate the security against differential-linear attacks for the lightweight cryptographic algorithms.

Differential [11] and linear [24] attacks are two of the most fundamental techniques of cryptanalysis. It is usually very difficult to find some long enough differentials and linear approximations for these ciphers which are well designed against differential and linear attacks. However, in some cases, with a short differential and linear approximation, an effective attack might be launched. In 1994, Langford and Hellman [20] firstly showed that a differential of E_0 and a highly biased linear approximation of E_1 could be combined into a distinguisher for the entire cipher E where E was divided into two subciphers E_0 and E_1 such that $E = E_1 \circ E_0$ by a technique called *differential-linear cryptanalysis*. Biham et al. [9] extended and improved this technique to obtain wider scope of applications. In 2017, Blondeau et al. [12] applied the link between differential and linear attacks and developed a concise theory of the differential-linear cryptanalysis. Then they gave an exact expression of the bias under the assumption that the two parts of the cipher were independent. Bar-on et al. [3], in EUROCRYPT 2019, presented the *Differential-Linear Connectivity Table* (DLCT) to take into account the dependency between two parts of the cipher, and showed that in many cases, the adversary could exploit it to launch more effective attacks. Besides, they derived that the DLCT could be constructed effectively using the Fast Fourier Transform. In CRYPTO 2020, Beierle et al. [6] presented several improvements in the context of the differential-linear attacks of ARX ciphers and successfully applied them to Chaskey and ChaCha. Recently, Liu et al. [22] studied differential-linear cryptanalysis from an algebraic perspective by introducing a technique called *Differential Algebraic Transitional Form* (DATF). Based on DATF, they developed a new theory of estimation of bias and techniques for key-recovery in the differential-linear cryptanalysis, which were applied to Ascon, Serpent and Grain v1. So far, the differential-linear technique has been used to attack many cryptographic primitives, such as the block cipher Serpent [10, 17, 22, 23], the stream cipher ChaCha [2, 6, 14, 15], the MAC algorithm Chaskey [6, 21], and the lightweight authenticated encryption Ascon [16, 22].

KNOT [29] is designed by Zhang et al., which is a family of bit-slice lightweight Authenticated Encryption with Associated Data (AEAD) and hashing algorithms. This family is based on the KNOT permutations which iteratively apply an SPN round transformation. There are both four members in KNOT-AEAD and KNOT-Hash and both of their primary members have a state of 256 bits. In 2019, KNOT was selected by NIST as one of the 32 candidates in the second round of lightweight cryptography (LWC) standardization process. In the specification of KNOT [29], the designers evaluated the security of

KNOT permutation against various attacks, such as (impossible) differential, linear, division cryptanalysis etc. Later, they [30] further updated the results of security analysis of KNOT-AEAD and KNOT-Hash. As far as we know, there is no third-party security analysis yet.

1.1   Our Contributions

In this paper, we evaluate the security for the initialization phase of two members of the KNOT-AEAD family by some techniques of differential-linear cryptanalysis. Our attacks significantly improve the previous analysis results on them.

To relieve in certain extent the influence of the dependency between differential and linear parts in the differential-linear cryptanalysis, the targeted cipher E is usually divided as $E = E'_l \circ E_m \circ E_d$. Since the diffusion layers of KNOT permutations are very simple, for E_m of up to 8 rounds, the determined output difference at a single bit can be observed when the input difference has only one non-zero bit. To obtain a differential-linear distinguisher which covers as many rounds as possible and has higher correlation, our strategy is to restrict the input difference and output linear mask of E_m to be single-bit. The detailed procedure of searching such differential-linear distinguisher is presented in Sect. 4.1. In addition, to amplify the correlation, some condition equations are imposed to make the differential of E_d determined which might be key-dependent. Then the correlation of conditional differential-linear distinguisher on the targeted cipher E can be treated as the one on a degraded cipher $E'_l \circ E_m$. Further, the key-recovery attacks are launched based on the conditional differential-linear distinguishers. We apply these cryptanalytic techniques to KNOT-AEAD(128,256,64) and KNOT-AEAD(128,384,192), of which the former is the primary member recommended by the designers. As a result, for 15-round KNOT-AEAD(128,256,64) (out of 52 full rounds) our attack takes $2^{48.8}$ time complexity and $2^{47.5}$ blocks to recover the full 128-bit key. With regard to 17-round KNOT-AEAD(128,384,192) (out of 76 full rounds), we require time complexity of $2^{59.2}$ and data complexity of $2^{58.2}$ to launch a key-recovery attack.

Comparison of Results. Next, we compare our attacks with the known analysis against KNOT-AEAD(128,256,64) and KNOT-AEAD(128,384,192), which are summarized in Table 1.

In [30], the designers of KNOT give the security analysis of KNOT-AEAD and KNOT-Hash. Especially, for KNOT-AEAD(128,256,64), they presented a 14-round distinguishing attack of complexity $O(2^{62.2})$ by considering a truncated difference propagation and a 12-round key-recovery attack of complexity $O(2^{60})$ through a linear approximation involving one key bit. Similarly, for KNOT-AEAD(128,384,192), they showed a 13-round distinguishing attack of complexity $O(2^{60.8})$ by considering a truncated difference propagation and a 12-round key-recovery attack of complexity $O(2^{60})$ through a linear approximation involving one key bit. In a distinguishing attack, the algorithm (or distinguisher) allows to distinguish the ciphertext produced by the target cipher from a random permutation with high probability, but no information of the secret key

Table 1. Summary of attacks on KNOT-AEAD

Cipher	Rounds	Type of attack	Time	Data	Ref.
† KNOT-AEAD v1	14	Distinguisher	$O(2^{62.2})$	$O(2^{62.2})$	[30]
	12	Key-recovery attack	$O(2^{60})$	$O(2^{60})$	[30]
	15	Key-recovery attack	$2^{48.8}$	$2^{47.5}$	Sect. 4.2
† KNOT-AEAD v2	13	Distinguisher	$O(2^{60.8})$	$O(2^{60.8})$	[30]
	12	Key-recovery attack	$O(2^{60})$	$O(2^{60})$	[30]
	17	Key-recovery attack	$2^{59.2}$	$2^{58.2}$	Sect. 4.3

† Here we adopt the notations used by designers in [30], i.e., KNOT-AEAD(128,256,64) and KNOT-AEAD(128,384,192) denoted by KNOT-AEAD v1 and KNOT-AEAD v2 respectively.
$ In our attacks, we can recover the full 128-bit secret key for 15-round KNOT-AEAD v1, and one bit of the secret key for 17-round KNOT-AEAD v2. In the previous analysis, only one bit of the secret key can be recovered for 12-round KNOT-AEAD v1 and v2.

can be obtained. Using the conditional differential-linear attacks, we obtain the key-recovery attack of 15-round KNOT-AEAD(128,256,64) which is three more rounds compared with their result. A key-recovery attack for 17-round KNOT-AEAD(128,384,192) is derived by our cryptanalytic techniques, and it is five rounds better than their analysis. For the detail of time and data complexities, please refer to Table 1.

1.2   Paper Organization

This paper is organized as follows. In Sect. 2, we describe the KONT-AEAD algorithms and review some basic notations and MILP-based automatic search method for differential and linear trails. In Sect. 3, an overview of the classic differential-linear attack is showed, followed by some recent developments on it. We present the details of the conditional differential-linear attacks against KNOT-AEAD in Sect. 4. First, we show the procedure of our strategy for searching good differential-linear distinguishers in Sect. 4.1. Then we carry out our key-recovery attacks against 15-round KNOT-AEAD(128,256,64) and 17-round KNOT-AEAD(128,384,192) in Sect. 4.2 and Sect. 4.3 respectively. Finally in Sect. 5, we give a brief summary of this paper.

2   Preliminaries

In this section we firstly describe the KNOT-AEAD algorithms and their underlying permutations. Then we provide an overview of some basic notations and MILP-based automatic search method for differential and linear trails.

2.1 Description of KNOT-AEAD

The KNOT family is designed by Zhang et al., which includes bit-slice lightweight AEAD and hashing algorithms [29]. In this subsection, we give firstly a brief specification of KNOT-AEAD on which our differential-linear attacks are applied.

The underlying permutation of each KNOT member iteratively applies an SPN-based round transformation. There are three round transformations which are different only in the size b of block, $b = 256, 384, 512$. Each of the round transformations consists of three steps: $AddRoundConstant_b$, $SubColumn_b$ and $ShiftRow_b$. Let p_b denote a round transformation and $p_b = ShiftRow_b \circ SubColumn_b \circ AddRoundConstant_b(S)$, where S is the b-bit state. As done in [29], a b-bit state is pictured as a $4 \times \frac{b}{4}$ rectangular array of bits. The first $\frac{b}{4}$ bits are arranged in 0-th row, denoted by a_0, the next $\frac{b}{4}$ bits are arranged in 1-st row, denoted by a_1, and so on. The j-th bit of i-th row is denoted by $a_{i,j}$ or $a_i[j]$. In the following, a cipher state is described in a two-dimensional way, as illustrated in Fig. 1.

$$\begin{bmatrix} a_{0,\frac{b}{4}-1} & \cdots & a_{0,1} & a_{0,0} \\ a_{1,\frac{b}{4}-1} & \cdots & a_{1,1} & a_{1,0} \\ a_{2,\frac{b}{4}-1} & \cdots & a_{2,1} & a_{2,0} \\ a_{3,\frac{b}{4}-1} & \cdots & a_{3,1} & a_{3,0} \end{bmatrix}$$

Fig. 1. A cipher state

The AddRoundConstant_b Transformation. It consists of a simple bitwise XOR of a d-bit round constant generated by the corresponding d-bit LFSR to the first d bits of the intermediate state, with $d = 6, 7, 8$. Since we can ignore this transformation in our attacks, we omit the detailed description of round constants here.

The SubColumn_b Transformation. It is composed of $\frac{b}{4}$ parallel applications of S-boxes to the 4 bits in the same column. The S-box used in KNOT is a 4-bit to 4-bit S-box $S : \{0,1\}^4 \rightarrow \{0,1\}^4$. The action of this S-box in hexadecimal notation is given in Table 2. Let x_0, x_1, x_2, x_3 and y_0, y_1, y_2, y_3 respectively denote the input and output of the KNOT S-box, where x_0 and y_0 are the least significant bits respectively. The algebraic normal form (ANF) of the S-box is the following:

Table 2. The S-box of KNOT

x	0	1	2	3	4	5	6	7	8	9	A	B	C	D	E	F
$S(x)$	4	0	A	7	B	E	1	D	9	F	6	8	5	2	C	3

$$y_0 = x_0x_1 \oplus x_2 \oplus x_0x_2 \oplus x_3 \oplus x_1x_3 \oplus x_0x_1x_3 \oplus x_2x_3$$
$$y_1 = x_1 \oplus x_2 \oplus x_0x_3 \oplus x_2x_3 \oplus x_1x_2x_3$$
$$y_2 = 1 \oplus x_0 \oplus x_1 \oplus x_2 \oplus x_1x_2 \oplus x_3$$
$$y_3 = x_1 \oplus x_0x_1 \oplus x_2 \oplus x_3.$$

The $ShiftRow_b$ Transformation. It makes up of a left rotation to each row over different offsets. The 0-th row is not rotated, i-th row is left rotated over c_i bit for $1 \leq i \leq 3$. The parameters (c_1, c_2, c_3) are $(1,8,25)$, $(1,8,55)$, $(1,16,25)$ for $b = 256, 384, 512$ respectively.

There are 4 members in KNOT-AEAD family whose modes are based on Duplex mode MonkeyDuplex [8]. Let KNOT-AEAD(k,b,r) denote a KNOT-AEAD member with k-bit key, b-bit state and r-bit rate. Note that the key length, the nonce length and the tag length are all equal to k bits for each member. In the following, we only concentrate on two members KNOT-AEAD(128,256,64) which is the primary member and KNOT-AEAD(128,384,192). Each member of KNOT-AEAD has 4 phases: initialization, processing associated data, encryption and finalization, which is illustrated in Fig. 2.

The authenticated encryption process is initialized by loading the key K and the nonce N, $S = K||N$ for KNOT-AEAD(128,256,64) and $S = (0^{128}||K||N) \oplus (1||0^{383})$ for KNOT-AEAD(128,384,192). Then the initial state is processed by $p[nr_0]$, i.e., nr_0 rounds of the round transformation, where $nr_0 = 52$ for KNOT-AEAD(128,256,64) and $nr_0 = 76$ for KNOT-AEAD(128,384,192). The associated data block A_i is XORed and then $p[nr]$ is applied to the intermediate state in sequence for $i = 0, \cdots, u-1$. The constant $1||0^{c-1}$ is XORed to the capacity part of state after the last $p[nr]$ in the process of associated data. Each plaintext block P_i is processed similarly to A_i for $i = 0, \cdots, v-1$, while the corresponding ciphertext block C_i is the output. In the finalization, $p[nr_f]$ is applied and the tag T is the output. The data, i.e., the blocks of processed plaintext and associated data, is limited to 2^{64} for both member by the designers of KNOT.

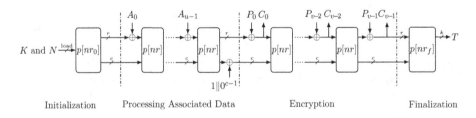

Initialization   Processing Associated Data   Encryption   Finalization

Fig. 2. The encryption of KNOT-AEAD

2.2 Notations

In this subsection, some basic notations are presented, followed by a fundamental lemma—Piling-up Lemma.

Let $\mathbb{F}_2 = \{0, 1\}$ be the finite field with two elements. The correlation of a binary random variable x is defined as $Cor(x) = \Pr[x = 0] - \Pr[x = 1] = 2\Pr[x = 0] - 1$. Similarly, the correlation of a Boolean function on an input with some distribution can be defined as following.

Definition 1. *The correlation of a Boolean function* $f : \mathbb{F}_2^n \to \mathbb{F}_2$ *is defined as* $Cor(f) = \Pr[f(X) = 0] - \Pr[f(X) = 1]$, *where* $X = (x_0, \cdots, x_{n-1})$ *is a vector of binary random variables.*

Lemma 1 (Piling-up Lemma [24]). *Let* $x_0, \cdots, x_{n-1}$ *be* n *independent binary random variables with probability* $\Pr[x_i = 0] = p_i$. *Then the following holds*

$$\Pr[x_0 \oplus \cdots \oplus x_{n-1} = 0] = \frac{1}{2} + 2^{n-1} \prod_{i=0}^{n-1} (p_i - \frac{1}{2}),$$

or alternatively, $Cor(x_0 \oplus \cdots \oplus x_{n-1}) = \prod_{i=0}^{n-1} Cor(x_i)$.

2.3 MILP-Based Automatic Search for Differential and Linear Trails

In this subsection, we give a brief description about the Mixed Integer Linear Programming (MILP)-based automatic search method for differential and linear trails and how we apply it to the KNOT permutations. For more details of this method, please refer to [27,28].

In [25], Mouha et al. introduced the MILP model to count the number of active S-boxes for those word-oriented block ciphers. In ASIACRYPT 2014, Sun et al. [28] extended the framework to bit-oriented ciphers. Let x_i denote the difference variable for the i-th bit. That is, $x_i = 1$ if the difference at the i-th bit is active; otherwise, $x_i = 0$.

Suppose the two vectors $(x_0, x_1, \cdots, x_{\omega-1})$ and $(y_0, y_1, \cdots, y_{\nu-1})$ are the input and output bit differences of an $\omega \times \nu$ S-box S_t. Let the bit variable A_t denote the activity of this S-box. That is to say, $A_t = 1$ if S_t is active, and $A_t = 0$ otherwise. The following constraints can be used to ensure that non-zero input difference of the S-box must active it:

$$\begin{cases} A_t - x_k \geq 0, \ k = 0, \ldots, \omega - 1, \\ -A_t + \sum_{j=0}^{\omega-1} x_j \geq 0. \end{cases} \tag{1}$$

Let a discrete point $(x_0, \cdots, x_{\omega-1}, y_0, \cdots, y_{\nu-1}) \in \mathbb{R}^{\omega+\nu}$ denote the input-output differential pattern of an S-box, and then we can get a finite set of discrete points Q, which includes all possible differential patterns of the S-box. By computing the H-Representation of the convex hull of Q, many linear inequalities are obtained, each of which can be used to remove some impossible differential patterns of the S-box. In [27], they presented the greedy algorithm to select a subset of the H-Representation of the convex hull with less inequalities, which can be used to exactly describe the differential patterns of the S-box.

The objective function can be to minimize the sum of all variables $\sum_t A_t$, which indicates the number of the active S-boxes appearing in the schematic description of the encryption. Using any MILP optimizer such as Gurobi, the model can be solved and good differential characteristics are returned.

For the S-box of the KNOT permutations, since there are 3 possible probabilities, i.e., 1, 2^{-2}, 2^{-3}, we append two extra bits (p, q) to encode the probability of the propagation. Therefore, a vector $(x_0, \cdots, x_3, y_0, \cdots, y_3, p, q) \in \mathbb{R}^{10}$ can describe a differential pattern with probability for the S-box. Then with the help of SageMath, 543 inequalities are derived through computing the H-Representation of the convex hull and the number of inequalities is reduced to 23 by the greedy algorithm in [27]. Since the linear layer of KNOT makes up of the left rotation, there is no need to introduce new inequalities. Besides, we can ignore the bitwise XOR of constants in the differential trail.

The objective function is minimization of the formula $\sum_t (p_t + 2q_t)$, which means the total probability of the differential trail through the encryption algorithm.

With regard to searching for linear trails, the modeling process is similar with the aforementioned.

3   The Framework of Differential-Linear Attacks

We begin with an overview of the classical differential-linear attack, and then we recall some recent developments on it.

3.1   The Classic Differential-Linear Attack

Let E be an entire cipher that can be decomposed into two subciphers E_d and E_l such that $E = E_l \circ E_d$ where the differential and linear cryptanalyses are applied into E_d and E_l respectively. More precisely, assume that a differential $\Delta_{in} \xrightarrow{p} \Delta_m$ for E_d holds with probability $\Pr[E_d(X) \oplus E_d(X \oplus \Delta_{in}) = \Delta_m] = p$, and a linear approximation $\Gamma_m \xrightarrow{q} \Gamma_{out}$ for E_l holds with probability $\Pr[\Gamma_m \cdot X = \Gamma_{out} \cdot E_l(X)] = \frac{1}{2}(1 + q)$ (or with correlation q), where $\cdot$ denotes the inner product between two vectors. The differential-linear attack combines the above two distinguishers and the procedure of new distinguisher is presented in the following.

Procedure of the Differential-Linear Distinguisher. To distinguish E from a random permutation R, the adversary samples N plaintext pairs (P, P') such that $P \oplus P' = \Delta_{in}$ and checks whether the corresponding ciphertext pairs (C, C') agree on the parity of output subset of bits in Γ_{out} one by one. The detailed procedure is presented as Algorithm 1.

In the case that the differential in E_d fails, the equality $\Gamma_{out} \cdot E(X) = \Gamma_{out} \cdot E(X \oplus \Delta_{in})$ is usually assumed to hold in approximately half. Under the assumption that E_d and E_l are independent, the probability of differential-linear distinguisher can be natively estimated using Piling-up Lemma, $\Pr[\Gamma_{out} \cdot E(X) =$

$\Gamma_{out} \cdot E(X \oplus \Delta_{in})] = p(\frac{1}{2}(1 + q^2)) + (1 - p)\frac{1}{2} = \frac{1}{2}(1 + pq^2)$ (assuming that $\Gamma_m \cdot \Delta_m = 0$). Therefore, by preparing $N = O(p^{-2}q^{-4})$ chosen plaintext pairs $(P, P \oplus \Delta_{in})$, one can distinguish the cipher E from a random permutation using Algorithm 1 (refer to [12,26] for the details about the data complexity and success probability).

Algorithm 1. Procedure of the differential-linear distinguisher

---

Ensure: The cipher E or random permutation R.
1: Set a counter T to 0.
2: **for** N plaintext pairs $(P, P \oplus \Delta_{in})$ **do**
3:    Increment T if $\Gamma_{out} \cdot (O(P) \oplus O(P \oplus \Delta_{in})) = 0$, where O is a encryption oracle E or R.
4: **end for**
5: **if** $\frac{2T}{N} - 1$ deviates enough from 0 **then**
6:    The data is draw from the cipher E.
7: **else**
8:    A random permutation R.
9: **end if**

In Theorem 2 of [26], Selçuk showed the analytical results of the success probability of a key-recovery attack in linear cryptanalysis. The main difference between the linear context and the differential-linear context is that the sign of the bias in the latter case is unaffected by any key bit (as all the affected key bits are used twice and thus canceled). In [12], Blondeau et al. adapted the framework of [26] and gave the success probability of a key-recovery attack in the differential-linear context as

$$P_S = \Phi(2\sqrt{N}|p_{dl} - \frac{1}{2}| - \Phi^{-1}(1 - 2^{-a})), \tag{2}$$

where Φ is the cumulative distribution function of the standard normal distribution, p_{dl} is the probability of differential-linear distinguisher, N is the number of chosen plaintext pairs and a is the advantage of the attack as defined in [26].

Exact Analysis for the Correlation of Differential-Linear Distinguisher. In [12], Blondeau et al. showed an exact expression of the correlation by *differential-linear hull*. With the following notations, the result is presented as Theorem 1.

$$\mathcal{E}_{\Delta_{in}, \Gamma_{out}} = 2\Pr[\Gamma_{out} \cdot (E(X) \oplus E(X \oplus \Delta_{in})) = 0] - 1$$
$$\varepsilon_{\Delta_{in}, \Gamma_m} = 2\Pr[\Gamma_m \cdot (E_d(X) \oplus E_d(X \oplus \Delta_{in})) = 0] - 1$$
$$c_{\Gamma_m, \Gamma_{out}} = 2\Pr[\Gamma_m \cdot X = \Gamma_{out} \cdot E_l(X)] - 1$$

Theorem 1 (Differential-Linear Hull [12]). *Assume that the part E_d and E_l of the block cipher $E = E_l \circ E_d$ are independent. Using the notation defined in the above, for all $\Delta_{in} \in \{0,1\}^n \setminus 0^n$ and $\Gamma_{out} \in \{0,1\}^n \setminus 0^n$, we have*

$$\mathcal{E}_{\Delta_{in}, \Gamma_{out}} = \sum_{\Gamma_m \in \{0,1\}^n} \varepsilon_{\Delta_{in}, \Gamma_m} c^2_{\Gamma_m, \Gamma_{out}}. \tag{3}$$

In Eq. (3) all the linear approximation trails are taken into account when estimating the correlation of the differential-linear approximation. Of course, it is usually hard to evaluate the correlation by the above expression. In practice, one mostly has to make the assumption of one *strong* linear approximation in E_l or *supporting subset* in the intermediate layer, and verify the results experimentally.

3.2   Recent Improvements

In practice, the assumption of independence between E_d and E_l might arise a problem that results in wrong estimation for the correlation. Currently, the only way to get some evidence of this independence assumption is to experimentally compute the correlation of differential-linear approximation over a reduced number of rounds of the cipher. As done in recent works [3,6,18,21], the subcipher E_l is further divided to two parts E_l' and E_m to obtain a more accurate estimation for the correlation of differential-linear distinguisher. That is the cipher is divided as $E = E_l' \circ E_m \circ E_d$ and the overall attack framework is depicted in Fig. 3. Bar-On et al. [3] introduced a theoretical method called DLCT to cover the middle part E_m. Moreover, they showed that the DLCT could be efficiently constructed using the Fast Fourier Transform. With the DLCT, they further improved the differential-linear attacks on ICEPOLE and 8-round DES. In CRYPTO 2021, Liu et al. [22] studied the differential-linear cryptanalysis from an algebraic perspective by introducing a technique called DATF. Then they developed a new theory of estimation of bias and techniques for key-recovery in the differential-linear cryptanalysis. The techniques were applied to Ascon, Serpent and Grain v1.

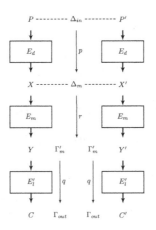

Fig. 3. The structure of differential-linear distinguisher

Subsequently, Beierle et al. [6] presented several improvements of the differential-linear attacks against ARX ciphers and successfully applied them to Chaskey and ChaCha. In their work, the correlation of middle part E_m is experimentally evaluated. Let r denote the correlation of the middle part E_m of the cipher, i.e., $r = Cor[\Gamma'_m \cdot (E_m(X) \oplus E_m(X \oplus \Delta_m))]$. Similarly, under the assumption of independence between the subciphers, the probability of differential-linear distinguisher can be simply estimated using Piling-up Lemma, $\Pr[\Gamma_{out} \cdot E(X) = \Gamma_{out} \cdot E(X \oplus \Delta_{in})] = \frac{1}{2}(1 + prq^2)$, and one can distinguish the cipher E from random permutation using $N = O(p^{-2}r^{-2}q^{-4})$ chosen plaintext pairs $(P, P \oplus \Delta_{in})$ using Algorithm 1. We pay attention to the part E_d where a differential $\Delta_{in} \xrightarrow{p} \Delta_m$ holds with probability $\Pr[E_d(X) \oplus E_d(X \oplus \Delta_{in}) = \Delta_m] = p$. Let $\mathbb{X}_d$ denote the set of all input values that define the right pairs for the differential, i.e., $\mathbb{X}_d = \{X \in \{0,1\}^n | E_d(X) \oplus E_d(X \oplus \Delta_{in}) = \Delta_m\}$. To amplify the correlation of differential-linear distinguisher, Beierle et al. [6] exploited the special structure of E_d called *fully or probabilistic independent parts* which could be rather likely observed in many ARX ciphers, such as ChaCha and Chaskey. With the help of *fully or probabilistic independent parts*, given one element $X \in \mathbb{X}_d$, one can generate many other elements in $\mathbb{X}_d$ for free or with some probability (almost 1), independently of the secret key. However, we can not use this method for a general permutation E_d due to that an arbitrary permutation might not have this special structure.

4   Differential-Linear Cryptanalysis of KNOT-AEAD

In this section, we present the details of the conditional differential-linear attacks against KNOT-AEAD. The KNOT's design document [29] shows, if the length of the associated data is zero, then no padding is applied and no associated data is processed. In our attacks, we omit the processing associated data phase, and our attack target is the initialization of KNOT-AEAD where nr'_0 rounds of the round transformation are applied to the initial state. In the following, we denote the targeted procedure by nr'_0-round KNOT-AEAD(k, b, r) which is shown in Fig. 4. Our attacks are performed in known plaintext attack scenario, i.e., P_0 and C_0 can be accessed. Only single-key model is taken into account in which the input difference is restricted on the nonce N which can be controlled by the adversary, and the output linear mask is restricted on the first 64 or 192 bits of a state, i.e., the rate part of a state.

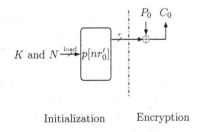

Fig. 4. The targeted procedure of KNOT-AEAD

4.1   Searching Differential-Linear Distinguishers

The diffusion layers of KNOT permutations are very simple and only make up of a left rotation to each row. For example, for 8-round E_m (from 3-rd to 10-th round), when the single-bit input difference is at 0-th bit of 2-nd row, the output difference at 55-th bit of 2-nd row is determined to be 1. To make the analysis cover as many rounds as possible and observe higher correlation, we only consider single-bit input difference and output linear mask of E_m. For obtaining a good differential-linear distinguisher, the procedure of our strategy is presented in the following:

STEP 1. Search the best difference trail given an arbitrary single-bit output difference on E_d by using the MILP-aided (differential trail) searching method. The best difference is denoted by $\Delta_{in} \rightarrow \Delta_m$ with the weight restriction $wt(\Delta_m) = 1$.

STEP 2. For all the single-bit input difference Δ_m, exhaustively search the best output linear mask whose weight is restricted to 1 on E_m by experiment-based correlation estimation method. The best differential-linear characteristic is denoted by $\Delta_m \rightarrow \Gamma'_m$ with the weight restriction $wt(\Delta_m) = wt(\Gamma'_m) = 1$.

STEP 3. Final, for all the single-bit input linear mask, exhaustively search the best linear trail on E'_l by using MILP-aided (linear trail) searching method. The best linear approximation is denoted by $\Gamma'_m \rightarrow \Gamma_{out}$ with the weight restriction $wt(\Gamma'_m) = 1$.

Then many differential-linear distinguishers are generated by combining results in the above three steps and the best one is chosen to launch our attacks.

4.2   Attack on 15-Round KNOT-AEAD(128,256,64)

In this subsection, we firstly show how to find the differential-linear distinguisher of 15-round KNOT-AEAD(128,256,64). Then a key-recovery attack is presented based on this distinguisher.

Differential-Linear Distinguisher. Since the (differential-linear) characteristics of KNOT are rotation-invariant within a 64-bit word, all the single-bit differences (or linear masks) can be classified into four cases. For each case, we search the best result separately.

   We searched all the differential trails of E_d up to 8 round in which the weight of output difference is restricted 1. But, there are three possible effective differential trails which can be used in our attacks, two 1-round trails with probability 2^{-3} and output difference at words of 0/2-th row, one 2-round trail with probability 2^{-6} and output difference at word of 2-nd row. To increase the number of rounds attacked as much as possible, we choose the 2-round trail in the following analysis, which is shown in Table 3. In the presentation of trails, the row ordering is from right to left, then from top-down, i.e., 0, 1, 2 and 3-th row respectively.

Table 3. A 2-round differential trail with probability 2^{-6}

Round	Difference
Input	0x0100000000000000 0x0100000000000000
	0x0000000000000000 0x0000000000000000
1st round	0x0000000000000000 0x0100000000000000
	0x0000000000000000 0x0000000000000000
2nd round	0x0000000000000000 0x0000000000000000
	0x0000000000000000 0x0000000000000001

To amplify the correlation, some condition equations are imposed to make the differential of E_d determined. Similar techniques are appeared in conditional differential cryptanalysis [7,19]. Then the correlation of conditional differential-linear distinguisher on the targeted cipher $E = E'_l \circ E_m \circ E_d$ can be treated as the one on a degraded cipher $E'_l \circ E_m$. With the symbolic computation in SageMath, the following 6 condition equations are imposed to make the differential trail in Table 3 determined, i.e., 3 bits of 1-st round $\Delta a_0^{(1)}[56] = n_0[56]k_1[56] \oplus n_0[56] \oplus n_1[56]k_1[56] \oplus n_1[56] \oplus k_0[56] \oplus 1 = 1$, $\Delta a_1^{(1)}[57] = k_0[56]k_1[56] \oplus k_1[56] \oplus 1 = 0$, $\Delta a_3^{(1)}[17] = n_0[56] \oplus n_1[56] = 0$, and 3 bits of 2-nd round $\Delta a_0^{(2)}[56] = a_1^{(1)}[56]a_3^{(1)}[56] \oplus a_1^{(1)}[56] \oplus a_2^{(1)}[56] = 0$, $\Delta a_1^{(2)}[57] = a_3^{(1)}[56] = 0$, $\Delta a_3^{(2)}[17] = a_1^{(1)}[56] = 0$, where $a_i^{(r)}[j]$ ($\Delta a_i^{(r)}[j]$) denotes the (difference) expression of the j-th bit of i-th 64-bit word of r-th round, $k_i[j]$ and $n_i[j]$ are the j-th bit of i-th 64-bit word of the secret K and nonce N respectively. Generally, we impose the 6 condition equations to make the corresponding differential trails determined, i.e., $\Delta a_0^{(1)}[i] = 1$, $\Delta a_1^{(1)}[(i+1) \bmod 64] = 0$, $\Delta a_3^{(1)}[(i+25) \bmod 64] = 0$, and $\Delta a_0^{(2)}[i] = 0$, $\Delta a_1^{(2)}[(i+1) \bmod 64] = 0$, $\Delta a_3^{(2)}[(i+25) \bmod 64] = 0$, for $0 \leq i \leq 63$, which are simplified as the below:

$$k_0[i] = 0,$$
$$k_1[i] = 1,$$
$$n_0[i] \oplus n_1[i] = 0,$$
$$n_0[i-1]k_1[i-1] \oplus (n_1[i-1] \oplus 1)k_0[i-1]k_1[i-1] \oplus n_1[i-1] \oplus k_0[i-1] = 0,$$
$$n_0[i-8] = (n_1[i-8] \oplus 1)k_0[i-8] \oplus n_1[i-8] \oplus k_1[i-8] \oplus 1,$$
$$(n_0[i-25] \oplus 1)n_1[i-25] = k_0[i-25] \oplus k_1[i-25]$$

(4)

where indices should be modulo 64 which denote the order of bits in a word. In the following, we will set the above condition equations to be satisfied and perform sampling experiments of correlation estimation of E_m.

For the subcipher E'_l, we searched all the linear trails up to 5 round in which the weight of input linear mask is restricted 1. But there is only one possible effective linear trail which can be used in our attacks, a 1-round trail with correlation 2^{-2} and input linear mask at word of 2-nd row, which is shown in Table 4.

Table 4. A 1-round linear trail with correlation 2^{-2}

Round	Linear mask
Input	0x0000000000000000 0x0000000000000000
	0x0000000000000000 0x0000000000000001
1st round	0x0000000000000000 0x0000000000000001
	0x0000000000000000 0x0000000000000000

Targeting the result of 15-round KNOT-AEAD(128,256,64), we exhaustively searched all the 64 single-bit output linear masks at word of 2-nd row for E_m of 12 rounds under the condition that the above difference equations in Eq. (4) are satisfied. We use at most 2^{35} random nonces for each of the 2^4 random keys, so we can only measure a correlation of about $|Cor| > c \cdot 2^{-17.5} = 2^{-14}$ (where $c \approx \sqrt{128}$ for a reasonable estimation error). For the input difference showed in Table 3 (i.e., $i = 56$), the best output linear mask is at 27-th bit of 2-nd row with correlation $-2^{-11.9}$. Furthermore, once one or more condition equations of Eq. (4) are not satisfied, we can not detect any correlation. As a result, we obtain a differential-linear distinguisher of correlation $-2^{-15.9}$ for 15-round KNOT-AEAD(128,256,64) by splicing the above 1-round linear trail.

Key-Recovery Attack. As defined in [19], conditions that control the difference propagations can be classified into three types in a chosen plaintext/initial value (IV) attack scenario, Type 0 conditions only involving bits of IV, Type 1 conditions only involving bits of IV and the secret key, Type 2 conditions only involving bits of the secret key. Note that the adversary can impose the condition equations of Type 0 for free in a chosen plaintext/IV attack scenario. Since condition equations might be key-dependent (only considering Type 1), we need guess the values of expressions that consist of bits of the secret key and choose the value of corresponding IV bits according to the condition equations. For the case of Type 2, the differential-linear cryptanalysis might degrade into a weak key-recovery attack. Assume that there are $l = l_1 + l_2$ independent expressions of key bits, l_1 conditions of Type 1 and l_2 conditions of Type 2. The general procedure of the conditional differential-linear attack is summarized as follows.

Procedure of the Conditional Differential-Linear Attack. For each guess of expressions of key bits in Type 1, like in Algorithm 1, the adversary samples N pairs of initial state (X, X') such that $X \oplus X' = \Delta_{in}$ and counts how many times the corresponding ciphertext pairs agree on the parity of output subset of bits in Γ_{out}. To make the differential propagation in E_d determined, some bits of IV called conditional IV bits are set according to the guessed values of expressions of key bits and the condition equations (containing Type 0). Besides, the sampled pairs of initial state should be generated by flipping non-conditional IV bits. In order to obtain an effective distinguisher, there must be enough non-conditional IV bits to generate initial states to observe the correlation of differential-linear distinguisher. In Algorithm 2, the details of this procedure are presented and the complexity of Algorithm 2 is $2^{l_1+1}N$. Note that we ignore the conditions of Type 2 in Algorithm 2, additional 2^{l_2} executions of Algorithm 2 are needed if there are enough other differential-linear distinguishers.

Algorithm 2. Procedure of the conditional differential-linear attack

---

Ensure: Set of candidates for some expressions of key bits of the cipher E.
1: **for** All 2^{l_1} possible values of expressions of key bits imposed in E_d **do**
2:     Set the conditional IV bits according to the condition equations.
3:     Prepare N pairs of initial states $(X, X \oplus \Delta_{in})$ by varying non-conditional IV bits.
4:     Set a counter T to 0.
5:     **for** N initial states $(X, X \oplus \Delta_{in})$ **do**
6:         Increment T if $\Gamma_{out} \cdot (E(X) \oplus E(X \oplus \Delta_{in})) = 0$.
7:     **end for**
8:     **if** $\frac{2T}{N} - 1$ deviates enough from 0 **then**
9:         Keep the current value of expressions of key bits in C_K as a candidate.
10:     **end if**
11: **end for**
12: Reduce the system of expressions of key bits in C_K and return the solutions.

For 15-round KNOT-AEAD(128,256,64), we launch the key-recovery attack by Algorithm 2. Among Eq. (4), 1 of 6 belongs to Type 0 conditions, 3 of 6 belong to Type 1 conditions and 2 of 6 belong to Type 2 conditions. First, we impose the Type 0 condition $n_0[i] \oplus n_1[i] = 0$ for free. And the value of $n_0[i-25]$ is set to zero (or $n_1[i-25] = 1$) to prevent the corresponding condition equation to degrade into a Type 2 condition. In Algorithm 2, the conditional IV bits are chosen as $CIV = \{n_0[i], n_0[i-25]\} \cup \{n_1[i-1], n_0[i-8], n_1[i-25]\}$ and $l_1 = 3$. Once the values of the flipped bits $FIV = \{n_0[i-1] = 0, n_1[i-8]\}$ are given, we can distinguish $k_0[i] = 0, k_1[i] = 1$ from the other cases using Algorithm 2 with the time and data complexities $2^{l_1+1}N = 2^{3+1+37.3} = 2^{41.3}$ and the success probability is almost 1 according to the formula in [12], Eq. (2). On average, we will succeed by repeatedly executing Algorithm 2 for $2^{l_2} = 4$ times with the index i varying which identifies the differential-linear distinguisher. In the case $k_0[i] = 0, k_1[i] = 1$, three or four extra expressions of key bits can be recovered, i.e., $k_0[i-1] = k_1[i-1] = 1$ or $k_0[i-1] = c_1$ (when $k_0[i-1]k_1[i-1] = 0$), $(v \oplus 1)k_0[i-8] \oplus v \oplus k_1[i-8] \oplus 1 = c_2$, $k_0[i-25] \oplus k_1[i-25] = c_3$, where $n_0[i-1] = 0$ and v is the value of $n_1[i-8]$. Note that when $k_0[i-1] = k_1[i-1] = 1$, the corresponding condition equation holds no matter what the value of $n_1[i-1]$ is. With the additional complexity of $2^{1+1+37.3} = 2^{39.3}$, one or two equations of key bits can be derived by flipping the value of FIV bit by bit, i.e., $k_1[i-1] \oplus k_0[i-1] = c_1'$ (when $k_0[i-1]k_1[i-1] = 0$), $(\overline{v} \oplus 1)k_0[i-8] \oplus \overline{v} \oplus k_1[i-8] \oplus 1 = c_2'$.

Therefore, we can totally obtain 7 independently linear equations of key bits in the case $k_0[i] = 0, k_1[i] = 1$.

For i ($0 \leq i \leq 63$), we can perform the above process 64 times and obtain some equations of key bits. On average, there are 16 indices i's such that $k_0[i] = 0, k_1[i] = 1$, and $16 \times 7 = 112$ equations of key bits can be derived in total. We have checked that the above linear system has on average 80 independently linear equations by thousands of experiments. In conclusion, we can recover the 128-bit secret key for 15-round KNOT-AEAD(128,256,64) with the expected time complexity of $(64 \times 2^{41.3} + 16 \times 2 \times 2^{39.3}) + 2^{48} = 2^{48.8}$ and data complexity of $64 \times 2^{41.3} + 16 \times 2 \times 2^{39.3} = 2^{47.5}$.

4.3   Attack on 17-Round KNOT-AEAD(128,384,192)

Similar to the attack of the primary AEAD member, we present the key-recovery attack against KNOT-AEAD(128,384,192) in the following.

Differential-Linear Distinguisher. We searched all the differential trails with single-bit output difference for E_d up to 9 round. But there are only two possible effective differential trails, two 1-round trails with probability 2^{-3} and output difference at words of 0/2-th row respectively. Note that the constants of initial state are treated as variables in our MILP-aided differential trail searching method. In the following attack, we choose the 1-round differential trail which is shown in Table 5.

Table 5. A 1-round differential trail with probability 2^{-3}

Round	Difference
Input	0x000000000000000000000000 0x010000000000000000000000
	0x000000000000000000000000 0x000000000000000000000000
1st round	0x000000000000000000000000 0x000000000000000000000000
	0x000000000000000000000000 0x000000000000000000000001

Taking the constants of initial state into account, we recompute the propagation of the above 1-round differential trail by SageMath. When the input difference is at i-th bit of 0-row ($0 \leq i \leq 94$), a single-bit output difference at $((i+8) \bmod 96)$-th bit of 2-nd row can be observed with probability 2^{-1} or 2^{-2}. The difference propagation will be certain when the below condition equations of difference are satisfied.

$$\begin{aligned}
n_{i+96} &= 0, & k_{i+64} &= 0, \ 0 \leq i \leq 31, \\
k_{i-32} &= 0, & k_{i+96} &= 0, \ 32 \leq i \leq 63, \\
k_{i-32} &= 0, & & 64 \leq i \leq 94.
\end{aligned} \tag{5}$$

For the subcipher E_m of 13 rounds, all the single-bit output linear masks are exhaustively searched when the input difference is at 0-th bit of 2-nd row. As a result, we detected high correlation at 14-th bit of 0-th row with $2^{-12.6}$.

For the subcipher E'_l, we searched all the linear trails up to 7 round in which the weight of input linear mask is restricted 1. Consequently, some rounds can be expanded forward when the single-bit input linear mask is at 0-th row or 2-nd row. From them, we choose three effective linear trails which can be used in our attacks, trails for 1/2/3 round(s) with correlation $2^{-2}/2^{-5}/2^{-7}$ respectively and input linear masks at words of 0-th row for them. By splicing the 3-round linear trail which is shown in Table 6, we obtain a differential-linear trail of correlation $2^{-26.6}$ for 17-round KNOT-AEAD(128,384,192).

Table 6. A 3-round linear trail with correlation 2^{-7}

Round	Linear mask
Input	0x00000000000000000000000 0x00000000000000000000001
	0x00000000000000000000000 0x00000000000000000000000
1st round	0x00000000000000000000000 0x00000000000000000000001
	0x00000000000000000000000 0x00000000000000000000100
2nd round	0x00000000000000000000000 0x00000000000000000000101
	0x00000000000000000000000 0x00000000000000000000100
3rd round	0x00000000000000000000202 0x00000000000000000000100
	0x00000000000000000000000 0x00000000000000000000000

Key-Recovery Attack. In the case $k_{i-32} = 0$ ($64 \le i \le 94$), the high correlation can be observed with time and data complexities of $2^{1+57.2} = 2^{58.2}$ with success probability of almost 1 by Algorithm 2 where no key expression needs to be guessed. We will succeed on average by repeatedly running Algorithm 2 for 2 times with different indices. In conclusion, with the time complexity of $2^{1+58.2} = 2^{59.2}$ and data complexity of $2^{58.2}$, we can on average distinguish 17-round KNOT-AEAD(128,384,192) from random permutation and recover one bit of the secret key. Similar analysis can be obtained for any $i \in [0, \cdots, 63]$.

5 Conclusion

In this paper, by some techniques of differential-linear cryptanalysis, we focus on the security for the initialization phase of two members of the KNOT-AEAD family. Based on an observation that the diffusion layers of KNOT permutations are very simple, our strategy is to restrict the input difference and output linear mask of E_m to be single-bit such that we can obtain a differential-linear distinguisher which covers as many rounds as possible and has higher correlation. In addition, to amplify the correlation, some condition equations are imposed to make the differential of E_d determined which might be key-dependent. Then we can carry the key-recovery attacks based on the conditional differential-linear distinguishers. We apply these cryptanalytic techniques to KNOT-AEAD(128,256,64) and KNOT-AEAD(128,384,192). As a result, our attacks significantly improve the previous analysis results on them.

Acknowledgements. We are very grateful to Wentao Zhang for her helpful suggestions on this paper. We also thank the anonymous reviewers for their valuable comments.

References

1. Aagaard, M., Al Tawy, R., Gong, G., Mandal, K., Rohit, R., Zidaric, N.: Wage: an authenticated cipher submission to the NIST LWC competition. https://csrc.nist.gov/CSRC/media/Projects/lightweight-cryptography/documents/round-2/spec-doc-rnd2/wage-spec-round2.pdf

2. Aumasson, J.-P., Fischer, S., Khazaei, S., Meier, W., Rechberger, C.: New features of Latin dances: analysis of salsa, chacha, and rumba. In: Nyberg, K. (ed.) FSE 2008, LNCS, vol. 5086, pp. 470–488. Springer, Heidelberg (2008). https://doi.org/10.1007/978-3-540-7-71039-4_30

3. Bar-On, A., Dunkelman, O., Keller, N., Weizman, A.: DLCT: a new tool for differential-linear cryptanalysis. In: Ishai, Y., Rijmen, V. (eds.) EUROCRYPT 2019. LNCS, vol. 11476, pp. 313–342. Springer, Cham (2019). https://doi.org/10.1007/978-3-030-17653-2_11

4. Beierle, C., et al.: Schwaemm and Esch: lightweight authenticated encryption and hashing using the sparkle permutation family. https://csrc.nist.gov/CSRC/media/Projects/lightweight-cryptography/documents/round-2/spec-doc-rnd2/sparkle-spec-round2.pdf

5. Beierle, C., et al.: Skinny-Aead and skinny-hash v1.1. https://csrc.nist.gov/CSRC/media/Projects/lightweight-cryptography/documents/round-2/SKINNY-spec-round2.pdf

6. Beierle, C., Leander, G., Todo, Y.: Improved differential-linear attacks with applications to ARX ciphers. In: Micciancio, D., Ristenpart, T. (eds.) CRYPTO 2020. LNCS, vol. 12172, pp. 329–358. Springer, Cham (2020). https://doi.org/10.1007/978-3-030-56877-1_12

7. Ben-Aroya, I., Biham, E.: Differential cryptanalysis of lucifer. In: Stinson, D.R. (ed.) CRYPTO 1993. LNCS, vol. 773, pp. 187–199. Springer, Heidelberg (1993). https://doi.org/10.1007/3-540-48329-2_17

8. Bertoni, G., Daemen, J., Peeters, M., Van Assche, G.: Permutation-based encryption, authentication and authenticated encryption. Directions in Authenticated Ciphers, pp. 159–170 (2012)

9. Biham, E., Dunkelman, O., Keller, N.: Enhancing differential-linear cryptanalysis. In: Zheng, Y. (ed.) ASIACRYPT 2002. LNCS, vol. 2501, pp. 254–266. Springer, Heidelberg (2002). https://doi.org/10.1007/3-540-36178-2_16

10. Biham, E., Dunkelman, O., Keller, N.: Differential-linear cryptanalysis of serpent. In: Johansson, T. (ed.) FSE 2003. LNCS, vol. 2887, pp. 9–21. Springer, Heidelberg (2003). https://doi.org/10.1007/978-3-540-39887-5_2

11. Biham, E., Shamir, A.: Differential cryptanalysis of des-like cryptosystems. In: Menezes, A., Vanstone, S.A. (eds.) CRYPTO 1990. LNCS, vol. 537, pp. 2–21. Springer, Heidelberg (1990). https://doi.org/10.1007/3-540-38424-3_1

12. Blondeau, C., Leander, G., Nyberg, K.: Differential-linear cryptanalysis revisited. J. Cryptol. **30**(3), 859–888 (2017)

13. Canteaut, A., et al.: Saturnin: a suite of lightweight symmetric algorithms for post-quantum security. https://csrc.nist.gov/CSRC/media/Projects/lightweight-cryptography/documents/round-2/spec-doc-rnd2/saturnin-spec-round2.pdf

14. Choudhuri, A.R., Maitra, S.: Significantly improved multi-bit differentials for reduced round salsa and chacha. IACR Trans. Symmetric Cryptol. **2016**(2), 261–287 (2016)

15. Coutinho, M., Souza Neto, T.C.: New multi-bit differentials to improve attacks against chacha. IACR Cryptol. ePrint Arch. **2020**, 350 (2020)

16. Dobraunig, C., Eichlseder, M., Mendel, F., Schläffer, M.: Cryptanalysis of ASCON. In: Nyberg, K. (ed.) CT-RSA 2015. LNCS, vol. 9048, pp. 371–387. Springer, Cham (2015). https://doi.org/10.1007/978-3-319-16715-2_20

17. Dunkelman, O., Indesteege, S., Keller, N.: A differential-linear attack on 12-round serpent. In: Chowdhury, D.R., Rijmen, V., Das, A. (eds.) INDOCRYPT 2008. LNCS, vol. 5365, pp. 308–321. Springer, Heidelberg (2008). https://doi.org/10.1007/978-3-540-89754-5_24

18. Gutiérrez, A.F., Leurent, G., Naya-Plasencia, M., Perrin, L., Schrottenloher, A., Sibleyras, F.: New results on Gimli: full-permutation distinguishers and improved collisions. In: Moriai, S., Wang, H. (eds.) ASIACRYPT 2020. LNCS, vol. 12491, pp. 33–63. Springer, Cham (2020). https://doi.org/10.1007/978-3-030-64837-4_2

19. Knellwolf, S., Meier, W., Naya-Plasencia, M.: Conditional differential cryptanalysis of NLFSR-based cryptosystems. In: Abe, M. (ed.) ASIACRYPT 2010. LNCS, vol. 6477, pp. 130–145. Springer, Heidelberg (2010). https://doi.org/10.1007/978-3-642-17373-8_8

20. Langford, S.K., Hellman, M.E.: Differential-linear cryptanalysis. In: Desmedt, Y. (ed.) CRYPTO 1994. LNCS, vol. 839, pp. 17–25. Springer, Heidelberg (1994). https://doi.org/10.1007/3-540-48658-5_3

21. Leurent, G.: Improved differential-linear cryptanalysis of 7-round Chaskey with partitioning. In: Fischlin, M., Coron, J.-S. (eds.) EUROCRYPT 2016. LNCS, vol. 9665, pp. 344–371. Springer, Heidelberg (2016). https://doi.org/10.1007/978-3-662-49890-3_14

22. Liu, M., Lu, X., Lin, D.: Differential-linear cryptanalysis from an algebraic perspective. In: Malkin, T., Peikert, C. (eds.) CRYPTO 2021, Part III. LNCS, vol. 12827, pp. 247–277. Springer Cham (2021). https://doi.org/10.1007/978-3-030-84252-9_9

23. Lu, J.: A methodology for differential-linear cryptanalysis and its applications. Des. Codes Cryptogr. **77**(1), 11–48 (2015)

24. Matsui, M.: Linear cryptanalysis method for DES cipher. In: Helleseth, T. (ed.) EUROCRYPT 1993. LNCS, vol. 765, pp. 386–397. Springer, Heidelberg (1993). https://doi.org/10.1007/3-540-48285-7_33

25. Mouha, N., Wang, Q., Gu, D., Preneel, B.: Differential and linear cryptanalysis using mixed-integer linear programming. In: Wu, C., Yung, M., Lin, D. (eds.) Inscrypt 2011. LNCS, vol. 7537, pp. 57–76. Springer, Heidelberg (2011). https://doi.org/10.1007/978-3-642-34704-7_5

26. Selçuk, A.A.: On probability of success in linear and differential cryptanalysis. J. Cryptol. **21**(1), 131–147 (2008)

27. Sun, S., et al.: Towards finding the best characteristics of some bit-oriented block ciphers and automatic enumeration of (related-key) differential and linear characteristics with predefined properties. Cryptology ePrint Archive, Report 2014/747 (2014). https://ia.cr/2014/747

28. Sun, S., Hu, L., Wang, P., Qiao, K., Ma, X., Song, L.: Automatic security evaluation and (related-key) differential characteristic search: application to Simon, present, lblock, DES(L) and other bit-oriented block ciphers. In: Sarkar, P., Iwata, T. (eds.) ASIACRYPT 2014, Part I. LNCS, vol. 8873, pp. 158–178. Springer, Heidelberg (2014). https://doi.org/10.1007/978-3-662-45611-8_9

29. Zhang, W., et al.: KNOT: algorithm specifications and supporting document. https://csrc.nist.gov/CSRC/media/Projects/lightweight-cryptography/documents/round-2/spec-doc-rnd2/knot-spec-round.pdf

30. Zhang, W., Ding, T., Zhou, C., Ji, F.: Security analysis of KNOT-AEAD and KNOT-HASH. https://csrc.nist.gov/CSRC/media/Events/lightweight-cryptography-workshop-2020/documents/papers/security-analysis-of-KNOT-lwc2020.pdf

Revisit Two Memoryless State-Recovery Cryptanalysis Methods on A5/1

Mingxing Wang[1,2] and Yonglin Hao[1(✉)]

[1] State Key Laboratory of Cryptology, P.O. Box 5159, Beijing 100878, China
haoyonglin@yeah.net
[2] The 6th Research Institute of China Electronics Corporation,
Beijing 100083, China

Abstract. At ASIACRYPT 2019, Zhang proposes a near collision attack on A5/1. He claims that such an attack method can recover the 64-bit A5/1 state with a time complexity around 2^{32} cipher ticks and requires negligible memory complexities. Soon after its proposal, Zhang's near collision attack is severely challenged by Derbez et al. who claim that Zhang's attack cannot have a time complexity lower than Golic's memoryless guess-and-determine attack dating back to EUROCRYPT 1997. In this paper, we study both the guess-and-determine and the near collision attacks for recovering A5/1 states with negligible memory complexities. In order to make a fair comparison, we recover the state s^0 using both methods. We propose a new guessing technique that can construct linear equation filters in a more efficient manner. When evaluating time complexities, we take the filtering strength of the linear equation systems into account making the complexities more convincing. According to our detailed analysis, the new guess-and-determine attack can recover the state s^0 with a time complexity of $2^{43.91}$ simple operations. The time complexity for the near collision attack is $2^{50.57}$ simple operations.

Keywords: Stream ciphers · A5/1 · Guess-and-determine · Near collision attack

1 Introduction

A5/1 is a typical LFSR-based stream cipher with an irregular clocking mechanism designed in 1980's for the GSM standard. Ever since its proposal, A5/1 has been attacked with various cryptanalytic methods such as time/memory/data tradeoff attacks, guess-and-determine attacks, near collision attack (NCA) etc. [1–8] Most of the practical attacks on A5/1 requires large precomputed rainbow table which significantly increases the memory complexities [9–11]. Since the implementation of high-memory-requirement attacks are usually quite expensive, the attacks with negligible memory complexities, which we refer in this paper as the "memoryless" attacks, are usually preferable.

The 1st memoryless state-recovery attack on A5/1 is proposed by Golic [1] at EUROCRYPT 1997. The basic guess-and-determine attack in [1] requires $2^{43.15}$

© Springer Nature Switzerland AG 2021
Y. Yu and M. Yung (Eds.): Inscrypt 2021, LNCS 13007, pp. 191–211, 2021.
https://doi.org/10.1007/978-3-030-88323-2_10

steps, where each step in this attack is much more complicated, since it is based on the solution of a linear system as pointed out in [9]. The latest memoryless result on A5/1 is proposed at Asiacrypt 2019 where Zhang [8] claims that, by utilizing some near collision properties, the complexity of A5/1 state recovery can be lowered to only around 2^{32} cipher ticks with a negligible memory requirement. Soon after its proposal, Zhang's result is challenged severely: Derbez et al. point out in [12] that since the attack in [8] is not fully implemented, according to their practical verification, the non-randomness claimed by Zhang in [8] do not even exist. Therefore, Derbez et al. draw the conclusion that Zhang's near collision attack in [8] cannot have a complexity lower than that of Golic's basic guess-and-determine attack in [1]. However, Derbez et al. has not fully implemented the Zhang's near collision attack either making it unknown whether the near collision method can still be regarded as an effective cryptanalysis tool for A5/1 state recovery.

It is also noticeable that both Golic's attack and Zhang's attack use a system of linear equations as a filter for wrong guesses. But neither Golic nor Zhang has ever evaluated the strength of such a filter in practice. Therefore, the complexities of both the guess-and-determine and near collision attacks should be reevaluated in a more detailed manner.

Our Contributions. In this paper, we revisit the memoryless attacks on A5/1 using both the guess-and-determine and the near collision methods. We first propose a new guessing technique: instead of guessing the clock bits directly, we guess the encoded move patterns so the linear systems can be constructed more efficiently. With this method, we are able to acquire a new guess-and-determine attack that can recover the initial state with a time complexity of $2^{43.91}$ simple operations. Then, we analyze the near collision attack given by Zhang in [8] only to find that the complexities in [8] are somewhat optimistic. We point out the mistakes made in [8] and give corrections. According to our detailed analysis, the near collision attack has a time complexity $2^{50.57}$ simple operations. The C++ source codes for computing the statistics in this paper are available online[1].

This paper is organized as follows. Section 2 provides brief introduction to the A5/1 stream cipher and general process of the two memoryless state-recovery attacks. Section 3 introduces a new guessing technique: the move pattern guessing technique. Section 4 introduces our move-guessing based guess-and-determine attack on A5/1. Section 5 revisits Zhang's near collision attack: we point out the mistakes made in [8] and provide new collision attacks with correct complexities. Section 6 conclude the paper and point out some future works.

2   Preliminary

In Sect. 2.1, we give a brief introduction to the keystream generation phase of the A5/1 stream cipher. In Sect. 2.2, we briefly review the main idea of Golic's guess-and-determine attack [1]. In Sect. 2.3, we give the general process of Zhang's near collision attack [8].

---

[1] https://github.com/peterhao89/A51Attacks.

2.1   The Keystream Generation Procedure of A5/1

A5/1 has a 64-bit internal state consisting of 3 registers of sizes 19, 22, 23 respectively. We denote the 64-bit state at time t $(t = 0, 1, 2, \ldots)$ as

$$
\begin{aligned}
s^t &= (R1^t, R2^t, R3^t) \\
&= (s^t[0, \ldots, 18], s^t[19, \ldots, 40], s^t[41, \ldots, 63]) \\
&= (R1^t[0, \ldots, 18], R2^t[0, \ldots, 21], R3^t[0, \ldots, 22])
\end{aligned}
\tag{1}
$$

Before generating the output bit z^t, A5/1 round function will update the internal state $s^t \rightarrow s^{t+1}$ in a stop-and-go manner as follows:

1. Compute maj^t as

$$
\begin{aligned}
maj^t &= (R1^t[8] \cdot R2^t[10]) \oplus (R1^t[8] \cdot R3^t[10]) \oplus (R2^t[10] \cdot R3^t[10]) \\
&= (s^t[8] \cdot s^t[29]) \oplus (s^t[8] \cdot s^t[51]) \oplus (s^t[29] \cdot s^t[51])
\end{aligned}
\tag{2}
$$

2. If $R1^t[8] = s^t[8] \neq maj^t$, $R1^{t+1} \leftarrow R1^t$, otherwise, call updateR1 as follows:

$$
R1^{t+1}[i] \leftarrow
\begin{cases}
R1^t[i-1] & i \in [1, 18] \\
R1^t[18] \oplus R1^t[17] \oplus R1^t[16] \oplus R1^t[13]
\end{cases}
\tag{3}
$$

3. If $R2^t[10] = s^t[29] \neq maj^t$, $R2^{t+1} \leftarrow R2^t$, otherwise, call updateR2 as follows:

$$
R2^{t+1}[i] \leftarrow
\begin{cases}
R2^t[i-1] & i \in [1, 21] \\
R2^t[21] \oplus R2^t[20]
\end{cases}
\tag{4}
$$

4. If $R3^t[10] = s^t[51] \neq maj^t$, $R3^{t+1} \leftarrow R3^t$, otherwise, call updateR3 as follows:

$$
R3^{t+1}[i] \leftarrow
\begin{cases}
R3^t[i-1] & i \in [1, 22] \\
R3^t[22] \oplus R3^t[21] \oplus R3^t[20] \oplus R3^t[7]
\end{cases}
\tag{5}
$$

Then, the output keystream bit z^t is generated as

$$
\begin{aligned}
z^t &= R1^{t+1}[18] \oplus R2^{t+1}[21] \oplus R3^{t+1}[22] \\
&= s^{t+1}[18] \oplus s^{t+1}[40] \oplus s^{t+1}[63]
\end{aligned}
\tag{6}
$$

In the remainder of this paper, we uniformly use $s^t[i]$ to represent the i-th bit of the whole state and avoid using $R1[j], R2[k], R3[\ell]$'s.

2.2   A Brief Review of Golic's Guess-and-Determine Attack

In Golic's guess-and-determine model [1], the adversary aims at recovering the initial state s^1: the state right before the generation of z^0. For each step $i = 1, 2 \ldots$, whether the registers $R1, R2, R3$ are updated or not depends on the three clock bits $s^i[8, 29, 51]$. With the knowledge of $s^i[8, 29, 51]$, each bit of s^{i+1}

can be represented as a linear combination of s^i bits. For each guess $s^i[8, 29, 51] = (\rho, \varrho, \sigma) \in \mathbb{F}_2^3$, the adversary can deduce 3 linear equations:

$$\begin{cases} s^i[8] = \rho \\ s^i[29] = \varrho \\ s^i[51] = \sigma \end{cases}$$

According to the output z^i, the adversary can further deduce 1 linear equation:

$$z^i = s^{i+1}[18] \oplus s^{i+1}[40] \oplus s^{i+1}[63]$$

In other words, by guessing 3 clock bits $s^i[8, 29, 51]$, the adversary can deduce 4 linear equations of state bits. Therefore, in [1], Golic propose a basic attack that guess $3t$ clock bits $s^1[8, 29, 51] \ldots s^t[8, 29, 51]$. Based on the output bits $z^0, \ldots, z^{t+1}$, the adversary can deduce a system of averaging $1 + 3t + \frac{4}{3}t$ linear equations. According to [1], for $t \geq 14.38$, the system consisting of $1 + 3t + \frac{4}{3}t \geq 63.32$ equations can identify the correct guess uniquely with high probability. Although such a "high probability" is never actually evaluated, the complexity of Golic's attack is usually believed as $2^{3t} \geq 2^{43.15}$ steps where each step needs the solution of a linear system.

2.3 The General Process of Zhang's Near Collision Attack

Unlike Golic's recovering s^1, Zhang's near collision attack in [8] aims at recovering the init state s^0. They divide the 64 s^0 bits into constraint part (CP) and the rest part (RP). The CP part consists of 33 bits related to the 5 output bits $z^0, \ldots, z^4$. The other 31 bits are all categorized as RP.

The most crucial step in Zhang's attack in [8] is the recovery of the 33-bit CP based on the first 5 keystream bits $z^0, \ldots, z^4$. Such a CP-recovery step can be summarized as the list-merging process in Fig. 1. In Fig. 1, the list $L_{z^i \ldots z^j}$ ($i < j$) contains the state s^i's whose state bits are only partially known: for each $s^i \in L_{z^i \ldots z^j}$, the known bits are at positions $\lambda \subseteq [0, 63]$ s.t. the knowledge of $s^i[\lambda]$ can produce the consecutive output bits $z^i, \ldots, z^j$ following the A5/1 keystream generation process. Specifically, for a list $L_{z^i z^{i+1}}$ at Level 1, 2 consecutive keystream bits $z^i z^{i+1}$ can be related to at most 15 state bits at positions λ_0 in (7).

$$\lambda_0 = \{7, 8, 16, 17, 18, 28, 29, 38, 39, 40, 50, 51, 61, 62, 63\} \tag{7}$$

The number of known state bits for 3, 4 and 5 consecutive keystream bits will grow to at most 21, 27 and 33 respectively. Therefore, finally at Level 4, it is claimed by Zhang in [8] each element $s^0 \in L_{z^0 z^1 z^2 z^3}$ should contain 33 bits. When merging two lists at the same level, the known bits at the overlapped positions are to be used as filters: only the elements share the same value at the overlapped positions can be merged as an element in the list in the next level. Since each element in the lists contains at most 33 known bits, it is estimated in [8] that

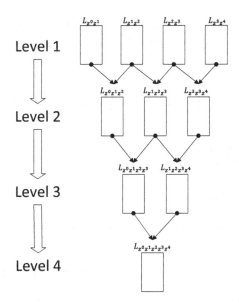

Fig. 1. The general process of Zhang's attack in [8]

the elements in all lists can be stored with 5 bytes of memory. However, the merging process in Fig. 1 is not fully implemented, only the process from Level 1 to 2 is implemented as can be seen from the source codes[2]. Without detailed analysis, Zhang theoretically estimated that the whole list merging process could be finished with a time complexity $2^{28.3}$ cipher ticks and the final list $L_{z^0z^1z^2z^3z^4}$ only contains $2^{16.6}$ elements.

Another feature of Zhang's attack is the construction of the 4 initial lists: they employ the idea of near collision to construct the lists $L_{z^0z^1}, \ldots, L_{z^3z^4}$. They consider the low-hamming-weight internal state difference (ISD) Δs as follows:

$$\mathcal{D}_2 := \{\Delta s | hw(\Delta s) \leq 2 \text{ and } \Delta s[i] = 0 \text{ for all } i \notin \lambda_1\} \tag{8}$$

Apparently, there are $\binom{15}{0} + \binom{15}{1} + \binom{15}{2} = 121$ elements in the ISD set $\mathcal{D}_2$ in (8). But only 99 ISDs in $\mathcal{D}_2$ can result in the 2-bit output difference 0x3. Therefore, the adversary only needs to store such 99 low-hamming-weight ISD's in a table $\mathcal{T}$ defined in (9).

$$\mathcal{T} := \{\Delta s \in \mathcal{D}_2 | \exists s^0 \Rightarrow z^0z^1(s^0) \oplus z^0z^1(s^0 \oplus \Delta s) = \text{0x3}\} \tag{9}$$

For a static 2-bit output z^0z^1, Algorithm 1 is proposed to generate list of states $L_{z^0z^1}$, making sure that all elements in the list can result in z^0z^1 directly. In Zhang's attack, the adversary sets the number limit $T = 4 \cdot 2^{15}/99 = 1323$ which results in the output list size 7963 and the correct state can be covered by $L_{z^0z^1}$ with probability $p_1 = 0.9835$. In order to improve the probability that the list

---

[2] https://github.com/martinzhangbin/gsmencryption.

contains the correct state, a distilling process is further proposed. For positive integers η and ζ, the distilling process first generate $\eta \times \zeta$ lists with Algorithm 1; then, intersection and union operations are carried out as (10).

$$L_{z^0 z^1} \leftarrow U(\eta, \zeta) = \bigcup_{i=1}^{\eta} \left(\bigcap_{j=1}^{\zeta} L_{z^0 z^1}^{i,j} \right) \text{ where } L_{z^0 z^1}^{i,j} \leftarrow \text{getList}(z^0 z^1, T) \quad (10)$$

According to [8], when $\eta = 2, \zeta = 6$, the correct state can be covered by $L_{z^0 z^1}$ with probability 0.9903.

Algorithm 1. Generate the internal states resulting in the given 2-bit output

---

1: **procedure** getList(output bits $z^0 z^1 \in \mathbb{F}_2^2$, the number limit T)
2:     Initialize an empty list $L_{z^0 z^1} \leftarrow \phi$
3:     Declare $\hat{z}_0 \hat{z}_1 \leftarrow z^0 z^1 \oplus \text{0x3}$
4:     Generate T states $\hat{s}^0$ that only have non-zero elements at positions λ_1 and can result in the output $\hat{z}_0 \hat{z}_1$
5:     **for** $\Delta s \in T$ **do**
6:         Construct state s^0
7:         **if** s^0 can result in the output $z^0 z^1$ **then**
8:             Update $L_{z^0 z^1} \leftarrow L_{z^0 z^1} \cup \{s^0\}$
9:         **end if**
10:     **end for**
11:     **Return** $L_{z^0 z^1}$
12: **end procedure**

After the CP-recovery phase, the adversary has already acquire $2^{16.6}$ s^0's in $L_{z^0 z^1 z^2 z^3}$. For each such s^0, the corresponding s^5 can be directly computed with the knowledge of 33 bits in CP. For RP-recovery, Zhang guess the $3y$ clock bits in (11) and construct linear equations of unknown RP bits according both guesses and output bits $z^5, \ldots, z^{5+y-1}$.

$$s^5[8, 29, 51], \ldots, s^{5+y-1}[8, 29, 51] \quad (11)$$

They claim that the RP bits can be recovered with complexity approximately 2^{32} cipher tickes which is also the overall time complexity of the whole attack. But there is no further details on how the different y's can affect the complexities. It is unknown how effective the linear equation system can be in filtering wrong states. It is also unknown which y should be used to identify the uniquely correct internal state s^0.

We are to show that Zhang's claims above are not accurate enough in Sect. 5.1. The analysis of y-effects are to be analyzed in detail in Sect. 5.2 only to find that Zhang's complexity analysis is underestimated due to the inaccurate parameters.

2.4   Unit of the Time Complexity

It is noticeable that the main operation of Golic's attack in [1] is solving the linear equation systems. Therefore, they use the time of solving the linear equation system solving by once as the unit of the time complexity. On the contrary, Zhang's near collision attack in [8] regard the cipher tick as the unit of time complexity. However, the linear equation system solving process in Zhang's attack is not strictly transformed to cipher ticks. In fact, the number of cipher ticks for solving a linear equation system depends on the numbers of both the variables and the equations in the system. The numbers of variables and equations are dynamic values depending on the bit guesses so an accurate transformation between the two units is quite difficult. Therefore, in this paper, we use Golic's time complexity unit in Golic's attack, which is the time of solving the linear equation system by once, and cipher ticks as time complexity units when talking about the attack in [8].

3   The Move Pattern Guessing Technique

In the Sect. 3.1, we introduce the concept of the move pattern and our move guessing technique. Section 3.2 compares the move guessing with the conventional clock guessing technique.

3.1   The Basic Concepts of the Move Pattern

For all 2^3 $\boldsymbol{s}^t[8, 29, 51]$ values, there are 4 possible move patterns denoted as Move 0, 1, 2 and 3. Each movement corresponds to 2 $\boldsymbol{s}^t[8, 29, 51]$ values and can also be represented as linear equations of state bits. Move 0–3 and their equations are defined as follows:

Move 0. updateR1 in (3), updateR2 in (4) and updateR3 in (5) are all called. The $\boldsymbol{s}^t[8, 29, 51]$ values are $(0, 0, 0)$ and $(1, 1, 1)$. The linear equations are:

$$\begin{cases} \boldsymbol{s}^t[8] \oplus \boldsymbol{s}^t[29] = 0 \\ \boldsymbol{s}^t[8] \oplus \boldsymbol{s}^t[51] = 0 \end{cases} \Leftrightarrow \begin{cases} \boldsymbol{R1}^t[8] = \boldsymbol{R2}^t[10] \\ \boldsymbol{R1}^t[8] = \boldsymbol{R3}^t[10] \end{cases} \tag{12}$$

Move 1. Only updateR2 and updateR3 are called. The $\boldsymbol{s}^t[8, 29, 51]$ values are $(0, 1, 1)$ and $(1, 0, 0)$. The equations are:

$$\begin{cases} \boldsymbol{s}^t[8] \oplus \boldsymbol{s}^t[29] = 1 \\ \boldsymbol{s}^t[8] \oplus \boldsymbol{s}^t[51] = 1 \end{cases} \Leftrightarrow \begin{cases} \boldsymbol{R1}^t[8] = \boldsymbol{R2}^t[10] \oplus 1 \\ \boldsymbol{R1}^t[8] = \boldsymbol{R3}^t[10] \oplus 1 \end{cases} \tag{13}$$

Move 2. Only updateR1 and updateR3 are called. The $\boldsymbol{s}^t[8, 29, 51]$ values are $(1, 0, 1)$ and $(0, 1, 0)$. The equations are:

$$\begin{cases} \boldsymbol{s}^t[8] \oplus \boldsymbol{s}^t[29] = 1 \\ \boldsymbol{s}^t[8] \oplus \boldsymbol{s}^t[51] = 0 \end{cases} \Leftrightarrow \begin{cases} \boldsymbol{R1}^t[8] = \boldsymbol{R2}^t[10] \oplus 1 \\ \boldsymbol{R1}^t[8] = \boldsymbol{R3}^t[10] \end{cases} \tag{14}$$

Move 3. Only `updateR1` and `updateR2` are called. The $s^t[8, 29, 51]$ values are $(1, 1, 0)$ and $(0, 0, 1)$. The equations are:

$$\begin{cases} s^t[8] \oplus s^t[29] = 0 \\ s^t[8] \oplus s^t[51] = 1 \end{cases} \Leftrightarrow \begin{cases} R1^t[8] = R2^t[10] \\ R1^t[8] = R3^t[10] \oplus 1 \end{cases} \tag{15}$$

We denote the movement $s^t \to s^{t+1}$ as $m^t \in \mathbb{F}_2^2 = \{0, 1, 2, 3\}$. So the movements before generating the output keystream bits $z^0, \ldots, z^t$ are $m^0, \ldots, m^t$. In our guess and determine attack, we first guess the movement m^t corresponding to $s^t \to s^{t+1}$ and maintains a linear equation set $\mathcal{BC}$ by adding new equations corresponding to the new movement m^t and the output z^t. For each step t, there are 3 linear equations: 2 are from one of (12), (13), (14), (15) according to the move guess and the rest is from the output z^t as

$$s^{t+1}[18] \oplus s^{t+1}[40] \oplus s^{t+1}[63] = z^t \tag{16}$$

So each move guess can deduce 3 equations. In Sect. 4, we guess the moves $m^0, \ldots, m^{t-1}$ and maintain a linear equations system to distinguish the correct state s^0 from the wrong ones.

3.2   Move Guessing vs. Clock Guessing

Our move guessing method differs from the previous guessing strategies. In previous A5/1 cryptanalysis, the adversary guesses directly the 3 clock bits $s^t[8, 29, 51]$ rather than the 2-bit move m^t. Apparently, our 2 move bits can be deduced from the 3 clock bits. Let $m^t[0, 1] = (\mu, \nu) \in \mathbb{F}_2^2$ and the corresponding clock bits are $s^t[8, 29, 51] = (\rho, \varrho, \sigma) \in \mathbb{F}_2^3$, the two bits (μ, ν) can be deduced from (ρ, ϱ, σ) as (17)

$$\begin{aligned} \mu &= \bar{\rho}\bar{\varrho}\sigma \oplus \bar{\rho}\varrho\sigma \oplus \rho\bar{\varrho}\bar{\sigma} \oplus \rho\varrho\bar{\sigma} \\ \nu &= \bar{\rho}\bar{\varrho}\sigma \oplus \bar{\rho}\varrho\bar{\sigma} \oplus \rho\bar{\varrho}\sigma \oplus \rho\varrho\bar{\sigma} \end{aligned} \tag{17}$$

where $\bar{x}$ is the NOT operation equivalent to $x \oplus 1$. From the linear equation point of view, a 3-bit guess $s^t[8, 29, 51] = (\rho, \varrho, \sigma)$ is naturally 3 equations. The 3 equations are also equivalent to 2 move-oriented equations and 1 bit value equation $s^t[8] = \rho$. For example, if the clock bit values are of the form $s^t[8, 29, 51] = (\rho, \rho, \rho)$, which corresponds to the Move 0, the 3 equations can also be regarded as adding $s^t[8] = \rho$ to the Move 0 constraints in (12) as shown in (18).

$$\begin{cases} s^t[8] = \rho \\ s^t[29] = \rho \\ s^t[51] = \rho \end{cases} \Leftrightarrow \begin{cases} s^t[8] = \rho \\ \begin{cases} s^t[8] \oplus s^t[29] = 0 \\ s^t[8] \oplus s^t[51] = 0 \end{cases} \end{cases} \tag{18}$$

Such an equivalence is also true for other clock bit values and move patterns. Adding the linear equations of the output in (16), we know that each 3-bit guess of the clock bits $s^t[8, 29, 51]$ can deduce 4 equations while each of our 2-bit guess of m^t can deduce 3 equations. On average, our move guessing method seems more efficient because each move bit guess can result in 1.5 equations while the number of linear equations for each clock bit guess is no more than 1.34. But it remains to be checked whether the clock-oriented equations can also be better filters for eliminating wrong internal states. To make fair comparison between the two strategies, we apply both move and clock guessing strategy in the RP-recovery phase of Zhang's near collision attack in [8]. The results show that move guessing can result in slightly lowered complexities than its clock counterpart. Details can be seen later in Sect. 5.2 and Sect. 5.3.

4   Guess-and-Determine Attack Based on the Move Guessing Technique

Instead of Golic's recovering s^1, we propose a state recovery attack on A5/1 targeting at s^0 so as to make a fair comparison with the near collision attack in [8]. As can be seen, the move equations (12), (13), (14), (15) and the output equation (16) correspond to the internal state at different time instances. But our attack is targeted to recovering the initial state s^0. Therefore, we need to represent the internal states at different time instance t with s^0 so that the equations are represented by s^0 bits as well. With the knowledge of $m^0, \ldots, m^{t-1}$, s^t can be iteratively deduced from s^0 and each s^t bit can be expressed as a linear combination of s^0 bits. Since a linear combination of s^0 bits can also be regarded as a inner-product of s^0 and a 64-bit word $w \in \mathbb{F}_2^{64}$, we can track each $s^0, \ldots, s^t$ bits with 64-bit words denoted as $W^0, \ldots, W^t \in (\mathbb{F}_2^{64})^{64}$. The initial W^0 corresponds to s^0 is defined naturally as (19)

$$W^0 = (e_0, \ldots, e_{63}), \text{ where } e_i[j] = \begin{cases} 1 & i = j \\ 0 & j \in [0, 63] \setminus \{i\} \end{cases} \text{ for } i = 0, \ldots, 63 \quad (19)$$

so as to make sure $W^0[i] \cdot s^0 = e_i \cdot s^0 = s^0[i]$ for $i = 0, \ldots, 63$. With $W^0, \ldots, W^{t-1}$, the word vector W^t can be deduced from W^{t-1} according to the movement $m^{t=1}$ by calling $W^t \leftarrow \text{UpdW}(m^{t-1}, W^{t-1})$ described in Algorithm 2. With the knowledge of W^t, each state bit of s^t can be uniformly expressed as a linear combination of s^0 bits as

$$s^t[i] = W^t[i] \cdot s^0, i = 0, \ldots, 63 \quad (20)$$

For t consecutive movements $m^0, \ldots, m^{t-1}$ and the corresponding output $z^0, \ldots, z^{t-1}$, we can deduce the corresponding linear equations set $\mathcal{BC}$ as

$$\mathcal{BC} \leftarrow \text{getBC}((m^0, \ldots, m^{t-1}), (z^0, \ldots, z^{t-1}))$$

where getBC is defined as Algorithm 3. The linear equations set $\mathcal{BC}$ can be regarded as a linear equation system in (21)

$$Ax^T = b^T, \text{ where } A \in \mathbb{F}_2^{3t \times 64}, x \in \mathbb{F}_2^{64}, b \in \mathbb{F}_2^{3t} \quad (21)$$

and the solutions to the linear system in (21) is exactly the possible values of the internal state s^0's resulting in the output keystream bits $z^0, \ldots, z^{t-1}$. The number of solutions to (21) depends on the rank of the matrix A and its extended matrix

$$E = [A, b^T] \qquad (22)$$

If $rank(A) = rank(E)$, there will be $2^{64-rank(A)}$ solutions; otherwise, there will be no solutions at all. Apparently, the matrix A and the vector b are both deduced according to the move guesses $m^0, \ldots, m^{t-1}$ and the output bits $z^0, \ldots, z^{t-1}$. For the correct guess of $m^0, \ldots, m^{t-1}$, the relation $rank(A) = rank(E)$ holds constantly; for the wrong guesses, however, there should be a probability $1 - \alpha_t$ $(0 \le \alpha_t \le 1)$ that $rank(A) \ne rank(E)$. Based on such a finding, the general process of our state-recovery attack can be divided naturally into 3 main steps:

S1. Guess moves $m^0, \ldots, m^{t-1}$ and maintain a linear system in (21)
S2. Do the matrix rank test and discard the wrong guesses satisfying $rank(A) \ne rank(E)$
S3. Deduce the remaining s^0 candidates and identify the correct s^0 with additional output bits $z^t, \ldots, z^{\ell-1}$ generated by the encryption oracle

Therefore, the detailed description of our move-guessing-based state-recovery attack is as follows:

1. Query the A5/1 encryption oracle for ℓ keystream bits $z^0, \ldots, z^{\ell-1}$
2. Initialize an empty set S of s^0 candidates
3. For some $t < \ell$, we guess the 2^{2t} movement values of $(m^0, \ldots, m^{t-1})$, acquire the equations $\mathcal{BC} \leftarrow \texttt{getBC}((m^0, \ldots, m^{t-1}), (z^0, \ldots, z^{t-1}))$ by calling Algorithm 3 (**S1**) and do the following substeps:
   (a) Deduce the A and b in (21) according to $\mathcal{BC}$ and compute the extended matrix E in (22)
   (b) Compute $rank(A)$ and $rank(E)$, if $rank(A) \ne rank(E)$, such a movement guess is wrong, go back to Step 3 for the next movement guess (**S2**)
   (c) For all $2^{64-rank(A)}$ solutions to $Ax^T = b^T$, set $\hat{s}^0 \leftarrow x$ and generate the keystream bits $\hat{z}^0, \ldots, \hat{z}^{t-1}, \hat{z}^t, \ldots, \hat{z}^{\ell-1}$
   (d) If $(\hat{z}^t, \ldots, \hat{z}^{\ell-1}) = (z^t, \ldots, z^{\ell-1})$, add such $\hat{s}^0$ into S (**S3**)
4. Return S

When ℓ is large enough, there should be only 1 element in S which is exactly the correct internal state s^0.

Complexity Analysis. In Step 3, there are 2^{2t} candidate moves $(m^0, \ldots, m^{t-1})$ and not all of them can pass the $rank(A) = rank(E)$ test Step 3.(b). We suppose that there is a positive number $0 \le \alpha_t \le 1$ that averaging $\alpha_t \cdot 2^{2t}$ candidate moves can pass the test. We further denote the averaging $rank(A)$ as β_t. With α_t, β_t, the averaging time complexity can be computed as follow:

$$Comp = 2^{2t} + \alpha_t \cdot 2^{2t+64-\beta_t} = 2^{2t} + 2^{2t+64-\beta_t+\log \alpha_t} \qquad (23)$$

We randomly select 2^{30} $((m^0, \ldots, m^{t-1}), (z^0, \ldots, z^{t-1}))$ pairs and do the 3.(b) test to compute the averaging α_t and β_t for t's. We find that when $t < 14$, α_t are larger than 0.5 ($\log \alpha_t \geq -1$) and $\beta_t \leq 3t$ so the overall complexity is constantly larger than 2^{50}. For $14 \leq t \leq 29$, the α_t, β_t and $Comp$ are listed in Table 1. As can be seen, the lowest time complexity appears at $t = 21$ with $Comp = 2^{43.91}$. As can be seen in Table 1, the order β_t has already climbed to almost 64 for $t = 27$. So we can safely set $\ell = 32$ to filter the wrong move guesses. According to our experiment, $\ell = 32$ is well enough to identify the correct s^0 so the data complexity of our attack is only 32 bits. The memory complexity is only $\mathcal{BC}$ and the corresponding matrix A as well as its extended matrix E in (21) and (22). The memory complexity is only $O(t)$ and, to be more specific, $2 \cdot (64+1) \cdot 3t \leq 12480$ bits which is bounded by $2\,\mathrm{KB}$. So the memory complexity is practical and negligible in comparison with previous attacks.

The Effect of the Branching Technique. In both Golic's and Zhang's attacks, they claim to have used a "branching" technique when deducing equations [1,8]. The branching technique based on the fact that, with the current $\mathcal{BC}$, some of the state bits are known and the following clock bits can be deduced from such known bits. Such a technique can be applied at the beginning of Step 3 so that some of the 2^{2t} do not need to be guessed so Step 3.(a) may only need to process $\gamma 2^{2t}$ moves where $\gamma \leq 1$. Although different γ values may be deduces from different bit guesses, the number of candidate moves passing Step 3.(a) is still averaging $\alpha_t 2^{2t}$ so the size of γ is lower bounded by α_t. Therefore, taking the effect of branching technique into account, the complexity in (23) can reformulated as

$$Comp = 2^{2t+\log \gamma} + 2^{2t+64-\beta_t+\log \alpha_t} \geq 2^{2t+\log \alpha_t} + 2^{2t+64-\beta_t+\log \alpha_t} \qquad (24)$$

Without doubt, the branching technique has some effects for lowering the complexity but, as can be seen in Table 1 it cannot change dominating factor of the overall complexities. In [1], based on the assumption that $\mathcal{BC}$ acts like a randomly constructed system, the α_t in Golic's attack is extremely small resulting in an

Table 1. The averaging α_t and β_t in (23) with 2^{30} random tests

t	β_t	$\log \alpha_t$	$\log Comp$	t	β_t	$\log \alpha_t$	$\log Comp$
14	41.959	−0.028	50.013	22	61.604	−3.971	44.417
15	44.868	−0.095	49.037	23	62.781	−5.915	46.055
16	47.683	−0.231	48.085	24	63.433	−8.420	48.006
17	50.381	−0.468	47.151	25	63.755	−11.173	50.001
18	52.955	−0.813	46.233	26	63.904	−14.060	52.000
19	55.409	−1.270	45.330	27	63.967	−17.027	54.000
20	57.734	−1.852	44.481	28	63.990	−20.021	56.000
21	59.860	−2.671	**43.914**	29	63.997	−23.117	58.000

overestimation to the effect of the branching technique. Such wrong evaluations are applied directly by Zhang in [8].

5   Revisit Zhang's Near Collision Attack

As has been briefly mentioned in Sect. 2.3, the CP-recovery phase of the near collision attack has not been fully implemented: only the 1st step from Level 1 to 2 is implemented [8]. The details of the following CP-recovery steps and the whole RP-recovery phase are absent, leaving it unknown whether the whole attack can work as claimed.

To verify their attack, we fully implement it only to find several mistakes and the complexity evaluation of the whole attack is underestimated. Section 5.1 points out the inaccurate evaluations of several crucial parameters in [8]. Section 5.2 supplements Zhang's attack with all the missing details in the CP- and RP-recovery phases and gives a correct complexity evaluation to the original attack in [8]. Section 5.3 replaces Zhang's clock-guess-based RP-recovery with our move-guess-based one to show the advantage of our technique.

5.1   Inaccurate Evaluations of Some Attack Parameters

There are 2 kinds of attack parameters being inaccurately evaluated in [8]: the p_1 used in the distilling phase along with the success probability deduced from p_1; the 4 parameters related to the complexities of the CP-Recovery process.

p_1 **and the Success Probability.** In [8], it is stated that, for $T = 4 \cdot 2^{15}/99$, a randomly constructed list $L_{z^0 z^1} \leftarrow \text{getList}(z^0 z^1, T)$ acquired by calling Algorithm 1 is of size 7963 and the correct internal state lies in $L_{z^0 z^1}$ with probability $p_1 = 0.9835$. However, we repeat the experiment 10^6 times and the correct state lies in $L_{z^0 z^1}$ for only 972436 times. So it is safe for us to claim that the actual p_1 is 0.9725: Zhang's evaluation in [8] is inaccurate. The reason why Zhang made such a mistake is unknown. Maybe their using RC4 as the source of randomness is not so qualified. Our experiments have tried various random generators including Snow-V [13], AES [14] etc. All these experiments reveal that the actual p_1 is 0.9725 rather than 0.9835.

With the corrected p_1, the probability for a distilled list U in (10) to cover the correct state should be reevaluated. Our corrected evaluation and Zhang's are both shown in Table 2. We read the source codes[3] corresponding to [8] carefully only to find that the $|U|$ parameter is wrong because of wrong implementation: when they try to get (η, ζ), they actually do ζ intersect operations so they actually acquire the $U(\eta, \zeta + 1)$ instead. As a consequence, the size $|U|$'s are smaller than expected. Since the attack can only succeed when the correct internal state lies in U, so the parameter Prob. in Table 2 is actually the success probability to the whole attack. Therefore, the success probability of Zhang's attack should be revised as well.

---

[3] https://github.com/martinzhangbin/gsmencryption.

Table 2. Our evaluation (left) v.s. Zhang et al.'s (right, quoted from [8])

η	ζ	$|U|$	Prob.	η	ζ	$|U|$	Prob.
2	3	8109	0.9935	2	3	8065	0.9940
2	4	8050	0.9887	2	4	7989	0.9927
2	5	8009	0.9830	2	5	7934	0.9912
2	6	7948	0.9761	2	6	7835	0.9903

4 Parameters Related to the CP-Recovery Process. Since the attack in [8] has not been fully implemented, the estimation of 4 related parameters are inaccurate. Both our and Zhang's evaluations of the 4 parameters are listed in Table 3. We provide detailed explanations as follows.

Table 3. 4 parameters related to the CP-recovery process: Zhang evaluation v.s. Ours

Parameter	Zhang's eval. [8]	Our eval
Cipher ticks for the merging process in Fig. 1	$2^{28.3}$	$2^{40.92}$†
The number of $L_{z^0 z^1 z^2 z^3 z^4}$ candidates	$2^{16.6}$	$2^{24.21}$
Bytes for storing a $L_{z^0 z^1 z^2 z^3 z^4}$ element	5	9
The number of known bits for each $L_{z^0 z^1 z^2 z^3 z^4}$ element	33	30.14

†: quadratic time implementations

Since the merging of two lists L_1, L_2 requires $|L_1| \cdot |L_2|$ (the time complexity of the merging algorithm in [8] is $|L_1| + |L_2|$) operations, it is impossible to get an exact evaluation to the complexities without actually knowing the sizes of all the lists. According to our implementation, the sizes of the lists are as follows:

$$
\begin{aligned}
|L_{z^i z_{i+1}}| &\approx 2^{12.95}, && \text{for } i = 0, 1, 2, 3 \\
|L_{z^i z_{i+1} z^{i+2}}| &\approx 2^{16.70}, && \text{for } i = 0, 1, 2 \\
|L_{z^i z_{i+1} z^{i+2} z^{i+3}}| &\approx 2^{20.46}, && \text{for } i = 0, 1 \\
|L_{z^0 z^1 z^2 z^3 z^4}| &\approx 2^{24.21}
\end{aligned}
\tag{25}
$$

Therefore, the complexity of the merging process is dominated by Level 3 to 4 which is approximately $2^{20.46 \times 2} = 2^{40.92}$ using the C++ implementation: far beyond $2^{28.3}$. The size of $L_{z^0 z^1 z^2 z^3 z^4}$ is $2^{24.21} > 2^{16.6}$. The reason is that the middle lists are used more than once in the merging phase, while in the original near collision attack, each list directly generated can only be used once.

The merging process in Fig. 1 takes two lists denoted as L_t and L_{t+1}. L_t contains the partial states of s^t while L_{t+1} consists of partial states of s^{t+1}. According to Sect. 3, a s^t should take a move $m^t \in \{0, 1, 2, 3\}$ before reaching s^{t+1} and that move m^t is decided by the three clock bits $s^t[8, 29, 51]$. So the merging step $\tilde{L}_t \leftarrow \text{merge}(L_t, L_{t+1})$ is as follows:

1. Initialize the merged list as empty $\tilde{L}_t \leftarrow \phi$.
2. For each $(s^t, s^{t+1}) \in L_t \times L_{t+1}$, do the following steps:
   (a) Identify the positions of the known bits in s^t denoted as $\lambda_0 \subseteq [0, 63]$.
   (b) Determine the move m^t according to 3 known clock bits $s^t[8, 29, 51]$.
   (c) Determine the state $\hat{s}^t$ s.t. $\hat{s}^t \xrightarrow{m^t} s^{t+1}$
   (d) Identify the positions of the known bits in $\hat{s}^t$ denoted as $\lambda_1 \subseteq [0, 63]$
   (e) If $\hat{s}^t[\lambda_0 \cap \lambda_1] = s^t[\lambda_0 \cap \lambda_1]$, store the vector $\tilde{s}^t \leftarrow \hat{s}^t \vee s^t$ in $\tilde{L}_t$ where $\vee$ is bitwise OR. The known bits of the newly generated $\tilde{s}^t$ is $\tilde{\lambda} \leftarrow \lambda_0 \cup \lambda_1$.
3. Return $\tilde{L}_t$

According to the description above, any element $s \in L$ should not only contain the value but the positions, denoted as λ, of the known bits as well. At Level 1, since all list are generated through Algorithm 1, all elements share the same known-bit positions in (7). But the following Example 1 shows that different moves will result in different known bit positions. Example 1 indicates that the known bits of the merged partial state $\tilde{s}^t$ may not be exactly the 21 bits given in [8]: they are also likely to be subsets of the 21 bits.

Example 1. Let $(s^0, s^1) \in L_{z^0 z^1} \times L_{z^1 z^2}$. We have $\lambda_0 = \lambda$ in (7). If the move $m^0 = 0$ ($s^0[8, 29, 51] \in \{(0, 0, 0), (1, 1, 1)\}$ according to (17) in Sect. 3.2), the known bit positions for s^1 should be

$$\lambda_1 := \{7 - 1, 8 - 1, 16 - 1, 17 - 1, 18 - 1, 28 - 1, 29 - 1, 38 - 1, 39 - 1, 40 - 1, 50 - 1, 51 - 1, 61 - 1, 62 - 1, 63 - 1\}.$$

and $\tilde{\lambda} = \lambda_0 \cup \lambda_1$ is of size $|\tilde{\lambda}| = 21$. If the move is $m^0 = 1$ ($s^0[8, 29, 51] \in \{(1, 0, 0), (0, 1, 1)\}$), we have

$$\lambda_1 := \{7, 8, 16, 17, 18, 28 - 1, 29 - 1, 38 - 1, 39 - 1, 40 - 1, 50 - 1, 51 - 1, 61 - 1, 62 - 1, 63 - 1\}.$$

and $|\tilde{\lambda}| = 19$.

In order to keep merging the lists in Level 2–4, $\tilde{\lambda}$ containing the known bit positions should also be stored which takes the same size of the partial states. Since the lists in Level 4 contain partial states of 33 bits, the $\tilde{\lambda}$'s are of the same size of 33 bits. So the elements in the lists requires at most $\lceil 2 \cdot 33/8 \rceil = 9$ bytes. Same with Example 1, the $\tilde{\lambda}$ for $\tilde{s}^0 \in L_{z^0 z^1 z^2 z^3 z^4}$ are more likely to be subsets of the 33 bits. In fact, according to our experiments, the number of known bits of $L_{z^0 z^1 z^2 z^3 z^4}$ elements are usually $|\tilde{\lambda}| \approx 30.14$, which is below 33. $|\tilde{\lambda}|$ can only be 33 when $m^0 = \ldots = m^4 = 0$. Such an event can happen with probability 2^{-10}.

5.2 Near Collision Attack with Original Clock-Guess-Based RP-Recovery

We have supplemented all the details of the list merging operations in Sect. 5.1. The whole CP-recovery phase in Fig. 1 can now be carried out. At the end of CP-recovery, the adversary have got the list $L_{z^0 z^1 z^2 z^3 z^4}$. Each $\tilde{s}^0 \in L_{z^0 z^1 z^2 z^3 z^4}$ corresponds to a set $\tilde{\lambda} \subseteq [0, 63]$ containing the positions of known state bits and it guarantees that the first 5 keystream bits are exactly $z^0, \ldots, z^4$. The known bits $\tilde{s}^0[\tilde{\lambda}]$ can deduce directly the first 5 moves $m^0, \ldots, m^4$. Therefore, the equations for each $\tilde{s}^0$ is simply $\mathcal{BC} \leftarrow \texttt{getBC}((m^0, \ldots, m^4), (z^0, \ldots, z^4))$ adding the bit value constraints of $\tilde{s}^0[\tilde{\lambda}]$. The number of equations is $15 + |\tilde{\lambda}|$.

Then, according to Zhang in [8], the RP part is to be recovered by guessing the unknown bits of $\tilde{s}^0$ corresponding to the clock bits $s^i[8, 29, 51]$ for $i = 5, 6, \ldots, t-1$ (equivalent to setting y in (11) as $y = t - 5$) and construct the corresponding linear equation system according to the clock bits and the output bits $z^0, \ldots, z^{t-1}$ as in (21). According to the analysis in Sect. 3.2, the clock guessing strategy is equivalent to adding bit value constraint to the corresponding move-oriented equations. Therefore, for the guesses of the $3(t-5)$ bits $s^5[8, 29, 51], \ldots, s^{t-1}[8, 29, 51]$, the number of deduced equations is $4(t-5)$. So the whole process of Zhang's near collision attack can now be summarized as follows:

1. Query the A5/1 encryption oracle for ℓ keystream bits $z^0, \ldots, z^\ell$
2. Run the merging process in Fig. 1 and acquire the list of candidates $L_{z^0z^1z^2z^3z^4}$ for the CP part of A5/1.
3. Initialize an empty set $\mathcal{S}$ of s^0 candidates
4. For each $\tilde{s}^0 \in L_{z^0z^1z^2z^3z^4}$ (**RP-Recovery**)
   (a) Deduce the 5 moves $(m_0, \ldots, m_4)$ and the known bit position set $\tilde{\lambda}$
   (b) For some $t \in [6, \ell - 1]$, we guess the $3(t-5)$ clock bits corresponding to $s^5[8, 29, 51], \ldots, s^{t-1}[8, 29, 51]$ and do the following substeps:
      i Deduce the move guesses $m^5, \ldots, m^{t-1}$ and deduce the equations

$$\mathcal{BC} \leftarrow \texttt{getBC}((m^5, \ldots, m^{t-1}), (z^5, \ldots, z^{t-1}))$$

      ii For all $i \in \tilde{\lambda}$, add the linear equations $x_i = \tilde{s}^0[i]$ to $\mathcal{BC}$
      iii For $s^i[8]$ ($i = 5, \ldots, t-1$), add the bit value constraint $W^i[8] \cdot x = s^i[8]$ to $\mathcal{BC}$
      iv Deduce the A and b in (21) according to $\mathcal{BC}$ and compute the extended matrix E in (22)
      v Compute $rank(A)$ and $rank(E)$, if $rank(A) \neq rank(E)$, such a clock guess is wrong, go back to Step (b) for the next guess of $s^5[8, 29, 51], \ldots, s^{t-1}[8, 29, 51]$
      vi For all $2^{64-rank(A)}$ solutions to $Ax^T = b^T$, set $\hat{s}^0 \leftarrow x$ and generate the keystream bits $\hat{z}^0, \ldots, \hat{z}^{t-1}, \hat{z}^t, \ldots, \hat{z}^{\ell-1}$
      vii If $(\hat{z}^t, \ldots, \hat{z}^{\ell-1}) = (z^t, \ldots, z^{\ell-1})$, add such $\hat{s}^0$ into $\mathcal{S}$
5. Return $\mathcal{S}$

Complexity Analysis. According to (25), there are $2^{24.21}$ candidate $\tilde{s}^0$ in $L_{z^0z^1z^2z^3z^4}$. In Step 4.(b), there are 2^{3t-15} possible guesses and we assume that only $\alpha_t \cdot 2^{3t-15}$ of them can pass the $rank(A) = rank(E)$ test at Step 4.(b).v where $0 \leq \alpha_t \leq 1$. We denote the averaging $rank(A)$ as β_t. The analysis in Sect. 5.1, the merging process in Step 2 has complexity $2^{40.92}$ using the quadratic time implementation, anyway this part is not dominated even with the linear time method in [8]. With α_t, β_t, the averaging time complexity can be computed as (27).

$$Comp = 2^{40.92} + 2^{24.21+3t-15} + \alpha_t \cdot 2^{24.21+3t-15+64-\beta_t}$$
$$= 2^{40.92} + 2^{9.21+3t} + 2^{73.21+3t+\log \alpha_t - \beta_t} \tag{26}$$

Same with Sect. 3, we randomly select 2^{30} $\left(\tilde{s}^0, s^5[8,29,51], \ldots, s^{t-1}[8,29,51], (z^5, \ldots, z^m)\right)$ triplets and do the 4.(b).v test to compute the averaging α_t and β_t for different t's. For $5 \le t \le 21$, the α_t, β_t and $Comp$ are listed in Table 5. As can be seen, the complexities are constantly larger than 2^{52}, indicating that Zhang's complexity evaluation in [8] is inaccurate and is no better than the new guess-and-determine attack in Sect. 4. The lowest time complexity is $2^{52.159}$ and it appears at $t = 12$. The memory complexity is dominated by the size of $L_{z^0 z^1 z^2 z^3 z^4}$ which is $2^{24.21}$ according to (25). Zhang has already claimed that the attack can only succeed when the exact s^i lies in the corresponding list $L_{z^i z_{i+1}}$ for $i = 0, 1, 2, 3$ in Fig. 1. According to the Sect. 5.1, the success probability can be evaluated as $p_1^4 \approx 0.8942$.

The Effect of the Branching Technique. Same with the analysis in Sect. 4, the branching technique can also be applied to Step 4 and the complexity in (26) can be reformulated as

$$Comp = 2^{40.92} + 2^{9.21+3t+\log \gamma} + 2^{73.21+3t+\log \alpha_t - \beta_t}$$
$$\ge 2^{40.92} + 2^{9.21+3t+\log \alpha_t} + 2^{73.21+3t+\log \alpha_t - \beta_t}$$

It does not affect the dominating factor of the whole attack so the overall complexity remains unchanged.

Table 4. The averaging α_t and β_t in (26) with 2^{30} random tests

t	β_t	$\log \alpha_t$	$\log Comp$	t	β_t	$\log \alpha_t$	$\log Comp$
6	33.443	−0.256	57.511	14	59.715	−0.989	54.646
7	37.424	−0.285	56.501	15	60.510	−1.455	56.560
8	41.423	−0.300	55.487	16	61.388	−2.586	58.223
9	45.421	−0.307	54.482	17	62.273	−4.668	60.387
10	49.415	−0.357	53.438	18	62.975	−7.000	63.233
11	53.470	−0.430	52.311	19	63.501	−9.483	66.213
12	56.494	−0.570	**52.159**	20	63.834	−12.293	69.210
13	58.436	−0.752	53.073	21	63.980	−15.476	72.210

5.3   Improved Near Collision Attack with Move-Based RP-Recovery

According to the relationship between our move guess and the conventional clock guess strategies revealed in Sect. 3.2, Zhang's clock-guess-based RP-recovery in Sect. 5.2 can be replaced with our move-guess-based strategy. We simply rewrite the RP-recovery phase of this modified attack as follows:

4. For each $\tilde{s}^0 \in L_{z^0 z^1 z^2 z^3 z^4}$ (**RP-Recovery**)
   (a) Deduce the 5 moves $(m_0, \ldots, m_4)$ and the known bit position set $\tilde{\lambda}$
   (b) For some $t \in [5, \ell-1]$, we guess the $2^{2(t-5)}$ movements $(m^5, \ldots, m^{t-1})$, we acquire the equations $\mathcal{BC} \leftarrow \mathtt{getBC}((m^0, \ldots, m^{t-1}), (z^0, \ldots, z^{t-1}))$ and do the following substeps:
      i For all $i \in \tilde{\lambda}$, add the linear equations $x_i = \tilde{s}^0[i]$ to $\mathcal{BC}$
      ii Deduce the A and b in (21) according to $\mathcal{BC}$ and compute the extended matrix E in (22)
      iii Compute $rank(A)$ and $rank(E)$, if $rank(A) \neq rank(E)$, such a movement guess is wrong, go back to Step (b) for the next guess of moves $m^5, \ldots, m^{t-1}$
      iv For all $2^{64-rank(A)}$ solutions to $Ax^T = b^T$, set $\hat{s}^0 \leftarrow x$ and generate the keystream bits $\hat{z}^0, \ldots, \hat{z}^{t-1}, \hat{z}^t, \ldots, \hat{z}^{\ell-1}$
      v If $(\hat{z}^t, \ldots, \hat{z}^{\ell-1}) = (z^t, \ldots, z^{\ell-1})$, add such $\hat{s}^0$ into $\mathcal{S}$

Complexity Analysis. In Step 4.(b), there are 2^{2t-10} candidate moves $(m^0, \ldots, m^t)$ and we assume that only $\alpha_t \cdot 2^{2t-10}$ moves can pass the $rank(A) = rank(E)$ test at Step 4.(b).iii where $0 \leq \alpha_t \leq 1$. We denote the averaging $rank(A)$ as β_t. According to (25), the size of $L_{z^0 z^1 z^2 z^3 z^4}$ is approximately $2^{24.21}$. The analysis in Sect. 5.1, the merging process in Step 2 has complexity $2^{40.92}$. With α_t, β_t, the averaging time complexity can be computed as (27).

$$Comp = 2^{40.92} + 2^{24.21+2t-10} + \alpha_t \cdot 2^{24.21+2t-10+64-\beta_t}$$
$$= 2^{40.92} + 2^{14.21+2t} + 2^{78.21+2t+\log \alpha_t - \beta_t} \tag{27}$$

For $6 \leq t \leq 21$, the α_t, β_t and $Comp$ are listed in Table 5. As can be seen, the complexities are constantly larger than 2^{50} which is no better than our guess-and-determine attack in Sect. 4 but is lower than Zhang 's original one in Sect. 5.2. The lowest possible complexity is $2^{50.567}$ and it appears at $t = 16$. The memory complexity and the success probability are identical to those of Zhang 's original attack which are $2^{24.21}$ and 0.8942 respectively. It is noticeable that the β_t in

Table 5. The averaging α and β in (27) with 2^{30} random tests

t	β_t	$\log \alpha_t$	$\log Comp$	t	β_t	$\log \alpha_t$	$\log Comp$
6	31.957	−0.160	58.094	14	54.675	−0.524	51.016
7	34.683	−0.203	57.325	15	56.735	−0.848	50.643
8	37.584	−0.217	56.409	16	58.302	−1.415	**50.567**
9	40.548	−0.223	55.438	17	59.485	−2.202	50.789
10	43.515	−0.234	54.461	18	60.401	−3.194	51.427
11	46.457	−0.259	53.494	19	61.146	−4.403	52.635
12	49.371	−0.300	52.540	20	61.788	−5.736	54.330
13	52.159	−0.370	51.682	21	62.365	−7.287	56.238

Algorithm 2. Deduce the equation word set according to a movement

---

1: **procedure** UpdW(movement $m^t \in \{0, 3\}$, words $W^t \in (\mathbb{F}_2^{64})^{64}$)
2:     **if** $m^t = 0$ **then**
3:         $A^t \leftarrow$ UpdWR($W^t, 1$)
4:         $B^t \leftarrow$ UpdWR($A^t, 2$)
5:         $W^{t+1} \leftarrow$ UpdWR($B^t, 3$)
6:     **end if**
7:     **if** $m^t = 1$ **then**
8:         $B^t \leftarrow$ UpdWR($W^t, 2$)
9:         $W^{t+1} \leftarrow$ UpdWR($B^t, 3$)
10:     **end if**
11:     **if** $m^t = 2$ **then**
12:         $A^t \leftarrow$ UpdWR($W^t, 1$)
13:         $W^{t+1} \leftarrow$ UpdWR($A^t, 3$)
14:     **end if**
15:     **if** $m^t = 3$ **then**
16:         $A^t \leftarrow$ UpdWR($W^t, 1$)
17:         $W^{t+1} \leftarrow$ UpdWR($A^t, 2$)
18:     **end if**
19:     **Return** W^{t+1}
20: **end procedure**

1: **procedure** UpdWR(words $W \in (\mathbb{F}_2^{64})^{64}$, register number $n \in \{1, 2, 3\}$)
2:     Initialize $X \in (\mathbb{F}_2^{64})^{64}$ as $X \leftarrow W$
3:     **if** $n = 1$ **then**
4:         **for** $i = 1, \ldots, 18$ **do**
5:             Update the i-th entry of X as $X[i] \leftarrow W[i-1]$
6:         **end for**
7:         Compute the 0-th entry of X as $X[0] \leftarrow W[18] \oplus W[17] \oplus W[16] \oplus W[13]$
    according to (3)
8:     **end if**
9:     **if** $n = 2$ **then**
10:         **for** $i = 20, \ldots, 40$ **do**
11:             Update the i-th entry of X as $X[i] \leftarrow W[i-1]$
12:         **end for**
13:         Compute the 19-th entry of X as $X[19] \leftarrow W[40] \oplus W[39]$ according to (4)
14:     **end if**
15:     **if** $n = 3$ **then**
16:         **for** $i = 42, \ldots, 63$ **do**
17:             Update the i-th entry of X as $X[i] \leftarrow W[i-1]$
18:         **end for**
19:         Compute the 41-th entry of X as $X[19] \leftarrow W[63] \oplus W[62] \oplus W[61] \oplus W[48]$
    according to (5)
20:     **end if**
21:     **Return** X
22: **end procedure**

Algorithm 3. Deduce the set of equations according to the given moves and output bits

---

1: **procedure** getBC(movements $(m^0, \ldots, m^{t-1}) \in \{0,3\}^t$, output bits $(z^0, \ldots, z^{t-1}) \in \mathbb{F}_2^t$)

2:    Initialize the words $W^0 \leftarrow (e_0, \ldots, e_{63})$ according to (19)

3:    Initialize the linear equations set as empty: $\mathcal{BC} \leftarrow \phi$

4:    Initialize $x = (x_0, \ldots, x_{63})$ as vector of 63 unknown boolean variables corresponding to the 64 state bits of s^0

5:    **for** $i = 0, 1, \ldots, t-1$ **do**

6:        **if** $m^i = 0, 1, 2, 3$ **then**

7:            Update $\mathcal{BC}$ by adding the following equations corresponding to (12),(13),(14),(15):
$$\begin{cases} (W^i[8] \oplus W^i[29]) \cdot x = \delta(m^i) \\ (W^i[8] \oplus W^i[51]) \cdot x = \varrho(m^i) \end{cases}$$
where $(\delta(m^i), \varrho(m^i)) = (0,0), (1,1), (1,0), (0,1)$ for $m_i = 0, 1, 2, 3$ respectively

8:        **end if**

9:        Deduce W^{i+1} according to W^i by calling $W^{i+1} \leftarrow$ UpdW(m^i, W^i) defined in Algorithm 2

10:        Update $\mathcal{BC}$ by adding the following linear equations corresponding to (16)
$$(W^{i+1}[18] \oplus W^{i+1}[40] \oplus W^{i+1}[63]) \cdot x = z^i$$

11:    **end for**

12:    **Return** $\mathcal{BC}$

13: **end procedure**

Table 4 grows faster than that in Table 5, indicating that clock guess can result in a faster growth in the order of matrix in (21). But such a growth cannot guarantee a better filter when applied to state-recovery attacks: this is a fact that can only be discovered by solid experiments and accurate implementations.

The Effect of the Branching Technique. Same with the analysis in Sect. 4, the branching technique can also be applied to Step 4 and the complexity in (27) can be reformulated as

$$Comp = 2^{40.92} + 2^{14.21+2t+\log \gamma} + 2^{78.21+2t+\log \alpha_t - \beta_t}$$
$$\geq 2^{40.92} + 2^{14.21+2t+\log \alpha_t} + 2^{78.21+2t+\log \alpha_t - \beta_t}$$

It does not affect the dominating factor of the whole attack so the overall complexity remains unchanged.

6   Conclusion and Future Works

In this paper, we revisit 2 memoryless state-recovery methods on A5/1 stream cipher namely the guess-and-determine attack and the near collision attack. For the guess-and-determine attack, we propose a new guessing technique and provides a new attack with practically verified complexities. For the near collision attack, we revisit Zhang's attack in [8]. We point out the mistake in [8] and provide correct complexity evaluations. According to our analysis, the Zhang's near collision attack can work for A5/1 but does not have an advantage over the new guess-and-determine attack method.

About future works, it is noticeable that we propose a new guess-and-determine attack to recover the state s^0 while Golic's original one targets at s^1 [1]. According to the analysis in Sect. 4, the filtering strength of the deduced linear equation system $\mathcal{BC}$ may not be as good as that of a random system. Since Golic constantly regards the $\mathcal{BC}$'s of wrong guesses as random systems, it is highly likely that the time complexity of Golic's original guess-and-determine attack be wrongly evaluated, as pointed out by some previous literature. In order to acquire the correct time complexity evaluation, one has to practically compute the α_t and β_t's following Golic's guessing strategy, which is an obvious direction for future works.

Acknowledgement. The authors thank the anonymous reviewers and the shepherd Bin Zhang for careful reading and many helpful comments. Mingxing Wang is sponsored by the open project of State Key Laboratory of Cryptology. Yonglin Hao is supported by National Natural Science Foundation of China (Grant No. 62002024), National Key Research and Development Program of China (No. 2018YFA0306404).

References

1. Golic, J.D.: Cryptanalysis of alleged A5 stream cipher. In: Fumy, W. (ed.) EURO-CRYPT 1997. LNCS, vol. 1233, pp. 239–255. Springer, Heidelberg (1997). https://doi.org/10.1007/3-540-69053-0_17

2. Biham, E., Dunkelman, O.: Cryptanalysis of the A5/1 GSM stream cipher. In: Roy, B.K., Okamoto, E. (eds.) INDOCRYPT 2000. LNCS. vol. 1977, pp. 43–51. Springer, Heidelberg (2000). https://doi.org/10.1007/3-540-44495-5_5

3. Shah, J., Mahalanobis, A.: A new guess-and-determine attack on the A5/1 stream cipher. Cryptology ePrint Archive, Report 2012/208 (2012). http://eprint.iacr.org/2012/208

4. Maximov, A., Johansson, T., Babbage, S.: An improved correlation attack on A5/1. In: Handschuh, H., Hasan, A. (eds.) SAC 2004. LNCS, vol. 3357, pp. 1–18. Springer, Heidelberg (2004). https://doi.org/10.1007/978-3-540-30564-4_1

5. Li, Z.: Optimization of rainbow tables for practically cracking GSM A5/1 based on validated success rate modeling. In: Sako, K. (ed.) CT-RSA 2016. LNCS, vol. 9610, pp. 359–377. Springer, Heidelberg (2016). https://doi.org/10.1007/978-3-319-29485-8_21

6. Gendrullis, T., Novotný, M., Rupp, A.: A real-world attack breaking A5/1 within hours. In: Oswald, E., Rohatgi, P. (eds.) CHES 2008. LNCS, vol. 5154, pp. 266–282. Springer, Heidelberg (2008). https://doi.org/10.1007/978-3-540-85053-3_17

7. Barkan, E., Biham, E.: Conditional estimators: an effective attack on A5/1. In: Preneel, B., Tavares, S. (eds.) SAC 2005. LNCS, vol. 3897, pp. 1–19. Springer, Heidelberg (2006). https://doi.org/10.1007/11693383_1

8. Zhang, B.: Cryptanalysis of GSM encryption in 2G/3G networks without rainbow tables. In: Galbraith, S.D., Moriai, S. (eds.) ASIACRYPT 2019, Part III. LNCS, vol. 11923, pp. 428–456. Springer, Heidelberg (2019). https://doi.org/10.1007/978-3-030-34618-8_15
9. Biryukov, A., Shamir, A., Wagner, D.: Real time cryptanalysis of A5/1 on a PC. In: Schneier, B. (ed.) FSE 2000. LNCS, vol. 1978, pp. 1–18. Springer, Heidelberg (2001). https://doi.org/10.1007/3-540-44706-7_1
10. Pornin, T., Stern, J.: Software-hardware trade-offs: application to A5/1 cryptanalysis. In: Koç, Ç.K., Paar, C. (eds.) CHES 2000. LNCS, vol. 1965, pp. 318–327. Springer, Heidelberg (2000). https://doi.org/10.1007/3-540-44499-8_25
11. Lu, J., Li, Z., Henricksen, M.: Time-memory trade-off attack on the GSM A5/1 stream cipher using commodity GPGPU - (extended abstract). In: Malkin, T., Kolesnikov, V., Lewko, A.B., Polychronakis, M. (eds.) ACNS 2015. LNCS, vol. 9092, pp. 350–369. Springer, Heidelberg (2015). https://doi.org/10.1007/978-3-319-28166-7_17
12. Derbez, P., Fouque, P., Mollimard, V.: Fake near collisions attacks. IACR Trans. Symmetric Cryptol. **2020**(4), 88–103 (2020)
13. Ekdahl, P., Johansson, T., Maximov, A., Yang, J.: A new SNOW stream cipher called SNOW-V. IACR Trans. Symmetric Cryptol. **2019**(3), 1–42 (2019)
14. Standards, N.: Specification for the advanced encryption standard (AES). FIPS-197 (2001)

More Accurate Division Property Propagations Based on Optimized Implementations of Linear Layers

Chunlei Hong, Shasha Zhang[✉], Siwei Chen, Da Lin, and Zejun Xiang

Faculty of Mathematics and Statistics, Hubei Key Laboratory of Applied Mathematics, Hubei University, Wuhan, China
{hongchunlei,linda}@stu.hubu.edu.cn, xiangzejun@hubu.edu.cn

Abstract. As a generalized integral property, the division property can be used to search integral distinguishers of symmetric ciphers by taking the advantage of automatic tools, such as Mixed Integer Linear Programming (MILP) and Boolean Satisfiability Problem (SAT) solvers. In this case, the accuracy of corresponding models will influence the resulting distinguishers. In this paper, we present a new technique to characterize the division property propagation of linear layers. Firstly, we study the impact of a linear layer implementation on its division property propagations. We found that division trails derived from an optimized implementation of a linear layer can be more accurate than the S method, and different implementations can eliminate some different invalid division trails. Thus, we can eliminate a large number of invalid division trails by combining different implementations. As an application of our technique, we have searched distinguishers for Midori64, Skinny64 and LED. As a result, we can obtain the same longest distinguishers as the $\mathcal{ZR}$ method and the $\mathcal{HW}$ method, which are the exact modeling of linear layers. Moreover, our method can be used with both MILP and SAT, while the $\mathcal{HW}$ method can only work with SAT. In addition, the number of constraints with the $\mathcal{HW}$ method increases quadratically, however it increases linearly with our method.

Keywords: Division property · Linear layer · Optimized implementation · Integral attack · Automatic tool

1 Introduction

Differential cryptanalysis [1], linear cryptanalysis [2] and integral cryptanalysis [3] are the most effective methods for attacking iterative block ciphers so far. In 1997, Daemen *et al.* proposed Square [4] block cipher and introduced a new method named Square attack to analyze the security of Square cipher. This attack method is the earliest form of integral attack. Afterwards, integral attack [3] was formally proposed by Knudsen and Wagner at FSE 2002. The core idea of integral attack is to find an integral distinguisher so that the adversary

© Springer Nature Switzerland AG 2021
Y. Yu and M. Yung (Eds.): Inscrypt 2021, LNCS 13007, pp. 212–232, 2021.
https://doi.org/10.1007/978-3-030-88323-2_11

can use this distinguisher to achieve a distinguishing attack or a key-recovery attack on the objective cipher. Thus, the most essential step in integral attacks is to construct effective integral distinguishers.

Currently, the most effective way to find a distinguisher is to study the evolution of integral properties in the encryption process and then judge whether there exists balanced bits in the corresponding output state. The division property (DP) [5], which was proposed as a generalized integral property by Todo at EUROCRYPT 2015, can be applied to search for longer integral distinguishers. With this technique, Todo constructed a new integral distinguisher and presented the full-round attack on MISTY1 in [6]. Afterwards, a more accurate DP called bit-based division property (BDP) [7] was introduced by Todo and Morii at FSE 2016. However, the BDP is only adapted to ciphers whose block sizes are upper bounded by 32 due to the huge time and memory complexities. In order to overstride this barrier, Xiang et al. [8] applied MILP method to search for integral distinguishers based on BDP at ASIACRYPT 2016, which allowed us to analyze primitives whose block sizes are larger than 32 using BDP. Thanks to this automatic method, what we need to do when searching for distinguishers is to construct an MILP model to characterize the propagation of BDP and use off-the-shelf solvers like Gurobi[1] to solve the model. Naturally, it is worth studying how to achieve the accurate description of the propagation of BDP in the MILP model, since the more accurate the corresponding MILP model is, the more balanced bits or longer distinguishers might be obtained.

The description of BDP propagations of non-linear layers (e.g., Sboxes [8], AND [8,9] and modular addition [10] operations) has been discussed extensively. For linear layers, there are three main ways to constrain the BDP propagation.

$\mathcal{S}$ **method** [9]. It was proposed by Sun et al. for a matrix $M \in \mathbb{F}_2^{n \times n}$, and the core of this method is to decompose a complex matrix into a series of COPY and XOR operations and then model these basic operations with some auxiliary variables. The modeling rules of COPY and XOR have been already handled in [8]. The advantage of this method is that the number of constraints is only $2n$ and it is universal to all the types of linear layers, but its shortcoming is that it might introduce some invalid division trails, which will cause the balance property of output bits to lose more quickly.

$\mathcal{ZR}$ **method** [11]. For an invertible matrix $M \in \mathbb{F}_{2^m}^{s \times s}$, Zhang and Rijmen constructed a one-to-one relation between a division trail of M and the invertibility of a sub-matrix of M, which is uniquely determined by this division trail. Specifically, a division trail is valid if and only if the corresponding sub-matrix is invertible. The number of constraints will be $m \cdot (2^s - 1)$ when constructing an MILP model. This method is completely accurate, but it cannot be applied to non-binary and non-invertible matrices because of the huge scale of constraints.

$\mathcal{HW}$ **method** [12]. Inspired by the $\mathcal{ZR}$ method, Hu et al. noticed that a matrix $M \in \mathbb{F}_2^{n \times n}$ is invertible if and only if there is a matrix $M' \in \mathbb{F}_2^{n \times n}$ such that

---

[1] https://www.gurobi.com/.

$M \times M'$ equals to an identity matrix. Thus, they introduced an auxiliary matrix and constrained the multiplication of this auxiliary matrix and the original matrix to be an identity matrix. If it is a solution, then the corresponding division trail is valid. This method is as accurate as the $\mathcal{ZR}$ method and is not limited by the invertibility of M. Note that the number of constraints is n^2, and it contains 4-degree constraints, thus it is only solvable for SMT/SAT solvers. In addition, when the scale of M is large, the model will be quite heavy, which may cause the infeasibility to solvers.

Recently, Elsheikh and Youssef [13] (ACISP 2021) proposed a method to optimize the precision of the BDP propagation of linear layers, which is based on the $\mathcal{ZR}$ method. In short, for a given input DP of linear layers, this method aims to search for the corresponding output DP such that the derived sub-matrix has full rank. Therefore, the first step is to determine the input DP and this process will take a lot of precomputations. The precomputations are time-consuming and hardly practical with the round increasing because of the huge amount of the input DP. Thus, the authors in [13] only succeed in applying this method to the first round. However, the above three methods and our method are all general descriptions of linear layers, without considering the specific input DP of linear layers.

1.1   Our Contributions

As mentioned above, the off-the-shelf methods to characterize the BDP propagation of complex linear layers have their advantages and limitations. In brief, the $\mathcal{S}$ method is applicable to various linear layers but not accurate enough. The $\mathcal{ZR}$ and the $\mathcal{HW}$ methods are completely accurate, but both of them are limited by the size of the linear matrix and the former is also limited by the invertibility of the matrix. Therefore, it is significant to consider how to reach a balance between the feasibility and the accuracy. In order to find this trade-off, in this paper, we introduce a new method to achieve a more accurate as well as applicable MILP-aided description of the BDP propagation of complex linear layers. This method is inspired by optimizing implementations of matrices, and combines several optimizing tools with the existing COPY and XOR modeling rules. Concretely, given a matrix $M \in \mathbb{F}_2^{n \times n}$, we first respectively use three algorithms **Paar** [14], **BP** [15] and **XZ** [16] to optimize the implementation of M. Next, we apply both COPY and XOR modeling rules to constrain each optimized implementation. Finally, we simultaneously add all the constraints to an MILP model to characterize the BDP propagation of M. In order to intuitively evaluate the number of constraints, we convert the optimized implementations to the simplest form like c = a $\oplus$ b, i.e., one equation contains only one XOR operation (see Eq. (2) in Sect. 3). Then, the upper bound on the number of constraints is 3N, where N denotes the total number of the linear equations or the XOR operations in the optimized implementations. Based on this new method, we propose a framework as depicted in Algorithm 1 to automatically generate a system of inequalities. Compared with the $\mathcal{S}$ method, it is more accurate since the

$\mathcal{S}$ method corresponds to the D-xor [23] metric of a linear matrix and this metric is far from optimal to represent the real cost of implementing a matrix. Thus, modeling these optimized implementations can effectively decrease the number of invalid division trails. We present a detailed discussion in Sect. 3 and prove that our technique is never worse than the $\mathcal{S}$ method. Moreover, it is more applicable than the $\mathcal{ZR}$ method thanks to its non-limitation on the type of matrices and more lightweight constraints even if it is not completely accurate. It is worth noting that this new method can also be implemented based on SMT/SAT, since all constraints are linear. Moreover, the number of the generated constraints is small compared with that of the $\mathcal{HW}$ method. As an illustration, we apply this method to search for integral distinguishers for three block ciphers Midori64 [17], Skinny64 [18] and LED [19], and compare our results with the previous works as summarized in Table 1. The related results[2] and source codes are available at https://github.com/hcl21/More-Accurate-BDP-for-LinearLayer.

1.2 Organization of the Paper

The rest of this paper is organized as follows. In Sect. 2, we briefly review the definition and propagation rules of division property and several heuristics for implementing linear layers. In Sect. 3, we introduce the new method proposed in this paper and give a discussion on the comparison between this method and the $\mathcal{S}$ method. In Sect. 4, we present applications of our new method to some block ciphers. We conclude this paper in Sect. 5.

2 Preliminaries

We first introduce some notations that appear frequently in this paper. Denote $\mathbb{F}_2$ the finite field that contains only two elements (0 and 1) and $\boldsymbol{a} \in \mathbb{F}_2^n$ an n-bit vector where $a_i \in \mathbb{F}_2$ denotes the i-th bit of $\boldsymbol{a}$. The Hamming weight of $\boldsymbol{a} \in \mathbb{F}_2^n$, denoted by $wt(\boldsymbol{a})$, is defined as $wt(\boldsymbol{a}) = \#\{i : a_i = 1, 0 \leq i \leq n - 1\}$. Let $\boldsymbol{k}$ and $\boldsymbol{k}'$ be two vectors in $\mathbb{F}_2^n$, we define $\boldsymbol{k} \succeq \boldsymbol{k}'$ if $k_i \geq k_i'$ for all i, otherwise $\boldsymbol{k} \not\succeq \boldsymbol{k}'$.

Bit Product Functions. Let $\pi_{\boldsymbol{u}} : \mathbb{F}_2^n \rightarrow \mathbb{F}_2$ be a function for any $\boldsymbol{u} \in \mathbb{F}_2^n$. Let $\boldsymbol{x} \in \mathbb{F}_2^n$ be an input of $\pi_{\boldsymbol{u}}$, then $\pi_{\boldsymbol{u}}(\boldsymbol{x})$ is defined as

$$\pi_{\boldsymbol{u}}(\boldsymbol{x}) := \prod_{i=0}^{n-1} x_i^{u_i}.$$

---

[2] Note that these ciphers' MixColumns are composed of 16-bit matrix. In order to exhibit the universality of our method, we also experimented on AES, and we respectively took about 5 and 10 min to find 4- and 5-round integral distinguishers in the key-dependent scenario. Our distinguishers are consistent with that of the $\mathcal{HW}$ method, but we took less time. Unfortunately, we can not obtain these results when using the $\mathcal{S}$ method.

Table 1. Comparison of our results with the previous works.

Ciphers	#Rounds	log₂(Data)	#Balanced Bits	Time	Ref.
Midori64	5	12	4	-	[9]
	5	12	**7**	12 s	Sect. 4.2
	6	45	16	–	[9]
	6	45	**19**	140 s	Sect. 4.2
	7	63	64	–	[11]
	7†	63	64	427 s	Sect. 4.2
Skinny64	8	56	40	–	[9]
	8	56	**64**	< 2 s	Sect. 4.2
	10	60	64	–	[11]
	10	60	64	5.5 s	Sect. 4.2
LED	6	52	– ‡	–	[9]
	6	52	64	15 min	[12]
	6	52	64	<4 h	Sect. 4.3
	7	63	64	14 min	[12]
	7	63	64	<5 h	Sect. 4.3

† In [9], Sun *et al.* presented the 7-round distinguisher with 61 active input bits and 16 balanced output bits. We also found this distinguisher and failed to explore more balanced bits using 61 active bits. For the case of setting 63 active input bits, [9] does not give the relevant result.
‡ For the data of 2^{52}, their model did not return any results.

Algebraic Normal Form. Any Boolean function $f : \mathbb{F}_2^n \to \mathbb{F}_2$ can be represented in its Algebraic Normal Form (ANF) as:

$$f(\boldsymbol{x}) = \bigoplus_{\boldsymbol{u} \in \mathbb{F}_2^n} a_{\boldsymbol{u}}^f \left(\prod_{i=0}^{n-1} x_i^{u_i} \right) = \bigoplus_{\boldsymbol{u} \in \mathbb{F}_2^n} a_{\boldsymbol{u}}^f \pi_{\boldsymbol{u}}(\boldsymbol{x}),$$

where $a_{\boldsymbol{u}}^f \in \mathbb{F}_2$ is a constant depending on f and $\boldsymbol{u}$.

2.1 (Bit-Based) Division Property and Its MILP-aided Applications

At EUROCRYPT 2015, division property [5] was proposed by Todo as a generalization of the integral property, which was originally defined at word level. Later, the bit-based division property [7] was introduced by Todo and Morii to investigate the DP at bit level. Note that the BDP is composed of two members, two-subset BDP and three-subset BDP. In this paper, we only focus on the two-subset BDP, thus we straightforwardly use BDP to represent the two-subset BDP for short. The definition of BDP is presented as follows.

Definition 1 (Bit-Based Division Property [7]). *Let* $\mathbb{X}$ *be a multiset whose elements belong to* $\mathbb{F}_2^n$ *and* $\mathbb{K}$ *be a set of n-bit vectors whose elements take the* *value 0 or 1. Then we call the multiset* $\mathbb{X}$ *has the division property* $\mathcal{D}_{\mathbb{K}}^{1^n}$ *if it fulfills the following conditions for any* $\boldsymbol{u} \in \mathbb{F}_2^n$:

$$\bigoplus_{\boldsymbol{x} \in \mathbb{X}} \pi_{\boldsymbol{u}}(\boldsymbol{x}) = \begin{cases} unknown & if \ there \ exists \ \boldsymbol{k} \in \mathbb{K} \ s.t. \ \boldsymbol{u} \succeq \boldsymbol{k}, \\ 0 & otherwise. \end{cases}$$

As a more accurate DP, the BDP can be applied to search for better integral distinguishers. However, the application of BDP is greatly limited by its high time and memory complexities, which caused the fact that the BDP was only applicable to the ciphers with block sizes no more than 32. In order to overcome this drawback, Xiang *et al.* [8] first adopted MILP-aided method, which has shown its great power in cryptanalysis such as [20,21], to automatically search for integral distinguishers based on BDP. Moreover, the concept of *division trail* was introduced to describe the BDP propagation and the MILP-aided modeling rules were proposed. In this paper, we devote our attention to modeling linear layers, thus we only revisit the modeling rules of XOR and COPY operations as well as the definition of division trail as follows. One can refer to [8,9] for more details about the modeling rules of AND operation and Sboxes.

Definition 2 (Division Trail [8]). *Let* f_r *denote the round function of an iterated block cipher with size of* n. *Assume the input multiset to the block cipher has initial division property* $\mathcal{D}_{\mathbb{K}_0}^{1^n}$, *and denote the division property after* i-*round propagation through* f_r *by* $\mathcal{D}_{\mathbb{K}_i}^{1^n}$. *Thus, we have the following chain of division property propagations:*

$$\{\boldsymbol{k}\} \stackrel{\triangle}{=} \mathbb{K}_0 \xrightarrow{f_r} \mathbb{K}_1 \xrightarrow{f_r} \mathbb{K}_i \xrightarrow{f_r} \cdots \mathbb{K}_r.$$

Moreover, for any vector $\boldsymbol{k}_i^*$ *in* $\mathbb{K}_i^*$, *there must exist a vector* $\boldsymbol{k}_{i-1}^*$ *in* $\mathbb{K}_{i-1}^*$ *such that* $\boldsymbol{k}_{i-1}^*$ *can propagate to* $\boldsymbol{k}_i^*$ *by division property propagation rules. Furthermore, for* $(\boldsymbol{k}_0, \boldsymbol{k}_1, \cdots, \boldsymbol{k}_r) \in \mathbb{K}_0 \times \mathbb{K}_1 \times \cdots \times \mathbb{K}_r$, *if* $\boldsymbol{k}_{i-1}$ *can propagate to* $\boldsymbol{k}_i$ *for all* $i \in \{1, 2, \cdots, r\}$ *we call* $(\boldsymbol{k}_0, \boldsymbol{k}_1, \cdots, \boldsymbol{k}_r)$ *an* r-*round division trail.*

Proposition 1 (MILP Modeling Rule for COPY [9]). *Denote a* $\xrightarrow{COPY}$ $(b_0, b_1, \cdots, b_{m-1})$ *a division trail of COPY function, the following inequalities are sufficient to describe the division propagation of COPY:*

$$\begin{cases} a - b_0 - b_1 - \cdots - b_{m-1} = 0, \\ a, b_0, b_1, \cdots, b_{m-1} \ are \ binaries. \end{cases}$$

Proposition 2 (MILP Modeling Rule for XOR [9]). *Denote* $(a_0, a_1, \cdots, a_{m-1}) \xrightarrow{XOR} b$ *a division trail of XOR function, the following inequalities can describe the division propagation of XOR:*

$$\begin{cases} a_0 + a_1 + \cdots + a_{m-1} - b = 0, \\ a_0, a_1, \cdots, a_{m-1}, b \ are \ binaries. \end{cases}$$

For the sake of convenience, we name the combined utilization of COPY and XOR rules as **CX** rules in this paper. Note that the S method is based on the **CX** rules to model the BDP propagation of linear layers.

2.2 Heuristics for Optimizing the Implementations of Linear Layers

The linear layer of a symmetric cipher can be represented as a matrix over $\mathbb{F}_2$, whose implementation is a sequence of XOR operations. Thus, the implementation cost of a linear layer can be estimated by the number of XOR gates required to implement the corresponding matrix. In order to find an optimized implementation of a given matrix with fewer XOR gates, several heuristics have been proposed, the widely used three of which are introduced in [14–16] respectively.

The Paar Algorithm [14]. Taking the matrix over $\mathbb{F}_2$ as the input, in each step, the **Paar** algorithm chooses a pair of columns from the matrix exhaustively and calculates the bitwise AND of these two columns, the pair of columns whose AND reaches the largest Hamming weight will be kept and their bitwise AND will be added to the matrix as a new column. Before choosing the next two columns from the new matrix, we should update the matrix by XORing the selected two columns with the newly added column. The above steps will be repeated until each row of the matrix has exactly one "1" .

Note that the **Paar** heuristic is *cancellation-free*, it means that the operands of any operation given by this method share no common variables. Each time the matrix is updated, both the AND of the last column and the updated two columns will lead to zero vectors. Therefore, these columns will never be selected as the operands of any operation in the subsequent implementation, i.e., if $a = b \oplus c$ is one of the operations, the operations such as $a \oplus b, a \oplus c$ and $b \oplus c$ will never appear afterwards.

The BP Algorithm [15]. Given a matrix $M_{m \times n}$ over $\mathbb{F}_2$, let $wt(M_i)$ be the Hamming weight of the i-th row of M, where $i \in [0, m-1]$. Firstly, the **BP** algorithm defines a base S and a vector dist[]. The base S is initialized as the set of all input bits of M, i.e., $S = \{x_0, x_1, \cdots, x_{n-1}\}$. The distance vector is initialized as $dist = \{wt(M_0)-1, wt(M_1)-1, \cdots, wt(M_{m-1})-1\}$. Then, pick two elements $S[i]$ and $S[j](i \neq j)$ from S in each step and treat the XOR of $S[i]$ and $S[j]$ as a possible element which might be added to S, update the distance vector as the minimum number of XOR gates required for calculating the output bits according to the elements from S. Keep the XOR of two elements selected from base that minimizes the sum of the distance vector and add it to the base S as a new element. If there are multiple candidates, choose the one that maximizes the Euclidean Norm of the updated distance vector. Repeat the above steps until all the elements in $dist[]$ are zero.

The XZ Algorithm [16]. Inspired by Gauss-Jordan elimination, Xiang *et al.* proposed several strategies to decompose an invertible matrix over $\mathbb{F}_2$ into a product of a sequence of type-1 and type-3 elementary matrices. A type-1 elementary matrix costs no XOR gate since it is produced by exchanging two rows/columns of an identity matrix, while a type-3 elementary matrix is produced by adding a row/column of an identity matrix to another row/column and thus costs one XOR gate. Thus, the matrix decomposition theory builds a relationship between the cost for implementing an invertible matrix and the number of type-3 elementary matrices in its decomposition. In order to further reduce the number of type-3 elementary matrices, they summarized seven reduction rules and combined with the rules of exchanging the order of two adjacent elementary matrices, they designed a heuristic to search implementations of a given matrix, which can obtain fewer XOR gates by running the algorithm multiple times.

In this paper, we utilize the source codes to implement those algorithms given in [16] and [22].

3   BDP Propagations Based on Linear Layer Optimization

In this section, we propose a new method to characterize BDP propagations of linear layers which is based on the **CX** rules and the optimized implementations of matrices. Firstly, we start by introducing an example to intuitively show the details and effects of the new method. Then we discuss and analyze the results obtained by using different optimized implementations to model linear transformation. Finally, we give a theoretical argument to prove that our new method will never be worse than the $\mathcal{S}$ method. This paper mainly considers three heuristics for optimizing the implementations of matrices, i.e., the **Paar**, the **BP** and the **XZ** algorithms. For convenience, we use the **Paar + CX** to represent the combination of the **Paar** algorithm with the **CX** rules. Other heuristics combined with the **CX** rules are also denoted similarly.

3.1   Construct BDP Propagation Models of Linear Layers

We will begin with a small example listed in the following to illustrate our idea.

Example 1. Let $L : (x_0, x_1, x_2, x_3) \mapsto (x_1 \oplus x_2 \oplus x_3, x_0 \oplus x_2 \oplus x_3, x_0 \oplus x_1 \oplus x_3, x_0 \oplus x_1 \oplus x_2)$ be a linear transformation on $\mathbb{F}_2^4$, the corresponding matrix M is as follows:

$$M = \begin{pmatrix} 0 & 1 & 1 & 1 \\ 1 & 0 & 1 & 1 \\ 1 & 1 & 0 & 1 \\ 1 & 1 & 1 & 0 \end{pmatrix}.$$

Assuming that $(u_0, u_1, u_2, u_3) \rightarrow (v_0, v_1, v_2, v_3)$ is a division trail through L. We compute and list all possible division trails of M according to the $\mathcal{S}$ method, $\mathcal{ZR}$ method and our technique.

(1) **The $\mathcal{S}$ method**: Based on the theory of the $\mathcal{S}$ method to characterize linear layers, we introduce s_k's as auxiliary binary variables, and the inequalities within the model are as follows:

$$\begin{cases} u_0 - s_0 - s_1 - s_2 = 0 \\ u_1 - s_3 - s_4 - s_5 = 0 \\ u_2 - s_6 - s_7 - s_8 = 0 \\ u_3 - s_9 - s_{10} - s_{11} = 0 \\ v_0 - s_3 - s_6 - s_9 = 0 \\ v_1 - s_0 - s_7 - s_{10} = 0 \\ v_2 - s_1 - s_4 - s_{11} = 0 \\ v_3 - s_2 - s_5 - s_8 = 0 \end{cases} . \tag{1}$$

Among them, $u_i, v_j, s_k (0 \leq i, j \leq 3, \ 0 \leq k \leq 11)$ are binary variables. By solving the above inequalities, the division trails of M can be obtained. The results are listed in Table 2.

Table 2. Division trails of different method. The trails highlighted in bold are invalid.

Input	S method	Our method	$\mathcal{ZR}$ method
$0x0$	$0x0$	$0x0$	$0x0$
$0x1$	$0x2, 0x4, 0x8$	$0x2, 0x4, 0x8$	$0x2, 0x4, 0x8$
$0x2$	$0x1, 0x4, 0x8$	$0x1, 0x4, 0x8$	$0x1, 0x4, 0x8$
$0x3$	$0x3, 0x5, 0x6, 0x9, 0xA, \mathbf{0xC}$	$0x3, 0x5, 0x6, 0x9, 0xA$	$0x3, 0x5, 0x6, 0x9, 0xA$
$0x4$	$0x1, 0x2, 0x8$	$0x1, 0x2, 0x8$	$0x1, 0x2, 0x8$
$0x5$	$0x3, 0x5, 0x6, 0x9, \mathbf{0xA}, 0xC$	$0x3, 0x5, 0x6, 0x9, 0xC$	$0x3, 0x5, 0x6, 0x9, 0xC$
$0x6$	$0x3, 0x5, 0x6, \mathbf{0x9}, 0xA, 0xC$	$0x3, 0x5, 0x6, 0xA, 0xC$	$0x3, 0x5, 0x6, 0xA, 0xC$
$0x7$	$\mathbf{0x7}, 0xB, 0xD, 0xE$	$0xB, 0xD, 0xE$	$0xB, 0xD, 0xE$
$0x8$	$0x1, 0x2, 0x4$	$0x1, 0x2, 0x4$	$0x1, 0x2, 0x4$
$0x9$	$0x3, 0x5, \mathbf{0x6}, 0x9, 0xA, 0xC$	$0x3, 0x5, 0x9, 0xA, 0xC$	$0x3, 0x5, 0x9, 0xA, 0xC$
$0xA$	$0x3, \mathbf{0x5}, 0x6, 0x9, 0xA, 0xC$	$0x3, 0x6, 0x9, 0xA, 0xC$	$0x3, 0x6, 0x9, 0xA, 0xC$
$0xB$	$0x7, \mathbf{0xB}, 0xD, 0xE$	$0x7, 0xD, 0xE$	$0x7, 0xD, 0xE$
$0xC$	$\mathbf{0x3}, 0x5, 0x6, 0x9, 0xA, 0xC$	$0x5, 0x6, 0x9, 0xA, 0xC$	$0x5, 0x6, 0x9, 0xA, 0xC$
$0xD$	$0x7, 0xB, \mathbf{0xD}, 0xE$	$0x7, 0xB, 0xE$	$0x7, 0xB, 0xE$
$0xE$	$0x7, 0xB, 0xD, \mathbf{0xE}$	$0x7, 0xB, 0xD$	$0x7, 0xB, 0xD$
$0xF$	$0xF$	$0xF$	$0xF$

(2) **Our method**: Our new method to model the BDP propagation of M needs to combine optimized implementations of M with the **CX** rules. Thus, we first need to obtain optimized implementations of M, then use the **CX** rules to model its BDP propagations. We detail this process in the following two phases.

Implementating Phase: In this phase, we use the algorithms of the **Paar**, the **BP** and the **XZ** to get the optimized implementations of M. The implementations of M are listed in Eq. (2), where the first set of inequalities denotes the direct implementation and others are implemented by the **Paar**, the **BP** and the **XZ**, respectively.

$$
\begin{cases} y_0 = x_1 \oplus x_2 \oplus x_3 \\ y_1 = x_0 \oplus x_2 \oplus x_3 \\ y_2 = x_0 \oplus x_1 \oplus x_3 \\ y_3 = x_0 \oplus x_1 \oplus x_2 \end{cases}
\begin{cases} t_0 = x_0 \oplus x_1 \\ t_1 = x_2 \oplus x_3 \\ y_0 = x_1 \oplus t_1 \\ y_1 = x_0 \oplus t_1 \\ y_2 = x_3 \oplus t_0 \\ y_3 = x_2 \oplus t_0 \end{cases}
\begin{cases} t_0 = x_0 \oplus x_2 \\ y_3 = x_1 \oplus t_0 \\ y_1 = x_3 \oplus t_0 \\ t_1 = y_3 \oplus y_1 \\ y_2 = x_0 \oplus t_1 \\ y_0 = t_0 \oplus y_2 \end{cases}
\begin{cases} t_0 = x_1 \oplus x_2 \\ t_1 = x_0 \oplus x_3 \\ y_1 = x_2 \oplus t_1 \\ y_0 = x_3 \oplus t_0 \\ y_2 = t_0 \oplus y_1 \\ y_3 = t_1 \oplus y_0 \end{cases}.
$$

$$(2)$$

Modeling Phase: We combine the **CX** rules with the three optimized implementations of M listed in Eq. (2) to model BDP propagations of M. This process needs to introduce binary auxiliary variables s_k's. These three set of inequalities contained in Eq. (3) are the constraints, which are constructed according to the **Paar**, the **BP** and the **XZ** implementations respectively. In order to illustrate the modeling details, we take the **Paar**'s implementation as an example. From the implementation, we know that x_0 and x_1 both appear twice, thus we need to copy u_0 and u_1 to two pieces: s_0, s_1 and s_2, s_3, where the variable u_i denotes the DP of x_i. This corresponds to the inequalities $u_0 - s_0 - s_1 = 0$ and $u_1 - s_2 - s_3 = 0$. The variable s_4 denotes the DP of the intermediate variable t_0 and s_4 is generated by the XOR operation of the copied DP from u_0 and u_1, i.e., s_0 and s_2, thus $s_2 + s_0 - s_4 = 0$. Note that t_0 is reused in the 5-th and 6-th equations. Thus, we need to copy s_4 to two pieces: s_{12} and s_{13}, which corresponds to the inequality $s_4 - s_{12} - s_{13} = 0$. Other equations can be modeled in a similar way.

$$
\begin{cases} u_0 - s_0 - s_1 = 0 \\ u_1 - s_2 - s_3 = 0 \\ s_2 + s_0 - s_4 = 0 \\ u_2 - s_5 - s_6 = 0 \\ u_3 - s_7 - s_8 = 0 \\ s_7 + s_5 - s_9 = 0 \\ s_9 - s_{10} - s_{11} = 0 \\ s_{10} + s_3 - v_0 = 0 \\ s_{11} + s_1 - v_1 = 0 \\ s_4 - s_{12} - s_{13} = 0 \\ s_{12} + s_8 - v_2 = 0 \\ s_{13} + s_6 - v_3 = 0 \end{cases}
\begin{cases} u_0 - s_{14} - s_{15} = 0 \\ u_2 + s_{14} - s_{16} = 0 \\ s_{16} - s_{17} - s_{18} = 0 \\ s_{19} - v_3 - s_{20} = 0 \\ s_{17} + u_1 - s_{19} = 0 \\ s_{18} - s_{21} - s_{22} = 0 \\ s_{23} - v_1 - s_{24} = 0 \\ s_{21} + u_3 - s_{23} = 0 \\ s_{24} + s_{20} - s_{25} = 0 \\ s_{26} - v_2 - s_{27} = 0 \\ s_{25} + s_{15} - s_{26} = 0 \\ s_{27} + s_{22} - v_0 = 0 \end{cases}
\begin{cases} u_2 - s_{28} - s_{29} = 0 \\ s_{28} + u_1 - s_{30} = 0 \\ u_3 - s_{31} - s_{32} = 0 \\ s_{31} + u_0 - s_{33} = 0 \\ s_{33} - s_{34} - s_{35} = 0 \\ s_{36} - v_1 - s_{37} = 0 \\ s_{34} + s_{29} - s_{36} = 0 \\ s_{30} - s_{38} - s_{39} = 0 \\ s_{40} - v_0 - s_{41} = 0 \\ s_{38} + s_{32} - s_{40} = 0 \\ s_{37} + s_{39} - v_2 = 0 \\ s_{41} + s_{35} - v_3 = 0 \end{cases}.
$$

$$(3)$$

Among them, $u_i, v_j, s_k (0 \leq i, j \leq 3, 0 \leq k \leq 41)$ are binary variables. The procedure for constructing the model by our method is shown in Algorithm 1.

Algorithm 1 traverses each row of a given matrix implementation and models it one by one. We explain Algorithm 1 in the following three steps. **Step 1:** Traverse the right side of an XOR operation within the matrix implementation from Line 11 to 31. If there is a variable reused in the subsequent matrix implementation, its DP needs to be copied and we should model this using the COPY rule (Proposition 1 in Subsect. 2.1). During this process, two new variables are generated, and the first new variable replaces the first occurrence of the considered variable's DP which is copied. Note that if a variable is reused in the subsequent matrix implementation, its DP may be reused for multiple times. We do not count the exact occurrences of this variable. We instead add a new term $temp[L[i][j]] = t_1$ into the dictionary. With this new term, we can make sure that $L[i][j]$ will be reused in the subsequent matrix implementation and its DP has been copied earlier. Thus, each time we have to check if $L[i][j]$ is an index of the dictionary, if this is the case, we should use the copied piece stored in the dictionary instead. **Step 2:** Traverse the left side variable of an XOR operation within the implementation from Line 32 to 41. If this variable is equal to an output bit of the matrix and reused in the subsequent implementation of a matrix, the variable's DP is copied. During the COPY operation, this will generate two new variables, the first new variable replaces the first occurrence's DP and the second new variable will be used to model the following occurrence's DP as in Step 1. **Step 3:** Line 42 performs an XOR operation on the updated variables in each line and adds them into the model. Finally, this algorithm will return an entire model $\mathcal{M}$ from Line 44.

Note that Line 33 and 36 are quite different, this is because if an output bit is reused, we should use one piece of the COPY operation to represent the output DP, as the other piece will be used to compute the following output bits.

3.2 Division Trails of Different Models

With the help of automatic solvers, such as Gurobi, Eq. (1) and (3) can be solved and the obtained solutions are division trails. Table 2 and 3 list the division trails of various methods, in which the binary representation of division trails is equivalent to the hexadecimal representation, denoted as: $(u_0, u_1, u_2, u_3) = (1, 0, 0, 0) \stackrel{\triangle}{=} 0x8$.

Comparing the division trails obtained by various methods in Table 2 and 3, it can be found that the division trails obtained using the **Paar + CX** are less than those obtained by the $\mathcal{S}$ method. For the **BP + CX** and the **XZ + CX**, both methods can eliminate some (invalid) division trails. However, they will also introduce some new (invalid) division trails at the same time.

Note that Zhang and Rijmen [11] presented a theoretical technique to determine if a division trail is valid, which computes the determinant of the sub-matrix defined by the input and the output DP, or equivalently checks if the ANF of the output (defined by the output DP) contains the input monomial (defined by the

Algorithm 1. Construct the MILP model of linear layer BDP propagation

---

Input: A matrix implementation
Output: The MILP model of BDP propagation $\mathcal{M}$
1: $count = 0$;
2: $L \leftarrow$ Read the matrix implementation by row, add the variables of each row to the corresponding row of the two-dimensional list L from left to right;
3: $temp \leftarrow$ dict(); //Initialized as an empty dictionary
4: **function** $Get\_new\_var(\ )$
5:     $new\_var = s_{count}$;
6:     $count = count + 1$;
7:     **return** new_var;
8: **end function**
9: $\mathcal{M}.var \leftarrow u_i, v_i, new\_var$; //$u_i$ and v_i represent the input and output division property, new_var denotes a newly generated binary variable
10: **for** $i = 0$; $i < len(L)$ **do**
11:     **for** $j = 1$; $j < len(L[i])$ **do**
12:         **if** $L[i][j]$ appears in the k-th$(k > i)$ row of L **then**
13:             **if** $L[i][j]$ is not an index of $temp$ **then**
14:                 $t_0 = Get\_new\_var(\ )$;
15:                 $t_1 = Get\_new\_var(\ )$;
16:                 $\mathcal{M}.con \leftarrow L[i][j]' = t_0 + t_1$; //$L[i][j]'$ represent the DP of $L[i][j]$
17:                 $temp[L[i][j]] = t_1$;
18:                 $L[i][j]' = t_0$;
19:             **else**
20:                 $t_0' = Get\_new\_var(\ )$;
21:                 $t_1' = Get\_new\_var(\ )$;
22:                 $\mathcal{M}.con \leftarrow temp[L[i][j]] = t_0' + t_1'$;
23:                 $temp[L[i][j]] = t_1'$;
24:                 $L[i][j]' = t_0'$;
25:             **end if**
26:         **else**
27:             **if** $L[i][j]$ in an index of $temp$ **then**
28:                 $L[i][j] = temp[L[i][j]]$;
29:             **end if**
30:         **end if**
31:     **end for**
32:     **if** $L[i][0] =$ Output **then**
33:         **if** $L[i][0]$ appears in the k-th$(k > i)$ row of L **then**
34:             $t_0 = Get\_new\_var(\ )$;
35:             $t_1 = Get\_new\_var(\ )$;
36:             $\mathcal{M}.con \leftarrow t_0 = L[i][0]' + t_1$; //$L[i][0]'$ represent the DP of $L[i][0]$
37:             $temp[L[i][j]] = t_1$;
38:             $temp \leftarrow$ Store $[L[i][0], t_1]$ in $temp$;
39:             $L[i][0]' = t_0$;
40:         **end if**
41:     **end if**
42:     $\mathcal{M}.con \leftarrow L[i][0]' = L[i][1]' + L[i][2]'$;
43: **end for**
44: **return** $\mathcal{M}$;

Table 3. Division trails of different implementations. The trails highlighted in bold are invalid.

Input	Paar + CX	BP + CX	XZ + CX
0x0	0x0	0x0	0x0
0x1	0x2, 0x4, 0x8	0x2, 0x4, 0x8	**0x1**, 0x2, 0x4, 0x8
0x2	0x1, 0x4, 0x8	0x1, **0x2**, 0x4, 0x8	0x1, **0x2**, 0x4, 0x8
0x3	0x3, 0x5, 0x6, 0x9, 0xA	0x3, 0x5, 0x6, 0x9, 0xA, **0xC**	0x3, 0x5, 0x6, 0x9, 0xA, **0xC**
0x4	0x1, 0x2, 0x8	0x1, 0x2, 0x8	0x1, 0x2, 0x8
0x5	0x3, 0x5, 0x6, 0x9, **0xA**, 0xC	0x3, 0x5, 0x6, 0x9, 0xC	0x3, 0x5, 0x6, 0x9, **0xA**, 0xC
0x6	0x3, 0x5, 0x6, **0x9**, 0xA, 0xC	0x3, 0x5, 0x6, **0x9**, 0xA, 0xC	0x3, 0x5, 0x6, 0xA, 0xC
0x7	**0x7**, 0xB, 0xD, 0xE	0xB, 0xD, 0xE	**0x7**, 0xB, 0xD, 0xE
0x8	0x1, 0x2, 0x4	0x1, 0x2, 0x4, **0x8**	0x1, 0x2, 0x4
0x9	0x3, 0x5, **0x6**, 0x9, 0xA, 0xC	0x3, 0x5, **0x6** , 0x9, 0xA, 0xC	0x3, 0x5, 0x9, 0xA, 0xC
0xA	0x3, **0x5**, 0x6, 0x9, 0xA, 0xC	0x3, 0x6, 0x9, 0xA, 0xC	0x3, **0x5** , 0x6, 0x9, 0xA, 0xC
0xB	0x7, **0xB**, 0xD, 0xE	0x7, 0xD, 0xE	0x7, **0xB**, 0xD, 0xE
0xC	0x5, 0x6, 0x9, 0xA, 0xC	**0x3**, 0x5, 0x6, 0x9, 0xA, 0xC	**0x3**, 0x5, 0x6, 0x9, 0xA, 0xC
0xD	0x7, 0xB, **0xD**, 0xE	0x7, 0xB, **0xD**, 0xE	0x7, 0xB, 0xE
0xE	0x7, 0xB, 0xD, **0xE**	0x7, 0xB, 0xD	0x7, 0xB, 0xD
0xF	0xF	0xF	0xF

input DP). Since the $\mathcal{S}$ method corresponds to direct implementation of a matrix, and our technique uses an optimized implementation, division trails obtained by these methods are reasonable characterizations of BDP propagations (in the sense that this may introduce invalid division trails). Thus, we can conclude that all increased division trails using our method are invalid trails compared with the $\mathcal{S}$ method. Let's consider the division trail $0x2 \xrightarrow{M} 0x2$ obtained by the **BP + CX**. This is a newly increased trail compared with the $\mathcal{S}$ method. The output bit defined by the output DP is y_2, which equals to $x_0 \oplus x_1 \oplus x_3$ according to the matrix. Obviously, the ANF of this output bit does not contain x_2, which indicates that $0x2 \xrightarrow{M} 0x2$ is an invalid trail. However, we can get a deeper look of this trail. According to the implementation returned by the **BP** algorithm, y_2 is computed as $t_0 = x_0 \oplus x_2, y_3 = x_1 \oplus t_0, y_1 = x_3 \oplus t_0, t_1 = y_3 \oplus y_1, y_2 = x_0 \oplus t_1$. The input DP of the matrix is $0x2$, thus the DP of x_2 is 1 which can propagate to t_0, and this can further propagate to y_3 and y_1, which finally propagate to y_2. This leads to the increased invalid division trail.

On the other hand, since each set of inequalities as listed in Eq. (1) and (3) can describe the BDP propagation of M in a non-accurate way, all decreased division trails of our method are all invalid trails. Let's take the division trail $0xC \xrightarrow{M} 0x3 \triangleq (1,1,0,0) \xrightarrow{M} (0,0,1,1)$ as an example. According to the matrix implementation of Eq. (2), we can compute the ANF of y_2y_3, i.e., $y_2y_3 = (x_0 \oplus x_1 \oplus x_3)(x_0 \oplus x_1 \oplus x_2) = x_0 \oplus x_0x_1 \oplus x_0x_2 \oplus x_0x_1 \oplus x_1 \oplus x_1x_2 \oplus x_0x_3 \oplus x_1x_3 \oplus x_2x_3$. It is easy to find that x_0x_1 appears twice, and the monomial will be cancelled after the XOR operation, then y_2y_3 does not include x_0x_1, so the input DP $(1,1,0,0)$ can not propagate to the output DP $(0,0,1,1)$. Therefore, this trail is not a valid propagation according to Zhang and Rijmen's theory. Similarly, it can be concluded that all decreased trails are invalid.

Since the **Paar + CX** method reduces two invalid trails, and both the **BP + CX** and **XZ + CX** methods introduce new invalid trails at the same time when reducing invalid trails. It seems that one should prefer the **Paar + CX** to the **BP + CX** and the **XZ + CX**. However, the **Paar + CX** method only reduces two trails which is not satisfactory. In the following, we combine all of the three methods. Note that each method (**Paar, BP, XZ + CX**) can describe the BDP propagation of M (in a non-accurate way), which means all valid trails of M should be contained in the trail set obtained by each of the three methods. Thus, the intersection of the three trail sets can characterize the BDP propagation. This has the advantage that each invalid trail eliminated by one of the methods will not be included in the intersection, thus eliminated. In practice, the trail set of each method is obtained by solving the corresponding system of inequalities. Therefore, we can gather the latter three sets of the inequalities listed in Eq. (2) as a whole, and the solutions of this model are the common solutions of the three methods, that is, the intersection of the solutions as desired. The column marked with "our method" in Table 2 lists the results of this combination. The results show that it can reduce a large number of invalid trails, which are fully identical to results by the $\mathcal{ZR}$ method as shown in the 4-th column of Table 2. In Table 3, we can clearly see that the optimized implementations of different algorithms can eliminate some different invalid trails. Due to the randomness of these algorithms and the linearly growth of modeling implementations using the **CX** rules, it is possible to use these algorithms multiple times to obtain multiple matrix implementations, and add the corresponding inequalities into the model to get a more accurate propagation, which enables us to search for more available integral properties.

3.3   On the Effectiveness of Our Method

The example discussed in Subsect. 3.2 shows that the **BP + CX** or the **XZ+ CX** method would possibly introduce some new invalid trails, even though they could eliminate several invalid trails at the same time. Thus, we can not conclude that the **BP + CX** or the **XZ + CX** method is better than the $\mathcal{S}$ method. As we discussed in Subsect. 3.2, the division trail $0x2 \xrightarrow{M} 0x2$ is a newly introduced invalid trail, and this happens because two x_2's are involved in the computation of y_2 and they will be cancelled by XOR. According to the computation process of the **Paar** algorithm described in Subsect. 2.2, this algorithm outputs *cancellation-free* implementations. That is, x_2 will never appear in the computation of y_2. Moreover, we can find in the example listed in Subsect. 3.2 that the **Paar + CX** method only eliminates invalid trails and no new invalid trails are introduced compared with the $\mathcal{S}$ method. We will discuss in this subsection and conclude that the **Paar + CX** method is always superior to the $\mathcal{S}$ method, i.e., the trail set computed by the **Paar + CX** method is a subset of the trail set obtained by the $\mathcal{S}$ method.

Let's first revisit Zhang and Rijmen's theory and the $\mathcal{S}$ method.

Theorem 1 ([11]). *Let $M = (a_{i,j})$ be the $n \times n$ matrix of an invertible linear transform. Let $(\boldsymbol{u}, \boldsymbol{v}) = (u_1, \cdots, u_n, v_1, \cdots, v_n) \in \mathbb{F}_2^n \times \mathbb{F}_2^n$, $I_u = \{i, u_i = 1\} = \{i_1, \cdots, i_{wt(u)}\}$, $I_v = \{j, v_j = 1\} = \{j_1, \cdots, j_{wt(v)}\}$. Then $(\boldsymbol{u}, \boldsymbol{v})$ is a valid division trail if and only if the order $wt(\boldsymbol{u})$ sub-matrix whose rows indices are taken from I_u and columns indices are taken from I_v is invertible.*

Let $P = (p_{i,j})_{n \times n}$ and $Q = (q_{i,j})_{n \times n}$ be two $n \times n$ matrices, we denote $P\&Q = (p_{i,j} \times q_{i,j})_{n \times n}$ an $n \times n$ matrix which is the element-wise AND of P and Q. In the following, we say that P contains Q or Q is contained in P if $P\&Q = Q$. Given the modeling process of the $\mathcal{S}$ method, we can easily deduce the following proposition.

Proposition 3. *Let $M = (a_{i,j})$ be the $n \times n$ matrix of an invertible linear transform. Let $(\boldsymbol{u}, \boldsymbol{v}) = (u_1, \cdots, u_n, v_1, \cdots, v_n) \in \mathbb{F}_2^n \times \mathbb{F}_2^n$, $I_u = \{i, u_i = 1\} = \{i_1, \cdots, i_{wt(u)}\}$, $I_v = \{j, v_j = 1\} = \{j_1, \cdots, j_{wt(v)}\}$. Then $(\boldsymbol{u}, \boldsymbol{v})$ is a division trail of the $\mathcal{S}$ method if and only if the order $wt(\boldsymbol{u})$ sub-matrix whose rows indices are taken from I_u and columns indices are taken from I_v contains a permutation matrix.*

From Theorem 1 and Proposition 3, we can conclude that each valid division trail (indicated by Theorem 1) is a division trail of the $\mathcal{S}$ method, since each invertible matrix must contain a permutation matrix. Conversely, each division trail of the $\mathcal{S}$ method is not necessarily a valid division trail. Consider a matrix whose all elements being 1. This matrix is not an invertible matrix, however this matrix contains the identity matrix as a permutation matrix.

Since the **Paar** algorithm is *cancellation-free*, if we compute an output bit y_i from the reverse order of a given implementation, input variables that are not contained in the ANF of y_i will never appear. For example, if we compute y_2 from the **Paar** implementation in Eq. (2), $y_2 = x_3 \oplus t_0 = x_0 \oplus x_1 \oplus x_3$. Thus, x_2 is not involved. However, if we consider y_2 from the **BP** implementation, $y_2 = x_0 \oplus t_1 = x_0 \oplus x_1 \oplus x_3 \oplus x_0 \oplus x_2 \oplus x_0 \oplus x_2$, and x_2 is involved. Given the *cancellation-free* property of the **Paar** algorithm, it can be easily concluded.

Property 1. *If an output bit has the division property of 1, one of the inputs involved in its ANF has the division property of 1.*

Moreover, assuming that two output bits y_i and y_j share several common input bits, and both y_i and y_j have input DP of 1. According to Property 1, the DP of y_i and y_j being 1 will indicate two input bits taking the DP of 1. Moreover, these two input bits cannot be the same. This is due to the fact that if any input bit x_k is involved in the ANFs of y_i and y_j, we should use the COPY operation to split the DP of x_k, and both y_i and y_j will take a piece of x_k. Thus, if y_i indicates that x_k has the DP of 1, which means the piece of x_k fed to y_i has DP of 1. Thus, the other piece fed to y_j will never take the DP of 1.

Property 2. *Different output bits taking the division property of 1 will indicate different input bits taking the division property of 1.*

Given a division trail $\boldsymbol{u} \rightarrow \boldsymbol{v}$ deduced from the **Paar + CX** method, let w denote the Hamming weight of $\boldsymbol{u}$ (and $\boldsymbol{v}$), and $i_1, \cdots, i_w (i_1 < i_2 < \cdots < i_w), j_1, \cdots, j_w (j_1 < j_2 < \cdots < j_w)$ denote the indices of $\boldsymbol{u}$ and $\boldsymbol{v}$ whose corresponding coordinates take the DP of 1. According to Property 2, we can pair $x_{i_1}, \cdots, x_{i_w}$ and $y_{j_1}, \cdots, y_{j_w}$, where x_{i_w} and y_{i_w} denote the input and out variables. For the sake of simplicity, assume that x_{i_s} and y_{j_s} form a pair, which means x_{i_s} is involved in the ANF of y_{j_s}. Thus, $M[j_s][i_s] = 1$ where $M[j_s][i_s]$ denotes the element in the j_s-th row and i_s-th column of M. Let $M_{v,u}$ denote the $w \times w$ sub-matrix of M as explained in Proposition 3, then this matrix contains the identity matrix as a permutation matrix, which means each division trail deduced from the **Paar + CX** method is a division trail of the $\mathcal{S}$ method.

Furthermore, we consider the case where the **Paar** algorithm will generate a new column with Hamming weight greater than 1, which denotes that there is at least one $x_i \oplus x_j$ for $i < j$ appears at least twice in the ANFs of $y_0, \cdots, y_{n-1}$. Without loss of generality, assume that $x_0 \oplus x_1$ appears both in y_0 and y_1, then the sub-matrix of M with the 1st, 2nd row and 1st, 2nd column must be a 2×2 matrix with all elements being 1. It is not invertible because it contains the 2×2 identity matrix as a permutation matrix. Then the division trail $(1, 1, \cdots, 0, 0) \longrightarrow (1, 1, \cdots, 0, 0)$ can be deduced from the $\mathcal{S}$ method by Proposition 3. But it must not be deduced from the **Paar + CX** method, since the

DP 1 of the intermediate variable $t = x_0 \oplus x_1$ can not be copied to two pieces both with DP 1, i.e., the DP of y_0 and y_1 cannot both be 1. This means that the **Paar** $+$ **CX** method must eliminate some invalid division trails which can be deduced from the $\mathcal{S}$ method.

Proposition 4. *For any given matrix M, division trails deduced from the* **Paar** $+$ **CX** *method are all division trails of the $\mathcal{S}$ method. Moreover, when the* **Paar** *algorithm generates some new columns with Hamming weight greater than 1, division trails deduced from the* **Paar** $+$ **CX** *method must be less than division trails deduced from the $\mathcal{S}$ method.*

The above proposition guarantees that the **Paar** $+$ **CX** method is never worse than the $\mathcal{S}$ method. In other words, the **Paar** $+$ **CX** method will never introduce newly invalid trails compared with the $\mathcal{S}$ method. Moreover, it can be inferred from Proposition 4 and the above discussion that a more optimized implementation by the **Paar** algorithm may result in more accurate propagations. Even though we have used a highly optimized implementation for both the **BP** $+$ **CX** and the **XZ** $+$ **CX** methods, the propagation of these two methods can eliminate some invalid trails, and however introduce some new invalid trails in the meanwhile, compared with the $\mathcal{S}$ method. Thus, we can never say that the **BP** $+$ **CX** or the **XZ** $+$ **CX** method alone is more accurate than the $\mathcal{S}$ method. In fact, we have experimented on two different implementations returned by the **BP** algorithm on LED cipher. Interestingly, the number of trails (both valid and invalid) of the better implementation (i.e., with a smaller XOR count) is larger than the worse implementation. Thus, if one wants to use an implementation of the **BP** or the **XZ** in the division propagation, there is no need to get a highly optimized implementation as this does not always indicate a more accurate propagation. However, we can simply consider the combination of these algorithms, which is absolutely more accurate than using only one of these algorithms.

4   Applications of Our New Technique

In this section, we show the applications of our technique to Midori64, Skinny64 and LED. Meanwhile, we also have reproduced the results of 4- and 5-round dependent-key integral distinguishers AES as reported in [12]. Our new technique mainly focuses on efficiently modeling BDP propagations of the linear layer. Table 4 partially lists division trails of linear layers of these block ciphers by the $\mathcal{S}$ method, the $\mathcal{ZR}$ method, the $\mathcal{HW}$ method and our method. The main results for integral characteristics of these block ciphers can be found in Table 1.

Some special notations will be used in this section. $\mathcal{A}$, $\mathcal{B}$ and $\mathcal{U}$ indicate that a certain nibble is active, balanced and unknown, respectively. The little letters a, b and u indicate the active bit, the balanced bit and the unknown bit respectively. And we use nR to generally denote an n-round encryption where R denotes a one-round encryption.

Table 4. Comparison of the number of division trails by different methods.

Ciphers	Hamming weight [†]	$\mathcal{S}$ method	$\mathcal{ZR}/\mathcal{HW}$ method	Our method
Midori64	3	12160	11280	11458
Skinny64	all [‡]	1500624	1185921	1185921
	3	144053	101938	123195

[†] The Hamming weight of the input DP. In our experiment, it can hardly to calculate the number of division trails when we traverse all the cases of the Hamming weight of the input DP for Midori64 and LED. Therefore, we only list the division trails that the Hamming weight of the input DP is 3 for Midori64 and LED.

[‡] Traverse all the cases of the Hamming weight of the input DP.

4.1 Application to Midori64

In [9], Sun $et\ al.$ obtained the longest 7-round integral distinguisher of Midori64. Although our method deduces distinguishers as long as the current longest one, but more balanced output bits can be obtained by our method. The 5-, 6- and 7-round distinguishers obtained by using the $\mathcal{S}$ method are shown as follows.

$$
\begin{bmatrix} A & C & C & C \\ C & A & C & C \\ C & C & A & C \\ C & C & C & C \end{bmatrix}
\overset{5R}{\Longrightarrow}
\begin{bmatrix} uubu & \mathcal{U} & \mathcal{U} & \mathcal{U} \\ uubu & \mathcal{U} & \mathcal{U} & \mathcal{U} \\ uubu & \mathcal{U} & \mathcal{U} & \mathcal{U} \\ uubu & \mathcal{U} & \mathcal{U} & \mathcal{U} \end{bmatrix}
\begin{bmatrix} A & A & C & accc \\ A & A & A & C \\ C & A & A & A \\ A & C & A & A \end{bmatrix}
\overset{6R}{\Longrightarrow}
\begin{bmatrix} uubu & uubu & uubu & uubu \\ uubu & uubu & uubu & uubu \\ uubu & uubu & uubu & uubu \\ uubu & uubu & uubu & uubu \end{bmatrix}
$$

$$
\begin{bmatrix} A & A & A & A \\ A & A & A & A \\ A & A & A & A \\ A & A & A & ccac \end{bmatrix}
\overset{7R}{\Longrightarrow}
\begin{bmatrix} uubu & uubu & uubu & uubu \\ uubu & uubu & uubu & uubu \\ uubu & uubu & uubu & uubu \\ uubu & uubu & uubu & uubu \end{bmatrix}
$$

Our 5-, 6- and 7-round distinguishers of Midori64 are shown as follows.

$$
\begin{bmatrix} A & C & C & C \\ C & A & C & C \\ C & C & A & C \\ C & C & C & C \end{bmatrix}
\overset{5R}{\Longrightarrow}
\begin{bmatrix} uubu & \mathcal{U} & \mathcal{U} & \mathcal{U} \\ uubu & \mathcal{U} & \mathcal{U} & \mathcal{U} \\ uubu & \mathcal{U} & \mathcal{U} & \mathcal{U} \\ \mathcal{B} & \mathcal{U} & \mathcal{U} & \mathcal{U} \end{bmatrix}
\begin{bmatrix} A & A & C & accc \\ A & A & A & C \\ C & A & A & A \\ A & C & A & A \end{bmatrix}
\overset{6R}{\Longrightarrow}
\begin{bmatrix} uubu & uubu & uubu & uubu \\ uubu & uubu & uubu & uubu \\ uubu & uubu & uubu & uubu \\ \mathcal{B} & uubu & uubu & uubu \end{bmatrix}
$$

$$
\begin{bmatrix} aaca & A & A & A \\ A & A & A & A \\ A & A & A & A \\ A & A & A & A \end{bmatrix}
\overset{7R}{\Longrightarrow}
\begin{bmatrix} \mathcal{B} & \mathcal{B} & \mathcal{B} & \mathcal{B} \\ \mathcal{B} & \mathcal{B} & \mathcal{B} & \mathcal{B} \\ \mathcal{B} & \mathcal{B} & \mathcal{B} & \mathcal{B} \\ \mathcal{B} & \mathcal{B} & \mathcal{B} & \mathcal{B} \end{bmatrix}
$$

The experimental results show that for 5-round integral distinguisher of Midori64, we can get 3 more balanced bits than the $\mathcal{S}$ method by setting 12 active bits. For 6-round integral distinguisher, we can also get 3 more balanced bits than the $\mathcal{S}$ method by setting 45 active bits. In addition, our 7-round distinguisher is consistent with that of the $\mathcal{ZR}$ method as in [11].

4.2 Application to Skinny64

By applying our new technique to Skinny64, we get a 10-round integral distinguisher by setting 60 active bits. However, as shown in [11], when using the $\mathcal{S}$ method, only 9-round integral distinguisher can be obtained by setting 63 active bits. Our 9- and 10-round integral distinguishers are shown as follows.

$$
\begin{bmatrix} \mathcal{C} & \mathcal{A} & \mathcal{A} & \mathcal{A} \\ \mathcal{A} & \mathcal{A} & \mathcal{A} & \mathcal{A} \\ \mathcal{A} & \mathcal{A} & \mathcal{A} & \mathcal{A} \\ \mathcal{A} & \mathcal{A} & \mathcal{A} & \mathcal{A} \end{bmatrix} \xrightarrow{9R} \begin{bmatrix} \mathcal{B} & \mathcal{B} & \mathcal{B} & \mathcal{B} \\ \mathcal{B} & \mathcal{B} & \mathcal{B} & \mathcal{B} \\ \mathcal{B} & \mathcal{B} & \mathcal{B} & \mathcal{B} \\ \mathcal{B} & \mathcal{B} & \mathcal{B} & \mathcal{B} \end{bmatrix} \quad \begin{bmatrix} \mathcal{C} & \mathcal{A} & \mathcal{A} & \mathcal{A} \\ \mathcal{A} & \mathcal{A} & \mathcal{A} & \mathcal{A} \\ \mathcal{A} & \mathcal{A} & \mathcal{A} & \mathcal{A} \\ \mathcal{A} & \mathcal{A} & \mathcal{A} & \mathcal{A} \end{bmatrix} \xrightarrow{10R} \begin{bmatrix} \mathcal{B} & \mathcal{B} & \mathcal{B} & \mathcal{B} \\ \mathcal{B} & \mathcal{B} & \mathcal{B} & \mathcal{B} \\ \mathcal{B} & \mathcal{B} & \mathcal{B} & \mathcal{B} \\ \mathcal{B} & \mathcal{B} & \mathcal{B} & \mathcal{B} \end{bmatrix}
$$

The experimental results show that our method inputs 56 active bits and obtains 64 balanced bits for the 9-round integral distinguisher, where fewer active bits are needed compared with the distinguishers obtained by $\mathcal{S}$ method. For 10-round integral distinguisher, there are 60 active input bits and 64 balanced output bits, which is consistent with the result by $\mathcal{ZR}$ method in [11].

4.3 Application to LED

In [9], Sun *et al.* can only search for 6-round integral distinguisher of LED. But using our method, 7-round integral distinguisher can be got which are consistent with the result by $\mathcal{HW}$ method in [12] and are expressed as follows.

$$
\begin{bmatrix} \mathcal{A} & aaac & \mathcal{A} & \mathcal{A} \\ \mathcal{A} & \mathcal{A} & \mathcal{A} & \mathcal{A} \\ \mathcal{A} & \mathcal{A} & \mathcal{A} & \mathcal{A} \\ \mathcal{A} & \mathcal{A} & \mathcal{A} & \mathcal{A} \end{bmatrix} \xrightarrow{7R} \begin{bmatrix} \mathcal{B} & \mathcal{B} & \mathcal{B} & \mathcal{B} \\ \mathcal{B} & \mathcal{B} & \mathcal{B} & \mathcal{B} \\ \mathcal{B} & \mathcal{B} & \mathcal{B} & \mathcal{B} \\ \mathcal{B} & \mathcal{B} & \mathcal{B} & \mathcal{B} \end{bmatrix}
$$

The experimental results show that our method can find one more round integral distinguisher than the $\mathcal{S}$ method, and when setting 63 active input bits, the distinguisher is same as the result obtained by the $\mathcal{HW}$ method.

5 Conclusion

In this paper, we propose a new technique to improve the accuracy of modeling BDP propagations of complex linear layers, whose core idea is to combine the optimized implementations of matrices and the modeling rules for COPY and XOR (**CX** rules). In particular, we use three heuristics (**Paar**, **BP** and **XZ**) to obtain optimized implementations of a matrix and then model these implementations based on the **CX** rules simultaneously to generate a system of inequalities.

Moreover, we theoretically prove that this new method is always superior to the $\mathcal{S}$ method, which straightforwardly ultilizes the **CX** rules to model the direct implementation of a matrix. In order to exhibit the effect of this new method, we apply it to several block ciphers. As a result, we can obtain longer distinguishers or more balanced bits for Midori64, Skinny64 and LED than that of the $\mathcal{S}$ method. Additionally, what we need emphasize is that our method is not completely accurate compared with the $\mathcal{ZR}$ and $\mathcal{HW}$ methods. However, our results are consistent with that of the $\mathcal{ZR}$ and $\mathcal{HW}$ methods. Furthermore, our method can be implemented based on MILP as well as SMT/SAT, and the constraints are fully linear, thus simple. In consequence, for modeling the BDP propagation of linear layers based on very large and complex matrices, our method may be more practical among these existing methods.

Acknowledgements. We would like to thank the anonymous reviewers for their helpful comments. This work was supported by the Application Foundation Frontier Project of Wuhan Science and Technology Bureau (NO. 2020010601012189), the National Natural Science Foundation of China (NO. 61802119) and the Research Foundation of Department of Education of Hubei Province, China (No. D2020104).

References

1. Biham, E., Shamir, A.: Differential cryptanalysis of DES-like cryptosystems. In: Menezes, A.J., Vanstone, S.A. (eds.) CRYPTO 1990. LNCS, vol. 537, pp. 2–21. Springer, Heidelberg (1991). https://doi.org/10.1007/3-540-38424-3_1
2. Matsui, M.: Linear cryptanalysis method for DES cipher. In: Helleseth, T. (ed.) EUROCRYPT 1993. LNCS, vol. 765, pp. 386–397. Springer, Heidelberg (1994). https://doi.org/10.1007/3-540-48285-7_33
3. Knudsen, L., Wagner, D.: Integral cryptanalysis. In: Daemen, J., Rijmen, V. (eds.) FSE 2002. LNCS, vol. 2365, pp. 112–127. Springer, Heidelberg (2002). https://doi.org/10.1007/3-540-45661-9_9
4. Daemen, J., Knudsen, L., Rijmen, V.: The block cipher Square. In: Biham, E. (ed.) FSE 1997. LNCS, vol. 1267, pp. 149–165. Springer, Heidelberg (1997). https://doi.org/10.1007/BFb0052343
5. Todo, Y.: Structural evaluation by generalized integral property. In: Oswald, E., Fischlin, M. (eds.) EUROCRYPT 2015. LNCS, vol. 9056, pp. 287–314. Springer, Heidelberg (2015). https://doi.org/10.1007/978-3-662-46800-5_12
6. Todo, Y.: Integral cryptanalysis on full MISTY1. In: Gennaro, R., Robshaw, M. (eds.) CRYPTO 2015. LNCS, vol. 9215, pp. 413–432. Springer, Heidelberg (2015). https://doi.org/10.1007/978-3-662-47989-6_20
7. Todo, Y., Morii, M.: Bit-based division property and application to SIMON family. In: Peyrin, T. (ed.) FSE 2016. LNCS, vol. 9783, pp. 357–377. Springer, Heidelberg (2016). https://doi.org/10.1007/978-3-662-52993-5_18
8. Xiang, Z., Zhang, W., Bao, Z., Lin, D.: Applying MILP method to searching integral distinguishers based on division property for 6 lightweight block ciphers. In: Cheon, J.H., Takagi, T. (eds.) ASIACRYPT 2016. LNCS, vol. 10031, pp. 648–678. Springer, Heidelberg (2016). https://doi.org/10.1007/978-3-662-53887-6_24
9. Sun, L., Wang, W., Wang, M.Q.: MILP-aided bit-based division property for primitives with non-bit-permutation linear layers. IET Inf. Secur. **14**, 12–20 (2020). https://doi.org/10.1049/iet-ifs.2018.5283

10. Sun, L., Wang, W., Liu, R., Wang, M.Q.: Milp-aided bit-based division property for ARX ciphers. Sci. China Inf. Sci. **61**, 118102:1-118102:3 (2018). https://doi.org/10.1007/s11432-017-9321-7

11. Zhang, W.Y., Rijmen, V.: Division cryptanalysis of block ciphers with a binary diffusion layer. IET Inf. Secur. **13**, 87–95 (2019). https://doi.org/10.1049/iet-ifs.2018.5151

12. Hu, K., Wang, Q.J., Wang, M.Q.: Finding bit-based division property for ciphers with complex linear layers. IACR Trans. Symmetric Cryptol. **2020**, 396–424 (2020). https://doi.org/10.13154/tosc.v2020.i1.396-424

13. Elsheikh M., Youssef A.: On MILP-based automatic search for bit-based division property for ciphers with (large) linear layers (Submitted to ACISP 2021) (2021). https://eprint.iacr.org/2021/643

14. Paar, C.: Optimized arithmetic for reed-solomon encoders. In: Proceedings of IEEE International Symposium on Information Theory 1997, p. 250 (1997). https://doi.org/10.1109/ISIT.1997.613165

15. Boyar, J., Matthews, P., Peralta, R.: Logic minimization techniques with applications to cryptology. J. Cryptol. **26**, 280–312 (2013). https://doi.org/10.1007/s00145-012-9124-7

16. Xiang, Z.J., Zeng, X.Y., Lin, D., Bao, Z.Z., Zhang, S.S.: Optimizing implementations of linear layers. IACR Trans. Symmetric Cryptol. **2020**, 120–145 (2020). https://doi.org/10.13154/tosc.v2020.i2.120-145

17. Banik, S., et al.: Midori: a block cipher for low energy. In: Iwata, T., Cheon, J.H. (eds.) ASIACRYPT 2015. LNCS, vol. 9453, pp. 411–436. Springer, Heidelberg (2015). https://doi.org/10.1007/978-3-662-48800-3_17

18. Beierle, C.: The SKINNY family of block ciphers and its low-latency variant MANTIS. In: Robshaw, M., Katz, J. (eds.) CRYPTO 2016. LNCS, vol. 9815, pp. 123–153. Springer, Heidelberg (2016). https://doi.org/10.1007/978-3-662-53008-5_5

19. Guo, J., Peyrin, T., Poschmann, A., Robshaw, M.: The LED block cipher. In: Preneel, B., Takagi, T. (eds.) CHES 2011. LNCS, vol. 6917, pp. 326–341. Springer, Heidelberg (2011). https://doi.org/10.1007/978-3-642-23951-9_22

20. Mouha, N., Wang, Q., Gu, D., Preneel, B.: Differential and linear cryptanalysis using mixed-integer linear programming. In: Wu, C.-K., Yung, M., Lin, D. (eds.) Inscrypt 2011. LNCS, vol. 7537, pp. 57–76. Springer, Heidelberg (2012). https://doi.org/10.1007/978-3-642-34704-7_5

21. Sun, S., Hu, L., Wang, P., Qiao, K., Ma, X., Song, L.: Automatic security evaluation and (related-key) differential characteristic search: application to SIMON, PRESENT, LBlock, DES(L) and other bit-oriented block ciphers. In: Sarkar, P., Iwata, T. (eds.) ASIACRYPT 2014. LNCS, vol. 8873, pp. 158–178. Springer, Heidelberg (2014). https://doi.org/10.1007/978-3-662-45611-8_9

22. Kranz, T., Leander, G., Stoffelen, K., Wiemer, F.: Shorter linear straight-line programs for MDS matrices. IACR Trans. Symmetric Cryptol. **2017**, 188–211 (2017). https://doi.org/10.13154/tosc.v2017.i4.188-211

23. Khoo, K., Peyrin, T., Poschmann, A.Y., Yap, H.: FOAM: searching for hardware-optimal SPN structures and components with a fair comparison. In: Batina, L., Robshaw, M. (eds.) CHES 2014. LNCS, vol. 8731, pp. 433–450. Springer, Heidelberg (2014). https://doi.org/10.1007/978-3-662-44709-3_24

Asymmetric Cryptanalysis

Security Analysis on an ElGamal-Like Multivariate Encryption Scheme Based on Isomorphism of Polynomials

Yasuhiko Ikematsu[1]([✉]), Shuhei Nakamura[2], Bagus Santoso[3],
and Takanori Yasuda[4]

[1] Institute of Mathematics for Industry, Kyushu University, 744, Motooka, Nishi-ku,
Fukuoka 819–0395, Japan
ikematsu@imi.kyushu-u.ac.jp
[2] Department of Liberal Arts and Basic Sciences, Nihon University, 1-2-1 Izumi-cho,
Narashino, Chiba 275-8575, Japan
nakamura.shuhei@nihon-u.ac.jp
[3] Department of Computer and Network Engineering, The University
of Electro-Communications, 1-5-1 Chofugaoka, Chofu, Tokyo 182-8585, Japan
santoso.bagus@uec.ac.jp
[4] Institute for the Advancement of Higher Education,
Okayama University of Science, 1-1 Ridaicho, Kitaku, Okayama 700-0005, Japan
tyasuda@bme.ous.ac.jp

Abstract. Isomorphism of polynomials with two secrets (IP2S) problem was proposed by Patarin et al. at Eurocrypt 1996 and the problem is to find two secret linear maps filling in the gap between two polynomial maps over a finite field. At PQC 2020, Santoso proposed a problem originated from IP2S, which is called block isomorphism of polynomials with circulant matrices (BIPC) problem. The BIPC problem is obtained by linearizing IP2S and restricting secret linear maps to linear maps represented by circulant matrices. Using the commutativity of products of circulant matrices, Santoso also proposed an ElGamal-like encryption scheme based on the BIPC problem. In this paper, we give a new security analysis on the ElGamal-like encryption scheme. In particular, we introduce a new attack (called linear stack attack) which finds an equivalent key of the ElGamal-like encryption scheme by using the linearity of the BIPC problem. We see that the attack is a polynomial-time algorithm and can break some 128-bit proposed parameters of the ElGamal-like encryption scheme within 10 h on a standard PC.

Keywords: Public key cryptography · Post quantum cryptography (PQC) · Multivariate public key cryptography (MPKC) · Isomorphism of Polynomials

1 Introduction

RSA and ECC are widely-used public key cryptosystems and are based on hard computational problems such as integer factorization problem and discrete

© Springer Nature Switzerland AG 2021
Y. Yu and M. Yung (Eds.): Inscrypt 2021, LNCS 13007, pp. 235–250, 2021.
https://doi.org/10.1007/978-3-030-88323-2_12

logarithm problem, respectively. In 1997, P. Shor [19] showed polynomial-time quantum algorithms to solve these problems using a large scale quantum computer. Therefore, before a large scale quantum computer gets realized, we need to develop cryptosystems having a resistance to quantum computer attacks. The research area to study such cryptosystems is called post quantum cryptography (PQC) [2].

Multivariate public key cryptography (MPKC) [7] is considered as one of the main candidates of PQC and is constructed based on hard computational problems on multivariate polynomials over finite fields. A main hard computational problem is the MQ problem, which finds a solution to a system of multivariate quadratic equations over a finite field. So far, there have been proposed various schemes based on the MQ problem. In particular, regarding signature schemes, Rainbow [8], GeMSS [4] and MQDSS [18] were selected as second round candidates of NIST PQC standardization project [12]. (Rainbow recently became a finalist of the project [6].) However, it is considered that there is no notable multivariate encryption scheme since most of the proposed schemes were not secure or had a large public key size.

Isomorphism of polynomials with two secrets (IP2S) problem is another problem in MPKC and was proposed by Patarin et al. at Eurocrypt 1996 [13]. The IP2S problem is to find two secret invertible linear maps representing the isomorphism between two multivariate polynomial maps over a finite field. Similar to the zero-knowledge interactive proof of graph isomorphism, Patarin proposed an interactive proof based on the IP2S problem. An authentication scheme based on the interactive proof scheme with its proof against impersonation attack is proposed in [15] and the security of the signature scheme based on the authentication scheme against quantum adversary in quantum random oracle model is proven in [17]. When the secret solutions of the IP2S problem are not restricted to invertible maps, we get another computational problem called Morphism of Polynomials (MP) problem which is proven to be an NP-hard problem [14]. Wang et al. [21] proposed a paradigm of constructing a public key encryption (PKE) scheme by using the Diffie-Hellman like algebraic structure derived from restricting the secrets/solutions of the MP problem into circulant matrices to obtain the commutativity. However, as the circulant matrices can be represented with few variables, it suffers from degradation of complexity as one can obtain a sufficient system of equations to solve the problem efficiently. Using this fact, Chen et al. [5] proposed an algebraic attack algorithm.

At PQC 2020, Santoso [16] proposed a new computational problem originated from the IP2S problem, which is called block isomorphism of polynomials with circulant matrices (BIPC) problem. The BIPC problem is obtained by linearizing IP2S and restricting secret linear maps to linear maps represented by circulant matrices. Moreover, similar to Wang et al.'s idea, using the commutativity of products of circulant matrices, Santoso proposed an ElGamal-like BIPC encryption scheme [16] and provided a security proof of the scheme based on the hardness of a Computational Diffie-Hellman (CDH)-like problem derived from the BIPC problem. In the BIPC problem, the secret solution is in the form of pairs of circulant matrices, instead of only one pair of matrices as in the IP2S problem. Therefore, although the secret solutions are circulant matrices, the number of variables can be adjusted to be sufficiently large to avoid Chen et al.'s algebraic attack. In [16], Santoso gave two attacks against the BIPC problem and selected four types of parameters which are called (a) conservative, (b) alternative, (c) extremely aggressive, and (d) moderately aggressive.

In this paper, we analyze the security of the ElGamal-like BIPC encryption scheme. We discuss a new attack, which is to find an equivalent key of the ElGamal-like encryption scheme by using the linearity of the BIPC problem (called *linear stack attack*). Our core idea is to show that there exists in fact an equivalent secret solution of the CDH-BIPC problem which consists of a set of pairs of circulant matrices. Note that the target of the linear stack attack is not for the BIPC problem but for the CDH-BIPC problem. Based on this idea, we can construct an equivalent key by randomly choosing enough set of pairs of circulant matrices and taking appropriately their scalar multiplications. We show that the linear stack attack is a polynomial-time algorithm and confirm that the attack is efficient for the proposed parameters (a),(b),(c) and (d). In fact, our experimental results showed that the 128-bit security parameters [16] in (b),(c) and (d) were broken within 10 h with a standard PC. Regarding (a), the 128-bit security parameter [16] did not finish within a week. Instead, we performed experiments for the 80-bit security parameter in (a) and confirmed that it was broken within 5 days.

As far as our knowledge, our attack[1] is the first algorithm which successfully breaks the ElGamal-like BIPC encryption scheme proposed in PQC 2020 [16]. Later, in an independent work [10], Hashimoto proposed a different attack algorithm that solves the BIPC problem directly. It should be noted that the attack algorithm in [10] is specifically developed for BIPC since it relies heavily on algebraic techniques which use the circulant properties of BIPC as the core. On the other hand, our attack algorithm is more simple and general, as we do not use the circulant properties of BIPC as the core of our algorithm. Therefore, at least in principle, our attack algorithm is more generalizable compared to the one in [10] and it may contribute to the future cryptanalysis of other IP2S based encryption schemes.

Our paper is organized as follows. In Sect. 2, we briefly recall the IP2S problem, the BIPC problem and the ElGamal-like encryption scheme. Moreover, we review the previous security analysis against the BIPC problem. In Sect. 3, we describe the linear stack attack and perform experiments for the proposed parameters in [16]. Finally, we conclude our paper in Sect. 4.

2   IP2S and BIPC Problems

In this section, we mainly recall the IP2S and BIPC problems. In Subsection 2.1, we review the IP2S problem proposed by Patarin et al. in [13]. In Subsection 2.2, we describe the BIPC problem proposed by Santoso [16] as a problem originated

---

[1] The earlier draft of our attack is published as a preprint in IACR Cryptology ePrint Archive [11].

from IP2S. Moreover, we recall the encryption scheme associated to the BIPC problem, which is our main concern in this paper. In Subsection 2.3, we revisit the previous security analysis against the BIPC problem following the original paper [16].

2.1   IP2S Problem

Let $\mathbb{F}$ be a finite field with q elements and let n and m be positive integers. We denote by $\mathbb{F}[x_1, \ldots, x_n]$ the polynomial ring in n variables over the finite field $\mathbb{F}$. We also denote by $\mathrm{GL}_n(\mathbb{F})$ the general linear group over $\mathbb{F}$ with size n. Any element of $\mathrm{GL}_n(\mathbb{F})$ can be considered as a linear map from $\mathbb{F}^n$ to $\mathbb{F}^n$. In order to describe the IP2S problem, we need the following set:

$$\mathcal{MQ}(n, m) := \left\{ \mathbf{f} = (f_1, \ldots, f_m) \,\middle|\, \begin{array}{l} f_i \in \mathbb{F}[x_1, \ldots, x_n] \ (1 \leq i \leq m) \\ \text{quadratic polynomial} \end{array} \right\}.$$

Namely, $\mathcal{MQ}(n, m)$ is the set of multivariate quadratic polynomial maps from $\mathbb{F}^n$ to $\mathbb{F}^m$. Any $\mathbf{f} = (f_1, \ldots, f_m) \in \mathcal{MQ}(n, m)$ is said to be *homogeneous* if all $f_1, \ldots, f_m$ are homogeneous. We define the operation of $\mathrm{GL}_n(\mathbb{F})$ and $\mathrm{GL}_m(\mathbb{F})$ to $\mathcal{MQ}(n, m)$:

$$(S, T) \cdot \mathbf{f} := T \circ \mathbf{f} \circ S, \qquad (S, T) \in \mathrm{GL}_n(\mathbb{F}) \times \mathrm{GL}_m(\mathbb{F}).$$

It is clear that for any $S \in \mathrm{GL}_n(\mathbb{F})$ and $T \in \mathrm{GL}_m(\mathbb{F})$,

$$\mathbf{f} \in \mathcal{MQ}(n, m) \implies (S, T) \cdot \mathbf{f} \in \mathcal{MQ}(n, m).$$

Namely, the operation of $\mathrm{GL}_n(\mathbb{F})$ and $\mathrm{GL}_m(\mathbb{F})$ holds the set $\mathcal{MQ}(n, m)$. Then, the IP2S problem is defined as follows:

Isomorphism of polynomials with two secrets (IP2S) [13]

Given two quadratic polynomial maps $\mathbf{f}, \mathbf{g} \in \mathcal{MQ}(n, m)$, find two linear maps $S \in \mathrm{GL}_n(\mathbb{F})$ and $T \in \mathrm{GL}_m(\mathbb{F})$ such that

$$\mathbf{g} = (S, T) \cdot \mathbf{f}. \tag{1}$$

In [13], Patarin proposed the basic idea of an authentication scheme and a signature scheme based on the IP2S problem. The concrete authentication scheme is refined in [15] and the security against quantum adversary in quantum random oracle model is proven in [17].

2.2   BIPC Problem and ElGamal-Like BIPC Encryption Scheme

In this subsection, we recall a problem originated from IP2S (called BIPC) and an ElGamal-like public key encryption scheme, which were proposed by Santoso at PQC 2020 [16].

Let $M_n(\mathbb{F})$ be the matrix ring with size $n \times n$ over $\mathbb{F}$. We also denote by $C_n(\mathbb{F})$ the subalgebra of circulant matrices in $M_n(\mathbb{F})$. Thus, any element A in $C_n(\mathbb{F})$ is written by

$$A = \begin{pmatrix} a_{11} & a_{12} & \cdots & a_{1n} \\ a_{1n} & a_{11} & \cdots & a_{1n-1} \\ \vdots & \vdots & \ddots & \vdots \\ a_{12} & a_{13} & \cdots & a_{11} \end{pmatrix}.$$

Note that $C_n(\mathbb{F})$ is a commutative ring, that is,

$$A, B \in C_n(\mathbb{F}) \implies AB = BA.$$

To describe the BIPC problem, we need the following definition:

Definition 1. *Let* k *be a positive integer and let* $\mathbf{f} = (\mathbf{f}_{[1]}, \ldots, \mathbf{f}_{[k]}) \in \mathcal{MQ}(n, m)^k$ *be a* k-*tuple of elements of* $\mathcal{MQ}(n, m)$. *For any two* k-*tuples* $\mathcal{A} = (A_1, \ldots, A_k) \in C_n(\mathbb{F})^k$ *and* $\mathcal{B} = (B_1, \ldots, B_k) \in C_m(\mathbb{F})^k$, *we define the operation*

$$(\mathcal{A}, \mathcal{B}) * \mathbf{f} := \begin{pmatrix} \sum_{j=1}^{k} B_j \circ \mathbf{f}_{[j \bmod k]} \circ A_j \\ \sum_{j=1}^{k} B_j \circ \mathbf{f}_{[j+1 \bmod k]} \circ A_j \\ \vdots \\ \sum_{j=1}^{k} B_j \circ \mathbf{f}_{[j+k-1 \bmod k]} \circ A_j \end{pmatrix}^T$$

$$= \begin{pmatrix} B_1 \circ \mathbf{f}_{[1]} \circ A_1 + B_2 \circ \mathbf{f}_{[2]} \circ A_2 + \cdots + B_k \circ \mathbf{f}_{[k]} \circ A_k \\ B_1 \circ \mathbf{f}_{[2]} \circ A_1 + B_2 \circ \mathbf{f}_{[3]} \circ A_2 + \cdots + B_k \circ \mathbf{f}_{[1]} \circ A_k \\ \vdots \\ B_1 \circ \mathbf{f}_{[k]} \circ A_1 + B_2 \circ \mathbf{f}_{[1]} \circ A_2 + \cdots + B_k \circ \mathbf{f}_{[k-1]} \circ A_k \end{pmatrix}^T$$

It is clear that $(\mathcal{A}, \mathcal{B}) * \mathbf{f}$ is also an element of $\mathcal{MQ}(n, m)^k$.

Remark 1. The operation $*$ does not hold the associativity. That is, in general

$$(\mathcal{A}, \mathcal{B}) * ((\mathcal{A}', \mathcal{B}') * \mathbf{f}) \neq (\mathcal{A}\mathcal{A}', \mathcal{B}\mathcal{B}') * \mathbf{f},$$

where $\mathcal{A}\mathcal{A}' = (A_1 A_1', \ldots, A_k A_k')$, $\mathcal{B}\mathcal{B}' = (B_1 B_1', \ldots, B_k B_k')$. Thus, the operation $*$ is not an action of $C_n(\mathbb{F})^k \times C_m(\mathbb{F})^k$ to $\mathcal{MQ}(n, m)^k$.

In the same way as IP2S, the BIPC problem is defined as follows:

Block isomorphism of polynomials with circulant matrices (BIPC) [16]
   Let k be a positive integer. Given two k-tuples of quadratic polynomial maps $\mathbf{f}, \mathbf{g} \in \mathcal{MQ}(n, m)^k$, find two k-tuples of circulant matrices $\mathcal{A} \in C_n(\mathbb{F})^k$ and $\mathcal{B} \in C_m(\mathbb{F})^k$ such that

$$\mathbf{g} = (\mathcal{A}, \mathcal{B}) * \mathbf{f}. \tag{2}$$

We can consider that the BIPC problem is obtained by linearizing the IP2S problem and restricting secret linear maps to linear maps represented by circulant matrices.

To construct an ElGamal-like encryption scheme based on BIPC, we need to see that the operation $*$ is commutative:

Lemma 1 *[16, Lemma1]. For any* $\mathbf{f} \in \mathcal{MQ}(n,m)^k$ *and* $\mathcal{A}, \mathcal{A}' \in C_n(\mathbb{F})^k$ *and* $\mathcal{B}, \mathcal{B}' \in C_m(\mathbb{F})^k$, *we have*

$$(\mathcal{A}, \mathcal{B}) * ((\mathcal{A}', \mathcal{B}') * \mathbf{f}) = (\mathcal{A}', \mathcal{B}') * ((\mathcal{A}, \mathcal{B}) * \mathbf{f}).$$

This lemma follows from the definition of $*$ and the commutativity of products of circulant matrices.

Before we recall the construction of the ElGamal-like encryption scheme, we define a subset of $\mathcal{MQ}(n,m)$, which is useful to reduce the key size of the encryption scheme. Let ℓ be a divisor of k. We define the set

$$\mathcal{MQ}(n,m)_\ell^k := \left\{ (\mathbf{f}_{[1]}, \dots, \mathbf{f}_{[k]}) \in \mathcal{MQ}(n,m)^k \,\middle|\, \begin{array}{l} \mathbf{f}_{[i]} = \mathbf{f}_{[i \bmod \ell]} \\ \forall i = 1, \dots, k \end{array} \right\}.$$

In particular, if $\ell = 1$, then we have $\mathbf{f}_{[1]} = \mathbf{f}_{[2]} = \cdots = \mathbf{f}_{[k]}$. It is clear that the size of an element of $\mathcal{MQ}(n,m)_\ell^k$ is $1/\ell$ of that of an element of $\mathcal{MQ}(n,m)^k$. Moreover, we have

$$\mathbf{f} \in \mathcal{MQ}(n,m)_\ell^k \implies (\mathcal{A}, \mathcal{B}) * \mathbf{f} \in \mathcal{MQ}(n,m)_\ell^k$$

for $\mathcal{A} \in C_n(\mathbb{F})^k$ and $\mathcal{B} \in C_m(\mathbb{F})^k$. Thus, we can define the variant of the BIPC problem by replacing $\mathcal{MQ}(n,m)^k$ with $\mathcal{MQ}(n,m)_\ell^k$, which reduces the size of the instance $(\mathbf{f}, \mathbf{g})$ to $1/\ell$.

In the following, we describe the construction of the ElGamal-like BIPC encryption scheme [16] based on the hardness of the BIPC computational problem.

ElGamal-like BIPC encryption scheme [16]

- Public parameters : $n, m, k, \ell \in \mathbb{N}$.
- Secret Key: $(\mathcal{A}, \mathcal{B}) \in C_n(\mathbb{F})^k \times C_m(\mathbb{F})^k$.
- Public Key: $\mathbf{f}, \mathbf{g} \in \mathcal{MQ}(n,m)_\ell^k$ such that $\mathbf{g} = (\mathcal{A}, \mathcal{B}) * \mathbf{f}$.
- Encryption: to encrypt a plaintext $\mathbf{h} \in \mathcal{MQ}(n,m)_\ell^k$, one chooses a random $(\mathcal{A}', \mathcal{B}') \in C_n(\mathbb{F})^k \times C_m(\mathbb{F})^k$ and computes:

$$\mathbf{c}_0 \leftarrow (\mathcal{A}', \mathcal{B}') * \mathbf{f}, \qquad \mathbf{c}_1 \leftarrow \mathbf{h} + (\mathcal{A}', \mathcal{B}') * \mathbf{g}.$$

The ciphertext is given by $\mathbf{c} = (\mathbf{c}_0, \mathbf{c}_1)$.
- Decryption: to decrypt a ciphertext $\mathbf{c} = (\mathbf{c}_0, \mathbf{c}_1)$, using the secret key $(\mathcal{A}, \mathcal{B}) \in C_n(\mathbb{F})^k \times C_m(\mathbb{F})^k$, one computes:

$$\nu \leftarrow \mathbf{c}_1 - (\mathcal{A}, \mathcal{B}) * \mathbf{c}_0.$$

The decryption result is ν.

It is clear from Lemma 1 that the decryption process produces the correct plaintext, that is, $\nu = \mathbf{h}$.

In [16], it is proven that the ElGamal-like encryption scheme is proven secure against OW-CPA attacks under the assumption that the CDH-BIPC problem is hard.

Computational Diffie-Hellman (CDH) BIPC problem

Let k be a positive integer. Given three k-tuples of quadratic polynomial maps $\mathbf{f}, \mathbf{g}, \mathbf{h} \in \mathcal{MQ}(n, m)_{\ell}^{k}$ such that $\mathbf{g} = (\mathcal{A}, \mathcal{B}) * \mathbf{f}$, $\mathbf{h} = (\mathcal{A}', \mathcal{B}') * \mathbf{f}$, then compute

$$(\mathcal{A}, \mathcal{B}) * ((\mathcal{A}', \mathcal{B}') * \mathbf{f}).$$

One can actually easily see that as similar to the case of ElGamal encryption scheme and the CDH problem, the converse is also true, i.e., if the CDH-BIPC problem is easy then breaking the ElGamal-like BIPC encryption scheme is also easy.

2.3   Previous Analysis

In this subsection, we recall the security analysis against the BIPC problem in the original paper [16]. In [16], two attacks were proposed under the assumption the finite field $\mathbb{F} = \mathbb{F}_2$. The first one (i) is by using the result of Bouillaguet et al. [3], and the second one (ii) is an algebraic attack using a Gröbner basis algorithm.

(i) **First attack:** The first attack is based on the work by Bouillaguet et al. [3] on breaking a homogeneous IP2S instance, which we summarize as follows. Given a homogeneous IP2S instance $(\mathbf{f}, \mathbf{g})$ described in (1), Bouillaguet et al. [3] attempt to find a pair of vectors α, $\beta \in \mathbb{F}^n$ such that $S^{-1}\alpha = \beta$. Under the assumption $\mathbb{F} = \mathbb{F}_2$, Bouillaguet et al. [3] showed how to obtain such α, β in high probability using a graph theory based algorithm with the complexity $\mathcal{O}(n^5 2^{n/2})$. Once such a pair α, β is discovered, we can define $(\mathbf{f}', \mathbf{g}')$, i.e., $\mathbf{f}'(x) = \mathbf{f}(x + \alpha)$ and $\mathbf{g}'(x) = \mathbf{g}(x + \beta)$, which have the same isomorphism as $(\mathbf{f}, \mathbf{g})$ but are no longer homogeneous. Thus, we can easily find the isomorphism between $\mathbf{f}'$ and $\mathbf{g}'$ using the algorithm of Faugére and Perret [9] on solving inhomogeneous instances of IP2S.

Now, we explain the first attack in [16] against a BIPC instance $(\mathbf{f}, \mathbf{g})$ described in (2). Assume that $\mathbf{g}$ is written as

$$\mathbf{g} = (\mathbf{g}_{[1]}, \ldots, \mathbf{g}_{[k]}) = (\mathcal{A}, \mathcal{B}) * \mathbf{f},$$

$$\mathbf{g}_{[i]} = \sum_{j=1}^{k} B_j \circ \mathbf{f}_{[j+i-1 \bmod k]} \circ A_j,$$

and each A_j is invertible. Then, the first attack finds vectors $\alpha_j, \beta_j \in \mathbb{F}^n$ ($1 \leq j \leq k$) such that $A_j^{-1}\alpha_j = \beta_j$, i.e., $\alpha_j = A_j\beta_j$. In [16], it is estimated that such vectors can be found with the complexity $\mathcal{O}(k^2 n^5 2^{nk/(k+1)})$ combining Bouillaguet et al. [3] and Suzuki et al. [20]. (See [16] for the detail.)

In [16], it is described that the next step is to apply the algorithm of Faugére and Perret [9] on solving inhomogeneous instances of IP2S. However, we point out in this paper that actually such step is not necessary, since A_j is a circulant matrix. Namely, by solving the linear equation $\alpha_j = A_j \beta_j$ with respect to components of A_j, we can easily recover the circulant matrix A_j. Therefore, we conclude that the complexity of the first attack against the BIPC problem is given by

$$\mathcal{O}(k^2 n^5 2^{nk/(k+1)}).$$

(ii) Second attack: Here, we review the algebraic attack using a Gröbner basis algorithm in [16]. In [16], it is assumed that there exist circulant matrices $\widetilde{B}_1, \ldots, \widetilde{B}_k$ such that the BIPC instance $(\mathbf{f}, \mathbf{g})$ satisfies the following:

$$\sum_{j=1}^{k} \widetilde{B}_j \circ \mathbf{g}_{[i]} = \sum_{j=1}^{k} \mathbf{f}_{[j+i-1 \bmod k]} \circ A_j, \quad (i = 1, \ldots, k). \tag{3}$$

Note that $B_1, \ldots, B_k$ can be computed easily once we obtain $A_j, \widetilde{B}_j$ for all $j = 1, \ldots, k$. If we identify each component of $A_j, \widetilde{B}_j$ as variables, then we obtain the system of at most $n(n+1)mk/2$ quadratic equations in $(n+m)k$ variables. In [16], it is estimated based on [1] that the complexity to solve the system with a Gröbner basis algorithm is given by

$$\mathcal{O}(2^{k \log(nm)/(4m)}).$$

However, it should be noted that we do not know exactly whether we can construct the system of quadratic equations shown in (3) since so far there is no proof for the existence of such circulant matrices $\widetilde{B}_1, \ldots, \widetilde{B}_k$.

Remark 2. In the IP2S problem (1), we have

$$\mathbf{g} = (S, T) \cdot \mathbf{f} \implies (1_n, T^{-1}) \cdot \mathbf{g} = (S, 1_m) \cdot \mathbf{f}$$

since the operation $\cdot$ holds the associativity. Similarly, if the operation $*$ satisfies the associativity, then we have

$$\mathbf{g} = (\mathcal{A}, \mathcal{B}) * \mathbf{f} \implies (1_n^k, \mathcal{B}^{-1}) * \mathbf{g} = (\mathcal{A}, 1_m^k) * \mathbf{f},$$

where we have set $\mathcal{B}^{-1} = (B_1^{-1}, \ldots, B_k^{-1})$, $1_n^k = (1_n, \ldots, 1_n)$ and $1_m^k = (1_m, \ldots, 1_m)$. Then (3) holds as $\widetilde{B}_i = B_i^{-1}$. However, as we stated in Remark 1, the operation $*$ does not hold the associativity.

Selected Parameters: Based on two attacks (i) and (ii) against the BIPC problem, the paper [16] sets four types of parameters:

(a) **Conservative Type:** In this type, $\mathbf{f}_{[1]}, \ldots, \mathbf{f}_{[k]}$ are chosen randomly (namely $\ell = k$) and the parameters are set such that the estimated complexity of performing first attack (i) and that of second attack (ii) are both larger than the targeted complexity for security. More precisely, here $n, m, k = \ell$ are set such that the following holds:

$$k^2 n^5 2^{nk/(k+1)} \geqq 2^\lambda, \quad 2^{k \log(nm)/(4m)} \geqq 2^\lambda,$$

where λ is the targeted bit security.

(b) **Alternative Type:** In this type, $\mathbf{f}_{[1]}, \ldots, \mathbf{f}_{[k]}$ are chosen randomly and the parameters are set such that the complexity of performing only second attack (ii) is larger than the targeted complexity for security. More precisely, here $n, m, k = \ell$ are set such that the followings holds:

$$2^{k \log(nm)/(4m)} \geqq 2^\lambda,$$

where λ is the targeted bit security.

(c) **Extremely Aggressive Type:** In this type, the multivariate quadratic polynomials $\mathbf{f}_{[1]}, \ldots, \mathbf{f}_{[k]}$ are set such that $\mathbf{f}_{[1]} = \mathbf{f}_{[2]} = \cdots = \mathbf{f}_{[k]}$, i.e., $\ell = 1$. The other parameters n, m, k are set based on the conservative type.

(d) **Moderately Aggressive Type:** In this type, we assume that k is an even number and set $\ell = 2$. The multivariate quadratic polynomials $\mathbf{f}_{[1]}, \ldots, \mathbf{f}_{[k]}$ are set such that $\mathbf{f}_{[1]} = \mathbf{f}_{[3]} = \cdots = \mathbf{f}_{[2i-1]}$ and $\mathbf{f}_{[2]} = \mathbf{f}_{[4]} = \cdots = \mathbf{f}_{[2i]}$ hold for $i \in [1, k/2]$. The other parameters are set based on the conservative type.

Below, we summarize the recommended parameters in [16] according to each type mentioned above for 128- and 256-bit security. Here, the finite field $\mathbb{F}$ was taken as $\mathbb{F}_2$.

Table 1. 128-bit security parameters proposed in [16]

Type	n	m	k	ℓ	Public key size (KByte)	Secret key size (KByte)
(a) Conservative	84	2	140	140	241	1.4
(b) Alternative	16	2	205	205	12.8	0.45
(c) Extremely aggressive	84	2	140	1	1.7	1.4
(d) Moderately aggressive	84	2	140	2	3.4	1.4

3   Linear Stack Attack

In this section, we propose a new attack (called linear stack attack) for the ElGamal-like BIPC encryption scheme in Subsect. 2.2. In Subsect. 3.1, we show a key lemma to propose the linear stack attack. In Subsect. 3.2, we describe the algorithm of the linear stack attack based on the key lemma. In Subsect. 3.3, we estimate the complexity of the linear stack attack and show some experimental results.

Table 2. 256-bit security parameters proposed in [16]

Type	n	m	k	ℓ	Public key size (KByte)	Secret key size (KByte)
(a) Conservative	206	2	236	236	2445	5.9
(b) Alternative	16	2	410	410	25.6	0.9
(c) Extremely aggressive	206	2	236	1	10.3	5.9
(d) Moderately aggressive	206	2	236	2	20.7	5.9

3.1   Key Lemma

In this subsection, we give a key lemma to propose the linear stack attack. Let $(\mathbf{f}, \mathbf{g})$ be a public key of the ElGamal-like encryption scheme in Subsect. 2.2. To break the encryption scheme, an attacker only has to compute a pair $(\mathcal{A}', \mathcal{B}') \in C_n(\mathbb{F})^k \times C_m(\mathbb{F})^k$ such that $\mathbf{g} = (\mathcal{A}', \mathcal{B}') * \mathbf{f}$, namely, an equivalent key. However, by the following lemma, we show that there are other kinds of equivalent keys.

Lemma 2. *Let $(\mathbf{f}, \mathbf{g})$ be an public key of the ElGamal-like encryption scheme. If there are an integer $t \in \mathbb{N}$ and a t-tuple $(\mathcal{A}_i, \mathcal{B}_i)_{i=1,\ldots,t} \in \left(C_n(\mathbb{F})^k \times C_m(\mathbb{F})^k \right)^t$ such that*

$$\mathbf{g} = \sum_{i=1}^{t} (\mathcal{A}_i, \mathcal{B}_i) * \mathbf{f},$$

then the t-tuple $(\mathcal{A}_i, \mathcal{B}_i)_{i=1,\ldots,t}$ works as an equivalent key for the public key $(\mathbf{f}, \mathbf{g})$.

Proof. Let $\mathbf{c}_0 = (\mathcal{A}', \mathcal{B}') * \mathbf{f}$ and $\mathbf{c}_1 = \mathbf{h} + (\mathcal{A}', \mathcal{B}') * \mathbf{g}$ be an ciphertext of the ElGamal-like encryption scheme as in Subsect. 2.2. To recover the plaintext $\mathbf{h}$, an attacker computes secret information $(\mathcal{A}', \mathcal{B}') * \mathbf{g}$ from known information $(\mathcal{A}_i, \mathcal{B}_i)_{i=1,\ldots,t}$ and $\mathbf{c}_0$ as follows:

$$\sum_{i=1}^{t} (\mathcal{A}_i, \mathcal{B}_i) * \mathbf{c}_0 = \sum_{i=1}^{t} (\mathcal{A}_i, \mathcal{B}_i) * ((\mathcal{A}', \mathcal{B}') * \mathbf{f})$$

$$= \sum_{i=1}^{t} (\mathcal{A}', \mathcal{B}') * ((\mathcal{A}_i, \mathcal{B}_i) * \mathbf{f})$$

$$= (\mathcal{A}', \mathcal{B}') * \left(\sum_{i=1}^{t} (\mathcal{A}_i, \mathcal{B}_i) * \mathbf{f} \right)$$

$$= (\mathcal{A}', \mathcal{B}') * \mathbf{g}$$

Thus, the attacker can compute the plaintext $\mathbf{h}$ by

$$\mathbf{c}_1 - \sum_{i=1}^{t} (\mathcal{A}_i, \mathcal{B}_i) * \mathbf{c}_0.$$

Therefore, the t-tuple $(\mathcal{A}_i, \mathcal{B}_i)_{i=1,\ldots,t}$ is an equivalent key.   □

In the next subsection, we show a concrete procedure to construct such an equivalent key $(\mathcal{A}_i, \mathcal{B}_i)_{i=1,\ldots,t}$.

3.2 The Algorithm of the Linear Stack Attack

We propose an attack to find an equivalent key, which is called linear stack attack, based on Lemma 2. The attack takes a public key $(\mathbf{f}, \mathbf{g})$ and a positive integer t as input, and a t-tuple $(\mathcal{A}_i, \mathcal{B}_i)_{i=1,\ldots,t} \in \left(C_n(\mathbb{F})^k \times C_m(\mathbb{F})^k \right)^t$ as output. The strategy of the algorithm is the following:

Linear stack attack

Step 1. Randomly choose tk elements $(A_1, B_1), \cdots, (A_{tk}, B_{tk})$ from $C_n(\mathbb{F}) \times C_m(\mathbb{F})$.

Step 2. Let $\alpha_1, \ldots, \alpha_{tk}$ be variables over $\mathbb{F}$. Set t-tuples as follows:

$$
\begin{aligned}
\mathcal{A}_1 &\leftarrow (A_1, \ldots, A_k) & \mathcal{B}_1 &\leftarrow (\alpha_1 B_1, \ldots, \alpha_k B_k) \\
\mathcal{A}_2 &\leftarrow (A_{k+1}, \ldots, A_{2k}) & \mathcal{B}_2 &\leftarrow (\alpha_{k+1} B_{k+1}, \ldots, \alpha_{2k} B_{2k}) \\
&\vdots & &\vdots \\
\mathcal{A}_t &\leftarrow (A_{tk-k+1}, \ldots, A_{tk}) & \mathcal{B}_t &\leftarrow (\alpha_{tk-k+1} B_{tk-k+1}, \ldots, \alpha_{tk} B_{tk})
\end{aligned}
$$

Step 3. Find a solution to the following linear equations in variables $\alpha_1, \ldots, \alpha_{tk}$:

$$
\mathbf{g} = \sum_{i=1}^{t} (\mathcal{A}_i, \mathcal{B}_i) * \mathbf{f} \tag{4}
$$

Step 4. If there is a solution $(\alpha_1, \ldots, \alpha_{tk})$, then output the t-tuple

$$
(\mathcal{A}_i, \mathcal{B}_i)_{i=1,\ldots,t}. \qquad \square
$$

The linear stack attack is able to find an equivalent key by linearly stacking $(\mathcal{A}_i, \mathcal{B}_i) * \mathbf{f}$. In the following theorem, we discuss the probability that one trial of the linear stack attack succeeds for the input number t.

Theorem 1. *Set $t = \lceil \frac{1}{2} n(n + 1) m\ell/k \rceil$ in the linear stack attack. Then one trial of the linear stack attack can find an equivalent key with the probability of at least $1/4$.*

Proof. We prove that when $t = \lceil \frac{1}{2} n(n+1) m\ell/k \rceil$, the linear Eq. (4) has a solution with the probability $\geq 1/4$.

The vector space $\mathcal{MQ}(n, m)$ is of dimension $\frac{1}{2} n(n + 1) m$ over $\mathbb{F}$, and $\mathcal{MQ}(n, m)_\ell^k$ is the vector space with dimension $\frac{1}{2} n(n + 1) m\ell$. Thus, the subspace

$$
V := \mathrm{Span}_{\mathbb{F}} \left\{ (\mathcal{A}, \mathcal{B}) * \mathbf{f} \in \mathcal{MQ}(n, m)_\ell^k \mid \mathcal{A} \in C_n(\mathbb{F})^k, \mathcal{B} \in C_m(\mathbb{F})^k \right\}
$$

in $\mathcal{MQ}(n,m)_\ell^k$ is at most of dimension $\frac{1}{2}n(n+1)m\ell$. The linear Eq. (4)

$$\mathbf{g} = \sum_{i=1}^{t}(\mathcal{A}_i,\mathcal{B}_i) * \mathbf{f}$$

in Step 3 has tk variables and $\dim_k V$ equations. We can consider that the probability that the linear Eq. (4) has a solution is equal to the probability that a uniformly chosen random matrix over $\mathbb{F}$ with size $tk \times \dim_k V$ has rank $\geq \dim_k V$. We conservatively assume that $\dim_k V = \frac{1}{2}n(n+1)m\ell$. Since we have $tk \risingdotseq \frac{1}{2}n(n+1)m\ell$, such a probability is given by the probability that a uniformly chosen random square matrix with size tk is nonsingular, which is $\prod_{i=1}^{tk}(1 - \frac{1}{q^i})$. Here,

$$\prod_{i=1}^{tk}(1 - \tfrac{1}{q^i}) = (1 - \tfrac{1}{q})^2(1 + \tfrac{1}{q})\prod_{i=3}^{tk}(1 - \tfrac{1}{q^i}) \geq (1 - \tfrac{1}{q})^2(1 + \tfrac{1}{q^{tk-2}}).$$

The latter inequality follows from $(1 + \frac{1}{q^j})(1 - \frac{1}{q^i}) \geq (1 + \frac{1}{q^{j+1}})$ for $j < i$. Since $q \geq 2$, we have $\prod_{i=1}^{tk}(1 - \frac{1}{q^i}) \geq (1 - \frac{1}{q})^2 \geq 1/4$. $\qquad\square$

If a trial of the linear stack attack fails for a parameter, then we retry the linear stack attack for the parameter. The above theorem implies that the linear stack attack succeed in around four trials. Note that according to our experiments below, the linear stack attack alway succeeded in one trail as $t = \lceil \frac{1}{2}n(n+1)m\ell/k \rceil$.

Remark 3. If we take $t > \lceil \frac{1}{2}n(n+1)m\ell/k \rceil$, the probability that a uniformly chosen random matrix over $\mathbb{F}$ with size $tk \times \dim_k V$ has rank $\geq \dim_k V$ can be raised. As a result, the success probability of one trial of the linear stack attack can be raised. On the other hand, since $\dim_k V$ is less than $\frac{1}{2}n(n+1)m\ell$ in general, the probability should be larger than $1/4$ even if we set $t = \lceil \frac{1}{2}n(n+1)m\ell/k \rceil$. In fact, according to our experiments below, the linear stack attack *alway* succeeded in one trial as $t = \lceil \frac{1}{2}n(n+1)m\ell/k \rceil$ on each experiment.

Remark 4. It should be noted that the linear stack attack does not break the BIPC problem. However, as we explained in Subsect. 2.2, in order to break the ElGamal-like encryption scheme, it is sufficient for an attacker to break the CDH-BIPC problem, that the linear stack attack actually does efficiently.

3.3   Complexity and Experimental Results

In this subsection, we estimate the complexity of our attack proposed in Subsect. 3.1 and show some experimental results.

Proposition 1. *The complexity of the linear stack attack is given by at most*

$$\mathcal{O}(n^6 m^3 \ell^3).$$

Proof. It is clear that the dominant part is Step 3. In Step 3, we need to compute tk composites $B_i \circ \mathbf{f}_{[j]} \circ A_i$ $(i = 1, \ldots, tk, j = 1, \ldots, \ell)$. The number of multiplications of $\mathbb{F}$ in each composite is at most

$$2n^3 + \tfrac{1}{2}n(n+1)m^2.$$

Since $tk \fallingdotseq \tfrac{1}{2}n(n+1)m\ell$, the complexity is

$$\mathcal{O}\left((2n^3 + \tfrac{1}{2}n(n+1)m^2) \cdot (\tfrac{1}{2}n(n+1)m\ell)\right) \leq \mathcal{O}(n^5 m^3 \ell).$$

In Step 3, we also solve the linear system with size $tk \fallingdotseq \tfrac{1}{2}n(n+1)m\ell$. Then the complexity is

$$\mathcal{O}((\tfrac{1}{2}n(n+1)m\ell)^\omega) \leq \mathcal{O}(n^6 m^3 \ell^3),$$

where $2 < \omega \leq 3$ is a linear algebra constant.

As a result, we conclude that the total complexity of the linear stack attack is at most

$$\mathcal{O}(n^6 m^3 \ell^3). \qquad \square$$

This proposition indicates that our attack is a polynomial-time algorithm. In Tables 3 and 4, we show the complexity of the proposed parameters in Tables 1 and 2 against our linear stack attack. Each complexity is given by the product of $n^6 m^3 \ell^3$ and the inverse of success probability $(1/4)^{-1}$.

Table 3. The complexity of the linear stack attack in Sect. 3 for the 128-bit security parameters proposed in [16]

Type	n	m	k	ℓ	Linear stack attack (bits)
(a) Conservative	84	2	140	140	**64.7**
(b) Alternative	16	2	205	205	**54.0**
(c) Extremely aggressive	84	2	140	1	**43.3**
(d) Moderately aggressive	84	2	140	2	**46.3**

Table 4. The complexity of the linear stack attack in Sect. 3 for the 256-bit security parameters proposed in [16]

Type	n	m	k	ℓ	Linear stack attack (bits)
(a) Conservative	206	2	236	236	**74.7**
(b) Alternative	16	2	410	410	**55.0**
(c) Extremely aggressive	206	2	236	1	**51.1**
(d) Moderately aggressive	206	2	236	2	**54.1**

Experimental Results

We confirm experimentally that our attack is valid and efficient enough to break the ElGamal-like encryption scheme. All experiments were performed on a 3.5 GHz 8 Core Intel Xeon W with Magma V2.25-7. Table 5 is the experimental results. We basically performed our attack on the 128-bit security parameters in Table 1. However, the attack against the conservative type (a) did not finish within a week, since its complexity against the linear stack attack is around 64.7 bits. Instead, we chose the 80-bit security parameter $(q, n, m, k, l) = (2, 42, 2, 102, 102)$ following the security analysis in [16], and confirmed that our attack is valid for such a conservative type (a). We note that the complexity of the linear stack attack against the parameter $(q, n, m, k, l) = (2, 42, 2, 102, 102)$ is 57.4 bits.

Table 5 shows the average time of 5 experiments on the linear stack attack for each type as $t = \lceil \frac{1}{2} n(n+1)m\ell/k \rceil$. According to our experiments, the success probability of one trial of the linear stack attack is 100% for each parameter.

Table 5. The average time (seconds) of 5 experiments on the linear stack attack for the 80-bit security parameter in (a) and the 128-bit security parameters [16] (b),(c),(d) in Table 1.

Type	n	m	k	ℓ	Average time (sec)
(a) Conservative	42	2	102	102	419408.490
(b) Alternative	16	2	205	205	35963.190
(c) Extremely aggressive	84	2	140	1	1732.240
(d) Moderately aggressive	84	2	140	2	6801.210

4   Conclusion

At PQC 2020, Santoso proposed an ElGamal-like public key encryption scheme based on the BIPC problem, which is a problem originated from the IP2S problem. The BIPC problem is obtained by linearizing IP2S and restricting secret linear maps to linear maps represented by circulant matrices. Moreover, the ElGamal-like encryption scheme was constructed by utilizing the commutativity of products of circulant matrices. Santoso gave four types of practical parameters which are called (a) conservative, (b) alternative, (c) extremely aggressive, and (d) moderately aggressive. In this paper, we proposed a new attack against the ElGamal-like encryption scheme, which is called linear stack attack. The linear stack attack finds equivalent keys of the ElGamal-like encryption scheme by using the linearity of the BIPC problem. We showed that the linear stack attack is polynomial time and confirmed that the attack is valid and efficient for the proposed parameters (a),(b),(c) and (d). Our experimental results showed that the 128-bit security parameter in (b),(c) and (d) were broken within 10 h. While the 128-bit security parameter in (a) did not finish within a week, instead, the 80-bit security parameter in (a) was broken within 5 days.

We stress that our attack algorithm consists of only basic simple linear algebraic techniques. Therefore, there is a possibility that we can further generalize our algorithm to solve more general computational problems beyond BIPC related ones. As future work, we aim to extend our attack algorithm to solve more general computational problems such as the general IP2S problem which is the foundation of many multivariate cryptographic schemes.

Acknowledgements. This work was supported by JST CREST Grant Number JPMJ CR14D6, JSPS KAKENHI Grant Number JP19K20266, JP20K19802, JP20K03741, JP18H01438, and JP18K11292

References

1. Bardet, M., Faugére, J.C., Salvy, B.: Complexity of gröbner basis computation for semi-regular overdetermined sequences over $\mathbb{F}_2$ with solutions in $\mathbb{F}_2$. techreport 5049. Institut National de Recherche en Informatique et en Automatique (INRIA) (2003)
2. Fauzi, P., Hovd, M.N., Raddum, H.: A practical adaptive key recovery attack on the LGM (GSW-like) cryptosystem. In: Cheon, J.H., Tillich, J.-P. (eds.) PQCrypto 2021 2021. LNCS, vol. 12841, pp. 483–498. Springer, Cham (2021). https://doi.org/10.1007/978-3-030-81293-5_25
3. Bouillaguet, C., Faugère, J.C., Fouque, P.A., Perret, L.: Isomorphism of polynomials: New results (2011)
4. Casanova, A., Faugere, J.-C., Macario-Rat, G., Patarin, J., Perret, L., Ryckeghem, J.: Gemss, technical report, national institute of standards and technology (2019). https://csrc.nist.gov/projects/post-quantum-cryptography/round-2-submissions
5. Chen, J., Tan, C.H., Li, X.: Practical cryptanalysis of a public key cryptosystem based on the morphism of polynomials problem. Tsinghua Sci. Technol **23**(6), 671–679 (2018)
6. Ding, J., Chen, M.S., Petzoldt, A., Schmidt, D., Yang, B.Y.: Rainbow, technical report, national institute of standards and technology (2020). https://csrc.nist.gov/projects/post-quantum-cryptography/round-3-submissions
7. Ding, J., Petzoldt, A., Schmidt, D.S.: Multivariate Public Key Cryptosystems. AIS, vol. 80. Springer, New York (2020). https://doi.org/10.1007/978-1-0716-0987-3
8. Ding, J., Chen, M.S., Petzoldt, A., Schmidt, D., Yang, B.Y.: Rainbow, technical report, national institute of standards and technology (2019). https://csrc.nist.gov/projects/post-quantum-cryptography/round-2-submissions
9. Faugère, J.-C., Perret, L.: Polynomial equivalence problems: algorithmic and theoretical aspects. In: Vaudenay, S. (ed.) EUROCRYPT 2006. LNCS, vol. 4004, pp. 30–47. Springer, Heidelberg (2006). https://doi.org/10.1007/11761679_3
10. Hashimoto, Y.: Solving the problem of blockwise isomorphism of polynomials with circulant matrices. IACR Cryptol. ePrint Arch. **2021**, 385 (2021)
11. Ikematsu, Y., Nakamura, S., Santoso, B., Yasuda, T.: Security analysis on an elgamal-like multivariate encryption scheme based on isomorphism of polynomials. IACR Cryptol. ePrint Arch. **2021**, 169 (2021)
12. National Institute of Standards and Technology. Report on post quantum cryptography. nistir draft 8105 (2019). https://csrc.nist.gov/csrc/media/publications/nistir/8105/final/documents/nistir_8105_draft.pdf

13. Patarin, J.: Hidden fields equations (HFE) and isomorphisms of polynomials (IP): two new families of asymmetric algorithms. In: Maurer, U. (ed.) EUROCRYPT 1996. LNCS, vol. 1070, pp. 33–48. Springer, Heidelberg (1996). https://doi.org/10.1007/3-540-68339-9_4

14. Patarin, J., Goubin, L., Courtois, N.: Improved algorithms for isomorphisms of polynomials. In: Nyberg, K. (ed.) EUROCRYPT 1998. LNCS, vol. 1403, pp. 184–200. Springer, Heidelberg (1998). https://doi.org/10.1007/BFb0054126

15. Santoso, B.: Reviving identification scheme based on isomorphism of polynomials with two secrets: a refined theoretical and practical analysis. IEICE Trans. **101**–**A**(5), 787–798 (2018)

16. Santoso, B.: Generalization of isomorphism of polynomials with two secrets and its application to public key encryption. In: Ding, J., Tillich, J.-P. (eds.) PQCrypto 2020. LNCS, vol. 12100, pp. 340–359. Springer, Cham (2020). https://doi.org/10.1007/978-3-030-44223-1_19

17. Santoso, B., Su, C.: Provable secure post-quantum signature scheme based on isomorphism of polynomials in quantum random oracle model. In: Okamoto, T., Yu, Y., Au, M.H., Li, Y. (eds.) ProvSec 2017. LNCS, vol. 10592, pp. 271–284. Springer, Cham (2017). https://doi.org/10.1007/978-3-319-68637-0_17

18. Samardjiska, S., Chen, M.S., Hulsing, A., Rijneveld, J., Schwabe, P.: Mqdss, technical report, national institute of standards and technology (2019). https://csrc.nist.gov/projects/post-quantum-cryptography/round-2-submissions

19. Shor, P.W.: Polynomial-time algorithms for prime factorization and discrete logarithms on a quantum computer. SIAM J. Comput. **26**(5), 1484–1509 (1997)

20. Suzuki, K., Tonien, D., Kurosawa, K., Toyota, K.: Birthday paradox for multi-collisions. In: Rhee, M.S., Lee, B. (eds.) ICISC 2006. LNCS, vol. 4296, pp. 29–40. Springer, Heidelberg (2006). https://doi.org/10.1007/11927587_5

21. Wang, H., Zhang, H., Mao, S., Wu, W., Zhang, L.: New public-key cryptosystem based on the morphism of polynomials problem. Tsinghua Sci. Technol **21**(3), 302–311 (2016)

Attacking ECDSA Leaking Discrete Bits with a More Efficient Lattice

Shuaigang Li[1,2,3], Shuqin Fan[2(✉)], and Xianhui Lu[1,2,3]

[1] SKLOIS, Institute of Information Engineering, CAS, Beijing, China
lishuaigang@iie.ac.cn
[2] State Key Laboratory of Cryptology, P.O. Box 5159, Beijing 100878, China
fansq@sklc.org
[3] School of Cyber Security, University of Chinese Academy of Sciences,
Beijing, China

Abstract. A lattice attack on the Elliptic Curve Digital Signature Algorithm (ECDSA) implementation constructs a lattice related to the secret key by utilizing the information leaked and then recovers the secret key by finding a certain short lattice vector. When the information leaked is discrete bits, Fan et al. (CCS 2016) constructed an efficient lattice by translating the problem of recovering the secret key to the Extended Hidden Number Problem (EHNP). Following their works, we propose two new techniques to construct a more efficient lattice which has a lower dimension and a shorter target vector. Moreover, we further improve the success probability of the secret key recovery by adjusting the lattice. Therefore, it is much easier to recover the secret key. Specifically, injecting our techniques into the existing lattice attacks, we recover the secret key with fewer signatures or a higher success probability.

Keywords: ECDSA · Discrete leaked bits · Lattice attack · EHNP · Efficient lattice

1 Introduction

Elliptic Curve Digital Signature Algorithm (ECDSA) [11] is an elliptic curve variant of Digital Signature Algorithm [18]. Due to the high security and small key size, it is implemented in many applications, such as TLS, smart card, OpenSSL, TPM 2.0, etc.

The computational intractability of the elliptic curve discrete logarithm problem (ECDLP) is the mathematical foundation for the security of ECDSA. However, in actual implementations, information in the ephemeral key can be leaked due to the secret-dependent physical behaviors of certain computing devices. These information can be extracted by side-channel attacks, for example, cache attacks [7,17,20] and time attacks [5,12,15].

In most situations, side-channel attacks can only obtain partial information of the ephemeral key, which implies partial information of the secret key is

© Springer Nature Switzerland AG 2021
Y. Yu and M. Yung (Eds.): Inscrypt 2021, LNCS 13007, pp. 251–266, 2021.
https://doi.org/10.1007/978-3-030-88323-2_13

also known. Therefore, with sufficiently many signatures under the same secret key, knowing a few bits of each ephemeral key allows an attacker to recover the full secret key. To recover the full secret key, a lattice attack on ECDSA implementation constructs a lattice related to the secret key and then recovers the secret key by lattice reduction algorithms [1,6,13].

According to the types of the information leaked, the lattice attack recovering the ECDSA secret key can be divided into two categories. One [9,10,15,16, 19] translates the problem of recovering the secret key to the Hidden Number Problem (HNP) proposed by Boneh and Venkatesan [4]. This attack is efficient when the leaked bits are consecutive, for example, several least significant bits are leaked. However, it can't make full use of the discrete leaked bits, e.g., the positions of the digits in a representation of the ephemeral key. To efficiently deal with the discrete leaked bits, the other attack, using signatures to construct an instance of the Extended Hidden Number Problem (EHNP) [8], was proposed by Fan et al. [7]. Then the HNP/EHNP is used to construct a lattice, where the information of the ephemeral keys and the secret key is embedded into a short lattice vector, i.e., the target vector. Once the target vector is found by lattice reduction algorithms (e.g., BKZ), the secret key can be recovered.

For the second lattice attack, efficient methods, including elimination, merging, most significant digit (MSD) recovering and enumeration, were proposed to decrease the dimension of the lattice in [7]. Furthermore, Micheli et al. [14] selected signatures with a certain feature to improve the success probability of the secret key recovery. In addition, they experimentally demonstrated that the secret key can be recovered even though a small number of errors exist in the information leaked. Therefore, we only consider the situation that the side-channel attacks extract the information without any error in this paper.

Attackers hope to recover the secret key with fewer signatures, a higher success probability and less time. These depend on the following two aspects:

1. The amount of the information leaked;
2. The structure of the lattice related to the secret key.

In this paper, we focus on the second aspect. In the lattice constructed to attack ECDSA, finding the target vector $\mathbf{w}$ can be considered as the approximate Shortest Vector Problem (SVP). According to the works in [2,3], to construct a more efficient n-dimensional lattice Λ, the following skills can be used:

1. Reducing the dimension of the lattice;
2. Reducing the value of the root-Hermit factor $\delta_0 = (\frac{\|\mathbf{w}\|}{\det^{\frac{1}{n}}(\Lambda)})^{\frac{1}{n}}$;
3. Reducing the number of lattice vectors shorter than the target vector.

According to the skills above, the efficiency of the lattices constructed in [7,14] is limited because of the following problems:

1. The dimension of the lattice is not small enough. The reason is that the target vector contains zero elements which can't be used to recover the secret key;

2. The target vector is not short enough. The reason is that the information leaked is not fully utilized, for example, as [7] claimed, "In fact, there are h bits among the $(h + 1)w + h$ unknown bits being known, but we just do not know how to utilize it".

To efficiently recover the ECDSA secret key, it is an interesting direction to solve the above problems and construct a more efficient lattice.

1.1   Contributions

In this paper, we solve the above problems by proposing two new techniques used to construct a more efficient lattice. Moreover, we provide another new technique to improve the success probability of the secret key recovery. Based on these new techniques, it is much easier to recover the ECDSA secret key.

We solve the above problems by the following two skills:

1. Eliminate the zero elements in the target vector by rewriting the signature equations, solving the first problem. Therefore, the dimension of the lattice is reduced;
2. Reconstruct the target vector by making full use of the information leaked, solving the second problem. Consequently, the target vector is shorter.

In the new lattice with a lower dimension and a shorter target vector, it's much easier to recover the secret key by finding the target vector related to the secret key. Moreover, we improve the success probability of the secret key recovery by adjusting the lattice.

To demonstrate the efficiency of our techniques, we consider the same information leaked as the lattice attacks in [7] and [14]. Injecting our techniques into these two attacks, we recover the secret key with fewer signatures or a higher success probability (see Table 1). Compared with the lattice attack in [7], we

Table 1. The efficiency of the new techniques. In this table, "N" represents the number of signatures, "Technique-1" represents the techniques (MSD recovering and enumeration) introduced in [7] and "Technique-2" represents the technique of selecting the signatures with a certain feature introduced in [14]. In addition, for a fixed lattice, "block", a parameter of BKZ, determines the time complexity of BKZ.

Attack	N	Technique-1	Technique-2	block	probability
[7]	4	Yes	No	25	8%
[7] + our techniques	3	Yes	No	35	0.2%
[14]	4	No	No	35	4%
[14] + our techniques	4	No	No	35	14.6%
[14]	3	No	Yes	35	0.2%
[14] + our techniques	3	No	Yes	35	4.1%

recover the secret key with only 3 signatures which reaches the theoretical optimal bound. Compared with the lattice attack in [14], we significantly improve the success probability of the secret key recovery. Specifically, we increase the success probability by at least 20 (resp., 3) times when the number of signatures is 3 (resp., 4).

1.2 Roadmap

In Sect. 2, we introduce some background knowledge of recovering the ECDSA secret key. Then we show how a lattice attack translates the problem of recovering the secret key to the approximate SVP in Sect. 3. In Sect. 4, we provide some new techniques to construct a more efficient lattice and then improve the success probability of the secret key recovery. To demonstrate the efficiency of our techniques, we compare the experimental results obtained by our lattice attack with that obtained by other lattice attacks in Sect. 5.

2   Preliminaries

In this section, we briefly introduce the lattice attack of recovering the ECDSA secret key and provide some corresponding background knowledge.

2.1   The Lattice Attack of Recovering the ECDSA Secret Key

According to the types of the information obtained by side-channel attacks, the lattice attack of recovering the secret key can be divided into two categories (see Fig. 1). The first (resp., second) attack utilizing the signatures to construct an instance of the HNP (resp., EHNP) is effective when the leaked bits are consecutive (resp., discrete). Then the HNP or EHNP is reduced to approximate SVP by constructing a corresponding lattice, where the target vector related to the secret key is a short lattice vector. Once the target vector is found by lattice reduction algorithms (e.g., BKZ), the secret key can be recovered. In this paper, our works focus on the structure of the lattice in the second attack.

Fig. 1. The lattice attack of recovering the ECDSA secret key.

2.2 Elliptic Curve Digital Signature Algorithm (ECDSA)

ECDSA is an elliptic curve variant of Digital Signature Algorithm (DSA) [18] by replacing the prime subgroup in DSA with a group of points on an elliptic curve. ECDSA first chooses an elliptic curve E and a fixed point $G \in E$ of a big prime order q. Based on the public parameters G and q, the secret key α is randomly selected from $\mathbb{Z}_q^*$ and the public key is the elliptic curve point $Q = \alpha G$. To sign a message m, the signature pair (r, s) can be obtained by the following steps:

1. Randomly choose an ephemeral key $k \in (0, q)$ and compute kG;
2. Define r as the x-coordinate of kG. If $r = 0$, then go back to the first step;
3. Compute $s = k^{-1}(H(m) + \alpha r) \mod q$, where H is a given hash function. If $s = 0$, then go back to the first step.

To verify the signature, one needs to compute

$$(x, y) = kG = H(m)s^{-1}G + rs^{-1}Q.$$

The signature is valid if $r = x \mod q$. For attackers, the signature pair (s, r) and the message m are known, if attackers can get the ephemeral key k, the secret key α can be obtained by computing

$$\alpha = (sk - H(m))r^{-1} \mod q. \tag{1}$$

2.3 The Information Leaked

Since the scalar multiplication kG is often the most time-consuming in ECDSA implementation, the windowed non-adjacent form (wNAF) representation is proposed to speed up the operation. Given a scalar k, the wNAF algorithm (see Algorithm 1) chooses a window size w and then obtains the wNAF representation of k: $e_1, e_2, \cdots, e_l$, where $e_i \in \{0, \pm 1, \pm 3, \cdots, \pm(2^w - 1)\}$ and $k = \sum_{i=1}^{l} e_i \cdot 2^i$. In the wNAF representation, any two non-zero digits e_i and e_j satisfy $i - j \geq w + 1$. For example, the wNAF presentation of $k = 59$ with a window size 3 is

$$(-5, 0, 0, 0, 0, 0, 1) \text{ because } 59 = (-5) \cdot 2^0 + 2^6.$$

According to [7], attackers can judge whether e_i is zero with a high success probability. In this paper, we assume that the information can be obtained without any error.

2.4 The Extended Hidden Number Problem (EHNP)

According to Sect. 2.1, given the information leaked, the problem of recovering the ECDSA secret key can be translated to the EHNP.

Algorithm 1. The wNAF Algorithm

Input: Scalar k and widow size w
Output: wNAF representation of k: $e_1, e_2, \cdots, e_l$
1: $i = 1$
2: **while** $k > 0$ **do**
3:　　**if** $k \mod 2 = 1$ **then**
4:　　　$e_i = k \mod 2^{w+1}$
5:　　　**if** $e_i \geq 2^w$ **then**
6:　　　　$e_i = e_i - 2^{w+1}$
7:　　　**end if**
8:　　　$k = k - e_i$
9:　　**else**
10:　　　$e_i = 0$
11:　　**end if**
12:　　$k = k/2$
13:　　$i = i + 1$
14: **end while**

The EHNP introduced in [8] was originally used to recover the DSA secret key and then was used to recover the ECDSA secret key [7]. Let q be a prime number, given u congruences

$$\alpha r_i - \sum_{j=1}^{l_i} a_{i,j} k_{i,j} \equiv_q c_i, 1 \leq i \leq u,$$

where $\alpha \in \mathbb{Z}_q^*$ and $k_{i,j} \in [0, 2^{\epsilon_{i,j}}]$ are unknown integers, r_i, l_i, $a_{i,j}$, c_i and $\epsilon_{i,j}$ are all known. The EHNP is to find the unknown number α (the hidden number).

2.5　The Approximate Shortest Vector Problem (SVP)

According to Sect. 2.1, attackers need to convert the EHNP to the approximate SVP by constructing a suitable lattice. Once the target vector in the lattice is found by lattice reduction algorithms, the secret key can be recovered.

In a lattice, the SVP is to find the shortest lattice vector (i.e., the target vector). According to [2,3], to find the target vector $\mathbf{w}$ in the n-dimensional lattice Λ, the following skills can be used:

1. Reducing the dimension of the lattice;
2. Reducing the value of the root-Hermite factor $\delta_0 = (\frac{\|\mathbf{w}\|}{\det^{\frac{1}{n}}(\Lambda)})^{\frac{1}{n}}$.

In the lattice constructed to attack ECDSA, the target vector may not be the shortest lattice vector, therefore, finding the target vector is an approximate SVP. In this case, attackers can also consider the third skill, i.e.,

3. Reducing the number of lattice vectors shorter than the target vector.

3 Basis Attack

In this section, assuming that side-channel attacks exactly obtain the positions of all non-zero digits in the wNAF representation with a window size $w = 3$, we show how the lattice attack in [7] utilizes the information leaked to recover the ECDSA secret key.

3.1 Extracting Information

Assuming that the number of the non-zero digits is l and the position of the i-th non-zero digit k_i' is λ_i $(1 \leq i \leq l)$, the ephemeral key k can be written as

$$k = \sum_{i=1}^{l} k_i' \cdot 2^{\lambda_i},$$

where $k_i' \in \{-7, -5, -3, -1, 1, 3, 5, 7\}$, l and λ_i's are known and k_i's are unknown.

Defining $k_i' = 2k_i^* - 7$, where $k_i^* \in \{0, 1, 2, 3, 4, 5, 6, 7\}$, the ephemeral key k can be rewritten as

$$k = \sum_{i=1}^{l} (2k_i^* - 7) \cdot 2^{\lambda_i} = \bar{k} + \sum_{i=1}^{l} k_i^* \cdot 2^{\lambda_i + 1}, \tag{2}$$

where $\bar{k} = -7 \cdot \sum_{i=1}^{l} 2^{\lambda_i}$.

In a wNAF representation with $w = 3$, there are approximately

$$(\lfloor logq \rfloor + 1)/(w + 2) - 1 = 50.4$$

non-zero digits of a 257-bit ephemeral key k. Because each non-zero digit k_i^* has 3 bits unknown, the number of all the unknown bits is $50.4 * 3 = 151.2$, i.e., $257 - 151.2 = 105.8$ bits are known on average. Theoretically, to uniquely determine the secrete key, the number of needed signatures is at least 3, since 3 is the least integer t such that $105.8 \cdot t > 257$.

3.2 Reducing the Problem of Recovering the Secret Key to the EHNP

Given u signature pairs (r_i, s_i)'s of messages m_i's under the same secret key α, how to get an instance of EHNP is shown in this section.

According to Equation (1), the signature equations are

$$\alpha r_i - s_i k_i + H(m_i) = 0 \mod q, \ 1 \leq i \leq u.$$

Combining with Equation (2), the above equations can be written as

$$\alpha r_i - \sum_{j=1}^{l_i^*}(2^{\lambda_{i,j}^*+1}s_ik_{i,j}^*) + (H(m_i) - s_i\bar{k}_i) + h_i^*q = 0, \ 1 \le i \le u, \qquad (3)$$

where $k_{i,j}^*$ is the j-th non-zero element in the wNAF representation of the i-th ephemeral key k_i, the position of $k_{i,j}^*$ is $\lambda_{i,j}^*$ and $\bar{k}_i = -7 \cdot \sum_{j=1}^{l_i^*} 2^{\lambda_{i,j}^*} \mod q$. In the equations, the parameters (α, $k_{i,j}^*$'s and h_i^*'s) are unknown and the others are known. Finding the secret key α in Eqs. (3) is an EHNP. Therefore, the problem of recovering the ECDSA secret key is reduced to the EHNP.

Moreover, to reduce the number of the unknown parameters, Fan et al. [7] proposed the methods: elimination and merging.

Using the method of elimination, the secret key α in Eqs. (3) is eliminated and thus Eqs. (3) are rewritten as

$$\sum_{j=1}^{l_1^*}(\gamma_{i-1,j}^*k_{1,j}^*) + \sum_{m=1}^{l_i^*}(c_{i-1,m}^*k_{i,m}^*) + \beta_{i-1} + h_{i-1}q = 0, \ 2 \le i \le u, \qquad (4)$$

where $\gamma_{i-1,j}^* = 2^{\lambda_{1,j}^*+1}s_1r_i \mod q$, $c_{i-1,m}^* = -2^{\lambda_{i,m}^*+1}s_ir_1 \mod q$ and $\beta_{i-1} = r_1(H(m_i) - s_i\bar{k}_i) - r_i(H(m_1) - s_1\bar{k}_1) \mod q$ are known, and $k_{i,j}^*$'s, h_{i-1}'s are unknown. Compared with Eqs. (3), the number of the unknown parameters is reduced by 1.

Compared with the method of elimination, the method of merging reduces more unknown parameters. Specifically, for any $k_{i,p}^*$ satisfying $\lambda_{i,p}^* - \lambda_{i,p-1} > 4$, the method of merging will merge $h_{i,j} + 1$ consecutive digits $k_{i,p}^*, \cdots, k_{i,p+h_{i,j}}^*$ into a new digit

$$k_{i,j} = k_{i,p}^* + 2^4 \cdot k_{i,p+1}^* + \cdots + 2^{4 \cdot h_{i,j}} \cdot k_{i,p+h_{i,j}}^*,$$

where $h_{i,j}$ is the biggest integer t such that $\lambda_{i,p+t}^* - \lambda_{i,p}^* = 4 \cdot t$. In this case, the new digit $k_{i,j}$ reduces $h_{i,j}$ unknown parameters. Based on the new digit $k_{i,j}$, its position $\lambda_{i,j} = \lambda_{i,p}^*$ and the number l_i of the new digits in the new representation of k_i, Eqs. (4) are rewritten as

$$\sum_{j=1}^{l_1}(\gamma_{i-1,j}k_{1,j}) + \sum_{m=1}^{l_i}(c_{i-1,m}k_{i,m}) + \beta_{i-1} + h_{i-1}q = 0, \ 2 \le i \le u, \qquad (5)$$

where $\gamma_{i-1,j} = 2^{\lambda_{1,j}+1}s_1r_i \mod q$ and $c_{i-1,m} = -2^{\lambda_{i,m}+1}s_ir_1 \mod q$. In the equations, the parameters $k_{i,j}$'s and h_{i-1}'s are unknown, and other parameters are known.

3.3   Reducing the EHNP to the Approximate SVP

Let $d_{i,j} = 2^{4 \cdot h_{i,j}+3}$, $\max_{i,j} d_{i,j} = d$ and $b_{i,j} = d/d_{i,j}$. Based on Eqs. (5), the basis of the lattice constructed in [7] is

$$
\mathbf{B} = \begin{pmatrix}
q \\
& \ddots \\
& & q \\
\gamma_{1,1} & \cdots & \gamma_{u-1,1} & b_{1,1} \\
\vdots & & \vdots & & \ddots \\
\gamma_{1,l_1} & \cdots & \gamma_{u-1,l_1} & & & b_{1,l_1} \\
c_{1,1} & & & & & & b_{2,1} \\
\vdots & & & & & & & \ddots \\
c_{1,l_2} & & & & & & & & b_{2,l_2} \\
& \ddots \\
& & c_{u-1,1} & & & & & & & & b_{u,1} \\
& & \vdots & & & & & & & & & \ddots \\
& & c_{u-1,l_u} & & & & & & & & & & b_{u,l_u} \\
\beta_1 & \cdots & \beta_{u-1} & -\frac{d}{2} & \cdots & -\frac{d}{2} & -\frac{d}{2} & \cdots & -\frac{d}{2} & \cdots & -\frac{d}{2} & \cdots & -\frac{d}{2} & \frac{d}{2}
\end{pmatrix}. \tag{6}
$$

The ephemeral keys are contained in the target vector (a short lattice vector)

$$
\begin{aligned}
\mathbf{w} &= (h_1, \cdots, h_{u-1}, k_{1,1}, \cdots, k_{i,j}, \cdots, k_{u,l_u}, 1)\mathbf{B} \\
&= (0, \cdots, 0, b_{1,1} \cdot k_{1,1} - \tfrac{d}{2}, \cdots, b_{i,j} \cdot k_{i,j} - \tfrac{d}{2}, \cdots, b_{u,l_u} \cdot k_{u,l_u} - \tfrac{d}{2}, \tfrac{d}{2}).
\end{aligned}
$$

Finding the target vector $\mathbf{w}$ is an approximate SVP, thus the EHNP is reduced to the approximate SVP. Once the short target vector $\mathbf{w}$ is found by lattice reduction algorithms, the ephemeral keys k_i's and the secret key α can be recovered, for

$$
k_i = \bar{k} + \sum_{i=1}^{l_i}(k_{i,j} \cdot 2^{\lambda_{i,j}+1}) \text{ and } \alpha = (s_i k_i - H(m_i)) \cdot r_i^{-1} \mod q.
$$

The methods of elimination and merging, reducing the dimension of the lattice by reducing the number of the unknown parameters, are efficient according to the first skill in Sect. 2.5. Moreover, the choices of $b_{i,j}$ and $\frac{d}{2}$, reducing the value of $\delta_0 = (\frac{\|\mathbf{w}\|}{\det^{\frac{1}{n}}(\mathbf{B})})^{\frac{1}{n}}$, are also efficient according to the second skill in Sect. 2.5. Therefore, attackers using the lattice constructed in [7] can recover the ECDSA secret key easier. Moreover, for ephemeral keys with a fixed bit length, Fan et al. [7] proposed the other two methods of MSD recovering and enumeration to reduce the dimension of the lattice.

4   Constructing a More Efficient Lattice

To recover the secret key, attackers need to solve the approximate SVP. According to the skills in Sect. 2.5, we observe that the efficiency of the lattices constructed in [7,14] is limited because of the following problems:

1. The dimension of the lattice is not small enough. The reason is that the target vector contains zero elements which can't be used to recover the secret key;

2. The target vector is not short enough. The reason is that the information leaked is not fully utilized, for example,
   - When $k_{i,j}$ belongs to $\{0, 1, 2, 3, 4, 5, 6, 7\}$, the corresponding element in **w** belonging to $\{-4, -3, -2, -1, 0, 1, 2, 3\}$ is asymmetric;
   - When $h + 1$ digits are merged, as [7] claimed, "In fact, there are h bits among the $(h + 1)w + h$ unknown bits being known, but we just do not know how to utilize it".

We propose two new techniques to solve the problems above and obtain a more efficient lattice. Specifically, we solve the first problem in Sect. 4.1 and the second problem in Sect. 4.2. The new lattice has a lower dimension and a shorter target vector, which makes it much easier to find the target vector. In addition, we propose another new technique to improve the success probability of the secret key recovery in Sect. 4.3.

4.1   Reducing the Dimension of the Lattice

In this section, we solve the first problem by eliminating the zero elements in the target vector, which reduces the dimension of the lattice. According to the first skill in Sect. 2.5, we thus construct a more efficient lattice.

To eliminate the zero elements in the target vector **w**, we rewrite Eq. (5) as

$$k_{i,1} = \sum_{j=1}^{l_1} (\gamma'_{i-1,j} k_{1,j}) + \sum_{m=2}^{l_i} (c'_{i-1,m} k_{i,m}) + \beta'_{i-1} + h'_{i-1} q, \ 2 \leq i \leq u, \quad (7)$$

where $\gamma'_{i-1,j} = -\gamma_{i-1,j} \cdot c^{-1}_{i-1,1}$, $c'_{i-1,m} = -c_{i-1,m} \cdot c^{-1}_{i-1,1}$ and $\beta'_{i-1} = -\beta_{i-1} \cdot c^{-1}_{i-1,1}$. In the equations, the parameters ($k_{i,j}$'s and h'_{i-1}'s) are unknown and the others are known. According to Eq. (7), we obtain the new lattice of which the basis is

$$\mathbf{B}' = \begin{pmatrix} q \cdot b_{2,1} & & & & & & & & & & & & \\ & \ddots & & & & & & & & & & & \\ & & q \cdot b_{u,1} & & & & & & & & & & \\ \gamma'_{1,1} \cdot b_{2,1} & \cdots & \gamma'_{u-1,1} \cdot b_{u,1} & b_{1,1} & & & & & & & & & \\ \vdots & & \vdots & & \ddots & & & & & & & & \\ \gamma'_{1,l_1} \cdot b_{2,1} & \cdots & \gamma'_{u-1,l_1} \cdot b_{u,1} & & & b_{1,l_1} & & & & & & & \\ c'_{1,2} \cdot b_{2,1} & & & & & & b_{2,2} & & & & & \\ \vdots & & & & & & & \ddots & & & & & \\ c'_{1,l_2} \cdot b_{2,1} & & & & & & & & b_{2,l_2} & & & & \\ & \ddots & & & & & & & & \ddots & & & \\ & & c'_{u-1,2} \cdot b_{u,1} & & & & & & & & b_{u,2} & & \\ & & \vdots & & & & & & & & & \ddots & \\ & & c'_{u-1,l_u} \cdot b_{u,1} & & & & & & & & & & b_{u,l_u} \\ \beta'_1 \cdot b_{2,1} - \frac{d}{2} & \cdots & \beta'_{u-1} \cdot b_{u,1} - \frac{d}{2} & -\frac{d}{2} & \cdots & -\frac{d}{2} & -\frac{d}{2} & \cdots & -\frac{d}{2} & \cdots & -\frac{d}{2} & \cdots & -\frac{d}{2} & \frac{d}{2} \end{pmatrix}. \quad (8)$$

The new target vector

$$
\begin{aligned}
\mathbf{w} &= (h_1', \cdots, h_{u-1}', k_{1,1}, \cdots, k_{1,l_1}, k_{2,2}, \cdots, k_{2,l_2}, \cdots, k_{u,2}, \cdots, k_{u,l_u}, 1)\mathbf{B}' \\
&= (b_{2,1} \cdot k_{2,1} - \tfrac{d}{2}, \cdots, b_{u,1} \cdot k_{u,1} - \tfrac{d}{2}, b_{1,1} \cdot k_{1,1} - \tfrac{d}{2}, \cdots, b_{1,l_1} \cdot k_{1,l_1} - \tfrac{d}{2}, \\
&\quad\ b_{2,2} \cdot k_{2,2} - \tfrac{d}{2}, \cdots, b_{2,l_2} \cdot k_{2,l_2} - \tfrac{d}{2}, \cdots, b_{u,2} \cdot k_{u,2} - \tfrac{d}{2}, \cdots, b_{u,l_u} \cdot k_{u,l_u} - \tfrac{d}{2}, \tfrac{d}{2})
\end{aligned}
$$

eliminates the first $u - 1$ zero elements in the old target vector. Compared with the lattice in Eq. (6),

1. The dimension of the new lattice is reduced by $u - 1$;
2. The determinant and the length of the target vector remain unchanged, which means that the new lattice has a smaller value of $\delta_0 = (\frac{\|\mathbf{w}\|}{\det^{\frac{1}{n}}(\mathbf{B}')})^{\frac{1}{n}}$.

According to the first and second skills in Sect. 2.5, we obtain a more efficient lattice by solving the first problem.

4.2   Reducing the Length of the Target Vector

To solve the second problem, we reconstruct the lattice by making full use of the information leaked. In the new lattice, the target vector $\mathbf{w}$ is shorter while the determinant $\det(\mathbf{B}')$ remains unchanged, which reduces the value of $\delta_0 = (\frac{\|\mathbf{w}\|}{\det^{\frac{1}{n}}(\mathbf{B}')})^{\frac{1}{n}}$. According to the second skill in Sect. 2.5, we thus obtain a more efficient lattice.

To reduce the value of δ_0, there are two commonly used methods:

1. Reducing the value of $\|\mathbf{w}\|$ while maintaining the value of $\det(\mathbf{B}')$;
2. Changing the values of $\|\mathbf{w}\|$ and $\det(\mathbf{B}')$ simultaneously.

The square of the length of the target vector is

$$
\|\mathbf{w}\|^2 = \sum_{p=1}^{n} \mathbf{w}_p^2,
$$

where $\mathbf{w}_p = b_{i,j} \cdot k_{i,j} - \tfrac{d}{2}$. The determinant of the lattice is $det(\mathbf{\Lambda}) = q^{u-1} \prod_{i,j} b_{i,j} \cdot d/2$. To change the value of $\|\mathbf{w}\|$, one needs to change the expectation of $\mathbf{w}_p^2$, i.e., $E(\mathbf{w}_p^2)$. To change the determinant of the lattice, one needs to change the values of the diagonal elements in the lattice basis $\mathbf{B}'$. We propose a technique to reduce the value of δ_0 and apply it to the lattice $\mathbf{B}'$.

In the target vector $\mathbf{w}$, the choice of the parameters $b_{i,j}$ and $\tfrac{d}{2}$ in [7] reduces the value of δ_0 by the second method, i.e., increasing the values of $\|\mathbf{w}\|$ and $\det(\mathbf{B}')$. To clearly show how our technique reduces the value of $\|\mathbf{w}\|$, we consider the parameters $b_{i,j}$ and $\tfrac{d}{2}$ after introducing the technique. In this case, assuming that $\mathbf{w}_p$ merges $h_{i,j} + 1$ digits, we have

$$
\mathbf{w}_p = k_{i,j} - 2^{4 \cdot h_{i,j} + 2} = \sum_{m=0}^{h_{i,j}} (2^{4 \cdot m} \cdot \frac{k_{i,m+m_1}' + 7}{2}) - 2^{4 \cdot h_{i,j} + 2}, \tag{9}
$$

where m_1 is a definite integer and $k'_{i,m+m_1} \in \{-7, -5, -3, -1, 1, 3, 5, 7\}$. To decrease $E(\mathbf{w}_p^2)$, we recenter the target vector and obtain the new one $\mathbf{w}$, where

$$\mathbf{w}_p = \sum_{m=0}^{h_{i,j}} (2^{4 \cdot m} \cdot \frac{k'_{i,m+m_1} + 7}{2}) - \frac{7}{2} \cdot \sum_{m=0}^{h_{i,j}} 2^{4 \cdot m} = \sum_{m=0}^{h_{i,j}} (2^{4 \cdot m} \cdot \frac{k'_{i,m+m_1}}{2}). \quad (10)$$

In the process of constructing the new target vector, every bit of the information leaked is used to recenter $\mathbf{w}_p$. Therefore, the new $\mathbf{w}_p$ is more balanced and $E(\mathbf{w}_p^2)$ is smaller.

Based on the works in [7] and the above technique, the process of reducing the value of $E(\mathbf{w}_p^2)$ can be summarized as the following two steps:

1. Rewrite the signature equations by defining a new integer variable $k^*_{i,j} = \frac{k'_{i,j} - a}{b}$, where $k'_{i,j}$ is the original unknown digit (see Sect. 3.1), and a and b are integers because they appear in the signature equations;
2. Obtain the target vector $\mathbf{w}$ of which the element is $\mathbf{w}_p = k^*_{i,j} - c$, where c is a real number.

Based on the above process, we provide a general method to minimize $E(\mathbf{w}_p^2)$ in Theorem 1, where we consider $k'_{i,j}$ as the variable x.

Theorem 1. *Assume that x is a uniformly distributed random variable on the set of integers $\{x_1, x_2, \cdots, x_n\}$ in ascending order. For integers a, b satisfying $\frac{x-a}{b}$ is an integer and a real number c, we can minimize*

$$E((\frac{x-a}{b} - c)^2)$$

when $b = \gcd(x_2 - x_1, \cdots, x_n - x_{n-1})$ and $c = \frac{E(x) - a}{b}$. To guarantee $\frac{x-a}{b}$ is an integer, we can let $a = x_0$.

Proof. Let $b_{max} = \gcd(x_2 - x_1, \cdots, x_n - x_{n-1})$. Because $\frac{x_i - a}{b}$ and $\frac{x_j - a}{b}$ are integers $(i, j \in [1, n])$, we have $\frac{x_i - a}{b} - \frac{x_j - a}{b} = \frac{x_i - x_j}{b}$ is also an integer. Therefore, the integer b must be a factor of b_{max}. Moreover, to minimize

$$E((\frac{x-a}{b} - c)^2) = \frac{D(x)}{b^2} + E^2(\frac{x-a}{b} - c),$$

where $D(x)$ is the variance of the variable x, the optimal b and c are b_{max} and $\frac{E(x) - a}{b}$ respectively. Finally, to guarantee $\frac{x-a}{b}$ is a integer, a can be x_0. □

As shown in Eq. (9), $\mathbf{w}_p = \sum_{m=0}^{h_{i,j}} (2^{4 \cdot m} \cdot \frac{k'_{i,m+m_1} + 7}{2}) - 2^{4 \cdot h_{i,j} + 2}$, where $k'_{i,m+m_1} \in \{-7, -5, -3, -1, 1, 3, 5, 7\}$. According to the Theorem 1, the new $\mathbf{w}_p$ in Eq. (10) is the optimal. Based on the optimal $\mathbf{w}_p$, we obtain a new lattice, whose lattice basis is

$$
\begin{pmatrix}
q \cdot b_{2,1} & & & & & & & & & & & \\
& \ddots & & & & & & & & & & \\
& & q \cdot b_{u,1} & & & & & & & & & \\
\gamma'_{1,1} \cdot b_{2,1} & \cdots & \gamma'_{u-1,1} \cdot b_{u,1} & b_{1,1} & & & & & & & & \\
\vdots & & \vdots & & \ddots & & & & & & & \\
\gamma'_{1,l_1} \cdot b_{2,1} & \cdots & \gamma'_{u-1,l_1} \cdot b_{u,1} & & & b_{1,l_1} & & & & & & \\
c'_{1,2} \cdot b_{2,1} & & & & & & b_{2,2} & & & & & \\
\vdots & & & & & & & \ddots & & & & \\
c'_{1,l_2} \cdot b_{2,1} & & & & & & & & b_{2,l_2} & & & \\
& \ddots & & & & & & & & \ddots & & \\
& & c_{u-1,2} \cdot b_{u,1} & & & & & & & & b_{u,2} & \\
& & \vdots & & & & & & & & & \ddots \\
& & c'_{u-1,l_u} \cdot b_{u,1} & & & & & & & & & b_{u,l_u} \\
\beta'_1 \cdot b_{1,1} + e_{2,1} & \cdots & \beta'_{u-1} \cdot b_{u,1} + e_{u,1} & e_{1,1} & \cdots & e_{1,l_1} & e_{2,2} & \cdots & e_{2,l_2} & \cdots & e_{u,2} & \cdots & e_{u,l_u} & \frac{d}{2}
\end{pmatrix}, \quad (11)
$$

where $e_{i,j} = -b_{i,j} \cdot E(k_{i,j}) = -\frac{7}{2} \cdot b_{i,j} \cdot \sum_{m=0}^{h_{i,j}} 2^{4 \cdot m}$. Compared with the lattice in Equation (8), the new lattice contains a shorter target vector by making full use of the information leaked. Therefore, we solve the second problem and obtain a more efficient lattice.

4.3 Improving the Success Probability

The method of merging in [7] merges $h_{i,j} + 1$ consecutive digits $k^*_{i,p}, \cdots, k^*_{i,p+h_{i,j}}$ into a new digit $k_{i,j}$, where $k^*_{i,p}$ satisfies $\lambda^*_{i,p} - \lambda^*_{i,p-1} > 4$ and $h_{i,j}$ is the biggest integer t such that $\lambda^*_{i,p+t} - \lambda^*_{i,p} = 4 \cdot t$.

To obtain a new method of merging, we modify the method in [7] when $h_{i,j} > m_u$, where m_u is an adjustable integer. In this case, we decompose the digit

$$
k_{i,j} = k^*_{i,p} + 2^4 \cdot k^*_{i,p+1} + \cdots + 2^{4 \cdot h_{i,j}} k_{i,p+h_{i,j}}
$$

into $n = \lceil \frac{h_{i,j}+1}{m_u+1} \rceil$ new digits

$$
k^*_{i,p} + \cdots + 2^{4 \cdot m_u} k^*_{i,p+m_u}, \cdots, k^*_{i,n_1-m_u} + \cdots + 2^{4 \cdot m_u} k^*_{i,n_1}, k^*_{i,n_1+1} + \cdots + 2^{4 \cdot (h_{i,j}-n_1-1)} k^*_{i,h_{i,j}},
$$

where $n_1 = p + (n-1) \cdot (m_u + 1) - 1$. The new method of merging increases the dimension of the lattice, however, it reduces the length of the target vector. Therefore, the lattice constructed based on the new method of merging may also be effective.

We observe that the lattices with different m_u's are probable to recover different secret keys, which can be used to improve the success probability of the ECDSA secret key recovery.

5   Experiments

We take 4 signatures as an example to demonstrate the efficiency of each new technique (see Table 2). In this table, the signatures are chosen based on the technique in [14], satisfying that, for any i and j, $\lambda_{i,j+4} - \lambda_{i,j} > 16$. The experimental results show that each new technique improves the success probability, which demonstrates the effectiveness of each new technique. Combining with all new techniques, we increase the success probability in [14] by 12 times.

Table 2. The efficiency of our techniques. In this table, "A", "B" and "C" represent the technique in Sect. 4.1, the technique in Sect. 4.2 and the technique in Sect. 4.3, respectively. "N" represents the number of signatures, "m_u" represents the maximum number of digits merged (see Sect. 4.3). In addition, for a fixed lattice, "block", a parameter of BKZ, determines the time complexity of BKZ. The results are from 1000 experiments with 1000 random secret keys.

Attack	N	block	m_u	probability
[14]	4	25	3	0.5%
[14] + A	4	25	3	2.3%
[14] + A + B	4	25	3	3.5%
[14] + A + B + C	4	25	0,1,2,3	6%

Moreover, we compare our results with the best results in the lattice attacks [7,14] (see Table 1). The difference between the two attacks is whether to use the methods (MSD recovering and enumeration) introduced in [7] and the method of selecting the signatures with a certain feature introduced in [14]. By injecting all the new techniques into the lattice attack in [7], we recover the secret key with fewer signatures. By injecting all the new techniques into the lattice attack in [14], we significantly improve the success probability. Specifically, we increase the success probability by at least 20 (resp., 3) times when the number of signatures are 3 (resp., 4).

6   Conclusion

In this paper, to recover the secret key of ECDSA leaking discrete bits, we construct a more efficient lattice which has a lower dimension and a shorter target vector by proposing two new techniques. Moreover, we improve the success probability by using the lattices merging different numbers of digits. Therefore, our attack is much easier to recover the secret key. Compared with the existing lattice attacks, we recover the secret key with fewer signatures or a higher success probability.

Acknowledgements. We thank the anonymous reviewers for their helpful comments and suggestions. Xianhui Lu and Shuaigang Li are supported by the National Natural Science Foundation of China (Grant No. 61972391).

References

1. Albrecht, M.R., Ducas, L., Herold, G., Kirshanova, E., Postlethwaite, E.W., Stevens, M.: The general sieve kernel and new records in lattice reduction. In: Ishai, Y., Rijmen, V. (eds.) EUROCRYPT 2019. LNCS, vol. 11477, pp. 717–746. Springer, Cham (2019). https://doi.org/10.1007/978-3-030-17656-3_25
2. Albrecht, M.R., Göpfert, F., Virdia, F., Wunderer, T.: Revisiting the expected cost of solving uSVP and applications to LWE. In: Takagi, T., Peyrin, T. (eds.) ASIACRYPT 2017. LNCS, vol. 10624, pp. 297–322. Springer, Cham (2017). https://doi.org/10.1007/978-3-319-70694-8_11
3. Alkim, E., Ducas, L., Pöppelmann, T., Schwabe, P.: Post-quantum key exchange - a new hope. In: USENIX Security Symposium, pp. 327–343. USENIX Association (2016)
4. Boneh, D., Venkatesan, R.: Hardness of computing the most significant bits of secret keys in Diffie-Hellman and related schemes. In: Koblitz, N. (ed.) CRYPTO 1996. LNCS, vol. 1109, pp. 129–142. Springer, Heidelberg (1996). https://doi.org/10.1007/3-540-68697-5_11
5. Brumley, B.B., Tuveri, N.: Remote timing attacks are still practical. In: Atluri, V., Diaz, C. (eds.) ESORICS 2011. LNCS, vol. 6879, pp. 355–371. Springer, Heidelberg (2011). https://doi.org/10.1007/978-3-642-23822-2_20
6. Chen, Y., Nguyen, P.Q.: BKZ 2.0: better lattice security estimates. In: Lee, D.H., Wang, X. (eds.) ASIACRYPT 2011. LNCS, vol. 7073, pp. 1–20. Springer, Heidelberg (2011). https://doi.org/10.1007/978-3-642-25385-0_1
7. Fan, S., Wang, W., Cheng, Q.: Attacking openssl implementation of ECDSA with a few signatures. In: CCS, pp. 1505–1515. ACM (2016)
8. Hlaváč, M., Rosa, T.: Extended hidden number problem and its cryptanalytic applications. In: Biham, E., Youssef, A.M. (eds.) SAC 2006. LNCS, vol. 4356, pp. 114–133. Springer, Heidelberg (2007). https://doi.org/10.1007/978-3-540-74462-7_9
9. Howgrave-Graham, N., Smart, N.P.: Lattice attacks on digital signature schemes. Des. Codes Cryptogr. **23**(3), 283–290 (2001)
10. Jancar, J., Sedlacek, V., Svenda, P., Sýs, M.: Minerva: The curse of ECDSA nonces systematic analysis of lattice attacks on noisy leakage of bit-length of ECDSA nonces. IACR Trans. Cryptogr. Hardw. Embed. Syst. **2020**(4), 281–308 (2020)
11. Johnson, D., Menezes, A., Vanstone, S.A.: The elliptic curve digital signature algorithm (ECDSA). Int. J. Inf. Sec. **1**(1), 36–63 (2001)
12. Kocher, P.C.: Timing attacks on implementations of Diffie-Hellman, RSA, DSS, and Other Systems. In: Koblitz, N. (ed.) CRYPTO 1996. LNCS, vol. 1109, pp. 104–113. Springer, Heidelberg (1996). https://doi.org/10.1007/3-540-68697-5_9
13. Lenstra, A.K., Lenstra, H.W., Lovász, L.: Factoring polynomials with rational coefficients. Mathematische Annalen 261(4) (1982)
14. De Micheli, G., Piau, R., Pierrot, C.: A tale of three signatures: practical attack of ECDSA with wNAF. In: Nitaj, A., Youssef, A. (eds.) AFRICACRYPT 2020. LNCS, vol. 12174, pp. 361–381. Springer, Cham (2020). https://doi.org/10.1007/978-3-030-51938-4_18
15. Moghimi, D., Sunar, B., Eisenbarth, T., Heninger, N.: TPM-FAIL: TPM meets timing and lattice attacks. In: USENIX Security Symposium, pp. 2057–2073. USENIX Association (2020)
16. Nguyen, P.Q., Shparlinski, I.E.: The insecurity of the digital signature algorithm with partially known nonces. J. Cryptol. **15**(3), 151–176 (2002)

17. Page, D.: Theoretical use of cache memory as a cryptanalytic side-channel. IACR Cryptol. ePrint Arch. **2002**, 169 (2002)
18. Schnorr, C., Euchner, M.: Digital signature standard (dss) FIPS, 186–3 (2013)
19. Wang, W., Fan, S.: Attacking openssl ECDSA with a small amount of side-channel information. Sci. China Inf. Sci. **61**(3), 032105:1–032105:14 (2018)
20. Weiser, S., Schrammel, D., Bodner, L., Spreitzer, R.: Big numbers - big troubles: systematically analyzing nonce leakage in (EC)DSA implementations. In: USENIX Security Symposium, pp. 1767–1784. USENIX Association (2020)

Cryptographic Protocols

A Simple Post-Quantum Non-interactive Zero-Knowledge Proof from Garbled Circuits

Hongrui Cui and Kaiyi Zhang[(⊠)]

Department of Computer Science, Shanghai Jiao Tong University,
Shanghai 200240, China
{rickfreeman,kzoacn}@sjtu.edu.cn

Abstract. We construct a simple public-coin zero-knowledge proof system solely based on symmetric primitives, from which we can apply the Fiat-Shamir heuristic to make it non-interactive. Our construction can be regarded as a simplified cut-and-choose-based malicious secure two-party computation for the zero-knowledge functionality. Our protocol is suitable for pedagogical purpose for its simplicity (code is only 728 lines).

Keywords: Zero-knowledge · Garbled circuit · Post-quantum

1 Introduction

Zero-knowledge proof (ZK) is a fundamental cryptographic primitive which allows a prover to convince a verifier of the membership of an instance x in any $\mathcal{NP}$ language without revealing any information about its witness w [14]. Due to its theoretical significance and practical applications (e.g., the use of ZK in nuclear disarmament [13]), ZK is also a central topic in cryptographic research. In particular, a rich body of research [7,11,15,16,21,25,27,30] (and many others) has successfully constructed *succinct* argument systems with proof size and verification complexity sub-linear in the size of the statement.

Despite the achievements, many current efficient ZK protocols have high prover complexity in order to facilitate the succinct property. While this captures the performance requirement in most cases, we argue that a lightweight prover is crucial for some applications as well. Imagine the following scenario: An computationally weak IoT device captures possibly sensitive data (e.g., biometric) from its sensors and need to prove some properties on the captured data to a powerful server. Due to the privacy requirement, it cannot simply send the data to the server. In this case, a zero-knowledge protocol that has low prover's complexity would be ideal.

1.1 Our Construction

Here we briefly introduce the intuitions of our construction in Fig. 1. We consider ZK as a special case of malicious secure two-party computation. Therefore we

© Springer Nature Switzerland AG 2021
Y. Yu and M. Yung (Eds.): Inscrypt 2021, LNCS 13007, pp. 269–280, 2021.
https://doi.org/10.1007/978-3-030-88323-2_14

Prove$(1^\kappa, C_x, w)$	**Verify**$(1^\kappa, C_x, \pi)$
for $i := 1$ **to** 2κ **do**	$b := H(\{GC_i, d_i\})$
$\quad (GC_i, e_i, d_i) \leftarrow \mathsf{Gb}(1^\kappa, C_x)$	**for** $i := 1$ **to** 2κ **do**
endfor	$\quad$ **if** $b_i = 0$ **then**
$b := H(\{GC_i, d_i\})$	$\quad\quad$ **if** $\mathsf{Ve}(GC_i, e_i, d_i, C_x) = 0$ **then**
$z := \{\}$	$\quad\quad\quad$ **return false**
for $i := 1$ **to** 2κ **do**	$\quad\quad$ **fi**
$\quad$ **if** $b_i = 0$ **then**	$\quad$ **fi**
$\quad\quad z \leftarrow z \cup e_i$	$\quad$ **if** $b_i = 1$ **then**
$\quad$ **elseif** $b_i = 1$ **then**	$\quad\quad$ **if** $\mathsf{De}(d_i, \mathsf{Ev}(GC_i, W_i)) = 0$ **then**
$\quad\quad W_i := \mathsf{En}(e_i, w)$	$\quad\quad\quad$ **return false**
$\quad\quad z \leftarrow z \cup W_i$	$\quad\quad$ **fi**
$\quad$ **fi**	$\quad$ **fi**
endfor	**endfor**
return $\pi = (\{GC_i, d_i\}, z)$	**return true**

Fig. 1. Our post quantum NIZK in a nutshell, where H is a random oracle, $\mathcal{G} = (\mathsf{Gb}, \mathsf{En}, \mathsf{De}, \mathsf{Ev}, \mathsf{ev}, \mathsf{Ve})$ is a garbling scheme. κ is the security parameter.

try to optimize cut-and-choose-based 2PC by utilizing features specific to the zero-knowledge setting.

Informally, a cut-and-choose-based 2PC consists of those steps: Firstly, the garbler generates garbled circuits and sends them to the evaluator. The evaluator randomly chooses a subset of garbled circuits and asks the garbler to open them. On receiving the seeds, the evaluator checks those garbled circuits are generated correctly. Then the two parties execute some oblivious transfers (OT) in order to let the evaluator obtain the garbled label corresponding to his private input. The evaluator also needs additional operations to make sure the garbler's inputs are consistent. Finally, the evaluator accepts the majority outcome of garbled circuits.

Let us try to apply this protocol to zero-knowledge proof directly. Unlike previous constructions [20], we let the prover and verifier be the garbler and evaluator respectively. This change gives rise to several advantages:

1. We no longer need OT because the verifier has no private input. This eliminates public key encryption and leaves only symmetric primitives. We can also get rid of the selective failure attack.
2. We do not have to check the input consistency since the ZK property does not require multiple witnesses to be the same as long as they are valid.
3. We can accept if and only if all outputs are the same instead of accepting the majority. In a 2PC setting, choosing the majority is to avoid one-bit leakage

from abortion, however, the verifier is not required to prevent this attack because he has no private inputs.
4. Finally we can see that the protocol is public-coin, i.e., the verifier has no private randomness in this protocol. Therefore we can apply Fiat-Shamir heuristic to this ZK protocol to make it non-interactive.

1.2 Related Works

Here we only briefly review those works related to universal post-quantum non-interactive zero-knowledge proof systems.

zk-STARK. This protocol was proposed and first realized by Ben-Sasson et al. in [5]. zk-STARK offers universal, transparent, scalable and post-quantum secure zero-knowledge proof system in the interactive oracle proofs (IOP) model.

MPC-in-the-Head. Ishai et al. [19] first introduce the "MPC-in-the-head" paradigm from which one can construct a ZK from the black-box use of a secure multiparty computation protocol. Later, this approach was first implemented by ZKBoo [12]. Some subsequent works [1,9] also follow this paradigm.

Garbled Circuit. Garbled Circuit (GC) is a cryptographic tool which is widely used in secure multiparty computation. It was invented by Yao [28] in 1986. Recent years, garbled circuits are improved quickly, like point-and-permute [3], row-reduction [24], free-XOR [22], half gate [29] and stacked garbling [18].

ZK from GC. Jawurek et al. proposed the first ZK protocol based on garbled circuits [20]. Their construction focuses on the advantage of garbled circuits, namely its efficiency at evaluating non-algebraic functions (e.g., a circuit for block cipher), and thus achieves good performance. Nevertheless, their protocol is not public-coin and cannot be made non-interactive using the standard Fiat-Shamir transformation.

2 Preliminaries

A negligible function, denoted by $\mathsf{negl}(n)$, represents a function $f : \mathbb{N} \to \mathbb{R}$ that for any constant c, there exists an integer N such that for all $n > N$, $f(n) \leq n^{-c}$. We also use $\mathsf{poly}(n)$ to denote *some* polynomial. For integer $n \in \mathbb{N}$ let $[n]$ to denote the set $\{1, 2, ..., n\}$. We use the common definitions of computational and statistical indistinguishable distribution ensembles. Throughout this work, we use κ to denote security parameters. We use PPT to indicate probabilistic polynomial-time and sometimes use the term "efficient" and PPT interchangeably.

An $\mathcal{NP}$ relation $\mathcal{R}$ is defined by a circuit family $\{C_i\}_{i \in \mathbb{N}}$ whose size is bounded by some polynomial. An instance-witness pair (x, w) is included in the relation iff. $C_{|x|}(x, w) = 1$. We use $L(\mathcal{R})$ to denote the language induced by the relation, i.e., $L(\mathcal{R}) = \{x | \exists w, (x, w) \in \mathcal{R}\}$.

2.1   Zero Knowledge Proof

We follow the standard definition of zero knowledge [17], which we recall as follows.

Definition 1. *A protocol π is a sigma protocol for relation R if it's a three-round public-coin protocol satisfying the following three properties:*

Completeness. *If P and V follow the protocol on public input x and private input w where $(x, w) \in R$ then V always accepts.*

Special soundness. *There exists an efficient PPT algorithm A such that given any x and any pair of accepting transcript (a, e, z) and (a, e', z') for x where $e \neq e'$ extracts w such that $(x, w) \in R$.*

Honest-verifier zero-knowledge. *There exists a PPT simulator S which on input x, e generates a transcript (a, e, z) such that for any $(x, w) \in R$ the transcript is identically distributed as in the real execution.*

2.2   Garbled Circuit

We follow the definition of garbled circuit in [20], which is derived from the standard definitions [4]. We first explain the syntax of a garbling scheme and then list the properties of a garbling scheme that is required in this paper.

Definition 2. *A garbling scheme is defined by a tuple $\mathcal{G} = (Gb, En, De, Ev, ev, Ve)$:*

- *The garbled circuit generation function Gb is a randomized algorithm that on input a security parameter 1^{κ} and the description of a Boolean function $C : \{0,1\}^n \to \{0,1\}$, outputs a triple of strings (GC, e, d).*
- *The plaintext evaluation algorithm ev evaluates the function described by C i.e., $ev(C, w) = C(w)$.*
- *The encoding function En is a deterministic function that uses e to map an input w to a garbled input W.*
- *The garbled evaluation function Ev is a deterministic function that evaluates a garbled circuit GC on an encoded input W to get an encoded output Z.*
- *The decoding function De, using the string d, decodes the encoded output Z into a plaintext output z.*
- *In addition to the standard algorithms, a verifiable garbled scheme has an extra procedure Ve that, on input garbled circuit GC, a description of a Boolean function C, and the encoding information e, outputs 1 (accept) or 0 (reject).*

We require the following standard properties of a garbling scheme.

Definition 3 (Correctness). *Let $\mathcal{G}$ be a garbling scheme described as above. We say that $\mathcal{G}$ enjoys correctness if for all $C : \{0,1\}^n \to \{0,1\}, w \in \{0,1\}^n$ such that $C(w) = 1$, the following probablity is negligible in paramter κ:*

$$\Pr[(GC, e, d) \leftarrow Gb(1^{\kappa}, C), W \leftarrow En(e, w) : De(d, Ev(GC, W)) \neq 1] \qquad (1)$$

Definition 4 (Privacy). *Let $\mathcal{G}$ be a garbling scheme described as above. We say that $\mathcal{G}$ enjoys privacy if for all $C : \{0,1\}^n \to \{0,1\}$ there exists a PPT algorithm Gb.Sim such that given plaintext output y, generates the garbled circuit, decoding information, and garbled input that is indistinguishable from a real execution. In particular, the following two distributions are computationally indistinguishable for any input w.*

- $\{(GC, e, d) \leftarrow \mathsf{Gb}(1^\kappa, C), W \leftarrow \mathsf{En}(e, w) : (GC, d, W)\}$
- $\{y \leftarrow \mathsf{ev}(C, w), (GC, d, W) \leftarrow \mathsf{Gb.Sim}(C, y) : (GC, d, W)\}$

Remark 1. In order to facilitate the security proof of our construction, we require the following two additional requirements on the encoding function $\mathsf{En}(e, w)$.

Projective. Fixing s, suppose the function En maps an n-bit string to an $n\ell$-bit one, then the map $f : w \mapsto \mathsf{En}(e, w)$ can be "decomposed" into n functions $f_1, ..., f_n$ such that $f(x) = f_1(w_1), ..., f_n(w_n)$ where w_i is the ith bit of w.
Injective. Let e be generated from $(GC, e, d) \leftarrow \mathsf{Gb}(C)$, the map $f : w \mapsto \mathsf{En}(e, w)$ is injective with high probability over the randomness of Gb.

The first property is standard [4] and is closely related to the application of garbled circuits in secure two-party computation. The second one is naturally satisfied by some natural constructions. For example, let $W = \mathsf{PRF}(s, w)$ where PRF is a pseudorandom function with a large enough range, then the probability of a collision is negligible.

The two properties listed above facilitates an efficient extraction procedure $\mathsf{Gb.Ext}$ that outputs w given e and encoded input W—the projective property allows us to extract bit-by-bit while the injective property guarantees the uniqueness of the extraction. In particular, for every input position i, the extractor test whether the output block corresponds to 0 or 1 and sets the results accordingly, as shown in Fig. 2.

Finally, we require the following verifiability property of a garbling scheme, which ensures the correctness of the garbling process by the verification algorithm. Jumping ahead, this guarantees the effectiveness of witness extraction given two accepting transcripts.

Definition 5 (Verifiability). *Let $\mathcal{G}$ be a garbling scheme described as above. We say that $\mathcal{G}$ enjoys verifiability if for all $C : \{0,1\}^n \to \{0,1\}$, for all PPT $\mathcal{A}$, the following probability is negligible in parameter κ.*

$$\Pr\left[\begin{matrix} (GC, e, d, W) \leftarrow \mathcal{A}(1^\kappa, C) \\ \mathsf{Ve}(C, GC, e) = 1 \wedge \mathsf{De}(d, \mathsf{Ev}(GC, W)) = 1 \end{matrix} : \mathsf{ev}(C, \mathsf{Gb.Ext}(e, W)) \neq 1\right] \quad (2)$$

We note that the above definition differs from the verifiability definition in [20]. Nevertheless, we show that under the assumption that the encoding function is injective and projective (i.e., efficient extraction is possible), Definition 5 is implied by the original one, which we recall below.

```
Gb.Ext(e, W)
─────────────────────────────
for i := 1 to n do
    if Wᵢ = Enᵢ(e, 0) then
        wᵢ := 0
    elseif Wᵢ = Enᵢ(e, 1) then
        wᵢ := 1
    else
        return ⊥
    endif
endfor
return w₁, ..., wₙ
```

Fig. 2. The input extraction procedure of an injective and projective garbling scheme $\mathcal{G}$. n is the input length and En_i is the ith output block of En.

Definition 6 (Verifiability from [20]). *A garbling scheme $\mathcal{G}$ enjoys verifiability if for all $C : \{0,1\}^n \to \{0,1\}$ and $x, y \in \{0,1\}^n$, for all PPT $\mathcal{A}$, the following probability is negligible in parameter κ.*

$$\Pr\left[\begin{matrix} (GC, e) \leftarrow \mathcal{A}(1^\kappa, C) \\ X = \mathsf{En}(e, x), Y = \mathsf{En}(e, y) \end{matrix} : \begin{matrix} \mathsf{Ve}(C, GC, e) = 1 \;\wedge \\ \mathsf{Ev}(GC, X) \neq \mathsf{Ev}(GC, Y) \end{matrix} \right] \tag{3}$$

Lemma 1. *Let $\mathcal{G}$ be a garbling scheme and the encoding function En is injective and projective, then Definition 6 implies Definition 5.*

Proof. Suppose a garbling scheme $\mathcal{G}$ satisfies Definition 6 but does not satisfy Definition 5. Consider the adversary $\mathcal{A}$ that returns (GC, e, d, W) on input C. The encoded input W satisfies that $\mathsf{De}(d, \mathsf{Ev}(GC, W)) = 1$ while the value returned from the extraction procedure $\mathsf{Gb.Ext}$—denoted as w—evalautes to 0 on C.[1]

Let $W' = \mathsf{En}(e, w)$. From the correctness and the deterministic property of the decoding procedure we conclude that $\mathsf{Ev}(GC, W) \neq \mathsf{Ev}(GC, W')$. Since all other requirements in Definition 6 are met, this forms a contradiction.

3   Construction

In this section, we present our construction of a public-coin zero-knowledge proof system based on garbled circuits.

---

[1] We ignore the case of $\mathsf{Gb.Ext}$ returning "$\bot$" since the *authenticity* property of the garbling scheme (which is standard and not presented in this paper) guarantees that an adversary cannot generate such malformed encoded input that evaluates to well-formed encoded output.

3.1   ZK in the Standard Model

In contrast to the well-known JKO protocol [20], we let the prover perform garbling in order to acquire a public-coin protocol. The protocol, which is shown in Fig. 3, is a cut-and-choose style sigma protocol where the prover first sends two garblings of a circuit C_x using independent random coins. When considering an $\mathcal{NP}$ relation $\mathcal{R}$ such that $(x, w) \in \mathcal{R}$ iff. $C(x, w) = 1$, we let the circuit C_x "hard-wire" the public information x, i.e., $C_x(w) = C(x, w)$.

Then the verifier samples a challenge $b \leftarrow \{0, 1\}$ and sends it to the prover. The prover reveals the coins specified by this index and sends input encodings W corresponding to the unopened circuit. Finally, the verifier accepts the proof if the random coin r_b successfully generates GC_b and the outputs induced by GC_{1-b} and X is 1.

Prover	Verifier
$(GC_0, e_0, d_0) \leftarrow \mathsf{Gb}(1^\kappa, C_x)$	
$(GC_1, e_1, d_1) \leftarrow \mathsf{Gb}(1^\kappa, C_x)$	
$\xrightarrow{\quad GC_0, d_0, GC_1, d_1 \quad}$	
	$b \leftarrow \{0, 1\}$
$\xleftarrow{\qquad b \qquad}$	
$W \leftarrow \mathsf{En}(e_{1-b}, w)$	
$\xrightarrow{\quad e_b, W \quad}$	
	The verifier accepts if
	$\mathsf{Ve}(GC_b, e_b, C_x) = 1 \wedge$
	$\mathsf{De}(d_{1-b}, \mathsf{Ev}(GC_{1-b}, W)) = 1$

Fig. 3. A public coin zero-knowledge in the standard model.

We prove the special soundness and honest-verifier zero-knowledge properties of this scheme in the following theorem.

Theorem 1. *Let $\mathcal{R}$ be a NP relation defined by circuit family $\{C'\}$ s.t. for every instance $(a, b) \in \mathcal{R}, C'(a, b) = 1$. For any instance $a \in L(\mathcal{R})$, define circuit family $C(w) = C'(a, w)$. Let $\mathcal{G} = (\mathsf{Gb}, \mathsf{En}, \mathsf{De}, \mathsf{Ev}, \mathsf{ev}, \mathsf{Ve})$ be a garbling scheme. The sigma protocol in Fig. 3 is a computational honest-verifier zero-knowledge protocol with special soundness for the relation $\mathcal{R}$.*

Proof. The completeness of the protocol follows from the correctness of the garbling scheme. We then prove the honest-verifier zero-knowledge property by explaining the procedure for generating an accepting verifier's transcript.

The procedure for generating an accepting transcript from input (x, b) is as follows:

- First generate $(GC_b, e_b, d_b) \leftarrow \mathsf{Gb}(1^\kappa, C_x)$ as an honest prover.
- Then generate the other garbled circuit and input by invoking the simulation algorithm for the garbling scheme: $(GC_{1-b}, W, d_{1-b}) \leftarrow \mathsf{Gb.Sim}(C_x, 1)$.
- Outputs the transcript $(GC_0, d_0, GC_1, d_1, b, e_b, W)$.

The effectiveness of the simulator $\mathsf{Gb.Sim}$ for the garbling scheme, which is implied by the privacy of the garbling scheme (Definition 4), guarantees the computational indistinguishability between a real accepting transcript and one generated from the above procedure (without the knowledge of input w), which implies computational zero-knowledge.

Next we argue the special soundness of the above scheme. Recall that this property requires that a valid input can be extracted from two transcripts (a, e, z) and (a, e', z') such that $e \neq e'$. Consider the two transcripts

- $(GC_0, d_0, GC_1, d_1, b, e_b, W)$
- $(GC_0, d_0, GC_1, d_1, b', e_{b'}, W')$

where without loss of generality we many assume $b = 0$ and $b' = 1$. Notice that for both indices, the condition $\mathsf{Ve}(GC, e, d, C_x) = 1 \wedge \mathsf{De}(d, \mathsf{Ev}(GC, W))$ holds. From the verifiability property (Definition 5) of the garbling scheme, we conclude that with non-negligible probability we can extract input w such that $\mathsf{ev}(C_x, w) = 1$ for either transcript.

We note that the above proof does not require rewinding and thus in the quantum random oracle model (QROM) the security properties hold against quantum adversaries [10, 23]. □

Next, we apply the standard techniques, namely parallel repetition and Fiat-Shamir transform, to the basic sigma protocol in Fig. 3, in order to acquire a non-interactive zero-knowledge proof with negligible soundness error in the random oracle model.

Corollary 1. *Let H be a random oracle and $\lambda \in \mathbb{N}$ be an integer. Then by running the protocol in Fig. 3 for λ times in parallel and generating each challenge by hashing all κ first messages using the random oracle H, one can acquire a non-interactive zero-knowledge proof with honest-verifier zero-knowledge and soundness error $2^{-\lambda}$ against PPT adversary.*

Optimizations. Notice that in our protocol a large overhead originates from the application of the cut-and-choose technique. Indeed, to achieve soundness error $2^{-\kappa}$, the prover needs to send 2κ garbled circuits where only one is actually evaluated. And therefore it is natural to apply the optimizations targeted at the cut-and-choose technique, commonly found in the malicious two-party computation setting.

- Instead of sending the garbled circuit, the prover can only send *commitments* in the first round. Then in the third round, the prover sends the coins for garbling and commitment for the selected index and decommitment information for the other index. This can reduce the communication complexity roughly by half.

Recall that a large overhead of the protocol in this subsection is caused by the need to verify that the prover faithfully garbles the correct circuit. Notwithstanding, a trusted party (e.g., a judiciary department) may exist in some scenarios, and can distribute some input-independent "raw-material" to both parties before the actual proof process begins. This is captured by the "Common Reference String" model in the next subsection.

3.2 ZK in the CRS Model

In this setting, a third party garbles the verification circuit and distributes the input encoding information to the prover and garbled circuit to the verifier faithfully. Notice that since the garbled circuit is guaranteed to be correct by the model, we can remove the expensive cut-and-choose step, and the proof message consists of only the garbled input (which is trivially non-interactive). This is captured in the algorithms in Fig. 4.

$\mathsf{CRS.Gen}(1^n)$	$\mathsf{Prove}(e, x)$	$\mathsf{Verify}(GC, d, X)$
$(GC, e, d) \leftarrow \mathsf{Gb}(C, 1^n)$	$X \leftarrow \mathsf{En}(e, x)$	$y \leftarrow \mathsf{De}(d, \mathsf{En}(GC, X))$
return $((GC, d), e)$	**return** X	**return** y

Fig. 4. Zero-knowledge protocol in the common reference string model.

3.3 Discussion

Recall that in the construction we proposed, the prover's computation is essentially garbling and encoding. From a theoretical perspective, this paradigm can be viewed as an application of the randomized encoding technique [2], where the prover essentially performs the encoder's job. When instantiated with the garbled circuit, the prover's computation is in $\mathcal{NC}1$—the class of functions that can be completed by a $O(\log n)$-depth circuit family. This characterization could inspire further applications, such as utilizing parallelism or delegation of computation.

4 Implementation and Experiments

We implement the protocol in Sect. 3 for the SHA256 relation defined as follows:

$$\mathcal{R}^{\mathrm{hash}}(y; x) : y = \mathtt{SHA256}(x), \text{ where } x \in \{0,1\}^{512}, \text{ and } y \in \{0,1\}^{256}.$$

Throughout the experiment, we use the specific SHA256 circuit in the works of Campanelli et al. [8] which has optimized the AND gate count. The total number of gates is 117,016 and the number of AND gates is 22,272.

To counter the Grover quantum attack, we extend the size of a garbled label to 256 bit. To achieve 2^{-128} soundness error, the repetition count is 128.

The proving time is 3.0 s. The verification time is 2.2 s. The proof is 379 MB.

We run the experiments on a Ubuntu 20.04 LTS machine with AMD Ryzen 5 3600 CPU and 16 GB of RAM. Our implementation is only 728 lines in C++ with dependency on OpenSSL.

5 Conclusion

We admit the proof size of our construction is large. However, in comparison with other post-quantum NIZK, our construction requires minimum knowledge. This scheme can be taught to undergraduate students right after they understand garbled circuits. Unlike zk-STARK, which requires plenty of efforts on complexity theory, or MPC-in-the-head paradigm, which requires secure multiparty computation in advance. Our implementation is only 728 lines, which is suitable as a course work for beginners.

Second, our construction is highly parallel. Not only cut-and-choose can be parallel, but also garbling itself. That means the execution time can be reduced by multiprocessor significantly.

On the other hand, our construction benefits from the improvements on garbled circuits. For example, Heath et al. recently purpose stacked garbling [18], indicating that our approach works potentially better than others on some specific tasks like evaluating a decision tree.

References

1. Ames, S., Hazay, C., Ishai, Y., Venkitasubramaniam, M.: Ligero: lightweight sublinear arguments without a trusted setup. In: Thuraisingham et al. [26], pp. 2087–2104. https://doi.org/10.1145/3133956.3134104
2. Applebaum, B.: Garbled circuits as randomized encodings of functions: a primer. Cryptology ePrint Archive, Report 2017/385 (2017). http://eprint.iacr.org/2017/385
3. Beaver, D., Micali, S., Rogaway, P.: The round complexity of secure protocols. In: Proceedings of the Twenty-Second Annual ACM Symposium on Theory of Computing, pp. 503–513 (1990)
4. Bellare, M., Hoang, V.T., Rogaway, P.: Foundations of garbled circuits. In: Yu, T., Danezis, G., Gligor, V.D. (eds.) ACM CCS 2012, pp. 784–796. ACM Press (Oct 2012). https://doi.org/10.1145/2382196.2382279

5. Ben-Sasson, E., Bentov, I., Horesh, Y., Riabzev, M.: Scalable, transparent, and post-quantum secure computational integrity. Cryptology ePrint Archive, Report 2018/046 (2018). https://eprint.iacr.org/2018/046
6. Boldyreva, A., Micciancio, D. (eds.): CRYPTO 2019, Part II, LNCS, vol. 11693. Springer, Heidelberg (2019)
7. Bootle, J., Cerulli, A., Chaidos, P., Groth, J., Petit, C.: Efficient zero-knowledge arguments for arithmetic circuits in the discrete log setting. In: Fischlin, M., Coron, J.S. (eds.) EUROCRYPT 2016, Part II. LNCS, vol. 9666, pp. 327–357. Springer, Heidelberg (May 2016). https://doi.org/10.1007/978-3-662-49896-5_12
8. Campanelli, M., Gennaro, R., Goldfeder, S., Nizzardo, L.: Zero-knowledge contingent payments revisited: Attacks and payments for services. In: Thuraisingham et al. [26], pp. 229–243. https://doi.org/10.1145/3133956.3134060
9. Chase, M., et al.: Post-quantum zero-knowledge and signatures from symmetric-key primitives. In: Thuraisingham et al. [26], pp. 1825–1842. https://doi.org/10.1145/3133956.3133997
10. Don, J., Fehr, S., Majenz, C., Schaffner, C.: Security of the Fiat-Shamir transformation in the quantum random-oracle model. In: Boldyreva and Micciancio [6], pp. 356–383. https://doi.org/10.1007/978-3-030-26951-7_13
11. Gennaro, R., Gentry, C., Parno, B., Raykova, M.: Quadratic span programs and succinct NIZKs without PCPs. In: Johansson, T., Nguyen, P.Q. (eds.) EUROCRYPT 2013. LNCS, vol. 7881, pp. 626–645. Springer, Heidelberg (2013). https://doi.org/10.1007/978-3-642-38348-9_37
12. Giacomelli, I., Madsen, J., Orlandi, C.: ZKBoo: faster zero-knowledge for Boolean circuits. In: Holz, T., Savage, S. (eds.) USENIX Security 2016, pp. 1069–1083. USENIX Association, August 2016
13. Glaser, A., Barak, B., Goldston, R.J.: A zero-knowledge protocol for nuclear warhead verification. Nature **510**(7506), 497–502 (2014)
14. Goldreich, O.: Foundations of Cryptography: Basic Applications, vol. 2. Cambridge University Press, Cambridge (2004)
15. Goldwasser, S., Kalai, Y.T., Rothblum, G.N.: Delegating computation: interactive proofs for muggles. In: Ladner, R.E., Dwork, C. (eds.) 40th ACM STOC, pp. 113–122. ACM Press, May 2008. https://doi.org/10.1145/1374376.1374396
16. Groth, J.: Short pairing-based non-interactive zero-knowledge arguments. In: Abe, M. (ed.) ASIACRYPT 2010. LNCS, vol. 6477, pp. 321–340. Springer, Heidelberg (Dec 2010). https://doi.org/10.1007/978-3-642-17373-8_19
17. Hazay, C., Lindell, Y.: Efficient Secure Two-Party Protocols - Techniques and Constructions. ISC, Springer, Heidelberg (2010). https://doi.org/10.1007/978-3-642-14303-8
18. Heath, D., Kolesnikov, V.: Stacked garbling - garbled circuit proportional to longest execution path. In: Micciancio, D., Ristenpart, T. (eds.) CRYPTO 2020, Part II. LNCS, vol. 12171, pp. 763–792. Springer, Heidelberg (Aug 2020). https://doi.org/10.1007/978-3-030-56880-1_27
19. Ishai, Y., Kushilevitz, E., Ostrovsky, R., Sahai, A.: Zero-knowledge from secure multiparty computation. In: Johnson, D.S., Feige, U. (eds.) 39th ACM STOC. pp. 21–30. ACM Press (Jun 2007). https://doi.org/10.1145/1250790.1250794
20. Jawurek, M., Kerschbaum, F., Orlandi, C.: Zero-knowledge using garbled circuits: how to prove non-algebraic statements efficiently. In: Sadeghi, A.R., Gligor, V.D., Yung, M. (eds.) ACM CCS 2013. pp. 955–966. ACM Press (Nov 2013). https://doi.org/10.1145/2508859.2516662

21. Kilian, J.: A note on efficient zero-knowledge proofs and arguments (extended abstract). In: 24th ACM STOC. pp. 723–732. ACM Press (May 1992). https://doi.org/10.1145/129712.129782

22. Kolesnikov, V., Schneider, T.: Improved garbled circuit: Free XOR gates and applications. In: Aceto, L., Damgård, I., Goldberg, L.A., Halldórsson, M.M., Ingólfsdóttir, A., Walukiewicz, I. (eds.) ICALP 2008, Part II. LNCS, vol. 5126, pp. 486–498. Springer, Heidelberg (Jul 2008). https://doi.org/10.1007/978-3-540-70583-3_40

23. Liu, Q., Zhandry, M.: Revisiting post-quantum Fiat-Shamir. In: Boldyreva and Micciancio [6], pp. 326–355. https://doi.org/10.1007/978-3-030-26951-7_12

24. Malkhi, D., Nisan, N., Pinkas, B., Sella, Y.: Fairplay - secure two-party computation system. In: Blaze, M. (ed.) USENIX Security 2004, pp. 287–302. USENIX Association, August 2004

25. Micali, S.: CS proofs (extended abstracts). In: 35th FOCS, pp. 436–453. IEEE Computer Society Press, November 1994. https://doi.org/10.1109/SFCS.1994.365746

26. Thuraisingham, B.M., Evans, D., Malkin, T., Xu, D. (eds.): ACM CCS 2017. ACM Press, October/November 2017

27. Xie, T., Zhang, J., Zhang, Y., Papamanthou, C., Song, D.: Libra: Succinct zero-knowledge proofs with optimal prover computation. In: Boldyreva, A., Micciancio, D. (eds.) CRYPTO 2019, Part III. LNCS, vol. 11694, pp. 733–764. Springer, Heidelberg (2019). https://doi.org/10.1007/978-3-030-26954-8_24

28. Yao, A.C.C.: How to generate and exchange secrets (extended abstract). In: 27th FOCS, pp. 162–167. IEEE Computer Society Press, October 1986. https://doi.org/10.1109/SFCS.1986.25

29. Zahur, S., Rosulek, M., Evans, D.: Two halves make a whole - reducing data transfer in garbled circuits using half gates. In: Oswald, E., Fischlin, M. (eds.) EUROCRYPT 2015, Part II. LNCS, vol. 9057, pp. 220–250. Springer, Heidelberg (2015). https://doi.org/10.1007/978-3-662-46803-6_8

30. Zhang, J., Xie, T., Zhang, Y., Song, D.: Transparent polynomial delegation and its applications to zero knowledge proof. In: 2020 IEEE Symposium on Security and Privacy, pp. 859–876. IEEE Computer Society Press, May 2020. https://doi.org/10.1109/SP40000.2020.00052

Improved Zero-Knowledge Argument of Encrypted Extended Permutation

Yi Liu[1,3]🆔, Qi Wang[1,2(✉)]🆔, and Siu-Ming Yiu[3]

[1] Guangdong Provincial Key Laboratory of Brain-inspired Intelligent Computation,
Department of Computer Science and Engineering, Southern University of Science
and Technology, Shenzhen 518055, China
liuy7@mail.sustech.edu.cn, wangqi@sustech.edu.cn
[2] National Center for Applied Mathematics (Shenzhen),
Southern University of Science and Technology, Shenzhen 518055, China
[3] Department of Computer Science, The University of Hong Kong,
Pokfulam, Hong Kong SAR, China
smyiu@cs.hku.hk

Abstract. Extended permutation (EP) is a generalized notion of the
standard permutation. Unlike the one-to-one correspondence mapping
of the standard permutation, EP allows to replicate or omit elements
as many times as needed during the mapping. EP is useful in the area
of secure multi-party computation (MPC), especially for the problem of
private function evaluation (PFE). As a special class of MPC problems,
PFE focuses on the scenario where a party holds a private circuit C
while all other parties hold their private inputs $x_1, \ldots, x_n$, respectively.
The goal of PFE protocols is to securely compute the evaluation result
$C(x_1, \ldots, x_n)$, while any other information beyond $C(x_1, \ldots, x_n)$ is hidden. EP here is introduced to describe the topological structure of the
circuit C, and it is further used to support the evaluation of C privately.

For an actively secure PFE protocol, it is crucial to guarantee that
the private circuit provider cannot deviate from the protocol to learn
more information. Hence, we need to ensure that the private circuit
provider correctly performs an EP. This seeks the help of the so-called
zero-knowledge argument of encrypted extended permutation protocol. In
this paper, we provide an improvement of this protocol. Our new protocol can be instantiated to be non-interactive while the previous protocol
should be interactive. Meanwhile, compared with the previous protocol,
our protocol is significantly (*e.g.*, more than 3.4×) faster, and the communication cost is only around 24% of that of the previous one.

Keywords: Elgamal encryption · Extended permutation · Private
function evaluation · Zero-knowledge

1 Introduction

The notion of *extended permutation* (EP) is a generalized notion of the standard permutation. Different from the one-to-one correspondence mapping of the

© Springer Nature Switzerland AG 2021
Y. Yu and M. Yung (Eds.): Inscrypt 2021, LNCS 13007, pp. 281–298, 2021.
https://doi.org/10.1007/978-3-030-88323-2_15

standard permutation, EP allows replication and omission of elements during the mapping. An EP π maps elements in a set $\{1, \ldots, M\}$ to a set $\{1, \ldots, N\}$ for positive integers M and N. Here, for every $y \in \{1, \ldots, N\}$, there exists exactly one $x \in \{1, \ldots, M\}$, such that $\pi(x) = y$. We note that π may not be a function, while π^{-1} is indeed a function.

EP is a very useful notion in many areas. In particular, EP is implicitly or explicitly used in the area of secure multi-party computation (MPC) [27]. In the setting of MPC, EP could be introduced to illustrate the topological structure of circuits. More concretely, EP can be used to describe the connections between wires of a circuit, and thus the topology of the circuit. To describe a circuit using EP, we divide the wires of the circuit into two types: *incoming* wires (IW) and *outgoing* wires (OW). All input wires of gates in the circuit are incoming wires, while the input wires of the circuit and the output wires of gates are outgoing wires. An example for a circuit C using such a naming rule is given in Fig. 1. It is easy to see that every incoming wire connects to exactly one outgoing wire. Meanwhile, an outgoing wire may connect to one or multiple incoming wires, or has no connection to any incoming wires. It is clear that for a circuit, its outgoing wires correspond to the domain of an EP, and its incoming wires correspond to the range of an EP. Therefore, after indexing the incoming wires and outgoing wires of a circuit, we can extract an EP that describes the topology of the circuit. In Fig. 2, we provide the corresponding EP for the circuit C in Fig. 1. [1] Moreover, given an EP (together with the numbers of gates, inputs, and outputs), we can easily reconstruct the topological structure of the corresponding circuit.

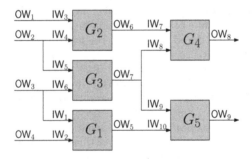

Fig. 1. An illustration of a circuit C, where wires are denoted by incoming wires (IW) and outgoing wires (OW).

EP is especially useful for the problem of (general-purpose) private function evaluation (PFE) [1]. PFE is a special class of MPC problems. It focuses on designing a protocol for the scenario where a party holds a private circuit C, while other parties possess their own private inputs $x_1, \ldots, x_n$. The goal of PFE is to privately evaluate C on $x_1, \ldots, x_n$, *i.e.*, to compute the evaluation result

---

[1] Since OW_8 and OW_9, as output wires of the circuit C, have no connections to other wires, we can simply omit them in the EP.

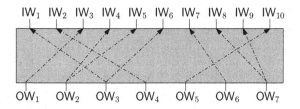

Fig. 2. The extended permutation corresponding to the circuit C in Fig. 1.

$C(x_1, \ldots, x_n)$. After the execution of PFE, parties receive the evaluation result $C(x_1, \ldots, x_n)$ while information beyond $C(x_1, \ldots, x_n)$ is hidden. Note that this is different from traditional secure function evaluation problem, in which the circuit C is publicly known. In fact, PFE problem can be reduced to securely evaluating a universal circuit [2,13,18,19,22,23,26,28], such that the description of the circuit C is used as inputs to the universal circuit. However, using universal circuits leads to a logarithmic blow-up. In other words, the universal circuit for evaluating a circuit C with size n has size at least $\Theta(n \log n)$, where the constant factor (*e.g.*, 12) and the low-order terms are significant. Starting from the original work of Katz and Malka [17], another line of research focuses on designing PFE protocols while avoiding the usage of universal circuits, such as [4,5,15,20,24,25]. This line of work has *linear* complexity in the size of the circuit n. It was shown [15,17] that they outperformed the state-of-the-art PFE protocol based on universal circuits theoretically and experimentally. The basic idea for this line of work is to use EP. More concretely, the party holding the private circuit C derives an EP from C, and *obliviously* performs an EP on a set of outgoing wires to establish the connections between outgoing wires and incoming wires. Then parties are able to follow the results from the EP to evaluate C on private inputs while keeping C hidden.

Although this line of work usually has good performance, only the work in [25] is secure against malicious adversaries, and all other results only work in the semi-honest model. One of the main challenges for designing an actively secure PFE protocol is to guarantee that the private function owner performs a valid EP on elements representing outgoing wires. In the setting of [25], the private circuit owner performs an EP on a set of encrypted elements locally and re-randomizes all encrypted elements in the resulting list. Then the private circuit owner is required to publish the resulting encrypted list and prove that the resulting encrypted list is derived from a valid EP on the encrypted elements in a zero-knowledge manner. The protocol for proving the validity of this result is called *zero-knowledge argument of encrypted extended permutation*, and it is also the efficiency bottleneck of the protocol [25].

1.1 Contribution

In this paper, we provide an improved version of the zero-knowledge argument of encrypted extended permutation protocol. Both our protocol and the original protocol in [25] are designed based on the ElGamal encryption scheme [11]. It is possible to extend our ideas to other encryption schemes. We note that our protocol can be instantiated to be non-interactive while the previous protocol should be interactive. Compared with the original work [25], the communication cost of our protocol is only around 24% of that of [25]. For computation cost, our protocol is significantly (e.g., more than $3.4\times$) faster than the previous protocol. Moreover, protocols based on our protocol, such as the linear actively secure PFE protocol in [25], can also gain better performance.

1.2 Overview of Our Idea

Before the full description of our protocol, we here briefly provide an overview of our idea. We denote the EP π by a mapping $\pi : \{1, \ldots, M\} \to \{1, \ldots, N\}$. Informally, given two lists of ciphertexts $\boldsymbol{\alpha} = [\alpha_1, \ldots, \alpha_M]$ and $\boldsymbol{c} = [c_1, \ldots, c_N]$, the goal of the prover in our protocol is to prove that there exists an EP π, such that the encrypted element of c_i is the same as the encrypted element of $\alpha_{\pi^{-1}(i)}$. A formal definition for the relation corresponding to our protocol will be given in Sect. 2. The idea of our protocol is to decompose a valid EP into four steps: extension, placement, replication, and finalization, and then the prover shows their validity respectively. The four steps are described in the following.

Extension. If $M < N$, we know that the length of the resulting ciphertext list $\boldsymbol{c}$ is longer than that of the original ciphertext list $\boldsymbol{\alpha}$. Therefore, all parties append $N - M$ ciphertexts at the end of $\boldsymbol{\alpha}$ as dummy ciphertexts. To ensure that the dummy ciphertexts are meaningless while the resulting new list is derived from a valid EP performed on the original list, all parties could append $N - M$ ciphertext α_1 at the end of $\boldsymbol{\alpha}$. If $M \geq N$, we can safely skip this extension step.

Placement. If the encrypted element of a ciphertext in $\boldsymbol{\alpha}$ does not appear in the resulting list $\boldsymbol{c}$ (in an encrypted form), i.e., this element is omitted according to the mapping of the EP π, the prover can label this ciphertext also as a dummy ciphertext. The prover now permutes the list, such that for each ciphertext encrypting the (non-omitted) element in the original list, if it is mapped to k different outputs according to π, $k - 1$ dummy ciphertexts are placed after this ciphertext. If $M > N$, extra dummy ciphertexts are moved to the end of the list. Then all ciphertexts are re-randomized.

Replication. The prover replaces all dummy ciphertexts except extra dummy ciphertexts with their first non-dummy ciphertext. In other words, if a non-omitted element is mapped to k different outputs according to π, its corresponding ciphertext is replicated $k - 1$ times thereafter. Then all ciphertexts are re-randomized.

Finalization. If $M > N$, parties can remove the last $M - N$ extra dummy ciphertexts from the list. Now the prover can permute the list to their final place according to π. Finally, all ciphertexts are re-randomized to derive $\boldsymbol{c}$.

Then the prover is required to prove that each step is executed correctly in the protocol. We give an illustration of these four steps for the EP corresponding to the circuit C (Fig. 1) in Fig. 3, where we use β_i's to denote the encrypted elements of ciphertexts in the list $\boldsymbol{\alpha}$.

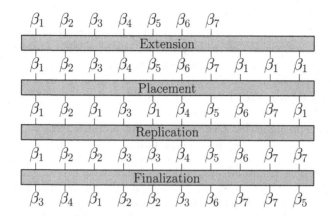

Fig. 3. The four steps for the proof corresponding to the circuit C in Fig. 1.

The organization for the rest of this paper is as follows. In Sect. 2, we present preliminaries for our further presentation. Then we provide a formal description for our main protocol in Sect. 3. Subsequently, sub-protocols inside our main protocol are given in Sect. 4. Finally, performance of our protocol and comparisons between our protocol and the original work [25] are presented in Sect. 5, from both communication and computation aspects.

2   Preliminaries

In this paper, the security of protocols is proved under standard security definitions (see [14,21] for more information). This paper mainly focuses on constructing a public-coin honest-verifier zero-knowledge protocol (see [12]). Note that this kind of protocols can be compiled by the Fiat-Shamir heuristic [9] to be non-interactive and secure against malicious verifiers with *low overhead*.

We use the notation $\|S\|$ to denote the number of bits required to represent elements in the set S. We write $x \leftarrow_\$ S$ to indicate that an element x is uniformly sampled from the set S. Define $[n] = \{1, \ldots, n\}$. The function $\max(\cdot, \cdot)$ takes as input two values and returns the maximum of these two values. We say that a function f in a variable κ mapping natural numbers to $[0, 1]$ is *negligible* if $f(\kappa) = \mathcal{O}(\kappa^{-c})$ for every constant $c > 0$.

We give the formal definition of EP in the following.

Definition 1 (Extended Permutation [24]). *For positive integers M and N, a mapping $\pi : [M] \to [N]$ is an extended permutation (EP) if for every $y \in [N]$, there exists exactly one $x \in [M]$, such that $\pi(x) = y$. We often denote x by $\pi^{-1}(y)$.*

Here, we give a brief description of the ElGamal encryption scheme [11]. This encryption scheme is over a cyclic group $\mathbb{G} = \langle g \rangle$ of prime order q. It is semantically secure under the decisional Diffie-Hellman (DDH) assumption (see [16]) for $\mathbb{G}$. The description of the scheme is in the following.

Key Generation. The algorithm KGen takes as input the security parameter 1^κ, picks $s \leftarrow_{\$} \mathbb{Z}_q$, and sets $h \leftarrow g^s$. Then the algorithm outputs the public key $\mathsf{pk} \leftarrow (\mathbb{G}, q, g, h)$ and the private key $\mathsf{sk} \leftarrow s$.

Encryption. The algorithm Enc takes as input a message $m \in \mathbb{G}$ and a public key pk, and returns the ciphertext $c \leftarrow (c^{(0)} = g^r, c^{(1)} = mh^r)$ for a random coin $r \leftarrow_{\$} \mathbb{Z}_q$.

Decryption. The algorithm Dec takes as input a ciphertext $c = (c^{(0)}, c^{(1)})$ and a key pair $(\mathsf{pk}, \mathsf{sk})$, and returns the plaintext $m \leftarrow c^{(1)}/(c^{(0)})^s$.

Remark 1. For the ElGamal encryption scheme with $\mathsf{pk} = (\mathbb{G}, q, g, h)$, it is easy for a prover to prove in zero-knowledge that two ElGamal ciphertexts encrypt the same value. Without loss of generality, we denote two ciphertexts by $c_1 = (c_1^{(0)}, c_1^{(1)}) = (g^{r_1}, mh^{r_1})$ and $c_2 = (c_2^{(0)}, c_2^{(1)}) = (g^{r_2}, mh^{r_2})$, such that they encrypt the same value m.

When we compute $c_3 \leftarrow (c_1^{(0)}(c_2^{(0)})^{-1}, c_1^{(1)}(c_2^{(1)})^{-1}) = (g^{r_1-r_2}, h^{r_1-r_2})$, the resulting ciphertext c_3 indeed encrypts 1. Therefore, c_1 and c_2 encrypt the same value if and only if c_3 encrypts 1. Let $r = r_1 - r_2$. If a prover knows r, she is able to prove that c_1 and c_2 encrypt the same value via proving that $(g, h, c_3^{(0)}, c_3^{(1)})$ is a Diffie-Hellman (DH) tuple. More concretely, it is equivalent for the prover to prove in zero-knowledge that there exists a value $r \in \mathbb{Z}_q$, such that $c_3^{(0)} = g^r$ and $c_3^{(1)} = h^r$.

In this paper, we aim to provide a zero-knowledge protocol for the relation R_{EncEP} based on the ElGamal encryption scheme:

$$R_{\mathsf{EncEP}} = \{(\mathbb{G}, q, g, h, \{(\alpha_i^{(0)}, \alpha_i^{(1)})\}_{i \in [M]}, \{(c_i^{(0)}, c_i^{(1)})\}_{i \in [N]}) \mid \exists \{r_i\}_{i \in [N]}, \pi, s.t.$$
$$c_i^{(0)} = \alpha_{\pi^{-1}(i)}^{(0)} g^{r_i} \wedge c_i^{(1)} = \alpha_{\pi^{-1}(i)}^{(1)} h^{r_i} \wedge \pi \text{ is an extended permutation}\}$$

Our construction utilizes a zero-knowledge protocol $\Pi_{\mathsf{zk}}^{\mathsf{Shuffle}}$ for the relation R_{Shuffle} based on the ElGamal encryption scheme:

$$R_{\mathsf{Shuffle}} = \{(\mathbb{G}, q, g, h, \{(c_i^{(0)}, c_i^{(1)})\}_{i \in [\ell]}, \{(c_i'^{(0)}, c_i'^{(1)})\}_{i \in [\ell]}) \mid \exists \{r_i\}_{i \in [\ell]}, \pi, s.t.$$
$$c_i'^{(0)} = c_{\pi(i)}^{(0)} g^{r_i} \wedge c_i'^{(1)} = c_{\pi(i)}^{(1)} h^{r_i} \wedge \pi \text{ is a permutation}\}$$

We note that there exist efficient (non-interactive) protocols with sub-linear communication cost that can be used to instantiate $\Pi_{\mathsf{zk}}^{\mathsf{Shuffle}}$, such as the protocol in [3].

3 Our Main Protocol

Based on the idea introduced in Sect. 1.2, we provide a full description of our main protocol in this section. The sub-protocols inside our protocol are given in Sect. 4.

The zero-knowledge protocol $\Pi_{zk}^{\mathsf{EncEP}}$ for R_{EncEP} between a prover P and a verifier V is given as follows.

Public Inputs: A group $\mathbb{G}$ of order q with generator g, where DDH assumption holds. The public key of the ElGamal encryption scheme $\mathsf{pk} = (\mathbb{G}, q, g, h)$. Two lists of ElGamal ciphertexts $\boldsymbol{\alpha} = [\alpha_1, \ldots, \alpha_M]$ and $\boldsymbol{c} = [c_1, \ldots, c_N]$ corresponding to pk. Each ciphertext α_i (resp. c_i) is of the form $\alpha_i = (\alpha_i^{(0)}, \alpha_i^{(1)}) \in \mathbb{G}^2$ (resp. $c_i = (c_i^{(0)}, c_i^{(1)}) \in \mathbb{G}^2$).

Witness: An EP $\pi : [M] \to [N]$ and a list $R = [r_1, \ldots, r_N]$, where $r_i \in \mathbb{Z}_q$.

Statement: There exists an EP π and a list $R = [r_1, \ldots, r_N]$, such that $c_i^{(0)} = \alpha_{\pi^{-1}(i)}^{(0)} g^{r_i}$ and $c_i^{(1)} = \alpha_{\pi^{-1}(i)}^{(1)} h^{r_i}$.

Protocol Description

1. **Extension.** Both parties append $\max(N - M, 0)$ ciphertexts α_1 to the list $\boldsymbol{\alpha}$ as dummy ciphertexts. The new list is denoted by $\boldsymbol{e} = [e_1, \ldots, e_N]$. Let $N' = \max(M, N)$.

2. **Placement.** If the index i of a ciphertext in $\boldsymbol{e}$ satisfies $i \leq M$ and $\{j \mid i = \pi^{-1}(j)\} = \emptyset$, i.e., this encrypted element is omitted after the EP, P also labels this ciphertext as a dummy ciphertext. P now permutes the list $\boldsymbol{e}$, such that for each non-dummy ciphertext in $\boldsymbol{e}$ with index j, if $|\pi(j)| = k$, $k - 1$ dummy ciphertexts are placed after this ciphertext. The condition $|\pi(j)| = k$ means that this encrypted element is mapped to k different outputs according to π. If $M > N$, extra dummy ciphertexts are moved to the end of the list. This permutation is denoted by π' and the resulting list of ciphertexts is denoted by $\hat{\boldsymbol{p}} = [\hat{p}_1, \ldots, \hat{p}_{N'}]$, where $\hat{p}_i = e_{\pi'(i)}$.
   Then P picks $r_i' \leftarrow_{\$} \mathbb{Z}_q$ for $i \in [N']$ and computes the ElGamal ciphertext $p_i \leftarrow (\hat{p}_i^{(0)} g^{r_i'}, \hat{p}_i^{(1)} h^{r_i'})$ for $i \in [N']$. We denote the resulting list by $\boldsymbol{p} = [p_1, \ldots, p_{N'}]$. P sends $\boldsymbol{p}$ to V.

3. **Replication.** P replaces all dummy ciphertexts except extra dummy ciphertexts by the nearest non-dummy ciphertexts before each of them. In other words, if a non-omitted element is mapped to k different outputs according to π, its corresponding ciphertext is replicated $k - 1$ times thereafter. We define a function $\omega : [N] \to [N]$ that maps an input index i to the index of a non-dummy ciphertext j, such that j is the maximum index of non-dummy ciphertext in $\boldsymbol{p}$ that satisfies $j \leq i$. We note that for a dummy ciphertext with index i, $\omega(i)$ is the index of the ciphertext that replaces it during this replication procedure.
   Let the resulting list be $\hat{\boldsymbol{\rho}} = [\hat{\rho}_1, \ldots, \hat{\rho}_{N'}]$. We have $\hat{\rho}_i = p_{\omega(i)}$ for $i \in [N]$. P picks $r_i'' \leftarrow_{\$} \mathbb{Z}_q$, and computes the ElGamal ciphertext $\rho_i \leftarrow (\hat{\rho}_i^{(0)} g^{r_i''}, \hat{\rho}_i^{(1)} h^{r_i''})$

for each $i \in [N]$. This resulting list is denoted by $\rho = [\rho_1, \ldots, \rho_{N'}]$. Note that if $N - M < 0$, the last $N - M$ ciphertext are still the extra dummy ciphertexts in p. P sends (the first N elements of) ρ to V.

4. **Finalization.** V obtains ρ. If $N - M < 0$, both parties remove the last $M - N$ extra ciphertexts from ρ. No matter whether we need to remove extra ciphertexts or not, we denote the current list of ciphertexts by ρ'. P permutes all ciphertexts to their final location as prescribed by π. We denote this permutation by π'' and the resulting list by $\hat{f} = [\hat{f}_1, \ldots, \hat{f}_N]$, where $\hat{f}_i = \rho_{\pi''(i)}$. Then P computes $\hat{r}_i \leftarrow r_i - r''_{\pi''(i)} - r'_{\omega(\pi''(i))} \bmod q$ for $i \in [N]$. It is easy to verify that $(\hat{f}_i^{(0)} g^{\hat{r}_i}, \hat{f}_i^{(1)} h^{\hat{r}_i}) = c_i$.

The remaining work is to show that these four steps are executed correctly. Since the extension step is done by both parties, P only needs to show that what she has done is correct in the last three steps. Namely, P needs to prove in zero-knowledge that p and c are derived from valid shuffles applied to e and ρ', respectively, and ρ is derived from a valid dummy ciphertext replacement (replication) applied to p. Hence, P and V together follow the detailed procedure below to prove the correctness of P's operations in these last three steps.

5. P uses the protocol $\Pi_{zk}^{\mathsf{Shuffle}}$ to prove that p is derived from a valid shuffle applied to e with witness $(\{r'_i\}_{i \in [N']}, \pi')$.
6. P uses the protocol $\Pi_{zk}^{\mathsf{Shuffle}}$ to prove that c is derived from a valid shuffle applied to ρ' with witness $(\{\hat{r}_i\}_{i \in [N]}, \pi'')$.
7. To prove that ρ is derived from a valid dummy ciphertext replacement from p, P needs to prove that the plaintext of ρ_1 is equal to p_1, and that the plaintext of each ρ_i is equal to that of ρ_{i-1} or that of p_i for $i = 2, \ldots, N$. According to Remark 1, the goal can be translated to prove the correctness of the corresponding DH tuple. Both parties compute two ciphertexts

$$\gamma_{i,0} \leftarrow (\rho_i^{(0)}(\rho_{i-1}^{(0)})^{-1}, \rho_i^{(1)}(\rho_{i-1}^{(1)})^{-1})$$

and

$$\gamma_{i,1} \leftarrow (\rho_i^{(0)}(p_i^{(0)})^{-1}, \rho_i^{(1)}(p_i^{(1)})^{-1})$$

for $i = 2, \ldots, N$, together with

$$\gamma_{1,0} = \gamma_{1,1} \leftarrow (\rho_1^{(0)}(p_1^{(0)})^{-1}, \rho_1^{(1)}(p_1^{(1)})^{-1}).$$

For $i = 2, \ldots, N$, if the plaintext of ρ_i is equal to that of ρ_{i-1}, the random coin of $\gamma_{i,0}$ is $\nu_{i,0} = r''_i - r''_{i-1} \bmod q$, and we let $b_i = 0$. If the plaintext of ρ_i is equal to that of p_i, the random coin of $\gamma_{i,1}$ is $\nu_{i,1} = r''_i$, and we let $b_i = 1$. In addition, the random coin for both $\gamma_{1,0}$ and $\gamma_{1,1}$ is $\nu_{1,0} = \nu_{1,1} = r''_1$. P computes $\{\nu_{i,b_i}\}_{i \in [N]}$ and uses the protocol Π_{zk}^{DH} to prove the following statement:

There exists a set of elements $\{\nu_{i,b_i}\}_{i \in [N]}$, where $b_i \in \{0, 1\}$ and $\nu_{i,b_i} \in \mathbb{Z}_q$, such that $\gamma_{i,b_i}^{(0)} = g^{\nu_{i,b_i}}$ and $\gamma_{i,b_i}^{(1)} = h^{\nu_{i,b_i}}$ for all $i \in [N]$.

8. If all the executions of $\Pi_{zk}^{\text{Shuffle}}$ and Π_{zk}^{DH} output accept, V outputs accept. Otherwise, V outputs reject.

In what follows, we present a theorem for the security of the protocol Π_{zk}^{EncEP}.

Theorem 1. *The protocol Π_{zk}^{EncEP} is a zero-knowledge argument of knowledge for the relation R_{EncEP}.*

Proof. It is easy to verify the completeness of the protocol. We first show that $(\hat{f}_i^{(0)} g^{\hat{r}_i}, \hat{f}_i^{(1)} h^{\hat{r}_i}) = c_i$. More concretely, we can verify that

$$
\begin{aligned}
\hat{f}_i^{(0)} g^{\hat{r}_i} &= \rho_{\pi''(i)}^{(0)} g^{r_i - r''_{\pi''(i)} - r'_{\omega(\pi''(i))}} \\
&= \rho_{\pi''(i)}^{(0)} g^{-r''_{\pi''(i)}} g^{-r'_{\omega(\pi''(i))}} g^{r_i} \\
&= \hat{\rho}_{\pi''(i)}^{(0)} g^{r''_{\pi''(i)}} g^{-r''_{\pi''(i)}} g^{-r'_{\omega(\pi''(i))}} g^{r_i} \\
&= \hat{\rho}_{\pi''(i)}^{(0)} g^{-r'_{\omega(\pi''(i))}} g^{r_i} \\
&= p_{\omega(\pi''(i))}^{(0)} g^{-r'_{\omega(\pi''(i))}} g^{r_i} \\
&= \hat{p}_{\omega(\pi''(i))}^{(0)} g^{r'_{\omega(\pi''(i))}} g^{-r'_{\omega(\pi''(i))}} g^{r_i} \\
&= \hat{p}_{\omega(\pi''(i))}^{(0)} g^{r_i} \\
&= e_{\pi'(\omega(\pi''(i)))}^{(0)} g^{r_i} \\
&= \alpha_{\pi^{-1}(i)}^{(0)} g^{r_i}
\end{aligned}
$$

Similarly, we have $\hat{f}_i^{(1)} g^{\hat{r}_i} = \alpha_{\pi^{-1}(i)}^{(1)} h^{r_i}$. Then, if the prover P honestly proves that all the operations conducted in the four steps are correct using related parameters derived in the operations, the completeness of the protocol directly follows from the completeness of the protocols $\Pi_{zk}^{\text{Shuffle}}$ and Π_{zk}^{DH}.

Then we show that the protocol achieves the zero-knowledge property. For an adversary $\mathcal{A}$ controlling the verifier V, we construct a simulator $\mathcal{S}$ that internally runs V and simulates V's view. $\mathcal{S}$ firstly sets $N' \leftarrow \max(M, N)$ as in the protocol. For the step of placement, $\mathcal{S}$ randomly picks $p_i \leftarrow_\$ \mathbb{G}^2$ for $i \in [N']$ and sends the list $\boldsymbol{p} = [p_1, \ldots, p_{N'}]$ to $\mathcal{A}$. For the step of replication, $\mathcal{S}$ randomly generates $\rho_i \leftarrow_\$ \mathbb{G}^2$ for $i \in [N']$ and sends $\boldsymbol{\rho} = [\rho_1, \ldots, \rho_{N'}]$ to $\mathcal{A}$. Then $\mathcal{S}$ invokes the simulator $\mathcal{S}_{\text{Shuffle}}$ for the protocol $\Pi_{zk}^{\text{Shuffle}}$ twice, for both Steps 5 and 6, to simulate the view of $\mathcal{A}$ in the execution of $\Pi_{zk}^{\text{Shuffle}}$. $\mathcal{S}$ computes elements of $\{\gamma_{i,b}\}_{i \in [N], b \in \{0,1\}}$ as in the protocol and uses the simulator $\mathcal{S}_{\text{DH}}$ for the protocol Π_{zk}^{DH} to simulate the view of $\mathcal{A}$ in the execution of Π_{zk}^{DH}. Finally, $\mathcal{S}$ outputs what $\mathcal{A}$ outputs to complete the simulation.

In the simulation, we note that elements in the lists $\boldsymbol{p}$ and $\boldsymbol{\rho}$ are all randomly generated ciphertexts, while those elements in a real execution are based on the extended permutation π. However, since the ElGamal encryption scheme in the protocol is semantically secure under the DDH assumption, all computationally bounded adversaries cannot distinguish these simulated ciphertexts from ciphertexts generated in a real execution except for a negligible probability. The other difference between the simulation and the real execution of the protocol is for the sub-protocols $\Pi_{zk}^{Shuffle}$ and Π_{zk}^{DH}. Because both the sub-protocols $\Pi_{zk}^{Shuffle}$ and Π_{zk}^{DH} are also zero-knowledge, $\mathcal{A}$'s view simulated by the corresponding simulators $\mathcal{S}_{Shuffle}$ and $\mathcal{S}_{DH}$ is computationally indistinguishable from a real execution. Therefore, the protocol is zero-knowledge.

We analyze the soundness of the protocol as follows. The prover P follows the four steps to perform the extended permutation on the original list of ciphertexts $\boldsymbol{\alpha}$ and derive the list of resulting ciphertexts $\boldsymbol{c}$. Intuitively, the protocols $\Pi_{zk}^{Shuffle}$ and Π_{zk}^{DH} guarantee that no new ciphertexts except encrypted values inside $\boldsymbol{\alpha}$ are added to the resulting list of ciphertexts $\boldsymbol{c}$, and thus a valid extended permutation is performed on the encrypted values in $\boldsymbol{\alpha}$. Our goal now is to extract the extended permutation π and random coins $\{r_i\}_{i\in[N]}$. In the following, we construct an extractor $\mathcal{E}$ that internally runs the prover P* and extracts the corresponding witness.

The extractor $\mathcal{E}$ runs the prover P* as a subroutine. Then $\mathcal{E}$ uses the extractor $\mathcal{E}_{Shuffle}$ for the sub-protocol $\Pi_{zk}^{Shuffle}$ in Steps 5 and 6 to extract the witness in these two execution of $\Pi_{zk}^{Shuffle}$. Namely, $\mathcal{E}$ uses $\mathcal{E}_{Shuffle}$ to extract witness $(\{r_i'\}_{i\in[N']}, \pi')$ and $(\{\hat{r}_i\}_{i\in[N]}, \pi'')$ in Steps 5 and 6, respectively. Meanwhile, $\mathcal{E}$ invokes the extractor $\mathcal{E}_{DH}$ for the sub-protocol Π_{zk}^{DH} in Step 7 to extract the random coins $\{\nu_{i,b_i}\}_{i\in[N]}$ of the ciphertexts $\{\gamma_{i,b_i}\}_{i\in[N]}$ (encrypting 1) and corresponding $\{b_i\}_{i\in[N]}$.

$\mathcal{E}$ can reconstruct the corresponding mapping ω. Then $\mathcal{E}$ iteratively assigns the value of $\omega(i)$ as follows. Let $\omega(1) = 1$. Then for $i = 2, \ldots, N$, let

$$\omega(i) = \begin{cases} \omega(i-1) & \text{if } b_i = 0, \\ i & \text{if } b_i = 1. \end{cases}$$

Meanwhile, $\mathcal{E}$ can effectively compute the random coins $\{r_i''\}_{i\in[N]}$. Firstly, $\mathcal{E}$ sets $r_1'' \leftarrow \nu_{1,b_1}$. Then $\mathcal{E}$ iteratively assigns the value of r_i'' as follows. For $i = 2, \ldots, N$,

$$r_i'' = \begin{cases} r_{i-1}'' + \nu_{i,b_i} \bmod q & \text{if } b_i = 0, \\ \nu_{i,b_i} & \text{if } b_i = 1. \end{cases}$$

Now, $\mathcal{E}$ can derive all the random coins for the extended permutation via computing

$$r_i = \hat{r}_i + r_{\pi''(i)}'' + r_{\omega(\pi''(i))}' \bmod q$$

for $i \in [N]$. Since $\mathcal{E}$ has obtained π', π'', and ω, $\mathcal{E}$ can reconstruct the extended permutation π as

$$\pi(i) = \pi''^{-1} \circ \omega^{-1} \circ \pi'^{-1}(i).$$

Therefore, the extractor successfully derives the extended permutation π and the list $R = [r_1, \ldots, r_N]$, and the soundness of the protocol is then proved. □

4 Sub-Protocols

As we have mentioned in Sect. 2, there exist efficient (non-interactive) protocols with sub-linear communication cost that can be used to instantiate the zero-knowledge protocol for shuffle ($\Pi_{zk}^{Shuffle}$). In this paper, we use the protocol in [3] as $\Pi_{zk}^{Shuffle}$.

Now we provide the sub-protocol Π_{zk}^{DH} inside our main protocol. We note that this zero-knowledge protocol Π_{zk}^{DH} is for the relation R_{DH}:

$$R_{DH} = \{(\mathbb{G}, q, g, h, \{(\gamma_i^{(0)}, \gamma_i^{(1)})\}_{i \in [\ell]} \mid \exists \{\nu_{i,b_i}\}_{i \in [\ell]}, \text{where } b_i \in \{0,1\} \text{ s.t.}$$
$$\forall i \ (\gamma_{i,b_i}^{(0)} = g^{\nu_{i,b_i}} \wedge \gamma_{i,b_i}^{(1)} = h^{\nu_{i,b_i}})\}.$$

In the following, we describe the protocol Π_{zk}^{DH} for the relation R_{DH} between a prover P and a verifier V utilizing the idea introduced in [7] and [8]. This protocol is honest-verifier zero-knowledge and can be compiled by the Fiat-Shamir heuristic [9] to be non-interactive and secure against malicious verifiers as we have mentioned in Sect. 2.

Public Inputs: A group $\mathbb{G} = \langle g \rangle$ of order q. Another generator h for $\mathbb{G}$. A set of elements $\{(\gamma_{i,b}^{(0)}, \gamma_{i,b}^{(1)})\}_{i \in [\ell], b \in \{0,1\}}$, where $(\gamma_{i,b}^{(0)}, \gamma_{i,b}^{(1)}) \in \mathbb{G}^2$.

Witness: A list $[\nu_{1,b_1}, \ldots, \nu_{\ell,b_\ell}]$, where $\nu_{i,b_i} \in \mathbb{Z}_q$ and $b_i \in \{0,1\}$.

Statement: Given ciphertexts $\{(\gamma_{i,b}^{(0)}, \gamma_{i,b}^{(1)})\}_{i \in [\ell], b \in \{0,1\}}$, there exist $\{\nu_{i,b_i}\}_{i \in [\ell]}$, where $\nu_{i,b_i} \in \mathbb{Z}_q$ and $b_i \in \{0,1\}$, such that $\gamma_{i,b_i}^{(0)} = g^{\nu_{i,b_i}}$ and $\gamma_{i,b_i}^{(1)} = h^{\nu_{i,b_i}}$ for all $i \in [\ell]$.

Protocol Description

1. For $i \in [\ell]$:
   (a) P picks $e_{i,1-b_i} \leftarrow_\$ \mathbb{Z}_q$ and $z_{i,1-b_i} \leftarrow_\$ \mathbb{Z}_q$.
   (b) P computes

$$a_{i,1-b_i}^{(0)} \leftarrow g^{z_{i,1-b_i}} (\gamma_{i,1-b_i}^{(0)})^{-e_{i,1-b_i}}$$

   and

$$a_{i,1-b_i}^{(1)} \leftarrow h^{z_{i,1-b_i}} (\gamma_{i,1-b_i}^{(1)})^{-e_{i,1-b_i}}$$

   to simulate a valid transcript.
   (c) P picks $x_{i,b_i} \leftarrow_\$ \mathbb{Z}_q$. Then P computes $a_{i,b_i}^{(0)} = g^{x_{i,b_i}}$ and $a_{i,b_i}^{(1)} = h^{x_{i,b_i}}$.
   P sends $\{(a_{i,b}^{(0)}, a_{i,b}^{(1)})\}_{i \in [\ell], b \in \{0,1\}}$ to V.
2. V chooses $e, \theta \leftarrow_\$ \mathbb{Z}_q$ and sends them to P.
3. For $i \in [\ell]$:
   (a) P computes $e_{i,b_i} \leftarrow e - e_{i,1-b_i} \mod q$.
   (b) P computes $z_{i,b_i} \leftarrow x_{i,b_i} + \nu_{i,b_i} e_{i,b_i} \mod q$.
   (c) P computes $z_0 \leftarrow \sum_{i=1}^{\ell} z_{i,0} \theta^i \mod q$ and $z_1 \leftarrow \sum_{i=1}^{\ell} z_{i,1} \theta^i \mod q$.
   P sends $\{e_{i,b}\}_{i \in [\ell], b \in \{0,1\}}$, z_0, and z_1 to V.

4. V verifies the following equations:

$$e_{i,0} + e_{i,1} \equiv e \bmod q$$

for $i \in [\ell]$, and

$$g^{z_b} = \prod_{i=1}^{\ell} (a_{i,b}^{(0)} (\gamma_{i,b}^{(0)})^{e_{i,b}})^{\theta^i}$$

and

$$h^{z_b} = \prod_{i=1}^{\ell} (a_{i,b}^{(1)} (\gamma_{i,b}^{(1)})^{e_{i,b}})^{\theta^i}$$

for $b \in \{0,1\}$. If all equations hold, V outputs accept. Otherwise, V outputs reject.

Theorem 2. *The protocol Π_{zk}^{DH} is an honest-verifier zero-knowledge proof of knowledge for the relation R_{DH}.*

Proof. For the completeness of the protocol, we can verify that:

$$\begin{aligned}
g^{z_{i,b_i}} &= g^{x_{i,b_i} + \nu_{i,b_i} e_{i,b_i}} \\
&= g^{x_{i,b_i}} g^{\nu_{i,b_i} e_{i,b_i}} \\
&= a_{i,b_i}^{(0)} (\gamma_{i,b_i}^{(0)})^{e_{i,b_i}}
\end{aligned}$$

and

$$\begin{aligned}
h^{z_{i,b_i}} &= h^{x_{i,b_i} + \nu_{i,b_i} e_{i,b_i}} \\
&= h^{x_{i,b_i}} h^{\nu_{i,b_i} e_{i,b_i}} \\
&= a_{i,b_i}^{(1)} (\gamma_{i,b_i}^{(1)})^{e_{i,b_i}}.
\end{aligned}$$

Meanwhile, for the verification related to $1 - b_i$ in Step 4, values $z_{i,1-b_i}$, $e_{i,1-b_i}$, $a_{i,1-b_i}^{(0)}$, and $a_{i,1-b_i}^{(1)}$ generated in Step 1 are specified to satisfy the equation for the verification. Therefore, we have

$$\begin{aligned}
g^{z_b} &= g^{\sum_{i=1}^{\ell} z_{i,b} \theta^i} \\
&= \prod_{i=1}^{\ell} (g^{z_{i,b}})^{\theta^i} \\
&= \prod_{i=1}^{\ell} (a_{i,b}^{(0)} (\gamma_{i,b}^{(0)})^{e_{i,b}})^{\theta^i}
\end{aligned}$$

and

$$h^{z_b} = h^{\sum_{i=1}^{\ell} z_{i,b}\theta^i}$$

$$= \prod_{i=1}^{\ell} (h^{z_{i,b}})^{\theta^i}$$

$$= \prod_{i=1}^{\ell} (a_{i,b}^{(1)} (\gamma_{i,b}^{(1)})^{e_{i,b}})^{\theta^i}$$

for $b \in \{0,1\}$. Now, it is easy to see that the protocol is complete.

To show that the protocol achieves the honest-verifier zero-knowledge property, we construct a simulator $\mathcal{S}$ to simulate the view of the verifier V. The simulator $\mathcal{S}$ first picks the challenges $e, \theta \leftarrow_\$ \mathbb{Z}_q$. Then $\mathcal{S}$ selects $e_{i,0} \leftarrow_\$ \mathbb{Z}$ and computes $e_{i,1} \leftarrow e - e_{i,0} \bmod q$. $\mathcal{S}$ generates $z_{i,b} \leftarrow_\$ \mathbb{Z}$ and computes

$$a_{i,b}^{(0)} \leftarrow g^{z_{i,b}} (\gamma_{i,b}^{(0)})^{-e_{i,b}}$$

and

$$a_{i,b}^{(1)} \leftarrow g^{z_{i,b}} (\gamma_{i,b}^{(1)})^{-e_{i,b}}$$

for $i \in [\ell]$ and $b \in \{0,1\}$. $\mathcal{S}$ also computes $z_0 \leftarrow \sum_{i=1}^{\ell} z_{i,0}\theta^i$ and $z_1 \leftarrow \sum_{i=1}^{\ell} z_{i,1}\theta^i$. We note that the distribution of

$$(\{(a_{i,b}^{(0)}, a_{i,b}^{(1)})\}_{i\in[\ell],b\in\{0,1\}}, e, \theta, \{e_{i,b}\}_{i\in[\ell],b\in\{0,1\}}, z_0, z_1)$$

in this simulation is perfectly indistinguishable from that of a real execution. This is due to the fact that given random $e, \theta \in \mathbb{Z}_q$, elements in $\{z_{i,b}\}_{i\in[\ell],b\in\{0,1\}}$ are uniformly random both in a real execution and in the simulation. Meanwhile, the distributions of each pair $(e_{i,0}, e_{i,1})$ satisfying $e_{i,0} + e_{i,1} \equiv e \bmod q$ in a real execution and in the simulation are identical. Conditioned on these values, z_0, z_1, and elements in $\{(a_{i,b}^{(0)}, a_{i,b}^{(1)})\}_{i\in[\ell],b\in\{0,1\}}$ are uniquely determined by the verification equations. Thus, the distribution of simulated proofs is identical to that of real proofs.

For soundness, we construct an extractor $\mathcal{E}$ that internally runs P* and executes the protocol with P*. If the transcript is accepting, $\mathcal{E}$ has to extract a witness. Therefore, $\mathcal{E}$ rewinds P* to the challenge phase (Step 2) and runs it again with different challenges to obtain ℓ pair of accepting transcripts with the same $\{(a_{i,b}^{(0)}, a_{i,b}^{(1)})\}_{i\in[\ell],b\in\{0,1\}}$, such that each pair is with different $\{\theta_{[j]}\}_{j\in[\ell]}$, and both transcripts in each pair are with challenges e and $\bar{e}(\neq e)$, respectively. Note that the rewinding scheme follows the strategy used in [6]. Let these pairs be of the form

$$(\{(a_{i,b}^{(0)}, a_{i,b}^{(1)})\}_{i\in[\ell],b\in\{0,1\}}, e, \theta_{[j]}, \{e_{i,b}^{[j]}\}_{i\in[\ell],b\in\{0,1\}}, \{z_b^{[j]}\}_{b\in\{0,1\}})$$

and

$$(\{(a_{i,b}^{(0)}, a_{i,b}^{(1)})\}_{i\in[\ell],b\in\{0,1\}}, \bar{e}, \theta_{[j]}, \{\bar{e}_{i,b}^{[j]}\}_{i\in[\ell],b\in\{0,1\}}, \{\bar{z}_b^{[j]}\}_{b\in\{0,1\}})$$

for $j \in [\ell]$. Note that the extractor $\mathcal{E}$ will obtain 2ℓ transcripts, and it runs in expected polynomial time. Since $e \neq \bar{e}$, for each $j \in [\ell]$, we must have $e_{i,0}^{[j]} \neq \bar{e}_{i,0}^{[j]}$ or $e_{i,1}^{[j]} \neq \bar{e}_{i,1}^{[j]}$. Let b_i be the value that $e_{i,b_i}^{[j]} \neq \bar{e}_{i,b_i}^{[j]}$ for $i \in [\ell]$. If we have both $e_{i,0}^{[j]} \neq \bar{e}_{i,0}^{[j]}$ and $e_{i,1}^{[j]} \neq \bar{e}_{i,1}^{[j]}$, b_i could be equal to either 0 or 1. According to the accepting transcripts, we have

$$g^{z_b^{[j]}} = \prod_{i=1}^{\ell} (a_{i,b}^{(0)}(\gamma_{i,b}^{(0)})^{e_{i,b}^{[j]}})^{\theta_{[j]}^i}, \quad h^{z_b^{[j]}} = \prod_{i=1}^{\ell} (a_{i,b}^{(1)}(\gamma_{i,b}^{(1)})^{e_{i,b}^{[j]}})^{\theta_{[j]}^i},$$

for $j \in [\ell]$ and $b \in \{0,1\}$. Therefore, there should be some $\{z_{i,b}^{[j]}\}_{i \in [\ell]}$, such that

$$a_{i,b}^{(0)}(\gamma_{i,b}^{(0)})^{e_{i,b}^{[j]}} = g^{z_{i,b}^{[j]}} \text{ for } i \in [\ell], \text{ and } z_b^{[j]} = \sum_{i=1}^{\ell} z_{i,b}^{[j]}\theta_{[j]}^i.$$

For the system of equations $z_b^{[j]} = \sum_{i=1}^{\ell} z_{i,b}^{[j]}\theta_{[j]}^i$ for $j \in [\ell]$, we can efficiently solve the unique solution $\{z_{i,b}^{[j]}\}_{i \in [\ell]}$. This is due to the fact that the corresponding Vandermonde matrix of θ is of full rank. It is straightforward to see that this unique solution $\{z_{i,b}^{[j]}\}_{i \in [\ell]}$ should also satisfy $a_{i,b}^{(1)}(\gamma_{i,b}^{(1)})^{e_{i,b}^{[j]}} = h^{z_{i,b}^{[j]}}$. Hence, we obtain $\{z_{i,b}^{[j]}\}_{i \in [\ell]}$ for $b \in \{0,1\}$. Similarly, we know that

$$g^{\bar{z}_b^{[j]}} = \prod_{i=1}^{\ell} (a_{i,b}^{(0)}(\gamma_{i,b}^{(0)})^{\bar{e}_{i,b}^{[j]}})^{\theta_{[j]}^i}, \quad h^{\bar{z}_b^{[j]}} = \prod_{i=1}^{\ell} (a_{i,b}^{(1)}(\gamma_{i,b}^{(1)})^{\bar{e}_{i,b}^{[j]}})^{\theta_{[j]}^i}$$

for $j \in [\ell]$. We can use the same approach to computing $\{\bar{z}_{i,b}^{[j]}\}_{i \in [\ell]}$ for $b \in \{0,1\}$, such that

$$a_{i,b}^{(0)}(\gamma_{i,b}^{(0)})^{\bar{e}_{i,b}^{[j]}} = g^{\bar{z}_{i,b}^{[j]}}, \quad a_{i,b}^{(1)}(\gamma_{i,b}^{(1)})^{\bar{e}_{i,b}^{[j]}} = h^{\bar{z}_{i,b}^{[j]}}, \quad \text{and } \bar{z}_b^{[j]} = \sum_{i=1}^{\ell} \bar{z}_{i,b}^{[j]}\theta_{[j]}^i.$$

Given a pair of equations $a_{i,b_i}^{(0)}(\gamma_{i,b_i}^{(0)})^{e_{i,b_i}^{[j]}} = g^{z_{i,b_i}^{[j]}}$ and $a_{i,b_i}^{(0)}(\gamma_{i,b_i}^{(0)})^{\bar{e}_{i,b_i}^{[j]}} = g^{\bar{z}_{i,b_i}^{[j]}}$, there should be some x_{i,b_i} and ν_{i,b_i}, such that

$$a_{i,b_i}^{(0)} = g^{x_{i,b_i}}, \quad \gamma_{i,b_i}^{(0)} = g^{\nu_{i,b_i}},$$

and

$$x_{i,b_i} + \nu_{i,b_i}e_{i,b_i} = z_{i,b_i}, \quad x_{i,b_i} + \nu_{i,b_i}\bar{e}_{i,b_i} = \bar{z}_{i,b_i}.$$

According to the assignment of b_i, we know $e_{i,b_i} \neq \bar{e}_{i,b_i}$. Thus, the extractor $\mathcal{E}$ can easily compute x_{i,b_i} and ν_{i,b_i} from the last two equations, and finally obtain $\{x_{i,b_i}\}_{i \in [\ell]}$ and $\{\nu_{i,b_i}\}_{i \in [\ell]}$ from pairs of equations for all $i \in [\ell]$. It is easy to verify that these extracted elements also satisfy

$$a_{i,b_i}^{(1)} = h^{x_{i,b_i}}, \quad \gamma_{i,b_i}^{(1)} = h^{\nu_{i,b_i}}.$$

Hence, the extractor $\mathcal{E}$ successfully extracts $\{\nu_{i,b_i}\}_{i \in [\ell]}$, where $b_i \in \{0,1\}$ and $\nu_{i,b_i} \in \mathbb{Z}_q$, such that $\gamma_{i,b_i}^{(0)} = g^{\nu_{i,b_i}}$ and $\gamma_{i,b_i}^{(1)} = h^{\nu_{i,b_i}}$ for all $i \in [\ell]$. The soundness of the protocol follows. $\qquad \square$

5 Analysis

In this section, we analyze the performance of our protocol. In Table 1, we present the communication cost for one execution of Π_{zk}^{EncEP} with parameters M, N and $N' = \max(M, N)$. We give the communication cost of the two executions of the sub-protocol $\Pi_{zk}^{Shuffle}$ inside Π_{zk}^{EncEP}, respectively. The row of "remaining" is for the communication cost of Π_{zk}^{EncEP} excluding the cost of sub-protocols $\Pi_{zk}^{Shuffle}$ and Π_{zk}^{DH}. We note that $\|\mathbb{G}\| > \|\mathbb{Z}_q\|$.

Table 1. Communication cost of each part in our protocol Π_{zk}^{EncEP} with parameter M, N and $N' = \max(M, N)$.

Protocol	From P to V	From V to P
1st $\Pi_{zk}^{Shuffle}$ [3]	$(11\sqrt{N'} + 5)\|\mathbb{G}\| + (5\sqrt{N'} + 9)\|\mathbb{Z}_q\|$	$8\|\mathbb{Z}_q\|$
2nd $\Pi_{zk}^{Shuffle}$ [3]	$(11\sqrt{N} + 5)\|\mathbb{G}\| + (5\sqrt{N} + 9)\|\mathbb{Z}_q\|$	$8\|\mathbb{Z}_q\|$
Π_{zk}^{DH}	$4N\|\mathbb{G}\| + (2N + 2)\|\mathbb{Z}_q\|$	$2\|\mathbb{Z}_q\|$
Remaining	$(2N' + 2N)\|\mathbb{G}\|$	0

In Table 2, we then present the comparison of communication cost between our protocol and the previous protocol [25] (in the honest-verifier zero-knowledge setting). Here our comparison follows the fact that the parameters satisfy $N > M$ in most applications of Π_{zk}^{EncEP}. Therefore, we simply let $N' = \max(M, N) = N$ in the comparison. We remark that the protocol in [25] is not public-coin, and interaction is needed for the protocol execution. Alternatively, in our protocol, all messages sent from the verifier are uniformly random, *i.e.*, the protocol is public-coin. Therefore, we can simply leverage the Fiat-Shamir heuristic to make our protocol non-interactive. Now the communication cost of our protocol only involves the bits sent from the prover P to the verifier V. From Table 2, we can see that the (non-interactive) communication cost of our protocol is around $8N\|\mathbb{G}\|$, while the total communication cost of the (interactive) protocol in [25] is around $34N\|\mathbb{G}\|$ bits. Therefore, the communication cost of our protocol is only around 24% of that of the protocol in [25].

Table 2. Communication cost comparison between the original protocol [25] and the protocol Π_{zk}^{EncEP} is this paper with parameters M and N.

Protocol	From P to V	From V to P
[25]	$\sim (32N\|\mathbb{G}\| + 12N\|\mathbb{Z}_q\|)$	$\sim (2N\|\mathbb{G}\| + 10N\|\mathbb{Z}_q\|)$
This paper	$\sim ((8N + 22\sqrt{N})\|\mathbb{G}\| + (2N + 10\sqrt{N})\|\mathbb{Z}_q\|)$	$18\|\mathbb{Z}_q\|$

Note that in our protocol, we use the protocol in [3] as the zero-knowledge protocol for shuffle twice, while the protocol in [25] adopts the zero-knowledge

Table 3. Comparison of computation cost between the original protocol [25] and the protocol $\Pi_{\mathsf{zk}}^{\mathsf{EncEP}}$ in this paper with parameters M and N except zero-knowledge protocols for shuffle.

Protocols	Time P Expos	Time V Expos
[25]	$\sim 37N$	$\sim 32N$
This paper	$\sim 10N$	$\sim 4N$

protocol for shuffle introduced in [10] twice (for ElGamal ciphertext list of the same length N). We denote the protocols in [3] and [10] by BG and FS, respectively. It is shown [3] that BG significantly outperforms FS from both communication and computation aspects. According to the analysis in [3], BG's argument size is only 1/94 that of FS's, and BG has 3.4× faster running time. We count the total number of exponentiations in $\mathbb{G}$ performed by P and V for the original protocol [25] and our protocol, except those performed by the zero-knowledge protocols for shuffle, in Table 3. We can see that without considering the zero-knowledge protocols for shuffle, the computation cost of our protocol is about 27% of that of the protocol in [25] for provers and 12.5% of that for verifiers. Therefore, our protocol should be much faster than the original protocol in [25]. In addition, we would like to note that the communication cost from FS in [10] is around $(10N\|\mathbb{G}\| + 4N\|\mathbb{Z}_q\|)$ bits. This means that the communication cost of our whole protocol outperforms that of the protocol in [10] even when the communication cost of FS in [10] is not considered.

Acknowledgments. We thank the reviewers for their detailed and helpful comments. Y. Liu and Q. Wang partially supported by the Shenzhen fundamental research programs under Grant no. 20200925154814002 and Guangdong Provincial Key Laboratory (Grant No. 2020B121201001). Y. Liu and S.-M. Yiu were also partially supported by ITF, Hong Kong (ITS/173/18FP).

References

1. Abadi, M., Feigenbaum, J.: Secure circuit evaluation. J. Cryptol. **2**(1), 1–12 (1990)
2. Alhassan, M.Y., Günther, D., Kiss, Á., Schneider, T.: Efficient and scalable universal circuits. J. Cryptol. **33**(3), 1216–1271 (2020)
3. Bayer, S., Groth, J.: Efficient zero-knowledge argument for correctness of a shuffle. In: Pointcheval, D., Johansson, T. (eds.) EUROCRYPT 2012. LNCS, vol. 7237, pp. 263–280. Springer, Heidelberg (2012). https://doi.org/10.1007/978-3-642-29011-4_17
4. Bicer, O., Bingol, M.A., Kiraz, M.S., Levi, A.: Highly efficient and re-executable private function evaluation with linear complexity. IEEE Trans. Depend. Secure Comput., 1 (2020)
5. Bingöl, M.A., Biçer, O., Kiraz, M.S., Levi, A.: An efficient 2-party private function evaluation protocol based on half gates. Comput. J. **62**(4), 598–613 (2019)

6. Bootle, J., Cerulli, A., Chaidos, P., Groth, J., Petit, C.: Efficient zero-knowledge arguments for arithmetic circuits in the discrete log setting. In: Fischlin, M., Coron, J.-S. (eds.) EUROCRYPT 2016. LNCS, vol. 9666, pp. 327–357. Springer, Heidelberg (2016). https://doi.org/10.1007/978-3-662-49896-5_12

7. Chaum, D., Pedersen, T.P.: Wallet databases with observers. In: Brickell, E.F. (ed.) CRYPTO 1992. LNCS, vol. 740, pp. 89–105. Springer, Heidelberg (1993). https://doi.org/10.1007/3-540-48071-4_7

8. Cramer, R., Damgård, I., Schoenmakers, B.: Proofs of partial knowledge and simplified design of witness hiding protocols. In: Desmedt, Y.G. (ed.) CRYPTO 1994. LNCS, vol. 839, pp. 174–187. Springer, Heidelberg (1994). https://doi.org/10.1007/3-540-48658-5_19

9. Fiat, A., Shamir, A.: How to prove yourself: practical solutions to identification and signature problems. In: Odlyzko, A.M. (ed.) CRYPTO 1986. LNCS, vol. 263, pp. 186–194. Springer, Heidelberg (1987). https://doi.org/10.1007/3-540-47721-7_12

10. Furukawa, J., Sako, K.: An efficient scheme for proving a shuffle. In: Kilian, J. (ed.) CRYPTO 2001. LNCS, vol. 2139, pp. 368–387. Springer, Heidelberg (2001). https://doi.org/10.1007/3-540-44647-8_22

11. ElGamal, T.: A public key cryptosystem and a signature scheme based on discrete logarithms. In: Blakley, G.R., Chaum, D. (eds.) CRYPTO 1984. LNCS, vol. 196, pp. 10–18. Springer, Heidelberg (1985). https://doi.org/10.1007/3-540-39568-7_2

12. Goldreich, O.: The Foundations of Cryptography - Volume 1: Basic Techniques. Cambridge University Press, Cambridge (2001)

13. Günther, D., Kiss, Á., Schneider, T.: More efficient universal circuit constructions. In: Takagi, T., Peyrin, T. (eds.) ASIACRYPT 2017. LNCS, vol. 10625, pp. 443–470. Springer, Cham (2017). https://doi.org/10.1007/978-3-319-70697-9_16

14. Hazay, C., Lindell, Y.: Efficient Secure Two-Party Protocols - Techniques and Constructions. Information Security and Cryptography, Springer, Heidelberg (2010). https://doi.org/10.1007/978-3-642-14303-8

15. Holz, M., Kiss, Á., Rathee, D., Schneider, T.: Linear-complexity private function evaluation is practical. In: Chen, L., Li, N., Liang, K., Schneider, S. (eds.) ESORICS 2020. LNCS, vol. 12309, pp. 401–420. Springer, Cham (2020). https://doi.org/10.1007/978-3-030-59013-0_20

16. Katz, J., Lindell, Y.: Introduction to Modern Cryptography, 2nd edn. CRC Press, Boca Raton (2014)

17. Katz, J., Malka, L.: Constant-round private function evaluation with linear complexity. In: Lee, D.H., Wang, X. (eds.) ASIACRYPT 2011. LNCS, vol. 7073, pp. 556–571. Springer, Heidelberg (2011). https://doi.org/10.1007/978-3-642-25385-0_30

18. Kiss, Á., Schneider, T.: Valiant's universal circuit is practical. In: Fischlin, M., Coron, J.-S. (eds.) EUROCRYPT 2016. LNCS, vol. 9665, pp. 699–728. Springer, Heidelberg (2016). https://doi.org/10.1007/978-3-662-49890-3_27

19. Kolesnikov, V., Schneider, T.: A practical universal circuit construction and secure evaluation of private functions. In: Tsudik, G. (ed.) FC 2008. LNCS, vol. 5143, pp. 83–97. Springer, Heidelberg (2008). https://doi.org/10.1007/978-3-540-85230-8_7

20. Laud, P., Willemson, J.: Composable oblivious extended permutations. In: Cuppens, F., Garcia-Alfaro, J., Zincir Heywood, N., Fong, P.W.L. (eds.) FPS 2014. LNCS, vol. 8930, pp. 294–310. Springer, Cham (2015). https://doi.org/10.1007/978-3-319-17040-4_19

21. Lindell, Y.: Parallel coin-tossing and constant-round secure two-party computation. J. Cryptol. 16(3), 143–184 (2003)

22. Lipmaa, H., Mohassel, P., Sadeghian, S.S.: Valiant's universal circuit: improvements, implementation, and applications. IACR Cryptol. ePrint Arch. **2016**, 17 (2016). http://eprint.iacr.org/2016/017

23. Liu, H., Yu, Y., Zhao, S., Zhang, J., Liu, W.: Pushing the limits of valiant's universal circuits: Simpler, tighter and more compact. IACR Cryptol. ePrint Arch. **2020**, 161 (2020). https://eprint.iacr.org/2020/161

24. Mohassel, P., Sadeghian, S.: How to hide circuits in MPC an efficient framework for private function evaluation. In: Johansson, T., Nguyen, P.Q. (eds.) EUROCRYPT 2013. LNCS, vol. 7881, pp. 557–574. Springer, Heidelberg (2013). https://doi.org/10.1007/978-3-642-38348-9_33

25. Mohassel, P., Sadeghian, S., Smart, N.P.: Actively secure private function evaluation. In: Sarkar, P., Iwata, T. (eds.) ASIACRYPT 2014. LNCS, vol. 8874, pp. 486–505. Springer, Heidelberg (2014). https://doi.org/10.1007/978-3-662-45608-8_26

26. Valiant, L.G.: Universal circuits (preliminary report). In: Chandra, A.K., Wotschke, D., Friedman, E.P., Harrison, M.A. (eds.) Proceedings of the 8th Annual ACM Symposium on Theory of Computing, Hershey, Pennsylvania, USA, 3–5 May 1976, pp. 196–203. ACM (1976)

27. Yao, A.C.: Protocols for secure computations (extended abstract). In: 23rd Annual Symposium on Foundations of Computer Science, Chicago, Illinois, USA, 3–5 November 1982, pp. 160–164. IEEE Computer Society (1982)

28. Zhao, S., Yu, Yu., Zhang, J., Liu, H.: Valiant's universal circuits revisited: an overall improvement and a lower bound. In: Galbraith, S.D., Moriai, S. (eds.) ASIACRYPT 2019. LNCS, vol. 11921, pp. 401–425. Springer, Cham (2019). https://doi.org/10.1007/978-3-030-34578-5_15

Mathematical Foundations

Isomorphism and Equivalence of Galois Nonlinear Feedback Shift Registers

Wenhui Kong[1,2], Jianghua Zhong[1(✉)], and Dongdai Lin[1]

[1] State Key Laboratory of Information Security, Institute of Information Engineering, Chinese Academy of Sciences, Beijing 100093, China
`zhongjianghua@iie.ac.cn`
[2] School of Cyber Security, University of Chinese Academy of Science, Beijing 100049, China

Abstract. Nonlinear feedback shift registers (NFSRs) have been used in many recent stream ciphers. They are generally classified as Fibonacci NFSRs and Galois NFSRs in terms of their implementation configurations. Two NFSRs are said to be isomorphic if their state diagrams are isomorphic, and two NFSRs are equivalent if their sets of output sequences are equal. Equivalent NFSRs must be isomorphic NFSRs, but not the vice versa. Previous work has been done on the isomorphism and equivalence of Fibonacci NFSRs. This paper continues this research for Galois NFSRs. It first gives some characterizations for several kinds of isomorphic Galois NFSRs, which improves and generalizes the previous corresponding results for Fibonacci NFSRs. It then presents some characterizations for two kinds of equivalent Galois NFSRs, helpful to the design of NFSR-based stream ciphers.

Keywords: Nonlinear feedback shift register · Boolean function · Stream cipher · Isomorphism · Equivalence.

1 Introduction

Nonlinear feedback shift registers (NFSRs) have been used as the main building blocks in many stream ciphers, such as the finalists Grain [1] and Trivium [2] in the eSTREAM project. An NFSR can be generally implemented in Fibonacci or Galois configuration. In Fibonacci configuration, the feedback is only applied to the last bit, while in the Galois configuration, the feedback can be applied to every bit. NFSRs in Fibonacci configuration are called Fibonacci NFSRs, and those in Galois configuration are called Galois NFSRs. Compared to Fibonacci NFSRs, Galois NFSRs may shorten propagation time and improve throughput [3]. Notably, the foregoing stream ciphers Grain and Trivium use the Galois NFSRs. Precisely, both are Galois NFSRs with terminal bits, which have the first several bits involved only shifts.

An NFSR has the same mathematical model as a Boolean network, which is a finite automaton evolving through Boolean functions. Boolean networks have

© Springer Nature Switzerland AG 2021
Y. Yu and M. Yung (Eds.): Inscrypt 2021, LNCS 13007, pp. 301–315, 2021.
https://doi.org/10.1007/978-3-030-88323-2_16

been well developed in the community of systems and control [4] via a powerful mathematical tool called semi-tensor product of matrices [5]. As mentioned in literature [6–10], NFSRs can be regarded as Boolean networks, and their cryptographic properties can be facilitated to some extent to analyze by using the semi-tensor product based Boolean network theory.

Two NFSRs are said to be isomorphic if their state diagrams are isomorphic, and two NFSRs are said to be equivalent if their sets of output sequences are equal. Equivalent NFSRs must be isomorphic, but not the vice versa. Some kinds of isomorphic Fibonacci NFSRs were studied and the relation between their feedback functions were revealed [9]. Some isomorphic Galois NFSRs equivalent to Fibonacci ones were found [11].

Some work has been done on the equivalence of NFSRs. A Fibonacci NFSR can be equivalent to "uniform" Galois NFSRs [3], and their initial states were matched in [12]. "Lower triangular" Galois NFSRs [13] and cascade connections of two Fibonacci NFSRs [14] were found equivalent to Fibonacci NFSRs. In addition, some characterizations of the feedback of Galois NFSRs equivalent to Fibonacci ones were revealed [15]. The Galois NFSRs with terminal bits that are equivalent to Fibonacci ones were enumerated [16].

Contribution. This paper considers the isomorphism and equivalence of Galois NFSRs. It first presents several kinds of isomorphic Galois NFSRs and reveals the relation of their feedbacks, which improves and generalizes the corresponding results for Fibonacci NFSRs. It then gives some characterizations of two kinds of Galois NFSRs equivalent to Fibonacci ones from the perspective of feedbacks and numbers, benefiting the design of NFSR-based stream ciphers.

Organization. The paper is organized as follows. Section 2 gives some preliminaries, including some basic concepts and related results on Boolean networks and NFSRs. Our main results on isomorphism and equivalence of Galois NFSRs are presented in Sects. 3 and 4, respectively. The paper concludes in Sect. 5.

2   Preliminaries

In this section, we review some basic concepts and related results on the semi-tensor product of matrices and NFSRs. Before that, we first introduce some notations used throughout the paper.

Notations: $\mathbb{F}_2$ denotes the binary Galois field, and $\mathbb{F}_2^n$ is an n-dimensional vector space over $\mathbb{F}_2$. $\mathbb{N}$ is the set of nonnegative integers. δ_n^i stands for the i-th column of the $n \times n$ identity matrix I_n. The set of all columns of I_n is denoted by Δ_n. Let $\mathcal{L}_{n \times m}$ be the set of all $n \times m$ matrices whose columns belong to the set Δ_n. For a matrix $A = [\delta_n^{i_1} \ \delta_n^{i_2} \ \cdots \ \delta_n^{i_m}] \in \mathcal{L}_{n \times m}$, we simply denote it as $A = \delta_n[i_1 \ i_2 \ \cdots \ i_m]$. The operators $+, -$ and $\times$, respectively, denote the ordinary addition, subtraction and multiplication in the real field. The operations $\oplus$ and $\odot$, respectively, represent the addition and multiplication over $\mathbb{F}_2$.

2.1   Boolean Network

Definition 1 ([17]). *For an $n \times m$ matrix $A = (a_{ij})$ and a $p \times q$ matrix B, their Kronecker product is defined as*

$$A \otimes B = \begin{bmatrix} a_{11}B & a_{12}B & \cdots & a_{1m}B \\ a_{21}B & a_{22}B & \cdots & a_{2m}B \\ \vdots & \vdots & & \vdots \\ a_{n1}B & a_{n2}B & \cdots & a_{nm}B \end{bmatrix}.$$

Definition 2 ([5]). *For an $n \times m$ A and a $p \times q$ matrix B, let α be the least common multiple of m and p. The semi-tensor product of A and B is defined as*

$$A \ltimes B = (A \otimes I_{\frac{\alpha}{m}})(B \otimes I_{\frac{\alpha}{p}}). \tag{1}$$

We can easily observe that if $m = p$ in Definition 2 , then the semi-tensor product is degenerated into the conventional matrix product.

An n-variable Boolean function f is a function from $\mathbb{F}_2^n$ to $\mathbb{F}_2$. The decimal number of a binary $(i_1, i_2, \ldots, i_n)$ is $i = i_1 2^{n-1} + i_2 2^{n-2} + \cdots + i_n$. We simply write $f(i_1, i_2, \ldots, i_n)$ as $f(i)$. $[f(2^n - 1), f(2^n - 2), \cdots, f(0)]$ is called the *truth table* of f, arranged in the reverse alphabet order. The matrix

$$F = \begin{bmatrix} f(2^n - 1) & f(2^n - 2) & \cdots & f(0) \\ 1 - f(2^n - 1) & 1 - f(2^n - 2) & \cdots & 1 - f(0) \end{bmatrix} \tag{2}$$

is named the *structure matrix* of f [4,18]. The function $\mathbf{f} = [f_1 \ f_2 \ \cdots \ f_n]^T$ is called a *vectorial function* if all f_is are Boolean functions.

The Hamming weight of a binary string α of finite length is the number of ones in α, denoted by $wt(\alpha)$. The Hamming weight of a Boolean function f, denoted by $wt(f)$, is the Hamming weight of its truth table. The Hamming weight is one of the most basic properties of a Boolean function, and is a crucial criterion in cryptography [19]. If an n-variable Boolean function f satisfies $wt(f) = 2^{n-1}$, then the Boolean function f is said to be balanced. An n-variable Boolean function f is said to be linear with respect to the variable X_i if $f(X_1, X_2, \cdots, X_n) = X_i \oplus \tilde{f}(X_1, X_2, \cdots, X_{i-1}, X_{i+1}, \cdots, X_n)$ for some i satisfying $1 \leq i \leq n$. If a Boolean function f is linear with respect to some variable, then it is balanced.

A Boolean network with n nodes and m outputs can be described in general as the nonlinear system:

$$\begin{cases} \mathbf{X}(t + 1) = \mathbf{g}(\mathbf{X}(t)), \\ \mathbf{Y}(t) = \mathbf{h}(\mathbf{X}(t)), t \in \mathbb{N}, \end{cases} \tag{3}$$

where $\mathbf{X} = [X_1 \ X_2 \ \ldots \ X_n]^T \in \mathbb{F}_2^n$ is the state, and the vectorial function $\mathbf{g} = [g_1 \ g_2 \ \cdots \ g_n]^T : \mathbb{F}_2^n \to \mathbb{F}_2^n$ is the state transition function, and $\mathbf{h} = [h_1 \ h_2 \ \ldots \ h_n]^T : \mathbb{F}_2^n \to \mathbb{F}_2^m$ is the output function.

Lemma 1 ([4]). *For any state* $\mathbf{X} = [X_1 \ X_2 \ \cdots \ X_n]^T \in \mathbb{F}_2^n$, *let* $\mathbf{x} = [X_1 \ X_1 \oplus 1]^T \ltimes [X_2 \ X_2 \oplus 1]^T \ltimes \cdots \ltimes [X_n \ X_n \oplus 1]^T$. *Then* $\mathbf{x} = \delta_{2^n}^j \in \Delta_{2^n}$ *with* $j = 2^n - (2^{n-1}X_1 + 2^{n-2}X_2 + \cdots + X_n)$.

From Lemma 1, we can easily see that the state $\mathbf{X} = [X_1 \ X_2 \ \cdots \ X_n]^T \in \mathbb{F}_2^n$ and the state $\mathbf{x} = \delta_{2^n}^j \in \Delta_{2^n}$ with $j = 2^n - (2^{n-1}X_1 + 2^{n-2}X_2 + \cdots + X_n)$ are one-to-one correspondence.

Boolean network (3) can be equivalently expressed as the linear system (4):

$$\begin{cases} \mathbf{x}(t+1) = L\mathbf{x}(t), \\ \mathbf{y}(t) = H\mathbf{x}(t), \ t \in \mathbb{N}, \end{cases} \tag{4}$$

with the state $\mathbf{x} \in \Delta_{2^n}$, the output $\mathbf{y} \in \Delta_{2^m}$, the state transition matrix $L \in \mathcal{L}_{2^n \times 2^n}$, and the output matrix $H \in \mathcal{L}_{2^m \times 2^n}$. The j-th column of L satisfies

$$Col_j(L) = Col_j(G_1) \otimes Col_j(G_2) \otimes \cdots \otimes Col_j(G_n), \ j = 1, 2, \ldots, 2^n, \tag{5}$$

with G_i being the the structure matrix of the i-th component g_i of the vectorial function $\mathbf{g}$ in (3) for any $i \in \{1, 2, \ldots, n\}$. The j-th column of H can be computed in a similar way.

2.2 Nonlinear Feedback Shift Register

Figure 1 shows the diagram of an n-stage Galois NFSR, in which each small square represents a binary storage device, also called *bit*. The content of bit i is labelled as X_i. All X_is together form the Galois NFSR's state $[X_1 \ X_2 \ \ldots \ X_n]^T$. Every bit i has its own feedback function f_i. They all form the Galois NFSR's feedback $\mathbf{f} = [f_1 \ f_2 \ \cdots \ f_n]^T$. At each periodic interval determined by a master clock, the content X_i is updated by the value of f_i taking at the previous contents of all X_is. The n-stage Galois NFSR can be described by the nonlinear system:

$$\begin{cases} X_1(t+1) = f_1(X_1(t), X_2(t), \ldots, X_n(t)), \\ X_2(t+1) = f_2(X_1(t), X_2(t), \ldots, X_n(t)), \\ \quad \vdots \\ X_n(t+1) = f_n(X_1(t), X_2(t), \ldots, X_n(t)), \end{cases} \tag{6}$$

where $t \in \mathbb{N}$ represents time instant.

If a Galois NFSR's feedback $\mathbf{f} = [f_1 \ f_2 \ \cdots \ f_n]^T$ satisfies $f_i(X_1, X_2, \cdots, X_n) = X_{i+1}$ for all $i = 1, 2, \cdots, n-1$, then the n-stage Galois NFSR becomes an n-stage Fibonacci NFSR. Figure 2 describes an n-stage Fibonacci NFSR, which is nonsingular if and only if its feedback function f is nonsingular, that is, $f = X_1 \oplus \tilde{f}(X_2, X_3, \cdots, X_n)$ [20].

The state diagram of an n-stage NFSR is a directed graph consisting of 2^n vertices and 2^n edges, in which each vertex represents a state of the NFSR, and each edge represents a transition between two states. Precisely, if state $\mathbf{X}$ is updated to state $\mathbf{Y}$, then there is an edge from state $\mathbf{X}$ to state $\mathbf{Y}$. In this case,

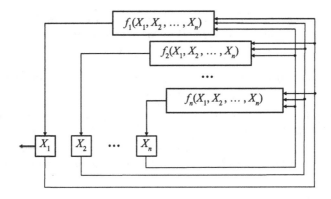

Fig. 1. An n-stage Galois NFSR.

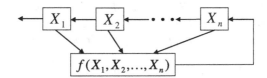

Fig. 2. An n-stage Fibonacci NFSR.

$\mathbf{X}$ is a *predecessor* of $\mathbf{Y}$, and $\mathbf{Y}$ is the *successor* of $\mathbf{X}$. Consecutive distinct states $\mathbf{X}_1, \mathbf{X}_2, \ldots, \mathbf{X}_p$ and their edges between them form a *cycle* of length p if $\mathbf{X}_1$ is the successor of $\mathbf{X}_p$.

For any $X \in \mathbb{F}_2$, denote $\bar{X} = X \oplus 1$. Let $G_i = (V_i, A_i)$ with $i \in \{1, 2\}$, be the state diagram of an n-stage NFSRi, where V_i is the set of states, while A_i is the set of edges. G_1 and G_2 are said to be *isomorphic* if there exists a bijective mapping $\varphi : V_1 \to V_2$ such that for any edge $E_1 \in A_1$ from state $\mathbf{X}$ to state $\mathbf{Y}$, there exists an edge $E_2 \in A_2$ from $\varphi(\mathbf{X})$ to $\varphi(\mathbf{Y})$. In this case, NFSR1 and NFSR2 are said to be *isomorphic NFSRs*. Furthermore, if the bijective mapping φ satisfies $\varphi = D : [X_1 \ X_2 \ \ldots \ X_n]^T \mapsto [\bar{X}_1 \ \bar{X}_2 \ \ldots \ \bar{X}_n]^T$, then G_1 and G_2 are said to be *dual isomorphic*, denoted by $G_2 = DG_1$; if φ satisfies $\varphi = R : [X_1 \ X_2 \ \ldots \ X_n]^T \mapsto [X_n \ X_{n-1} \ \ldots \ X_1]^T$, then G_1 and G_2 are said to be *anti-isomorphic*, denoted by $G_2 = RG_1$; if φ satisfies $\varphi = DR : [X_1 \ X_2 \ \ldots \ X_n]^T \mapsto [\bar{X}_n \ \bar{X}_{n-1} \ \ldots \ \bar{X}_1]^T$, then G_1 and G_2 are said to be *dual anti-isomorphic*, denoted by $G_2 = DRG_1$.

Lemma 2 ([9]). *For an n-stage Fibonacci NFSR1 with feedback function f,*

1. *if the state diagram of an n-stage Fibonacci NFSR2 is dual isomorphic to that of the Fibonacci NFSR1, then the feedback function of the Fibonacci NFSR2 is D_f satisfying $D_f(X_1, X_2, \ldots, X_n) = \overline{f(\bar{X}_1, \bar{X}_2, \ldots, \bar{X}_n)}$;*

2. *if the state diagram of an n-stage Fibonacci NFSR2 is anti-isomorphic to that of the Fibonacci NFSR1, then the feedback function of the Fibonacci NFSR2 is R_f satisfying $R_f(X_1, X_2, \ldots, X_n) = f(X_n, X_{n-1}, \ldots, X_1)$;*

3. *if the state diagram of an n-stage Fibonacci NFSR2 is dual anti-isomorphic to that of the Fibonacci NFSR1, then the feedback function of the Fibonacci NFSR2 is DR_f satisfying $DR_f(X_1, X_2, \ldots, X_n) = \bar{f}(\bar{X}_n, \bar{X}_{n-1}, \ldots, \bar{X}_1)$.*

Lemma 3 ([21]). *If an n-stage Fibonacci NFSR and an n-stage Galois NFSR are equivalent, then their state diagrams are isomorphic.*

Definition 3 ([16]). *For a positive integer τ satisfying $1 \leq \tau \leq n-1$, an n-stage Galois NFSR with feedback $\mathbf{f} = [f_1 \ f_2 \ \cdots \ f_n]^T$ is said to have the terminal bit τ if $f_i(\mathbf{X}) = X_{i+1}$ for all $i = 1, 2, \ldots, \tau$ and for all $\mathbf{X} = [X_1 \ X_2 \ \cdots \ X_n]^T \in \mathbb{F}_2^n$. Such an NFSR with terminal bit τ is called an n-stage τ-terminal-bit Galois NFSR.*

Lemma 4 ([16]). *Suppose τ to be a positive integer satisfying $1 \leq \tau \leq n-1$. An n-stage τ-terminal-bit Galois NFSR represented by a nonlinear system $\mathbf{X}(t+1) = \mathbf{f}(\mathbf{X}(t))$ with state $\mathbf{X} \in \mathbb{F}_2^n$ is equivalent to an n-stage Fibonacci NFSR represented by a nonlinear system $\mathbf{Y}(t+1) = \mathbf{h}(\mathbf{Y}(t))$ with state $\mathbf{Y} \in \mathbb{F}_2^n$, if and only if there exists a bijective mapping $\varphi : \mathbf{X} \mapsto \mathbf{Y}$ such that $\varphi(\mathbf{f}(\mathbf{X})) = \mathbf{h}(\varphi(\mathbf{X}))$ and*

$$diag(\underbrace{1\ 1\cdots 1}_{\tau+1}\ 0\cdots 0)\varphi(\mathbf{X}) = diag(\underbrace{1\ 1\cdots 1}_{\tau+1}\ 0\cdots 0)\mathbf{X} \qquad (7)$$

for all $\mathbf{X} \in \mathbb{F}_2^n$, where $diag(\cdot)$ denotes a diagonal matrix with diagonal elements of 1 and 0.

Lemma 5 ([15]). *An n-stage Galois NFSR with feedback $\mathbf{f} = [f_1 \ f_2 \cdots f_n]^T$ can be equivalently expressed as a linear system:*

$$\mathbf{x}(t+1) = L_g \mathbf{x}(t), t \in \mathbb{N},$$

where $\mathbf{x} \in \Delta_{2^n}$ is the state, and $L_g = \delta_{2^n}[\xi_1 \ \xi_2 \ \cdots \ \xi_{2^n}] \in \mathcal{L}_{2^n \times 2^n}$ is the state transition matrix, satisfying

$$\xi_i = 2^n - 2^{n-1}f_1(2^n - i) - 2^{n-2}f_2(2^n - i) - \cdots - 2f_{n-1}(2^n - i) - f_n(2^n - i),$$
$$j = 1, 2, \cdots, 2^n.$$

Lemma 6 ([10]). *An n-stage Fibonacci NFSR with a feedback function f, can be expressed as the following linear system:*

$$\mathbf{x}(t+1) = L\mathbf{x}(t), \ t \in \mathbb{N},$$

where $\mathbf{x} \in \Delta_{2^n}$ is the state, $L \in \mathcal{L}_{2^n \times 2^n}$ is the state transition matrix, satisfying

$$L = \delta_{2^n}[\eta_1 \ \cdots \ \eta_{2^{n-1}} \ \eta_{2^{n-1}+1} \ \cdots \ \eta_{2^n}]$$

with

$$\begin{cases} \eta_i = 2i - s_i, \ i = 1, 2, \cdots, 2^{n-1}, \\ \eta_{2^{n-1}+i} = 2i - s_{2^{n-1}+i}, \end{cases}$$

and $[s_1, s_2, \cdots, s_{2^n}]$ being the truth table of f, arranged in the reverse alphabet order.

3   Isomorphism of Galois NFSRs

In this section, we will reveal some characterizations of several kinds of isomorphic Galois NFSRs.

Theorem 1. *For an n-stage Galois NFSR1 with feedback* $\mathbf{f} = [f_1 \; f_2 \; \cdots \; f_n]^T$,

1. *the state diagram of an n-stage Galois NFSR2 is dual isomorphic to that of Galois NFSR1, if and only if the feedback* $D_{\mathbf{f}}$ *of the Galois NFSR2 satisfies*

$$D_{\mathbf{f}} = [\overline{f_1(\bar{X}_1, \bar{X}_2, \cdots, \bar{X}_n)} \quad \overline{f_2(\bar{X}_1, \bar{X}_2, \cdots, \bar{X}_n)} \quad \cdots \quad \overline{f_n(\bar{X}_1, \bar{X}_2, \cdots, \bar{X}_n)}]^T;$$
(8)

2. *the state diagram of an n-stage Galois NFSR3 is anti-isomorphic to that of Galois NFSR1, if and only if the feedback* $R_{\mathbf{f}}$ *of the Galois NFSR3 satisfies*

$$R_{\mathbf{f}} = [f_n(X_n, X_{n-1}, \ldots, X_1) \quad f_{n-1}(X_n, X_{n-1}, \ldots, X_1) \quad \cdots \quad f_1(X_n, X_{n-1}, \ldots, X_1)]^T.$$
(9)

3. *the state diagram of an n-stage Galois NFSR4 is dual anti-isomorphic to that of Galois NFSR1, if and only if the feedback* $DR_{\mathbf{f}}$ *of the Galois NFSR4 satisfies*

$$DR_{\mathbf{f}} = [\overline{f_n(\bar{X}_n, \bar{X}_{n-1}, \ldots, \bar{X}_1)} \quad \overline{f_{n-1}(\bar{X}_n, \bar{X}_{n-1}, \ldots, \bar{X}_1)} \quad \cdots \quad \overline{f_1(\bar{X}_n, \bar{X}_{n-1}, \ldots, \bar{X}_1)}]^T.$$
(10)

Proof. Let $[a_0 \quad a_1 \quad \ldots \quad a_n]^T$ be a vertex in the state diagram of Galois NFSR1. Then, there is an edge from $[a_0 \quad a_1 \quad \ldots \quad a_n]^T$ to $[f_1(a_1, a_2, \ldots, a_n) \quad f_2(a_1, a_2, \ldots, a_n) \quad \ldots \quad f_n(a_1, a_2, \ldots, a_n)]^T$ in the state diagram of Galois NFSR1.

Case 1: If the state diagram of the Galois NFSR2 is dual isomorphic to that of the Galois NFSR1, then there is an edge from $[\bar{a}_1 \quad \bar{a}_2 \quad \ldots \quad \bar{a}_n]^T$ to $[\overline{f_1(a_1, a_2, \ldots, a_n)} \quad \overline{f_2(a_1, a_2, \ldots, a_n)} \quad \ldots \quad \overline{f_n(a_1, a_2, \ldots, a_n)}]^T$ in the state diagram of the Galois NFSR2. Let $b_i = \bar{a}_i$ for all $i = 1, 2, \cdots, n$. Then, there is an edge from $[b_1 \quad b_2 \quad \ldots \quad b_n]^T$ to $[\overline{f_1(\bar{b}_1, \bar{b}_2, \cdots, \bar{b}_n)} \quad \overline{f_2(\bar{b}_1, \bar{b}_2, \cdots, \bar{b}_n)} \quad \cdots \quad \overline{f_n(\bar{b}_1, \bar{b}_2, \cdots, \bar{b}_n)}]^T$ in the state diagram of Galois NFSR2. Thus, the feedback $D_{\mathbf{f}}$ of Galois NFSR2 satisfies Eq. (8).

Conversely, if the feedback $D_{\mathbf{f}}$ of Galois NFSR2 satisfies Eq. (8), then there is an edge from $[b_1 \quad b_2 \quad \ldots \quad b_n]^T$ to $[\overline{f_1(\bar{b}_1, \bar{b}_2, \cdots, \bar{b}_n)} \quad \overline{f_2(\bar{b}_1, \bar{b}_2, \cdots, \bar{b}_n)} \quad \cdots \quad \overline{f_n(\bar{b}_1, \bar{b}_2, \cdots, \bar{b}_n)}]^T$ in the state diagram of Galois NFSR2. Let $a_i = \bar{b}_i$ for all $i = 1, 2, \cdots, n$. Then there is an edge from $[\bar{a}_1 \quad \bar{a}_2 \quad \ldots \quad \bar{a}_n]^T$ to $[\overline{f_1(a_1, a_2, \ldots, a_n)} \quad \overline{f_2(a_1, a_2, \ldots, a_n)} \quad \ldots \quad \overline{f_n(a_1, a_2, \ldots, a_n)}]^T$ in the state diagram of Galois NFSR2. Therefore, the state diagram of Galois NFSR2 is dual isomorphic to that of Galois NFSR1.

Case 2: If the state diagram of Galois NFSR3 is anti-isomorphic to that of Galois NFSR1, then there is an edge from $[a_n \quad a_{n-1} \quad \ldots \quad a_1]^T$ to $[f_n(a_1, a_2, \ldots, a_n) \quad f_{n-1}(a_1, a_2, \ldots, a_n) \quad \cdots \quad f_1(a_1, a_2, \ldots, a_n)]^T$ in the state diagram of the Galois NFSR3. Let $b_i = a_{n-i+1}$ for all

$i = 1, 2, \ldots, n$. Then, there is an edge from $[b_1 \quad b_2 \quad \ldots \quad b_n]^T$ to $[f_n(b_n, b_{n-1}, \ldots, b_1) \quad f_{n-1}(b_n, b_{n-1}, \ldots, b_1) \quad \ldots \quad f_1(b_n, b_{n-1}, \ldots, b_1)]^T$ in the state diagram of the Galois NFSR3. Thereby, the feedback R_f of Galois NFSR3 satisfies Eq. (9).

Conversely, if the feedback R_f of Galois NFSR3 satisfies Eq. (9), then there is edge from $[b_1 \quad b_2 \quad \ldots \quad b_n]^T$ to $[f_n(b_n, b_{n-1}, \ldots, b_1) \quad f_{n-1}(b_n, b_{n-1}, \ldots, b_1)$ $\ldots \quad f_1(b_n, b_{n-1}, \ldots, b_1)]^T$ in the state diagram of the Galois NFSR3. Let $a_i = b_{n-i+1}$ for all $i = 1, 2, \ldots, n$. Thus, there is an edge from $[a_n \quad a_{n-1} \quad \ldots \quad a_1]^T$ to $[f_n(a_1, a_2, \ldots, a_n) \quad f_{n-1}(a_1, a_2, \ldots, a_n) \quad \cdots \quad f_1(a_1, a_2, \ldots, a_n)]^T$ in the state diagram of Galois NFSR3. Therefore, the state diagram of Galois NFSR3 is anti-isomorphic to that of Galois NFSR1.

Case 3: From Cases 1 and 2, we can easily follow Case 3.   □

Theorem 1 generalizes the results of Lemma 2 for Fibonacci NFSRs to Galois ones, and improves the necessary condition to the necessary and sufficient condition, using the proof method similar to that in [9].

Theorem 2. *For an n-stage nonsingular Galois NFSR1 with feedback* $\mathbf{f}$*, the state diagram of an n-stage nonsingular Galois NFSR2 has a direction opposite to that of the Galois NFSR1, if and only if Galois NFSR2 has the feedback* $\mathbf{f}^{-1}$*.*

Proof. Since the Galois NFSR1 is nonsingular, its feedback $\mathbf{f}$ is invertible, and each state has unique predecessor and unique successor.

If the state diagram of an n-stage nonsingular Galois NFSR2 has a direction opposite to that of NFSR1, then for any state $\mathbf{X}$, its successor $\mathbf{Y}$ (i.e., $\mathbf{Y} = \mathbf{f}(\mathbf{X})$) in the state diagram of NFSR1 becomes its predecessor (i.e., $\mathbf{X} = \mathbf{f}^{-1}(\mathbf{Y})$) in the sate diagram of NFSR2. Due to the arbitrariness of state $\mathbf{X}$, we can infer that the Galois NFSR2 has the feedback $\mathbf{f}^{-1}$.

Conversely, if Galois NFSR2 has the feedback $\mathbf{f}^{-1}$, then the for any state $\mathbf{Y}$, its successor $\mathbf{X}$ (i.e., $\mathbf{X} = \mathbf{f}^{-1}(\mathbf{Y})$) in the state diagram of NFSR2 becomes its predecessor (i.e., $\mathbf{Y} = \mathbf{f}(\mathbf{X})$)) in the sate diagram of NFSR1. Due the arbitrariness of state $\mathbf{Y}$, we can conclude that the state diagram of Galois NFSR2 has a direction opposite to that of NFSR1.   □

Corollary 1. *For an n-stage nonsingular Fibonacci NFSR1 with feedback function* $f = X_1 + \tilde{f}(X_2, X_3, \cdots, X_n)$*, the state diagram of an n-stage Galois NFSR2 has a direction opposite to that of NFSR1 if and only if the Galois NFSR2 has the feedback* $\mathbf{g} = [g_1 \quad g_2 \quad \ldots \quad g_n]^T$ *satisfying*

$$\begin{cases} g_1 = X_n + \tilde{f}(X_1, X_2, \cdots, X_{n-1}), \\ g_2 = X_1, \\ g_3 = X_2, \\ \quad \vdots \\ g_n = X_{n-1}. \end{cases} \tag{11}$$

Proof. As a particular nonsingular Galois NFSR, the nonsingular Fibonacci NFSR1 with feedback function $f = X_1 + \tilde{f}(X_2, X_3, \cdots, X_n)$ has the feedback $\mathbf{f} = [f_1 \ f_2 \ \cdots \ f_n]^T$ satisfying

$$\begin{cases} f_1 = X_2, \\ f_2 = X_3, \\ \vdots \\ f_{n-1} = X_n, \\ f_n = X_1 \oplus f(X_2, X_3, \ldots, X_n). \end{cases}$$

By direct computation, we can deduce that $\mathbf{f}^{-1} = \mathbf{g}$ satisfying Eq. (11). Then the result follows from Theorem 2. $\square$

Remark 1. The n-stage Galois NFSR2 with feedback $\mathbf{g} = [g_1 \ g_2 \ \cdots \ g_n]^T$ satisfying (11) is actually an n-stage Fibonacci NFSR with feedback function $R_f(X_1, X_2, \ldots, X_n) = f(X_n, X_{n-1}, \ldots, X_1)$, where f is the feedback function of the Fibonacci NFSR in Corollary 1. It implies that two n-stage anti-isomorphic Fibonacci NFSRs, actually, have their state diagrams with directions opposite to each other.

4   Equivalence of Galois NFSRs

In this section, we give some characterizations for two kinds of equivalent Galois NFSRs.

Theorem 3. *If an n-stage τ-terminal-bit Galois NFSR with feedback $\mathbf{f} = [f_1 \ f_2 \ \cdots \ f_n]^T$ is equivalent to an n-stage Fibonacci NFSR, then its feedback function $f_{\tau+1}$ satisfies*

$$wt\left([f_{\tau+1}(2^n - 1), f_{\tau+1}(2^n - 2), \cdots, f_{\tau+1}(2^n - 2^{n-\tau-1})]\right)$$
$$= wt\left([f_{\tau+1}(2^n - 2^{n-\tau-1} - 1), f_{\tau+1}(2^n - 2^{n-\tau-1} - 2), \cdots, f_{\tau+1}(2^n - 2^{n-\tau})]\right)$$
$$= \cdots$$
$$= wt\left([f_{\tau+1}(2^{n-\tau-1} - 1), f_{\tau+1}(2^{n-\tau-1} - 2), \cdots, f_i(0)]\right) = 2^{n-\tau-2}.$$

Proof. We use the semi-tensor product based Boolean network theory. Then, the Galois NFSR represented by nonlinear system $\mathbf{X}(t + 1) = \mathbf{f}(\mathbf{X}(t))$ with $\mathbf{X} \in \mathbb{F}_2^n$ has a linear system representation $\mathbf{x}(t + 1) = L_g\mathbf{x}(t)$ with $\mathbf{x} \in \Delta_{2^n}$, and the Fibonacci NFSR represented by nonlinear system $\mathbf{Y}(t+1) = \mathbf{h}(\mathbf{Y}(t))$ with state $\mathbf{Y} \in \mathbb{F}_2^n$ has a linear system representation $\mathbf{y}(t + 1) = L_f\mathbf{y}(t)$ with $\mathbf{y} \in \Delta_{2^n}$.

If the n-stage τ-terminal-bit Galois NFSR is equivalent to an n-stage Fibonacci NFSR, then according to Lemma 4, there exists a bijection $\varphi : \mathbf{X} \mapsto \mathbf{Y}$ such that $\varphi(\mathbf{f}(\mathbf{X})) = \mathbf{h}(\varphi(\mathbf{X}))$ and Eq. (7) holds. It means there is a transformation $\mathbf{y} = P\mathbf{x}$ such that $L_g = P^T L_f P$, and $P = \delta_{2^n}[j_1 \ j_2 \ \cdots \ j_{2^n}]$ satisfies $1 \le j_i \le 2^{n-\tau-1}, 1 + 2^{n-\tau-1} \le j_{2^{n-\tau-1}+i} \le 2^{n-\tau}, \cdots, 1 + 2^n - 2^{n-\tau-1} \le j_{2^n-2^{n-\tau-1}+i} \le 2^n$ for all $i = 1, 2, \cdots, 2^{n-\tau-1}$.

Let $L_f = \delta[\eta_1 \ \eta_2 \ \cdots \ \eta_{2^n}]$ and $L_g = \delta_{2^n}[\xi_1 \ \xi_2 \ \cdots \ \xi_{2^n}]$. Then,

$$L_g = P^T L_f P = P^T \delta_{2^n}[\eta_1 \ \eta_2 \ \cdots \ \eta_{2^n}]\delta_{2^n}[j_1 \ j_2 \ \cdots \ j_{2^n}]$$
$$= (\delta_{2^n}[j_1 \ j_2 \ \cdots \ j_{2^n}])^T \delta[\eta_{j_1} \ \eta_{j_2} \ \cdots \ \eta_{j_{2^n}}],$$

which yields,

$$\delta_{2^n}^{\xi_i} = (\delta[j_1 \ j_2 \ \cdots \ j_{2^n}])^T \delta_{2^n}^{\eta_{j_i}}, i = 1, 2, \cdots, 2^n,$$

that is,

$$[0 \ \cdots \ 0 \ 1 \ 0 \ \cdots \ 0]^T = (\delta_{2^n}[j_1 \ j_2 \ \cdots \ j_{2^n}])^T [0 \ \cdots \ 0 \ 1 \ 0 \ \cdots \ 0]^T .$$
$$\underset{\xi_i-th}{} \qquad\qquad\qquad\qquad\qquad \underset{\eta_{j_i}-th}{}$$

From the above equation, we can see that the column vector $[0 \ \cdots \ 0 \ 1 \ 0 \ \cdots \ 0]^T$
$$\underset{\xi_i-th}{}$$
is just a row permutation of $[0 \ \cdots \ 0 \ 1 \ 0 \ \cdots \ 0]^T$ via the permutation
$$\underset{\eta_{j_i}-th}{}$$
$(j_1 \ j_2 \ \cdots j_{2^n})$. Clearly, if $1 \le j_i \le 2^{n-\tau-1}$, then $1 \le \eta_{j_i} \le 2^{n-\tau-1}$ and thereby $1 \le \xi_i \le 2^{n-\tau-1}$. Similarly, if $1 + k2^{n-\tau-1} \le j_i \le (k+1)2^{n-\tau-1}$, then $1+k2^{n-\tau-1} \le \eta_{j_i} \le (k+1)2^{n-\tau-1}$ and thereby $1+k2^{n-\tau-1} \le \xi_i \le (k+1)2^{n-\tau-1}$ for all $k = 0, 1, 2, \cdots, 2^{\tau+1} - 1$.

According to Lemma 6, we deduce that there are $2^{n-\tau-2}$ η_is satisfying $1 \le \eta_i \le 2^{n-\tau-1}$, and $2^{n-\tau-2}$ η_is satisfying $1 + 2^{n-\tau-1} \le \eta_i \le 2^{n-\tau}$ with $1 \le i \le 2^{n-\tau-1}$. Similarly, there are $2^{n-\tau-2}$ η_is satisfying $1 + k2^{n-\tau-1} \le \eta_i \le (k+1)2^{n-\tau-1}$, $2^{n-\tau-2}$ η_is satisfying $1 + (k+1)2^{n-\tau-1} \le \eta_i \le (k+2)2^{n-\tau-1}$ with $1+k2^{n-\tau-1} \le i \le (k+1)2^{n-\tau-1}$ and $k = 0, 1, 2, \cdots, 2^{\tau+1} - 1$. Hence, there are $2^{n-\tau-2}$ ξ_is satisfying $1+k2^{n-\tau-1} \le \xi_i \le (k+1)2^{n-\tau-1}$, $2^{n-\tau-2}$ ξ_is satisfying $1 + (k+1)2^{n-\tau-1} \le \xi_i \le (k+2)2^{n-\tau-1}$, with $1+k2^{n-\tau-1} \le i \le (k+1)2^{n-\tau-1}$ and $k = 0, 1, 2, \cdots, 2^{\tau+1} - 1$.

From Lemma 5, we know

$$\xi_i = 2^n - 2^{n-1}f_1(2^n - i) - 2^{n-2}f_2(2^n - i) - \cdots - 2f_{n-1}(2^n - i) - f_n(2^n - i)$$

for all $j = 1, 2, \cdots, 2^n$. Clearly, $1 \le \xi_i \le 2^{n-\tau-1}$ yields

$$2^n - 2^{n-\tau-1} \le 2^{n-1}f_1(2^n - i) + 2^{n-2}f_2(2^n - i) + \cdots + f_n(2^n - i) \le 2^n - 1.$$

It means $f_{\tau+1}(2^n - i) = 1$. Similarly, if $1 + 2^{n-\tau-1} \le \xi_i \le 2^{n-\tau}$, then $f_{\tau+1}(2^n - i) = 0$; and if $1+2^{n-\tau} \le \xi_i \le 3 \times 2^{n-\tau-1}$, then $f_{\tau+1}(2^n-i) = 1$. Keeping the same reasoning, we can infer that, if $1 + (2^{\tau+1} - 2)2^{n-\tau-1} \le \xi_i \le (2^{\tau+1} - 1)2^{n-\tau-1}$, then $f_{\tau+1}(2^n - i) = 0$, and if $1 + (2^{\tau+1} - 1)2^{n-\tau-1} \le \xi_i \le 2^n$, then $f_{\tau+1}(2^n - i) = 1$. Therefore, there are $2^{n-\tau-2}$ ones in $[f_{\tau+1}(2^{n-\tau-1} - 1), f_{\tau+1}(2^{n-\tau-1} - 2), \cdots, f_{\tau+1}(0)]$, and in $[f_{\tau+1}(2^{n-\tau} - 1), f_{\tau+1}(2^{n-\tau} - 2), \cdots, f_{\tau+1}(2^{n-\tau-1})]$, till in $[f_{\tau+1}(2^n - 1), f_{\tau+1}(2^n - 2), \cdots, f_{\tau+1}(2^n - 2^{n-\tau-1})]$. $\qquad \square$

Table 1. The truth table of f_3 tables.

X	1111	1110	1101	1100	1011	1010	1001	1000
$f_3(\mathbf{X})$	0	1	1	0	1	0	1	0
X	0111	0110	0101	0100	0011	0010	0001	0000
$f_3(\mathbf{X})$	1	0	1	0	1	0	1	0

Example 1. Consider a 4-stage 2-terminal-bit Galois NFSR with feedback $\mathbf{f} = [f_1 \ f_2 \ f_3 \ f_4]^T$ satisfying

$$\begin{cases} f_1 = X_2, \\ f_2 = X_3, \\ f_3 = X_4 \oplus X_1 X_2 X_3, \\ f_4 = 1 \oplus X_1 \oplus X_2 \oplus X_2 X_3 \oplus X_2 X_4 \oplus X_1 X_2 X_3. \end{cases}$$

This Galois NFSR is equivalent to a 4-stage Fibonacci NFSR with feed back function $f = 1 \oplus X_1 \oplus X_2 \oplus X_2 X_3 \oplus X_2 X_4 \oplus X_2 X_3 X_4$. We can get the truth table of f_3, listed in Table 1.

It satisfies $wt([f_3(15), f_3(14)]) = wt([f_3(13), f_3(12)]) = \cdots = wt([f_3(1), f_3(0)]) = 1$, consistent with the result in Theorem 3.

The following result gives some Boolean functions satisfying the necessary condition of Theorem 3.

Proposition 1. *The Boolean function*

$$f(X_1, X_2, \cdots, X_n) = X_{i+1} \oplus g(X_{i+2}, X_{i+3}, \cdots, X_n) \ \ or$$

$$f(X_1, X_2, \cdots, X_n) = X_{i+1} \oplus u(X_1, X_2, \cdots, X_i, X_{i+2}, \cdots, X_n)$$

satisfies

$$wt([f(2^n - 1), \cdots, f(2^n - 2^{n-i})]) = \cdots = wt([f(2^{n-i} - 1), \cdots, f(0)]) = 2^{n-i-1}.$$

Proof. For the first case of $f(X_1, X_2, \cdots, X_n) = X_{i+1} \oplus g(X_{i+2}, X_{i+3}, \cdots, X_n)$, we note that f is actually not relative to $X_1, X_2, \ldots, X_i$. For this case, we set $Y_j = X_{i+j}$ for all $j = 1, 2, \cdots, n - i$, and set $h = f$. Then, $h(Y_1, Y_2, \cdots, Y_{n-i}) = Y_1 \oplus g(Y_2, Y_3, \cdots, Y_{n-i})$. The function h is, clearly, an $(n - i)$-variable function and is linear with respect to the variable Y_1. Hence, h is balanced, and thereby $wt(h) = 2^{n-i-1}$.

On the other hand, note that $f(2^n - 1), f(2^n - 2), \cdots, f(2^n - 2^{n-i})$ are the possible values of $f(1, 1, \cdots, 1, 1, X_{i+1}, \cdots, X_n)$. Similarly, we can get $f(2^n - 2^{n-i} - 1), f(2^n - 2^{n-i} - 2), \cdots, f(2^n - 2 \times 2^{n-i})$ are the possible values of $f(1, 1, \cdots, 1, 0, X_{i+1}, \cdots, X_n)$. By the same reasoning, we have $f(2^{n-2} - 1), f(2^{n-2} - 2), \cdots, f(0)$ are the possible values of $f(0, 0, \cdots, 0, 0, X_{i+1}, \cdots, X_n)$. Together considering $f(1, 1, \cdots, 1, 1, X_{i+1}, \cdots, X_n) = f(1,$

$1, \cdots, 1, 0, X_{i+1}, \cdots, X_n) = \cdots = f(0, 0, \cdots, 0, 0, X_{i+1}, \cdots, X_n)$, we can infer that the result holds for the first case.

For the second case of $f(X_1, X_2, \ldots, X_n) = X_{i+1} \oplus u(X_1, X_2, \ldots, X_i, X_{i+2}, \ldots, X_n)$, any one of $\{u(1, 1, \cdots, 1, 1, X_{i+2}, \cdots, X_n), u(1, 1, \cdots, 1, 0, X_{i+2}, \cdots, X_n), \cdots, u(0, 0, \cdots, 0, 0, X_{i+2}, \cdots, X_n)\}$ has a function $g(X_{i+2}, X_{i+3}, \cdots, X_n)$ equal to it. Keeping the reasoning similar to the first case, we can prove the result holds for the second case.   □

Let a sequence set $S = \{(s_i)_{i \geq 1} | s_i \in \mathbb{F}_2\}$, and $\bar{S} = \{(\bar{s}_i)_{i \geq 1} | (s_i)_{i \geq 1} \in S\}$. $\bar{S}$ is called the *complementary set* of S.

Proposition 2. *The output sequence set S of an n-stage Fibonacci NFSR is equal to its complementary set $\bar{S}$, if and only if the feedback function f of the Fibonacci NFSR satisfies $f = D_f$.*

Proof. Clearly, an output sequence $(s_i)_{i \geq 1} \in S$ if and only if $(\bar{s}_i)_{i \geq 1} \in \bar{S}$. In an n-stage Fibonacci NFSR, $S_i = [s_i \quad s_{i+1} \quad \cdots \quad s_{i+n-1}]^T$ with $i \geq 1$ is a state of the Fibonacci NFSR. Therefore, $S = \bar{S}$ means that, there is a path $S_1, S_2, \cdots, S_k (k \leq 2^n)$ in a Fibonacci state diagram if and only if there is also a path $\bar{S}_1, \bar{S}_2, \cdots, \bar{S}_k$. The mapping $D : S_r \mapsto \bar{S}_r$ with $1 \leq r \leq k$ is a dual mapping. Therefore, we can get the Fibonacci NFSR's state diagram G satisfies $G = DG$, where DG is a dual graph of G. According to Theorem 1, the result follows.   □

Remark 2. From the security perspective, a Fibonacci NFSR with output sequence set equal to its complementary set should be avoided in the design of NFSR-based stream ciphers, due to the "bad" randomness of output sequences.

Example 2. For a 3-bit Fibonacci NFSR with feedback function $f(X_1, X_2, X_3) = X_1 X_2 \oplus X_2 X_3 \oplus X_1 X_3$, we get its state diagram as:

$$110 \to 101 \to 011 \to 111 \circlearrowleft;$$
$$001 \to 010 \to 100 \to 000 \circlearrowleft.$$

Obviously, the feedback function f of the Fibonacci NFSR satisfies $f = D_f$, and its output sequence set is equal to its complementary set, consistent with the result in Proposition 2.

Corollary 2. *For two n-stage Fibonacci NFSRs with feedback functions f and f' satisfying $f' = f \oplus 1$. If one Fibonacci NFSR satisfies its output sequence set equal to its complementary set, then the other also satisfies this property.*

Proof. Without loss of generality, we assume the Fibonacci NFSR with feedback function f satisfies its output sequence set equal to its complementary set. Then, according to Proposition 2, we know $D_f = f$. Together taking into consideration $f' = f \oplus 1$, we have

$$D_{f'}(X_1, X_2, \cdots, X_n) = \overline{f'(\bar{X}_1, \bar{X}_2, \cdots, \bar{X}_n)} = f(\bar{X}_1, \bar{X}_2, \cdots, \bar{X}_n)$$
$$= D_f(X_1, X_2, \cdots, X_n) \oplus 1 = f(X_1, X_2, \cdots, X_n) \oplus 1 = f'(X_1, X_2, \cdots, X_n).$$

According to Proposition 2 again, we know Corollary 2 holds.   □

Proposition 3. *Suppose an n-stage Fibonacci NFSR represented by a nonlinear system $\mathbf{Y}(t+1) = \mathbf{h}(\mathbf{Y}(t))$ with $\mathbf{Y} \in \mathbb{F}_2^n$ satisfies its output sequences set equal to its the complementary set. An n-stage Galois NFSR represented by a nonlinear system $\mathbf{X}(t+1) = \mathbf{f}(\mathbf{X}(t))$ with $\mathbf{Y} \in \mathbb{F}_2^n$ is equivalent to the n-stage Fibonacci NFSR if and only if there exists a bijective mapping $\varphi : \mathbf{X} \mapsto \mathbf{Y}$ such that $\varphi(\mathbf{f}(\mathbf{X})) = \mathbf{h}(\varphi(\mathbf{X}))$ and $[1 \quad 0 \quad \ldots \quad 0]\varphi(\mathbf{X}) = \mathbf{X}$ or $[1 \quad 0 \quad \ldots \quad 0]\varphi(\mathbf{X}) = \mathbf{X} \oplus 1$ for all $\mathbf{X} \in \mathbb{F}_2^n$.*

Proof. Let S be the set of output sequences of the n-stage Fibonacci NFSR. Then $S = \bar{S}$ means for any sequence $(s_i)_{i \geq 1} \in S$, we have $(s_i \oplus 1)_{i \geq 1} \in S$ as well, denoted by **Property 1**.

Necessity: Clearly, for each $\mathbf{X} \in \mathbb{F}_2^n$, there exists an edge from state $\mathbf{X}$ to state $\mathbf{f}(\mathbf{X})$ in the state diagram of the Galois NFSR. Similarly, for each $\mathbf{Y} \in \mathbb{F}_2^n$, there exists an edge from state $\mathbf{Y}$ to state $\mathbf{h}(\mathbf{Y})$ in the state diagram of the Fibonacci NFSR. If a Galois NFSR is equivalent to a Fibonacci NFSR, then according to Lemma 3, their state diagrams are isomorphic, which is equivalent to that there exists a bijective mapping $\varphi : \mathbf{X} \mapsto \mathbf{Y}$ such that $\varphi(\mathbf{f}(\mathbf{X})) = \mathbf{h}(\mathbf{Y}) = \mathbf{h}(\varphi(\mathbf{X}))$ for all $\mathbf{X} \in \mathbb{F}_2^n$. Note that an NFSR usually uses the content of the lowest bit as its output. Together taking into consideration Property 1, we can infer that the mapping φ must make the first component $\mathbf{Y}$ equal or complementary to the first component of $\mathbf{X}$, that is, $[1 \quad 0 \quad \ldots \quad 0]\varphi(\mathbf{X}) = \mathbf{X}$ or $[1 \quad 0 \quad \ldots \quad 0]\varphi(\mathbf{X}) = \mathbf{X} \oplus 1$ for all $\mathbf{X} \in \mathbb{F}_2^n$.

Sufficiency: If there exists a bijective mapping $\varphi : \mathbf{X} \mapsto \mathbf{Y}$ such that $\varphi(\mathbf{f}(\mathbf{X})) = \mathbf{h}(\varphi(\mathbf{X}))$, then according to the necessity proof, the state diagrams of the Galois NFSR and the Fibonacci NFSR are isomorphic. Moreover, if the bijection φ satisfies $[1 \quad 0 \quad \ldots \quad 0]\varphi(\mathbf{X}) = \mathbf{X}$ or $[1 \quad 0 \quad \ldots \quad 0]\varphi(\mathbf{X}) = \mathbf{X} \oplus 1$ for all $\mathbf{X} \in \mathbb{F}_2^n$, then their sets of output sequences of both NFSRs are equal provided that Property 1 holds. Therefore, the Galois NFSR and the Fibonacci NFSR are equivalent. $\square$

Theorem 4. *If an n-stage Fibonacci NFSR satisfies its output sequences set equal to its the complementary set, then there are $2 \times (2^{n-1}!)^2$ Galois NFSRs are equivalent to the Fibonacci NFSR.*

Proof. Different diagrams correspond to different Galois NFSRs. According to Proposition 3, we can only count the number of bijective mappings φ. Suppose the bijective mapping $\varphi : \mathbf{X} \mapsto \mathbf{Y}$ making the first component $\mathbf{Y}$ equal to the first component of $\mathbf{X}$. Thereby, if the first component of $\mathbf{X}$ is given, then the first component of $\mathbf{Y}$ is given as well. Clearly, the first component of $\mathbf{X}$ has two possible forms: 0 or 1, say, $\mathbf{X} = [0 \ X_2 \ \ldots \ X_n]^T$. Then $\mathbf{Y} = [0 \ Y_2 \ \ldots \ Y_n]^T$. The mapping $\varphi : \mathbf{X} = [0 \ X_2 \ \ldots \ X_n]^T \mapsto \mathbf{Y} = [0 \ Y_2 \ \ldots \ Y_n]^T$ has $(2^{n-1}!)$ possible forms. Thus, the bijective mapping $\varphi : \mathbf{X} \mapsto \mathbf{Y}$ making the first component of $\mathbf{Y}$ equal to the first component of $\mathbf{X}$ has $(2^{n-1}!)^2$ possible forms. Similarly, we can easily observe that the bijective mapping $\varphi : \mathbf{X} \mapsto \mathbf{Y}$ making the first component $\mathbf{Y}$ complementary to the first component of $\mathbf{X}$ has $(2^{n-1}!)^2$ possible forms as well. Therefore, the result follows. $\square$

5   Conclusion

This paper considered the isomorphism and equivalence of Galois NFSRs. It characterized the feedback of several kinds of isomorphic Galois NFSRs. In addition, the characterizations of two kinds of equivalent Galois NFSRs were revealed from the perspectives of their feedback functions and numbers. In the future, it will be interesting to find more characterizations of isomorphic and/or equivalent Galois NFSRs to benefit the design of NFSR-based stream ciphers.

Acknowledgments. This work was supported by the National Natural Science Foundation of China under Grant Nos. 61772029 and 61872359.

References

1. Hell, M., Johansson, T., Maximov, A., Meier, W.: The grain family of stream ciphers. In: Robshaw, M., Billet, O. (eds.) New Stream Cipher Designs. LNCS, vol. 4986, pp. 179–190. Springer, Heidelberg (2008). https://doi.org/10.1007/978-3-540-68351-3_14

2. De Cannière, C., Preneel, B.: Trivium. In: Robshaw, M., Billet, O. (eds.) New Stream Cipher Designs. LNCS, vol. 4986, pp. 244–266. Springer, Heidelberg (2008). https://doi.org/10.1007/978-3-540-68351-3_18

3. Dubrova, E.: A transformation from the Fibonacci to the Galois NLFSRs. IEEE Trans. Inf. Theory **55**(11), 5263–5271 (2009)

4. Cheng D., Qi H., Li Z.: Analysis and Control of Boolean Networks. Springer, London (2011) https://doi.org/10.1007/978-0-85729-097-7

5. Cheng D., Qi H., Zhao Y.: An Introduction To Semi-Tensor Product of Matrices And Its Applications. World Scientific Publishing Company, Singapore (2012)

6. Zhao, D., Peng, H., Li, L., Hui, S., Yang, Y.: Novel way to research nonlinear feedback shift register. Sci. China Inf. Sci. **57**(9), 1–14 (2014)

7. Zhong, J., Lin, D.: Driven stability of nonlinear feedback shift registers. IEEE Trans. Commun. **64**(6), 2274–2284 (2016)

8. Zhong, J., Lin, D.: On minimum period of nonlinear feedback shift registers in Grainlike structure. IEEE Trans. Inf. Theory **64**(9), 6429–6442 (2018)

9. Wan Z., Dai Z., Liu M. et al.: Nonlinear Shift Register (in Chinese), Science Press, Beijing, China (1978)

10. Zhong, J., Lin, D.: A new linearization method of nonlinear feedback shift registers. J. Comput. Syst. Sci. **81**(4), 783–796 (2015)

11. Zhao, X.-X., Zheng, Q.-X., Wang, Z.-X., Qi, W.-F.: On a class of isomorphic NFSRs. Des. Codes Cryptogr. **88**(6), 1205–1226 (2020)

12. Dubrova, E.: Finding matching initial states for equivalent NLFSRs in the Fibonacci and the Galois configurations. IEEE Trans. Inf. Theory **56**(6), 2961–2966 (2010)

13. Lin Z.: The transformation from the Galois NLFSR to the Fibonacci Configuration. In: EI-DWT 2013, USA, NJ, Piscataway: IEEE Press, pp. 335–339 (2013)

14. Mykkeltveit, J., Siu, M.-K., Ton, P.: On the cylcle structure of some nonlinear shift register sequences. Inf. Control **43**(2), 202–215 (1979)

15. Zhong, J., Pan, Y., Lin, D.: On Galois NFSRs equivalent to Fibonacci ones. In: Wu, Y., Yung, M. (eds.) Inscrypt 2020. LNCS, vol. 12612, pp. 433–449. Springer, Cham (2021). https://doi.org/10.1007/978-3-030-71852-7_29

16. Pan Y., Zhong J. and Lin D.: On Galois NFSRs with terminal bits. In: 2021 IEEE International Symposium on Information Theory (ISIT 2021), to appear
17. Roger A.H., Johnson C.R.: Topics in Matrix Analysis. Cambridge University Press, UK (1991)
18. Qi, H., Cheng, D.: Logic and logic-based control. J. Contr. Theory Appl. **6**(1), 123–133 (2008)
19. Barbier, M., Cheballah, H., Le Bars, J.-M.: On the computation of the Mobius transform. Theor. Comput. Sci. **809**, 171–188 (2020)
20. Golomb S. W.: Shift Register Sequences. Holden-Day, Laguna Hills, CA, USA (1967)
21. Zhong J. and Lin D.: Decomposition of nonlinear feedback shift registers based on Boolean networks. Sci. China Inf. Sci. **62**(3), 39110:1–39110:3 (2019)

Elliptic Curve and Integer Factorization

Zhizhong Pan[1,2(✉)] and Xiao Li[1,2]

[1] State Key Laboratory of Information Security, Institute of Information Engineering, Chinese Academy of Sciences, Beijing 100093, People's Republic of China
`panzhizhong@iie.ac.cn`
[2] School of Cyber Security, University of Chinese Academy of Science, Beijing 100093, People's Republic of China

Abstract. Suppose that we want to factor an integer D where $D = pq$, and p, q are two distinct odd primes. Assuming the parity conjecture and BSD conjecture hold, we reduce the problem of integer factorization to computing the generators of the Mordell-Weil group of $E_{Dr} : y^2 = x^3 - Drx$, where r is a suitable integer with $(r, D) = 1$. Then for the sake of deciding whether the point of E_{Dr} can factor D, it is shown that we need to compute the 2-Selmer group of E_{Dr}. Finally, we give a method to compute the 2-Selmer group of E_{Dr} and conduct some experiments to illustrate our method.

Keywords: Elliptic curve · Integer factorization · 2-Selmer group

1 Introduction

In 2003, Burhanuddin and Huang [2,3], related a subproblem of integer factoring to the problem of computing the Mordell-Weil group of an elliptic curve from a special family. Specially, they considered the family of elliptic curves $E = E_D : y^2 = x^3 - Dx$, where $D = pq$ with p and q distinct prime integers, $p \equiv q \equiv 3 \bmod 16$, and $\left(\frac{p}{q}\right) = 1$. Furthermore they speculated that the problem of integer factorization and the problem of computing the rational points of the elliptic curve can be polynomial-time equivalent. This method is completely different from the Lenstra's method of factoring integers by computing the order of elliptic curve over finite field, and provides a new idea for integer factorization.

Later, in 2014 Li and Zeng [6] studied a family of elliptic curve $E = E_{2Dr} : y^2 = x^3 - 2Drx$, where $D = pq$ is a product of two distinct odd primes and $2Dr$ is square-free. They proved that there are infinitely many $r \geq 1$ such that E_{2Dr} has conjectural rank one and $v_p(x(kP)) \neq v_q(x(kP))$ for any odd integer k, where P is the generator of $E_{2Dr}(\mathbb{Q})/E_{2Dr}(\mathbb{Q})_{tors}$. Furthermore, assuming the Generalized Riemann hypothesis holds, the minimal value of r is in $O(\log^4(D))$.

In this paper, we focus on a larger family of elliptic curve $E = E_{Dr} : y^2 = x^3 - Drx$, where $D = pq$ is the integer we want to factor and r is an arbitrary integer. Employing the method of two-descent, we reduce the problem of factoring integer to computing the Mordell-Weil group of $E_{Dr} : y^2 = x^3 - Drx$. This method is

© Springer Nature Switzerland AG 2021
Y. Yu and M. Yung (Eds.): Inscrypt 2021, LNCS 13007, pp. 316–330, 2021.
https://doi.org/10.1007/978-3-030-88323-2_17

different from Burhanuddin and Li, and is simpler and more intuitive. Moreover, it can be found that not only the points on the elliptic curve with rank 1 can be used to factor D, but also the points on the elliptic curve with higher ranks can. But for simplicity, we only discuss the situation of rank one. The conclusions are as follows.

Theorem 1. *Assuming $D = pq$ is a product of two distinct odd primes, suppose the parity conjecture is true, then*

(1) *There exists infinity many integer r, such that the rank of E_{Dr} is greater or equal to one.*

(2) *When the rank of E_{Dr} is greater or equal to one, and $S'(\phi) = \{1, A, \frac{-Dr}{A}, \overline{-Dr}\}$, $S(\phi) = \{1, \overline{Dr}\}$, where $\overline{-Dr}$ means $-Dr$ with the square factors removed, A is divisible by only one of p or q, $S'(\phi)$ and $S(\phi)$ are defined in Definition 2, then E_{Dr} has conjectural rank one. At that time, $v_p(x(kP)) \neq v_q(x(kP))$ for any odd integer k, in which P is the generator of $E_{Dr}(\mathbb{Q})/E_{Dr}(\mathbb{Q})_{tors}$. Then we can factor D.*

Remark 1. In the case $S'(\phi) = \{1, \overline{-Dr}\}$, $S(\phi) = \{1, A, \frac{Dr}{A}, \overline{Dr}\}$, both of $E_{Dr}(\mathbb{Q})$ and its dual curve $E_{-4Dr}(\mathbb{Q})$ have rank one. And for any odd integer k, we have $v_p(x(k\widehat{P})) \neq v_q(x(k\widehat{P}))$, where $\widehat{P}$ is the generator of $E_{-4Dr}(\mathbb{Q})/E_{-4Dr}(\mathbb{Q})_{tors}$. So we can factor D by using the points on $E_{-4Dr}(\mathbb{Q})$.

So the next question is how to compute $S(\phi)$ and $S'(\phi)$. Burhanuddin and Huang computed the 2-Selmer group of a family of elliptic curves $E = E_D : y^2 = x^3 - Dx$, where $D = pq$ with p and q distinct prime integers, $p \equiv q \equiv 3 \bmod 16$, and $\left(\frac{p}{q}\right) = 1$. Accurately, $S(\phi) = \{1, pq\}, S'(\phi) = \{1, p, -q, -pq\}$. At that time, the rank of E_D is one, and we can factor D.

Then Li and Zeng developed the method of computing the 2-Selmer group of a family of elliptic curve $E = E_{2Dr} : y^2 = x^3 - 2Drx$, where $D = pq$ is a product of two distinct odd primes and $2Dr$ is square-free. They concluded that when r meets certain conditions, $S(\phi) = \{1, 2Dr\}, S'(\phi) = \{1, A, \frac{-2Dr}{A}, -2Dr\}$, in which A is divisible by only one of p or q. At that time, the rank of E_{2Dr} is one, and we can factor D.

The second work of this article is to improve their method of calculating 2-Selmer group. We give a way to compute the 2-Selmer group of a family of elliptic curve $E = E_{Dr} : y^2 = x^3 - Drx$, where $D = pq$ is a product of two distinct odd primes and r is an arbitrary integer. The theorem is as follows.

Theorem 2. *Let $C_d : w^2 = d + \frac{D}{d}z^4, where D = (-1)^m 2^n \prod p_i \prod q_j^2 \prod r_k^3, p_i, q_j, r_k$ are distinct primes, d is square-free and $d \mid D$, we have*

(1) *When $m = 0$, $C_d(\mathbb{Q}_\infty) \neq \Phi \Leftrightarrow d > 0$.*
   When $m = 1$, $C_d(\mathbb{Q}_\infty) \neq \Phi$ holds for any d.
(2) 1) *When $2 \nmid d$*
   i) *If $n = 0$, $C_d(\mathbb{Q}_2) \neq \Phi \Leftrightarrow d \equiv 1 \bmod 8$ or $d + \frac{D}{d} \equiv 0 \bmod 16$ or $d + \frac{D}{d} \equiv 4 \bmod 32$ or $\frac{D}{d} \equiv 1 \bmod 8$.*

$ii)$ If $n = 1$, $C_d(\mathbb{Q}_2) \neq \Phi \Leftrightarrow d \equiv 1 \bmod 8$ or $d + \frac{D}{d} \equiv 1 \bmod 8$.

$iii)$ If $n = 2$, $C_d(\mathbb{Q}_2) \neq \Phi \Leftrightarrow d \equiv 1 \bmod 8$ or $d + \frac{D}{d} \equiv 1 \bmod 8$ or $\frac{D}{4d} \equiv 1 \bmod 4$.

$iv)$ If $n = 3$, $C_d(\mathbb{Q}_2) \neq \Phi \Leftrightarrow d \equiv 1 \bmod 8$.

2) When $2 \mid d$

$i)$ If $n = 1$, $C_d(\mathbb{Q}_2) \neq \Phi \Leftrightarrow d + \frac{D}{d} \equiv 1 \bmod 8$ or $\frac{D}{d} \equiv 1 \bmod 8$.

$ii)$ If $n = 2$, $C_d(\mathbb{Q}_2) \neq \Phi \Leftrightarrow \frac{d}{2} + \frac{D}{2d} \equiv 0 \bmod 32$ or $\frac{d}{2} + \frac{D}{2d} \equiv 2 \bmod 16$ or $\frac{d}{2} + \frac{D}{2d} \equiv 8 \bmod 32$.

$iii)$ If $n = 3$, $C_d(\mathbb{Q}_2) \neq \Phi \Leftrightarrow \frac{D}{4d} \equiv 1 \bmod 4$.

(3) $\forall t \mid d$, t is prime

1) When $t = p_i$, $C_d(\mathbb{Q}_t) \neq \Phi \Leftrightarrow (\frac{D/d}{t}) = 1$.

2) When $t = q_j$, $C_d(\mathbb{Q}_t) \neq \Phi \Leftrightarrow (\frac{-d^2/D}{t})_4 = 1$.

3) When $t = r_k$, $C_d(\mathbb{Q}_t) \neq \Phi \Leftrightarrow (\frac{D/dt^2}{t}) = 1$.

(4) $\forall t \nmid d$, t is prime

1) When $t = p_i$, $C_d(\mathbb{Q}_t) \neq \Phi \Leftrightarrow (\frac{d}{t}) = 1$.

2) When $t = q_j$, $C_d(\mathbb{Q}_t) \neq \Phi \Leftrightarrow (\frac{d}{t}) = 1$ or $(\frac{D/dt^2}{t}) = 1$.

3) When $t = r_k$, $C_d(\mathbb{Q}_t) \neq \Phi \Leftrightarrow (\frac{d}{t}) = 1$.

Remark 2. In [6], Li has proved theorem when D is an even square-free integer. On the basis of her theory, we have proved theorem can be applied to the larger family curves where D is an arbitrary integer.

Thus according to Theorem 2, we can compute $S(\phi)$ and $S'(\phi)$. The specific calculation process is in Sect. 4.

This paper is organized as follows. In Sect. 2 we do some preprocess to our elliptic curve and introduce the theorem to compute the torsion subgroup. By applying the parity conjecture, we also prove Theorem 1(1). In Sect. 3 we briefly introduced the process and principle of the two-descent method. In Sect. 4 we explain how to reduce the problem of factoring integer to computing the Mordell-Weil subgroup of $E_{Dr} : y^2 = x^3 - Drx$, and prove Theorem 1(2). In Sect. 5 we prove Theorem 2. Finally, in Sect. 6, we give a few examples to illustrate our results.

2   Torsion Subgroups and Parity Conjecture

2.1   Notations

At the beginning, we fix some notations. For elliptic curve $E_D : y^2 = x^3 - Dx$, if $D = A^4 D'$, that is $y^2 = x^3 - A^4 D'x$. Divide both sides by A^6 to obtain $\frac{y^2}{A^6} = \frac{x^3}{A^6} - D'\frac{x}{A^2}$. Let $x' = \frac{x}{A^2}$, $y' = \frac{y}{A^3}$, and we get a new curve $E_{D'} : y'^2 = x'^3 - D'x'$. So the relation gives a one-to-one correspondence $(x, y) \leftrightarrow (\frac{x}{A^2}, \frac{y}{A^3})$ of the points between E_D and $E_{D'}$.

According to that, we begin to preprocess the elliptic curve. By removing r's quartic factors, we obtain the new elliptic curve $E_{Dr} : y^2 = x^3 - Drx$, where

$r = (-1)^m 2^n \prod p_i \prod q_j^2 \prod r_k^3$, and p_i, q_j, r_k are distinct primes, and $(r, p) = (r, q) = 1$, $n = 0, 1, 2, 3$, $m = 0, 1$. We denote this curve by E. At the same time we consider its dual curve $E_{-4Dr} : y^2 = x^3 + 4Drx$, using the same method, removing its quartic factors, and denote the new curve by $\widehat{E}$.

Remark 3. In fact, when $r \in \mathbb{Q}$, we can also simplify the curve to the above situation.

2.2   Torsion Subsubgroups

The question about the structure of the torsion subgroup of an elliptic curve is relatively simple, especially when the elliptic curve is defined over $\mathbb{Q}$, we have the following theorem:

Theorem 3 *(see [7]). Let $D \in \mathbb{Z}$ is quartic-free, $E_D : y^2 = x^3 - Dx$ is defined over $\mathbb{Q}$, then*

$$E_{D,tors}(\mathbb{Q}) \cong \begin{cases} \mathbb{Z}/4\mathbb{Z} & if\, D = -4, \\ \mathbb{Z}_2 \oplus \mathbb{Z}_2 & if\ D\ is\ the\ square\ integer, \\ \mathbb{Z}_2 & otherwise, \end{cases} \tag{1}$$

where $E_{D,tors}$ *is the torsion subgroup of* E_D.

By Theorem 3, we know that the torsion subgroup of E_{Dr} is $\mathbb{Z}_2$, two elements of which are ∞ and $(0, 0)$. We will denote $(0, 0)$ by T from now on.

2.3   Parity Conjecture

Let E be an elliptic curve defined over $\mathbb{Q}$ with conductor N_E. By the Modularity Theorem, the L-function can be analytically extended to the entire complex plane and satisfies the functional equation

$$\Lambda_E(2 - s) = w_E \lambda_E(s), \quad \text{where } \lambda_E(s) = (2\pi)^{-s} N_E^{s/2} \Gamma(s) L_E(s) \tag{2}$$

and $w_E = \pm 1$ is called the global root number.

Let r_E^{an} and r_E be the analytic rank and arithmetic rank of E respectively, where r_E^{an} is the order of vanishing of $L_E(s)$ at $s = 1$ and r_E is the rank of the abelian group $E(\mathbb{Q})$. The famous BSD conjecture says that $r_E^{an} = r_E$. On the other hand for the parity of r_E, there is another conjecture:

Conjecture 1 (Parity conjecture, see [1,5]). We have $(-1)^{r_E} = w_E$.

From this, we obtain the following:

Corollary 1. *Let elliptic curve $E_D : y^2 = x^3 - Dx$ be defined over $\mathbb{Q}$ with $4 \nmid D$ and D quartic-free. We denote the rank of E_D by r_E. Then $(-1)^{r_E} = w_E = w_\infty \cdot w_2 \cdot \prod_{p^2 \| D} w_p$, in which*

$$w_\infty = sgn(-D),$$

$$w_2 = \begin{cases} -1 & D \equiv 1,3,11,13 \ mod \ 16, \\ 1 & otherwise, \end{cases}$$

$$w_p = (\frac{-1}{p}) = \begin{cases} -1 & p \equiv 3 \ mod \ 4, \\ 1 & p \equiv 1 \ mod \ 4. \end{cases}$$

So when $w_E = -1$, we can infer that r_E is an odd number. At this point we can claim that the rank of the elliptic curve is greater than 1.

Consider our elliptic curve $E_{Dr} : y^2 = x^3 - Drx$, where $D = pq$ and $r = (-1)^m 2^n \prod p_i \prod q_j^2 \prod r_k^3$. When $m = 0$ and $n = 1$, $w_\infty = -1$, $w_2 = 1$, only the product of the square factors in r congruents to 1 modulo 4 is needed. When $m = 1$ and $n = 1$, $w_\infty = 1$, $w_2 = 1$, the product of the square factors in r congruents to 3 modulo 4 will guarantee $w_E = -1$. Other conditions are similar to before.

According to Dirichlet's density theorem, there are infinitly many integers r such that the rank of E_{Dr} is greater than or equal to 1. So we finish the prove of Theorem 1(1).

3   A Brief Introduction to Two-Descent Method

In this section we analyze the specific curve by the two-descent method. Considering the elliptic curve $E_{Dr} : y^2 = x^3 - Drx$, where $D = pq$ and $r = (-1)^m 2^n \prod p_i \prod q_j^2 \prod r_k^3$. Denote it by E, and denote its dual curve E_{-4Dr} : $y^2 = x^3 + 4Drx$ by $\widehat{E}$.

Theorem 4 (see [4]). (1) There exists a map ϕ from E to $\widehat{E}$, such that $\phi(P) = (\frac{y^2}{x^2}, \frac{y(x^2+Dr)}{x^2})$, $\phi(\infty) = \phi(T) = \hat{\infty} \in \widehat{E}(\mathbb{Q})$. In fact, ϕ is a group homomorphism whose kernel is $\{\infty, T\}$.

(2) There exists a map $\hat{\phi}$ from $\widehat{E}$ to E, such that $\hat{\phi}(\hat{P}) = (\frac{\hat{y}^2}{4\hat{x}^2}, \frac{\hat{y}(\hat{x}^2-4Dr)}{8\hat{x}^2})$, $\hat{\phi}(\hat{\infty}) = \hat{\phi}(\hat{T}) = \infty \in E(\mathbb{Q})$. In fact, $\hat{\phi}$ is a group homomorphism whose kernel is $\{\hat{\infty}, \hat{T}\}$.

(3) $\phi \circ \hat{\phi}(\hat{P}) = 2\hat{P}$, $\hat{\phi} \circ \phi(P) = 2P$. So ϕ is an isogeny from E to $\widehat{E}$, and $\hat{\phi}$ is its dual isogeny. They are two-isogenies.

Definition 1 (see [4]). Define the two-descent map

$$\alpha : E(\mathbb{Q}) \longrightarrow \mathbb{Q}^\times / \mathbb{Q}^{\times^2}$$
$$(x, y) \longmapsto \bar{x}$$
$$\infty \longmapsto 1$$
$$T \longmapsto \overline{-Dr}$$

$$\hat{\alpha} : \hat{E}(\mathbb{Q}) \longrightarrow \mathbb{Q}^{\times}/\mathbb{Q}^{\times^2}$$
$$(\hat{x}, \hat{y}) \longmapsto \tilde{\hat{x}}$$
$$\hat{\infty} \longmapsto 1$$
$$\hat{T} \longmapsto \overline{Dr}$$

where $\overline{x}$ means x with the square factors removed.

Proposition 1 (see [4]). *For α and $\hat{\alpha}$, we have the following properties:*

(1) α and $\hat{\alpha}$ are group homomorphisms.
(2) $Im\alpha \subseteq < -1, b_i >$, where $b_i | Dr$.
   $Im\hat{\alpha} \subseteq < -1, b'_i >$, where $b'_i | 4Dr'$.
(3) If $b \in Im\alpha$, then $\overline{\frac{-Dr}{b}} \in Im\alpha$.
   If $b \in Im\hat{\alpha}$, then $\overline{\frac{Dr}{b}} \in Im\hat{\alpha}$.
(4) $\{1, \overline{-Dr}\} \subseteq Im\alpha$ and $\{1, \overline{Dr}\} \subseteq Im\hat{\alpha}$.
(5) $|Im\alpha| \cdot |Im\hat{\alpha}| = 2^{r_E+2}$.

Remark 4. We define $r' = (-1)^m 2^{(n+2) \bmod 4 - 2}$ in $4Dr'$, in order to remove the quartic factor of 2 in $4Dr$.

From Proposition 1, we know that as long as $Im\alpha$ and $Im\hat{\alpha}$ are determined, we can compute the rank of E_{Dr}. At the same time, through the inverse maps of α and $\hat{\alpha}$, we can also calculate the points on $E(\mathbb{Q})$ and $\hat{E}(\mathbb{Q})$. So the next step is how to calculate $Im\alpha$ and $Im\hat{\alpha}$.

Let $S = \{\infty\} \bigcup \{b_i \mid b_i \text{ is the prime factor of } Dr\}$, $Q(S, 2)$ be the subgroup generated by -1 and S in $\mathbb{Q}^{\times}/\mathbb{Q}^{\times^2}$. Simultaneously, let $\hat{S} = \{\infty\} \bigcup \{b_i \mid b_i \text{ is the prime factor of } 4Dr'\}$, $\hat{Q}(\hat{S}, 2)$ be the subgroup generated by -1 and $\hat{S}$ in $\mathbb{Q}^{\times}/\mathbb{Q}^{\times^2}$, where r' is defined in Remark 4.

Theorem 5 (see [4]). *(1) $\forall b \in Q(S, 2)$, $b \in Im\alpha \Leftrightarrow C'_b : w^2 = b - \frac{Dr}{b}z^4$ has solutions in $\mathbb{Q}$.*
(2) $\forall b \in \hat{Q}(\hat{S}, 2)$, $b \in Im\hat{\alpha} \Leftrightarrow C_b : w^2 = b + \frac{4Dr'}{b}z^4$ has solutions in $\mathbb{Q}$.

Theorem 5 gives the conditions to be satisfied by the elements in $Im\alpha$ and $Im\hat{\alpha}$. Because there are finitely many elements in $Q(S, 2)$ and $\hat{Q}(\hat{S}, 2)$, we only need to check both elements in $Q(S, 2)$ and $\hat{Q}(\hat{S}, 2)$ one by one. In fact, according to Proposition 1(3), we only need to check half of the elements in $Q(S, 2)$ and $\hat{Q}(\hat{S}, 2)$. But deciding whether C_b and C'_b have solutions in $\mathbb{Q}$ is a difficult problem, so instead we consider whether they have solutions on local field $\mathbb{Q}_p$ ($p \leq \infty$). Furthermore, according to [7], we only need to consider whether C_b and C'_b have solutions in $\mathbb{Q}_p$ ($p \mid 2Dr$ or $p = \infty$). Now we give the definition of 2-Selmer group.

Definition 2 (see [8]). *(1) Define $S'(\phi) \triangleq \{b \in Q(S, 2) \mid C'_b(\mathbb{Q}_p) \neq \Phi, \forall p \in S \bigcup \{\infty\}\}$, which is an abelian group, called 2-Selmer group of $E(\mathbb{Q})$.*
(2) Define $S(\phi) \triangleq \{b \in \hat{Q}(\hat{S}, 2) \mid C_b(\mathbb{Q}_p) \neq \Phi, \forall p \in \hat{S} \bigcup \{\infty\}\}$, which is an abelian group, called 2-Selmer group of $\hat{E}(\mathbb{Q})$.

From Definition 2, we know that $Im\alpha \subseteq S'(\phi)$ and $Im\hat{\alpha} \subseteq S(\phi)$, the opposite sides are not necessarily true. In order to measure the gaps between them, we give the following definition.

Definition 3 *(see [8]). (1) Define* $\text{III}'(\phi) \triangleq S'(\phi)/Im\alpha$, *called the 2-Shafarevich group of* $E(\mathbb{Q})$,
    (2) Define $\text{III}(\phi) \triangleq S(\phi)/Im\hat{\alpha}$, *called the 2-Shafarevich group of* $\hat{E}(\mathbb{Q})$.

To end this section, we briefly give the 2-descent method to calculate the rank and generator of $E_{Dr} : y^2 = x^3 - Drx$:

step1 : Give $E_{Dr} : y^2 = x^3 - Drx$ and its 2-isogeny dual curve $E_{-4Dr} : y^2 = x^3 + 4Drx$, generate $Q(S, 2)$ and $\hat{Q}(\hat{S}, 2)$.

step2 : For $d \in Q(S, 2)$, determine whether $C'_d : w^2 = d - \frac{Dr}{d}z^4$ has a solution on $\mathbb{Q}^2$. If there is a solution (z_0, w_0), then $d \in Im\alpha$, and $(\frac{d}{z_0^2}, \frac{dw_0}{z_0^3})$ is a point on $E(\mathbb{Q})$, and there is $-\frac{Dr}{d} \in Im\alpha$ at the same time.
    For $d \in \hat{Q}(\hat{S}, 2)$, determine whether $C_d : w^2 = d + \frac{4Dr'}{d}z^4$ has a solution on $\mathbb{Q}^2$. If there is a solution (z_0, w_0), then $d \in Im\hat{\alpha}$, and $(\frac{d}{z_0^2}, \frac{dw_0}{z_0^3})$ is a point on $\hat{E}(\mathbb{Q})$, and there is $\frac{4Dr'}{d} \in Im\hat{\alpha}$ at the same time, where r' is defined in Remark 4.

step3 : According to $|Im\alpha| \cdot |Im\hat{\alpha}| = 2^{r_E+2}$, we can compute the rank of E_{Dr}, meanwhile determine the generator from the point calculated in step 2.

4   Integer Factorization and the Mordell-Weil Group

With the above preparations, let's consider a special case, the case in Theorem 1 (2).

Theorem 6. *Suppose* $r_E \geq 1$, $|S'(\phi)| = 4$, $|S(\phi)| = 2$ *or* $|S'(\phi)| = 2, |S(\phi)| = 4 \Leftrightarrow \text{III}'(\phi) = \text{III}(\phi) = 1$ *and* $r_E = 1$.

Proof. ($\Rightarrow$) Because $r_E \geq 1$, then $|Im\alpha| \cdot |Im\hat{\alpha}| = 2^{r_E+2} \geq 8$, and in view of $Im\alpha \subseteq S'(\phi)$, $Im\hat{\alpha} \subseteq S(\phi)$, we have $|Im\alpha| \cdot |Im\hat{\alpha}| \leq |S'(\phi)| \cdot |S(\phi)| = 8$.

It follows that $|Im\alpha| \cdot |Im\hat{\alpha}| = 8$. So $r_E = 1$, and $Im(\alpha) = S'(\phi)$, $Im(\hat{\alpha}) = S(\phi)$, $\text{III}'(\phi) = \text{III}(\phi) = 1$.
    ($\Leftarrow$) Obviously.   □

Let's assume that $|S'(\phi)| = 4$, $|S(\phi)| = 2$, and the case where $|S'(\phi)| = 2$, $|S(\phi)| = 4$ is similar.

As $\{1, \overline{-Dr}\} \subseteq S'(\phi)$, $\{1, \overline{Dr}\} \subseteq S(\phi)$, we can assume that $S'(\phi) = \{1, A, \overline{\frac{-Dr}{A}}, \overline{-Dr}\}$, $S(\phi) = \{1, \overline{Dr}\}$.

Proposition 2. *When $r_E \geq 1$, if $S'(\phi) = \{1, A, \frac{-Dr}{A}, \overline{-Dr}\}$, $S(\phi) = \{1, \overline{Dr}\}$, then $r_E = 1$. At that time, the map α and $\hat{\alpha}$ can be written as:*

$$\alpha : E(\mathbb{Q}) \longrightarrow \mathbb{Q}^{\times}/\mathbb{Q}^{\times^2}$$
$$\infty \longmapsto 1$$
$$T \longmapsto \overline{-Dr}$$
$$(2k+1)P \longmapsto A \text{ or } \frac{-Dr}{A}$$
$$(2k+1)P + T \longmapsto \frac{-Dr}{A} \text{ or } A$$
$$2kP \longmapsto 1$$
$$2kP + T \longmapsto \overline{-Dr}$$

$$\hat{\alpha} : \hat{E}(\mathbb{Q}) \longrightarrow \mathbb{Q}^{\times}/\mathbb{Q}^{\times^2}$$
$$\hat{\infty} \longmapsto 1$$
$$\hat{T} \longmapsto \overline{Dr}$$
$$k\hat{P} \longmapsto 1$$
$$k\hat{P} + \hat{T} \longmapsto \overline{Dr}$$

where P and $\hat{P}$ are the generators of $E(\mathbb{Q})$ and $\hat{E}(\mathbb{Q})$ respectively.

Proof. This result can be obtained immediately by the property that the X-coordinate of the even multiple point of the elliptic curve is a square number and Proposition 1. □

From the map α, we see that if A can only be divided by p (resp q), then $v_p(x((2k+1)P))$ is an odd number (resp even number) and the corresponding $v_q(x((2k+1)P))$ is an even number (resp odd number). It follows that $v_p(x((2k+1)P)) \neq v_q(x((2k+1)P))$, and then we can use $x((2k+1)P)$ to factor D. So we finished the prove of Theorem 1(2).

Remark 5. The case of $|S'(\phi)| = 2$, $|S(\phi)| = 4$ is similar to the above. But at this time, the points on $\hat{E}(\mathbb{Q})$ can used to factor D. Since there is a two-isogeny map between E and $\hat{E}$, it can actually be summarized to the points on E to do the factorization.

In the end we only have one question left, and that is how to find $Im\alpha$ and $Im\hat{\alpha}$. According to Theorem 6, we know that when $|S'(\phi)| = 4$, $|S(\phi)| = 2$ or $|S'(\phi)| = 2$, $|S(\phi)| = 4$, we have $Im(\alpha) = S'(\phi)$, $Im(\hat{\alpha}) = S(\phi)$. So in this case, it suffices to give a method to compute $S'(\phi)$ and $S(\phi)$.

5   Compute $S'(\phi)$ and $S(\phi)$

To prove Theorem 2, we first recall the Hensel's Lemma.

Lemma 1 *(Hensel's Lemma, see [8]). Let R be a ring that is complete with respect to a discrete valuation v, $f(x_1, \cdots, x_n) \in R[x_1, \cdots, x_n]$. Suppose there exists a point $(a_1, \cdots, a_n) \in R^n$ satisfying*

$$v(f(a_1, \cdots, a_n)) > 2v \frac{\partial f}{\partial x_k}(a_1, \cdots, a_n), \quad (\exists k, 1 \le k \le n). \tag{3}$$

Then $f(x_1, \cdots, x_n)$ has a solution in R^n.

With Hensel's lemma, let's start the proof of Theorem 2.

Proof. For convenience, we denote $f(z, w) = w^2 - \frac{D}{d}z^4 - d$.

(1) Obviously.

(2) 1) When $2 \nmid d$

i) If $n = 0$

($\Rightarrow$) $C_d(\mathbb{Q}_2) \ne \Phi$, we have $2v_2(w) \ge min\{v_2(d), v_2(\frac{D}{d}) + 4v_2(z)\} = min\{0, 4v_2(z)\}$.

When $v_2(z) > 0$, $v_2(w) = 0$, so $1 \equiv w^2 \equiv d + \frac{D}{d}z^4 \equiv d \bmod 8$.

When $v_2(z) = 0$, $v_2(w) > 0$, so $z^4 \equiv 1$ *or* $17 \bmod 32$, $w^2 \equiv 0$ *or* 4 *or* $16 \bmod 32$, so we have $d + \frac{D}{d} \equiv 0 \bmod 32$, or $d + 17\frac{D}{d} \equiv 0 \bmod 32$, or $d + \frac{D}{d} \equiv 4 \bmod 32$, or $d + 17\frac{D}{d} \equiv 4 \bmod 32$, or $d + \frac{D}{d} \equiv 16 \bmod 32$, or $d + 17\frac{D}{d} \equiv 16 \bmod 32$. Combine them together we have $d + \frac{D}{d} \equiv 0 \bmod 16$ or $d + \frac{D}{d} \equiv 4 \bmod 32$.

When $v_2(z) < 0$, $v_2(w) = 2v_2(z)$, assume $z = 2^{-i}z'$, $w = 2^{-2i}w'$, where $i > 0$, $v_2(z') = v_2(w') = 0$, then we have $2^{-4i}w'^2 = d + \frac{D}{d}2^{-4i}z'^4$, Simplify to get $w'^2 = 2^{4i}d + \frac{D}{d}z'^4$, so $1 \equiv w'^2 \equiv 2^{4i}d + \frac{D}{d}z'^4 \equiv \frac{D}{d} \bmod 8$.

($\Leftarrow$) If $d \equiv 1 \bmod 8$, consider $v_2(f(0,1)) = v_2(1 - d) \ge 3$, $v_2(\frac{\partial f}{\partial w}(0,1)) = v_2(2) = 1$, so $v_2(f(0,1)) > 2v_2(\frac{\partial f}{\partial w}(0,1))$. according to Hensel lemma, $f(z, w)$ has root in $\mathbb{Q}_2^2$, which is said that $C_d(\mathbb{Q}_2) \ne \Phi$.

If $d + \frac{D}{d} \equiv 0 \bmod 16$, first we have $d + \frac{D}{d} \equiv 0 \bmod 32$, consider $v_2(f(1,0)) = v_2(-d - \frac{D}{d}) \ge 5$, $v_2(\frac{\partial f}{\partial z}(1,0)) = v_2(\frac{4D}{d}) = 2$, so $v_2(f(1,0)) > 2v_2(\frac{\partial f}{\partial z}(1,0))$. Or we have $d + \frac{D}{d} \equiv 16 \bmod 32$, consider $v_2(f(1,4)) = v_2(16 - d - \frac{D}{d}) \ge 5$, $v_2(\frac{\partial f}{\partial z}(1,4)) = v_2(\frac{4D}{d}) = 2$, so $v_2(f(1,4)) > 2v_2(\frac{\partial f}{\partial z}(1,4))$.

If $d + \frac{D}{d} \equiv 4 \bmod 32$, consider $v_2(f(1,2)) = v_2(4 - d - \frac{D}{d}) \ge 5$, $v_2(\frac{\partial f}{\partial z}(1,2)) = v_2(\frac{4D}{d}) = 2$, so $v_2(f(1,2)) > 2v_2(\frac{\partial f}{\partial z}(1,2))$.

If $\frac{D}{d} \equiv 1 \bmod 8$, consider $v_2(f(\frac{1}{2}, \frac{1}{4})) = v_2(\frac{1}{16} - d - \frac{D}{16d}) \ge min\{v_2(d), v_2(\frac{1}{16}(1 - \frac{D}{d}))\} \ge -1$, $v_2(\frac{\partial f}{\partial w}(\frac{1}{2}, \frac{1}{4})) = v_2(\frac{1}{2}) = -1$, so $v_2(f(\frac{1}{2}, \frac{1}{4})) > 2v_2(\frac{\partial f}{\partial w}(\frac{1}{2}, \frac{1}{4}))$.

ii) If $n = 1$

($\Rightarrow$) $C_d(\mathbb{Q}_2) \neq \Phi$, we have $2v_2(w) \geq min\{v_2(d), v_2(\frac{D}{d}) + 4v_2(z)\} = min\{0, 1 + 4v_2(z)\}$.

When $v_2(z) > 0$, $v_2(w) = 0$, so $1 \equiv w^2 \equiv d + \frac{D}{d}z^4 \equiv d$ mod 8.

When $v_2(z) = 0$, $v_2(w) = 0$, so $1 \equiv w^2 \equiv d + \frac{D}{d}z^4 \equiv d + \frac{D}{d}$ mod 8.

($\Leftarrow$) If $d \equiv 1$ mod 8, consider $v_2(f(0,1)) > 2v_2(\frac{\partial f}{\partial w}(0,1))$.

If $d + \frac{D}{d} \equiv 1$ mod 8, consider $v_2(f(1,1)) > 2v_2(\frac{\partial f}{\partial w}(1,1))$.

iii) If $n = 2$

($\Rightarrow$) $C_d(\mathbb{Q}_2) \neq \Phi$, we have $2v_2(w) \geq min\{v_2(d), v_2(\frac{D}{d}) + 4v_2(z)\} = min\{0, 2 + 4v_2(z)\}$.

When $v_2(z) \geq 0$, $v_2(w) = 0$, then $1 \equiv w^2 \equiv d + \frac{D}{d}z^4$ mod 8, so $d \equiv 1$ mod 8 or $d + \frac{D}{d} \equiv 1$ mod 8.

When $v_2(z) < 0$, $v_2(w) = 1 + 2v_2(z)$, assume $z = 2^{-i}z'$, $w = 2^{-2i+1}w'$, where $i > 0$, $v_2(z') = v_2(w') = 0$, then we have $2^{-4i+2}w'^2 = d + \frac{D}{d}2^{-4i}z'^4$, simplify to get $w'^2 = 2^{4i-2}d + \frac{D}{4d}z'^4$, so $1 \equiv w'^2 \equiv 2^{4i-2}d + \frac{D}{4d}z'^4 \equiv \frac{D}{4d}$ mod 4.

($\Leftarrow$) If $d \equiv 1$ mod 8, consider $v_2(f(2,1)) = v_2(1 - d - \frac{16D}{d}) \geq min\{v_2(1-d), v_2(\frac{16D}{d})\} \geq 3$, $v_2(\frac{\partial f}{\partial w}(2,1)) = 1$.

If $d + \frac{D}{d} \equiv 1$ mod 8, consider $v_2(f(1,1)) = v_2(1 - d - \frac{D}{d}) \geq min\{v_2(1-d), v_2(\frac{D}{d})\} \geq 3$, $v_2(\frac{\partial f}{\partial w}(1,1)) = 1$.

If $\frac{D}{4d} \equiv 1$ mod 4, consider $v_2(f(\frac{1}{2}, \frac{1}{2})) = v_2(\frac{1}{4} - d - \frac{D}{16d}) \geq min\{v_2(d), v_2(1 - \frac{D}{4d}) - 2\} \geq 0$, $v_2(\frac{\partial f}{\partial z}(\frac{1}{2}, \frac{1}{2})) = v_2(\frac{D}{2d}) = -1$.

iv) If $n = 3$

($\Rightarrow$) $C_d(\mathbb{Q}_2) \neq \Phi$, we have $2v_2(w) \geq min\{v_2(d), v_2(\frac{D}{d}) + 4v_2(z)\} = min\{0, 3 + 4v_2(z)\}$. At this time $v_2(z) \geq 0$, $v_2(w) = 0$, so $1 \equiv w^2 \equiv d + \frac{D}{d}z^4 \equiv d$ mod 8.

($\Leftarrow$) If $d \equiv 1$ mod 8, consider $v_2(f(0,1)) = v_2(1 - d) \geq 3$, $v_2(\frac{\partial f}{\partial w}(0,1)) = 1$.

2) When $2 \mid d$

i) If $n = 1$

($\Rightarrow$) $C_d(\mathbb{Q}_2) \neq \Phi$, we have $2v_2(w) \geq min\{v_2(d), v_2(\frac{D}{d}) + 4v_2(z)\} = min\{1, 4v_2(z)\}$.

When $v_2(z) = 0$, $v_2(w) = 0$, so $1 \equiv w^2 \equiv d + \frac{D}{d}z^4 \equiv d + \frac{D}{d}$ mod 8.

When $v_2(z) < 0$, $v_2(w) = 2v_2(z)$, assume $z = 2^{-i}z'$, $w = 2^{-2i}w'$, where $i > 0$, $v_2(z') = v_2(w') = 0$, then we have $2^{-4i}w'^2 = d + \frac{D}{d}2^{-4i}z'^4$, simplify to get $w'^2 = 2^{4i}d + \frac{D}{d}z'^4$, so $1 \equiv w'^2 \equiv 2^{4i}d + \frac{D}{d}z'^4 \equiv \frac{D}{d}$ mod 8.

($\Leftarrow$) If $d + \frac{D}{d} \equiv 1$ mod 8, consider $v_2(f(1,1)) > 2v_2(\frac{\partial f}{\partial w}(1,1))$.

If $\frac{D}{d} \equiv 1$ mod 8, consider $v_2(f(\frac{1}{2}, \frac{1}{4})) = v_2(\frac{1}{16} - d - \frac{D}{16d}) \geq min\{v_2(d), v_2(\frac{1}{16}(1 - \frac{D}{d}))\} \geq -1$, $v_2(\frac{\partial f}{\partial w}(\frac{1}{2}, \frac{1}{4})) = v_2(\frac{1}{2}) = -1$.

ii) If $n = 2$

($\Rightarrow$) $C_d(\mathbb{Q}_2) \neq \Phi$, we have $2v_2(w) \geq min\{v_2(d), v_2(\frac{D}{d}) + 4v_2(z)\} = min\{1, 1 + 4v_2(z)\}$. At this time $v_2(z) = 0$, $v_2(w) > 0$, so $z^4 \equiv 1$ or 17 mod 32, $\frac{w^2}{2} \equiv 0$ or 2 or 8 or 18 mod 32. Then we have

$\frac{d}{2} + \frac{D}{2d} \equiv 0 \ mod \ 32$, or $\frac{d}{2} + 17\frac{D}{2d} \equiv 0 \ mod \ 32$, or $\frac{d}{2} + \frac{D}{2d} \equiv 2 \ mod \ 32$, or $\frac{d}{2} + 17\frac{D}{2d} \equiv 2 \ mod \ 32$, or $\frac{d}{2} + \frac{D}{2d} \equiv 8 \ mod \ 32$, or $\frac{d}{2} + 17\frac{D}{2d} \equiv 8 \ mod \ 32$, $\frac{d}{2} + \frac{D}{2d} \equiv 18 \ mod \ 32$, or $\frac{d}{2} + 17\frac{D}{2d} \equiv 18 \ mod \ 32$. Combine them together we have $\frac{d}{2} + \frac{D}{2d} \equiv 0 \ mod \ 32$ or $\frac{d}{2} + \frac{D}{2d} \equiv 2 \ mod \ 16$ or $\frac{d}{2} + \frac{D}{2d} \equiv 8 \ mod \ 32$.

($\Leftarrow$) Let $f'(z,w) = \frac{w^2}{2} - \frac{d}{2} - \frac{D}{2d}z^4$, then $f(z,w)$ has root in $\mathbb{Q}_2^2$ $\Leftrightarrow$ $f'(z,w)$ has root in $\mathbb{Q}_2^2$.

If $\frac{d}{2} + \frac{D}{2d} \equiv 0 \ mod \ 32$, consider $v_2(f'(1,0)) = v_2(-\frac{d}{2} - \frac{D}{2d}) \geq 5$, $v_2(\frac{\partial f'}{\partial z}(1,0)) = v_2(\frac{2D}{d}) = 2$.

If $\frac{d}{2} + \frac{D}{2d} \equiv 2 \ mod \ 32$, consider $v_2(f'(1,2)) = v_2(2 - \frac{d}{2} - \frac{D}{2d}) \geq 5$, $v_2(\frac{\partial f'}{\partial z}(1,2)) = v_2(\frac{2D}{d}) = 2$.

If $\frac{d}{2} + \frac{D}{2d} \equiv 8 \ mod \ 32$, consider $v_2(f'(1,4)) = v_2(8 - \frac{d}{2} - \frac{D}{2d}) \geq 5$, $v_2(\frac{\partial f'}{\partial z}(1,4)) = v_2(\frac{2D}{d}) = 2$.

If $\frac{d}{2} + \frac{D}{2d} \equiv 18 \ mod \ 32$, consider $v_2(f'(1,6)) = v_2(18 - \frac{d}{2} - \frac{D}{2d}) \geq 5$, $v_2(\frac{\partial f'}{\partial z}(1,6)) = v_2(\frac{2D}{d}) = 2$.

$iii)$ If $n = 3$

($\Rightarrow$) $C_d(\mathbb{Q}_2) \neq \Phi$, we have $2v_2(w) \geq min\{v_2(d), v_2(\frac{D}{d}) + 4v_2(z)\} = min\{1, 2 + 4v_2(z)\}$. Then $v_2(z) < 0$, $v_2(w) = 1 + 2v_2(z)$, assume $z = 2^{-i}z'$, $w = 2^{-2i+1}w'$, where $i > 0$, $v_2(z') = v_2(w') = 0$, so we get $2^{-4i+2}w'^2 = d + \frac{D}{d}2^{-4i}z'^4$, simplify to get $w'^2 = 2^{4i-2}d + \frac{D}{4d}z'^4$, that is $1 \equiv w'^2 \equiv 2^{4i-2}d + \frac{D}{4d}z'^4 \equiv \frac{D}{4d} \ mod \ 8$.

($\Leftarrow$) If $\frac{D}{4d} \equiv 1 \ mod \ 8$, consider $v_2(f(\frac{1}{2}, \frac{1}{2})) = v_2(\frac{1}{4} - d - \frac{D}{16d}) \geq min\{v_2(d), v_2(1 - \frac{D}{4d}) - 2\} \geq 1$, $v_2(\frac{\partial f}{\partial w}(\frac{1}{2}, \frac{1}{2})) = v_2(1) = 0$.

(3) $\forall t | d$, t is prime

1) When $t = p_i$

($\Rightarrow$) $C_d(\mathbb{Q}_t) \neq \Phi$, we have $2v_t(w) \geq min\{v_t(d), v_t(\frac{D}{d}) + 4v_t(z)\} = min\{1, 4v_t(z)\}$. Then $v_t(z) \leq 0$, $v_t(w) = 2v_t(z)$, assume $z = t^{-i}z'$, $w = t^{-2i}w'$, where $i \geq 0$, $v_t(z') = v_t(w') = 0$, then we get $t^{-4i}w'^2 = d + \frac{D}{d}t^{-4i}z'^4$, simplify to get $w'^2 = t^{4i}d + \frac{D}{d}z'^4$, so $w'^2 \equiv t^{4i}d + \frac{D}{d}z'^4 \ mod \ t$, that is $(\frac{D/d}{t}) = 1$.

($\Leftarrow$) If $(\frac{D/d}{t}) = 1$, then $\exists a, S.t. a^2 \equiv \frac{D}{d} \ mod \ t$, consider $v_t(f(1,a)) \geq min\{v_t(a^2 - \frac{D}{d}), v_t(d)\} \geq 1$, $v_t(\frac{\partial f}{\partial w}(1,a)) = v_t(2a) = 0$, so $v_t(f(1,a)) > 2v_t(\frac{\partial f}{\partial w}(1,a))$.

2) When $t = q_j$

($\Rightarrow$) $C_d(\mathbb{Q}_t) \neq \Phi$, we have $2v_t(w) \geq min\{v_t(d), v_t(\frac{D}{d}) + 4v_t(z)\} = min\{1, 1 + 4v_t(z)\}$. Then $v_t(z) = 0$, $v_t(w) \geq 1$, meanwhile $\frac{w^2}{t} = \frac{d}{t} + \frac{D}{dt}z^4$, so $0 \equiv \frac{w^2}{t} \equiv \frac{d}{t} + \frac{D}{dt}z^4 \ mod \ t \Rightarrow \frac{-d^2}{D} \equiv z^4 \ mod \ t$, that is said $(\frac{-d^2/D}{t})_4 = 1$.

($\Leftarrow$) If $(\frac{-d^2/D}{t})_4 = 1$, then $\exists a$ such that $a^4 \equiv \frac{-d^2}{D} \ mod \ t$, consider $f'(z,w) = \frac{w^2}{t} - \frac{d}{t} - \frac{D}{dt}z^4$, then $f'(a,t) \equiv 0 - \frac{D}{dt} \cdot \frac{-d^2}{D} - \frac{d}{t} \equiv 0 \ mod \ t$, then we get $v_t(f'(a,t)) \geq 1$, and $v_t(\frac{\partial f'}{\partial w}(a,t)) = 0$. So $v_t(f'(a,t)) > 2v_t(\frac{\partial f'}{\partial w}(a,t))$, according to Hensel Lemma, $f'(z,w)$ has root in $\mathbb{Q}_t^2$, that is equivalence to $f(z,w)$ has root in $\mathbb{Q}_t^2$, $C_d(\mathbb{Q}_t) \neq \Phi$.

3) When $t = r_k$

($\Rightarrow$) $C_d(\mathbb{Q}_t) \neq \varPhi$, we have $2v_t(w) \geq min\{v_t(d), v_t(\frac{D}{d}) + 4v_t(z)\} = min\{1, 2 + 4v_t(z)\}$. Then $v_t(z) < 0$, $v_t(w) = 1 + 2v_t(z)$, assume $z = t^{-i}z'$, $w = t^{-2i+1}w'$, where $i < 0$, $v_t(z') = v_t(w') = 0$, so we get $t^{-4i+2}w'^2 = d + \frac{D}{d}t^{-4i}z'^4$, simplify to get $w'^2 = t^{4i-2}d + \frac{D}{dt^2}z'^4$, so $w'^2 \equiv t^{4i-2}d + \frac{D}{dt^2}z'^4 \mod t$, that is $(\frac{D/dt^2}{t}) = 1$.

($\Leftarrow$) If $(\frac{D/dt^2}{t}) = 1$, then $\exists a, S.t.a^2 \equiv \frac{D}{dt^2} \mod t$, consider $v_t(f(\frac{a}{t}, \frac{1}{t})) \geq min\{-2 + v_t(a^2 - \frac{D}{dt^2}), v_t(d)\} \geq -1$, $v_t(\frac{\partial f}{\partial w}(\frac{a}{t}, \frac{1}{t})) = v_t(\frac{a}{t}) = -1$, so $v_t(f(\frac{a}{t}, \frac{1}{t})) > 2v_t(\frac{\partial f}{\partial w}(\frac{a}{t}, \frac{1}{t}))$.

(4) $\forall t \nmid d$, t is prime

1) When $t = p_i$

($\Rightarrow$) $C_d(\mathbb{Q}_t) \neq \varPhi$, we have $2v_t(w) \geq min\{v_t(d), v_t(\frac{D}{d}) + 4v_t(z)\} = min\{0, 1 + 4v_t(z)\}$. Then $v_t(z) \leq 0$, $v_t(w) = 0$, so we get $w^2 \equiv d + \frac{D}{d}z^4 \mod t \Rightarrow w^2 \equiv d \mod t \Rightarrow (\frac{d}{t}) = 1$.

($\Leftarrow$) If $(\frac{d}{t}) = 1$, then $\exists a, S.t.a^2 \equiv d \mod t$, consider $v_t(f(0, a)) = v_t(a^2 - d) \geq 1$, $v_t(\frac{\partial f}{\partial w}(0, a)) = v_t(2a) = 0$.

2) When $t = q_j$

($\Rightarrow$) $C_d(\mathbb{Q}_t) \neq \varPhi$, we have $2v_t(w) \geq min\{v_t(d), v_t(\frac{D}{d}) + 4v_t(z)\} = min\{0, 2 + 4v_t(z)\}$.

When $v_t(z) \geq 0$, $v_t(w) = 0$, so $w^2 \equiv d + \frac{D}{d}z^4 \mod t \Rightarrow w^2 \equiv d \mod t \Rightarrow (\frac{d}{t}) = 1$.

When $v_t(z) < 0$, $v_t(w) = 1 + 2v_t(z)$, assume $z = t^{-i}z'$, $w = t^{-2i+1}w'$, where $i < 0$, $v_t(z') = v_t(w') = 0$, then we get $t^{-4i+2}w'^2 = d + \frac{D}{d}t^{-4i}z'^4$, simplify to get $w'^2 = t^{4i-2}d + \frac{D}{dt^2}z'^4$, so $w'^2 \equiv t^{4i-2}d + \frac{D}{dt^2}z'^4 \mod t$, that is $(\frac{D/dt^2}{t}) = 1$.

($\Leftarrow$) If $(\frac{d}{t}) = 1$, then $\exists a, S.t.a^2 \equiv d \mod t$, consider $v_t(f(0, a)) = v_t(a^2 - d) \geq 1$, $v_t(\frac{\partial f}{\partial w}(0, a)) = v_t(2a) = 0$.

If $(\frac{D/dt^2}{t}) = 1$, then $\exists a, S.t.a^2 \equiv \frac{D}{dt^2} \mod t$, consider $v_t(f(\frac{a}{t}, \frac{1}{t})) \geq min\{-2 + v_t(a^2 - \frac{D}{dt^2}), v_t(d)\} \geq -1$, $v_t(\frac{\partial f}{\partial w}(\frac{a}{t}, \frac{1}{t})) = v_t(\frac{a}{t}) = -1$.

3) When $t = r_k$

($\Rightarrow$) $C_d(\mathbb{Q}_t) \neq \varPhi$, we have $2v_t(w) \geq min\{v_t(d), v_t(\frac{D}{d}) + 4v_t(z)\} = min\{0, 3 + 4v_t(z)\}$. Then $v_t(z) \geq 0$, $v_t(w) = 0$, so $w^2 \equiv d + \frac{D}{d}z^4 \mod t \Rightarrow w^2 \equiv d \mod t \Rightarrow (\frac{d}{t}) = 1$.

($\Leftarrow$) If $(\frac{d}{t}) = 1$, then $\exists a, S.t.a^2 \equiv d \mod t$, consider $v_t(f(0, a)) = v_t(a^2 - d) \geq 1$, $v_t(\frac{\partial f}{\partial w}(0, a)) = v_t(2a) = 0$.

$\square$

6 Examples

Example 1. When $r = 1$, $p \equiv q \equiv 3 \mod 16$, and $(\frac{p}{q}) = 1$, the dual curve of $E_D : y^2 = x^3 - Dx$ is $E_{-4D} : y^2 = x^3 + 4Dx$, then we have $r_E = 1$, and $v_p(x((2k+1)P)) \neq v_q(x((2k+1)P))$.

Proof. According to Corollary 1, we can get $(-1)^{r_E} = w_\infty \cdot w_2 \cdot w_p = -1 \cdot 1 \cdot 1 = -1$, so $r_E \geq 1$.

(1) For $E_D : y^2 = x^3 - Dx$, $S = \{\infty\} \bigcup \{p, q\}$, $Q(S, 2) = <-1, p, q> \bigcup \{\infty\}$.
$\forall d \in Q(S, 2)$, apply Theorem (2) to investigate the local solution of C'_d :
$w^2 = d - \frac{D}{d} z^4$.
Because of $(\frac{q}{q}) = (-1)^{\frac{p-1}{2}}(-1)^{\frac{q-1}{2}}(\frac{p}{q}) = -1 \Rightarrow C_{pq}(\mathbb{Q}_p) = \Phi$, so $-1, pq \notin S'(\phi)$.
Because of $(\frac{q}{p}) = (-1)^{\frac{p-1}{2}}(-1)^{\frac{q-1}{2}}(\frac{p}{q}) = -1 \Rightarrow C_{-p}(\mathbb{Q}_p) = \Phi$, so $-p, q \notin S'(\phi)$.
Because of $p - \frac{D}{p} \equiv 0 \bmod 16 \Rightarrow C_p(\mathbb{Q}_2) \neq \Phi$; $(\frac{-q}{p}) = (-1)^{\frac{p-1}{2}}(\frac{p}{q}) = 1 \Rightarrow$
$C_p(\mathbb{Q}_p) \neq \Phi$; $(\frac{p}{q}) = 1 \Rightarrow C_p(\mathbb{Q}_q) \neq \Phi$, so $p, -q \in S'(\phi)$.
Thus $S'(\phi) = \{1, p, -q, -pq\}$.

(2) For $E_{-4D} : y^2 = x^3 + 4Dx$, $\widehat{S} = \{\infty\} \bigcup \{2, p, q\}$, $\widehat{Q}(\widehat{S}, 2) = <-1, 2, p, q>$
$\bigcup \{\infty\}$. $\forall d \in \widehat{Q}(\widehat{S}, 2)$, apply Theorem (2) to investigate the local solution of
$C_d : w^2 = d + \frac{4D}{d} z^4$.
Because of $4D > 0$, so $-1, -2, -p, -q, -2p, -2q, -2pq \notin S(\phi)$.
Because of $(\frac{2}{p}) = (-1)^{\frac{p-1}{2}} = -1 \Rightarrow C_2(\mathbb{Q}_p) = \Phi$, so $2, 2pq \notin S(\phi)$.
Because of $p \equiv 3 \bmod 4$, $\frac{4D}{4p} \equiv q \equiv 3 \bmod 4 \Rightarrow C_p(\mathbb{Q}_2) = \Phi$, so $p, q \notin S(\phi)$.
Because of $2p + \frac{D}{2p} \equiv 2p + 2q \equiv 12 \bmod 16 \Rightarrow C_{2p}(\mathbb{Q}_2) = \Phi$, so $2p, 2q \notin S(\phi)$.
Thus $S(\phi) = \{1, pq\}$.

So from Theorem 6 we can get $r_E = 1$. Then from Property 2 we obtain that $v_p(x((2k+1)P)) \neq v_q(x((2k+1)P))$. At this point, we can use the points on E_D to factor D.   □

Remark 6. This is the result of Burhanuddin and Huang [2,3].

Example 2. When the elliptic curve is $E_{2Dr} : y^2 = x^3 - 2Drx$, where r is an odd prime integer. Its dual curve is $E_{-8Dr} : y^2 = x^3 + 8Drx$. In this case, the points on E_{2Dr} can be used to decompose D as shown in the following table 1.

When p, q, r meet the conditions in the Table 1, we have $r_E = 1$, and $v_p(x((2k+1)P)) \neq v_q(x((2k+1)P))$. At this point, we can use the points on E_{2Dr} to factor D.

Proof. The proof is similar to Example 1. We can prove it by applying Theorem 2, Theorem 6 and Proposition 2.   □

Remark 7. This is the result of Li and Zeng [6]. At the same time, the above method can be used to analyze any elliptic curve $E_{Dr} : y^2 = x^3 - Drx$, where r is an arbitrary integer.

Next, we will give a specific curve to illustrate our theory.

Example 3. Suppose we want to factor $D = 295927$, select $r = 3$, then $E_{2Dr} :$
$y^2 = x^3 - 1775562x$, use Magma to compute its generator as $(1623, 37329)$. And $GCD(1623, 295927) = 541$. It can just factor D at this time.

We can also get the above conclusions by checking Table 1.

Table 1. r is odd prime integer

D	r	p,q,r
$D \equiv 1 \bmod 8$	$r \equiv 1 \bmod 8$	$p \equiv 5,7 \bmod 8$ and $\left(\frac{D}{r}\right) = -1$
	$r \equiv 3 \bmod 8$	$p \equiv 3,7 \bmod 8$ and $\left(\frac{D}{r}\right) = -1$
	$r \equiv 7 \bmod 8$	$p \equiv 3,5 \bmod 8$ and $\left(\frac{D}{r}\right) = -1$
$D \equiv 3 \bmod 8$	$r \equiv 1 \bmod 8$	$p \equiv 5,7 \bmod 8$ and $\left(\frac{D}{r}\right) = -1$
	$r \equiv 3 \bmod 8$	$p \equiv 5,7 \bmod 8$
	$r \equiv 5 \bmod 8$	$p \equiv 1 \bmod 8$ and $\left(\frac{r}{p}\right) = -1$
		$p \equiv 3 \bmod 8$ and $\left(\frac{r}{q}\right) = -1$
		$p \equiv 5 \bmod 8$ and $\left(\frac{r}{q}\right) = 1$
		$p \equiv 7 \bmod 8$ and $\left(\frac{r}{p}\right) = 1$
	$r \equiv 7 \bmod 8$	$p \equiv 1,5 \bmod 8$ and $\left(\frac{r}{p}\right) = -1$
		$p \equiv 3,7 \bmod 8$ and $\left(\frac{r}{q}\right) = -1$
$D \equiv 5 \bmod 8$	$r \equiv 1 \bmod 8$	$p \equiv 3,7 \bmod 8$ and $\left(\frac{D}{r}\right) = -1$
	$r \equiv 3 \bmod 8$	$p \equiv 1,7 \bmod 8$ and $\left(\frac{r}{p}\right) = -1$
		$p \equiv 3,5 \bmod 8$ and $\left(\frac{r}{q}\right) = -1$
	$r \equiv 5 \bmod 8$	$p \equiv 3,7 \bmod 8$
	$r \equiv 7 \bmod 8$	$p \equiv 1 \bmod 8$ and $\left(\frac{r}{p}\right) = -1$
		$p \equiv 3 \bmod 8$ and $\left(\frac{r}{p}\right) = 1$
		$p \equiv 5 \bmod 8$ and $\left(\frac{r}{q}\right) = -1$
		$p \equiv 7 \bmod 8$ and $\left(\frac{r}{q}\right) = 1$
$D \equiv 7 \bmod 8$	$r \equiv 1 \bmod 8$	$p \equiv 3,5 \bmod 8$ and $\left(\frac{D}{r}\right) = -1$
	$r \equiv 3 \bmod 8$	$p \equiv 1 \bmod 8$ and $\left(\frac{r}{p}\right) = -1$
		$p \equiv 3 \bmod 8$ and $\left(\frac{r}{q}\right) = 1$
		$p \equiv 5 \bmod 8$ and $\left(\frac{r}{p}\right) = 1$
		$p \equiv 7 \bmod 8$ and $\left(\frac{r}{q}\right) = -1$
	$r \equiv 5 \bmod 8$	$p \equiv 1 \bmod 8$ and $\left(\frac{r}{p}\right) = -1$
		$p \equiv 3 \bmod 8$ and $\left(\frac{r}{p}\right) = 1$
		$p \equiv 5 \bmod 8$ and $\left(\frac{r}{q}\right) = 1$
		$p \equiv 7 \bmod 8$ and $\left(\frac{r}{q}\right) = -1$

References

1. Birch, B.J., Stephens, N.M.: The parity of the rank of the mordell-weil group. Topology **5**(4), 295–299 (1966)
2. Burhanuddin, I.A., Huang, M.: Factoring integers and computing elliptic curve rational points. Usc Computer Science (2012)
3. Burhanuddin, I.A., Huang, M.: On the equation $y^2 = x^3 - pqx$. J. Numb. **2014**(193), 1–5 (2014). Accessed 16 July 2014
4. Cohen, H.: Number Theory: Volume I: Tools and Diophantine Equations. Springer, New York (2008). https://doi.org/10.1007/978-0-387-49923-9

5. Dokchitser, T.: Notes on the Parity Conjecture. Springer, Basel (2010). https://doi.org/10.1007/978-3-0348-0618-3_5
6. Li, X.M., Zeng, J.X.: On the elliptic curve $y^2 = x^3 - 2rdx$ and factoring integers. Sci. China **2014**(04), 719–728 (2014)
7. Silverman, J.H.: The Arithmetic of Elliptic Curves. Springer, New York (2009). https://doi.org/10.1007/978-0-387-09494-6
8. Washington, L.C.: Elliptic curves: Number Theory and Cryptography, 2nd edn. CRC Press, Inc., Boca Raton (2008)

On the Linear Complexity of Feedforward Clock-Controlled Sequence

Yangpan Zhang$^{(\boxtimes)}$ and Maozhi Xu

School of Mathematical Sciences, Peking University, Beijing 100871, China
zyp94@pku.edu.cn

Abstract. As a research field of stream ciphers, the pursuit of a balance of security and practicality is the focus. The conditions for security usually have to satisfy at least high period and high linear complexity. Because the feedforward clock-controlled structure can provide quite a high period and utility, many sequence ciphers are constructed based on this structure. However, the past study of its linear complexity only works when the controlled sequence is an m-sequence. Using the theory of matrix over the ring and block matrix in this paper, we construct a more helpful method. It can estimate the lower bound of the linear complexity of the feedforward clock-controlled sequence. Even the controlled sequence has great linear complexity.

Keywords: Stream cipher · Clock-controlled · Linear complexity · Block matrix

1 Introduction

A clock-controlled structure is a structure that uses one sequence generator as a clock to control another sequence generator (or control itself) to generate a new sequence. The sequences generated by this structure have a large linear complexity and are widely used in stream cipher design.

The first proposal of the clock-controlled structure dates back to 1980 when Jennings [12] and Kjeldsen [14] proposed a similar structure, respectively. In 1984, T. Beth and F. C. Piper [1] first introduced the concept of "clock-controlled."

The subsequent studies [11] divided the clock-controlled structure into two categories, i.e., feedforward and feedback clock-controlled. The basic feedforward clock-controlled structure refers to using a regular sequence generator to control the clock of another sequence generator. For the feedback clock-controlled structure, it uses the output of the pseudo-random sequence generator to clock-control itself. In practice, the feedback structure makes it challenging to analyze the security from the theory, so most of the clock-controlled sequences are of feedforward structure.

The feedforward clock-controlled structure has a mathematically more apparent structure and better theoretical analysis results for its periodic and statistical properties [13]. However, the study of linear complexity is not as clear.

© Springer Nature Switzerland AG 2021
Y. Yu and M. Yung (Eds.): Inscrypt 2021, LNCS 13007, pp. 331–348, 2021.
https://doi.org/10.1007/978-3-030-88323-2_18

The upper bound on the linear complexity is nq [20], where the order n is the linear complexity of the controlled sequence, and q is the period of the control sequence. However, the conditions for the linear complexity to reach the upper bound are pretty demanding.

By analyzing irreducible polynomials over a finite field, assuming that the controlled sequence is an m-sequence, Li finds a sufficient condition for the linear complexity to reach an upper bound [20]. In contrast, Golic J.D analyzes it from a probabilistic point of view in 1988 [10]. The probability of the linear complexity reaching the upper bound tends to 1 as n grows. When the controlled sequence is an m-sequence of order n, the step sum M is less than 2^n.

The above studies were published around 1990. However, in the last years of the 20th century, stream cryptanalysis tools such as linear analysis [5,16], correlation analysis [9,17], and algebraic attacks [6] were widely researched and developed. The discovery of these analysis tools has made the traditional sequence cryptosystem based on LFSR design less secure. People gradually abandoned the design approach using LFSRs as linear drivers and shifted to nonlinear design schemes. In this way, the above-mentioned linear complexity study of clock-controlled sequences based on m-sequences was rendered useless.

Furthermore, when the controlled sequence is nonlinear, its minimal polynomials are often reducible and irregular. Even the linear complexity is unknown. Therefore, in practical analysis, people tend to use less rigorous experimental analysis methods. That is, analyze the actual linear complexity in the degenerate case with shortened register. Then the nondegenerate case is reasonably guessed by the relationship between register length and linear complexity. Such as the LILI-128 algorithm [7].

In this paper, we make a new method to estimate the lower bound of linear complexity of a feedforward clock-controlled sequence. This new method can estimate better when the clock-controlled sequence is under a nonlinear driver. Unlike the current result, this paper does not analyze the polynomial reducibility. However, it estimates the lower bound of the matrix rank of the sequence-generating circulant matrix after a proper transformation. Our approach method gives a better bound on the linear complexity of the feedforward clock-controlled sequence. Unlike the current results in the papers [10,19,20], this method does not require the controlled sequence to be an m-sequence. It is, therefore, suitable for feedforward clock-controlled sequences in a general sense.

The article is structured as follows. Section 2 will give the basic concepts in the study and some mathematical tools for the study of block matrices. With the help of these tools, we give in Sect. 3 an estimation method for the lower bound of the linear complexity of the feedforward clock-controlled sequence. Section 4 proposes its improved algorithm LIFI-128 based on the LILI-128 algorithm and estimates its linear complexity very well. A summary of the whole paper is given in Sect. 5.

2   Pre-requisite Knowledge

2.1   Feedforward Clock-Controlled Sequence

The paper [11] is a good review of clock-controlled shift registers, after which the definition of a basic feedforward clock-controlled sequence generator can be given as follows.

Definition 1 (Basic clock-controlled sequence generator).

Input: *a Control Sequence Generator A with period T_1; a Controlled Sequence Generator B with period T_2; a step map $f_L : output_A \rightarrow Z_{T_2}$. where $output_A$ represents the set of possible states of the output of generator A at any moment.*

Key: *the initial states of the two sequence generators A and B.*

Process: *Denote the initial state moment as $t = 0$. For $t = 1, 2, \cdots$, complete the following actions step by step.*

   – *1 Run sequence generator A for one time, after which the current output state of sequence generator A is recorded as a_t, and $f_L(a_t)$ is calculated.*
   – *2 Run the sequence generator B for a total of $f_L(a_t)$ times, after which the state b_{σ_t} of the output of B is set to the output state $c_t = b_{\sigma_t}$ of the clock-controlled sequence generator at moment t. where b_i is the output state of generator B after continuous running i times since the initial state, $\sigma_t = \sum_{i=1}^{t}(f_L(a_i))$.*

Output: *clock-controlled sequence $\{c_t\}_{t=1}^{\infty}$.*

In the above definition, we call the sequence generated by A under the action of f_L a Control Sequence and the sequence generated by B under the control of a regular clock a Controlled Sequence.

This definition can also be reduced to a binary pseudo-random sampling sequence as follows.

Definition 2 (Binary pseudo-random sampling sequence).

Input: *given a binary periodic sequence $\{b_t\} = (b_0, b_1, \cdots,)$, where $b_i \in F_2$; given a pseudo-random sampling subscript sequence $\{\sigma_t\} = (\sigma_1, \sigma_2, \cdots)$, where $\sigma_i \in N$.*

Output: *a new set of binary sequences $\{c_t\} = (b_{\sigma_1}, b_{\sigma_2}, \cdots)$. Call it a pseudo-random sampling sequence.*

For the period of the clock-controlled sequence, the following result is obtained.

Theorem 1 [2]. *Denote $S = \sum_{i=1}^{T_1}(f_L(a_i))$, i.e., $S = \sigma_{T_1}$. When $gcd(S, T_2) = 1$, i.e., when the integer S is coprime with the period T_2. The minimum positive period of the clock-controlled sequence $\{c_t\}_{t=1}^{\infty}$ is $T_3 = T_1 T_2$, which reaches a maximum period.*

For clock-controlled sequence algorithms, the maximum period is always preferred in practical applications. Therefore, all the sequence models for clock control that appear below in this paper are chosen to reach the maximum period.

2.2   Linear Complexity and Circulant Matrix

In recent years, the LFSR structure is no longer directly used to construct stream cipher regimes. However, the linear complexity also measures the resistance of a sequence to many linear-based attacks. Therefore, linear complexity is still a very important metric in measuring stream cipher security.

An equivalent definition of linear complexity is given below after the definition of circulant matrix.

Definition 3. *On a field* $\mathbb{K}$, *a matrix of the following shape is called a* $n \times n$ *r-circulant matrix. where* $r \in K$.

$$
\begin{pmatrix}
a_1 & a_2 & a_3 & \cdots & a_{n-1} & a_n \\
ra_n & a_1 & a_2 & \cdots & a_{n-2} & a_{n-1} \\
ra_{n-1} & ra_n & a_1 & \cdots & a_{n-3} & a_{n-2} \\
\vdots & \vdots & \vdots & \vdots & \vdots & \vdots \\
ra_2 & ra_3 & ra_4 & \cdots & ra_n & a_1
\end{pmatrix}_{n \times n}
\tag{1}
$$

For convenience, it can be generally shortened to $Cir_n^r (a_1, a_2, \cdots, a_n)$. *Specially, if* $r = 1$, *we call it circulant matrix.*

For a purely periodic sequence $A = (a_1, a_2, \cdots)$ of period n over a field $\mathbb{K}$. Denote $Cir_n^1 (a_1, a_2, \cdots, a_n)$ by $M_{cir}(A)$.

Theorem 2 [18]. *A is a purely periodic sequence on a field* $\mathbb{K}$ *with period* n. *Then, for* $M_{cir} (A)$, *there is such a property. That is, the rank of* $M_{cir} (A)$ *is equal to the linear complexity* $L (A)$ *of the sequence* A *over the field* $\mathbb{K}$.

When the sequence $B = (b_1, b_2, \cdots)$, is regular sampled from the sequence $A = (a_1, a_2, \cdots)$, with a period of l. That is, for any $i \geq 1$, we have $b_i = a_{s+l \cdot (i-1)}$, where $b_1 = a_s$ is called the starting sampling point. It can be denoted briefly as $B = A(s, l)$. If A is a sequence of period n and satisfies $gcd(l, n) = 1$, then the following corollary can be obtained using Theorem 2.

Corollary 1. *Assume A is a purely periodic sequence over a field* $\mathbb{K}$ *with period* n. *And the sequence* $B = A(s, l)$ *is a sequence of regular samples of the sequence* A. *If* $gcd(l, n) = 1$, *then: (1) the period of sequence* B *is* n; *(2)* $L(A) = L(B)$.

The proof of the corollary is simple; it only requires a proper primary rows and columns swap for $M_{cir} (A)$ to become $M_{cir} (B)$. Therefore, the two sequences have the same linear complexity.

For any r-circulant matrix over a number field $\mathbb{K}$, there is a very important theorem.

Theorem 3 [4]. *Let* $M = Cir_n^r (w_1, w_2, \cdots, w_n)$ *be an r-circulant matrix over field* $\mathbb{K}$. *Denote the function* $w(x) = \sum_{i=0}^{n-1} w_{i+1} x^i$. *If the set of all roots of the equation* $x^n - r = 0$ *over field* $\mathbb{K}$ *can be written as* $\{\theta \xi^i \mid i = 0, 1, \cdots, n-1\}$, *where* $\theta^n = r$. *Then the set of all characteristic roots of the matrix* M *is* $\{w(\theta \xi^i) \mid i = 0, 1, \cdots, n-1\}$.

2.3   Block Matrix and Matrix over Ring

Let $\mathbb{K}$ be a field, denote the ring of all $mn \times mn$ matrices over field $\mathbb{K}$ by $M_{mn \times mn}(\mathbb{K})$. Mark matrix ring R as subring of $M_{n \times n}(\mathbb{K})$. Suppose a matrix A belongs to $M_{m \times m}(R)$, then A also belongs to $M_{mn \times mn}(\mathbb{K})$. Let $[A]_{i,j}^R$ denote the i,jth block of A, $a_{i,j}$ denote the i,jth entry of A when over $M_{mn \times mn}(\mathbb{K})$. It's easy to see that

$$
A = \begin{pmatrix} a_{1,1} & a_{1,2} & \cdots & a_{1,mn} \\ a_{2,1} & a_{2,2} & \cdots & a_{2,mn} \\ \vdots & \vdots & \ddots & \vdots \\ a_{mn,1} & a_{mn,2} & \cdots & a_{mn,mn} \end{pmatrix} = \begin{pmatrix} A_{1,1} & A_{1,2} & \cdots & A_{1,m} \\ A_{2,1} & A_{2,2} & \cdots & A_{2,m} \\ \vdots & \vdots & \ddots & \vdots \\ A_{m,1} & A_{m,2} & \cdots & A_{m,m} \end{pmatrix} = A^R
$$

The above sliced matrix A is called the block matrix, In particular, when we discuss A as a element of $M_{m \times m}(R)$, we use A^R to denote A, and the corner marks are used only for distinction.

For a general commutative ring R, Brown W C [3] studied relevant properties about matrices over the ring R. Including the determinant $det_R(A^R)$, rank $rank_R(A^R)$, modulus, diagonalization. Based on the definitions and results given in the book, we got the following remarkable theorems.

Theorem 4. Let $A \in M_{m \times m}(R)$, where $R = \{\sum_{i=0}^{\infty} k_i S^i | k_i \in \mathbb{K}\}$ is a subalgebra of $M_{n \times n}(\mathbb{K})$. In particular, the minimal polynomial $f(x) = p^r(x)$ of $S \in M_{n \times n}(\mathbb{K})$ is an power of an irreducible polynomial $p(x)$ over the field $\mathbb{K}$. Thus,

$$
rank_R\left(A^R\right) = k \Rightarrow rank_{\mathbb{K}}(A) \geq kn, 0 \leq k \leq m
$$

Clearly, when the commutative ring R satisfies the conditions in the above theorem, R is isomorphic to the residue class ring $H = \mathbb{K}[x]/(p^r(x))$. This means that the equation $rank_R(A^R) = rank_H(A^H)$ will hold automatically under isomorphism.

Denote another ring of residue classes $\overline{H} = \mathbb{K}[x]/(p(x))$, it's easy to see $\overline{H}$ is a field. At the same time, there exists a subjective homomorphism mapping π from H to $\overline{H}$. The image of A^H under the action of π is written as $\overline{A} \in M_{m \times m}(\overline{H})$. We have the following theorem.

Theorem 5.
$$
rank_H\left(A^H\right) = rank_{\overline{H}}\left(\overline{A}\right)
$$

These two theorems provide theoretical support for our estimate of the lower bound on linear complexity. The proof procedure is complex and unproductive for this paper. For logical reasons, the exact process of their proof is omitted.

3   Linear Complexity Estimation Model for Feedforward Clock-Controlled Sequences

This section we will show you how to use the basic model of pseudo-random sampling. And transform sequences' circulant matrix. Finally estimate the rank of block matrix.

Denote two period sequence $\{a_i\}_\infty$ and $\{b_i\}_\infty$, where $a_i \in \mathbb{N}$ and $b_i \in \mathbb{F}_2$. Denote $\sum_{i=1}^{k} a_i$ by s_k. By sampling $\{b_i\}_\infty$ with index sequence $\{s_i\}_\infty$, we get a new sequence $C = \{c_i\}_\infty$, where $c_i = b_{s_i}$. We call $\{c_i\}_\infty$ a clock-controlled sequence generated by $\{a_i\}_\infty$ controlling $\{b_i\}_\infty$.

In general case, people prefer to use maximal period sequences as them have good statistical properties. So we always assume s_m is coprime with the period n in follow discussion.

3.1   Primary Transformation of the Circulant Matrix $M_{cir}(C)$

It's hard to direct calculate rank of $M_{cir}(C)$, so we do some row operations and column operations on $M_{cir}(C)$ and denote the matrix after operations by $\overline{C}$:

$$
\begin{array}{c}
\\ 1 \\ 2 \\ 3 \\ \vdots \\ mn
\end{array}
\begin{array}{c}
\begin{array}{ccccc} 1 & 2 & 3 & \cdots & mn \end{array} \\
\left(\begin{array}{ccccc}
c_1 & c_2 & c_3 & \cdots & c_{mn} \\
c_{mn} & c_1 & c_2 & & c_{mn-1} \\
c_{mn-1} & c_{mn} & c_1 & & c_{mn-2} \\
\vdots & & & \ddots & \vdots \\
c_2 & c_3 & c_4 & \cdots & c_1
\end{array}\right)
\end{array}
\Rightarrow
\begin{array}{c}
\\ I_1 \\ I_2 \\ I_3 \\ \vdots \\ I_m
\end{array}
\begin{array}{c}
\begin{array}{ccccc} I_1 & I_2 & I_3 & \cdots & I_m \end{array} \\
\left(\begin{array}{ccccc}
C_{1,1} & C_{1,2} & C_{1,3} & & C_{1,m} \\
C_{2,1} & C_{2,2} & C_{2,3} & \cdots & C_{2,m} \\
C_{3,1} & C_{3,2} & C_{3,3} & & C_{3,m} \\
\vdots & & & \ddots & \vdots \\
C_{m,1} & C_{m,2} & C_{m,3} & \cdots & C_{m,m}
\end{array}\right)
\end{array}
$$

where the index set $I_i = \{i, m+i, 2m+i, \cdots, (n-1)m+i\}$, and the submatrix $C_{i,j}$ was construct by entries from I_i's rows and I_j's columns of $M_{cir}(C)$. Assume $t = (j - i + 1) \bmod mn$, then:

$$
C_{i,j} =
\begin{array}{c}
\\ i \\ m+i \\ 2m+i \\ \vdots \\ (n-1)m+i
\end{array}
\begin{array}{c}
\begin{array}{ccccc} j & m+j & 2m+j & \cdots & (n-1)m+j \end{array} \\
\left(\begin{array}{ccccc}
c_t & c_{t+m} & c_{t+2m} & & c_{t+(n-1)m} \\
c_{t+(n-1)m} & c_t & c_{t+m} & \cdots & c_{t+(n-2)m} \\
c_{t+(n-2)m} & c_{t+(n-1)m} & c_t & & c_{t+(n-3)m} \\
\vdots & & & \ddots & \vdots \\
c_{t+m} & c_{t+2m} & c_{t+3m} & \cdots & c_t
\end{array}\right)
\end{array}
$$

It's easy to show that $C_{i,j}$ was a circulant matrix, and for two submatrices $C_{i,j}$ and $C_{i',j'}$, $C_{i,j} = C_{i',j'}$ if and only if $j - i = j' - i'$.

Consider subsequence $C^t = \{c_{t+m \cdot i}\}_\infty$, this sequence has a period of n. In fact, C^t equals to $\{b_{s_t+s_m \cdot i}\}_\infty$, it's a sampling sequence of $\{b_i\}_\infty$ with s_m step length. Further, assume $v = (s_m)^{-1} \bmod n$ and $l_t = v(s_t - s_1)$, C^t equals to C^1 start from l_tth position.

Using the fact that $C_{i,j}$ is a circulant matrix, $C_{i,j}$ equals to $M_{cir}(C^t)$. Thus, there is a formula:

$$C_{i,j} = M_{cir}(C^t) = M_{cir}(C^1) \cdot D^{l_t} \tag{2}$$

D is a primitive circulant matrix with dimension n, as shown in follow:

$$D = \begin{pmatrix} 0\,1\,0\,0 & & 0 \\ 0\,0\,1\,0 & \cdots & 0 \\ 0\,0\,0\,1 & & 0 \\ \vdots & \ddots & \\ 1\,0\,0\,0 & \cdots & 0 \end{pmatrix}.$$

Turn back to $C_{i,j}$, if $j \geq i$, then $t = j - i + 1$, if $j < i$, then $t = j - i + 1 + mn$. So

$$C_{i,j} = M_{cir}(C^1) \cdot D^{l_t} = M_{cir}(C^1) \cdot D^{v(s_t - s_1)}.$$

Denote D^v by T, denote $M_{cir}(C^1) \cdot T^{-s_1}$ by $\hat{C}$. Notice that $T^n = I$, we denote $s_{-i} = s_{m-i} - s_m$. When $j \geq i$, $C_{i,j} = \hat{C} \cdot T^{s_j - i + 1}$; when $j < i$, $C_{i,j} = \hat{C} \cdot T^{s_j - i + 1 + s_m n} = \hat{C} \cdot T^{s_j - i + 1} = \hat{C} \cdot T^{s_{m+j-i+1} - s_m} = \hat{C} \cdot T^{s_{m+j-i+1}} \cdot D^{-1}$. Different premise get same result.

Thus,

$$\overline{C} = \begin{pmatrix} \hat{C}T^{s_1} & \hat{C}T^{s_2} & \hat{C}T^{s_3} & & \hat{C}T^{s_m} \\ \hat{C}T^{s_m}D^{-1} & \hat{C}T^{s_1} & \hat{C}T^{s_2} & \cdots & \hat{C}T^{s_{m-1}} \\ \hat{C}T^{s_{m-1}}D^{-1} & \hat{C}T^{s_m}D^{-1} & \hat{C}T^{s_1} & & \hat{C}T^{s_{m-2}} \\ & \vdots & & \ddots & \vdots \\ \hat{C}T^{s_2}D^{-1} & \hat{C}T^{s_3}D^{-1} & \hat{C}T^{s_4}D^{-1} & \cdots & \hat{C}T^{s_1} \end{pmatrix}.$$

3.2 Decomposition of the Matrix over the Ring

In this part, some Lemmas are needed to decompose the matrix over the ring $R =< S >= \{\sum_{i=0}^{\infty} k_i S^i \big| k_i \in \mathbb{K}, i = 0, 1, \cdots \}$.

Let $R =< S >= \{\sum_{i=0}^{\infty} k_i S^i | k_i \in \mathbb{K}, i = 0, 1, \cdots \}$, where S is an element of $M_{n \times n}(\mathbb{K})$. It's obvious that R is a commutative(multiplication) subalgebra of $M_{n \times n}(\mathbb{K})$

Denote S's minimal polynomial over $\mathbb{K}$ by $f(x) = \sum_{i=0}^{l} f_i x^i$, where $l \leq n$ and $f_i \in \mathbb{K}(f_l = 1)$. Thus,

$$< S >= \{\sum_{i=0}^{l-1} k_i S^i | k_i \in \mathbb{K}, i = 0, 1, \cdots, l-1\}.$$

Given $U, V \in < S >$, where $U = \sum_{i=0}^{l-1} u_i S^i, V = \sum_{i=0}^{l-1} v_i S^i$. It's obvious that $U = V$ if and only if $u_i = v_i, \forall i = 0, 1, \cdots, l-1$.

Lemma 1. *Suppose that $S \in M_{n \times n}(\mathbb{K})$ is a matrix over the field $\mathbb{K}$, where the minimal polynomial of S is $f(x)$. And the unique factorization of $f(x)$ over field K is $f(x) = \prod_{i=1}^{d} p_i^{r_i}(x)$, $p_i(x)$ is irreducible and $p_i(x) \neq p_j(x)$ when $i \neq j$.*

Thus, there exists a non-singular matrix $P \in M_{n \times n}(\mathbb{K})$, and matrices S_i for $1 \leq i \leq d$. Where the minimal polynomial of S_i is $p_i^{r_i}(x)$. Such that:

$$S = P^{-1} \cdot \begin{pmatrix} S_1 & & & \\ & S_2 & & \\ & & \ddots & \\ & & & S_d \end{pmatrix} \cdot P$$

In the classical theory of linear algebra, this lemma can be easily proved by analyzing the invariant subspace of the linear transformation.

Corollary 2. *For any $U = \sum_{i=0}^{l-1} u_i S^i \in R = < S >$, exist mapping $g(U) = P \cdot U \cdot P^{-1}$, from $R = < S >$ to $\overline{R} = < PSP^{-1} >$. And,*

$$g(U) = \begin{pmatrix} \sum_{i=0}^{l-1} u_i S_1^i & & \\ & \ddots & \\ & & \sum_{i=0}^{l-1} u_i S_d^i \end{pmatrix}$$

Extend the mapping g from $M_{n \times n}(\mathbb{K})$ to $M_{m \times m}(M_{n \times n}(\mathbb{K}))$. Define a mapping G on $M_{m \times m}(M_{n \times n}(\mathbb{K}))$. for any element $T \in M_{m \times m}(M_{n \times n}(\mathbb{K}))$, T can be written as block matrix $T^{M_{n \times n}(\mathbb{K})} = (T_{ij})_{m \times m}$, where $T_{ij} \in M_{n \times n}(\mathbb{K})$. The mapping G is defined as:

$$G((T_{ij})_{m \times m}) = (g(T_{ij}))_{m \times m}.$$

Obviously, G is a self-isomorphism on $M_{m \times m}(M_{n \times n}(\mathbb{K}))$. And $M_{m \times m}(R)$ is isomorphic to $M_{m \times m}(\overline{R})$ under the action of G, and for $\forall A \in M_{m \times m}(R)$, $rank_{\mathbb{K}}(A) = rank_{\mathbb{K}}(G(A))$.

Return to $M_{m \times m}(R)$. According to corollary 2, suppose $A \in M_{m \times m}(R)$, $G(A) \in M_{m \times m}(\overline{R})$. Thus, every entry of $G(A)$ must have a diagonal shape like:

$$[G(A)]_{i,j}^{\overline{R}} = \begin{pmatrix} S_1^{i,j} & & & \\ & S_2^{i,j} & & \\ & & \ddots & \\ & & & S_d^{ij} \end{pmatrix}.$$

Further, if

$$[A]_{i,j}^R = f_{i,j}(S) = \sum_{t=0}^{l-1} a_t S^t,$$

then

$$[G(A)]_{i,j}^{\overline{R}} = g([A]_{i,j}^R) = P \cdot f_{i,j}(S) \cdot P^{-1} = \sum_{t=0}^{l-1} a_t (PSP^{-1})^t.$$

It's trivial that $S_k^{i,j} = f_{i,j}(S_k)$ for all $i, j = 1, 2, \cdots, m$; $k = 1, 2, \cdots, d$.

Thus, by some row operations and column operations, we can transform $G(A)$ into a quasi-diagonal matrix over $M_{mn \times mn}(\mathbb{K})$:

$$\Gamma_0 \cdot G(A) \cdot \Gamma_1 = \begin{pmatrix} A_1 & & & \\ & A_2 & & \\ & & \ddots & \\ & & & A_d \end{pmatrix}.$$

Γ_0 and Γ_1 are products of some elementary matrix over $M_{mn \times mn}(\mathbb{K})$. $A_t \in M_{mn_t \times mn_t}(\mathbb{K})$ was constructed by $S_t^{i,j}$ as follow:

$$A_t = \begin{pmatrix} S_t^{1,1} & S_t^{1,2} & \cdots & S_t^{1,m} \\ S_t^{2,1} & S_t^{2,2} & & \vdots \\ \vdots & & \ddots & \\ S_t^{m,1} & \cdots & & S_t^{mm} \end{pmatrix}.$$

So $A_t \in M_{m \times m}(< S_t >)$, and we arrive at the conclusion that:

$$rank_{\mathbb{K}}(A) = rank_{\mathbb{K}}(G(A)) = \sum_{t=1}^{d} rank_{\mathbb{K}}(A_t).$$

3.3   Linear Complexity Estimation Model

Let $R =< D > \in M_{n \times n}$, D is a primitive circulant matrix with dimension n.

Obviously, the minimal polynomials of D is $f(x) = x^n + 1$. Assume $f(x)$ have unique factorization $f(x) = \prod_{i=1}^{d} p_i^{2^{\sigma}}(x)$, where $n/2^{\sigma}$ is exactly an odd integer.

From the conclusion of Subsect. 3.1, the linear complexity of the clock-controlled sequence $L(C) = rank_{\mathbb{K}}(\overline{C})$. At the same time, $\overline{C} \in M_{m \times m}(R)$. Combining the matrix decomposition conclusions of Subsect. 3.2, we know that

$$rank_{\mathbb{K}}(\overline{C}) = rank_{\mathbb{K}}(G(\overline{C})) = \sum_{t=1}^{d} rank_{\mathbb{K}}(\overline{C}_t)$$

At the same time, $\overline{C}_t$ is very similar to $\overline{C}$ and has the following form:

$$\overline{C}_t = \begin{pmatrix} \hat{C}_t & O & \cdots & O \\ O & \hat{C}_t & & O \\ \vdots & & \ddots & \\ O & O & \cdots & \hat{C}_t \end{pmatrix} \cdot \begin{pmatrix} T_t^{s_1} & T_t^{s_2} & T_t^{s_3} & & T_t^{s_m} \\ T_t^{s_m} D_t^{-1} & T_t^{s_1} & T_t^{s_2} & \cdots & T_t^{s_{m-1}} \\ T_t^{s_{m-1}} D_t^{-1} & T_t^{s_m} D_t^{-1} & T_t^{s_1} & & T_t^{s_{m-2}} \\ \vdots & & & \ddots & \vdots \\ T_t^{s_2} D_t^{-1} & T_t^{s_3} D_t^{-1} & T_t^{s_4} D_t^{-1} & \cdots & T_t^{s_1} \end{pmatrix}$$

where

$$P \cdot D \cdot P^{-1} = \begin{pmatrix} D_1 & & & \\ & D_2 & & \\ & & \ddots & \\ & & & D_d \end{pmatrix}.$$

and $T_t = D_t^v$, where $v \times s_m \equiv 1 \mod n$.

D_t's minimal polynomial is $p_t^{2^\sigma}(x)$, D_t generate a commutative subalgebra, denote it by $R_t =< D_t >$. Recall the theory of block-matrix, we know $R_t \cong \mathbb{F}_2[x]/(p_t^{2^\sigma}(x)) \triangleq H_t$. Set up ϕ_t to be the isomorphism function from R_t to $\mathbb{F}_t[x]/(p_t^{2^\sigma}(x))$, denote $\phi_t(D_t)$ by α_t, denote $\phi_t(T_t)$ by β_t. Thus, $\beta_t = \alpha^v \mod p_t^{2^\sigma}(x)$. Furthermore, consider the projection δ_t from $\mathbb{F}_2[x]/(p_t^{2^\sigma}(x))$ to field $\mathbb{F}_2[x]/(p_t(x)) \triangleq \overline{H_t}$:

$$\delta_t(\overline{h(x)}) = \overline{(h(x) \mod p_t(x))}$$

Let $\delta_t(\alpha_t) = \overline{\alpha_t}$, $\delta_t(\beta_t) = \overline{\beta_t}$.

Denoted matrix $M_t \in M_{m \times m}(R_t)$ and $\overline{M_t} \in M_{m \times m}(\overline{H_t})$:

$$M_t^{R_t} = \begin{pmatrix} T_t^{s_1} & T_t^{s_2} & T_t^{s_3} & & T_t^{s_m} \\ T_t^{s_m}D_t^{-1} & T_t^{s_1} & T_t^{s_2} & \cdots & T_t^{s_{m-1}} \\ T_t^{s_{m-1}}D_t^{-1} & T_t^{s_m}D_t^{-1} & T_t^{s_1} & & T_t^{s_{m-2}} \\ & \vdots & & \ddots & \vdots \\ T_t^{s_2}D_t^{-1} & T_t^{s_3}D_t^{-1} & T_t^{s_4}D_t^{-1} & \cdots & T_t^{s_1} \end{pmatrix}$$

$$\overline{M_t} = \begin{pmatrix} \overline{\beta_t}^{s_1} & \overline{\beta_t}^{s_2} & \overline{\beta_t}^{s_3} & & \overline{\beta_t}^{s_m} \\ \overline{\beta_t}^{s_m}\overline{\alpha_t}^{-1} & \overline{\beta_t}^{s_1} & \overline{\beta_t}^{s_2} & \cdots & \overline{\beta_t}^{s_{m-1}} \\ \overline{\beta_t}^{s_{m-1}}\overline{\alpha_t}^{-1} & \overline{\beta_t}^{s_m}\overline{\alpha_t}^{-1} & \overline{\beta_t}^{s_1} & & \overline{\beta_t}^{s_{m-2}} \\ & \vdots & & \ddots & \vdots \\ \overline{\beta_t}^{s_2}\overline{\alpha_t}^{-1} & \overline{\beta_t}^{s_3}\overline{\alpha_t}^{-1} & \overline{\beta_t}^{s_4}\overline{\alpha_t}^{-1} & \cdots & \overline{\beta_t}^{s_1} \end{pmatrix}$$

Since Theorem 4,

$$rank_{\mathbb{K}}(\overline{C}_t) \geq rank_{\mathbb{K}}(\hat{C}_t) \times rank_{R_t}(M_t^{R_t}).$$

Since Theorem 5,

$$rank_{\mathbb{K}}(\overline{C}_t) \geq rank_{\mathbb{K}}(\hat{C}_t) \times rank_{R_t}(M_t^{R_t}) = rank_{\mathbb{K}}(\hat{C}_t) \times rank_{\overline{H_t}}(\overline{M_t}).$$

Finally, we get a Linear complexity lower bound estimation inequality.

Theorem 6.

$$L(C) = \sum_{t=1}^{d} rank_{\mathbb{K}}(\overline{C}_t) \geq \sum_{t=1}^{d} rank_{\mathbb{K}}(\hat{C}_t) \times rank_{\overline{H_t}}(\overline{M_t})$$

The last problem turns into how to estimate $rank_{\mathbb{K}}(\hat{C}_t)$ and $rank_{\overline{H_t}}(\overline{M_t})$.

Estimate $rank(\hat{C}_t)$ over F_2: Since $C^1 = \{c_{1+m \cdot i}\}_{i=0}^{\infty}$, so $\hat{C} = M_{cir}(C^1) \cdot T^{-s_1} = \left(\sum_{i=0}^{n-1} c_{1+m \cdot i}D^i \right) \cdot D^{-s_1 v}$. Thus:

$$\hat{C}_t = \left(\sum_{i=0}^{n-1} c_{1+m \cdot i}D_t^i \right) \cdot D_t^{-s_1 v}$$

That means, $rank_{F_2}(\hat{C}_t)$ equals to rank of matrix $\sum_{i=0}^{n-1} c_{1+m\cdot i} D_t^i$.

Let the formal power series $F^1(x) = \sum_{i=0}^{\infty} c_{1+m\cdot i} x^i$, be the generating function of the sequence C^1, and let $H(x) \in F_2[x]$, be the minimum generator Polynomial of C^1. The order of $H(x)$ is equal to the linear complexity of C^1. There exists polynomial $P(x) \in F_2[x]$ with number less than l such that the following constant equation holds, $H(x)$ and $P(x)$ are coprime [8].

$$F^1(x) = \frac{P(x)}{H(x)}$$

Let $\overline{F^1}(x) = \sum_{i=0}^{n-1} c_{1+m\cdot i} x^i$, then the power series of the form

$$F^1(x) = \frac{\overline{F^1}(x)}{1 + x^n}$$

and $H(x)|1 + x^n$. This is a conclusion that comes from the minimal property of $H(x)$.

Thus,

$$\overline{F^1}(x) \cdot H(x) = P(x) \cdot (1 + x^n)$$

The equation no longer needs to be discussed under the formal power series sense and goes back to the polynomial ring $F_2[x]$.

As we know, $x^n + 1 = \prod_{i=1}^{d} p_i^{2^\delta}(x)$ and $H(x)|(1 + x^n)$. Assume $H(x) = \prod_{i=1}^{d} p_i^{h_i}(x)$, where $0 \le h_i \le 2^\sigma$. Then:

$$\overline{F^1}(x) = P(x) \cdot \prod_{i=1}^{d} p_i^{2^\delta - h_i}(x)$$

- When $h_t = 0$, Since the characteristic(minimal) polynomial of the matrix D_t is $p_t^{2^\delta}(x)$, $p_t^{2^\delta}(D_t)$ is a zero square matrix. Led to

$$\overline{F^1}(D_t) = P(D_t) \cdot \prod_{i \ne t} p_i^{2^\delta - h_i}(D_i) \cdot p_t^{2^\delta}(D_t) = O$$

$$rank\left(\hat{C}_t\right) = rank(\overline{F^1}(D_t)) = 0$$

- When $h_t > 0$, Since $H(x)$ is coprime to $P(x)$, $p_t(x)$ is coprime to $P(x)$. Therefore, $P(D_t)$ is still a full-rank square (because the root sets of $P(x) = 0$ does not include any characteristic root of D_t). Thus,

$$rank\left(\hat{C}_t\right) = rank\left(\overline{F^1}(D_t)\right) = rank\left(p_t^{2^\delta - h_t}(D_t)\right) \ge h_t \times deg(p_t(x))$$

Combining these two cases, the following inequalities can be derived.

$$rank\left(\hat{C}\right) = \sum_{t=1}^{d} rank\left(\hat{C}_t\right) \ge \sum_{t=1}^{d} (h_t \times deg(p_t(x))) = deg(H(x))$$

Notice that both left and right of the inequality are equal to the $L\left(C^1\right)$, so the inequality equal sign holds constant. That is, for $\forall 1 \le t \le d$, we have

$$rank\left(\hat{C}_t\right) = h_t \times deg\left(p_t\left(x\right)\right).$$

Estimate $Rank_{\overline{H_t}}(\overline{M_t})$: It's easy to see that $\overline{M_t}$ is an $\overline{\alpha_t}^{-1}$-circulant matrix over field $\overline{H_t}$. Let $E_t(x) = \sum_{i=0}^{m-1} \overline{\beta_t}^{s_{i+1}} x^i \in \overline{H_t}[x]$, $J_t(x) = x^m + \overline{\alpha_t}^{-1} \in \overline{H_t}[x]$. Use Theorem 3, denote The degree of the greatest common factor of $E_t(x)$ and $J_t(x)$ by g_t, then

$$rank_{\overline{H_t}}(\overline{M_t}) = m - g_t.$$

In summary, we get a final inequality of rank:

$$rank\left(M_t\right) \ge rank\left(\hat{C}_t\right) \cdot rank_{R_t}\left(\overline{M_t}^{R_t}\right) = h_t \times deg\left(p_t\left(x\right)\right) \times \left(m - g_t\right)$$

After accumulation:

Theorem 7.

$$L(C) \ge \sum_{t=1}^{d} h_t \times deg\left(p_t\left(x\right)\right) \times \left(m - g_t\right)$$

3.4   Section Summary

This section analyzed the lower bound on the linear complexity of the basic feedforward clock-controlled sequence.

The first step is to correspond the linear complexity to the rank of the cyclic matrix. After that, the matrix is organized according to a particular sampling law. In this way, the matrix becomes a matrix on a circulant matrix ring.

However, the matrix on a normal commutative ring is not easy to count the rank. So further quasi-diagonalization is performed for each matric block at the same time. Then the goal becomes to compute the sum of the ranks of all matrices M_t on the diagonal.

Using Theorem 4 and Theorem 5, we can successfully estimate the rank of the matrix M_t.

Through such a series of transformations, we decompose the problem to each subfield. In this way, the enormous problem of overall linear complexity becomes a collection of several minor problems. Finally, we obtained a valuable conclusion.

The following section gives a new stream cipher LIFI-128 using a nonlinear drive module reference to the LILI-128 algorithm. This kind of stream cipher's complexity is impossible to be estimated by traditional results. However, our new method can solve its linear complexity problem.

4 LIFI-128, and It's Linear Complexity

4.1 Description of LIFI-128

We give an example that was set up to follow the LILI-128 algorithm. The clock-control subsystem uses a pseudorandom binary sequence produced by a regularly clocked LFSR, $LFSR_a$, of length 39, and a function, f_a, operating on some contents of $LFSR_a$ to produce a pseudorandom integer sequence, $A = \{a_i\}_\infty$, and $a_i \in \{1, 2, 3, 4\}$. The feedback polynomial of $LFSR_a$ is chosen to be a primitive polynomial. Moreover, the initial state of $LFSR_a$ must not be all zero. It follows that $LFSR_a$ produces a maximum-length sequence of period $m = 2^{39} - 1$. Set f_a to be boolean balance function every bit, so $s_m = 2^{39-1}(2^2+1)-1$.

The data-generation subsystem uses the integer sequence A to control the clocking of a binary FCSR[15], $FCSR_b$, of length 89. The lowest content bit of $FCSR_b$ will generate a binary sequence $B = \{b_i\}_\infty$. The feedback integer of $FCSR_b$ is chosen to be a safe prime integer $q = 2p + 1$, where p is a prime, $\lfloor \log_2(q) \rfloor = 89$. And the initial state of $FCSR_b$ is not zero, 2 is a primitive elements of $\mathbb{F}_q^*$. It follows that $FCSR_b$ produces a nonlinear binary sequence with period $n = 2p$, linear complexity $L(B) = p + 1$. Specially, in this example, we assume 2 also is a primitive elements of $\mathbb{F}_p^*$, and $gcd(p - 1, 39) = 1$.

Notice that $n = 2p$ is coprime with $s_m = 2^{39-1}(2^2 + 1) - 1$. Define the clock-controlled sequence $C = \{c_i = b_{s_i}\}_\infty$ as the keystream, thus C get a maximum-length of period $mn = (2^{39} - 1) \times (2p) \approx 2^{128}$ (Fig. 1).

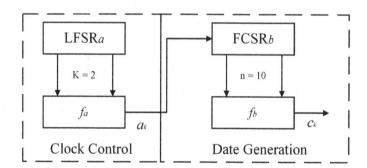

Fig. 1. The structure of LIFI-128

4.2 Linear Complexity

We are going to prove that the linear complexity of C has a lower bound $(L(B) - 2)m + 2 = (p - 1)(2^{39} - 1) + 2$.

Consider the $n \times n$ circulant matrices ring R which was generated by D. It's easy to show that R is a commutative algebra over $\mathbb{F}_2$, thus, for any period n

sequence S, $M_{cir}(S) \in R$. As this result, the clock-matrix is a $m \times m$ matrix over R.

It is obvious that the minimal polynomial of D equals to $f(x) = x^n + 1$. $f(x)$ has a decomposition over $\mathbb{F}_2$:

$$f(x) = x^{2p} + 1 = (x^p + 1)^2 = (x+1)^2 \left(\sum_{i=0}^{p-1} x^i\right)^2.$$

As 2 is a primitive elements of $\mathbb{F}_p^*$, $\sum_{i=0}^{p-1} x^i$ is reduced in $\mathbb{F}_2[x]$. Assume $f(x) = p_1^2(x)p_2^2(x)$, where $p_1(x) = x + 1$, $p_2(x) = \sum_{i=0}^{p-1} x^i$. Thus, we can find a $n \times n$ nonsingular matrix P over $\mathbb{F}_2$ such that $P \cdot S \cdot P^{-1}$ is a quasi-diagonalization on $S \in R$.

$$P \cdot S \cdot P^{-1} = \begin{pmatrix} Q_1 & O \\ O & Q_2 \end{pmatrix}$$

In above formula Q_1 is the factor relates to $p_1^2(x)$, Q_2 is factor relates to $p_2^2(x)$. As $degree(p_1) = 1$, $degree(p_2) = p - 1$, $Q_1 \in M_{2\times 2}(\mathbb{F}_2)$, $Q_2 \in M_{2(p-1)\times 2(p-1)}(\mathbb{F}_2)$.

Notice that $\hat{C}, T, D \in R$, we denote:

$$P\hat{C}P^{-1} = \begin{pmatrix} \hat{C}_1 & O \\ O & \hat{C}_2 \end{pmatrix}, \quad PTP^{-1} = \begin{pmatrix} T_1 & O \\ O & T_2 \end{pmatrix}, \quad PDP^{-1} = \begin{pmatrix} D_1 & O \\ O & D_2 \end{pmatrix}$$

By theory of FCSR[15], the minimial generator Polynomial of sequence $B' = \{b_{s_m i+1}\}_{i=0}^{\infty}$ is $H(x) = (x+1)(x^p+1) = p_1^2(x)p_2(x)$. Thus $rank(\hat{C}_1) = 2$, $rank(\hat{C}_2) = p - 1$.

In field $F_2[x]/(x+1) = F_2$, $\overline{\alpha_1} = \overline{\beta_1} = \overline{1}$. Then:

$$\overline{M_1} = \begin{pmatrix} \overline{\beta_1}^{s_1} & \overline{\beta_1}^{s_2} & \overline{\beta_1}^{s_3} & & \overline{\beta_1}^{s_m} \\ \overline{\beta_1}^{s_m}\overline{\alpha_1}^{-1} & \overline{\beta_1}^{s_1} & \overline{\beta_1}^{s_2} & \cdots & \overline{\beta_1}^{s_{m-1}} \\ \overline{\beta_1}^{s_{m-1}}\overline{\alpha_1}^{-1} & \overline{\beta_1}^{s_m}\overline{\alpha_1}^{-1} & \overline{\beta_1}^{s_1} & & \overline{\beta_1}^{s_{m-2}} \\ \vdots & & & \ddots & \vdots \\ \overline{\beta_1}^{s_2}\overline{\alpha_1}^{-1} & \overline{\beta_1}^{s_3}\overline{\alpha_1}^{-1} & \overline{\beta_1}^{s_4}\overline{\alpha_1}^{-1} & \cdots & \overline{\beta_1}^{s_1} \end{pmatrix} = \begin{pmatrix} \overline{1}\,\overline{1}\cdots\overline{1} \\ \overline{1}\,\overline{1}\cdots\overline{1} \\ \vdots\,\vdots\,\ddots\,\vdots \\ \overline{1}\,\overline{1}\cdots\overline{1} \end{pmatrix}.$$

It's easy to see $rank(\overline{M_1}) = 1$.

Next, we are going to count follow matrix $\overline{M_2}$.

$$\overline{M_2} = \begin{pmatrix} \overline{\beta_2}^{s_1} & \overline{\beta_2}^{s_2} & \overline{\beta_2}^{s_3} & & \overline{\beta_2}^{s_m} \\ \overline{\beta_2}^{s_m}\overline{\alpha_2}^{-1} & \overline{\beta_2}^{s_1} & \overline{\beta_2}^{s_2} & \cdots & \overline{\beta_2}^{s_{m-1}} \\ \overline{\beta_2}^{s_{m-1}}\overline{\alpha_2}^{-1} & \overline{\beta_2}^{s_m}\overline{\alpha_2}^{-1} & \overline{\beta_2}^{s_1} & & \overline{\beta_2}^{s_{m-2}} \\ \vdots & & & \ddots & \vdots \\ \overline{\beta_2}^{s_2}\overline{\alpha_2}^{-1} & \overline{\beta_2}^{s_3}\overline{\alpha_2}^{-1} & \overline{\beta_2}^{s_4}\overline{\alpha_2}^{-1} & \cdots & \overline{\beta_2}^{s_1} \end{pmatrix}$$

$\overline{\beta_2} = \overline{\alpha_2}^v$, where $v \times s_m \equiv 1 \mod n$.

Notice that $\overline{M_2}$ is a $m \times m$ matrix over field $\mathbb{F}_2[x]/(p_2(x))$, in particular, $\overline{M_2}$ is a $\overline{\alpha_2}^{-1}$-circulant matrix.

With the help of Theorem 3, we know $\overline{M_2}$ is non-singular if and only if $w(x) = \sum_{i=1}^{m} \overline{\beta_2}^{s_i} x^{i-1}$ doesn't have common root with $x^m - \overline{\alpha_2}^{-1} = 0$, or $\overline{M_2}$ has a zero eigenvalue.

As m is coprime with the order p of $\overline{\alpha_2}^{-1}$, there is a integer k such that $(\overline{\alpha_2}^k)^m = \overline{\alpha_2}^{-1}$. Assume $\{\xi^i | i = 0, 1, \cdots, m-1\}$ is all roots of equation $x^m - 1 = 0$, then roots set of $x^m - \overline{\alpha_2}^{-1} = 0$ is $\{\xi^i \overline{\alpha_2}^k | i = 0, 1, \cdots, m-1\}$. If $\xi^j \overline{\alpha_2}^k$ is a root of $w(x)$, which means:

$$w(\xi^j \overline{\alpha_2}^k) = \sum_{i=1}^{m} \overline{\beta_2}^{s_i} (\xi^j \overline{\alpha_2}^k)^{i-1}$$

$$= \sum_{i=1}^{m} \overline{\alpha_2}^{s_i v + (i-1)k} (\xi^j)^{i-1}$$

Define another function $g(x) = \sum_{i=1}^{m} \overline{\alpha_2}^{s_i v + (i-1)k} x^{i-1}$, it's easy to see that $gcd(w(x), x^m - \overline{\alpha_2}^{-1}) \neq 1$ equals to $gcd(g(x), x^m - 1) \neq 1$.

The proof is by contradiction, suppose that there is $0 \leq i' \leq m-1$, $\xi' = \xi^{i'}$ is a common root of $g(x)$ and $x^m - 1$. Notice that $\xi'^{m+1} = \xi'^{2^{39}} = \xi'$, we calculate the 2^{39}th power of $g(\xi')$. It shows:

$$0 = (g(\xi'))^{2^{39}}$$

$$= \sum_{i=1}^{m} \overline{\alpha_2}^{(s_i v + (i-1)k) \times 2^{39}} (\xi'^{2^{39}})^{i-1}$$

$$= \sum_{i=1}^{m} (\overline{\alpha_2}^{2^{39}})^{s_i v + (i-1)k} \xi'^{i-1}$$

Define function

$$h(\overline{\alpha_2}) = \sum_{i=1}^{m} \xi'^{i-1} (\overline{\alpha_2})^{(s_i v + (i-1)k \mod p)}$$

$$= \sum_{i=0}^{p-1} [\sum_{s_j v + (j-1)k \equiv i} \xi'^j] \overline{\alpha_2}^i$$

Above formula shows that if $\overline{\alpha_2}$ is a root of $h(\overline{\alpha_2}) = 0$, then $\overline{\alpha_2}^{2^{39}}$ will also be a root of $h(\overline{\alpha_2}) = 0$. Now we get a set $\Omega = \{\overline{\alpha_2}^{2^{39i}} | i = 0, 1, \cdots \}$, any elements of this set would be a root of $h(\overline{\alpha_2}) = 0$. Recall that $\overline{\alpha_2}$'s order is p, and 2 is a primitive element of $\mathbb{F}_p^*$, so $\overline{\alpha_2}^{2^{39a}} = \overline{\alpha_2}^{2^{39b}}$ if and only if $39a \equiv 39b \mod (p-1)$. Thus $\#|\Omega| = p - 1$. As degree of $h(\overline{\alpha_2})$ less than or equal to $p - 1$, Ω must be all roots set of $h(\overline{\alpha_2}) = 0$. Thus, $h(\overline{\alpha_2}) = \xi^* \prod_{i=0}^{p-1} (\overline{\alpha_2} - \overline{\alpha_2}^{2^{39i}})$, ξ^* is a constant.

Denote $\sum_{s_j v + (j-1)k \equiv i} \xi'^j$ by ε_i, $h(\overline{\alpha_2}) = \sum_{i=0}^{p-1} \varepsilon_i \overline{\alpha_2}^i$ and $\xi^* = \varepsilon_{p-1} \neq 0$. Notice $\Omega \subseteq \mathbb{F}_2[x]/p_2(x)$, suppose that $\varepsilon_{i_0} \neq 0$, then ε_{i_0}/ξ^* must be an element in field $\mathbb{F}_2[x]/p_2(x)$, as it is represented as an element generated by Ω over field $\mathbb{F}_2[x]/p_2(x)$. Denote this field by $\mathbb{F}_{2^{p-1}}$.

In the same way,

$$\varepsilon_{i_0}/\xi^* = [\sum_{s_j v+(j-1)k \equiv i_0} \xi'^j]/[\sum_{s_j v+(j-1)k \equiv p-1} \xi'^j].$$

In fact, we can show that $\#\{1 \le j \le m | s_j v + (j-1)k \equiv i_0 \mod p\} \le 1$ for any i_0. Suppose there are $1 \le j < j' \le m$ such that $s_j v + (j-1)k \equiv s_{j'} v + (j'-1)k \mod p$. Thus, $s_m m(s_{j'} - s_j)v + s_m m(j'-j)k \equiv 0 \mod p$, equals to $(s_{j'} - s_j)m - s_m(j'-j) \equiv 0 \mod p$. Notice that

$$
\begin{aligned}
|(s_{j'} - s_j)m - s_m(j'-j)| &\le |(s_{j'} - s_j)m| + |s_m(j'-j)| \\
&\le 4(j'-j)m + s_m(j'-j) \\
&= (5 \times 2^{38} + 3)(j'-j) \\
&\le 2^{41} \times 2^{39} \\
&= 2^{80} < p.
\end{aligned}
$$

Thus $(s_{j'} - s_j)m = s_m(j'-j)$. Because $gcd(m, s_m) = gcd(2^{39}-1, 5 \times 2^{38}-1) = 1$, we get $m|(j'-j)$, conflicts with $1 \le j'-j \le m-1$ and implies $\#\{1 \le j \le m | s_j v + (j-1)k \equiv i_0 \mod p\} \le 1$.

This fact shows that $\varepsilon_{i_0}/\xi^* = 0$, or $\varepsilon_{i_0}/\xi^* = \xi'^s$ for an integer s. As $\varepsilon_{i_0}/\xi^* \in \mathbb{F}_{2^p-1}$, $\xi'^m = 1$ and $gcd(m, 2^{p-1}-1) = 1$, those facts led to $\xi'^s = 1$. But it's easy to confirm that $g(\xi') = g(1) \neq 0$. This result conflicts with $g(\xi') = 0$. Based on these facts, $g(x)$ doesn't have common root with $x^m - 1$, $\overline{M_2}$ is non-singular, $rank(\overline{M_2}) = m$

Thus, recall Theorem 7,

$$
\begin{aligned}
L(C) &\ge \sum_{t=1}^{2} h_t \times deg(p_t(x)) \times (m - g_t) \\
&= 2 \times 1 \times 1 + 1 \times (p-1) \times m \\
&= m(p-1) + 2.
\end{aligned}
$$

C's rank greater then $(p-1)m + 2 = (p-1)(2^{39} - 1) + 2$, we get a linear complexity lower bound of clock-controlled sequence $\{c_i\}_\infty$.

4.3   Section Summary

This section modifies the LILI-128 algorithm so that its controlled sequence becomes nonlinearly driven with extremely high linear complexity. We call the new algorithm LIFI-128.

None of the published linear complexity analysis methods give a good result for LIFI-128. However, our new model can solve this type of problem very well. The practical value of the linear complexity lower bound estimation method proposed in this paper is fully illustrated.

5   Conclusion

The feedforward clock control structure is a hardware-friendly and widely used structure for designing sequence encryption algorithms. Its basic structure is that two sequence generators connect in series. The first generator is regular output and the second generator clock-controlled by the output of the first generator.

In this paper, we research the feedforward clock-controlled sequence structure by new methods such as circulant matrix and matrix over the ring. Finally, the resulting complexity estimation inequalities can widely apply to the analysis of cryptographic properties of the clock-controlled structure. The traditional result base on cyclotomic polynomials over finite fields is not practical when the controlled sequence is nonlinear. The results presented in this paper can be exactly effective for the analysis of clock-controlled cryptographic systems whether the drive module is linear or nonlinear.

Acknowledgements. We thank the anonymous reviewers for their helpful comments. This work was supported by the National Natural Science Foundation of China(Grant No.6207211, No.61672059) and the National Key R&D Program of China 2017YFB0802000.

References

1. Beth, T., Piper, F.C.: The stop-and-go-generator. In: Beth, T., Cot, N., Ingemarsson, I. (eds.) EUROCRYPT 1984. LNCS, vol. 209, pp. 88–92. Springer, Heidelberg (1985). https://doi.org/10.1007/3-540-39757-4_9
2. Blakley, G., Purdy, G.B.: A necessary and sufficient condition for fundamental periods of cascade machines to be products of the fundamental periods of their constituent finite state machines. Inf. Sci. **24**(1), 71–91 (1981)
3. Brown, W.C.: Matrices Over Commutative Rings. Marcel Dekker, Inc., New York (1993)
4. Cline, R., Plemmons, R., Worm, G.: Generalized inverses of certain toeplitz matrices. Linear Algebra Appl. **8**(1), 25–33 (1974)
5. Coppersmith, D., Halevi, S., Jutla, C.: Cryptanalysis of stream ciphers with linear masking. In: Yung, M. (ed.) CRYPTO 2002. LNCS, vol. 2442, pp. 515–532. Springer, Heidelberg (2002). https://doi.org/10.1007/3-540-45708-9_33
6. Courtois, N.T., Meier, W.: Algebraic attacks on stream ciphers with linear feedback. In: Biham, E. (ed.) EUROCRYPT 2003. LNCS, vol. 2656, pp. 345–359. Springer, Heidelberg (2003). https://doi.org/10.1007/3-540-39200-9_21
7. Dawson, E., Clark, A., Golic, J., Millan, W., Penna, L., Simpson, L.: The lili-128 keystream generator. In: Proceedings of first NESSIE Workshop. Citeseer (2000)
8. Denguo, F., Dingyi, P.: Cryptography Guide. Science Press, Beijing (1999)
9. Golić, J.D.: Correlation properties of a general binary combiner with memory. J. Cryptol. **9**(2), 111–126 (1996). https://doi.org/10.1007/BF00190805
10. Golic, J.D., Zivkovic, M.V.: On the linear complexity of nonuniformity decimated pn-sequences. IEEE Trans. Inf. Theory **34**(5), 1077–1079 (1988)
11. Gollmann, D., Chambers, W.G.: Clock-controlled shift registers: a review. IEEE J. Sel. Areas Commun. **7**(4), 525–533 (1989)

12. Jennings, S.M.: A special case of binary sequences. Ph.D. thesis, University of London (1980)
13. Kholosha, A.: Investigations in the design and analysis of key-stream generators (2004)
14. Kjeldsen, K., Andresen, E.: Some randomness properties of cascaded sequences (corresp.). IEEE Trans. Inf. Theory **26**, 227–232 (1980)
15. Klapper, A., Goresky, M.: 2-adic shift registers. In: Anderson, R. (ed.) FSE 1993. LNCS, vol. 809, pp. 174–178. Springer, Heidelberg (1994). https://doi.org/10.1007/3-540-58108-1_21
16. Matsui, M.: Linear cryptanalysis method for DES cipher. In: Helleseth, T. (ed.) EUROCRYPT 1993. LNCS, vol. 765, pp. 386–397. Springer, Heidelberg (1994). https://doi.org/10.1007/3-540-48285-7_33
17. Meier, W., Staffelbach, O.: Correlation properties of combiners with memory in stream ciphers (extended abstract). In: Damgård, I.B. (ed.) EUROCRYPT 1990. LNCS, vol. 473, pp. 204–213. Springer, Heidelberg (1991). https://doi.org/10.1007/3-540-46877-3_18
18. Schaub, T.: A linear complexity approach to cyclic codes (1990)
19. Xiangang, L.: Analysis of clock-controlled sequences. In: Information Security and Communications Privacy, vol. 2 (1991)
20. Xiangang, L., Zengfa, W., Guozhen, X.: The complexity of some pseudo-random decimated sequences. J. China Inst. Commun. **11**(2), 1–6 (1990)

Symmetric Cryptography

On Characterization of Transparency Order for (n, m)-functions

Yu Zhou[1]([✉]), Yongzhuang Wei[2], Hailong Zhang[3], Luyang Li[4], Enes Pasalic[5], and Wenling Wu[6]

[1] Science and Technology on Communication Security Laboratory,
Chengdu 610041, China
zhouyu.zhy@tom.com
[2] Guilin University of Electronic Technology, Guilin 541004, China
[3] State Key Laboratory of Information Security, Institute of Information
Engineering, Chinese Academy of Sciences, Beijing 100093, China
zhanghailong@iie.ac.cn
[4] National Engineering Laboratory for Wireless Security, Xi'an University of Post
and Telecommunications, Xi'an 710061, China
[5] University of Primorska, FAMNIT & IAM, Koper, Slovenia
[6] TCA Laboratory, SKLCS, Institute of Software, Chinese Academy of Sciences,
Beijing 100190, China
wwl@tca.iscas.ac.cn

Abstract. The *transparency order* (denoted by $\mathcal{TO}$) is a useful measure of the robustness of (n, m)-functions (cryptographic S-boxes as mappings from $GF(2)^n$ to $GF(2)^m$) to multi-bits Differential Power Analysis (DPA). An improved version of transparency order (denoted by $\mathcal{RTO}$), based on the use of cross-correlation coefficients, was also introduced recently. For the first time, we resolve this open problem which (n, m)-functions reach the upper bound on $\mathcal{TO}$ for odd n (m is a power of 2). We also investigate the tightness of upper and lower bounds related to $\mathcal{RTO}$ and derive its relationship to main cryptographic characterizations of (n, m)-functions (such as nonlinearity, the sum-of-square indicator and algebraic immunity). Finally, concerning S-boxes of size 4×4, the distributions of $\mathcal{RTO}$ for all 302 balanced S-boxes (up to affine equivalence) and 16 equivalence classes of optimal S-boxes are given.

Keywords: (n, m)-functions · Transparency order · Nonlinearity · Auto-correlation · Cross-correlation

1 Introduction

S-box is an important non-linear component of cryptographic algorithms. A careful selection of an S-box is required for ensuring cryptographic robustness of block (or stream) ciphers, at the same time aiming at efficient implementation. In fact, most attacks on symmetric algorithms choose S-box as the target. For example, in side channel attacks, the secret key (used in the implementation of

© Springer Nature Switzerland AG 2021
Y. Yu and M. Yung (Eds.): Inscrypt 2021, LNCS 13007, pp. 351–370, 2021.
https://doi.org/10.1007/978-3-030-88323-2_19

symmetric algorithms) can be recovered by analyzing the relationship between its leakages and the output of an S-box. For the first time, at CRYPTO 1999, Kocher et al. proposed differential power analysis (DPA) [5]. Then, the security of S-boxes against DPA was analyzed [1,10]. At FSE 2005, the transparency order $(\mathcal{TO})$ based on the auto-correlation coefficients of (n, m)-functions was proposed by Prouff [10]. According to the definition of $\mathcal{TO}$, (n, m)-functions with smaller $\mathcal{TO}$ are more secure against DPA attacks. At INDOCRYPT 2005, Carlet obtained a lower bound of $\mathcal{TO}$ for highly non-linear (n, m)-functions. Besides, he also deduced a relationship between $\mathcal{TO}$ and the non-linearity for any (n, m)-function [1]. Later, Fan et al. proposed a fast computation technique for $\mathcal{TO}$ [4]. Then, Picek et al. proposed a genetic algorithm to find some Boolean functions with better $\mathcal{TO}$ values [9]. Mazumdar et al. also focused on the search of S-boxes with better $\mathcal{TO}$ values [7].

Recently, Chakraborty et al. proposed a revised definition of the transparency order (denoted by $\mathcal{RTO}$) based on the cross-correlation coefficients of (n, m)-functions (thus not only auto-correlation) in [3]. Consequently, cryptographically strong S-boxes, apart from satisfying standard cryptographic criteria such as high algebraic degree, high nonlinearity and good differential properties, also need to possess relatively large $\mathcal{RTO}$ to withstand DPA-like attacks. However, the analysis in [3] does not provide a thorough treatment regarding the properties of $\mathcal{RTO}$, thus no tight lower and upper bounds are given and its relation to other cryptographic criteria was not elaborated. A tight upper bound on $\mathcal{RTO}$ for Boolean functions was established in [13] and it was additionally shown that the lower bound directly depends on the nonlinearity. The latter result can be interpreted as a negative trade-off between nonlinearity and $\mathcal{RTO}$, stating that Boolean functions (as coordinate functions of an (n, m)-function or S-box) with high nonlinearity also have larger transparency order which is not a desirable feature in the context of DPA attacks. This also implies that the design of S-boxes satisfying all the cryptographic criteria including a low $\mathcal{RTO}$ becomes even a more demanding task.

So far, little has been done about addressing the problems related to identification of (n, m)-functions reaching the bounds on the (revised) transparency order and even less efforts have been made towards theoretical design of (n, m)-functions having relatively good transparency order and at the same time satisfying other cryptographic criteria. In this article, we address some open problems related to both definitions of transparency order. Firstly, whereas some instances of (n, m)-functions reaching the upper bound for even n were given in [10], we consider the problem of specifying (n, m)-functions achieving the upper bound on $\mathcal{TO}$ (thus the worst possible case concerning DPA) which was left open in [10] for odd n. We explicitly specify those classes of (n, m)-functions having the maximum possible $\mathcal{TO}$ when m is a power of 2. Secondly, to further elaborate on the design of robust (n, m)-functions with respect to the $\mathcal{RTO}$ indicator [3], we establish some important connections between $\mathcal{RTO}$ and other cryptographic properties such as the *sum-of-square indicator*, *algebraic immunity* (AI), and *nonlinearity* of the coordinate functions of (n, m)-functions. In particular, it is shown that not only the nonlinearity impacts $\mathcal{RTO}$ but also the sum-of-square indicator (as expected) has a direct influence on the resistance to DPA attacks.

Furthermore, the established connection between the algebraic immunity and transparency order essentially indicates (along with other trade-offs) that the design of cryptographically secure (n, m)-functions is hard to achieve if the protection against DPA attacks is taken into account. In this direction, it would be interesting to establish a similar connection between differential properties of (n, m)-functions and $\mathcal{RTO}$.

Finally, concerning the upper and lower bounds on $\mathcal{RTO}$, for the first time their tightness has been confirmed through explicit examples. Moreover, we have also computed the transparency order for all S-boxes of size 4×4 (up to affine equivalence) which gives a complete insight in their properties related to $\mathcal{RTO}$.

This paper is organized as follows. In Sect. 2, some notations and definitions related to Boolean functions are given. Besides, we recall two different notions of transparency order. In Sect. 3, in connection to the transparency order introduced by Prouff [10], we provide certain classes of (n, m)-functions reaching the upper bound of $\mathcal{TO}$. We also specify several connections between the recently introduced $\mathcal{RTO}$ indicator and some main cryptographic parameters, and additionally derive a tight lower and upper bound on $\mathcal{RTO}$. In Sect. 4, we provide distributions of the transparency order for all S-boxes of size 4×4 (up to affine equivalence). Finally, some concluding remarks are given in Sect. 5.

2 Preliminaries

In this section, we give some definitions of Boolean functions and the transparency order, and introduce some indicators for Boolean functions.

2.1 Definition of Boolean Functions

The set of n-variable Boolean functions is denoted by $\mathbb{B}_n$, where any $f \in \mathbb{B}_n$ is simply a mapping $f : \mathbb{F}_2^n \to \mathbb{F}_2$. We denote by $\oplus$ the addition modulo two performed in $\mathbb{F}_2$ and the vector space $\mathbb{F}_2^n$. Every Boolean function $f \in \mathbb{B}_n$ admits a unique representation called the algebraic normal form (ANF) which is a multivariate polynomial over $\mathbb{F}_2$:

$$f(x_1, \ldots, x_n) = a_0 \oplus \bigoplus_{1 \leq i \leq n} a_i x_i \oplus \bigoplus_{1 \leq i < j \leq n} a_{i,j} x_i x_j \oplus \cdots \oplus a_{1,\ldots,n} x_1 x_2 \cdots x_n,$$

where the coefficients $a_0, a_i, a_{i,j}, \cdots, a_{1,\ldots,n} \in \mathbb{F}_2$. The algebraic degree, $deg(f)$, is the largest length of the monomial(s) with non-zero coefficients.

Let $supp(f) = \{(x_1, \ldots, x_n) \in \mathbb{F}_2^n \mid f(x_1, \ldots, x_n) = 1\}$ and $wt(f)$ be the Hamming weight of f, then $wt(f) = |supp(f)|$. Furthermore, if $wt(f) = 2^{n-1}$ for any $f \in \mathbb{B}_n$, then f is said to be balanced. We denote by $\mathbb{A}_n$ the set of affine functions, that is, $deg(f) \leq 1$ in this set.

In this paper, let $\mathbf{0}^n = \underbrace{\{0, \ldots, 0\}}_{n}$ and $\mathbf{1}^n = \underbrace{\{1, \ldots, 1\}}_{n}$ denote the all-zero and all-one vectors, respectively.

2.2   Some Indicators for Boolean Functions

Nonlinearity is an important indicator to measure the linearity of Boolean functions. Boolean functions with higher nonlinearity are more resistant to linear attacks.

Definition 1. *Let $f \in \mathbb{B}_n$. The nonlinearity of f can be computed using*

$$N_f = 2^{n-1} - \frac{1}{2} \max_{\alpha \in \mathbb{F}_2^n} | \mathcal{F}(f \oplus \varphi_\alpha) |,$$

where $\mathcal{F}(f \oplus \varphi_\alpha)$ is the Walsh spectral value of f at point $\alpha \in \mathbb{F}_2^n$ computed as:

$$\mathcal{F}(f \oplus \varphi_\alpha) = \sum_{x \in \mathbb{F}_2^n} (-1)^{f(x) \oplus \varphi_\alpha(x)},$$

where $\varphi_\alpha(x) = \alpha \cdot x = \alpha_1 x_1 \oplus \cdots \oplus \alpha_n x_n$.

Based on the nonlinearity of $f \in \mathbb{B}_n$ and the well-known Parseval's equation, we know that f is a *bent* function [11] if $N_f = 2^{n-1} - 2^{n/2-1}$ for even n.

The cross-correlation and the auto-correlation functions play an important role in this paper. For any $f, g \in \mathbb{B}_n$, the cross-correlation function is defined as

$$\triangle_{f,g}(\alpha) = \sum_{x \in \mathbb{F}_2^n} (-1)^{f(x) \oplus g(x \oplus \alpha)}, \alpha \in \mathbb{F}_2^n.$$

If $f = g$ in the above formula, then the auto-correlation function of f is given by $\triangle_f(\alpha) = \sum_{x \in \mathbb{F}_2^n} (-1)^{f(x) \oplus f(x \oplus \alpha)}, \alpha \in \mathbb{F}_2^n$.

In order to measure the correlation between two Boolean functions, we recall the definition of perfectly uncorrelated functions. Two Boolean functions $f, g \in \mathbb{B}_n$ are said to be perfectly uncorrelated if $\triangle_{f,g}(\alpha) = 0$, for any $\alpha \in \mathbb{F}_2^n$. Sarkar et al. [12] proved that $\mathcal{F}(f \oplus \varphi_\alpha)\mathcal{F}(g \oplus \varphi_\alpha) = 0$ for any $\alpha \in \mathbb{F}_2^n$ if and only if f and g are perfectly uncorrelated. Later, Pasalic et al. [8] proved that f and g are disjoint spectra functions (meaning that $\mathcal{F}(f \oplus \varphi_\alpha) = 0$ implies that $\mathcal{F}(g \oplus \varphi_\alpha) \neq 0$ or vice versa) if and only if f and g are perfectly uncorrelated. In order to better prove some conclusions in this paper, we give the definition of *almost perfectly uncorrelated* functions.

Definition 2. *Let $f, g \in \mathbb{B}_n$. f and g are almost perfectly uncorrelated, if $\triangle_{f,g}(\alpha) = 0$ for any $\alpha \in \mathbb{F}_2^{n*}$, where $\mathbb{F}_2^{n*} = \mathbb{F}_2^n \setminus 0^n$.*

Definition 2 implies that f and g are almost perfectly uncorrelated if f and g are perfectly uncorrelated.

In order to characterize the so-called global avalanche property, Zhang et al. [14] introduced an indicator based on the auto-correlation function of a Boolean function.

Definition 3. *Let $f \in \mathbb{B}_n$. The global avalanche characteristics (GAC) of f is given by:*

$$\sigma_f = \sum_{\alpha \in \mathbb{F}_2^n} [\triangle_f(\alpha)]^2, \qquad \triangle_f = \max_{\alpha \in \mathbb{F}_2^n, \alpha \neq 0^n} | \triangle_f(\alpha) |.$$

In 2010, Zhou et al. [16] generalized Definition 3, and presented the notions of the *absolute indicator* and the *sum-of-squares indicator* (defined below respectively) based on the cross-correlation function for two Boolean functions $f, g \in \mathbb{B}_n$:

$$\triangle_{f,g} = \max_{\alpha \in \mathbb{F}_2^n, wt(\alpha) \neq 0} |\triangle_{f,g}(\alpha)|, \qquad \sigma_{f,g} = \sum_{\alpha \in \mathbb{F}_2^n} [\triangle_{f,g}(\alpha)]^2.$$

2.3 Definition of (n, m)-functions and the Transparency Order

In this paper, we study some properties of the transparent order properties for (n, m)-functions, therefore we first give the definition of (n, m)-functions.

Let $f_i \in \mathbb{B}_n (i = 1, 2, \ldots, m)$. If $F = (f_1, \ldots, f_m) : \mathbb{F}_2^n \to \mathbb{F}_2^m$, then F is called an (n, m)-function. An (n, m)-function F is balanced if and only if its *component functions* are balanced, meaning that for every nonzero $v \in \mathbb{F}_2^m$ the Boolean function $v \cdot F$ is balanced. Thus, the balanced (n, n)-functions are the permutations on $\mathbb{F}_2^n$.

Based on the auto-correlation and cross-correlation functions and the definition of (n, m)-functions, Prouff [10] introduced the concept of transparency order.

Definition 4 *[10]. Let $F = (f_1, \ldots, f_m)$ be an (n, m)-function. The transparency order is defined by:*

$$\mathcal{TO}(F) = \max_{\beta \in \mathbb{F}_2^m} \{| m - 2wt(\beta) | - \frac{1}{2^{2n} - 2^n} \sum_{a \in \mathbb{F}_2^{n*}} | \sum_{i=1}^{m} (-1)^{\beta_i} \triangle_{f_i}(a)|\}. \qquad (1)$$

Later, Chakraborty et al. [3] revised this definition by using cross-correlation properties, which then reflects DPA attacks in the Hamming weight model in a more transparent manner. In order to be consistent with (n, m)-functions in Definition 4 and to address the properties of (n, m)-functions in general, we extend the original definition of balanced (n, m)-functions to any (n, m)-functions.

Definition 5 *[3]. Let $F = (f_1, \ldots, f_m)$ be an (n, m)-function. The transparency order of F is defined by:*

$$\mathcal{RTO}(F) = \max_{\beta \in \mathbb{F}_2^m} \{m - \frac{1}{2^{2n} - 2^n} \sum_{a \in \mathbb{F}_2^{n*}} \sum_{j=1}^{m} | \sum_{i=1}^{m} (-1)^{\beta_i \oplus \beta_j} \triangle_{f_i, f_j}(a)|\}. \qquad (2)$$

The above expression can be further manipulated to give

$$\mathcal{RTO}(F) = \max_{\beta \in \mathbb{F}_2^m} \{m - \frac{1}{2^{2n} - 2^n} \sum_{a \in \mathbb{F}_2^{n*}} \sum_{j=1}^{m} | \sum_{i=1}^{m} \triangle_{f_i \oplus \beta_i, f_j \oplus \beta_j}(a)|\}.$$

The following quantities, for a given $\beta \in \mathbb{F}_2^m$, will be proved useful in the sequel:

$$\Gamma_F^\beta = m - \nu_{F,\beta}. \qquad (3)$$

$$\nu_{F,\beta} = \frac{1}{2^{2n} - 2^n} \sum_{a \in \mathbb{F}_2^{n*}} \sum_{j=1}^{m} | \sum_{i=1}^{m} \triangle_{f_i \oplus \beta_i, f_j \oplus \beta_j}(a) |. \qquad (4)$$

3   Cryptographic Properties of $\mathcal{RTO}$

In this section, we give the existence of (n, m)-functions reaching the upper bound m on $\mathcal{TO}$, then we provide tight upper and lower bounds on $\mathcal{RTO}$ and deduce some cryptographic properties of $\mathcal{RTO}$.

3.1   The Existence of (n, m)-functions Reaching the Upper Bound m on $\mathcal{TO}$

For the standard definition of transparency order given by Definition 4, Prouff [10] showed that the maximum value of $\mathcal{TO}$ of an (n, m)-function F equals to m when n is even, and it can be easily achieved if every coordinate function is a bent function. On the other hand, it was left as an open problem to specify a class of vectorial (n, m)-functions satisfying $\mathcal{TO}(F) = m$ when n is odd. The solution to this problem is given below, so that the existence of (n, m)-functions or S-boxes (for m being a power of two), regardless the parity of n, having the largest possible transparency order (the worst case regarding the resistance to DPA) is now asserted.

Theorem 1. *Let $F = (f_1, \ldots, f_m)$ be an (n, m)-function.*

1) If n is even, then defining f_i to be a bent function for all $1 \leq i \leq m$ implies that $\mathcal{TO}(F) = m$.

2) For $n \geq 4$ and $m = 2^k$, where $n \geq m$ and $k \geq 2$, let $g \in \mathcal{B}_{n-k}$ be a bent function (thus $n - k$ is even). Define $F = (f_1, \ldots, f_m)$ through its coordinate functions given by,

$$f_i(x, y) = g(x) \oplus \omega_i \cdot y, \quad x \in \mathbb{F}_2^{n-k}, y \in \mathbb{F}_2^k,$$

where $\omega_i \in \mathbb{F}_2^k$ for $1 \leq i \leq m = 2^k$ and $\omega_i \neq \omega_j$ when $i \neq j$. Then, $\mathcal{TO}(F) = m$.

Proof. 1) This result is proved in [10].

2) For any $\omega_i, \gamma \in \mathbb{F}_2^k$ and $\alpha \in \mathbb{F}_2^{n-k}$, we compute the auto-correlation of f_i as:

$$
\begin{aligned}
\triangle_{f_i}(\alpha, \gamma) &= \sum_{x \in \mathbb{F}_2^{n-k}, y \in \mathbb{F}_2^k} (-1)^{f_i(x,y) \oplus f_i(x \oplus \alpha, y \oplus \gamma)} \\
&= \sum_{x \in \mathbb{F}_2^{n-k}, y \in \mathbb{F}_2^k} (-1)^{g(x) \oplus \omega_i \cdot y \oplus g(x \oplus \alpha) \oplus \omega_i \cdot (y \oplus \gamma)} \\
&= \sum_{y \in \mathbb{F}_2^k} (-1)^{\omega_i \cdot y \oplus \omega_i \cdot (y \oplus \gamma)} \sum_{x \in \mathbb{F}_2^{n-k}} (-1)^{g(x) \oplus g(x \oplus \alpha)} \\
&= 2^k (-1)^{\omega_i \cdot \gamma} \sum_{x \in \mathbb{F}_2^{n-k}} (-1)^{g(x) \oplus g(x \oplus \alpha)} \\
&= \begin{cases} 2^n (-1)^{\omega_i \cdot \gamma}, & \alpha = 0^{n-k}; \\ 0, & \alpha \neq 0^{n-k}. \end{cases}
\end{aligned}
$$

For $\beta = (\beta_1, \ldots, \beta_m) \in \mathbb{F}_2^m$, we can express $\mathcal{TO}(F)$ as:

$$\mathcal{TO}(F) = \max_{\beta \in \mathbb{F}_2^m} \{| m - 2wt(\beta) | - \frac{1}{2^{2n} - 2^n} \sum_{a=(\alpha,\gamma) \in \mathbb{F}_2^{n*}} |\sum_{i=1}^{m} \triangle_{f_i \oplus \beta_i}(a)|\}$$

$$= \max_{\beta \in \mathbb{F}_2^m} \{|m - 2wt(\beta) | - \frac{2^n}{2^{2n} - 2^n} \sum_{\gamma \in \mathbb{F}_2^{k*}} |(-1)^{\omega_1 \cdot \gamma \oplus \beta_1} + \cdots +$$

$$(-1)^{\omega_m \cdot \gamma \oplus \beta_m}|\}$$

$$= \max_{\beta \in \mathbb{F}_2^m} \{|m - 2wt(\beta) | - \frac{2^n}{2^{2n} - 2^n} \sum_{\gamma \in \mathbb{F}_2^{k*}} |\sum_{i=1}^{m}(-1)^{\omega_i \cdot \gamma \oplus \beta_i}|\}. \tag{5}$$

When $wt(\beta) = m$ or $wt(\beta) = 0$, then

$$\mathcal{TO}(F) = \max_{\beta \in \mathbb{F}_2^m} \{m - \frac{2^n}{2^{2n} - 2^n} \sum_{\gamma \in \mathbb{F}_2^{k*}} |\sum_{i=1}^{m}(-1)^{\omega_i \cdot \gamma}|\}.$$

Noting that $\sum_{i=1}^{m}(-1)^{\omega_i \cdot \gamma} = 0$, for $\gamma \in \mathbb{F}_2^{k*}$, we obtain

$$\mathcal{TO}(F) = \max_{\beta \in \mathbb{F}_2^m} \{m - 0\} = m. \qquad \blacksquare$$

Example 1. *Let $F = (f_1, \ldots, f_4)$ be an $(n, 4)$ function whose coordinate functions are defined as:*

$$f_1(x, y_1, y_2) = g(x) \oplus y_1 \oplus y_2, \quad f_2(x, y_1, y_2) = g(x) \oplus y_1,$$
$$f_3(x, y_1, y_2) = g(x) \oplus y_2, \quad f_4(x, y_1, y_2) = g(x),$$

where g is a bent $(n - 2)$-variable function and n is even. Then $\mathcal{TO}(F) = 4$, which can be confirmed with help of the auto-correlation coefficients of f_i given in Table 1, where $\gamma \in \mathbb{F}_2^{n-2}$ and $\gamma_1, \gamma_2 \in \mathbb{F}_2$.

Then using (5) and the auto-correlation values in Table 1, it can be easily verified that for $\beta = (1, 1, 1, 1)$ or $\beta = (0, 0, 0, 0)$, we have $\mathcal{TO}(F) = \max_{\beta \in \mathbb{F}_2^4} \{| 4 - 2wt(\beta) | - 0\} = 4$.

Table 1. Auto-correlation values of the coordinate functions of F in Example 1

$\alpha = (\gamma, \gamma_1, \gamma_2)$	$(0^{n-2}, 0, 0)$	$(0^{n-2}, 0, 1)$	$(0^{n-2}, 1, 0)$	$(0^{n-2}, 1, 1)$	else
$\triangle_{f_1}(\alpha)$	2^n	-2^n	-2^n	2^n	0
$\triangle_{f_2}(\alpha)$	2^n	2^n	-2^n	-2^n	0
$\triangle_{f_3}(\alpha)$	2^n	-2^n	2^n	-2^n	0
$\triangle_{f_4}(\alpha)$	2^n	2^n	2^n	2^n	0

A similar analysis can be performed for odd n, defining for simplicity two coordinate functions for $(x, y) \in \mathbb{F}_2^{n-1} \times \mathbb{F}_2$:

$$f_1(x, y) = g(x) \oplus y, \ f_2(x, y) = g(x),$$

where $g(x)$ is a bent function so that $n - 1$ is even. Again, $F = (f_1, f_2)$ reaches the upper bound on $\mathcal{TO}$, thus $\mathcal{TO}(F) = 2$.

Example 1 of Theorem 1 illustrates the specification of (n, m)-functions achieving the upper bound on $\mathcal{TO}$.

Remark 1. *There are several observations worth of noticing in connection to Theorem 1. In the first place, none of these $f_i(x, y) = g(x) + \omega_i y$ is a bent function and therefore this method differs substantially from the result in [10]. It can be easily verified that f_i and f_j are disjoint spectra functions. Furthermore, when n is odd (which necessarily implies that k is odd) the result of Theorem 1 essentially solves the open problem in [10] of finding (n, m) functions reaching the upper bound on $\mathcal{TO}$ if m is a power of 2. The nonlinearity of the coordinate functions given by $2^{n-1} - \frac{1}{2} \times 2^{\frac{n-k}{2}} 2^k = 2^{n-1} - 2^{\frac{n+k}{2}-1}$ is rather high which confirms its negative impact on $\mathcal{TO}$.*

In the following, we perform a detailed theoretical analysis of the revised transparency order $\mathcal{RTO}$ [3]. We first provide sharp and general lower and upper bound of $\mathcal{RTO}$ for a class of almost perfectly uncorrelated functions and specify the instances of S-boxes achieving these bounds. In addition, we derive some useful connections that relate $\mathcal{RTO}$ to other cryptographic notions such as nonlinearity, algebraic immunity and cross-correlation coefficients. A general conclusion is that attaining a low $\mathcal{RTO}$ indicator (thus offering a higher resistance to side-channel cryptanalysis) induces a certain worsening of other cryptographic criteria. Therefore, providing an optimal design of cryptographic S-boxes that possess sufficient robustness to both standard cryptanalytic attacks as well as to side-channel cryptanalysis appears to be a quite demanding task.

3.2   The Upper and Lower Bounds on $\mathcal{RTO}(F)$

In this section, we give the upper and lower bounds on $\mathcal{RTO}$ by using almost perfectly uncorrelated functions. Based on Definition 5 of the transparency order, a lower bound on $\mathcal{RTO}$ was derived in [3] in terms of the Walsh spectrum of the coordinate functions of (n, m)-functions. Before we provide a tight lower and upper bound on $\mathcal{RTO}$, employing the concept of almost perfectly uncorrelated functions, we give some simple preparatory results.

Lemma 1. *Let $F = (f_1, \ldots, f_m)$ be a balanced (n, m)-function, where $x \in \mathbb{F}_2^n$. Then, $F \oplus \beta = (f_1 \oplus \beta_1, \ldots, f_m \oplus \beta_m)$ is also a balanced (n, m)-function for any $\beta = (\beta_1, \ldots, \beta_m) \in \mathbb{F}_2^m$.*

Proof. The fact that $F = (f_1, \ldots, f_m)$ is a balanced vectorial Boolean function, implies that $v \cdot F$ is a balanced Boolean function for any $v \in \mathbb{F}_2^{n*}$ and the result follows. ∎

Lemma 2. *Let $F = (f_1, \ldots, f_m)$ be a balanced (n, m)-function. Then, f_i and f_j are almost perfectly (or perfectly) uncorrelated for any $1 \leq i < j \leq m$ if and only if $f_i \oplus \beta_i$ and $f_j \oplus \beta_j$ are (almost) perfectly uncorrelated for any $1 \leq i < j \leq m$, where $\beta = (\beta_1, \ldots, \beta_m) \in \mathbb{F}_2^m$.*

Proof. For any $\beta = (\beta_1, \ldots, \beta_m) \in \mathbb{F}_2^m$ and $\alpha \in \mathbb{F}_2^n$ we have

$$\triangle_{f_i \oplus \beta_i, f_j \oplus \beta_j}(\alpha) = \sum_{x \in \mathbb{F}_2^n} (-1)^{f_i(x) \oplus \beta_i \oplus f_j(x \oplus \alpha) \oplus \beta_j}$$

$$= (-1)^{\beta_i \oplus \beta_j} \sum_{x \in \mathbb{F}_2^n} (-1)^{f_i(x) \oplus f_j(x \oplus \alpha)}$$

$$= (-1)^{\beta_i \oplus \beta_j} \triangle_{f_i, f_j}(\alpha).$$

Thus, $f_i(x) \oplus \beta_i$ and $f_j(x) \oplus \beta_j$ are (almost) perfectly uncorrelated if and only if $f_i(x)$ and $f_j(x)$ are (almost) perfectly uncorrelated for any $1 \leq i < j \leq m$, $\alpha \in \mathbb{F}_2^n$ and $\beta \in \mathbb{F}_2^n$. ∎

Theorem 2. *Let $F = (f_1, \ldots, f_m)$ be an (n, m)-function, $F : \mathbb{F}_2^n \to \mathbb{F}_2^m$. If f_i and f_j are almost perfectly uncorrelated functions for $1 \leq i \neq j \leq m$, then*

$$0 \leq \mathcal{RTO}(F) \leq m.$$

Especially, $\mathcal{RTO}(F) = m$ if and only if $\triangle_{f_i}(\alpha) = 0$ for any $\alpha \in \mathbb{F}_2^{n*}$ and $1 \leq i \leq m$. Also, $\mathcal{RTO}(F) = 0$ if and only if $\mid \triangle_{f_i}(\alpha) \mid = 2^n$ for any $\alpha \in \mathbb{F}_2^{n*}$ and $1 \leq i \leq m$.

Proof. Since f_i and f_j are almost perfectly uncorrelated for any $1 \leq i \neq j \leq m$, we have $\triangle_{f_i, f_j}(a) = 0$ for any $a \in \mathbb{F}_2^{n*}$. Then,

$$\Gamma_F^\beta = m - \frac{1}{2^{2n} - 2^n} \sum_{a \in \mathbb{F}_2^{n*}} \sum_{j=1}^{m} \mid \sum_{i=1}^{m} \triangle_{f_i \oplus \beta_i, f_j \oplus \beta_j}(a) \mid$$

$$= m - \frac{1}{2^{2n} - 2^n} \sum_{a \in \mathbb{F}_2^{n*}} \sum_{j=1}^{m} \mid \triangle_{f_1 \oplus \beta_1, f_j \oplus \beta_j}(a) + \cdots$$

$$+ \triangle_{f_j \oplus \beta_j, f_j \oplus \beta_j}(a) + \cdots + \triangle_{f_m \oplus \beta_m, f_j \oplus \beta_j}(a) \mid$$

$$= m - \frac{1}{2^{2n} - 2^n} \sum_{a \in \mathbb{F}_2^{n*}} \sum_{j=1}^{m} \mid \triangle_{f_j \oplus \beta_j, f_j \oplus \beta_j}(a) \mid$$

$$= m - \frac{1}{2^{2n} - 2^n} \sum_{a \in \mathbb{F}_2^{n*}} \sum_{j=1}^{m} \mid \triangle_{f_j \oplus \beta_j}(a) \mid$$

For any $f_j(x) \oplus \beta_j$, with $1 \leq j \leq m$, we know that $0 \leq \mid \triangle_{f_j \oplus \beta_j}(a) \mid \leq 2^n$. Thus, $0 \leq \Gamma_F^\beta \leq m$, that is, $0 \leq \mathcal{RTO}(F) \leq m$.

In particular, we have $\mathcal{RTO}(F) = m$ if and only if $\mid \triangle_{f_j \oplus \beta_j}(a) \mid = 0$, for any $\alpha \in \mathbb{F}_2^{n*}$ and $1 \leq i \leq m$. Similarly, $\mathcal{RTO}(F) = 0$ if and only if $\mid \triangle_{f_i}(\alpha) \mid = 2^n$, for any $\alpha \in \mathbb{F}_2^n \setminus \mathbf{0}^n$ and $1 \leq i \leq m$. ∎

Example 2. *Let $F = (f_1, f_2)$ be a $(4, 2)$-function whose coordinate functions are bent and given by:*

$$f_1(x) = x_1 x_2 \oplus x_3 x_4, \quad f_2(x) = x_1 x_2 \oplus x_3 x_4 \oplus 1.$$

We deduce that $\triangle_{f_i}(a) = 0$ and $\triangle_{f_i, f_j}(a) = 0$ for any $a \in \mathbb{F}_2^{n*}$. We have

$$\Gamma_F^\beta = m - \frac{1}{2^{2n} - 2^n} \sum_{a \in \mathbb{F}_2^{n*}} \sum_{j=1}^{m} \mid \sum_{i=1}^{m} \triangle_{f_i \oplus \beta_i, f_j \oplus \beta_j}(a) \mid = m - 0 = m,$$

so that $\mathcal{RTO}(F) = m = 2$.

Example 3. *Let $F = (f_1, \ldots, f_4)$ be an $(8, 4)$-function, thus $F : \mathbb{F}_2^8 \to \mathbb{F}_2^4$, with its coordinate (linear) functions specified as:*

$$f_1(x) = x_1 \oplus x_2, \quad f_2(x) = x_3 \oplus x_4, \quad f_3(x) = x_5 \oplus x_6, \quad f_4(x) = x_7 \oplus x_8.$$

It is easily verified that $\mid \triangle_{f_i}(a) \mid = 2^n$ and $\triangle_{f_i, f_j}(a) = 0$ for any $a \in \mathbb{F}_2^{n*}$, where $n = 8$. Then,

$$\Gamma_F^\beta = m - \frac{1}{2^{2n} - 2^n} \sum_{a \in \mathbb{F}_2^{n*}} \sum_{j=1}^{m} \mid \sum_{i=1}^{m} \triangle_{f_i \oplus \beta_i, f_j \oplus \beta_j}(a) \mid = m - \frac{m 2^n (2^n - 1)}{2^{2n} - 2^n} = 0,$$

implying that $\mathcal{RTO}(F) = 0$.

Example 2 and Example 3 illustrate the specification of (n, m)-functions achieving the upper bound on $\mathcal{RTO}$ in Theorem 2, respectively.

Remark 2. *If we take f to be bent and let $F = (f, 1 \oplus f)$, we deduce that $\mathcal{RTO}(F) = 2$, thus reaching the upper bound on $\mathcal{RTO}$ of $(n, 2)$-functions when n is even. This confirms that using bent functions corresponds to the worst case with respect to DPA, whereas linear S-boxes offer the highest resistance to DPA.*

3.3 Relating $\mathcal{RTO}$ to the Absolute Cross-Correlation Indicator

An upper bound on $\mathcal{RTO}$ can be also stated in terms of the absolute indicator (computed at zero for particular shifts of input functions) which is then useful for two purposes. In the first place, employing the fact that for certain classes of Boolean functions the values of this indicator are known, one can easily specify certain S-boxes reaching the upper bound. Moreover, a similar reasoning allows us to also specify S-boxes (of certain size) whose transparency order is provably smaller than the upper bound.

Lemma 3 *[16]. For two Boolean functions $f, g \in \mathbb{B}_n$, the following holds:*

$$\sum_{\alpha \in \mathbb{F}_2^n} \triangle_{f,g}(\alpha) = (2^n - 2wt(f))(2^n - 2wt(g)).$$

Using Lemma 3, for (n, m)-functions, one can deduce an upper bound on $\mathcal{RTO}(F)$ that depends on $\triangle_{f_i \oplus \beta_i, f_j \oplus \beta_j}(\mathbf{0^n})$.

Theorem 3. *Let $F = (f_1, \ldots, f_m)$ be an (n, m)-function and $wt(f_i) = 2^{n-1}(1 \leq i \leq m)$. Then*

$$\mathcal{RTO}(F) \leq m - \frac{1}{2^{2n} - 2^n}\Big|\sum_{j=1}^{m}\sum_{i=1}^{m}[\triangle_{f_i \oplus \beta_i, f_j \oplus \beta_j}(\mathbf{0^n})]\Big|,$$

where $\beta = (\beta_1, \ldots, \beta_m) \in \mathbb{F}_2^m$.

Proof. Using the inequality $\sum_{i=1}^{m}|a_i| \geq |\sum_{i=1}^{m}a_i|$ for any $a_i \in \mathbb{R}$, we have

$$\nu_{F,\beta} = \frac{1}{2^{2n} - 2^n}\sum_{a \in \mathbb{F}_2^{n*}}\sum_{j=1}^{m}\sum_{i=1}^{m}\Big|\sum \triangle_{f_i \oplus \beta_i, f_j \oplus \beta_j}(a)\Big|$$

$$\geq \frac{1}{2^{2n} - 2^n}\sum_{a \in \mathbb{F}_2^{n*}}\Big|\sum_{j=1}^{m}\sum_{i=1}^{m}\triangle_{f_i \oplus \beta_i, f_j \oplus \beta_j}(a)\Big|$$

$$\geq \frac{1}{2^{2n} - 2^n}\Big|\sum_{a \in \mathbb{F}_2^{n*}}\sum_{j=1}^{m}\sum_{i=1}^{m}\triangle_{f_i \oplus \beta_i, f_j \oplus \beta_j}(a)\Big|$$

$$= \frac{1}{2^{2n} - 2^n}\Big|\sum_{j=1}^{m}\sum_{i=1}^{m}\sum_{a \in \mathbb{F}_2^{n*}}[\triangle_{f_i \oplus \beta_i, f_j \oplus \beta_j}(a)]\Big|$$

$$= \frac{1}{2^{2n} - 2^n}\Big|\sum_{j=1}^{m}\sum_{i=1}^{m}[\sum_{a \in \mathbb{F}_2^{n}}[\triangle_{f_i \oplus \beta_i, f_j \oplus \beta_j}(a)] - \triangle_{f_i \oplus \beta_i, f_j \oplus \beta_j}(\mathbf{0^n})]\Big|.$$

Since f_i is a balanced function for $1 \leq i \leq m$, by Lemma 3, we have

$$\nu_{F,\beta} \geq \frac{1}{2^{2n} - 2^n}\Big|\sum_{j=1}^{m}\sum_{i=1}^{m}[[2^n - 2wt(f_i \oplus \beta_i)][2^n - 2wt(f_j \oplus \beta_j)] -$$

$$\triangle_{f_i \oplus \beta_i, f_j \oplus \beta_j}(\mathbf{0^n})]\Big|$$

$$= \frac{1}{2^{2n} - 2^n}\Big|\sum_{j=1}^{m}\sum_{i=1}^{m}[-\triangle_{f_i \oplus \beta_i, f_j \oplus \beta_j}(\mathbf{0^n})]\Big|$$

$$= \frac{1}{2^{2n} - 2^n}\Big|\sum_{j=1}^{m}\sum_{i=1}^{m}[\triangle_{f_i \oplus \beta_i, f_j \oplus \beta_j}(\mathbf{0^n})]\Big|,$$

which proves the result. ∎

If f_i and f_j are perfectly uncorrelated functions for $1 \leq i \neq j \leq m$, then $\triangle_{f_i \oplus \beta_i, f_j \oplus \beta_j}(a) = 0$ for any $1 \leq i \neq j \leq m$. From the proof of Theorem 3, we have

$$\nu_{F,\beta} \geq \frac{1}{2^{2n} - 2^n}\Big|\sum_{j=1}^{m}\sum_{i=1}^{m}[\triangle_{f_i \oplus \beta_i, f_j \oplus \beta_j}(\mathbf{0^n})]\Big|$$

$$= \frac{1}{2^{2n} - 2^n} | \sum_{i=1}^{m} [\Delta_{f_i \oplus \beta_i, f_i \oplus \beta_i}(\mathbf{0}^n)] |$$

$$= \frac{m \times 2^n}{2^{2n} - 2^n}$$

$$= \frac{m}{2^n - 1}.$$

Corollary 1. *Let* $F = (f_1, \ldots, f_m)$ *be an* (n, m)*-function and* $wt(f_i) = 2^{n-1} (1 \le i \le m)$. *If the coordinate functions* f_i *and* f_j *are perfectly uncorrelated for* $1 \le i \ne j \le m$, *then*

$$\mathcal{RTO}(F) \le m - \frac{m}{2^n - 1}.$$

The following example illustrate the possibility of specifying (n, m)-functions whose transparency order $\mathcal{RTO}$ is smaller than the upper bound.

Example 4. *Let* $F = (f_1, f_2)$ *be an* $(n, 2)$*-function, and define* f_i *as:*

$$f_1(x, y_1, y_2) = g(x) \oplus y_1 \oplus y_2, \quad f_2(x, y_1, y_2) = g(x) \oplus y_1,$$

where n *is even,* $x \in \mathbb{F}_2^{n-2}, y_1, y_2 \in \mathbb{F}_2$, $g \in \mathbb{B}_{n-2}$ *is a bent function. Then,* $TO(F) = 2 - \frac{6}{2^n - 1}$. *The distribution of auto-correlation coefficients of* f_i *are given in Table 2.*

Table 2. Distribution of auto-correlation and cross-correlation functions of $F(x, y_1, y_2)$

$\alpha = (\gamma, \gamma_1, \gamma_2)$	$(\mathbf{0}^{n-2}, 0, 0)$	$(\mathbf{0}^{n-2}, 0, 1)$	$(\mathbf{0}^{n-2}, 1, 0)$	$(\mathbf{0}^{n-2}, 1, 1)$	else
$\Delta_{f_1}(\alpha)$	2^n	-2^n	-2^n	2^n	0
$\Delta_{f_2}(\alpha)$	2^n	2^n	-2^n	-2^n	0
$\Delta_{f_1, f_2}(\alpha)$	0	0	0	0	0

Using Table 2, we obtain

$$\Gamma_F^\beta = 2 - \frac{1}{2^{2n} - 2^n} \sum_{a \in \mathbb{F}_2^{n*}} \sum_{j=1}^{2} | \sum_{i=1}^{2} \Delta_{f_i \oplus \beta_i, f_j \oplus \beta_j}(a) |$$

$$= 2 - \frac{1}{2^{2n} - 2^n} \sum_{a \in \mathbb{F}_2^{n*}} \sum_{j=1}^{2} | \Delta_{f_1 \oplus \beta_1, f_j \oplus \beta_j}(a) + \Delta_{f_2 \oplus \beta_2, f_j \oplus \beta_j}(a) |$$

$$= 2 - \frac{1}{2^{2n} - 2^n} \sum_{a \in \mathbb{F}_2^{n*}} [| \Delta_{f_1 \oplus \beta_1, f_1 \oplus \beta_1}(a) + \Delta_{f_2 \oplus \beta_2, f_1 \oplus \beta_1}(a) |$$

$$+ | \Delta_{f_1 \oplus \beta_1, f_2 \oplus \beta_2}(a) + \Delta_{f_2 \oplus \beta_2, f_2 \oplus \beta_2}(a) |]$$

$$= 2 - \frac{1}{2^{2n} - 2^n} \sum_{a \in \mathbb{F}_2^{n*}} [| \Delta_{f_1 \oplus \beta_1, f_1 \oplus \beta_1}(a) | + | \Delta_{f_2 \oplus \beta_2, f_2 \oplus \beta_2}(a) |]$$

$$= 2 - \frac{1}{2^{2n} - 2^n} \sum_{a \in \mathbb{F}_2^{n*}} [|(-1)^{\beta_1 \oplus \beta_1} \triangle_{f_1, f_1}(a)| + |(-1)^{\beta_2 \oplus \beta_2} \triangle_{f_2, f_2}(a)|]$$

$$= 2 - \frac{6 \times 2^n}{2^{2n} - 2^n}$$

$$= 2 - \frac{6}{2^n - 1}.$$

Thus, $\mathcal{RTO}(F) = 2 - \frac{6}{2^n - 1} < 2 - \frac{2}{2^n - 1}$, where the right-hand side value is the bound in Theorem 3.

On the other hand, again using bent functions in the background, the derived disjoint spectra Boolean functions easily give rise to S-boxes reaching the upper bound of Corollary 1 (see Example 5).

Example 5. Let n be an odd and $F = (f_1, f_2)$ be an $(n, 2)$-function with f_i given by $x \in \mathbb{F}_2^{n-1}$, $y \in \mathbb{F}_2$. If $F(x, y)$ is expressed as:

$$f_1(x, y) = g(x) \oplus y, \quad f_2(x, y) = g(x), \quad (x, y) \in \mathbb{F}_2^{n-1} \times \mathbb{F}_2,$$

where $g \in \mathbb{B}_{n-1}$ is a bent function. Then, based on the fact that f_1 and f_2 are disjoint spectra functions (see e.g. [8]), it can be easily verified that $\mathcal{RTO}(F) = 2 - \frac{2}{2^n - 1}$.

3.4 The Relationships Between $\mathcal{RTO}$ and Other Cryptographic Properties

To design robust S-boxes for cryptographic applications (referring mainly to their use in block ciphers), not only the transparency order should be moderately low but also the considered S-box should satisfy other cryptographic criteria such as good differential properties, low sum-of-square indicator, high nonlinearity, and high algebraic immunity and degree. Thus, the relationships between $\mathcal{RTO}$ and other cryptographic criteria is quite important. In the first place, the bounds on $\mathcal{RTO}$ that depend on these quantities might give us a useful insight whether it is possible at all to design cryptographically robust S-boxes unifying all the relevant criteria.

The following result describes the relationship between $\mathcal{RTO}$ and the sum-of-square indicator.

Theorem 4. Let $F = (f_1, \ldots, f_m)$ be a balanced (n, m)-function. If f_i and f_j are not almost perfectly uncorrelated for $1 \leq i \neq j \leq m$, then

$$\mathcal{RTO}(F) \geq m - \frac{1}{2^n} \sqrt{\frac{m}{2^n - 1}} \sum_{j=1}^{m} \left[\sum_{i=1}^{m} \sqrt{\sigma_{f_i} \sigma_{f_j}} \right]^{1/2}.$$

Proof. By using the Cauchy's inequality, for $\beta = (\beta_1, \cdots, \beta_m) \in \mathbb{F}_2^m$ we have

$$\sum_{a \in \mathbb{F}_2^{n*}} \left| \sum_{i=1}^{m} \triangle_{f_i \oplus \beta_i, f_j \oplus \beta_j}(a) \right| \leq [(2^n - 1) \sum_{a \in \mathbb{F}_2^{n*}} (\sum_{i=1}^{m} \triangle_{f_i \oplus \beta_i, f_j \oplus \beta_j}(a))^2]^{1/2}$$

$$= [(2^n - 1) \sum_{a \in \mathbb{F}_2^n} [(\sum_{i=1}^{m} \triangle_{f_i \oplus \beta_i, f_j \oplus \beta_j}(a))^2$$

$$- (\sum_{i=1}^{m} \triangle_{f_i \oplus \beta_i, f_j \oplus \beta_j}(\mathbf{0}^n))^2]]^{1/2}$$

$$= [(2^n - 1) \sum_{a \in \mathbb{F}_2^n} (\sum_{i=1}^{m} \triangle_{f_i \oplus \beta_i, f_j \oplus \beta_j}(a))^2]^{1/2}.$$

Furthermore, we know

$$\sum_{a \in \mathbb{F}_2^n} (\sum_{i=1}^{m} \triangle_{f_i \oplus \beta_i, f_j \oplus \beta_j}(a))^2 \le m \sum_{a \in \mathbb{F}_2^n} \sum_{i=1}^{m} [\triangle_{f_i \oplus \beta_i, f_j \oplus \beta_j}(a)]^2.$$

Thus,

$$\sum_{a \in \mathbb{F}_2^{n*}} \sum_{j=1}^{m} \sum_{i=1}^{m} |\sum \triangle_{f_i \oplus \beta_i, f_j \oplus \beta_j}(a)| \le \sum_{j=1}^{m} [m(2^n - 1) \sum_{a \in \mathbb{F}_2^n} \sum_{i=1}^{m} [\triangle_{f_i \oplus \beta_i, f_j \oplus \beta_j}(a)]^2]^{1/2}$$

$$= \sum_{j=1}^{m} [m(2^n - 1) \sum_{i=1}^{m} \sum_{a \in \mathbb{F}_2^n} [\triangle_{f_i \oplus \beta_i, f_j \oplus \beta_j}(a)]^2]^{1/2}$$

$$= \sum_{j=1}^{m} [m(2^n - 1) \sum_{i=1}^{m} \sigma_{f_i \oplus \beta_i, f_j \oplus \beta_j}]^{1/2}$$

$$\le \sum_{j=1}^{m} [m(2^n - 1) \sum_{i=1}^{m} \sqrt{\sigma_{f_i \oplus \beta_i} \sigma_{f_j \oplus \beta_j}}]^{1/2}$$

$$= \sum_{j=1}^{m} [m(2^n - 1) \sum_{i=1}^{m} \sqrt{\sigma_{f_i} \sigma_{f_j}}]^{1/2},$$

which gives a lower bound on $\mathcal{RTO}(F)$. ∎

Theorem 4 gives the relationship between $\mathcal{RTO}(F)$ and $\sigma_{f_i}(1 \le i \le m)$, implying that the smaller the σ_{f_i} the larger is $\mathcal{RTO}(F)$. Using the fact that for any $f \in \mathbb{B}_n$, we have $\sigma_f \le 2^n[\mathcal{L}_f]^2$ [15], where $\mathcal{L}_{f_i} = \max_{\alpha \in \mathbb{F}_2^n} |\mathcal{F}(f_i \oplus \varphi_\alpha)|$, one can easily deduce the following result.

Corollary 2. Let $F = (f_1, \ldots, f_m)$ be a balanced (n, m)-function. If f_i and f_j are not almost perfectly uncorrelated for $1 \le i \ne j \le m$, then

$$\mathcal{RTO}(F) \ge m - \sqrt{\frac{m}{2^n(2^n - 1)}} \sum_{j=1}^{m} \left[\sum_{i=1}^{m} \mathcal{L}_{f_i} \mathcal{L}_{f_j} \right]^{1/2}.$$

Remark 3. *Using Theorem 4 and Corollary 2, one may also derive the relationship between $\mathcal{RTO}(F)$ and the nonlinearity of the coordinate functions N_{f_i}; alternatively between $\mathcal{RTO}(F)$ and the algebraic immunity $AI(f_i)$, where $1 \leq i \leq m$.*

1) The relationship between $\mathcal{RTO}(F)$ and $N_{f_i} (1 \leq i \leq m)$.

$$\mathcal{RTO}(F) \geq m - \sqrt{\frac{m}{2^n(2^n-1)}} \sum_{j=1}^{m} \left[\sum_{i=1}^{m} (2^n - 2N_{f_i})(2^n - 2N_{f_j}) \right]^{1/2}.$$

2) The relationship between $\mathcal{RTO}(F)$ and $AI(f_i)(1 \leq i \leq m)$.

$$\mathcal{RTO}(F) \geq m - \sqrt{\frac{m}{2^n(2^n-1)}} \sum_{j=1}^{m} \left\{ \sum_{i=1}^{m} \left[2^n - 4 \sum_{k=0}^{AI(f_i)-2} \binom{n-1}{k} \right] \left[2^n - 4 \sum_{l=0}^{AI(f_j)-2} \binom{n-1}{l} \right] \right\}^{1/2},$$

which easily follows from the bound $N_f \geq 2 \sum_{i=0}^{AI(f)-2} \binom{n-1}{i}$ for $f \in \mathbb{B}_n$, see [2, pp. 331].

In other words, the negative impact on $\mathcal{RTO}$ is again confirmed, thus the larger the N_{f_i} (or $AI(f_i)$), the larger is the $\mathcal{RTO}(F)$.

Finally, one can also deduce a lower bound on $\mathcal{RTO}$ which uses other cross-correlation properties of the coordinate functions.

Theorem 5. *Let $F = (f_1, \ldots, f_m)$ be a balanced (n, m)-function. If f_i and f_j are not almost perfectly uncorrelated for $1 \leq i \neq j \leq m$, then*

$$\mathcal{RTO}(F) \geq m - \frac{1}{2^n} \sum_{j=1}^{m} \sum_{i=1}^{m} (2^n - Num_{\triangle_{f_i,f_j}})(2^n - Num_{\mathcal{F}_{f_i,f_j}}),$$

where $Num_{\triangle_{f_i,f_j}} = | \{ u \in \mathbb{F}_2^n : \triangle_{f_i,f_j}(u) = 0 \} |$, $Num_{\mathcal{F}_{f_i,f_j}} = | \{ u \in \mathbb{F}_2^n : \mathcal{F}(f_i \oplus \varphi_u)\mathcal{F}(f_j \oplus \varphi_u) = 0 \} |$.

Proof. From [12], we know

$$\max_{a \in \mathbb{F}_2^n} \triangle_{f,g}(a) \leq (2^n - Num_{\triangle_{f,g}})(2^n - Num_{\mathcal{F}_{f,g}}).$$

Thus,

$$\sum_{a \in \mathbb{F}_2^{n*}} | \sum_{i=1}^{m} \triangle_{f_i \oplus \beta_i, f_j \oplus \beta_j}(a) | \leq \sum_{a \in \mathbb{F}_2^{n*}} \sum_{i=1}^{m} | \triangle_{f_i \oplus \beta_i, f_j \oplus \beta_j}(a) |$$

$$\leq (2^n - 1) \sum_{i=1}^{m} \max_{a \in \mathbb{F}_2^n} | \triangle_{f_i \oplus \beta_i, f_j \oplus \beta_j}(a) |$$

$$\leq (2^n - 1) \sum_{i=1}^{m} (2^n - Num_{\triangle_{f_i,f_j}})(2^n - Num_{\mathcal{F}_{f_i,f_j}})$$

$$= (2^n - 1) \sum_{i=1}^{m} (2^n - Num_{\triangle_{f_i, f_j}})(2^n - Num_{\mathcal{F}_{f_i, f_j}}).$$

∎

Remark 4. *In terms of the above results it is uncertain whether a design of cryptographic S-boxes satisfying all the relevant criteria (including the resistance to DPA attacks) is actually possible after all. The problem of giving a theoretical evidence regarding the existence of S-boxes with overall good properties remains open however. More specifically, the question is whether the induced trade-offs are acceptable from the security margins viewpoint or not.*

4 $\mathcal{RTO}$ of S-Boxes of Size 4×4

For efficient hardware implementation, small sized bijective S-boxes (as confusion primitives in block ciphers that use substitution permutation framework) are commonly preferable in practical applications. The number of bijective mappings $F : \mathbb{F}_2^4 \to \mathbb{F}_2^4$, up to affine equivalence (when a cryptographic property remains invariant under affine transformations; affine equivalent S-boxes share the same cryptographic properties), was determined. In [3], it was pointed out that $\mathcal{RTO}$ is affine invariant for $F \circ A$, where $A \in A_n$ is an affine permutation, and $\mathcal{RTO}$ is not affine invariant for $B \circ F$ under some affine permutation $B \in A_n$. The exact number of equivalence classes of 4×4 S-boxes is 302 among which only 10 S-boxes have nonlinearity 4, degree 3 and absolute auto-correlation value 8, which are the optimal values of these parameters for this particular size of the ambient space. For this reason the authors in [3] only provided the $\mathcal{RTO}$ values for these 10 equivalence classes of S-boxes. On the other hand, in [6], all optimal 4-bit S-boxes were classified and up to affine equivalence there are only 16 different classes (here "optimal" means that 16 classes S-boxes satisfy: 1) the linearity is 8; 2) the difference is 8; 3) the algebraic degree is 3), where the term optimal refers to those S-boxes that achieve the best differential property and nonlinearity.

4.1 $\mathcal{RTO}$ of 302 Affine Equivalent Representative $(4, 4)$ S-Box

We here compute the transparency order of all 302 (representative) S-boxes of size 4×4 and give a somewhat better insight in the behaviour of this parameter, especially with respect to randomly selected S-boxes. Our simulations show (see also [17]) that the transparency order is confined within the range $0 \leq \mathcal{RTO}(F) \leq 2.767$, having a single (affine) S-box, say F, for which $\mathcal{RTO}(F) = 0$. We summarize the distribution of transparency order values for $(4, 4)$ S-boxes in Table 3, omitting the case of affine S-boxes.

Table 3. Distribution of $\mathcal{RTO}$ for 302 $(4,4)$ S-boxes [17]

$\mathcal{RTO}$	$Number$	$Per(\%)$	$\mathcal{RTO}$	$Number$	$Per(\%)$
0.467	1	0.331	2.133	6	1.656
0.800	1	0.331	2.167	2	0.662
1.067	1	0.331	2.200	2	0.662
1.133	1	0.331	2.233	1	0.331
1.267	1	0.331	2.267	6	1.656
1.333	3	0.993	2.300	5	1.656
1.400	1	0.331	2.333	22	7.285
1.533	1	0.331	2.367	15	4.967
1.600	1	0.331	2.400	22	7.285
1.733	2	0.662	2.433	21	6.954
1.800	4	1.325	2.467	30	9.934
1.833	1	0.331	2.500	31	10.265
1.867	5	1.656	2.533	30	9.934
1.900	1	0.331	2.567	26	8.609
1.933	8	2.649	2.600	20	6.623
1.967	3	0.993	2.633	9	2.980
2.000	2	0.662	2.667	7	2.318
2.033	1	0.331	2.700	1	0.331
2.067	3	0.993	2.733	1	0.331
2.100	2	0.662	2.767	1	0.331

Remark 5. *The number of affine equivalence classes whose transparency order lies in the range $\mathcal{RTO}_{(4,4)} = [2.333, 2.600]$ equals to $217 = 22 + 15 + 22 + 21 + 30 + 31 + 30 + 26 + 20$, which corresponds to about 71.85% of their total number. This simply means that for a randomly selected $(4, 4)$ S-box, the probability that its transparency order is in the range $\mathcal{RTO}_{(4,4)}$ is approximately 71.85%, which is quite high.*

4.2 $\mathcal{RTO}$ of $A \circ G_i$ for 16 Optimal S-Box G_i

From [6], we know that there are 16 different class (denoted by $G_0, G_1, \cdots, G_{15}$) in all optimal 4-bit S-boxes up to affine equivalence. Since $\mathcal{RTO}(S \circ A) = \mathcal{RTO}(S)$ for any (n, n) S-box S and any affine permutation $A \in A_n$ [3], thus, we only analyse the distribution of $\mathcal{RTO}(A \circ G_i)(i = 0, 1, \cdots, 15)$. The number of affine permutation $A \in A_4$ is 20160, thus we calculate 20160 $\mathcal{RTO}(A \circ G_i)$ for every $G_i(i = 0, 1, \cdots, 15)$. Because the calculation method for the distribution of $\mathcal{RTO}(A \circ G_i)$ is similar for any $G_i(i = 0, 1, \cdots, 15)$, due to page limits, here we give the distribution of $\mathcal{RTO}(A \circ G_{15})$, where $G_{15} = \{0, 1, 2, 13, 4, 7, 15, 6, 8, 14, 12, 11, 9, 3, 10, 5\}$ [6], see Table 4.

Table 4. Distribution of $\mathcal{RTO}$ for $A \circ G_{15}$ S-boxes

Case	$\mathcal{RTO}$	Number	$Per(\%)$
1	2.133	24	0.119
2	2.167	72	0.357
3	2.200	144	0.714
4	2.233	312	1.55
5	2.267	144	0.714
6	2.300	432	2.143
7	2.333	600	2.976
8	2.367	1248	6.19
9	2.400	1848	9.167
10	2.433	2040	10.119
11	2.467	3000	14.881
12	2.500	2616	12.976
13	2.533	2904	14.404
14	2.567	1872	9.286
15	2.600	1296	6.429
16	2.633	672	3.333
17	2.667	360	1.786
18	2.700	288	1.429
19	2.733	144	0.714
20	2.767	48	0.238
21	2.800	24	0.119
22	2.867	48	0.238
23	2.900	24	0.119
–	–	20160	100

Remark 6. *From Table 4, we can find that there are 23 different value for* $\mathcal{RTO}(A \circ G_{15})$. *The range of* $\mathcal{RTO}(A \circ G_{15})$ *is* $[2.133, 2.900]$, *but* $\mathcal{RTO}(G_{15}) = 2.500$. *This shows that some affine permutation* A *makes* $\mathcal{RTO}(A \circ G_i) > \mathcal{RTO}(G_i)$, *certain* A *make* $\mathcal{RTO}(A \circ G_i) < \mathcal{RTO}(G_i)$, *and it can happen that* $\mathcal{RTO}(A \circ G_i) = \mathcal{RTO}(G_i)$ *for* $i = 0, 1, \cdots, 15$. *This further implies that* $\mathcal{RTO}$ *is not an invariant with respect to an affine permutation. This fact is consistent with the results in [6].*

5   Conclusions

This article further addresses some relevant results related to $\mathcal{TO}$ and $\mathcal{RTO}$. We answer the open problem regarding the existence of (n, m)-functions that reach the upper bound on $\mathcal{TO}$ for odd n, and give tight upper and lower bounds $\mathcal{RTO}$. Then, we derive its relationship to main cryptographic characterizations of (n, m)-functions (such as nonlinearity, the sum-of-square indicator and algebraic immunity). Finally, the distributions of $\mathcal{RTO}$ for 302 4-bit S-boxes and $\mathcal{RTO}$ of $A \circ G_i$ for 16 optimal S-box G_i are given as theoretical verification. These results improve the theoretical results for $\mathcal{RTO}$ of S-boxes, and lay a theoretical foundation for how to construct S-boxes with smaller $\mathcal{RTO}$ in the next step.

Acknowledgments. Yu Zhou is supported in part by the Sichuan Science and Technology Program (2020JDJQ0076). Yongzhuang Wei is supported by the National Natural Science Foundation of China (61872103), the Guangxi Science and Technology Foundation (Guike AB18281019) and the Guangxi Natural Science Foundation (2019GXNS-FGA245004). Hailong Zhang is supported by the National Natural Science Foundation of China (61872040). Enes Pasalic is supported in part by the Slovenian Research Agency (research program P1-0404 and research projects J1-9108, J1-1694, N1-0159, J1-2451). Luyang Li is supported by the Natural Science Foundation of Shaanxi Provincial Department of Education (20JK0911).

References

1. Carlet, C.: On highly nonlinear S-boxes and their inability to thwart DPA attacks. In: Maitra, S., Veni Madhavan, C.E., Venkatesan, R. (eds.) INDOCRYPT 2005. LNCS, vol. 3797, pp. 49–62. Springer, Heidelberg (2005). https://doi.org/10.1007/11596219_5
2. Carlet, C.: Boolean Functions for Cryptography and Coding Theory. Cambridge University Press, New York (2020)
3. Chakraborty, K., Sarkar, S., Maitra, S., Mazumdar, B., Mukhopadhyay, D., Prouff, E.: Redefining the transparency order. Designs Codes Cryptogr. **82**(1–2), 95–115 (2017)
4. Fan, L., Zhou, Y., Feng, D.: A fast implementation of computing the transparency order of S-Boxes. In: The 9th International Conference of Young Computer Scientists, 2008, ICYCS 2008, pp. 206–211. IEEE (2008)
5. Kocher, P., Jaffe, J., Jun, B.: Differential power analysis. In: Wiener, M. (ed.) CRYPTO 1999. LNCS, vol. 1666, pp. 388–397. Springer, Heidelberg (1999). https://doi.org/10.1007/3-540-48405-1_25
6. Leander, G., Poschmann, A.: On the classification of 4 bit S-boxes. In: International Workshop on Arithmetic of Finite Fields (WAIFI 2007), pp. 159–176 (2007)
7. Mazumdar, B., Nyjgioadgtat, D., Sengupta, I.: Constrained search for a class of good bijective S-boxes with improved DPA resistivity. IEEE Trans. Inf. Forensics Secur. **8**(12), 2154–2163 (2013)
8. Pasalic, E., Maitra, S., Johansson, T., Sarkar, P.: New constructions of resilient and correlation immune boolean functions achieving upper bound on nonlinearity. Electron. Notes Disc. Math. **6**, 158–167 (2001)

9. Picek, S., Batina, L., Jakobovic, D.: Evolving DPA-resistant boolean functions. In: Bartz-Beielstein, T., Branke, J., Filipič, B., Smith, J. (eds.) PPSN 2014. LNCS, vol. 8672, pp. 812–821. Springer, Cham (2014). https://doi.org/10.1007/978-3-319-10762-2_80

10. Prouff, E.: DPA attacks and S-boxes. In: Fast Software Encryption: 12th International Workshop, FSE 2005, Paris, France, 21–23 February 2005, Revised Selected Papers, pp. 424–441 (2005)

11. Rothaus, O.S.: On bent functions. J. Comb. Theory A **20**, 300–305 (1976)

12. Sarkar, P., Maitra, S.: Cross-correlation analysis of cryptographically useful boolean functions and S-boxes. Theory Comput. Syst. **35**(1), 39–57 (2002)

13. Wang, Q., Stănică, P.: Transparency order for Boolean functions: analysis and construction. Designs Codes Cryptogr. **87**, 2043–2059 (2019)

14. Zhang, X., Zheng, Y.: GAC - the criterion for global avalance characteristics of cryptographic functions. J. Univ. Comput. Sci. **1**(5), 320–337 (1995)

15. Zheng, Y., Zhang, X.: On plateaued functions. IEEE Trans. Inf. Theory **47**(3), 1215–1223 (2001)

16. Zhou, Y., Xie, M., Xiao, G.: On the global avalanche characteristics between two Boolean functions and the higher order nonlinearity. Inf. Sci. **180**(2), 256–265 (2010)

17. Zhou, Y., Wei, Y., Zhang, H., Zhang, W.: On the modified transparency order of (n, m)-functions. Secur. Commun. Netw., Article ID 6640099, p. 14 (2021). https://doi.org/10.1155/2021/6640099

Binary Sequences Derived from Monomial Permutation Polynomials over $\mathrm{GF}(2^p)$

Qun-Xiong Zheng[1,2], Yupeng Jiang[3(✉)], Dongdai Lin[2], and Wen-Feng Qi[1]

[1] PLA Strategic Support Force Information Engineering University,
Zhengzhou 450001, China
wenfeng.qi@263.net

[2] State Key Laboratory of Information Security, Institute of Information
Engineering, Chinese Academy of Sciences, Beijing 100093, China
ddlin@iie.ac.cn

[3] School of Cyber Science and Technology, Beihang University, Beijing 100191, China
jiangyupeng@amss.ac.cn

Abstract. In this paper, we propose a class of binary sequences induced by monomial permutation polynomials over $\mathrm{GF}(2^p)$ and study the period property and the shift-equivalence of these binary sequences. In particularly, we give a necessary and sufficient condition for such a sequence to have maximal period. Moreover, we also give a necessary and sufficient condition for two such sequences to be shift equivalent.

Keywords: Mersenne prime · Permutation polynomial · Pseudorandom sequence · Periodicity · Shift equivalence

1 Introduction

Pseudo-random number generators (PRNGs) are widely used in cryptography, communication, statistical sampling, Monte Carlo simulation, etc. Different applications have different requirements for PRNGs. For the application of stream ciphers, it is usually required that a PRNG should have a sufficiently large period, as well as a "good" nonlinear structure in order to effectively resist correlation attacks and algebraic attacks. Nonlinear feedback shift registers (NFSRs) are a most popular PRNGs for stream cipher design. However, some critical properties of NFSRs, such as the period properties, are still hard to be analyzed. In this paper, we propose a new PRNG based on permutation polynomials of finite fields. Our main idea is first to generate sequences with controllable periods by a suitable permutation polynomial over finite fields, and then to prove that the

This work was supported by NSF of China (Nos. 61872383). The work of Qun-Xiong Zheng was also supported by Young Elite Scientists Sponsorship Program by CAST (2016QNRC001) and by National Postdoctoral Program for Innovative Talents (BX201600188) and by China Postdoctoral Science Foundation funded project (2017M611035).

© Springer Nature Switzerland AG 2021
Y. Yu and M. Yung (Eds.): Inscrypt 2021, LNCS 13007, pp. 371–383, 2021.
https://doi.org/10.1007/978-3-030-88323-2_20

induced coordinate sequences also have sufficiently large periods. The nonlinear iterative approach naturally imply that the induced coordinate sequences are nonlinear. More importantly, since there are many choices of bases for a finite field, a variety of coordinate sequences can be derived.

Let $\mathrm{GF}(2^n)$ be a finite field with 2^n elements. A polynomial $f \in \mathrm{GF}(2^n)[x]$ is called a permutation polynomial of $\mathrm{GF}(2^n)$ if the associated mapping $x \mapsto f(x)$ from $\mathrm{GF}(2^n)$ into $\mathrm{GF}(2^n)$ is a permutation of $\mathrm{GF}(2^n)$. It is well-known that the monomial polynomial x^e is a permutation polynomial of $\mathrm{GF}(2^n)$ if and only if $\gcd(e, 2^n - 1) = 1$. Permutation polynomials have wide applications in many areas of mathematics and engineering such as coding theory, cryptography and combinatorial designs. We refer the reader to [1, Ch.7], [2, Ch.8], [3] and the references therein for a detailed exposition of permutation polynomials. We also refer the reader to [4–6] for some constructions of permutation polynomials. For some recent advances such as complete permutation polynomials over finite fields, [7–9] are recommended.

Let f be a permutation polynomial of $\mathrm{GF}(2^n)$. Given an initial value $a \in \mathrm{GF}(2^n)$, one can obtain a sequence $\underline{a} = (a, f(a), f^2(a), \ldots)$ over $\mathrm{GF}(2^n)$, where $f^t(a) = f(f^{t-1}(a))$ for any integer $t \geq 1$ and $f^0(a) = a$. For convenience, we say that $\underline{a}$ is a sequence induced by f with a being the initial value. If there exists a positive integer T such that $f^T(a) = a$, then $\underline{a}$ is called a **periodic sequence**. The minimum of such T is called the period of $\underline{a}$ and is denoted by $\mathrm{per}(\underline{a})$. Because of the fact that the associated mapping $x \mapsto f(x)$ from $\mathrm{GF}(2^n)$ into $\mathrm{GF}(2^n)$ is a bijection of $\mathrm{GF}(2^n)$, any sequence induced by f is periodic.

Let $\{\alpha_0, \alpha_1, \ldots, \alpha_{n-1}\}$ be a basis of $\mathrm{GF}(2^n)$ over $\mathrm{GF}(2)$. Each element $a \in \mathrm{GF}(2^n)$ can be uniquely represented as

$$a = [a]_0 \cdot \alpha_0 + [a]_1 \cdot \alpha_1 + \cdots + [a]_{n-1} \cdot \alpha_{n-1} \text{ with } [a]_i \in \mathrm{GF}(2) \text{ for } 0 \leq i \leq n-1,$$

where $[a]_i$ is called the i-th coordinate of a w.r.t. $\{\alpha_0, \alpha_1, \ldots, \alpha_{n-1}\}$. Let

$$\underline{a} = (a, f(a), f^2(a), \ldots)$$

be a sequence over $\mathrm{GF}(2^n)$. If each $f^t(a)$, $t \geq 0$, is uniquely represented as

$$f^t(a) = [f^t(a)]_0 \cdot \alpha_0 + [f^t(a)]_1 \cdot \alpha_1 + \cdots + [f^t(a)]_{n-1} \cdot \alpha_{n-1},$$

where $[f^t(a)]_i \in \mathrm{GF}(2)$ for $0 \leq i \leq n-1$, then one can simultaneously obtain n binary sequences $[\underline{a}]_0, [\underline{a}]_1, \ldots, [\underline{a}]_{n-1}$, where

$$[\underline{a}]_i = ([a]_i, [f(a)]_i, [f^2(a)]_i, \ldots) \text{ for } 0 \leq i \leq n-1.$$

For convenience, $[\underline{a}]_i$ is called the i-th **coordinate sequence** of $\underline{a}$ w.r.t. $\{\alpha_0, \alpha_1, \ldots, \alpha_{n-1}\}$. The idea of using permutation polynomials to derive coordinate sequences can be traced back to Niederreiter [10], where pseudorandom vectors are generated by the inversive method. The method of using coordinate vectors to describe pseudorandom numbers is driven by paralleized simulation methods. For details of applications in paralleized simulation methods, Anderson

[11], Bhavsar and Isaac [12], and Eddy [13] are recommended. It is worth noticing that the period of each coordinate sequence strictly divides the period of the original sequence. Then a natural problem has arisen—that is, if $\underline{a}$ is a sequence induced by a nonlinear permutation polynomial f with period large enough, do all of its coordinate sequences have period large enough? In particular, all have the same period as $\underline{a}$. If so, these coordinate sequences may be of potential interest to many applications, such as the design of stream ciphers, since it is a challenging work to design nonlinear sequences with controllable periods. However, the above problem is of independent interest in theory, regardless of its potential applications.

In this paper, we focus ourself on the monomial permutation polynomials over $\mathrm{GF}(2^n)$. Let $f = x^e$ be a monomial permutation polynomial over $\mathrm{GF}(2^n)$ and let $\underline{a} = (a, f(a), f^2(a), \ldots)$ be a sequence over $\mathrm{GF}(2^n)$ induced by f. It is easy to see that the maximum possible period for $\underline{a}$ is $2^n - 2$. If per $(\underline{a}) = 2^n - 2$, then $\underline{a}$ is called an MLM-sequence (maximal length monomial sequence). Firstly, it is shown that $\underline{a}$ is an MLM-sequence if and only if $2^n - 1$ is a Mersenne prime and e is a primitive root modulo $2^n - 1$. Secondly, the periods of coordinate sequences of an MLM-sequence $\underline{a}$ are studied. Let $[\underline{a}]_0, [\underline{a}]_1, \ldots, [\underline{a}]_{n-1}$ be n binary coordinate sequences of $\underline{a}$ w.r.t. a given basis $\{\alpha_0, \alpha_1, \ldots, \alpha_{n-1}\}$ of $\mathrm{GF}(2^n)$ over $\mathrm{GF}(2)$. It is shown that per $([\underline{a}]_i) = 2^n - 2$ if and only if $\beta_i \neq 1$; and per $([\underline{a}]_i) = (2^n - 2)/n$ if and only if $\beta_i = 1$, where $1 \leq i \leq n$ and $\{\beta_0, \beta_1, \ldots, \beta_{n-1}\}$ is the dual basis of $\{\alpha_0, \alpha_1, \ldots, \alpha_{n-1}\}$. In particular, per $([\underline{a}]_0) = $ per $([\underline{a}]_1) = \cdots = $ per $([\underline{a}]_{n-1}) = 2^n - 2$ if $\{\alpha_0, \alpha_1, \ldots, \alpha_{n-1}\}$ is chosen to be a normal basis of $\mathrm{GF}(2^n)$ over $\mathrm{GF}(2)$. Finally, the shift-equivalence of $[\underline{a}]_0, [\underline{a}]_1, \ldots, [\underline{a}]_{n-1}$ is further studied. For $0 \leq i < j \leq n-1$, it is shown that $[\underline{a}]_i = L^s[\underline{a}]_j$ for some positive integer s if and only if $\beta_j = \beta_i^{2^k}$ and $e^s \equiv 2^k \bmod 2^n - 1$ for some $0 \leq k \leq n - 1$, where $L^s[\underline{a}]_j$ is the s-shift of $[\underline{a}]_j$. Particularly, if $\{\alpha_0, \alpha_1, \ldots, \alpha_{n-1}\}$ is chosen to be a normal basis of $\mathrm{GF}(2^n)$ over $\mathrm{GF}(2)$, then there always exists a positive integer $s_j = u_j(2^n - 2)/n$ with $1 \leq u_j \leq n - 1$ such that $[\underline{a}]_0 = L^{s_j}[\underline{a}]_j$. Moreover, $s_1, s_s, \ldots, s_{n-1}$ run exactly through the set $\{(2^n - 2)/n, 2(2^n - 2)/n, \ldots, (n-1)(2^n - 2)/n\}$.

The rest of this paper is organized as follows. In Sect. 2, we first recall the definition of dual bases and their basic properties, and then we give a necessary and sufficient condition for MLM-sequences. In Sect. 3, we study the periodicity and the shift-equivalence of coordinate sequences derived from MLM-sequences. Finally, we conclude this paper in Sect. 4.

2   Preliminaries

2.1   Dual Bases

Let $n > 1$ and let $\{\alpha_0, \alpha_1, \ldots, \alpha_{n-1}\}$ and $\{\beta_0, \beta_1, \ldots, \beta_{n-1}\}$ be two bases of $\mathrm{GF}(2^n)$ over $\mathrm{GF}(2)$. Then $\{\alpha_0, \alpha_1, \ldots, \alpha_{n-1}\}$ and $\{\beta_0, \beta_1, \ldots, \beta_{n-1}\}$ are said to be dual bases if for $0 \leq i, j \leq n - 1$ we have

$$\mathrm{Tr}(\alpha_i \beta_j) = \begin{cases} 0 \text{ if } i \neq j, \\ 1 \text{ if } i = j, \end{cases}$$

where $\mathrm{Tr}(y) = y + y^2 + \cdots + y^{2^{n-1}}$ is the trace function from $\mathrm{GF}(2^n)$ to $\mathrm{GF}(2)$. It is known that given a basis $\{\alpha_0, \alpha_1, \ldots, \alpha_{n-1}\}$ of $\mathrm{GF}(2^n)$ over $\mathrm{GF}(2)$, its dual basis $\{\beta_0, \beta_1, \ldots, \beta_{n-1}\}$ always exists and is uniquely determined by $\{\alpha_0, \alpha_1, \ldots, \alpha_{n-1}\}$. Moreover, for $0 \leq i \leq n-1$, it is easy to check that

$$[y]_i = \mathrm{Tr}(\beta_i y) \text{ for all } y \in \mathrm{GF}(2^n), \tag{1}$$

where $[y]_i$ is the i-th coordinate of y w.r.t. $\{\alpha_0, \alpha_1, \ldots, \alpha_{n-1}\}$. For more details of dual bases, we refer to [1].

2.2   Maximal Length Monomial Sequences

Let n be an integer greater than 1 and e a positive integer coprime with $2^n - 1$. Let $f = x^e$ be a monomial permutation polynomial over $\mathrm{GF}(2^n)$ and $\underline{a} = (a, f(a), f^2(a), \ldots)$ a sequence over $\mathrm{GF}(2^n)$ induced by f. It is clear that $\underline{a}$ is an all-zero sequence with $\mathrm{per}(\underline{a}) = 1$ if $a = 0$; and $\underline{a}$ is an all-one sequence with $\mathrm{per}(\underline{a}) = 1$ if $a = 1$; and $\underline{a}$ is a periodic sequence with $\mathrm{per}(\underline{a}) \leq 2^n - 2$ if $a \in \mathrm{GF}(2^n) \backslash \{0, 1\}$.

Definition 1 *(MLM-sequences). Let $f = x^e$ be a monomial permutation polynomial over $\mathrm{GF}(2^n)$, where e is a positive integer coprime with $2^n - 1$. Let $\underline{a} = (a, f(a), f^2(a), \ldots)$ be a sequence over $\mathrm{GF}(2^n)$ induced by f. If $\mathrm{per}(\underline{a}) = 2^n - 2$, then $\underline{a}$ is called a maximal length monomial sequence (called MLM-sequence in short).*

Remark 1. If $a \notin \{0, 1\}$, then $f^t(a) = a^{e^t} \notin \{0, 1\}$ for any integer $t \geq 0$. Therefore, $a, f(a), f^2(a), \ldots f^{2^n-3}(a)$ run exactly through the set $\mathrm{GF}(2^n) \backslash \{0, 1\}$ if $\underline{a}$ is an MLM-sequence over $\mathrm{GF}(2^n)$.

We recall that a prime number of the form $2^n - 1$ is called a Mersenne prime. It is necessary that n is prime if $2^n - 1$ is a Mersenne prime. We also recall that a positive integer e coprime to $2^n - 1$ is called a **primitive root** modulo $2^n - 1$, if the multiplicative order of e modulo $2^n - 1$ (the smallest positive integer k with $e^k \equiv 1 \bmod 2^n - 1$) is equal to $\varphi(2^n - 1)$, where $\varphi(\cdot)$ is the Euler's totient function. There are totally $\varphi(\varphi(2^n - 1))$ primitive roots modulo $2^n - 1$ for $1 < e < 2^n - 1$.

Next we will give a necessary and sufficient condition for MLM-sequences.

Theorem 1. *Let $f = x^e$ be a monomial permutation polynomial over $\mathrm{GF}(2^n)$, where e is a positive integer coprime with $2^n - 1$. Let $a \in \mathrm{GF}(2^n) \backslash \{0, 1\}$. Then $\underline{a} = (a, f(a), f^2(a), \ldots)$ is an MLM-sequence over $\mathrm{GF}(2^n)$ if and only if $2^n - 1$ is a Mersenne prime and e is a primitive root modulo $2^n - 1$.*

Proof. ($\Leftarrow$) We note that $f^t(a) = a^{e^t}$ for any integer $t \geq 0$. If there exists an integer $1 \leq t \leq 2^n - 3$ such that $f^t(a) = a$, then $a^{e^t} = a$, and so

$$a^{e^t - 1} = 1. \tag{2}$$

Since $2^n - 1$ is a Mersenne prime, every element belongs to $\mathrm{GF}(2^n)\backslash\{0,1\}$ is a primitive element of $\mathrm{GF}(2^n)$. It naturally follows that a is a primitive element of $\mathrm{GF}(2^n)$. Now (2) implies that $e^t \equiv 1 \bmod 2^n - 1$, which is a contradiction since by assumption e is a primitive root modulo $2^n - 1$. Therefore,

$$f^t(a) \neq a \text{ for } 1 \leq t \leq 2^n - 3,$$

and so per $(\underline{a}) \geq 2^n - 2$. On the other hand, it is obvious that per $(\underline{a}) \leq 2^n - 2$. Altogether, we have shown that per $(\underline{a}) = 2^n - 2$, or equivalently, that $\underline{a}$ is an MLM-sequence over $\mathrm{GF}(2^n)$.

($\Rightarrow$) We recall that the nonzero elements of $\mathrm{GF}(2^n)$ form a cyclic group of order $2^n - 1$ under multiplication. Let $\mathrm{ord}(a)$ denote the order of a. Then $\mathrm{ord}(a) \mid 2^n - 1$. On the other hand, it follows from Remark 1 that $a, a^e, a^{e^2}, \ldots, a^{e^{2^n-3}}$ run exactly through the set $\mathrm{GF}(2^n)\backslash\{0,1\}$. This implies that $\mathrm{ord}(a) > 2^n - 2$. Now, together with $\mathrm{ord}(a) \mid 2^n - 1$, we get $\mathrm{ord}(a) = 2^n - 1$. Since

$$a^{e^{2^n-2}} = f^{2^n-2}(a) = a \text{ but } a^{e^t} = f^t(a) \neq a \text{ for } 1 \leq t \leq 2^n - 3, \qquad (3)$$

by applying $\mathrm{ord}(a) = 2^n - 1$ to (3) we obtain

$$e^{2^n-2} \equiv 1 \bmod 2^n - 1 \text{ but } e^t \not\equiv 1 \bmod 2^n - 1 \text{ for } 1 \leq t \leq 2^n - 3,$$

and hence the multiplicative order of e modulo $2^n - 1$ is equal to $2^n - 2$. This happens only if $2^n - 1$ is a Mersenne prime and e is a primitive root modulo $2^n - 1$.

3   Properties of Coordinate Sequences Derived from MLM-sequences

Throughout this section, we always assume that $2^p - 1$ is a Mersenne prime (p is, of course, a prime number) and e is a primitive root modulo $2^p - 1$.

We will study two properties of coordinate sequences derived from MLM-sequences. Before proceeding, we first give two concrete examples.

Example 1. It can be verified that 2^5-1 is a Mersenne prime and 11 is a primitive root modulo $2^5 - 1$. Let $\mathrm{GF}(2^5) = \mathrm{GF}(2)[x]/(x^5 + x^3 + 1)$, where $x^5 + x^3 + 1$ is an irreducible polynomial of degree 5 over $\mathrm{GF}(2)$. Let $\alpha \in \mathrm{GF}(2^5)$ be a root of $x^5 + x^3 + 1$. Then $\{1, \alpha, \alpha^2, \alpha^3, \alpha^4\}$ is a polynomial basis of $\mathrm{GF}(2^5)$ over $\mathrm{GF}(2)$. Set $f = x^{11}$ and $a = \alpha$. By Theorem 1, $\underline{a} = (a, f(a), f^2(a), \ldots)$ is an MLM-sequence over $\mathrm{GF}(2^5)$ with per $(\underline{a}) = 30$. In fact, it can be checked that

$$\begin{aligned}
\underline{a} = (&\alpha, \alpha^3 + \alpha^2 + \alpha + 1, \alpha^2 + 1, \alpha^3 + \alpha, \alpha^4 + \alpha^3 + \alpha^2 + 1, \alpha^4 + \alpha, \alpha^4, \\
&\alpha^4 + \alpha^2 + 1, \alpha^4 + \alpha^3 + \alpha + 1, \alpha^3 + \alpha^2 + \alpha, \alpha^3 + 1, \alpha^4 + \alpha^3 + \alpha^2, \\
&\alpha^3 + \alpha^2, \alpha^4 + \alpha^2 + \alpha + 1, \alpha + 1, \alpha^4 + \alpha^2, \alpha^4 + \alpha^3 + \alpha^2 + \alpha + 1, \alpha^3, \quad (4) \\
&\alpha^2, \alpha^2 + \alpha + 1, \alpha^4 + 1, \alpha^4 + \alpha^2 + \alpha, \alpha^4 + \alpha^3 + 1, \alpha^4 + \alpha^3 + \alpha^2 + \alpha, \\
&\alpha^4 + \alpha^3 + \alpha, \alpha^3 + \alpha + 1, \alpha^3 + \alpha^2 + 1, \alpha^2 + \alpha, \alpha^4 + \alpha + 1, \alpha^4 + \alpha^3, \ldots),
\end{aligned}$$

and so the 5 coordinate sequences of $\underline{a}$ w.r.t. $\{1, \alpha, \alpha^2, \alpha^3, \alpha^4\}$ are as follows:

$[\underline{a}]_0 = (0,1,1,0,1,0,0,1,1,0,1,0,0,1,1,0,1,0,0,1,1,0,1,0,0,1,1,0,1,0,\dots),$

$[\underline{a}]_1 = (1,1,0,1,0,1,0,0,1,1,0,0,0,1,1,0,1,0,0,1,0,1,0,1,1,1,0,1,1,0,\dots),$

$[\underline{a}]_2 = (0,1,1,0,1,0,0,1,0,1,0,1,1,1,0,1,1,0,1,1,0,1,0,1,0,0,1,1,0,0,\dots),$

$[\underline{a}]_3 = (0,1,0,1,1,0,0,0,1,1,1,1,1,0,0,0,1,1,0,0,0,0,1,1,1,1,1,0,0,1,\dots),$

$[\underline{a}]_4 = (0,0,0,0,1,1,1,1,1,0,0,1,0,1,0,1,1,0,0,0,1,1,1,1,1,0,0,0,1,1,\dots).$

It can be seen that

$$\mathrm{per}\,([\underline{a}]_0) = 6, \mathrm{per}\,([\underline{a}]_1) = \mathrm{per}\,([\underline{a}]_2) = \mathrm{per}\,([\underline{a}]_3) = \mathrm{per}\,([\underline{a}]_4) = 30.$$

Consequently, among the 5 coordinate sequences, only 4 of them attain the maximum period. It also can be seen that

$$[\underline{a}]_1 = L^{18}[\underline{a}]_2 \text{ and } [\underline{a}]_3 = L^{12}[\underline{a}]_4,$$

where $L^k \underline{z}$ denotes the k-shift of $\underline{z}$ (i.e., $L^k \underline{z} = (z(t+k))_{t\geq0}$ if $\underline{z} = (z(t))_{t\geq0}$). This implies that $[\underline{a}]_1$ and $[\underline{a}]_2$ (or $[\underline{a}]_3$ and $[\underline{a}]_4$) are shift equivalent. However, it can be checked that $[\underline{a}]_1$ (or $[\underline{a}]_2$) and $[\underline{a}]_3$ (or $[\underline{a}]_4$) are shift distinct.

Example 2. Let $\mathrm{GF}(2^5)$ and α be as in Example 1. Let $\beta = \alpha^3 + 1$. Then

$$\beta^2 = \alpha^4 + \alpha + 1, \beta^4 = \alpha^4 + \alpha^3 + \alpha^2 + \alpha + 1, \beta^8 = \alpha^4 + \alpha^3 + \alpha^2 + 1, \beta^{16} = \alpha^4 + \alpha^3 + 1,$$

and so $\{\beta, \beta^2, \beta^4, \beta^8, \beta^{16}\}$ is a normal basis of $\mathrm{GF}(2^5)$ over $\mathrm{GF}(2)$. Let $\underline{a}$ be as in (4). Then the 5 coordinate sequences of $\underline{a}$ w.r.t. $\{\beta, \beta^2, \beta^4, \beta^8, \beta^{16}\}$ are as follows:

$[\underline{a}]_0 = (0,1,1,0,0,1,1,0,0,0,1,1,0,0,1,1,0,0,0,1,0,1,0,1,1,1,1,0,0,1,\dots),$

$[\underline{a}]_1 = (0,0,1,1,0,0,0,1,0,1,0,1,1,1,1,0,0,1,0,1,1,0,0,1,1,0,0,0,1,1,\dots),$

$[\underline{a}]_2 = (1,1,1,0,0,1,0,1,1,0,0,1,1,0,0,0,1,1,0,0,1,1,0,0,0,1,0,1,0,1,\dots),$

$[\underline{a}]_3 = (1,0,0,0,1,1,0,0,1,1,0,0,0,1,0,1,0,1,1,1,1,0,0,1,0,1,1,0,0,1,\dots),$

$[\underline{a}]_4 = (0,1,0,1,0,1,1,1,1,0,0,1,0,1,1,0,0,1,1,0,0,0,1,1,0,0,1,1,0,0,\dots).$

It can be seen that

$$\mathrm{per}\,([\underline{a}]_0) = \mathrm{per}\,([\underline{a}]_1) = \mathrm{per}\,([\underline{a}]_2) = \mathrm{per}\,([\underline{a}]_3) = \mathrm{per}\,([\underline{a}]_4) = 30.$$

Moreover, any two of $[\underline{a}]_0, [\underline{a}]_1, [\underline{a}]_2, [\underline{a}]_3, [\underline{a}]_4$ are shift equivalent. In fact, we have

$$[\underline{a}]_0 = L^{18}[\underline{a}]_1 = L^6[\underline{a}]_2 = L^{24}[\underline{a}]_3 = L^{12}[\underline{a}]_4.$$

Examples 1 and 2 above have shown that the properties of coordinate sequences are closely related to the choice of a basis. In the rest of this section, we will discuss more details. In Subsect. 3.1, we will completely determine the periods of coordinate sequences of MLM-sequences. In particular, a necessary and sufficient condition is given for coordinate sequences whose periods attain the maximum. In Subsect. 3.2, we will give a necessary and sufficient condition for coordinate sequences of MLM-sequences who are shift equivalent.

3.1 Period Properties of the Coordinate Sequences

Lemma 1. *Let $f = x^e \in \mathrm{GF}(2^p)[x]$, where e is a primitive root modulo $2^p - 1$. Let $\underline{a} = (a, f(a), f^2(a), \ldots)$ be an MLM-sequence over $\mathrm{GF}(2^p)$, and let $[\underline{a}]_i$, $0 \leq i \leq p - 1$, be the i-th coordinate sequence of $[\underline{a}]$ w.r.t. $\{\alpha_0, \alpha_1, \ldots, \alpha_{p-1}\}$, where $\{\alpha_0, \alpha_1, \ldots, \alpha_{p-1}\}$ is a basis of $\mathrm{GF}(2^p)$ over $\mathrm{GF}(2)$. Suppose $\{\beta_0, \beta_1, \ldots, \beta_{p-1}\}$ is the dual basis of $\{\alpha_0, \alpha_1, \ldots, \alpha_{p-1}\}$. Then $\mathrm{per}\,([\underline{a}]_i) \mid T$ if and only if*

$$\mathrm{Tr}\left(\beta_i\left(y^{e^T} + y\right)\right) = 0 \text{ for all } y \in \mathrm{GF}(2^p), \tag{5}$$

where T is a positive integer.

Proof. It is clear that $\mathrm{per}\,([\underline{a}]_i) \mid T$ if and only if

$$\left[f^{t+T}(a)\right]_i = \left[f^t(a)\right]_i \text{ for any integer } t \geq 0,$$

that is, if and only if

$$\left[\left(a^{e^t}\right)^{e^T}\right]_i = \left[a^{e^t}\right]_i \text{ for any integer } t \geq 0. \tag{6}$$

Since $a, a^e, a^{e^2}, \ldots, a^{e^{2^p - 3}}$ run exactly through the set $\mathrm{GF}(2^p)\backslash\{0, 1\}$ by Remark 1, the equality (6) is equivalent to

$$\left[y^{e^T}\right]_i = [y]_i \text{ for all } y \in \mathrm{GF}(2^p)\backslash\{0, 1\}.$$

Observe that $\left[y^{e^T}\right]_i = [y]_i$ naturally holds for $y \in \{0, 1\}$, and so (6) is also equivalent to

$$\left[y^{e^T}\right]_i = [y]_i \text{ for all } y \in \mathrm{GF}(2^p),$$

or equivalently,

$$\left[y^{e^T} + y\right]_i = 0 \text{ for all } y \in \mathrm{GF}(2^p). \tag{7}$$

Combining (6) and (7), we get that $\mathrm{per}\,([\underline{a}]_i) \mid T$ if and only if

$$\left[y^{e^T} + y\right]_i = 0 \text{ for all } y \in \mathrm{GF}(2^p).$$

Now (1) already gives the desired result.

Remark 2. Lemma 1 implies that if $\mathrm{per}\,([\underline{a}]_i) = T$, then T is the least positive integer for which the equality (5) holds.

Lemma 2. *Let $0 \neq \beta \in \mathrm{GF}(2^p)$ and $1 \leq d \leq 2^p - 1$. Then $\mathrm{Tr}\left(\beta\left(y^d + y\right)\right) = 0$ for all $y \in \mathrm{GF}(2^p)$ if and only if either $d = 1$ or $\beta = 1$ and $d = 2^k$ for some $1 \leq k \leq p - 1$.*

Proof. ($\Leftarrow$) The result is obvious since $\mathrm{Tr}\left(\beta\left(y+y\right)\right) = 0$ and $\mathrm{Tr}\left(y^{2^k}+y\right) = \mathrm{Tr}\left(y^{2^k}\right) + \mathrm{Tr}\left(y\right) = 0$.

($\Rightarrow$) Let us view y as a variable over $\mathrm{GF}(2^p)$. Let $g(y)$ be the (unique) remainder of $\mathrm{Tr}\left(\beta\left(y^d+y\right)\right)$ modulo $y^{2^p}+y$. It is clear that $g(y)$ is a zero polynomial by assumption. We claim that

$$d = 2^k \text{ for some } 0 \le k \le p-1. \tag{8}$$

Otherwise, $d = 2^{k_1} + \cdots + 2^{k_w}$ for some $2 \le w \le p-1$. For convenience, we say that y^d has weight w. Note that the remainder of $\mathrm{Tr}\left(\beta y^d\right)$ modulo $y^{2^p}+y$ is a polynomial consisting of p terms, each of which has weight w, while the remainder of $\mathrm{Tr}\left(\beta y\right)$ modulo $y^{2^p}+y$ is a polynomial consisting of p terms, each of which has weight 1. Thus the remainder of $\mathrm{Tr}\left(\beta\left(y^d+y\right)\right) = \mathrm{Tr}\left(\beta y^d\right) + \mathrm{Tr}\left(\beta y\right)$ modulo $y^{2^p}+y$ is a nonzero polynomial, a contradiction. Therefore, we have proven the claim. If $d \ne 1$, then $d = 2^k$ for some $1 \le k \le p-1$. Now

$$0 = \mathrm{Tr}\left(\beta\left(y^d+y\right)\right) = \mathrm{Tr}\left(\beta\left(y^{2^k}+y\right)\right) = \mathrm{Tr}\left(\left(\beta^{2^{p-k}}+\beta\right)y\right)$$

implies that $\beta^{2^{p-k}} + \beta = 0$ since $\mathrm{Tr}\left(\cdot\right)$ maps $\mathrm{GF}(2^p)$ onto $\mathrm{GF}(2)$, and so $\beta \in \mathrm{GF}(2^{p-k})$. Since by assumption $0 \ne \beta \in \mathrm{GF}(2^p)$, we have

$$0 \ne \beta \in \mathrm{GF}(2^p) \cap \mathrm{GF}(2^{p-k}) = \mathrm{GF}(2),$$

and hence $\beta = 1$. This completes the proof.

With the above two lemmas, we can now completely determine the periods of coordinate sequences of MLM-sequences. In particular, we can give a necessary and sufficient condition for coordinate sequences whose periods attain the maximum.

Theorem 2. *Let $f = x^e \in \mathrm{GF}(2^p)[x]$, where e is a primitive root modulo 2^p-1. Let $\underline{a} = (a, f(a), f^2(a), \ldots)$ be an MLM-sequence over $\mathrm{GF}(2^p)$, and let $[\underline{a}]_i$, $0 \le i \le p-1$, be the i-th coordinate sequence of $[\underline{a}]$ w.r.t. $\{\alpha_0, \alpha_1, \ldots, \alpha_{p-1}\}$, where $\{\alpha_0, \alpha_1, \ldots, \alpha_{p-1}\}$ is a basis of $\mathrm{GF}(2^p)$ over $\mathrm{GF}(2)$. Suppose $\{\beta_0, \beta_1, \ldots, \beta_{p-1}\}$ is the dual basis of $\{\alpha_0, \alpha_1, \ldots, \alpha_{p-1}\}$. Then:*

(i) $\mathrm{per}\left([\underline{a}]_i\right) = 2^p - 2$ if and only if $\beta_i \ne 1$; and
(ii) $\mathrm{per}\left([\underline{a}]_i\right) = \left(2^p-2\right)/p$ if and only if $\beta_i = 1$.

Proof. We note that $y^{2^p} = y$ for all $y \in \mathrm{GF}(2^p)$, and so for a given integer T we have $y^{e^T} = y^d$ for all $y \in \mathrm{GF}(2^p)$, where $e^T \equiv d \mod 2^p - 1$ with $1 \le d \le 2^p - 2$. Then by applying Lemmas 1 and 2, we get $\mathrm{per}\left([\underline{a}]_i\right) \mid T$ if and only if

$$e^T \equiv 1 \mod 2^p - 1 \text{ or } \beta_i = 1 \text{ and } e^T \equiv 2^k \mod 2^p - 1 \tag{9}$$

for some $1 \le k \le p-1$. We also note that

$$e^{(2^p-2)/p} \equiv 2^k \mod 2^p - 1 \text{ for some } 1 \le k \le p-1. \tag{10}$$

This is because $e^{2^p-2} \equiv 1 \bmod 2^p - 1$ and $\{2, 2^2, \ldots, 2^{p-1}\}$ is exactly the set of primitive p-th roots of unity (i.e. the roots of $x^p = 1$ except for 1) over $\mathrm{GF}(2^p-1)$, the prime field with $2^p - 1$ elements.

(i) To prove the necessity of (i), suppose, on the contrary, that $\beta_i = 1$. If we set $T = (2^p - 2)/p$, then (10) implies that the latter condition of (9) is satisfied, and so per $([\underline{a}]_i) \mid (2^p - 2)/p$, a contradiction. Therefore, we have $\beta_i \neq 1$. Conversely, set $T = $ per $([\underline{a}]_i)$. It is clear that $T \mid 2^p - 2$. Since by assumption $\beta_i \neq 1$, the latter condition of (9) is not satisfied, and so we get $e^T \equiv 1 \bmod 2^p - 1$. Then the desired result follows from the fact that e is a primitive root modulo $2^p - 1$.

(ii) The necessity of (ii) is an immediate consequence of (i). If $\beta_i = 1$, we set $T = (2^p - 2)/p$. Then it has been shown in proving the necessity part of (i) that per $([\underline{a}]_i) \mid (2^p - 2)/p$. The equality per $([\underline{a}]_i) = (2^p - 2)/p$ holds simply because $e^s \neq 2^k \bmod 2^p - 1$ for any $1 \leq k \leq p - 1$ if $1 \leq s < (2^p - 2)/p$.

Remark 3. Theorem 2 has shown that the coordinate sequences of MLM-sequences have desirable period properties. In detail, since $\{\beta_0, \beta_1, \ldots, \beta_{p-1}\}$ is a basis of $\mathrm{GF}(2^p)$ over $\mathrm{GF}(2)$, there are at least $p - 1$ elements among $\beta_0, \beta_1, \ldots, \beta_{p-1}$ who are not equal to 1. It follows immediately that, among $[\underline{a}]_0, [\underline{a}]_1, \ldots, [\underline{a}]_{p-1}$, there are at least $p - 1$ coordinate sequences whose periods attain the maximum $2^p - 2$. Although the period of the remaining one may not attain the maximum, it still not less than $(2^p - 2)/p$.

In the rest of this subsection, we will give two further results for two special types of bases. The first one is for polynomial bases, and the second one is for normal bases.

Corollary 1. *Let f and $\underline{a}$ be as in Theorem 2. Let $[\underline{a}]_i$, $0 \leq i \leq p-1$, be the i-th coordinate sequence of $[\underline{a}]$ w.r.t. $\{1, \alpha, \alpha^2, \ldots, \alpha^{p-1}\}$, where $\{1, \alpha, \alpha^2, \ldots, \alpha^{p-1}\}$ is a polynomial basis of $\mathrm{GF}(2^p)$ over $\mathrm{GF}(2)$. Then per $([\underline{a}]_i) = 2^p - 2$ for $1 \leq i \leq p - 1$; and*

$$\text{per}\,([\underline{a}]_0) = \begin{cases} (2^p - 2)/p & \text{if } \mathrm{Tr}(\alpha^j) = 0 \text{ for } 1 \leq j \leq p-1, \\ 2^p - 2 & \text{otherwise.} \end{cases}$$

Proof. Let $\{\beta_0, \beta_1, \ldots, \beta_{p-1}\}$ be the dual basis of $\{1, \alpha, \alpha^2, \ldots, \alpha^{p-1}\}$. It is clear that $\beta_i \neq 1$ for $1 \leq i \leq p-1$, since otherwise there is an integer $j \in \{1, 2, \ldots, p-1\}$ such that $\beta_j = 1$, and then $\mathrm{Tr}(\beta_j \cdot 1) = \mathrm{Tr}(1) = 1 \neq 0$, a contradiction to the fact that $\{\beta_0, \beta_1, \ldots, \beta_{p-1}\}$ is the dual basis of $\{1, \alpha, \alpha^2, \ldots, \alpha^{p-1}\}$. Therefore, the first result immediately follows from Theorem 2. To prove the second result, it suffices to show that

$$\beta_0 = 1 \text{ if and only if } \mathrm{Tr}(\alpha^j) = 0 \text{ for } 1 \leq j \leq p - 1. \tag{11}$$

The necessity of (11) is obvious from the definition of the dual basis.

Next we will prove the sufficiency part of (11). Since by the definition of the dual basis, we have

$$\mathrm{Tr}(\alpha^j \beta_0) = \begin{cases} 1 \text{ for } j = 0, \\ 0 \text{ for } 1 \le j \le p - 1. \end{cases}$$

Combining it with the condition that $\mathrm{Tr}(\alpha^j) = 0$ for $1 \le j \le p - 1$, we get

$$\mathrm{Tr}(\alpha^j (\beta_0 - 1)) = 0 \text{ for } 0 \le j \le p - 1.$$

Note that $\{1, \alpha, \alpha^2, \dots, \alpha^{p-1}\}$ is a basis of $\mathrm{GF}(2^p)$ over $\mathrm{GF}(2)$, and so we obtain the desired result that $\beta_0 = 1$. This completes the proof.

Corollary 2. *Let f and $\underline{a}$ be as in Theorem 2. Let $[\underline{a}]_i$, $0 \le i \le p - 1$, be the i-th coordinate sequence of $[\underline{a}]$ w.r.t. $\{\alpha, \alpha^2, \dots, \alpha^{2^{p-1}}\}$, where $\{\alpha, \alpha^2, \dots, \alpha^{2^{p-1}}\}$ is a normal basis of $\mathrm{GF}(2^p)$ over $\mathrm{GF}(2)$. Then*

$$\mathrm{per}\,([\underline{a}]_i) = 2^p - 2 \text{ for } 0 \le i \le p - 1.$$

Proof. Let $\{\beta_0, \beta_1, \dots, \beta_{p-1}\}$ be the dual basis of $\{\alpha, \alpha^2, \dots, \alpha^{2^{p-1}}\}$. By Theorem 2, it suffices to show that $\beta_i \ne 1$ for $0 \le i \le p - 1$. This result follows from the fact that $\{\beta_0, \beta_1, \dots, \beta_{p-1}\}$ is also a normal basis of $\mathrm{GF}(2^p)$ over $\mathrm{GF}(2)$ (see, for example, [14]) and that any element of a normal basis is not equal to 1.

3.2   Shift-Equivalence of the Coordinate Sequences

We recall that two periodic sequences $\underline{a}$ and $\underline{b}$ are called shift equivalent if $\underline{a} = L^s \underline{b}$ for some nonnegative integer s, where $L^s \underline{b}$ is the s-shift of $\underline{b}$. Otherwise, $\underline{a}$ and $\underline{b}$ are called shift distinct.

Lemma 3. *With the notation of Theorem 2, let $0 \le i < j \le p - 1$. Then $[\underline{a}]_i = L^s [\underline{a}]_j$ for some positive integer s if and only if $\mathrm{Tr}\left(\beta_i y + \beta_j y^{e^s}\right) = 0$ for all $y \in \mathrm{GF}(2^p)$.*

Proof. Firstly, we show that $[\underline{a}]_i = L^s [\underline{a}]_j$ if and only if

$$\mathrm{Tr}\,(\beta_i y) = \mathrm{Tr}\left(\beta_j y^{e^s}\right) \text{ for all } y \in \mathrm{GF}(2^p) \backslash \{0, 1\}. \tag{12}$$

We note that $\underline{a} = (a, f(a), f^2(a), \dots)$, where $f^t(a) = a^{e^t}$ for any integer $t \ge 0$, and so by (1) we have

$$[f^t(a)]_i = \mathrm{Tr}\left(\beta_i a^{e^t}\right) \text{ and } [f^{t+s}(a)]_j = \mathrm{Tr}\left(\beta_j \left(a^{e^t}\right)^{e^s}\right) \text{ for any integer } t \ge 0.$$

Therefore, $[\underline{a}]_i = L^s [\underline{a}]_j$ if and only if

$$\mathrm{Tr}\left(\beta_i a^{e^t}\right) = \mathrm{Tr}\left(\beta_j \left(a^{e^t}\right)^{e^s}\right) \text{ for any integer } t \ge 0,$$

if and only if

$$\mathrm{Tr}\left(\beta_i y\right) = \mathrm{Tr}\left(\beta_j y^{e^s}\right) \text{ for all } y \in \mathrm{GF}(2^p)\backslash\{0,1\}.$$

The last equality follows from the fact that $a, a^e, a^{e^2}, \ldots, a^{e^{2^p-3}}$ run exactly through the set $\mathrm{GF}(2^p)\backslash\{0,1\}$ and $a^{e^{2^p-2}} = a$.

For $y = 0$, the equality holds obviously. Since the trace functions are balanced, the equality must hold for $y = 1$ too. This completes the proof.

The main result of this subsection can be described explicitly in the following Theorem.

Theorem 3. *With the notation of Theorem 2, let* $0 \le i < j \le p-1$. *Then* $[\underline{a}]_i = L^s[\underline{a}]_j$ *for some positive integer* s *if and only if* $\beta_j = \beta_i^{2^k}$ *and* $e^s \equiv 2^k \bmod 2^p-1$ *for some* $0 \le k \le p-1$.

Proof. By Lemma 3, it suffices to show that $\mathrm{Tr}\left(\beta_i y + \beta_j y^{e^s}\right) = 0$ for all $y \in \mathrm{GF}(2^p)$ if and only if

$$\beta_j = \beta_i^{2^k} \text{ and } e^s \equiv 2^k \bmod 2^p - 1 \text{ for some } 0 \le k \le p-1.$$

If $\beta_j = \beta_i^{2^k}$ and $e^s \equiv 2^k \bmod 2^p - 1$ for some $0 \le k \le p-1$, then it is clear that

$$\mathrm{Tr}\left(\beta_i y + \beta_j y^{e^s}\right) = \mathrm{Tr}\left(\beta_i y + \beta_i^{2^k} y^{2^k}\right) = \mathrm{Tr}\left(\beta_i y + (\beta_i y)^{2^k}\right) = 0$$

holds for all $y \in \mathrm{GF}(2^p)$.

Conversely, suppose $\mathrm{Tr}\left(\beta_i y + \beta_j y^{e^s}\right) = 0$ for all $y \in \mathrm{GF}(2^p)$. An argument similar to that leading to (8) shows that

$$e^s \equiv 2^k \bmod 2^p - 1 \text{ for some } 0 \le k \le p-1.$$

Consequently,

$$
\begin{aligned}
0 &= \mathrm{Tr}\left(\beta_i y + \beta_j y^{e^s}\right) \\
&= \mathrm{Tr}\left(\beta_i y + \beta_j y^{2^k}\right) \\
&= \mathrm{Tr}\left(\beta_i y + \left(\beta_j y^{2^k}\right)^{2^{p-k}}\right) \\
&= \mathrm{Tr}\left(\left(\beta_i + \beta_j^{2^{p-k}}\right) y\right)
\end{aligned}
$$

holds for all $y \in \mathrm{GF}(2^p)$, which immediately implies that $\beta_i = \beta_j^{2^{p-k}}$, or, equivalently, that $\beta_j = \beta_i^{2^k}$.

For normal bases, we have a more concrete result, which is stated in the following Corollary.

Corollary 3. *Let f and $\underline{a}$ be as in Theorem 2. Let $[\underline{a}]_j$, $0 \leq j \leq p-1$, be the i-th coordinate sequence of $[\underline{a}]$ w.r.t. $\{\alpha, \alpha^2, \ldots, \alpha^{2^{p-1}}\}$, where $\{\alpha, \alpha^2, \ldots, \alpha^{2^{p-1}}\}$ is a normal basis of $\mathrm{GF}(2^p)$ over $\mathrm{GF}(2)$. Then for $1 \leq j \leq p-1$, there exists an integer $s_j = u_j(2^p - 2)/p$ with $1 \leq u_j \leq p-1$ such that $[\underline{a}]_0 = L^{s_j}[\underline{a}]_j$. Moreover, $s_1, s_2, \ldots, s_{p-1}$ run exactly through the set*

$$\{(2^p - 2)/p, 2(2^p - 2)/p, \ldots, (p-1)(2^p - 2)/p\}.$$

Proof. Let $\{\beta_0, \beta_1, \ldots, \beta_{p-1}\}$ be the dual basis of $\{\alpha, \alpha^2, \ldots, \alpha^{2^{p-1}}\}$. Since the dual basis of a normal base is also a normal base, it immediately follows that $\beta_j = \beta_0^{2^j}$ for $0 \leq j \leq p-1$. Furthermore,

$$e^{(2^p-2)/p} \equiv 2^k \bmod 2^p - 1 \text{ for some } 1 \leq k \leq p-1 \tag{13}$$

by (10). Let u_j be the least nonnegative residue of $k^{-1}j$ modulo p for $1 \leq j \leq p-1$, that is $u_j = k^{-1}j \bmod p$, where k^{-1} is the inverse of k modulo p. Then (13) yields

$$e^{u_j(2^p-2)/p} \equiv 2^{u_j k} \equiv 2^j \bmod 2^p - 1. \tag{14}$$

By setting $i = 0$ and applying (13) and (14) to Theorem 3, the first desired result immediately follows. The second desired result follows from the fact that $u_j = k^{-1}j \pmod{p}$ runs through the set $\{1, 2, \ldots, p-1\}$ if j runs through $\{1, 2, \ldots, p-1\}$.

4   Conclusions

Binary sequences with desirable properties have important applications in cryptography, communication, Monte Carlo simulation and so on. In this paper, a class of binary sequences induced by monomial permutation polynomials over $\mathrm{GF}(2^n)$ is proposed, and the period property and the shift-equivalence of these binary sequences are studied. In particularly, a necessary and sufficient condition is given such that they have the maximum possible period. Moreover, a necessary and sufficient condition is also given for two sequences who are shift equivalent. The results of this paper imply that these binary sequences should be potential interested for several applications such as stream ciphers.

How to generate a pseudo-random sequence with desirable properties is a classical problem. Although our new proposed PRNG can be viewed as a Galois NFSR, it should be pointed out that its actual performance cannot be compared with NFSR since the power operations over finite fields are usually resource-consuming. How to improve the performance of the proposed PRNG or how to design other type of PRNGs with desirable properties and performance deserves further study.

Acknowledgement. The authors would like to thank the anonymous referees for their helpful comments and suggestions.

References

1. Lidl, R., Niederreiter, H.: Finite Fields. Encyclopedia of Mathematics and Its Applications, vol. 20. Cambridge University Press, Cambridge (1997)
2. Mullen, G.L., Panario, D.: Handbook of Finite Fields. CRC Press, Boca Raton (2013)
3. Hou, X.D.: Permutation polynomials over finite fields - a survey of recent advances. Finite Fields Appl. **32**, 82–119 (2015)
4. Tu, Z., Zeng, X.: A class of permutation trinomials over finite fields of odd characteristic. Cryptogr. Commun **11**(4), 563–583 (2018). https://doi.org/10.1007/s12095-018-0307-4
5. Tu, Z.R., Zeng, X.Y., Jiang, Y.P.: Two classes of permutation polynomials having the form $(x^{2^m} + x + \delta)^s + x$. Finite Fields Appl. **53**, 99–112 (2018)
6. Wang, L.B., Wu, B.F.: General constructions of permutation polynomials of the form $(x^{2^m} + x + \delta)^{i(2^m-1)+1} + x$ over $F_{2^{2m}}$. Finite Fields Appl. **52**, 137–155 (2018)
7. Feng, X.T., Lin, D.D., Wang, L.P., Wang, Q.: Further results on complete permutation monomials over finite fields. Finite Fields Appl. **57**, 47–59 (2019)
8. Xu, X.F., Feng, X.T., Zeng, X.Y.: Complete permutation polynomials with the form $(x^{p^m} - x + \delta)^s + ax^{p^m} + bx$ over F_{p^n}. Finite Fields Appl. **57**, 309–343 (2019)
9. Wu, B.F., Lin, D.D.: On constructing complete permutation polynomials over finite fields of even characteristic. Disc. Appl. Math. **184**, 213–222 (2015)
10. Niederreiter, H.: Pseudorandom vector generation by the inversive method. ACM Trans. Model. Comput. Simul. **4**(2), 191–212 (1994)
11. Anderson, S.L.: Random number generators on vector supercomputers and other advanced architectures. SIAM Rev. **32**, 221–251 (1990)
12. Bhavsar, V.C., Isaac, J.R.: Design and analysis of parallel Monte Carlo algorithms. SIAM J. Sci. Stat. Comput. **8**, s73–s95 (1987)
13. Eddy, W.F.: Random number generators for parallel processors. J. Comput. Appl. Math. **31**, 63–71 (1986)
14. Menezes, A.J., Blake, I.F., et al.: Applications of Finite Fields. Kluwer Academic Publishers, New York (1993)

On the Provable Security Against Truncated Impossible Differential Cryptanalysis for AES in the Master-Key Setting

Xueping Yan, Lin Tan[✉], Hong Xu, and Wenfeng Qi

PLA Strategic Support Force Information Engineering University, Zhengzhou, China

Abstract. Impossible differential cryptanalysis is a powerful cryptanalysis technique of block ciphers. Length of impossible differentials is important for the security evaluation of a block cipher against impossible differential cryptanalysis. Many previous studies on finding impossible differentials of AES assumed that round keys are independent and uniformly random. There are few results on security evaluation of AES in the master-key setting. In ASIACRYPT 2020, Hu et al. redefined impossible differential with the key schedule considered, and showed that there exists no one-byte active input and one-byte active output impossible differential for 5-round AES-128 even considering the relations of 3-round keys. In this paper, we prove theoretically that even though the relations of all round keys are considered, there do not exist three kinds of truncated impossible differentials for 5-round AES: (1) the input truncated differences are nonzero only in any diagonal and the output truncated differences are nonzero only in any inverse diagonal; (2) the input truncated differences are nonzero only in any two diagonals and the output truncated differences are nonzero only in any inverse diagonal; (3) the input truncated differences are nonzero only in any diagonal and the output truncated differences are nonzero only in any two inverse diagonals. Furthermore, for any given truncated differentials of these three kinds, the lower bounds of the number of master keys such that the truncated differentials are possible for 5-round AES-128 are presented.

Keywords: AES · Truncated impossible differential · Provable security · Master-key setting

1 Introduction

Impossible differential cryptanalysis [4,20] is a powerful cryptanalysis technique of block ciphers. The differentials with probability 0 are used to distinguish round-reduced block ciphers and discard the wrong keys in the key recovery attack. Truncated impossible differentials are usually used in the impossible differential cryptanalysis of block ciphers, such as AES [1,5,6,9,13,21,28], Crypton

© Springer Nature Switzerland AG 2021
Y. Yu and M. Yung (Eds.): Inscrypt 2021, LNCS 13007, pp. 384–398, 2021.
https://doi.org/10.1007/978-3-030-88323-2_21

[6,9], Camellia [6,7], SIMON [7], CLEFIA [7,25] and XTEA [8]. AES is the most widely used block cipher and its security has been studied worldwide in the last twenty years. Many cryptanalysis techniques have been applied to distinguish or attack the round-reduced variants of AES, such as integral [12], impossible differential [6], zero-correlation linear [17,23], subspace trail [15], mixture differential [2,14], multiple-of-8 [16], meet-in-the-middle [10], yoyo [22], exchange [3] and boomerang [11]. The first impossible differential distinguisher on 4-round AES was proposed to attack 5-round AES in [5]. Then based on 4-round impossible differential distinguishers, many impossible differential attacks on 6 rounds and 7 rounds of AES were proposed [1,6,9,21,28]. As we know, the best key recovery attacks on AES-128 in the secret-key model cover 7 rounds. In EUROCRYPT 2021, Gaëtan et al. [13] gave new representations of the AES key schedule and improved the impossible differential attack on 7-round AES-128. The length of truncated impossible differentials used in these known attacks is 4 rounds. To some extent, the longer truncated impossible differentials can be found, the more rounds can be attacked. Whether there exist 5-round truncated impossible differentials is one of important problems for the security evaluation of AES.

In [24], Sun et al. proved that there exists no 5-round impossible differential for the AES structure, where the details of S-boxes are not considered. Under the assumption that round keys are independent and uniformly random, Wang et al. showed that there exists no 5-round truncated impossible differential even considering the details of the AES S-box [26], and further proved that any concrete differential is possible for 5-round AES [27]. These results are not true for the real AES, because the round keys are dependent under the key schedule. In ASIACRYPT 2020, Hu et al.[18] redefined impossible differential with the key schedule considered, and proposed a SAT-based automatic search tool for impossible differentials. With the help of the automatic search tool, it was shown that there exists no one-byte active input and one-byte active output impossible differential for 5-round AES even taking the relations of the middle 3-round keys into account. It is the first result on the provable security evaluation of AES against impossible differential cryptanalysis with the key schedule considered.

In this paper, we study three kinds of truncated differentials for 5-round AES in the master-key setting.

- **Set 1**: the input truncated differences are nonzero only in any diagonal and the output truncated differences are nonzero only in any inverse diagonal.
- **Set 2**: the input truncated differences are nonzero only in any two diagonals and the output truncated differences are nonzero only in any inverse diagonal.
- **Set 3**: the input truncated differences are nonzero only in any diagonal and the output truncated differences are nonzero only in any two inverse diagonals.

By investigating the properties of the key schedule, we prove theoretically that there do not exist the three kinds of truncated impossible differentials for 5-round AES even considering the relations of all round keys. Furthermore, for any given truncated differentials in the three sets, the lower bounds of the number of master keys such that the truncated differentials are possible for 5-round AES-128 are presented.

This paper is organized as follows. In Sect. 2, the description of AES and the definitions related to truncated differential are recalled. In Sect. 3, three kinds of truncated differentials for 5-round AES in the master-key setting are studied. Section 4 concludes the paper.

2 Preliminaries

2.1 Brief Description of AES

AES is a Substitution-Permutation Network cipher with 128-bit block. The 128-bit state can be described as a 4×4 matrix over the finite field $\mathbb{F}_{2^8}$, and the order of bytes in the state matrix is showed in Fig. 1. The number of rounds N_r depends on the length of master key, that is, $N_r = 10$ for 128-bit key, $N_r = 12$ for 192-bit key and $N_r = 14$ for 256-bit key. The round transformation of AES consists of the following four operations.

1. *SubBytes(SB)*: applies the same 8-bit S-box to 16 bytes of the state parallelly. The S-box is composed of the multiplicative inverse transformation over $\mathbb{F}_{2^8}$ and an affine function over $\mathbb{F}_2$, i.e., $S(x) = L(x^{-1}) + b$, $x \in \mathbb{F}_{2^8}$.
2. *ShiftRows(SR)*: shifts the i-th row by i bytes to the left circularly for $i = 0, 1, 2, 3$.
3. *MixColumns(MC)*: multiplies each column by the following MDS matrix over $\mathbb{F}_{2^8}$.

$$\begin{bmatrix} 02 & 03 & 01 & 01 \\ 01 & 02 & 03 & 01 \\ 01 & 01 & 02 & 03 \\ 03 & 01 & 01 & 02 \end{bmatrix}$$

4. *AddRoundKey(AK)*: XORs the state with a 128-bit round key, which is generated from a master key by the key schedule.

An additional AK is applied before the first round and the MC is omitted in the last round. Let K_r denote the r-th round key, and AK_r denote the AddRoundKey operation with K_r. The r-th round transformation can be written as $AK_r \circ MC \circ SR \circ SB$. When interchanging the order of MC and AK, we can get the equivalent round transformation $MC \circ AK'_r \circ SR \circ SB$, where AK'_r denotes XORing the equivalent round key $K'_r = MC^{-1}(K_r)$. Denote by $K_{r,j}$ the j-th byte of K_r. When considering several bytes $j_1, j_2, ..., j_n$ of K_r simultaneously, we denote by $K_{r,\{j_1,j_2,...,j_n\}}$. In this paper, we focus on AES-128. The key schedule of AES-128 can be described as follows.

$$\begin{aligned} K_{r,0} &= K_{r-1,0} + S(K_{r-1,13}) + C_r, \\ K_{r,1} &= K_{r-1,1} + S(K_{r-1,14}), \\ K_{r,2} &= K_{r-1,2} + S(K_{r-1,15}), \\ K_{r,3} &= K_{r-1,3} + S(K_{r-1,12}), \\ K_{r,j} &= K_{r-1,j} + K_{r,j-4}, \quad 4 \le j \le 15, \end{aligned}$$

where K_0 is the master key, and C_r is the round constant, $1 \le r \le 10$.

0	4	8	12
1	5	9	13
2	6	10	14
3	7	11	15

Fig. 1. The order of bytes in the state matrix

2.2 Definitions

Definition 1. *Given a vectorial Boolean function $f : \mathbb{F}_2^n \to \mathbb{F}_2^n$, for an input difference $\Delta X \in \mathbb{F}_2^n$ and an output difference $\Delta Y \in \mathbb{F}_2^n$, the differential probability is defined as*

$$DP(\Delta X \xrightarrow{f} \Delta Y) = \frac{1}{2^n} \# \{ X \in \mathbb{F}_2^n \mid f(X) + f(X + \Delta X) = \Delta Y \}.$$

Definition 2. *Given a keyed function $f_K : \mathbb{F}_2^n \times K \to \mathbb{F}_2^n$, for an input difference $\Delta X \in \mathbb{F}_2^n$ and an output difference $\Delta Y \in \mathbb{F}_2^n$, the expected differential probability over all keys is defined as*

$$EDP(\Delta X \xrightarrow{f_K} \Delta Y) = \frac{1}{\#K} \sum_{k \in K} DP(\Delta X \xrightarrow{f_k} \Delta Y).$$

If $EDP(\Delta X \xrightarrow{f_K} \Delta Y)$ is too small to distinguish f_K from random permutations for any differential $\Delta X \to \Delta Y$, then f_K is provably secure against differential cryptanalysis. If $EDP(\Delta X \xrightarrow{f_K} \Delta Y) = 0$, then $\Delta X \to \Delta Y$ is called an impossible differential of f_K. In the following we recall the definitions related to truncated differential introduced in [19].

Definition 3. *For $x \in \mathbb{F}_{2^m}$, define the function χ as*

$$\chi(x) = \begin{cases} 0, & \text{if } x = 0; \\ 1, & \text{if } x \neq 0. \end{cases}$$

For $X = (x_1, x_2, \ldots, x_n) \in \mathbb{F}_{2^m}^n$, define $\chi(X) = (\chi(x_1), \chi(x_2), \ldots, \chi(x_n))$.

Definition 4. *Given a function $f : \mathbb{F}_{2^m}^n \to \mathbb{F}_{2^m}^n$, for an input truncated difference $\overline{\Delta X} \in \mathbb{F}_2^n$ and an output truncated difference $\overline{\Delta Y} \in \mathbb{F}_2^n$, the truncated differential probability is defined as*

$$DP(\overline{\Delta X} \xrightarrow{f} \overline{\Delta Y}) = \frac{\displaystyle\sum_{\substack{\Delta X, \Delta Y \in \mathbb{F}_{2^m}^n, \\ \chi(\Delta X) = \overline{\Delta X}, \chi(\Delta Y) = \overline{\Delta Y}}} DP(\Delta X \xrightarrow{f} \Delta Y)}{\# \{ \Delta X \in \mathbb{F}_{2^m}^n \mid \chi(\Delta X) = \overline{\Delta X} \}}.$$

Definition 5. *Given a keyed function $f_K : \mathbb{F}_{2^m}^n \times K \to \mathbb{F}_{2^m}^n$, for an input truncated difference $\overline{\Delta X} \in \mathbb{F}_2^n$ and an output truncated difference $\overline{\Delta Y} \in \mathbb{F}_2^n$, the expected truncated differential probability over all keys is defined as*

$$EDP(\overline{\Delta X} \xrightarrow{f_K} \overline{\Delta Y}) = \frac{1}{\#K} \sum_{k \in K} DP(\overline{\Delta X} \xrightarrow{f_k} \overline{\Delta Y}).$$

If $EDP(\overline{\Delta X} \xrightarrow{f_K} \overline{\Delta Y}) = 0$, then $\overline{\Delta X} \to \overline{\Delta Y}$ is called a truncated impossible differential of f_K. To prove that truncated differential $\overline{\Delta X} \to \overline{\Delta Y}$ is possible for f_K, we need to find at least a key $k \in K$ and a differential $\Delta X \to \Delta Y$ such that $\chi(\Delta X) = \overline{\Delta X}$, $\chi(\Delta Y) = \overline{\Delta Y}$, and $DP(\Delta X \xrightarrow{f_k} \Delta Y) > 0$.

3   Main Results

Let $\overline{\Delta X}, \overline{\Delta W} \in \mathbb{F}_2^{4 \times 4}$ be the input and output truncated differences respectively. In this section, we reveal some properties of the key schedule of AES-128, and prove theoretically that in the master-key setting there do not exist the following three kinds of truncated impossible differentials for 5-round AES.

- **Set 1:** $\overline{\Delta X}$ is nonzero only in any diagonal and $\overline{\Delta W}$ is nonzero only in any inverse diagonal;
- **Set 2:** $\overline{\Delta X}$ is nonzero only in any two diagonals and $\overline{\Delta W}$ is nonzero only in any inverse diagonal;
- **Set 3:** $\overline{\Delta X}$ is nonzero only in any diagonal and $\overline{\Delta W}$ is nonzero only in any two inverse diagonals.

We note that the input (output) truncated differences being nonzero in some diagonals (inverse diagonals) means that there exists at least a nonzero bit in each corresponding diagonal (inverse diagonal).

Five rounds of AES can be written as

$$AK_5 \circ SR \circ SB \circ AK_4 \circ G \circ AK_1' \circ SR \circ SB \circ AK_0,$$

where $G = MC \circ SR \circ SB \circ AK_3 \circ MC \circ SR \circ SB \circ MC \circ AK_2' \circ SR \circ SB \circ MC$. To prove the results, it is sufficient to prove that the following three kinds of truncated differentials $\overline{\Delta X'} \to \overline{\Delta W'}$ are all possible for G even considering the relation of K_2' and K_3.

1. $\overline{\Delta X'}$ is nonzero only in any column and $\overline{\Delta W'}$ is nonzero only in any column;
2. $\overline{\Delta X'}$ is nonzero only in any two columns and $\overline{\Delta W'}$ is nonzero only in any column;
3. $\overline{\Delta X'}$ is nonzero only in any column and $\overline{\Delta W'}$ is nonzero only in any two columns.

Since SB and SR are applied on each byte independently, we can interchange their order in the last $SR \circ SB$ of G. Then decompose G as

$$G = f \circ (SR \circ AK_3) \circ g \circ (AK_2' \circ SR) \circ h,$$

where $h = SB \circ MC$, $g = MC \circ SR \circ SB \circ MC$, and $f = MC \circ SB$ are key-independent.

Lemma 1. *For any nonzero truncated difference $\overline{\Delta y} \in \mathbb{F}_2^4$, there exists difference $\Delta x \in (\mathbb{F}_{2^8}^*)^4$ such that $\chi(MC(\Delta x)) = \overline{\Delta y}$, where $\mathbb{F}_{2^8}^*$ denotes the multiplicative group of nonzero elements of $\mathbb{F}_{2^8}$.*

Proof. Let c be the Hamming weight of $\overline{\Delta y}$. If $c = 1$, then for any Δy with $\chi(\Delta y) = \overline{\Delta y}$, we have $MC^{-1}(\Delta y) \in (\mathbb{F}_{2^8}^*)^4$ since the MC matrix is MDS. If $2 \le c \le 4$, then the number of Δy such that $\chi(\Delta y) = \overline{\Delta y}$ is 255^c. But the number of Δy such that $\chi(\Delta y) = \overline{\Delta y}$ and $MC^{-1}(\Delta y) \notin (\mathbb{F}_{2^8}^*)^4$ is at most $4 \cdot (255)^{c-1}$. Therefore, there exists difference $\Delta x \in (\mathbb{F}_{2^8}^*)^4$ such that $\chi(MC(\Delta x)) = \overline{\Delta y}$. □

Lemma 2. (See [27].) *If $SB \circ MC$ is regarded as a function on $\mathbb{F}_{2^8}^4$, then for any nonzero input truncated difference $\overline{\Delta x} \in \mathbb{F}_2^4$ and any output difference $\Delta y \in (\mathbb{F}_{2^8}^*)^4$, there exists input difference Δx such that $\chi(\Delta x) = \overline{\Delta x}$ and*

$$SB \circ MC(x) + SB \circ MC(x + \Delta x) = \Delta y$$

for some $x \in \mathbb{F}_{2^8}^4$.

Lemma 3. *Suppose the master keys of AES-128 are independent and uniformly random. Then any inverse diagonal of K_r' and any diagonal of K_{r+1} are independent, and for any given values of the eight bytes there are 2^{64} master keys under the key schedule of AES-128, $0 \le r \le 9$.*

Proof. By the assumption, the 16 bytes of K_r are independent and uniformly random. Let $(p, q, s, t) \in \{(0, 7, 10, 13), (1, 4, 11, 14), (2, 5, 8, 15), (3, 6, 9, 12)\}$ be any inverse diagonal. Since $K_r' = MC^{-1}(K_r)$, four bytes in the p-th inverse diagonal of K_r' can be represented by the bytes of K_r as follows.

$$
\begin{aligned}
K_{r,p}' &= a_0 K_{r,0} + a_1 K_{r,1} + a_2 K_{r,2} + a_3 K_{r,3}, \\
K_{r,q}' &= a_4 K_{r,4} + a_5 K_{r,5} + a_6 K_{r,6} + a_7 K_{r,7}, \\
K_{r,s}' &= a_8 K_{r,8} + a_9 K_{r,9} + a_{10} K_{r,10} + a_{11} K_{r,11}, \\
K_{r,t}' &= a_{12} K_{r,12} + a_{13} K_{r,13} + a_{14} K_{r,14} + a_{15} K_{r,15},
\end{aligned}
\tag{1}
$$

where $a_j \in \{0B, 0D, 0E, 09\}$ is a constant dependent on (p, q, s, t), $0 \le j \le 15$. From the key schedule, the four diagonals of K_{r+1} can be represented by the bytes of K_r as the following four systems of equations respectively.

$$
\begin{aligned}
K_{r+1,0} &= K_{r,0} + S(K_{r,13}) + C_{r+1}, \\
K_{r+1,5} &= K_{r,5} + K_{r,1} + S(K_{r,14}), \\
K_{r+1,10} &= K_{r,10} + K_{r,6} + K_{r,2} + S(K_{r,15}), \\
K_{r+1,15} &= K_{r,15} + K_{r,11} + K_{r,7} + K_{r,3} + S(K_{r,12}).
\end{aligned}
\tag{2}
$$

$$
\begin{aligned}
K_{r+1,3} &= K_{r,3} + S(K_{r,12}), \\
K_{r+1,4} &= K_{r,4} + K_{r,0} + S(K_{r,13}) + C_{r+1}, \\
K_{r+1,9} &= K_{r,9} + K_{r,5} + K_{r,1} + S(K_{r,14}), \\
K_{r+1,14} &= K_{r,14} + K_{r,10} + K_{r,6} + K_{r,2} + S(K_{r,15}).
\end{aligned}
\tag{3}
$$

$$K_{r+1,2} = K_{r,2} + S(K_{r,15}),$$
$$K_{r+1,7} = K_{r,7} + K_{r,3} + S(K_{r,12}),$$
$$K_{r+1,8} = K_{r,8} + K_{r,4} + K_{r,0} + S(K_{r,13}) + C_{r+1},$$
$$K_{r+1,13} = K_{r,13} + K_{r,9} + K_{r,5} + K_{r,1} + S(K_{r,14}).$$
(4)

$$K_{r+1,1} = K_{r,1} + S(K_{r,14}),$$
$$K_{r+1,6} = K_{r,6} + K_{r,2} + S(K_{r,15}),$$
$$K_{r+1,11} = K_{r,11} + K_{r,7} + K_{r,3} + S(K_{r,12}),$$
$$K_{r+1,12} = K_{r,12} + K_{r,8} + K_{r,4} + K_{r,0} + S(K_{r,13}) + C_{r+1}.$$
(5)

We claim that for any given values of $K'_{r,\{p,q,s,t\}}$ and any diagonal of K_{r+1}, the number of solutions of K_r is 2^{64}. For $K_{r+1,\{0,5,10,15\}}$, we can take the eight bytes $K_{r,\{0,1,4,6,9,11,14,15\}}$ as free variables in the system of (1) and (2). When the free variables are determined the other eight bytes of K_r have unique solution. Similarly, for $K_{r+1,\{3,4,9,14\}}$, we also take $K_{r,\{0,1,4,6,9,11,14,15\}}$ as free variables in the system of (1) and (3). For $K_{r+1,\{2,7,8,13\}}$, we take $K_{r,\{0,2,4,5,9,11,12,13\}}$ as free variables in the system of (1) and (4). For $K_{r+1,\{1,6,11,12\}}$, we take $K_{r,\{0,2,4,5,9,11,14,15\}}$ as free variables in the system of (1) and (5). Since $K'_{r,\{p,q,s,t\}}$ and any diagonal of K_{r+1} can take arbitrary values, they are independent. Furthermore, for their any given values there are 2^{64} master keys under the key schedule of AES-128.   □

Theorem 1. *For any input truncated difference $\overline{\Delta X}$ with one diagonal nonzero and any output truncated difference $\overline{\Delta W}$ with one inverse diagonal nonzero, there are at least 2^{66} master keys such that $\overline{\Delta X} \to \overline{\Delta W}$ is possible for 5-round AES-128.*

Proof. It is sufficient to prove that for any input truncated difference $\overline{\Delta X'}$ with one column nonzero and any output truncated difference $\overline{\Delta W'}$ with one column nonzero, there are at least 2^{66} master keys such that

$$DP(\overline{\Delta X'} \xrightarrow{G} \overline{\Delta W'}) > 0.$$

Let the i-th column of $\overline{\Delta X'}$ and the j-th column of $\overline{\Delta W'}$ be nonzero, $0 \le i, j \le 3$. From the definition of truncated differential probability, we just need to find a differential $\Delta X' \to \Delta W'$ such that $\chi(\Delta X') = \overline{\Delta X'}$, $\chi(\Delta W') = \overline{\Delta W'}$, and

$$DP(\Delta X' \xrightarrow{G} \Delta W') > 0.$$

The propagation of the differential is shown in Fig. 2. We recall

$$G = f \circ (SR \circ AK_3) \circ g \circ (AK'_2 \circ SR) \circ h,$$

where $h = SB \circ MC$, $g = MC \circ SR \circ SB \circ MC$, and $f = MC \circ SB$.

From Lemma 1, there exist ΔZ with only four bytes in the j-th column nonzero and $\Delta W'$ with $\chi(\Delta W') = \overline{\Delta W'}$ such that $f(Z) + f(Z + \Delta Z) = \Delta W'$, where $Z \in \mathbb{F}_{2^8}^{4 \times 4}$ and the bytes except the j-th column of Z can take arbitrary

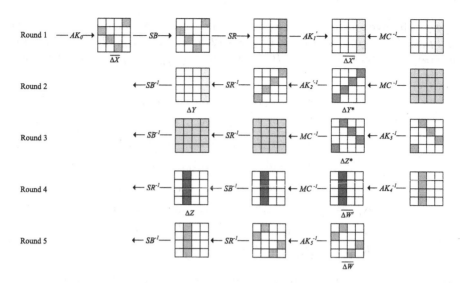

Fig. 2. The propagation of the differential in Set 1

values. Let $\Delta Z^* = SR^{-1}(\Delta Z)$, then $SR^{-1} \circ MC^{-1}(\Delta Z^*) \in (\mathbb{F}_{2^8}^*)^{4\times 4}$. From Lemma 2, there exists input difference ΔY^* with only four bytes in the i-th inverse diagonal nonzero such that $g(Y^*) + g(Y^* + \Delta Y^*) = \Delta Z^*$ for some $Y^* \in \mathbb{F}_{2^8}^{4\times 4}$. Let $\Delta Y = SR^{-1}(\Delta Y^*)$. From Lemma 2 again, there exists input difference $\Delta X'$ such that $\chi(\Delta X') = \overline{\Delta X'}$ and $h(X') + h(X' + \Delta X') = \Delta Y$, where $X' \in \mathbb{F}_{2^8}^{4\times 4}$ and the bytes except the i-th column of X' can take arbitrary values. Denote $Y = h(X')$, then the bytes except the i-th column of Y can take arbitrary values.

Taking $K_2' = SR(Y) + Y^*$ or $K_2' = SR(Y) + Y^* + \Delta Y^*$, the output states of $SR \circ h$ and the input states of g are connected. Because the bytes except the i-th column of Y can take arbitrary values, the bytes except the i-th inverse diagonal of K_2' can take arbitrary values. Denote $Z^* = g(Y^*)$. Taking $K_3 = Z^* + SR^{-1}(Z)$ or $K_3 = Z^* + SR^{-1}(Z) + \Delta Z^*$, the output states of g and the input states of $f \circ SR$ are connected. Since the bytes except the j-th column of Z can take arbitrary values, the bytes except the j-th diagonal of K_3 can take arbitrary values.

The i-th inverse diagonal of K_2' and the j-th diagonal of K_3 have at least two possible values respectively. From Lemma 3, for any given values of these eight bytes, there are 2^{64} master keys under the key schedule of AES-128. Thus there are at least 2^{66} master keys such that $\overline{\Delta X'} \to \overline{\Delta W'}$ is possible for G. This completes the proof. □

Lemma 4. *Suppose the master keys of AES-128 are independent and uniformly random. Then any two inverse diagonals of K_r' and any diagonal of K_{r+1} are independent, and for any given values of the twelve bytes there are 2^{32} master keys under the key schedule of AES-128, $0 \le r \le 9$.*

Proof. The bytes of K_r are independent and uniformly random. Let (p, q, s, t), $(p', q', s', t') \in \{(0, 7, 10, 13), (1, 4, 11, 14), (2, 5, 8, 15), (3, 6, 9, 12)\}$ are any two inverse diagonals. Since $K'_r = MC^{-1}(K_r)$, $K'_{r,\{p,p',q,q',s,s',t,t'\}}$ can be represented by the bytes of K_r as follows.

$$
\begin{aligned}
K'_{r,p} &= a_0 K_{r,0} + a_1 K_{r,1} + a_2 K_{r,2} + a_3 K_{r,3}, \\
K'_{r,p'} &= a'_0 K_{r,0} + a'_1 K_{r,1} + a'_2 K_{r,2} + a'_3 K_{r,3}, \\
K'_{r,q} &= a_4 K_{r,4} + a_5 K_{r,5} + a_6 K_{r,6} + a_7 K_{r,7}, \\
K'_{r,q'} &= a'_4 K_{r,4} + a'_5 K_{r,5} + a'_6 K_{r,6} + a'_7 K_{r,7}, \\
K'_{r,s} &= a_8 K_{r,8} + a_9 K_{r,9} + a_{10} K_{r,10} + a_{11} K_{r,11}, \\
K'_{r,s'} &= a'_8 K_{r,8} + a'_9 K_{r,9} + a'_{10} K_{r,10} + a'_{11} K_{r,11}, \\
K'_{r,t} &= a_{12} K_{r,12} + a_{13} K_{r,13} + a_{14} K_{r,14} + a_{15} K_{r,15}, \\
K'_{r,t'} &= a'_{12} K_{r,12} + a'_{13} K_{r,13} + a'_{14} K_{r,14} + a'_{15} K_{r,15}.
\end{aligned}
\tag{6}
$$

where $a_j, a'_j \in \{0B, 0D, 0E, 09\}$ are constants dependent respectively on (p, q, s, t) and (p', q', s', t'), $0 \leq j \leq 15$. Note that four diagonals of K_{r+1} are represented by the bytes of K_r in (2), (3), (4) and (5). We combine (6) with (2),(3), (4) and (5) respectively, and $K_{r,\{4,5,12,13\}}$ can be taken as free variables in the four combined systems of equations. When the free variables are determined the other twelve bytes of K_r have unique solution. Thus, for any given values of $K'_{r,\{p,p',q,q',s,s',t,t'\}}$ and any diagonal of K_{r+1}, the number of solutions of K_r is 2^{32}. Since the twelve bytes can take arbitrary values, they are independent. Furthermore, for any given values of the twelve bytes there are 2^{32} master keys under the key schedule of AES-128. □

Theorem 2. *For any input truncated difference $\overline{\Delta X}$ with two diagonals nonzero and any output truncated difference $\overline{\Delta W}$ with one inverse diagonal nonzero, there are at least 2^{34} master keys such that $\overline{\Delta X} \rightarrow \overline{\Delta W}$ is possible for 5-round AES-128.*

Proof. It is sufficient to prove that for any input truncated difference $\overline{\Delta X'}$ with two columns nonzero and any output truncated difference $\overline{\Delta W'}$ with one column nonzero, there are at least 2^{34} master keys such that

$$
DP(\overline{\Delta X'} \xrightarrow{G} \overline{\Delta W'}) > 0.
$$

Let the i_1-th and i_2-th columns of $\overline{\Delta X'}$ and the j-th column of $\overline{\Delta W'}$ be nonzero, $i_1 \neq i_2$, $0 \leq i_1, i_2, j \leq 3$. We need to find a differential $\Delta X' \rightarrow \Delta W'$ such that $\chi(\Delta X') = \overline{\Delta X'}$, $\chi(\Delta W') = \overline{\Delta W'}$, and

$$
DP(\Delta X' \xrightarrow{G} \Delta W') > 0.
$$

The propagation of the differential is shown in Fig. 3. Similar to the proof of Theorem 1, there exist ΔZ with only four bytes in the j-th column nonzero and $\Delta W'$ with $\chi(\Delta W') = \overline{\Delta W'}$ such that $f(Z) + f(Z + \Delta Z) = \Delta W'$, where

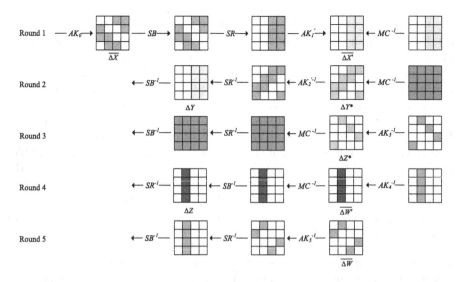

Fig. 3. The propagation of the differential in Set 2

$Z \in \mathbb{F}_{2^8}^{4\times4}$ and the bytes except the j-th column of Z can take arbitrary values. Let $\Delta Z^* = SR^{-1}(\Delta Z)$, and then $SR^{-1} \circ MC^{-1}(\Delta Z^*) \in (\mathbb{F}_{2^8}^*)^{4\times4}$. From Lemma 2, there exists ΔY^* with only eight bytes in the i_1-th and i_2-th inverse diagonals nonzero such that $g(Y^*) + g(Y^* + \Delta Y^*) = \Delta Z^*$ for some $Y^* \in \mathbb{F}_{2^8}^{4\times4}$. Let $\Delta Y = SR^{-1}(\Delta Y^*)$. By Lemma 2 again, there exists input difference $\Delta X'$ such that $\chi(\Delta X') = \overline{\Delta X'}$ and $g(X') + g(X' + \Delta X') = \Delta Y$, where $X' \in \mathbb{F}_{2^8}^{4\times4}$ and the bytes except the i_1-th and i_2-th columns of X' can take arbitrary values. Denote $Y = h(X')$, the bytes except the i_1-th and i_2-th columns of Y can take arbitrary values.

Taking $K_2' = SR(Y) + Y^*$ or $K_2' = SR(Y) + Y^* + \Delta Y^*$, then the output states of $SR \circ h$ and the input states of g are connected. The bytes except the i_1-th and i_2-th inverse diagonals of K_2' can take arbitrary values. Denote $Z^* = g(Y^*)$. Taking $K_3 = Z^* + SR^{-1}(Z)$ or $K_3 = Z^* + SR^{-1}(Z) + \Delta Z^*$, then the output states of g and the input states of $f \circ SR$ are connected. The bytes except the j-th diagonal of K_3 can take arbitrary values. From Lemma 4, for any given values of the i_1-th and i_2-th inverse diagonals of K_2' and the j-th diagonal of K_3, there are 2^{32} master keys under the key schedule of AES-128. Thus there are at least 2^{34} master keys such that $\overline{\Delta X'} \to \overline{\Delta W'}$ is possible for G.   □

Lemma 5. *Suppose the master keys of AES-128 are independent and uniformly random. Then any inverse diagonal of K_r' and any two diagonals of K_{r+1} are independent, and for any given values of the twelve bytes there are 2^{32} master keys under the key schedule of AES-128, $0 \le r \le 9$.*

Proof. By the assumption, the 16 bytes of K_r are independent and uniformly random. Let $(p,q,s,t) \in \{(0,7,10,13),(1,4,11,14),(2,5,8,15),(3,6,9,12)\}$ be any inverse diagonal. Then $K'_{r,\{p,q,s,t\}}$ can be represented by the bytes of K_r in (1). Note that four diagonals of K_{r+1} are represented by the bytes of K_r in (2), (3), (4) and (5) respectively. We combine (1) with any two of (2), (3), (4) and (5) to form 6 systems of equations. For each system, there are four bytes of K_r that can be taken as free variables. That is, $K_{r,\{5,6,12,13\}}$ are free variables in the system of (1), (2) and (3). $K_{r,\{7,13,14,15\}}$ are free variables in the system of (1), (2) and (4). $K_{r,\{2,7,12,13\}}$ are free variables in the system of (1), (2) and (5). $K_{r,\{1,5,12,14\}}$ are free variables in the system of (1), (3) and (4). $K_{r,\{0,12,13,14\}}$ are free variables in the system of (1), (3) and (5). $K_{r,\{0,4,13,14\}}$ are free variables in the system of (1), (4) and (5). When the free variables are determined the other bytes of K_r have unique solution in each combined system of equations. Since $K'_{r,\{p,q,s,t\}}$ and any two diagonals of K_{r+1} can take arbitrary values, they are independent. Furthermore, for their any given values there are 2^{32} master keys under the key schedule of AES-128. $\qquad\square$

Theorem 3. *For any input truncated difference $\overline{\Delta X}$ with one diagonal nonzero and any output truncated difference $\overline{\Delta W}$ with two inverse diagonals nonzero, there are at least 2^{34} master keys such that $\overline{\Delta X} \to \overline{\Delta W}$ is possible for 5-round AES-128.*

Proof. It is sufficient to prove that for any input truncated difference $\overline{\Delta X'}$ with one column nonzero and any output truncated difference $\overline{\Delta W'}$ with two columns nonzero, there are at least 2^{34} master keys such that

$$DP(\overline{\Delta X'} \xrightarrow{G} \overline{\Delta W'}) > 0.$$

Let the i-th column of $\overline{\Delta X'}$ and the j_1-th and j_2-th columns of $\overline{\Delta W'}$ be nonzero, $j_1 \neq j_2$, $0 \leq i, j_1, j_2 \leq 3$. We just need to find a differential $\Delta X' \to \Delta W'$ such that $\chi(\Delta X') = \overline{\Delta X'}$, $\chi(\Delta W') = \overline{\Delta W'}$, and

$$DP(\Delta X' \xrightarrow{G} \Delta W') > 0.$$

The propagation of the differential is shown in Fig. 4. From Lemma 1, there exists $\Delta W'$ such that $\chi(\Delta W') = \overline{\Delta W'}$ and the eight bytes in the j_1-th and j_2-th columns of $MC^{-1}(\Delta W')$ are nonzero. Let $f(Z) + f(Z + \Delta Z) = \Delta W'$, where $Z \in \mathbb{F}_{2^8}^{4 \times 4}$ and the bytes except the j_1-th and j_2-th columns of Z can take arbitrary values. By the differential distribution of S-box, each byte in the j_1-th and j_2-th columns of ΔZ has 127 possible values. Denote $\Delta Z^* = SR^{-1}(\Delta Z)$, then each column of ΔZ^* has two nonzero bytes and each nonzero byte has 127 possible values. That is, the number of ΔZ^* is 127^8. But the number of ΔZ^* such that $MC^{-1}(\Delta Z^*) \notin (\mathbb{F}_{2^8}^*)^{4 \times 4}$ is at most $(127 \cdot 4)^4$. So there exists ΔZ^* such that $MC^{-1}(\Delta Z^*) \in (\mathbb{F}_{2^8}^*)^{4 \times 4}$, and then $SR^{-1} \circ MC^{-1}(\Delta Z^*) \in (\mathbb{F}_{2^8}^*)^{4 \times 4}$. From Lemma 2, there exists input difference ΔY^* with only four bytes in the i-th inverse diagonal nonzero such that $g(Y^*) + g(Y^* + \Delta Y^*) = \Delta Z^*$ for some $Y^* \in \mathbb{F}_{2^8}^{4 \times 4}$. Let $\Delta Y = SR^{-1}(\Delta Y^*)$. From Lemma 2 again, there exists input difference $\Delta X'$ such that $\chi(\Delta X') = \overline{\Delta X'}$ and $h(X') + h(X' + \Delta X') = \Delta Y$,

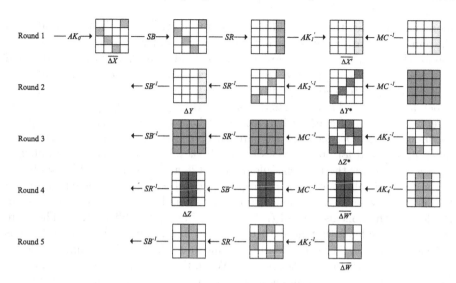

Fig. 4. The propagation of the differential in Set 3

where $X' \in \mathbb{F}_{2^8}^{4 \times 4}$ and the bytes except the i-th column of X' can take arbitrary values. Denote $Y = h(X')$, then the bytes except the i-th column of Y can take arbitrary values.

Taking $K_2' = SR(Y) + Y^*$ or $K_2' = SR(Y) + Y^* + \Delta Y^*$, the output states of $SR \circ h$ and the input states of g are connected. Denote $Z^* = g(Y^*)$. Taking $K_3 = Z^* + SR^{-1}(Z)$ or $K_3 = Z^* + SR^{-1}(Z) + \Delta Z^*$, then the output states of g and the input states of $f \circ SR$ are connected. The bytes except the i-th inverse diagonal of K_2' as well as the bytes except the j_1-th and j_2-th diagonals of K_3 can take arbitrary values. From Lemma 5, for any given values of the i-th inverse diagonal of K_2' and the j_1-th and j_2-th diagonals of K_3, there are 2^{32} master keys under the key schedule of AES-128. Thus there are at least 2^{34} master keys such that $\overline{\Delta X'} \to \overline{\Delta W'}$ is possible for G. □

From the view of provable security, we can get the following theorem. The result also holds for AES-192 and AES-256 because their master keys have larger degrees of freedom.

Theorem 4. *There do not exist truncated impossible differentials in Set 1, Set 2 and Set 3 for 5-round AES even considering the key schedule. That is, for any truncated differential $\overline{\Delta X} \to \overline{\Delta W}$ in Set 1, Set 2 or Set 3, we have*

$$EDP(\overline{\Delta X} \xrightarrow{5-round\ AES} \overline{\Delta W}) > 0.$$

4 Conclusion

In this paper, we prove theoretically that there do not exist three kinds of truncated impossible differentials for 5-round AES in the master-key setting. Furthermore, for any given truncated differentials of the three kinds, the lower bounds of the number of master keys such that the truncated differentials are possible for 5-round AES-128 are given. The lower bounds could be improved by more detailed analysis. These results improve the provable security evaluation of the real AES. It seems difficult to study the differentials in the master-key setting, because the dependence of round keys affects the propagation of states. Thanks to the simple algebraic relation of consecutive two-round keys in the key schedule, we prove the independence between the key bytes involved for the three kinds of truncated differentials. And for any given values of the key bytes involved, the number of master keys under the key schedule of AES-128 are also presented by analysing the number of solutions of the corresponding systems of algebraic equations. In the master-key setting, the nonexistence of r-round impossible differentials can not lead to the nonexistence of $(r + 1)$-round impossible differentials. There are still many problems that need to be studied in the future. For example, it is not clear that whether other kinds of truncated differentials are impossible for 5-round AES in the master-key setting. When the concrete differentials are considered, whether they are impossible for round-reduced AES in the master-key setting.

Acknowledgements. The authors are grateful to the anonymous reviewers for their helpful comments and suggestions. This work was supported by the National Cryptography Development Fund of China under grant numbers MMJJ20170103 and MMJJ20180204.

References

1. Bahrak, B., Aref, M.R.: Impossible differential attack on seven-round AES-128. IET Inf. Secur. **2**(2), 28–32 (2008)
2. Bar-On, A., Dunkelman, O., Keller, N., Ronen, E., Shamir, A.: Improved key recovery attacks on reduced-round AES with practical data and memory complexities. J. Cryptol. **33**(3), 1003–1043 (2020)
3. Bardeh, N.G., Rønjom, S.: The exchange attack: *how to distinguish six rounds of AES with $2^{88.2}$ chosen plaintexts*. In: Galbraith, S.D., Moriai, S. (eds.) ASIACRYPT 2019. LNCS, vol. 11923, pp. 347–370. Springer, Cham (2019). https://doi.org/10.1007/978-3-030-34618-8_12
4. Biham, E., Biryukov, A., Shamir, A.: Cryptanalysis of Skipjack reduced to 31 rounds using impossible differentials. In: Stern, J. (ed.) EUROCRYPT 1999. LNCS, vol. 1592, pp. 12–23. Springer, Heidelberg (1999). https://doi.org/10.1007/3-540-48910-X_2
5. Biham, E., Keller, N.: Cryptanalysis of reduced variants of Rijndael. In: The 3rd AES Conference (2000)
6. Boura, C., Lallemand, V., Naya-Plasencia, M., Suder, V.: Making the impossible possible. J. Cryptol. **31**(1), 101–133 (2018)
7. Boura, C., Naya-Plasencia, M., Suder, V.: Scrutinizing and improving impossible differential attacks: applications to CLEFIA, Camellia, LBlock and SIMON. In: Sarkar, P., Iwata, T. (eds.) ASIACRYPT 2014. LNCS, vol. 8873, pp. 179–199. Springer, Heidelberg (2014). https://doi.org/10.1007/978-3-662-45611-8_10

8. Chen, J., Wang, M., Preneel, B.: Impossible differential cryptanalysis of the lightweight block ciphers TEA, XTEA and HIGHT. In: Mitrokotsa, A., Vaudenay, S. (eds.) AFRICACRYPT 2012. LNCS, vol. 7374, pp. 117–137. Springer, Heidelberg (2012). https://doi.org/10.1007/978-3-642-31410-0_8

9. Cheon, J.H., Kim, M.J., Kim, K., Jung-Yeun, L., Kang, S.W.: Improved impossible differential cryptanalysis of Rijndael and Crypton. In: Kim, K. (ed.) ICISC 2001. LNCS, vol. 2288, pp. 39–49. Springer, Heidelberg (2002). https://doi.org/10.1007/3-540-45861-1_4

10. Derbez, P., Fouque, P.-A., Jean, J.: Improved key recovery attacks on reduced-round AES in the single-key setting. In: Johansson, T., Nguyen, P.Q. (eds.) EUROCRYPT 2013. LNCS, vol. 7881, pp. 371–387. Springer, Heidelberg (2013). https://doi.org/10.1007/978-3-642-38348-9_23

11. Dunkelman, O., Keller, N., Ronen, E., Shamir, A.: The retracing boomerang attack. In: Canteaut, A., Ishai, Y. (eds.) EUROCRYPT 2020. LNCS, vol. 12105, pp. 280–309. Springer, Cham (2020). https://doi.org/10.1007/978-3-030-45721-1_11

12. Ferguson, N., et al.: Improved cryptanalysis of Rijndael. In: Goos, G., Hartmanis, J., van Leeuwen, J., Schneier, B. (eds.) FSE 2000. LNCS, vol. 1978, pp. 213–230. Springer, Heidelberg (2001). https://doi.org/10.1007/3-540-44706-7_15

13. Leurent, G., Pernot, C.: New representations of the AES key schedule. In: Canteaut, A., Standaert, F.-X. (eds.) EUROCRYPT 2021. LNCS, vol. 12696, pp. 54–84. Springer, Cham (2021). https://doi.org/10.1007/978-3-030-77870-5_3

14. Grassi, L.: Mixture differential cryptanalysis: New approaches for distinguishers and attacks on round-reduced AES. IACR Trans. Symmetric Cryptol. 2018(2), 133–160 (2018)

15. Grassi, L., Rechberger, C., Rønjom, S.: Subspace trail cryptanalysis and its applications to AES. IACR Trans. Symmetric Cryptol. 2016(2), 192–225 (2016)

16. Grassi, L., Rechberger, C., Rønjom, S.: A new structural-differential property of 5-round AES. In: Coron, J.-S., Nielsen, J.B. (eds.) EUROCRYPT 2017. LNCS, vol. 10211, pp. 289–317. Springer, Cham (2017). https://doi.org/10.1007/978-3-319-56614-6_10

17. Hu, K., Cui, T., Gao, C., Wang, M.: Towards key-dependent integral and impossible differential distinguishers on 5-round AES. In: Cid, C., Jacobson, M., Jr. (eds.) SAC 2018. LNCS, vol. 11349, pp. 139–162. Springer, Cham (2019). https://doi.org/10.1007/978-3-030-10970-7_7

18. Hu, X., Li, Y., Jiao, L., Tian, S., Wang, M.: Mind the propagation of states. In: Moriai, S., Wang, H. (eds.) ASIACRYPT 2020. LNCS, vol. 12491, pp. 415–445. Springer, Cham (2020). https://doi.org/10.1007/978-3-030-64837-4_14

19. Kanda, M., Matsumoto, T.: Security of camellia against truncated differential cryptanalysis. In: Matsui, M. (ed.) FSE 2001. LNCS, vol. 2355, pp. 286–299. Springer, Heidelberg (2002). https://doi.org/10.1007/3-540-45473-X_24

20. Knudsen, L.R.: DEAL - a 128-bit cipher. Technical report, Department of Informatics, University of Bergen, Norway (1998)

21. Mala, H., Dakhilalian, M., Rijmen, V., Modarres-Hashemi, M.: Improved impossible differential cryptanalysis of 7-round AES-128. In: Gong, G., Gupta, K.C. (eds.) INDOCRYPT 2010. LNCS, vol. 6498, pp. 282–291. Springer, Heidelberg (2010). https://doi.org/10.1007/978-3-642-17401-8_20

22. Rønjom, S., Bardeh, N.G., Helleseth, T.: Yoyo tricks with AES. In: Takagi, T., Peyrin, T. (eds.) ASIACRYPT 2017. LNCS, vol. 10624, pp. 217–243. Springer, Cham (2017). https://doi.org/10.1007/978-3-319-70694-8_8

23. Sun, B., Liu, M., Guo, J., Qu, L., Rijmen, V.: New insights on AES-Like SPN ciphers. In: Robshaw, M., Katz, J. (eds.) CRYPTO 2016. LNCS, vol. 9814, pp. 605–624. Springer, Heidelberg (2016). https://doi.org/10.1007/978-3-662-53018-4_22

24. Sun, B., Liu, M., Guo, J., Rijmen, V., Li, R.: Provable security evaluation of structures against impossible differential and zero correlation linear cryptanalysis. In: Fischlin, M., Coron, J.-S. (eds.) EUROCRYPT 2016. LNCS, vol. 9665, pp. 196–213. Springer, Heidelberg (2016). https://doi.org/10.1007/978-3-662-49890-3_8

25. Tsunoo, Y., Tsujihara, E., Shigeri, M., Saito, T., Suzaki, T., Kubo, H.: Impossible differential cryptanalysis of CLEFIA. In: Nyberg, K. (ed.) FSE 2008. LNCS, vol. 5086, pp. 398–411. Springer, Heidelberg (2008). https://doi.org/10.1007/978-3-540-71039-4_25

26. Wang, Q., Jin, C.: Upper bound of the length of truncated impossible differentials for AES. Des. Codes Crypt. **86**(7), 1541–1552 (2017). https://doi.org/10.1007/s10623-017-0411-z

27. Wang, Q., Jin, C.: More accurate results on the provable security of AES against impossible differential cryptanalysis. Des. Codes Crypt. **87**(12), 3001–3018 (2019). https://doi.org/10.1007/s10623-019-00660-7

28. Zhang, W., Wu, W., Feng, D.: New results on impossible differential cryptanalysis of reduced AES. In: Nam, K.-H., Rhee, G. (eds.) ICISC 2007. LNCS, vol. 4817, pp. 239–250. Springer, Heidelberg (2007). https://doi.org/10.1007/978-3-540-76788-6_19

Adaptive Side-Channel Analysis Model and Its Applications to White-Box Block Cipher Implementations

Yufeng Tang[1], Zheng Gong[1(✉)], Tao Sun[2], Jinhai Chen[1], and Fan Zhang[3,4]

[1] School of Computer Science, South China Normal University, Guangzhou, China
[2] China Information Technology Security Evaluation Center (Guangdong Office),
Guangzhou, China
[3] College of Computer Science and Technology, Zhejiang University,
Hangzhou, China
[4] Key Laboratory of Blockchain and Cyberspace Governance of Zhejiang Province,
Hangzhou, China

Abstract. White-box block cipher (WBC) aims at protecting the secret key of a block cipher even if an adversary has full control over the implementations. At CHES 2016, Bos *et al.* proved that WBC are also threatened by *side-channel analysis* (SCA), e.g., *differential fault analysis* (DFA) and *differential computation analysis* (DCA). Therefore, advanced countermeasures have been proposed by Lee *et al.* for resisting DFA and DCA, such as table redundancy and improved masking methods, respectively. In this paper, we introduce a new *adaptive side-channel analysis* model which assumes that an adversary adaptively collects the intermediate values of a specific function and can mount the DFA/DCA attack with chosen inputs. In the adaptive SCA model, both theoretical analysis and experimental results show that Lee *et al.*'s proposed methods are vulnerable to DFA and DCA attacks. Moreover, a negative proposition is also demonstrated on the corresponding *high-order* countermeasures under our new model.

Keywords: White-box block cipher · Adaptive side-channel analysis · Differential fault analysis · Differential computation analysis

1 Introduction

The concept of *white-box attack context* was introduced in 2002 by Chow, Eisen, Johnson, and van Oorschot (CEJO) [14,15]. It assumes that an adversary can analyze the details of a cryptosystem with full control over its execution. White-box block cipher (WBC) aims at preventing the secret key of a block cipher algorithm from being extracted in a white-box environment. The first two attempts of WBC were white-box AES [15] (CEJO-WBAES) and DES [14] proposed by CEJO. The fundamental idea of them is to convert the operations of a cryptographic algorithm with a secret key into look-up tables (LUTs) and apply

© Springer Nature Switzerland AG 2021
Y. Yu and M. Yung (Eds.): Inscrypt 2021, LNCS 13007, pp. 399–417, 2021.
https://doi.org/10.1007/978-3-030-88323-2_22

linear and non-linear encodings to protect the intermediate values. In 2004, Billet *et al.* [7] presented an algebraic attack which was named BGE attack against CEJO-WBAES. From then on, although several improvements on white-box AES [13,23,35] were mentioned to resist cryptanalysis, all of them were subsequently broken [16–18].

In addition to algebraic attacks, *side-channel analysis* (SCA) has been demonstrated on WBC. At CHES 2016, Bos et al. [9,12] proposed to use *differential fault analysis* (DFA) and *differential computation analysis* (DCA) to attack white-box implementations. DFA induces faults in intermediate values and analyzing the differential equations with faulty and unencoded ciphertexts. DCA adapts a statistical technique of *differential power analysis* (DPA) but uses software computation traces consisting of noise-free intermediate values and accessed data. These attacks perform statistical analysis on the intermediate values such that avoid a time-consuming reverse engineering step and can be implemented automatically. SCA attacks are the major threats to white-box implementations as shown in the security assessment of the submissions of WhibOx 2017/19 competition [11,22].

Advanced SCA Methods on WBC. At CHES 2017, Banik *et al.* [6] developed *zero difference enumeration* attack which records software traces for pairs of selected plaintexts and performs an analysis on the difference of traces. Bock *et al.* [10] analyzed the ineffectiveness of internal encoding on white-box implementations under DCA attack. Amadori *et al.* [4] presented a new DFA attack that combines the techniques of DFA and BGE on a class of white-box AES implementation with 8-bit external encodings. At CHES 2019, Rivain and Wang [30] investigated *mutual information analysis* and *collision attack* to defeat the internal encoding. Another DCA-like approach, called *statistical bucketing attack*, was published by Zeyad *et al.* [36] for recovering the key by capturing computation traces based on the cryptanalysis technique introduced by Chow *et al.* [14]. For mitigating DFA, Lee *et al.* proposed a table redundancy method [26] which replaces the comparison step for fault detection with an exclusive-or (XOR) operation based on the white-box diversity and linearity of encodings. For countering DCA, Lee *et al.* [28] proposed the masking technique to the key-dependent value before applying encodings in the table generating phase. However, Rivain and Wang [30] described a 2-byte key guessing model of DCA and analyzed the first-round output of which the state is unmasked. To thwart the existing DCA attacks, Lee and Kim [27] improved their proposed scheme [28] by extending the masking to the round outputs.

Our Contribution. The main contributions of this paper are summarized as follows. (1) Based on the abilities of a white-box attacker and the efficiency of SCA attacks on white-box implementations, we introduce an adaptive SCA model for WBC. (2) The instantiation of adaptive DFA and DCA attacks are presented to break Lee *et al.*'s table redundancy [26] and improved masking [27] white-box implementations, respectively. The adaptive DFA replaces the ninth-round inputs with the adaptively collected states to bypass the XOR phase for fault detection. And the adaptive DCA exploits the collision of output mask to choose the plaintexts which have the same mask at the first-round output. (3) The higher-order table redundancy and improved masking are also discussed. Moreover, the adaptive higher-order DFA and DCA attacks are extended to defeat such countermeasures. The comparison between the applications of traditional and adaptive SCA models is shown in Table 1.

Table 1. The comparison between the applications of traditional and adaptive SCA models.

Method	SCA	Adaptive SCA
(Higher-order) Table redundancy [26]	(Higher-order) DFA resisted	DFA succeed, adaptively chosen ninth-round inputs (Sect. 3.2, 5)
(Higher-order) Improved masking [27]	(Higher-order) DCA resisted	DCA succeed, adaptively chosen plaintexts (Sect. 3.3, 5)

Organization. The remainder of this paper is organized as follows. Section 2 reviews the table redundancy [26] and improved masking [27] for white-box implementation. Section 3 describes the core idea of the adaptive SCA model on WBC. And then we provide instances of adaptive DFA and DCA attacks against table redundancy and improved masking methods. Afterward, Sect. 4 shows the experimental results of the adaptive DFA and DCA attacks, and Sect. 5 extends the attacks to the higher-order countermeasures. Section 6 concludes this paper.

2   Preliminaries

In this section, we briefly recall CEJO-WBAES and its SCA attacks. The state-of-the-art countermeasures on those SCA attacks are also reviewed.

2.1   CEJO-WBAES

In 2002, Chow *et al.* [15] defined the *white-box attack context* and introduced CEJO-WBAES to resist key extraction in cryptographic implementations. The basic idea is to convert the round functions of AES into a series of LUTs and apply secret invertible encodings to protect the intermediate values. Let T denote a LUT, f and g be random bijective mappings. Then the encoded LUT T' is defined as $T' = g \circ T \circ f^{-1}$, where f^{-1} and g are called the input and output encoding, respectively. To maintain the functionality of AES, the input and output encodings of consecutive rounds should be constructed as pairwise invertible mappings. Therefore, the input encoding can also play a role as input decoding since it decodes the previous encoded output to recover the secret state. Let an encoded LUT R' be defined as $R' = h \circ R \circ g^{-1}$ such that a networked encoding can be depicted as $R' \circ T' = (h \circ R \circ g^{-1}) \circ (g \circ T \circ f^{-1}) = h \circ (R \circ T) \circ f^{-1}$.

The basic principles of CEJO-WBAES are recalled as follows. Note that an AES state is represented by a byte array such that the index is ranked from 0 to 15. By means of *partial evaluation*, for each round, AddRoundKey and SubBytes operations are composed as 16 8-bit bijective key-dependent LUTs which are defined as T-boxes as follows.

$$T_i^r(x) = S(x \oplus \hat{k}_i^{r-1}), \qquad \text{for } i \in [0, 15] \text{ and } r \in [1, 9],$$
$$T_i^{10}(x) = S(x \oplus \hat{k}_i^9) \oplus \hat{k}_i^{10}, \text{ for } i \in [0, 15],$$

where S denotes the Sbox, $\hat{k}^r$ represent the result of applying ShiftRows to the byte array of round key. With *matrix partitioning*, the multiplication of MixColumns can be decomposed into four 32-bit vectors.

$$\begin{bmatrix} 02 & 03 & 01 & 01 \\ 01 & 02 & 03 & 01 \\ 01 & 01 & 02 & 03 \\ 03 & 01 & 01 & 02 \end{bmatrix} \begin{bmatrix} x_0 \\ x_1 \\ x_2 \\ x_3 \end{bmatrix} = x_0 \begin{bmatrix} 02 \\ 01 \\ 01 \\ 03 \end{bmatrix} \oplus x_1 \begin{bmatrix} 03 \\ 02 \\ 01 \\ 01 \end{bmatrix} \oplus x_2 \begin{bmatrix} 01 \\ 03 \\ 02 \\ 01 \end{bmatrix} \oplus x_3 \begin{bmatrix} 01 \\ 01 \\ 03 \\ 02 \end{bmatrix}$$
$$= Ty_0(x_0) \oplus Ty_1(x_1) \oplus Ty_2(x_2) \oplus Ty_3(x_3).$$

Ty_j for $0 \leq j \leq 3$ denote the 8 bits to 32 bits mappings for the decomposition of MixColumns. For rounds $1 \leq r \leq 9$, the T-boxes and Ty_j are then merged together to construct 16 TMC_i^r for $0 \leq i \leq 15$. Each TMC_i^r is defined as follows.

$$\text{TMC}_i^r = Ty_j \circ T_i^r, \text{ for } 0 \leq i \leq 15 \text{ and } j = i \bmod 4.$$

To add *diffusion* and *confusion* to each key-dependent intermediate value, the Mixing Bijections and Nibble Encodings are applied to all inputs and outputs of tables. An 8×8-bit linear transformation L_i^r and a 32×32-bit one MB are inserted before and after TMC_i^r, respectively. Subsequently, 4-bit non-linear encodings N are applied to the table inputs and outputs. The resulting encoded TMC_i^r are denoted by *TypeII* which is defined as follows.

$$TypeII: N \circ \text{MB} \circ \text{TMC}_i^r \circ L_i^r \circ N^{-1}.$$

To cancel out the effect of MB and convert it to $(L_i^{r+1})^{-1}$ to from the networked encoding, a *TypeIII* table is introduced accordingly and shown in below. Note that the table is generated by the technique of *matrix partitioning* as well.

$$TypeIII: N \circ (L_i^{r+1})^{-1} \circ \text{MB}^{-1} \circ N^{-1}.$$

Besides, all the XOR operations between encoded values are conducted by *TypeIV* tables which decode two 4-bit inputs and provides a 4-bit encoded XOR result. The combination of the outputs of *TypeII* is aptly named *TypeIV_II* while the one of *TypeIII* is aptly named *TypeIV_III*. Due to the linearity of XOR, the encoding and decoding phases of *TypeIV* only consist of non-linear encodings. Combining these tables, one can obtain an encoded fixed-key white-box AES such that $G \circ AES \circ F^{-1}$, where F^{-1} and G denote the external input and output encodings respectively. Since the external encoding lacks of compatibility, most of the theoretical analyses and constructions have not taken it into consideration (e.g., WhibOx 2017/19 competitions [1,2]). We note that every 4 bytes of CEJO-WBAES can also be interpreted as a column vector of 4×4 state matrix. For a detailed description of CEJO-WBAES, please refer to the tutorial paper [29].

2.2 Differential Fault Analysis

Following the ninth-round DFA attack model [19], Teuwen *et al.* [34] applied fault attacks against CEJO-WBAES. The attack injects a byte fault into the steps between the eighth-round and ninth-round MixColumns. Suppose that a fault is injected at the first byte $x \in \mathbb{F}_2^8$ of the ninth-round inputs. Let $\delta, \delta' \in \mathbb{F}_2^8$ denote the difference between the original byte and the faulty one before and after SubBytes, respectively. Such that $\delta' = S(x) \oplus S(x \oplus \delta)$, where S denotes the Sbox of SubBytes. The 4-byte difference after the MixColumn is represented by $(2\delta', \delta', \delta', 3\delta')$, where 2, 1, 1, 3 are the coefficients of MixColumns. Let S^{-1} be the inverse SubBytes. For the fault-free ciphertexts $C_0...C_7...C_{10}...C_{13}$ ($C_i \in \mathbb{F}_2^8$, $i \in [0, 15]$) and the faulty ciphertexts $C_0^*...C_7^*...C_{10}^*...C_{13}^*$ ($C_i^* \in \mathbb{F}_2^8$, $i \in \{0, 7, 10, 13\}$, $C_j \in \mathbb{F}_2^8$, $j \in [0, 15] \backslash \{i\}$), the following equations can be listed to find the tenth-round subkey candidate K_i^* ($i \in \{0, 7, 10, 13\}$). By injecting two such faults, the tenth-round 4-byte subkey can be determined by the differential equations. The other subkeys can be recovered by the similar analysis.

$$2\delta' = S^{-1}(C_0 \oplus K_0^*) \oplus S^{-1}(C_0^* \oplus K_0^*),$$
$$\delta' = S^{-1}(C_7 \oplus K_7^*) \oplus S^{-1}(C_7^* \oplus K_7^*),$$
$$\delta' = S^{-1}(C_{10} \oplus K_{10}^*) \oplus S^{-1}(C_{10}^* \oplus K_{10}^*),$$
$$3\delta' = S^{-1}(C_{13} \oplus K_{13}^*) \oplus S^{-1}(C_{13}^* \oplus K_{13}^*).$$

2.3 The Table Redundancy Method Against DFA

As introduced by Lee *et al.* [26], table redundancy method uses multiple branches of LUTs for the vulnerable rounds (e.g., the sixth to ninth rounds) and XOR the outputs to obfuscate the fault injection. The description of the scheme can be shown in three parts as follows. (1) Sharing the LUTs from Round 1 to 5. (2) Transforming independently in parallel with two sets of LUTs from the sixth round to ninth-round *TypeII*. These two computations are constructed with different sets of LUTs built by different encodings. (3) Sharing the LUTs from ninth-round *TypeIV_II* to Round 10. Note that the basic technique for constructing the LUTs is followed by CEJO-WBAES [15].

Let $\mathrm{MB}_l \in \mathbb{F}_2^{32 \times 32}$ and $\mathrm{MB}_r \in \mathbb{F}_2^{32 \times 32}$ (l (resp. r) represents the left (resp. right) part of the two computations) be the 32-bit Mixing Bijections of the ninth-round *TypeII*. The $x_l \in \mathbb{F}_2^8$ and $x_r \in \mathbb{F}_2^8$ denote the two unencoded bytes of ninth-round inputs. Such that $\text{TMC}(x_l)$ and $\text{TMC}(x_r)$ represent the outputs of SubBytes and MixColumns from x_l and x_r, respectively. The outputs of the two computations XOR with each other by a type of *TypeIV* followed by the shared *TypeIV_II*. Let $x \in \mathbb{F}_2^8$ be the original state at ninth-round inputs of standard AES, the XOR process can be shown as

$$\text{MB}_l \cdot \text{TMC}(x_l) \oplus \text{MB}_r \cdot \text{TMC}(x_r) =$$
$$(\text{MB}_l \oplus \text{MB}_r) \cdot \text{TMC}(x), \text{ iff } x_l = x_r = x.$$

Hence, the inverse Mixing Bijection $\text{MB}^{-1} \in \mathbb{F}_2^{32 \times 32}$ in ninth-round *TypeIII* can be depicted as

$$\text{MB}^{-1} = (\text{MB}_l \oplus \text{MB}_r)^{-1}.$$

The Mixing Bijections can be combined with $\oplus$ because both of them are linear transformations and the underlying state x is fault-free. Once x_l or x_r is injected by a fault, the XOR cannot lead to a valid differential equation.

2.4   Differential Computation Analysis

At CHES 2016, Bos *et al.* [12] introduced DCA as the software counterpart of DPA [25] to break white-box implementations. DCA divides the measurement traces in two distinct sets according to the value of one of the bits of Sbox output. Let x_i be an input, v_i be the collected traces, $b = S_j(x_i \oplus k)$ denote the j-th bit of Sbox. For each j and k, sorting the traces v_i into two sets b_0 and b_1 based on the value of b. The mean trace is defined as

$$\bar{b}_{\{0,1\}} = \frac{\sum_{v \in b_{\{0,1\}}} v}{|b_{\{0,1\}}|}.$$

And the difference of means is calculated as

$$\Delta = |\bar{b}_0 - \bar{b}_1|.$$

Let Δ^j denote the difference of means trace obtained at j-th bit for a key hypothesis k^h. Let denote the best target bit which has the highest peak for k^h by $\Delta^{j'}$. Then $\Delta^{j'}$ is selected as the best difference of means trace for k^h and is denoted as Δ^h. The final step is to select the best difference which has the highest peak among all Δ^h and it is denoted as $\Delta^{h'}$. Such that the hypothesis $k^{h'}$ corresponding to $\Delta^{h'}$ is the most probably correct key.

2.5   The Improved Masking Method Against DCA

To thwart DCA, Lee *et al.* presented the improved masking method [27] which applies the random masks to the round outputs. When building *TypeII*, the masks are randomly picked for each input, and each output of Ty_j XOR with the random mask. The 8×8 linear transformations L are applied to the masks to form the mask table. The outputs of masked *TypeII* continue to feed the following tables of the first round (i.e., *TypeII_IV*, *TypeIII*, and *TypeIII_IV*). Both the masked *TypeII* and mask table are combined as *TypeII_MO* as shown in Fig. 1.

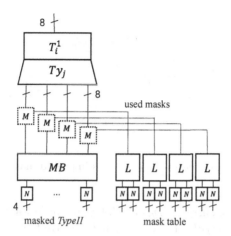

Fig. 1. *TypeII_MO* table in the first round. The input encoding is omitted because of the absence of external encoding.

For clarity, let *vs* (value state) and *ms* (mask state) denote the round outputs of masked state and mask table itself, respectively. The *TypeII* table in the second round takes each corresponding byte of *vs* and *ms* as inputs. Thus, *vs* and *ms* are combined by XOR to unmask in the input decoding phase of the second round to form the *TypeII_MIMO* table as illustrated in Fig. 2. Since the unmasking is combined with the input decoding phase of *TypeII_MIMO* table in the second round, the intermediate values of the first round are all masked with the random masks. Figure 3 shows the look-up sequence from the first column of

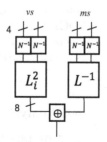

Fig. 2. The input decoding phase of *TypeII_MIMO* table in the second round. The following TMC_i^2 and the output encodings are omitted.

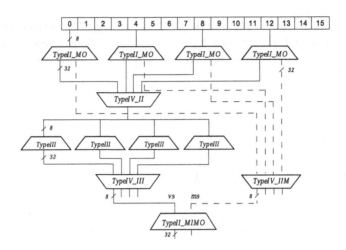

Fig. 3. LUT sequences of Lee *et al.*'s improved masking method.

plaintexts to the first entry of *TypeII_MIMO* in the second round. *TypeIV_IIM* represents a type of *TypeIV* table to XOR the outputs of mask table.

The solid line in Fig. 3 denotes the masked intermediate values in the first round while the dotted line represents the encoded masks. Hence, the collected traces of the encoded first-round Sbox are independent of the hypothetical values due to the presence of random masks. For a detailed description of the improved masking method, one can refer to the original proposal [27].

3   Adaptive Side-Channel Analysis Model and Its Applications

In the previous section, we recall the two proposed countermeasures for protecting against DFA and DCA on CEJO-WBAES. The table redundancy method [26] exploits the white-box diversity to combine the redundant computations with fault detection. The improved masking technique [27] randomizes the output value of key-dependent LUTs before encodings. Although the two proposals can mitigate the original DFA and DCA attacks, the designer did not take into account the ability of a white-box adversary. For concerning a white-box attacker with the technique of SCA, an adaptive SCA model on WBC is proposed in this section.

3.1   The Adaptive Side-Channel Analysis Model on WBC

Compared with the algebraic attacks [7, 16–18] which need to retrieve the encodings, SCA on WBC has been proved to reduce the time complexity of recovering the secret key of the implementation with limited knowledge (e.g., side-channel

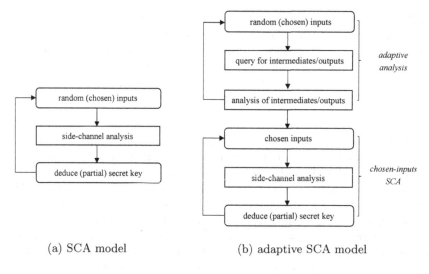

(a) SCA model   (b) adaptive SCA model

Fig. 4. The flowchart of SCA and adaptive SCA models.

information). The main benefits of SCA attack are that it do not need knowledge of particular implementation and the effort of reverse engineering. WBC is more vulnerable to SCA attacks even if it is intended to thwart a more powerful attack in the white-box setting (i.e., with full control of the implementation). The steps of an SCA attack in a white-box scenario can be informally described as follows, which are also illustrated in Fig. 4(a).

1. The adversary invokes the white-box implementation many times with random (chosen) inputs.
2. During each execution, the adversary performs a modeling analysis on the side-channel information (e.g., intermediate values) for deducing the (partial) secret key.

Note that the modification and record of side-channel information can be implemented with the help of *dynamic binary instrumentation* tools, such as Intel PIN [3]. For mitigating the SCA attacks, the side-channel countermeasure (e.g., table redundancy and improved masking) prevents the generalized SCA attacks by introducing a newly generated component (e.g., redundant computation and mask table). In practice, an adversary can extend the technique of SCA attacks with the powerful ability in the white-box attack context. An attacker can analyze the correlation between the original and newly generated component to collect the inputs which will contribute to a successful SCA attack. Such a new attack extends the efficiency of generalized SCA and is adapted to the dedicated countermeasure. Now, we introduce an *Adaptive Side-Channel Analysis* model to break the side-channel countermeasure for WBC implementations. The steps of an adaptive SCA attack are divided into two phases: *adaptive analysis* and *chosen-inputs SCA* as informally described as follows, which are also illustrated in Fig. 4(b).

- *Adaptive analysis.* The adversary pinpoints the entry of a specific function and queries it with random (chosen) inputs for collecting intermediates/outputs. The adversary then performs an analysis on the intermediates/outputs to choose inputs for repeating query or for the following SCA attack.
- *Chosen-inputs SCA.* The adversary makes her choice of the inputs to the cryptographic algorithm and mounts the generalized SCA attacks to retrieve the secret key.

The attacker can pinpoint a dedicated region by the exploitation of *data dependency analysis* [21] and fault attacks [4,5,8]. The concrete steps and time complexity are related to the code obfuscation techniques used in the white-box implementation. Since the obscurity of the location of a function in a WBC implementation cannot provide the security on the algorithm itself, our adaptive SCA model assumes that an entry can be pinpointed with affordable complexity. After the adaptive analysis phase, chosen-inputs SCA can be mounted automatically with the help of practical SCA tools [31,32]. Moreover, we note that an adaptive SCA adversary is capable of all known SCA attacks on WBC.

The main difference between SCA and adaptive SCA model is that an adaptive SCA attacker needs to obtain a set of target inputs before an SCA attack. The previous work [24] described an adversary with the ability of choosing inputs for SCA attacks. But it follows the gray-box model instead of the white-box model and is out of scope for this work. The adaptive SCA model in a gray-box setting is left as future work. In the next section, we will show the adaptive DFA and DCA attacks against Lee *et al.*'s table redundancy [26] and improved masking methods [27].

3.2   Adaptive DFA on the Table Redundancy Method

To break the table redundancy method [26], the fault needs to be simultaneously induced at both the original and redundant computations and thus their underlying states are the same value. Concerning the fault-free process of table redundancy method, the decoded states of both sides always keep the equal values since both of the two computations are the same AES encryption. Although the diversity of WBC is considered in the redundant design, the internal encodings are fixed when the implementation is running. So the intermediate input values of the ninth-round *TypeII* always appear pairwise. Let $y_{l_i} \in \mathbb{F}_2^8$ and $y_{r_i} \in \mathbb{F}_2^8$ ($i \in [0, 15]$) be an 8-bit input value of the two ninth-round *TypeII*, respectively. Let $x_i \in \mathbb{F}_2^8$ ($i \in [0, 15]$) be an 8-bit unencoded input state of the ninth round. The P_{l_i} and P_{r_i} ($i \in [0, 15]$) denote an 8-bit input decoding on $\mathbb{F}_2^8$ (i.e., Mixing Bijections and non-linear encodings) of y_{l_i} and y_{r_i}, respectively. For the decoding process of the ninth-round inputs , we have

$$x_i = P_{l_i}(y_{l_i}) = P_{r_i}(y_{r_i}), \; i \in [0, 15].$$

Since x_i have 256 different values and the mappings of input decoding (i.e., P_{l_i} and P_{r_i}) are bijections, each pair of (y_{l_i}, y_{r_i}) can be collected from the corresponding inputs of the ninth round. Let $\mathcal{T}$ be a set of pairwise values, such that

$$\mathcal{T}_i = \{(y_{li}, y_{ri}) \mid y_{li} \in \mathbb{F}_2^8, \ y_{ri} \in \mathbb{F}_2^8\}, \ with \ \#\mathcal{T}_i = 256, \ i \in [0, 15].$$

Based on the ninth-round DFA attack model [19], the fault can be injected at one of the four bytes of a column to recover the four-byte subkey in the tenth round. Such that $\mathcal{T}_j$ for $j = 0, 4, 8, 12$ are sufficient for obtaining the tenth-round key. For simplicity, the index j is discarded and the injection on one byte of the ninth round can be concluded by the following steps. The other locations of the ninth-round inputs are similar to this example.

1. Querying for the pairwise values at the original and redundant ninth-round inputs by repeatedly running the implementation with random plaintexts to form the set $\mathcal{T}$.
2. Getting a fault-free ciphertext by running with a random plaintext and denoting the pairwise values at the ninth-round inputs as (y_l, y_r).
3. Replacing (y_l, y_r) with other pairs in $\mathcal{T} \backslash (y_l, y_r)$ which are denoted as (y_l^*, y_r^*) and collecting the faulty ciphertexts by running the cryptographic program with the same plaintext.
4. Repeating Step 3 and using the DFA tools to perform the analysis between the fault-free and faulty ciphertexts.

Let $x^* \in \mathbb{F}_2^8$ be the underlying state of the faulty pairs (y_l^*, y_r^*). The decoding P_l and P_r are fixed into the parts of LUTs in the encryption, thus x will be tampered as x^* if (y_l, y_r) are replaced with (y_l^*, y_r^*). The modification from x to x^* represents that the faults are injected successfully at the ninth-round inputs. This process simultaneously modifies the underlying states of the two computations into other ones by replacing the pairwise values at the ninth-round inputs with the other pairs in $\mathcal{T}$. In this way, MB can be combined in the XOR process since the decoded states after the ninth-round TMC are identical to each other between two computations. Note that $\mathcal{T}$ can be collected with overwhelming probability because of the splendid confusion and diffusion of the first 8-round AES. Concerning the practical analysis, the subkey can be recovered by only two faults in the same location, thus $\mathcal{T}$ need not be a full set. In this way, the adaptive DFA attack on the table redundancy method exploits the replacement on the ninth-round inputs to bypass the elaborately designed XOR phases of *TypeII*. Thus, the vulnerability of table redundancy under DFA attack is identical to CEJO-WBAES [15]. The adaptive DFA can also be extended to break a table redundant white-box implementation with 8-bit external encodings since we assume that the attacker knows the technique of existing DFA attack [4].

3.3 Adaptive DCA on the Improved Masking Method

Since the improved masking conceals the key-dependent outputs of the first round by introducing the random masks, DCA fails to analyze the correlation between the intermediate and hypothesis values. In the following text, Q_i and

Q_i' for $0 \leq i \leq 3$ denote bijective mapping on $\mathbb{F}_2^8$ and are referred to as output encodings of vs and ms (refer to Sect. 2.5), respectively. Let $y_i, y_i' : (\mathbb{F}_2^8)^4 \rightarrow \mathbb{F}_2^8$ for $0 \leq i \leq 3$ be the functions of the mappings from plaintexts to vs and ms, $k_i \in \mathbb{F}_2^8$ for $0 \leq i \leq 3$ be the subkeys in the first round, and $(x_0, x_1, x_2, x_3) \in (\mathbb{F}_2^8)^4$ denote the first column of plaintexts. Such that the function of vs in the first column which is depicted by solid line in Fig. 3 can be shown as follows.

$$y_i(x_0, x_1, x_2, x_3) = Q_i \circ (mc_{i,0} \cdot S(x_0 \oplus k_0) \oplus mc_{i,1} \cdot S(x_1 \oplus k_1)$$
$$\oplus\, mc_{i,2} \cdot S(x_2 \oplus k_2) \oplus mc_{i,3} \cdot S(x_3 \oplus k_3) \oplus M_i).$$

The corresponding function of ms which is depicted by the dotted line in Fig. 3 can be represented in below.

$$y_i'(x_0, x_1, x_2, x_3) = Q_i' \circ (M_i).$$

Note that M_i denote the mask used and take all the values on $\mathbb{F}_2^8$, mc_i denote the MixColumns coefficient, $0 \leq i \leq 3$ denotes the index of states.

Mentioned by Lee et al. [27], each M_i is independently generated for different inputs such that its randomness and uniformity help to mask the key-dependent output of y_i. However, since M_i need to be annihilated between the outputs of y_i and y_i', the underlying M_i used in the function of vs and ms for the same (x_0, x_1, x_2, x_3) are identical to each other. Due to the fact that the encodings Q_i' are fixed bijective mapping, a collision in an encoded byte $Q_i'(x)$ corresponds with a collision in the decoded byte x as well. Thus, one can sort the inputs by the identical outputs of y_i', i.e., to get the set

$$\mathcal{P}_i = \{(x_0, x_1, x_2, x_3) \mid y_i'(x_0, x_1, x_2, x_3) = c\},$$

where c is a constant and i denotes the index of entry. For simplicity, the following analysis takes $i = 0$. Based on the 2-byte key guessing model [30], we suppose that $(\alpha, \beta, 0, 0), (\alpha', \beta', 0, 0) \in \mathcal{P}_0$ such that $y_0'(\alpha, \beta, 0, 0) = y_0'(\alpha', \beta', 0, 0)$, which also implies that $Q_0'(M_0) = Q_0'(M_0')$. In this way, $M_0 = M_0'$, thus $(\alpha, \beta, 0, 0)$ and $(\alpha', \beta', 0, 0)$ have the same mask value M_0. Once the underlying mask of y_i are constant for different plaintexts, DCA can recover the secret key for analyzing the correlation between the computation traces and hypothesis outputs. The detailed attack can be represented by the following steps on recovering the first two bytes of the first-round key. The steps for other key bytes are similar to this one.

1. Querying for the plaintexts as the set $\mathcal{P}_0$ which have the same output of y_0' by enumerating the first two bytes of the inputs and fixing the other bytes of y_0' (e.g., $y_0'(x_0, x_1, 0, 0)$).
2. Collecting the bit traces v which include the values of the outputs of y_0 by choosing the plaintexts in $\mathcal{P}_0$.
3. Selecting the XOR of the first two outputs of MixColumns as the hypothetical value b, that is

$$b = mc_{i,0} \cdot S(x_0 \oplus k_0') \oplus mc_{i,1} \cdot S(x_1 \oplus k_1'),$$

where k_0' and k_1' are key guesses.

4. Mounting the DCA attack on analyzing the correlation between v and b to recover k_0 and k_1.

For k_2 and k_3, the attack needs to enumerate x_2 and x_3 and fix the other bytes. The key recovery of other columns is similar to this example. Note that the collected y_0' need not be set as a pre-defined value since any constant on $\mathbb{F}_2^8$ can help to sort the plaintexts. For a practical attack, the number of plaintexts in $\mathcal{P}_0$ depends on the number of traces that are exploited by the original DCA.

Suppose that the mask value is fixed as a constant m, such that

$$y_0(x_0, x_1, 0, 0) = Q_0 \circ (mc_{i,0} \cdot S(x_0 \oplus k_0) \oplus mc_{i,1} \cdot S(x_1 \oplus k_1) \oplus \gamma \oplus m),$$

where the constant $\gamma = mc_{i,2} \cdot S(0 \oplus k_2) \oplus mc_{i,3} \cdot S(0 \oplus k_3)$. Note that the XOR phase of constant can be combined with the linear part of the encoding Q_0 to form a new encoding $\widetilde{Q}_0$. Thus, $y_0(x_0, x_1, 0, 0) = \widetilde{Q}_0 \circ (mc_{i,0} \cdot S(x_0 \oplus k_0) \oplus mc_{i,1} \cdot S(x_1 \oplus k_1))$. Because of the ineffectiveness of internal encodings [10], the strong correlations can be computed between v and b.

The adaptive DCA attack on the improved masking method utilizes the collision on y' to sort the plaintexts which have the same mask. Such that the elaborately designed masking can be bypassed since a constant mask cannot prevent the leakage of a secret key. In this way, the vulnerability of improved masking under DCA attack is identical to CEJO-WBAES [15].

4   Theoretical Analysis and Experimental Results

This section performs the practical attacks on table redundancy and improved masking based on the adaptive SCA model. Following such a model, a white-box adversary can directly locate and modify any intermediate values in an implementation. Such that for efficiency, the experiment collects the target values during the table look-up operations by modifying the corresponding source code of encryption. Our attack is conducted on a PC with Intel Core i5-6200U processor @2.3 GHz, 12 GB RAM. The compiler for building a shared library is GCC 8.2.0, while "-O2" optimization is enabled. All the counts have been measured 100,000 times to get the averages. For verifying our results, the crucial components of our experiments are open-sourced[1].

4.1   Results of the Adaptive DFA on the Table Redundancy Method

The experiment firstly generates the sets $\mathcal{T}_j$ for $j = 0, 4, 8, 12$ consisting of pairwise bytes of the ninth-round inputs between which one is the original state and the other is the redundant one. The result shows that each $\mathcal{T}_j$ can be fully filled up by 1,548 executions, encrypting with random plaintexts. Due to the fact that two faults injection at the first byte of a column in the ninth round can help to recover a 4-byte subkey of the tenth round, $\mathcal{T}_j$ can only be collected by three

---

[1] https://github.com/scnucrypto/Adaptive-SCA.

pairwise states instead of a full set. Note that, the first element of T_j can be found by the first encryption and the corresponding plaintext can be recorded as the one for the fault injection. Such that the replacement for adaptive DFA attack only relies on another two elements of T_j which can be collected by extra 2 executions with random plaintexts based on our further experiment. The correlation between the number of plaintexts and the number of the adaptively chosen elements of T_j is illustrated in Fig. 5. Note that each T_j has 256 elements at most.

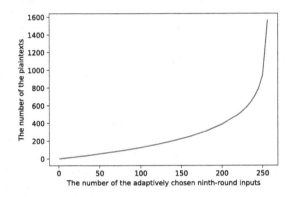

Fig. 5. The number of the plaintexts used to adaptively choose the pairwise ninth-round inputs to form the elements of T_j.

Subsequently, the pairwise states at the first byte in each of four columns are collected to form four corresponding T_j. The adaptive replacement between the original pairwise state at ninth-round inputs and the elements in T_j is performed to yield a result as the fault injection. After the fault-free ciphers and faulty ciphertexts are recorded, the tools Jean Grey [32] is invoked to solve the differential equations and recover the tenth-round key. The main key can be obtained from the tenth-round key by using the key scheduling reversers supported by Stark [33] tools. To sum up, at least 5 executions (3 times for collecting T_j and 2 times for the replacement of fault injection) of the white-box implementation can recover the 4-byte subkey of the tenth round. Totally at least 20 executions of encryption can extract the 16-byte tenth-round key.

4.2   Results of the Adaptive DCA on the Improved Masking Method

The experiment focuses on collecting P_0 as an example. The collision of y'_0 for $(x_0, x_1, 0, 0)$ can help to choose the plaintexts of which the mask value are identical to each other. Such that DCA can recover k_0 and k_1 based on the 2-byte key guessing model [30]. Similarly, the collision of $y'_0(0, 0, x_2, x_3)$ for all x_2 and x_3 helps to choose the plaintexts to retrieve k_2 and k_3 by DCA. Note that the collision relies on the mapping on $(\mathbb{F}_2^8)^2 \rightarrow \mathbb{F}_2^8$. Based on the randomness and uniformity of the mask, for each constant $c \in \mathbb{F}_2^8$, there are 256 possible inputs for $y_0'(x_0, x_1, 0, 0) = c$. This implies that 256 plaintexts (also 256 traces with the same mask) at most help to recover a 2-byte key. The result shows that 53,884 executions with the enumeration of $(x_0, x_1) \in (\mathbb{F}_2^8)^2$ can collect all 256 inputs which map to a same constant through the function y_0' to form the set $\mathcal{P}_0$. Subsequently, the elements in $\mathcal{P}_0$ are adaptively chosen as plaintexts for the white-box implementation and thus the DCA attack can be mounted by the tools [20, 31].

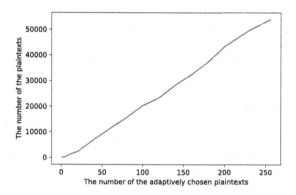

Fig. 6. The number of the plaintexts used to adaptively choose the target plaintexts which have a same mask value in y_0 to form the elements of $\mathcal{P}_0$.

In practice, a 2-byte key leakage attack can be captured under DCA by analyzing less than 256 traces. Our experimental result shows that at least 25 plaintexts in $\mathcal{P}_0$ can successfully help to recover the 2-byte key with the traces that are composed of y_0. Figure 6 shows the relation between the number of the elements in $\mathcal{P}_0$ and the number of required plaintexts. The plaintexts are adaptively chosen by enumerating $(x_0, x_1) \in (\mathbb{F}_2^8)^2$. Note that each $\mathcal{P}_0$ has 256 elements at most because of the uniform distribution with random mask. As illustrated in Fig. 6, nearly 3,240 executions of encryption can help to collect 25 elements of $\mathcal{P}_0$. Note that each 2-byte key is obtained by DCA with chosen 4-byte plaintexts. Such that, in summary, at least about 3,265 executions (3,240 times for obtaining $\mathcal{P}_j$ corresponding to four 4-byte plaintexts and 25 times for collecting computation traces which comprises the outputs of y_j, for $j = 0, 4, 8, 12$) of the white-box implementation can recover four 2-byte subkeys of the first round. Totally at least about 6,530 executions of encryption can extract the 16-byte first-round key.

5   Adaptive SCA on Lee *et al.*'s Higher-Order Countermeasures

In [26], Lee *et al.* also discussed an enhancement on the security of the table redundancy method for protecting against DFA. The proposal increases the number of redundant computations and is introduced as the higher-order version of the table redundancy method in this paper. Higher-order table redundancy consists of more than one redundant computation. This implies that the faults need to be injected simultaneously on every state so that the combination of the original and redundant computations still can induce the available faulty ciphers. The higher-order adaptive DFA attack exploits the sets of pre-collected intermediate values at the ninth-round inputs to implement a replacement between the fault-free and faulty states. Such fault injection takes place in the ninth-round inputs which are not affected by the XOR phase of table redundancy. The required times of encryption for the adaptive DFA on higher-order table redundancy does not increase due to the identical collection as the attack on the one redundant computation.

Higher-order improved masking consists of more than one mask to enhance the security for protecting against DCA attack. The higher-order adaptive DCA needs to successfully find the collisions of ms (refer to Sect. 2.5) to obtain the target plaintexts which have the same masks. Subsequently, the attacker can mount a successful DCA attack by the chosen plaintexts and collecting the software traces which include the value of vs (refer to Sect. 2.5). This process requires the adaptive DCA attacker to collect the plaintexts from each mask table in turn. The theoretical result shows that, to attack a third-order improved masking, $2^{32} + 2^{24} + 2^{16}$ lookups of the mask tables can obtain 2^8 plaintexts which have the same masks. However, it is worth noting that, the higher-order improved masking is not practical for white-box implementations because the multiple inputs of $TypeII\_MIMO$ (refer to Fig. 2) will result in an exponential increase in the space footprint.

6   Conclusion

In this paper, a novel SCA model has been proposed for introducing the *adaptive analysis* and *chosen-inputs SCA* phases to traditional SCA attacks on WBC. The new adaptive model is applied to Lee *et al.*'s improved countermeasures. For the practical security of WBC, our results motivate to explore new SCA countermeasures on WBC by concerning the abilities of adaptive SCA attacker. In future work, it is interesting to build an adaptive algebraic analysis model to break the state-of-the-art countermeasures of algebraic attacks (e.g., BGE attack) on WBC.

Acknowledgments. We are grateful to the anonymous reviewers for their insightful comments. This work was supported in part by National Key R&D Program of China (2020AAA0107700), National Natural Science Foundation of China (62072192, 62072398), and National Cryptography Development Fund (MMJJ20180206). Fan Zhang was also supported by Alibaba-Zhejiang University Joint Institute of Frontier Technologies, by Zhejiang Key R&D Plan (2021C01116).

References

1. CHES 2017 capture the flag challenge - the WhibOx contest, an encrypt white-box cryptography competition. https://whibox.io/contests/2017/. Accessed 1 June 2021
2. CHES 2019 capture the flag challenge - the WhibOx contest edition 2. https://whibox.io/contests/2019/. Accessed 1 June 2021
3. Pin - a dynamic binary instrumentation tool. https://software.intel.com/content/www/us/en/develop/articles/pin-a-dynamic-binary-instrumentation-tool.html. Accessed 1 June 2021
4. Amadori, A., Michiels, W., Roelse, P.: A DFA attack on white-box implementations of AES with external encodings. In: Paterson, K.G., Stebila, D. (eds.) SAC 2019. LNCS, vol. 11959, pp. 591–617. Springer, Cham (2020). https://doi.org/10.1007/978-3-030-38471-5_24
5. Amadori, A., Michiels, W., Roelse, P.: Automating the BGE attack on white-box implementations of AES with external encodings. In: 2020 IEEE 10th International Conference on Consumer Electronics (ICCE-Berlin), pp. 1–6. IEEE (2020). https://doi.org/10.1109/ICCE-Berlin50680.2020.9352195
6. Banik, S., Bogdanov, A., Isobe, T., Jepsen, M.: Analysis of software countermeasures for whitebox encryption. IACR Trans. Symmetric Cryptol. 307–328 (2017). https://doi.org/10.13154/tosc.v2017.i1.307-328
7. Billet, O., Gilbert, H., Ech-Chatbi, C.: Cryptanalysis of a white box AES implementation. In: Handschuh, H., Hasan, M.A. (eds.) SAC 2004. LNCS, vol. 3357, pp. 227–240. Springer, Heidelberg (2004). https://doi.org/10.1007/978-3-540-30564-4_16
8. Biryukov, A., Udovenko, A.: Attacks and countermeasures for white-box designs. In: Peyrin, T., Galbraith, S. (eds.) ASIACRYPT 2018. LNCS, vol. 11273, pp. 373–402. Springer, Cham (2018). https://doi.org/10.1007/978-3-030-03329-3_13
9. Bock, E.A., et al.: White-box cryptography: don't forget about grey-box attacks. J. Cryptol. 32(4), 1095–1143 (2019). https://doi.org/10.1007/s00145-019-09315-1
10. Alpirez Bock, E., Brzuska, C., Michiels, W., Treff, A.: On the ineffectiveness of internal encodings - revisiting the DCA attack on white-box cryptography. In: Preneel, B., Vercauteren, F. (eds.) ACNS 2018. LNCS, vol. 10892, pp. 103–120. Springer, Cham (2018). https://doi.org/10.1007/978-3-319-93387-0_6
11. Bock, E.A., Treff, A.: Security assessment of white-box design submissions of the CHES 2017 CTF challenge. IACR Cryptology ePrint Archive 2020, 342 (2020). https://eprint.iacr.org/2020/342
12. Bos, J.W., Hubain, C., Michiels, W., Teuwen, P.: Differential computation analysis: hiding your white-box designs is not enough. In: Gierlichs, B., Poschmann, A.Y. (eds.) CHES 2016. LNCS, vol. 9813, pp. 215–236. Springer, Heidelberg (2016). https://doi.org/10.1007/978-3-662-53140-2_11
13. Bringer, J., Chabanne, H., Dottax, E.: White box cryptography: Another attempt. IACR Cryptology ePrint Archive 2006, 468 (2006). https://eprint.iacr.org/2006/468
14. Chow, S., Eisen, P., Johnson, H., van Oorschot, P.C.: A white-box DES implementation for DRM applications. In: Feigenbaum, J. (ed.) DRM 2002. LNCS, vol. 2696, pp. 1–15. Springer, Heidelberg (2003). https://doi.org/10.1007/978-3-540-44993-5_1

15. Chow, S., Eisen, P., Johnson, H., Van Oorschot, P.C.: White-box cryptography and an AES implementation. In: Nyberg, K., Heys, H. (eds.) SAC 2002. LNCS, vol. 2595, pp. 250–270. Springer, Heidelberg (2003). https://doi.org/10.1007/3-540-36492-7_17

16. De Mulder, Y., Roelse, P., Preneel, B.: Cryptanalysis of the Xiao – Lai white-box AES implementation. In: Knudsen, L.R., Wu, H. (eds.) SAC 2012. LNCS, vol. 7707, pp. 34–49. Springer, Heidelberg (2013). https://doi.org/10.1007/978-3-642-35999-6_3

17. De Mulder, Y., Roelse, P., Preneel, B.: Revisiting the BGE attack on a white-box AES implementation. IACR Cryptology ePrint Archive 2013, 450 (2013). https://eprint.iacr.org/2013/450

18. De Mulder, Y., Wyseur, B., Preneel, B.: Cryptanalysis of a perturbated white-box AES implementation. In: Gong, G., Gupta, K.C. (eds.) INDOCRYPT 2010. LNCS, vol. 6498, pp. 292–310. Springer, Heidelberg (2010). https://doi.org/10.1007/978-3-642-17401-8_21

19. Dusart, P., Letourneux, G., Vivolo, O.: Differential fault analysis on A.E.S. In: Zhou, J., Yung, M., Han, Y. (eds.) ACNS 2003. LNCS, vol. 2846, pp. 293–306. Springer, Heidelberg (2003). https://doi.org/10.1007/978-3-540-45203-4_23

20. Fakub: White-box DPA processing: Scripts for trace acquisition, filtering, processing and displaying results. https://github.com/fakub/White-Box-DPA-Processing. Accessed 1 June 2021

21. Goubin, L., Paillier, P., Rivain, M., Wang, J.: How to reveal the secrets of an obscure white-box implementation. J. Cryptogr. Eng. **10**(1), 49–66 (2019). https://doi.org/10.1007/s13389-019-00207-5

22. Goubin, L., Rivain, M., Wang, J.: Defeating state-of-the-art white-box countermeasures with advanced gray-box attacks. IACR Trans. Cryptogr. Hardware Embedded Syst. **2020**(3), 454–482 (2020). https://doi.org/10.13154/tches.v2020.i3.454-482

23. Karroumi, M.: Protecting white-box AES with dual ciphers. In: Rhee, K.-H., Nyang, D.H. (eds.) ICISC 2010. LNCS, vol. 6829, pp. 278–291. Springer, Heidelberg (2011). https://doi.org/10.1007/978-3-642-24209-0_19

24. Keren, O., Polian, I.: IPM-RED: combining higher-order masking with robust error detection. J. Cryptogr. Eng. **11**(2), 147–160 (2020). https://doi.org/10.1007/s13389-020-00229-4

25. Kocher, P., Jaffe, J., Jun, B.: Differential power analysis. In: Wiener, M. (ed.) CRYPTO 1999. LNCS, vol. 1666, pp. 388–397. Springer, Heidelberg (1999). https://doi.org/10.1007/3-540-48405-1_25

26. Lee, S., Jho, N.S., Kim, M.: Table redundancy method for protecting against fault attacks. IEEE Access **9**, 92214–92223 (2021). https://doi.org/10.1109/ACCESS.2021.3092314

27. Lee, S., Kim, M.: Improvement on a masked white-box cryptographic implementation. IEEE Access **8**, 90992–91004 (2020). https://doi.org/10.1109/ACCESS.2020.2993651

28. Lee, S., Kim, T., Kang, Y.: A masked white-box cryptographic implementation for protecting against differential computation analysis. IEEE Trans. Inf. Forensics Secur. **13**(10), 2602–2615 (2018). https://doi.org/10.1109/TIFS.2018.2825939

29. Muir, J.A.: A tutorial on white-box AES. In: Kranakis, E. (eds.) Advances in Network Analysis and Its Applications. MATHINDUSTRY, vol. 18, pp. 209–229. Springer, Heidelberg (2012). https://doi.org/10.1007/978-3-642-30904-5_9

30. Rivain, M., Wang, J.: Analysis and improvement of differential computation attacks against internally-encoded white-box implementations. IACR Trans. Cryptogr. Hardware Embedded Syst. 225–255 (2019). https://doi.org/10.13154/tches.v2019. i2.225-255

31. Side-Channel-Marvels: Deadpool: Repository of various public white-box cryptographic implementations and their practical attacks. https://github.com/SideChannelMarvels/Deadpool. Accessed 1 June 2021

32. Side-Channel-Marvels: JeanGrey: A tool to perform differential fault analysis attacks (DFA). https://github.com/SideChannelMarvels/JeanGrey. Accessed 1 June 2021

33. Side-Channel-Marvels: Stark: Repository of small utilities related to key recovery. https://github.com/SideChannelMarvels/Stark. Accessed 1 June 2021

34. Teuwen, P., Hubain, C.: Differential fault analysis on white-box AES implementations. https://blog.quarkslab.com/differential-fault-analysis-on-white-box-aes-implementations.html. Accessed 1 June 2021

35. Xiao, Y., Lai, X.: A secure implementation of white-box AES. In: 2009 2nd International Conference on Computer Science and its Applications, pp. 1–6. IEEE (2009). https://doi.org/10.1109/CSA.2009.5404239

36. Zeyad, M., Maghrebi, H., Alessio, D., Batteux, B.: Another look on bucketing attack to defeat white-box implementations. In: Polian, I., Stöttinger, M. (eds.) COSADE 2019. LNCS, vol. 11421, pp. 99–117. Springer, Cham (2019). https://doi.org/10.1007/978-3-030-16350-1_7

Public Key Cryptography

Fully Secure Lattice-Based ABE
from Noisy Linear Functional Encryption

Geng Wang$^{(\boxtimes)}$, Ming Wan, Zhen Liu, and Dawu Gu

School of Electronic Information and Electrical Engineering, Shanghai Jiao Tong
University, Shanghai 100072, People's Republic of China
wanggxx@sjtu.edu.cn

Abstract. Constructing lattice-based fully secure attribute-based
encryption (ABE) has always been a challenging task. Although there
are many selective secure ABE schemes from the hardness of learning
with errors (LWE) problem, it is hard to extend them to fully security,
since the dual system technique in pairing-based cryptography cannot
be applied to lattice-based constructions.

In this paper, we take a different approach: constructing fully secure
ABE from another primitive called noisy linear functional encryption
(NLinFE) which can be constructed from LWE problem. We give a fully
secure ciphertext-policy ABE scheme for CNF formulae which security
relies on the security of NLinFE and hardness of LWE. Since current
constructions for NLinFE only satisfy bounded collusion security, our
resulting scheme is also bounded collusion only, but it can be easily
extended into unbounded security if unbounded NLinFE can be shown
to exist. Also, since existing NLinFE schemes are inefficient, we give a
new construction for NLinFE with better efficiency, hence our ABE construction is more efficient than other existing bounded collusion ABE/FE
schemes.

Keywords: Attribute-based encryption · Noisy linear functional
encryption · LWE · Lattice-based cryptography

1 Introduction

Attribute-based Encryption (ABE for short) was first brought by Sahai and
Waters in 2005 [37]. In an ABE scheme, the decryption is correct only if the
provided attribute set satisfies a certain access policy. By using different types
of access policies, ABE can handle flexible access control matters, without using
complex key distribution techniques. There are mainly two types of ABE, one
is called key-policy ABE (KP-ABE) [25], other is called ciphertext-policy ABE
(CP-ABE) [10]. In KP-ABE, the access policy is embedded in the decryption
key, while the ciphertext is related to a set of attributes; in CP-ABE, the access
policy is embedded in the ciphertext, and attributes are related to the decryption
key, held by the users. In [13], ABE is considered as a special case of a more generalized primitive called functional encryption (FE), which given an encrypted

© Springer Nature Switzerland AG 2021
Y. Yu and M. Yung (Eds.): Inscrypt 2021, LNCS 13007, pp. 421–441, 2021.
https://doi.org/10.1007/978-3-030-88323-2_23

data $Enc(x)$, calculate the function output $f(x)$ of an encrypted message for a certain class of function class $f \in \mathcal{F}$.

Most of these early ABE schemes [10,19,25,33,36,41] are from a weak security model, which is called selective security. In a selective security model, the adversary must first give the challenge policy (for CP-ABE) or challenge attribute set (for KP-ABE) before it was allowed to get the public key and query for secret keys. It is easy to see that the selective security model greatly restricts the ability of the adversary, and cannot handle many types of real world attacks.

Many researchers focus on removing the restriction to get full security for ABE schemes. Many different approaches have been proposed, but the most successful one among them is the dual-system encryption method, given by Waters in 2009 [40]. Although the original method is for IBE and HIBE, which are only simplified versions of ABE, it was soon used to construct fully secure ABE schemes for various access policies, as in [9,18,27–30,42].

The schemes above are constructed in bilinear groups, which suffer from quantum attacks. Recently, many researchers have been working on constructing ABE schemes using lattice assumptions, such as learning with error (LWE) problem [3,4,14]. Lattice-based ABE schemes are not only quantum secure, but also more powerful than schemes in bilinear groups, as they support much richer classes of access policies, even for arbitrary circuits [12,16,23].

However, the existing schemes are only selective secure, except for some recent works [26,38] that can only support a quite weak class of access policies. Since the original dual-system method is highly related to the properties of pairing in bilinear groups, it was not known whether there exists an analogue for dual-system in lattice, which could be used to prove the full security of lattice-based ABE schemes. This question has been raised in many earlier works, and has been considered as a long time open problem in lattice-based cryptography. In this paper, we present a similar method for constructing fully secure lattice-based ABE schemes using noisy linear functional encryption (NLinFE), also give a CP-ABE scheme supporting CNF policies and prove its full security in the standard model.

The security properties of our constructed CP-ABE scheme rely on the security properties of the underlying NLinFE scheme. With bounded collusion public-key NLinFE in [7] (eprint version), and secret-key NLinFE in [1,6], we get both a fully secure bounded collusion CP-ABE and a fully secure secret-key CP-ABE from lattice assumptions. We also give a construction for NLinFE with weaker security which only supports random key queries, but outperforms [7] in the ciphertext size, hence get a bounded collusion CP-ABE which has shorter ciphertexts. If public key unbounded NLinFE can be proven to exist, we can simply construct a fully secure unbounded CP-ABE supporting CNF policies, which beats all current results.

1.1 Related Works

There are currently a few researches working on lattice-based fully secure identity-based encryption (IBE) [2,15,17,43], which can be considered as ABE which access policy is point function. These security proofs rely on various primitives, such as admissible hash or pseudorandom functions. It is not known how these techniques can be used for other access policies. In [23], the authors claimed that using a result from [11], the selective security of the scheme can be extended to full security assuming the subexponential hardness of LWE. Despite the non-standardness of the hardness assumption, it seems that this method cannot be extended into CP-ABE schemes. In [16,24], the authors focused on semi-adaptive security of ABE schemes. Although stronger than selective security, it is still weaker than full security.

In [38], the author gave the first fully secure ABE scheme (other than IBE) from standard LWE assumption using a new primitive called conforming cPRF, which is a huge step forward. However, the access policy is only t-CNF for a constant t, which means that each clause exactly contains t literals. A similar construction is from [26] which supports inner products. These are weaker than our access policy, which is (unrestricted) CNF. The authors claimed that the access policy is only related to the expressibility of the conforming cPRF, however, constructing conforming cPRF supporting various access policies seems to be extremely difficult. Despite the complexity in the conforming cPRF itself, the function needs to be evaluated through key-homomorphic encryption [12], which makes the scheme almost impossible for implementation, while our scheme is more simple and efficient for implementation.

In [39], a fully secure decentralized ABE is constructed from inner product encryption based on LWE assumption [5]. The idea of using NLinFE in our scheme is partly borrowed from the use of (non-approximate) IPE in their work. Their construction is also with bounded collusion. We note that our result highly overlaps with this work. (Using similar techniques, it seems that our scheme can also be made decentralized, but we will not discuss that in this paper.) However, the number of calls to IPE is related to the vector dimension of IPE, hence the number of key queries, while our number of calls to NLinFE is only related to the access policy, which leads to a more efficient scheme.

It seems that fully secure ABE with bounded collusion can also be instantiated by fully secure functional encryption with bounded collusion as in [5,7,21,22]. However, since these constructions are for arbitrary polynomial circuits, their schemes have larger ciphertexts, and are more complex and hard to implement compared with ours.

The Table 1 below compares the ciphertext size between this work and other ABE or FE schemes with bounded collusion, where Q is the number of key queries. We also point out that in [8], the authors introduced a new technique on any bounded collusion schemes, such that the ciphertext size which is polynomial in Q becomes polynomial in the security parameter λ and linear in Q (e.g. the ciphertext size of our construction becomes $O(Q\lambda \log \lambda)$ instead of $O(Q \log Q)$). This does not change the fact that our ciphertext size is smaller than others.

Table 1. Compare with other bounded collusion ABE and FE

	Supporting functions	Ciphertext size	CT Size with [AV19]
GVW12 [22]	P/poly	$O(Q^4)$	$O(Q\lambda^4)$
AR17 [7]	P/poly	$O(Q^2)$	$O(Q\lambda^2)$
WFL19 [39]	0-1 LSSS	$O(Q^2 \log Q)$	$O(Q\lambda^2 \log \lambda)$
This work	CNF	$O(Q \log Q)$	$O(Q\lambda \log \lambda)$

2   Preliminaries

Notations. $x \leftarrow \chi$ for a distribution χ means that x is sampled from χ. $x \leftarrow X$ for a set X means that x is uniformly random chosen from X. For any odd modulus q, $\mathbb{Z}_q$ and the operation mod q takes value from $[-\frac{q-1}{2}, \frac{q-1}{2}]$. We say that ϵ is negligible in λ, if $\epsilon < 1/\Omega(\lambda^c)$ for any $c > 0$ for sufficiently large λ. For two distributions X, Y, let $\Delta(X, Y)$ be the statistical distance between X and Y. $\|.\|$ is the 2-norm, while $\|.\|_\infty$ is the infinity norm.

2.1   Conjunctive Normal Form

Definition 2.1. *Let* $\mathbf{L}$ *be a set of literals (a literal is either* α *or* $\neg\alpha$ *for some variable* α*), and* $T_1, ..., T_k \subseteq \mathbf{L}$ *be a set of* clauses.

A conjunctive normal form (CNF) is a boolean function $f = \bigwedge_{i=1}^k (\bigvee T_i)$*, which inputs a set of literals* $L \subseteq \mathbf{L}$ *(for each variable* α*,* α *and* $\neg\alpha$ *not both in* L*), and outputs the value* $f(L) = \bigwedge_{i=1}^k (\bigvee T_i(L))$*. Here* $\bigvee T_i(L) = 1$ *if and only if* $T_i \cap L \neq \emptyset$*.*

Let $l = |\mathbf{L}|$*, and we label the literals in* $\mathbf{L}$ *by 1 to* l*.*

Note that we do not consider the relationship between α and $\neg\alpha$, and simply let them be two different elements. Such representation does not lower the expressibility of CNF policy. In fact, our definition is stronger than boolean formulas: for an attribute (literal) set L, we allow that both α and $\neg\alpha$ are not in L, which means that we "do not care" the value of α, as in [19].

2.2   Ciphertext-Policy Attribute-Based Encryption

Definition 2.2. *A CP-ABE scheme for CNF formula* f *consists of four algorithms* (Setup, Enc, KeyGen, Dec)*:*

- Setup$(1^\lambda) \rightarrow$ (mpk, msk)*: The setup algorithm gets as input the security parameter* λ*, and outputs the public parameter* mpk*, and the master key* msk*.*
- Enc(mpk, f, m) $\rightarrow$ ct$_f$*: The encryption algorithm gets as input* mpk*, a CNF formula* f*, and a message* $m \in \mathcal{M}$*. It outputs a ciphertext* ct$_f$*. Note that the policy is known if we know the ciphertext.*

- KeyGen(msk, L) → sk$_L$: *The key generation algorithm gets as input* msk *and a set of literals L. It outputs a secret key* sk$_L$.
- Dec(sk$_L$, ct$_f$) → m: *The decryption algorithm gets as input a secret key and a ciphertext, and outputs either* ⊥ *or a message* $m \in \mathcal{M}$.

The CP-ABE scheme is correct if and only if the decryption algorithm returns the correct message when $f(L) = 1$, and returns ⊥ when $f(L) = 0$.

Definition 2.3. *A CP-ABE scheme is fully secure, if for any adversary, the advantage of winning the following CPA-CP-ABE game is negligible:*

Setup. *The challenger runs* **Setup** *and gives the adversary* mpk.

Phase 1. *The adversary submits a set of literals L for a* **KeyGen** *query. These queries can be repeated adaptively.*

Challenge. *The adversary submits two messages m_0 and m_1 of equal length, and a CNF formula f, and $f(L) = 0$ for all previously queried L. The challenger chooses a random bit $b \in \{0, 1\}$, and encrypts m_b under f. The encrypted ciphertext* ct$_f$ *is returned to the adversary.*

Phase 2. *The adversary repeats* **Phase 1** *to get more secret keys. Each queried L must have $f(L) = 0$.*

Guess. *The adversary outputs a guess b' for b.*

The advantage of an adversary $\mathcal{A}$ in the CPA-CP-ABE game is defined by $\mathsf{Adv}_{\mathcal{A}}^{\mathrm{ABE}}(\lambda) = |Pr[b' = b] - 1/2|$.

2.3 Lattice and Smoothing Parameters

Definition 2.4. *Let $\mathbf{b}_1, ..., \mathbf{b}_n$ be a set of vectors in $\mathbb{R}^m$ for $m \geq n$. A lattice Λ is defined as $\{\sum_{i=1}^{n} c_i \mathbf{b}_i : c_1, ..., c_n \in \mathbb{Z}\}$, and $\mathbf{b}_1, ..., \mathbf{b}_n$ is called a basis of Λ.*

Definition 2.5 [34].

Given its center $\mathbf{c} \in \mathbb{Z}^m$, for vector $\mathbf{x} \in \mathbb{Z}^m$, let $\rho_{s,\mathbf{c}}(\mathbf{x}) = \exp(-\pi\|\mathbf{x} - \mathbf{c}\|^2/s^2)$.

For a lattice Λ and $\mathbf{c} \in \mathbb{Z}^m$, the discrete Gaussian distribution $D_{\Lambda,s,\mathbf{c}}$ is defined as:

$$D_{\Lambda,s,\mathbf{c}}(\mathbf{x}) = \frac{\rho_{s,\mathbf{c}}(\mathbf{x})}{\sum_{\mathbf{v} \in \Lambda} \rho_s(\mathbf{v})}.$$

$D_{\Lambda,s,\mathbf{c}}$ *is sometimes also written as $D_{\Lambda+\mathbf{c},s}$, $\Lambda + \mathbf{c}$ is a lattice coset. We also write $\rho_s(\Lambda) = \sum_{\mathbf{v} \in \Lambda} \rho_s(\mathbf{x})$.*

There is an important property for lattice called smoothing parameter, defined as below:

Definition 2.6 [32]. *For any n-dimensional lattice Λ and $\epsilon > 0$, the smoothing parameter $\eta_\epsilon(\Lambda)$ is the smallest s such that $\rho(\Lambda^* - \{0\}) \leq \epsilon$, where $\Lambda^* = \{\mathbf{x} \in \mathbb{R}^n : \forall \mathbf{v} \in \Lambda, \langle \mathbf{x}, \mathbf{v} \rangle \in \mathbb{Z}\}$.*

The following properties for lattice are related to its smoothing parameter, and will be used in our proof.

Lemma 2.1 [20]. *For any n-dimensional lattice Λ, $\epsilon > 0$, and any $\omega(\sqrt{\log n})$ function, there is a negligible $\epsilon(n)$ for which $\eta_\epsilon(\Lambda) \leq \omega(\sqrt{\log n})/\lambda_1^\infty(\Lambda^*)$, $\lambda_1^\infty(\Lambda^*)$ is the length of shortest non-zero vector in Λ^*.*

Lemma 2.2 [20]. *For any n-dimensional lattice Λ, $\mathbf{c} \in \text{span}(\Lambda)$, real $\epsilon \in (0, 1)$, and $s \geq \eta_\epsilon(\Lambda)$, $Pr_{\mathbf{x} \leftarrow D_{\Lambda,s,\mathbf{c}}}[\|\mathbf{x} - \mathbf{c}\| > s\sqrt{n}] \leq \frac{1+\epsilon}{1-\epsilon} \cdot 2^{-n}$.*

Lemma 2.3 [38]. *Let $y \in \mathbb{Z}$, the statistical difference between $D_{\mathbb{Z},\sigma}$ and $D_{\mathbb{Z},\sigma} + y$ is at most $|y|/\sigma$.*

2.4   Lattice Trapdoor and Learning with Error

The following lemma in [20,31] shows that there exists a trapdoor and a preimage sampling algorithm for discrete Gaussian distribution.

Lemma 2.4 [20,31]. *There is an efficient algorithm $\mathsf{TrapSamp}(1^n, 1^m, q)$ that, given $n \geq 1$, $q \geq 2$, $m = \Omega(n \log q)$, outputs $\mathbf{A} \in \mathbb{Z}_q^{n \times m}$ and a "trapdoor" T such that the distribution of $\mathbf{A}$ is $\text{negl}(n)$-close to uniform.*

Moreover, let $\Lambda_\mathbf{u}^\perp(\mathbf{A}) = \{\mathbf{x} : \mathbf{A}\mathbf{x} = \mathbf{u}\}$ (which is a lattice coset). Then there is an efficient randomized algorithm $\mathsf{SamplePre}$ that for any $\mathbf{u} \in \mathbb{Z}_q^n$, $s = \Omega(\sqrt{n \log q})$, $\mathsf{SamplePre}(\mathbf{A}, \mathsf{T}, \mathbf{u}, s)$ outputs a vector $\mathbf{r} \in \mathbb{Z}^m$, which distribution is statistically close to $D_{\Lambda_\mathbf{u}^\perp(\mathbf{A}),s}$ (with negligible distance).

We sometimes omit the parameter s if there is no confusion.

The following lemma is required for our security proof:

Lemma 2.5. *Let $(\mathbf{A}, \mathsf{T}) \leftarrow \mathsf{TrapSamp}(1^n, 1^m, q)$, $(\mathbf{A}', \mathsf{T}') \leftarrow \mathsf{TrapSamp}(1^{n'}, 1^m, q)$, $n' > n$, and we write $\mathbf{A}' = \begin{pmatrix} \bar{\mathbf{A}} \\ \tilde{\mathbf{A}} \end{pmatrix}$, $\bar{\mathbf{A}} \in \mathbb{Z}_q^{n \times m}$, and $\tilde{\mathbf{A}} \in \mathbb{Z}_q^{(n'-n) \times m}$. Then there exists $s > 0$ such that the following two distribution are statistically indistinguishable:*

- $\mathbf{A}, \mathbf{x} \leftarrow \mathsf{SamplePre}(\mathbf{A}, \mathsf{T}, \mathbf{u}, s)$;
- $\bar{\mathbf{A}}, \bar{\mathbf{x}} \leftarrow \mathsf{SamplePre}(\mathbf{A}', \mathsf{T}', \begin{pmatrix} \mathbf{u} \\ \mathbf{b} \end{pmatrix}, s)$, *where $\mathbf{b} \leftarrow \mathbb{Z}_q^{n'-n}$.*

Proof. See Appendix A.   □

Now we introduce our hardness assumption: the (decisional) learning with error (LWE) problem, first introduced in [35]. It has the nice property called worst-case to average-case reduction: solving LWE on the average is as hard as (quantumly) solving GapSVP and SIVP problems in the worst case.

Definition 2.7 (LWE problem) *[35]. For a vector $\mathbf{s} \in \mathbb{Z}_q^n$ called the secret, the LWE distribution $A_{\mathbf{s},\chi}$ over $\mathbb{Z}_q^n \times \mathbb{Z}_q$ is sampled by choosing $\mathbf{a} \leftarrow \mathbb{Z}_q^n$ uniformly at random, choosing $e \leftarrow \chi$, and outputting $(\mathbf{a}, b = \mathbf{s}^T\mathbf{a} + e \bmod q)$.*

The decisional learning with errors (LWE) problem $\mathsf{LWE}_{n,q,\chi,m}$ is that given m independent samples $(\mathbf{a}_i, b_i) \in \mathbb{Z}_q^n \times \mathbb{Z}_q$ where the samples are distributed according to either $A_{\mathbf{s},\chi}$ for a uniformly random $\mathbf{s}$ or the uniform distribution, distinguish which is the case with non-negligible advantage.

For parameters, it is often required that $m = \text{poly}(n)$, $q = O(2^{n^{\epsilon}})$ for some $\epsilon > 0$, and χ is the discrete Gaussian. We say that the distribution χ is β-bounded, if $|\chi| \leq \beta$ with overwhelming probability. We can choose appropriate parameters for χ to be β-bounded given $\beta = \text{poly}(\lambda)$ such that $\mathsf{LWE}_{n,q,\chi,m}$ is hard.

We give a lemma which will be used in our proof:

Lemma 2.6. *For* $\mathbf{s} \leftarrow \mathbb{Z}_q^n$, *let* $\{(\mathbf{a}_i, b_i)\}_{i \in [m]}$ *be sampled from* $A_{\mathbf{s},\chi}$. *Let* $M \subseteq [m]$, *and* $\{(\mathbf{a}_i', b_i')\}_{i \in [m]}$ *be defined as: for* $i \in M$, $(\mathbf{a}_i', b_i') \leftarrow A_{\mathbf{s},\chi}$, *otherwise* $(\mathbf{a}_i', b_i')$ *is uniformly random. Then* $\{(\mathbf{a}_i, b_i)\}_{i \in [m]}$ *and* $\{(\mathbf{a}_i', b_i')\}_{i \in [m]}$ *are indistinguishable assuming the hardness of* $\mathsf{LWE}_{n,q,\chi,m}$.

Proof. Let $\{(\mathbf{a}_i^*, b_i^*)\}_{i \in [m]}$ be a set of m uniformly random samples, then it is indistinguishable with $\{(\mathbf{a}_i, b_i)\}_{i \in [m]}$ from the hardness of $\mathsf{LWE}_{n,q,\chi,m}$. For those $i \in M$, we replace only $(\mathbf{a}_i^*, b_i^*)$ by LWE samples from $A_{\mathbf{s},\chi}$ to get $\{(\mathbf{a}_i', b_i')\}_{i \in [m]}$, and the two are also indistinguishable from the hardness of $\mathsf{LWE}_{n,q,\chi,m}$. $\qquad\square$

Below we also use another assumption called mheLWE [5], which hardness can be reduced to the standard LWE assumption.

Definition 2.8 [5]. *Let* q, m, t *be integers,* σ *be a real and* τ *be a distribution over* $\mathbb{Z}^{t \times m}$, *all of them functions of a parameter* n. *The multi-hint extended-LWE problem* $\mathsf{mheLWE}_{n,q,\sigma,m,t,\tau}$ *is to distinguish between the distributions of the tuples:* $(\mathbf{A}, \mathbf{A} \cdot \mathbf{s} + \mathbf{e}, \mathbf{Z}, \mathbf{Z} \cdot \mathbf{e})$ *and* $(\mathbf{A}, \mathbf{u}, \mathbf{Z}, \mathbf{Z} \cdot \mathbf{e})$, *where* $\mathbf{A} \leftarrow \mathbb{Z}_q^{m \times n}$, $\mathbf{s} \leftarrow \mathbb{Z}_q^n$, $\mathbf{u} \leftarrow \mathbb{Z}_q^m$, $\mathbf{e} \leftarrow D_{\mathbb{Z},\sigma}^m$, *and* $\mathbf{Z} \leftarrow \tau$.

Lemma 2.7 [5]. *Let* $n \geq 100$, $q \geq 2$, $t < n$ *and* m *with* $m = \Omega(n \log n)$ *and* $m \leq n^{O(1)}$. *There exists* $\xi \leq O(n^4 m^2 \log 5/2n)$ *and a distribution* τ *over* $\mathbb{Z}^{t \times m}$ *such that the following statements hold:*

- *There is a reduction from* $\mathsf{LWE}_{n-t,q,\sigma,m}$ *in dimension to* $\mathsf{mheLWE}_{n,q,\sigma\xi,m,t,\tau}$ *that reduces the advantage by at most* $2^{\Omega(t-n)}$;
- *It is possible to sample from* τ *in time polynomial in* n;
- *Each entry of matrix* τ *is an independent discrete Gaussian* $\tau_{i,j} = D_{\mathbb{Z},\sigma_{i,j},c_{i,j}}$ *for some* $c_{i,j} \in \{0,1\}$ *and* $\sigma_{i,j} \geq \Omega(\sqrt{mn \log m})$;
- *All rows from a sample from* τ *have norms* $\leq \xi$ *without a negligible probability.*

3 Noisy Linear Functional Encryption with Bounded Collusion

In this section, we construct an indistinguishability-based secure noisy linear functional encryption scheme with random key queries. Our construction is similar to the inner-product encryption scheme in [5].

Definition 3.1. *An NLinFE scheme consists of the following algorithms:*

- $\mathsf{Setup}(1^\lambda, 1^l)$: *output a pair* (PK, MSK).
- $\mathsf{KeyGen}(MSK, \mathbf{x})$: *for* $\mathbf{x} \in \mathbb{Z}_q^l$, *output a secret key* $sk_{\mathbf{x}}$.

- $\mathsf{Enc}(PK, \mathbf{y})$: *for* $\mathbf{y} \in \mathbb{Z}_q^l$, *output a ciphertext* $ct_{\mathbf{y}}$.
- $\mathsf{Dec}(ct_{\mathbf{y}}, sk_{\mathbf{x}})$: *Output an approximate inner product for* $\mathbf{y}, \mathbf{x}$.

An NLinFE scheme is γ-*correct if for any* $ct_{\mathbf{y}} \leftarrow \mathsf{Enc}(PK, \mathbf{y})$ *and* $sk_{\mathbf{x}} \leftarrow \mathsf{KeyGen}$ $(MSK, \mathbf{x})$, $|\mathsf{Dec}(ct_{\mathbf{y}}, sk_{\mathbf{x}}) - \langle \mathbf{y}, \mathbf{x} \rangle| \mod q \leq \gamma$ *except for a negligible probability.*

Now we give our construction for NLinFE with random keys.

- $\mathsf{Setup}(1^\lambda, 1^l)$: Let τ be a distribution over $\mathbb{Z}^{(l+1) \times m}$ as in the definition of mheLWE. Sample $\mathbf{A} \leftarrow \mathbb{Z}_q^{m \times n}$ and $\mathbf{Z} \leftarrow \tau$ (as defined in Lemma 2.7), compute $\mathbf{U} = \mathbf{Z} \cdot \mathbf{A} \in \mathbb{Z}_q^{(l+1) \times n}$. Let $PK = (\mathbf{A}, \mathbf{U})$ and $MSK = \mathbf{Z}$.
- $\mathsf{KeyGen}(MSK, \mathbf{x})$: Given a vector $\mathbf{x} \in \mathbb{Z}^l$ which is indistinguishable from $D_{\mathbb{Z}^l, \sigma}$, let $\bar{\mathbf{x}} = \binom{\mathbf{x}}{0}$, return the secret key $sk_{\mathbf{x}} = (\mathbf{x}, \mathbf{z}_{\mathbf{x}} := \bar{\mathbf{x}}^T \mathbf{Z} \in \mathbb{Z}^m)$.
- $\mathsf{Enc}(PK, \mathbf{y})$: To encrypt a vector $\mathbf{y} \in \mathbb{Z}_q^l$, let $\bar{\mathbf{y}} = \binom{\mathbf{y}}{\alpha}$, $\alpha \leftarrow \mathbb{Z}_q$. Sample $\mathbf{s} \in \mathbb{Z}_q^n$, $\mathbf{e}_0 \leftarrow D_{\mathbb{Z}, \sigma}^m$, $\mathbf{e}_1 \leftarrow D_{\mathbb{Z}, \sigma'}^{l+1}$, and compute $ct = (\mathbf{c}_0 = \mathbf{A} \cdot \mathbf{s} + \mathbf{e}_0, \mathbf{c}_1 = \mathbf{U} \cdot \mathbf{s} + \mathbf{e}_1 + \bar{\mathbf{y}})$.
- $\mathsf{Dec}(ct, sk_{\mathbf{x}})$: Let $ct = (\mathbf{c}_0, \mathbf{c}_1)$, compute $\mu = \langle \mathbf{x}, \mathbf{c}_1 \rangle - \langle \mathbf{z}_{\mathbf{x}}, \mathbf{c}_0 \rangle$.

Note that we add restrictions on $\mathbf{x}$ in each KeyGen query, such that $\mathbf{x}$ is indistinguishable from a specific distribution: say, $D_{\mathbb{Z}^l, \sigma}$. This limits the usage of our NLinFE scheme. However, it is enough to construct the required ABE scheme.

Correctness. Since $\langle \mathbf{x}, \mathbf{y} \rangle = \langle \bar{\mathbf{x}}, \bar{\mathbf{y}} \rangle$, we see that $(\langle \bar{\mathbf{x}}, \mathbf{c}_1 \rangle - \langle \mathbf{z}_{\mathbf{x}}, \mathbf{c}_0 \rangle) - \langle \mathbf{x}, \mathbf{y} \rangle = \langle \bar{\mathbf{x}}, \mathbf{e}_1 \rangle - \langle \mathbf{z}_{\mathbf{x}}, \mathbf{e}_0 \rangle$. By Lemma 2.2, we have that $\|\bar{\mathbf{x}}\| \leq \sigma\sqrt{l}$, $\|\mathbf{z}_{\mathbf{x}}\| \leq \sigma \max\{\sigma_{i,j}\} l \sqrt{m}$, $\|\mathbf{e}_0\| \leq \sigma\sqrt{m}$, $\|\mathbf{e}_1\| \leq \sigma'\sqrt{l}$. So the scheme is γ-correct for $\gamma \geq \sigma\sigma' l + \sigma^2 \max\{\sigma_{i,j}\} lm$.

We define the fully indistinguishability-based security by the following interactive game:

Definition 3.2. *An NLinFE scheme with random keys is fully* β-*indistinguishability-based secure, if for any adversary, the advantage of winning the following game is negligible:*

*Setup. The challenger runs the **Setup** algorithm and gives the adversary* PK.

Phase 1. The adversary submits a vector $\mathbf{x}$ *for a **KeyGen** query which distribution is indistinguishable from* $D_{\mathbb{Z}^l, \sigma}$. *The challenger answers with a secret key* $sk_{\mathbf{x}}$ *for* $\mathbf{x}$. *These queries can be repeated adaptively.*

Challenge. The adversary chooses two challenge messages $\mathbf{y}_0, \mathbf{y}_1$ *and gives it to the challenger. The challenger first checks whether for all queried* $\mathbf{x}$, *there is* $|\langle \mathbf{x}, \mathbf{y}_0 - \mathbf{y}_1 \rangle| \leq \beta$. *If this does not hold, then the challenger aborts. Otherwise, it chooses a random bit* $b \in \{0, 1\}$, *and returns* $ct_{\mathbf{y}} = \mathsf{Enc}(PK, \mathbf{y}_b)$ *to the adversary.*

Phase 2. The adversary repeats Phase 1, under the restriction that each queried $\mathbf{x}$ *satisfies that* $|\langle \mathbf{x}, \mathbf{y}_0 - \mathbf{y}_1 \rangle| \leq \beta$.

Guess. The adversary outputs a guess b' *for* b, *and the winning advantage is defined as* $|\Pr[b' = b] - 1/2|$.

Theorem 3.1. *For some properly chosen* $\sigma, \tau, \sigma', q, n$, $l < n$ *and* $m = \Theta(n \log q)$, *the NLinFE scheme above is fully indistinguishability-based secure with* k-*bounded collusion for* $k \leq l/3$, *assuming the hardness of* $\mathsf{mheLWE}_{n,q,\sigma,m,l,\tau}$.

Proof. The proof of this theorem is similar to the proof in [5]. We refer the readers to Appendix B.

We see that the number of maximal key queries can be bounded by $l/3$ where l is the vector dimension, hence the vector dimension must grow linearly in Q. We note that in order to successfully decrypt, the modulus q should also grow polynomially in the vector dimension, so it leads to a ciphertext size of $O(Q \log Q)$. This is better than [7] where the modulus q grows exponentially in the vector dimension, which leads to $O(Q^2)$ ciphertext size.

4   Fully Secure CP-ABE Scheme for CNF Policies

4.1   Construction

Let NLinFE be γ-correct and β-indistinguishability-based secure as in Sect. 3. We choose a β-bounded error distribution χ, and $\beta/\gamma = O(2^{-\lambda^\epsilon})$ for some $\epsilon > 0$. The CP-ABE scheme is constructed as follows:

- Setup($1^\lambda, 1^l$): Let l be the maximal number of literals. Sample $l+1$ uniformly random matrixes in $\mathbb{Z}_q^{n \times m}$ along with trapdoor: $(\mathbf{A}_1, \mathbf{T}_1), ..., (\mathbf{A}_l, \mathbf{T}_l), (\mathbf{A}, \mathbf{T})$, and a uniformly random vector $\mathbf{u} \in \mathbb{Z}_q^n$. Run NLinFE.Setup $l+1$ times to generate $(PK_1, MSK_1), ..., (PK_l, MSK_l), (PK, MSK)$. Output $mpk = (\mathbf{A}_1, ..., \mathbf{A}_l, \mathbf{A}, \mathbf{u}, PK_1, ..., PK_l, PK)$, and $msk = (\mathbf{T}_1, ..., \mathbf{T}_l, \mathbf{T}, MSK_1, ..., MSK_l, MSK)$.
- KeyGen(msk, L): Randomly choose $\mathbf{a} \in \mathbb{Z}_q^n$. Sample $\mathbf{x} \in \mathbb{Z}^m$ such that $\mathbf{A}\mathbf{x} = \mathbf{a} + \mathbf{u}$, and use NLinFE.KeyGen($MSK, \mathbf{x}$) to generate an NLinFE secret key K. For each literal $i \in L$, sample $\mathbf{x}_i \in \mathbb{Z}^m$ such that $\mathbf{A}_i \mathbf{x}_i = \mathbf{a}$, and use NLinFE.KeyGen($MSK_i, \mathbf{x}_i$) to generate an NLinFE secret key K_i. Return the secret key $K, \{K_i\}_{i \in L}$.
- Enc(mpk, f, μ): Let $T_1, ..., T_k$ be clauses in f. Generate uniform $\mathbf{s}_1, ..., \mathbf{s}_k \in \mathbb{Z}_q^n$. For each $j \in T_i$, let $C_{i,j} = $ NLinFE.Enc($PK_j, \mathbf{s}_i^T \mathbf{A}_j$). Let $C = $ NLinFE.Enc $(PK, (\sum_{i=1}^k \mathbf{s}_i)^T \mathbf{A})$, and $C' = (\sum_{i=1}^k \mathbf{s}_i)^T \mathbf{u} + \mu \lfloor q/2 \rfloor + \bar{e}, \bar{e} \leftarrow \chi$. Return the ciphertext $(\{C_{i,j}\}_{i \in [k], j \in T_i}, C, C')$.
- Dec(ct_f, sk_L): First check if L satisfy the policy f. If $f(L) = 1$, then for each $i \in [k]$, there is at least one literal $l_i \in L \cap T_i$, let $d_i = $ NLinFE.Dec(K_{l_i}, C_{i,l_i}). Let $d = $ NLinFE.Dec(K, C). Calculate $(\sum_{i=1}^k d_i) - d + C'$, if the value is close to 0, return 0; if the value is close to $q/2$, return 1.

Theorem 4.1. *Let $q > 4(l+1)\gamma + 4\beta$, and NLinFE is γ-correct. Then the CP-ABE scheme above is correct.*

Proof. First, by the correctness of NLinFE, for $j \in L \cap T_i$, $d_i = \mathbf{s}_i^T \mathbf{A}_j \mathbf{x}_i + e_i = \mathbf{s}_i^T \mathbf{a} + e_j, |e_j| \leq \gamma$. Also, $d = (\sum_{i=1}^k \mathbf{s}_i)^T \mathbf{A}\mathbf{x} + e = (\sum_{i=1}^k \mathbf{s}_i)^T (\mathbf{a} + \mathbf{u}) + e, |e| \leq \gamma$.

So $(\sum_{i=1}^k d_i) - d + C' = \mu \lfloor q/2 \rfloor + \sum_{i=1}^k e_i - e + \bar{e}$, which is $(l+1)\gamma + \beta$-close to 0 or $\lfloor q/2 \rfloor$. Since $(l+1)\gamma + \beta < q/4$, we can get the correct message. $\square$

Now we give the security result of the scheme above.

Theorem 4.2. *The construction above is fully secure under bounded collusion, assuming the existence of an indistinguishability-based secure NLinFE scheme with bounded collusion and the hardness of LWE problem.*

We combine Theorem 4.2, Theorem 3.1 and Lemma 2.7, and immediately get the following result:

Corollary 4.3. *The construction above is fully secure under bounded collusion, assuming the hardness of LWE problem.*

4.2 Hyper-functional Keys and Semi-functional Ciphertexts

Now we are ready to prove Theorem 4.2. But before we start the security proof, we first define hyper-functional secret keys and semi-functional ciphertexts.

Hyper-functional Key. For a hyper-functional key, we not only change the key generation algorithm, but also the setup algorithm. In Setup, instead of generating $\mathbf{A}$ along with its trapdoor, we generate $\mathbf{A}' \in \mathbb{Z}_q^{(n+1)\times m}$ along with its trapdoor $\mathbf{T}'$. We write the first n rows of $\mathbf{A}'$ as $\mathbf{A}$, and the last row as $\tilde{\mathbf{a}}^T$, which means that $\mathbf{A}' = \left(\begin{smallmatrix}\mathbf{A}\\\tilde{\mathbf{a}}^T\end{smallmatrix}\right)$. $\mathbf{A}$ is included in the public key as normal. We also generate $\mathbf{t} \leftarrow \mathbb{Z}_q^n$.

For KeyGen queries, we first sample $e', e \leftarrow \chi$. Let $\mathbf{x} \leftarrow \mathsf{SamplePre}(\mathbf{A}', \mathbf{T}', \left(\begin{smallmatrix}\mathbf{a}+\mathbf{u}\\\mathbf{t}^T(\mathbf{a}+\mathbf{u})+e'+\bar{e}+e\end{smallmatrix}\right))$. Then we have $(\tilde{\mathbf{a}}^T - \mathbf{t}^T\mathbf{A})\mathbf{x} = e' + \bar{e} + e \approx 0$. Let $K \leftarrow \mathsf{NLinFE.KeyGen}(MSK, \mathbf{x})$ and other key elements generated the same as normal. We say that the secret key is hyper-functional related to $\tilde{\mathbf{a}}^T - \mathbf{t}^T\mathbf{A}$.

Note that we also say that a the secret key is "normal", if $\mathbf{x} \leftarrow \mathsf{SamplePre}(\mathbf{A}', \mathbf{T}', \left(\begin{smallmatrix}\mathbf{a}+\mathbf{u}\\b\end{smallmatrix}\right))$ for $b \leftarrow \mathbb{Z}_q$.

For the indistinguishability between hyper-functional and normal keys, we have the following lemma:

Lemma 4.4. *Let $(\mathbf{A}_0, \mathbf{T}_0) \leftarrow \mathsf{TrapSamp}(1^n, 1^m, q)$. For $i \in [Q]$ and $\mathbf{a}^i \leftarrow \mathbb{Z}_q^n$, $\mathbf{x}_0^i = \mathsf{SamplePre}(\mathbf{A}_0, \mathbf{T}_0, \mathbf{a}^i)$. Let $(\mathbf{A}', \mathbf{T}') \leftarrow \mathsf{TrapSamp}(1^{n+1}, 1^m, q)$, $\mathbf{x}_1^i = \mathsf{Sample Pre}(\mathbf{A}', \mathbf{T}', \left(\begin{smallmatrix}\mathbf{a}^i\\a'^i+e^i\end{smallmatrix}\right))$, where $\mathbf{A}' = \left(\begin{smallmatrix}\mathbf{A}_1\\\tilde{\mathbf{a}}\end{smallmatrix}\right)$, $e^i \leftarrow \chi$, $a'^i \in \mathbb{Z}_q$. Then $(\mathbf{A}_0, \{\mathbf{x}_0^i\}_{i\in[Q]})$ is computationally indistinguishable from $(\mathbf{A}_1, \{\mathbf{x}_1^i\}_{i\in[Q]})$ assuming the hardness of LWE.*

Proof. We prove the lemma by showing the following distributions are pairwise indistinguishable (either statistical or computational).

- (1) Let $(\mathbf{A}'', \mathbf{T}'') \leftarrow \mathsf{TrapSamp}(1^{2n+1}, 1^m, q)$, $\mathbf{A}''^T = (\mathbf{A}_2^T|\bar{\mathbf{A}}^T|\bar{\mathbf{a}}^T)$. Let $\mathbf{x}_2^i = \mathsf{SamplePre}(\mathbf{A}'', \mathbf{T}'', (\mathbf{a}^{i^T}|\bar{\mathbf{b}}^{i^T}|\bar{b}^i)^T)$, where $\bar{\mathbf{b}}^i \leftarrow \mathbb{Z}_q^n$ and $\bar{b}^i \leftarrow \mathbb{Z}_q$. By Lemma 2.5, $(\mathbf{A}_0, \{\mathbf{x}_0^i\}_{i\in[Q]})$ is statistically indistinguishable from $(\mathbf{A}_2, \{\mathbf{x}_2^i\}_{i\in[Q]})$.

- (2) We first choose $\tilde{b}^i \leftarrow \mathbb{Z}_q^n$ and write $\bar{b}^i = \tilde{b}^i + a'^i$. This does not change the distribution.
- (3) We first choose $\mathbf{s} \leftarrow \mathbb{Z}_q^n$, let $\bar{b}'^i = \mathbf{s}^T \bar{b}^i + e^i + a'^i$, and let $\mathbf{x}_2'^i = \mathsf{SamplePre}(\mathbf{A}'', \mathbf{T}'', (\mathbf{a}^{i^T}|\bar{\mathbf{b}}^{i^T}|\bar{b}'^i)^T)$. By the hardness of LWE problem, any adversary cannot distinguish between $\bar{b}^i, \tilde{b}^i$ and $\bar{b}^i, \mathbf{s}^T \bar{b}^i + e^i$, hence cannot distinguish between $\mathbf{x}_2^i$ and $\mathbf{x}_2'^i$.
- (4) Let $\tilde{\mathbf{a}} = \bar{\mathbf{a}} - \bar{\mathbf{A}}^T \mathbf{s}$, and we have $\tilde{\mathbf{a}}^T \mathbf{x}_2'^i = a'^i + e^i$.
- (5) This time we write $\mathbf{A}''^T = (\mathbf{A}_2^T|\bar{\mathbf{A}}^T|\tilde{\mathbf{a}}^T)$, and set $\mathbf{x}_2''^i = \mathsf{SamplePre}(\mathbf{A}'', \mathbf{T}'', (\mathbf{a}^{i^T}|\bar{\mathbf{b}}^{i^T}|a'^i + e^i)^T)$. Then $\mathbf{x}_2'^i$ and $\mathbf{x}_2''^i$ are from the same distribution.
- (6) By Lemma 2.5, $(\mathbf{A}_2, \{\mathbf{x}_2''^i\}_{i \in [Q]})$ is statistically indistinguishable from $(\mathbf{A}_1, \{\mathbf{x}_1^i\}_{i \in [Q]})$.

$\square$

Semi-functional Ciphertext. A ciphertext is semi-functional, if the ciphertext element C is $\mathsf{NLinFE.Enc}(PK, (\sum_{i=1}^k \mathbf{s}_i - \mathbf{t})^T \mathbf{A} + \tilde{\mathbf{a}})$ instead of $\mathsf{NLinFE.Enc}(PK, (\sum_{i=1}^k \mathbf{s}_i)^T \mathbf{A})$.

It follows directly from the indistinguishable security of NLinFE that a semi-functional ciphertext element is indistinguishable from a normal one if all secret keys are hyper-functional.

Along with hyper-functional keys and semi-functional ciphertexts, we also define temporary hyper-functional keys and i-temporary semi-functional ciphertexts, which will be used in our security proof. We note that in our definition, "hyper-functional" and "temporary hyper-functional" form two independent dimensions: a temporary hyper-functional key can be either normal or hyper-functional.

Temporary Hyper-functional Key. Let l be the number of literals. Like the definition of hyper-functional keys, we not only change the key generation algorithm, but also the setup algorithm. In Setup, instead of generating $\mathbf{A}_j$, $j \in [l]$ along with its trapdoor, we generate $\mathbf{A}_j' \in \mathbb{Z}_q^{(n+1) \times m}$ along with its trapdoor $\mathbf{T}_j'$. We write the first n rows of $\mathbf{A}_j'$ as $\mathbf{A}_j$, and the last row as $\tilde{\mathbf{a}}_j^T$, which means that $\mathbf{A}_j' = \begin{pmatrix} \mathbf{A}_j \\ \tilde{\mathbf{a}}_j^T \end{pmatrix}$. $\mathbf{A}_j$ is included in the public key as normal.

For KeyGen queries, let L be the queried literal set. For $j \in L$, let $\mathbf{x}_j \leftarrow \mathsf{SamplePre}(\mathbf{A}_j', \mathbf{T}_j', (\begin{smallmatrix} \mathbf{a} \\ \mathbf{t}^T \mathbf{a} + e' + e_j \end{smallmatrix}))$, where $e_j \leftarrow \chi$, and if the key is normal, we sample $e' \leftarrow \chi$, if the key is hyper-functional, we use the same e' as in the generation of $\mathbf{x}$. Then we have $(\tilde{\mathbf{a}}_j^T - \mathbf{t}^T \mathbf{A}_j)\mathbf{x}_j = e' + e_j \approx 0$. Let $K_j \leftarrow \mathsf{NLinFE.KeyGen}(MSK_j, \mathbf{x}_j)$. We say that the secret key is temporary hyper-functional related to $\{\tilde{\mathbf{a}}_j^T - \mathbf{t}^T \mathbf{A}_j\}_{j \in S}$.

We can also use Lemma 4.4 to prove the indistinguishability between normal/hyper-functional keys and temporary hyper-functional keys.

i-Temporary Semi-functional Ciphertext. A ciphertext is i-temporary semi-functional, if each ciphertext element $C_{i,j}$ is $\mathsf{NLinFE.Enc}(PK_j, (\mathbf{s}_i - \mathbf{t})^T \mathbf{A}_j + \tilde{\mathbf{a}}_j)$ instead of $\mathsf{NLinFE.Enc}(PK_j, \mathbf{s}_i^T \mathbf{A}_j)$.

It follows directly from the indistinguishability-based security of NLinFE that a temporary semi-functional ciphertext element is indistinguishable from a semi-functional one if all secret keys but those $sk_L, L \cap T_i = \emptyset$ are temporary hyper-functional.

4.3   Security Proof

We first give the outline of our proof.

- Switch all queried secret keys into hyper-functional keys.
- Switch the challenge ciphertext into semi-functional ciphertext.
- For the p-th query in Phase 1 which challenge literal set is L:
    - Switch all secret keys into temporary hyper-functional secret keys.
    - Switch the ciphertext into i-temporary semi-functional ciphertext such that $L \cap T_i = \emptyset$.
    - Switch the p-th secret key into a normal one using LWE assumption.
    - Switch the ciphertext into a non-temporary semi-functional ciphertext.
    - Switch all secret keys into non-temporary normal or hyper-functional secret keys.
- For queries in Phase 2, and $i \in [k]$, k is the maximal number of clauses:
    - Switch all secret keys into temporary hyper-functional secret keys.
    - Switch the ciphertext into i-temporary semi-functional ciphertext.
    - Switch all Phase 2 secret keys such that $L \cap T_i = \emptyset$ into a normal one using LWE assumption.
    - Switch the ciphertext into a non-temporary semi-functional ciphertext.
    - Switch all secret keys into non-temporary normal or hyper-functional secret keys.
- Now C is uniformly random, independent with any queried secret keys. We further switch C' into a uniformly random element, and thus have our result.

Now we define the game sequence.

Game 0 is the original game.

Game 1: Each queried secret key is a hyper-functional key. **Game 0** and **Game 1** are indistinguishable by Lemma 4.4.

Game 2: The challenge ciphertext is semi-functional. We first define **Game 1a** and **Game 2a** as follows:

- The Setup phase and Phase 1 are the same as Game 1 or Game 2.
- Let Q_2 be the maximal number of Phase 2 queries. In the Challenge phase, before the challenge ciphertext is given, for each $r \in [Q_2]$, we generate $\mathbf{a}^r \leftarrow \mathbb{Z}_q^n$, $e'^r, e^r \leftarrow \chi$, and $\mathbf{x}^r \leftarrow \mathsf{SamplePre}(\mathbf{A}', \mathbf{T}', \left(_{\mathbf{t}^T(\mathbf{a}^r+\mathbf{u})+e'^r+\bar{e}+e^r}^{\mathbf{a}^r+\mathbf{u}}\right))$. Let $K^r = \mathsf{NLinFE.KeyGen}(MSK, \mathbf{x}^r)$.

- In Game 1a, the challenger returns a normal ciphertext, and in Game 2a, it returns a semi-functional one.
- In the r-th Phase 2 query, we let $e' = e'^r$, $e = e^r$, $\mathbf{a} = \mathbf{a}^r$, and the key element $K = K^r$. Other key elements are generated as before.

It is easy to see that **Game 1** and **Game 1a**; **Game 2** and **Game 2a** are the same from the adversary's point of view. We now show that **Game 1a** and **Game 2a** are indistinguishable.

For the challenger, instead of generating all Ks and C itself, it now runs a indistinguishable game for NLinFE, get K by the KeyGen query of NLinFE, and get C as the challenge ciphertext of NLinFE. Because $|(\tilde{\mathbf{a}}^T - \mathbf{t}^T\mathbf{A})\mathbf{x}| \leq 3\beta$ and $\beta/\gamma = O(2^{-\lambda^\epsilon})$, we have the indistinguishable result by Theorem 3.1.

Game 2(p), $p \in [Q_1 + 1]$, Q_1 is the number of phase 1 queries: The first $p - 1$ Phase 1 keys are normal, and the rest of the keys are hyper-functional; the challenge ciphertext is semi-functional. Then **Game 2(1)** is **Game 2**, and in **Game 2($Q_1 + 1$)**, all Phase 1 keys are normal. We prove the following result:

Lemma 4.5. *Game 2(p) and Game 2(p + 1) are indistinguishable assuming the security of NLinFE and the hardness of LWE.*

Proof. We prove this by the following game sequence:

Game 2-1(p): **Game 2-1(p)** is same as **Game 2(p)**, except that we change all keys into temporary hyper-functional keys. **Game 2-1(p)** is indistinguishable from **Game 2(p)** according to Lemma 4.4.

Let L be the challenge literal set in the p-th query of Phase 1. So there must be clause T_i such that $L \cap T_i = \emptyset$. This i will be used in the following games.

Game 2-2(p, j): **Game 2-2(p, j)** is same as **Game 2-1(p)**, except that for any $C_{i,j'}$ such that $j' \leq j$ and $j' \in T_i$, $C_{i,j'}$ is generated as $\mathsf{NLinFE.Enc}(PK_{j'}, (\mathbf{s}_i - \mathbf{t})^T\mathbf{A}_{j'} + \tilde{\mathbf{a}}_{j'}^T)$. So **Game 2-2(p, 0)** is **Game 2-1(p)**, and in **Game 2-2(p, l)**, the ciphertext is i-temporary semi-functional. We now show that **Game 2-2(p, j − 1)** is indistinguishable from Game 2-2(p, j).

We define **Game 2-2a(p, j)** and **Game 2-2b(p, j)** as follows:

Game 2-2a(p, j): The game is the same as **Game 2-2(p, j)**, except that:

- In the Challenge phase, before the challenge ciphertext is given, we first check whether $j + 1 \in T_i$. If $j + 1 \notin T_i$, the game proceeds as **Game 2-2(p, j)**. If $j + 1 \in T_i$, for each $r \in [Q_2]$, we generate $\mathbf{a}^r \leftarrow \mathbb{Z}_q^n$, $e'^r, e_{j+1}^r \leftarrow \chi$, and $\mathbf{x}_{j+1}^r \leftarrow \mathsf{SamplePre}(\mathbf{A}_{j+1}', \mathbf{T}_{j+1}', (\mathbf{t}^T\mathbf{a}^r + e'^r + e_{j+1}^r))$. Let $K_{j+1}^r = \mathsf{NLinFE.KeyGen}(MSK_{j+1}, \mathbf{x}_{j+1}^r)$.
- In the r-th Phase 2 query, if $j + 1 \in T_i$, we let $e' = e'^r$, $e_{j+1} = e_{j+1}^r$, $\mathbf{a} = \mathbf{a}^r$, and the key element $K_{j+1} = K_{j+1}^r$. Then, generate other key elements as in **Game 2-2(p, j)**.

Game 2-2b(p, j): The game is the same as **Game 2-2(p, j)**, except that:

- In the Challenge phase, before the challenge ciphertext is given, we first check whether $j \in T_i$. If $j \notin T_i$, the game proceeds as **Game 2-2(p,j)**. If $j \in T_i$, for each $r \in [Q_2]$, we generate $\mathbf{a}^r \leftarrow \mathbb{Z}_q^n$, $e'^r, e_j^r \leftarrow \chi$, and $\mathbf{x}_j^r \leftarrow$ SamplePre$(\mathbf{A}_j', \mathbf{T}_j', \binom{\mathbf{a}^r}{\mathbf{t}^T \mathbf{a}^r + e'^r + e_j^r})$. Let $K_j^r =$ NLinFE.KeyGen$(MSK_j, \mathbf{x}_j^r)$.

- In the r-th Phase 2 query, if $j \in T_i$, we let $e' = e'^r$, $e_j = e_j^r$, $\mathbf{a} = \mathbf{a}^r$, and the key element $K_j = K_j^r$. Then, generate other key elements as in **Game 2-2(p,j)**.

It is easy to see that **Game 2-2(p,j)**, **Game 2-2a(p,j)** and **Game 2-2b(p,j)** are the same from the adversary's point of view. We now show that **Game 2-2a(p, j − 1)** and **Game 2-2b(p,j)** are indistinguishable.

For the challenger, instead of generating all K_js and $C_{i,j}$ itself, it now runs a indistinguishable game for NLinFE, get K_j by the KeyGen query of NLinFE, and get $C_{i,j}$ as the challenge ciphertext of NLinFE. Since $|(\tilde{\mathbf{a}}_j^T - \mathbf{t}^T \mathbf{A}_j)\mathbf{x}_j| \leq 2\beta$ and $\beta/\gamma = O(2^{-\lambda^\epsilon})$ by assumption, we only need to show that the NLinFE game can proceed correctly. If $j \in T_i$, all KeyGen queries are made before the challenge ciphertext, which is legal in the NLinFE game. If $j \notin T_i$, the NLinFE challenge ciphertext is never required, so all KeyGen queries can be made correctly. Thus we have the indistinguishable result by Theorem 3.1.

Thus we have that **Game 2-1(p)** is indistinguishable from **Game 2-2(p,l)**.

Game 2-3(p): The game is the same as **Game 2-2(p,l)**, except that:

- In the challenge phase, we generate $\bar{\mathbf{s}} \leftarrow \mathbb{Z}_q^n$, $\{\mathbf{s}_{i'}\}_{i' \neq i} \leftarrow \mathbb{Z}_q^n$, and write $C_{i,j}$ for any $j \in T_i$ as NLinFE.Enc$(PK_j, (\bar{\mathbf{s}} - \sum_{i' \neq i} \mathbf{s}_{i'})^T \mathbf{A}_j + \tilde{\mathbf{a}}_j)$.
- We also write $C =$ NLinFE.Enc$(PK, \bar{\mathbf{s}}^T \mathbf{A} + \tilde{\mathbf{a}}^T)$, and $C' = (\bar{\mathbf{s}} + \mathbf{t})^T \mathbf{u} + \mu \lfloor q/2 \rfloor + \bar{e}$.

Note that in **Game 2-3(p)**, we implicitly set $\mathbf{s}_i = \bar{\mathbf{s}} + \mathbf{t} - \sum_{i' \neq i} \mathbf{s}_{i'}$, so that for the adversary, **Game 2-3(p)** is the same as **Game 2-2(p,l)**. Now we see that $\mathbf{t}$ only occurs in C' and in KeyGen queries. All these occurrences of $\mathbf{t}$ take the form of LWE samples: $\mathbf{t}^T \mathbf{a} + e'$, and $\mathbf{t}^T \mathbf{u} + \bar{e}$.

Game 2-4(p): For the p-th query, we choose a uniformly random $\tilde{b} \leftarrow \mathbb{Z}_q$, and $\mathbf{x} \leftarrow$ SamplePre$(\mathbf{A}', \mathbf{T}', \binom{\mathbf{a}}{\tilde{b} + \mathbf{t}^T \mathbf{u} + \bar{e} + e})$. For $i \in [l]$, $\mathbf{x}_i \leftarrow$ SamplePre$(\mathbf{A}_i', \mathbf{T}_i', \binom{\mathbf{a}}{\tilde{b} + e_i})$.

Game 2-3(p) and **Game 2-4(p)** are indistinguishable using Lemma 2.6, by the hardness of LWE problem. We also define **Game 2-4a(p)**, which removes $\bar{\mathbf{s}}$, and $\mathbf{s}_i$ is uniformly sampled in the challenge phase. **Game 2-4a(p)** is the same as **Game 2-4(p)** from the adversary's point of view.

Game 2-5(p,j): **Game 2-5(p,j)** is same as **Game 2-4a(p)**, except that for any $C_{i,j'}$ such that $j' \leq j$ and $j' \in T_i$, $C_{i,j'}$ is generated as NLinFE.Enc$(PK_{j'}, \mathbf{s}_i^T \mathbf{A}_{j'})$. So **Game 2-5(p,0)** is **Game 2-4a(p)**, and in **Game 2-5(p,l)**, the ciphertext is (non-temporary) semi-functional.

The indistinguishability between **Game 2-5(p, j − 1)** and **Game 2-5(p,j)** is nearly the same as **Game 2-2(p, j − 1)** and **Game 2-2(p,j)**, except that this time, for the p-th query with literal set L, $|(\tilde{\mathbf{a}}_j^T - \mathbf{t}^T \mathbf{A}_j)\mathbf{x}_j|$ may not be small. However, since $L \cap T_i = \emptyset$, for each $j \in T_i$ where it is required to generate the ciphertext element $C_{i,j}$, the corresponding key element $\mathbf{x}_j$ does not occur. So the ciphertext can be generated correctly in the reduction. Now we have that **Game 2-4a(p)** is indistinguishable from **Game 2-5(p,l)**.

Game 2-6(p): **Game 2-6(p)** is same as **Game 2-5(p,l)** except that in the p-th KeyGen query, instead of generating random $\tilde{b}$, we sample $b \leftarrow \mathbb{Z}_q$, and set $\tilde{b} = b - \mathbf{t}^T \mathbf{u} - \bar{e} - e$. **Game 2-6($p$)** is same as **Game 2-5(p,l)** from the adversary's point of view. We can see that **Game 2-6(p)** is indistinguishable from **Game 2($p+1$)** from Lemma 4.4. $\qquad\qquad\Box$

Game 3(i), $i \in [k+1]$, k is the number of clauses in the challenge access policy: The Phase 1 keys are normal, and for the Phase 2 keys which challenge literal set is L, the key is normal iff there exists $i' < i$ such that $L \cap T_{i'} = \emptyset$. Game 3(1) is the same as Game 2($Q_1 + 1$). Since L must not satisfy the access policy, it is easy to see that in **Game 3($k+1$)**, all keys are normal.

Lemma 4.6. *Game 3(i) and Game 3(i + 1) are indistinguishable assuming the security of NLinFE and the hardness of LWE.*

Proof. The proof is essentially the same as Lemma 4.5. We omit the details here. $\qquad\qquad\Box$

Game 4: **Game 4** is same as **Game 3($k+1$)**, except that all secret keys are temporary hyper-functional keys. **Game 4** is indistinguishable from **Game 3($k+1$)** by Lemma 4.4.

Game 5: **Game 5** is same as **Game 4**, except that the challenge ciphertext is 1-temporary semi-functional. Using similar discussion from **Game 2-2(p,j)** in Lemma 4.5, we have that **Game 4** and **Game 5** are indistinguishable by Theorem 3.1.

Game 6: The game is the same as **Game 5**, except that:

- In the challenge phase, we generate $\bar{\mathbf{s}} \leftarrow \mathbb{Z}_q^n$, $\{\mathbf{s}_{i'}\}_{i' \neq 1} \leftarrow \mathbb{Z}_q^n$, and write $C_{1,j}$ for any $j \in T_1$ as $\mathsf{NLinFE.Enc}(PK_j, (\bar{\mathbf{s}} - \sum_{i' \neq 1} \mathbf{s}_{i'})^T \mathbf{A}_j + \tilde{\mathbf{a}}_j)$.
- We also write $C = \mathsf{NLinFE.Enc}(PK, \bar{\mathbf{s}}^T \mathbf{A} + \tilde{\mathbf{a}}^T)$, and $C' = (\bar{\mathbf{s}} + \mathbf{t})^T \mathbf{u} + \mu\lfloor q/2 \rfloor + \bar{e}$.

Game 6 is the same as **Game 5** from the adversary's point of view. Note that this time, $\mathbf{t}^T \mathbf{u}$ only occurs in C'.

Game 7: The game is the same as **Game 6**, except that in the challenge phase, C' is generated by $\bar{\mathbf{s}}^T \mathbf{u} + v + \mu\lfloor q/2 \rfloor$, $v \leftarrow \mathbb{Z}_q$. **Game 7** is indistinguishable from **Game 6** by Lemma 2.6 from LWE assumption.

Game 8: The game is the same as **Game 7**, except that in the challenge phase, we let $v' \leftarrow \mathbb{Z}_q$, and $v = v' - \bar{\mathbf{s}}^T \mathbf{u} - \mu\lfloor q/2 \rfloor$, so $C' = v'$. **Game 7** and **Game 8** are the same from the adversary's point of view. Then in **Game 8**, the ciphertext contains no information on μ, so the advantage for any adversary is $1/2$. Thus we finish our proof.

5   Conclusion and Future Works

In this paper, we give a construction for lattice-based fully secure ABE schemes from noisy linear functional encryption, which can be considered as a lattice version of the widely used dual-system method from pairing-based cryptography. Our scheme supports CNF formula as its access policy, and any predetermined number of key queries. Compared with other methods for constructing bounded collusion fully secure ABE, our scheme is simpler and has smaller ciphertext size. Since dual-system encryption has shown to be useful in pairing-based cryptography, we hope that we can also extend our scheme for richer functionalities.

Although our scheme supports only bounded collusion, it is easy to see that it can be extended into unbounded case if there exists an unbounded NLinFE scheme. Although in [1], a secret key version of unbounded NLinFE has been introduced, it is currently unknown how to transform it into a public key scheme. This shall be our future work.

Acknowledgements. This work is partially supported by the National Natural Science Foundation of China (No. 62072305, No. 61672339), the National Cryptography Development Fund (No. MMJJ20170111), and the Foundation of Science and Technology on Information Assurance Laboratory (No. KJ-17-109).

A   Proof of Lemma 2.5

We first give the following lemma which is proven in [20,32].

Lemma A.1 [20].
    For any $\epsilon \in (0,1)$, there exists $\eta > 0$, such that for $s \geq \eta$, $\rho_s(\Lambda_{\mathbf{u}}^{\perp}(\mathbf{A})) \in [\frac{1-\epsilon}{1+\epsilon}, 1] \cdot \rho_s(\Lambda_{\mathbf{0}}^{\perp}(\mathbf{A}))$.

By Lemma 2.1, we have that the distribution of $\mathbf{x}$ is statistically close to $D_{\Lambda_{\mathbf{u}}^{\perp}(\mathbf{A}),s}$. So we only need to show that the distribution of $\mathbf{x}'$ is statistically close to $D_{\Lambda_{\mathbf{u}}^{\perp}(\mathbf{A}'),s}$.

It is easy to see that $\{\Lambda_{(\mathbf{u}^T|\mathbf{b}^T)^T}^{\perp}(\mathbf{A}')\}_{\mathbf{b} \in \mathbb{Z}_q^{n'-n}}$ forms a partition of the lattice co-set $\Lambda_{\mathbf{u}}^{\perp}(\bar{\mathbf{A}})$. So by the definition of discrete Gaussian, we have that, for any $\mathbf{c} \in \Lambda_{\mathbf{u}}^{\perp}(\mathbf{A}')$, let $\mathbf{b} = \tilde{\mathbf{A}}\mathbf{c}$, we have $Pr(\mathbf{x} = \mathbf{c}) = q^{-(n'-n)}\rho_s(\mathbf{c})/\rho_s(\Lambda_{(\mathbf{u}^T|\mathbf{b}^T)^T}^{\perp}(\mathbf{A}'))$. For a negligible ϵ, we choose s satisfies Lemma A.1. Then we have that for any $\mathbf{b}'$, $\rho_s(\Lambda_{(\mathbf{u}^T|\mathbf{b}^T)^T}^{\perp}(\mathbf{A}'))/\rho_s(\Lambda_{(\mathbf{u}^T|\mathbf{b}'^T)^T}^{\perp}(\mathbf{A}')) \in [\frac{1-\epsilon}{1+\epsilon}, \frac{1+\epsilon}{1-\epsilon}]$.

By definition, we have:

$$D_{\Lambda_{\mathbf{u}}^{\perp}(\mathbf{A}'),s}(\mathbf{c}) = \frac{\rho_s(\mathbf{c})}{\rho_s(\Lambda_{\mathbf{u}}^{\perp}(\bar{\mathbf{A}}))} = \frac{\rho_s(\mathbf{c})}{\sum_{\mathbf{b}'^T \in \mathbb{Z}_q^{n'-n}} \rho_s(\Lambda_{(\mathbf{u}^T|\mathbf{b}^T)^T}^{\perp}(\mathbf{A}'))}.$$

So:

$$\frac{1-\epsilon}{1+\epsilon} \cdot \frac{\rho_s(\mathbf{c})}{q^{n'-n}\rho_s(\Lambda_{(\mathbf{u}^T|\mathbf{b}^T)^T}^{\perp}(\mathbf{A}'))} \leq D_{\Lambda_{\mathbf{u}}^{\perp}(\mathbf{A}'),s}(\mathbf{c}) \leq \frac{1+\epsilon}{1-\epsilon} \cdot \frac{\rho_s(\mathbf{c})}{q^{n'-n}\rho_s(\Lambda_{(\mathbf{u}^T|\mathbf{b}^T)^T}^{\perp}(\mathbf{A}'))}.$$

Now we have that the statistical distance between the two distributions is no more than 2ϵ, thus we have our result.

B   Proof of Theorem 3.1

We prove this by a sequence of interactive games. Let Game 0 be the full security game defined above.

Game 1: Instead of $c_1 = U \cdot s + e_1 + y_\beta$, we compute $c_1 = Z \cdot c_0 - Z \cdot e_0 + e_1 + y_\beta$. Game 1 is the same as Game 0.

Game 2: In Game 2, c_0 is chosen uniform randomly from $\mathbb{Z}_q^m$ instead of $As + e_0$. Game 2 is indistinguishable from Game 1 by the hardness of mheLWE.

Now, we remain to prove that in Game 2, the distinguishing advantage for any adversary is negligible. Let $x_1, ..., x_\kappa$ be the largest set of independent vectors in the key query, and we write $X = (x_1|...|x_\kappa)$, and $\kappa \leq k$. We write the ciphertext $ct_\beta = (c_0, c_1^\beta)$. By the construction of our scheme, we only need to show that any adversary cannot distinguish between $(A, ZA, X, XZ, c_0, c_1^0)$ and $(A, ZA, X, XZ, c_0, c_1^1)$ with non-negligible probability.

Let $y = c_1^0 - c_1^1 = \binom{y_0 - y_1}{\alpha_0 - \alpha_1}$ for $\alpha_0, \alpha_1 \leftarrow \mathbb{Z}_q$. Since the last row of X is 0, so y is linearly independent with X except for a negligible probability. We find a short solution t, such that $X^T t = 0$, $y^T t \neq 0$, the coefficients of t is co-prime, and $\|t\| = O(\text{poly}(n))$. The solution exists by Siegel's Lemma. We append vectors orthogonal to t, y and linear independent with X to form a invertible $n \times n$ matrix (modulus q), written as $\bar{X} = (X|y|X')$.

Given the invertible matrix $\bar{X}$, we have that $(A, ZA, X, XZ, c_0, c_1^0)$ and $(A, ZA, X, XZ, c_0, c_1^1)$ are indistinguishable if and only if $(A, ZA, X, XZ, c_0, \bar{X}^T c_1^0)$ and $(A, ZA, X, XZ, c_0, \bar{X}^T c_1^1)$ are indistinguishable.

We then write $\bar{X}^T c_1^\beta$ as $(X^T c_1^\beta, X'^T c_1^\beta, y^T c_1^\beta)$. By the choice of X', we have that $X'^T c_1^0 = X'^T c_1^1$.

By the definition of β-indistinguishability-based security, we have that $|\langle x_i, y_0 \rangle - \langle x_i, y_0 \rangle| \leq \beta$. So we have that $X^T c_1^0 = X^T Z(c_0 - e_0) + X^T e_1 + X^T y_0 = X^T Z(c_0 - e_0) + X^T e_1 + X^T y_1 + b$ where $\|b\|_\infty \leq \beta$. By the lemma below, we show that $X^T e_1$ is indistinguishable from $X^T e_1 + b$.

Lemma B.1. *Given $A \in \mathbb{Z}^{n \times m}$, where each row of A is independently sampled from $D_{\mathbb{Z}^m, \sigma}$, $\sigma = O(\text{poly}(n))$, $m \geq 3n$, $b \in \mathbb{Z}^n$, and $\|b\|_\infty \leq \beta = O(\text{poly}(n))$. Then there exists $x \in \mathbb{Z}^m$ and $\|x\|_\infty \leq \delta = O(\text{poly}(n))$ such that $Ax = b$ except for a negligible probability.*

Proof. This proof is using standard methods in linear algebra and number theory, we only give a proof sketch due to the page limits.

The proof consists of the several steps:

- For $A \in \mathbb{Z}^{n \times m}$, show that $Ax = b$ has an integer solution iff the determinants of all $n \times n$ sub-matrixes of A are co-prime. This is proven by constructing the elementary row/column transformations that transform A into $I|0$.
- Show that for A sampled as defined and each prime $p < q$, the probability that the determinants of all $n \times n$ sub-matrixes of A are a multiple of p is negligible, hence the probability of $Ax = b$ has no integer solution is negligible. This is

proven by induction on n: as long as there is at least one $(k-1) \times (k-1)$ sub-matrix of $\mathbf{A}$ which determinant is not a multiple of p, there is at least one $k \times k$ sub-matrix which determinant is not a multiple of p except for a negligible probability.

- We write $\mathbf{A}_0$ as the first $n-1$ rows of $\mathbf{A}$, and $\mathbf{a}^T$ as the last row of $\mathbf{A}$. Using Siegel's lemma, $\mathbf{A}_0 \mathbf{x} = \mathbf{0}$ has a set of linear independent solutions with norm at most $\text{poly}(n)$, we write them as $\mathbf{x}_1, ..., \mathbf{x}_{m-n+1}$. Let $c_i = \mathbf{a}^T \mathbf{x}_i$, then $c_i = \text{poly}(n)$ and $c_1, ..., c_{m-n+1}$ are co-prime (otherwise there is no integer solution for $\mathbf{A}\mathbf{x} = \mathbf{e}_n$, $\mathbf{e}_n = (0, ..., 0, 1)^T$). By Bezout's lemma, we construct $d_1, ..., d_{m-n+1}$ such that $d_i = \text{poly}(n)$ and $c_1 d_1 + ... + c_{m-n+1} d_{m-n+1} = 1$, so $d_1 \mathbf{x}_1 + ... + d_{m-n+1} \mathbf{x}_{m-n+1}$ is an integer solution of $\mathbf{A}\mathbf{x} = \mathbf{e}_n$ with norm at most $\text{poly}(n)$.

- Similarly, we construct integer solutions for $\mathbf{A}\mathbf{x} = \mathbf{e}_i$ for $i \in [n]$, and use them to construct a solution for $\mathbf{A}\mathbf{x} = \mathbf{b}$ with norm at most $\text{poly}(n)$.

$\square$

Now we find $\mathbf{r}$ such that $\mathbf{X}^T \mathbf{r} = \mathbf{b}$ and $\|\mathbf{r}\|_\infty \leq \delta$, and we can write $\mathbf{X}^T \mathbf{e}_1 + \mathbf{b}$ as $\mathbf{X}^T(\mathbf{e}_1 + \mathbf{r})$. So we only need to show that $\mathbf{e}_1$ and $\mathbf{e}_1 + \mathbf{r}$ are indistinguishable. By Lemma 2.3, we can choose large enough σ' such that $\mathbf{e}_1$ is statistical indistinguishable from $\mathbf{e}_1 + \mathbf{r}$.

We write $\mathbf{X}_{top} = (\mathbf{X}|\mathbf{X}')$. Now we only need to show that given $\mathbf{A}, \mathbf{ZA}, \mathbf{X}, \mathbf{X}^T$ $\mathbf{Z}, \mathbf{c}_0, \mathbf{X}_{top}^T \mathbf{c}_1^0, \mathbf{y}^T \mathbf{c}_1^0$ is indistinguishable from $\mathbf{y}^T \mathbf{c}_1^1$. The discussion is exactly the same as Theorem 2 in [5], except that the vector orthogonal to $\mathbf{X}_{top}$ here is $\mathbf{t}$, instead of $\mathbf{y}$. We omit the details here due to the page limits.

References

1. Agrawal, S.: Indistinguishability obfuscation without multilinear maps: new methods for bootstrapping and instantiation. In: Ishai, Y., Rijmen, V. (eds.) EUROCRYPT 2019. LNCS, vol. 11476, pp. 191–225. Springer, Cham (2019). https://doi.org/10.1007/978-3-030-17653-2_7

2. Agrawal, S., Boneh, D., Boyen, X.: Lattice basis delegation in fixed dimension and shorter-ciphertext hierarchical IBE. In: Rabin, T. (ed.) CRYPTO 2010. LNCS, vol. 6223, pp. 98–115. Springer, Heidelberg (2010). https://doi.org/10.1007/978-3-642-14623-7_6

3. Agrawal, S., Boyen, X., Vaikuntanathan, V., Voulgaris, P., Wee, H.: Functional encryption for threshold functions (or fuzzy IBE) from lattices. In: Fischlin, M., Buchmann, J., Manulis, M. (eds.) PKC 2012. LNCS, vol. 7293, pp. 280–297. Springer, Heidelberg (2012). https://doi.org/10.1007/978-3-642-30057-8_17

4. Agrawal, S., Freeman, D.M., Vaikuntanathan, V.: Functional encryption for inner product predicates from learning with errors. In: Lee, D.H., Wang, X. (eds.) ASIACRYPT 2011. LNCS, vol. 7073, pp. 21–40. Springer, Heidelberg (2011). https://doi.org/10.1007/978-3-642-25385-0_2

5. Agrawal, S., Libert, B., Stehlé, D.: Fully secure functional encryption for inner products, from standard assumptions. In: Robshaw, M., Katz, J. (eds.) CRYPTO 2016. LNCS, vol. 9816, pp. 333–362. Springer, Heidelberg (2016). https://doi.org/10.1007/978-3-662-53015-3_12

6. Agrawal, S., Pellet-Mary, A.: Indistinguishability obfuscation without maps: attacks and fixes for noisy linear FE. In: Canteaux, A., Ishai, Y. (eds.) EURO-CRYPT 2020. LNCS, vol. 12105, pp. 110–140. Springer, Cham (2020). https://doi.org/10.1007/978-3-030-45721-1_5

7. Agrawal, S., Rosen, A.: Functional encryption for bounded collusions, revisited. In: Kalai, Y., Reyzin, L. (eds.) TCC 2017. LNCS, vol. 10677, pp. 173–205. Springer, Cham (2017). https://doi.org/10.1007/978-3-319-70500-2_7

8. Ananth, P., Vaikuntanathan, V.: Optimal bounded-collusion secure functional encryption. In: Hofheinz, D., Rosen, A. (eds.) TCC 2019. LNCS, vol. 11891, pp. 174–198. Springer, Cham (2019). https://doi.org/10.1007/978-3-030-36030-6_8

9. Attrapadung, N.: Dual system encryption via doubly selective security: framework, fully secure functional encryption for regular languages, and more. In: Nguyen, P.Q., Oswald, E. (eds.) EUROCRYPT 2014. LNCS, vol. 8441, pp. 557–577. Springer, Heidelberg (2014). https://doi.org/10.1007/978-3-642-55220-5_31

10. Bethencourt, J., Sahai, A., Waters, B.: Ciphertext-policy attribute-based encryption. In: IEEE Symposium on Security and Privacy, pp. 321–334 (2007)

11. Boneh, D., Boyen, X.: Efficient selective-ID secure identity-based encryption without random oracles. In: Cachin, C., Camenisch, J.L. (eds.) EUROCRYPT 2004. LNCS, vol. 3027, pp. 223–238. Springer, Heidelberg (2004). https://doi.org/10.1007/978-3-540-24676-3_14

12. Boneh, D., et al.: Fully key-homomorphic encryption, arithmetic circuit ABE and compact garbled circuits. In: Nguyen, P.Q., Oswald, E. (eds.) EUROCRYPT 2014. LNCS, vol. 8441, pp. 533–556. Springer, Heidelberg (2014). https://doi.org/10.1007/978-3-642-55220-5_30

13. Boneh, D., Sahai, A., Waters, B.: Functional encryption: definitions and challenges. In: Ishai, Y. (ed.) TCC 2011. LNCS, vol. 6597, pp. 253–273. Springer, Heidelberg (2011). https://doi.org/10.1007/978-3-642-19571-6_16

14. Boyen, X.: Attribute-based functional encryption on lattices. In: Sahai, A. (ed.) TCC 2013. LNCS, vol. 7785, pp. 122–142. Springer, Heidelberg (2013). https://doi.org/10.1007/978-3-642-36594-2_8

15. Boyen, X., Li, Q.: Towards tightly secure lattice short signature and id-based encryption. In: Cheon, J.H., Takagi, T. (eds.) ASIACRYPT 2016. LNCS, vol. 10032, pp. 404–434. Springer, Heidelberg (2016). https://doi.org/10.1007/978-3-662-53890-6_14

16. Brakerski, Z., Vaikuntanathan, V.: Circuit-ABE from LWE: unbounded attributes and semi-adaptive security. In: Robshaw, M., Katz, J. (eds.) CRYPTO 2016. LNCS, vol. 9816, pp. 363–384. Springer, Heidelberg (2016). https://doi.org/10.1007/978-3-662-53015-3_13

17. Cash, D., Hofheinz, D., Kiltz, E., Peikert, C.: Bonsai trees, or how to delegate a lattice basis. In: Gilbert, H. (ed.) EUROCRYPT 2010. LNCS, vol. 6110, pp. 523–552. Springer, Heidelberg (2010). https://doi.org/10.1007/978-3-642-13190-5_27

18. Chen, J., Gong, J., Kowalczyk, L., Wee, H.: Unbounded ABE via bilinear entropy expansion, revisited. In: Nielsen, J.B., Rijmen, V. (eds.) EUROCRYPT 2018. LNCS, vol. 10820, pp. 503–534. Springer, Cham (2018). https://doi.org/10.1007/978-3-319-78381-9_19

19. Cheung, L., Newport, C.: Provably secure ciphertext policy ABE. In: Proceedings of the 14th ACM conference on Computer and Communications Security, pp. 456–465 (2007)

20. Gentry, C., Peikert, C., Vaikuntanathan, V.: Trapdoors for hard lattices and new cryptographic constructions. In: Symposium on the Theory of Computing, pp. 197–206 (2008)

21. Goldwasser, S., Kalai, Y.T., Popa, R.A., Vaikuntanathan, V., Zeldovich, N.: Reusable garbled circuits and succinct functional encryption. In: Symposium on Theory of Computing Conference, STOC 2013, pp. 555–564 (2013)
22. Gorbunov, Sergey, Vaikuntanathan, Vinod, Wee, Hoeteck: Functional encryption with bounded collusions via multi-party computation. In: Safavi-Naini, Reihaneh, Canetti, Ran (eds.) CRYPTO 2012. LNCS, vol. 7417, pp. 162–179. Springer, Heidelberg (2012). https://doi.org/10.1007/978-3-642-32009-5_11
23. Gorbunov, S., Vaikuntanathan, V., Wee, H.: Attribute-based encryption for circuits. In: Symposium on the Theory of Computing, pp. 545–554 (2013)
24. Goyal, R., Koppula, V., Waters, B.: Semi-adaptive security and bundling functionalities made generic and easy. In: Hirt, M., Smith, A. (eds.) TCC 2016. LNCS, vol. 9986, pp. 361–388. Springer, Heidelberg (2016). https://doi.org/10.1007/978-3-662-53644-5_14
25. Goyal, V., Pandey, O., Sahai, A., Waters, B.: Attribute-based encryption for fine-grained access control of encrypted data. In: Proceedings of the 13th ACM Conference on Computer and Communications Security 2006, pp. 89–98 (2006)
26. Katsumata, S., Nishimaki, R., Yamada, S., Yamakawa, T.: Adaptively secure inner product encryption from LWE. In: Moriai, S., Wang, H. (eds.) ASIACRYPT 2020. LNCS, vol. 12493, pp. 375–404. Springer, Cham (2020). https://doi.org/10.1007/978-3-030-64840-4_13
27. Kowalczyk, L., Lewko, A.B.: Bilinear entropy expansion from the decisional linear assumption. In: Gennaro, R., Robshaw, M. (eds.) CRYPTO 2015. LNCS, vol. 9216, pp. 524–541. Springer, Heidelberg (2015). https://doi.org/10.1007/978-3-662-48000-7_26
28. Kowalczyk, L., Wee, H.: Compact adaptively secure ABE for NC^1 from k-Lin. In: Ishai, Y., Rijmen, V. (eds.) EUROCRYPT 2019. LNCS, vol. 11476, pp. 3–33. Springer, Cham (2019). https://doi.org/10.1007/978-3-030-17653-2_1
29. Lewko, A., Okamoto, T., Sahai, A., Takashima, K., Waters, B.: Fully secure functional encryption: attribute-based encryption and (hierarchical) inner product encryption. In: Gilbert, H. (ed.) EUROCRYPT 2010. LNCS, vol. 6110, pp. 62–91. Springer, Heidelberg (2010). https://doi.org/10.1007/978-3-642-13190-5_4
30. Lewko, A., Waters, B.: New proof methods for attribute-based encryption: achieving full security through selective techniques. In: Safavi-Naini, R., Canetti, R. (eds.) CRYPTO 2012. LNCS, vol. 7417, pp. 180–198. Springer, Heidelberg (2012). https://doi.org/10.1007/978-3-642-32009-5_12
31. Micciancio, D., Peikert, C.: Trapdoors for lattices: simpler, tighter, faster, smaller. In: Pointcheval, D., Johansson, T. (eds.) EUROCRYPT 2012. LNCS, vol. 7237, pp. 700–718. Springer, Heidelberg (2012). https://doi.org/10.1007/978-3-642-29011-4_41
32. Micciancio, D., Regev, O.: Worst-case to average-case reductions based on Gaussian measures. SIAM J. Comput. **37**(1), 267–302 (2007)
33. Ostrovsky, R., Sahai, A., Waters, B.: Attribute-based encryption with non-monotonic access structures. In: Proceedings of the 14th ACM Conference on Computer and Communications Security, pp. 195–203 (2007)
34. Regev, O.: New lattice-based cryptographic constructions. J. ACM (JACM) **51**(6), 899–942 (2004)
35. Regev, O.: On lattices, learning with errors, random linear codes, and cryptography. J. ACM **56**(6), 34 (2009)
36. Rouselakis, Y., Waters, B.: Practical constructions and new proof methods for large universe attribute-based encryption. In: Proceedings of the 2013 ACM SIGSAC Conference on Computer & Communications Security, pp. 463–474 (2013)

37. Sahai, A., Waters, B.: Fuzzy identity-based encryption. In: Cramer, R. (ed.) EURO-CRYPT 2005. LNCS, vol. 3494, pp. 457–473. Springer, Heidelberg (2005). https://doi.org/10.1007/11426639_27

38. Tsabary, R.: Fully secure attribute-based encryption for t-CNF from LWE. In: Boldyreva, A., Micciancio, D. (eds.) CRYPTO 2019. LNCS, vol. 11692, pp. 62–85. Springer, Cham (2019). https://doi.org/10.1007/978-3-030-26948-7_3

39. Wang, Z., Fan, X., Liu, F.-H.: FE for inner products and its application to decentralized ABE. In: Lin, D., Sako, K. (eds.) PKC 2019. LNCS, vol. 11443, pp. 97–127. Springer, Cham (2019). https://doi.org/10.1007/978-3-030-17259-6_4

40. Waters, B.: Dual system encryption: realizing fully secure IBE and HIBE under simple assumptions. In: Halevi, S. (ed.) CRYPTO 2009. LNCS, vol. 5677, pp. 619–636. Springer, Heidelberg (2009). https://doi.org/10.1007/978-3-642-03356-8_36

41. Waters, B.: Ciphertext-policy attribute-based encryption: an expressive, efficient, and provably secure realization. In: Catalano, D., Fazio, N., Gennaro, R., Nicolosi, A. (eds.) PKC 2011. LNCS, vol. 6571, pp. 53–70. Springer, Heidelberg (2011). https://doi.org/10.1007/978-3-642-19379-8_4

42. Wee, H.: Dual system encryption via predicate encodings. In: Lindell, Y. (ed.) TCC 2014. LNCS, vol. 8349, pp. 616–637. Springer, Heidelberg (2014). https://doi.org/10.1007/978-3-642-54242-8_26

43. Yamada, S.: Adaptively secure identity-based encryption from lattices with asymptotically shorter public parameters. In: Fischlin, M., Coron, J.-S. (eds.) EURO-CRYPT 2016. LNCS, vol. 9666, pp. 32–62. Springer, Heidelberg (2016). https://doi.org/10.1007/978-3-662-49896-5_2

Revocable Identity-Based Encryption with Server-Aided Ciphertext Evolution from Lattices

Yanhua Zhang[1(✉)], Ximeng Liu[2], Yupu Hu[3], and Huiwen Jia[4]

[1] Zhengzhou University of Light Industry, Zhengzhou 450001, China
yhzhang@email.zzuli.edu.cn
[2] Fuzhou University, Fuzhou 350108, China
[3] Xidian University, Xi'an 710071, China
yphu@mail.xidian.edu.cn
[4] Guangzhou University, Guangzhou 510006, China
hwjia@gzhu.edu.cn

Abstract. Revocable identity-based encryption (RIBE) with server-aided ciphertext evolution (RIBE-CE), recently proposed by Sun et al. at TCS 2020, offers significant advantages over previous identity (or key) revocation mechanisms when considering the scenario of a secure data sharing in the cloud setting. In this new system model, the user (i.e., a recipient) can utilize the current short-term decryption key to decrypt all ciphertexts sent to him, meanwhile, the ciphertexts in the cloud evolve to new ones with the aided of the cloud server and the old ones are completely deleted, and thus, the revoked users cannot access to both the previously and subsequently shared data.

In this paper, inspired by Sun et al.'s work, we propose the first lattice-based RIBE-CE. Our scheme is more efficient and secure than the existing constructions of lattice-based RIBE. Simultaneously, the private key generator (PKG) maintains a binary tree (BT) to handle key revocation only with a logarithmic complexity workload in time key update, not growing linearly in the numbers of system users N, which serves as one solution to the challenge proposed by Sun et al. and based on the hardness of the learning with errors (LWE) problem, we prove that our first scheme is selectively secure in the standard model. Subsequently, based on the main techniques for lattice basis delegation with hierarchical IBE (HIBE), we construct our second lattice-based RIBE-CE scheme with decryption key exposure resistance (DKER), a default security requirement for RIBE, which has not been considered by Sun et al.

Keywords: IBE · Lattices · Key revocation · Ciphertext evolution

1 Introduction

Identity-based encryption (IBE), a seminal notion envisaged by Shamir [25] at Crypto 1984, can eliminate the needs for providing a public-key infrastructure in

© Springer Nature Switzerland AG 2021
Y. Yu and M. Yung (Eds.): Inscrypt 2021, LNCS 13007, pp. 442–465, 2021.
https://doi.org/10.1007/978-3-030-88323-2_24

conventional public-key cryptosystems. Until 2001, the first realizations of IBE based on pairings and on quadratic residual problem were introduced by Boneh and Franklin [5] and Cocks [8], respectively. In addition, Boneh and Franklin [5] also suggested a naive solution to the issue of identity (or key) revocation in IBE, that is, each non-revoked user needs to be periodically reassigned a private key by communicating with the private key generator (PKG) per time epoch via a *secret* channel. Obviously, this solution is inefficient for a large-scale IBE system, because the PKG's workload grows linearly in the number of system users N.

The first scalable IBE with key revocation, or simply revocable IBE (RIBE) was set forth by Boldyreva et al. [4] at CCS 2008, whose scheme is designed by adopting a binary tree (BT) based revocation method [19] and PKG's workload is only logarithmic in N. Though the time key updating process of [4] can be exactly executed for all the non-revoked users over a *public* channel, each non-revoked user still requires different time keys to accomplish ciphertexts decryption for different time periods, and each user in IBE should store a series of time update keys which grow linearly in the whole periods. Additionally, when considering a practical application of RIBE, there is a problem that ciphertexts generated for a user, but prior to the user's revocation, remain available to the revoked user. This problem may be undesirable for some applications, such as the scenario of a secure data sharing in the cloud setting.

To solve both the aforementioned two problems simultaneously in a practical manner, Sun et al. [27] recently introduced revocable identity-based encryption with server-aided ciphertext evolution (RIBE-CE) - a new revocation method in which the user (i.e., a recipient) has to utilize the current short-term decryption key to decrypt all ciphertexts sent to him, meanwhile, the ciphertexts in the cloud evolve to new ones with the aided of the cloud server and old ones are completely deleted, and thus, the revoked users cannot access to both the previously and subsequently shared data. To be more specific, an RIBE-CE scheme should be carried out as follows: once the system is set up, PKG issues a long-term private key to user. A time update key is generated by PKG and sent to the cloud server (and all users) via a *public* channel at each time period. The cloud server should do ciphertext evolution on the encrypted data which may be just uploaded by a data owner or have been stored in the cloud for some time to new ciphertexts by using the time update key, and the old ciphertexts are deleted. Because only the non-revoked user can obtain a valid short-term decryption key, any revoked users cannot decrypt the ciphertexts (including the former ciphertexts) sent to him. In [27], apart from introducing this new RIBE model, Sun et al. also described a generic construction and the pairing-based instantiations of RIBE-CE.

In this paper, inspired by the clear advantages of RIBE-CE, we bring it into the world of lattice-based cryptograph which has faster arithmetic operations and is believed to the most promising candidate for post-quantum cryptography.

RELATED WORKS. The first scalable RIBE scheme was introduced by Boldyreva et al. [4], whose scheme is constructed by combining a fuzzy IBE scheme [23] and a subset cover framework [19]. Subsequently, an adaptive-id secure RIBE and RIBE with decryption key exposure resistance (DKER) from bilinear groups were proposed by Libert and Vergnaud [15] and Seo and Emura [24], respectively.

Lattice-based cryptography, believed to be secure in a quantum computer attack environment, enjoys some competive advantages over conventional number-theoretic cryptography, such as simpler arithmetic operations and proven secure based on the *worst-case* hardness assumptions. Following the model of [4], the first lattice-based RIBE scheme without DKER, the first schemes with bounded DKER and unbounded DKER and an adaptively secure scheme in the quantum random oracle model were proposed by Chen et al. [7], Takayasu and Watanabe [29], Katsumata et al. [11] and Takayasu [28], respectively.

Cloud-based technology, including cloud computing and cloud storage, etc., has already created a new generation of computing paradigm, and with a flexible assistance of cloud (e.g., irrespective of time and location), many conventional costly computations and bulky storages can be performed with ease. Therefore, introducing cloud computing services into RIBE is an interesting idea to alleviate the workloads of PKG and each user. The study of outsourcing RIBE (O-RIBE) was initiated by Li et al. [13], in which a semi-trusted key update cloud service provider is adopted to update each user's time key. Though Liang et al. [14] attempted to solve the same problems as in this work with proxy re-encryption technique, their scheme is insecure to resist the re-encryption key forgery attack and collusion attack [30]. To overcome the decryption challenges for users only with limited resources, Qin et al. [21] introduced a new revocation method called server-aided RIBE (SA-RIBE), contrary to previous O-RIBE, all workloads on the users side are outsourced to the cloud server. Inspired by these two new models, Nguyen et al. [20] and Dong et al. [9] respectively designed the first lattice-based SA-RIBE scheme and the first lattice-based O-RIBE scheme. Recently, the generic constructions of RIBE with complete subset (CS) method and subset difference (SD) method were respectively proposed by Ma and Lin [16] and Lee [12].

OUR CONTRIBUTIONS. In this paper, we introduce two (and the first) constructions of lattice-based RIBE-CE. We inherit and extend the main efficiency and security advantages of Sun et al.'s model for RIBE: the system users do not have to store each time update key, as they can utilize the current short-term decryption key to decrypt all ciphertexts sent to him, meanwhile, the revoked users cannot access to both the previously and subsequently shared data in the cloud. Furthermore, PKG maintains a BT and adopts the CS method to handle key revocation with a logarithmic complexity workload in time key update, not growing linearly in the numbers of system users as in Sun et al. [27]. As for previous lattice-based RIBE schemes [7,11,20,28,29], our two constructions only work for one-bit message, but the multi-bit version can be achieved by adopting a standard transformation technique showed in [1,10]. As in [7,9,11,28,29], the public parameters almost enjoy the same asymptotic efficiency, though the bit-size of our final ciphertext in our two schemes is linear in the length of identity id, while all ciphertexts (the secure data) are stored in cloud, thus for the local users the storage cost is not a challenge. More startlingly, our two schemes are naturally SA-RIBE as [20] in which the recipient does not need to communicate with PKG for time update key, thus the recipient enjoys a lower decryption cost.

As in [20], each user's long-term private key of our second scheme is a trapdoor matrix, thus having a relatively large bit-size, but constant in the number of system users. In particular, the later scheme satisfies DKER, a default security requirement for RIBE, which is not considered by Sun et al. A detailed comparison among the schemes [7,11,20,28,29] and ours is shown in Table 1.

As a high level, the design method of our first lattice-based RIBE-CE scheme is similar to the pairing-based concrete construction of Sun et al., and a double encryption mechanism is also adopted as the core building block. In our second scheme, instead of only using a conventional IBE scheme as in Sun et al., a lattice-based two-level hierarchical IBE (HIBE) scheme [1] is introduced, from which the PKG can issue a long-term private key (a trapdoor matrix, not a vector) to each user id. This technique enables a user id with a long-term private key to derive partial short-term decryption key corresponding to his identity id and time t all by himself, and thus achieving DKER.

Table 1. Comparison of lattice-based RIBE schemes.

Schemes	$\lvert pp\rvert$	$\lvert sk_{id}\rvert$	$\lvert uk_t\rvert$	$\lvert dk_{id,t}\rvert$	$\lvert ct_{id,t}\rvert$	CE	DKER	Model
[7]	$\widetilde{O}(n^2)$	$\widetilde{O}(n^2)$	$O(r\log\frac{N}{r})\cdot\widetilde{O}(n)$	$\widetilde{O}(n)$	$\widetilde{O}(n)$	no	no	Standard
[20]	$\widetilde{O}(n^2)$	$\widetilde{O}(n^2)$	$O(r\log\frac{N}{r})\cdot\widetilde{O}(n)$	$\widetilde{O}(n)$	$\widetilde{O}(n)$	no	Unbounded	Standard
[29]	$\widetilde{O}(n^2)$	$d\cdot\widetilde{O}(n^2)$	$O(r\log\frac{N}{r})\cdot\widetilde{O}(n)$	$\widetilde{O}(n)$	$\widetilde{O}(n)$	no	Bounded	Standard
[11]	$\widetilde{O}(n^2)$	$\widetilde{O}(n^2)$	$O(r\log\frac{N}{r})\cdot\widetilde{O}(n)$	$\widetilde{O}(n)$	$\widetilde{O}(n)$	no	Unbounded	Standard
[28]	$\widetilde{O}(n^2)$	$d\cdot\widetilde{O}(n^2)$	$O(r\log\frac{N}{r})\cdot\widetilde{O}(n)$	$\widetilde{O}(n)$	$\widetilde{O}(n)$	no	Bounded	Quantum ROM
Ours-1	$\widetilde{O}(n^2)$	$\widetilde{O}(n)$	$O(r\log\frac{N}{r})\cdot\widetilde{O}(n)$	$\widetilde{O}(n)$	$\widetilde{O}(n^2)$	yes	no	Standard
Ours-2	$\widetilde{O}(n^2)$	$\widetilde{O}(n^2)$	$O(r\log\frac{N}{r})\cdot\widetilde{O}(n)$	$\widetilde{O}(n)$	$\widetilde{O}(n^2)$	yes	Unbounded	Standard

Note: n is a security parameter, $N = 2^n$ is the maximum numbers of system users, r is the number of revoked users, d is the number of private keys stored in each node over path(id); $\lvert\cdot\rvert$ denotes the bit-size, pp is public parameters, sk_{id} is long-term private key, uk_t is time update key, $dk_{id,t}$ is short-term decryption key, and $ct_{id,t}$ is ciphertext; CE denotes ciphertext evolution and ROM denotes random oracle model.

Furthermore, looking into the details on time key update. The PKG in Sun et al. [27] issues a time update key for each non-revoked user with a conventional IBE scheme, and thus the workload of PKG grows linearly in the numbers of the non-revoked users. Instead, we adapt the classical BT-based revocation mechanism [19] to obtain a logarithmic complexity workload of PKG which serves as one solution to the challenge proposed by Sun et al., and an extended ciphertext design technique recently employed by Ma and Lin [16], which works as follows: the sender encrypts a message under a HIBE scheme and an IBE scheme corresponding to the time and node pairs (t, θ) where $\theta \in$ path(id) and the recipient id is assigned to a leaf node in BT. Given a user revocation list (RL), PKG computes the time update key under the IBE scheme corresponding to the time and node pairs (t, θ') where $\theta' \in$ KUNode(BT, RL, t) denotes all the non-revoked children of revoked id with t, only a non-revoked id at t can derive a short-term decryption key consisting of two parts, which are corresponding to the two-level HIBE and the unique node $\theta \in$ path(id) $\cap$ KUNode(BT, RL, t). Unfortunately, the bit-size of final ciphertext in our constructions is linear in the length of id.

The security of our lattice-based RIBE-CE schemes rely on a lattice-based IBE scheme [1] and a lattice-based double encryption scheme employed by Nguyen et al. [20] in the design of lattice-based SA-RIBE. The constructions are selectively secure in the standard model for our two schemes based on the hardness assumption of the learning with errors (LWE) problem.

ORGANIZATION. The organization of the paper is as follows. In Sect. 2, we review the definition of RIBE-CE and some background knowledge on lattices. A lattice-based RIBE-CE scheme without DKER and a scheme with DKER in the standard model are described and analyzed in Sects. 3 and 4, respectively. In the final Sect. 5, we conclude our whole paper.

2   Definition and Security Model

Table 2 refers to the notations used in this paper.

Table 2. Notations of this paper.

Notation	Definition
$\mathbf{a}, \mathbf{A}$	Vectors, matrices
$\xleftarrow{\$}$	Sampling uniformly at random
$\|\cdot\|, \|\cdot\|_\infty$	Euclidean norm ℓ_2, infinity norm ℓ_∞
$\lceil e \rceil, \lfloor e \rceil$	The smallest integer not less than e, the integer closet to e
$\mathcal{O}, \tilde{\mathcal{O}}, \omega$	Standard asymptotic notations
$\log e$	Logarithm of e with base 2
ppt	Probabilistic polynomial-time

2.1   RIBE with Server-Aided Ciphertext Evolution

We first review the definition and security model of RIBE-CE introduced by Sun et al. [27]. An RIBE-CE is an extension of RIBE that supports key revocation, and additionally it delegates ciphertext evolution to a cloud server (Cloud). A trusted center first issues a master secret key (msk) and public parameters (pp). The PKG issues a long-term private key sk_{id} for each system user id and a time update key uk_t with time t by using msk, meanwhile, it distributes uk_t to Cloud (and all users) and maintains a revocation list (RL) to record the state information on revoked users. The Cloud periodically transforms a ciphertext for id with t into a new one for $t' > t$ by using uk_t. To decrypt a ciphertext which specifies an identity id and a time t, the non-revoked recipient combines his long-term private

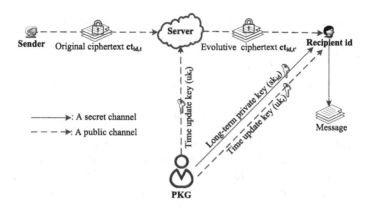

Fig. 1. System model of RIBE-CE.

key $\mathsf{sk}_{\mathsf{id}}$ and current time update key uk_t to derive a short-term decryption key $\mathsf{dk}_{\mathsf{id},\mathsf{t}}$. The system model of RIBE-CE is shown in Fig. 1.

Definition 1. *An RIBE-CE scheme involves four distinct entities: PKG, a cloud server Cloud, sender and recipient, associated with identity space $\mathcal{I}$, time space $\mathcal{T}$ (time is treated as discrete and the size of $\mathcal{T}$ is polynomial in the security parameter) and message space $\mathcal{M}$, and consists of eight polynomial-time (pt) algorithms which are described as follows:*

- Setup($1^n, N$): *The setup algorithm is run by PKG, and it takes as input a security parameter n and the maximal number of system users N. It outputs a master secret key msk, the public parameters pp, a user revocation list RL (initially empty), and a state st. Note: msk is kept in secret by PKG and pp is made public and as an implicit input of all other algorithms.*
- PriKeyGen(msk, id): *The key generation algorithm is run by PKG, and it takes as input an identity id, and the master secret key msk. It outputs a long-term private key $\mathsf{sk}_{\mathsf{id}}$. Note: $\mathsf{sk}_{\mathsf{id}}$ is sent to the recipient via a secret channel.*
- KeyUpd(RL, t, msk, st): *The key update algorithm is run by Cloud, and it takes as input current revocation list RL, a time t, the master secret key msk, and a state st. It outputs a time update key uk_t. Note: uk_t is sent to Cloud and all users via a public channel.*
- DecKeyGen($\mathsf{sk}_{\mathsf{id}}$, uk_t, t): *The decryption key derivation algorithm is run by the recipient id, and it takes as input a long-term private key $\mathsf{sk}_{\mathsf{id}}$, a corresponding time update key uk_t (or $\perp$), and the current time t. It outputs a short-term decryption key $\mathsf{dk}_{\mathsf{id},\mathsf{t}}$ (or $\perp$ indicating that the recipient id was revoked).*
- Encrypt(id, t, m): *The encryption algorithm is run by the sender, and it takes as input a recipient's identity id, an encryption time t, and a message m. It outputs a ciphertext $\mathsf{ct}_{\mathsf{id},\mathsf{t}}$.*
- Evolve($\mathsf{ct}_{\mathsf{id},\mathsf{t}}$, t', uk_t): *The ciphertext evolution algorithm is run by Cloud, and it takes as input a ciphertext $\mathsf{ct}_{\mathsf{id},\mathsf{t}}$ with identity id and time t, a new time t' > t, and the current time update key uk_t. It outputs a new ciphertext $\mathsf{ct}_{\mathsf{id},\mathsf{t}'}$. Note: If id has been revoked at time t, the ciphertext remains unchanged.*

- Decrypt($dk_{id',t'}$, $ct_{id,t}$): *The decryption algorithm is run by the recipient, and it takes as input a ciphertext $ct_{id,t}$ and a decryption key $dk_{id',t'}$. It outputs a message* $m \in \mathcal{M}$, *or a symbol* $\perp$.
- Revoke(id, t, RL, st): *The revocation algorithm is run by* PKG, *and it takes as input the current revocation list* RL, *an identity* id, *a revoked time* t, *and a state* st. *It outputs an updated revocation list* $RL = RL \cup \{(id, t)\}$. *Note: a copy of* RL *will be sent to* Cloud *via a public channel.*

The correctness of an RIBE-CE scheme is described as follows: for all pp, msk, RL, and st generated by Setup(1^n, N), sk_{id} generated by PriKeyGen(msk, id, st) for id $\in \mathcal{I}$, uk_t generated by KeyUpd(RL, t, msk, st) for t $\in \mathcal{T}$ and RL, $ct_{id,t}$ generated by Encrypt(id, t, m) for id $\in \mathcal{I}$, t $\in \mathcal{T}$ and m $\in \mathcal{M}$, and $ct_{id,t'}$ generated by Evolve($ct_{id,t}$, t', uk_t), then it is required that:

- If $(id, t') \notin$ RL for all $t' \leq t$, then DecKeyGen(sk_{id}, uk_t, t) = $dk_{id,t}$.
- If $(id, t') \notin$ RL for all $t' < t$, then Evolve($ct_{id,t'}$, t, uk_t) = $ct_{id,t}$.
- If $(id = id') \wedge (t = t')$, then Decrypt($dk_{id',t'}$, $ct_{id,t}$) = m.

Since RIBE-CE is an extension of RIBE, the indistinguishability under chosen-plaintext attack (ind-cpa) security of RIBE must be satisfied to guarantee message hiding security against an inside attacker $\mathcal{A}_0$ who owns a long-term private key (e.g., a revoked user), and an outside attacker $\mathcal{A}_1$ who knows all time update keys (e.g., the cloud server Cloud).

Sun et al. [27] defined the security against adaptive-revocable-identity-time chosen-plaintext attacks for RIBE-CE. Here, we only consider selective-revocable-identity-time security (a weaker notion initially was suggested in RIBE by Boldyreva et al. [4], subsequently by Chen et al. [7], Nguyen et al. [20] and Katsumata et al. [11], in which an adversary $\mathcal{A}$ ($\mathcal{A}_0$ or $\mathcal{A}_1$) sends a challenge identity and time pair (id*, t*) to the challenger $\mathcal{C}$ before the execution of Setup(1^n, N). A slight difference is that we formalize the ind-cpa security adopting a game capturing a stronger privacy property called *indistinguishable from random* as defined in [1] and a stronger security property called DKER defined in [24].

In our ind-cpa security model of RIBE-CE, the attacker can request long-term private key, time update key, revocation, short-term decryption key (as in Sun et al., in our first construction, there is also no this query), and ciphertext evolution queries. One of the most restrictions of this model is that if the attacker has requested a long-term private key for the challenge identity id*, then id* must be revoked before (or at) the time update key query of challenge time t*. Finally, the goal of the attacker is to determine that the challenge ciphertxet is completely random, or correctly encrypted on the challenge m* corresponding to (id*, t*). A detailed definition is described as follows:

Definition 2. *The* ind-cpa *security of* RIBE-CE *is shown in the following game:*

- Intial: *The adversary* $\mathcal{A}$ *first declares a challenge identity and time pair* (id*, t*).

- Setup: *The challenger $\mathcal{C}$ runs* Setup$(1^n, N)$ *to obtain* $(\mathsf{msk}, \mathsf{pp}, \mathsf{RL}, \mathsf{st})$. *Note: RL is initially empty, $\mathcal{C}$ keeps* msk *in secret by himself and provides* pp *to $\mathcal{A}$.*
- Query phase 1: *The query-answer between $\mathcal{A}$ and $\mathcal{C}$ is described in Table 3. Remark:* PriKenGen$(\cdot)$, KeyUpd$(\cdot)$, Revoke$(\cdot)$, DecKeyGen$(\cdot)$ *and* CE *share* st *and the queries should be with some restrictions defined later. The* DecKeyGen$(\cdot)$ *oracle is used to define* DKER *for our second scheme, which has not been provided by Sun et al.*
- Challenge: *$\mathcal{A}$ submits a message* $\mathsf{m}^* \in \mathcal{M}$. *$\mathcal{C}$ samples a bit $b \xleftarrow{\$} \{0,1\}$. If $b = 0$, $\mathcal{C}$ returns a challenge ciphertext* $\mathsf{ct}^*_{\mathsf{id}^*, \mathsf{t}^*}$ *by running* Encrypt$(\mathsf{id}^*, \mathsf{t}^*, \mathsf{m}^*)$, *otherwise, a random* $\mathsf{ct}^*_{\mathsf{id}^*, \mathsf{t}^*} \xleftarrow{\$} \mathcal{U}$.
- Query phase 2: *$\mathcal{A}$ can continue to make additional queries as before with the same restrictions.*
- Guess: *$\mathcal{A}$ outputs a bit $b^* \in \{0, 1\}$, and wins if $b^* = b$.*

  In the above game, the following restrictions should be satisfied:
  - KeyUpd$(\cdot)$ *and* Revoke$(\cdot)$ *must be queried in a non-decreasing order of time.*
  - Revoke$(\cdot)$ *cannot be queried at* t *if* KeyUpd$(\cdot)$ *has been queried at* t.
  - Revoke$(\cdot)$ *must be queried on* $(\mathsf{id}^*, \mathsf{t})$ *for* $\mathsf{t} \le \mathsf{t}^*$ *if* PriKenGen$(\cdot)$ *has been queried on* id^*.
  - DecKeyGen$(\cdot)$ *cannot be queried at* t *if* KeyUpd$(\cdot)$ *was not queried at* t.
  - DecKeyGen$(\cdot)$ *cannot be queried on* $(\mathsf{id}^*, \mathsf{t}^*)$, *and in* CE *query,* $\mathsf{t}' > \mathsf{t}$.

$\mathcal{A}$'s advantage is defined as $\mathsf{Adv}^{\mathsf{ind\text{-}cpa}}_{\mathsf{RIBE\text{-}CE}, \mathcal{A}}(n) = |\Pr[b^* = b] - 1/2|$. An RIBE-CE scheme is secure if $\mathsf{Adv}^{\mathsf{ind\text{-}cpa}}_{\mathsf{RIBE\text{-}CE}, \mathcal{A}}(n)$ is negligible in the security parameter n.

Table 3. The query-answer between $\mathcal{A}$ and $\mathcal{C}$.

	PriKenGen$(\cdot)$	KeyUpd$(\cdot)$	Revoke$(\cdot)$	DecKeyGen$(\cdot)$	CE
$\mathcal{A}$	id	RL, t	RL, id, t	id, t	$\mathsf{ct}_{\mathsf{id}, \mathsf{t}}, \mathsf{t}, \mathsf{t}'$
$\mathcal{C}$	$\mathsf{sk}_{\mathsf{id}}$	uk_{t}	RL = RL $\cup$ $\{(\mathsf{id}, \mathsf{t})\}$	$\mathsf{dk}_{\mathsf{id}, \mathsf{t}}$	$\mathsf{ct}_{\mathsf{id}, \mathsf{t}'}$

2.2 Lattices

In this subsection, we recall the knowledge on integer lattices.

Definition 3. *Given n, m, $q \ge 2$, a random $\mathbf{A} \in \mathbb{Z}_q^{n \times m}$, and $\mathbf{u} \in \mathbb{Z}_q^n$, the m-dimensional q-ary orthogonal lattice $\Lambda_q^{\perp}(\mathbf{A})$ (and its shift $\Lambda_q^{\mathbf{u}}(\mathbf{A})$) is defined as:*
$$\Lambda_q^{\perp}(\mathbf{A}) = \{\mathbf{e} \in \mathbb{Z}^m \mid \mathbf{A} \cdot \mathbf{e} = \mathbf{0} \bmod q\} \text{ and } \Lambda_q^{\mathbf{u}}(\mathbf{A}) = \{\mathbf{e} \in \mathbb{Z}^m \mid \mathbf{A} \cdot \mathbf{e} = \mathbf{u} \bmod q\}.$$

The discrete Gaussian distribution over Λ with the center $\mathbf{c} \in \mathbb{Z}^m$ and a Gaussian parameter $s > 0$ is denoted as $\mathcal{D}_{\Lambda, s, \mathbf{c}}$, and we omit the subscript and denote it as $\mathcal{D}_{\Lambda, s}$ if $\mathbf{c} = \mathbf{0}$.

Lemma 1 ([10]). *For integers n, $q \geq 2$, $m \geq 2n\lceil \log q \rceil$, assume that the columns of a random $\mathbf{A} \in \mathbb{Z}_q^{n \times m}$ generates $\mathbb{Z}_q^n$, let $\epsilon \in (0, 1/2)$ and $s \geq \eta_\epsilon(\Lambda^\perp(\mathbf{A}))$, then the followings hold:*

1. *For $\mathbf{e} \xleftarrow{\$} \mathcal{D}_{\mathbb{Z}^m, s}$, the statistical distance between $\mathbf{u} = \mathbf{A} \cdot \mathbf{e} \bmod q$ and $\mathbf{u}' \xleftarrow{\$} \mathbb{Z}_q^n$ is at most 2ϵ.*
2. *For $\mathbf{e} \xleftarrow{\$} \mathcal{D}_{\mathbb{Z}^m, s}$, then $\Pr[\|\mathbf{e}\|_\infty \leq \lceil s \cdot \log m \rceil]$ holds with a larger probability.*
3. *The min-entropy of $\mathcal{D}_{\mathbb{Z}^m, s}$ is at least $m - 1$.*

A ppt trapdoor generation algorithm returning a statistically close to uniform $\mathbf{A} \in \mathbb{Z}_q^{n \times m}$ together with a low Gram-Schmidt norm basis for $\Lambda_q^\perp(\mathbf{A})$ plays a key role in lattice-based cryptography. The algorithm was first introduced by Ajtai [2], and two improvements were investigated in [3,18].

Lemma 2 ([2,3,18]). *Let $n \geq 1$, $q \geq 2$, $m = 2n\lceil \log q \rceil$, there is a ppt algorithm $\mathsf{TrapGen}(q, n, m)$ that returns $\mathbf{A} \in \mathbb{Z}_q^{n \times m}$ statistically close to an uniform matrix in $\mathbb{Z}_q^{n \times m}$ and a trapdoor $\mathbf{R_A}$ for $\Lambda_q^\perp(\mathbf{A})$.*

Gentry et al. [10] showed an algorithm to sample short vectors (or matrices) from a discrete Gaussian distribution, and an improvement was given in [18]. Meanwhile, to delegate a trapdoor for a super-lattice was given in [6].

Lemma 3 ([10,18]). *Let $n \geq 1$, $q \geq 2$, $m = 2n\lceil \log q \rceil$, given $\mathbf{A} \in \mathbb{Z}_q^{n \times m}$, a trapdoor $\mathbf{R_A}$ for $\Lambda_q^\perp(\mathbf{A})$, a parameter $s = \omega(\sqrt{n \log q \log n})$, and a vector $\mathbf{u} \in \mathbb{Z}_q^n$, there is a ppt algorithm $\mathsf{SamplePre}(\mathbf{A}, \mathbf{R_A}, \mathbf{u}, s)$ returning a shorter vector $\mathbf{e} \in \Lambda_q^\mathbf{u}(\mathbf{A})$ sampled from a distribution statistically close to $\mathcal{D}_{\Lambda_q^\mathbf{u}(\mathbf{A}), s}$.*

Lemma 4 ([6]). *Let $q \geq 2$, $m = 2n\lceil \log q \rceil$, given $\mathbf{A} \in \mathbb{Z}_q^{n \times m}$ who can generate $\mathbb{Z}_q^n$, a basis $\mathbf{R_A} \in \mathbb{Z}^{m \times m}$ for $\Lambda_q^\perp(\mathbf{A})$, a random $\mathbf{A}' \in \mathbb{Z}_q^{n \times m'}$, there is a deterministic algorithm $\mathsf{ExtBasis}(\mathbf{R_A}, \mathbf{A}^* = \mathbf{A}|\mathbf{A}')$ returning a basis $\mathbf{R_{A^*}} \in \mathbb{Z}^{(m+m') \times (m+m')}$ for $\Lambda_q^\perp(\mathbf{A}^*)$, especially, $\mathbf{R_A}$, $\mathbf{R_{A^*}}$ are with equal Gram-Schmidt norm. Note: the result holds for any given permutation of all columns of $\mathbf{A}^*$.*

Lemma 5 ([6]). *Let $n \geq 1$, $q \geq 2$, $m = 2n\lceil \log q \rceil$, $s \geq \|\widetilde{\mathbf{R_A}}\| \cdot \omega(\sqrt{\log n})$, $\mathbf{R_A} \in \mathbb{Z}^{m \times m}$ is a basis for $\Lambda_q^\perp(\mathbf{A})$, there is a ppt algorithm $\mathsf{RandBasis}(\mathbf{R_A}, s)$ returning a new basis $\mathbf{R_A}' \in \mathbb{Z}^{m \times m}$ and $\|\mathbf{R_A}'\| \leq s \cdot \sqrt{m}$. In particular, for two basis matrices $\mathbf{R_A}^{(1)}$ and $\mathbf{R_A}^{(2)}$ for $\Lambda_q^\perp(\mathbf{A})$, and $s \geq \max\{\|\widetilde{\mathbf{R_A}^{(1)}}\|, \|\widetilde{\mathbf{R_A}^{(2)}}\|\} \cdot \omega(\sqrt{\log n})$, $\mathsf{RandBasis}(\mathbf{R_A}^{(1)}, s)$ is statistically close to $\mathsf{RandBasis}(\mathbf{R_A}^{(2)}, s)$.*

Lemma 6 ([1]). *Let $q > 2$, $m > n$, $\mathbf{A} \in \mathbb{Z}_q^{n \times m}$, $\mathbf{A}' \in \mathbb{Z}_q^{n \times m'}$, and $s > \|\widetilde{\mathbf{R_A}}\| \cdot \omega(\sqrt{\log(m + m')})$, given a trapdoor $\mathbf{R_A}$ for $\Lambda_q^\perp(\mathbf{A})$ and $\mathbf{u} \in \mathbb{Z}_q^n$, there is a ppt algorithm $\mathsf{SampleLeft}(\mathbf{A}|\mathbf{A}', \mathbf{R_A}, \mathbf{u}, s)$ returning a shorter $\mathbf{e} \in \mathbb{Z}^{2m}$ sampled from a distribution statistically close to $\mathcal{D}_{\Lambda_q^\mathbf{u}(\mathbf{A}|\mathbf{A}'), s}$.*

Lemma 7 ([1]). *Let $q > 2$, $m > n$, $\mathbf{A}$, $\mathbf{B} \in \mathbb{Z}_q^{n \times m}$, $s > \|\widetilde{\mathbf{R_B}}\| \cdot \mathcal{O}(\sqrt{m}) \cdot \omega(\sqrt{\log m})$, given a trapdoor $\mathbf{R_B}$, a low-norm $\mathbf{R} \in \{-1, 1\}^{m \times m}$, and $\mathbf{u} \in \mathbb{Z}_q^n$, there is a ppt algorithm $\mathsf{SampleRight}(\mathbf{A}, \mathbf{B}, \mathbf{R}, \mathbf{R_B}, \mathbf{u}, s)$ returning a shorter $\mathbf{e} \in \mathbb{Z}^{2m}$ distributed statistically close to $\mathcal{D}_{\Lambda_q^\mathbf{u}(\mathbf{F}), s}$, where $\mathbf{F} = [\mathbf{A}|\mathbf{AR} + \mathbf{B}]$.*

We recall the learning with errors (LWE) problem introduced by Regev [22].

Definition 4. *The* LWE *problem is defined as follows: given* $\mathbf{s} \xleftarrow{\$} \mathbb{Z}_q^n$, *a distribution* χ *over* $\mathbb{Z}$, *let* $\mathcal{A}_{\mathbf{s},\chi}$ *be the distribution* $(\mathbf{A}, \mathbf{A}^\top \mathbf{s} + \mathbf{e})$ *where* $\mathbf{A} \xleftarrow{\$} \mathbb{Z}_q^{n \times m}$, $\mathbf{e} \xleftarrow{\$} \chi^m$, *and to make distinguish between* $\mathcal{A}_{\mathbf{s},\chi}$ *and* $\mathcal{U} \xleftarrow{\$} \mathbb{Z}_q^{n \times m} \times \mathbb{Z}_q^m$. *Let* $\beta \geq \sqrt{n} \cdot \omega(\log n)$, *for a prime power* q, *given a* β-*bounded* χ, *the* LWE *problem is as least as hard as the shortest independent vectors problem* SIVP$_{\widetilde{\mathcal{O}}(nq/\beta)}$.

An injective encoding function $\mathcal{H} : \mathbb{Z}_q^n \to \mathbb{Z}_q^{n \times n}$ is adopted for our RIBE-CE schemes. An explicit design called encoding with full-rank differences (FRD) was proposed by Agrawal et al. [1].

Definition 5. *Let* $n > 1$, *prime* $q \geq 2$, *an injective encoding function* $\mathcal{H} : \mathbb{Z}_q^n \to \mathbb{Z}_q^{n \times n}$ *is called* FRD *if:*

1. *For* $\forall \mathbf{e}_1, \mathbf{e}_2 \in \mathbb{Z}_q^n$, $\mathbf{e}_1 \neq \mathbf{e}_2$, $\mathcal{H}(\mathbf{e}_1) - \mathcal{H}(\mathbf{e}_2) \in \mathbb{Z}_q^{n \times n}$ *is full-rank.*
2. $\mathcal{H}$ *can be computed in a polynomial time, i.e.,* $\mathcal{O}(n \log q)$.

Two followings two facts will be used in the security proofs of this work.

Lemma 8 ([1]). *Let* $n \geq 1$, *prime* $q > 2$, $m > (n+1)\log q + \omega(\log n)$, $\mathbf{A} \xleftarrow{\$} \mathbb{Z}_q^{n \times m}$, $\mathbf{B} \xleftarrow{\$} \mathbb{Z}_q^{n \times k = poly(n)}$, *and* $\mathbf{R} \xleftarrow{\$} \{-1, 1\}^{m \times k} \bmod q$. *Then, for all* $\mathbf{w} \in \mathbb{Z}_q^m$, $(\mathbf{A}, \mathbf{A}\mathbf{R}, \mathbf{R}^\top \mathbf{w})$ *is statistically close to* $(\mathbf{A}, \mathbf{B}, \mathbf{R}^\top \mathbf{w})$.

Lemma 9 ([1]). *Let* $\mathbf{R} \xleftarrow{\$} \{-1, 1\}^{m \times m}$ *and* $\mathbf{w} \in \mathbb{R}^m$, $\Pr[\|\mathbf{R} \cdot \mathbf{w}\|_\infty > \|\mathbf{w}\|_\infty \cdot \sqrt{m} \cdot \omega(\sqrt{\log m})] < negl(m)$.

3   Our Lattice-Based RIBE-CE Scheme Without DKER

Our first RIBE-CE scheme adopts a lattice-based IBE scheme [1] from which the PKG issues a long-term private key to each user id and a time update key to Cloud for ciphertext evolution, a classical BT revocation mechanism [19] to alleviate the load of PKG (a logarithmic complexity and a user id is viewed as a leaf node of BT, each node in BT has an identifier which is a fixed and unique binary string[1], and an extended ciphertext design method [16] to resolve the problem of the same state information of BT is used in PriKeyGen(·) and KeyUpd(·).

---

[1] Set an identifier of the root node (root) as 0, and an identifier of other node is assigned as follows: each edge in BT is assigned with 0 or 1 depending on whether it is connected to a left or right child node, thus an identifier of each node is defined as all labels of edges in the path from root to this node. Obviously, each user id $= (0, id_1, id_2, \cdots, id_{\log N}) \in 0 \| \{0,1\}^{\log N}$ is with a path path(id), where N is the maximal number of system users. Additionally, the detailed description of KUNodes(BT,RL,t) algorithm is omitted in this paper and any interested readers please refer to [4, 7, 9, 20, 21, 24].

3.1 Description of the Scheme

As in Sun et al. [27], our lattice-based RIBE-CE scheme also consists of eight pt algorithms: Setup, PriKeyGen, KeyUpd, DecKeyGen, Encrypt, Evolve, Decrypt and Revoke. The main algorithms are described as follows:

- Setup($1^n, N$): On input a security parameter n and the maximal number of users $N = 2^n$, set prime modulus $q = \widetilde{\mathcal{O}}(n^3)$, dimension $m = 2nk$ where $k = \lceil \log q \rceil$, Gaussian parameter $s = \widetilde{\mathcal{O}}(m)$ and norm bound $\beta = \widetilde{\mathcal{O}}(\sqrt{n})$ for a distribution χ. PKG specifies the following steps:
    1. Let identity space $\mathcal{I} = 0||\{0,1\}^n$, time space $\mathcal{T} \subset 0||\{0,1\}^n$, and message space $\mathcal{M} = \{0,1\}$.
    2. Run TrapGen(q, n, m) to generate $\mathbf{A} \in \mathbb{Z}_q^{n \times m}$ with a trapdoor $\mathbf{R_A}$, and $\mathbf{B} \in \mathbb{Z}_q^{n \times m}$ with a trapdoor $\mathbf{R_B}$.
    3. Sample a collision-resistance hash function $\mathcal{G} : \{0,1\}^* \to \mathbb{Z}_q^n$, and an FRD function $\mathcal{H} : \mathbb{Z}_q^n \to \mathbb{Z}_q^{n \times n}$.
    4. Sample $\mathbf{A_0}, \mathbf{A_1}, \mathbf{B_0}, \mathbf{B_1} \xleftarrow{\$} \mathbb{Z}_q^{n \times m}$, $\mathbf{v} \xleftarrow{\$} \mathbb{Z}_q^n$, and $\mathbf{U} \xleftarrow{\$} \mathbb{Z}_q^{n \times k}$.
    5. Set the sate st = BT that BT is with at least N leaf nodes, and the initial revocation list RL = $\emptyset$.
    6. Set pp = $(\mathbf{A}, \mathbf{A_0}, \mathbf{A_1}, \mathbf{B}, \mathbf{B_0}, \mathbf{B_1}, \mathbf{v}, \mathbf{U}, \mathcal{G}, \mathcal{H})$, and msk = $(\mathbf{R_A}, \mathbf{R_B})$.
    7. Output (pp, msk, RL, st) where msk is kept in *secret* by PKG, and pp is made *public* and as an implicit input of all other algorithms.
- PriKeyGen(msk, id): On input an identity id $\in \mathcal{I}$ and the master secret key msk. PKG specifies the following steps:
    1. View id as an unassigned leaf node of BT, thus, id $\in 0||\{0,1\}^n$.
    2. Define $\mathbf{A_{id}} = [\mathbf{A}|\mathbf{A_0} + \mathcal{H}(\mathcal{G}(\text{id}))\mathbf{A_1}] \in \mathbb{Z}_q^{n \times 2m}$.
    3. Run SampleLeft($\mathbf{A_{id}}, \mathbf{R_A}, \mathbf{v}, s$) to generate $\mathbf{e_{id}} \in \mathbb{Z}^{2m}$ satisfying $\mathbf{A_{id}} \cdot \mathbf{e_{id}} = \mathbf{v} \bmod q$.
    4. Output $\text{sk}_{\text{id}} = \mathbf{e_{id}}$. *Note*: sk_{id} is sent to user id via a *secret* channel.
- KeyUpd(RL, t, msk, st): On input a time t $\in \mathcal{T}$, the master secret key msk, a revocation list RL and the state st. PKG specifies the following steps:
    1. For $\theta \in$ KUNodes(BT, RL, t), define $\mathbf{B_{t_\theta}} = [\mathbf{B}|\mathbf{B_0} + \mathcal{H}(\mathcal{G}(\text{t}||\theta))\mathbf{B_1}] \in \mathbb{Z}_q^{n \times 2m}$.
    2. Run SampleLeft($\mathbf{B_{t_\theta}}, \mathbf{R_B}, \mathbf{U}, s$) to generate $\mathbf{E_\theta} \in \mathbb{Z}^{2m \times k}$ satisfying $\mathbf{B_{t_\theta}} \cdot \mathbf{E_\theta} = \mathbf{U} \bmod q$.
    3. Output $\text{uk}_t = (\theta, \mathbf{E_\theta})_{\theta \in \text{KUNodes(BT,RL,t)}}$.
- DecKeyGen(sk_{id}, uk_t, t): On input a long-term private key $\text{sk}_{\text{id}} = \mathbf{e_{id}}$, a time t and current time update key $\text{uk}_t = (\theta, \mathbf{E_\theta})_{\theta \in \text{KUNodes(BT,RL,t)}}$. The recipient id specifies the following steps:
    1. If path(id) $\cap$ KUNodes(BT, RL, t) = $\emptyset$, return $\bot$ and abort.
    2. Otherwise, select $\theta \in$ (path(id) $\cap$ KUNodes(BT, RL, t)) (only one θ exists).
    3. Return $\text{dk}_{\text{id,t}} = (\mathbf{e_{id}}, \mathbf{E_\theta})$.
- Encrypt(id, t, m): On input an identity id $\in \mathcal{I}$, a time t $\in \mathcal{T}$, and a message m $\in \{0,1\}$. The sender will specify the following steps:
    1. Let $\mathbf{A_{id}} = [\mathbf{A}|\mathbf{A_0} + \mathcal{H}(\mathcal{G}(\text{id}))\mathbf{A_1}] \in \mathbb{Z}_q^{n \times 2m}$.
    2. For $\theta \in$ path(id), define $\mathbf{B_{id_\theta,t}} = [\mathbf{B}|\mathbf{B_0} + \mathcal{H}(\mathcal{G}(\text{t}||\theta))\mathbf{B_1}] \in \mathbb{Z}_q^{n \times 2m}$.

3. Sample $s_0, s_0' \xleftarrow{\$} \mathbb{Z}_q^n$, $e_0 \xleftarrow{\$} \chi$, $e_0' \xleftarrow{\$} \chi^k$, $e_1, e_1' \xleftarrow{\$} \chi^m$, and $\mathbf{R}_1, \mathbf{R}_2 \xleftarrow{\$} \{1, -1\}^{m \times m}$.

4. Let $c_0 = \mathbf{v}^{\mathrm{T}} s_0 + e_0 + m\lfloor \frac{q}{2} \rfloor \bmod q \in \mathbb{Z}_q$, $\mathbf{c}_1 = \mathbf{A}_{\mathsf{id}}^{\mathrm{T}} s_0 + \begin{bmatrix} e_1 \\ \mathbf{R}_1^{\mathrm{T}} e_1 \end{bmatrix} \in \mathbb{Z}_q^{2m}$.

5. Let $\mathbf{c}_0' = \mathbf{U}^{\mathrm{T}} s_0' + e_0' + \mathsf{bin}(c_0)\lfloor \frac{q}{2} \rfloor \bmod q \in \mathbb{Z}_q^k$, $\mathbf{c}_{2,\theta} = \mathbf{B}_{\mathsf{id}_\theta, t}^{\mathrm{T}} s_0' + \begin{bmatrix} e_1' \\ \mathbf{R}_2^{\mathrm{T}} e_1' \end{bmatrix} \in \mathbb{Z}_q^{2m}$. *Note*: a binary decomposition function $\mathsf{bin} : \mathbb{Z}_q \to \{0, 1\}^k$ is adopted here, and for all $\mathbf{e} \in \mathbb{Z}_q$ we have that $\mathbf{e} = (1, 2, \cdots, 2^{k-1}) \cdot \mathsf{bin}(\mathbf{e})$.

6. Output $\mathsf{ct}_{\mathsf{id}, t} = (\mathsf{id}, t, \mathbf{c}_0', \mathbf{c}_1, (\mathbf{c}_{2,\theta})_{\theta \in \mathsf{path}(\mathsf{id})}) \in (0 || \{0, 1\}^n)^2 \times \mathbb{Z}_q^k \times (\mathbb{Z}_q^{2m})^{n+2}$.

- Evolve($\mathsf{ct}_{\mathsf{id}, t}, t', \mathsf{uk}_t$): On input a ciphertext $\mathsf{ct}_{\mathsf{id}, t} = (\mathsf{id}, t, \mathbf{c}_0', \mathbf{c}_1, (\mathbf{c}_{2,\theta})_{\theta \in \mathsf{path}(\mathsf{id})})$, a new $t' > t$, and the current time update key $\mathsf{uk}_t = (\theta, \mathbf{E}_\theta)_{\theta \in \mathsf{KUNodes}(\mathsf{BT}, \mathsf{RL}, t)}$. The Cloud specifies the following steps:
  1. If the recipient of $\mathsf{ct}_{\mathsf{id}, t}$ has been revoked before (or at) time t, set $\mathsf{ct}_{\mathsf{id}, t'} = \mathsf{ct}_{\mathsf{id}, t}$.
  2. Otherwise, compute $\mathbf{w}_0 = \mathbf{c}_0' - \mathbf{E}_\theta^{\mathrm{T}} \cdot \mathbf{c}_{2,\theta} \bmod q \in \mathbb{Z}_q^k$, here, $\theta \in (\mathsf{path}(\mathsf{id}) \cap \mathsf{KUNodes}(\mathsf{BT}, \mathsf{RL}, t))$.
  3. Compute $c_0 = (1, 2, \cdots, 2^{k-1}) \cdot \lfloor \frac{2}{q} \mathbf{w}_0 \rfloor \in \mathbb{Z}_q$.
  4. Sample $s_0'' \xleftarrow{\$} \mathbb{Z}_q^n$, $e_0'' \xleftarrow{\$} \chi^k$, $e_1'' \xleftarrow{\$} \chi^m$, and $\mathbf{R}_2' \xleftarrow{\$} \{1, -1\}^{m \times m}$.
  5. For $\theta \in \mathsf{path}(\mathsf{id})$, define $\mathbf{B}_{\mathsf{id}_\theta, t'} = [\mathbf{B} | \mathbf{B}_0 + \mathcal{H}(\mathcal{G}(t' || \theta))\mathbf{B}_1] \in \mathbb{Z}_q^{n \times 2m}$.
  6. Let $\mathbf{c}_0'' = \mathbf{U}^{\mathrm{T}} s_0'' + e_0'' + \mathsf{bin}(c_0)\lfloor \frac{q}{2} \rfloor \bmod q \in \mathbb{Z}_q^k$, and $\mathbf{c}_{2,\theta}' = \mathbf{B}_{\mathsf{id}_\theta, t'}^{\mathrm{T}} s_0'' + \begin{bmatrix} e_1'' \\ \mathbf{R}_2'^{\mathrm{T}} e_1'' \end{bmatrix} \bmod q \in \mathbb{Z}_q^{2m}$.
  7. Output $\mathsf{ct}_{\mathsf{id}, t'} = (\mathsf{id}, t', \mathbf{c}_0'', \mathbf{c}_1, (\mathbf{c}_{2,\theta}')_{\theta \in \mathsf{path}(\mathsf{id})}) \in (0 || \{0, 1\}^n)^2 \times \mathbb{Z}_q^k \times (\mathbb{Z}_q^{2m})^{n+2}$.

- Decrypt($\mathsf{dk}_{\mathsf{id}', t'}, \mathsf{ct}_{\mathsf{id}, t}$): On input a ciphertext $\mathsf{ct}_{\mathsf{id}, t} = (\mathsf{id}, t, \mathbf{c}_0', \mathbf{c}_1, (\mathbf{c}_{2,\theta})_{\theta \in \mathsf{path}(\mathsf{id})})$ and a decryption key $\mathsf{dk}_{\mathsf{id}', t'}$. The recipient id' specifies the following steps:
  1. If $(\mathsf{id} \neq \mathsf{id}') \vee (t \neq t')$, return $\perp$ and abort.
  2. Otherwise, compute $\mathbf{w}_0 = \mathbf{c}_0' - \mathbf{E}_\theta^{\mathrm{T}} \cdot \mathbf{c}_{2,\theta} \bmod q \in \mathbb{Z}_q^k$, here, $\theta \in (\mathsf{path}(\mathsf{id}) \cap \mathsf{KUNodes}(\mathsf{BT}, \mathsf{RL}, t))$.
  3. Compute $c_0 = (1, 2, \cdots, 2^{k-1}) \cdot \lfloor \frac{2}{q} \mathbf{w}_0 \rfloor \in \mathbb{Z}_q$, and $w = c_0 - \mathbf{e}_{\mathsf{id}}^{\mathrm{T}} \mathbf{c}_1 \in \mathbb{Z}_q$.
  4. Output $\lfloor \frac{2}{q} w \rceil \in \{0, 1\}$.

- Revoke($\mathsf{id}, t, \mathsf{RL}, \mathsf{st}$): On input current revocation list RL, an identity id, a time t, and a state $\mathsf{st} = \mathsf{BT}$. PKG specifies the following steps:
  1. Add (id, t) to RL for all nodes associated with id.
  2. Output an updated $\mathsf{RL} = \mathsf{RL} \cup \{(\mathsf{id}, t)\}$.

3.2 Analysis

We analysis the efficiency, correctness and security of our lattice-based RIBE-CE scheme without DKER.

Efficiency: The efficiency aspect of our lattice-based RIBE-CE without DKER with $N = 2^n$ is as follows:

- The bit-size of public parameters pp is $(6nm + n + nk + 2n) \log q = \tilde{\mathcal{O}}(n^2)$.
- The long-term private key $\mathsf{sk_{id}}$ has a short vector of bit-size $\tilde{\mathcal{O}}(n)$.
- The time update key $\mathsf{uk_t}$ has bit-size $\mathcal{O}(r \log \frac{N}{r}) \cdot \tilde{\mathcal{O}}(n)$ where r is the number of revoked users.
- The ciphertext $\mathsf{ct_{id,t}}$ has bit-size $2(n+1) + (k + 2m(n+2)) \log q = \tilde{\mathcal{O}}(n^2)$.
- The short-term decryption key $\mathsf{dk_{id,t}}$ has bit-size $\tilde{\mathcal{O}}(n)$.

Correctness: If the first lattice-based RIBE-CE scheme is operated correctly as specified, and a recipient id is not revoked at time $\mathsf{t} \in \mathcal{T}$, then $\mathsf{dk_{id,t}} = (\mathbf{e_{id}}, \mathbf{E}_\theta)$ satisfies $\mathbf{A_{id}} \cdot \mathbf{e_{id}} = \mathbf{v} \bmod q$ and $\mathbf{B_{t_\theta}} \cdot \mathbf{E_\theta} = \mathbf{U} \bmod q$. In the decryption algorithm, the non-revoked id tries to derive m by using $\mathsf{dk_{id,t}}$:

Given a ciphertext (no matter an original or evolutive ciphertext) $\mathsf{ct_{id,t}} = (\mathsf{id}, \mathsf{t}, \mathbf{c_0'}, \mathbf{c_1}, (\mathbf{c_{2,\theta}})_{\theta \in \mathsf{path(id)}})$.

1. Parse $\mathbf{c_{2,\theta}} = \begin{bmatrix} \mathbf{c_{2,0}} \\ \mathbf{c_{2,1}} \end{bmatrix}$ where $\mathbf{c_{2,i \in \{0,1\}}} \in \mathbb{Z}_q^m$, $\theta \in$ (path(id) $\cap$ KUNodes(BT, RL, t)).

2. Compute

$$\mathbf{w_0} = \mathbf{c_0'} - \mathbf{E_\theta^T} \mathbf{c_{2,\theta}} = \mathbf{U^T} \mathbf{s_0'} + \mathbf{e_0'} + \mathsf{bin}(c_0) \lfloor \frac{q}{2} \rfloor - \mathbf{E_\theta^T} \begin{bmatrix} \mathbf{c_{2,0}} \\ \mathbf{c_{2,1}} \end{bmatrix}$$

$$= \mathsf{bin}(c_0) \lfloor \frac{q}{2} \rfloor + \underbrace{\mathbf{e_0'} - \mathbf{E_\theta^T} \begin{bmatrix} \mathbf{e_1'} \\ \mathbf{R_2^T} \mathbf{e_1'} \end{bmatrix}}_{\text{error}'}$$

According to our parameters settings, it can be checked that the error term error$'$ is bounded by $q/5$ (i.e., $\|\text{error}'\|_\infty < q/5$), thus, we have the conclusion $(1, 2, \cdots, 2^{k-1}) \cdot \lfloor \frac{2}{q} \mathbf{w_0} \rceil = c_0$ with overwhelming probability.

3. Parse $\mathbf{c_1} = \begin{bmatrix} \mathbf{c_{1,0}} \\ \mathbf{c_{1,1}} \end{bmatrix}$ where $\mathbf{c_{1,i \in \{0,1\}}} \in \mathbb{Z}_q^m$, and compute

$$w = c_0 - \mathbf{e_{id}^T} \mathbf{c_1} = \mathbf{v^T} \mathbf{s_0} + e_0 + m \lfloor \frac{q}{2} \rfloor - \mathbf{e_{id}^T} \begin{bmatrix} \mathbf{c_{1,0}} \\ \mathbf{c_{1,1}} \end{bmatrix} = m \lfloor \frac{q}{2} \rfloor + \underbrace{e_0 - \mathbf{e_{id}^T} \begin{bmatrix} \mathbf{e_1} \\ \mathbf{R_1^T} \mathbf{e_1} \end{bmatrix}}_{\text{error}}$$

According to our parameters settings, it can be checked that the error term error is bounded by $q/5$ (i.e., $\|\text{error}\|_\infty < q/5$), thus, we have the conclusion $\lfloor \frac{2}{q} w \rceil = m$ with overwhelming probability.

Theorem 1. *Our lattice-based* RIBE-CE *without* DKER *is* ind-cpa *secure if the* LWE *assumption holds.*

Proof. To proof this theorem, we define a list of games where the first one is identical to the original ind-cpa game as in Definition 2 and show that a ppt adversary $\mathcal{A}$ has advantage zero in the last game. We show that $\mathcal{A}$ cannot distinguish between these games, and thus $\mathcal{A}$ has negligible advantage in winning the original ind-cpa game. In particular, the LWE hardness assumption is adopted to prove that Game 2 and Game 3 are indistinguishable.

Let id^* be a challenge identity and t^* be a challenge time, we consider two types of adversaries:

- Type-0: An inside adversary $\mathcal{A}_0$ who requests a long-term private key on the challenge identity id^*. In this case, id^* must be revoked at $t \le t^*$.
- Type-1: An outside adversary $\mathcal{A}_1$ who only requests a long-term private key on the identity $id \ne id^*$.

For Type-0 adversary, we simulate the game as follow:

Game 0. It is the original ind-cpa game defined in Definition 2.

Game 1. We slightly change the way that $\mathcal{C}_0$ generates $\mathbf{B}_0$ in pp. $\mathcal{C}_0$ samples $\mathbf{R}_2^* \xleftarrow{\$} \{1, -1\}^{m \times m} \bmod q$ at the setup phase, and defines $\mathbf{B}_0 = \mathbf{BR}_2^* - \mathcal{H}(\mathcal{G}(t^*\|\theta))\mathbf{B}_1 \bmod q$. For the remainders, they are unchanged and identical to those in Game 0. Next, we show that Game 0 and Game 1 are indistinguishable. In Game 1, $\mathbf{R}_2^*$ is used only in the designs of $\mathbf{B}_0, \mathbf{R}_2^{*\mathrm{T}}\mathbf{e}_1'$. According to Lemma 8, $(\mathbf{B}, \mathbf{BR}_2^*, \mathbf{R}_2^{*\mathrm{T}}\mathbf{e}_1')$ is statistically close to $(\mathbf{B}, \mathbf{C}_0, \mathbf{R}_2^{*\mathrm{T}}\mathbf{e}_1')$, where $\mathbf{C}_0 \xleftarrow{\$} \mathbb{Z}_q^{n \times m}$. In $\mathcal{A}_0$'s view, $\mathbf{BR}_2^*$ is statistically close to uniform, and thus $\mathbf{B}_0$ is close to uniform. Hence, $\mathbf{B}_0$ in Game 1 and Game 0 are indistinguishable.

Game 2: We redesign $\mathbf{B}$ and $\mathbf{B}_1$. $\mathcal{C}_0$ samples $\mathbf{B} \xleftarrow{\$} \mathbb{Z}_q^{n \times m}$ and runs TrapGen(q, n, m) to obtain $\mathbf{B}_1$ with a trapdoor $\mathbf{R}_{\mathbf{B}_1}$. Let $\mathbf{B}_{t_\theta} = [\mathbf{B}|\mathbf{BR}_2^* + (\mathcal{H}(\mathcal{G}(t\|\theta)) - \mathcal{H}(\mathcal{G}(t^*\|\theta^*)))\mathbf{B}_1]$, due to the collision-resistance property of $\mathcal{G}$ and the main property of FRD, $\mathcal{H}(\mathcal{G}(t\|\theta)) - \mathcal{H}(\mathcal{G}(t^*\|\theta^*))$ is full-rank, and $\mathbf{R}_{\mathbf{B}_1}$ is also a trapdoor for $\Lambda_q^\perp((\mathcal{H}(\mathcal{G}(t\|\theta)) - \mathcal{H}(\mathcal{G}(t^*\|\theta^*)))\mathbf{B}_1)$. $\mathcal{C}_0$ responds a time update key query for any $t \ne t^*$ (id^* has been revoked before or at t^*) by running SampleRight$(\mathbf{B}, (\mathcal{H}(\mathcal{G}(t\|\theta)) - \mathcal{H}(\mathcal{G}(t^*\|\theta^*)))\mathbf{B}_1, \mathbf{R}_2^*, \mathbf{R}_{\mathbf{B}_1}, \mathbf{U}, s)$ that returns $\mathbf{E}_{\theta \in \mathsf{KUNodes}(\mathsf{BT},\mathsf{RL},t)}$. Additionally, the parameter $s = \tilde{\mathcal{O}}(m)$ is sufficiently large. According to Lemma 7, $\mathbf{E}_\theta$ is statistically close to that in Game 1. For the remainders, they are unchanged and identical to those in Game 1. Because $\mathbf{B}$ and $\mathbf{B}_1$ are statistically close to those in Game 1, the advantage of $\mathcal{A}_0$ in Game 2 is at most negligibly different from that in Game 1.

Game 3: We redesign the partial challenge ciphertexts $\mathbf{c}_0'^*$ and $\mathbf{c}_{2,\theta}^*$, and the remainders (including $\mathbf{c}_1^*$) are unchanged and identical to those in Game 2. $\mathcal{C}_0$ samples $\mathbf{c}_0'^* \xleftarrow{\$} \mathbb{Z}_q^k$ and $\mathbf{c}_{2,\theta}^* \xleftarrow{\$} \mathbb{Z}_q^{2m}$. Because $\mathbf{c}_0'^*$ and $\mathbf{c}_{2,\theta}^*$ are always random, the advantage of $\mathcal{A}_0$ in returning a correct c_0 is zero, and the same advantage zero for the message $\mathsf{m} = \lfloor \frac{2}{q}(c_0 - \mathbf{e}_{id^*}^\mathrm{T}\mathbf{c}_1^*) \rceil$ is returned correctly.

A reduction from the LWE problem will be given to show that Game 2 and Game 3 are computationally indistinguishable for a ppt adversary.

A reduction from LWE: Assume that there is a ppt adversary $\mathcal{A}_0$ distinguishing Game 2 and Game 3 with non-negligible advantage, then we use $\mathcal{A}_0$ to design an algorithm $\mathcal{B}_0$ to solve the LWE problem defined in Definition 4.

Given an LWE instance, a fresh pair $(\mathbf{a}_i, b_i) \in \mathbb{Z}_q^n \times \mathbb{Z}_q$ for $i = 1, \cdots, m(n + 1) + k$, from a sampling oracle, which is truly random $\mathcal{R}_\$$ or noisy pseudo-random

$\mathcal{R}_{\mathbf{s}'_0}$ for a secret vector $\mathbf{s}'_0 \in \mathbb{Z}^n_q$. The target of $\mathcal{B}_0$ is to distinguish between the two oracles by utilizing $\mathcal{A}_0$ as follows:

Instance: $\mathcal{B}_0$ receives an LWE instance (i.e., $(\mathbf{a}_i, b_i), i = 1, \cdots, m(n+1) + k$).

Setup: $\mathcal{B}_0$ does as follows:

1. Assemble $\mathbf{B} \in \mathbb{Z}^{n \times m}_q$ from m of the given LWE samples, that is, define $\mathbf{B} = [\mathbf{a}_1 | \mathbf{a}_2 | \cdots | \mathbf{a}_m]$.

2. Assemble $\mathbf{U} \in \mathbb{Z}^{n \times k}_q$ from the unused samples, define $\mathbf{U} = [\mathbf{a}_{m+1} | \cdots | \mathbf{a}_{m+k}]$.

3. Run $\mathsf{TrapGen}(q, n, m)$ to generate $\mathbf{A} \in \mathbb{Z}^{n \times m}_q$ and a trapdoor $\mathbf{R_A}$, sample $\mathbf{A}_0, \mathbf{A}_1 \xleftarrow{\$} \mathbb{Z}^{n \times m}_q, \mathbf{v} \xleftarrow{\$} \mathbb{Z}^n_q$.

4. Design the remainders of public matrices, $\mathbf{B}_0, \mathbf{B}_1 \in \mathbb{Z}^{n \times m}_q$, as in Game 2 by using $\mathsf{id}^*, \mathbf{t}^*$, and $\mathbf{R}^*_2$.

5. Sample a collision-resistance hash function $\mathcal{G} : \{0, 1\}^* \to \mathbb{Z}^n_q$, and an FRD function $\mathcal{H} : \mathbb{Z}^n_q \to \mathbb{Z}^{n \times n}_q$.

6. Let $\mathsf{pp} = (\mathbf{A}, \mathbf{A}_0, \mathbf{A}_1, \mathbf{B}, \mathbf{B}_0, \mathbf{v}, \mathbf{B}_1, \mathbf{U}, \mathcal{G}, \mathcal{H})$, and send pp to $\mathcal{A}_1$.

Queries: $\mathcal{B}_0$ answers a time update key query for $\mathbf{t}$ as in Game 2. As $\mathcal{B}_0$ knows the master secret key $\mathbf{R_A}$, it can answer a long-term private key query for id (a shorter vector $\mathbf{e}_{\mathsf{id}}$) as in the real game.

Challenge: Once receive a message $\mathsf{m}^* \in \mathcal{M}$, $\mathcal{B}_0$ computes a challenge ciphertext for id^* and $\mathbf{t}^*$ as follows:

1. Let $\mathbf{A}_{\mathsf{id}^*} = [\mathbf{A} | \mathbf{A}_0 + \mathcal{H}(\mathcal{G}(\mathsf{id}^*))\mathbf{A}_1] \in \mathbb{Z}^{n \times 2m}_q$.

2. Sample $\mathbf{s}_0 \xleftarrow{\$} \mathbb{Z}^n_q, e_0 \xleftarrow{\$} \chi, \mathbf{e}_1 \xleftarrow{\$} \chi^m$, and $\mathbf{R}_1 \xleftarrow{\$} \{1, -1\}^{m \times m}$.

3. Let $c^*_0 = \mathbf{v}^\mathsf{T}\mathbf{s}_0 + e_0 + \mathsf{m}^*\lfloor \frac{q}{2} \rfloor \bmod q \in \mathbb{Z}_q, \mathbf{c}^*_1 = \mathbf{A}^\mathsf{T}_{\mathsf{id}^*}\mathbf{s}_0 + \begin{bmatrix} \mathbf{e}_1 \\ \mathbf{R}^\mathsf{T}_1\mathbf{e}_1 \end{bmatrix} \in \mathbb{Z}^{2m}_q$.

4. Assemble $\mathbf{e}'^*_{1,\theta}$ from m of the given LWE samples, define $\mathbf{e}'^*_{1,\theta} = \begin{bmatrix} b_{|\theta|m+1} \\ \vdots \\ b_{|\theta|m+m} \end{bmatrix}$,

$\mathbf{b}^* = \begin{bmatrix} b_{m(n+1)+1} \\ \vdots \\ b_{m(n+1)+k} \end{bmatrix}$, where $\theta \in \mathsf{path}(\mathsf{id}^*)$ and $|\theta|$ denotes the length of θ.

5. Blind the message string by defining $\mathbf{c}'^*_0 = \mathbf{b}^* + \mathsf{bin}(c^*_0)\lfloor \frac{q}{2} \rfloor \in \mathbb{Z}^k_q$, and $\mathbf{c}^*_{2,\theta} = \begin{bmatrix} \mathbf{e}'^*_{1,\theta} \\ \mathbf{R}^{*\mathsf{T}}_2\mathbf{e}'^*_{1,\theta} \end{bmatrix} \in \mathbb{Z}^{2m}_q$.

6. Send $\mathsf{ct}_{\mathsf{id}^*, \mathbf{t}^*} = (\mathsf{id}^*, \mathbf{t}^*, \mathbf{c}'^*_0, \mathbf{c}^*_1, (\mathbf{c}^*_{2,\theta})_{\theta \in \mathsf{path}(\mathsf{id}^*)})$ to $\mathcal{A}_0$.

We first show that if the LWE instance is from a noisy pseudo-random $\mathcal{R}_{\mathbf{s}'_0}$, so $(\mathbf{c}^*_0, \mathbf{c}^*_1) \in \mathsf{ct}_{\mathsf{id}^*, \mathbf{t}^*}$ enjoys a distribution exactly as in Game 2. First, it can be checked that $\mathbf{B}_{\mathsf{id}^*_\theta, \mathbf{t}^*} = [\mathbf{B} | \mathbf{B}\mathbf{R}^*_2]$. Second, it can be checked that $\mathbf{e}'^*_{1,\theta} = \mathbf{B}^\mathsf{T}\mathbf{s}'_0 + \mathbf{e}'_1 \bmod q$ where $\mathbf{e}'_1 \xleftarrow{\$} \chi^m$. Thus, $\mathbf{c}^*_{2,\theta}$ enjoys the following structure:

$$\mathbf{c}^*_{2,\theta} = \begin{bmatrix} \mathbf{e}'^*_{1,\theta} \\ \mathbf{R}^{*\mathsf{T}}_2\mathbf{e}'^*_{1,\theta} \end{bmatrix} = \begin{bmatrix} \mathbf{B}^\mathsf{T}\mathbf{s}'_0 + \mathbf{e}'_1 \\ (\mathbf{B}\mathbf{R}^*_2)^\mathsf{T}\mathbf{s}'_0 + \mathbf{R}^{*\mathsf{T}}_2\mathbf{e}'_1 \end{bmatrix} = \mathbf{B}^\mathsf{T}_{\mathsf{id}^*_\theta, \mathbf{t}^*}\mathbf{s}'_0 + \begin{bmatrix} \mathbf{e}'_1 \\ \mathbf{R}^{*\mathsf{T}}_2\mathbf{e}'_1 \end{bmatrix} \bmod q,$$

which implies that $\mathbf{c}_{2,\theta}^*$ is exactly the $\mathbf{c}_{2,\theta}$ part of a valid challenge ciphertext in Game 2.

We then show that if the LWE instance is from a truly random $\mathcal{R}_{\$}$, then $(\mathbf{c}_0'^*, (\mathbf{c}_{2,\theta}^*)_{\theta \in \mathsf{path}(\mathsf{id}^*)}) \in \mathsf{ct}_{\mathsf{id}^*, t^*}$ enjoys a distribution exactly as in Game 3. It can be checked that $\mathbf{b}^*$ is unform over $\mathbb{Z}_q^k$, and $\mathbf{e}_{1,\theta}'^*$ are unform over $\mathbb{Z}_q^m$. Thus, $\mathbf{c}_{2,\theta}^*$ is unform and independent over $\mathbb{Z}_q^{2m}$, which implies that $\mathbf{c}_{2,\theta}^*$ is exactly the $\mathbf{c}_{2,\theta}$ part of a valid challenge ciphertext in Game 3.

Guess: After making some additional queries, $\mathcal{A}_0$ returns a guess for which challenger, Game 2 or Game 3, it is interacting with. Then, $\mathcal{B}_0$ returns the guess of $\mathcal{A}_0$ as an answer to the given LWE instance.

According to the above analysis, if the LWE instance is from $\mathcal{R}_{\mathbf{s}_0'}$, $\mathcal{A}_0$'s view is as in Game 2, and if the LWE instance is from $\mathcal{R}_{\$}$, $\mathcal{A}_0$'s view is as in Game 3, and thus, the advantage of $\mathcal{B}_0$ in solving the LWE problem is the same as that of $\mathcal{A}_0$ in distinguishing Game 2 and Game 3.

For Type-1 adversary, we simulate the game as follow:

Game 0. It is the original ind-cpa game defined in Definition 2.

Game 1. We slightly change the way that $\mathcal{C}_1$ generates $\mathbf{A}_0$ in pp. $\mathcal{C}_1$ samples $\mathbf{R}_1^* \xleftarrow{\$} \{1, -1\}^{m \times m}$ at the setup phase, let $\mathbf{A}_0 = \mathbf{A}\mathbf{R}_1^* - \mathcal{H}(\mathcal{G}(\mathsf{id}^*))\mathbf{A}_1 \bmod q$. For the remainders, they are unchanged and identical to those in Game 0. Next, we show that Game 0 and Game 1 are indistinguishable. In Game 1, $\mathbf{R}_1^*$ is used only in the designs of $\mathbf{A}_0$ and $\mathbf{R}_1^{*\mathrm{T}}\mathbf{e}_1$. So, according to Lemma 10, $(\mathbf{A}, \mathbf{A}\mathbf{R}_1^*, \mathbf{R}_1^{*\mathrm{T}}\mathbf{e}_1)$ is statistically close to $(\mathbf{A}, \mathbf{C}_1, \mathbf{R}_1^{*\mathrm{T}}\mathbf{e}_1)$, where $\mathbf{C}_1 \xleftarrow{\$} \mathbb{Z}_q^{n \times m}$. In $\mathcal{A}_1$'s view, $\mathbf{A}\mathbf{R}_1^*$ is statistically close to uniform, and thus $\mathbf{A}_0$ is close to uniform. Hence, $\mathbf{A}_0$ in Game 1 and Game 0 are indistinguishable.

Game 2: We redesign $\mathbf{A}, \mathbf{A}_1$. $\mathcal{C}_2$ samples $\mathbf{A} \xleftarrow{\$} \mathbb{Z}_q^{n \times m}$ and runs $\mathsf{TrapGen}(q, n, m)$ to get $\mathbf{A}_1$ with trapdoor $\mathbf{R}_{\mathbf{A}_1}$. Let $\mathbf{A}_{\mathsf{id}} = [\mathbf{A} | \mathbf{A}\mathbf{R}_0^* + (\mathcal{H}(\mathcal{G}(\mathsf{id})) - \mathcal{H}(\mathcal{G}(\mathsf{id}^*)))\mathbf{A}_1]$, and due to the collision-resistance property of $\mathcal{G}$ and the main property of FRD, $\mathcal{H}(\mathcal{G}(\mathsf{id}) - \mathcal{H}(\mathcal{G}(\mathsf{id}^*))$ is full-rank, $\mathbf{R}_{\mathbf{A}_1}$ is a trapdoor for $\varLambda_q^\perp((\mathcal{H}(\mathcal{G}(\mathsf{id})) - \mathcal{H}(\mathcal{G}(\mathsf{id}^*)))\mathbf{A}_1)$. $\mathcal{C}_1$ can respond a long-term private key query for any $\mathsf{id} \neq \mathsf{id}^*$ by running $\mathsf{SampleRight}(\mathbf{A}_{\mathsf{id}}, (\mathcal{H}(\mathcal{G}(\mathsf{id})) - \mathcal{H}(\mathcal{G}(\mathsf{id}^*)))\mathbf{A}_1, \mathbf{R}_1^*, \mathbf{R}_{\mathbf{A}_1}, \mathbf{v}, s)$ to generate a short vector $\mathbf{e}_{\mathsf{id}} \in \mathbb{Z}^{3m}$. The parameter $s = \tilde{\mathcal{O}}(m)$ is sufficiently large, and according to Lemma 7, $\mathbf{e}_{\mathsf{id}}$ is statistically close to that in Game 1. The remainders are unchanged and identical to those in Game 1. $\mathbf{A}$ and $\mathbf{A}_1$ are statistically close to those in Game 1, the advantage of $\mathcal{A}_1$ in Game 2 is at most negligibly different from that in Game 1.

Game 3: We redesign the partial challenge ciphertexts $\mathbf{c}_1^*$ and $\mathbf{c}_0'^*$, and the remainders (including $\mathbf{c}_{2,\theta}^*$) are unchanged and identical to those in Game 2. $\mathcal{C}_1$ first samples $c_0^* \xleftarrow{\$} \mathbb{Z}_q$ and $\mathbf{c}_1^* \xleftarrow{\$} \mathbb{Z}_q^{3m}$, then set $\mathbf{c}_0'^* = \mathbf{U}^{\mathrm{T}}\mathbf{s}_0' + \mathbf{e}_0' + \mathsf{bin}(c_0^*)\lfloor \frac{q}{2} \rfloor \bmod q \in \mathbb{Z}_q^k$. Because c_0^* and $\mathbf{c}_1^*$ are always random, the advantage of $\mathcal{A}_1$ in returning a correct c_0^* is zero, and the same advantage zero for the message m is returned correctly.

A reduction from the LWE problem will be given to show that Game 2 and Game 3 are computationally indistinguishable for a ppt adversary.

A reduction from LWE: Assume that there is a ppt $\mathcal{A}_1$ distinguishing Games 2 and 3 with non-negligible advantage, then we use $\mathcal{A}_1$ to design an algorithm $\mathcal{B}_1$ to solve the LWE problem defined in Definition 4.

Given an LWE instance, a fresh pair $(\mathbf{a}_i, b_i) \in \mathbb{Z}_q^n \times \mathbb{Z}_q$ for $i = 1, 2, \cdots, m+1$, from a sampling oracle, which is truly random $\mathcal{R}_\$$ or noisy pseudo-random $\mathcal{R}_{\mathbf{s}_0}$ for a secret vector $\mathbf{s}_0 \in \mathbb{Z}_q^n$. The target of $\mathcal{B}_1$ is to distinguish between the two oracles by utilizing $\mathcal{A}_1$ as follows:

Instance: $\mathcal{B}_1$ receives an LWE instance (i.e., $(\mathbf{a}_i, b_i), i = 1, 2, \cdots, m+1$).
Setup: $\mathcal{B}_1$ does as follows:

1. Assemble $\mathbf{A} \in \mathbb{Z}_q^{n \times m}$ from m of the given samples, define $\mathbf{A} = [\mathbf{a}_1 | \cdots | \mathbf{a}_m]$.
2. Assemble $\mathbf{v} \in \mathbb{Z}_q^n$ from the unused samples, that is, define $\mathbf{v} = \mathbf{a}_{m+1}$.
3. Run TrapGen(q, n, m) to generate $\mathbf{A}_1 \in \mathbb{Z}_q^{n \times m}$ and a trapdoor $\mathbf{R}_{\mathbf{A}_1}$, $\mathbf{B} \in \mathbb{Z}_q^{n \times m}$ and a trapdoor $\mathbf{R}_{\mathbf{B}}$, sample $\mathbf{U} \xleftarrow{\$} \mathbb{Z}_q^{n \times k}$, $\mathbf{B}_0, \mathbf{B}_1 \xleftarrow{\$} \mathbb{Z}_q^{n \times m}$.
4. Design $\mathbf{A}_0 \in \mathbb{Z}_q^{n \times m}$, as in Game 2 by using id* and R_1^*.
5. Sample a collision-resistance hash function $\mathcal{G} : \{0, 1\}^* \to \mathbb{Z}_q^n$, and an FRD function $\mathcal{H} : \mathbb{Z}_q^n \to \mathbb{Z}_q^{n \times n}$.
6. Let $\mathsf{pp} = (\mathbf{A}, \mathbf{A}_0, \mathbf{A}_1, \mathbf{B}, \mathbf{B}_0, \mathbf{v}, \mathbf{B}_1, \mathbf{U}, \mathcal{G}, \mathcal{H})$, and send pp to $\mathcal{A}_1$.

Queries: $\mathcal{B}_1$ answers a long-term private key query for id $\neq$ id* as in Game 2. As $\mathcal{B}_1$ knows the master secret key $\mathbf{R}_{\mathbf{B}}$, it can answer a time update key query for any t (a list of shorter matrices $(\mathbf{E}_\theta)_{\theta \in \mathsf{KUNodes}(\mathsf{BT}, \mathsf{RL}, \mathsf{t})}$) as in the real game.

Challenge: Once receive m*, $\mathcal{B}_1$ computes a challenge for id* and t* as follows:

1. Assemble $\mathbf{e}_1^*$ from m of the samples, define $\mathbf{e}_1^* = \begin{bmatrix} b_1 \\ \vdots \\ b_m \end{bmatrix}$, and $v^* = b_{m+1}$.

2. Blind m* by defining $c_0^* = v^* + \mathsf{m}^* \lfloor \frac{q}{2} \rfloor \in \mathbb{Z}_q$, and $\mathbf{c}_1^* = \begin{bmatrix} \mathbf{e}_1^* \\ \mathbf{R}_1^{*\mathrm{T}} \mathbf{e}_1^* \end{bmatrix} \in \mathbb{Z}_q^{2m}$.

3. For $\theta \in \mathsf{path}(\mathsf{id}^*)$, define $\mathbf{B}_{\mathsf{id}_\theta^*, \mathsf{t}^*} = [\mathbf{B} | \mathbf{B}_0 + \mathcal{H}(\mathcal{G}(\mathsf{t}^* || \theta))\mathbf{B}_1] \in \mathbb{Z}_q^{n \times 2m}$.

4. Sample $\mathbf{s}_0' \xleftarrow{\$} \mathbb{Z}_q^n$, $\mathbf{e}_0' \xleftarrow{\$} \chi^k$, $\mathbf{e}_1' \xleftarrow{\$} \chi^m$, and $\mathbf{R}_2 \xleftarrow{\$} \{1, -1\}^{m \times m}$.

5. Let $\mathbf{c}_0'^* = \mathbf{U}^{\mathrm{T}} \mathbf{s}_0' + \mathbf{e}_0' + \mathsf{bin}(c_0^*) \lfloor \frac{q}{2} \rfloor$, and $\mathbf{c}_{2,\theta}^* = \mathbf{B}_{\mathsf{id}_\theta^*, \mathsf{t}}^{\mathrm{T}} \mathbf{s}_0' + \begin{bmatrix} \mathbf{e}_1' \\ \mathbf{R}_2^{\mathrm{T}} \mathbf{e}_1' \end{bmatrix} \in \mathbb{Z}_q^{2m}$.

6. Send $\mathsf{ct}_{\mathsf{id}^*, \mathsf{t}^*} = (\mathsf{id}^*, \mathsf{t}^*, \mathbf{c}_0'^*, \mathbf{c}_1^*, (\mathbf{c}_{2,\theta}^*)_{\theta \in \mathsf{path}(\mathsf{id}^*)})$ to $\mathcal{A}_1$.

Obviously, c_0^* can be derived from $(\mathbf{c}_0'^*, (\mathbf{c}_{2,\theta}^*)_{\theta \in \mathsf{path}(\mathsf{id}^*)})$ by using a time update key $(\mathbf{E}_\theta)_{\theta \in \mathsf{KUNodes}(\mathsf{BT}, \mathsf{RL}, \mathsf{t}^*)}$. We first show that if the LWE instance is from a noisy pseudo-random $\mathcal{R}_{\mathbf{s}_0}$, so $(c_0^*, \mathbf{c}_1^*)$ enjoys a distribution exactly as in Game 2. First, it can be checked that $\mathbf{A}_{\mathsf{id}^*} = [\mathbf{A} | \mathbf{A}\mathbf{R}_1^*] \in \mathbb{Z}_q^{n \times 2m}$. Second, it can be checked that $\mathbf{e}_1^* = \mathbf{A}^{\mathrm{T}} \mathbf{s}_0 + \mathbf{e}_1 \bmod q$, where $\mathbf{e}_1 \xleftarrow{\$} \chi^m$. Thus, $\mathbf{c}_1^*$ enjoys the following structure:

$$\mathbf{c}_1^* = \begin{bmatrix} c\mathbf{e}_1^* \\ \mathbf{R}_1^{*\mathrm{T}} \mathbf{e}_1^* \end{bmatrix} = \begin{bmatrix} \mathbf{A}^{\mathrm{T}} \mathbf{s}_0 + \mathbf{e}_1 \\ (\mathbf{A}\mathbf{R}_1^*)^{\mathrm{T}} \mathbf{s}_0 + \mathbf{R}_1^{*\mathrm{T}} \mathbf{e}_1 \end{bmatrix} = \mathbf{A}_{\mathsf{id}^*}^{\mathrm{T}} \mathbf{s}_0 + \begin{bmatrix} \mathbf{e}_1 \\ \mathbf{R}_1^{*\mathrm{T}} \mathbf{e}_1 \end{bmatrix} \bmod q,$$

which implies that $\mathbf{c}_1^*$ is exactly the $\mathbf{c}_1$ part of a valid challenge in Game 2.

We then show that if the LWE instance is from a truly random $\mathcal{R}_\$$, so $(c_0^*, \mathbf{c}_1^*)$ enjoys a distribution exactly as in Game 3. It can be checked that v^* is unform over $\mathbb{Z}_q$, and $\mathbf{e}_1^*$ is unform over $\mathbb{Z}_q^m$. Thus, $\mathbf{c}_1^*$ is unform and independent over $\mathbb{Z}_q^{2m}$, which implies that $\mathbf{c}_1^*$ is exactly the $\mathbf{c}_1$ part of a valid challenge ciphertext in Game 3.

Guess: After making some additional queries, $\mathcal{A}_1$ returns a guess for which challenger, Game 2 or Game 3, it is interacting with. Then, $\mathcal{B}_1$ returns the guess of $\mathcal{A}_1$ as an answer to the given LWE instance.

According to the above analysis, if the LWE instance is from $\mathcal{R}_{\mathbf{s}_0}$, $\mathcal{A}_1$'s view is as in Game 2, and if the LWE instance is from $\mathcal{R}_\$$, $\mathcal{A}_1$'s view is as in Game 3, and thus, the advantage of $\mathcal{B}_1$ in solving the LWE problem is the same as that of $\mathcal{A}_1$ in distinguishing Game 2 and Game 3. This completes the proof.

4   Our Lattice-Based RIBE-CE Scheme with DKER

Our RIBE-CE scheme with DKER in the standard model is a combination of a two-level lattice-based HIBE scheme and an IBE scheme [1] from which the PKG still issues a long-term private key to each system user id, yet this private key is a trapdoor matrix, not a shorter vector as in our first scheme. This trapdoor matrix ensures each user id computing a short-term decryption key (a shorter vector) for any time period on their own. Similarly, the BT revocation mechanism is adopted to alleviate the workload of PKG.

4.1   Description of the Scheme

As in our first scheme, our lattice-based RIBE-CE with DKER in the standard model consists of eight pt algorithms: Setup, PriKeyGen, KeyUpd, DecKeyGen, Encrypt, Evolve, Decrypt and Revoke. The algorithms are described as follows:

- Setup$(1^n, N)$: On input a security parameter n and the maximal number of users $N = 2^n$, parameters q, m, k, s and $\beta = \widetilde{\mathcal{O}}(\sqrt{n})$ are the same as in our first scheme. PKG specifies the same steps as in our first scheme except it additionally samples $\mathbf{A}_2 \xleftarrow{\$} \mathbb{Z}_q^{n \times m}$, and thus:
  1. Set pp $= (\mathbf{A}, \mathbf{A}_0, \mathbf{A}_1, \mathbf{A}_2, \mathbf{B}, \mathbf{B}_0, \mathbf{B}_1, \mathbf{v}, \mathbf{U}, \mathcal{G}, \mathcal{H})$, and msk $= (\mathbf{R}_\mathbf{A}, \mathbf{R}_\mathbf{B})$.
  2. Output (pp, msk, RL, st) where msk is kept in $secret$ by PKG, and pp is made $public$ and as an implicit input of all other algorithms.
- PriKeyGen(msk, id): On input an identity id $\in \mathcal{I}$ and the master secret key msk. PKG specifies the following steps:
  1. View id as an unassigned leaf node of BT, thus, id $\in 0 \| \{0, 1\}^n$.
  2. Define $\mathbf{A}_{\mathsf{id}} = [\mathbf{A} | \mathbf{A}_0 + \mathcal{H}(\mathcal{G}(\mathsf{id}))\mathbf{A}_2] \in \mathbb{Z}_q^{n \times 2m}$.
  3. Run RandBasis(ExtBasis$(\mathbf{R}_\mathbf{A}, \mathbf{A}_{\mathsf{id}}), s$) to generate a trapdoor $\mathbf{R}_{\mathbf{A}_{\mathsf{id}}}$ for $\Lambda_q^\perp(\mathbf{A}_{\mathsf{id}})$.
  4. Output $\mathsf{sk}_{\mathsf{id}} = \mathbf{R}_{\mathbf{A}_{\mathsf{id}}}$.

- KeyUpd$(\mathsf{RL}, \mathsf{t}, \mathsf{msk}, \mathsf{st})$: The same as in our first scheme.
- DecKeyGen$(\mathsf{sk}_{\mathsf{id}}, \mathsf{uk}_{\mathsf{t}}, \mathsf{t})$: On input a long-term private key $\mathsf{sk}_{\mathsf{id}} = \mathbf{R}_{\mathbf{A}_{\mathsf{id}}}$, a time t and current time update key $\mathsf{uk}_{\mathsf{t}} = (\theta, \mathbf{E}_\theta)_{\theta \in \mathsf{KUNodes}(\mathsf{BT}, \mathsf{RL}, \mathsf{t})}$. The recipient id specifies the following steps:
  1. If $\mathsf{path}(\mathsf{id}) \cap \mathsf{KUNodes}(\mathsf{BT}, \mathsf{RL}, \mathsf{t}) = \emptyset$, return $\perp$ and abort.
  2. Otherwise, define $\mathbf{A}_{\mathsf{id},\mathsf{t}} = [\mathbf{A}_{\mathsf{id}} | \mathbf{A}_1 + \mathcal{H}(\mathcal{G}(\mathsf{t}))\mathbf{A}_2] \in \mathbb{Z}_q^{n \times 3m}$.
  3. Run SampleLeft$(\mathbf{A}_{\mathsf{id},\mathsf{t}}, \mathbf{R}_{\mathbf{A}_{\mathsf{id}}}, \mathbf{v}, s)$ to generate $\mathbf{e}_{\mathsf{id},\mathsf{t}} \in \mathbb{Z}^{3m}$ satisfying $\mathbf{A}_{\mathsf{id},\mathsf{t}} \cdot \mathbf{e}_{\mathsf{id},\mathsf{t}} = \mathbf{v} \bmod q$.
  4. Select $\theta \in (\mathsf{path}(\mathsf{id}) \cap \mathsf{KUNodes}(\mathsf{BT}, \mathsf{RL}, \mathsf{t}))$, and return $\mathsf{dk}_{\mathsf{id},\mathsf{t}} = (\mathbf{E}_\theta, \mathbf{e}_{\mathsf{id},\mathsf{t}})$.
- Encrypt$(\mathsf{id}, \mathsf{t}, m)$: On input an identity $\mathsf{id} \in \mathcal{I}$, a time $\mathsf{t} \in \mathcal{T}$, and a message $m \in \{0, 1\}$. The sender will specify the following steps:
  1. Let $\mathbf{A}_{\mathsf{id},\mathsf{t}} = [\mathbf{A} | \mathbf{A}_0 + \mathcal{H}(\mathcal{G}(\mathsf{id}))\mathbf{A}_2 | \mathbf{A}_1 + \mathcal{H}(\mathcal{G}(\mathsf{t}))\mathbf{A}_2] \in \mathbb{Z}_q^{n \times 3m}$.
  2. For $\theta \in \mathsf{path}(\mathsf{id})$, define $\mathbf{B}_{\mathsf{id}_\theta,\mathsf{t}} = [\mathbf{B} | \mathbf{B}_0 + \mathcal{H}(\mathcal{G}(\mathsf{t} \| \theta))\mathbf{B}_1] \in \mathbb{Z}_q^{n \times 2m}$.
  3. Sample $\mathbf{s}_0, \mathbf{s}_0' \xleftarrow{\$} \mathbb{Z}_q^n$, $e_0 \xleftarrow{\$} \chi$, $\mathbf{e}_0' \xleftarrow{\$} \chi^k$, $\mathbf{e}_1, \mathbf{e}_1' \xleftarrow{\$} \chi^m$, and $\mathbf{R}_0, \mathbf{R}_1, \mathbf{R}_2 \xleftarrow{\$} \{1, -1\}^{m \times m}$.
  4. Let $c_0 = \mathbf{v}^{\mathrm{T}}\mathbf{s}_0 + e_0 + m\lfloor \frac{q}{2} \rfloor \bmod q \in \mathbb{Z}_q$, $\mathbf{c}_1 = \mathbf{A}_{\mathsf{id},\mathsf{t}}^{\mathrm{T}}\mathbf{s}_0 + \begin{bmatrix} \mathbf{e}_1 \\ \mathbf{R}_0^{\mathrm{T}}\mathbf{e}_1 \\ \mathbf{R}_1^{\mathrm{T}}\mathbf{e}_1 \end{bmatrix} \in \mathbb{Z}_q^{3m}$.
  5. Let $\mathbf{c}_0' = \mathbf{U}^{\mathrm{T}}\mathbf{s}_0' + \mathbf{e}_0' + \mathsf{bin}(c_0)\lfloor \frac{q}{2} \rfloor \in \mathbb{Z}_q^k$, and $\mathbf{c}_{2,\theta} = \mathbf{B}_{\mathsf{id}_\theta,\mathsf{t}}^{\mathrm{T}}\mathbf{s}_0' + \begin{bmatrix} \mathbf{e}_1' \\ \mathbf{R}_2^{\mathrm{T}}\mathbf{e}_1' \end{bmatrix} \in \mathbb{Z}_q^{2m}$.
  6. Output $\mathsf{ct}_{\mathsf{id},\mathsf{t}} = (\mathsf{id}, \mathsf{t}, \mathbf{c}_0', \mathbf{c}_1, (\mathbf{c}_{2,\theta})_{\theta \in \mathsf{path}(\mathsf{id})}) \in (0\|\{0,1\}^n)^2 \times \mathbb{Z}_q^k \times \mathbb{Z}_q^{3m} \times (\mathbb{Z}_q^{2m})^{n+1}$.
- Evolve$(\mathsf{ct}_{\mathsf{id},\mathsf{t}}, \mathsf{t}', \mathsf{uk}_{\mathsf{t}})$: On input an original ciphertext $\mathsf{ct}_{\mathsf{id},\mathsf{t}} = (\mathsf{id}, \mathsf{t}, \mathbf{c}_0', \mathbf{c}_1, (\mathbf{c}_{2,\theta})_{\theta \in \mathsf{path}(\mathsf{id})})$ or an evolutive ciphertext $\mathsf{ct}_{\mathsf{id},\mathsf{t}} = (\mathsf{id}, \mathsf{t}'', \mathsf{t}, \mathbf{c}_0', \mathbf{c}_1, (\mathbf{c}_{2,\theta})_{\theta \in \mathsf{path}(\mathsf{id})})$, a new time $\mathsf{t}' > \mathsf{t} > \mathsf{t}''$, and the current time update key $\mathsf{uk}_{\mathsf{t}} = (\theta, \mathbf{E}_\theta)_{\theta \in \mathsf{KUNodes}(\mathsf{BT}, \mathsf{RL}, \mathsf{t})}$. The Cloud specifies the following steps:
  1. If the recipient has been revoked before (or at) time t, set $\mathsf{ct}_{\mathsf{id},\mathsf{t}'} = \mathsf{ct}_{\mathsf{id},\mathsf{t}}$.
  2. Otherwise, compute $\mathbf{w}_0 = \mathbf{c}_0' - \mathbf{E}_\theta^{\mathrm{T}} \cdot \mathbf{c}_{2,\theta} \bmod q \in \mathbb{Z}_q^k$, here, $\theta \in (\mathsf{path}(\mathsf{id}) \cap \mathsf{KUNodes}(\mathsf{BT}, \mathsf{RL}, \mathsf{t}))$.
  3. Compute $c_0 = (1, 2, \cdots, 2^{k-1}) \cdot \lfloor \frac{2}{q}\mathbf{w}_0 \rceil \in \mathbb{Z}_q$.
  4. Sample $\mathbf{s}_0'' \xleftarrow{\$} \mathbb{Z}_q^n$, $\mathbf{e}_0'' \xleftarrow{\$} \chi^k$, $\mathbf{e}_1'' \xleftarrow{\$} \chi^m$, and $\mathbf{R}_2' \xleftarrow{\$} \{1, -1\}^{m \times m}$.
  5. For $\theta \in \mathsf{path}(\mathsf{id})$, define $\mathbf{B}_{\mathsf{id}_\theta,\mathsf{t}'} = [\mathbf{B} | \mathbf{B}_0 + \mathcal{H}(\mathcal{G}(\mathsf{t}' \| \theta))\mathbf{B}_1] \in \mathbb{Z}_q^{n \times 2m}$.
  6. Let $\mathbf{c}_0'' = \mathbf{U}^{\mathrm{T}}\mathbf{s}_0'' + \mathbf{e}_0'' + \mathsf{bin}(c_0)\lfloor \frac{q}{2} \rfloor \in \mathbb{Z}_q^k$, $\mathbf{c}_{2,\theta}' = \mathbf{B}_{\mathsf{id}_\theta,\mathsf{t}'}^{\mathrm{T}}\mathbf{s}_0'' + \begin{bmatrix} \mathbf{e}_1'' \\ \mathbf{R}_2'^{\mathrm{T}}\mathbf{e}_1'' \end{bmatrix} \in \mathbb{Z}_q^{2m}$.
  7. Output $\mathsf{ct}_{\mathsf{id},\mathsf{t}'} = (\mathsf{id}, \mathsf{t}(\text{or } \mathsf{t}''), \mathsf{t}', \mathbf{c}_0'', \mathbf{c}_1, (\mathbf{c}_{2,\theta}')_{\theta \in \mathsf{path}(\mathsf{id})}) \in (0\|\{0,1\}^n)^3 \times \mathbb{Z}_q^k \times \mathbb{Z}_q^{3m} \times (\mathbb{Z}_q^{2m})^{n+1}$.
- Decrypt$(\mathsf{dk}_{\mathsf{id}',\mathsf{t}'}, \mathsf{ct}_{\mathsf{id},\mathsf{t}})$: On input an original ciphertext $\mathsf{ct}_{\mathsf{id},\mathsf{t}} = (\mathsf{id}, \mathsf{t}, \mathbf{c}_0', \mathbf{c}_1, (\mathbf{c}_{2,\theta})_{\theta \in \mathsf{path}(\mathsf{id})})$ or an evolutive ciphertext $\mathsf{ct}_{\mathsf{id},\mathsf{t}} = (\mathsf{id}, \mathsf{t}'', \mathsf{t}, \mathbf{c}_0'', \mathbf{c}_1, (\mathbf{c}_{2,\theta}')_{\theta \in \mathsf{path}(\mathsf{id})})$, and a decryption key $\mathsf{dk}_{\mathsf{id}',\mathsf{t}'}$. The recipient id' needs to specify the following steps:

  1. For the original ciphertext $\mathsf{ct}_{\mathsf{id},\mathsf{t}} = (\mathsf{id}, \mathsf{t}, \mathbf{c}_0', \mathbf{c}_1, (\mathbf{c}_{2,\theta})_{\theta \in \mathsf{path}(\mathsf{id})})$:

   1.1. If $(\mathsf{id} \neq \mathsf{id}') \vee (\mathsf{t} \neq \mathsf{t}')$, return $\perp$ and abort.

   1.2. Otherwise, compute $\mathbf{w}_0 = \mathbf{c}_0' - \mathbf{E}_\theta^{\mathrm{T}} \cdot \mathbf{c}_{2,\theta} \bmod q \in \mathbb{Z}_q^k$, here, $\theta \in$ $(\mathsf{path}(\mathsf{id}) \cap \mathsf{KUNodes}(\mathsf{BT}, \mathsf{RL}, \mathsf{t}))$.

   1.3. Compute $c_0 = (1, 2, \cdots, 2^{k-1}) \cdot \lfloor \frac{2}{q} \mathbf{w}_0 \rceil \in \mathbb{Z}_q$, $w = c_0 - \mathbf{e}_{\mathsf{id},\mathsf{t}}^{\mathrm{T}} \mathbf{c}_1 \in \mathbb{Z}_q$.

   1.4. Output $\lfloor \frac{2}{q} w \rceil \in \{0, 1\}$.

 2. For the evolutive ciphertext $\mathsf{ct}_{\mathsf{id},\mathsf{t}} = (\mathsf{id}, \mathsf{t}'', \mathsf{t}, \mathbf{c}_0', \mathbf{c}_1, (\mathbf{c}_{2,\theta})_{\theta \in \mathsf{path}(\mathsf{id})})$:

   2.1. If $(\mathsf{id} \neq \mathsf{id}') \vee (\mathsf{t} \neq \mathsf{t}')$, return $\perp$ and abort.

   2.2. Otherwise, compute $\mathbf{w}_0 = \mathbf{c}_0'' - \mathbf{E}_\theta^{\mathrm{T}} \cdot \mathbf{c}_{2,\theta} \bmod q \in \mathbb{Z}_q^k$, here, $\theta \in$ $(\mathsf{path}(\mathsf{id}) \cap \mathsf{KUNodes}(\mathsf{BT}, \mathsf{RL}, \mathsf{t}))$.

   2.3. Compute $c_0 = (1, 2, \cdots, 2^{k-1}) \cdot \lfloor \frac{2}{q} \mathbf{w}_0 \rceil \in \mathbb{Z}_q$.

   2.4. Define $\mathbf{A}_{\mathsf{id},\mathsf{t}''} = [\mathbf{A}_{\mathsf{id}} | \mathbf{A}_1 + \mathcal{H}(\mathcal{G}(\mathsf{t}'')) \mathbf{A}_2] \in \mathbb{Z}_q^{n \times 3m}$.

   2.5. Run $\mathsf{SampleLeft}(\mathbf{A}_{\mathsf{id},\mathsf{t}''}, \mathbf{R}_{\mathbf{A}_{\mathsf{id}}}, \mathbf{v}, s)$ to generate $\mathbf{e}_{\mathsf{id},\mathsf{t}''} \in \mathbb{Z}^{3m}$ satisfying $\mathbf{A}_{\mathsf{id},\mathsf{t}''} \cdot \mathbf{e}_{\mathsf{id},\mathsf{t}''} = \mathbf{v} \bmod q$.

   2.6. Define $w = c_0 - \mathbf{e}_{\mathsf{id},\mathsf{t}''}^{\mathrm{T}} \mathbf{c}_1 \bmod q \in \mathbb{Z}_q$.

   2.7. Output $\lfloor \frac{2}{q} w \rceil \in \{0, 1\}$.

– Revoke$(\mathsf{id}, \mathsf{t}, \mathsf{RL}, \mathsf{st})$: The same as in our first scheme.

4.2 Analysis

We analysis the efficiency, correctness and security of our lattice-based RIBE-CE scheme with DKER in the standard model.

Efficiency: The efficiency aspect of our lattice-based RIBE-CE scheme with DKER in the standard model and $N = 2^n$ is as follows:

– bit-size of public parameters pp is $(7nm + n + nk + 2n) \log q = \widetilde{\mathcal{O}}(n^2)$.

– The long-term private key $\mathsf{sk}_{\mathsf{id}}$ has a trapdoor matrix of bit-size $\widetilde{\mathcal{O}}(n^2)$.

– The time update key uk_t has bit-size $\mathcal{O}(r \log \frac{N}{r}) \cdot \widetilde{\mathcal{O}}(n)$ where r is the number of revoked users.

– The ciphertext $\mathsf{ct}_{\mathsf{id},\mathsf{t}}$ has bit-size $2(n+1) + (k + 3m + 2m(n+1)) \log q = \widetilde{\mathcal{O}}(n^2)$.

– The short-term decryption key $\mathsf{dk}_{\mathsf{id},\mathsf{t}}$ has bit-size $\widetilde{\mathcal{O}}(n)$.

Correctness: If the first lattice-based RIBE-CE with DKER in the standard model is operated correctly as specified, and a recipient id is not revoked at time t, then $\mathsf{dk}_{\mathsf{id},\mathsf{t}} = (\mathbf{E}_\theta, \mathbf{e}_{\mathsf{id},\mathsf{t}})$ satisfies $\mathbf{B}_{\mathsf{t}_\theta} \cdot \mathbf{E}_\theta = \mathbf{U} \bmod q$ and $\mathbf{A}_{\mathsf{id},\mathsf{t}} \cdot \mathbf{e}_{\mathsf{id},\mathsf{t}} = \mathbf{v} \bmod q$. In the decryption algorithm, the non-revoked id tries to derive m by using $\mathsf{dk}_{\mathsf{id},\mathsf{t}}$ (sometimes, id also needs to use the long-term private key to derive a new shorter vector according to a new time):

– If the given ciphertext is an original ciphertext, $\mathsf{ct}_{\mathsf{id},\mathsf{t}} = (\mathsf{id}, \mathsf{t}, \mathbf{c}_0', \mathbf{c}_1,$ $(\mathbf{c}_{2,\theta})_{\theta \in \mathsf{path}(\mathsf{id})})$.

   1. Parse $\mathbf{c}_{2,\theta} = \begin{bmatrix} \mathbf{c}_{2,0} \\ \mathbf{c}_{2,1} \end{bmatrix}$ where $\mathbf{c}_{2,i \in \{0,1\}} \in \mathbb{Z}_q^m$ and $\theta \in (\mathsf{path}(\mathsf{id}) \cap$ $\mathsf{KUNodes}(\mathsf{BT}, \mathsf{RL}, \mathsf{t}))$.

2. Compute

$$\mathbf{w}_0 = \mathbf{c}'_0 - \mathbf{E}_\theta^T \mathbf{c}_{2,\theta} = \mathbf{U}^T \mathbf{s}'_0 + \mathbf{e}'_0 + \mathsf{bin}(c_0)\lfloor\tfrac{q}{2}\rfloor - \mathbf{E}_\theta^T \begin{bmatrix} \mathbf{c}_{2,0} \\ \mathbf{c}_{2,1} \end{bmatrix} = \mathsf{bin}(c_0)\lfloor\tfrac{q}{2}\rfloor + \underbrace{\mathbf{e}'_0 - \mathbf{E}_\theta^T \begin{bmatrix} \mathbf{e}'_1 \\ \mathbf{R}_2^T \mathbf{e}'_1 \end{bmatrix}}_{\text{error}'}$$

According to our parameters settings, it can be checked that the error term error$'$ is bounded by $q/5$ (i.e., $\|\text{error}'\|_\infty < q/5$), thus, we have the conclusion $(1,2,\cdots,2^{k-1})\cdot\lfloor\tfrac{2}{q}\mathbf{w}_0\rceil = c_0$ with overwhelming probability.

3. Parse $\mathbf{c}_1 = \begin{bmatrix} \mathbf{c}_{1,0} \\ \mathbf{c}_{1,1} \\ \mathbf{c}_{1,2} \end{bmatrix}$ where $\mathbf{c}_{1,i\in\{0,1,2\}} \in \mathbb{Z}_q^m$, and compute

$$w = c_0 - \mathbf{e}_{\mathsf{id},t}^T \mathbf{c}_1 = \mathbf{v}^T \mathbf{s}_0 + e_0 + m\lfloor\tfrac{q}{2}\rfloor - \mathbf{e}_{\mathsf{id},t}^T \begin{bmatrix} \mathbf{c}_{1,0} \\ \mathbf{c}_{1,1} \\ \mathbf{c}_{1,2} \end{bmatrix} = m\lfloor\tfrac{q}{2}\rfloor + \underbrace{e_0 - \mathbf{e}_{\mathsf{id},t}^T \begin{bmatrix} \mathbf{e}_1 \\ \mathbf{R}_0^T \mathbf{e}_1 \\ \mathbf{R}_1^T \mathbf{e}_1 \end{bmatrix}}_{\text{error}}$$

According to our parameters settings, it can be checked that the error term error is bounded by $q/5$ (i.e., $\|\text{error}\|_\infty < q/5$), thus, we have the conclusion $\lfloor\tfrac{2}{q}w\rceil = m$ with overwhelming probability.

- If the given ciphertext is an evolutive ciphertext, $\mathsf{ct}_{\mathsf{id},t} = (\mathsf{id}, t'', t, c''_0, \mathbf{c}_1, (\mathbf{c}'_{2,\theta})_{\theta\in\mathsf{path}(\mathsf{id})})$,

  1. Parse $\mathbf{c}'_{2,\theta} = \begin{bmatrix} \mathbf{c}'_{2,0} \\ \mathbf{c}'_{2,1} \end{bmatrix}$ where $\mathbf{c}'_{2,i\in\{0,1\}} \in \mathbb{Z}_q^m$ and $\theta \in (\mathsf{path}(\mathsf{id}) \cap$ KUNodes(BT, RL, t)).

  2. Compute

$$\mathbf{w}_0 = \mathbf{c}''_0 - \mathbf{E}_\theta^T \mathbf{c}'_{2,\theta} = \mathbf{U}^T \mathbf{s}''_0 + \mathbf{e}''_0 + \mathsf{bin}(c_0)\lfloor\tfrac{q}{2}\rfloor - \mathbf{E}_\theta^T \begin{bmatrix} \mathbf{c}'_{2,0} \\ \mathbf{c}'_{2,1} \end{bmatrix} = \mathsf{bin}(c_0)\lfloor\tfrac{q}{2}\rfloor + \underbrace{\mathbf{e}''_0 - \mathbf{E}_\theta^T \begin{bmatrix} \mathbf{e}''_1 \\ \mathbf{R}'_2^T \mathbf{e}''_1 \end{bmatrix}}_{\text{error}''}$$

According to our parameters settings, it can be checked that the error term error$''$ is bounded by $q/5$ (i.e., $\|\text{error}''\|_\infty < q/5$), thus, we have the conclusion $(1,2,\cdots,2^{k-1})\cdot\lfloor\tfrac{2}{q}\mathbf{w}_0\rceil = c_0$ with overwhelming probability.

  3. Let $\mathbf{A}_{\mathsf{id},t''} = [\mathbf{A}_{\mathsf{id}}|\mathbf{A}_1 + \mathcal{H}(\mathcal{G}_1(t''))\mathbf{A}_2] \in \mathbb{Z}_q^{n\times 3m}$.
  4. Run SampleLeft$(\mathbf{A}_{\mathsf{id},t''}, \mathbf{R}_{\mathbf{A}_{\mathsf{id}}}, \mathbf{v}, s)$ to generate $\mathbf{e}_{\mathsf{id},t''} \in \mathbb{Z}^{3m}$ satisfying $\mathbf{A}_{\mathsf{id},t''} \cdot \mathbf{e}_{\mathsf{id},t''} = \mathbf{v} \bmod q$.

  5. Parse $\mathbf{c}_1 = \begin{bmatrix} \mathbf{c}_{1,0} \\ \mathbf{c}_{1,1} \\ \mathbf{c}_{1,2} \end{bmatrix}$ where $\mathbf{c}_{1,i\in\{0,1,2\}} \in \mathbb{Z}_q^m$, and compute

$$w = c_0 - \mathbf{e}_{\mathsf{id},t''}^T \mathbf{c}_1 = \mathbf{v}^T \mathbf{s}_0 + e_0 + m\lfloor\tfrac{q}{2}\rfloor - \mathbf{e}_{\mathsf{id},t''}^T \begin{bmatrix} \mathbf{c}_{1,0} \\ \mathbf{c}_{1,1} \\ \mathbf{c}_{1,2} \end{bmatrix} = m\lfloor\tfrac{q}{2}\rfloor + \underbrace{e_0 - \mathbf{e}_{\mathsf{id},t''}^T \begin{bmatrix} \mathbf{e}_1 \\ \mathbf{R}_0^T \mathbf{e}_1 \\ \mathbf{R}_1^T \mathbf{e}_1 \end{bmatrix}}_{\text{error}}$$

According to our parameters settings, it can be checked that the error term error is bounded by $q/5$ (i.e., $\|\text{error}\|_\infty < q/5$), thus, we have the conclusion $\lfloor\tfrac{2}{q}w\rceil = m$ with overwhelming probability.

Theorem 2. *Our* RIBE-CE *scheme with* DKER *in the standard model is* ind-cpa *secure if the* LWE *assumption holds.*

Proof. The proof is similar to that in Theorem 1, and due to the limited space, the details are presented in the full paper.

5   Conclusion

In this paper, we propose two (and the first) lattice-based RIBE schemes with server-aided ciphertext evolution. In comparison with previous lattice-based constructions of RIBE, our two schemes enjoy a significant advantage in terms of ciphertext security when considering the scenario of a secure data (i.e., ciphertext) sharing in the cloud setting and the revoked users cannot access to both the previously and subsequently shared data. The BT revocation mechanism is adopted for time key update, thus our three schemes only obtain a logarithmic complexity workload of the PKG, which serves as one solution to the challenge posed by Sun et al. In particular, we remedy the security model and introduce DKER property into RIBE-CE, a default security requirement for RIBE, which has not been considered by Sun et al. Our first and second lattice-based RIBE-CE schemes are without DKER in the standard model and with DKER in the standard model, respectively.

Acknowledgments. The authors would like to thank the anonymous reviewers of Inscrypt 2021 for their helpful comments and this research was supported by National Natural Science Foundation of China (Grant No. 61802075), Guangxi key Laboratory of Cryptography and Information Security (Grant No. GCIS201907) and Natural Science Foundation of Henan Province (Grant No. 202300410508.

References

1. Agrawal, S., Boneh, D., Boyen, X.: Efficient Lattice (H)IBE in the standard model. In: Gilbert, H. (ed.) EUROCRYPT 2010. LNCS, vol. 6110, pp. 553–572. Springer, Heidelberg (2010). https://doi.org/10.1007/978-3-642-13190-5_28
2. Ajtai, M.: Generating Hard Instances of Lattice Problems (Extended Abstract). In: STOC, pp. 99–108. ACM (1996). https://doi.org/10.1145/237814.237838
3. Alwen, J., Peikert, C.: Generating shorter bases for hard random lattices. Theor. Comput. Sys. **48**(3), 535–553 (2011). https://doi.org/10.1007/s00224-010-9278-3
4. Boldyreva, A., Goyal, V., Kumar, V.: Identity-based encryption with efficient revocation. In: CCS, pp. 417–426. ACM (2008). https://doi.org/10.1145/1455770.1455823
5. Boneh, D., Farnklin, M.: Identity-based encryption from the weil pairing. In: Kilian, J. (ed.) CRYPTO 2001. LNCS, vol. 2139, pp. 213–229. Springer, Heidelberg (2001). https://doi.org/10.1007/3-540-44647-8_13
6. Cash, D., Hofheinzy, D., Kiltz, E., et al.: Bonsai trees, or how to delegate a lattice basis. In: Gilbert, H. (ed.) EUROCRYPT 2010. LNCS, vol. 6110, pp. 523–552. Springer, Heidelberg (2010). https://doi.org/10.1007/978-3-642-13190-5_27

7. Chen, J., Lim, H.W., Ling, S., Wang, H., Nguyen, K.: Revocable identity-based encryption from lattices. In: Susilo, W., Mu, Y., Seberry, J. (eds.) ACISP 2012. LNCS, vol. 7372, pp. 390–403. Springer, Heidelberg (2012). https://doi.org/10.1007/978-3-642-31448-3_29

8. Cocks, C.: An identity based encryption scheme based on quadratic residues. In: Honary, B. (ed.) Cryptography and Coding 2001. LNCS, vol. 2260, pp. 360–363. Springer, Heidelberg (2001). https://doi.org/10.1007/3-540-45325-3_32

9. Dong, C., Yang, K., Qiu, J., et al.: Outsouraced revocable identity-based encryption from lattices. Trans. Emerging Tel. Tech. e3529 (2018). https://doi.org/10.1002/ett.3529

10. Gentry, C., Peikert, C., Vaikuntanathan, V.: Trapdoor for hard lattices and new cryptographic constructions. In: STOC, pp. 197–206. ACM (2008). https://doi.org/10.1145/1374376.1374407

11. Katsumata, S., Matsuda, T., Takayasu, A.: Lattice-based revocable (Hierarchical) IBE with decryption key exposure resistance. In: Lin, D., Sako, K. (eds.) PKC 2019. LNCS, vol. 11443, pp. 441–471. Springer, Cham (2019). https://doi.org/10.1007/978-3-030-17259-6_15

12. Lee, K.: A generic construction for revocable identity-based encryption with subset difference methods. PLOS ONE **15**(9), e0239053 (2020). https://doi.org/10.1371/journal.pone.o239053

13. Li, J., Li, J., Chen, X., et al.: Identity-based encryption with outsourced revocation in cloud computing. IEEE Trans. Comput. **64**(2), 426–437 (2015). https://doi.org/10.1109/TC.2013.208

14. Liang, K., Liu, J.K., Wong, D.S., Susilo, W.: An efficient cloud-based revocable identity-based proxy re-encryption scheme for public clouds data sharing. In: Kutyłowski, M., Vaidya, J. (eds.) ESORICS 2014. LNCS, vol. 8712, pp. 257–272. Springer, Cham (2014). https://doi.org/10.1007/978-3-319-11203-9_15

15. Libert, B., Vergnaud, D.: Adaptive-ID secure revocable identity-based encryption. In: Fischlin, M. (ed.) CT-RSA 2009. LNCS, vol. 5473, pp. 1–15. Springer, Heidelberg (2009). https://doi.org/10.1007/978-3-642-00862-7_1

16. Ma, X., Lin, D.: Generic constructions of revocable identity-based encryption. In: Liu, Z., Yung, M. (eds.) Inscrypt 2019. LNCS, vol. 12020, pp. 381–396. Springer, Cham (2020). https://doi.org/10.1007/978-3-030-42921-8_22

17. Micciancio, D., Peikert, C.: Hardness of SIS and LWE with small parameters. In: Canetti, R., Garay, J.A. (eds.) CRYPTO 2013. LNCS, vol. 8042, pp. 21–39. Springer, Heidelberg (2013). https://doi.org/10.1007/978-3-642-40041-4_2

18. Micciancio, D., Peikert, C.: Trapdoors for lattices: simpler, tighter, faster, smaller. In: Pointcheval, D., Johansson, T. (eds.) EUROCRYPT 2012. LNCS, vol. 7237, pp. 700–718. Springer, Heidelberg (2012). https://doi.org/10.1007/978-3-642-29011-4_41

19. Naor, D., Naor, M., Lotspiech, J.: Revocation and tracing schemes for stateless receivers. In: Kilian, J. (ed.) CRYPTO 2001. LNCS, vol. 2139, pp. 41–62. Springer, Heidelberg (2001). https://doi.org/10.1007/3-540-44647-8_3

20. Nguyen, K., Wang, H., Zhang, J.: Server-aided revocable identity-based encryption from lattices. In: Foresti, S., Persiano, G. (eds.) CANS 2016. LNCS, vol. 10052, pp. 107–123. Springer, Cham (2016). https://doi.org/10.1007/978-3-319-48965-0_7

21. Qin, B., Deng, R.H., Li, Y., Liu, S.: Server-aided revocable identity-based encryption. In: Pernul, G., Ryan, P.Y.A., Weippl, E. (eds.) ESORICS 2015. LNCS, vol. 9326, pp. 286–304. Springer, Cham (2015). https://doi.org/10.1007/978-3-319-24174-6_15

22. Regev, O.: On lattices, learning with errors, random linear codes, and cryptography. In: STOC, pp. 84–93. ACM (2005). https://doi.org/10.1145/1060590.1060603
23. Sahai, A., Waters, B.: Fuzzy identity-based encryption. In: Cramer, R. (ed.) EURO-CRYPT 2005. LNCS, vol. 3494, pp. 457–473. Springer, Heidelberg (2005). https://doi.org/10.1007/11426639_27
24. Seo, J.H., Emura, K.: Revocable identity-based encryption revisited: security model and construction. In: Kurosawa, K., Hanaoka, G. (eds.) PKC 2013. LNCS, vol. 7778, pp. 216–234. Springer, Heidelberg (2013). https://doi.org/10.1007/978-3-642-36362-7_14
25. Shamir, A.: Identity-based cryptosystems and signature schemes. In: Rabin, T. (ed.) CRYPTO 2010. LNCS, vol. 6223, pp. 98–115. Springer, Heidelberg (2010). https://doi.org/10.1007/978-3-642-14623-7_6
26. Shor, P.: Polynomial-time algorithms for prime factorization and dislogarithms on a quantum computer. SIAN J. Comput. **26**(5), 1485–1509 (1997). https://doi.org/10.1016/j.tcs.2020.02.03
27. Sun, Y., Mu, Y., Susilo, W., et al.: Revocable identity-based encryption with server-aided ciphertext evolution. Theor. Comput. Sci. **2020**(815), 11–24 (2020). https://doi.org/10.1016/j.tcs.2020.02.03
28. Takayasu, A.: Adaptively secure lattice-based revocable IBE in the QROM: compact parameters, tight security, and anonymity. Des. Codes Cryptogr. (2021). https://doi.org/10.1007/s10623-021-00895-3
29. Takayasu, A., Watanabe, Y.: Lattice-based revocable identity-based encryption with bouned decryption key exposure resistance. In: Pieprzyk, J., Suriadi, S. (eds.) ACISP 2017. LNCS, vol. 10342, pp. 184–204. Springer, Cham (2017). https://doi.org/10.1007/978-3-319-60055-0_10
30. Wang, C., Fang, J., Li, Y.: An improved cloud-based revocable identity-based proxy re-rncryption scheme. In: Niu, W., Li, G., Liu, J., et al. (eds.) ATIS 2015. LNCS, vol. 557, pp. 14–26. Springer, Heidelberg (2015). https://doi.org/10.1007/978-3-662-48683-2_2

Homomorphic Modular Reduction and Improved Bootstrapping for BGV Scheme

Ruiqi Li[1] and Chunfu Jia[1,2(✉)]

[1] College of Cyber Science, Nankai University, Tianjin 300350, China
lrq@mail.nankai.edu.cn, cfjia@nankai.edu.cn
[2] Tianjin Key Laboratory of Network and Data Security Technology,
Tianjin 300350, China

Abstract. Bootstrapping is a crucial subroutine of fully homomorphic encryption (FHE), where a homomorphic encryption scheme evaluates its own decryption circuits. Homomorphic modular reduction is a crucial part of bootstrapping a BGV ciphertext.

In this paper, we investigate the homomorphic modular reduction technique. We propose a new homomorphic modular reduction algorithm based on the idea of "blind rotation". This new homomorphic modular reduction procedure requires no basic homomorphic operations, hence it has lower noise accumulation and more suitable for implementing. Furthermore, we also resort to the blind rotation to construct a new bootstrapping procedure for the BGV scheme. We analyze the noise performance and the computational complexity of our scheme. The results illustrate that our new bootstrapping scheme achieves low noise accumulation so that the lattice approximation factor for the underlying worst-case lattice assumption is smaller than that of Chen and Zhang's work. Meanwhile, the complexity of our bootstrapping scheme is comparable with their scheme.

Keywords: Homomorphic encryption · Bootstrapping · Modular reduction

1 Introduction

Fully homomorphic encryption (FHE) is an emerging cryptographic primitive that enables homomorphic computations on encrypted data without decryption. In 2009, Gentry [17,18] proposed the blueprint for achieving fully homomorphism and constructed the first FHE scheme. After Gentry's breakthrough, many FHE schemes emerge [3,5,7,13,15,23,27].

Almost all existing HE schemes include "noise" in ciphertexts, and the "noise" accumulates during homomorphic operations. When the "noise" rises up to some extent, ciphertexts cannot be decrypted correctly. To address this problem, Gentry proposed a technique called bootstrapping in [17] to refresh

© Springer Nature Switzerland AG 2021
Y. Yu and M. Yung (Eds.): Inscrypt 2021, LNCS 13007, pp. 466–484, 2021.
https://doi.org/10.1007/978-3-030-88323-2_25

ciphertexts. Generally, a bootstrapping procedure is to evaluate decryption function homomorphically on encryptions of secret key. Bootstrapping is a computationally fairly expensive procedure, and it is the main bottleneck of making FHE schemes practical. Therefore, there are many studies aimed at improving the efficiency of bootstrapping to make FHE faster.

Currently, researches of improving bootstrapping are pursued following two main approaches. The first approach, studied in [2,4,6,9,16,22,30], is to present bootstrapping techniques for HE schemes based on the Gentry-Sahai-Waters (GSW) scheme [23]. These schemes try to decrease the cost of bootstrapping a single ciphertext as much as possible, even at the expense of having to perform bootstrapping after evaluating every gate of the circuit. However, the above schemes have some limitations that the bootstrapping procedure has to be performed for essentially every gate of the circuit, and do not support packing several messages into a single ciphertext. The only exception is [30], since it first packs a number of LWE ciphertexts into an RLWE ciphertext and then refresh it.

Another approach explored in [1,8,11,12,14,19–21,24,25,31] aims at providing bootstrapping techniques for FHE schemes that can pack several messages into one ciphertext and refresh them in parallel. At present, BGV (Brakerski-Gentry-Vaikuntanathan) HE schemes [5,21] are one class of the most efficient somewhat homomorphic encryption (SWHE) schemes that support batching. Since BGV schemes can encrypt a ring element rather than a single bit in one ciphertext, they naturally support packing a number of messages into independent "slots" and performing Single-Instruction-Multiple-Data (SIMD) operations using the techniques based on Chinese Remainder Theorem (CRT) [33]. Therefore, many bootstrapping techniques for BGV scheme are studied. While bootstrapping such kind of schemes may be costly, it can simultaneously refresh plenty of messages in a single bootstrapping execution. Though the bootstrapping schemes of the first approach can reduce the runtime of bootstrapping a single ciphertext as much as possible, bootstrapping methods of the batched BGV scheme still have much better amortized per-bit runtime.

However, in the BGV scheme, the noise of ciphertext grows quadratically after every homomorphic multiplication, therefore these schemes essentially incur quasi-polynomial noise when decryption circuits have polynomial multiplication levels, and consequently require worst-case lattice assumptions with superpolynomial approximation factors. [14] is an exception among these works, which utilizes the techniques of [2] to refresh BGV ciphertexts. These techniques allow their construction to achieve worst-case assumptions with polynomial approximation factors. A smaller approximation factor leads to a weaker assumption. Relying on such weaker assumption allows us to use a smaller dimension lattice to achieve the same security level, and hence the efficiency of the scheme can be improved.

The decryption function of the BGV scheme can be represented as

$$\mathbf{Dec}(c, sk) = \mu + te \mod (q, \Phi_m(X)) \tag{1}$$

where c is the encryption of message μ under the secret key sk, t is a plaintext modulus, q is a modulus and $\Phi_m(X)$ is a cyclotomic polynomial modulus. Therefore, a bootstrapping procedure of BGV scheme consists of two steps: homomorphic polynomial arithmetic and homomorphic modular reduction. This indicates that we can make homomorphic modular reduction algorithm more practical so as to obtain a bootstrapping procedure which has better performance.

Our Results. In this paper, we investigate the homomorphic modular reduction algorithm in the procedure of bootstrapping a BGV ciphertext. We propose a new homomorphic modular reduction algorithm based on the idea of blind rotation used in the FHEW-like scheme [16,29]. Our new algorithm is suitable for all RLWE-based HE schemes whose decryption circuits satisfy Eq. 1. We obtain a new bootstrapping procedure for the BGV scheme. We analyze the noise growth and the computational complexity. Theoretic analysis results show that our scheme can bootstrap BGV ciphertexts with polynomial noise and has lower noise accumulation than Chen and Zhang's work [14], hence we can achieve smaller lattice approximation factor for the underlying worst-case lattice assumption. Meanwhile, the computational complexity is comparable with that of [14].

2   Preliminaries

In this paper, we use lower case letters to denote scalers including integers, reals, e.g. a, and use italic bold lower case letters to denote polynomials, e.g. $\boldsymbol{a}$. We use $\overrightarrow{a}$ to denote a vector. We write the ceiling, floor and rounding functions as $\lceil \cdot \rceil$, $\lfloor \cdot \rfloor$, and $\lfloor \cdot \rceil$, respectively. For integers n, t, $[n]_t$ represents the reduction of n modulo t, and $[n]_t \in (-\lfloor t/2 \rfloor, \lfloor t/2 \rfloor]$.

We use $a \leftarrow \chi$ to denote sampling a according to the distribution χ, and use $U(S)$ to denote a uniform distribution whose support is a finite set S. We denote by χ_{key} a ternary distribution, which samples a value from $\{-1, 0, 1\}$. χ_{err} is used to denote a discrete Gaussian distribution with a standard deviation σ_{err}. All logarithms in this paper are base two, unless stated otherwise.

2.1   Cyclotomic Rings

In this paper, BGV schemes and our bootstrapping procedure are supposed to perform over power-of-two cyclotomic rings.

Let N be a power of two, we denote the $2N$-th cyclotomic ring by $\mathcal{R} := \mathbb{Z}[X]/(X^N + 1)$ and its quotient ring by $\mathcal{R}_q := \mathcal{R}/q\mathcal{R}$. For a polynomial $\boldsymbol{a} \in \mathcal{R}$, we write $\boldsymbol{a} = a_0 + a_1 X + \cdots a_{N-1} X^{N-1}$, and denote its coefficient vector by $\overrightarrow{a} = (a_0, a_1, \ldots, a_{N-1})$. We denote the ℓ_∞ norm of $\boldsymbol{a}$ as $\|\boldsymbol{a}\|_\infty = \|\overrightarrow{a}\|_\infty = \max_{0 \leq i < N} \{|a_i|\}$. There exists a constant $\delta_{\mathcal{R}}$ such that $\|\boldsymbol{a} \cdot \boldsymbol{b}\|_\infty \leq \delta_{\mathcal{R}} \|\boldsymbol{a}\|_\infty \|\boldsymbol{b}\|_\infty$ for any $\boldsymbol{a}, \boldsymbol{b} \in \mathcal{R}$, and we use the bound $\delta_{\mathcal{R}} = 2\sqrt{N}$ for $\mathcal{R} = \mathbb{Z}[X]/(X^N + 1)$.

Let $a = a_0 + a_1 X + \cdots a_{N-1} X^{N-1}$ be a polynomial in $\mathcal{R}$ and m be a positive integer less than N. Notice that

$$a \cdot X^m \bmod (X^N + 1)$$
$$= -a_{N-m} - \cdots - a_{N-1} X^{m-1} + a_0 X^m + \cdots + a_{N-1-m} X^{N-1}$$

The above equation implies that $a \cdot X^m$ is a cyclic rotation of a with the cycled entries negated, and that the ℓ_∞-norm of $a \cdot X^m$ is equal to that of a.

2.2 (Ring) LWE Problems and Ciphertexts

We now introduce the LWE problem and the ring-LWE problem. Firstly, we bring in the definition of B-bounded distribution.

Definition 1 (B-bounded distribution). *A distribution ensemble $\{\chi_n\}_{n\in\mathbb{N}}$, supported over the integers or polynomial rings, is called B-bounded if*

$$\Pr_{e \leftarrow \chi_n}[\|e\|_\infty > B] = \mathrm{negl}(n).$$

The LWE problem was firstly introduced by Regev in [32].

Definition 2 (Decisional LWE (DLWE) [32]). *For security parameter λ, let $n = n(\lambda), q = q(\lambda)$ be integers, and let $\chi = \chi(\lambda)$ be a distribution over $\mathbb{Z}$. The decisional LWE problem (denoted by $DLWE_{n,q,\chi}$) is to distinguish the following two distributions: In the first distribution, one first draws a secret vector $s \in \mathbb{Z}_q^n$ uniformly, and then samples tuples $(b_i, a_i) \in \mathbb{Z}_q \times \mathbb{Z}_q^n$ by choosing $a_i \leftarrow \mathbb{Z}_q^n$ uniformly at random and a noise term $e_i \leftarrow \chi$, and setting $b_i = \langle a_i, s \rangle + e_i$. In the second distribution, one samples (b_i, a_i) uniformly from $\mathbb{Z}_q^{n+1}$.*

The RLWE problem was firstly introduced by Lyubashevsky et al. in [28].

Definition 3 (Decisional RLWE (DRLWE) [28]). *Let K be a number field and R be the ring of integers of K. $R^\vee \subset K$ is the dual fractional ideal of R. Let χ be a distribution over $K_\mathbb{R} = K \otimes_\mathbb{Q} \mathbb{R}$. The decisional version of RLWE problem (denoted by $DRLWE_{q,\chi}$) is to distinguish the following two distributions: In the first distribution, one first draws $s \leftarrow R_q$ uniformly at random, and samples (a, b) by sampling $a \leftarrow R_q$ uniformly, and a noise term $e \leftarrow \chi$, and setting $b = a \cdot s + e$. In the second distribution, one samples (a, b) uniformly over $R_q \times K \otimes_\mathbb{Q} \mathbb{R}$.*

The theorem below captures reductions from ideal lattice GapSVP (or GapSIVP) to RLWE, and we state the result in terms of B-bounded distributions.

Theorem 1 (Adapted from [14]). *Let R be the m-th cyclotomic ring, and $n = \phi(m)$. Let $q = q(n)$, $q \equiv 1 \bmod m$ be an integer and $B = \omega(\sqrt{n \log n})$. Let χ be a B-bounded distribution. There is a polynomial time quantum reduction from $n^{\omega(1)} q/B$-approximate SVP on ideal lattices in R to $DRLWE_{q,\chi}$.*

In the following, we introduce two forms of ciphertexts based on LWE problem and RLWE problem.

Definition 4 (LWE ciphertexts). *Let n, q be positive integers. An LWE ciphertext of $m \in \mathbb{Z}$ under the secret key $\vec{s} \in \mathbb{Z}^n$ is defined as*

$$LWE_{\vec{s}, q}(m, e) := (\vec{a}, b) = (\vec{a}, -\langle \vec{a}, \vec{s} \rangle + e + m) \in \mathbb{Z}_q^{n+1}$$

where $\vec{a} \leftarrow U(\mathbb{Z}_q^n)$ and e is a small error.

Definition 5 (Ring-LWE ciphertexts). *Let Q be a positive integer and N be a power of 2. An RLWE ciphertext of $m \in \mathcal{R}$ under the secret key $s \in \mathcal{R}$ is defined as*

$$RLWE_{s, Q}(m) := (a, b) = (a, -a \cdot s + e + m) \in \mathcal{R}_Q^2$$

where $a \leftarrow U(\mathcal{R}_Q)$ and e is a small error.

Sample Extraction (adapted from [9,29]). A RLWE ciphertext consists of two polynomials with N coefficients in $\mathcal{R}$ and it is easy to homomorphically extract a coefficient as a scalar LWE ciphertext with the same key. Let $(a, b) = RLWE_{s,q}(m, e)$ be an RLWE ciphertext. Multiplication of two polynomials a and s in $\mathcal{R}$ can be written as:

$$s \cdot a = \sum_{i=0}^{N-1} \left(\sum_{j=0}^{i} s_j \cdot a_{i-j} - \sum_{j=i+1}^{N-1} s_j \cdot a_{i-j+N} \right) X^i$$

Let $\vec{s} = (s_0, \ldots, s_{N-1}) \in \mathbb{Z}^N$ be a vector of coefficients of s. We can extract LWE ciphertexts $LWE_{\vec{s}, q}(m_i, e_i) = (\vec{a}^{(i)}, b_i)$ for $0 \leq i < N$ from a, where

$$\vec{a}^{(i)} = (a_i, a_{i-1}, \ldots, a_0, -a_{N-1}, -a_{N-2}, \ldots, -a_{i+1}).$$

We denote this procedure as $(\vec{a}^{(i)}, b_i) \leftarrow \mathbf{Extract}_i((a, b))$, and we simply write $\mathbf{Extract}((a, b))$ when $i = 0$.

2.3   BGV Scheme

The BGV scheme [5,20] is one of frequently-used RLWE-based HE schemes. In the BGV scheme, n is the degree of underlying cyclotomic polynomial, t is the plaintext modulus, and q is the coefficient modulus. In this paper, we assume that the BGV scheme is defined over $R = \mathbb{Z}[X]/(X^n + 1)$ where n is a power of 2. The plaintext space is $R_t = R/tR$, and the secret key s is an element of $R_q = R/qR$. In practice, each coefficient of s is usually sampled from the ternary distribution χ_{key}. A BGV ciphertext is a pair (a, b) of elements in R_q.

Specifically, the BGV scheme is essentially parameterized by a sequence of decreasing moduli $q_L \gg q_{L-1} \gg \cdots \gg q_0$. For $0 \leq \ell \leq L$, a level-ℓ ciphertext $(a^{(\ell)}, b^{(\ell)})$ of a message $m \in R_t$ under the key $s^{(\ell)} \in R$ satisfies

$$\mathbf{Dec}(a^{(\ell)}, s^{(\ell)}) = m + t \cdot e^{(\ell)} \bmod (q_\ell, \Phi(X))$$

where $e^{(\ell)}$ is the *noise* of the ciphertext $(a^{(\ell)}, b^{(\ell)})$ and $t \cdot \|e^{(\ell)}\|_{\infty} \ll q_{\ell}$. After each homomorphic operation, modulus q_{ℓ} of level ℓ needs to be switched to $q_{\ell-1}$ of level $\ell - 1$ by *Modulus Switching*, and the corresponding key is also switched by *Key Switching*. When the level comes to 0, we cannot perform any more homomorphic operations and thus require the bootstrapping procedure, i.e. we have to refresh the ciphertext to obtain a new one with a level-L secret key.

In this paper, we denote a BGV ciphertext of $m \in R_t$ under the secret key s as $\mathbf{BGV}_{s,q}^t(m, e) \in R_q^2$, where e is an error. Notice that $\mathbf{BGV}_{s,q}^t(m, e)$ is in fact an RLWE ciphertext $\mathbf{RLWE}_{s,q}(m, t \cdot e)$. Therefore, the properties of RLWE ciphertexts introduced in Sect. 2.2 also work for BGV ciphertexts.

2.4 A Ring Variant of the GSW Scheme

In this section, we adapt the definitions of $\mathbf{RLWE}'$ and $\mathbf{RGSW}$ from [26, 29] to describe a ring variant of the GSW HE scheme [2, 23] over $\mathcal{R}$.

Let $\overrightarrow{g} = (g_0, g_1, \ldots, g_{d-1}) \in \mathbb{Z}^d$ be a gadget vector. Let $h \in \mathcal{R}_Q$ be a polynomial and $g^{-1}(h) = (h_0, h_1, \ldots, h_{d-1}) \in \mathcal{R}^d$ be a gadget decomposition of h such that $h = \sum_{i=0}^{d-1} g_i \cdot h_i$. For a power of two modulus Q, we will use a power gadget vector $(1, B, B^2, \ldots, B^{d-1})$ with a power of two B.

For a gadget vector $\overrightarrow{g} \in \mathbb{Z}^d$, we define

$$\mathbf{RLWE}'_{s,Q}(m) := (\mathbf{RLWE}_{s,Q}(g_0 \cdot m, e_0), \ldots, \mathbf{RLWE}_{s,Q}(g_{d-1} \cdot m, e_{d-1})) \in \mathcal{R}_Q^{2 \times d}.$$

In order to explain the homomorphic scalar multiplication, we firstly introduce the multiplication between a scalar and an RLWE ciphertext. Let $c \in \mathcal{R}_Q$ be a scalar and $\mathbf{RLWE}_{s,Q}(m, e) := (a, b)$. The multiplication between c and $\mathbf{RLWE}_{s,Q}(m, e)$ is defined as

$$c \cdot \mathbf{RLWE}_{s,Q}(m, e) := (c \cdot a, c \cdot b) = \mathbf{RLWE}_{s,Q}(c \cdot m, c \cdot e).$$

In the rest of this paper, we regard an RLWE ciphertext as a single element in the procedure of the scalar multiplication, so we can further generalize the multiplication between a scalar and an RLWE ciphertext to "inner product" between a vector of scalars and a vector of RLWE ciphertexts.

On the basis of the above discussion, the homomorphic scalar multiplication between $\mathbf{RLWE}'_{s,Q}(m)$ and a polynomial $h \in \mathcal{R}_Q$ is defined as

$$h \odot \mathbf{RLWE}'_{s,Q}(m)$$
$$= \langle g^{-1}(h), (\mathbf{RLWE}_{s,Q}(g_0 \cdot m, e_0), \cdots, \mathbf{RLWE}_{s,Q}(g_{d-1} \cdot m, e_{d-1})) \rangle$$
$$= \sum_{i=0}^{d-1} h_i \cdot \mathbf{RLWE}_{s,Q}(g_i \cdot m, e_i)$$
$$= \mathbf{RLWE}_{s,Q}(\sum_{i=0}^{d-1} g_i \cdot h_i \cdot m, \sum_{i=0}^{d-1} h_i \cdot e_i)$$
$$= \mathbf{RLWE}_{s,Q}(h \cdot m, e') \in \mathcal{R}_Q^2$$

The procedure of the homomorphic scalar multiplication $h \odot \mathbf{RLWE}'_{s,Q}(m)$ produces an RLWE ciphertext $\mathbf{RLWE}_{s,Q}(h \cdot m, e')$ where $e' = \sum_{i=0}^{d-1} h_i \cdot e_i$. The following lemma states the computational complexity of the homomorphic scalar multiplication and the upper bound of the error of the resulting ciphertext.

Lemma 1. *Let E be an upper bound of error in $\mathbf{RLWE}'_{s,Q}(m)$. The homomorphic scalar multiplication between $\mathbf{RLWE}'_{s,Q}(m)$ and an element $h \in \mathcal{R}_Q$ can be computed in time $\tilde{O}(dN)$, and the error of the resulting RLWE ciphertext is bounded by $2d\sqrt{N}BE$.*

Proof. Note that computing $h_i \cdot \mathbf{RLWE}_{s,Q}(g_i \cdot m, e_i)$ requires 2 multiplications of two elements in $\mathcal{R}$, so the whole procedure requires $2d$ multiplications. In addition, the complexity of multiplications for ring elements of $\mathcal{R}$ by FFT (Fast Fourier Transform) is $O(N \log N)$. Generally, the time complexity of the homomorphic scalar multiplication is no more than $\tilde{O}(dN)$.

The error of the output RLWE ciphertext is $e' = \sum_{i=0}^{d-1} h_i \cdot e_i$, and $\|h_i\|_\infty \le B, \|e_i\|_\infty \le E$. Therefore, the error of the output ciphertext is bounded by $2d\sqrt{N}BE$. $\square$

The form of ciphertexts of our RGSW scheme is defined as follows.

Definition 6 (RGSW ciphertexts). *Let Q be a positive integer and N be a power of 2. Let $\overrightarrow{g} \in \mathbb{Z}^d$ be a gadget vector. An RGSW encryption $m \in \mathcal{R}$ under the secret key $s \in \mathcal{R}$ is defined as*

$$\mathbf{RGSW}_{s,Q}(m) := (\mathbf{RLWE}'_{s,Q}(s \cdot m), \mathbf{RLWE}'_{s,Q}(m)) \in \mathcal{R}_Q^{4 \times d}$$

We can define an external product between an RLWE ciphertext and an RGSW ciphertext, similar to [9,10].

Lemma 2 (External Product). *Let $\mathbf{RLWE}_{s,Q}(m_1, e) = (a, b)$ be an RLWE ciphertext and $g^{-1}(a) = (a_i)_{0 \le i \le d-1}, g^{-1}(b) = (b_i)_{0 \le i \le d-1}$. Let*

$$\mathbf{RGSW}_{s,Q}(m_2)$$
$$= (\mathbf{RLWE}'_{s,Q}(s \cdot m_2), \mathbf{RLWE}'_{s,Q}(m_2))$$
$$= ((\mathbf{RLWE}_{s,Q}(g_i \cdot s \cdot m_2, e_{1,i}))_{0 \le i \le d-1}, (\mathbf{RLWE}_{s,Q}(g_i \cdot m_2, e_{2,i}))_{0 \le i \le d-1})$$

be an RGSW ciphertext. The external product between these two ciphertexts is computed by

$$\mathbf{RLWE}_{s,Q}(m_1, e) \times \mathbf{RGSW}_{s,Q}(m_2) = a \odot \mathbf{RLWE}'_{s,Q}(s \cdot m_2) + b \odot \mathbf{RLWE}'_{s,Q}(m_2).$$

in time $\tilde{O}(dN)$ and produces an RLWE ciphertext $\mathbf{RLWE}_{s,Q}(m_1 \cdot m_2, e')$ where $e' = m_2 \cdot e + \sum_{i=0}^{d-1} a_i e_{1,i} + b_i e_{2,i}$. If we assume that $m_2 = X^v$ with some integer v, $\|e\|_\infty \le E_1$ and $\|e_{1,i}\|_\infty, \|e_{2,i}\|_\infty \le E_2$, then $\|e'\|_\infty \le E_1 + 4\sqrt{N}dBE_2$.

Proof. The external product is computed as

$$a \odot \mathbf{RLWE}'_{s,Q}(s \cdot m_2) + b \odot \mathbf{RLWE}'_{s,Q}(m_2)$$

$$= \mathbf{RLWE}_{s,Q}\left(a \cdot s \cdot m_2, \sum_{i=0}^{d-1} a_i \cdot e_{1,i}\right) + \mathbf{RLWE}_{s,Q}\left(b \cdot m_2, \sum_{i=0}^{d-1} b_i \cdot e_{2,i}\right)$$

$$= \mathbf{RLWE}_{s,Q}\left((a \cdot s + b) \cdot m_2, \sum_{i=0}^{d-1} a_i \cdot e_{1,i} + b_i \cdot e_{2,i}\right)$$

$$= \mathbf{RLWE}_{s,Q}\left(m_1 \cdot m_2 + e \cdot m_2, \sum_{i=0}^{d-1} a_i \cdot e_{1,i} + b_i \cdot e_{2,i}\right)$$

$$= \mathbf{RLWE}_{s,Q}\left(m_1 \cdot m_2, m_2 \cdot e + \sum_{i=0}^{d-1} a_i \cdot e_{1,i} + b_i \cdot e_{2,i}\right) \in \mathcal{R}_Q^2$$

In fact, the external product is computed by two homomorphic scalar multiplications. Hence, according to Lemma 1, we know the time complexity of the external product procedure is within $\tilde{O}(dN)$.

Since the error of the output ciphertext can be written as $e' = m_2 \cdot e + \sum_{i=0}^{d-1} a_i \cdot e_{1,i} + b_i \cdot e_{2,i}$, then we have $\|e'\|_\infty \leq E_1 + 4\sqrt{N}dBE_2$.

3   New Homomorphic Modular Reduction Algorithm

3.1   The Basic Idea

The basic idea of our homomorphic modular reduction is inspired by the "blind rotation" technique used in [9,10,16].

Notice that $\langle X \rangle = \{1, X, \ldots, X^{N-1}, -1, \ldots, -X^{N-1}\}$ forms a cyclic group in $\mathcal{R} = \mathbb{Z}[X]/(X^N + 1)$. If we set $q = 2N$, then $\mathbb{Z}_q \cong \langle X \rangle$. This means that we can map an integer $v \in \mathbb{Z}_q$ to an element X^v of the group $\langle X \rangle$. Note that the degree of a test polynomial is at most N in $\mathcal{R}$, but there are $q = 2N$ possible values for $v \in \mathbb{Z}_q$, and we have to verify every possible value of v to obtain $[v]_t$. Therefore, we cannot use the test polynomials similar to the one proposed in [9].

Let w_i be the constant term of $X^{-v} \cdot X^i$ for $v \in [0, q-1]$ and $i \in [0, N-1]$. We observe that

$$w_i = \begin{cases} 1, & i = v, \\ -1, & i = v - q/2, \\ 0, & \text{otherwise.} \end{cases}$$

holds. This result can be used to find v from the range $\{0, 1, \ldots, q-1\}$. However, this fact is not sufficient yet, since there are two possible non-zero values of the constant term of $X^{-v} \cdot X^i$ (i.e., 1 or -1). What we want is that the constant term of $X^{-v} \cdot X^i$ is equal to 1 whenever $i = v$ or $i = v - q/2$. Fortunately, we find that if we set α_i as the constant term of $\lfloor \frac{1}{2}X^i \cdot X^{-v} + \frac{1}{4} \rceil$ and β_i as the constant term of $\lfloor -\frac{1}{2}X^i \cdot X^{-v} + \frac{1}{4} \rceil$ for $0 \le i < N$ and $v \in \{0, 1, \ldots, q-1\}$, then we have

$$\alpha_i = \begin{cases} \lfloor \frac{3}{4} \rceil = 1, & i = v, \\ \lfloor -\frac{1}{4} \rceil = 0, & i = v - q/2, \\ \lfloor \frac{1}{4} \rceil = 0, & \text{otherwise.} \end{cases} \qquad \beta_i = \begin{cases} \lfloor -\frac{1}{4} \rceil = 0, & i = v, \\ \lfloor \frac{3}{4} \rceil = 1, & i = v - q/2, \\ \lfloor \frac{1}{4} \rceil = 0, & \text{otherwise.} \end{cases}$$

Utilizing the above equations, we can design the following method to obtain $[v]_t$ for $v \in \{0, 1, \ldots, q-1\}$:

$$\sum_{i=0}^{N-1} (\alpha_i \cdot [i]_t + \beta_i \cdot [i+N]_t) = [v]_t$$

As a toy example, let $q = 2N = 8$ and $v = 5$. We can obtain that $\alpha_0 = \lfloor \frac{1}{4} \rceil = 0$, $\alpha_1 = \lfloor -\frac{1}{4} \rceil = 0$, $\alpha_2 = \lfloor \frac{1}{4} \rceil = 0$, $\alpha_3 = \lfloor \frac{1}{4} \rceil = 0$, and that $\beta_0 = \lfloor \frac{1}{4} \rceil = 0$, $\beta_1 = \lfloor \frac{3}{4} \rceil = 1$, $\beta_2 = \lfloor \frac{1}{4} \rceil = 0$, $\beta_3 = \lfloor \frac{1}{4} \rceil = 0$. Hence, we have that

$$\sum_{i=0}^{3} (\alpha_i \cdot [i]_t + \beta_i \cdot [i+N]_t) = \beta_1 \cdot [1+4]_t = [5]_t.$$

3.2   Homomorphic Modular Reduction

In this subsection, we elaborate our new homomorphic modular reduction algorithm. The entire **HomModRed** procedure is formalized in Algorithm 1. Lemma 3 states the correctness of the homomorphic modular reduction and the noise performance of this procedure.

Algorithm 1. The **HomModRed** Algorithm

Input: An RLWE ciphertext $\mathbf{RLWE}_{2s,Q}(X^{-v}, 2te) = (a, b) \in \mathcal{R}_{2N}^2$
Output: An LWE ciphertext $\mathbf{LWE}_{\vec{s},Q}([v]_t, e')$ $//\vec{s}$ is the coefficient vector of s
1: $(\vec{a}, b) \leftarrow (\vec{0}, 0)$;
2: **for** $i = 1$ to $N - 1$ **do**
3:     $(a, b) \leftarrow X \cdot (a, b)$;
4:     $(c, d) \leftarrow (a, \lfloor \frac{1}{2}b + \frac{1}{4} \rceil)$, $(c', d') \leftarrow (-a, \lfloor -\frac{1}{2}b + \frac{1}{4} \rceil)$;
5:     $(\vec{c}, d) \leftarrow \mathbf{Extract}((c, d))$, $(\vec{c}', d') \leftarrow \mathbf{Extract}((c', d'))$;
6:     $(\vec{a}, b) \leftarrow (\vec{a}, b) + [i]_t \cdot (\vec{c}, d) + [i+N]_t \cdot (\vec{c}', d')$;
7: **end for**
8: **return** $(\vec{a}, b)$;

Lemma 3. *Let* $\boldsymbol{RLWE}_{2s,Q}(X^{-v}, 2te) = (\boldsymbol{a}, \boldsymbol{b})$ *where* $0 \leq v \leq 2N - 1$ *and* $\|e\|_\infty \leq E$. *There exists an algorithm* $\boldsymbol{HomModRed}$ *that on input* $(\boldsymbol{a}, \boldsymbol{b})$, *outputs an LWE ciphertext* $\boldsymbol{LWE}_{\overrightarrow{s},Q}([v]_t, te')$ *in time* $O(N^2)$, *where* $|e'| \leq tNE/2$.

Proof. At the i-th loop, we have that

$$(\boldsymbol{c}, \boldsymbol{d}) = (\boldsymbol{a} \cdot X^i, \left\lfloor \frac{1}{2}(-\boldsymbol{a} \cdot X^i \cdot 2s + 2te \cdot X^i + X^{-v} \cdot X^i) + \frac{1}{4} \right\rceil)$$

$$= (\boldsymbol{a} \cdot X^i, -\boldsymbol{a} \cdot X^i \cdot s + te \cdot X^i + \left\lfloor \frac{1}{2}X^{-v} \cdot X^i + \frac{1}{4} \right\rceil),$$

$$(\boldsymbol{c}', \boldsymbol{d}') = (-\boldsymbol{a} \cdot X^i, \left\lfloor -\frac{1}{2}(-\boldsymbol{a} \cdot X^i \cdot 2s + 2te \cdot X^i + X^{-v} \cdot X^i) + \frac{1}{4} \right\rceil)$$

$$= (-\boldsymbol{a} \cdot X^i, \boldsymbol{a} \cdot X^i \cdot s - te \cdot X^i + \left\lfloor -\frac{1}{2}X^{-v} \cdot X^i + \frac{1}{4} \right\rceil).$$

Hence, we have that $(\overrightarrow{c}, d)$ and $(\overrightarrow{c}', d')$ satisfy

$$(\overrightarrow{c}, d) = (\overrightarrow{c}, -\langle \overrightarrow{c}, \overrightarrow{s} \rangle + te + \alpha),$$
$$(\overrightarrow{c}', d') = (\overrightarrow{c}', -\langle \overrightarrow{c}', \overrightarrow{s} \rangle - te + \beta),$$

where $\overrightarrow{s}$ is the coefficient vector of s, e is the constant term of $e \cdot X^i$, α is the constant term of $\lfloor \frac{1}{2}X^{-v} \cdot X^i + \frac{1}{4} \rceil$ and β is the constant term of $\lfloor -\frac{1}{2}X^{-v} \cdot X^i + \frac{1}{4} \rceil$.

Therefore, after $N - 1$ iterations, $(\overrightarrow{a}, b)$ can be represented as

$$\overrightarrow{a} = \sum_{i=1}^{N-1} [i]_t \overrightarrow{c} + [i+N]_t \overrightarrow{c}',$$

$$b = -\langle \overrightarrow{a}, \overrightarrow{s} \rangle + t \sum_{i=1}^{N-1} ([i]_t - [i+N]_t) e_i + \sum_{i=1}^{N-1} ([i]_t \alpha_i + [i+N]_t \beta_i).$$

According to the discussion in Sect. 3.1, we have that

$$b = -\langle \overrightarrow{a}, \overrightarrow{s} \rangle + te' + [v]_t$$

where $e' = \sum_{i=1}^{N-1}([i]_t - [i+N]_t)e_{i,0}$, therefore $(\overrightarrow{a}, b)$ is an LWE ciphertext of $[v]_t$ under the key $\overrightarrow{s}$.

In one loop, Step 3 in Algorithm 1 is just to perform cyclic rotation with the cycled entries negated on coefficients of $\boldsymbol{a}, \boldsymbol{b}$, and Step 5 is just to extract and shuffle several coefficients from polynomials. We think these two steps hardly contribute to the computational complexity of the whole algorithm. Step 4 in Algorithm 1 is to perform scalar multiplications in $\mathcal{R}$, and the computational complexity of scalar multiplications in $\mathcal{R}$ is $O(N)$. Step 6 requires two multiplications between a scalar and a vector of integers and an addition of two vectors of integers, hence the complexity of this step is $O(N)$. Therefore, the whole algorithm runs in time $O(N^2)$.

Now we start to analyze the noise performance. Based on the properties of power-of-two cyclotomic ring described in Sect. 2.1, we can get that $\|e \cdot X^i\|_\infty = \|e\|_\infty \leq E$, so $|e_i| \leq \|e \cdot X^i\|_\infty \leq E$. In addition we know $|[i]_t - [i+N]_t| \leq t/2$. Therefore, $|e'| \leq tNE/2$.

4 Improved Bootstrapping for BGV Scheme

Let the BGV ciphertext to be bootstrapped is $\mathbf{BGV}^t_{s,q_0}(m,e) \in R^2_{q_0}$. The blueprint of our bootstrapping procedure is described below and illustrated in Fig. 1.

Modulus Switching. One fixes a power of two N and compute a new ciphertext $\mathbf{BGV}^t_{s,2N}(m,\tilde{e})$ which encrypts the same plaintext m but has smaller size. In addition, it needs to be stressed that $\|m + t\tilde{e}\|_\infty \leq N$.

Extraction. $\mathbf{BGV}^t_{s,2N}(m,\tilde{e})$ is in fact an RLWE ciphertext $\mathbf{RLWE}_{s,2N}(m, t\tilde{e})$. Here we use **Extract** to obtain n LWE ciphertexts $\{\mathbf{LWE}_{\overrightarrow{s},2N}(m_i, t\tilde{e}_i)\}_{0 \leq i < n}$ from $\mathbf{RLWE}_{s,2N}(m, t\tilde{e})$, where $\overrightarrow{s}$ is the coefficient vector of s.

Blind Rotation. For an LWE ciphertext $\mathbf{LWE}_{\overrightarrow{s},2N}(m_i, t\tilde{e}_i) = (\overrightarrow{a}, b)$, we use a blind rotation procedure to get an RLWE ciphertext $\mathbf{RLWE}_{2z,Q}(X^{-\tilde{m}_i}, 2t\tilde{e}_i)$, where $\tilde{m} = b + \sum_{j=0}^{n-1} a_j \cdot s_j$. The output of this step is n RLWE ciphertexts of the form $\mathbf{RLWE}_{2z,Q}(X^{-\tilde{m}_i}, t\tilde{e}_i)$.

Homomorphic Modular Reduction. When the above steps are done, we obtain n RLWE ciphertexts. Then, we will apply Algorithm 1 to each of RLWE ciphertexts, resulting in n LWE ciphertexts $\{\mathbf{LWE}_{\overrightarrow{z},Q}([\tilde{m}_i]_t, t\tilde{e}_i)\}_{0 \leq i < n}$.

Repacking. Finally, we repack the LWE ciphertexts output by the previous step into one single ciphertext which encrypts m.

In the following, we will elaborate the blind rotation procedure and the repacking procedure.

4.1 Blind Rotation

After the **Extraction** procedure, we obtain n LWE ciphertexts. Each of these ciphertexts can be represented as $\mathbf{LWE}_{\overrightarrow{s},2N}(m, te) = (\overrightarrow{a}, b)$ satisfying

$$b + \langle \overrightarrow{a}, \overrightarrow{s} \rangle = b + \sum_{i=0}^{n-1} a_i \cdot s_i = m + te \bmod 2N.$$

For an LWE ciphertext $\mathbf{LWE}_{\overrightarrow{s},2N}(m, te) = (\overrightarrow{a}, b)$, we start the blind rotation with $\mathbf{ACC} \leftarrow \mathbf{RLWE}_{2z,Q}(X^{-b}, 0)$ (For simplicity, we set $\mathbf{RLWE}_{2z,Q}(X^{-b}, 0) = (0, X^{-b})$. To homomorphically compute $X^{-b-\sum_{i=0}^{n-1} a_i \cdot s_i}$, we need encryptions of s_i, which form the alleged *bootstrapping key*). The bootstrapping key is $\mathbf{bk} = \{\mathbf{RGSW}_{2z,Q}(s_i^+), \mathbf{RGSW}_{2z,Q}(s_i^-)\}$, where

$$\begin{cases} s_i^+ = 1, & s_i = 1 \\ s_i^+ = 0, & \text{otherwise} \end{cases}, \quad \begin{cases} s_i^- = 1, & s_i = -1 \\ s_i^- = 0, & \text{otherwise} \end{cases} \quad \text{for } i \in [0, N-1]$$

$$\mathbf{BGV}^t_{s,q_0}(\boldsymbol{m},\boldsymbol{e})$$

$$\downarrow \; \textbf{Modulus Switching}$$

$$\mathbf{BGV}^t_{s,2N}(\boldsymbol{m},\tilde{\boldsymbol{e}})$$

$$\downarrow \; \textbf{Extraction}$$

$$\mathbf{LWE}_{\bar{s},2N}(m_0,t\tilde{e}_0), \; \mathbf{LWE}_{\bar{s},2N}(m_1,t\tilde{e}_1),..., \; \mathbf{LWE}_{\bar{s},2N}(m_{n-1},t\tilde{e}_{n-1})$$

$$\downarrow \; \textbf{Blind Rotation}$$

$$\mathbf{RLWE}_{2z,Q}(X^{-\tilde{m}_0},2t\tilde{e}_0), \; \mathbf{RLWE}_{2z,Q}(X^{-\tilde{m}_1},2t\tilde{e}_1),..., \; \mathbf{RLWE}_{2z,Q}(X^{-\tilde{m}_{n-1}},2t\tilde{e}_{n-1})$$

$$\downarrow \; \textbf{Homomorphic Modular Reduction}$$

$$\mathbf{LWE}_{z,Q}([\tilde{m}_0]_t,t\overline{e}_0), \; \mathbf{LWE}_{z,Q}([\tilde{m}_1]_t,t\overline{e}_1),..., \; \mathbf{LWE}_{z,Q}([\tilde{m}_{n-1}]_t,t\overline{e}_{n-1})$$

$$\downarrow \; \textbf{Repacking}$$

$$\mathbf{BGV}^t_{s_L,q_L}(\boldsymbol{m},\boldsymbol{e}')$$

Fig. 1. Bootstrapping procedure

We iteratively compute

$$\mathbf{RGSW}_{2z,Q}(X^{-a_i \cdot s_i})$$
$$= \mathbf{I}_2 \otimes \overrightarrow{g} + (X^{-a_i}-1) \cdot \mathbf{RGSW}_{2z,Q}(s_i^+) + (X^{a_i}-1) \cdot \mathbf{RGSW}_{2z,Q}(s_i^-)$$

where $\mathbf{I}_2$ is a 2×2 identity matrix and $\otimes$ means tensor product. (In fact, $\mathbf{I}_2 \otimes \overrightarrow{g}$ is a trivial RGSW encryption of 1 under any key.) The above equation is correct since $s_i \in \{-1,0,1\}$ and at least one of s_i^+ and s_i^- is zero. Then we update $\mathbf{ACC} \leftarrow \mathbf{ACC} \odot \mathbf{RGSW}_{2z,Q}(X^{-a_i \cdots s_i})$.

After **ACC** is updated iteratively, the result is

$$\mathbf{RLWE}_{2z,Q}(X^{-b-a_0 s_0 - \cdots - a_{n-1}s_{n-1}}, 2t\tilde{e}) = \mathbf{RLWE}_{2z,Q}(X^{-(m+te)}, 2t\tilde{e})$$

The **BlindRotate** algorithm is described in Algorithm 2.

The following lemma concludes the noise growth and computational complexity of Algorithm 2.

Lemma 4. *Let* $\mathbf{LWE}_{\overrightarrow{s},2N}(m,te) = (\overrightarrow{a},b) \in \mathbb{Z}_{2N}^{n+1}$ *be an LWE ciphertext and* $\mathbf{bk} = \{\mathbf{RGSW}_{2z,Q}(s_i^+), \mathbf{RGSW}_{2z,Q}(s_i^-)\}$ *be a bootstrapping key. There exists a **BlindRotate** algorithm that on input* $\mathbf{LWE}_{\overrightarrow{s},2N}(m,te) = (\overrightarrow{a},b) \in \mathbb{Z}_{2N}^{n+1}$ *and* $\mathbf{bk}$*, outputs an RLWE ciphertext* $\mathbf{RLWE}_{2z,Q}(X^{-(m+te)}, 2t\tilde{e})$ *in time* $\tilde{O}(dN^2)$*, and* $\|\tilde{e}\|_\infty$ *is bounded by* $4n\sqrt{N}dBE_{bk}$ *if error of the bootstrapping key is bounded by* E_{bk}*.*

Algorithm 2. The **BlindRotate** Algorithm

Input: An LWE ciphertext $\mathbf{LWE}_{\vec{s},2N}(m, te) = (\vec{a}, b) \in \mathbb{Z}_{2N}^{n+1}$;
   A bootstrapping key $\mathbf{bk} = \{\mathbf{RGSW}_{2z,Q}(s_i^+), \mathbf{RGSW}_{2z,Q}(s_i^-)\}\}$;
Output: An RLWE ciphertext $\mathbf{RLWE}_{2z,Q}(X^{-(m+te)}, 2t\tilde{e})$;
 1: $\mathbf{ACC} \leftarrow (0, X^{-b})$;
 2: **for** $i = 0$ to $n - 1$ **do**
 3:    $\mathbf{ACC} \leftarrow \mathbf{ACC} \odot \mathbf{RGSW}_{2z,Q}(X^{-a_i \cdot s_i})$;
 4: **end for**
 5: **return** $\mathbf{ACC}$;

Proof. The correctness of this algorithm is stated above. Here we mainly prove the computational complexity and the noise performance. The cost of this algorithm is dominated by Step 3 of Algorithm 2, and the operation is essentially an external product. By Lemma 2, we know the cost of Step 3 is $\tilde{O}(dN)$ and error e_i of $\mathbf{ACC}_i$ at i-th loop satisfies $\|e_i\|_\infty \leq \|e_{i-1}\|_\infty + 4\sqrt{N}dBE_{bk}$. Therefore, the computational cost of the whole algorithm is no more than $\tilde{O}(dnN)$, and the error of the output ciphertext is bounded by $4n\sqrt{N}dBE_{bk}$.

4.2   Repacking

As described at the beginning of Sect. 4, we need a procedure to repack several LWE ciphertexts into a BGV ciphertext, so we resort to the repacking technique proposed in [30]. The **Repack** algorithm is formalized in Algorithm 3, and Lemma 5 illustrates the correctness of the repacking algorithm and the error growth during this procedure.

Algorithm 3. The **Repack** Algorithm

Input: $\{\mathbf{LWE}_{\vec{z},Q}(m_i, te_i) = (\vec{a}_i, b_i)\}_{0 \leq i < n}$;
   $\mathbf{rpk} = \{\mathbf{BGV}_{s,q}^t(z_j \cdot g_k, e_{j,k})\}_{0 \leq j < N, 0 \leq k < d}$;
Output: $\mathbf{BGV}_{s,q}^t(m, e)$; $//m(X) = \sum_{i=0}^{n-1} m_i X^i$
 1: $b = \sum_{i=0}^{n-1} b_i X^i$;
 2: **for** $j = 0$ to $n - 1$ **do**
 3:    $a_j = \sum_{i=0}^{n-1} a_{i,j} X^i$;
 4:    $(a_{j,0}, \ldots, a_{j,d-1}) \leftarrow g^{-1}(a_j)$
 5: **end for**
 6: $(\tilde{a}, \tilde{b}) \leftarrow (0, b) + \sum_{j,k} a_{j,k} \cdot \mathbf{BGV}_{s,q}^t(z_j \cdot g^k, e_{j,k})$;
 7: **return** $(\tilde{a}, \tilde{b})$;

Lemma 5. *Algorithm 3 is an algorithm that on input* $\mathbf{LWE}_{\vec{z},Q}(m_i, te_i) = (\vec{a}_i, b_i)$ *for* $0 \leq i < n$ *with error* E, *and a repacking key*

$$\mathbf{rpk} = \{\mathbf{BGV}_{s,q}^t(z_j \cdot g_k, e_{j,k})\}_{0 \leq j < N, 0 \leq k < d} = \{(c_{j,k}, d_{j,k})\}_{0 \leq j < N, 0 \leq k < d}$$

with error E_{repack}, outputs a BGV ciphertext $\mathbf{BGV}_{s,q}^{t}(\boldsymbol{m}, \boldsymbol{e})$ encrypting $\boldsymbol{m} = \sum_{i=0}^{n-1} m_i X^i$ in time $\tilde{O}(dnN)$, with error at most $E + 2\sqrt{nd}NE_{\text{repack}}$.

Proof. For an LWE ciphertext $\mathbf{LWE}_{\vec{z},Q}(m_i, te_i) = (\vec{a}_i, b_i)$, we have that $b_i + \langle \vec{a}_i, \vec{z} \rangle = m_i + te_i$, i.e., $b_i + \sum_{j=0}^{N-1} a_{i,j} \cdot z_j = m_i + te_i$. We also have that $\sum_{i=0}^{n-1} a_{i,j} X^i = \sum_{k=0}^{d-1} \boldsymbol{a}_{j,k} \cdot g^k$, and

$$\mathbf{BGV}_{s,q}^{t}(z_j \cdot g_k, \boldsymbol{e}_{j,k}) = (\boldsymbol{c}_{j,k}, \boldsymbol{d}_{j,k}) = (\boldsymbol{c}_{j,k}, -\boldsymbol{c}_{j,k}\boldsymbol{s} + t\boldsymbol{e}_{j,k} + z_j \cdot g^k)$$

Hence, it holds that

$$\tilde{\boldsymbol{a}} = \mathbf{0} + \sum_{j,k} \boldsymbol{a}_{j,k} \boldsymbol{c}_{j,k} = \sum_{j,k} \boldsymbol{a}_{j,k} \boldsymbol{c}_{j,k}$$

$$\begin{aligned}
\tilde{\boldsymbol{b}} &= \boldsymbol{b} + \sum_{j,k} \boldsymbol{a}_{j,k} \cdot \boldsymbol{d}_{j,k} \\
&= \boldsymbol{b} + (-\sum_{j,k} \boldsymbol{a}_{j,k}\boldsymbol{c}_{j,k}\boldsymbol{s} + t\sum_{j,k} \boldsymbol{a}_{j,k}\boldsymbol{e}_{j,k} + \sum_{j,k} z_j \cdot g^k \cdot \boldsymbol{a}_{j,k}) \\
&= \boldsymbol{b} + (-\sum_{j,k} \boldsymbol{a}_{j,k}\boldsymbol{c}_{j,k}\boldsymbol{s} + t\sum_{j,k} \boldsymbol{a}_{j,k}\boldsymbol{e}_{j,k} + \sum_{j=0}^{N-1}\sum_{i=0}^{n-1} a_{i,j}X^i \cdot z_j) \\
&= -\sum_{j,k} \boldsymbol{a}_{j,k}\boldsymbol{c}_{j,k}\boldsymbol{s} + t\sum_{j,k} \boldsymbol{a}_{j,k}\boldsymbol{e}_{j,k} + \sum_{i=0}^{n-1}(\sum_{j=0}^{N-1} a_{i,j} \cdot z_j)X^i + \sum_{i=0}^{n-1} b_i X^i \\
&= -\sum_{j,k} \boldsymbol{a}_{j,k}\boldsymbol{c}_{j,k}\boldsymbol{s} + t\sum_{j,k} \boldsymbol{a}_{j,k}\boldsymbol{e}_{j,k} + \sum_{i=0}^{n-1}(m_i + te_i)X^i \\
&= -\sum_{j,k} \boldsymbol{a}_{j,k}\boldsymbol{c}_{j,k}\boldsymbol{s} + t\sum_{j,k} \boldsymbol{a}_{j,k}\boldsymbol{e}_{j,k} + t\sum_{i=0}^{N-1} e_i X^i + \boldsymbol{m}
\end{aligned}$$

Therefore, we have that $(\tilde{\boldsymbol{c}}, \tilde{\boldsymbol{d}})$ is a BGV ciphertext $\mathbf{BGV}_{s,q}^{t}(\boldsymbol{m}, \sum_{j,k} \boldsymbol{a}_{j,k}\boldsymbol{e}_{j,k} + \sum_{i=0}^{N-1} e_i X^i)$, which encrypts $\boldsymbol{m} = \sum_i m_i X^i$.

Notice that error of the output ciphertext can be written as $\boldsymbol{e} = \sum_i e_i X^i + \sum_{j,k} \boldsymbol{a}_{j,k}\boldsymbol{e}_{j,k}$. Since $|e_i| \leq E$ for $0 \leq i < n$, we have $\|\sum_{i=0}^{n-1} e_i X^i\|_\infty \leq E$. Using $\|\boldsymbol{e}_{j,k}\|_\infty \leq E_{\text{repack}}$, we get that $\|\sum_{j,k} \boldsymbol{a}_{j,k}\boldsymbol{e}_{j,k}\|_\infty \leq 2\sqrt{nd}NE_{\text{repack}}$ Therefore, the error of the output is at most $E + 2\sqrt{nd}NE_{\text{repack}}$.

Step 6 of Algorithm 3 dominates the computational complexity of the entire algorithm. In this step, main operations consist of scalar multiplications and additions in R. Therefore, the runtime of this algorithm is no more than $\tilde{O}(dnN)$.

4.3 Bootstrapping

Combining **HomModRed** described in Sect. 3.2 with **BlindRotate** and **Repack**, we can obtain an improved bootstrapping procedure for BGV scheme.

Let a BGV ciphertext to be bootstrapped be parameterized by a plaintext modulus t, a modulus cyclotomic polynomial $X^n + 1$ with a power of two n, a modulus q_ℓ. The blueprint of our bootstrapping procedure is formalized by Algorithm 4.

Algorithm 4. The **Bootstrap** Algorithm

Input: A BGV ciphertext $\mathbf{BGV}^t_{s,q_\ell}(m,e) = (a,b)$;
       A bootstrapping key $\mathbf{bk} = \{\mathbf{RGSW}_{2z,q_L}(s_i^+), \mathbf{RGSW}_{2z,Q}(s_i^-)\}_{0 \le i < n}$;
       A repacking key $\mathbf{rpk} = \{\mathbf{BGV}^t_{s^{(L)},q_L}(z_j \cdot g_k, e_{j,k})\}_{0 \le j < N, 0 \le k < d}$;
Output: A level-L BGV-type ciphertext $\mathbf{BGV}^t_{s^{(L)},q_L}(m,\tilde{e})$;
1:   $\mathbf{BGV}^t_{s^{(\ell)},2N}(m,e') \leftarrow \mathbf{ModSwitch}(\mathbf{BGV}^t_{s^{(\ell)},q_\ell}(m,e))$;
2: **for** $i = 0$ to $n - 1$ **do**
3:     $\mathbf{LWE}_{\vec{s},2N}(m_i, te_i) \leftarrow \mathbf{Extract}_i(\mathbf{BGV}^t_{s^{(\ell)},2N}(m,e'))$;
4:     $\mathbf{RLWE}_{2z,q_L}(X^{-\tilde{m}_i}, e_i) \leftarrow \mathbf{BlindRotate}(\mathbf{LWE}_{\vec{s},2N}(m_i, te_i), \mathbf{bk})$;
      $//\tilde{m}_i = m_i + te_i$;
5:     $\mathbf{LWE}_{\vec{z},q_L}(m_i, e'_i) \leftarrow \mathbf{HomModRed}(\mathbf{RLWE}_{2z,q_L}(X^{-\tilde{m}_i}, e_i))$;
6: **end for**
7: $(\tilde{a}, \tilde{b}) \leftarrow \mathbf{Repack}(\{\mathbf{LWE}_{\vec{z},Q}(m_i, e'_i), \mathbf{rpk}\})$;
8: **return** $(\tilde{a}, \tilde{b})$;

In the following, we state two theorems to show the noise growth and computational complexity of the entire bootstrapping procedure based on our new homomorphic modular reduction algorithm. For parameters used in our bootstrapping procedure, we set $t = O(1)$, $N = \Theta(n)$, $q_L = \mathrm{poly}(n)$, $B = O(1)$ and $d = O(\log n)$.

Noise Analysis. The noise performance of the entire bootstrapping method is analyzed by the following theorem.

Theorem 2. *Given a bootstrapping key with initial noise E_{bk} and a repacking key with initial noise E_{rpk}, we can bootstrap BGV homomorphic encryption scheme within $\tilde{O}((n^{2.5}E_{\mathrm{bk}} + n^{1.5}E_{\mathrm{rpk}}))$.*

Proof. According to Lemma 4, the output ciphertext of **BlindRotate** has an error bounded by $4n\sqrt{N}dBE_{\mathrm{bk}}$. By Lemma 1, the error of the output ciphertext of **HomModRed** is bounded by $tN/2 \cdot E$, where E is an upper bound of the output of **BlindRotate**. Based on Lemma 5, we know that **Repack** outputs a ciphertext whose error is within $E' + 2\sqrt{n}dNE_{\mathrm{rpk}}$, where E' is an upper bound of the output of **HomModRed**. In conclusion, Algorithm 4 output a ciphertext whose error is within $2nN^{1.5}dBE_{\mathrm{bk}} + 2n^{0.5}dNE_{\mathrm{rpk}} = \tilde{O}(n^{2.5}E_{\mathrm{bk}} + n^{1.5}E_{\mathrm{rpk}})$.

Computational Complexity. Computational complexity of our bootstrapping method is stated by the following theorem.

Theorem 3. *The computation complexity of bootstrapping procedure described in Algorithm 4 is no more than $\tilde{O}(n^3)$.*

Proof. By Lemma 3, 4, 5, we can easily get that the computation complexity of our bootstrapping procedure is no more than $\tilde{O}(nN^2 + dnN^2 + dn^2N) = \tilde{O}(n^3)$.

Asymptotic Parameters. In the worst case, to make decryption correct at level-L, we need to ensure that

$$\tilde{O}(n^{2.5}E_{\mathrm{bk}} + n^{1.5}E_{\mathrm{rpk}})^{M+1} \leq \frac{q_L}{2t}$$

Therefore $q_L = \tilde{O}(n^{2.5}E_{\mathrm{bk}} + n^{1.5}E_{\mathrm{rpk}})^{M+1}$, where M can be any positive constant integer that is chosen at first and independent of dimension n and security parameter λ. For instance, if we set $E_{\mathrm{bk}} = E_{\mathrm{rpk}} = \omega(\sqrt{n\log n})$ and $M = 1$, then $q_L = \tilde{O}(n^6)$ suffices. According to Theorem 3, the security of our scheme can be relied on the hardness of $\tilde{O}(n^{5.5})$-approximate SVP. The similar result in [14] is that the security of their scheme relies on $\tilde{O}(n^{6.5})$-approximate SVP. The following table illustrates the comparison results between Chen and Zhang's work and ours. The results show that the computational complexity of our bootstrapping procedure is almost the same with the CZ17 scheme in terms of algorithm complexity, but our scheme is more suitable for implementing than the CZ17 scheme. For noise performance, our bootstrapping scheme has lower noise accumulation than that of [14], hence it allows to use worst-case complexity assumption with lower approximation factors (Table 1).

Table 1. Comparison with CZ17 scheme.

	Time complexity	Noise growth	Assumption
Our scheme	$\tilde{O}(n^3)$	$\tilde{O}(n^6)$	GapSVP$_{\tilde{O}(n^{5.5})}$
CZ17	$\tilde{O}(n^3)$	$\tilde{O}(n^7)$	GapSVP$_{\tilde{O}(n^{6.5})}$

5   Conclusion

Bootstrapping technique is a pivotal component to construct a fully homomorphic encryption scheme. The computational cost of bootstrapping procedure has a major influence on the performance of the entire FHE scheme. Meanwhile, it is vital for a bootstrapping scheme to incur polynomial noise since it requires worst-case lattice assumptions with polynomial approximation factors. Therefore, it is worthy to study a better bootstrapping procedure with polynomial noise.

In this paper, we investigate the homomorphic modular reduction algorithm in the procedure of bootstrapping BGV scheme. We use the idea of blind rotation to design a new homomorphic modular reduction algorithm and apply it to bootstrapping BGV scheme. We carry out an analysis of the noise accumulation and the computational cost. The results show that our bootstrapping scheme incurs polynomial noise accumulation and has lower noise growth, therefore our improvement decreases the approximate factor for the underlying worst-case lattice assumption from $\tilde{O}(n^{6.5})$ to $\tilde{O}(n^{5.5})$. Moreover, our new homomorphic modular reduction can be applied independently to other applications where one needs to perform modular reduction homomorphically.

Acknowledgements. We would like to thank all anonymous reviewers for their helpful advice and comments. This work was supported by National Key R&D Program of China (2018YFA0704703); National Natural Science Foundation of China (61972215, 61972073); Natural Science Foundation of Tianjin (20JCZDJC00640).

References

1. Alperin-Sheriff, J., Peikert, C.: Practical bootstrapping in quasilinear time. In: Canetti, R., Garay, J.A. (eds.) CRYPTO 2013. LNCS, vol. 8042, pp. 1–20. Springer, Heidelberg (2013). https://doi.org/10.1007/978-3-642-40041-4_1

2. Alperin-Sheriff, J., Peikert, C.: Faster bootstrapping with polynomial error. In: Garay, J.A., Gennaro, R. (eds.) CRYPTO 2014. LNCS, vol. 8616, pp. 297–314. Springer, Heidelberg (2014). https://doi.org/10.1007/978-3-662-44371-2_17

3. Brakerski, Z.: Fully homomorphic encryption without modulus switching from classical GapSVP. In: Safavi-Naini, R., Canetti, R. (eds.) CRYPTO 2012. LNCS, vol. 7417, pp. 868–886. Springer, Heidelberg (2012). https://doi.org/10.1007/978-3-642-32009-5_50

4. Bonnoron, G., Ducas, L., Fillinger, M.: Large FHE gates from tensored homomorphic accumulator. In: Joux, A., Nitaj, A., Rachidi, T. (eds.) AFRICACRYPT 2018. LNCS, vol. 10831, pp. 217–251. Springer, Cham (2018). https://doi.org/10.1007/978-3-319-89339-6_13

5. Brakerski, Z., Gentry, C., Vaikuntanathan, V.: (Leveled) fully homomorphic encryption without bootstrapping. In: Proceedings of the 3rd Innovations in Theoretical Computer Science 2012, pp. 309–325. ACM (2012)

6. Biasse, J.-F., Ruiz, L.: FHEW with efficient multibit bootstrapping. In: Lauter, K., Rodríguez-Henríquez, F. (eds.) LATINCRYPT 2015. LNCS, vol. 9230, pp. 119–135. Springer, Cham (2015). https://doi.org/10.1007/978-3-319-22174-8_7

7. Brakerski, Z., Vaikuntanathan, V.: Efficient fully homomorphic encryption from (standard) LWE. In: IEEE 52nd Annual Symposium on Foundations of Computer Science, pp. 97–106 (2011)

8. Chen, H., Chillotti, I., Song, Y.: Improved bootstrapping for approximate homomorphic encryption. In: Ishai, Y., Rijmen, V. (eds.) EUROCRYPT 2019. LNCS, vol. 11477, pp. 34–54. Springer, Cham (2019). https://doi.org/10.1007/978-3-030-17656-3_2

9. Chillotti, I., Gama, N., Georgieva, M., Izabachène, M.: Faster fully homomorphic encryption: bootstrapping in less than 0.1 S. In: Cheon, J.H., Takagi, T. (eds.) ASIACRYPT 2016. LNCS, vol. 10031, pp. 3–33. Springer, Heidelberg (2016). https://doi.org/10.1007/978-3-662-53887-6_1

10. Chillotti, I., Gama, N., Georgieva, M., Izabachne, M.: TFHE: fast fully homomorphic encryption over the torus. J. Cryptol. **33**(1), 34–91 (2020)

11. Chen, H., Han, K.: Homomorphic lower digits removal and improved FHE bootstrapping. In: Nielsen, J.B., Rijmen, V. (eds.) EUROCRYPT 2018. LNCS, vol. 10820, pp. 315–337. Springer, Cham (2018). https://doi.org/10.1007/978-3-319-78381-9_12

12. Cheon, J.H., Han, K., Kim, A., Kim, M., Song, Y.: Bootstrapping for approximate homomorphic encryption. In: Nielsen, J.B., Rijmen, V. (eds.) EUROCRYPT 2018. LNCS, vol. 10820, pp. 360–384. Springer, Cham (2018). https://doi.org/10.1007/978-3-319-78381-9_14

13. Cheon, J.H., Kim, A., Kim, M., Song, Y.: Homomorphic encryption for arithmetic of approximate numbers. In: Takagi, T., Peyrin, T. (eds.) ASIACRYPT 2017. LNCS, vol. 10624, pp. 409–437. Springer, Cham (2017). https://doi.org/10.1007/978-3-319-70694-8_15

14. Chen, L., Zhang, Z.: Bootstrapping fully homomorphic encryption with ring plaintexts within polynomial noise. In: Okamoto, T., Yu, Y., Au, M.H., Li, Y. (eds.) ProvSec 2017. LNCS, vol. 10592, pp. 285–304. Springer, Cham (2017). https://doi.org/10.1007/978-3-319-68637-0_18

15. van Dijk, M., Gentry, C., Halevi, S., Vaikuntanathan, V.: Fully homomorphic encryption over the integers. In: Gilbert, H. (ed.) EUROCRYPT 2010. LNCS, vol. 6110, pp. 24–43. Springer, Heidelberg (2010). https://doi.org/10.1007/978-3-642-13190-5_2

16. Ducas, L., Micciancio, D.: FHEW: bootstrapping homomorphic encryption in less than a second. In: Oswald, E., Fischlin, M. (eds.) EUROCRYPT 2015. LNCS, vol. 9056, pp. 617–640. Springer, Heidelberg (2015). https://doi.org/10.1007/978-3-662-46800-5_24

17. Gentry, C.: A fully homomorphic encryption scheme. Thesis (2009). http://www.pqdtcn.com/thesisDetails/289F3CEC4CD0013B0C9716D3BED41535

18. Gentry, C.: Fully homomorphic encryption using ideal lattices. In: Proceedings of the 41st Annual ACM Symposium on Theory of Computing, STOC 2009, pp. 169–178. ACM (2009)

19. Gentry, C., Halevi, S., Peikert, C., Smart, N.P.: Ring switching in BGV-Style homomorphic encryption. In: Visconti, I., De Prisco, R. (eds.) SCN 2012. LNCS, vol. 7485, pp. 19–37. Springer, Heidelberg (2012). https://doi.org/10.1007/978-3-642-32928-9_2

20. Gentry, C., Halevi, S., Smart, N.P.: Better bootstrapping in fully homomorphic encryption. In: Fischlin, M., Buchmann, J., Manulis, M. (eds.) PKC 2012. LNCS, vol. 7293, pp. 1–16. Springer, Heidelberg (2012). https://doi.org/10.1007/978-3-642-30057-8_1

21. Gentry, C., Halevi, S., Smart, N.P.: Fully homomorphic encryption with polylog overhead. In: Pointcheval, D., Johansson, T. (eds.) EUROCRYPT 2012. LNCS, vol. 7237, pp. 465–482. Springer, Heidelberg (2012). https://doi.org/10.1007/978-3-642-29011-4_28

22. Gama, N., Izabachène, M., Nguyen, P.Q., Xie, X.: Structural lattice reduction: generalized worst-case to average-case reductions and homomorphic cryptosystems. In: Fischlin, M., Coron, J.-S. (eds.) EUROCRYPT 2016. LNCS, vol. 9666, pp. 528–558. Springer, Heidelberg (2016). https://doi.org/10.1007/978-3-662-49896-5_19

23. Gentry, C., Sahai, A., Waters, B.: Homomorphic encryption from learning with errors: conceptually-simpler, asymptotically-faster, attribute-based. In: Canetti, R., Garay, J.A. (eds.) CRYPTO 2013. LNCS, vol. 8042, pp. 75–92. Springer, Heidelberg (2013). https://doi.org/10.1007/978-3-642-40041-4_5

24. Halevi, S., Shoup, V.: Algorithms in HElib. In: Garay, J.A., Gennaro, R. (eds.) CRYPTO 2014. LNCS, vol. 8616, pp. 554–571. Springer, Heidelberg (2014). https://doi.org/10.1007/978-3-662-44371-2_31

25. Halevi, S., Shoup, V.: Bootstrapping for HElib. In: Oswald, E., Fischlin, M. (eds.) EUROCRYPT 2015. LNCS, vol. 9056, pp. 641–670. Springer, Heidelberg (2015). https://doi.org/10.1007/978-3-662-46800-5_25

26. Kim A., Deryabin M., Eom J., et al.: General bootstrapping approach for RLWE-based homomorphic encryption. IACR Cryptology ePrint Archive (2021). https://eprint.iacr.org/2021/691

27. López-Alt, A., Tromer, E., Vaikuntanathan, V.: On-the-fly multiparty computation on the cloud via multikey fully homomorphic encryption. In: Proceedings of the 44th Symposium on Theory of Computing Conference, STOC 2012, pp. 1219–1234. ACM (2012)

28. Lyubashevsky, V., Peikert, C., Regev, O.: On ideal lattices and learning with errors over rings. In: Gilbert, H. (ed.) EUROCRYPT 2010. LNCS, vol. 6110, pp. 1–23. Springer, Heidelberg (2010). https://doi.org/10.1007/978-3-642-13190-5_1

29. Micciancio, D., Polyakov, Y.: Bootstrapping in FHEW-like cryptosystems. IACR Cryptology ePrint Archive (2020). https://eprint.iacr.org/2020/086

30. Micciancio, D., Sorrell, J.: Ring packing and amortized FHEW bootstrapping. In: 45th International Colloquium on Automata, Languages, and Programming, vol. 107, pp. 100:1–100:14. Schloss Dagstuhl - Leibniz-Zentrum für Informatik (2018)

31. Orsini, E., van de Pol, J., Smart, N.P.: Bootstrapping BGV ciphertexts with a wider choice of p and q. In: Katz, J. (ed.) PKC 2015. LNCS, vol. 9020, pp. 673–698. Springer, Heidelberg (2015). https://doi.org/10.1007/978-3-662-46447-2_30

32. Regev, O.: On lattices, learning with errors, random linear codes, and cryptography. In: Gabow, H.N., Fagin, R. (eds.) Proceedings of the 37th Annual ACM Symposium on Theory of Computing, pp. 84–93. ACM (2005)

33. Smart, N.P., Vercauteren, F.: Fully homomorphic SIMD operations. Des. Codes Crypt. **71**(1), 57–81 (2014). https://doi.org/10.1007/s10623-012-9720-4

Real World Cryptography

Privacy Preserving OpenPGP Public Key Distribution with Spamming Resistance

Wenyuan Li[1,2], Wei Wang[1,3]($\boxtimes$), Jingqiang Lin[4], Qiongxiao Wang[1,2], and Wenjie Wang[1,2]

[1] State Key Laboratory of Information Security, Institute of Information Engineering, Chinese Academy of Sciences, Beijing 100089, China
wangwei@iie.ac.cn
[2] School of Cyber Security, University of Chinese Academy of Sciences, Beijing 100089, China
[3] Data Assurance and Communication Security Research Center, CAS, Beijing 100089, China
[4] School of Cyber Security, University of Science and Technology of China, Hefei 230027, Anhui, China

Abstract. OpenPGP public key distribution via Synchronizing Key-Servers (SKS) is facing the challenges of user privacy leakage caused by keyword search behaviors and service unavailability of OpenPGP software caused by OpenPGP certificate spamming attack (CVE-2019-13050). Most existing solutions to the problem dispense with the necessary features and functions of SKS or Web of Trust (WoT) for attack mitigation. In this paper, we put forward a solution which is privacy-preserving and spamming-resistant, while maintaining the functionalities of SKS and WoT. Considering the characteristics of our scenario, we protect user privacy by introducing a third-party server, and propose a specific third party-based private set intersection protocol to improve usability of OpenPGP software. Our protocol helps users filter out the required key data by intersection computation between *unbalanced* sets of keywords. We also propose an enhanced scheme for multi-key query and further privacy protection. We evaluate the usability and privacy of our schemes. Experimental results show that our scheme can largely reduce unnecessary data download with appropriate filter parameters. The proposed solution relies on the security of Elliptic Curve Diffie–Hellman, HMAC-based Key Derivation Function, Bloom filter and symmetric cryptographic encryption to defend against semi-honest adversaries.

Keywords: Pretty Good Privacy · Key distribution · Keyword search · Private set intersection

This work was supported by National Key R&D Program of China (Grant No. 2020YFB1005800) and National Natural Science Foundation of China (Grant No. 61772518).

© Springer Nature Switzerland AG 2021
Y. Yu and M. Yung (Eds.): Inscrypt 2021, LNCS 13007, pp. 487–506, 2021.
https://doi.org/10.1007/978-3-030-88323-2_26

1 Introduction

Pretty Good Privacy (PGP) is an encryption program that provides cryptographic privacy and authentication for end-to-end data communication especially for e-mail communication. OpenPGP is a standard for e-mail encryption originally derived from PGP. PGP adopts Web of Trust (WoT) structure for distributed key management. Besides Public Key Infrastructure (PKI) with Certificate Authorities (CA), WoT is another mechanism for verifying digital identities on the Internet. In WoT, any entity can certify another entity by signing a certification signature for the binding relationship between a public key and the signee's identity. Certification signatures are the basis of WoT. Researchers have investigated the properties of WoT [37] which is similar to Online Social Network (OSN) such as Facebook and Twitter.

Since the beginning of year 2000, a write-only keyserver pool named Synchronizing KeyServers (SKS) has been employed to OpenPGP public key distribution. To date, SKS has provided over 6 million OpenPGP public keys[1] for users to query without restriction. Other major key distribution approaches include Web Key Directory (WKD) [24] and DNS-Based Authentication of Named Entities (DANE) [39]. WKD over HTTPS only provides keys without signatures. DANE simplifies key content by adding only a few signatures that are considered helpful. OpenPGP public key distribution via SKS has two disadvantages. One disadvantage is user privacy leakage caused by query behaviors. The other is low availability of OpenPGP software caused by OpenPGP certificate spamming attack.

On the one hand, the behaviors of users to query OpenPGP public keys from SKS will reveal the privacy of users. The attackers may infer the identity of users on the basis of the query information and the properties of WoT. Querying OpenPGP public keys via SKS can be regarded as a fundamental database operation called Keyword Search (KS) [15]. KS involves two parties: i) a server, holding a database comprised of a set of payloads and associated keywords. ii) a client, who may send queries consisting of keywords and receive the payloads associated with these keywords. Searchable encryption [4] is a positive way to protect sensitive data of users, which supports keyword search on encrypted data. However, the huge amount of legacy data which is already known to SKS in plain text renders the searchable encryption approach unrealistic.

On the other hand, the attackers of OpenPGP certificate spamming attack [1] expanded the size of OpenPGP public keys in SKS by spamming a quantity of signatures or large size signatures. The attack caused the failure of key import in OpenPGP software such as GNU Privacy Guard (GPG) and other usability issues. To mitigate the negative effects of the attack, GPG has updated a new version [23] to ignore all the signatures except self-signatures received from SKS. A draft [17] has proposed several simple mitigation methods

---

[1] https://pool.sks-keyservers.net/pks/lookup?op=stats

mainly from the perspective of keyservers. Moreover, a new keyserver named keys.openpgp.org [2] separates an OpenPGP public key into identity information and non-identity information. Identity information is only distributed with consent, and certification signatures in non-identity information are not distributed via keys.openpgp.org. Most of the mitigation recommendations and measures above suggest to obsolete SKS, eliminate the features of WoT, and put restrictions on user behaviors, which goes against the original intention of PGP developers.

For privacy protection, we first reconstruct the database in SKS into pairs of payloads and associated keywords, and split certification signatures and other key information by disparate keywords. Then we introduce a third-party server which helps users to search on encrypted pairs in SKS with encrypted keywords in requests. To mitigate OpenPGP public key distribution attack with the reservation of SKS and WoT, one solution is to give users the option to filter the OpenPGP public key data before downloading by computing intersection between sets of keywords in the user requests and in the database.

The research efforts of Private Set Intersection (PSI) focus on protocols [7, 20,22] for the case where two parties holding sets compare encrypted versions of these sets in order to compute the intersection. While these protocols turn out to be impractical for use-cases like OpenPGP public key distribution with SKS. In our scenario, the PSI protocol needs a third-party server and should be suitable for *unbalanced* sets when keys queried have been spammed. We propose a third party-based PSI protocol specially for our scenario, and apply Elliptic Curve Diffie–Hellman (ECDH), HMAC-based Key Derivation Function (HKDF), Bloom filter, and symmetric cryptographic encryption to ensure security. The third-party server for PSI computation in our scheme is called PSI Proxy. In summary, we frame our key contributions as follows:

- We solve the problems of OpenPGP public key distribution with SKS on the basis of the original features and normal functions of SKS and WoT for key validation and verification.
- We first propose an OpenPGP public key distribution scheme for private preserving and spamming resistance with a third party-based PSI protocol, and an enhanced scheme with better privacy protection.
- We evaluate our schemes in terms of usability through user behavior simulations and privacy in the semi-honest model. Our scheme can largely reduce unnecessary data download, and has the high ability to resist various attacks.

The remainder of this paper is structured as follows. We review our research background in Sect. 2. In Sect. 3, we describe the problem in brief, and give our design principles and threat model afterwards. In Sect. 4, we describe our basic and enhanced schemes for OpenPGP public key distribution with a third party-based PSI protocol. We provide an evaluation of our scheme in terms of usability and privacy in Sect. 5. Finally, we summarize related work in Sect. 6, and give a conclusion in Sect. 7.

2   Background

To start, we focus on the status quo and properties of OpenPGP public key distribution, and introduce cryptographic building blocks that are required for the remainder of this work.

2.1   OpenPGP and Web of Trust

OpenPGP is a standard [12,13] for providing end-to-end security for e-mail communication. In OpenPGP, User ID (including a user name and e-mail address) identifies a user, and is associated with a public/private key pair (either DSA/ElGamal or RSA) held by the user. Users can issue certification signatures to each other by signing the binding relationship between a public key and an identity with their private keys. These certification signatures are a significant part of a valid OpenPGP public key. An OpenPGP public key consists of a number of records called packets. OpenPGP packets are assembled into sequences in order to transfer keys. There is a public key ID in each Public-Key packet and an issuer key ID in each Signature packet. The essential elements of a transferable OpenPGP public key are as follows:

- One Public-Key packet (each contains a public key ID)
- Zero or more revocation signatures
- One or more User ID packets
- After each User ID packet, zero or more Signature packets (each contains an issuer key ID)
- Zero or more User Attribute packets
- After each User Attribute packet, zero or more Signature packets
- Zero or more Subkey packets
- After each Subkey packet, one Signature packet, plus optionally a revocation.

In PGP environment [40], a key that is not revoked or expired is valid if it is users own key, or it is certified(signed) by other valid and trusted keys. Certification signatures are shared on keyservers, and show that the issuer is sure about the signee's identity. While trust is only locally (by users themselves) and not shared, and defines whose certification signatures users trust for validating other's keys. In GPG, the trust model is similar, but the trust information is specifically stored in a local file named *trustdb*. Users sign each other's keys and progressively build a web of public keys interconnected by these certification signatures which is so-called WoT [3].

2.2   Synchronizing Keyservers

SKS is widely used for OpenPGP public key distribution, and typically exists as a keyserver pool which consists of several keyservers. The main innovation of SKS is a highly-efficient set reconciliation algorithm [28] for keeping the keyservers synchronized. The algorithm reconciles two similar sets held by different hosts.

OpenPGP users communicate with SKS using OpenPGP HTTP Keyserver Protocol (HKP) [35]. Developers have primitively designed SKS to be write-only, so that the government can not forcibly delete or tamper the key data in SKS. The original design purposes of SKS and WoT are necessary for key validation and trust transitivity, which results in the difficulty to deal with OpenPGP certificate spamming attack. The reasons for the attack are as follows: i) OpenPGP does not restrict the maximal amount of signatures in an OpenPGP public key. ii) SKS only writes and does not validate the correctness and completeness of uploaded keys or signatures. Any user can verify a key in SKS and upload a certification signature to SKS without authentication. iii) GPG or other OpenPGP software has limitations on the size of the keys imported. The software may crash when the imported data blocks become too large. iv) SKS runs a reconciliation algorithm implemented as a software developed in Ocaml which is complex to maintain.

2.3   Private Set Intersection

PSI is a cryptographic technique of secure multiparty computation (MPC). It allows two parties holding sets to compare encrypted versions of these sets in order to compute the intersection. In traditional scenario, neither party reveals anything to the counterparty except for the elements in the intersection. While in the server-client scenario, only the client learns the intersection of her set with the set of the server, without the server learning intersection of his set with the clients [32]. A naive solution of PSI has been proposed that both parties apply a cryptographic hash function to their inputs and compare these hash values, which is efficient but insecure. The researchers have proposed a variety of advanced PSI protocols based on public key, oblivious transfer, circuit, third party and so on. Inbar et al. [20] implemented PSI based on secret sharing and Garbled Bloom Filter (GBF) as a variant of Bloom filter. Chen et al. [7] constructed a fast PSI protocol with a small amount of communication between two parties using full homomorphic encryption. This protocol is specially designed for the application scenario when one of the two sets is much smaller than the other. These two sets are named *unbalanced* sets. Third Party-Based PSI [22] realized a multi-party PSI protocol aided by a third-party server.

2.4   Bloom Filter

Bloom filter is a data structure that was conceived by Burton Howard Bloom in 1970 to retrieve whether an element is in a collection [5]. Bloom filter will tell either "possibly in set" or "definitely not in set", and the degree of false positive rate can be configured. Bloom filter represents a set X of n elements by an array of m bits, and uses k independent hash functions. We describe below the initial, add and check process of Bloom filter.

1) Before initialization, the generation parameters of Bloom filter m and k are calculated according to n and an intended false positive rate p.

$$m = -\frac{n \times \ln p}{(\ln 2)^2} \qquad k = \ln 2 \times \frac{m}{n} \tag{1}$$

2) During initialization, an array with the length of m bits is generated, and each bit is initialized to 0.
3) When adding an element s of X to Bloom filter, s is hashed with k hash functions to get k indices and set 1 to these indices of Bloom filter.
4) When checking whether an element s' belongs to X, s' is hashed with k hash functions to get k indices. If all these indices of Bloom filter are 1 then s' is considered to probably in X, otherwise s' is not in X.

2.5 HMAC-Based Key Derivation Function

HKDF [25] is a special Key derivation function (KDF) [6] based on HMAC. HKDF function is divided into two phases: Extract and Expand. The Extract phase converts the input key into a short key that satisfies the pseudo-random nature. The Expand phase expands the pseudo-random key to the desired length. The inputs of HKDF function contain a hash function, a source key material, a extractor salt (which may be null or constant), a number of key bits to be produced by HKDF, and a "context information" string (which may be null) [26]. The number and length of the output key depend on the particular cryptographic algorithm that requires the key.

3   Assumptions and Goals

To present our proposal, we introduce the existing system of OpenPGP public key distribution with SKS in brief, and point out its drawbacks. Based on the issues in the existing system, we establish our design principles and threat model.

3.1   Problem Description

We provide the existing system of OpenPGP public key distribution via SKS in Fig. 1. Users are able to connect to SKS by setting an access point such as pool.sks-keyservers.net in their OpenPGP software, and retrieve keys from SKS with *keyword* like Key ID, User ID or Fingerprint. After sending a query request to one of the keyservers, users will receive a response with *payload* (which is usually a complete OpenPGP public key) associated with *keyword* in OpenPGP format from the keyserver. Users can import *payload* into local keyring by using an OpenPGP software if needed. In the above-mentioned system, usability is lessened when users download or import *payload* with a quantity of signatures which have been spammed into keys. Upon most occasions, a tiny minority of these signatures are helpful for key validation or trust transitivity. At the same time, user privacy is revealed when a user query SKS with *keyword*. All the OpenPGP public keys in SKS are retrievable to users with no authentication mechanisms. Moreover, the user communicates with SKS using HKP protocol, which is considered insecure. There is probably a relationship between the user and the owner of the key associated with *keyword*. The attackers may infer the user's identity on the basis of the query information and the properties of WoT.

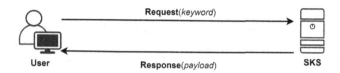

Fig. 1. Existing OpenPGP public key distribution system

3.2   Design Principles

Considering the privacy and usability issues of the existing OpenPGP public key distribution system, our scheme aims to achieve the following goals.

1) **Compatible:** Users can continue to use the original functions of SKS and WoT for key validation and trust transitivity. There is no modification required to the configuration of OpenPGP software for users to retrieve *payload* which contains certification signatures.

2) **Efficient:** Users can filter *payload* before downloading with specific filter conditions. The filtration can reduce user downloads of *payload* which further mitigates OpenPGP certificate spamming attack. Users can only import useful signatures for key validation and trust transitivity (For example, issuer key ID of a signature and Key ID of an introducer in *trustdb* are the same). We allow a moderate number of false positives to be introduced to hide the accurate number of filter conditions.

3) **Anonymous:** Attackers including semi-honest SKS and PSI Proxy can not obtain any private data in the query or filter requests of users, and thus are incapable of inferring the attributes of a user.

3.3   Threat Model

We develop our threat model with semi-honest adversaries including SKS and PSI Proxy. There is no collusion between SKS and PSI Proxy. An attacker seeks to learn the private information of a user. The private information consists of *keyword* of query requests, filter conditions (like *trustdb*) and identity information (like User ID). We list four types of possible attacks in the key distribution process. An attacker can first perform a dictionary attack, an eavesdropping attack or/and a replay attack to obtain the query or filter information, and then perform an attribute inference attack to infer user identity or other attributes. While the IP address tied to requests, a user can rely on a mix network such as Tor. IP address issue is out of scope of our threat model.

Dictionary Attack: In OpenPGP, the data type and length of *keyword* have been explicitly defined. Key ID is defined as a fixed eight-octet scalar. User ID is an UTF-8 text with no restrictions on its content. The fingerprint of a key is a MD5 hash which has been deprecated or a 160-bit SHA-1 hash. Given the format and length of *keyword*, a dictionary can be pre-computed by an attacker. The attacker can create requests with *keyword* in the dictionary, and attempt to collide with the query or filter information of any other users with these requests.

Eavesdropping or Replay Attack: In an eavesdropping attack, an attacker may take advantage of unsecure network communications to access the request and response of a query between users, SKS, and PSI Proxy. In a replay attack, an attacker can intercept a request of a user and re-transmit it to acquire *payload*. As all the *payload* in SKS and the local trust information of the user are constantly updated, the attacker can compare the present data to the previous ones, and may learn the private information of the user from the delta data.

Attribute Inference Attack: In attribute inference attack [19] towards OSN, an attacker aims to propagate attribute information of social network users with publicly visible attributes to users with missing or incomplete attribute data. Further, attackers can identify users in OSN with limited information [38]. In attribute inference attack towards WoT, an attacker may infer user identity on the strength of *keyword* and filter conditions. There may be a relationship between the user and the owner of the key queried or trusted. Based on the relationships and the characteristics of WoT, the user's attributes such as OpenPGP public key ID, User ID or its circle of friends can be inferred. Attackers can take advantage of these attributes to attack not only the user but also their friends through spam, XSS, phishing or malware which have occurred in OSN [14].

4   Scheme

Refer to our design principles, we propose an OpenPGP public key distribution system which introduces a third-party server PSI Proxy for PSI computation in Fig. 2. When a user sends a query request with *keyword* to SKS, SKS sends processed *payload* associated with *keyword* to PSI Proxy. Then the user sends a filter request with filter conditions such as *trustdb* to PSI Proxy. PSI Proxy filters *payload* by running a specific PSI protocol between the sets of *keyword* in *trustdb* and *payload*, and returns filtered *payload* to the user.

Our design relies on a combination of ECDH[2], HKDF, Bloom filter[3] to address all the risks outlined in our threat model. Here, we explain the reason why the existing PSI protocols can not be directly used in our scenario. Then we depict our basic scheme with a PSI protocol dedicated to OpenPGP

---

[2] Our scheme can use other key exchange algorithms such as Diffie-Hellman (DH).

[3] Bloom filter can be replaced by Cuckoo filter [11]. Both filters are very fast and compact, and may return false positives as answers to set-membership queries.

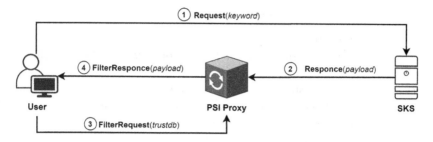

Fig. 2. Privacy Preserving and spamming resisting OpenPGP public key distribution system

public key distribution, and detail the data exchanged between a user, SKS, and PSI Proxy. We also present a strengthened scheme for further privacy protection, and provide suggestions for optimization to improve compatibility and availability.

4.1 Protocol Selection

The PSI protocol in our scheme should meet two requirements. The first one is filtering *payload* to reduce downloads. The second one is hiding the query and filter information both in content and in number. We observe the characteristics of our scenario, and classify our scenario into one of PSI application scenarios. All the *payload* in SKS is openly searchable. Thus we need to select the PSI protocols that apply to the server-client scenario. In addition, when a key suffers from a certificate spamming attack, the number of signatures spammed into the key is much larger than the number of introducers in *trustdb*. Therefore, PSI protocols for *unbalanced* sets are proper for our scenario.

We focus on several existing PSI protocols which may fulfill our requirements. The PSI protocol using secret sharing and GBF requires users to receive complete data, which can not achieve the purpose of filtering. When applying the PSI protocol using full homomorphic encryption for *unbalanced* sets to our scenario, users still need to send the intersection results as *keyword* to get associated *payload* from SKS. SKS can learn the filter information from the intersection. The PSI protocols using a third party can hide the query information from SKS, but the third-party server simply computes the intersection and can not index *keyword* to the corresponding *payload*. Thus, we design a PSI protocol that is proposed specifically for OpenPGP public key distribution scenario.

4.2 Scheme Details

Our scheme consists of two main phases: Query phase and Filter phase. In Query phase, a user sends a query request with *keyword* to SKS. SKS processes the *payload* and associated *keyword*, and sends them to PSI Proxy. In Filter phase, the user sends *trustdb* in a filter request to PSI Proxy. PSI Proxy filters the

Table 1. Notation list

Symbol	Description
H	A public set that contains n hash functions, $H = \{h_1, h_2, h_3, \ldots, h_n\}$
K	A symmetric key generated by ECDH
IV	An initialization vector for symmetric encryption
qid	An auto-increment ID in a long int type for each query
L	A number of key bits produced by HKDF
XTS	A secret extractor salt of HKDF
$CTXinfo$	A "context information" string of HKDF
err_rate	An intended false positive rate of Bloom filter
n_h	A number of hash functions of Bloom filter
m	A length of Bloom filter
pid_i	Public key ID of ith key
$sid_{i,j}$	Issuer key ID of jth signature in i^{th} key
tid_i	Key ID of ith introducer in $trustdb$
$info_i$	Other key information except signatures in i^{th} key
$sig_{i,j}$	j^{th} signature in i^{th} key
$info\_pair_i$	The pair of $info_i$ and associated pid_i, $info\_pair_i = (pid_i, info_i)$
$sig\_pair_{i,j}$	The pair of $sig_{i,j}$ and associated Key IDs (including pid_i and $sid_{i,j}$), $sig\_pair_{i,j} = ((pid_i, sid_{i,j}), sig_{i,j})$
S_1	The database of $info\_pair_i$ in SKS
S_2	The database of $sig\_pair_{i,j}$ in SKS
S	The entire database in SKS, $S = S_1 \cup S_2$

processed *payload* by running a PSI protocol between the sets of *keyword* in *trustdb* and database. We define the variants in our scheme, and list them in Table 1. We reconstruct the database S in SKS as two kinds of pairs: $info\_pair_i$ represented as $(pid_i, info_i)$, and $sig\_pair_{i,j}$ represented as $((pid_i, sid_{i,j}), sig_{i,j})$. Before querying, the user and SKS generate K, and then safely transmit other parameters including IV, qid, n_h ($n_h \leq n$), L and XTS with K.

Query Phase: When querying an OpenPGP public key $\hat{pk}$, an user sends public key ID $\hat{pid}$ of $\hat{pk}$ as *keyword*[4]. SKS finds the pairs (both $info\_pair_i$ and $sig\_pair_{i,j}$) having $\hat{pid}$ as *keyword*. For these pairs, SKS calculates HKDF values $SKD_{i,j}$ of issuer key IDs, and encrypts all the *payload* using Algorithm 1 to complete the data processing in Eq. (2). SKS uses $sid_{i,j}$ as SKM and qid as $CTXinfo$ for HKDF function. After processing, SKS sends qid, $enc_{\hat{i}}$, and the set of processed pairs $Sig\_pair_{\hat{i}}$ to PSI Proxy.

$$((pid_i, sid_{i,j}), sig_{i,j}) \rightarrow ((pid_i, SKD_{i,j}), Enc_K(sig_{i,j})) \tag{2}$$

---

[4] We choose Key ID as *keyword* to make our solution more concise. Users can also use User ID or fingerprint in the implementation.

Algorithm 1. ProcessData

Input: $S_1, S_2, IV, H, n_h, XTS, qid, L$
Output: $enc_{\hat{i}}, Sig\_pair_{\hat{i}}$
1: **for** $(pid_i, info_i) \in S_1$ **do**
2:   **if** $pid_i = \hat{pid}$ **then**
3:     $\hat{i} \leftarrow i$
4:     $enc_{\hat{i}} \leftarrow Enc_K(info_{\hat{i}})$
5:     **for** $j = 1; j \leq n_{s_{\hat{i}}}; j++$ **do**
6:       **for** $k = 1; k \leq n_h; k++$ **do**
7:         $SKD_{\hat{i},j}[k] \leftarrow HKDF(h_k, XTS, sid_{\hat{i},j}, qid, L)$
8:       **end for**
9:       $enc_{\hat{i},j} \leftarrow Enc_K(sig_{\hat{i},j})$
10:      $Sig\_pair_{\hat{i}}[j] \leftarrow ((pid_{\hat{i}}, SKD_{\hat{i},j}), enc_{\hat{i},j})$
11:    **end for**
12: **end if**
13: **end for**

Filter Phase: The user locally adds tid_i to Bloom filter BF_c by HKDF values TKD_i of tid_i in $trustdb$, which is outlined in Algorithm 2. The user uses tid_i as SKM and qid as $CTXinfo$ for HKDF function. Then the user sends qid, BF_c, and n_h in a filter request to PSI Proxy. m and n_h of BF_c are calculated by err_rate and the set size n_t of $trustdb$ using Eq. (1) in Sect. 2.4. PSI Proxy searches $Sig\_pair_{\hat{i}}$ according to qid as the input of Algorithm 3. The output Sig which contains n_{sf} signatures is sent to the user together with $enc_{\hat{i}}$ as $payload$. All the data received by the user can be decrypted with K and IV, and imported into local keyring.

Algorithm 2. CreateFilterRequest

Input: $err\_rate, n_t, H, n_h, XTS, trustdb, qid, L$
Output: BF_c
1: $initial(BF_c, err\_rate, n_t)$
2: **for** $tid_i \in trustdb$ **do**
3:   **for** $k = 1; k \leq n_h; k++$ **do**
4:     $TKD_i[k] \leftarrow HKDF(h_k, XTS, tid_i, qid, L)$
5:     $add(BF_c, TKD_i[k])$
6:   **end for**
7: **end for**

4.3 Extension to Public Key IDs

Our scheme applies for single-key queries, and can not hide public key IDs queried from SKS. We suggest users to rely on Tor to query. On the basis of our scheme, we propose an enhanced scheme shown in Fig. 3 by applying a "double filtration" solution. As the number of keys queried is far less than the amount of keys in SKS, the PSI computation for issuer key IDs can also be applied to public

---

Algorithm 3. ComputeSetIntersection

Input: BF_c, Sig_pair_i
Output: Sig, n_{sf}
1: **for** $j = 1, n_{sf} = 1; j \leq n_{s_i}; j + +$ **do**
2:     $iscontian \leftarrow check(BF_c, SKD_{i,j})$
3:     **if** $iscontian == 1$ **then**
4:         $\hat{j} \leftarrow j$
5:         $Sig[n_{sf} + +] \leftarrow Enc_k\left(Sig_{i,j}\right)$
6:     **end if**
7: **end for**

---

key IDs. Especially when the user queries multiple keys in a query, this extension can further enhance privacy protection with a few downloads of *payload*.

In Query phase, SKS needs to shuffle the orders of pairs before processing (in case semi-honest PSI Proxy acts as a user to get the indices of all the data). Then as shown in Eq. (3) and Eq. (4), SKS computes HKDF values PKD_i of pid_i, and processes all the pairs in S. SKS sends PKD_i and the processed database to PSI Proxy.

$$(pid_i, info_i) \rightarrow (PKD_i, Enc_K\left(info_i\right)) \tag{3}$$

$$((pid_i, sid_{i,j}), sig_{i.j}) \rightarrow ((PKD_i, SKD_{i,j}), Enc_K\left(sig_{i,j}\right)) \tag{4}$$

In Filter phase, when querying n_q keys with a set of public key IDs named *qlist*, the user uses Algorithm 2 to add these keys into Bloom filter BF_q by HKDF values PKD_i (*err_rate* of BF_q can differ from that of BF_c). The user then sends BF_q to PSI Proxy. PSI Proxy uses Algorithm 3 to filter *info_pair$_i$* in S_1 with BF_q as the first level of filtration, finding n_{kf} public key IDs that may be involved in *qlist*. PSI Proxy then performs Filter phase of the basic scheme towards *sig_pair$_{i,j}$* having the same *keyword pid$_i$* in S_2 with BF_c as the second level of filtration, and sends the output as *payload* to the user. The user encrypts the filter result with K and IV, and selects the desired *payload* by *qlist*. While the limitation of this solution is for each query, SKS is required to process the entire database S, including HKDF calculation of all the *keyword* and symmetric encryption of all the *payloads*.

4.4   Optimization

On top of our scheme, several optimizations can be carried out to improve compatibility and availability. With no need to modify the original functions of SKS, one or more proxy servers can be deployed on SKS side. The proxy server takes charge of SKS for the interactions with users or PSI Proxy and *payload* processing to improve compatibility. Simplifying HKDF function to simple Hash function in our scheme helps decrease computation of SKS, which may suffer from a dictionary attack. However, the employ of Bloom filter still introduces false positives to hide the set size and content of *keyword*. By adjusting the

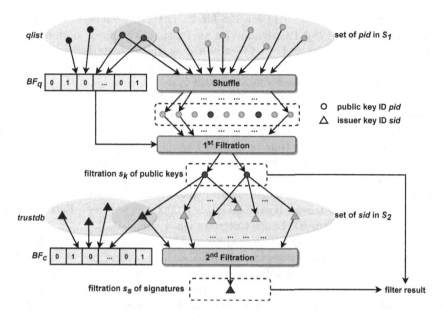

Fig. 3. An extended scheme to enhance privacy protection which applies two levels of filtration. Before filtering, SKS shuffles all the OpenPGP public keys in the database, and users generate BF_q with *qlist* and BF_c with *trustdb*. In first filtration, PSI Proxy filters *pid* with BF_q to get the intersection s_k of public keys. In second filtration, PSI Proxy filters *sid* which has certified *sid* in s_k with BF_c to get the intersection s_s of signatures. With all the Key IDs in s_k and s_s as *keyword*, PSI Proxy sends encrypted *payload* as filter result to users.

parameter *err_rate* and L (not less than the hash function output length), the communication amount of HKDF values from SKS to PSI Proxy can be effectively reduced.

5   Evaluation

We evaluate our solutions in terms of usability and privacy. We set disparate benchmarks to evaluate the effect of filtering in the basic scheme. We also analyze the complexities and the storage required for the parties in both solutions. For the possible attacks in threat model, we evaluate the cryptographic operations and techniques in our scheme for the processing and transmission of sensitive data.

5.1   Experimental Settings

We implement our scheme including a GPG user, PSI Proxy, and one keyserver of SKS in Ubuntu 16.04 operating system and C++ programming language. We

use OpenSSL library (v. 1.1.1) for 128-bit ECDH key exchange, HKDF computation, and AES-128-CBC symmetric encryption. We need to simulate the
private information $qlist$ and $trustdb$ of users. As the characteristics of WoT are
similar to those of OSN, With reference [29] to the number of friends in OSN, the
number of key IDs in the user's local $trustdb$ is assumed to be in the range of 0
to 100. We randomly generate Key IDs in $qlist$ and $trustdb$ in the normal range.
We choose the main keyserver of SKS of which the URL is https:// pool. sks-
keyservers. net/. For an OpenPGP public key in SKS, the reasonable number
of signatures should be less than or around 1000 [34] which can be regarded as a
criterion for whether the key has been attacked. We find several representative
keys that have suffered from OpenPGP certificate spamming attack in SKS. The
user name of these keys are Yegor Timoshenko (174622 signatures), Robert J.
Hansen (149120 signatures), Ryan McGinnis (100002 signatures), Patrick Brun-
schwig (151491 signatures), Lance Cottrell (34391 signatures).

Our scheme also consider data updates in SKS and in users' $trustdb$. There
are constant updates on the key data in SKS such as revocations of the existing
keys or signatures or the uploading of fresh keys or signatures. In the implementation, users send a query request with a parameter of time range, and receive
the key data with updates in this time range from SKS. Users can modify the
trust information in $trustdb$ subjectively. When $trustdb$ changes, the parameters
of Bloom filter need to be modified by users to generate a new filter.

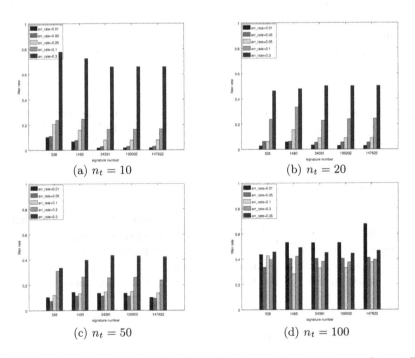

Fig. 4. Experimental results of filtration. We choose the set size n_t of $trustdb \in$
$\{10, 20, 50, 100\}$ and the average set size of signatures of the target keys $n_s \in$
$\{538, 1480, 34391, 100002, 147622\}$. We get the ratio *filter rate* of user downloads to
the original key size under different *err_rate*.

5.2   Usability Evaluation

We compare the filtering effect in the basic scheme under diverse set sizes of *keyword* through the experimental results. As shown in Fig. 4, the greater the disparity of the set sizes, the greater the mitigation effect of OpenPGP certificate spamming attack. Then we set different *err_rate* of Bloom filter to evaluate the impact of it on downloads. In most cases in Fig. 4, as *err_rate* reduces, the decrease of downloads becomes more pronounced. We suggest *err_rate* to be less than 0.3 whthin which the reduction of downloads can be more than half. Supposing the average size of signatures is s, regardless of the fact that the size of signatures can be exaggerated, we get the decline d of downloads which can be approximately calculated as $n_s(1-p)s$ theoretically if n_s is large enough.

For the basic solution in Sect. 4.2 and the improved solution in Sect. 4.3, we depict the computation and communication complexities of users and SKS, and the storage required by PSI Proxy during key distribution in Table 2. The complexities and storage are linear to the number of users. The computation complexity is expressed as the number of symmetric cryptographic operations (sym) and the number of HKDF operations (hkdf). ECDH operations which perform only once before each query are not represented in Table 2. The communication complexity of a user in our schemes is much lower than that in the existing system for the most part, and the computation complexity depends mainly on the number of symmetric encryption operations. The complexities of SKS depend on the number of signatures in the keys queried in the basic scheme. While they depend on the total amount of pairs in SKS in the improved scheme. In addition, the data volume that PSI Proxy needs to store is approximately equal to the communication amount transmitted by SKS.

Table 2. Complexities and storage for OpenPGP public key distribution (σ: bit size of the communication required for key exchange and data transmission before query; ℓ: bit size of qid; hkdf: HKDF operations; sym: symmetric cryptographic operations; n_k, n_{kf}: set sizes as defined in Sect. 4.2; n_s, n_{sf}: the average number of the signatures in each key and in the intersection; k, s: bit size of $info_i$ and $sig_{i,j}$ defined in Sect. 4.2; L: HKDF parameter; m, n_h: Bloom filter parameters).

Role	Type	Basic scheme	Improvement scheme
User	Computation (#ops hkdf/sym)	$n_t n_h$ hkdf $n_{sf}+1$ sym	$(n_t + n_q)n_h$ hkdf $(n_{sk}+1)n_{kf}$ sym
	Communication (bit)	$\sigma + m + \ell + k + n_{sf}s$	$\sigma + 2m + \ell + n_{kf}k + n_{kf}n_{sf}s$
SKS	Computation (#ops hkdf/sym)	$n_s n_h$ hkdf $n_s + 1$ sym	$n_s n_k n_h$ hkdf $(n_s + 1)n_k$ sym
	Communication (bit)	$\sigma + \ell + k + n_s s + n_s n_h L$	$\sigma + \ell + n_k k + n_k n_s s + n_s n_k n_h L$
PSI proxy	Storage (bit)	$m + \ell + k + n_s s + n_s n_h L$	$2m + \ell + n_k k + n_k n_s s + n_s n_k n_h L$

5.3   Privacy Evaluation

Before the privacy evaluation of our proposal, we explain the security of cryptographic algorithms and techniques used in our solution which consists of ECDH, HKDF, Bloom filter and symmetric encryption. ECDH is one of key exchange schemes based on ECC which provides the same cryptographic strength as the RSA system, but with much smaller keys. We apply HKDF function on the basis of the properties of the HMAC scheme both as extractor and pseudorandom function. In our solution, we further strengthen the security of HKDF with a secret salt. For Bloom filter, a query returns either "possibly in set" or "definitely not in set" rather than an exact element in the set. The apply of Bloom filter also automatically introduces false positives for filtering, which can hide the accurate set size and content. For each query, a key for symmetric encryption is pre-shared between users and SKS, and is invalidated each time the user decrypts the result. In both our basic and extended scheme, all the sensitive data and parameters between users, SKS, and PSI Proxy are transmitted in a non-plaintext form, except public key ID in the basic scheme. We carry out security analysis of our scheme towards possible attacks outlined in the threat model on the basis of the security of cryptographic algorithms and techniques.

Collision Resistant: The parameters of HKDF function are agreed between users and SKS in a secure channel. Without the parameters of other users, an attacker can not launch a dictionary attack by the computation of HKDF values for all the keywords. Although SKS can obtain the parameters and compute HKDF values, it can not create filter requests without *qlist* and *trustdb* of users. In our enhanced solution, we ask SKS to shuffle all the *payload* before processing to prevent semi-honest PSI Proxy. If SKS processes the *payload* in a fixed sequence, PSI Proxy can act as a user to query with all the keywords in the dictionary. Thus, PSI Proxy can learn the real data content by the sequential index. When a user filers *payload* through PSI Proxy, PSI Proxy can learn the privacy information of the user by the indices of filter results. After SKS shuffling all the keys, PSI Proxy can not learn the plaintext of *payload* by indices.

Eavesdropping and Replay Resistant: The attacker eavesdropping on users, SKS, and PSI Proxy can not learn any privacy information from the requests and responses which are all encrypted. Our schemes can also resist replay attacks by adding a query ID for each query. Query ID is auto-increment for each query and is associated with the symmetric key exchanged between users and SKS. The attacker can be detected by SKS or PSI Proxy when re-transmitting the query or filter requests with the same or uncorrect query ID.

Identity Anonymous: An attacker can not identify a user with no access to user privacy information particularly the filter information like *trustdb*. In the basic scheme, semi-honest SKS can only obtain *keyword* of the key queried. While SKS can not get either *qlist* as *keyword* and *trustdb* in the enhanced scheme. Other attackers like semi-honest PSI Proxy can not obtain all the sensitive information. Both *qlist* and *trustdb* are in the form of Bloom filter, and *payload* processed by SKS is in the form of ciphertext. Moreover, the parameters of Bloom filter are constantly modified by users to generate new filters, so that attackers are agnostic about the variation of *qlist* and *trustdb*.

6 Related Work

PSI protocols for *unbalanced* sets have been used to protect user privacy in many application scenarios. Thomas et al. [36] introducing a PSI protocol based on ECDH key Exchange which is used to mitigate credential stuffing attack. Kales et al. [21] implemented a PSI protocol based on Oblivious Pseudo-Random Function (OPRF) and Cuckoo filter to protect the privacy of contact information of mobile devices. Related to PSI, private keyword search which is also introduced as Oblivious Keyword Search (OKS) [31] has become another problem to solve for privacy protection of query. Kushilevitz and Ostrovsky [27] first suggests a single-server Private Information Retrieval (PIR) protocol for obtaining a semi-private Keyword Search (KS) protocol. PIR schemes allow a user to retrieve the ith bit of an n-bit database, without revealing to the database the value of i. There are two classes of PIR protocols. Information-theoretic PIR (IT-PIR) [9] provides security guarantees, and is usually more computationally efficient. However, any non-trivial IT-PIR requires multiple non-colluding servers. Chor et al. [8] proved that the trivial protocol in which clients are sent the entire database is communication optimal in the single-server setting. Computational PIR (cPIR) [10] can achieve sublinear communication with a single server, but is typically more computationally expensive as it usually involves cryptographic operations based on public-key primitives to be carried out on each element of the database. Other techniques for private keyword search are homomoephic encryption [16], oblivious transfer [33], oblivious-RAM (ORAM) [18], oblivious polynomial Evaluation [30] and searchable encryption [4].

7 Conclusion

In this paper, We first propose an OpenPGP public key distribution scheme with an effective third party-based PSI protocol for *unbalanced* sets to deal with user privacy leakage and certificate spamming attack. We enhance our scheme by applying a "double filtration" solution for further user privacy protection. Our schemes applies cryptographic operations and techniques to prevent privacy disclosure to defend against semi-honest adversaries. With appropriate filter parameters, our schemes can effectively reduce unnecessary user download to resist certificate spamming attack.

However, in our enhanced scheme, each query requires SKS to fully encrypt the database, which increases the computational and communication complexity. Future research may consider to combine PIR to remove the third party and perfect our proposal which can be implemented in a multi-user scenario.

References

1. CVE-2019-13050   (2019).   https:// nvd. nist. gov/ vuln/ detail/ CVE- 2019-13050
2. keys.openpgp.org (2019). https:// keys. openpgp. org
3. Abdul-Rahman, A.: The pgp trust model. EDI Forum J. Electron. Commer. **10**, 27–31 (1997)
4. Bellare, M., Boldyreva, A., O'Neill, A.: Deterministic and efficiently searchable encryption. In: Menezes, A. (ed.) CRYPTO 2007. LNCS, vol. 4622, pp. 535–552. Springer, Heidelberg (2007). https:// doi. org/ 10. 1007/ 978- 3- 540- 74143-5_30
5. Bloom, B.H.: Space/time trade-offs in hash coding with allowable errors. Commun. ACM **13**(7), 422–426 (1970)
6. Camenisch, J., Fischer-Hübner, S., Rannenberg, K.: Privacy and Identity Management for Life. Springer, Heidelberg (2011). https:// doi. org/ 10. 1007/ 978-3- 642- 20317- 6
7. Chen, H., Laine, K., Rindal, P.: Fast private set intersection from homomorphic encryption. In: Proceedings of the 2017 ACM SIGSAC Conference on Computer and Communications Security, pp. 1243–1255 (2017)
8. Chor, B., Gilboa, N., Naor, M.: Private information retrieval by keywords. Citeseer (1997)
9. Demmler, D., Herzberg, A., Schneider, T.: RAID-PIR: practical multi-server PIR. In: Proceedings of the 6th edition of the ACM Workshop on Cloud Computing Security, pp. 45–56 (2014)
10. Dong, C., Chen, L.: A fast single server private information retrieval protocol with low communication cost. In: Kutyłowski, M., Vaidya, J. (eds.) ESORICS 2014. LNCS, vol. 8712, pp. 380–399. Springer, Cham (2014). https:// doi. org/ 10. 1007/ 978- 3- 319- 11203- 9_22
11. Fan, B., Andersen, D.G., Kaminsky, M., Mitzenmacher, M.D.: Cuckoo filter: practically better than bloom. In: Proceedings of the 10th ACM International on Conference on Emerging Networking Experiments and Technologies, CoNEXT 2014, pp. 75–88. Association for Computing Machinery, New York (2014). https:// doi. org/ 10. 1145/ 2674005. 2674994
12. Finney, H., Donnerhacke, L., Callas, J., Thayer, R.L., Shaw, D.: OpenPGP Message Format. RFC 4880 (November 2007). https:// doi. org/ 10. 17487/ RFC4880, https:// rfc- editor. org/ rfc/ rfc4880. txt
13. Finney, H., Thayer, R.L., Donnerhacke, L., Callas, J.: OpenPGP Message Format. RFC 2440 (November 1998). https:// doi. org/ 10. 17487/ RFC2440, https:// rfc- editor. org/ rfc/ rfc2440. txt
14. Fire, M., Goldschmidt, R., Elovici, Y.: Online social networks: threats and solutions. IEEE Commun. Surv. Tutorials **16**(4), 2019–2036 (2014)
15. Freedman, M.J., Ishai, Y., Pinkas, B., Reingold, O.: Keyword search and oblivious pseudorandom functions. In: Kilian, J. (ed.) TCC 2005. LNCS, vol. 3378, pp. 303–324. Springer, Heidelberg (2005). https:// doi. org/ 10. 1007/ 978- 3- 540- 30576-7_17
16. Gentry, C., et al.: A Fully Homomorphic Encryption Scheme, vol. 20. Stanford University, Stanford (2009)
17. Gillmor, D.K.: Abuse-Resistant OpenPGP Keystores. Internet-Draft draft-dkg-openpgp-abuse-resistant-keystore-04, Internet Engineering Task Force (August 2019, work in progress). https:// datatracker. ietf. org/ doc/ html/ draft- dkg-openpgp- abuse- resistant- keystore- 04

18. Goldreich, O.: Towards a theory of software protection and simulation by oblivious rams. In: Proceedings of the 19th Annual ACM Symposium on Theory of Computing, pp. 182–194 (1987)
19. Gong, N.Z., Liu, B.: Attribute inference attacks in online social networks. ACM Trans. Priv. Secur. (TOPS) **21**(1), 1–30 (2018)
20. Inbar, R., Omri, E., Pinkas, B.: Efficient scalable multiparty private set-intersection via garbled bloom filters. In: Catalano, D., De Prisco, R. (eds.) SCN 2018. LNCS, vol. 11035, pp. 235–252. Springer, Cham (2018). https:// doi. org/ 10. 1007/ 978-3- 319- 98113- 0_13
21. Kales, D., Rechberger, C., Schneider, T., Senker, M., Weinert, C.: Mobile private contact discovery at scale. In: 28th USENIX Security Symposium (USENIX Security 19), pp. 1447–1464 (2019)
22. Kamara, S., Mohassel, P., Raykova, M., Sadeghian, S.: Scaling private set intersection to billion-element sets. In: Christin, N., Safavi-Naini, R. (eds.) FC 2014. LNCS, vol. 8437, pp. 195–215. Springer, Heidelberg (2014). https:// doi. org/ 10. 1007/ 978- 3- 662- 45472- 5_13
23. Koch, W.: Gnupg 2.2.17 released to mitigate attacks on keyservers (2019). https:// lists. gnupg. org/ pipermail/ gnupg- announce/ 2019q3/ 000439. html
24. Koch, W.: OpenPGP Web Key Directory. Internet-Draft draft-koch-openpgp-webkey-service-11, Internet Engineering Task Force (November 2020, work in progress). https:// datatracker. ietf. org/ doc/ html/ draft- koch- openpgp-webkey- service- 11
25. Krawczyk, D.H., Eronen, P.: HMAC-based Extract-and-Expand Key Derivation Function (HKDF). RFC 5869 (May 2010). https:// doi. org/ 10. 17487/ RFC5869, https:// rfc- editor. org/ rfc/ rfc5869. txt
26. Krawczyk, H.: Cryptographic extraction and key derivation: the HKDF scheme. In: Annual Cryptology Conference (2010)
27. Kushilevitz, E., Ostrovsky, R.: Replication is not needed: single database, computationally-private information retrieval. In: Proceedings 38th Annual Symposium on Foundations of Computer Science, pp. 364–373. IEEE (1997)
28. Minsky, Y., Trachtenberg, A.: Practical set reconciliation. In: 40th Annual Allerton Conference on Communication, Control, and Computing, vol. 248. Citeseer (2002)
29. Mislove, A., Marcon, M., Gummadi, K.P., Druschel, P., Bhattacharjee, B.: Measurement and analysis of online social networks. In: Proceedings of the 7th ACM SIGCOMM Conference on Internet Measurement, IMC 2007, pp. 29–42. Association for Computing Machinery, New York (2007). https:// doi. org/ 10. 1145/ 1298306. 1298311
30. Naor, M., Pinkas, B.: Oblivious polynomial evaluation. SIAM J. Comput. **35**(5), 1254–1281 (2006)
31. Ogata, W., Kurosawa, K.: Oblivious keyword search. J. Complex. **20**(2–3), 356–371 (2004)
32. Pinkas, B., Schneider, T., Segev, G., Zohner, M.: Phasing: private set intersection using permutation-based hashing. Cryptology ePrint Archive, Report 2015/634 (2015). https:// eprint. iacr. org/ 2015/ 634
33. Rabin, M.O.: How to exchange secrets with oblivious transfer. IACR Cryptology ePrint Archive 2005(187) (2005)
34. Richters, O., Peixoto, T.P.: Trust transitivity in social networks. PLOS ONE **6**(4), e18384 (2011)

35. Shaw, D.: The OpenPGP HTTP Keyserver Protocol (HKP). Internet-Draft draft-shaw-openpgp-hkp-00, Internet Engineering Task Force (March 2003, work in progress). https:// datatracker. ietf. org/ doc/ html/ draft- shaw- openpgp-hkp- 00

36. Thomas, K., et al.: Protecting accounts from credential stuffing with password breach alerting. In: 28th USENIX Security Symposium (USENIX Security 19), pp. 1556–1571 (2019)

37. Ulrich, A., Holz, R., Hauck, P., Carle, G.: Investigating the OpenPGP web of trust. In: Atluri, V., Diaz, C. (eds.) ESORICS 2011. LNCS, vol. 6879, pp. 489–507. Springer, Heidelberg (2011). https:// doi. org/ 10. 1007/ 978- 3- 642- 23822-2_27

38. Vesdapunt, N., Garcia-Molina, H.: Identifying users in social networks with limited information. In: 2015 IEEE 31st International Conference on Data Engineering, pp. 627–638 (2015). https:// doi. org/ 10. 1109/ ICDE. 2015. 7113320

39. Wouters, P.: DNS-Based Authentication of Named Entities (DANE) Bindings for OpenPGP. RFC 7929 (August 2016). https:// doi. org/ 10. 17487/ RFC7929, https:// rfc- editor. org/ rfc/ rfc7929. txt

40. Zimmermann, P.R.: The Official PGP User's Guide. MIT Press (1995)

Collaborative Verifiable Delay Functions

Liam Medley[✉] and Elizabeth A. Quaglia

Royal Holloway, University of London, London, UK
`liam.medley.2018@rhul.ac.uk`

Abstract. We propose and define a new primitive, collaborative verifiable delay functions (coVDFs), an extension to VDFs allowing multiple parties to jointly compute a publicly verifiable delay, whilst encapsulating a personal input from each party. These personal inputs can contain information such as a hash of a bid in an auction, or some public identifier of the solving party. We highlight the differences between the single-party and the multi-party settings, and discuss some applications facilitated by the additional properties offered by coVDFs.

We formalise this new primitive, as well as the relevant security properties, and we introduce the notions of *robustness* and *traceability*, which mitigate adversarial behaviour arising from the introduction of multiple parties. We propose two candidate constructions: the first is an extension of Wesolowski's VDF construction from EUROCRYPT 2019, relying on repeated squaring in a finite abelian group. We prove that this extension satisfies the traceability property, however it is not robust. Our second construction is based on the hashgraph protocol proposed by Baird in 2016, and involves each of the n parties repeatedly implementing a gossip protocol to one another and computing a hash each time they do. The construction results in every party producing a copy of the same graph, and is robust, meaning it runs correctly, in the presence of up to $n/3$ malicious parties.

Keywords: Verifiable delay functions · Repeated squaring · Hashgraph

1 Introduction

In recent years, the rapid growth of distributed ledger technology has fuelled research into proving effort has been expended. The most well-known case is the proof of work system used by Bitcoin [28], among other blockchains. However, this resource-intensive design has received widespread criticism due to its vast energy consumption and the associated impact on climate change. Alternative, more energy efficient methods of showing that computational effort has been expended have been proposed [12,13,20,26], among them verifiable delay functions (VDFs) [10,11,15,16].

VDFs, first formalised in [10] in 2018, have quickly become a very active research area [16,29,32]. They are used to show that some amount of clock time

© Springer Nature Switzerland AG 2021
Y. Yu and M. Yung (Eds.): Inscrypt 2021, LNCS 13007, pp. 507–530, 2021.
https://doi.org/10.1007/978-3-030-88323-2_27

has elapsed, by running a sequential algorithm resistant to massive parallelisation: regardless of how many cores each participant has access to, they must be able to reach the same solution at approximately the same time. VDFs enable a variety of applications including building resource efficient blockchains, public randomness beacons and timestamping mechanisms [10,13].

More formally, a VDF consists of a triple of algorithms, Setup, Eval and Verify. Setup takes security parameter λ and delay parameter t, and outputs public parameters which specify how to compute and verify the VDF. Eval takes an input and the public parameters, and provides an output y and a proof π. Verify uses π to efficiently verify that y is the correct output for x, implying that t steps have been calculated. A VDF must be sequential, efficiently verifiable, and have a unique output for any input. The sequentiality property links this computation to wall-clock time, by requiring that each step of the computation relies on the output of the previous step. This prevents the entire computation being parallelised, and is how a delay is achieved. Uniqueness ensures that work from one VDF instance cannot be re-used in another computation to circumvent the delay.

In this work, we extend VDFs to a group setting and define a collaborative verifiable delay function (coVDF), where n parties jointly compute the delay function. We additionally allow each party to embed a *personal input* into the computation. This gives the primitive additional functionality, allowing the delay to be utilised in a wider array of settings. A personal input can be a commitment to a vote or a bid, or it could be some public information showing the age of a document, or an indicator of how much work has been contributed by a single party.

Furthermore, with our new primitive we can take a VDF application such as timestamping and 'batch' it, allowing multiple parties to timestamp documents together in an either synchronised or sequential way. That is, we can either show multiple documents to all be the same age, or obtain an ordering of such documents, where documents are added incrementally. We discuss applications in greater detail in Sect. 1.2.

1.1 Related Work

VDFs were first introduced by Boneh et al. in 2018 [10], motivated by applications in decentralized systems, such as public randomness beacons, leadership elections in consensus protocols, and timestamping.

Three candidate VDF schemes were proposed soon after [16,29,32], based on repeated squaring in a group of unknown order, and on isogenies over elliptic curves. An intuitive approach to building a coVDF could be to use a single-party VDF and *split* the work between each of the n solvers. In practice, this is not necessarily easy as output proofs also need to be split, and some method is required to add personal inputs into the protocol. In Appendix A, we show that this intuition does work in specific cases, and, in particular, we extend Wesolowski's VDF [32] to a coVDF, giving a concrete instantiation from repeated squaring.

In EUROCRYPT 2020, Ephraim et al. introduced the notion of a continuous VDF (cVDF) [15], defined as a VDF which can be verified at regular intervals rather than at the end of the computation. This allows standard VDF applications such as timestamping or providing a randomness beacon to be outsourced, and also allows for another party to take over the computation at any verification point. Whilst cVDFs are similar to (a specific class of) coVDFs, the key difference is that coVDFs allow users to include a personal input, enabling more functionalities.

Extending a VDF to a multi-user setting can be seen as closely related to Multi-Party Computation (MPC), which allows evaluation of an arbitrary function on private inputs from multiple parties without revealing the inputs. In a coVDF, a group of parties jointly provide a set of private inputs, with a computational timestamp and proof of effort associated with the primitive's computation. One typical application of secure MPC is blind auctions, which we discuss in the next section as a potential application of coVDFs.

1.2 Applications of a coVDF

We next explore some use cases of coVDFs, distinguishing between two distinct classes of coVDFs, namely *sequential* and *parallel*, for which we provide a formal definition (Definition 2) in Sect. 2. Intuitively, in a sequential coVDF parties provide their personal input at various stages in the computation, while parallel coVDFs require parties to provide their personal input at the same time, i.e., at the beginning of the computation. This leads to separate applications arising in each setting, which we expand upon next.

Applications of Sequential coVDFs. In a sequential coVDF, parties take turns to calculate their part of the computation, before passing it on to another party to continue. In a trusted setting, the key advantage of a coVDF when compared with iterating a standard VDF is that only one verification procedure is required, rather than multiple, which can make a noticeable difference in practice: Attias et al. [1] showed that the proving time of Wesolowski and Pietrzak's VDFs is of the same order of evaluation.

Sequential coVDFs can find a natural application in the setting of collaborative work. Consider an entity such as an employer or teacher, who wants a group (such as employees or students) to complete some collaborative activity, which requires effort from all parties, but each part of this activity relies on the previous one being completed. In such a scenario, the use of a sequential coVDF can be used to provide evidence that the work has been done by each party, as well as providing the next party the required information to start their task. Alternatively, a coVDF can be used by a group of parties as a proof of expended effort, in return for access to some resource owned by a company. In particular, this can be done by parties who can only expend effort at certain times, for example at night when electricity is cheaper [6,19]. Upon verification, the company can then use this computation to implement a randomness beacon. In Appendix C, we outline how to achieve this using our sequential coVDF construction from Appendix A.

Applications of Parallel coVDFs. Using a parallel coVDF, n parties each submit a personal input, and together calculate a delay on this set of inputs. The knowledge that all parties submitted these inputs together, and before some particular event, can be useful in various settings. The example we focus on is decentralised blind auctions.

In a blind auction, each party submits a sealed bid, such that no bidder knows the bid of any other participant. The party with the highest bid wins the auction, and pays the price they submitted for the goods [14]. Blind auctions have been subject to recent study in the decentralised setting, for example [17] and [3] propose auctioneer-free sealed-bid protocols, using smart contracts on Ethereum and multi-party computation, respectively. However, in schemes such as those listed above, parties post their bids on a public bulletin board. The drawback of this is that those who bid later have knowledge of how many bids have been submitted, which can be construed as an advantage over those who bid first. This can also mean that bidders bid higher: when bidders have constant absolute risk aversion, the expected selling price in such auctions is higher when the bidders do not know how many other bidders there are, compared with when they do know this [27]. These two points provide an argument that an auction where all parties know n is fairer for the bidders.

coVDFs can be used to instantiate fair, blind auctions in a decentralised setting, in such a way that no private communication channels are required and all results are publicly verifiable. Running a coVDF will give each party an opportunity to bid simultaneously, whilst knowing n, and hence providing a fairer system. In Sect. 4, we provide a construction for a parallel coVDF, and in Appendix C, we show explicitly how our construction can be used in the context of blind auctions.

1.3   Our Contributions

In this paper we propose and formally define a collaborative VDF, a primitive in which a fixed number of parties n take an external input and a personal input and spend a certain amount of time t computing an output, using sequential calculations. Once this computation has been completed, it can be verified as correct by anybody in time $O(\text{polylog}(t))$. We define the security notions of correctness, soundness and sequentiality for coVDFs.

When moving to a trustless multi-party setting, one must consider malicious parties who wish to abort the protocol in order to learn some information [2,24]. To mitigate this problem, we introduce two properties: *traceability* - which allows malicious parties to be identified and removed from the protocol, allowing a successful rerun; and *robustness* - capturing the idea that the protocol still runs correctly even when some fraction of n is malicious. We model these properties formally in the context of our new primitive.

We propose two constructions: for our first, we show how to adapt an existing single-party VDF scheme [32], which is based on repeated squaring in a group of unknown order, to the multi-party setting. We describe a method for obtaining traceability, and prove its security.

Our second construction is based on gossip and sequential hashing, and satisfies robustness. For this construction we borrow techniques from the hashgraph consensus protocol proposed in [4][1]. Each hash, known as an event, is recorded in a graph. The n solvers repeatedly implement a gossip protocol, in which they "gossip about gossip": each time a party gossips to another, they tell the receiving party all the new events that they became aware of since the last sync between the two parties. The receiving party creates an event to represent this new sync, by hashing the most recent event from both parties. In this process, information spreads exponentially quickly through the n solvers, and each party ends up with a graph that is *consistent* with all other parties. We use the techniques of [4] to ensure that all parties obtain a copy of the same graph, and to show that our construction is robust, providing we have a 2/3 honest majority.

2   coVDFs: Definitions and Security Properties

A collaborative verifiable delay function (coVDF) allows users to jointly compute a delay, with the option of embedding a personal input. We begin by providing a formal definition for coVDFs, before categorising constructions as sequential or parallel. We define a coVDF, as well as the properties of *correctness, soundness* and *sequentiality* using syntax which covers both of these cases.

Notation. In what follows, we refer to two different types of input for each party: We denote the external input of party i by c_i, which is the standard input used to run the computation. This may come from another solving party, or from the third party who generates the instance. In particular, c_0 is the seed used at the start of each instance, and this should be generated independently of all solving parties. We denote by x_i the optional personal input as described in Sect. 1.2. We use N to refer to the set of all n solving parties. Finally, H denotes a collision resistant hash function.

Definition 1 (coVDF). *A collaborative verifiable delay function $V = $ (Setup, Eval, Verify) consists of the following triple of algorithms, implemented by an initiator, n solvers, and a verifier:*

Setup$(\lambda, t, n) \to \mathbf{pp} = $ (ek, vk) is ran by the initiator, taking a security parameter λ, delay parameter t, and the number of solvers n as inputs. Setup returns the following public parameters: an evaluation key ek and the corresponding verification key vk. Where appropriate, the public parameters also specify the input space $\mathcal{X}$ and the output space $\mathcal{Y}$.

Eval(ek, $c_i, x_i) \to (y_i, \pi_i)$ is an algorithm run by each solver, in which the solvers take an evaluation key ek, some external input $c_i \in \mathcal{X}$, and a possibly empty personal input $x_i \in \mathcal{X}$. Each solver then outputs $y_i \in \mathcal{Y}$ and a (possibly empty) proof π_i. The time taken for all solvers to run Eval, each using at most $O(poly(t, \lambda))$ processors, must be at least t.

---

[1] Baird introduced the Hashgraph in 2016 as a fair, fast consensus protocol. It has since been used as the basis for a cryptocurrency, Hedera Hashgraph [5].

Verify(vk, X, Y, Π) $\rightarrow$ {(Yes, aux), (No, aux)} is an algorithm running in time $O(polylog(t), \lambda, n)$, which takes the verification key vk, along with a set of inputs $X = (\{c_i\}_{i \in R}, \{x_i\}_{i \in S})$, a set of outputs $Y = \{y_i\}_{i \in U}$, and a set of proofs $\Pi = \{\pi_i\}_{i \in V}$, where R, S, U, V are each a subset of the n solving parties. Verify then outputs Yes or No, along with some (possibly empty) auxiliary information aux.

On comparison of our definition with that of the single-party case given in [10], one can see that the latter is a special case of the former. The multi-party definition contains the following additional information: the number of solvers n, an optional personal input x_i, and some optional auxiliary information, aux. Let $n = 1$, and remove the optional values of x_i and aux. Upon observing that each set X, Y, Π will contain at most a single element in the single-party case, we have an equivalent definition to that of [10].

In proposing this new primitive, we differentiate between two classes of coVDFs, sequential and parallel, distinguished as follows.

Definition 2 (Sequential vs Parallel coVDFs). *A collaborative verifiable delay function is* sequential *if the external input of each solver (excluding the first) depends on the output of a previous solver. If all parties share a common, fixed external input, we instead say it is* parallel. *For a sequential construction we require that the first solver take some fixed external input. We refer to this, as well as the common external input in the parallel case, as the* seed c_0.

A coVDF, whether sequential or parallel, must satisfy correctness, soundness, sequentiality, uniqueness and be efficiently verifiable.

2.1 Correctness, Soundness and Sequentiality

We provide formal security definitions in the widely adopted framework of provable security, which allows for formal security proofs. We start by defining correctness for a coVDF, which ensures that if the computation is performed correctly, then Verify will output Yes with overwhelming probability. We present the correctness game in Fig. 1.

Definition 3 (Correctness). *A collaborative VDF is* correct *if for any* **pp** *there exists a negligible function in λ,* **negl**(λ) *such that the Correctness Game in Fig. 1 outputs* Yes *with probability at least* $1 - $**negl**($\lambda$).

While correctness implies an honest evaluation overwhelmingly outputs Yes upon verification, the soundness property ensures that an incorrect evaluation of the protocol will not verify with overwhelming probability. We model this formally in Fig. 2.

$\mathbf{pp} = (\mathsf{ek}, \mathsf{vk}) \xleftarrow{\mathrm{R}} \mathsf{Setup}(\lambda, t, n)$
Setup is ran by the initiator
for i in $1{:}n$ **do**
    $(y_i, \pi_i) \leftarrow \mathsf{Eval}(\mathsf{ek}, c_i, x_i)$
All solving parties run the Eval algorithm

$\{\mathsf{Yes}, \mathsf{No}\} \leftarrow \mathsf{Verify}(\mathsf{vk}, X = \{c_0, x_1, \cdots, x_n\}, Y = \{y_1, \cdots, y_n\}, \Pi = \{\pi_1, \cdots, \pi_n\})$

Fig. 1. Correctness Game

In the soundness game, the adversary, on input the public parameters, outputs a subset of parties M to subvert. They provide a personal input x_j and an external input c_j for each party in M. Our model is generic enough to capture both the sequential and parallel setting, where c_j is the output of solver $j-1$ or a fixed input, respectively. The adversary wins the game if Verify outputs Yes, for a false evaluation.

$\mathbf{pp} \xleftarrow{\mathrm{R}} \mathsf{Setup}(\lambda, t, n)$
Setup is ran by the initiator.

$M \subseteq N \leftarrow \mathcal{A}(\mathbf{pp})$
Adversary outputs a subset M of parties to subvert

For $j \in M : (c_j, x_j) \leftarrow \mathcal{A}$
Adversary outputs an external and personal input for each subverted party.

For $j \in M : (y_j, \pi_j) \leftarrow \mathcal{A}(\mathbf{pp}, c_j, x_j)$
Adversary produces output and proof.

$\mathcal{A}$ wins if $\mathsf{Yes} \leftarrow \mathsf{Verify}(\mathsf{vk}, \{c_0, x_1, \cdots, x_n\}, \{y_1, \cdots, y_n\}, \{\pi_1, \cdots, \pi_n\}) \wedge (y_j, \pi_j) \neq \mathsf{Eval}(\mathsf{ek}, c_j, x_j)$, for any $j \in M$

Fig. 2. Soundness Game

Definition 4 (Soundness). *A collaborative VDF is sound if for any PPT adversary $\mathcal{A}$ there exists a negligible function in λ, negl(λ), such that $\mathcal{A}$ cannot win the Soundness Game with probability greater than negl(λ).*

Finally, we formalise the sequentiality property to capture how resistant a scheme is to parallelisation: an adversary with vast parallel resources should be able to evaluate the function no faster than αt, for some $\alpha \in (0, 1)$, close to 1.

In our game, shown in Fig. 3, an adversary is given the public parameters for precomputation, before choosing an index j to subvert. The adversary produces a personal input, and an external input for party j. Using these, along with the preprocessing Z, the adversary attempts to replicate the correct output of Eval. $\mathcal{A}$ wins the game if this can be achieved, and security relies on precomputation and parallelisation providing a negligible speed up.

Definition 5 (Sequentiality). *Take any pair of randomised algorithms $\mathcal{A}_0$ and $\mathcal{A}_1$, where $\mathcal{A}_0$ runs in time $O(poly(t, \lambda))$, and $\mathcal{A}_1$ runs either in time $\alpha(t)$ (for a parallel construction) or $\alpha(t/n)$ (for a sequential construction). We call a coVDF (p, α)-sequential if for any adversary $\mathcal{A} = (\mathcal{A}_0, \mathcal{A}_1)$, there exists a negligible function in λ, negl(λ), such that the Sequentiality Game cannot be won by $\mathcal{A}$ with probability greater than negl(λ) on at most p processors.*

$\mathbf{pp} \xleftarrow{\text{R}} \mathsf{Setup}(\lambda, t, n)$
Setup is ran by the initiator.

$(Z, j, c_j, x_j) \xleftarrow{\text{R}} \mathcal{A}_0(\mathbf{pp})$
Adversary preprocesses based on pp, and outputs an index j, an external
input c_j and a personal input x_j.

$(y_j, \pi_j) \leftarrow \mathcal{A}_1(Z, \mathbf{pp}, c_j, x_j)$
Adversary produces output and proof.

$\mathcal{A}$ wins if $(y_j, \pi_j) = \mathsf{Eval}(\mathsf{ek}, c_j, x_j)$.

Fig. 3. Sequentiality Game

Uniqueness and Efficient Verification. Additionally, a coVDF should satisfy uniqueness, and be efficiently verifiable. Similarly to a VDF [10], a coVDF satisfies uniqueness if the output of any one instance of a coVDF cannot be mangled into another, circumventing the delay. For a coVDF to have practical applications, a time gap is required between Eval and Verify. We define verification to be efficient if it runs in time $O(polylog(t), \lambda, n)$, where t is the time taken for all parties to run Eval. This is incorporated in Definition 1.

The properties we have presented above correspond to those required in a single-party VDF (cf. [10]). However, the presence of multiple parties introduces further security concerns, since some parties may not act honestly. As clock time is intrinsic to coVDFs and their applications, protocol aborts can be damaging. As such, we next define the additional properties of traceability and robustness, which help to prevent such aborts.

2.2   Security in a Trustless Setting

When used by a group of mutually trusting parties, the properties defined in Sect. 2.1 are sufficient for most applications. However, once we extend coVDFs to a trustless environment, e.g., for use in auctions (Sect. 1.2), we want to ensure that a malicious party can't simply abort the protocol, leading to the loss of computation. To achieve this, we introduce two new security properties for coVDFs: *traceability* and *robustness*.

Traceability. In order to provide incentives for good behaviour, we introduce *traceability*. The property of traceability has been used in a variety of primitives and protocols such as signature schemes and voting schemes [21,22], and it typically involves the use of a trace algorithm, whose goal is to allow an entity (such as an administrator) to discover some information about some or all parties. In our context, this property is useful as it allows us to use the technique of *punishable abort* [7,18], where each party first places a deposit on a blockchain, and can only reclaim it if they act honestly.

To define traceability, we extend the definition of a coVDF to include a Trace algorithm. We define this algorithm in such a way that the tracer discovers all parties who acted dishonestly. The property of traceability is captured by defining the correctness and soundness of the trace algorithm, which ensure that no honest parties are output, and all malicious parties are output, respectively.

Trace is run after Verify outputs No in a run of the protocol. The tracer obtains the inputs, computation outputs and proofs of each party from Eval, and runs the Trace algorithm, which outputs a list of dishonest parties. Trace is formally described as follows.

$M \leftarrow \mathsf{Trace}(\mathsf{vk}, (\{c_i\}, \{x_j\}), \{y_k\}, \{\pi_h\})$, where $M \subseteq N$, is a PPT algorithm which takes the verification key vk, along with a set of inputs $(\{c_i\}, \{x_j\})$, a set of outputs $\{y_k\}$, and a set of proofs $\{\pi_h\}$, which are each a subset of size at most n. Trace outputs a list of misbehaving parties, corresponding to indices in M.

In Fig. 4, we define the Trace *Correctness* Game where the trace algorithm is run on a coVDF instance where Verify outputs No. The tracer wins the Trace Correctness Game if no honest parties are output by Trace.

In Fig. 5, we define the Trace *Soundness* Game we again run the trace algorithm on a coVDF instance where Verify outputs No. The adversary chooses a subset M of parties to subvert, and wins the Trace Soundness Game if for any party $j \in M$, their output is different from $\mathsf{Eval}(\mathsf{ek}, c_j, x_j)$, and yet j is not included in the set output by Trace.

$\mathbf{pp} \xleftarrow{R} \mathsf{Setup}(\lambda, t, n)$
Setup is ran by the initiator.

Let X, Y, Π correspond to the inputs, outputs and proofs of all n solving parties.

$M \leftarrow \mathsf{Trace}(\mathsf{vk}, X, Y, \Pi)$
Tracer $\mathcal{C}$ runs trace.

$\mathcal{C}$ wins the game if $M \subseteq N \wedge \forall m \in M : (y_m, \pi_m) \neq \mathsf{Eval}(\mathsf{ek}, c_m, x_m)$

Fig. 4. Trace Correctness Game

Definition 6 (Traceability). *A collaborative VDF satisfies* traceability *if for any public parameters, and any PPT adversary* $\mathcal{A} = (\mathcal{A}_0, \mathcal{A}_1)$, *there exist negligible functions of* λ *such that the following hold*

1. *The tracer* $\mathcal{C}$ *wins the Trace Correctness Game with probability* $1 - negl_1(\lambda)$,
2. *Adversary* $\mathcal{A}$ *cannot win the Trace Soundness Game with probability greater than* $negl_2(\lambda)$.

Robustness. Many applications of coVDFs are time-sensitive, meaning the consequences of a protocol abort can be significant. We introduce *robustness* to capture the idea of a protocol being resistant to a fraction σ of malicious parties: if the number of dishonest parties is smaller than σn, the protocol can still run correctly, producing a time delay of t. We define robustness by letting the adversary control a fraction of the solvers, and causing Verify to fail on the set of honest users.

In Fig. 6 we let an adversary $\mathcal{A}$ choose a subset of malicious parties $M \subseteq N$, and allow them to run any PPT algorithm. $\mathcal{A}$ wins the game if set M is smaller than σn and Verify run on the honest solvers is caused to output No.

Definition 7 (Robustness). *We say a collaborative VDF* V *is* σ-robust *for some* $0 < \sigma < 1$ *if for any PPT adversary* $\mathcal{A}$ *there exists a negligible function* negl *such that* $\mathcal{A}$ *wins the Robustness Game in Fig. 6 with probability at most* $negl(\lambda)$.

$\mathbf{pp} \xleftarrow{\text{R}} \mathsf{Setup}(\lambda, t, n)$
Setup is ran by the initiator.

$M \subseteq N \leftarrow \mathcal{A}(\mathbf{pp})$
Adversary outputs a subset M of parties to subvert.

For $j \in M : (x_j, c_j) \leftarrow \mathcal{A}$
Adversary outputs a personal and external input for each subverted party.

For $j \in M : (y_j, \pi_j) \xleftarrow{\text{R}} \mathcal{A}(\mathbf{pp}, c_j, x_j)$
Adversary produces an output and proof for each subverted party.

Let X, Y, Π correspond to the inputs, outputs and proofs of all n parties.

$Z \leftarrow \mathsf{Trace}(\mathsf{vk}, X, Y, \Pi)$
Tracer $\mathcal{C}$ outputs set of cheating parties.

$\mathcal{A}$ wins the game if $Z \subseteq N \wedge (y_j, \pi_j) \neq \mathsf{Eval}(\mathsf{ek}, c_j, x_j) \wedge j \notin Z$ for any $j \in M$

Fig. 5. Trace Soundness Game

A scheme is robust if when the adversary corrupts a subset of the solvers, this corrupted subset can be identified and removed, with Verify outputting Yes on the subset of honest solvers. Note that this is distinguished from soundness, as $\mathcal{A}$ wins the soundness game (Fig. 2) if Verify outputs Yes when run on the set of *all* outputs and proofs, rather than just the honest subset.

$pp \xleftarrow{R} Setup(\lambda, t, n)$
Setup is ran by the initiator.

$M \subseteq N \leftarrow \mathcal{A}(pp)$
Adversary outputs a subset M of parties to corrupt.

For $k \in H = N \setminus M : (y_k, \pi_k) \leftarrow Eval(ek, c_k, x_k)$
The honest parties run Eval.

$\mathcal{A}$ wins if $|M| < \sigma n \wedge$
$(No, aux) \leftarrow Verify (vk, \{x_k\}_{k \in H}, \{y_k\}_{k \in H}, \{\pi_k\}_{k \in H})$

Fig. 6. Robustness Game

We note that our security model does not prevent an adversary from honestly computing multiple parts of a coVDF themselves. In doing so, however, they would expend significant effort, for no gain. Consider this in the applications given: In the collaborative work example, they would work on multiple parts, whereby a single part would be sufficient to provide access to some resource, meaning they have expended additional effort for no reason. Similarly, in an auction, this approach would mean making multiple bids, each requiring effort, where all but the largest bid is irrelevant. If a party wishes to compute the coVDF alone, then a standard VDF should be used instead.

We have now defined the properties of a coVDF. In the remainder of the paper we present our two candidate constructions for coVDFs: the first is a sequential construction which satisfies traceability but not robustness; this motivates our second, parallel construction, which is robust.

3   A Sequential coVDF

We propose a construction for a sequential coVDF based on Wesolowski's VDF [32], which we modify for the collaborative setting. In particular, we allow each party to embed the personal input x_i in the evaluation stage by multiplying x_i with the output of the underlying VDF computation. Furthermore, we design a trace algorithm to prove the honesty of each party in the case of an abort. This requires the addition of a second verification-style protocol, using the personal input instead of the external input. We present details of the construction and relevant security proofs in Appendix A.

4   A Robust coVDF Construction

In this section, we propose a parallel coVDF construction based on repeated hashing, which we will see achieves 1/3-robustness, i.e., it withstands up to $n/3$ malicious parties whilst still running correctly. Such a parallel scheme will be particularly useful in applications such as blind auctions, as discussed in Sect. 1.2 and discussed more in detail in Appendix C.

Sequential hashes have been used in a similar scenario: in [26], Mahmoody et al. provide a proof of sequential work based on a directed acyclic graph (DAG), in which a prover first creates a DAG, and then hashes all edges between the nodes of the graph. This creates a tree of hashes, which can be verified probabilistically by checking some fraction of the hashes. This construction naturally satisfies most of the properties of a verifiable delay function, however it does not satisfy uniqueness. This is because for a given solution, changing a single edge will provide a different output, whilst being unlikely to be picked up by random challenges.

In this section, we look at a method of mitigating this whilst extending the scheme to multiple parties. Rather than creating a suitable DAG prior to the hashing procedure, we instead create it during the hashing phase at random. This is achieved by solvers randomly syncing to another party, who then creates a hash to mark the event. This process stops once some parties have completed t hashes, achieving the required delay.

To ensure each party generates the same graph, and to enable us to prove security notions, we base our construction on the hashgraph consensus protocol proposed in [4].

The Hashgraph Consensus Protocol. The Swirlds hashgraph consensus protocol [4] is an asynchronous Byzantine Fault Tolerance consensus protocol which is proved to be fast and fair. Here we give a brief description of the key concepts of this protocol, and in the full version of this paper, we present the relevant definitions and results from [4] more formally. We refer the reader to [4] for a full description and proofs of the ideas presented.

Gossip About Gossip. The underlying idea of this protocol is that as often as possible each party runs a gossip protocol[2] in which they sync with another party, transmitting all the new events ('gossip') they have learned from previous syncs from other parties. Using this method, all information will spread exponentially fast through the group of parties. Each time a sync occurs, the party receiving the sync creates a new node, also known as an event, by hashing their most recent event concatenated with the most recent event of the party who initiated the sync. Through repeated syncing, each party will eventually end up with a copy of the same graph, up to a certain point in time.

Sequential hashing makes this scheme resistant to parallelisation, and the required delay is defined by the number of hashes computed by each solver.

---

[2] A gossip protocol is a procedure in which nodes propagate information through a group, based on the way epidemics spread; see [23].

4.1 coVDF from Repeated Hashing

In this construction, parties build a graph together, populating it with events, or nodes. It is necessary that all parties reach consensus on the ordering of nodes. This ensures that each party has a copy of the same graph, allowing for a single output which can be efficiently verified. To achieve a unique output, and to prove robustness, our protocol uses features from [4]. In this section we outline the major intuitive ideas, presenting the technical details in the security analysis provided in the full version of this paper.

We first write our coVDF as a triple of algorithms: $V_2 = ($Setup$_2$, Eval$_2$, Verify$_2$) as follows.

Setup. Setup$_2(\lambda, t, n) \rightarrow$ **pp** $= (H, \mathcal{G}, m)$ takes a security parameter λ, time delay t, and the number of solvers n; and outputs public parameters **pp** $= (H, \mathcal{G}, m)$, where H is a collision resistant hash function $H: \{0,1\}^{2m} \rightarrow \{0,1\}^m$, $\mathcal{G}$ is an empty directed acyclic graph, containing a random ordering of the n parties dictating where each party's events will sit on the graph, and m is used to define the hash function and the input space, $\mathcal{X} = \{0,1\}^m$. The output space is defined to be a populated graph of depth at least t. Additionally, we require each personal input x_i to be some data hashed by H.

Eval. The initiator randomly samples an external input $c_0 \in \{0,1\}^m$, and passes it to the solvers. Each of the n solvers runs Eval$_2($**pp**$, c_0, x_i) \rightarrow (\mathcal{G}, \mathcal{H})$ by taking the external input c_0, providing a personal input x_i, and doing as prescribed in Fig. 7. The output is $\mathcal{G}$, the completed directed graph up to the point where consensus has been reached, along with $\mathcal{H}$, the set of parties who agree with the output graph $\mathcal{G}$, voting Yes on Line 9 of Fig. 7.

1: Compute i's first event $H(x_i\|c_0)$.
2: Let $\mathcal{G}$ be the graph output by Setup$_2$.
3: **while** At least $n/3$ different parties have fewer than t nodes **do**
4:     Call Sync as both sender and receiver in parallel, with different parties.
5: **for** j in $1 : n/3$ **do**
6:     **if** $i = j$ **then**
7:         Output graph $\mathcal{G}_j$ up to consensus.
8:     **else**
9:         Vote Yes if graphs $\mathcal{G}_i$ and $\mathcal{G}_j$ are consistent, and No otherwise.
10:     If graph gets at least $2n/3$ votes, end Eval and output this graph.
11: Abort protocol.

Fig. 7. Eval$_2$

In the Eval$_2$ algorithm, each party first hashes their personal input with c_0, before repeatedly running a gossip protocol (Fig. 8). Each party then repeatedly syncs at random with other parties, creating a hash to record each sync. During

---

1: Let i be the sender, and let j be the receiver.
2: i sends j all new events since their previous sync.
3: j updates $\mathcal{G}$ with these new events, and creates a new event $H(x\|y)$, where x and y are the most recent events by j and i respectively.
4: j calls divideRounds
5: j calls decideFame
6: j calls findOrder
7: Output $\mathcal{G}_j$

Fig. 8. Sync

each sync, the syncing party, i, will tell the receiving party, j, all events that have been gossiped to i since the last sync between i and j. This sync is known as gossip.

This process will stop once at least $2n/3$ parties have computed t hashes (see Line 3). Any party who has calculated less than ϕt hashes will be dropped from the group prior to verification, where ϕ is a parameter representing the minimum amount of work required to not be considered lazy.

Next, parties vote on which graph to output. This is achieved as follows: Party 1 outputs their graph up to $(1 - \epsilon)t$ nodes (this is the point at which consensus has been reached on the graph - we go into greater detail on ϵ later). All parties check their copy of the graph is consistent with that of party 1. They then vote Yes or No accordingly. If at least $2n/3$ votes are Yes, this graph is output. If not, party 2 outputs their graph and repeats the process. This can be repeated up to $n/3$ times. If no graph receives enough votes by this point, the protocol is aborted.

Note that the last three lines of Fig. 8 are commands to run three new procedures, all of which can be found in the full version of this paper, as well as in [4]. These procedures are necessary to provide uniqueness and robustness, but not to provide an intuition of the scheme. In short, these three algorithms ensure that all parties have the same ordering on all events, by splitting the graph up into epochs, and marking the first node in each epoch as a witness. Witnesses which are quickly gossiped to more than $2n/3$ of parties are then called famous. divideRounds is used to determine the round of events in the previous round, decideFame is used to determine whether a witnesses in previous rounds are famous, findOrder is used to provide consensus on the ordering of events. The notions of a node being a witness, famous and having a round number are expanded on in the full version of this paper, as well as in [4]. In Appendix B, we provide an example to illustrate how the graph is built using Eval_2.

Verify. The verify algorithm $\mathsf{Verify}_2(H, c_0, \mathcal{G}, \mathcal{H}) \to \{\mathsf{Yes}, \mathsf{No}\}$ takes the hash function H, the external input c_0 and the graph $\mathcal{G}$, along with the subset $\mathcal{H}$ who voted Yes on the graph (Fig. 9).

1: On graph $\mathcal{G}$, choose $k(t)$ nodes created by each party in $\mathcal{H}$. These are the challenge nodes.
2: **for** All challenge nodes **do**
3:     Hash the two parents of each node together and compare with the node. If they are different, remove the node creator from $\mathcal{H}$.
4: **if** $\#\mathcal{H} > 2n/3$ **then**
5:     Output Yes.
6: **else**
7:     Output No.

Fig. 9. Verify$_2$

The verifier then checks $k(t) = \omega(\lambda) \log t$ hashes at random for each player, where $\omega(\lambda)$ is an increasing function which ensures the probability of any malicious party remaining in $\mathcal{H}$ is negligible with respect to the security parameter. Any party found to have incorrectly computed a hash will be removed from $\mathcal{H}$. If the number of parties remaining in $\mathcal{H}$ is greater than $2n/3$ after all checks are completed, the verifier outputs Yes.

Efficiency Remarks. This construction is based upon a fast, fair consensus protocol which makes very efficient use of bandwidth.

Setup$_2$ simply provides an ordering of the parties, as well as specifying a cryptographic hash function, and the size of inputs. This requires little computational overhead. Eval$_2$ repeatedly calls a subroutine Sync (Fig. 8), which involves one party i sending j the set of new events i learned since their precious sync. Importantly, sync is run in parallel, meaning all parties can act as both the receiver and the sender simultaneously. As soon as party j has completed the hash, and added the new events from the sync, they can receive another sync whilst running the procedures divideRounds, decideFame and findOrder. This ensures each party is continuously hashing new events. In [4] it is shown that the gossip protocol is very efficient in terms of bandwidth: each member will receive each transaction once, and also send each transaction on average once. The hashes for gossiped events don't have to be sent during the sync - it is sufficient to send the identity of the creator of the event, and the event number of its other parent, which can be stored in a single array.

4.2   Security of V_2

In the full version of this paper, we provide a detailed security analysis of our parallel coVDF construction V_2, showing it satisfies the properties of correctness, robustness, sequentiality and uniqueness. Due to lack of space, here we provide a brief intuition.

Correctness. If all parties run the Eval$_2$ algorithm, then they will construct a graph with a minimum depth of t, and all nodes will have been hashed correctly. Hence all checks will be correct, and Verify$_2$ will output Yes.

Robustness. For robustness to hold we require that provided at least $2n/3$ parties act honestly, the computation should be accepted by the verifier, regardless of the behaviour of the remaining parties. We analyse the possible behaviour of malicious parties, which include lack of participation, faking hash values, and dishonest gossiping. We utilise results from Baird [4] to show that in each case, we still get consistency under an honest majority of $2/3$.

Sequentiality. The sequentiality of this construction is based upon sequential hashing, which has been used previously as a proof of sequential work [26]. The sequentiality of V_2 follows directly from the assumption that iterated hashing is resistant to parallelisation.

Uniqueness. We show that assuming that we have a $2/3$ honest majority of parties, then an output graph cannot be mangled into another such graph. This is due to the graph relying directly on the set of personal inputs, which due to the collision resistance of the hash function cannot be recovered.

5   Concluding Remarks

In this work we introduced the idea of collaborative VDFs, extending the definitions of the single party case. We formalized the primitive and its security properties, and we categorised coVDFs as either sequential or parallel. We additionally defined the new properties of traceability and robustness to address the behaviour of dishonest solvers in the multi-party setting.

An approach to achieving a sequential construction is to take an existing VDF scheme and splitting the work into n parts, where each solver computes one such part before passing the work on to the next solver. We proved this is possible by giving a concrete extension of Wesolowski's VDF [32], additionally providing traceability. We then proposed a candidate parallel construction in which all parties build a graph together, using gossip and sequential hashing. These constructions show the flexibility of this primitive, and allow the use of coVDFs in a variety of applications.

A   A Sequential coVDF Construction

In this section we take the VDF scheme presented by Wesolowski [32], and extend it to a coVDF. Our construction incorporates both personal inputs from each party as well as traceability.

In the construction given by Wesolowski in [32], the prover takes as input a base element x, performs a hash H on it, and then calculates $H(x)^{2^t}$, where t is the delay parameter. This calculation has to be done in a particular type of finite group, $\mathbb{G}$ - see [11] for a discussion on concrete groups. The verifier then uses a public-coin succinct argument [31] to efficiently verify the output. We will use this scheme to construct a coVDF in the following way.

Recall that H is a collision resistant hash function, let $\mathsf{Primes}(\lambda)$ be the set containing the first $2^{2\lambda}$ prime numbers, and let N be the set of n solvers.

Let $\text{bin}(x)$ be the representation of an element x as a binary string. We define $V_1 = (\text{Setup}_1, \text{Eval}_1, \text{Verify}_1)$ as follows.

$\text{Setup}_1(\lambda, t, n)$ takes security parameter λ, time delay t, and the number of solvers n and outputs public parameters $\mathbf{pp}$, which consist of a finite abelian group of unknown order $\mathbb{G}$, a hash function H mapping any string s to $\mathbb{G}$, and a hash function H_{prime} mapping any string s to $\text{Primes}(\lambda)$. The public parameters also specify an ordering on the solvers.

The initiator randomly samples a seed $c_0 \in \mathbb{G}$, and passes it to the first solver. Each solver runs $\text{Eval}_1(\mathbf{pp}, c_i, x_i)$ on an external input c_i and their personal input x_i, to compute y_i and π_i, as described in Fig. 10. For the first solver, c_0 is used as the external input. For every other solver, $c_i \leftarrow y_{i-1}$ will be received from the previous solver.

Along with y_i, each solver also outputs three values which enable the trace algorithm to be non-interactive. These are z_i, τ_i and ω_i. τ_i and ω_i each consist of a tuple of the form (g^q, l), and are used to run Wesolowski's proof algorithm on the input x_i, and its inverse $z_i = x_i^{-1}$ respectively. These three values are only included for use in Trace, and are not used in Verify_1.

To verify the output computation, the verifier runs $\text{Verify}_1(\mathbf{pp}, X, Y, \Pi)$ on the set of inputs, X, the set of outputs Y and the set of proofs Π. Solver n and the verifier run an extension of Wesolowski's succinct argument as described in Fig. 12, and the verifier outputs either Yes or No.

We define the number of steps needed to be 2^{nt}, and split this into 2^t for each of the n solvers. During Eval_1, each player i computes 2^t modular exponentiations on c_i, and then multiplies this by x_i. The value $y_i \leftarrow x_i c_i^{2^t}$ is the output of player i, and the external input of player $i+1$. This value y_i will be raised to the power of $2^{(n-i)t}$ by the remaining solvers.

1: Check $c_i \in \mathbb{G}$, and abort if not.
2: Compute $y_i \leftarrow x_i \cdot c_i^{2^t}$.
3: Pass y_i to solver $i+1$.
4: Compute the inverse of the personal input: $z_i \leftarrow x_i^{-1}$.
5: Compute $\pi_i \leftarrow z_i^{2^{(n-i)t}}$.
6: Compute τ_i and ω_i by running the proof algorithm in Figure 11 on $(c_i, y_i \cdot z_i)$ and (z_i, π_i) respectively.
7: Output (y_i^*, π_i^*), where $y_i^* = (y_i, z_i)$, and $\pi_i^* = (\pi_i, \tau_i, \omega_i)$.

Fig. 10. Eval_1

1: Take a pair of inputs (g, h).
2: Sample a prime $l \leftarrow H_{\text{prime}}(\text{bin}(g)\|\text{bin}(h))$.
3: The solver finds a linear combination of h and l, such that $h = ql + r$, with $0 \leq r \leq l$.
4: Output (g^q, l).

Fig. 11. Proof algorithm

1: Solver n computes $y \leftarrow y_n \pi_1 \cdots \pi_n$.
2: The verifier checks $c_0, y \in \mathbb{G}$, and outputs No if not.
3: The verifier sends solver n a random prime $l \in \mathsf{Primes}(\lambda)$.
4: Solver n then finds a linear combination of 2^{nt} and l, such that $2^{nt} = ql + r$, with $0 \le r \le l$. $\tau := c_0^q$ is then sent to the verifier.
5: The verifier computes r from $2^{nt} \mod l$. If $\tau \in \mathbb{G}$ and $y = \tau^l c_0^r \in \mathbb{G}$, the verifier outputs Yes. If not, the verifier outputs No.

Fig. 12. Verify$_1$

The output of player n can be written as

$$c_0^{2^{nt}} x_n x_{n-1}^{2^t} \cdots x_1^{2^{nt}}.$$

We want to cancel out all terms apart from $c_0^{2^{nt}}$. We require all parties to compute $z_i \leftarrow x_i^{-1}$ to achieve this. The personal input of player i will be raised to the power of $2^{(n-i)t}$ subsequent solvers. Therefore, solver i must then raise z_i to the power of $2^{(n-i)t}$. This allows us to 'unwrap' each of the inputs, by cancelling the personal input out with the correct power of z_i.

z_i is output along with y_i to enable traceability, which we describe later. Similarly, Fig. 11 is run twice by each player i to compute proofs that both their output y_i, and their proof π_i are correct. This is to ensure a tracer has all the information needed to run the trace algorithm non-interactively, and the outputs τ_i and ω_i are not used in Verify$_1$.

In Verify$_1$, solver n multiplies their output y_n by each of the π_i values to obtain $y = c_0^{2^{nt}}$. This allows solver n and the verifier to run Wesolowski's succinct argument, which runs as follows.

The verifier first checks c_0 and y are in the group $\mathbb{G}$. The verifier then sends solver n a prime l taken from $\mathsf{Primes}(\lambda)$. Solver n writes 2^{nt} as a linear combination of l, such that $2^{nt} = ql + r$, with $r \le l$. Solver n then computes $\tau \leftarrow c_0^q$ and sends this to the verifier. The verifier checks this $\tau \in \mathbb{G}$ and computes the value r from $2^{nt} \mod l$. The verifier then computes $\tau^l c_0^r$. If all parties have acted honestly, this is equal to $(c_0^q)^l c_0^r = c_0^{ql+r} = c_0^{2^{nt}} = y$.

Note that Verify$_1$ can be made non-interactive using the Fiat-Shamir heuristic [8] by sampling primes using H_{prime}, as in Fig. 11.

Traceability. As discussed in Sect. 2.2, traceability allows one to remove dishonest parties prior to restarting the protocol. This allows a *punishable abort* [7,18] to be incorporated into the scheme, providing an incentive to good behaviour.

In Eval$_1$, each party first checks their external input is in $\mathbb{G}$, and aborts the computation if it is not. If party i triggers such an abort, we immediately know party $i - 1$ has acted dishonestly, removing the need for the trace algorithm.

In the case that all parties output $y_i, \pi_i \in \mathbb{G}$, but Verify$_1$ outputs No, we require a Trace algorithm. One way to obtain traceability is to run the succinct argument used in Verify$_1$ on each of the proofs and each of the outputs. Trace outputs all parties with an incorrect proof or output. In order to achieve this whilst ensuring that Trace is non-interactive, we have each solver compute τ_i and ω_i to allow a tracer to run the succinct argument twice on each player to ensure they acted correctly.

We define $M \leftarrow \mathsf{Trace}_1(X, Y, \Pi)$ as an algorithm run by the tracer $\mathcal{C}$ on the set of all inputs (private and external), the set of all outputs and the set of all proofs, as prescribed in Fig. 13. The output is the subset of dishonest parties, M.

1: Let M be an empty set.
2: **for** $i \in N$ **do**
3:     Compute prime $l \leftarrow H_{\mathsf{prime}}(\mathsf{bin}(c_i) \| \mathsf{bin}(y_i \cdot z_i))$.
4:     Compute r_i from $y_i \cdot z_i \mod l$.
5:     If $\tau_i \in \mathbb{G} \ \wedge \ y_i \cdot z_i = \tau_i^l c_i^{r_i} \in \mathbb{G}$ is not true, add i to M.
6:     Compute prime $k \leftarrow H_{\mathsf{prime}}(\mathsf{bin}(z_i) \| \mathsf{bin}(\pi_i))$.
7:     Compute a_i from $\pi_i \mod k$.
8:     If $\omega_i \in \mathbb{G} \ \wedge \ \pi_i = \omega_i^k z_i^{a_i} \in \mathbb{G}$ is not true, add i to M.
9: Output M.

Fig. 13. Trace_1

The tracer runs Wesolowski's succinct argument, acting as the prover, twice for each party. On line 4, τ_i is used to prove that y_i was calculated correctly, and on line 6, ω_i is used to prove that π_i was calculated correctly. This is done using an identical argument to that in Verify_1. The primes are reconstructed to ensure they were correctly sampled from $\mathsf{Primes}(\lambda)$.

We have presented an efficient coVDF with the traceability property. This construction allows for applications such as collaborative work, as described in Sect. 1.2. In Appendix C we show concretely how this construction can be used in such a setting. In the following section, we provide a security analysis of this construction.

A.1 Security of V_1

In the full version of this paper, we provide a detailed security analysis of our parallel coVDF construction V_1, showing it satisfies the properties of correctness, robustness, sequentiality and uniqueness. Due to lack of space, here we instead provide a brief intuition for our results.

Correctness. On a correct run of the protocol, the personal input and proof will cancel out, meaning the underlying verification protocol will run on c_0 and $c_0^{2^{nt}}$, and hence output 1.

Soundness. Consider an adversary $\mathcal{A}$ who chooses a set of parties M to corrupt, along with inputs c_j, and x_j for each $j \in M$. This adversary then runs some algorithm $\mathcal{A}_1 \neq \mathsf{Eval}_1$ for each j. To break the soundness property, they would have to output a pair (y_j, π_j) such that $c_j^{2^t}(x_j^{2^{n-j}}\pi_j) = y_j \neq 1_{\mathbb{G}}$ for each j. Even if $\mathcal{A}$ lets $x_j = \pi_j = 1$, then they still have to find a solution for t sequential squarings of c_j without running the squaring algorithm. This reduces to the adaptive root assumption of the underlying construction [32], and so has an overwhelmingly small probability of being correct.

Sequentiality. The sequentiality of this scheme directly relies upon the task of repeated squaring. This has been a base assumption for many time-lock constructions [25,30], and is considered a standard assumption.

Traceability. Trace correctness holds if all parties output by Trace have not run $\mathsf{Eval}_1(\mathbf{pp}, c_i, x_i)$. Any party who runs $\mathsf{Eval}_1(\mathbf{pp}, c_i, x_i)$ will have the correct values of τ_i and ω_i, as well as the correct values of z_i, π_i and y_i. This gives us trace correctness. Meanwhile, trace soundness holds if all parties j who output $(y_j^*, \pi_j^*) \neq \mathsf{Eval}_1(\mathbf{pp}, c_i, x_i)$ are output by Trace. Trace runs Wesolowski's succinct argument twice: once on the output y_j, and once on the proof π_j. As this procedure is deterministic, any party j who outputs $(y_j^*, \pi_j^*) \neq \mathsf{Eval}_1(\mathbf{pp}, c_i, x_i)$ will fail one of the succinct arguments, and so be output by Trace.

B   Example of Graph Built Using Eval_2

Each node is calculated from the hash of two previous nodes; the most recent node by the receiver of the sync, concatenated with the most recent node of the initiator of the sync. We refer to these two nodes as the *parents* of the new node. We will use the notation $k\|l$ to refer to the hashing of node k concatenated with node l. In Fig. 14, the two ingoing arrows to each node represent the parents.

In Fig. 14, we show the start of a graph with $n = 4$ being populated. Each party's first event, $\{1, 2, 3, 4\}$, is the result of hashing $x_i\|c_0$. After this, each party repeatedly syncs with other parties, and the receiving party creates a new node each time. For example node 5 is created by hashing $1\|2$, and node 8 is created by hashing $3\|6$.

We give an example of the next sync to occur after Fig. 14, leading to a new event (which would be node 14) being added to the graph: solver 1 (Blue) syncs with solver 2 (Green). We see that Blue knows every event, as each party's most recent event has been gossipped via $9 \to 10 \to 12 \to 13$.

In the most recent sync between Blue and Green, Green had events $\{1, 2, 3, 4, 5, 6\}$ in their graph. Therefore Blue sends the hash labels and corresponding parents for nodes $\{7, \cdots, 13\}$. Green now updates their graph and adds the new node 14 by hashing $9\|13$.

Now, if Red were to sync with Green, Red would also send events $\{4, 7, 10, 12\}$ as these are the events Red has learned since their previous sync with Green (which resulted in the creation of node 9). Green would check that these were consistent with those currently in their graph, and add event 15 by hashing $14\|12$.

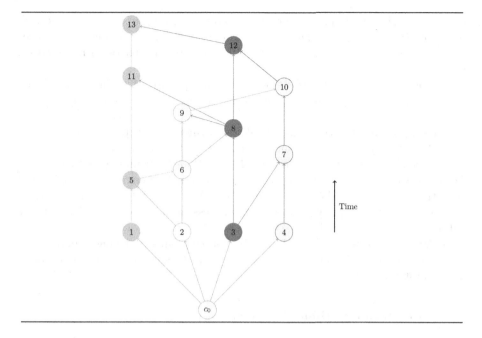

Fig. 14. Example (Color figure online)

C   Examples

We provide two concrete examples illustrating how to use each of our proposed coVDF constructions in the applications discussed in Sect. 1.2.

C.1   Collaborative Work

We consider a scenario where a group of n mutually distrusting parties wish to access a private resource owned by a company. In return for this access, the company asks the group to compute a coVDF in order to implement a randomness beacon.

The company wishes to ensure that only parties who contributed gain access, and parties all want to contribute the same amount of effort, whilst keeping their identity hidden from other parties. We assume that each party has a private communication channel with the company, and that each party deposits some funds on a blockchain, under the condition that this is returned only if they carry out the protocol honestly.

Let the required length of evaluation be nt, and let each party have some personal input $x_i \in \mathbb{G}$, obtained by hashing their public identifier. By setting these hashes as the personal inputs, we show how this group can together compute such a coVDF.

The company runs $\mathsf{Setup}_1(\lambda, t, n) \to \mathbf{pp} = (\mathbb{G}, H, H_{\mathsf{prime}})$, taking as input a chosen security parameter λ and time delay t, and the number of parties n. The outputs are the public parameters, which consist of a group $\mathbb{G}$, as well as hash functions H and H_{prime}, as described in Appendix A. The company then chooses some ordering on the parties, and provides the starting party with a seed c_0, sampled at random from $\mathbb{G}$.

Parties run Eval_1 in turns, as described in Appendix A, using their hashed identifiers x_i as personal inputs. The first party will use c_0 as their external input, and subsequent parties will use the output of the previous party, $c_i = y_{i-1}$. Then the final party and the company run Verify_1, which will output Yes or No.

If Verify outputs Yes, we can use Trace to allow parties to each privately reveal their identity to the company. This is done by running lines 6 to 8 of Trace on each party, to verify that x_i, was indeed the personal input of i, and then the party reveals their public identifier. After checking that this identifier hashes to x_i, The company will then give i access to the resource, and each party will receive their deposit back.

If Verify outputs No, Trace is ran by the company, and honest parties are refunded their deposit. The remaining funds can be split between the authority and honest parties.

C.2   Decentralised Blind Auctions

In our second example, we show how to instantiate a fair, decentralised blind auction using a parallel coVDF. Consider a seller who wishes to auction off some goods in a decentralised fashion, to avoid the fees associated with an auction house. Suppose this seller requires interested parties to show legitimate interest with a proof of effort (i.e. a delay of time t), to avoid fake bids. We allow the n interested parties place bids in this auction, as discussed in Sect. 1.2.

We can achieve this by using our proposed parallel coVDF, V_2. Parties all hash their bids concatenated with some randomness at the same time, and each compute t steps of iterated computation, serving as the proof of effort. This proceeds as follows:

Once the seller has advertised this auction and is ready to accept bids, they will run Setup_2 on the number of interested parties n. This means that when all parties bid, they have full transparency of the number of parties involved in this auction, providing a fair setting.

$\text{Setup}_2(\lambda, t, n) \rightarrow \mathbf{pp} = (H, \mathcal{G}, m)$ takes a security parameter λ, time delay t, and the number of solvers n; and outputs public parameters $\mathbf{pp} = (H, \mathcal{G}, m)$, which give the parties the necessary details to produce a hashgraph. Parties can now hash their bid using H to obtain their personal input x_i. The seller then randomly samples an element $c_0 \in \mathcal{G}$ as the external input allowing parties to use this c_0 and their personal inputs x_i to run Eval_2, together producing a graph of depth t.

We have now successfully instantiated an auction, and we can use standard techniques from secure multi party computation to calculate the highest bid, whilst keeping all others private. An example of this is Borealis [9], which is an efficient, low interaction protocol for secure computation of rank among integers.

References

1. Attias, V., Vigneri, L., Dimitrov, V.: Implementation study of two verifiable delay functions. In: Tokenomics (2020)
2. Aumann, Y., Lindell, Y.: Security against covert adversaries: efficient protocols for realistic adversaries. In: Vadhan, S.P. (ed.) TCC 2007. LNCS, vol. 4392, pp. 137–156. Springer, Heidelberg (2007). https://doi.org/10.1007/978-3-540-70936-7_8
3. Bag, S., Hao, F., Shahandashti, S.F., Ray, I.G.: SEAL: sealed-bid auction without auctioneers. IEEE Trans. Inf. Forensics Secur. **15**, 2042–2052 (2019)
4. Baird, L.: The swirlds hashgraph consensus algorithm: fair, fast, byzantine fault tolerance (2016)
5. Baird, L., Harmon, M., Madsen, P.: Hedera: a governing council & public hashgraph network (2018)
6. Bakos, G.: Energy management method for auxiliary energy saving in a passive-solar-heated residence using low-cost off-peak electricity. Energy Build. **31**(3), 237–241 (2000)
7. Bentov, I., Kumaresan, R.: How to use bitcoin to design fair protocols. In: Garay, J.A., Gennaro, R. (eds.) CRYPTO 2014. LNCS, vol. 8617, pp. 421–439. Springer, Heidelberg (2014). https://doi.org/10.1007/978-3-662-44381-1_24
8. Bernhard, D., Pereira, O., Warinschi, B.: How not to prove yourself: pitfalls of the Fiat-Shamir heuristic and applications to Helios. In: Wang, X., Sako, K. (eds.) ASIACRYPT 2012. LNCS, vol. 7658, pp. 626–643. Springer, Heidelberg (2012). https://doi.org/10.1007/978-3-642-34961-4_38
9. Blass, E.-O., Kerschbaum, F.: BOREALIS: building block for sealed bid auctions on blockchains. Cryptology ePrint Archive, Report 2019/276 (2019). https://eprint.iacr.org/2019/276
10. Boneh, D., Bonneau, J., Bünz, B., Fisch, B.: Verifiable delay functions. In: Shacham, H., Boldyreva, A. (eds.) CRYPTO 2018. LNCS, vol. 10991, pp. 757–788. Springer, Cham (2018). https://doi.org/10.1007/978-3-319-96884-1_25
11. Boneh, D., Bünz, B., Fisch, B.: A survey of two verifiable delay functions. IACR Cryptology ePrint Archive (2018). https://eprint.iacr.org/2018/712.pdf
12. Cohen, B., Pietrzak, K.: Simple proofs of sequential work. In: Nielsen, J.B., Rijmen, V. (eds.) EUROCRYPT 2018. LNCS, vol. 10821, pp. 451–467. Springer, Cham (2018). https://doi.org/10.1007/978-3-319-78375-8_15
13. Cohen, B., Pietrzak, K.: The Chia network blockchain (2019)
14. Coppinger, V.M., Smith, V.L., Titus, J.A.: Incentives and behavior in English, Dutch and sealed-bid auctions. Econ. Inq. **18**, 1–22 (1980)
15. Ephraim, N., Freitag, C., Komargodski, I., Pass, R.: Continuous verifiable delay functions. In: Canteaut, A., Ishai, Y. (eds.) EUROCRYPT 2020. LNCS, vol. 12107, pp. 125–154. Springer, Cham (2020). https://doi.org/10.1007/978-3-030-45727-3_5
16. De Feo, L., Masson, S., Petit, C., Sanso, A.: Verifiable delay functions from supersingular isogenies and pairings. In: Galbraith, S.D., Moriai, S. (eds.) ASIACRYPT 2019. LNCS, vol. 11921, pp. 248–277. Springer, Cham (2019). https://doi.org/10.1007/978-3-030-34578-5_10
17. Galal, H.S., Youssef, A.M.: Verifiable sealed-bid auction on the Ethereum blockchain. In: Zohar, A., et al. (eds.) FC 2018. LNCS, vol. 10958, pp. 265–278. Springer, Heidelberg (2019). https://doi.org/10.1007/978-3-662-58820-8_18
18. Gao, H., Ma, Z., Luo, S., Wang, Z.: BFR-MPC: a blockchain-based fair and robust multi-party computation scheme. IEEE Access **7**, 110439–110450 (2019)

19. Huisman, R., Huurman, C., Mahieu, R.: Hourly electricity prices in day-ahead markets. Energy Econ. **29**(2), 240–248 (2007)
20. Kiayias, A., Russell, A., David, B., Oliynykov, R.: Ouroboros: a provably secure proof-of-stake blockchain protocol. In: Katz, J., Shacham, H. (eds.) CRYPTO 2017. LNCS, vol. 10401, pp. 357–388. Springer, Cham (2017). https://doi.org/10.1007/978-3-319-63688-7_12
21. Kiayias, A., Tsiounis, Y., Yung, M.: Traceable signatures. In: Cachin, C., Camenisch, J.L. (eds.) EUROCRYPT 2004. LNCS, vol. 3027, pp. 571–589. Springer, Heidelberg (2004). https://doi.org/10.1007/978-3-540-24676-3_34
22. Ling, L., Liao, J.: Anonymous electronic voting protocol with traceability. In: 2011 International Conference for Internet Technology and Secured Transactions, pp. 59–66 (2011)
23. Li, H.C., et al.: BAR gossip. In: Proceedings of the 7th Symposium on Operating Systems Design and Implementation, pp. 191–204. USENIX Association (2006)
24. Lysyanskaya, A., Triandopoulos, N.: Rationality and adversarial behavior in multiparty computation. In: Dwork, C. (ed.) CRYPTO 2006. LNCS, vol. 4117, pp. 180–197. Springer, Heidelberg (2006). https://doi.org/10.1007/11818175_11
25. Mahmoody, M., Moran, T., Vadhan, S.: Time-lock puzzles in the random Oracle model. In: Rogaway, P. (ed.) CRYPTO 2011. LNCS, vol. 6841, pp. 39–50. Springer, Heidelberg (2011). https://doi.org/10.1007/978-3-642-22792-9_3
26. Mahmoody, M., Moran, T., Vadhan, S.: Publicly verifiable proofs of sequential work. In: Proceedings of the 4th Conference on Innovations in Theoretical Computer Science, pp. 373–388. Association for Computing Machinery (2013)
27. McAfee, P., McMillan, J.: Auctions with a stochastic number of bidders. J. Econ. Theor. **43**, 1–19 (1987)
28. Nakamoto, S.: Bitcoin: a peer-to-peer electronic cash system (2008)
29. Pietrzak, K.: Simple verifiable delay functions. In: 10th Innovations in Theoretical Computer Science Conference, ITCS 2019 (2019)
30. Rivest, R.L., Shamir, A., Wagner, D.A.: Time-lock puzzles and timed-release crypto (1996)
31. Smart, N.: Cryptography: An Introduction, vol. 3. McGraw-Hill, New York (2003)
32. Wesolowski, B.: Efficient verifiable delay functions. In: Ishai, Y., Rijmen, V. (eds.) EUROCRYPT 2019. LNCS, vol. 11478, pp. 379–407. Springer, Cham (2019). https://doi.org/10.1007/978-3-030-17659-4_13

SMCOS: Fast and Parallel Modular Multiplication on ARM NEON Architecture for ECC

Wenjie Wang[1,2], Wei Wang[1,3]($\boxtimes$), Jingqiang Lin[4,5]($\boxtimes$), Yu Fu[1,2],
Lingjia Meng[1,2], and Qiongxiao Wang[1,2]

[1] State Key Laboratory of Information Security, Institute of Information
Engineering, Chinese Academy of Sciences, Beijing 100089, China
wangwei@iie.ac.cn
[2] School of Cyber Security, University of Chinese Academy of Sciences,
Beijing 100089, China
[3] Data Assurance and Communication Security Research Center, CAS,
Beijing 100089, China
[4] School of Cyber Security, University of Science and Technology of China,
Hefei 230027, Anhui, China
linjq@ustc.edu.cn
[5] Beijing Institute, University of Science and Technology of China, Beijing, China

Abstract. Elliptic Curve Cryptography (ECC) is considered a more effective public-key cryptographic algorithm in some scenarios, because it uses shorter key sizes while providing a considerable level of security. Modular multiplication constitutes the "arithmetic foundation" of modern public-key cryptography such as ECC. In this paper, we propose the Cascade Operand Scanning for Specific Modulus (SMCOS) vectorization method to speed up the prime field multiplication of ECC on Single Instruction Multiple Data (SIMD) architecture. Two key features of our design sharply reduce the number of instructions. 1) SMCOS uses operands based on non-redundant representation to perform a "trimmed" Cascade Operand Scanning (COS) multiplication, which minimizes the cost of multiplication and other instructions. 2) One round of fast vector reduction is designed to replace the conventional Montgomery reduction, which consumes less instructions for reducing intermediate results of multiplication. Further more, we offer a general method for pipelining vector instructions on ARM NEON platforms. By this means, the prime field multiplication of ECC using the SMCOS method reaches an ever-fastest execution speed on 32-bit ARM NEON platforms. Detailed benchmark results show that the proposed SMCOS method performs modular multiplication of NIST P192, Secp256k1, and Numsp256d1 within only 205, 310 and 306 clock cycles respectively, which are roughly 32% faster than the Multiplicand Reduction method, and about 47% faster than the Coarsely Integrated Cascade Operand Scanning method.

This work was partially supported by Shandong Province Key Research & Development Plan/Major Science & Technology Innovation Project (Grant No. 2020CXGC010115).

© Springer Nature Switzerland AG 2021
Y. Yu and M. Yung (Eds.): Inscrypt 2021, LNCS 13007, pp. 531–550, 2021.
https://doi.org/10.1007/978-3-030-88323-2_28

Keywords: Public-key cryptography · Vector instructions · Modular multiplication · SIMD · ECC · ARM NEON

1 Introduction

Effective implementation of public-key cryptographic algorithms on general-purpose computing devices facilitates the application of cryptography in communication security. As a crucial component of modern public-key cryptography, the Elliptic Curve Cryptography (ECC) based on the discrete logarithm problem has been widely used, because of its shorter key sizes than other cryptographic algorithms (e.g. DSA and RSA). Despite more than three decades of research efforts, ECC defined over general fields of large prime characteristic is still considered computation-intensive due to underlying arithmetic operations performed between large integers, especially when executed on embedded processors. Multi-precision modular multiplication is a performance-critical building block in ECC, which demands careful optimization to achieve acceptable performance [27].

In recent years, an increasing number of commodity processors were equipped with co-processors that provide vector instruction set extensions to perform single instruction multiple data (SIMD) operations. Advanced Vector Extension (AVX), the vector instruction set provided by Intel, is mostly used for application optimization on large server hosts and PCs. In terms of embedded platforms, due to the limitation of their computing capability, more and more ARM embedded processors (e.g. ARM Cortex-A, Cortex-R series) start to use NEON vector instructions to execute a wide variety of compute-intensive applications. For conventional cryptosystems, the parallel computing power provided by the SIMD co-processor can readily be used to optimize the implementation of public-key cryptographic algorithms such as RSA and ECC. In order to improve the performance of cryptographic algorithms, the research community has studied ways to reduce the latency of multi-precision modular multiplication through SIMD vectorization.

In these designs, one of the most often vectorized modular reduction techniques is the Montgomery algorithm [3,10,17,22,25–27,31]. It was originally proposed in 1985 [19] and has been widely deployed in real-world applications. Montgomery modular multiplication, as a general modular multiplication design, has good execution efficiency and can be applied in multi-precision modular multiplication of cryptographic algorithms such as RSA and ECC. However, the Montgomery modular multiplication has the following two defects. One is that the instructions used by Montgomery reduction are usually expensive, which are roughly the same as the consumption of multiplication. On the other hand, a conditional subtraction could occur at the end of Montgomery modular multiplication in order to keep the result valid, which can be exploited in conventional timing-based side-channel attacks [15,25,29].

Besides, since the redundant representation suggested in [14] can handle carry propagation more easily, it is adopted by many vectorization solutions [2,5,10,11,13,16,24,25]. The redundant representation allows several products of big numbers to be summed up, without causing an overflow inside the "container" (usually, a register) that holds the accumulation result. The cumbersome handling of the carry propagation can therefore be avoided [10]. However, the redundant representation introduces more multiplication instructions to compute more partial products than the non-redundant representation. Also, when it is used for multiplicand or intermediate result reduction and carry propagation, the inconsistency of the size in bits of partial operands divided by redundant representation and the word size of the processors (32- or 64-bit) will cause additional overhead of instructions (e.g. *bic*, *shift* instruction) for handling reduction and carry.

In this paper, we propose an innovative design for ECC over the prime field $\mathbb{F}_p$, which uses non-redundant representation to implement a non-Montgomery form of vectorized modular multiplication, called Cascade Operand Scanning for Specific Modulus (SMCOS). Two key features of our design sharply reduce the number of instructions and pipeline stalls. 1) In a non-redundant representation, the multiplicands perform a "trimmed" Cascade Operand Scanning (COS) multiplication and obtain an intermediate result without carry propagation. COS vector multiplication was introduced in [27], which greatly eliminates Read-After-Write (RAW) dependencies in the instruction flow, and non-redundant representation reduces the number of multiplication instructions. When applied to SMCOS, the carry propagation at the end of COS is removed to avoid extra pipeline stalls due to sequential scalar operations in vector registers. 2) For the specific form of prime modulus in ECC, we introduce a fast vector reduction method in SMCOS to reduce the intermediate results of multiplication, instead of the general Montgomery reduction. The number of vector instructions consumed by this reduction is only about 12%−23% of the Montgomery reduction in [27] (see Sect. 4.2 for details). Furthermore, the SMCOS modular multiplication runs in constant time to resist certain types of side-channel attacks using timing and branch prediction.

On the Cortex-A9 platform, the SMCOS and two other fast vector modular multiplication methods for ARM NEON architecture, the Multiplicand Reduction (MR) [24] and the Coarsely Integrated Cascade Operand Scanning (CICOS) [27], are respectively integrated into the cryptographic algorithm library OpenSSL 1.1.1k [21], libsecp256k1 [23] and MSR ECCLib 2.0 [18]. After that, we make comprehensive comparisons of the execution time in terms of modular multiplication, point addition, point doubling, Elliptical Curve Diffie-Hellman (ECDH) for key exchange, Elliptic Curve Digital Signature Algorithm (ECDSA), etc. The detailed benchmark results indicate that SMCOS brings larger performance enhancements to all levels of ECC arithmetic. Taking ECDSA signature as an example, the signature performance of NIST P192 curve based on SMCOS, is about 17% faster than the MR method, 22% faster than the CICOS method, and 58% faster than the native OpenSSL signature. And for Secp256k1 curve, SMCOS's is roughly 10% faster than libsecp256k1 optimized by manual assembly language before, and 26% faster than CICOS. Also for Numsp256d1 curve, the signature performance using SMCOS is approximately 17% faster than CICOS and 25% faster than MSR ECCLib (see Sect. 5 for details).

The main contributions of our work are as follows.

- Firstly, a vector modular multiplication design based on specific modulus is proposed to fully exploit the computing power of SIMD co-processors for ECC. To the best of our knowledge, this is the first non-redundant representation and non-Montgomery form of vector modular multiplication design in the prime field $\mathbb{F}_p$.
- Secondly, due to the specific modulus of the prime field for ECC, we design a single round of fast vector reduction method to reduce the intermediate results of multiplication.
- Thirdly, we investigate the timing of ARM SIMD integer instructions and provide a general method of pipelining on 32-bit ARM NEON platforms.
- Finally, thanks to highly optimized multiplication in $\mathbb{F}_p$, the performance of ECC protocols obtains great enhancements on 32-bit ARM processors with NEON.

The rest of the paper is organized as follows. Section 2 surveys the related work. The preliminaries about ARM NEON and the representation of prime field elements are presented in Sect. 3. Sections 4 describes the design and implementation of our SMCOS modular multiplication. In Sect. 5, performance results of the SMCOS method and ECC implementations are given and compared with other works and cryptographic algorithm libraries. We conclude in Sect. 6.

2   Related Work

The first practice and evaluation of cryptographic algorithm on ARM NEON architecture belonged to Bernstein and Schwabe in CHES'12 [2]. The authors showed that NEON supports elliptic curve cryptography at surprised high speeds, and summarized useful instructions for vectorization of cryptographic algorithms. In 2013, Câmaraand et al. employed NEON's VMULL.P8 instruction to describe a novel vector implementation for 64-bit polynomial multiplication in ECC based on the binary field $\mathbb{F}_{2^m}$ [4]. [1,9,20,28,30] proposed accelerated implementations of applying NEON instructions to other cryptographic algorithms (e.g. AES, RSA, LWE, pairing-based and lattice-based cryptography, etc.). Despite recent research progress, for cryptographic algorithms, in particular public-key cryptography, the efficient implementation of multi-precision modular multiplication on the SIMD architecture is still an interesting and challenging topic.

The authors of [25] and [10] used Intel SSE and AVX2 vector instructions to implement Montgomery multiplication with redundant representation, and integrated them into RSA modular exponentiation. In SAC 2013, Bos et al. introduced a 2-way Montgomery modular multiplication, which uses non-redundant representation and splits the Montgomery modular multiplication into two parts: modular multiplication and reduction, being computed in parallel [3]. This is the first Montgomery modular multiplication parallel design with non-redundant representation, but its performance is compromised by the RAW dependencies in the instruction flow. Based on the work of Bos, Seo et al. proposed the Coarsely

Integrated Cascade Operand Scanning (CICOS) method in ICISC 2014 [27]. This method eliminates the RAW dependencies of the 2-way Montgomery modular multiplication in the carry propagation, thereby reducing the number of pipeline stalls and reaching record execution time.

In [24], the Multiplicand Reduction (MR) modular multiplication was introduced to implement NIST-recommended prime-field curves including P192 and P224. The design adopts the redundant representation suggested in [14], and uses a kind of fast reduction instead of the Montgomery reduction to reduce multiplicands in advance. It is significantly faster than some schoolbook multiplication with intermediate reduction methods [21].

3   Preliminaries

3.1   ARM NEON Architecture

The 32-bit RISC-based ARM architecture, which includes ARMv7, is the most popular in embedded devices. It features 13 general-purpose 32-bit registers (R0-R12), and additional three 32-bit registers which have special names and usage models: R13 for stack pointer, R14 for link register, as well as R15 for program counter. Its instruction sets support 32-bit operations or, in the case of Thumb and Thumb2, a mix of 16- and 32-bit operations [1].

Many ARM cores include NEON, a powerful 128-bit SIMD engine that comes with sixteen 128-bit registers (Q0-Q15) which can also be viewed as thirty-two 64-bit registers (D0-D31). The NEON instructions provide data processing and load/store operations, and are integrated into the ARM and Thumb instruction sets. NEON includes support for 128-, 16-, 8-, 4-, or 2-way SIMD operations using vectors of 1-, 8-, 16-, 32- and 64-bit integer elements respectively. The number of elements operated on is indicated by the specified register size. For example, VADD.U8 Q0, Q1, Q2 indicates an addition operation on 8-bit integer elements stored in 128-bit Q registers. This means that the addition operation is on sixteen 8-bit lanes in parallel. Some instructions can have different size input and output registers. For example, VMULL.U32 Q0, D2, D3 uses two pairs of 32-bit integers stored in two 64-bit D registers as inputs to generate a pair of 64-bit products and stores them in a 128-bit Q register. Similarly, there is a VMLAL.U32 instruction that executes a VMULL.U32 operation and adds the result to a 128-bit Q register (treated as two 64-bit integers). For more detailed information, refer to [12].

3.2   Representation of Prime Field Elements

The elements of $\mathbb{F}_p$ are usually represented by the integers in the range 0 to $p-1$ and the arithmetic operations remain as usual as in the integers except for the computation of a reduction modulo p at the end of each operation, which has the purpose of bringing the result within an original range. If p is a large integer of several hundreds or even thousands of bits, in order to store an $\mathbb{F}_p$ element in memory, an m-bit vector is needed, where m is the size of p in bits. However, the word size of prevailing processors is either $n = 32$ or $n = 64$ bits, which in any case is shorter than the size of the large integer p. Therefore, multi-precision arithmetic must be implemented to handle integers larger than the word of processors [8]. At present, there are two popular designs for representing elements in $\mathbb{F}_p$, which are used in multi-precision arithmetic to divide an m-bit large number.

The *non-redundant (full-radix) representation* divides an $\mathbb{F}_p$ element into several parts with the word size of processors. In this way, an element can be stored by s words of n bits, i.e. $s = \lceil \frac{m}{n} \rceil$. The advantage of this representation is that its storage is compact, which usually means that fewer iterations are required to complete a multi-precision operation. However, one of the disadvantages of using this representation on an n-bit architecture is that some arithmetic operations impose a sequential evaluation of integer operations, for example, in the modular addition, the carry bits must be propagated from the least- to the most-significant digits. If non-redundant representation, there will be no extra space to store these carry bits, which limits the opportunities for calculating additions in parallel [7].

The second representation, *redundant (reduced-radix) representation*, divides an $\mathbb{F}_p$ element into s' shorter slices than the word size of processors, where $s' = \lceil \frac{m}{n'} \rceil$, $n' \in \mathbb{R}^+$ and $n' < n$. Because it relies on the selection of a real number $n' < n$, each word will have enough bits to store the carry bits produced by several modular additions. This feature can delay the carry propagation to the end and facilitate the implementation of parallelization. However, as mentioned above, compared to the non-redundant representation, it needs more iterations ($s' \geq s$) for completing a multi-precision operation, so more instructions are consumed.

4   Modular Multiplication for ECC Using SIMD Extensions

In this section, we firstly describe the design of the Cascade Operand Scanning for Specific Modulus (SMCOS) method for the prime field multiplication in ECC and its implementation details on the ARM NEON architecture. Then, we analyze the expected performance of our design, and compare it with the Multiplicand Reduction (MR) method in [24] and the Coarsely Integrated Cascade Operand Scanning (CICOS) method in [27]. Finally, we offer a general method of pipelining on 32-bit ARM NEON platforms.

4.1   Cascade Operand Scanning for Specific Modulus on SIMD

"Trimmed" COS. The COS Multiplication was first proposed in [27]. As a multiplication using non-redundant representation, it eliminates RAW dependencies in the instruction flow and has preferable efficiency. When it is used in SMCOS, we remove the carry propagation at the end of multiplication, which produces more pipeline stalls due to sequential scalar operations in vector registers.

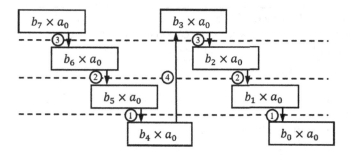

Fig. 1. Carry propagation in non-redundant representation. The lower bits are added to higher bits of lower intermediate results. The additions with same serial number are executed in parallel.

Taking the 32-bit word with 256-bit multiplication as an example, "trimmed" COS method is described in Algorithm 1. In the beginning, the algorithm conducts VTRN vector transpose instruction to re-organize and classify the operand $\bar{B}$ as groups $((b_7, b_3), (b_6, b_2), (b_5, b_1), (b_4, b_0))$ instead of the normal order $((b_7, b_6), (b_5, b_4), (b_3, b_2), (b_1, b_0))$. Next, in the first round, the products of (a_0, a_0) and elements in $((b_7, b_3), (b_6, b_2), (b_5, b_1), (b_4, b_0))$ are separately computed by VMLAL vector multiplication instruction, which supports 2-way multiplication in parallel. The partial product pairs are stored in $([L_7, L_3], [L_6, L_2], [L_5, L_1], [L_4, L_0])$, where each L_i is a 64-bit D register. Following which, the VTRN instruction is reused to separate the partial products into higher 32 bits $(63-32)$ and lower 32 bits $(31-0)$, generating eight pairs of 32-bit data stored in 16 D registers, L_0-L_7 and H_0-H_7. Finally, the lower bits are added to higher bits of lower intermediate results. For example, the lower 32 bits stored in $([L_7, L_3], [L_6, L_2], [L_5, L_1], L_4)$ are added to the corresponding higher 32 bits in $([H_6, H_2], [H_5, H_1], [H_4, H_0], H_3)$. By referring to Fig. 1, this operation uses 3 vector addition VADD and 1 ADD instruction. After addition, the least significant word c_0 (lowest 32 bits of $\bar{B} \times a_0$) is obtained, and other more significant words are stored in H_0 to H_7.

In the next round, we need to perform $\bar{B} \times a_1$, because a_1 is higher than a_0, the products of (a_1, a_1) and $((b_7, b_3), (b_6, b_2), (b_5, b_1), (b_4, b_0))$ happen to be accumulated to intermediate results in $([H_7, H_3], [H_6, H_2], [H_5, H_1], [H_4, H_0])$ of the first round, and we can perform a new round of operations in the same way. This process is repeated with operands (a_1-a_7) by seven times more, we get the intermediate result $\bar{C}$ of $\bar{B} \times \bar{A}$. Its lower 256 bits are eight 32-bit values c_0 to c_7, which are the least significant words output at the end of each round. And higher 256-bit intermediate results are in L_0 to L_7 after the last round, 64-bit C_8 to C_{15}. The higher 32 bits of them are carry bits to upper intermediate results.

After that, the original COS multiplication will carry out the final carry propagation to align. Because it conducts sequential scalar operations directly in vector registers, the RAW dependencies incur more pipeline stalls. But in SMCOS, we keep the intermediate results of the multiplication to the next stage and straightforwardly reduce the results without pipeline stalls.

Algorithm 1. "Trimmed" COS. This arithmetic performs $\bar{B} \times \bar{A}$ and obtains the intermediate result $\bar{C}$. Note that $\bar{C}$ consists of two parts, c_i with a range of $0 \sim 2^{32} - 1$ and C_i with a range of $0 \sim 2 \times (2^{32} - 1)$.

Input: Two multiplicand $\bar{A}$ and $\bar{B}$ such that $\bar{A} = \sum_{i=0}^{7} a_i 2^{32i}, \bar{B} = \sum_{i=0}^{7} b_i 2^{32i}, 0 \leq a_i, b_i < 2^{32}$.
Output: Multiplication intermediate result $\bar{C} = \sum_{i=0}^{7} c_i 2^{32i} + \sum_{j=8}^{15} C_j 2^{32j}$.
1: $\bar{B} \leftarrow \text{VTRN}(\bar{B})$
2: Initialize $L_i \leftarrow 0$ for all $i \in \{0, 1, ..., 7\}$
3: **for** $i = 0$ to 7 **do**
4:    **for** $j = 0$ to 3 **do**
5:        $[L_{j+4}, L_j] \leftarrow \text{VMLAL}([L_{j+4}, L_j], (a_i, a_i), (b_{j+4}, b_j))$
6:    **end for**
7:    Initialize $H_k \leftarrow 0$ for all $k \in \{0, 1, ..., 7\}$
8:    **for** $j = 0$ to 3 **do**
9:        $([L_{j+4}, L_j], [H_{j+4}, H_j]) \leftarrow \text{VTRN}([L_{j+4}, L_j], [H_{j+4}, H_j])$
10:    **end for**
11:    **for** $j = 0$ to 2 **do**
12:        $[H_{j+4}, H_j] \leftarrow \text{VADD}([L_{j+5}, L_{j+1}], [H_{j+4}, H_j])$
13:    **end for**
14:    $H_3 \leftarrow \text{ADD}(L_4, H_3)$
15:    $c_i \leftarrow (L_0)_{0..31}$
16:    Let $L_j \leftarrow H_j$ for all $j \in \{0, 1, ..., 7\}$
17: **end for**
18: Let $C_{i+8} \leftarrow L_i$ for all $i \in \{0, 1, ..., 7\}$
19: **return** $\bar{C}$

Fast Reduction for Specific Modulus. Unlike most solutions [3,17,26–28] that use Montgomery reduction, we design a fast vector reduction method for the characteristic that most prime fields for ECC have specific modulus, and gain great performance advantages. We take NIST P192 and Secp256k1 as examples to illustrate different use cases of fast vector reduction on different curves, and offer our reduction method for modulo $P = 2^{256} - 2^{32} - 977$ in Secp256k1, see Algorithm 2.

In the reduction process, we will reduce the intermediate results of "trimmed" COS multiplication. For NIST-standard prime-field curves, NIST primes are special primes which are of the form $2^m \pm 2^n - ... - 1$. The smallest prime among NIST primes is $p_{192} = 2^{192} - 2^{64} - 1$, then any number larger than this prime can be reduced by using the relation $2^{192} \equiv 2^{64} + 1 (\text{mod} p_{192})$. So for curves over NIST prime fields, we can use these relations to construct reduction for intermediate results of multiplication larger than NIST primes. Take NIST P192 as an example, as shown in Fig. 2, the intermediate results of 192-bit "trimmed" COS multiplication are separated into two groups. One group is the 32-bit c_0 to c_5 corresponding to $2^0, 2^{32}, ..., 2^{160}$ respectively, and they are less than p_{192}, so no reduction is required. We respectively store them in two 64-bit D registers on a Q register in pairs $((c_5, c_4), (c_3, c_2), (c_1, c_0))$. The second group is the 64-bit intermediate results C_6 to C_{11} that are larger than p_{192}. They are items

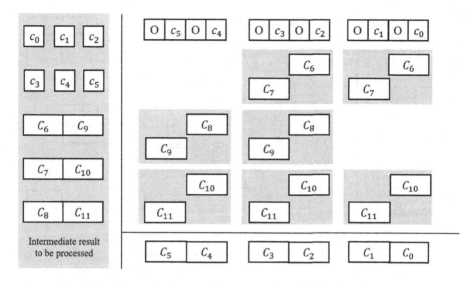

Fig. 2. One round of fast vector reduction for NIST P192. 32-bit S registers where "O" is located are cleared. The multiplication intermediate result to be processed is on the left, and the processing flow is on the right.

corresponding to $2^{192}, 2^{224}, ..., 2^{352}$. Using the above reduction relation, $C_6 \times 2^{192} \equiv C_6 \times 2^{64} + C_6 (\text{mod} p_{192})$. So, C_6 is reduced from 2^{192} to 2^{64} and 2^0, which correspond to the positions of c_2 and c_0 respectively.

In the same way, after reduction, the positions and times of C_7 to C_{11} can also be calculated, as shown in Fig. 2. We find that for the intermediate results of the multiplication, the reduction can be further performed in an additive and parallel manner. By referring to Algorithm 1, the value range of C_6 to C_{11} is $0-2 \times (2^{32} - 1)$. Accumulating them several times with c_0-c_5 will not result in an overflow of the 64-bit D register. We use the form of $([C_{11}, C_{10}], [C_9, C_8], [C_7, C_6])$ in pairs (the locations marked in Fig. 2) and add them to the corresponding positions to complete all the reductions. Only 7 VADD vector additions are consumed, and we get six 64-bit reduction results, C_0 to C_5.

For the elliptic curves over non-NIST primes, take Secp256k1 as an example. Although its modulo $P = 2^{256} - 2^{32} - 977$ is more irregular than NIST primes, the relation $2^{256} \equiv 2^{32} + 977 (\text{mod} P)$ still works. This relation results in some reduction items that may carry a multiplication factor, 977. As shown in Fig. 3, c_0 to c_7 are items less than modulo P, we store them in four Q registers in pairs $((c_7, c_3), (c_6, c_2), (c_5, c_1), (c_4, c_0))$. For C_8 to C_{15}, we can also execute the reduction relation of modulo P to find out the positions of reduction items. But unlike NIST primes, we must multiply some items with the constant 977 to further transform their reduction to the method of NIST primes. Since 32-bit ARM NEON platforms do not provide 64-bit multiplication and vector multiplication instructions, we skillfully adopt vector shift (e.g. VSHL, VSRA) and vector subtraction VSUB to construct the multiplication, based on the relation

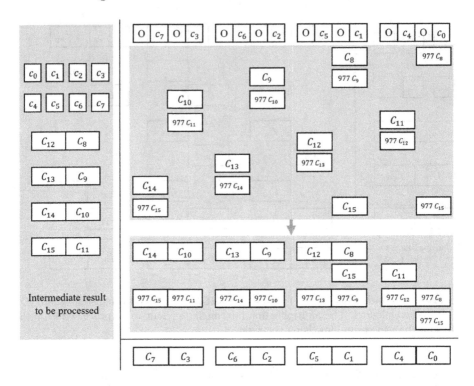

Fig. 3. One round of fast vector reduction for `Secp256k1`. 32-bit S registers where "O" is located are cleared. The multiplication intermediate result to be processed is on the left, and the processing flow is on the right.

of $977 = (2^{10} + 2^0) - (2^5 + 2^4)$. Fortunately, even if C_8 to C_{15} are multiplied by 977, they are far from beyond the range of the D register. Finally, after the multiplication with 977, we successfully conduct the reduction for modulo P in the similar manner with NIST primes, using 7 vector addition VADD and 3 ADD instructions.

For a more detailed description, see Algorithm 2, where VSHL is a vector shift left instruction, and VSRA is a vector shift right and accumulate instruction. In addition, for the third curve used in the experiment, `Numsp256d1`, the modulo P is $2^{256} - 189$. The reduction method in `Secp256k1` can be reused with a little transformation.

Final Alignment on Main Processor. SIMD co-processor is very effective in performing vector operations (e.g. parallel multiplication), but performs poorly for scalar operations like carry propagation and may pose more pipeline stalls [24]. Therefore, different from the previous vector modular multiplication designs [2,27,28], which deal directly with the final carry propagation and alignment in vector registers, we design SMCOS as SIMD co-processor and ARM main processor working together. Multiplication and reduction are implemented using

Algorithm 2. One round of fast vector reduction for Secp256k1. This arithmetic performs $\bar{C}' \equiv \bar{C}(\mathrm{mod}\,(2^{256} - 2^{32} - 977))$.

Input: Multiplication intermediate result $\bar{C}$ such that $\bar{C} = \sum_{i=0}^{7} c_i 2^{32i} + \sum_{j=8}^{15} C_j 2^{32j}, 0 \leq c_i < 2^{32}, 0 \leq C_j \leq 2 \times (2^{32} - 1)$.
Output: Reduction result $\bar{C}' = \sum_{k=0}^{7} C_k 2^{32k}$.
1: Initialize $C_i \leftarrow c_i$ for all $i \in \{0, 1, ..., 7\}$
2: **for** $i = 1$ to 3 **do**
3:    $[C_{i+4}, C_i] \leftarrow \mathtt{VADD}([C_{i+4}, C_i], [C_{i+11}, C_{i+7}])$
4: **end for**
5: $C_4 \leftarrow \mathtt{ADD}(C_4, C_{11})$
6: $C_1 \leftarrow \mathtt{ADD}(C_1, C_{15})$
7: **for** $i = 0$ to 3 **do**
8:    $[C'_{i+12}, C'_{i+8}] \leftarrow \mathtt{VSHL}([C_{i+12}, C_{i+8}], \#5)$
9:    $[C''_{i+12}, C''_{i+8}] \leftarrow \mathtt{VSHL}([C_{i+12}, C_{i+8}], \#10)$
10:    $[C'_{i+12}, C'_{i+8}] \leftarrow \mathtt{VSRA}([C'_{i+12}, C'_{i+8}], \#1)$
11:    $[C''_{i+12}, C''_{i+8}] \leftarrow \mathtt{VSRA}([C''_{i+12}, C''_{i+8}], \#10)$
12:    $[C_{i+12}, C_{i+8}] \leftarrow \mathtt{VSUB}([C''_{i+12}, C''_{i+8}], [C'_{i+12}, C'_{i+8}])$
13:    $[C_{i+4}, C_i] \leftarrow \mathtt{VADD}([C_{i+4}, C_i], [C_{i+12}, C_{i+8}])$
14: **end for**
15: $C_0 \leftarrow \mathtt{ADD}(C_0, C_{15})$
16: **return** $\bar{C}'$

NEON vector instructions, but the final alignment is migrated to scalar registers. This change effectively breaks RAW dependencies in the instruction flow and reduces pipeline stalls. When carry bits are propagated to the most significant coefficient, no matter whether the digit (higher 32 bits of C_7 in Fig. 3) larger than modulo P is 0, we will use reduction relations to perform a simple reduction and the second round of alignment, ensuring that SMCOS runs in constant time for resisting timing-based side-channel attacks.

4.2   Performance Analysis

In this section, we analyze the performance of our Cascade Operand Scanning for Specific Modulus (SMCOS) method, and compare it with the Multiplicand Reduction (MR) method in [24] and the Coarsely Integrated Cascade Operand Scanning (CICOS) method in [27].

For the clock cycle of instructions on the ARM NEON architecture, we denote 2-cycle instructions (e.g. VMULL, VMLAL, etc.) as X, and 1-cycle instructions (e.g. VADD, ADD, VTRN, etc.) as Y. For the modular multiplication in NIST P192, in the process of multiplication, the SMCOS and CICOS methods using non-redundant representation need to be executed 6 rounds. In each round they mainly conduct 3 VMLAL (VMULL), 3 VTRN, 2 VADD, and 1 ADD instructions, the instructions consumed in each round are equal to $3X+6Y$. Therefore, for the SMCOS and CICOS methods, their total instructions in the multiplication process are approximately $18X + 36Y$. The MR with redundant representation is 8 rounds in total, and

Table 1. Comparison of instructions for modular multiplication. X represents a 2-cycle instruction and Y represents a 1-cycle instruction.

Elliptic curve	Stage	MR [24][a]	CICOS [27]	Our SMCOS
NIST P192	Multiplication	$32X$	$18X + 36Y$	$18X + 36Y$
	Reduction	$35Y$	$18X + 36Y$	$7Y$
	Final Alignment	$48Y$	$12Y$	$12Y$
	Total	$32X + 83Y$	$36X + 84Y$	$18X + 55Y$
Secp256k1	Multiplication	–	$32X + 64Y$	$32X + 64Y$
	Reduction	–	$32X + 64Y$	$30Y$
	Final Alignment	–	$16Y$	$16Y$
	Total	–	$64X + 144Y$	$32X + 110Y$
Numsp256d1	Multiplication	–	$32X + 64Y$	$32X + 64Y$
	Reduction	–	$32X + 64Y$	$24Y$
	Final Alignment	–	$16Y$	$16Y$
	Total	–	$64X + 144Y$	$32X + 104Y$

[a] The MR method is not applicable to `Secp256k1` and `Numsp256d1`.

each round only conducts `VMULL` (`VMLAL`) four times, which is equal to $4X$, and its total execution instructions are about $32X$.

In the reduction stage, the SMCOS method only requires one round, seven `VADD` instructions, so the total number of instructions used is $7Y$. Each round of MR mainly requires 2 `VEXT`, 1 `BIC`, and 2 `ADD` instructions, 7 rounds in total, and the instructions can be represented as $35Y$. As for CICOS, its reduction and multiplication are all completed by a COS multiplication, so the instructions used for reduction are also about $18X + 36Y$. In the final alignment, the instructions consumed by the SMCOS and CICOS methods with non-redundant representation are mainly additions, and each alignment needs carry only six times, and the total instructions are about $12Y$. Compared with them, the MR using redundant representation also requires a *shift* and a *bic* instruction to complete carry, and each alignment executes 8 times, so the total instructions are roughly $48Y$.

Based on the same standard, we count the instructions of the SMCOS and CICOS methods at each stage, when they are applied to `Secp256k1` and `Numsp256d1`. As shown in Table 1, both 2-cycle instruction (X) and 1-cycle instruction (Y) used by SMCOS are significantly reduced compared to MR and CICOS methods. According to Table 1, it can be further estimated that clock cycles of the instructions conducted by the SMCOS method are reduced by about 38% compared with MR, and about 36%−42% compared with CICOS. In particular, for the vector modular multiplication designs implemented by NEON, the main 2-cycle instructions used are `VMULL` and `VMLAL` vector multiplication instructions. For the two instructions with larger execution cycles, the SMCOS method greatly reduces the frequency of their use, which is mainly reflected in the following two aspects. 1) In the multiplication stage, we use a non-redundant representation, which reduces the number of partial products compared to the MR method with redundant representation. Taking NIST P192 as an example, MR uses a radix-2^{24} representation (i.e. 24 bits per word) for 192-bit operands, the total number of partial products is $8 \times 8 = 64$, which requires 32 vector multiplication instructions. On the other hand, SMCOS uses non-redundant representation based on a radix of 2^{32}, and reduces the number of partial products to $6 \times 6 = 36$, only 18 vector multiplication instructions. Besides, there are also fewer other instructions for reduction and carry propagation, because the size in bits of operands separated in a non-redundant way is the same as the word size of ARM processors. 2) In the reduction stage, our choice is not the Montgomery reduction adopted by CICOS, because it consumes the same instructions as the multiplication stage. A fast vector reduction design is used by SMCOS, so that SMCOS does not need to use any multiplication and only requires some instructions (e.g. addition, shift, and subtraction) with smaller clock cycles to complete the reduction.

4.3   Making SMCOS Fully Pipelined

Data dependencies in the instruction flow may cause pipeline stalls during the execution of vector instructions. If an instruction about to be executed has to wait for the operands written by the previous instruction for several cycles, in the meantime no other instructions enter the pipeline, the cycles of SIMD co-processors will be wasted and the performance will be compromised [31]. This kind of data dependencies between instructions are called Read-After-Write (RAW) dependencies, and the purpose of pipelining is to reduce or avoid RAW dependencies. Due to a large number of pipeline stalls, the 2-way Montgomery modular multiplication in [3] even obtains lower performance than scalar methods, when they are all implemented on ARM. Therefore, in order to maximize the performance of SMCOS, we need to perform sophisticated pipelining. And we investigate the clock cycles and delay of the instructions used by SMCOS. The advanced SIMD integer instruction timing on ARM Cortex-A9 platforms is provided in [6], as shown in Table 2.

We conduct sophisticated pipelining in each stage of the SMCOS implementation. During the execution of SMCOS, every vector instruction will be performed in terms of the sequence in the assembly code, so we manually adjust the instruction sequence to avoid pipeline stalls. Take the construction of vector multiplication with 977 in Algorithm 2 as an example, the original assembly code is ASM Code 1 in Fig. 4. According to the timing of vector instructions in Table 2, the manually adjusted assembly code is ASM Code 2 in Fig. 4.

As described in Algorithm 2, ASM Code 1 uses 2 VSHL, 2 VSRA, and 1 VSUB instructions to construct a vector multiplication with constant 977 on four pairs of 64-bit data stored in Q8 to Q11. The processing code of Q8 is in lines 1 to 5 of ASM Code 1, and the codes of Q9 to Q11 can be deduced by analogy. There are a lot of RAW dependencies in the original assembly code. Even though the execution cycle of the 20 instructions in ASM Code 1 is only 20 clock cycles in total, in fact, according to Table 2, due to pipeline stalls caused by the

Table 2. Advanced SIMD integer instruction timing on ARM Cortex-A9 [6]

Instruction	Description	Issue cycles[a]	Available result[b]
VADD	Vector Addition	1	3
VDUP	Vector Duplication	1	2
VMOV	Vector Move	1	3
VSWP	Vector Swap	1	2
VSUB	Vector Subtraction	1	3
VEXT	Vector Extraction and Concatenate	1	2
VTRN	Vector Traspose	1	2
VSHL	Vector Shift Left	1	3
VSRA	Vector Shift Right with Addition	1	4
VMULL	Vector Multiplication	2	7
VMLAL	Vector Multiplication with Addition	2	7

[a] This is the number of issue cycles the particular instruction consumes.
[b] The Result field indicates the execution cycle when the result is ready.

instruction dependencies, it takes 50 cycles to complete execution and get all the results. This is absurd but true. In order to reduce pipeline stalls, we insert several independent instructions into any two data-dependent instructions to break these dependencies, so that the pipeline can be filled with new instructions again and fully utilized while an instruction is waiting for the result of the previous instruction. By referring to Table 2, we perform pipelining to ASM Code 1, the adjusted ASM Code 2 only takes 22 clock cycles to get all results, which is 44% of ASM Code 1.

5   Results

In this section, we conduct the experiments to evaluate our SMCOS method and ECC implementations on the 32-bit ARM Cortex-A9 processor and compare our results with related work and several ECC algorithm libraries, in terms of modular multiplication, point addition, point doubling, ECDH, and ECDSA.

5.1   Target Platforms

The ARM Cortex-A series are full implementations of the ARMv7, v8 architecture including NEON engine. The Cortex-A processors provide a series of application scenarios for devices using operating systems such as Linux or Android. These devices are used in various applications, from low-cost handheld devices to smartphones, tablets, set-top boxes, and corporate network devices. Among the Cortex-A series processors, we choose the Cortex-A9 on 32-bit ARMv7 architecture as the experimental platform, which is consistent with the previous implementations [1,3,16,17,27,28]. The Cortex-A9 processor is widely used in several

```
1    vshl.u64 q12, q8,  #5
2    vsra.u64 q12, q12, #1
3    vshl.u64 q8,  q8,  #10
4    vsra.u64 q8,  q8,  #10
5    vsub.u64 q8,  q8,  q12
6    vshl.u64 q13, q9,  #5
7    vsra.u64 q13, q13, #1
8    vshl.u64 q9,  q9,  #10
9    vsra.u64 q9,  q9,  #10
10   vsub.u64 q9,  q9,  q13
11   vshl.u64 q14, q10, #5
12   vsra.u64 q14, q14, #1
13   vshl.u64 q10, q10, #10
14   vsra.u64 q10, q10, #10
15   vsub.u64 q10, q10, q14
16   vshl.u64 q15, q11, #5
17   vsra.u64 q15, q15, #1
18   vshl.u64 q11, q11, #10
19   vsra.u64 q11, q11, #10
20   vsub.u64 q11, q11, q15
```

(a) ASM Code 1 (Original)

```
1    vshl.u64 q12, q8,  #5
2    vshl.u64 q8,  q8,  #10
3    vshl.u64 q13, q9,  #5
4    vshl.u64 q9,  q9,  #10
5    vshl.u64 q14, q10, #5
6    vshl.u64 q10, q10, #10
7    vshl.u64 q15, q11, #5
8    vshl.u64 q11, q11, #10
9    vsra.u64 q12, q12, #1
10   vsra.u64 q8,  q8,  #10
11   vsra.u64 q13, q13, #1
12   vsra.u64 q9,  q9,  #10
13   vsra.u64 q14, q14, #1
14   vsra.u64 q10, q10, #10
15   vsra.u64 q15, q15, #1
16   vsra.u64 q11, q11, #10
17   vsub.u64 q8,  q8,  q12
18   vsub.u64 q9,  q9,  q13
19   vsub.u64 q10, q10, q14
20   vsub.u64 q11, q11, q15
```

(b) ASM Code 2 (Adjusted)

Fig. 4. Two pieces of code for constructing vector multiplication with 977.

devices including iPad 2, iPhone4S, Galaxy S2, Galaxy S3, Galaxy Note 2, Kindle Fire, and NVIDIA Tegra T30. At the same time, the NEON instructions on its ARMv7 architecture are compatible with ARMv8.

5.2 Performance Comparison of Prime Field Multiplication

We perform the experiments on the Exynos 4412 development board equipped with the Cortex-A9 processor (1.4GHz), and clock cycles are measured by reading counter registers from Performance Monitoring Unit (PMU) inside CP15 co-processor of ARM. We select three elliptic curves over prime fields with different categories and security levels, NIST P192, Secp256k1, and Numsp256d1, to deploy the experiments. We implement the SMCOS, MR [24] and CICOS [27] vector modular multiplication methods in ARM assembly language, and integrate them into several ECC algorithm libraries for comparison. In order to control the variables, specifically, for NIST P192 curve, we choose OpenSSL 1.1.1k [21] to perform the replacements and evaluations of the above three vector methods on corresponding prime field. For Secp256k1 curve, libsecp256k1 [23], the fastest official algorithm library used for Bitcoin protocol implementations, is selected for method replacements. It is worth mentioning that its modular multiplication implementation is optimized by manual assembly before. As for Numsp256d1 curve, we choose the ECC algorithm library MSR ECCLib 2.0 [18] provided by Microsoft Research.

For our SMCOS method, MR method, CICOS method, and several ECC libraries, Table 3 summarizes the number of clock cycles required to perform one modular multiplication operation on the three curves. This result impressively demonstrates the efficiency of SMCOS for modular multiplication in ECC, and indirectly supports the performance analysis of Sect. 4.2, that is, SMCOS uses fewer instructions in the multiplication and reduction stages, and has higher performance.

Table 3. Comparison of clock cycles for modular multiplication[a]

Elliptic curve	Field	Implementation	Mod-Mul
NIST P192	$\mathbb{F}_{2^{192}-2^{64}-1}$	**Our SMCOS**	205
		MR [24]	301
		CICOS [27]	387
		OpenSSL [21]	1,079
Secp256k1	$\mathbb{F}_{2^{256}-2^{32}-977}$	**Our SMCOS**	310
		CICOS [27]	574
		libsecp256k1 [23]	434
		OpenSSL [21]	2,051
Numsp256d1	$\mathbb{F}_{2^{256}-189}$	**Our SMCOS**	306
		CICOS [27]	574
		MSR ECClib [18]	1,050

[a] Entries are clock cycles measured on a ARM Cortex-A9 processor.

The detailed results are as follows. For NIST P192 curve, our SMCOS method only needs 205 clock cycles to complete a modular multiplication operation, which is about 32% faster than MR, about 47% faster than CICOS, and more than five times as fast as the special NIST modular multiplication in OpenSSL. For Secp256k1 curve, the clock cycles of SMCOS is only 310, which is almost equal to the time to conduct a 256-bit multiplication in [27]. This result is roughly 46% faster than CICOS, 29% faster than the hand-optimized modular multiplication of libsecp256k1, and 85% faster than the Montgomery method used by OpenSSL. For Numsp256d1 curve, SMCOS also has an overwhelming advantage, about 47% faster than CICOS and about 71% faster than MSR ECClib. Moreover, for these ECC algorithm libraries, except for the modular multiplication of libsecp256k1, other libraries are implemented in C language on ARM platforms. This is why the performance of these libraries is much lower than that of several vector methods such as SMCOS.

5.3 Performance Comparison of Elliptic Curve Arithmetic

Point addition and point doubling based on underlying prime field arithmetic are the core operations of various ECC protocols. Table 4 shows the clock cycles of point addition and point doubling for each implementation. Profit from the better optimization of the prime field multiplication, the point addition and point doubling using the SMCOS method also gain better experimental results than other methods. In OpenSSL's NIST P192, our SMCOS method requires 6340 and 5755 clock cycles to perform point addition and point doubling, which are roughly 18% and 23% faster than MR, roughly 27% and 32% faster than CICOS. As for Secp256k1, SMCOS makes point addition and point doubling reach record-setting execution times on Cortex-A9 processors, they only consume 5853 and 2736 clock cycles, which are about 18% and 11% faster than libsecp256k1, also about 35% and 40% faster than CICOS. For Numsp256d1 curve, the point addition and point doubling on SMCOS require 7657 and 3297 clock cycles, which are about 36% faster than CICOS, and about three times as fast as MSR ECClib.

By referring to Table 4, compared to libsecp256k1 and MSR ECClib for 256-bit ECC, the performance of 192-bit NIST P192 in native OpenSSL is lower. So even if we use several vector methods to replace its prime field multiplication, point addition and point doubling do not gain good benchmark results. This is also the reason why we choose efficient dedicated libraries for Secp256k1 and Numsp256d1 curves. But even so, deploying our SMCOS method to OpenSSL still has a greater performance enhancement than other designs.

Table 4. Comparison of clock cycles for point addition and point doubling[a]

Elliptic curve	Implementation	Point addition	Point doubling
NIST P192	**Our SMCOS**	6,340	5,755
	MR [24]	7,692	7,409
	CICOS [27]	8,727	8,419
	OpenSSL [21]	17,003	14,860
Secp256k1	**Our SMCOS**	5,853	2,736
	CICOS [27]	9,017	4,563
	libsecp256k1 [23]	7,132	3,064
	OpenSSL [21]	25,840	24,751
Numsp256d1	**Our SMCOS**	7,657	3,297
	CICOS [27]	11,893	5,164
	MSR ECClib [18]	19,424	9,220

[a] Entries are clock cycles measured on a ARM Cortex-A9 processor.

5.4 Performance Results of ECDH and ECDSA

The ultimate goal of our SMCOS method is to reduce the computational complexity of ECC protocols such as ECDSA and ECDH, and improve their performance, so that they can be used more extensively on general-purpose computing devices, especially on embedded devices. As far as the performance of ECDSA and ECDH, to evaluate the impact of our implementation techniques, we compare SMCOS with two fast vector modular multiplication methods, MR and CICOS, and several ECC libraries.

Table 5. Comparison of clock cycles for ECDH and ECDSA[a]

Elliptic curve	Implementation	ECDH key exchange	ECDSA signature
NIST P192	**Our SMCOS**	2,282	2,852
	MR [24]	2,855	3,423
	CICOS [27]	3,117	3,672
	OpenSSL [21]	6,206	6,781
Secp256k1	**Our SMCOS**	950	1,291
	CICOS [27]	1,429	1,737
	libsecp256k1 [23]	1,103	1,438
	OpenSSL [21]	12,285	13,063
Numsp256d1	**Our SMCOS**	1,401	1,996
	CICOS [27]	2,085	2,418
	MSR ECClib [18]	3,816	2,653

[a] Entries are 10^3 clock cycles measured on a ARM Cortex-A9 processor.

Table 5 shows the benchmark results of ECDH key exchange and ECDSA signature based on several implementations. For ECDH key exchange, the SMCOS method is roughly 27%−34% faster than CICOS (all 3 curves), 20% faster than MR (NIST P192), 63% faster than OpenSSL (NIST P192), 14% faster than libsecp256k1 (Secp256k1), and 63% faster than MSR ECClib (Numsp256d1). Moreover, ECDSA signature using SMCOS is about 17%−26% faster than CICOS, 17% faster than MR, 58% faster than OpenSSL, 10% faster than libsecp256k1, and 25% faster than MSR ECClib. In summary, ECDSA signature and ECDH key exchange based on SMCOS obtain better performance on ARM Cortex-A9 platforms than other methods. There are two main reasons responsible for the results: 1) performing an ECDSA signature or ECDH key exchange often requires thousands or even tens of thousands of modular multiplication operations; 2) the SMCOS multi-precision modular multiplication has better performance than other methods for these ECC implementations.

6   Conclusions

In this paper, we introduce an optimization technique to improve the performance of multi-precision modular multiplication on ARM NEON platforms. More specifically, we propose a design and implementation of prime field multiplication for specific modulus, called SMCOS, to make full use of the computing power of SIMD co-processors for ECC. On the ARM Cortex-A9 platform, our SMCOS method performs modular multiplication of NIST P192, Secp256k1, and Numsp256d1 within only 205, 310 and 306 clock cycles, which are roughly 32% faster than MR method of Pabbuleti et al. and about 47% faster than CICOS method of Seo et al.

The SMCOS modular multiplication can be applied to other ECC algorithms as primitives. At the same time, one of the most obvious future work is to apply the proposed modular multiplication routines to Intel-AVX processors.

References

1. Azarderakhsh, R., Liu, Z., Seo, H., Kim, H.: NEON PQCRYTO: fast and parallel ring-LWE encryption on ARM NEON architecture. IACR Cryptol. ePrint Arch. **2015**, 1081 (2015)
2. Bernstein, D.J., Schwabe, P.: NEON crypto. In: Prouff, E., Schaumont, P. (eds.) CHES 2012. LNCS, vol. 7428, pp. 320–339. Springer, Heidelberg (2012). https://doi.org/10.1007/978-3-642-33027-8_19
3. Bos, J.W., Montgomery, P.L., Shumow, D., Zaverucha, G.M.: Montgomery multiplication using vector instructions. In: Lange, T., Lauter, K., Lisoněk, P. (eds.) SAC 2013. LNCS, vol. 8282, pp. 471–489. Springer, Heidelberg (2014). https://doi.org/10.1007/978-3-662-43414-7_24
4. Câmara, D., Gouvêa, C.P.L., López, J., Dahab, R.: Fast software polynomial multiplication on arm processors using the NEON engine. In: Cuzzocrea, A., Kittl, C., Simos, D.E., Weippl, E., Xu, L. (eds.) CD-ARES 2013. LNCS, vol. 8128, pp. 137–154. Springer, Heidelberg (2013). https://doi.org/10.1007/978-3-642-40588-4_10
5. Cheng, H., Großschädl, J., Tian, J., Rønne, P.B., Ryan, P.Y.A.: High-throughput elliptic curve cryptography using AVX2 vector instructions. In: Dunkelman, O., Jacobson, Jr., M.J., O'Flynn, C. (eds.) SAC 2020. LNCS, vol. 12804, pp. 698–719. Springer, Cham (2021). https://doi.org/10.1007/978-3-030-81652-0_27
6. ARM Cortex: A9 NEON media processing engine technical reference manual revision: r4p1 (2012)
7. Faz-Hernández, A., López, J.: Fast implementation of Curve25519 using AVX2. In: Lauter, K., Rodríguez-Henríquez, F. (eds.) LATINCRYPT 2015. LNCS, vol. 9230, pp. 329–345. Springer, Cham (2015). https://doi.org/10.1007/978-3-319-22174-8_18
8. Faz-Hernández, A., Lopez, J., Dahab, R.: High-performance implementation of elliptic curve cryptography using vector instructions. ACM Trans. Math. Softw. (TOMS) **45**(3), 1–35 (2019)
9. Grewal, G., Azarderakhsh, R., Longa, P., Hu, S., Jao, D.: Efficient implementation of bilinear pairings on arm processors. In: Knudsen, L.R., Wu, H. (eds.) SAC 2012. LNCS, vol. 7707, pp. 149–165. Springer, Heidelberg (2013). https://doi.org/10.1007/978-3-642-35999-6_11
10. Gueron, S., Krasnov, V.: Software implementation of modular exponentiation, using advanced vector instructions architectures. In: Özbudak, F., Rodríguez-Henríquez, F. (eds.) WAIFI 2012. LNCS, vol. 7369, pp. 119–135. Springer, Heidelberg (2012). https://doi.org/10.1007/978-3-642-31662-3_9
11. Hisil, H., Egrice, B., Yassi, M.: Fast 4 way vectorized ladder for the complete set of montgomery curves. IACR Cryptol. ePrint Arch. **2020**, 388 (2020)
12. Holdings, A.: Arm architecture reference manual, ARMV7-A AND ARMV7-R edition. Arm Holdings (2014)
13. Huang, J., Liu, Z., Hu, Z., Großschädl, J.: Parallel implementation of SM2 elliptic curve cryptography on Intel processors with AVX2. In: Liu, J.K., Cui, H. (eds.) ACISP 2020. LNCS, vol. 12248, pp. 204–224. Springer, Cham (2020). https://doi.org/10.1007/978-3-030-55304-3_11
14. Intel Corporation: Using streaming SIMD extensions (SSE2) to perform big multiplications, application note AP-941, July 2000. http://software.intel.com/sites/default/files/14/4f/24960

15. Kocher, P.C.: Timing attacks on implementations of Diffie-Hellman, RSA, DSS, and other systems. In: Koblitz, N. (ed.) CRYPTO 1996. LNCS, vol. 1109, pp. 104–113. Springer, Heidelberg (1996). https://doi.org/10.1007/3-540-68697-5_9

16. Longa, P.: FourQNEON: faster elliptic curve scalar multiplications on ARM processors. In: Avanzi, R., Heys, H. (eds.) SAC 2016. LNCS, vol. 10532, pp. 501–519. Springer, Cham (2017). https://doi.org/10.1007/978-3-319-69453-5_27

17. Márquez, R.C., Sarmiento, A.J.C., Sánchez-Solano, S.: Speeding up elliptic curve arithmetic on arm processors using neon instructions. Revista Ingeniería Electrónica, Automática y Comunicaciones **41**(3), 1–20 (2020). ISSN: 1815-5928

18. Microsoft Research: MSR Elliptic Curve Cryptography library (MSR ECClib) (2014). http://research.microsoft.com/en-us/projects/nums

19. Montgomery, P.L.: Modular multiplication without trial division. Math. Comput. **44**(170), 519–521 (1985)

20. Oder, T., Pöppelmann, T., Güneysu, T.: Beyond ecdsa and rsa: Lattice-based digital signatures on constrained devices. In: 2014 51st ACM/EDAC/IEEE Design Automation Conference (DAC). pp. 1–6. IEEE (2014)

21. OpenSSL: The open source toolkit for SSL. Download at https://www.openssl.org

22. Orisaka, G., Aranha, D.F., López, J.: Finite field arithmetic using AVX-512 for isogeny-based cryptography. In: Anais do XVIII Simpósio Brasileiro em Segurança da Informação e de Sistemas Computacionais, pp. 49–56. SBC (2018)

23. Wuille, P., et al.: libsecp256k1: Optimized C library for EC operations on curve Secp256k1 (2015)

24. Pabbuleti, K.C., Mane, D.H., Desai, A., Albert, C., Schaumont, P.: SIMD acceleration of modular arithmetic on contemporary embedded platforms. In: 2013 IEEE High Performance Extreme Computing Conference (HPEC), pp. 1–6. IEEE (2013)

25. Page, D., Smart, N.P.: Parallel cryptographic arithmetic using a redundant montgomery representation. IEEE Trans. Comput. **53**(11), 1474–1482 (2004)

26. Sánchez, A.H., Rodríguez-Henríquez, F.: NEON implementation of an attribute-based encryption scheme. In: Jacobson, M., Locasto, M., Mohassel, P., Safavi-Naini, R. (eds.) ACNS 2013. LNCS, vol. 7954, pp. 322–338. Springer, Heidelberg (2013). https://doi.org/10.1007/978-3-642-38980-1_20

27. Seo, H., Liu, Z., Großschädl, J., Choi, J., Kim, H.: Montgomery modular multiplication on ARM-NEON revisited. In: Lee, J., Kim, J. (eds.) ICISC 2014. LNCS, vol. 8949, pp. 328–342. Springer, Cham (2015). https://doi.org/10.1007/978-3-319-15943-0_20

28. Seo, H., Liu, Z., Großschädl, J., Kim, H.: Efficient arithmetic on ARM-NEON and its application for high-speed RSA implementation. Secur. Commun. Netw. **9**(18), 5401–5411 (2016)

29. Walter, C.D., Thompson, S.: Distinguishing exponent digits by observing modular subtractions. In: Naccache, D. (ed.) CT-RSA 2001. LNCS, vol. 2020, pp. 192–207. Springer, Heidelberg (2001). https://doi.org/10.1007/3-540-45353-9_15

30. Wang, J., Vadnala, P.K., Großschädl, J., Xu, Q.: Higher-order masking in practice: a vector implementation of masked AES for ARM NEON. In: Nyberg, K. (ed.) CT-RSA 2015. LNCS, vol. 9048, pp. 181–198. Springer, Cham (2015). https://doi.org/10.1007/978-3-319-16715-2_10

31. Zhao, Y., Pan, W., Lin, J., Liu, P., Xue, C., Zheng, F.: PhiRSA: exploiting the computing power of vector instructions on Intel Xeon Phi for RSA. In: Avanzi, R., Heys, H. (eds.) SAC 2016. LNCS, vol. 10532, pp. 482–500. Springer, Cham (2017). https://doi.org/10.1007/978-3-319-69453-5_26

Correction to: Differential-Linear Cryptanalysis of the Lightweight Cryptographic Algorithm KNOT

Shichang Wang, Shiqi Hou, Meicheng Liu, and Dongdai Lin

Correction to:
Chapter "Differential-Linear Cryptanalysis
of the Lightweight Cryptographic Algorithm KNOT"
in: Y. Yu and M. Yung (Eds.): *Information Security*
***and Cryptology*, LNCS 13007,**
https://doi.org/10.1007/978-3-030-88323-2_9

In an older version of this paper, there was an orthographical error in the title. This has been corrected.

The updated version of this chapter can be found at
https://doi.org/10.1007/978-3-030-88323-2_9

© Springer Nature Switzerland AG 2022
Y. Yu and M. Yung (Eds.): Inscrypt 2021, LNCS 13007, p. C1, 2022.
https://doi.org/10.1007/978-3-030-88323-2_29

Author Index

Printed in the United States
by Baker & Taylor Publisher Services